The Routledge Handbook of Lexicography

The Routledge Handbook of Lexicography provides a comprehensive overview of the major approaches to lexicography and their applications within the field. This *Handbook* features key case studies and cutting-edge contributions from an international range of practitioners, teachers, and researchers. Analysing the theory and practice of compiling dictionaries within the digital era, the 47 chapters address the core issues of:

- The foundations of lexicography and its interactions with other disciplines, including corpus linguistics and information science;
- Types of dictionaries, for purposes such as translation and teaching;
- Innovative specialized dictionaries such as the Oenolex wine dictionary and the Online Dictionary of New Zealand Sign Language;
- Lexicography and world languages, including Arabic, Hindi, Russian, Chinese, and Indonesian;
- The future of lexicography, including the use of the Internet, user participation, and dictionary portals.

The Routledge Handbook of Lexicography is essential reading for researchers and students working in this area.

Pedro A. Fuertes-Olivera is Full Professor at the University of Valladolid, Spain; Extraordinary Professor at the University of Stellenbosch, South Africa; and Tutor at UNED, Spain.

Routledge Handbooks in Linguistics

Routledge Handbooks in Linguistics provide overviews of a whole subject area or sub-discipline in linguistics, and survey the state of the discipline including emerging and cutting edge areas. Edited by leading scholars, these volumes include contributions from key academics from around the world and are essential reading for both advanced undergraduate and postgraduate students.

The Routledge Handbook of the English Writing System
Edited by Vivian Cook and Des Ryan

The Routledge Handbook of Metaphor and Language
Edited by Elena Semino and Zsófia Demjén

The Routledge Handbook of Systemic Functional Linguistics
Edited by Tom Bartlett and Gerard O'Grady

The Routledge Handbook of Heritage Language Education
From Innovation to Program Building
Edited by Olga E. Kagan, María M. Carreira and Claire Hitchins Chik

The Routledge Handbook of Language and Humor
Edited by Salvatore Attardo

The Routledge Handbook of Language and Dialogue
Edited by Edda Weigand

The Routledge Handbook of Language and Politics
Edited by Ruth Wodak and Bernhard Forchtner

The Routledge Handbook of Language and Media
Edited by Daniel Perrin and Colleen Cotter

The Routledge Handbook of Ecolinguistics
Edited by Alwin F. Fill and Hermine Penz

The Routledge Handbook of Lexicography
Edited by Pedro A. Fuertes-Olivera

Further titles in this series can be found online at www.routledge.com/series/RHIL

The Routledge Handbook of Lexicography

Edited by
Pedro A. Fuertes-Olivera

Routledge
Taylor & Francis Group
LONDON AND NEW YORK

First published 2018 by Routledge
2 Park Square, Milton Park, Abingdon, Oxon OX14 4RN

and by Routledge
605 Third Avenue, New York, NY 10017

First issued in paperback 2021

Routledge is an imprint of the Taylor & Francis Group, an informa business

Publisher's Note
The publisher has gone to great lengths to ensure the quality of this reprint but points out that some imperfections in the original copies may be apparent.

British Library Cataloguing-in-Publication Data
A catalogue record for this book is available from the British Library

Library of Congress Cataloging-in-Publication Data
A catalog record for this book has been requested

ISBN 13: 978-1-03-209626-1 (pbk)
ISBN 13: 978-1-138-94160-1 (hbk)

Typeset in Times New Roman
by Apex CoVantage, LLC

Contents

Figures

Tables

Acknowledgments

My sense of gratitude on the publication of this volume is deep, for its writing and editing have been a cooperative and collaborative process. First, I want to thank the contributors for their participation and for their tolerance of my editorial efforts. I would also like to express my thanks to the lexicographers acting as reviewers of chapters and ideas. Although their names are not mentioned (it was agreed that all chapters will be subjected to blind peer review), I do feel obliged to express my gratitude for their efforts and time.

My thanks to the copyright holders of dictionaries, some of whose articles are reproduced in the volume, either as edited examples or as images. My sincere thanks go to Akamai Technologies, Aranzadi, Ariel, Cambridge University Press, Duden, Farlex, Ediciones S-M., Pharos, Gredos, HarperCollins, Houghton Mifflin Harcourt, Indonesian National Language Body, John Wiley & Sons, Longman, Macmillan Publishers, Merriam-Webster, Miller Longman, Mouton De Gruyter, Nelson Education, Ordbogen, Oscar Brandstetter Verlag, Oxford University Press, Pearson, Real Academia Española de la Lengua, Reverso, SGEL, Spektrum Akademischer Verlag, Systrans, TLex Dictionaries, the Wikipedia Foundation, the Wordnik Foundation and WordReference.com. Every effort has been made to contact copyright holders. If any have been inadvertently overlooked, the publisher will be pleased to make the necessary arrangements at the first opportunity.

I am very much interested in acknowledging the work of Routledge staff, especially commissioning editor, Nadia Seemungal, who initially approached me to edit this *Handbook of Lexicography* and allowed me free rein to come up with my own authors and topics selection. I would also like to thank Helen Tredget, senior editorial assistant, with whom I worked closely during the two years of the project. Finally, I also want to thank the Spanish Ministerio de Economía y Competitividad for financial support (grant FFI2014-52462-P) and my colleagues at the Centre for Lexicography (University of Aarhus) and International Centre for Lexicography (University of Valladolid).

This book is dedicated to my family – wife, daughters and grandchildren – and my students for their inspiration, their motivation and their constructive criticism. For without them, there would be no book and no conceivable reason to have ever considered writing one.

Contributors

Andrea Abel is head of the Institute for Applied Linguistics at Eurac Research (Italy) and lecturer at several universities. Research interests include the modeling of language competence and linguistic variation (German as L1 and L2), research into learner and variety corpora, electronic and pedagogical lexicography, and sociolinguistic aspects of language contact. She is currently the president of EURALEX (European Association for Lexicography).

Heidi Agerbo, MA in English from Aarhus University, Denmark, and MA in Applied Corpus Linguistics from the University of Birmingham, UK, is a PhD candidate in Lexicography at Aarhus University. Her research project focuses on function-based information tools on sport and fitness, and she is using the conceptualisation of such tools to investigate the dictionary functions described and applied in the Function Theory of Lexicography. Some of the themes she is investigating in her PhD project are the under-researched functions operation and interpretation and the application of the function theory in the production of meaning explanations.

Collin F. Baker is Project Manager of the FrameNet Project at the International Computer Science Institute. His research interests include studying how the system of semantic frames developed for annotating English text can be extended to other languages around the world and other modalities such as speech and social media.

María Auxiliadora Barrios Rodríguez is Associate Professor of the Spanish Language Department at Universidad Complutense de Madrid (UCM, 2009) and member of the "Relaciones léxico-sintaxis" group of research (2004). She was awarded the National Research Fellowship (FPI) from the Spanish Ministry of Science and Innovation (2003–2007). After research stays at the University of Montreal (Canada), New England University (Australia), and Paris VII (France), she received a PhD degree with European mention from the UCM in 2008. Her research interests are at the intersection between lexicology and lexicography with natural language processing. Her scientific production includes over 60 publications in international conferences and journals. She has participated in eight international and national projects and lectured 50 courses in Spanish Language for undergraduate and postgraduate students. She is the founder of the Spanish as Second Language website (www.masalladelespanol.com).

Henning Bergenholtz was born in Copenhagen (1944). He obtained his MA in 1973 (Technical University of Berlin), his DrPhil in 1975 (University of Essen), his DrHabil in 1978 (University of Essen), a DrHC in 2009 (University of Valladolid), and his ProfHC in 2014

(University of Guangzhou). From 1973 he has taught at universities in Bonn, Essen, Cairo, Cologne, Bochum, and the Aarhus School of Business (Denmark). In 1984 he was the extraordinary professor for German linguistics at the University of Essen, from 1987 to 1992 a research professor, in 1992 a professor of bilingual specialized lexicography at the Aarhus School of Business, from 2005 the extraordinary professor at the University of Stellenbosch, from 2011 the extraordinary professor at the University in Pretoria at the Department for Information Science, from 1996 to 2013 the director of the Centre for Lexicography, Aarhus University, from 2013 professor emeritus at the Aarhus University, and from 2014 an honorary professor at the Jinan University, Guangzhou, China. He has published more than 300 scientific publications and has edited more than 50 dictionaries (printed and online).

Hans C. Boas is the Raymond Dickson, Alton C. Allen, and Dillon Anderson Centennial Professor in the Department of Germanic Studies and the Department of Linguistics at the University of Texas at Austin, Director of the Linguistics Research Center, German FrameNet, and the Texas German Dialect Project. His research focuses on syntax, lexical semantics, computational lexicography, language contact and variation, historical linguistics, pragmatics, morphology, phonology, documentary linguistics, contrastive linguistics, corpus linguistics, endangered languages and dialects, foreign language education, language policy and planning, intercultural communication, and history and philosophy of linguistics.

Bob Boelhouwer is a computer linguist working at the Instituut voor de Nederlandse Taal. He has worked on a number of dictionary projects. His main interests lie in lexicography and corpus linguistics. He obtained a doctorate with a dissertation in psycholinguistics, studying the role of the mental lexicon in auditory word recognition.

Ignacio Bosque is Honorary Professor of Spanish Linguistics at Complutense University (Madrid). His main research interests include Spanish grammar (syntax, morphology, and the lexicon–syntax interface), as well as theoretical linguistics, lexicography, lexicology, and grammar instruction. He coordinated two combinatory dictionaries of Spanish (*REDES. Diccionario combinatorio del español contemporáneo*, 2004; and *Diccionario combinatorio práctico del español contemporáneo*, 2006), as well as two comprehensive grammars of the Spanish language (*Gramática descriptiva de la lengua española*, 1999, with V. Demonte; and *Nueva gramática de la lengua española*, 2009). He has published extensively on collocations and other restrictive predicate–argument lexical relations. He is the author of *Las categorías gramaticales* (1989; 2nd edition in 2015) and *Sobre la negación* (1990); co-author, with J. Gutiérrez- Rexach, of *Fundamentos de sintaxis formal* (2009); and editor of *Indicativo y subjuntivo* (1990), *El sustantivo sin determinación* (1996), and *Advances in the Analysis of Spanish Exclamatives* (2017).

Theo J. D. Bothma is professor emeritus and contract professor in the Department of Information Science at the University of Pretoria, South Africa. Until his retirement on 30 June 2016, he was the Head of the Department (since 1 October 1995) and chairperson of the School of Information Technology (since 1 September 2008). His teaching and research focus on information organisation and retrieval (specifically in the fields of e-lexicography and information literacy), web development, and electronic publishing.

Lynne Bowker, PhD, is a Full Professor at the School of Translation and Interpretation of the University of Ottawa, Canada. Her teaching and research interests include terminology and language for special purposes, corpus linguistics, and translation technologies. She is a member of the editorial board of the *International Journal of Lexicography* and the *International Journal of Corpus Linguistics*.

Anne Condamines is a linguist and Director of Research at the French CNRS (National Center for Scientific Research) at Toulouse. Her research interests are language for specific purposes, terminology, and controlled natural languages. Her main aim is to bring studies of specialized corpora closer to corpus linguistics, taking into account the variation in terminology according to textual genre and to extra-linguistic needs. She has proposed tool-assisted methods in order to define fine-grained analysis of specialized corpora. In 1993, she co-founded the TIA group (Terminology and Artificial Intelligence) that still organizes an international conference every year. She has had many responsibilities in her university (head of the ERSS team, President of the Specialized Scientific College in Linguistics, elected member of the Research Commission, appointed member of the Valorisation Commission) and within the CNRS (elected member of the National Committee). She has evaluated numerous projects for several national and international research centers (French ANR, Belgian FNRS, Canadian CRSH, John Benjamins). Finally, she has published around 100 national or international articles.

Stefan Dollinger is Professor of English Linguistics at the University of Gothenburg and Associate Professor of English at UBC Vancouver (PhD in English Linguistics, Vienna University, 2006). He specializes in historical linguistics, dialectology, sociolinguistics, and the lexicography and lexicology of varieties of English. He is the author of more than 40 papers (http://gu-se.academia.edu/StefanDollinger). His books include *New-Dialect Formation in Canada* (2008), *The Written Questionnaire in Social Dialectology* (2015), and, as editor-in-chief, the new edition of *A Dictionary of Canadianisms on Historical Principles* (DCHP-2, www.dchp.ca/dchp2), as well as the digitized first edition of DCHP-1 (Avis et al. 1967), which is now available in open-access format (www.dchp.ca/dchp1).

Anne Dykstra (1949) has been affiliated with the Fryske Akademy (FA) since 1983. After his retirement in 2014 he continued to work for the FA's lexicographic department as an honorary research fellow. He worked on the scholarly multi-volume *Dictionary of the Frisian Language*, and in 2000 he published his Frisian-English dictionary. His main field of research is the history of (Frisian) lexicography. He obtained his doctorate with a dissertation on the nineteenth-century Frisian-Latin *Lexicon Frisicum*. He has been editor of *International Journal of Lexicography* until March 2017.

Anna Dziemianko is a university professor at Adam Mickiewicz University in Poznań, Poland. Her main research interests include English pedagogical lexicography, user studies, syntax in dictionaries, defining strategies as well as presentation and distribution of lexicographic data on dictionary websites. She has also researched the relative usefulness of paper and electronic dictionaries. In her current work the focus is on e-lexicography, especially issues connected with e-dictionary design and actual benefits of the electronic medium to dictionary users.

Gertrud Faaß is a computational and a corpus linguist; she works as a researcher and lecturer in the Institute of Information Science and Natural Language Processing at the University of Hildesheim, Germany, focusing inter alia on theory and applications of corpus linguistics utilized for information tools. She has published on corpora, grammar, and dictionaries describing African languages, specifically Northern Sotho and Zulu. Her latest list of research topics includes language learners' software and dictionaries for German as a foreign (scientific) language on the basis of corpus data.

Trinidad Fernández is Associate Professor at the Universidad Politécnica de Madrid where she lectures ESP to graduate and professional students in the Department of Applied Linguistics in Science and Technology. She is the author of various research papers on lexicography and second-language learning, and has designed a bilingualised thesaurus (English-Spanish) for architecture and construction (*BEST*). Her research interests include terminology, corpus compilation, specialized dictionaries, and second-language teaching.

Pedro A. Fuertes-Olivera is Full Professor at the University of Valladolid, Extraordinary Professor at the University of Stellenbosch (Department of Afrikaans and Dutch), and Tutor at UNED (Spanish Open University). He has also taught at Aarhus University (Visiting Professor 2007 and Velux Vising Professor 2011–2012). He has extensively published in the field of lexicography, for example, *Pedagogical Specialised Lexicography* (with Ascensión Arribas-Baño, 2008); *Theory and Practice of Specialised Online Dictionaries. Lexicography versus Terminography* (with Sven Tarp, 2014); *Specialised Dictionaries for Learners* (2010); and *e-Lexicography: The Internet, Digital Initiatives and Lexicography* (with H. Bergenholtz, 2011 and 2013). He is also editor of the *Diccionarios Valladolid-UVa*, a collection of 28 online dictionaries covering general Spanish (monolingual dictionaries), general Spanish and English (bilingual dictionaries), and accounting facts and languages (specialised English and Spanish accounting dictionaries).

Laura Giacomini is a teacher and researcher at the Institute of Translation and Interpretation of Heidelberg University (Germany) and currently a guest researcher at the Institute of Information Science and Natural Language Processing of Hildesheim University (Germany). Her research fields include lexicography, phraseology, specialised language, and translation studies. She is involved in different lexicographic projects and is now working at her habilitation thesis on LSP variation in the technical domain.

Rufus H. Gouws is Professor of Afrikaans linguistics in the Department of Afrikaans and Dutch at the University of Stellenbosch. His research focuses primarily on metalexicography, and he complements his work in theoretical lexicography with active participation in the lexicographic practice in his capacity as editor or co-editor of various dictionaries.

Orin Hargraves is an American lexicographer with 25 years of industry experience and the author of various English language reference books about clichés, American slang, and British and American differences. He has contributed to dictionaries from Oxford, Cambridge, Merriam-Webster, Collins, and others. He lectures at the University of Colorado.

Reinhard R. K. Hartmann was born in Wien/Vienna, Austria, where he studied economics, translation, and linguistics. He has worked at UMIST Manchester (1964–68), the University of Nottingham (1968–74), and the University of Exeter (1974–2001). He has held post-retirement visiting professorships and fellowships at the Universities of Exeter and Birmingham. His extensive publications, chiefly in linguistics and lexicography, include a *Dictionary of Language and Linguistics* (with F.C. Stork 1972), *A Reader on Language Variety* (with C.S. Butler 1976), *Contrastive Textology* (1980), *Lexicography. Principles and Practice* (with contributions from 18 authorities 1983), *LEXeter '83 Proceedings* (1984), *Dictionary of Lexicography* (with G. James 1998), *Teaching and Researching Lexicography* (2001), and *Lexicography: Critical Concepts* (3 volumes 2003).

Nathalie Hernandez is an associate professor in the Computer Science Department (Institut de Recherche en Informatique de Toulouse) of Toulouse 2 University. Her current research topics are ontology engineering, RDF triplet store querying, and natural language interfaces for the Semantic Web.

Reinhard Heuberger is an assistant professor in the Department of English at the University of Innsbruck. He was the co-director of the government-funded project SPEED (2006–2010) and co-directed its follow-up project EDD Online (2011–2016), both concerned with the digitization and investigation of Joseph Wright's *English Dialect Dictionary*. His research focuses on lexicography (pedagogical and online dictionaries) and ecolinguistics.

Aleš Horák is an Associate Professor of Informatics at Masaryk University, Brno, Czech Republic. His research concentrates on natural language processing, knowledge representation and reasoning, e-lexicography, and corpus linguistics.

John Humbley is emeritus professor of applied linguistics at Université Paris-Diderot, Sorbonne-Paris-Cité, member of the research group CLILLAC-ARP EA 3967, F-75205 Paris and associate member of Laboratoire Lexique, Dictionnaires, Informatique UMR 7187 CNRS, and guest professor at the University of Verona (2015–2018). His interests are in terminology and in particular aspects concerning neology and multilingualism, as well as translation and lexicology-lexicography. He is cofounder and coeditor, with Jean-François Sablayrolles, of the journal *Neologica* and associate editor of *Terminology* and is currently on the editorial board of *ASp*, *Les Cahiers de lexicologie*, *Fachsprache*, *Hermes*, *Lexis*, *Meta*. *LCS (Langues, cultures et sociétés)*, Publif@rum and *TOTh*.

Howard Jackson is Professor Emeritus of English Language and Linguistics in the School of English at Birmingham City University, United Kingdom, where he taught for over 40 years. He taught modules on lexicography and corpus linguistics, as well as on grammar and lexicology. He currently contributes to the MA in field linguistics at the British SIL training programme. He is the author of *Lexicography: An Introduction* (2002) and (with Etienne Zé Amvela) of *Words, Meaning and Vocabulary* (2nd edition, 2007). He also authored the 'Lexicography' article in the *Morphology* volume of the *HSK* (2004). In 2013 he edited *The Bloomsbury Companion to Lexicography*, a book devoted to the analysis of state-of-art lexicography at the coming of age of the Internet.

Olga M. Karpova is a Doctor of Philology, Professor, the Head of the English Philology Department at Ivanovo State University, Russia, and founder of Ivanovo Lexicographic School. She trained 33 PhD students. Professor Karpova specialises in theory and practice of English lexicography, being particularly interested in writers' dictionaries of different types with special reference to Shakespeare lexicography. She is the author of 22 books and 340 articles. Olga Karpova is a member of EURALEX with two Verbatim Awards (1993, 1997); International Society for Historical Lexicology and Lexicography (UK); National

Association of Applied Linguistics (NAAL) (Russia), etc. She has numerous awards for outstanding scientific achievements and initiatives. She is currently the Project Leader of the Dictionary for Guides and Tourists Florence in the Works of World Famous People created with support of Fondazione Romualdo Del Bianco® – Life Beyond Tourism®.

Alexander Koplenig is a research assistant in the Department for Lexical Studies at the Institute for the German Language in Mannheim. His research focuses on the quantitative analysis of empirical linguistic data.

Deny Arnos Kwary is the head of the English Department, Faculty of Humanities, Universitas Airlangga, Indonesia. He is also the Indonesian Language Manager at the Oxford Global Languages, Oxford University Press, University of Oxford, UK. His current research focuses on Indonesian lexicography, electronic lexicography, and corpus linguistics.

Patrick Leroyer, PhD, is Associate Professor of French and Danish LSP and Business Communication at the University of Aarhus, Faculty of Arts, School of Communication and Culture, and is attached to the Centre for Lexicography. He is also affiliated with the International Centre for Lexicography at the University of Valladolid, Spain. His current research is on theoretical lexicography in a broad, functional perspective and includes the development of specific theories for data access, selection, and presentation in connection with communicative and cognitive functions in lexicographic information tools (specialized dictionaries, tourist dictionaries, wine dictionaries, corporate dictionaries, bilingual dictionaries). He has published within the fields of LSP and Business Communication, Terminography, and Lexicography, and is also co-author of a number of mono- and bilingual specialized dictionaries, both in print and online.

Teresa Lino is a Full Professor with a PhD from Université de la Sorbone Nouvelle – Paris 3; she was President of the Scientific Board of the Department of Linguistics; she was also President of the Centre of Linguistics of *Universidade Nova de Lisboa*, where she created a research unit on Lexicology, Lexicography and Terminology and has been since in charge of that team. She has led and participated in national and international projects, she is a member of international research networks (Réseau LTT – Lexicologie, Terminologie et Tradction, REALITER – Réseau Panlatin de Terminologie, among others) and has participated in their Managing Committees. She teaches Lexicology and Lexicography, Terminology, Computational Linguistics, and French Linguistics. She has a large number of publications in Portugal and abroad. Her awards include the following: "Chevalier dans l'Ordre des Arts et des Lettres", an honour bestowed by the Ministère de la Culture de la République Française; and "Prix Spécial de Terminologie Eugen Wüster", an honour awarded by the University of Wien – A. Eugen Wüster, International Information Centre for Terminology – INFOTERM, UNESCO.

Przemysław Łozowski got his PhD in 1996 for the dissertation *Vagueness in Language: From Truth-Conditional Synonymy to Un-conditional Polysemy* (2000), and completed his habilitation in 2008 on the basis of the monograph *Language as Symbol of Experience: King Alfred's* cunnan, magan, *and* motan *in a Panchronic Perspective* (2008). His main research interests include cognitive linguistics, historical linguistics, and cultural linguistics, with semantics being the major field of investigation. Until 2016 he had been Head of the Institute of English Studies at Maria Curie-Skłodowska University, Lublin, and currently is Dean of the Faculty of Philology and Pedagogy at Kazimir Pułaski University, Radom, Poland.

José Mateo is Full Professor of English at the University of Alicante (Spain) and founder member of IPA (Academic and Professional English). His current research includes specialized lexicography, cognitive approaches to specialized translation, and business communication. He has authored and co-authored five specialized bilingual dictionaries.

Paul Achille Mavoungou (born in 1972) is an assistant professor of the Department of Language Sciences at the University Omar Bongo in Libreville (Gabon). Paul Achille is mainly interested in phraseology, core meaning, and dictionary topics for the African languages. He teaches lexicography, lexicology, African languages, and general linguistics to undergraduate and postgraduate students. His publications include more than 20 peer-reviewed journal articles, conference proceedings, and book chapters, as well as eight books published nationally and internationally, including two dictionaries *Dictionnaire Yilumbu-Français* (2010; co-author Bernard Plumel) and *Le dico des makaya et des mamadou. Dictionnaire des collocations et des locutions figurées du français du Gabon* (2015; co-authors Firmin Moussounda Ibouanga and Jean-Aimé Pambou), as well as the book entitled *Festschrift Rufus H. Gouws* (2013; co-authors: W. P. Botha and D. Nkomo). He received his Doctor Litteratum (PhD) degree under Rufus H. Gouws in 2003 at Stellenbosch University, South Africa.

Erin McKean is the founder of *Wordnik.com*, the world's biggest online dictionary. Before founding *Wordnik*, she was the editor-in-chief of American Dictionaries for Oxford University Press. She has a BA and MA in Linguistics from the University of Chicago. Her goal is to make every word in the English language "lookupable" – including the 52 percent of unique English words that aren't currently in any dictionary. Erin is the author of three *Weird and Wonderful Words* books, the best-selling novel *The Secret Lives of Dresses*, and (most recently) *The Hundred Dresses*, a field guide to dresses. She's written regular columns for *The Boston Globe* and the *Wall Street Journal*, and her writing has also appeared in *The New York Times*, *PAPER*, *Foreign Affairs*, and *Sew News*. She's served as an advisor to the American National Corpus, the journal *American Speech*, and the Wikimedia Foundation, and serves on the KPCB Design Council. She blogs at *dressaday.com* and tweets as @emckean. When you meet her, please tell her your favourite word.

David McKee is a Senior Lecturer and Director of the Deaf Studies Research Unit in the School of Linguistics and Applied Language Studies at Victoria University of Wellington. He is the managing editor of the Online Dictionary of NZSL and has extensive experience in teaching sign languages, in training sign language teachers and interpreters, and in lexicographical research on New Zealand Sign Language (NZSL).

Rachel McKee is an Associate Professor in the School of Linguistics and Applied Language Studies at Victoria University of Wellington. A professional background in sign language interpreting in New Zealand and the United States since 1985 led to an academic career in applied sign linguistics. Rachel has established teaching programmes for sign language interpreters, Deaf teachers of New Zealand Sign Language (NZSL), and hearing second-language learners of NZSL. Her research has spanned description of grammar, lexicon and sociolinguistic variation in NZSL, sign language interpreting, deaf education, ethnography of the New Zealand Deaf community, and language policy for NZSL.

Julia Miller, PhD, is a senior lecturer in the School of Education at the University of Adelaide, where she teaches academic skills and research communication. She has an honours degree in Modern and Medieval Languages from the University of Cambridge; a research MA on anglicisms in Portuguese from Flinders University (South Australia); and a PhD in pedagogical lexicography and phraseology from Flinders University. Her research interests are in lexicography, phraseology, phraseodidactics, and academic skills. She is an AustraLex committee member (2015–2017) and the founder of the English for Uni website (www.adelaide.edu.au/english-for-uni). This website has creative, innovative materials, together with video stories based on popular culture, all of which offer a research-based, humorous approach to transcultural language learning and teaching.

Christian M. Meyer is a senior researcher at the Ubiquitous Knowledge Processing (UKP) Lab of the Technische Universität Darmstadt, Germany, and a principal investigator in the research training group "Adaptive Preparation of Information from Heterogeneous Sources" (AIPHES). His current research focuses on intelligent writing assistance, user participation and collaborative lexicography, interactive machine learning, and computer-assisted approaches.

Karlheinz Mörth is director of the Austrian Centre for Digital Humanities (Austrian Academy of Sciences). Proceeding from a background in Middle Eastern Studies (with a focus on Arabic and Modern Persian), his recent research has been directed towards e-lexicography, digital standards for lexical data, and digital language resources.

Carolin Müller-Spitzer is a project manager at the Institute for the German Language in Mannheim. Her current research focuses on dictionary use, digital lexicography, and empirical methods in linguistics. She is a member of the editorial board of the *International Journal of Lexicography* (OUP).

Dion Nkomo is Associate Professor at the African Language Studies Section of the School of Languages and Literatures at Rhodes University. Among other courses, his teaching and research interests include language planning and policy, lexicography, terminology, and comparative Nguni studies. He holds a BA (Hons) in African Languages from the University of Zimbabwe, and an M.Phil. and a PhD in Lexicography from Stellenbosch University. He has worked as a language practitioner and lexicographer under the African Languages Lexical (ALLEX) Project (University of Zimbabwe) and the Multilingualism Education Project (University of Cape Town).

Sandro Nielsen is affiliated with the Department of English as well as Centre for Lexicography at School of Communication and Culture, Faculty of Arts, Aarhus University, Denmark, where he is associate professor, and is affiliated with the International Centre for Lexicography, University of Valladolid, Spain. He has an MA in English (LSP for translators and interpreters) from 1987 and was awarded his PhD degree in specialised lexicography in 1992. He has published extensively on theoretical and practical lexicography, and is the author of *The Bilingual LSP Dictionary. Principles and Practice for Legal Language* (1994); co-editor of *Lexicography in the 21st Century* (2009), *Lexicography at a Crossroads* (2009), a printed and two online bilingual law dictionaries, and three printed and more than twenty online accounting dictionaries; and a contributor to the *Manual of Specialised Lexicography*. His main research areas are principles for specialised online dictionaries, user guides in dictionaries, lexicographic information costs, and academic dictionary reviewing. Teaching interests focus on lexicography and legal translation for translators and interpreters.

Marta Niño Amo, PhD, is Associate Professor at the University of Valladolid, where she teaches accounting. She is currently the Head of Department of Accounting and Finance and the editor of the *Memento Contable*, a kind of users' guide of accounting matters documenting case studies and changes on accounting standards and regulations. She is also affiliated with the International Centre for Lexicography (University of Valladolid) and has been working on the *Accounting Dictionaries* since 2008.

Vincent Ooi is a faculty member at the Department of English Language and Literature, National University of Singapore. His main teaching and research interests include lexicology and lexicography, corpus linguistics, computer-mediated communication, and Asian varieties of English.

Jing Peng is currently associate professor of Guangdong University of Finance and Economics, with a master's degree from Southampton University. Her academic interests include diachronic lexicography, communicative lexicography, and business English. Her major publications include *Bilingual Lexicography from a Communicative Perspective* (co-authored with Heming Yong, 2007), *Chinese Lexicography: A History from 1046 BC to AD 1911* (co-authored with Heming Yong, 2008), *Chinese Dictionaries: Three Millennia (from 1046 BC to AD 1999)* (co-authored with Heming Yong, 2010), *A History of English Lexicography from Remote Times to the Present Day* (co-authored with Heming Yong, 2015), and *Government Foresighted Leading* (co-translator, 2017).

Pam Peters is a Fellow of the Australian Academy of the Humanities and an Emeritus Professor of Macquarie University, Sydney. Her research in Australian and international English usage is grounded in corpus linguistics and informs major publications such as the *Cambridge Guide to English Usage* (2004) and the *Cambridge Guide to Australian English Usage* (2007). She was Director of Macquarie University's Dictionary Research Centre (2000–2007) and led the compilation of reference corpora for researching Australian English morphosyntax. She now leads the *TermFinder* project, developing online termbanks in law and cancer medicine. Her most recent monograph is the *Cambridge Dictionary of English Grammar* (2013).

Danie Prinsloo is a professor in African languages at the University of Pretoria. His field of interest is African Language lexicography. He has published more than 100 articles, books, and chapters in books on this subject and delivered an equal number of papers at international conferences. He received several awards as outstanding academic achiever of the University and as a University of Pretoria Centenary leading mind.

Daniel Prinsloo is a senior Software Engineer and consultant at Entelect, a software development contracting firm. He completed his BSc Computer Science degree in 2009 at the University of Pretoria. He is a full-stack software developer with primarily NET and secondary Java experience, specializing in front-end web development, in particular

AngularJs and PhoneGap mobile applications. His main focus and interest is providing the most practical and useful systems as possible to end users. This resonates strongly with the main challenge faced by electronic dictionaries. His interest is in designing and implementing innovative systems and tools that transcend mere paper dictionaries into electronic format systems and tools that would greatly aid end users in language learning and text production.

Jacobus Prinsloo is a Computer Engineer at Aerosud. He completed his BEng. and BEng (Hons.) degree in Computer Engineering at the University of Pretoria. His main area of expertise is in C++ and embedded programming. Currently he is the software control system developer of the Aeroswift additive manufacturing project being developed at the Council for Scientific and Industrial Research (CSIR) National Laser Center. He has a keen interest in electronic dictionaries and electronic user support systems such as access on demand and systems linking electronic dictionaries to writing tools.

Adam Rambousek is a Research Assistant at the Faculty of Informatics, Masaryk University, Brno, Czech Republic. His main interests are computational lexicography, corpus linguistics, ontologies, and semantic networks.

Catherine Roussey is a researcher at IRSTEA, the French National Research Institute of Science and Technology for Environment and Agriculture. Her current research focuses on ontologies creation and reuse for publishing agricultural and sensor data on the Linked Open Data cloud.

Josef Ruppenhofer is group leader in the research project "Empirical Linguistics & Computational Language Modeling", which is jointly conducted by the Institute for German Language, Mannheim, and the Institute for Computational Linguistics at Heidelberg University. He works on corpus linguistics and computational linguistics, with a special interest in the development of lexical resources. Since his graduate studies at UC Berkeley, Josef Ruppenhofer has been intensely involved with the FrameNet project and Frame Semantics, a key theoretical cornerstone of FrameNet. More recently, he has focused on sentiment/subjectivity analysis with the goal of extending the FrameNet resource with information relevant for sentiment analysis.

Hindrik Sijens (1960) is a lexicographer working at the Fryske Akademy. He has worked on the scholarly multi-volume dictionary of the Frisian language, a two-volume monolingual Frisian concise dictionary, and the Taalweb-project, a web portal for Frisian language assistance. He is currently editor of the *Online Dutch-Frisian Dictionary*. His main fields of interest besides lexicography are neologisms and orthography.

Parman Singh holds a PhD degree in Linguistics from Banaras Hindu University and worked on Metaphoric Competence in Cognitive Linguistics Theory as a Post-Doctoral Fellow from the Department of Science and Technology, Government of India. He is the author of *Hindi Lexicography: Past, Present and Future* (2013) and *Culture, Cognition and Competence* (2017). Currently he is working as Senior Resource Person in the Scheme for Protection and Preservation of Endangered Languages (SPPEL) at the Central Institute of Indian Languages, Mysore.

Petra Storjohann is editor-in-chief of the corpus-based e-dictionary *Paronymwörterbuch* at the Institute for German Language in Mannheim (IDS). Her research focuses on the corpus-analytical study of lexical semantic relations in texts and discourse, methods in corpus linguistics and theory, and practices in e-lexicography. Her publications include the co-edited volume *Wort und Wortschatz* (2015) and an edited volume *Lexical-Semantic Relations* (2010).

Sven Tarp is Professor and Head of the Centre for Lexicography at the Aarhus University (Denmark). He is also Extraordinary Professor at the Department of Afrikaans and Dutch at the University of Stellenbosch (South Africa), Extraordinary Board Member of the International Centre for Lexicography at the University of Valladolid (Spain), Founding Member of the Sino-Danish Sindberg Centre of Lexicography, Translation and Business Communication at the Guangdong University of Finance (China), and Distinguished Visitor of the City of Santiago de Cuba (Cuba). With a PhD in specialised lexicography (1993) and a Doctor's Degree in learners' lexicography (2006), he is the editor or co-editor of several specialised dictionaries and has published a large number of contributions in journals and well-known series. He is the author of *Lexicography in the Borderland Between Knowledge and Non-knowledge* (2008), co-author of *Theory and Practice of Specialised Online Dictionaries* (2014), and co-editor of *Manual of Specialised Lexicography* (1995), *Lexicography at a Crossroads: Dictionaries and Encyclopedias Today, Lexicographical Tools Tomorrow* (2009), and *Lexicography in the 21st Century* (2009). He is one of the founders of the Function Theory of Lexicography.

Arimardan Kumar Tripathi, PhD, is a Computational Linguist and has done his PhD on Anaphora Resolution. He has been working for various research and academic institutions for the last 10 years in the field of Language Technology. Currently he is a Faculty Member at the Centre for Endangered Languages at Visva-Bharati Santiniketan, West Bengal (India).

Sascha Wolfer is a research assistant in the Department for Lexical Studies at the Institute for the German Language in Mannheim. His current research focuses on quantitative approaches in corpus linguistics, psycholinguistics, text comprehension, and lexicography.

Heming Yong is currently professor and president of Guangdong University of Finance and PhD supervisor at Suzhou University, China. After he got his master's degree at Suzhou University in 1992, he furthered his education at Macquarie University, Australia; the University of Massachusetts, United States; York University, Canada; and The University of Oxford, UK. He was awarded a doctoral degree in linguistics in 2001 by Macquarie University. His representative publications include *Bilingual Lexicography from a Communicative Perspective* (co-authored with Jing Peng, 2007), *A Contemporary Dictionary of English Prepositions* (chief editor, 2007), *Chinese Lexicography: A History from 1046 BC to AD 1911* (co-authored with Jing Peng, 2008), *Chinese Dictionaries: Three Millennia (from 1046 BC to AD 1999)* (coauthored with Jing Peng, 2010), *A History of English Lexicography from Remote Times to the Present Day* (co-authored with Jing Peng, 2015), and *Government Foresighted Leading* (translator, 2017). His academic interests include English grammar, diachronic lexicography, and communicative lexicography. He has completed six research projects funded by China National Social Sciences Research Foundation and The Humanities and Social Sciences Research Foundation of the Ministry of Education, China. His books have received considerable attention in international academic circles and have been reviewed by scholars in Denmark, UK, Holland, and Australia as well as in China and in various journals, like *Australian Journal of Linguistics*, *Australian Review of Applied Linguistics*, *International Journal of Lexicography*, *Terminology*, *Kinabladet* and *Lexicographical Studies*. He was awarded the title of Excellent Teacher of the Year by Guangdong Provincial Government in 1996, the title of The New Century Excellent Talent by China's Ministry of Education, and the title of Outstanding Expert for Special Government Allowances by China's State Council. He received the International Achievement Alumni Award for Distinguished Service from Macquarie University in August 2009 and was awarded the title of Honorary Professor by Murdoch University, Australia, in June 2011. He was Velux visiting professor at Aarhus University, Denmark, with sponsorship from Velux Foundation of Denmark.

Haïfa Zargayouna is an associate professor in the Computer Science Department (Laboratoire d'Informatique de Paris-Nord, LIPN) of Paris 13 University. Her main research focuses are text-based knowledge acquisition and semantic information retrieval.

Introduction

Lexicography in the Internet era

Pedro A. Fuertes-Olivera

This *Handbook* is a reference work covering key topics in lexicography. Each chapter provides an accessible introductory overview of an area of the field of lexicography. The book is intended for a diverse audience, but is firmly oriented towards newcomers: you, the reader, might be a researcher, a (graduate) student, an academic wanting to become familiar with the state of the art in the field of lexicography, or indeed a professional lexicographer looking for a way in to one or more of the several topics covered.

Lexicography

Lexicography is *the science concerned with the theory and practice of dictionaries, that is, dictionaries, encyclopaedias, lexica, glossaries, vocabularies, terminological knowledge bases, and other information tools covering areas of knowledge and its corresponding language* – in other words, reference and information tools dealing with "things", "facts", and "language". The forty-seven contributions in this volume together constitute a guide to what are, in the editor's view, the most significant contours in the lexicographical world, as well as offering a series of possible developments that might be influencing the near future of the field, which is clearly being subjected to *both* new developments and disruptive technologies. The coming of age of the Internet is the driving force of the Cambrian explosion lexicography is experiencing and which is felt in the design and construction of dictionaries, as well as in its new possible commercial applications and business models (Fuertes-Olivera 2016; Tarp and Fuertes-Olivera 2016).

The scope of this volume

Each chapter in this volume focuses on a specific area of lexicography. The chapters share broadly the same format, covering a history of the area, a critical discussion of its main current issues, and an indication of its emergent debates and theoretical and practical possibilities. Chapters conclude with a list of related topics in the volume. Each chapter has a section of further reading: a short annotated list of works that readers might consult for a more in-depth treatment of the area. Finally, bibliographical references appear at the end of each chapter, making them self-contained. In the field of lexicography, references usually come in two formats: (a) lexicographical journals and collections (e.g. *International Journal of Lexicography*) typically divide the reference lists into two parts: one for dictionaries and one for books, articles, and similar reference literature; and (b) other lexicographical journals and traditions (e.g. *Lexicographica*, quite often, and *Terminology*) just use only one list of references, which is orthographically organized. I have decided to maintain the reference list each author has prepared. This will benefit the intended reader of this *Handbook*, especially if he or she accesses it electronically.

In a collection of such size and diversity, there will be aspects to regard critically. Some readers will disapprove of the way authors have examined a particular topic. Others will take issue with the organization of the book. And others will inevitably find gaps. Clearly, and despite my intention to cover much ground, certain areas are not as fully dealt with as some might wish. However, I must say that this *Handbook* offers a balanced view of the main approaches to lexicography in general and to some of its specific aspects. This is manifest in the six parts of the volume, each devoted to key lexicographical issues, and prepared with the main aim of offering a red line that goes from the most abstract (Chapter 1) to the most concrete ones (Chapter 47).

Part I: Foundations of lexicography

This section contains chapters exploring the nature of lexicography as previously defined. It makes my case for editing a handbook which clearly differentiates and stands out in the academic field of lexicography. Although lexicography is frequently associated with (applied) linguistics – for example, this *Handbook* is included in the prestigious Routledge Handbooks in Linguistics series – the chapters in this part defend the proposition that lexicography is an independent science in its own right, with its own independent core and a big interdisciplinary vocation. The five chapters in this part reflect on the independent core of lexicography: dictionary making is an art and craft which can be transformed in a scientific activity by approaching it under the tenets of a lexicographical theory: the so-called *Function Theory of Lexicography* (Bergenholtz and Tarp 2003; Tarp 2008; Fuertes-Olivera and Tarp 2014).

Tarp's "Lexicography as an independent science" (Chapter 1) refers to the controversy on the disciplinary status of lexicography and makes his case for defending the scientific status of lexicography following Buhr and Klaus' (1971) concept of science. Lexicography is an independent science because it (a) "constitutes a system of knowledge growing out of social practice"; (b) "is developing on an ongoing basis"; (c) "is rooted in the form of concepts, categories, defined goals, theories and hypothesis"; (d) "comprises both the history of dictionaries and its own history"; (e) "contains independent contributions to methodology"; and (f) "includes dictionaries for practical action". Moreover, lexicography has its own research agenda, which should focus on dictionary management (Chapter 2), access (Chapter 3), meaning construction (Chapter 4), and criticism (Chapter 5) together with an array of topics that do not need to be dealt with separately (e.g. history, user needs and situations, empirical basis for the lexicographical data, treatment of lexicographical data, and so on); instead, these issues can be treated in specific circumstances, usually in connection with specific dictionaries or dictionary types, with the aim of extracting general trends from particular lexicographic activities. Hence, most chapters situate concepts and issues in a historical perspective and make provisions for specific user needs, situations, empirical basis, treatment of lexicographical data, and so on.

The importance of lexicography as an independent science is observed in Bergenholtz's "Dictionary management" (Chapter 2). He argues that there must be a lexicographer as editor-in-chief of the whole process, which cannot be in the hands of someone without expert knowledge in lexicography. He even claims that the editor-in-chief is responsible for seeing that everyone taking part in the project (e.g. IT expert, business controller, and so on) understands the underlying lexicographic principles. Gouws's "Dictionaries and access" (Chapter 3) also refers to the same view, which he explains by illustrating the possibilities of the *access structure* (he explains the working of some access structures such as the *rapid access structure* and the *access alphabet* within the general concept of the access process) and concludes his chapter by emphasizing that a lexicographer's main responsibility is to assure potential users easy and quick access to the lexicographical data, especially to the most important data in any dictionary type: *meaning items*, which are much more than traditional definitions, as explained in Agerbo's "Explaining meaning in lexicographical information tools" (Chapter 4). Agerbo's hypothesis and proposals illuminate possible outcomes in the online environment. They also explain why dictionary reviews must be more than accounts of language matters, also an idea defended in Nielsen's "Dictionary criticism" (Chapter 5), which offers a method of dictionary criticism that encompasses language and factual matters, as well as access to data in different use situations.

Part II: The interdisciplinary nature of lexicography

Although independent, lexicography clearly shows an interdisciplinary vocation, that is, cooperation between disciplines. Nielsen's initial chapter "Lexicography and interdisciplinarity" (Chapter 6) presents the basis of this cooperation by analyzing the key role interdisciplinarity plays in today's lexicography, especially as lexicography is complex by nature "due to its multi-faceted challenge of providing help to users in a wide range of extra-lexicographic situations" and must respond to challenges that are not restricted to one specific discipline. Hence, he clearly states that dictionaries are more than inventories of the words of a language (Hanks 2016); they are information tools, and as such different disciplines are of some help for lexicography. In particular, disciplines such as linguistics (applied linguistics and corpus linguistics), information science, terminology, cultural studies, discourse analysis, and natural language processing may be of help for compiling dictionaries. The relationship between these disciplines and lexicography is explored in this part, which defends the necessity of having lexicographic interdisciplinary networks, that is, several specialists working together, for compiling dictionaries in today's world.

Chapters by Peters and Fernández and Faaß (Chapters 7 and 8, respectively) describe cooperation between linguistics and lexicography. Peters and Fernández discuss the influence of applied linguistics (basically pedagogically oriented theories), whereas Faaß centres on corpus linguistics. These two chapters are complementary: Peters and Fernández focus their discussion on English and Spanish dictionaries – Hornby's *Oxford Advanced Learner's Dictionary* and Moliner's *Diccionario de uso del español* – and demonstrate that making pedagogical dictionaries like these for second-language learners demands the active cooperation and participation of linguists who are responsible for translating linguistic theories and analyses into lexicographic data. Faaß, however, adopts a broader view, which consists in (a) summarizing the basic requirements of corpora and (b) describing some corpus tools which can be used for compiling dictionaries. In other words, Peters and Fernández illustrate how applied linguistics has influenced the making of two exemplary dictionaries, whereas Faaß shows how several corpus ideas, tools, and methods are being used (or can be used) for lexicographic purposes. Both chapters are connected with several other chapters in the *Handbook*, especially chapters connected with pedagogically oriented language dictionaries (e.g. Chapters 19 and 22) and electronic dictionaries (e.g. Chapter 41).

Chapters by Bowker, Nkomo, and Łozowski limit cooperation to narrower aspects of lexicography: specialized vocabulary (Bowker's chapter), language planning (Nkomo's chapter), and the language–culture interface (Łozowski's chapter). These three chapters are related in the sense that they clearly show that dictionaries are also cultural products that record, say, technological innovations and developments, political dominance, and cultural heritage. Dictionaries must not only record these phenomena but also explain them, which may result in a political approach to reality.

Bowker's "Lexicography and terminology" (Chapter 9) is basically neutral. She claims that both disciplines are intimately related and that cooperation among them is increasing, especially as a consequence of technological innovations – she especially mentions *crowdsourcing* – and similar practical work (e.g. blending the object of study and adopting corpus-based methods). The chapter is adamant that the relationship between them will continue to blossom in the near future, perhaps up to a point in which distinctions between them will disappear as more and more users demand quality information tools, no matter if they centre on words, terms, or both.

Nkomo's "Dictionaries and language policy" (Chapter 10) is less neutral: Nkomo's main thesis is that dictionaries and language policies influence each other. This cooperation may have both positive and negative outcomes. For instance, he thinks that at a macro level this cooperation may have negative influences – certain languages may be marginalized. However, it also shows that lexicography may play a crucial role in the redressing of linguistic inequalities by contributing towards the development of previously marginalized languages. Cooperation at a micro level is subtler, as it is basically concerned with the advantages and disadvantages of prescription and description. He favours proscription – that is, recommendation (Bergenholtz 2003) – as a good way of eliminating the disadvantages of prescription and description while conserving their advantages.

Finally, Łozowski's "Dictionaries and culture" (Chapter 11) centres on illustrating how some key lexicographic components, especially definitions, can be (and they are typically so) ideological weapons; that is, they can show a "reality" according to a particular political, religious, racial, gendered, and so on worldview. Hence, lexicographic data such as definitions typically do not reflect an objective reality, but "what users mean by the words they use", and consequently words are only subjective symbols of humans' experience (i.e. social labels). This idea is really disturbing and calls into question the assumed (at least by many lexicographers) idea that lexicographers can really make definitions based on concordances and similar machine-led methods.

Chapters by Horák and Rambousek ("Lexicography and natural language processing"; Chapter 12); Bothma ("Lexicography and information science"; Chapter 13); and Roussey, Hernandez, and Zargayouna ("Domain ontologies"; Chapter 14) analyze cooperation that came to the fore very recently. These chapters could have been included in Part 6 of this volume: they also present methods, tools, technologies, resources, and so on that illustrate possible future outcomes in lexicography. By including them in this part, I want to emphasize that they are auxiliary and therefore cannot (or should not) modify the nature of lexicography, as the same is defined at the very beginning of this introduction. In other words, both natural language processing (NLP) and information science can play a significant role in lexicography if they are used as auxiliary elements in a lexicographic project. Conversely, they can ruin the project if they are the dominant part of it, especially when participants in the project seem to be more interested in presenting "illusions", that is, lexicographic projects without proper cost–benefit analysis, than making real dictionaries. These three chapters are complementary: Horák and Rambousek focus on connections between NLP and lexicography, Bothma reviews possible uses of information science for lexicographic purposes, and Roussey et al. illustrate how information science and NLP can join forces and develop domain ontologies, some of which may be of much use for lexicographers.

Horák and Rambousek's chapter introduces links between NLP and lexicography in both directions. First, they illustrate how lexicographic work benefits from techniques of natural language processing, especially from "word sense disambiguation", "semantic similarity measures", "named entity recognition", "relation extraction", and "corpus-based lexicographical activities", for example, for selecting "good examples". Second, they refer to the exploitation of lexicographic data (e.g. *Wiktionary*) for improving language engineering technologies, especially those used for creating lexical databases (e.g. *OWID*), developing ontologies and semantic networks (e.g. *WordNet*), and making use of linked (open) data. They also see the future of lexicography in connection with "user interface adaptation", that is, increased *individualization* (Fuertes-Olivera and Tarp 2014), and "crowdsourcing", that is, user-generated dictionaries, especially users manually annotating large datasets with syntactic and/or semantic information (see Chapter 29 of this *Handbook*).

Bothma's chapter argues that lexicography and information science have much to learn from each other, especially in terms of designing more innovative online dictionaries. He basically analyzes a host of disruptive technologies as they are currently used in information technology that can also be of much use in lexicography. In particular, he discusses topics such as "user information needs and behaviour" and "access to data and information" from the point of view of state-of-the-art information technology accepted principles and practices, with the aim of discussing their possible validity for the theory and practice of lexicography. For instance, technologies such as "searching and navigating", "filtering and profiling", "adaptive hypertext and hypermedia", and "data markup" can be used to improve access to lexicographic data and favour individualization, perhaps lexicographers' holy grail at the time of writing this introduction. He also looks to the future and claims that future cooperation between lexicography and information science may be in applying *relevance theory* – in my view a proxy synonym of lexicographic individualization – and favouring information and dictionary literacy (i.e. the skills needed to convert lexicographic data into useful information in a quick and easy way).

Roussey et al. offer a detailed description of ontologies in computer science (i.e. information systems that specify conceptualizations explicitly). They analyze domain ontologies from the point of view of computer science and define their key components (e.g. *terms, lexical relations, concept, terminological concept*, and so on) with two basic aims. The first one is to offer readers of this *Handbook* an easy-to-read and easy-to-understand approach to the same concept of *ontology* which permeates current knowledge systems; for example, it is being used in the development and creation of terminological knowledge bases (see Chapter 21 of this *Handbook*), which are usually presented as proxies of specialized dictionaries. The second one is to comment on some "resources" – *WordNet, VerbNet, Linked Open data*, etc. – that may be of use for lexicographers, although they seem not to be using them much yet (see Chapter 43 for a rather different view).

Part III: Types of dictionaries

Dictionary typologies exist in many sizes and shapes. There are three main types of classifications based on formal, structural, or functional criteria. The formal and structural classifications usually coincide on offering phenomenological divisions, for example, based on *range, perspective*, and *presentation* of dictionary articles (Malkiel 1962). Mel'čuk (1992), for instance, has proposed a classification of dictionaries which is based on *type of nomenclature* (e.g. general or specialized dictionaries), *arrangement of entries* (e.g. alphabetical or systematic dictionaries), *type of information* (e.g. synchronic or diachronic dictionaries), and *purpose of the dictionaries* (e.g. a research instrument or a teaching-learning tool). In my view, these typologies are rather confusing and are losing relevance in the Internet era. Hence, Part 3 of this *Handbook* offers a simpler approach, which rests on two main ideas.

First, dictionaries are utility tools. Tarp's "The concept of dictionary" (Chapter 15) indicates that they are "conceived for consultation with the genuine purpose of meeting punctual information needs experienced by specific types of potential users in specific types of extra-lexicographical context". Some of these extra-lexicographic contexts are reception (Chapter 16), production (Chapter 17), translation (Chapter 18), teaching-learning (Chapter 19), and LSP contexts (Chapters 20 and 21).

Second, the medium is influencing the practice of dictionary making in such a way that existing dictionary typologies must be discarded. For instance, Humbley (Chapter 20) convincingly argues that Wikipedia "has quickly become what is probably the world's most used specialised dictionary".

Leroyer's "Dictionaries for text reception" (Chapter 16), Fuertes-Olivera and Bergenholtz's "Dictionaries for text production" (Chapter 17), and Giacomini's "Dictionaries for translation" (Chapter 18) exemplify three types of dictionaries for meeting potential needs in these three extra-lexicographic situations: *reception* (e.g. someone is reading), *production* (e.g. someone is writing), and *translation* (e.g. someone is translating from L1 into L2 or from L2 into L1). These three chapters complement each other and follow Tarp's concept of dictionary (Chapter 15). Leroyer offers a more general perspective, as he analyzes "reception patterns", which also influence production and translation. Fuertes-Olivera and Bergenholtz review different types of existing dictionaries for production (although they are not traditionally identified as such; e.g. "grammar and spelling dictionaries") and also refer to a dictionary project which contemplates the making of several production dictionaries of Spanish. And Giacomini focuses on "bilingual dictionaries for translation", thus implying that "translation dictionary" and "bilingual dictionary" are different, although related, concepts.

Heuberger's "Dictionaries to assist teaching and learning" (Chapter 19) adopts a somewhat different approach: he interprets them by paying a lot of attention to monolingual English learners' dictionaries. Some of them (the so-called "big six") are also analyzed in Chapter 22, although from a rather different perspective. Heuberger focuses on their characteristics in terms of their usefulness in a teaching-learning situation. He also mentions "special types of learners' dictionaries" – in particular, he mentions the existence of "bilingualised learners' dictionaries" and "specialised learners' dictionaries". Heuberger thinks that the future of these dictionaries is in upgrading customization.

Humbley's "Specialised dictionaries" (Chapter 20) and Condamines's "Terminological knowledge bases" (Chapter 21) illustrate the earlier view by analyzing specialized dictionaries, that is, dictionaries that cover language, facts, and things outside general knowledge, from two perspectives or "academic traditions": (a) "terminological orientation" (Condamines) and (b) "functional lexicographical orientation" (Humbley).

Humbley reviews the main characteristics of print and electronic specialized dictionaries that follow the functional lexicographical orientation, also identified as "user-orientated".

These dictionaries show *degrees of specialization* depending on their target users (basically "total laypersons, educated laypersons or experts", *range of specialization, type of specialization*, and so on. He concludes that many "of the functions previously played by the specialised dictionary may well migrate to other environments: Wikipedia, translation memory". Although this conclusion may surprise the reader of this book, it has its merits, and therefore authors in this and in other parts of the *Handbook* are envisaging new "types of dictionaries" (see Chapter 29). Condamines describes the "terminological orientation" initiated by Wüster in the 1930s. In particular she focuses on the *terminological knowledge base*, which can be considered an attempt to offer better information tools, that is, tools that not only make more use of technological innovations but also take into account interdisciplinarity (e.g. IT experts, translators, and terminologists working together) and real users' needs. Condamines offers a linguist's viewpoint of the terminological knowledge base and indicates that these information tools are being replaced by *domain ontologies* (see Chapter 14 of this *Handbook*).

Part IV: Innovative dictionaries

Innovation is typically viewed as the application of better solutions to those traditionally considered and used at a particular period. Hence, innovation is associated with new ideas, devices, or methods that add value to a product, process, or service. It typically implies something disruptive coming into a particular market and "destroying" the existing status quo. The chapters in this part basically follow this view: all of them focus on lexicographical aspects that can be considered innovative and, at the same time, explain that innovation and tradition can be two sides of the same coin. In other words, these chapters show, first, that these dictionaries stand out and, second, that innovation and tradition are compatible and mutually reinforcing. There are no chapters devoted to "brand new projects" (e.g. *mined dictionaries*), basically because these projects typically refer to unfinished lexicographic projects. They may be leading a possible and future lexicographic revolution, but to the best of my knowledge, they are only "project dictionaries" at the time of editing this *Handbook*.

Lexicographic innovations concern data description, data access, and/or data presentation. Miller's "Learners' dictionaries of English" (Chapter 22) offers an analysis of English learners' dictionaries – the so-called big six – from the point of view of someone who is an English native speaker but lives and works "Down Under". From this point of view, her analysis is very interesting, especially her conclusions on some of the advantages and disadvantages of these big six dictionaries. Her analysis shows that these dictionaries stand out because they have introduced some far-reaching ideas into lexicography, the use of simplified vocabularies and corpus data being two of them. No one doubts that the use of corpora as a lexicographical empirical basis has influenced the practice of lexicography in the last thirty years and is still the major influence in today's lexicographic world (Atkins and Rundell 2008). She also offers some clues connected with two recent trends in e-lexicography: (a) the development of a new business model, which is based on free access and promotional practices and (b) users' active participation, either as "commentators" and/or "amateur lexicographers" (see Chapter 29 of this *Handbook*). To sum up, the chapter shows that these dictionaries exert a lot of influence in lexicography and therefore merit its inclusion in a part devoted to presenting innovative dictionaries.

Dollinger's "Revising the *Dictionary of Canadianisms* on Historical Principles" (Chapter 23) excels in four main aspects, which taken together makes this contribution an excellent example of real lexicographic innovations concerning not only "data description", "data access", and "data presentation", but also Considine's view (2010: 146) that "what matters is what has been achieved in the real world with real money". First, this chapter illustrates how scholarly dictionaries can be updated and adapted to users' changing life conditions and necessities. Second, it shows how editors can make use of previous work (i.e. we do not need to reinvent the lexicographical wheel at all times). Third, it explains how an historical dictionary can be completed with poor funding in a brief span of time. And finally, it also claims that the Internet can offer a lot of good lexicographic "solutions" provided certain "safe practices" are adopted. Similar principles are explained in McKee and McKee's "The *Online Dictionary of New Zealand Sign Language*" (Chapter 25). They also indicate that this online dictionary stems from previous printed versions, that it has used data from these printed versions, and that the "new" online dictionary is making use of "state-of-the-art" technology as well as lexicographic knowledge and practice. It is obvious that sign language dictionaries are not abundant and that their conceptualization and making demand approaching them innovatively. McKee and McKee explain the approach used in their dictionary and signal the way ahead in sign language lexicography: developing automated signing avatars, increasing the sophistication of sign language corpora and lexical databases, improving the usability of interfaces, and so on.

A somewhat different, but related, experience is described in Ruppenhofer, Boas, and Baker's "*FrameNet*" (Chapter 24) and Mateo's "The *Alicante Dictionaries*" (Chapter 26). These two chapters refer to dictionaries that were initiated in the 1990s and that stand out as exemplars of two different theoretical and practical frameworks, one which is only accessible on the Internet and one that is only found in printed format.

FrameNet is basically a lexicographic online database which is being compiled to put into practice Fillmore's ideas on language with the aim of assisting language researchers in different parts of the world. An analysis of the numbers of researchers and publications connected in one way or another with *FrameNet* reveals that this information tool is widely used: more than 1,000 research groups are using *FrameNet* in their research projects, many of which are basically connected with natural language processing; for example, it is used as a resource in a great number of applications, notably semantic role labelling and (semi-) automatic disambiguation (see Chapters 12, 14, and 43 of this *Handbook*). The *Alicante Dictionaries* are paper dictionaries that combine a lexicographic approach to dictionary making with a high interest on linguistic issues (e.g. their "normative" approach to loans, calques, and other foreign words). These dictionaries stand out as lexicographic milestones in Spanish-speaking countries and high-quality bilingual (English-Spanish/Spanish-English) specialized dictionaries covering different areas, domains, and sub-domains. They are innovative in several aspects that are difficult to find in paper specialized bilingual dictionaries. These dictionaries contain much more than equivalents; they also include meaning explanations, examples, collocations, sub-domain labels, grammar data, lexicographic notes, and geographical labels of either European or Latin American Spanish. They also illustrate a working methodology, which makes use of computers, corpora, existing dictionaries, handbooks, manuals, experts in the field, translators, and lexicographers.

Leroyer's "The *Oenolex wine dictionary*" (Chapter 27) and Fuertes-Olivera and Niño Amo's "The *Accounting Dictionaries*" (Chapter 28) are also specialized dictionaries that are different from the previous ones. The following four aspects are especially relevant: (a) they are totally inspired by a lexicographic approach to dictionary making, which leaves linguistic aspects of the same out of focus; (b) they are examples of interdisiciplinarity: experts in the field, IT personnel, private companies, and public institutions work side by side with lexicographers with the aim of making specialized dictionaries of around 8,000 lemmas in around two years' time; (c) they make use of state-of-the-art lexicographic innovations: idiosyncratic lexicographic databases; cloud computing management tools; integration of several retrieval systems; and so on; and (d) they offer several access possibilities, for example the *Accounting Dictionaries* include up to 27 different interfaces, including one with a "user-generated exploratory search route", which allows users to search when they "are uncertain of the exact form of the term to be searched for, or who want to explore the data of a particular term field, to generate their own searches and search strategies by using Boolean operators" (Fuertes-Olivera and Leroyer 2014). The main difference between these two dictionaries concerns their use of different empirical basis: the *Oenoelex Wine Dictionary* makes extensive use of corpus tools for generating, acquiring, and processing written and oral data sources; it even goes a step further: this dictionary shows how specialized corpora in lexicography can be integrated and become true functional components of the lexicographic tool. The *Accounting Dictionaries* use experts' knowledge and Google searches as an empirical basis, a combination that is worth investigating and using, as we have shown that this methodology is reliable, cheap, easy to use, and adequate for enhancing lexicographic productivity (Tarp and Fuertes-Olivera 2016).

McKean's "*Wordnik*" (Chapter 29) summarizes the possibilities innovation has in lexicography. First, it is a real lexicographic project which is using existing lexicographic data to create its own dictionary articles. Second, it is based on introspection (i.e. a lexicographer's knowledge of users' needs). Without resorting to user studies or corpus lexicography, *Wordnik* was conceived on the hypothesis that dictionaries do not usually include the words that users typically look up (McKean argues that existing dictionaries do not include 52 percent of the word stock of a language). Third, it was initially funded by seed capital; once it was found that its possible economic returns would not make it profitable, its business model changed: it is now under the aegis of a non-profit organization. This is influencing the concept of lexicographic crowdsourcing: users do contribute to dictionary making and do fund the project by, say, adopting a word. Fourth, it is using artificial intelligence technologies with the stated aim of collecting and sharing all the words of English. This can only be achieved by assuming that dictionaries are no longer products, but services, and that lexicographic issues such as lemma and/or equivalent selection, user studies, corpus lexicography, use of a particular definitional style, and so on are not as relevant as they are usually described in many publications. And finally, *Wordnik* started as a lexicographic project, based on lexicographic ideas (i.e. theories), and aimed at solving information needs, which are quite different from purely language needs.

Part V: Lexicography around the world: an overview

This part reviews the current state of lexicographic theory and practice in today's world. Due to space constraints, I have chosen three criteria for selecting the chapters included. First, I have chosen the lexicography of *world languages*; that is, they are the official languages of the United Nations (Arabic, Chinese, English, French, Russian, and Spanish). Second, I have selected languages whose lexicographic traditions have been and are dominant and much appreciated, especially in their "backyards" (i.e. areas of influence): German and Portuguese. Finally, I have selected several "lesser-resourced languages" (Prinsloo et al., this volume), that is, languages for which very limited lexicographic resources exist. In particular, I have chosen languages with a lot of political support (African languages, especially Bantu languages) or especial sociolinguistic situations: Hindi and Indonesian. These languages either coexist with powerful second languages within their geographical area (for instance, Afrikaans and English in South Africa), with a myriad of local languages (Indonesian), or a lot of language variation (Hindi). Some of the criteria can be applied to more than one language (e.g. English can be included in more than one of these groups). Taken together, this section analyzes the current lexicographic work published in languages that are spoken by around 75 percent of the world population, and therefore constitute a testbed for observing future lexicographic trends (e.g. how and when lexicographers of lesser-resourced languages will make the transition from printed to online lexicography). This section places these traditions in today's world with the aim of making reflections on the possible influence of the Internet on them.

Although the form and structure of the chapters in this part are uniform, their content is very different. This is due to four main factors: (a) the influence the Internet has had so far in each lexicography; (b) the authors' approach to writing the chapter; (c) the amount and quality of resources that can be used for lexicographic purposes; and (d) the role played by "commercial lexicography", that is, dictionaries made and paid for by publishing houses with the basic aim of making a profit. These factors are intimately related and permeate most, if not all, of the chapters of this section. Although the importance and amount of contents differ, the reader of the *Handbook* can obtain a complete picture of what is really happening in the world of lexicography around the globe. For instance, he or she will find that English and German lexicography are in the forefront of lexicographic innovations.

Prinsloo et al's chapter ("African lexicography in the Internet era"; Chapter 30) focuses on the state of the art in African online language dictionaries. By African they mean several Bantu languages (e.g. Sesotho, Tshivenda, Sepedi, isiNdebele, and so on). Their analysis shows that African lexicography is in full swing, although messy. It seems that African lexicographic development is being hindered by three main factors: (a) political meddling; (b) competition from information-related gadgets (e.g. Google); and (c) poor lexicographic culture and professional training. However, their chapter offers hope for the future of African lexicography (and, I will say, for other lesser-resourced languages): they illustrate how good lexicographers together with IT specialists can really improve the lexicographic resources of "lesser-resourced languages".

This conclusion is also defended in Singh and Tripathi's "Hindi lexicography in the Internet era" (Chapter 36) and in Kwary's "Indonesian lexicography in the Internet era" (Chapter 37). Both chapters illustrate the situation of two languages with many millions of native speakers but with important drawbacks for improving e-lexicography in their areas of influence. Some of the problems they mention seem to be related to IT infrastructure (however important, these difficulties will not be dealt with in this *Handbook*); some others stem from the situation of the language in their countries. For instance, Hindi is not used as a medium of instruction in higher education; Indonesian must compete with a plethora of local languages. The authors of both chapters are also optimistic about the future of Hindi and Indonesian e-lexicography. Indonesians are basically reproducing English methods and procedures and are benefiting from initiatives such as Oxford's project Oxford Global Languages, which aims "at building lexicographical resources for 100 of the world's languages, especially the languages which are both global and digitally under-represented". Hindi lexicographers are also inclined to follow the experiences of more developed places, for example, a focus on the user's paradigm, acceptance of the interdisciplinarity of lexicography – especially its needed cooperation with information science – and the concept of the dictionary as tool.

Indonesian and Hindi lexicographers may also benefit from Arabic lexicographers who, according to Mörth's chapter ("Arabic lexicography in the Internet era"; Chapter 31) have jumped onto the Internet wagon with enthusiasm and hard work. After presenting two particular features of the Arabic language – the highly conservative nature of the written language and the existence of quite divergent forms of spoken varieties – he describes the effect the digital world is having on Arabic lexicography: (a) compilation of digital corpora for lexicographic purposes; (b) creation of digital encoding standards; (c) creation of digital libraries, each providing large amounts of free accessible lexical data; and (d) creation of a plethora of online dictionaries, as well as dictionary portals with several types of dictionaries. He also sees the future of Arabic lexicography optimistically: both high-quality bilingual and dialect dictionaries (i.e. covering local spoken varieties) will be designed and made, thus filling a pressing gap in Arabic lexicography. If these projects are successfully completed, "Arabic must no longer be regarded as a technologically under-resourced language".

Jackson, Storjohann, and Mavongou describe "much-resourced languages", that is, languages spoken by millions of native and second-language speakers, living in politically and economically powerful and developed countries, having a standardized orthography, a lot of resources, and a well-attested dictionary culture. Although each chapter mainly focuses on the future of their online dictionaries, they also review and comment on general and much-debated issues in e-lexicography. For instance, Jackson's "English lexicography in the Internet era" (Chapter 33) refers to (a) the role of corpora in lexicography; (b) similarities and differences between printed and online dictionary typologies; (c) a better understanding of the interrelationship between search and access, especially for avoiding information overload and favouring customization; (d) the structure of presentation of dictionary articles, especially the necessity of creating dynamic dictionary articles; and (e) the role graphics, audio, and files should play in e-lexicography.

Storjohann's "German lexicography in the Internet era" (Chapter 35) also discusses many of these issues and widens the discussion by referring to some challenges lexicographers currently face. Whereas Jackson's study is basically concerned with commercial lexicography (nobody can forget the enormous influence of the publishing houses responsible for the making of the "big six" dictionaries; see Chapters 19 and 22 of this *Handbook*), Storjohann's also includes "academic lexicography" and "collaborative lexicography" in the centre of lexicographic debates. These differences may explain their different views on the future of lexicography. Whereas Jackson claims that lexicography as we know it today may be in real danger of extinction, Storjohann is more optimistic. She seems to believe in a future with new opportunities, provided that lexicographers work side by side with experts and users to increase their dictionary culture.

Mavongou's "French lexicography in the Internet era" (Chapter 34) takes for granted many of the topics discussed by Jackson and Storjohann. Instead of dealing with general issues affecting online French dictionaries, he gives a comprehensive overview of the various existing French electronic dictionaries, including machine translation systems and online corpora, and investigates some of their specific features and structures. He concludes that although French electronic dictionaries have greatly improved in the last two decades, there is still ample room for making them better and more user oriented. For instance, he claims that French online dictionaries must be updated more regularly and that they should make more use of existing Internet technologies.

Although Bosque and Barrios, Yong and Peng, Karpova, and Lino also report on "much-resourced languages", their analysis is much more restricted in scope than the one offered by Jackson, Storjohann, and Mavongou. Bosque and Barrios's "Spanish lexicography in the Internet era" (Chapter 40) offers a very comprehensive reference list of lexicographic publications and dictionaries, most of them printed and/or CD-dictionaries. They are categorized in "traditionally conceived" dictionary typologies together with metalexicographic publications, most of them in Spanish. Readers interested in the main issues and topics affecting Spanish lexicographers will find the chapter full of insightful information on, say, similarities and differences between Spanish dictionary typologies and other language dictionary typologies. For instance, in the Spanish-speaking world, "*thesauri* are compilations of dictionaries carried out with some chronological or geographical basis". Bosque and Barrios also refer to some online dictionaries compiled *ex novo*, although they are still projects (i.e. they have not been completed yet).

Yong and Peng's "Chinese lexicography in the Internet era" (Chapter 32) also offers a detailed history of Chinese lexicography, which may be mostly unknown for the target readers of this *Handbook*. This may have prompted them to write a chapter whose content is really different: the Internet is not much used in Chinese lexicography, and the authors do not document online Chinese dictionaries; both lexicographic theory and practice in China have followed a very different path from other traditions, especially Western ones. Hence, the chapter may interest readers who are eager to know how Chinese dictionaries have evolved from "ancient reading primers" to today's electronic dictionaries. For instance, Yong and Peng claim that the future of Chinese lexicography will be connected with the development of "chip dictionaries" (i.e. palm, pocket, or handheld electronic dictionaries), perhaps because the Internet is not so freely available in China as it is in many Western countries.

Karpova's "Russian lexicography in the Internet era" (Chapter 39) also offers a detailed review of Russian dictionaries – some of them (e.g. "author's dictionaries") are idiosyncratically Russian – and metalexicographic works. The chapter also focuses on printed dictionaries; yet it also mentions several institutional and private initiatives that aim to favour the making of Russian online dictionaries, most of them following English, French, and German influences. She mentions several recent lexicographic initiatives in Russia: (a) creation of different "websites with a set of dictionaries for general and special purposes which are mostly demanded by modern Russian users", (b) the publication of metalexicographic works has considerably increased, and (c) there are many ongoing projects centred on developing specialized dictionaries.

Lino's "Portuguese lexicography in the Internet era" (Chapter 38) also describes a similar lexicographic landscape to Karpova's. Indeed, she mentions several online specialized dictionary projects which are being developed in her university and research department. The philosophy underlying these projects is terminological (see Chapter 21 of this *Handbook*), for example, interest in including concept maps is explicitly mentioned. She also comments on the collaboration between public and private institutions located in different Portuguese-speaking countries, mainly Portugal and Brazil, which has achieved some important success (e.g. a spelling agreement has been signed by the Community of Portuguese Language Countries).

To sum up, these chapters show that e-lexicography is really making in-roads, that the lexicographic development in "lesser-resourced languages" follows known paths and methods (notably English), that its future will also depend on political and social scenarios that are well beyond lexicographers' reach, that some lexicographies – notably English and German – are leading lexicographic developments whereas some others lag behind, and that the making of online dictionaries needs *explicit* collaboration with other quarters, notably from information science, natural language processing, language engineering, and the like, as shown in Part 6.

Part VI: Looking to the future: lexicography in the Internet era

Contrary to what was analyzed in Part 2, the chapters in Part 6 describe specific tools, theories, methods, and so on that are changing the theory and practice of lexicography at a concrete level. In general, these are concerned with the role of the Internet in lexicography. Dziemianko's "Electronic dictionaries" (Chapter 41) emphasizes the integration of electronic dictionaries into educational software packages. She sees this, as well as customization, as the main driving force of lexicography in the Internet era. Dziemianko claims that both access to *personalized* or *customized* lexicographic data and assurance of its quality will influence the appearance of new business models and with them new types of dictionaries for human consumption. Dziemianko also adds that "electronic lexicography is not just a continuation of print lexicography. Nor does it mean merely making print dictionaries available online or on some data carrier".

Ooi's "Using the Web for lexicographic purposes" (Chapter 42) examines the interlinked concepts of "user", "data", and "access" that define online dictionaries and lexicographic tools on the Web nowadays. In terms of the user parameter, Ooi draws on Hoey's (2005) concept of *lexical priming* for providing "a coherent explanation of different construals in the mental lexicon of various users for the same term in different situations". For the data parameter, he revises the apparently contrastive use of the "Web-as-corpus" and "Web-for-corpus" and finds the idea of lexicographical corpus particularly useful. In terms of the access parameter, Ooi outlines the attendant issue that e-lexicography brings with it: "competitive lexicography" vs. "cooperative lexicography", the transference from p(rinted) to e(lectronic) formats and content adequacy. Hargraves's "Information retrieval for lexicographic purposes" (Chapter 43) enumerates several resources that can be used to facilitate lexicographers' work: the Sketch Engine, Google Ngram Viewer, WordNet, the Pattern Dictionary of English Verbs, VerbNet, FrameNet, Google Image Search, and so on. He illustrates the working of these systems and how they can be used in lexicography.

The coming of age of the Internet is also influencing the role users can have in lexicography, either as informants in online usage research or as amateur lexicographers in cooperative lexicography.

Müller-Spitzer, Koplenig, and Wolfer's "Dictionary usage research in the Internet era" (Chapter 44) argues that usage research is totally necessary and illustrates this hypothesis by commenting on the benefits of three online methods whose workings are detailed in full: using online questionnaires, employing eye tracking technologies, and interpreting log files.

Meyer and Abel's "User participation in the Internet era" (Chapter 45) focuses on user participation in lexicographic projects and comments that such an activity should be incorporated into the metalexicographic research environment, especially by introducing research questions related to, say, the "analysis and development of user participation, the meaningful selection and implementation of suitable methods when planning a product, and the evaluation of motivational factors, quality, legal restrictions, and effectiveness of user participation methods". They put their hypothesis to work and offer a unified framework for classifying user activities and contributions. This comprises three types of user participation: (a) direct user participation, (b) indirect user participation, and (c) accessory user participation.

The role of users in the era of the Internet is also dealt with in Boelhouwer, Dykstra, and Sijens' "Dictionary portals" (Chapter 46). They analyze Engelberg and Müller-Spitzer's (2013) typology of dictionary portals and comment on the results of a survey that has been conducted in the context of the European Network of e-Lexicography. The analysis of the results shows the main characteristics of the three types of dictionary portals identified so far: (a) dictionary nets, (b) dictionary search engines, and (c) dictionary collections. They finish their contribution by offering several proposals for making dictionary portals more useful for users. These are basically related to augmenting search systems and facilitating search in context.

The last chapter is a desideratum for the future of lexicography. Hartmann's "Towards an international directory of lexicography" (Chapter 47) shows the necessity of having a directory of lexicography where lexicographers, researchers, and publishing houses have access to lexicographers' names and addresses, lexicographic resources (e.g. journals), lexicographic institutions, research centres, publishers, conferences, and so on. I totally agree with Hartmann's view and therefore end this introduction by reproducing his main thesis: the time has come for a directory where all relevant and not-so-relevant lexicographic issues and matters are easily found.

References

Dictionaries

OALD = Hornby, A. S. (1948) *Oxford Advanced Learners Dictionary*. Oxford: Oxford University Press.

DUE = Moliner, María (1966) *Diccionario de uso del español*. Madrid: Gredos.

OWID: www.owid.de

VerbNet: https://verbs.colorado.edu/verb-index/

Wikipedia: www.wikipedia.org

Wiktionary: https://en.wiktionary.org/wiki/Wiktionary:Main_Page

WordNet: https://wordnet.princeton.edu

Other literature

Atkins, B.T.S. and M. Rundell (2008) *A Practical Guide to Lexicography*. Oxford: Oxford University Press.

Bergenholtz, H. (2003) "User-Oriented Understanding of Descriptive, Proscriptive and Prescriptive Lexicography", *Lexikos* 13: 65–80.

Bergenholtz, H. and S. Tarp (2003) "Two Opposing theories: On H.E. Wiegand's Recent Discovery of Dictionary Functions", *Hermes. Journal of Linguistics* 31: 171–196.

Buhr, M. and G. Klaus (eds.) (1971) *Philosophisches Wörterbuch: Band 1 and 2*. Berlin: Das europäische Buch.

Considine, J. (ed.) (2010) *Current Projects in Historical Lexicography*. Newcastle: Cambridge Scholars.

Engelberg, J. and C. Müller-Spitzer (2013) "Dictionary Portals", in R. H. Gouws, U. Heid, W. Schweickard and H. E. Wiegand (eds.), *Dictionaries: An International Encyclopedia of Lexicography*. Berlin: de Gruyter Mouton, pp. 1023–1035.

Fuertes-Olivera, P. A. (2016) "A Cambrian Explosion in Lexicography: Some Reflections for Designing and Constructing Specialised Online Dictionaries", *International Journal of Lexicography* 29 (2): 226–247.

Fuertes-Olivera, P. A. and P. Leroyer (2014) "User-Generated Exploratory Search Routes: ENCONTRAR UN TÉRMINO in the Accounting Dictionaries", in Josef Ruppenhoffer and Gertrud Faaß (eds.), *Proceedings of the 12th Edition of the Konvens Conference*. Hildesheim: University of Hildesheim, pp. 86–95. See at http://opus.bsz-bw.de/ubhi/volltexte/2014/289/pdf/konvens_proceedings.pdf [Last accessed 30 January 2017]

Fuertes-Olivera, P. A. and S. Tarp (2014) *Theory and Practice of Specialised Online Dictionaries: Lexicography Versus Terminography*. Berlin/Boston: de Gruyter.

Hanks, P. (2016) "Definitions", in Philip Durkin (ed.), *The Oxford Handbook of Lexicography*. Oxford: Oxford University Press, pp. 94–122.

Hoey, M. (2005) *Lexical Priming: A New Theory of Words and Language*. London: Routledge.

Linked Open Data. www.w3.org/wiki/SweoIG/TaskForces/CommunityProjects/LinkingOpenData

Malkiel, Y. (1962) "A Typological Classification of Dictionaries on the Basis of Distinctive Features", in F.W. Householder and Sol Saporta (eds.), *Problems in Lexicography*. Bloomington: Indiana University Press, pp. 3–24.

Mel'čuk, I. (1992) "Lexicon. An overview", in W. Bright (ed.), *International Encyclopaedia of Linguistics*. Oxford: Pergamon, pp. 332–334.

Tarp, S. (2008) *Lexicography in the Borderland Between Knowledge and Non-Knowledge*. Tübingen: Niemeyer.

Tarp, S. and P. A. Fuertes-Olivera (2016) "Advantages and Disadvantages in the Use of Internet as a Corpus: The Case of the Online Dictionaries of Spanish Valladolid-UVa", *Lexikos* 26: 273–295.

Part I

Foundations of lexicography

1

Lexicography as an independent science

Sven Tarp

1.1 Introduction

Lexicography is the discipline that deals with dictionaries and other reference works designed to be consulted in order to retrieve information. Although there is general agreement in the community about this short definition, much more controversial is the disciplinary status of lexicography. This is not surprising in a discipline based on a millenary cultural practice which has created works of very different types and covering almost all spheres of human activity and thinking. Hence, if we take the two words included in the title of this contribution (i.e. independent and science), the different opinions on whether or not lexicography can be regarded as independent (in relation to other disciplines) and a science can, roughly speaking, be divided into four big groups with no sharp dividing lines and much overlapping.

Lexicographers belonging to the first group simply consider their discipline to be "art and craft" (Landau 2001). They do not only deny that lexicography can be regarded as a science, they even reject the existence and possibility of lexicographical theories (Béjoint 2010). The only theories accepted are "an enormous body of linguistic theory which has the potential to help lexicographers to do their jobs more effectively" (Atkins and Rundell 2008: 4). In this understanding, the discipline is not independent but an "instance of applied linguistics" (Meier 2003: 307). At the outmost it can be considered a "scientific activity" if linguistics is "taken as a background" (Ten Hacken 2009: 399). This vision of lexicography is especially strong in the Anglo-Saxon community.

The second group characterizes lexicography as a science. Kempcke (1984: 733), for instance, defines it as "the science of the arrangement and explanation of the vocabulary in dictionaries and lexica". Similarly, Kudashev (2007: 159) regards it as "a branch of science which deals with presentation and description of lexical units of natural languages in the dictionaries". In this vision, the science of lexicography is understood, on the one hand, as a "special branch of linguistic science" (i.e. subordinated to linguistics) and, on the other hand, as "an independent discipline with its own theory, own tasks and own methods for their solution" (Sorokoletov 1982: 79). Scerba (1940) is the most renowned supporter of this vision of lexicography which has its roots in Eastern Europe and part of Asia.

The third group deems lexicography to be an independent discipline which is neither "applied linguistics" nor "a sub-discipline of linguistics" (Wiegand 2013: 29). The main figure in this group is the German researcher H. E. Wiegand who, like many other scholars, distinguishes between lexicography and metalexicography. In his view, lexicography may take the form of a "scientific practice", whereas metalexicography may be treated as a "scientific research area" which, however, does not yet fulfil all requirements, allowing it to be considered a science (Wiegand 1984, 1989, 1998). Given the many interdisciplinary relations, the scholars belonging to this group have recently started classifying "systematic metalexicography . . . as part of information science" (Wiegand 2013: 14).

The fourth group, which is mainly composed of supporters of the function theory, regards lexicography as a science with its own independent core and a big interdisciplinary vocation (Tarp 2008). This group has many characteristics common with the other groups. It shares both the view that dictionary making is "art and craft" and the view that this lexicographical practice can be transformed into a "scientific activity" when it is guided by an advanced theory (provided this theory is lexicographical). It endorses the statement that lexicography is a science and should be treated as "an independent discipline with its own theory, own tasks and own methods". In addition, and although it does not regard lexicography as a "special branch of linguistic science", it fully agrees with the idea that it "has a lot in common with information science" (Fuertes-Olivera and Tarp 2014: 30). This position is defended here.

If the scholarly literature is scrutinized, one will find a wide variety of opinions about the disciplinary status of lexicography. Wiegand (2013: 16–17), for instance, lists 40 different opinions expressed by various scholars, and the picture is not complete. Some of these opinions may fit into one of the four groups mentioned earlier, whereas others will share features with two or more of them. In this respect, it seems that a growing number of scholars tend to accept the distinction between lexicography as the practice of dictionary making and metalexicography as an area concerned with research into dictionaries as well as theory building. At the same time, there is a certain tendency to perceive this area as autonomous in its relation to linguistics.

Lew (2007: 212), for instance, understands metalexicography as the "theoretical foundation to lexicographic practice" and argues that "although undoubtedly new developments in linguistics bear some relevance to dictionary-making, metalexicography is less and less likely for the latter to be seen as just a part of linguistics, as it grows, branches out, and specializes". The same idea was expressed with other words by Zgusta (1992/93: 137) who wrote that "what is called the theory of lexicography is not something opposed to lexicographic practice, nor is it an endeavor that largely coincides with linguistics (theoretical or otherwise)".

At first glance, the wide variety of different and partially overlapping opinions observed may seem confusing. They can nonetheless be explained by the authors' different approaches to the existing empirical reality as well as their use of different concepts of science and theory. These two questions will be discussed in the following sections.

1.2 Core issues and topics

1.2.1 Empirical reality

Al-Kasimi (1977: 1) rightly observes that the "major motives behind the rise of lexicography differ from one culture to another" and that each culture therefore develops "dictionaries appropriate to its characteristic demands". To this can be added that dictionaries produced within each culture and historical period also vary widely in terms of their type, content and underpinning technology. During the centuries, these works have been produced with different techniques and made available on various platforms of very different natures, most recently on the Internet. They have covered hundreds of languages and most spheres of human activity and knowledge. Dictionaries are compiled with a huge variety of purposes. They transmit knowledge between generations and within each generation. They help people to communicate in their mother tongue and among language communities. They assist their users with advice and instructions in order to perform various types of actions. In this perspective, dictionaries play an important role in our cultural development (see Tarp 2010).

This rich cultural heritage cannot be reduced to some sort of applied linguistics. There *are* many lexicographical works where knowledge of linguistics has been requisite, but there *are also* many others where no such knowledge has been needed. The definitions in the *Oxford Dictionary of Economics*, for instance, are not based on linguistic theories but on expert knowledge of modern economics as explained by Hashimzade, Myles and Myles (2014), two of them authors of this dictionary. Besides, it should not be ignored that a modern e-dictionary project presupposes interdisciplinary teamwork and collaboration between experts with different types of knowledge and skills, above all lexicographical knowledge and skills, domain-specific knowledge, language and programming skills as well as knowledge about databases, Internet design, project management and finance.

Hence, in order to be based on healthy grounds, the discussion on lexicography's disciplinary status should first of all take its point of departure in the indicated empirical reality in its totality and not in any of its single component parts, for example, specific types of dictionaries or specific activities related to the production, presentation, usage and criticism of these works. If this is done, the existing empirical reality allows for the following three central statements to be formulated:

1 Lexicography is not a sub-discipline of linguistics or an instance of applied linguistics because there are thousands of dictionaries where knowledge of linguistics has not been requisite;
2 Lexicography is not a sub-discipline of any of the other disciplines with which it interacts because none of these disciplines have been relevant to all dictionaries produced;
3 Lexicography is characterized by a big interdisciplinary vocation and collaboration.

The idea that lexicography should be understood as subordinated to linguistics may be explained by a selective and partial approach to the empirical reality. If the concept of dictionary, for instance, is limited to dictionaries where linguistic knowledge is required, and if other types of dictionaries are excluded *a priori*, then the conclusions will necessarily be biased. It is thus a *sine qua non* that all types of dictionaries are taken into account in order to reach empirically grounded conclusions of scientific relevance.

The fact that the thousands of works published during the centuries can all be classified as dictionaries indicates that there must be something that unites them in spite of their big differences. This something cannot be any of the many disciplines with which lexicography interacts. If an abstraction is made from the specific content of all the elements and aspects taken from these disciplines, what remains is nothing but pure lexicography. In this perspective, lexicography can be characterized as a discipline in its own right, the core of which comprises the uniting elements and aspects that are common to all lexicographical products and not the ones separating them. The most important of these commonalities are:

1 Dictionaries are utility tools produced in order to satisfy human needs.
2 The category of needs to be satisfied by dictionaries are needs for punctual information.
3 The nature of the information needs depends first of all on the social situation where they occur as well as on the characteristics of the person experiencing them.
4 Dictionaries are designed to be consulted, not to be read from one end to another.
5 Dictionaries do not directly solve information needs, but provide access to carefully prepared data from which their users can retrieve the required information.
6 The retrieved information can then be used to solve the original need in the situation where it occurred.

These six axiomatic statements, based on observation of the empirical reality, express the main commonalities of all lexicographical products and are, at the same time, the fundamental statements underpinning the lexicographical function theory.

1.2.3 Subject matter (preliminary)

Another argument in favour of the independent nature of lexicography is its subject matter which differs completely from that of linguistics. The subject matter of linguistics is language, which is a natural phenomenon rooted in human genes and stimulated by social life, and without which *Homo sapiens* would not be *Homo sapiens*. By contrast, the subject matter of lexicography is dictionaries and other lexicographical reference works, that is, cultural products or artefacts produced by human beings in order to resolve specific types of information needs detected in society.

No other discipline shares this same subject matter. However, there is another discipline, information science, which also focuses on information and information systems, and with which lexicography would benefit from a much closer collaboration. This affinity has also been highlighted by a researcher from the field of information science:

> It is evident that there are a number of commonalities between information science and lexicography and a number of researchers have pointed this out in the recent past. This could imply that information science can learn from lexicography at the level of theory and practice, and vice versa. Obviously, however, these commonalities are not evident in all sub-disciplines of information science and of lexicography. In both cases, the eventual use of the data by end-users is the reason why the data is organized, in both cases the data are retrieved by end-users and in both cases, especially currently, e-technologies, that is, modern information and communication technologies, play an important role in how the data are organized and how they are retrieved. Both disciplines have used computers since their popularization in the 1980s to organize and retrieve data/information, in both cases moving from originally paper-based systems to digital systems, in both cases using database systems for organizing the data and search algorithms for retrieving the data.
>
> (Bothma 2015: 22)

Against this background, it seems reasonable to categorize lexicography as a discipline in its own right which, simultaneously, constitutes a special branch of information science, a branch that developed independently and produced marvellous works hundreds of years before information science came into the world in the first half of the twentieth century. Even then, the two disciplines "developed along parallel lines but with no or very little formal relation between them" until the first decade of the twenty-first century when a group of researchers from both disciplines started exploring the many similarities (see Bothma and Tarp 2012: 82).

1.2.4 Lexicographical theory

Theory is a central element in all philosophical definitions of science and will therefore briefly be treated in this section. In this respect, the scholarly literature on lexicography is full of references to general and specific theories, of which some are widely known among members of the lexicographical community. Here we will just mention a few: *Outline of a General Theory of Lexicography* (Scerba 1940); *General Theory of Lexicography* (Wiegand 1998); *Function Theory of Lexicography* (Bergenholtz and Tarp 2002, 2003); *Theory of Bilingual Lexicography* (Duda et al. 1986); *Theory of the Lexicographical Example* (Hausmann 1985); and *Theory of the Dictionary Form* (Wiegand and Morán 2009).

Bogaards (2010), the former editor of the *International Journal of Lexicography*, also confirms that many authors refer to theory in contributions published in this journal. With this in mind, it is surprising that a number of scholars deny not only the existence, but also the possibility, of a theory of lexicography. It is one thing to disagree with other scholars' theories, but a completely different thing to claim that they do not exist. Disagreements are absolutely normal and even welcome within the framework of a healthy academic discussion culture. It is perfectly legal to say that 'their theories are not my theories'. Denialism, however, is of another nature and can only be explained by the fact that different scholars refer to different concepts of theory.

In order to avoid unnecessary misunderstanding, the following discussion will thus be based on a widely accepted concept of theory taken from an encyclopaedic dictionary of philosophy. Ongoing from this concept, a theory is defined as a systematically organized set of statements about an area of objective reality or consciousness, that is, *logical structures reflecting the fact that certain things have certain properties, or that certain relationships exist between these things* (see Buhr and Klaus 1971: 155, 1083). Accordingly, the concept of *lexicographical theory* can be defined as "a systematically organized set of statements about dictionaries and their relationship with specific types of social need" (Tarp 2008: 9).

Although various lexicographers sustain that a theory of lexicography is not possible, only a few of them have tried to argue in favour of this position. One of them is Béjoint (2010: 381), who writes:

> A science has a theory, a craft does not. All natural phenomena need a theory, but how can there be a theory of the production of artefacts? There are theories of language, there may be theories of lexicology, but there is no theory of lexicography. Lexicography is about all a craft, the craft of preparing dictionaries, as well as an art.

These statements raise a number of relevant questions. As indicated earlier, the practical production of dictionaries is neither a science nor a theory but a millenarian cultural practice that can certainly be defined as a craft. However, this does not exclude that the craft of dictionary making – together with the needs giving rise to it, the resulting artefacts and the use made of these – can be subjected to observation, empirical studies and theoretical generalizations. In this sense, it is perfectly possible 1) to *observe and study* this craft in all its dimensions; 2) to isolate relevant *phenomena with certain properties*; 3) to establish the *relationships* existing between them; 4) to make *statements* about these phenomena and relationships; and 5) to *systematize* these statements. If this process is carried through, it will end up with a set of systematically organized statements which constitutes *a coherent theory of lexicography* in accordance with the concept of theory defined earlier (Tarp (2012: 326).

From this perspective, Béjoint's understanding of the question of theory and practice also goes against the position taken by many researchers from outside the Anglo-Saxon tradition. One such example is Yong and Peng (2008: 5) who, in a study on the history of Chinese lexicography, criticize the previous research in this field for being "purely linguistic" and stress the need for developing lexicographical theories:

> It is frequently apparent in their research that more emphasis is laid on the parts than on the whole, that more attention is paid to the isolated analysis of cases than to *theoretical generalizations*, and that more consideration is given to accumulation of practical experiences than to formulation of *lexicographical theories*.

Another objection to the possibility of formulating lexicographical theories is related to the principle of falsification. Among the few scholars who have raised this question are Farø and Gotlieb (2007) and Bogaards (2010). The latter, for instance, rejects that the lexicographical function theory can be considered a theory with the argument that it "lacks any form of empirically verifiable or falsifiable hypotheses" (Bogaards 2010: 316).

There is no doubt that falsification is an essential method within many disciplines where it is used to validate theories and make progress. However, the idea that each and every theory should be falsifiable links to a tradition that largely reduces the scope of science to natural phenomena and excludes many other phenomena from the world of science. Within social disciplines, for instance, there are many theories built on practice-based evidence. Such theories are indispensable in order to understand practice and take these disciplines forward even though they cannot be falsified with the same rigid criteria as theories concerning natural phenomena (see Bergenholtz, Bergenholtz and Tarp (2008).

In this respect, Fuertes-Olivera and Tarp (2014: 41) conclude:

> The idea that social sciences and humanities should be subjected to the same criteria as natural sciences is basically a reductionist one that does not take into account the special characteristics of these disciplines, reducing everything to natural phenomena. This reductionist view of science is in no way helpful for the development of lexicography.

The principle of falsification is closely related to the Popperian tradition, but the way in which it is introduced into lexicography by Farø and Gotlieb (2007) and Bogaards (2010) is not loyal to this tradition. Popper himself did not regard falsification as a method to judge whether or not a set of statements could qualify as a theory. On the contrary, he introduced the method as a means to distinguish between what he called scientific and unscientific theories. He never claimed that unfalsifiable theories should be disregarded as theories and that they were necessarily incorrect:

> Thus the problem which I tried to solve by proposing the criterion of falsifiability was neither a problem of meaningfulness or significance, nor a problem of truth or

> acceptability. It was a problem of drawing the line (as well as it can be done) between statements, or systems of statements, of the empirical sciences, and all other statements . . . The criterion of falsifiability is a solution to this problem of demarcation because it says that statements or systems of statements, in order to be ranked as scientific, must be capable of conflicting with possible, or conceivable, observations.
>
> (Popper 1963: 38)

It is a matter of course that the dismissal of falsification as a relevant method to evaluate lexicographical theories does not imply that the value and relevance of these theories should be left without being tested. On this matter, the evaluation criterion is, above all, *lexicographical practice* in its three main dimensions, namely the product, its production and quality: Is it possible to produce dictionaries with the foreseen characteristics, to reduce the time and resources employed and to raise their quality in terms of functionality and user satisfaction when guided by a specific theory? The two first questions can easily be answered by observation and simple measuring, whereas the third involves time-consuming qualitative methods (Fuertes-Olivera and Tarp 2014: 41). This kind of evaluation is much more appropriate to lexicography than the criterion of falsification. It shows above all the value of a specific theory (i.e. to which extent it is capable of guiding lexicographical practice and taking the discipline forward).

In this respect, a distinction should be made between *contemplative* and *transformative* lexicographical theories. Theories of the first type only describe the existing lexicographical reality and are mainly, but not exclusively, connected with the study of old dictionaries. By contrast, theories of the second type are formulated in such a way that they are capable of describing existing reality and simultaneously guiding the constant transformation of the discipline and improvement of the lexicographical products. It goes without saying that it is only transformative lexicographical theories that can be evaluated in lexicographical practice (i.e. through dictionary-making inspired by these theories). Transformative theories are the ones taking lexicography forward.

To summarize, lexicographical theories, which are based on the previously introduced concept of theory, *can exist* and *do exist* even if they are not falsifiable. Whether or not lexicographers will deem the existing theories to be scientific or unscientific depends on the concept of science which will be discussed in the next section.

1.2.5 Science of lexicography

Three of the four groups of opinion roughly sketched out in the beginning of this contribution view lexicography as an independent discipline, although two of them connect it to information science and one to linguistics. The same three groups accept the existence of lexicographical theories, whereas only two of them deem lexicography to be a science. The diverging opinions about lexicography's relation to other disciplines were explained by different approaches to the empirical reality, and those concerning the existence of lexicographical theories were related to different concepts of theory. Something similar holds true for lexicography's status as a science. In this case, the two divergent opinions are related to three different concepts of science.

The first of the two groups rejecting lexicography's status as a science is strongly embedded in an Anglo-Saxon academic tradition according to which science is only related to natural phenomena, whereas other phenomena are referred to the sphere of art and craft, among others. This point of view is, for instance, reflected in Béjoint's (2010) line of argumentation which was quoted earlier. This tradition is opposed to traditions in other countries, for instance, in Germany where university students can study various disciplines such as *cultural science* (*Kulturwissenschaft*), *art science* (*Kunstwissenschaft*), *literature science* (*Literaturwissenschaft*) and *religious science* (*Religionswissenschaft*), all of them sciences which would not be regarded as such if the underlying concept of science was the previous one.

The second group rejecting lexicography's status as a science is represented by Wiegand (1989, 1998). This group refers to a concept of science formulated by Posner (1988) and holds that lexicography does not yet fulfil 2 of 15 criteria which are required in order to be classified as a science in keeping with this concept. One of these criteria is the one discussed earlier, namely that "there is no consistent metalexicographical theory which is available in a falsifiable form and explains a large coherent part of the subject area" (Wiegand (1989: 261). The used concept of science links to a tradition according to which there is only one science divided into countless disciplines. This view also implies that many sciences taught at German and other universities cannot be regarded as such (Wiegand 1998). In this context, it should be added that the absence of falsification does not prevent Wiegand and other researchers from formulating lexicographical theories, thus being much more consequent in this respect than Farø and Gotlieb (2007) and Bogaards (2010).

By contrast, the two groups that deem lexicography to be a science ground their judgment on the same fundamental concept of science, but different from that of Posner. This concept can be summarized in the following way:

> A science is a system of knowledge growing out of social practice and developing on an ongoing basis, comprising the recognition of the most important properties, causal relationships and regularities of nature, society and philosophy; rooted in the form of concepts, categories, defined goals, laws, theories and hypotheses, and constituting the basis of Man's growing mastery of his natural and social environment. A science also consists of its own history, pre-theoretical ideas, contributions to methodology, directions for practical action etc.
>
> (see Buhr and Klaus 1971: 1083, 1169)

If this concept of science is taken as the basis and related to modern lexicographical research, it can easily be resolved that this discipline meets all requirements to be classified as a science (see Tarp 2008: 6):

1 It constitutes a system of knowledge growing out of social practice (i.e. the production and usage of dictionaries).
2 It is developing on an ongoing basis.
3 It is rooted in the form of concepts, categories, defined goals, theories and hypotheses.
4 It comprises both the history of dictionaries and its own history, including pre-theoretical ideas.
5 It contains independent contributions to methodology.
6 It includes directions for practical action.

In addition to these statements, it should not be forgotten that lexicography has its own singular subject matter, namely dictionaries. In this perspective, lexicography has undoubtedly all the characteristics of an independent science.

1.2.6 Subject matter (extended)

It is frequently claimed that lexicography is the discipline that deals with the theory and practice of dictionaries. The statement is not false, but neither is it complete as it does not cover the whole discipline which, in conformity with the concept of science introduced earlier, also comprises other elements than theory and practice. Something similar can be said about the frequent distinction between lexicography as a practice and metalexicography as a research area: Which component parts does metalexicography contain? What is the subject matter of metalexicographical research? What is meant by lexicographical practice? And how is the overall field of lexicography delimited in this respect?

Previously, the subject matter of lexicography was defined as dictionaries. This requires further specification. It is true that dictionaries make up the central focus area of lexicography. However, apart from these artefacts themselves, the subject matter also includes their planning, production, design and usage, as well as their close relationships with specific types of social need, namely punctual information needs.

In this regard, it is possible to identify three different areas that can be subjected to separate lexicographical studies. The first is the artefact itself (i.e. the dictionary), which can be studied exclusively in terms of its formal aspects such as structure, layout, accessibility, etc. (see for instance Wiegand and Morán 2009). The second area is the relationships between the artefact, on the one hand, and the needs it is supposed to solve and its usefulness in this regard, on the other hand, that is, its relationships with the potential and factual users (see for instance Tarp 2008). The third area of study is the activities related to the conception, planning, compilation, presentation and updating of the artefact (see for instance Atkins and Rundell 2008).

The information needs detected in society are the starting point for all lexicographical work, and they will therefore also be the starting point for the following discussion. In this respect, Bergenholtz, Bothma and Gouws (2015: 20) have proposed a model representing the various phases and steps in the overall information-search process. In a condensed version, this process encompasses the appearance of information needs in society, the decision to look for assistance, the selection and consultation of an information source, the retrieval of information and the subsequent use made of the retrieved information in order to solve the original needs.

As it is presented here, the information-search process is not a lexicographical one; nor are the activities carried out in connection with the process lexicographical activities. It is a process that took place millions of times before the first dictionary was ever produced, and it is a process that takes place millions of times each and every day without the information source being a dictionary or any other type of lexicographical work. From this perspective, the process is part of the general subject matter of information science. However, in some cases the nature of the information needs giving rise to the whole process allows for these to be solved by consulting a dictionary or another lexicographical information tool. In these cases, the process becomes lexicographically relevant and may therefore be subjected to studies in the framework of the science of lexicography and included in the subject matter of this discipline.

However, this does not imply that the different activities carried out in connection with the lexicographical information-search process can be regarded as lexicographical activities. The reading of a book, which is a typical situation where information needs may occur, is, for instance, not a lexicographical activity even though it is highly lexicographically relevant. And neither is the use of an equivalent in order to accomplish a translation task a lexicographical activity. The same holds true for dictionary consultation which is an absolutely essential part of the millenarian cultural practice related to lexicography and therefore also a central research area; but it is still not part of the discipline in the narrow sense of the word, among other things, because it does not presuppose any knowledge of lexicography whatsoever. The terms 'lexicographical practice' and 'scientific activity' are absurd in this context, also when potential users are trained in order to improve and speed up their search for information.

By contrast, all activities carried out in direct connection with the production of a dictionary are lexicographical activities, although to a different extent. These activities have a specific lexicographical goal, namely the creation of a dictionary with well-defined characteristics, and can be divided into two groups.

The first group encompasses the conception, compilation, presentation and updating of the dictionary as well as the composition of the empirical basis (Tarp 2014). All these activities require an interdisciplinary combination of lexicographical knowledge and domain-specific knowledge (i.e. knowledge of the subject-field or language treated in the dictionary). These activities are directly materialized in the final product, and they are also the ones that are most frequently discussed in the scholarly literature.

Apart from that, there is another group of lexicographical activities which are not directly materialized in the dictionary, although they are absolutely necessary for achieving a good result in terms of the production process as well as the final product. These activities are related to the necessary technological support and the overall management of lexicographical projects (see Chapter 2 of this *Handbook*). Apart from knowledge of lexicography, these central activities require, on the one hand, knowledge of databases, user interfaces and programming, and on the other hand, knowledge of project management including finances, work plans, team building and training of lexicographers. These activities, which presuppose interdisciplinary knowledge, are crucial to the success of any modern dictionary project, and it is therefore surprising how scarcely they have been represented in the lexicographical literature. Among the relative few contributions treating these questions are Fuertes-Olivera and Bergenholtz (2015), Tarp (2015) and Grundy and Rawlinson (2016). This lack of interest may be explained by the strong linguistic approach which many lexicographers have to their discipline.

1.2.7 Lexicographical research

Lexicographical research is frequently referred to as metalexicography or theoretical lexicography, although the latter, as already mentioned, is somewhat misleading as research comprises much more than the formulation of theories. In the scholarly literature there is a certain tradition of dividing dictionary-related research into several areas. Wiegand (1989), for instance, divides metalexicography into four main types of research, namely 1) systematic dictionary research, 2) historical dictionary research, 3) dictionary criticism and 4) research into dictionary usage. This typology may be relevant for certain purposes, but it is not unproblematic. Tarp (2017), for instance, has shown how dictionary criticism encroaches strongly on the three other research areas as they are defined by Wiegand. Even more problematic is the separation of systematic dictionary research (which includes the formulation of theories) as a research area of its own, thus ignoring the fact that theories are also formulated in a systematic way in relation to other areas of lexicographical research.

Various criteria can be used to distinguish between research areas. One of them is the defined goal of the research, that is, the expected outcome in terms of new knowledge about a specific subject matter. In principle, this implies that lexicography as an overall research field can be subdivided in different ways and that there is no absolute truth in this regard as long as the whole subject field is covered. In this respect, five main goals can be observed, namely to provide:

1 Knowledge of the lexicographically relevant information-search process, including the needs which can be solved by dictionaries and the usage made of these;
2 Knowledge of dictionary making, including the types of decisions to be taken, the methods applied and the different activities performed during this process;
3 Knowledge of dictionaries in terms of their formal aspects such as structures, access options, functionality and underpinning technology;
4 Knowledge of the usefulness of specific and general aspects of dictionaries, that is, how these aspects contribute to the satisfaction of the needs giving rise to dictionary consultation as well as the needs related to the consultation process itself;
5 Knowledge of the history of dictionaries and lexicography in general.

The research activities carried out with the objective of achieving these five types of knowledge represent different areas of lexicographical research. Some of the activities may be common to two or more areas, but each of them can nevertheless be clearly delimited due to the fact that the activities are always performed with a specific goal in mind. Accordingly, lexicographical research can be divided into the following five research areas: 1) research into the information-search process; 2) research into dictionary making; 3) research into the dictionary form; 4) research into the usefulness of dictionaries; and 5) research into the history of lexicography. As can be observed in the existing scholarly literature, the knowledge generated within these five research areas is rooted in the form of *lexicographical concepts*, *categories*, *goals*, *hypotheses* and *theories* in accordance with Buhr and Klaus' (1971) requirements for a science.

In this respect, it is pertinent to distinguish between *genuine* and *non-genuine lexicographical research*. The first type of research is the one that is based on lexicographical theories, concepts and categories, whereas the second one is outgoing from theories, concepts and categories taken in from other disciplines. This duality has its roots in the interdisciplinarity that characterizes most lexicographical activities (see Chapter 6 of this *Handbook*). Frequently, scholars from other areas of knowledge are interested in knowing how their discipline, or aspects of it, have been reflected in dictionaries. A considerable part of the academic literature on general dictionaries has been written by researchers from the field of linguistics who look at dictionaries from the point of view of their specialty and analyze how specific linguistic categories and phenomena have been treated and presented. Ten Hacken (2009), for instance, explicitly states that he approaches lexicography and the concept of dictionary from the perspective of Chomskyan linguistics.

This phenomenon can also be observed in the literature on specialized dictionaries. Within some disciplines there is a long tradition of using dictionaries as a privileged means to transmit the most advanced knowledge to a selected audience. Hence, today many researchers study dictionaries in order to see how specific categories and phenomena related to these disciplines have been defined and how they have developed over time. Besomi (2011), for instance, contains a number of contributions by specialists in the history of economics who discuss how the concepts of "crisis" and "business circle" are defined in 650 dictionaries and encyclopaedias published during the past 300 years. Similarly, Astigarraga, Zabalza and Almodovar (2001) analyze how political economy has been treated in dictionaries compiled in the Iberian Peninsula since the eighteenth century; Guidi (1994) does the same with Italian dictionaries published until 1861.

Many other examples of this class of research could be mentioned. It contributes highly relevant knowledge about the content of dictionaries, not only in terms of the disciplines treated (economics, linguistics, etc.) but also in terms of lexicography. As such, it constitutes *a sixth area of lexicographical research* in addition to the five other ones already discussed earlier, namely research into the dictionary content. However, as this class of research is mainly conducted through the prism of other disciplines and without taking necessary account of the specific lexicographical aspects, it does not classify as a genuine lexicographical research area, but "only" as a non-genuine one.

1.3 Looking to the future

In this contribution, lexicography has been defined as an independent science with a strong interdisciplinary vocation. By independent it is understood that dictionaries have a core of aspects and elements that are common to all of them and different from those of other disciplines. This does not mean that lexicography is isolated from these other disciplines. On the contrary, it has been argued that most activities related to the production of dictionaries presuppose knowledge of both lexicography and other disciplines and that the content of dictionaries most often is based upon these disciplines. In this sense, lexicography has a strong interdisciplinary vocation (see Part 2 of this *Handbook*).

Today, lexicography is in a process of adapting to digital media. The introduction of new disruptive computer and information technologies have opened completely new horizons to this 4,000-year-old discipline (see Part 6 of this *Handbook*). It can already be observed how the relationship between user and information tool is being turned upside down. The lexicographical product is becoming still more personalized. Some of the most advanced dictionaries now offer dynamic articles with lexicographical data that are increasingly adapted to their users' specific needs. Other dictionaries are getting still more integrated into various types of digital tools, some of which are designed to alert their users when they experience information needs without being aware of it. Alternative types of data access are also seeing the light together with the option to make use of the achieved information by a simple click or movement with the mouse or a finger.

As a consequence, the new techniques are completely changing the information-search process as it is described by Bergenholtz, Bothma and Gouws (2015) and thus justifying the definition of this process as a separate area of lexicographical research. The near future will probably see a further merging of lexicography and information science. It will become increasingly clear that lexicography is not an instance of applied linguistics and that it should rather be classified as an information-science discipline with its own singular core of concepts, categories, theories, defined goals and tasks.

Related topics

The concept of dictionary; dictionary criticism; dictionaries for text production; dictionaries for text reception; dictionaries for translation; dictionaries to assist teaching and learning.

Further reading

Dictionaries. *Journal of the Dictionary Society of North America*, 14, 1992/93.

This issue of Dictionaries contains a special section where various lexicographers with different opinions discuss the question of theory in relation to their discipline. It is mainly, but not exclusively, embedded in the Anglo-Saxon tradition.

Fuertes-Olivera, P. A. and H. Bergenholtz (eds.) (2011). *e-Lexicography: The Internet, Digital Initiatives and Lexicography*. London: Continuum.
In this book, various authors discuss the transition from printed to digital media and show how new technologies are transforming lexicography. It also contains many comments on the relationship between lexicography and information science.

Sorokoletov, F. P. (1982). "Traditionen der sowjetrussischen Lexikographie", in W. Wolski (ed.), *Aspekte der sowjetrussischen Lexikographie*. Tübingen: Niemeyer, pp. 63–88.
In this contribution, Sorokoletov discusses a number of basic ideas and principles characterizing lexicography in the Soviet period, many of which are still widely referred to in this part of the world.

Tarp, S. (2008). *Lexicography in the Borderland Between Knowledge and Non-Knowledge*. Tübingen: Niemeyer.
This book provides a comprehensive introduction to the function theory of lexicography and the relationship between information needs and dictionaries. It defends the idea that lexicography is an independent science with a big interdisciplinary vocation.

Wiegand, H. E. (1984). "On the Structure and Contents of a General Theory of Lexicography", in R.R.K. Hartmann (ed.), *LEXeter '83*. Tübingen: Max Niemeyer, pp. 13–30.
In this short English article, Wiegand introduces a series of ideas concerning the theory and status of lexicography which he subsequently develops in other contributions, most of them written in German.

References

Al-Kasimi, A. M. (1977) *Linguistics and Bilingual Dictionaries*. Leyden: E. J. Brill.

Astigarraga, J., J. Zabalza and A. Almodovar (2001) "Dictionaries and Encyclopaedias on Political Economy in the Iberian Peninsula (18th, 19th and 20th Centuries)", *Storia del Pensiero Economico* 41: 25–63.

Atkins, B.T.S. and M. Rundell (2008) *The Oxford Guide to Practical Lexicography*. Oxford: Oxford University Press.

Béjoint, H. (2010) *The Lexicography of English*. Oxford: Oxford University Press.

Bergenholtz, C., H. Bergenholtz and S. Tarp (2008) "Leksikografi i Videnskabsteoretisk Perspektiv: Sand, Falsk eller Irrelevant", *LexicoNordica* 15: 155–168.

Bergenholtz, H., T.D.J. Bothma and R. H. Gouws (2015) "Phases and Steps in the Access to Data in Information Tools", *Lexikos* 25: 1–30.

Bergenholtz, H. and S. Tarp (2002) "Die moderne lexikographische Funktionslehre. Diskussionsbeitrag zu neuen und alten Paradigmen, die Wörterbücher als Gebrauchsgegenstände verstehen", *Lexicographica* 18: 253–263.

Bergenholtz, H. and S. Tarp (2003) "Two Opposing Theories: On H.E. Wiegand's Recent Discovery of Lexicographic Functions", *Hermes. Journal of Linguistics* 31: 171–196.

Besomi, D. (ed.) (2011) *Crises and Cycles in Economic Dictionaries and Encyclopaedias*. London and New York: Routledge.

Bogaards, P. (2010) "Lexicography: Science Without Theory?", in G.M.D. Schryver (ed.), *A Way With Words: Recent Advances in Lexical Theory and Analysis*. Kampala: Menha Publishers, pp. 313–322.

Bothma, T.J.D. (2015) "Reflexiones sobre la interrelación entre lexicografía y ciencia de la información: una perspectiva personal", *Estudios de Lexicografía* 4: 21–30.

Bothma, T.J.D. and S. Tarp (2012) "Lexicography and the Relevance Criterion", *Lexikos* 22: 86–108.

Buhr, M. and G. Klaus (eds.) (1971) *Philosophisches Wörterbuch: Band 1 and 2*. Berlin: Das europäische Buch.

Duda, W., M. Frenzel, E. Wöller and T. Zimmermann (1986) *Zu einer Theorie der zweisprachigen Lexikographie: Überlegungen zu einen neuen russisch-deutschen Wörterbuch*. Berlin: Akademieverlag.

Farø, K. and H. Gottlieb (2007) "Socioleksikografi – eller: 'Det sekundære og afledte er ordbøgerne'. Ny dansk disputats", *LexicoNordica* 14: 189–199.
Fuertes-Olivera, P. A. and H. Bergenholtz (eds.) (2011) *e-Lexicography: The Internet, Digital Initiatives and Lexicography*. London: Continuum.
Fuertes-Olivera, P. A. and H. Bergenholtz (2015) "Los diccionarios en línea de español 'Universidad de Valladolid'". *Revista de Lexicografía* 4: 71–98.
Fuertes-Olivera, P. A. and S. Tarp (2014) *Theory and Practice of Specialised Online Dictionaries: Lexicography Versus Terminography*. Berlin and Boston: de Gruyter.
Grundy, V. and D. Rawlinson (2016) "The Practicalities of Dictionary Production; Planning and Managing Dictionary Projects; Training of Lexicographers", in P. Durkin (eds.), *The Oxford Handbook of Lexicography*. Oxford: Oxford University Press, pp. 561–578.
Guidi, M. L. (1994) "Economy and Political Economy in Italian Dictionaries and Encyclopedias" (1726–1861). In M. Albertone and A. Masoero (eds.), *Political Economy and National Realities*. Torino: Fondazione Luigi Einaudi, pp. 147–175.
Hashimzade, N., G. A. Myles and G. D. Myles (2014) "Can Authority Be Sustained While Balancing Accessibility and Formality?", *Hermes* 52: 11–24.
Hausmann, F. J. (1985) "Kollokationen im deutschen Wörterbuch. Ein Beitrag zur Theorie des lexikographischen Beispiels", in H. Bergenholtz and J. Mugdan (eds.), *Lexikographie und Grammatik*. Tübingen: Niemeyer, pp. 118–129.
Kempcke, G. (ed.) (1984) *Handwörterbuch der deutschen Gegenwartssprache: Band 1 and 2*. Berlin: Akademieverlag.
Kudashev, I. (2007) "Terminography vs. Lexicography Opposition Revisited", in N. Niemelä and E. Lehtinen (eds.), *Theory of Translation, LSP and Multilingualism*. Vasa: Vaasan yliopisto, pp. 157–166.
Landau, S. (2001) *Dictionaries: The Art and Craft of Lexicography*. Cambridge: Cambridge University Press.
Lew, R. (2007) "Linguistic Semantics and Lexicography: A Troubled Relationship", in M. Fabiszak (ed.), *Language and Meaning: Cognitive and Functional Perspectives*. Frankfurt am Main: Peter Lang, pp. 217–224.
Meier, H. H. (2003) "Lexicography as Applied Linguistics", in R.R.K. Hartmann (ed.), *Lexicography: Critical Concepts III*. London, New York: Routledge, pp. 307–318.
Popper, K.R.P. (1963) *Conjectures and Refutations*. London: Routledge and Kegan Paul.
Posner, R. (1988) "What Is an Academic Discipline?", in R. Claussen and R. Daube-Schackat (eds.), *Gedankenzeichen: Festschrift für Klaus Oehler zum 60. Geburtstag*. Tübingen: Stauffenburg Verlag, pp. 165–185.
Scerba, L. V. (1940) "Towards a General Theory of Lexicography", *International Journal of Lexicography* 8 (4) 1995: 315–350.
Sorokoletov, F. P. (1982) "Traditionen der sowjetrussischen Lexikographie", in W. Wolski (ed.), *Aspekte der sowjetrussischen Lexikographie*. Tübingen: Niemeyer, pp. 63–88.
Tarp, S. (2008) *Lexicography in the Borderland between Knowledge and Non-Knowledge*. Tübingen: Niemeyer.
Tarp, S. (2010) "Reflections on the Academic Status of Lexicography", *Lexikos* 20: 450–465.
Tarp, S. (2012) "Do We Need a (New) Theory of Lexicography?", *Lexikos* 22: 321–332.
Tarp, S. (2014) "Theory-Based Methods in a Functional Perspective: An Overview", *Lexicographica* 30: 58–76.
Tarp, S. (2015) "Structures in the Communication Between Lexicographer and Programmer: Database and Interface", *Lexicographica* 31: 217–246.
Tarp, S. (2017) "Dictionary Criticism and Lexicographical Function Theory", in M. Bielińska and S. J. Schierholz (eds.), *Wörterbuchkritik. Dictionary Criticism*. Berlin, Boston: De Gruyter.
Ten Hacken, P. (2009) "What Is a Dictionary? A View From Chomskyan Linguistics", *International Journal of Lexicography* 22(4): 399–421.

Wiegand, H. E. (1984) "On the Structure and Contents of a General Theory of Lexicography", in R.R.K. Hartmann (ed.), *LEXeter '83*. Tübingen: Max Niemeyer, pp. 13–30.

Wiegand, H. E. (1989) "Der gegenwärtige Status des Lexikographie und ihr Verhältnis zu anderen Disziplinen", in F. J. Hausmann, O. Reichmann, H. E. Wiegand and L. Zgusta (eds.), *Wörterbücher. Ein internationales Handbuch zur Lexikographie*. Berlin, New York: Walter de Gruyter, pp. 246–280.

Wiegand, H. E. (1998) *Wörterbuchforschung. Untersuchungen zur Wörterbuchbenutzung, zur Theorie, Geschichte, Kritik und Automatisierung der Lexikographie. 1. Teilband*. Berlin, New York: Walter de Gruyter.

Wiegand, H. E. (2013) "Lexikographie und Angewandte Linguistik", *Zeitschrift für angewandte Linguistik* 58(1): 13–39.

Wiegand, H. E. and M.T.F. Morán (2009) *Estructuras Lexicográficas: Aspectos Centrales de una Teoría de la Forma del Diccionario*. Granada: Tragacanto.

Yong, H. and J. Peng (2008) *Chinese Lexicography: A History From 1046 BC to AD 1911*. Oxford: Oxford University Press.

Zgusta, L. (1992/93) "Lexicography, Its Theory, and Linguistics', *Dictionaries* 14: 130–138.

2 Dictionary management

Henning Bergenholtz

2.1 Introduction

Managing a dictionary project is not an easy task. It is often quoted that only 25 percent of all lexicographic projects are finished with the presentation of a dictionary. And even worse, the finished dictionaries were not finished on time but took, on average, four times longer than planned. We have never seen any kind of documentation for this assertion. But looking at the many failed dictionary projects, it seems likely that we have a big scope of mismanagement in practical lexicography. If the assertion is correct, lexicographers should learn to avoid wasting time and money, e.g. by asking themselves if they can and should learn from management theories. Management theories highlight the fact that management of a project is of considerable economic importance (see e.g. Winter et al. (2006) and Svejvik and Andersen (2015: 278)).

2.2 Historical perspective: project management

It is easy to find short courses in management where the provider promises insight into the main management problems. You can also buy access to many professional presentations from world-leading management experts, for example, Stalks (2016). In this independent study, the subject is general management problems about, for example, risk management, team diversity, building a brand and corporate governance, with examples from big companies like Lego, Vodafone, Carlsberg, Kodak and Continental. It is not likely that such topics and such examples are always relevant for specific projects from all kinds of fields or in the same way for small and big projects. Each project is a time-constrained process designed to produce a unique product, and it is in contrast to business-as-usual actions. A project can run from a few weeks to a few years. It must never last more than 100 years, as some projects of national dictionaries usually do. For each project there is, or should be, a project management plan with at least a target, a concept, a timetable with milestones, the delegation of tasks, risk management and a deadline. This management plan is created (in cooperation with other project members), executed and controlled by the project manager. In the ideal case, the project manager is an expert in the field of project management and at the same time an expert in the content of the project. The different management contributions focus on the need of a professional from the field of management who is not an expert in the project content.

Many short recommendations with brief guidelines for project planning have been written. The following is a quote from a typical example written by an engineering company: CWP (2016). This private company describes ten steps to follow in order to create and control a good project plan:

1 Define the project goals.
2 Make a customer analysis.
3 Make a timetable with milestones.
4 Make a cost calculation.
5 Make a risk analysis.
6 Convince the main participants.
7 Publish the project plan.
8 Make a running quality and quantity control.
9 Revise the project plan – if needed.
10 Close the project.

To a lexicographer, this sounds convincing, but much too general. These guidelines do not mention any project manager though this person seems to be the recipient, cf. the use of the pronoun "you" in "so you construct and control a project plan" CWP (2016). Most lexicographers do not talk about a dictionary project manager; instead, they call this person editor-in-chief or dictionary director. The main question for a lexicographer, especially the dictionary manager, must be the following: Do we really need to be an expert or a semi-expert in management in addition to having expert knowledge of lexicography, the subject field, the language, knowledge about the language and economy planning? In the following, I will discuss these questions in connection with two recent dictionary projects.

2.3 Core issues and topics

2.3.1 Dictionary planning and making

Recent contributions about management of dictionary projects do not use the term *dictionary management*, but normally speak about dictionary planning and dictionary making (there is one exception, to which I will refer briefly in the next paragraph). There is a vast amount of contributions to the topic in many reports about ongoing or finished dictionary projects. Such contributions are much too specific and do not discuss the main management problems in a general way. More relevant are chapters about dictionary planning in lexicographical handbooks, but here we do not find any references to general project management theories as referred to in the first chapter.

The exception is Grundy and Rawlinson (2016: 562–563), with the promising title "Developments in Dictionary Project Management" given to section 2 of their contribution to the *Oxford Handbook of Lexicography*. This contribution mentions many of the relevant management problems, but in a very unsystematic way without any reference to general management theories. The authors begin their contribution with a key problem in dictionary management: "Time was, when the chief editor of a dictionary project presided, largely single-handedly, over the entire management of the project in hand" (Grundy and Rawlinson

2016: 562). Their main argument is that this situation has changed radically to a new ideal where the editor-in-chief should not use his time on the dictionary "content-neutral aspect of the project management" (Grundy and Rawlinson 2016: 562) but should leave this to experts in business administration and experts in computational tools and instead concentrate on the quality of the dictionaries (Grundy and Rawlinson 2016: 563). This standpoint is the complete opposite of the main thesis in this contribution: the editor-in-chief does not make every detailed decision and does not write the IT program, she or he does not make the salary calculations, etc., but she or he has to be the decision maker in the general planning and all the work phases – in some cases, this person has to overrule proposals from the business and IT experts if these proposals do not fit into the overall lexicographic concept. This reflects the ideal management policy, although, as has been shown, not all scholars share this opinion.

First of all it is important to focus on the starting point: Who came up with the idea to create this dictionary project? And is this person the one who should make the general decisions in the planning phase? There is no focus on that topic in most lexicographical handbooks. Meyer and Gurevych (2014) is an exception in their methodical discussion about collaborative dictionaries (dictionaries produced mainly through user contributions; see Chapters 29 and 45 of this *Handbook*). But as not all possible contributors can and will take part in the planning phase, the real difference between collaborative, semi-collaborative and noncollaborative dictionary projects does not exist. In all cases, you gather a group of lexicographers who discuss the planning. Is it necessary to have a project manager to make the last decisions, or are they made after a democratic voting? Meyer and Gurevych (2014: 191) claim that a general consensus between the group of lexicographers must take place before the lexicographical instructions can be written, but in special controversial cases, they demand an intensive discussion followed by a democratic vote. This sounds appealing, as democracy is a general demand for a better functioning society. However, it should be questioned whether this is a practical method in all projects. A dictionary project needs a clear conception from the very beginning. And it also requires a consistent use of the lexicographic instructions when the lexicographers involved place data in the different data fields. In particular we have to warn against fundamental changes in the instructions during a running project. Such instructions should have as a main rule that new instructions or changes in the instructions are possible, but on one condition: no finished dictionary article should need to be changed after such a change or addition. (Bergenholtz 1990)

In other words, this contribution argues for a planning and working phase with one main decision taker, a project manager, who should be a lexicographer, not, like Atkins and Rundell, who claim that publishers are the final decision makers:

> During this pre-lexicography stage, the decision-making process typically involves a dialogue between publisher and senior editor. The editor may have plenty of ideas about what she or he would like to do, but the final say rests with the publisher, who holds the purse string.
>
> (Atkins and Rundell 2008: 18)

I do not doubt that this happens, but it only happens rarely, although it should never happen. If the senior lexicographer, the project manager, from the very beginning gives away his influence, he is not the project manager anymore and cannot be the main lexicographer in a project that aims to produce an information tool for certain users with certain needs. Of course, we know about many poor dictionaries selling well and about high-quality dictionaries with low sales, but as a seriously working lexicographer, you cannot argue like that. You should try to produce a high-quality dictionary selling well by starting with an analysis of the dictionary functions and following that line throughout the whole process. Most commercial (not all dictionaries are commercial) dictionary projects start in another way; they begin with the concept and some first-test dictionary articles, which the lexicographer presents to a publisher, asking if he is interested in being the publisher of this dictionary. It happens that the following sequence of events takes place by the birth of a new dictionary, but this happens seldom and is not to be recommended:

1 The marketing department spots a 'gap' in the booksellers' shelves.
2 The marketing department specifies the type of dictionary needed.
3 The selling price and the budget are fixed.
4 The lexicographer specifies the needs of the end user; the needs of the end user determine the content of the dictionary.
5 The lexicographer writes the style guide (= lexicographic instructions).

(Atkins and Rundell 2008: 18)

Instead of this process, what we need in lexicography is a planning and working process directed by professional lexicographers. This person, of course, has to find and cooperate with a lexicographical publisher. But this senior lexicographer, the project manager, is or should be like the *chef du cuisine* (Bergenholtz and Gouws 2012), making all the important decisions – in cooperation with all the other lexicographers, IT specialists, layout/design specialists, marketing specialists, etc.

More realistic is the general overview for a dictionary project in Wiegand (1998: 135ff.). Wiegand calls the first phase the preparation phase, making a clear distinction between (1) the operational plan and (2) the development of a dictionary plan. For (1), Wiegand has a description of the following steps:

1 Financing.
2 Personal plan (number and qualifications of all persons to participate in the project).
3 Working plan (distribution of different tasks to different project participants).
4 Timetable with milestones.
5 Layout and printing plan.

Wiegand sees the layout and the printing phase as the last phase in the project. This is a natural sequence for printed dictionaries. For e-dictionaries, it is recommended to make the first draft of the user interface(s) shortly after having finished the first 50 to 100 cards in the database. This is especially important when you prepare several dictionaries extracted from the same database but with different user interfaces (dictionaries). With an early presentation of the planned user interfaces, it is possible for the involved lexicographers during the whole working phase to see how their distribution of data in the single database fields is presented to the end user.

For (2), the development of a dictionary plan, Wiegand (1998: 139) describes the following steps:

1 Development of a dictionary conception.
2 Selection of data for the empirical basis (corpus, other dictionaries, surveys, etc.).
3 Plan for the work with the empirical basis.

4 Lexicographical instructions.
5 Plan for the article structure.

However, in this description, two important steps are missing. The first one is the database development. Also in 1998, the year that Wiegand's book was published, most dictionary projects involved the use of a database in the lexicographical work. The number of database fields and the relation between them depend on the dictionary conception, but the database should be finished and ready to be used before the lexicographic instructions can be written. The most important missing step in Wiegand (1998) is the dictionary function. This is not the same as the dictionary conception, because every decision for the dictionary conception depends on the dictionary function (which information needs shall the dictionary cover and for which user group is it produced?). This topic is the starting point for every lexicographical decision: the dictionary conception; the selection of the database fields; the selection of data for the empirical basis; the selection of data for the different data fields; the presentation and sequencing of the data types in the dictionary or the dictionaries using the data in the planned database.

Despite this critique, Wiegand's discussion of dictionary planning and making is one of the most realistic discussions in the literature about dictionary management. That does not mean that his contribution can be recommended as a full first approach, as it is only written for printed dictionaries, it does not discuss the conception of a database and it does not discuss the possibility of having one database for several dictionaries. And neither does it discuss if one and the same lexicographer should write the whole dictionary article, or if the work tasks are divided between different lexicographers so that one lexicographer works with certain data fields and another one with other fields. And neither is there a discussion about a continuous learning process connected with an ongoing correction of the daily work with the database. In the following, you will find two examples of dictionary management taking some of these problems into account.

2.3.2 Examples of two dictionary projects

The first example discussed is a Danish text production dictionary started in August 1997, finished in August 1999 and published in 1999 as *DanskOrdbogen*. It is a printed dictionary with 1,175 pages. Dictionary projects carried out over a very long timespan quite often give a non-consistent result. In this case, the relatively short period of two years was only possible because of clear and strict project management and because one project manager made all the decisions after short discussions with the lexicographers involved in the project. The project was divided into related management steps:

August to December 1997

1 Choice of dictionary function (user needs and user type) leading to a first conception.
2 Financing and conception negotiations with a publisher.
3 Selection of the involved lexicographers, the IT expert and the layout designer.
4 Test dictionary articles and decision of the article structure.
5 Second and final dictionary conception.
6 Selection of fields for the database.
7 Construction of a database with 14 fields.
8 Lexicographic instructions.

9 Collection of empirical data (corpus and other dictionaries).
10 Lemma selection.
11 Distribution of work tasks to each lexicographer (which lexicographer works with which fields and in which sequence for each field type) connected to a timetable with milestones.

December 1997 to May 1999

12 Selecting of and inserting data in the data fields for each lemma.

May to August 1999

13 Proofreading.
14 Making the layout with some last proofreading corrections.
15 Printing.
16 The dictionary was delivered by the publisher to the bookshops.

If a project is planned well, and if you have found the right lexicographers, database specialists and layout designers, you can finish a project like this in two years. We were only four people working on the project: a senior lexicographer as the project manager, two lexicographers and one IT specialist, who also made the field for hyphenation items and the layout.

In this project, dictionary management included the following steps:

1 Dictionary functions and dictionary conception.
2 Business plan.
3 Timetable with milestones.
4 Making the database.
5 Dictionary making.
6 Layout and printing.

The second project example is a recent one, and it is still in progress. It is a project about monolingual general-language dictionaries produced at the University of Valladolid (Fuertes-Olivera and Bergenholtz 2015). The aim is to create seven Spanish e-dictionaries: (1) a grammar and spelling dictionary, (2) a synonym and antonym dictionary, (3) a text production dictionary, (4) a reception (meaning) dictionary, (5) a word finding dictionary (tell me the word I am looking for and want to use), (6) a dictionary of fixed expressions and (7) a comprehensive dictionary for communicative and cognitive needs (see Chapter 17 of this *Handbook*). The first six dictionaries are monofunctional (reception or text production for native speakers of Spanish), and the last one is a polyfunctional dictionary for communicative and cognitive needs of Spanish native speakers. All dictionaries are extracted from the same database; thus all the analyzed empirical data added to the database are selected and presented differently according to each of the seven dictionaries.

The project was planned and initiated with the following project phases:

January to June 2013

1 Developing the idea following the example of the similar Danish e-dictionaries.
2 Applying for research funding for the project.

3 Negotiating a contract with a company that distributes and sells e-dictionaries.
4 Selecting fields for the database, which should be able to cover the different dictionary functions of the seven dictionaries.
5 Developing a database with 25 fields, that is, the construction of an editor (described in Bergenholtz and Nielsen 2013).

November to December 2013

6 Advertising for four lexicographers for the project (in the advertisement it was mentioned that the lexicographical staff would include people with different backgrounds: (1) Spanish linguistics, (2) economics, (3) science and (4) engineering (for reasons not to employ only linguists, but also experts from different fields (see Bergenholtz 2013)).
7 Selecting 12 of 92 applicants to participate in a selection test.
8 Test where the 12 applicants were introduced to the database and explained how to used it after which they were asked to write a number of test articles.
9 Final selection of four lexicographers.
10 Lemma selection (about 105,000 lemmas).
11 The lexicographers start working on the project. They receive daily feedback to their work and a monthly briefing about problematic cases with suggested solutions.

April to June 2015

12 Plan for the sequence, the kinds of searches and the presentation in each user interface (dictionary).
13 Transformation of the plan presentation in single user interfaces.

October 2017

14 The seven e-dictionaries will be available on the Internet for free.

January 2018

15 The seven e-dictionaries can be accessed by subscribers, who pay a yearly sum for the use of one or more of the dictionaries.

2.4 Conclusion

I have discussed the difference between business as usual in small or large companies and in special projects as part of a large organization or as its own organization. A specific project is normally accomplished within a few months or within a maximum of five to six years. When we talk about dictionary projects, many of these take much longer to carry out, for example, the national dictionary projects in Norway, Sweden and South Africa, which are all projects that have already lasted for more than 100 years. We do not think that such long-lasting projects have followed a well-defined project plan. Bergenholtz (2010) argues that a dictionary project should be carried out within a maximum of five years. Of course, a dictionary can always be revised or/and expanded, but in such cases we recommend making a new project plan.

This contribution argues for the appointment of a professional lexicographer as the dictionary project manager. Such a manager could benefit from knowledge of management theories, but she or he should keep in mind that good dictionary making means planning, planning and planning combined with dictionary functions related to deciding, deciding and deciding. This is what should be called dictionary management.

The development of e-lexicography shows that IT experts have more and more influence on the conception and the continuous work with e-dictionaries. In many cases, we can see that IT experts have made the whole dictionary design without giving the dictionary project manager the possibility of having any influence. They have decided not to show the whole lemma list to the users. They have in other cases decided not to show synonyms or word formation items if those items were not lemmas already. In such cases – and these cases are not rare – the dictionary manager loses his ability to guarantee the quality of the dictionary, that is, to ensure that the dictionary shows the data in a way that meets the dictionary users' information needs and corresponds with the intended dictionary function. If a dictionary manager can accept that, she or he does not deserve this title, but should look for another job or, even better, hire other IT experts.

In this contribution, we have focused on the dictionary manager and stressed his or her responsibility to make the dictionary concept and control the use of that concept. This does not mean that it is a manager in a so-called top-down organization. The dictionary manager must ensure that the concept is followed, and she or he should also have steady contact with all project employees, especially the lexicographers. This also means that the manager should be open to new ideas from the lexicographers and pay attention to good practice in their work so that this can be told to and used by the other lexicographers in the project. A good project manager also has to ensure that the human relations in the project are positive and that the employees are motivated, for example, by writing a weekly or monthly newsletter about the ongoing work, providing suggestions or solutions to problems with specific dictionary entries. It is also very important that each single lexicographer as part of the day-to-day management gets feedback on his or her work, in the ideal case every day – not only about mistakes, but also about some particularly good solutions for certain items.

Related topics

Dictionaries for text production; lexicography as an independent science; the Accounting Dictionaries; using the Web for lexicographic purposes; user participation in the era of the Internet.

Further Reading

Larson, E. and R. Larson (2012). *10 Steps to Creating a Project Plan.* www.projecttimes.com/articles/10-steps-to-creating-a-project-plan.html (Accessed 15 January 2015)

The authors discuss ten steps to creating a project plan. They presume an already well-developed project plan with a clear concept and a roadmap for the project.

Svejvik, P. and P. Andersen (2015). "Rethinking Project Management: A Structured Literature Review With a Critical Look at the Brave New World", *International Journal of Project Management* 33: 278–290.

This paper contains a commented up-to-date literature list about project management. Especially relevant is the overview of classical project management compared with rethinking project management.

References

Atkins, B.T.S. and M. Rundell (2008) *The Oxford Guide to Practical Lexicography*. Oxford: Oxford University Press.

Bergenholtz, H. (1990) "Lexikographische Instruktionen für ein zweisprachiges Wörterbuch", *Zeitschrift für Phonetik, Sprachwissenschaft und Kommunikationsforschung* 43: 19–37.

Bergenholtz, H. (2010) *Discurso de Investidura como Doctor Honoris Cause de. D. Henning Bergenholtz. La Presentatión y el Acceso a los Datos Adaptados a las Necesidades de los Usuarios*. Valladolid: Universidad de Valladolid.

Bergenholtz, H. (2013) "The Role of Linguists in Planning and Making Dictionaries in Modern Information Society", in D. Kwary, N. Wulan, and L. Musyahda (eds.), *Lexicography and Dictionaries in the Information Age: Selected Papers From the 8th ASIALEX Conference*. Surabaya: Airlangga University Press, pp. 1–10.

Bergenholtz, H. and R. Gouws (2012) "Who Is a Lexicographer?", *Lexikon* 42: 68–78.

Bergenholtz, H. and J. S. Nielsen (2013) "What Is a Lexicographical Database?", *Lexikos* 23: 77–87. Reprinted in translation with the title Sözlükbilimi Nedir?, *Dil ve Edebiyat Araştırmaları* 2014: 39–53.

CWP (2016) "10 trin: Sådan udarbejder og styrer du en god projektplan". www.cwp-ing.dk/ (Accessed 15. January 2015).

DanskOrdbogen = Bergenholtz, H. J. Pedersen, V. Vrang and R. Almind (1999) *DanskOrdbogen*. Århus: Systime.

Fuertes-Olivera, P. A. and H. Bergenholtz (2015) "Los diccionarios en línea de español Universidad de Valladolid", *Estudios de Lexicografía. Revista de Lexicografía. ELex* 4: 71–98.

Grundy, V. and D. Rawlinson. (2016) "The Practicalities of Dictionary Production; Planning and Managing Dictionary Projects; Training of Lexicographers", in P. Durkin (ed.), *The Oxford Handbook of Lexicography*. Oxford: Oxford University Press, pp. 561–578.

Meyer, C. M. and I. Gurevych (2014) "Methoden bei kollaborativen Wörterbüchern", *Lexicographica* 30: 187–212.

Stalks, H. (2016) "The Business & Management Collection Video Lectures & Case Studies". https://hstalks.com/business/?utm_source=JangoMail&utm_medium=Email&utm_campaign=Management+Lectures+and+Case+Studies+(318319688)&utm_content= (Accessed 15 January 2015).

Svejvik, P. and P. Andersen (2015) "Rethinking Project Management: A Structured Literature Review with a Critical Look at the Brave New World", *International Journal of Project Management* 33: 278–290.

Wiegand, H. E. (1998) *Wörterbuchforschung. Untersuchungen zur Wörterbuchbenutzung, zur Theorie, Geschichte, Kritik und Automatisierung der Lexikographie*. Berlin: de Gruyter.

3

Dictionaries and access

Rufus H. Gouws

3.1 Introduction

As containers of knowledge (see McArthur 1986), dictionaries have to provide data that contribute to the satisfaction of the lexicographic needs of their intended target users. In order to achieve this, cognizance has to be taken of the real lexicographic needs and reference skills of a clearly identified intended target user group for each dictionary. No single dictionary can either satisfy all the lexicographic needs of a general and unidentified user group nor be everything to everyone. In the planning and compilation of their dictionaries lexicographers should therefore meticulously negotiate the typical user and usage situations of their envisaged dictionaries, and this should have a determining influence on the functions, contents and structures of these dictionaries.

In the field of metalexicography and dictionary research scholars strive to formulate theories that can help to prevent a haphazard and arbitrary approach in the lexicographic practice and can assist practical lexicographers with theoretically based models to be used in the planning and eventual compilation of dictionaries. The development of lexicographic theory should never be performed as an activity of theory for the sake of theory. It should be interpretable in terms of the practice and be directed at enhancing the quality of the lexicographic practice. Wiegand (1989d:251) already indicated that lexicography is a scientific activity that leads to the production of dictionaries so that a further activity (i.e. the cultural process of dictionary use can be activated). The success of any dictionary is not to be found primarily in the assessment given by lexicographers or metalexicographers but rather by those people utilising it as members of its intended target group in a typical usage situation. The response of the intended target users to the way in which the dictionary assisted them in their consultation procedures and the ease of retrieving the required information rapidly and unambiguously from the data on offer in the dictionary should indicate the degree of success of that dictionary as a practical instrument.

Because lexicographers should have a clear identification of the intended target users of their dictionary they should also be keenly aware of the envisaged function(s) of the dictionary. These functions are determined by the role the dictionary has to play within its user group. In order to achieve the function(s) foreseen for a given dictionary the appropriate data need to be selected and the necessary structures be employed to make the data accessible and the information retrievable by the intended target users. Access to the data on offer is an early and necessary step to ensure eventual successful dictionary consultation procedures.

This chapter will focus on one of the structures of dictionaries (i.e. the *access structure*), but will also go beyond the access structure by looking at the more comprehensive process of access in both printed and online dictionaries. Comprehensive and detailed discussions of the access structure can be found in Wiegand (2008) and Wiegand and Beer (2013). The current discussion does not attempt to go into the same detail. Some seminal issues discussed in these publications will be referred to in this chapter but in a brief and far less detailed way.

3.2 On the notion of *structure*

A significant feature of a structure is the arrangement of elements that are interrelated as components of a single system. In his definition of dictionary structures Wiegand emphasises ordering as a feature, e.g. the macrostructure (Wiegand and Gouws 2013:78) and microstructure (Wiegand and Smit 2013:159) that are ordering structures, but ordering is also a feature of access structures (Wiegand and Beer 2013:115). Looking at the access structure in printed dictionaries the arrangement and organisation of elements can be clearly identified. There is a linear order, for example, from the entries on the spine of a dictionary to a specific item in the dictionary article. In combination the outer and inner access structures determine the search route a user can follow from an extra-lexicographical situation where a lexicographic need is realised which lets the user turn to a dictionary. Depending on the familiarity of the specific user with the specific dictionary or with dictionaries in general, either the full search route or one or more sections of the search route could be followed to reach the destination which is the item from which the required information can be retrieved.

A user familiar with a specific dictionary may skip some phases in the external access process, whereas someone not familiar with the same dictionary needs to go through all the steps on the external search route before reaching the lemma sign of the article in which the item presenting the required data occurs. But even the most experienced user will need at least a part of a rapid access structure or the search words on the top of each page to reach the desired article stretch that contains the article with the required item. Irrespective of the steps followed or omitted, there is a linear ordering in the total number of steps, and a typical consultation proceeds in a specific ordering or partial ordering. A distinction has to be made between the full structure or a partial structure. The search route of a given user may consist of a part of the complete search route. That part is determined by a partial article structure, and any two or more subsequent components of the access structure represent a partial stretch in the access structure. The ordering, and therefore also a given partial access structure stretch, is not necessarily monodirectional because on the outer search route a user can pass the desired article stretch or the relevant search words and then has to page backwards. Even on the inner search route a user can move from the lemma sign as guiding element to a search zone beyond the zone that contains the required item. On the vertical search route the search direction may then be upwards instead of the default downward direction.

A valid question that arises, then, is whether the notion of an access structure also applies to online dictionaries. Is there still sufficient evidence of an interrelated arrangement of components that belong to a single system? Some e-dictionaries (e.g. dictionaries on CD that actually only are digital versions of printed dictionaries) do have an access structure similar to their printed counterparts. The question to be answered is not directed at these dictionaries but at those e-dictionaries available and accessible in online format. In principle online dictionaries also have an arrangement of components that could determine the access route a user follows to reach the required entry. However, all these stepping stones on the search route are not necessarily used when a user accesses a given dictionary. Some users rely on all or several components, whereas other users may utilise a minimum of these access markers. The fact that they still are there and still are available constitute the interrelated arrangement as a structure. The use of this arrangement of components cannot, however, be regarded as a compulsory phase in accessing a dictionary, and in online dictionaries new access possibilities emerge. I will look at some of these new possibilities in Section 3.5 (see Part VI of this *Handbook* as well as Chapters 27 and 28 for gaining more insight on the concept of access in online dictionaries).

3.3 Access structures – a brief historical perspective

It is a well-known fact that the lexicographic practice is much older than lexicographic theory or than attempts to formulate theoretical models to improve the quality of dictionaries (see Gouws 2005). During its early developments lexicographic theory primarily focused on a reflection of the contents, especially the linguistic contents, of prevailing dictionaries and on an analysis of dictionary typology (see Zgusta 1971). A subsequent phase in the development of lexicographic theory shifted the focus to an identification and discussion of dictionary structures (Gouws 2005). Macrostructures and microstructures were introduced and discussed by Rey-Debove (1971:21), and this identification and comprehensive discussion of a variety of structures were continued in publications like Wiegand (1989a; 1989b).

Throughout the ages of their existence dictionaries functioned as practical instruments, and the data in these dictionaries had been presented in ways that could be accessed by their target users. However, the focus in these dictionaries had been on the contents and not on the structures or the establishment of search routes to guide the user to the required entries. The emergence of lexicographic theory and its identification and analysis of dictionary structures should not be regarded as the introduction of these structures – they had been there before but had not been named as such or been analysed in theoretical discussions. One of the important contributions of the emergence of theoretical lexicography was the fact that it presented a mirror that enabled practical lexicographers to take a critical look at dictionaries, including the contents and presentation of data and the ways in which users are assisted or neglected in their consultation procedures. A further advantage was an identification of different components and structures of dictionaries and a discussion that helped enhance the future utilisation of these structures to improve the quality of dictionaries.

A historical perspective on dictionary access as given in this chapter is rather a historical perspective on some of the theoretical discussions of access structures than on the development of access routes prior to the formal identification of this structure type or on the way in which early lexicographers planned their dictionaries to assist users in quickly finding the required data. A real perspective on access prior to the identification of access structures would have had to look among others at the use of a thematic ordering in the early dictionaries by means of which words that refer to things belonging to the same theme were brought together, or one would have had to look at the transition to the system of alphabetical ordering and the implications it had for users when looking for a specific word and data regarding that word in a given dictionary. This will not be done in this chapter.

The concept of the access structure as one of the core dictionary structures was introduced by Hausmann and Wiegand (1989: 329). According to them the "access structure of the microstructure is called the inner access structure", whereas "(A)ll other access structures, above all the access structure of the central list, are called outer access structures". Unfortunately they fail to define the access structure as such but rather explain the outer and inner search paths. Wiegand (2008:213) stresses the need for a clear distinction between *access structure* and *search route/path*. The access structure is not the search route a user follows, but rather the structure that determines this search route. The outer access structure determines the search route from the entries on the spine of a dictionary up to the lemma sign. The inner access structure determines the search route within the dictionary article with the required item as final destination.

Since the early work by Hausmann and Wiegand (1989), advances in the discussion of the access structure are expressed by Wiegand in, among others, Wiegand (2008); Wiegand and Beer (2013), which gives a comprehensive discussion of a variety of types of access structures (all of which will not be discussed in this chapter); Engelberg and Lemnitzer (2009); and Svensén (2009). Bergenholtz and Gouws (2010) also focus on access to data but instead of using the term *access structure*, they refer to the *access process*.

3.4 Core issues and topics: dictionary structures and the role of access structure

Metalexicographic research of the last three decades often focussed on dictionary structures. Although a variety of structures have been identified and discussed individually in metalexicographic literature, especially by the prolific German metalexicographer Herbert Ernst Wiegand, e.g. Wiegand (1989a, 1989b, 1989c, 1996, 2003; Hausmann and Wiegand 1989) it is important to realise that no single structure functions in isolation. The nature of each structure is co-determined by the function(s) of the dictionary and the distribution and presentation of data, and the different structures often have an interactive relation with other structures. As an example of this interaction one could refer to the fact that the microstructure as a structure that presents an ordering of items within the dictionary article interacts with the article structure. The article structure contains text segments that can be divided into items and structural indicators. These structural indicators are not components of the microstructure but play an important role in the identification of the search zones in which the items are accommodated to ensure a successful microstructural ordering. An interactive relation also exists between the data distribution and the addressing structures of a dictionary. If the lexicographer opts for a complex system of addressing, e.g. lemmatic addressing completed by non-lemmatic addressing, the data distribution structure has to make provision for data allocated to subsections in search zones with a microstructural item and not the lemma sign as address.

With this chapter's focus on access, some aspects of interactive relations in which the access structure participates will also come to the fore. It is important to note that the access structure is not the only structure that plays a significant role in the envisaged dictionary user's access to the data on offer in the dictionary. In this regard the role of structures like the data distribution structure, the frame structure, the macrostructure, the microstructure and the article structure needs to be negotiated. In the following sections selected information about selected structures that are relevant for accessing the data in dictionaries are briefly discussed. It has to be mentioned that this is not a comprehensive or even balanced reflection of the nature and role of these structures, but it only looks at some of the issues relevant to the access process. The discussion of these aspects of other structures will be done whilst looking at various aspects of access and accessibility. However, one structure (i.e. the data distribution structure) needs to be dealt with before further attention to access.

3.4.1 The data distribution structure

One of the first structures to be employed in the compilation of a dictionary is the data distribution structure (Bergenholtz, Tarp and Wiegand 1999:1778). This structure determines the venues of all data to be included in a dictionary as a text compound or *big text*, also known as a carrier of text types (Kammerer and Wiegand 1998:224). Prior to the distribution of data in a dictionary, there has to be clarity on the different venues that are available to be populated by the data. The lexicographers need to decide on the overall structure, that is, the textual book structure in printed dictionaries (Hausmann and Wiegand 1989: 330) or the feature compound structure in online dictionaries (Klosa and Gouws 2015:149). The central list of the dictionary (i.e. the traditional alphabetical component of printed dictionaries) represents a search field that contains article stretches in which each article constitutes a search area and within each article different search zones exist (Wiegand, Beer and Gouws 2013: 63). Besides deciding on the data types to be distributed to the various search zones in the different types of articles (e.g. default single articles, cross-reference articles and synopsis articles), lexicographers should also negotiate the possibility of using outer texts, or outer features in online dictionaries, to accommodate additional data that supplement the default presentation. The more diverse the data venues determined by the data distribution structure are, the more complicated the access procedures that need to guide users to the different data entries. Where access is needed to data allocated to venues other than the dictionary articles, users need additional assistance to make them aware of these locations and to determine a search route to these venues that could ensure an optimal retrieval of information.

In the majority of discussions of access structures in printed dictionaries the focus has been on access to data in the central list – employing the outer and the inner access structure. Although access to items in the dictionary articles remain important, provision should also be made for systematic access to data presented in other venues of a given dictionary.

3.4.2 Significant features in access structure

Whether they have an underlying theoretical approach or not, the eventual success of any product in the lexicographic practice is co-determined by its accessibility. All ways and means employed to enhance access to the data on offer in a dictionary should be applauded, and both practical and theoretical lexicographers should strive to elevate the levels of accessibility to such an extent that even the most inexperienced member of the envisaged target user group of any dictionary can perform a successful dictionary consultation procedure by accessing the dictionary successfully, retrieving the necessary information and having the confidence that this information provides an unambiguous answer to the question that prompted the dictionary consultation. This constitutes the core objective of access in dictionaries.

In order to ensure such an increased accessibility, it is important to be familiar with some significant features of access, including features of access structures but also of some other dictionary structures. In this regard only four topics will be discussed: the type of macrostructure and its implications for the access structure, the rapid access structure, the access alphabet and the article structure.

3.4.2.1 The macrostructure

A dictionary can have one or more than one word list in its macrostructure. Where a dictionary has only one word list the macrostructure and the alphabetical access structure are identical (see Hausmann and Wiegand 1989: 328).

The macrostructure is an ordering structure that displays the lemmata as guiding elements of dictionary articles in a specific way. Different types of ordering lead to different access possibilities. In a straight-alphabetical macrostructure, all the lemmata are presented in a vertical order and the typical access will proceed downwards starting at the top of a page.

Due to especially space-saving efforts macrostructures in printed dictionaries often deviate from a straight-alphabetical order in favour of sinuous lemma files where vertical ordering is complemented by horizontal ordering. This leads to procedures of niching, i.e. where the horizontally ordered lemmata maintain the strict alphabetical ordering as in Figure 3.1, a partial article stretch from the *Pharos Woordeboek Dictionary* (Du Plessis 2005), or nesting, where the horizontally ordered lemma cluster shows deviation from the strict alphabetical ordering on morpho-semantic grounds, as in Figure 3.2, a partial article stretch from *Nasionale woordeboek* (De Villiers et al. 1987):

call-ing geroep; roepstem; beroep; roeping; beroeping (*deur gemeente)*
calling card (*Am.*) visitekaartjie
calling-off afgelasting

cal-li-o-pe (*Am. mus.*) stoomorrel
Cal-li-o-pe (*Gr. mit*) Kalliope, Kalliopë

cal-li-per (*Am.*) **caliper** (*dikw. mv., med.*) loopyster
inside callipers holpasser
outside callipers diktepasser
(*pair of*) *callipers* krom-, meetpasser, loopyster
rule callipers kaliberstok
calliper brake passerrem
calliper compasses krom-, meetpasser
calliper gauge speermaat
calliper splint (*med.*) loopyster

Figure 3.1 Example of niching

blaas I (blase) s.nw. 1. *dun vlies gevul met lug of gas.*
Lug-, seepblaas. 2. *rekbare spiersak in die menslike of dierlike liggaam gevul met vog.* Galblaas.
3. *voorwerp soos 'n blaas of daarvan gemaak.* Die
– van *'n* voetbal. Verfblaas. Vir *'n* – met ertjies op loop sit, *gou bang word, skrik.* **'blasie, blaas≈ agtig; blaaskruid, – vrug, – wier** (by 1); **blaasaandoening, – breuk, – geswel, – koliek, – kramp, – kwaal, – ontsteking, – steen, – stoornis** (by 2); **blaasbrand, – roes** (by 3).

Figure 3.2 Example of nesting

Compared to a dictionary with a straight-alphabetical ordering, difficulty of access is increased in a dictionary with a niched ordering (Figure 3.1) and even more in a dictionary with a nested ordering (Figure 3.2).

Because the access structure coincides with the main macrostructure, these different types of macrostructures lead to different types of access structures (i.e. a niching or a nesting access structure). The lexicographer's decision to opt for a niched or nested macrostructural ordering should not be done in a random way or merely on the grounds of space-saving attempts. This microstructural choice also has access implications. Niching, and especially nesting, increases the degree of textual condensation in the central list of a dictionary, and this could easily impede accessibility. Consequently, before choosing a macrostructure that deviates from the alphabetical ordering, the lexicographer needs to consider the reference skills of the intended user and the implications in terms of rapid access and successful information retrieval. For younger and less experienced users of printed dictionaries, a strict alphabetical ordering of macrostructural elements will be the preferred arrangement and will offer the best access possibilities.

The language in dictionary articles often displays a deviation from natural syntax because of different procedures of textual condensation. The more condensed the items in a dictionary article, the more cumbersome the access process becomes. This can also be seen on macrostructural level where space-saving procedures often lead to lemma clusters where the first stem of the lemmata have been substituted by a place-keeping symbol, downgrading these macrostructural elements to the level of sublemmata, that is, a lemma sign that can only be reached via the lemma sign that functions as guiding element of a preceding article (see Gouws and Prinsloo 2005:89). In the following example, Figure 3.3, from the Afrikaans dictionary *HAT5* (Odendal and Gouws 2005), the lemma *daklig* ('light in a roof') is presented in the condensed form *~lig* with its first stem substituted by the place-keeping symbol '~'. This lemma occurs in a niche, attached to the article of the main lemma *dak* ('roof'), and the niche contains a cluster of niched partial lemmata, preceded by a lemma part in lemma-external niche entrance position (Wolski 1989:365; Wiegand 1983), that is, the form *dak:*. The sublemma *daklig*, as is the case with all the sublemmata in this niche, cannot be accessed directly but only via the lemma sign *dak* and the subsequent lemma part in lemma-external niche entrance position. This is a complicated form of access, and lexicographers need to determine whether their users are qualified to access the data in such clusters successfully.

> **dak** *s.nw. [~ke, ~kie]*
>
> **1** Boonste, dekkende raamwerk van *'n* gebou; ook wel, die laag dekmateriaal wat op die raamwerk rus: *Af-, gewel-, saaldak. 'n Asfalt, pan-, plankies-, rietdak.*
> **2** Huis, woning: *Onder een dak woon,* in dieselfde huis.
> **3** Bedekking wat aan die dak van *'n* huis, laat dink: *Die dak van 'n bus, trem.*
> **Uitdr:** *Onder dak bly,* in die huis. *'n Dak bo jou kop hê, 'n* woning hê. *Iemand onder dak bring,* van huisvesting voorsien. *Dak natmaak (natgooi),* by die bou van *'n* huis, die werksmense trakteer sodra die eerste kap opgestel is. *Iets van die dakke of verkondig,* dit openbaar maak. *Onder dak wees,* beskerm teen wind en weer.
> **dak: ~balk, ~bedekking, ~dekker, ~geraamte, ~geut, ~gewel, ~helling, ~kap, ~lig, ~materiaal, ~raam, ~rand, ~strooi, ~timmerasie, ~venster.**

Figure 3.3 Example of place-keeping symbols for space saving

In some dictionaries a user can follow more than one route to eventually reach a specific lemma sign in the central list. Lexicographers can employ additional access possibilities to increase the routes to be followed. In this regard a distinction can be made between mono-accessible and poly-accessible dictionaries. In a mono-accessible dictionary the default outer access route will be the only way of reaching a lemma sign and continuing on the inner access route within the dictionary article. Poly-accessibility is realized, for example, when a dictionary has an index, and a given word can either be found via the macrostructure or via an entry in the index.

The Afrikaans dictionary *Grondslagfasewoordeboek* (Gouws, R. et al. 2010) has learners in the first three school years as target users. In the central list an alphabetical ordering prevails. A user already familiar with the alphabet may immediately go to the central word list and follow the default outer access route to reach a given lemma sign.

Users could also go to the back matter texts *List of words . . . Lys van woorde* where each word included as lemma in the dictionary and each word given as English equivalent for an Afrikaans lemma sign are presented in two separate lists. For each lemma or equivalent from the central list entered here these lists contain entries giving the page numbers where the relevant words can be found in the central list, and a user can proceed to the required lemma sign via the reference found in the back matter text.

In the word list each word typically has a reference to two different page numbers – the one to the central word list, and the other to a text in the front matter section. The front matter of this dictionary contains a thematic section in which different themes treated in the class room are presented by means of pictures and words.

Each smaller picture presented in the main picture is also given separately in columns next to the main picture with the Afrikaans and English words for the thing represented by the picture. Users consulting this dictionary during an early phase of their first school year when they are not yet fully familiar with reading can move from the main picture to the relevant smaller picture and from the word given there to the relevant lemma sign in the alphabetical section – where the same small picture precedes the lemma sign and functions, along with the relevant lemma sign, as a component of a combined guiding element. The limited dictionary-using skills of the target users of this dictionary are taken into consideration and yet another way of accessing the data is made available in this poly-accessible dictionary.

3.4.2.2 The rapid access structure

Hausmann and Wiegand (1989:338) already introduced the notion of a rapid access structure. Lexicographers employ different ways and methods to enhance the accessibility of their dictionaries and to ensure faster consultation procedures. This is done on the level of both the external and the internal access structure. Within the outer access structure the two main sections of a bidirectional bilingual dictionary, that is, the two alphabetical components within which each of the two treated languages respectively functions as source language, are often separated by means of a coloured page. Looking at the front edge of the dictionary this colour page divides the dictionary, and a user can easily see where the second alphabetical component of the dictionary commences. In a similar way the back matter texts or even texts inserted as middle matter within the alphabetical components are distinguished by means of coloured pages (see the *Macmillan English Dictionary* (Rundell 2002)) with its inner texts inserted into the alphabetical section and identified for rapid access by means of pages with coloured edges.

Also on the front edge of a dictionary lexicographers often employ thumb index markers to guide users to specific article stretches. In some dictionaries these indexes are explicitly marked for specific alphabet stretches, whereas some other dictionaries merely have a small block to indicate the start of a new stretch. The knowledgeable dictionary user is especially assisted by these aids as part of the rapid access structure of a dictionary. Whereas rapid access is a complementary access component of printed dictionaries, it can be regarded as a default approach in online dictionaries where the search does not have to proceed via search words, article stretches or even lemma signs as guiding elements of articles (see Section 3.5 of this chapter).

Search words, also referred to as alphabetised lemmatic running titles (see Wiegand and Beer 2013:132), constitute another form of rapid access on the external search route. Having reached a specific article stretch, either by means of a thumb index marker or by a mere guessing of where a given lemma is alphabetically positioned in a dictionary, a dictionary user can speed up the search for a lemma by looking at the search words given at the top of each page, above the presentation of the partial article stretch of the specific page. Dictionaries have different ways of ensuring this type of rapid access. The one way is to include a search word that represents the first lemma treated on the specific left-hand page of a dictionary in the top left corner of that page and the last lemma treated on the right-hand page in the top right corner of the right-hand page of that dictionary.

A more helpful way is to give a search word representing the first and last lemma treated on a single page in the top left and top right corner respectively of that single page – and to do it on every page.

These search words assist the user to determine whether the lemma sign he or she is looking for occurs on the specific page. If the required lemma sign does fall within the partial article stretch identified by the search words, the user can continue with the outer access by looking at the lemma signs on the specific page to find the one that is the guiding element of the article from which information needs to be retrieved.

3.4.2.3 The access alphabet

Wiegand and Beer (2013:111) indicate that the external data accessibility in printed dictionaries "is achieved by creating outer access structures." The macrostructure is one such structure, and the alphabetical ordering of lemmata in the macrostructure plays an important role in enhancing the accessibility of the dictionary. However, lemma candidates cannot always only be ordered, and therefore also accessed, by means of an alphabetical approach. Many lemma candidates contain both alphabetical and numerical elements (e.g. *4×4-vehicle, .38 gun, 18-wheeler*), lemmas including alphabetical elements as well as elements from other alphabets (e.g. *α-particle*) and even other orthographic elements like hyphens and letters marked for orthographic purposes with, for example, a circumflex or diaeresis. The Danish alphabet contains among others the letters *å æ* and *ø*, and in Sepedi the letter *š* has a frequent occurrence besides the normal *s*. Decisions need to be taken how and where words starting with or containing these letters should be ordered. A clearly explained system is needed to ensure quick and successful access to the relevant words. The lexicon of Afrikaans contains the following words: *leer, lêer* and *leër*. In which order should they be lemmatised?

Decisions that need to be taken to ensure a proper ordering of such lemma candidates led to the formulation of an access alphabet (see Bergenholtz, Tarp and Wiegand 1999:1813). In addition to the alphabet prevailing in a given language, lexicographers need to make provision for the ordering of and consequent access to lemma signs that deviate from the pure alphabetical form of the specific language. Such alphanumeric items or items with marked letters compel lexicographers to devise an access alphabet for their dictionaries that makes provision for a consistent and systematic ordering of these items as entries in the dictionary. An access alphabet is the set of elements according to which lemma signs are ordered in the macrostructure of a dictionary. Typical applications of access alphabets are as follows:

1 Numerical elements, both in numerical lemmata (e.g. *24/7*) and in combination with alphabetical elements (e.g. *4×4-vehicle*), as well as symbols in lemma signs (e.g. *α-particle*), are treated according to their 'word' value. 24/7 will be entered in the article stretch for the letter 'T' and in the position where the words *twenty four* would have been entered, whereas *4×4-vehicle* and *α-particle* would be treated in the alphabetically applicable positions in the article stretches of the letters 'F' (*four by four vehicle*) and 'A' (*alpha particle*) respectively.
2 Unmarked precedes marked, resulting in the ordering *leer, leër, lêer*, because in the first word both vowel signs are unmarked and in the second one the first vowel sign is unmarked.
3 A word without hyphen precedes a word with a hyphen, e.g. the Afrikaans word *sandaal* ('sandal') precedes *sand-aal* ('sand eel').
4 Blanks often do not play a role in the ordering of lemmata – the ordering only goes according to the signs (e.g. letters). Therefore *honey bear* precedes *honeybee* which precedes *honey beer*.

Dictionary users need to become familiar with these ordering principles because such a knowledge will enhance the speed of access to the lemma sign that is the destination of their outer search route.

3.4.2.4 The article structure

The access structure interacts with the article structure in a variety of ways but primarily to secure the best possible inner search route. Wiegand, Feinauer and Gouws (2013:317) indicate that a dictionary article is an accessible dictionary unit that shows at least one external access text element, is a constituent of a wordlist and consists of lexicographic data that are made accessible so that the dictionary user can unlock lexicographic information. The article structure plays a significant role in the accessibility of lexicographic data.

Articles contain text segments which can be divided into two types: items and indicators (see Wiegand 1989b:427–428). Items giving different types of data are presented in different search zones within the dictionary article as a search area (Wiegand, Beer and Gouws 2013:63). Each one of these search zones contains items from which information can be retrieved.

The inner access structure determines the inner search route that provides guidance for a user within the dictionary article. Whereas items are components of the microstructure, the structural indicators, both typographical and non-typographical indicators (see Wiegand 1989b:428), are not part of the microstructure but elements of the article structure. They mark specific search zones and specific items to assist users with access to the necessary data-carrying entry in a dictionary article. Especially in printed dictionaries the structural indicators ensure that the knowledgeable dictionary users do not have to read the whole article, but can directly access the search zone that contains the required items. Yet again, this rapid access implies that a user does not have to complete every step of the search route but may skip certain sections in order to quickly reach the desired search zone. The article structure should be devised in such a way that indicators enhance the search procedure and therefore add to the success of the dictionary consultation procedure. The following article from *HAT6* (Luther et al. 2015), Figure 3.4, displays clearly marked search zones. This article layout allows rapid access to the different items included in the article.

bos *s.nw. [~se, ~sie]*
1 groot klomp bome; woud: *'n natuurlike/inheemse/aangeplante bos* • *'n bos met geeldoringbome.*
2 (*botanie*) lae plantegroei; struik: *'n struikagtige bos* • *Die bitterbessie is 'n bossie met swart bessies.*
3 groep/bondel voorwerpe bymekaar/aanmekaar gebind: *'n bos blomme* • *'n bossie beet/wortels/spinasie/kruie* • *'n bos sleutels* • *'n dik/welige/wilde bos hare.*
◊**Uitdr:**
|*deur die bome die bos nie sien nie*
die geheel nie kan sien nie as gevolg van te veel kleinighede.
| *deur die hele bos loop om die kromste lat te sny*
gesê van 'n meisie wat baie vryers gehad het, maar met die treurigste van hulle getrou het.
(. . .)
|*voorste bos*
(*as antwoord op die vraag: Hoe gaan dit?*) baie goed.
▶ **bos: ~beampte, ~bewaarder, ~brand, ~navorsing, ~opsigter, ~pad, ~ryk, ~varing**
▶ **b*o*sagtig**

Figure 3.4 Example of structural indicators displaying clearly marked search zones

The ordering within the article and a clear marking of different subsections of the article also have to make provision for the treatment of the different part of speech occurrences of a given word. In this regard the lexicographer needs to decide whether the ordering of the treatment directed at the different part of speech occurrences is done in a random way, according to the usage frequency of the use of the different part of speech occurrences or in a fixed order, for example, the treatment of a word's occurrence as noun always precedes its treatment as a verb, etc. Here structural indicators could guide a user from one part of speech occurrence to the next. Compare the following article for the lemma sign *haat* (hate), Figure 3.5, from *HAT5*, where an arrow point is used as structural indicator to mark the different zones where the different part of speech occurrences are treated. This adds to the rapid access assistance of this dictionary.

haat

▷ *s.nw.* Gevoel van hewige afkeer, sterk vyandige gesindheid: *Geveinsde liefde is gevaarliker as openlike haat. Hy haat dit met 'n wrewelige haat. Haat en nyd skaad altyd. Iemand haat toedra. Haat jeens iemand hê.* ♦ *So vergeld hulle my met kwaad vir goed en haat vir liefde* (Ps. 109.5 NV).♦ *Dat liefde so tot haat kon skif. | . . . Haat wat sulke dun wei-water is*) N.P. van Wyk Louw). ♦ *Die grootste van die drie | bly nog die haat* (Emst van Heerden). ♦ *Regina het nie geweet dat haar haat so intens soos haar diep liefde was nie* (A.H.M. Scholtz). **≠liefde.**

▷ **ww. [gehaat]** *'n* Gevoel van hewige afkeer van iemand of iets hê, *'n* baie sterk wrok teen iemand of iets koester. *Jou vyande haat. Julle moet haat wat sleg is en liefhê wat goed is. 'n Gehate mededinger, diktator, tiran. . .* ♦ *Wie my haat, haat ook my Vader* (Joh. 15:23 NV).). **≠liefhê.**

Figure 3.5 Example of arrow being used as structural indicator to mark different zones

In online dictionaries, access to specific search zones is enhanced by the use of a multi-layered article structure (Gouws 2014:164). Figures 3.6 and 3.7 from *elexico* show a screen shot of the article of the lemma sign *Pferd* ('horse'). In the first screen shot the user can find search zones, for example, for orthography and etymology and an overview of the different subcomments on semantics.

Pferd

Lesartenübergreifende Angaben

⓿ **Orthographie**

Normgerechte Schreibung:	**Pferd**
Worttrennung:	**Dieses Wort ist nicht trennbar.**

⓿ **Herkunft und Wandel**

Etymologische Angaben:	*anzeigen* ☞
Wandel 1700 bis 1945:	–
Wandel seit 1945:	–

⓿ **Wortbildungsprodukte**

(automatisch ermittelt) *weiter* ☞

Lesartenbezogene Angaben ⓿

Lesart **'Reittier'** *weiter* ☞

Mit *Pferd* bezeichnet man ein großes Säugetier mit langen Beinen, das vom Menschen bevorzugt als Reittier und gelegentlich auch als Zug- und Lasttier genutzt wird.

Lesart **'Turngerät'** *weiter* ☞

Mit *Pferd* bezeichnet man ein Turngerät mit vier langen Beinen, einem ledernen Aufbau und zwei Griffen an der Oberseite.

Lesart **'Schachfigur'** *weiter* ☞

Mit *Pferd* bezeichnet man die Schachfigur, die als einzige über die anderen Figuren hinweg auf ein freies Feld bewegt werden kann.

Lesart **'Tierkreiszeichen'** *weiter* ☞

Mit *Pferd* bezeichnet man eines der zwölf Tierkreiszeichen des chinesischen Horoskops.

Figure 3.6 Search categories in online dictionaries

By clicking the zone of an item giving a polysemous sense, the user accesses that subcomment on semantics (cf. Figure 3.1). The internal access structure allows the user to be guided to other relevant search zones, for example, for collocations, constructions and grammar. The presentation in this screen shot enhances rapid access and contributes to successful dictionary consultation procedures.

Pferd

Lesart **'Reittier'**

❶ zur Übersichtsseite

Bedeutungs-erläuterung	Kollo-kationen	Konstruk-tionen	Sinnverwandte Wörter	Gebrauchs besonderheiten	Grammatik

❶ **Erläuterung der Bedeutung/Funktion**

Mit *Pferd* bezeichnet man ein großes Säugetier mit langen Beinen, das vom Menschen bevorzugt als Reittier und gelegentlich auch als Zug- und Lasttier genutzt wird.

□ Belege *anzeigen* ☞ □ Illustrationen *anzeigen* ☞

❶ Wortklasse: Individuativum

Figure 3.7 Accessing semantic subcomments in online dictionaries

3.5 Looking to the future: new possibilities in the digital era

The digital era has brought numerous new possibilities to the fore, including in fields like lexicography and information science. One of the most significant differences between printed and online dictionaries is the ease and speed of access. A user can start with a given lemma sign and then move into the article in a way comparable to the access in printed dictionaries. However, access does not only have to proceed via the lemma sign because a well-planned online dictionary makes it possible to have rapid access to individual items within a dictionary article. By entering a search string that contains, for example, two or more words from a fixed expression, the user can immediately be taken to that fixed expression as an item within a dictionary article. Where search zones are clearly identified they could be the immediate target of a specific consultation.

Svensén (2009:441) regards the access structure as the predominating structure in online dictionaries, although it functions differently compared to printed dictionaries. Searching in an online dictionary will often not be sequential. Svensén (2009:442) makes provision for different types of searching in online dictionaries (e.g. wildcard, incremental and fuzzy searching) but also searching several strings simultaneously by using Boolean operators. Access is also enhanced by means of a variety of linking procedures.

What is of paramount importance is that online dictionaries need to be planned and compiled in such a way that the structures, including the access structure, may be utilised effectively when accessing data. This yet again emphasises the need for a strong theoretical basis to ensure an optimal lexicographic practice.

3.6 Conclusion

Dictionaries are practical instruments and need to be planned and compiled in such a way that their target users can achieve a successful retrieval of information. This is only possible if they can access the data. As part of the responsibility to their users lexicographers need to devise the best possible access structures for both printed and online dictionaries. Innovative research to ensure successful access in new types of dictionaries should be a priority in the field of metalexicography in order to enhance the quality of the lexicographic practice.

Acknowledgement

This research is supported in part by the National Research Foundation of South Africa (grant specific unique reference number (UID) 85434). The Grantholder acknowledges that opinions, findings and conclusions or recommendations expressed in any publication generated by the NRF supported research are that of the author, and that the NRF accepts no liability whatsoever in this regard.

Related topics

Lexicography and information science; electronic dictionaries; dictionary portals; the Accounting Dictionaries.

Further reading

Further guidance on access and access structures can be found in, among others, Wiegand and Beer (2013), specifically a general theoretical discussion of access in printed dictionaries, Svensén (2009) for access in printed and online dictionaries, Engelberg and Lemnitzer (2009) for a discussion of a variety of topics regarding access and Bergenholtz and Gouws (2010) for terms to be used when referring to the access process and a discussion of case studies in dictionary access. Tarp (2015) deals with e-lexicography, examines the whole concept of *structure* and discusses some of the new ways in which lexicographical structures express themselves in the digital environment.

References

Dictionaries

De Villiers, M., J. Smuts, L.C. Eksteen and R.H. Gouws (eds.) (1987) *Nasionale woordeboek*. Cape Town: Nasou.

Du Plessis, M. (ed.) (2005) *Pharos Afrikaans-Engels/English-Afrikaans Woordeboek/Dictionary*. Cape Town: Pharos.

elexico: www.owid.de/wb/elexiko/start.html

Gouws, Ronél, L. Potgieter and S. Burgess (eds.) (2010) *Grondslagfasewoordeboek Afrikaans/English*. Cape Town: Maskew Miller Longman.

Luther, J., F. Pheiffer and R.H. Gouws (eds.) (2015) *HAT6: Handwoordeboek van die Afrikaanse Taal*. Cape Town: Pearson.

Odendal, F. F. and R. H. Gouws (2005) *HAT5: Handwoordeboek van die Afrikaanse Taal*. Cape Town: Pearson.

Rundell, M. (ed.) (2002) *Macmillan English Dictionary for Advanced Learners*. Oxford: Macmillan Education.

Other literature

Bergenholtz, H. and R.H. Gouws. (2010) "A New Perspective on the Access Process", *Hermes* 44: 103–127.

Bergenholtz, H., S. Tarp and H. E. Wiegand. (1999) "Datendistributionsstrukturen, Makro- und Mikrostrukturen in neueren Fachwörterbüchern", in L. Hoffmann, H. Kalverkämper and H. E. Wiegand (eds.) *Fachsprachen. Languages for Special Purposes: An International Handbook of Special-Language and Terminology Research*. Berlin: de Gruyter, pp. 1762–1832.

Engelberg, S. and L. Lemnitzer (2009) *Lexikographie und Wörterbuchforschung*. Tübingen: Stauffenburg.

Gouws, R.H. (2005) "Meilensteine auf dem historischen Weg der Metalexikographie". *Lexicographica* 21: 158–178.

Gouws, R. H. and D. J. Prinsloo. (2005) *Principles and Practice of South African Lexicography*. Stellenbosch: SunMedia.

Gouws, R. H., U. Heid, W. Schweickard and H.E. Wiegand. (eds.) (2013) *Dictionaries: An International Encyclopedia of Lexicography. Supplementary Volume: Recent Developments with Focus on Electronic and Computational Lexicography*. Berlin/New York: Walter de Gruyter.

Hausmann, F. J. and H. E. Wiegand. (1989) "Component Parts and Structures of General Monolingual Dictionaries: A Survey", in F. J. Hausmann, O. Reichmann, H. E. Wiegand and E. Zgusta. (eds.) (1989–1991): pp. 328–360.

Hausmann, F. J., O. Reichmann, H. E. Wiegand and E. Zgusta (eds.) (1989–1991) *Wörterbücher: Dictionaries. Dictionnaires. An International Encyclopedia of Lexicography*. Berlin/New York: de Gruyter.

Kammerer, M. and H.E. Wiegand. (1998) "Über die textuelle Rahmenstruktur von Wörterbüchern. Präzisierungen und weiterführende Überlegungen". *Lexicographica* 14: 224–238.

Klosa, A. and R.H. Gouws (2015) "Outer features in e-dictionaries". *Lexicographica* 31: 142–172.

McArthur, T. (1986) *Worlds of Reference*. Cambridge: Cambridge University Press.

Rey-Debove, J. (1971) *Étude linguistique et sémiotique des dictionnaires francais contemporains*. The Hague/Paris: Mouton.

Svensén, B. (2009) *A Handbook of Lexicography*. Cambridge: Cambridge University Press.

Tarp, S. (2015) "Structures in the communication between lexicographer and programmer: Database and interface". *Lexicographica* 31: 217–235

Wiegand, H. E. (1983) "Was ist eigentlich ein Lemma?", in H. E. Wiegand (ed.), *Studien zur neuhochdeutschen Lexikographie III* (Germanistische Linguistik 1–4/82). Hildesheim: George Olms, pp. 401–474.

Wiegand, H. E. (1989a) "Aspekte der Makrostruktur im allgemeinen einsprachigen Wörterbuch: alphabetische Anordnungsformen und ihre Probleme", in F. J. Hausmann et al. (eds.) (1989–1991), pp. 371–409.

Wiegand, H. E. (1989b) "Der Begriff der Mikrostruktur: Geschichte, Probleme, Perspektiven", in F. J. Hausmann et al. (eds.) (1989–1991), pp. 409–462.

Wiegand, H. E. (1989c) "Arten von Mikrostrukturen im allgemeinen einsprachigen Wörterbuch", in F. J. Hausmann et al. (eds.) (1989–1991), pp. 462–501.

Wiegand, H. E. (1989d) "Der gegenwärtige Status der Lexikographie", in F. J. Hausmann et al. (eds.), pp. 246–280.

Wiegand, H. E. (1996) "Das Konzept der semiintegrierten Mikrostrukturen: Ein Beitrag zur Theorie zweisprachiger Printwörterbücher", in H. E. Wiegand (ed.), *Wörterbücher in der Diskussion II*. Tübingen: Max Niemeyer Verlag, pp. 1–82.

Wiegand, H.E. (2003) "Überlegungen zur Typologie von Wörterbuchartikeln in Printwörterbüchern. Ein Beitrag zur Theorie der Wörterbuchform". *Lexicographica* 19: 169–313.
Wiegand, H. E. (2008) "Zugriffsstrukturen in Printwörterbüchern. Ein zusammenfassender Beitrag zu einem zentralen Ausschnitt einer Theorie der Wörterbuchform". *Lexicographica* 24: 209–315.
Wiegand, H. E. and S. Beer (2013) "Access Structures in Printed Dictionaries", in R. H. Gouws et al. (eds.) (2013), pp. 110–149.
Wiegand, H. E., S. Beer and R. H. Gouws. (2013) "Textual Structures in Printed Dictionaries: An Overview", in R. H. Gouws et al. (eds.) (2013), pp. 31–73.
Wiegand, H. E., I. Feinauer and R. H. Gouws (2013) "Types of Dictionary Articles in Printed Dictionaries", in R. H. Gouws et al. (eds.) (2013), pp. 314–366.
Wiegand, H. E. and R. H. Gouws (2013) "Macrostructures in Printed Dictionaries", in R. H. Gouws et al. (eds.) (2013), pp. 73–110.
Wiegand, H.E and M. Smit (2013) "Microstructures in printed dictionaries". In Gouws, R.H. et al. (eds.) 2013: 149–214.
Wolski, W. (1989) "Das Lemma und die verschiedenen Lemmatypen", in F. J. Hausmann et al. (eds.) (1989–1991), pp. 360–371.
Zgusta, L. (1971) *Manual of Lexicography*. The Hague: Mouton.

4

Explaining meaning in lexicographical information tools

Heidi Agerbo

4.1 Introduction

The definition is often considered the most important aspect of a dictionary both by dictionary users and lexicographers. This is, for example, expressed in the definition of *dictionary* in the *Longman Dictionary of Contemporary English* in which this is the only data type that is mentioned, "a book that gives a list of words in alphabetical order and explains their meanings in the same language, or another language" – though not all dictionaries are books, not all dictionaries explain meanings (definitions) and the lemmas are not necessarily alphabetically ordered. The salience given to definitions is also emphasized by Lombard (1991: 158), who argues that "[t]he lexicographical definition is still the most important entry in a dictionary article."

Definitions play an important role in supporting the dictionary function, and this is also why the literature on this topic is extensive. However, this chapter will argue that the word *definition* is problematic as it implies the existence of word boundaries, something that can easily be discarded. Instead, the chapter will make provisions for the concept of *meaning explanation*. Meanings blend into each other and overlap. Therefore, dictionaries cannot and should not provide definitions, that is, necessary conditions that express what is correct about a word, but instead typical features of a word. If 'chair' is described as furniture with a back and four legs, then a chair with only three legs would not be considered a chair if the mentioned characteristics were necessary conditions. The format of a dictionary unfortunately presents the human yearning to present the disorderliness of meanings in natural language as something that is tidy and discrete, but lexicographical representations of meaning should not seduce lexicographers into thinking that they are writing definitions; instead, they write meaning explanations of words. This chapter will furthermore argue that these meaning explanations should vary according to the given dictionary function, that is, that the lexicographer should write different explanations for different user types with different information needs in different extra-lexicographical situations.

4.2 Historical perspective: definitions and meaning explanations in lexicography

The term *definition* has been widely discussed not only in lexicography, but also in philosophy, logic and linguistics. Much classical literature describes the lexicographer's task as a search for the truth, which is an idea found in both philosophy and classical semantics. One of the oldest contributions to the concept of definition was provided by Aristotle (384–322 BC), who is famous for his formula for a good definition: that it should be described with a *genus proximus* and *differentia specifica*. Another important contribution he made in terms of later lexicographical influence was drawing the distinction between the essential properties of a category and its accidental properties. More than two millennia later, these two principles or approaches are still favoured and practiced by some lexicographers, among others the semanticist-lexicographer Anna Wierzbicka (1992: 46), who, like Aristotle searching for the essence, seeks to capture what she calls the *invariant* – the truth about a word's meaning,

> [t]he description about a word's meaning may vary, legitimately, in completeness from one work to another, but it should not differ in its basic content. A 'definition' is meant to represent the truth about a word's meaning, and there is only one such truth.

A way of identifying this distinct word meaning is to identify a unique set of necessary and sufficient conditions, cf. the classical (and later criticized) example of *bachelor* with the defining features human, male, adult and unmarried. This approach to definition writing, the so-called classical or analytic definition, is common in early lexicographical literature. However, both Aristotle and Wierzbicka are concerned with questions about concepts, not about words. This focus on concepts is also applied in terminology where terms are considered conceptual representations (Fuertes-Olivera 2012: 58). Definitions, however, may be categorized in different ways according to what they seek to describe: real definitions, nominal definitions and conceptual definitions of which the first define *things* (*objects* or *significates*), the second define *words* (*signs* or *symbols*) and the third define *concepts* (Robinson 1950: 11). In contemporary general lexicography, to a large extent, the focus has moved from concepts to words and senses. Lexicographers such as Sue Atkins, Patrick Hanks (2000; 2013) and Adam Kilgarriff (1997) argue that they do not believe in word senses and that if we look at the natural meaning of words instead of analysing the meaning of concepts, meanings can only be constructions. They argue that there is no point in searching for the true meaning of a word, as this is not possible to find in a lexicographical context.

Many lexicographers today therefore reject the use of definitions (both the term and that which it stands for) in lexicography and instead call this part of the dictionary article *meaning explanation*, though the number of terms applied is vast, for example:

- Dictionary definition (Ayto 1983)
- Lexicographic definition (Wiegand 1992)
- Lexicographic meaning description (Svensén 2009)
- Explanation (Hanks 1987)
- Meaning explanation (Bergenholtz and Agerbo 2014)
- Dictionary sense (Atkins and Rundell 2008)

This distinction between defining and explaining was also expressed by Bolinger (1965: 572), who half a century ago wrote that "[d]ictionaries do not exist to define, but to help people grasp meanings." However, in order to help people in a lexicographical context, lexicographers must look at the dictionary user and his or her lexicographical needs when writing meaning explanations instead of producing them in isolation. Already in the eighteenth century, it was demonstrated by the work of the German grammarian and philologist Johann Adelung that a meaning explanation should contain what the user needs, not what is considered the truth about a word. In his dictionary *Grammatisch-kritisches Wörterbuch der hochdeutschen Mundart* (published in 1774), he describes the word *Fisch* (En. *fish*) in one of its senses as all living animals that live in water as well as some animals that live on land (e.g. waterfowls), which people are allowed to eat during Lent. This is a rather unusual explanation in the eyes of a twenty-first-century lexicographer, but the reason behind this use of the word is that the members of the Roman church were allowed to eat fish during Lent, thus the more animals categorized as fish, the more they were allowed to eat. This is not a case of a true definition from a semantic or philosophical viewpoint, but an applicable explanation that can help dictionary users understand the word in this context.

Most lexicographers today agree that meaning explanations should be designed according to the user's needs and skills, for example, Darian (1982: 29), who writes that "[t]he complexity of a definition depends on the age, interests, purpose, and background knowledge of the audience" and Atkins and Rundell (2008: 5), who write that "every aspect of a dictionary must, centrally, take account of who the users will be and what they will use the dictionary for." However, the user is not the only important factor that must be considered when writing meaning explanations or working with other types of lexicographical data.

In the rest of the chapter I will frame my proposal of lexicographical meaning explanation within the framework of the *function theory of lexicography* (see e.g. Tarp 2008a, 2008b, 2012; Fuertes-Olivera and Tarp 2014), which defends that every aspect in the making of a dictionary should be based on two important factors: (1) a specific user type with certain linguistic, factual and cultural competences and (2) an extra-lexicographical situation in which the user comes across a problem that results in the occurrence of a lexicographically relevant need that can be solved by using a lexicographical information tool. For example, if a layman is reading a text and comes across a word that she or he thinks she or he understands and looks it up in a dictionary just to verify her or his assumption, the meaning explanation would not have to be as detailed as if it were in a reception situation where the user is not familiar with the word. Thus, it is not only with the user, but also the user situation as the point of departure that the lexicographer should select the meaning elements to include in a meaning explanation.

4.3 Core issues and topics: meaning explanation from a functional perspective

Within the framework of the function theory a *lexicographical meaning explanation* is:

> A description in the form of one or more words, a sound and/or an image of a word, phrase, idiom, collocation or some other language construction or of a non-linguistic sign, which is presented in a dictionary article, and which has been formulated, drawn or recorded to help satisfy the need of a specific user type in a specific extra-lexicographical user situation.

This definition of meaning explanation entails a number of points: First, no meaning explanation can serve all users in all situations. Second, no distinction can or should be made between semantic and encyclopaedic knowledge (Haiman 1980) in the selection and distribution of data. Third, a meaning explanation does not have to be presented in words, but could also or instead be presented as an image (e.g. for the colour word *red*) or a sound (e.g. for the sound word *thunder*), cf. Liu (2015). Finally, a meaning explanation may also describe a non-linguistic sign (e.g. the signal a referee makes to communicate *timeout* to the players, see Chapter 25 of this *Handbook*). The data incorporated into a meaning explanation in the form of meaning elements are selected from the empirical basis (see Section 4.4) based on their usefulness according to the relevant dictionary function (Bergenholtz and Agerbo 2014).

The above-mentioned definition of meaning explanation entails several lexicographical and technical aspects that will be analysed later in sub-sections dealing with dictionaries and databases, principles for writing meaning explanations under a functional approach to lexicography and several examples of the same.

4.3.1 Dictionaries and databases

A database and a dictionary are not the same (Bergenholtz and Nielsen 2013) – it is possible to extract more than one dictionary from the same database (see Chapter 28 of this *Handbook*). Therefore, if we extract a number of monofunctional and/or polyfunctional e-dictionaries from the same database, the question arises as to whether different meaning explanations should be written for the different dictionaries according to their function(s). In the project *The Danish Internet Dictionaries*, the database from which the six e-dictionaries (designed to help Danish laymen in different situations) are extracted contains only one meaning explanation that is used in all the six information tools, or more precisely, for the tools in which meaning explanations are incorporated. In terms of time and money in the working process, reusing the same meaning explanation for all situations is the best solution. In terms of usability, however, it may have been better if different meaning explanations depending on the function of each tool were produced and extracted from the database. Thus, in the case of e-dictionaries, instead of looking at meaning explanations as static, a more dynamic approach can be applied, as will be demonstrated in Sub-section 4.3.3.

4.3.2 Principles for writing meaning explanations

When working with meaning explanations (and all other data types) from a functional perspective, the concept of *relevance* is highly important:

> The lexicographic concept of relevance helps lexicographers when deciding which data to include in dictionaries, ensures that the data selected are actually connected with the dictionary function(s), and that the data are presented so as to minimise the comprehension-related information costs.
>
> (Nielsen 2010: 134)

As explained in Section 4.2, dictionary making is not about telling the full truth, but about selecting what is useful for the specific user in the specific user situation. If we take a dynamic approach to meaning explanations as suggested earlier, *relevance* becomes a very important concept, as this is what guides the lexicographer's selection of meaning elements for different users in different user situations, that is, the lexicographer must consider the following: What is relevant to tell this user type based on her or his competences *and* what is relevant to tell this user type in this type of situation? Nothing more and nothing less than what is needed should be provided in the meaning explanation. In case of more, the user may face information overload and give up her or his search. In case of less, the user will not get the help she or he needs, and the information tool is useless to this person.

A second principle is that the selected meaning elements must be *structured* or *distributed* in the explanation field in an order that aids the users understanding of the meaning explanation. For some words, there is a difference according to the dictionary function in how the meaning elements should be presented (e.g. compare the position of the meaning element *a player can only receive/be given the yellow card once* in the football meaning explanations of *yellow card* for receptive use and operative use, respectively, in Sub-section 4.3.3).

One of the traditional principles for writing meaning explanations is that the lexicographer must apply simple language; the language used to describe a word must be simpler than the word itself, cf. for example Zgusta (1971) and Landau (1984). Although this seems very reasonable, it would be better to say that the explanation has to be *easily understandable* from the viewpoint of the specific user type. For example, the language (vocabulary and syntax) used to describe the meaning of the word *aorta* to a semi-expert does not have to be simple, but it has to be easy to understand for semi-experts. For a layman, on the other hand, non-scientific terms should be applied, and the explanation should not be as scientifically detailed as to a semi-expert.

A fourth principle in writing meaning explanations is that the data must be *correct* and *reliable*, that is, the data should be derived from reliable empirical evidence (see Section 4.4). A difference between a search made with Google or some other search engine and a look-up in a dictionary is that the dictionary will contain carefully selected and reliable data, whereas an Internet search will result in a vast amount of data of which only some will be relevant to the user and of which a lot has not been produced by reliable sources. Notice that this principle of correctness is not the same as explaining the truth. Correct in this context means that the user must be able to trust that the data selected for her or him in the given situation is valid and not misleading.

A fifth principle is that the meaning explanation must be autonomous. The user should not have to make another look-up, and in case of polysemy, the user should not have to have read one or more of the previous explanations in order to understand the relevant one. For example, the explanation of *football* polysem 2 in *Collins English Dictionary* online, "the ball used in any of these games or their variants", is problematic as it relies on the explanation of polysem 1, which explains what "these games" are.

To sum up, the following five main principles must be adhered to when writing meaning explanations from a functional perspective:

1 The data must be lexicographically relevant.
2 The semantic elements must be placed in an order that supports the dictionary function.
3 The explanation must be easily understandable for the intended user type.
4 The data must be correct and reliable.
5 The meaning explanation must be autonomous.

4.3.3 Examples of writing function-based meaning explanations: yellow card

Many different theories or methods can be applied when writing meaning explanations, but in this sub-section, an application of the function theory will be described using the definition of *meaning explanation* presented earlier. This has only been attempted before to a limited extent and will therefore provide new insights into the production of meaning explanations (for example, Nielsen (2011) suggests applying the function theory to meaning explanations and presents some good points, but these are very general and not exemplified, and Kwary (2011) applies the function theory to form a typology of definitions for LSP dictionaries). Some of the points to consider using a function-theoretical approach to meaning explanations will be demonstrated with the term *yellow card.* First, meaning explanations of the lemma from three well-known online dictionaries are provided and briefly discussed, and second, different function-based meaning explanations are suggested. These meaning explanations are tentative, thus they are open for criticism and discussion and do not (yet) appear in a real information tool.

In *Cambridge Advanced Learner's Dictionary & Thesaurus* (CALDT), *Collins English Dictionary* (CED) and *Oxford British & World English Dictionary* (OBWED), the meaning explanations of *yellow card* are as follows (explanations (1), (2) and (3), respectively):

(1) CALDT:
> in football, and some other sports, a small yellow card that is shown to a player by the referee (= the official who is responsible for making certain the rules are followed) as a warning that the player has not obeyed a rule

(2) CED:
> a card of a yellow colour displayed by a referee to indicate that a player has been officially cautioned for some offence

(3) OBWED:
> (in soccer and some other games) a yellow card shown by the referee to a player being cautioned

A number of factual mistakes have been made in the production of these three meaning explanations as indicated with the following authentic examples (emphasis added):

- Example 1: UNH called time out at that point and gained a player advantage just seven seconds later when a BU player *was sent off the field* with **a yellow card.** → in field hockey
- Example 2: After a Foothill player was issued a yellow card, Coach Kaylee Navarette complained to the referee, who gave *the coach* **a yellow card** as well. → in lacrosse
- Example 3: Jack Colback intercepts the pass and Zaha is shown **a yellow card** *for diving.* → in football
- Example 4: Lauren Holiday *will be suspended* for the U.S. women's quarterfinal match against China, after she picked up **her second yellow card** in Canada. → in football

These four authentic examples demonstrate the following:

1 that the meaning explanations quoted from CALDT, CED, and OBWED are too narrow. They focus too much on specific sports such as football, thus they are not useful if a dictionary user wants to understand the word's meaning in some of the other sports in which yellow cards are used, cf. Examples 1 and 2;
2 that the yellow card can be shown not only to players, but (in some sports) also to team officials, cf. Example 2;

3 that the meaning explanations are too superficial. For example, they do not mention the specific situations or acts that may entail a yellow card, how many times a team or a player may receive a yellow card before it has consequences, or what the consequence of receiving this card is, cf. Examples 3 and 4;
4 and that some of the dictionaries do not focus on the relevant parts of the meaning or use of the word. CALDT explains who the referee is, but this is not relevant if the user looks up the term *yellow card* in order to understand what it means (this is probably a consequence of using a restricted defining vocabulary).

Lexicographers often only mention or describe words within the context(s) in which dictionary users will most often come across these words; for example, in the case of England, the most popular sport is football, thus, most investigated data will contain the term *yellow card* in a football context. This selection of the football sense of the term in dictionaries is based on the (high) frequency principle, that is, that only the most frequent uses of a word should be described in a dictionary. If we consider this from a function-perspective, it may be a fine strategy in a production dictionary for non-native speakers (if this dictionary contains meaning explanations) as this user type's active vocabulary will mainly consist of the most frequent uses of a word. However, in a reception dictionary for native speakers, this approach is questionable as the user will most likely know the most frequent uses of a word, but not the infrequent uses, thus it is the latter case that will result in an information need in a reception situation and therefore a need to look up the meaning in a dictionary. This means that in the latter situation, the meaning of *yellow card* in, for example, water polo and handball may be more important to incorporate in this dictionary than the meaning of the word in football.

None of the three dictionaries successfully narrow down the purpose of the dictionary. For example, on the Oxford online dictionaries webpage it says, "Oxforddictionaries.com is your destination whenever you need language guidance: every time you need to know the meaning or pronunciation of a word, how to translate it into another language, or whether you're using it correctly." OBWED is polyfunctional, and it is designed to be used in whatever situation a user needs language guidance. However, incorporating too much data – that is, data that has not been selected by the lexicographer based on its relevance for a given function – may lead to information overload (Gouws and Tarp 2016). In OBWED, the user is not only provided with a meaning explanation, but also with information on line breaks, audio pronunciation, part of speech, examples, a reference to *red card*, social share buttons and adverts, and in CED, the dictionary article contains grammatical data, audio pronunciation, phonetic transcriptions, synonyms, a Chinese translation, social share buttons, adverts and a list of words alphabetically related to the lemma. As this is not a polysemous term in English, these articles with *yellow card* are somewhat easy to read, but if we look this word up in a reception situation, much of the data is irrelevant – for this purpose, only the meaning explanation (and possibly the part of speech) is useful. Also, many dictionaries are today accessible on a mobile phone, which means that even monosemous words can be complicated to get an overview of and browse through if the article contains too much irrelevant data.

Following are provided some suggestions and considerations on how to incorporate meaning explanations in five different situations for laymen (other data types are not mentioned, but different types of data should be applied in different situations, e.g. for production, the user would also need, among other things, data on grammar and collocations, see Chapter 17 of this *Handbook*). These examples indicate that it is not just a question about length, but about what kinds of and how much data the user needs in the described user situations:

1 A person is reading a text and looks up a word in order to understand its meaning in this specific text (= **reception**). This person requires *a rather elaborate meaning explanation; the reader should be able to understand the meaning of the word in the given context. A general meaning explanation is not very useful – factual and cultural details are important.*
2 A person is writing a text and wants to check the inflection of a certain word so she or he uses a spelling and grammar dictionary (= **production**). This dictionary should contain meaning explanations in case of homonymy, as the user needs to be able to distinguish between the homonyms if the dictionary applies grammatical homonymy. This person requires *only a synonym if the person knows something about the relevant theme, but sometimes relevant synonyms do not exist; in the latter case, a simple meaning explanation will suffice (e.g. a short phrase).*
3 A person wants to know more than she or he already knows about a certain word or theme and therefore looks this up in a cognitive dictionary (= **cognition**). This person requires *a much more elaborate meaning explanation than for reception. This could be solved with a lexical note that elaborates on the meaning explanation of the lemma from the reception dictionary, that is, the lexicographer can show these two together in the cognitive dictionary instead of writing a different meaning explanation.*
4 A person cannot remember or does not know the word she or he is looking for when writing a text, but she or he knows its meaning (= **production**). For this purpose, a dictionary can be made in which the user can look for the word using Boolean operators and key search words. This person requires *a meaning explanation that can help her/him decide on the right word (if it exists) in the result list. If the user does not know the word, the explanation should be as elaborate as for reception; if the user cannot remember the word, but knows it, a short explanation is enough.*
5 A person is working on a translation and looks up an unknown word from the source text in a bilingual dictionary in order to find an equivalent (= **translation**). We have two situations: A) The person is not an advanced L2 speaker and does not know much about the relevant theme; and B) the person is an advanced L2 speaker and knows a lot about the relevant theme. In situation A, this person requires *a rather detailed meaning explanation so the translator knows exactly which equivalent to use if there are more than one equivalent. The explanation should be supplied in both L1 and L2*. In situation B, this person requires *only equivalents as the person has sufficient knowledge to distinguish between the equivalents without the help of meaning explanations.*

Agerbo (2015) considers whether there should be only one meaning explanation of a specific sports term in general and specialized dictionaries or if there should be an explanation for its use in each branch of sport. Even if you have the "same" words or terms in handball, football, hockey, etc., they are in reality different and are used quite differently within different sports (e.g. with different collocations and different synonyms). A lexicographer could write a general meaning explanation of *yellow card* for laymen as the one suggested next (resembling the explanations provided by the three dictionaries above):

> *yellow card, approximately 6 by 12 cm and made of plastic, used by the referee in certain sports to warn a player or team official that she or he has broken the rules of the*

game or competition (a mild offence) and that a similar act following this one will have greater consequences; in some sports, the player must leave the field for a short period of the game during which the team plays one man short

Proposal 1: general meaning explanation of **yellow card** to laymen for reception

However, this meaning explanation does not explain the meaning of the word in a handball context in the following example (translated from Danish) from an online discussion forum:

- Example 5: If an act is serious, it can result in a 2-minute penalty even though the team hasn't received three yellow cards yet.

Here, the writer says that you can be given a 2-minute-suspension instead of a yellow card (i.e. you are not given a warning before the penalty). Also, the example mentions that *the team* has received yellow cards, not *a person.* This does not fit with the general meaning explanation. The meaning explanation in handball could be formulated in the following way:

a small yellow card, which the referee in handball shows to a player or team official to tell him that he has broken one of the rules (a minor offence) of the game; the same person can only receive one yellow card in a game, which means that the second time this person violates the rules, he is given a 2-minute suspension; a team can only be given three yellow cards in total, which means that the next time someone from the same team breaks a rule, this person will get a 2-minute suspension; if a person commits a more serious foul, he can receive a 2-minute suspension even though he has not received a yellow card beforehand and even though his team has not received three yellow cards beforehand

Proposal 2: **handball** meaning explanation of **yellow card** to laymen for reception

The following example (translated from Danish) from a news website is also problematic if a layman is reading this article about football and wants to understand the meaning of *yellow card* using the above general meaning explanation:

- Example 6: There will be no relaxation of the quarantine rules for yellow cards in Champions League the next three years. Six players are not allowed to play in the final because they have all received three yellow cards.

The general meaning explanation does not explain that a yellow card in football may have consequences for the player not only in the relevant match, but also in the following matches. A meaning explanation in football could instead be:

a small yellow card, which the referee in football shows to a player to tell him that he has broken one of the more serious rules of the game; the same person can only receive one yellow card in a match without being ejected, which means that the second time this person violates the rules, the second yellow card is converted into a red card and the player must leave the match; in addition to this, in most tournaments, if a player is given a certain number of yellow cards over several matches, it results in disqualification of this offending player for a certain number of subsequent matches

Proposal 3: **football** meaning explanation of **yellow card** to laymen for reception

Of course, this approach to writing and presenting meaning explanations is difficult to apply in a paper dictionary because of the limited space, but in an online dictionary, it would be possible to provide different meaning explanations of the word according to its application in the different sports, for example, by showing them in a list as links:

lemma: *yellow card*
field hockey
football
handball
water polo
etc.
Proposal 4: Links to **yellow card** in different sports

But what if the user only needs a general meaning explanation of the term (e.g. if the person is checking its meaning in a production situation)? Then a general explanation as the one earlier will have to be made, but the lexicographer must decide whether the best solution would be to provide an explanation resembling the use in the most popular sports (i.e. according to frequency) or if it would be better to make an explanation that exemplifies the use in less famous sports (in an English corpus, this would, for example, be its use in *handball*). As explained earlier, this decision will depend on the target user.

Apart from communicative and cognitive situations, there are other situations in which meaning explanations should be applied: operative and interpretative situations. These are yet not well researched and are therefore rarely discussed in lexicographical literature, but see some examples in Bergenholtz and Bothma (2011) and Tarp and Bothma (2013). In an operative situation, the user seeks advice and instructions in order to perform some kind of mental or manual action, and in an interpretative situation, the user needs help to interpret signals and symbols in the surrounding world (Tarp 2008b: 185):

Operative situation:
In what situations and how do I give out a yellow card?
→ This is relevant if you are for example a referee

Interpretative situation:
What does the yellow card mean, and how should a player react to it?
→ This is relevant if you are for example a player or a spectator

A meaning explanation of *yellow card* provided for operative use to interested laymen and also for semi-experts could be:

This card must be presented by the referee to the wrongdoer straight after the foul has been committed. The card should be held straight up in the air and, if necessary, the referee should point at the wrongdoer to make it clear that he is the one given a warning. Following this, the referee should write the name of the wrongdoer on the back of the card or in a notebook so the referee remembers who has been given the card in the match. The referee can only give a player a yellow card once as a warning – the second time he gives the same player a yellow card, he must also show him the red card and exclude him from the match. Once the yellow card has been given to a player, this cannot be reversed.

Proposal 5: **football** meaning explanation of **yellow card** to laymen/semi-experts for operative use

There are authentic examples in which referees have made a mistake when giving someone a yellow card (emphasis added), which suggests that the operative situation is a topic that is worth investigating in more detail:

- Example 7: CSKA should have been down to 10 men as well as the ref gave **the yellow card** *to the wrong player*. → in football
- Example 8: Referee Graham Poll tagged Josip Simunic with **a yellow card** but *forgot to book him*. On Simunic's second offense, Poll again gave Simunic a yellow card. At this point, the referee should have had shown a red card and eject the offending player. But Poll forgot and failed to do so. It was only on Simunic's **third yellow card** that the mistake became apparent. → in football

The last situation to mention is the interpretative situation. Imagine a person not familiar with all the rules of the game handball watching a game in which the referee gives a player a yellow card or shows a player two V-shaped fingers. The TV viewer does not understand these non-linguistic signals and therefore needs an information tool that explains what they mean and why the players act the way they do according to these signals. One of the difficulties in producing a dictionary to satisfy this need can be the search options: if a spectator at a handball or basketball game is not familiar with one of the referee's signals, how can this person search for it in an information tool with an interpretative function? Some of the options are that the user can apply Boolean operators and search words to search for an image and/or written explanation of the signal in the dictionary, or she or he can take a photo of the referee making the signal and use a visual search in the dictionary as for example can be done with the Google Goggles mobile application. A sports dictionary could also provide a list of referee signals which the user could browse though this solution is not optimal as it may be time consuming.

As these different examples have demonstrated, when using a functional approach to meaning explanations, it is important for lexicographers to be familiar with each user type's competences and be aware of what she or he needs to know in the different situations. If we work with the three main user types as described in much modern lexicographical literature (layman, semi-expert and expert), we can stipulate the following for reception: An expert would not look up in a dictionary in order to understand the meaning of a word because a (true) expert would already know this. A semi-expert already knows a lot about the field and therefore seeks a more in-depth explanation. And a layman will need to know the most relevant things about the word. Such considerations about the different user types must also be applied to the other known situations.

When writing meaning explanations, it is not only important to consider the product, that is, the specific information tool(s), in which the explanations are to be used, but also the sources that are to be applied when looking for the needed lexicographical data (i.e. the empirical basis). Most corpus linguists argue that the only way to describe how language is used is by analysing texts in corpora and from this data interpret the relevant meaning, "it would be odd to find a major dictionary project anywhere in the world which did not take a corpus as its starting point" (Atkins and Rundell 2008: 25). The following section discusses the use of electronic corpora as well as other sources for finding lexicographical evidence to be used in meaning explanations.

4.4 Lexicographical data sources

The application of sources for collecting lexicographical evidence has changed from the lexicographer using his intuition combined with the use of manually gathering citations to using corpus evidence from which data such as collocations and examples are extracted and meaning explanations are extrapolated. According to Kilgarriff (1997: 101), "[c]omputerized language corpora changed how lexicographers think about meaning." Instead of relying on intuition and prescribing how language should be used, corpus linguists argue that dictionaries should contain descriptions of language in use; instead of making semantic analyses of words or providing definitions based on one's knowledge (subjective source of evidence), lexicographers should rely on corpus evidence (objective source of evidence) in order to distinguish between what is conventional and recurrent and that which is idiosyncratic.

There is no question that corpora play a central role in many dictionary projects, but corpora are not always useful for collecting data to write meaning explanations or some of the other data types for that matter (Fuertes-Olivera and Tarp 2014; Bergenholtz 2015). In Bergenholtz and Agerbo (2014: 510), a figure demonstrating the extraction and selection of meaning elements as well as the distribution and formulation of meaning elements is presented. The figure, among other things, shows that when a meaning item has been selected, the lexicographer investigates the empirical basis to find relevant data (i.e. meaning elements to include in the given meaning explanation). As examples of the empirical basis, the authors mention introspection, corpora, blogs, websites, dictionaries, handbooks and interviews with experts – they do not only use a corpus. However, the article does not go into detail with this part of the lexicographical work; it is not explained when which sources are used or if the lexicographers in the relevant dictionary project always use a corpus to begin with. Neither does it discuss what the authors mean when they talk about *corpora*. *The Danish Internet Dictionaries*, a number of general language dictionaries which the authors have co-produced and refer to in their article, have all been made using the Web as a corpus, not a compiled corpus. However, when corpus linguists talk about corpora, they typically refer to collections of texts compiled in order to be representative of a language or part of a language and in a machine-readable form. Thus, Bergenholtz and Agerbo (2014) apply a much broader definition of *corpus* as they consider the Web a vast, free and instantly available source of old as well as new language data (see Kilgarriff and Grefenstette (2003) for a discussion of using the Web as a corpus).

If we look at the role of experts as a source for lexicographical evidence, Fuertes-Olivera and Tarp (2014) and Bergenholtz (see Chapter 2 of this *Handbook*) argue that in the case of specialized lexicography, a team must always consist of at least a lexicographer, a field expert and an IT expert. The field expert is the one who writes the meaning explanations of the specialized terms (if he is competent for this task) or who verifies that the meaning explanation is correct – the work will not be based on a corpus analysis. When Henning Bergenholtz (lexicographer and dictionary editor) and Uwe Kaufmann (expert in gene technology) wrote the *Dictionary of Gene Technology* (published in 1992), Kaufmann wrote the meaning explanations and Bergenholtz revised them. A person writing a meaning explanation of *gene* to a semi-expert or an expert needs to be an expert himself on the topic. An expert will also be better at writing explanations of specialized terms to laymen, as she or he will, contrary to a non-expert, more likely have knowledge about certain differences between the applications of a term in general versus specialized language, though not all experts have the proper language skills to formulate such explanations.

When working with specialized language, a lexicographer needs to decide whether explanations of specialized words should be made with scientific precision and stringency, that is, according to scientists (experts), or if the explanation should be more flexible and prototype-based (Varantola 1993: 249–251; Hanks 2013: 342). If we look at a word such as *tomato*, corpus data show that many non-experts consider this a vegetable, but a biologist or a botanist would consider this a fruit. Thus, lexicographers must decide whether to describe language as it is used in a corpus of general language or in terms of scientific definitions. Though corpus linguists would argue that it is language in a corpus that should be described, a better answer to this would be: this will depend on the intended user and user situation. The scientific explanation involves a tomato being described as a fruit, but for a layman who wants to understand the use of this word in a specific text, the dictionary could mention that it is considered and eaten as a vegetable, for example, as in OBWED, "A glossy red, or occasionally yellow, pulpy edible fruit which is eaten as a vegetable or in salad." In a meaning explanation aimed at a layman, another solution is to write that this is a vegetable, but in a note write that scientifically speaking it is a fruit. For a semi-expert who wants to write a text and use the word *tomato*, the lexicographer could write in the meaning explanation that this is a fruit, but in a note write that it is often considered a vegetable amongst laymen (a solution very similar to the one used in OBWED) so the semi-expert will be aware of this if writing a text to laymen.

This example demonstrates that a corpus investigation is sometimes not enough to write a meaning explanation. At other times, it is not even useful (Fuertes-Olivera 2012; Bergenholtz 2016). If we consider geographical names, lexicographers do not use a corpus to describe words such as *London* or the *Danube*, but they apply their own knowledge, check handbooks and other dictionaries. The meaning explanation of *Danube* in OBWED is clearly not derived from an analysis of corpus data:

> A river which rises in the Black Forest in SW Germany and flows about 2,850 km (1,770 miles) into the Black Sea. It is the second-longest river in Europe after the Volga; the cities of Vienna, Budapest, and Belgrade are situated on it. German name Donau.

Indeed, for place names, it is stated in *Collins Dictionary of the English Language* that "[s]tatistical information about places has been obtained from the most up-to-date and reliable sources available. Population figures have been compiled from the most recent census available at the time of going to press" (1979: xv).

Therefore, when a lexicographer applies lexicographical sources in the process of writing meaning explanations, she or he must consider the relation between the explanation and the intended user type and user situation. The following figure (Figure 4.1) is a revised version of the one found in Bergenholtz (2016).

Figure 4.1 demonstrates how the lexicographer chooses what sources from the empirical basis to apply when searching for lexicographical evidence for a dictionary article. The point of departure is the genuine dictionary purpose, that is, a choice has to be made concerning the intended user type and user situation. Bergenholtz does not mention that type of language construction (e.g. a geographical name as in Figure 4.2) should also be considered when preparing meaning explanations. However, this is to be explained as this also

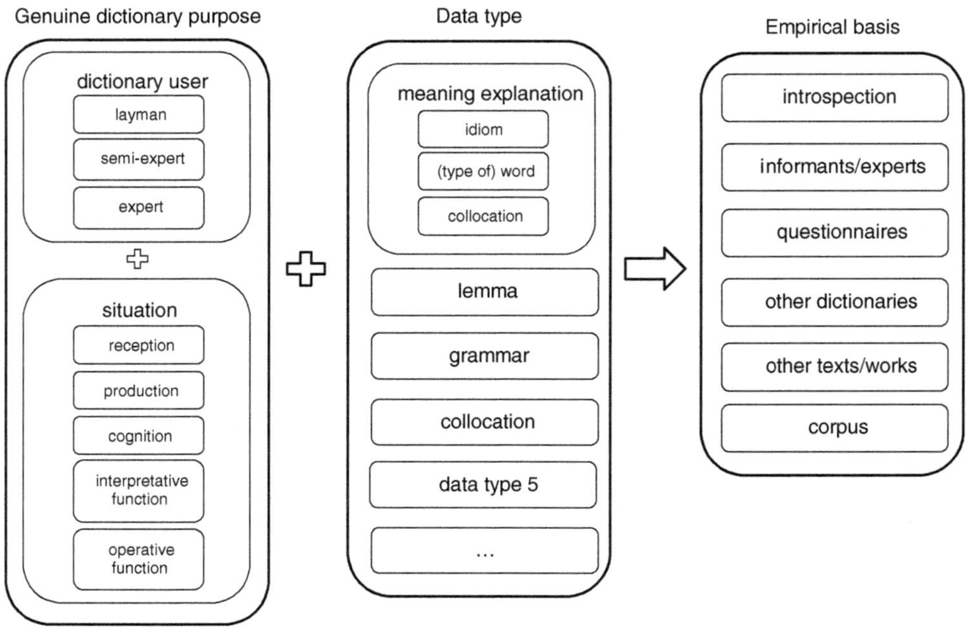

Figure 4.1 The application of the empirical basis based on the dictionary function

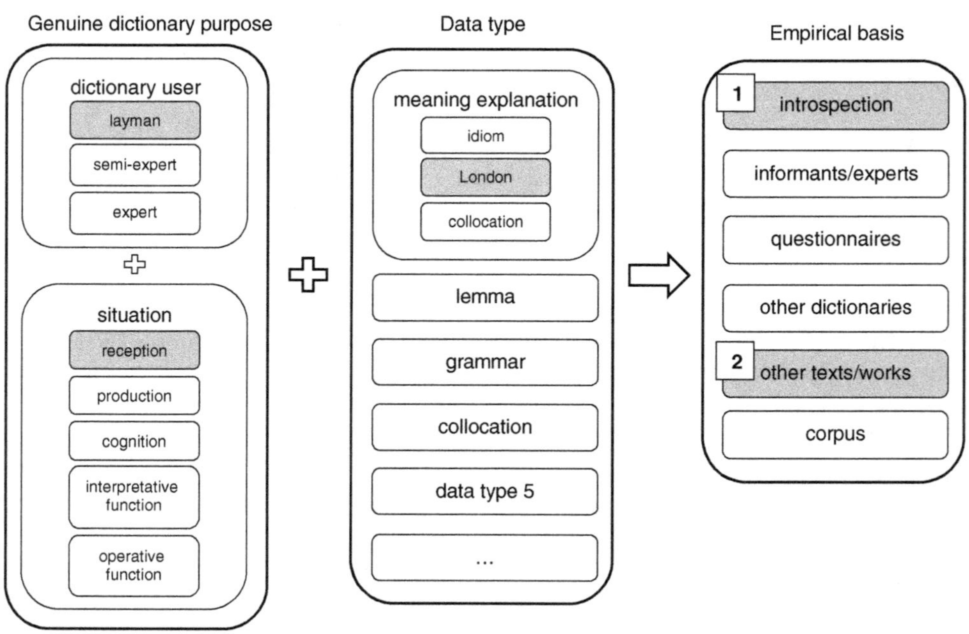

Figure 4.2 Sources applied in the explanation of *London*

influences what sources from the empirical basis should be used. Nor does he comment on the succession of the different sources (if different sources are used) during the process. Figures 4.2, 4.3 and 4.4 demonstrate how the elements USER + SITUATION + LANGUAGE CONSTRUCTION determine what source or sources should be applied in the collection of lexicographical evidence for the meaning explanation, and the numbers show the order in which the sources from the empirical basis are applied:

Figure 4.2 shows that if a lexicographer's task were to write the meaning explanation of *London* to laymen for reception, she or he would first apply her or his own knowledge (e.g. that London is the capital of England) and then look it up in an atlas in order to describe its geographical location and in a census in order to comment on the number of inhabitants. Figure 4.3 shows that if writing the meaning explanation of *yellow card* to laymen in an operative situation (see Sub-section 4.3.3), the lexicographer would first apply her or his own knowledge (e.g. if the lexicographer has knowledge about football, handball and/or other sports), then look in a corpus and in handbooks on sport and finally compare this explanation to other dictionary explanations. A corpus will typically only show the use of the word in the most popular sports, and therefore it would also be necessary to use handbooks on sport. It may be that handbooks should be consulted before a corpus, but introspection as the first source and other dictionaries as the final source should be applied in this order. In Figure 4.4, the word *gene* is to be explained to semi-experts, and in this case, the lexicographer would have to work together with experts or be an expert herself or himself and also use handbooks on genetics – a corpus would not be relevant for this task.

At the beginning of this section, it was described as a given that the purpose of an information tool is to describe language in use. However, if language in use means language in a

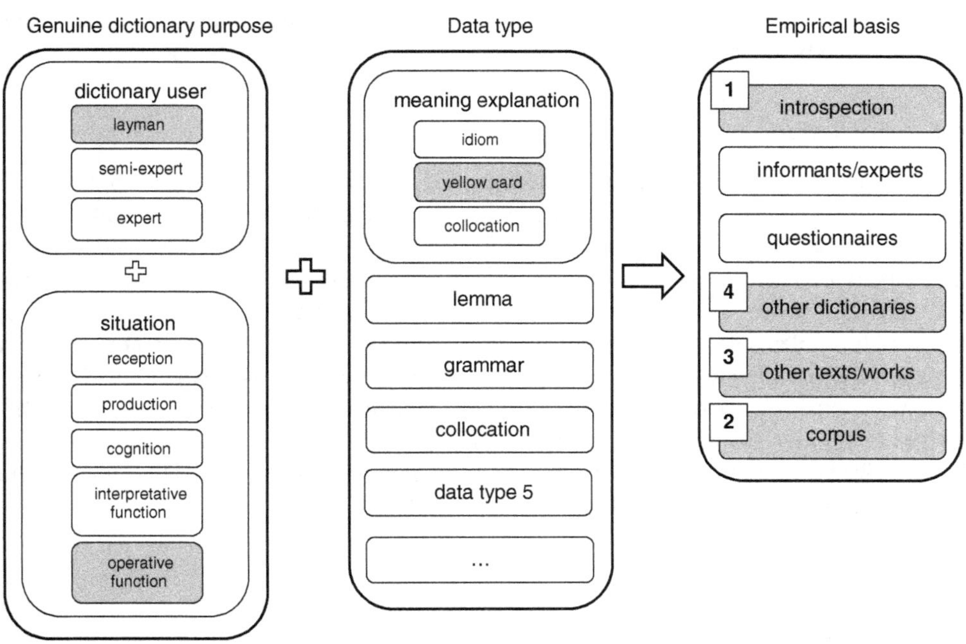

Figure 4.3 Sources applied in the explanation of *yellow card*

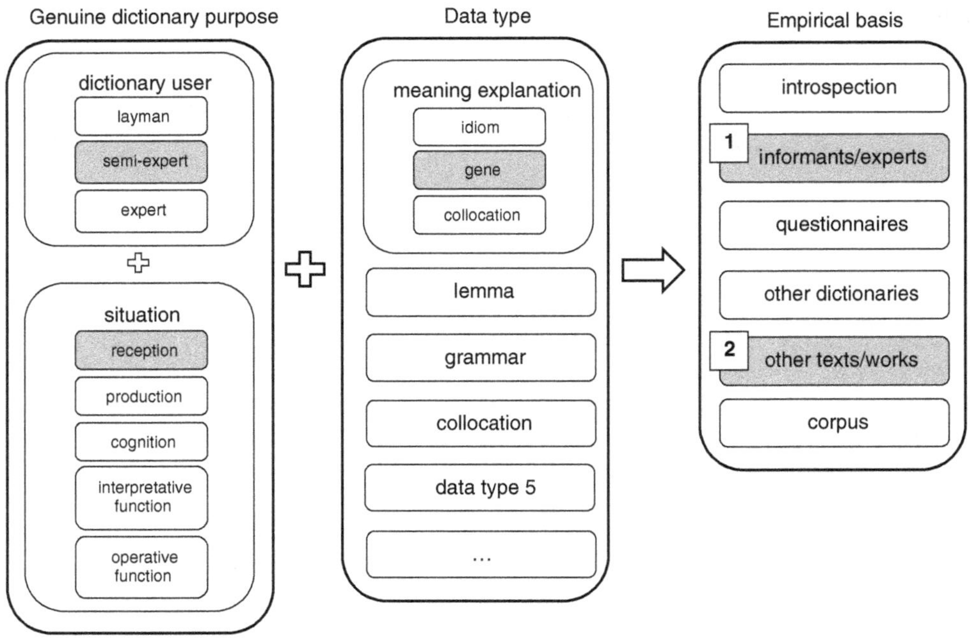

Figure 4.4 Sources applied in the explanation of *gene*

corpus, this statement should be questioned. When looking for data types such as examples and collocations, then yes, we do need a corpus because we cannot rely on our intuition. But as has been demonstrated in this section, when producing meaning explanations, (1) sometimes we should only use a corpus, (2) sometimes a corpus should supplement or be supplemented by other sources and (3) in other cases a corpus is simply not useful.

4.5 Conclusion

This chapter has demonstrated what meaning explanations look like when applying the function theory instead of using a linguistic theory. Whether discussing the content, form or structure of meaning explanations, they should always be produced in order to aid a certain user type with a certain information need that has occurred in a certain extra-lexicographical situation. When lexicographers write meaning explanations for e-tools, they are not faced with problems of space or primitive search options, and therefore they should take a dynamic approach to meaning explanations as demonstrated with the test word *yellow card* in Sub-section 4.3.3. Dictionaries today are mainly aimed at helping their users in communicative or cognitive situations, but future dictionaries may also be designed to aid their users in operative and interpretative situations. However, more research needs to be done into the nature of these functions in relation to the function theory.

Related topics

Lexicography as an independent science; dictionary management; lexicography and interdisciplinarity; lexicography and information science; dictionaries for text reception; using the Web for lexicographic purposes.

Further reading

Bergenholtz, H. and S. Tarp. (2003). "Two Opposing Theories: On HE Wiegand's Recent Discovery of Lexicographic Functions", *Hermes* 31: 171–196.
Section 2 in this article provides a good presentation of the function theory, though it does not comment on the operative and interpretative functions, as these were not mentioned in the lexicographical literature until 2007 and 2008, respectively. Unfortunately, very little research into these two functions has been performed, and therefore the literature on them is still scarce.

Hanks, P. (2016). "Definitions", in P. Durkin (ed.), *The Oxford Handbook of Lexicography*. Oxford: Oxford University Press, pp. 94–122.
This chapter provides an overview of the incorporation of definitions in lexicography from a historical perspective.

Nielsen, S. (2013). "Domain-Specific Knowledge in Lexicography: How It Helps Lexicographers and Users of Accounting Dictionaries Intended for Communicative Usage Situations", *Hermes* 50: 51–60.
This article argues that a lexicographer should have domain-specific knowledge when writing definitions of specialized words both in general and specialized dictionaries.

Riemer, N. (2015). "Word Meanings", in J. R. Taylor (ed.), *The Oxford Handbook of the Word*. Oxford: Oxford University Press, pp. 305–319.
This chapter discusses the concept *word meaning*, and the author supports the approach presented in this chapter as he argues that the correct explanation of a word is whatever works in the particular situation in which the explanation is needed. This argument is applicable both in everyday conversation and in a lexicographical context.

Tarp, S. (2013). "Lexicographic Functions", in R. H. Gouws, U. Heid, W. Schweickard and H. E. Wiegand (eds.) *Dictionaries: An International Encyclopedia of Lexicography: Supplementary Volume: Recent Developments With Focus on Electronic and Computational Lexicography*. Berlin: Walter de Gruyter, pp. 460–468.
This short chapter describes how the lexicographical function theory developed through the work of certain influential lexicographers from different schools of thought, and it describes the essence of this theory: the lexicographical functions.

References

Dictionaries

Cambridge (2013) *Cambridge Advanced Learner's Dictionary*. [online] Cambridge: Cambridge University Press. http://dictionary.cambridge.org/dictionary/english/ [Accessed 15 February 2016].

Collins (1979) *Collins Dictionary of the English Language*. London: Collins.

Collins (2014) *Collins English Dictionary*. [online] Glasgow: HarperCollins Publishers. www.collinsdictionary.com/dictionary/english [Accessed 15 February 2016].

Longman (2013) *Longman Dictionary of Contemporary English*. [online] Harlow: Longman. www.ldoceonline.com [Accessed 15 February 2016].

Ordbogen.com (2016) *Den Danske Netordbog*. [online] Odense: Ordbogen.com. www.ordbogen.com.

Oxford (2010) *Oxford Dictionary of English*. [online] New York: Oxford University Press. http://oxforddictionaries.com [Accessed 15 February 2016].

Other literature

Agerbo, H. (2015) "How to Describe Sports Terms in Information Tools for Laymen", *Estudios de Lexicografia* 4: 137–160.

Atkins, B. S. and M. Rundell. (2008) *The Oxford Guide to Practical Lexicography*. Oxford: Oxford University Press.

Ayto, J. R. (1983) "On Specifying Semantic Analysis and Dictionary Definitions", in R.R.K. Hartmann (ed.), *Lexicography: Principles and practice*. London: Academic, pp. 89–98.

Béjoint, H. (1988) "Scientific and technical words in general dictionaries", *International Journal of Lexicography* 1(4): 354–368.

Bergenholtz, H. (2016) "Eine Korpusanalyse ist eine überflüssige Zeremonie", in S. J. Schierholz, R. H. Gouws, Z. Hollós and W. Wolski (eds.), *Wörterbuchforschung und Lexicographie*. Berlin: Walter de Gruyter, pp. 155–168.

Bergenholtz, H. and H. Agerbo (2014) "Extraction, selection and distribution of meaning elements for monolingual information tools", *Lexicographica* 30: 488–510.

Bergenholtz, H. and J. S. Nielsen. (2013) "What Is a Lexicographical Database?", *Lexikos* 23: 77–87.

Bergenholtz, H. and S. Tarp (eds.) (1995) *Manual of Specialised Lexicography: The Preparation of Specialised Dictionaries*. Amsterdam: John Benjamins Publishing.

Bolinger, D. (1965) "The Atomization of Meaning", *Language* 41(4): 555–573.

Darian, S. (1982) "The Role of Definitions in Scientific and Technical Writing: Forms, Functions, and Properties", in J. Høedt, L. Lundquist, H. Picht and J. Qvistgaard (eds.), *Proceedings of the 3rd European Symposium on LSP. Copenhagen, August 1981. 'Pragmatics and LSP'*. Copenhagen: Erhvervsøkonomisk Forlag, pp. 27–47.

Fuertes-Olivera, P. A. (2012) "Lexicography and the internet as a (Re-)source", *Lexicographica* 28: 49–70.

Fuertes-Olivera, P. A. and S. Tarp. (2014) *Theory and Practice of Specialised Online Dictionaries: Lexicography Versus Terminography*. Berlin: de Gruyter.

Gouws, R. H., and S. Tarp (2016) "Information Overload and Data Overload in Lexicography", *International Journal of Lexicography*. ecw030. doi: 10.1093/ijl/ecw030

Haiman, J. (1980) "Dictionaries and Encyclopedias", *Lingua* 50(4): 329–357.

Hanks, P. (1987) "Definitions and Explanations", in J. M. Sinclair (ed.), *Looking Up: An Account of the COBUILD Project in Lexical Computing*. London: Collins, pp. 116–136.

Hanks, P. (2000) "Do Word Meanings Exist?", *Computers and the Humanities* 34(1): 205–215.

Hanks, P. (2013) *Lexical Analysis: Norms and Exploitations*. Cambridge: MIT Press.

Kilgarriff, A. (1997) "I Don't Believe in Word Senses", *Computers and the Humanities* 31(2): 91–113.

Kilgarriff, A., and G. Grefenstette. (2003) "Introduction to the Special Issue on the Web as Corpus", *Computational linguistics* 29(3): 333–347.

Kwary, D. (2011) "Towards a Typology of Definitions for LSP", *Journal of English Studies* 9: 55–74.

Landau, S. I. (1984) *Dictionaries: The Art and Craft of Lexicography*. New York: Charles Scribner's Sons.

Liu, X. (2015) "Multimodal Definition: the Multiplication of Meaning in Electronic Dictionaries", *Lexikos* 25: 210–232.

Lombard, F. J. (1991) "Die aard en aanbieding van die leksikografiese definisie", *Lexikos* 1: 158–182.

Nielsen, S. (2010) "The Relevance of Lexicographic Functions", in A. Aminova and N. Fattakhova (eds.), *Comparative Philology and Multilingualism: Materials of the International Scientific Conference*. Kazan: Academy of Science, pp. 132–135.

Nielsen, S. (2011) "Function-and User-Related Definitions in Online Dictionaries", in F. Kartashkova (ed.), *Ivanovskaya leksikografischeskaya shkola: traditsii i innovatsii*. Ivanovo: Ivanovo State University, pp. 197–219.

Robinson, R. (1950) *Definition*. Oxford: Oxford University Press.

Svensén, B. (2009) *Handbook of Lexicography: The Theory and Practice of Dictionary-Making*. Cambridge: Cambridge University Press.

Tarp, S. (2008a) *Lexicography in the Borderland between Knowledge and Non-knowledge: General Lexicographical Theory With Particular Focus on Learner's Lexicography*. Tübingen: Max Niemeyer Verlag.

Tarp, S. (2008b) "Revival of a Dusty Old Profession", *Hermes* 41: 175–188.

Tarp, S. (2012) "Do We Need a (New) Theory of Lexicography?", *Lexikos* 22: 321–332.

Tarp, S., and T. J. Bothma. (2013) "An Alternative Approach to Enlightenment Age Lexicography: The Universal Dictionary of Trade and Commerce", *Lexicographica* 29(1): 222–284.

Varantola, K. (1993) "Technical Vocabulary and Learners' Dictionaries", in R. Hiltunen, M. Gustafsson, K. Battarbee and L. Dahl (eds.), *English Far and Wide: A Festschrift for Inna Koskenniemi*. Turku: Turun Yliopisto, pp. 249–260.

Wiegand, H. E. (1992) "Elements of a Theory Towards a So-Called Lexicographic Definition", *Lexicographica* 8: 175–289.

Wierzbicka, A. (1992) "What Are the Uses of Theoretical Lexicography?", *Dictionaries: Journal of the Dictionary Society of North America* 14(1): 44–78.

Zgusta, L. (1971) *Manual of Lexicography*. The Hague: Mouton.

5 Dictionary criticism

Sandro Nielsen

5.1 Introduction

Dictionary criticism is an activity that goes back many years and has been exercised by a wide range of different people. The criticism has thus come in many shapes and sizes with focuses that tend to reflect the personal interests of individual critics. In order to provide general guidance on critiquing dictionaries a limited number of lexicographers have discussed various issues relevant for writing critiques, for example, by proposing lists of features to look for in dictionaries or criteria to follow to express opinions about their qualities. Ripfel (1989) discusses in detail criteria for evaluating monolingual dictionaries with a focus on semantic features in German dictionaries, whereas Chan and Loong (1999) and Chan and Taylor (2001) discuss evaluation criteria for monolingual learner's dictionaries with particular focus on morphological, phonological, syntactic, semantic and pragmatic data, and language of definitions. Pearsons and Nichols (2013) discuss a framework for evaluating online English dictionaries with a focus on usability issues and linguistic data, and Steiner (1979) provides guidelines for critiquing bilingual dictionaries mainly on the basis of their linguistic data. Despite several attempts to provide help to those who critique dictionaries, Swanepoel (2013: 594) concludes that "the whole topic of dictionary evaluation still requires extensive research."

Critiques of dictionaries can be unpublished writings such as exploratory analyses that form part of lexicographical research projects but are often published as dictionary reviews in various media. Popular media tend to contain relatively short reviews of dictionaries for the general public for instance with a view to drawing attention to new publications, whereas scholarly media contain relatively long reviews for academia. In general, good dictionary reviews may be seen as genuine contributions to the ongoing development of practical and theoretical lexicography, and this chapter focuses on dictionary criticism that can potentially contribute to the development of lexicographical practice and theory. Dictionary reviews are thus relevant writings for practitioners as well as researchers, and reviewers should engage critically with the subject, but what does criticism mean in this context? According to *Oxford Advanced Learner's Dictionary* the noun *criticism* has two meanings: "**1** the act of expressing disapproval of sb/sth and opinions about their faults or bad qualities

[. . . .] **2** the work or activity of making fair, careful judgements about the good and bad qualities of sb/sth." The latter sense refers to the relevant type of critique, and in order to establish what good dictionary reviews may contain, it is appropriate to define dictionary criticism as *the act of giving a fair presentation of a dictionary based on judgements about the qualities of the dictionary following an examination of it.*

This definition contains several elements that will be discussed here, and Section 5.2 examines dictionaries as the object of study and attempts to define the genuine purpose of dictionary criticism. Section 5.3 describes a procedure that can be used by reviewers and proposes three approaches to the task. In addition, it examines the qualitative requirements of dictionary reviews, and Section 5.4 provides a brief glimpse of the future of dictionary criticism.

5.2 Historical perspective: two fundamentals of dictionary criticism

Those who are engaged in writing should make sure that they have a sound base from which to proceed. This involves a clear idea of the nature of the object analysed, described and examined and a clear idea of the purpose of the review exercise, as discussed later.

5.2.1 Defining the object of study

There is no doubt that the objects to be studied and critiqued in dictionary reviews are dictionaries and, therefore, reviewers should have a clear picture of the nature of the social reality examined. This may seem obvious but as described by Tarp and Bothma (2013: 224), lexicography during the Enlightenment era aimed to disseminate knowledge about language and factual matters with a didactic element but this situation changed when lexicographers such as Samuel Johnson began to work "with a much narrower concept [of dictionary] than other authors from the same century. In his [Johnson's] view, a dictionary is apparently only about words" (Tarp and Bothma 2013: 225). Nielsen (2015a: 162–163) argues that it is a fallacy to say that dictionaries are only about language and attempts to show that modern lexicography has re-adopted a broad view describing dictionaries as lexicographical tools that deal with words, terms, facts and things.

The ontological assumptions reviewers make should not be underestimated. As claimed by Grix (2010: 60) "Your 'ontological position', whether you know it or not, is implicit even before you choose your topic of study", and a failure to address ontological assumptions "stems from vagueness, imprecision, or a failure to understand that there is more than one ontological perspective" (Mason 2002: 16). Dictionary reviews should comply with the general requirements of clarity, precision and transparency because the ontological assumptions of reviewers are directly linked to their understanding of the concept of dictionary as an object of analysis, examination and research. As implied earlier, not all lexicographers agree on what a dictionary is; for instance, Durkin (2016: 1) expresses little doubt when he writes that "Few people need to be told, in the broadest terms, what a dictionary is" and goes on to claim that "all dictionaries ultimately form part of an interconnected network of information about language and languages" (Durkin 2016: 2). An ontological position like this is not very helpful because it implies that many dictionaries including the *Oxford Dictionary of Economics* – which, according to Hashimzade, Myles and Myles (2014), is about concepts, terms, facts and skills – do not qualify as dictionaries because they are not about language. Other scholars describe dictionaries as reference works that contain words, their pronunciation, spelling and meaning, or as books that show words and their translations in other languages; see e.g. Crystal (2010: 112) and Sterkenburg (2003: 396). When they establish their ontological position, reviewers should note that dictionaries are about more than languages.

Reviewers should have an open mind and adopt a wide and complex ontological position when they critique dictionaries. Nielsen (2009a: 27–28; and 2009b: 215) suggest that dictionaries are information tools with a number of features that are visible to users in print or on screens, called surface features, such as user guides, wordlists, appendices, search sites and results sites, as well as three underlying features, the first of which is that dictionaries are designed to have one or more lexicographical functions. Following Bergenholtz and Tarp (2010: 30) a lexicographical function can be defined as the type of help a dictionary can give to a specific user type in a specific type of non-lexicographical situation in which a person may consult a dictionary; this includes communicative functions such as providing help to write, to understand or to translate texts, and cognitive functions such as to provide help to acquire knowledge independently of communicative activities. Second, dictionaries contain data that have been selected because they support the relevant function(s), and third, lexicographical structures present and link the data so that they support the dictionary function(s). Reviewers should not see these as isolated features, because a dictionary is made up of the totality of surface and underlying features and their interrelationships.

The proposed ontological position is wide and complex in the sense that it applies to dictionaries in general (see Chapter 14 of this *Handbook*). It includes, for instance, print and online dictionaries, monolingual and bilingual dictionaries, general and specialised dictionaries and learner's expert's dictionaries. The earlier function-oriented definition focuses on information needs of users and how lexicographers can respond to such needs, and the proposed ontological position allows reviewers to regard dictionaries as lexicographical tools that deal with words, terms, concepts, facts and practical matters. When they have clearly identified the functions, which types of data can support those functions and how the data are linked, reviewers will have a sound ontological position on which to proceed. However, the ontological position regarding the object of study must be linked to the purpose of dictionary criticism.

5.2.2 Defining the purpose of dictionary criticism

The ontological position affects the way in which reviewers treat the dictionaries under review, and their critique should comply with the purpose of dictionary reviewing. The existing literature contains various proposals for the purpose of dictionary criticism although lexicographers seem to agree that reviews should describe, analyse and examine dictionaries (e.g. Ripfel 1989: 31), which is in line with the general requirement of good writing being critical and analysing. Swanepoel (2008: 209) further argues that the two major goals of reviews are to guide readers to find the dictionaries that can best satisfy lexicographically relevant user needs and to guide lexicographers in improving the qualities of dictionaries.

Partly based on the earlier considerations and linking them to the object of dictionary criticism described in Section 5.2.1, a tentative definition of the purpose of dictionary reviews may read as follows: *The purpose of dictionary criticism is to give a fair presentation of dictionary function(s), dictionary data, presentation of the data, and accessibility of the data.* This fair presentation should be useful to existing and potential dictionary users, dictionary researchers, dictionary compilers, dictionary publishers and others interested in practical and theoretical lexicography in the following general types of situation: when they apply and develop theoretical and/or practical lexicographical principles; when they form opinions about dictionaries in theoretical and practical contexts; when they consult dictionaries as part of their theoretical and practical work; when they buy or contemplate buying dictionaries; and when they recommend or advise against dictionaries. Finally, it follows from this that reviewers can only provide a fair presentation if their depiction of a dictionary is complete in the sense that it takes the whole dictionary into account (i.e. surface and underlying features).

5.3 Core topics and issues: basic approaches to reviewing

All evaluations made by man have a subjective element through the exercise of judgement and the evaluation of dictionaries is no different. This may seem to contradict the general requirement of objectivity in, for example, research and critical analyses, but a closer look at the meaning of objectivity should dispel any fear:

> Objectivity refers primarily to the extent to which the scholar relies on external criteria, facts or evidence (including theoretical arguments) in making a choice or reaching a conclusion [. . . .] So objectivity is not related to whether or not you have exercised judgment, but rather to what you have based that judgment on.
>
> (Nygaard 2015: 45)

This means, first of all, that good dictionary reviews include judgements about dictionaries based on objective criteria and evidence. Second, without the subjective element, dictionary reviews would mainly be descriptions, and the subjective element is part of the critical analyses required of most serious work. Finally, this form of objectivity makes it possible to have different reviews of the same dictionary that are all correct but reflect different judgements, which is the reason why the purpose of dictionary criticism is to give *a* fair presentation and not *the* fair presentation of a dictionary.

Dictionary criticism is part of the ongoing lexicographical dialogue and should comply with generally accepted principles. Nielsen (2009a) proposes a general framework for reviewing online and print dictionaries and argues that due to the nature of the object of study the lexicographical, linguistic, and factual as well as other competences of reviewers play a key role in the review process. According to a function-based approach, reviewers should therefore evaluate dictionaries by examining the degree to which the data in the dictionary fulfil the intended function(s) and by relating individual data types to one or more particular functions.

The general framework allows reviewers to combine three basic approaches that match the object of study and the purpose of reviews. Reviewers should primarily use a lexicographical approach in line with the broad scope of modern lexicography where dictionaries have lexicographically relevant functions and are concerned with words, terms, concepts, facts and practical matters (see Chapters 1 and 15 of this *Handbook*). When using this approach, reviewers analyse, describe and evaluate the lexicographical practices and principles adopted by the lexicographers and may compare these with lexicographical practices and principles that were not adopted. The lexicographical approach requires knowledge of various lexicographical principles and practices for print and online dictionaries, including knowledge about lexicographical functions and their related extra-lexicographical use situations, for instance knowledge of the practice and principles of communicative, cognitive, interpretive and operative activities such as translation of fictional and non-fictional texts.

Another approach is the factual approach where reviewers analyse, describe and evaluate the factual data in the dictionary and relate the data to the relevant lexicographical function(s). Reviewers must possess semantic, encyclopaedic and domain-specific knowledge because general dictionaries usually contain domain-specific terms and because specialised dictionaries may treat more than one subject field.

The last approach may be called a linguistic approach and here reviewers analyse, describe and evaluate the language treated by the dictionary. The linguistic approach requires knowledge of language for general purposes and language for special purposes at, for example, sentence, phrase, word and term levels, and reviewers may also need additional linguistic competences depending on whether dictionaries are mono-, bi- or multilingual. In order to make their analyses, descriptions and evaluations as useful to readers as possible, reviewers should relate these three approaches to the surface and underlying features of dictionaries.

5.3.1 Using the lexicographical approach

Reviewers who use the lexicographical approach may address general issues that are relevant to all identified features. In order to give a fair presentation of a dictionary, reviewers should relate the dictionary to the ontological position described in Section 5.2.1, which seems to fit in well with the following statement: "To conclude, reviewing a dictionary means not only scrutinizing the lexical material which it provides, but also examining its front matter, back matter, covers, spine, jacket, and title, as well as the publisher's advertising for it" (Gold 1993: 305). This observation supports the claim that dictionaries are complex objects of study that contain a number of independent components and text types, such as user guides, grammar sections, subject-field components and wordlists. In print dictionaries, these components are related to each other through their data contents and the order in which they appear so that all the individual surface feature components constitute a coherent whole. Online dictionaries also contain several and often similar types of component in the form of text files, webpages and audio/visual material linked to search options or results pages and may even contain links to other websites as attempts to provide help to users in specific situations. Reviewers may then examine these components and relate the findings to the three underlying features of the dictionary. For example, reviewers who study dictionary functions will not only examine the separate components of the dictionary independently but should examine their relationship to each other and the wordlist (and its online equivalent).

In their evaluation of surface feature components, reviewers should focus on the data these components contain, the way in which the data are presented and how the data can be accessed by users. In its back matter, *Collins COBUILD Advanced Dictionary of English* has a component called "Brief Writer's Handbook" and one called "Brief Speaker's Handbook", which are relevant to the communicative activities writing and speaking, but the "Guide to Key Features" does not mention these two components. In such cases, reviewers may comment on this lack of reference because the data in the two components directly affect the help the dictionary provides to users in communicative situations. Furthermore, it seems reasonable to expect that user guides answer the following questions in relation to each dictionary component:

1 What is this component?
2 How does this component assist users in relation to the dictionary function(s)?
3 How does this component relate to and interact with the other components?

The general lack of attention to such surface feature components is discussed in Nielsen (2009b), who examined the evaluation of outside matter in reviews published in the journal *Lexikos* and found that reviewers define the object of study differently, with some excluding outside matter altogether from their reviews, and that the way in which outside matter is assessed differs considerably, from a mere mention to a detailed discussion of factual contents. One way in which to contribute to a fair presentation of the dictionary is to describe what each component is about, to explain why it is relevant for the function(s) of the dictionary and to examine how it interacts with the rest of the dictionary.

Lexicographical functions are the assistance lexicographers provide in an attempt to satisfy the needs of users in extra-lexicographical situations. Reviewers may examine the function(s) of dictionaries by analysing, describing and evaluating the functions a dictionary is designed to fulfil, for instance, communicative functions such as providing help to understand, write, edit and translate texts, and cognitive functions such as providing help to acquire knowledge about something in general or specific knowledge about a particular matter, to determine whether the dictionary data support the relevant function(s). For instance, specialised translation dictionaries for learners should help learners acquire knowledge about terms as well as help learners acquire knowledge about correct usage, such as domain-specific syntactic structures, genre conventions and translation strategies. In addition, Nielsen (2000) examines translation strategies for culture-specific genre conventions in bilingual specialised dictionaries and concludes that the lexicographers used translation strategies inconsistently, failed to inform users about different strategical solutions used within dictionary articles and often led users astray. Reviewers should consider addressing such issues when evaluating translation dictionaries because the issues are part and parcel of translating. The functional approach thus allows reviewers to show that dictionaries are suitable or not suitable for all or some of the functions and extra-lexicographical user situations mentioned in their meta-texts based on an examination of the data included.

As in most other situations, successful communication of data in dictionaries (i.e. the provision of help) depends on the way in which the data are presented. This means that lexicographers should present data in dictionaries that are easily accessible to and understandable by users, so reviewers may, for instance, examine whether dictionaries use full sentences and complex syntax in definitions, use textual condensation such as abbreviations or symbols, and use logical and navigable structures to present data in all dictionary components in print or on screen. In this context, reviewers may find it useful to distinguish between lexicographical data, which are data that provide help concerning the function(s) and use of dictionaries, and extra-lexicographical data, which are data that do not support the function(s) and use of dictionaries. Extra-lexicographical data in, for instance, online dictionaries include general informative data by publishers, advertisements on home pages and advertisements surrounding the main text body in onsite guides and results pages. Reviewers should prioritise lexicographical data because they directly support the functions and use of dictionaries and may discuss extra-lexicographical data if these affect the presentation of lexicographical data negatively or positively to a material extent (see Section 5.3.4).

Data can be presented in dictionary components in three general ways. First, data can be presented as written text shown as straight text, that is, long black text with or without signposts for users to follow, but can also be shown using white lines to separate text blocs causing the visual hierarchy of the main body text to stand out. Normally, such data are presented as black text on a white background, but may also be presented as polychrome text using different colours to highlight words or background that function as signposts for users, although some fonts and colours are easier to read than others. Furthermore, online dictionaries often allow users to change font sizes so that users can increase or decrease the font size of dictionary data or zoom in or out of a particular text part. Finally, online dictionaries may use a layered presentation format in that webpages often contain elements that need to be activated such as drop-down menus and hover-over explanations written in clear and readable text. Reviewers should examine to which extent written data are legible and presented so that they support the identified dictionary functions.

Second, print and online dictionaries often contain data presented as illustrations. Users can find drawings, graphs and photos in print dictionaries and online dictionaries may contain screenshots, video footage and multimedia features as well. Some types of illustration, such as video footage in sign language dictionaries, may have to be activated to be presented. The quality of such illustrations is important because poor factual and presentational quality may prevent users from understanding the purpose of such data. Reviewers should consider whether illustrations in dictionaries support surrounding text and identified dictionary functions, and should examine the factual and illustrative quality of the illustrations.

Third, data in dictionary components can be presented in audio format. At first glance, this would only apply to online dictionaries, but some print dictionaries come with CDs containing audio files such as audio pronunciation, and some publishers offer free online audio pronunciation support. However, most audio data are found in online dictionaries where, for instance, word pronunciation may be given as written text as well as audio pronunciation; this is also an example of multi-layered presentation of data because users will have to activate the sound files. Publishers may also cater for visually challenged users and include features that can read definitions and other text parts aloud, and video footage may be supported by sound tracks; both types of audio support may have adjustable volume and speed. Reviewers should examine to which extent audio data are presented in clearly articulated form and support identified dictionary functions.

An evaluation of data presentation in dictionaries can include the concept of lexicographical information costs, which are the efforts users believe or feel are associated with consulting a dictionary or any part of a dictionary. Comprehension-related information costs are the perceived ease or difficulty with which users can properly understand the data presented in dictionaries. For instance, complicated wording and complex syntax in user guides, subject-field components and definitions as well as illogical, blurred or otherwise faulty presentation of other types of data, such as data subject to a high degree of textual condensation (e.g. morphological data, collocations, example sentences, illustrations and audio pronunciations), are likely to result in high information costs to users, whereas data with clear wording, articulation and simple syntax adjusted to user competences will likely result in low information costs. The question is not which data types are included in dictionaries, but how the data types are presented to provide help in specific types of user situation.

An issue that is directly linked to the presentation of data in dictionaries is how users can search for the help they need. Access to data may depend on the medium and the type of help sought. Many print dictionaries have alphabetically arranged wordlists, whereas some have conceptually arranged wordlists supported by alphabetically arranged indexes. However, this description only concerns one or two dictionary components, and the access to data in, for example, writing sections, grammar sections, business resources sections, study sections and citation guides is equally important, especially the implicit and explicit links (i.e. cross-references) between data in different dictionary components that support identified functions. In order to assist users in finding help, print dictionaries often use signposts such as numbered section headings in subject-field components and grammar components, as well as other typographical means including boldface, italics, coloured text and symbols to guide users to specific types of data. Signposts are also often used in wordlists and inside dictionary articles to show the organisational arrangement of data types in articles, so that users can easily find inflectional data, definitions, collocations, example sentences, etc. Reviewers should examine how easy users can find help to understand words and terms encountered in texts, help to write texts with specific words and terms, help to translate specific words, terms and collocations, and help to acquire knowledge about something in general or something specific.

Online dictionaries may give users the same types of access to data but may also offer additional options. Rudimentary online dictionaries are mere electronic versions of print dictionaries, whereas genuine online dictionaries usually present users with a number of different search options where users fill in search boxes with strings of letters, for example words, parts of words, strings of words, and words in canonical or inflected form, in order to get access to help. Some online dictionaries even allow users to perform fuzzy searches and use wildcard characters, but no matter what users type in search boxes, the data presented as help are important. To what extent do the data satisfy user needs? Can users search for headwords only or can they also search in/for definitions, collocations, phrases, example sentences and various dictionary components? How easy is it to understand the functions, icons and guiding texts on dictionary search sites? Can users search for specific types of help, for example help to write a text using a specific word or help to translate a specific collocation? Reviewers should focus on how dictionaries give access to specific types of help in specific types of user situation and the ability of dictionaries to satisfy user needs through search options.

The concept of lexicographical information costs also pertains to the search for data in dictionaries. Search-related information costs are the actual or perceived efforts required to get access to the data users are looking for. This type of cost is directly relevant to the search activities necessary to use print, CD and online dictionaries. Users may incur search-related information costs when following cross-references that send users on apparently random tours of dictionaries, and the number of individual activities users have to perform before they find what they are looking for may also result in heavy information costs. Similarly, users who have to scroll vertically or horizontally may find it takes a lot of effort to find on-screen data, whereas users who have the option of searching for specific words instead of scrolling long lists and the option of searching for words in their inflected forms may find dictionary consultation effortless (for a detailed discussion of lexicographical information costs, see Nielsen 2008).

5.3.2 Using the factual approach

This approach focuses on the factual data in dictionaries and can be applied to general as well as specialised dictionaries. General and learners' dictionaries usually contain domain-specific terms and diatechnical labels; for example, the *Oxford Advanced Learner's Dictionary* contains subject labels such as 'finance', 'medical' and 'sport'. Few reviewers are experts in all the subject fields covered by multi-field dictionaries such as the typical business dictionary, so they may have to limit their analysis and description to selected subject fields or team up with lexicographers, linguists and subject-field experts when critiquing dictionaries. *Oxford Advanced Learner's Dictionary* and *Longman Dictionary of Contemporary English* both contain central legal terms, and even though both are based on large authoritative corpora neither contains the civil procedure terms introduced in UK law in 1999 but only the old terms they replaced (for a detailed discussion, see Nielsen 2015b).

Reviewers may examine how up to date dictionaries actually are and how they apparently use or fail to use relevant corpora as well as the correctness of definitions and other explanations contained in various dictionary components. For example, is the explanation of a specific concept in the subject-field component at odds with the definition of that concept in the word list or results page? Reviewers need considerable factual knowledge about terms and concepts contained in dictionaries so they can write reviews that contain useful information. The factual approach supplements the lexicographical approach and helps to give a fair presentation of dictionaries as defined in Section 5.2.2.

5.3.3 Using the linguistic approach

The linguistic approach also supplements the lexicographical approach and focuses on linguistic categories, principles, structures, etc. This approach is relevant to all underlying features of dictionaries and applies to all dictionaries whether general or special. For instance, the language of specialised subject fields often make frequent and special use of linguistic options not often found in normal, unmarked language, and reviewers may examine grammar data (e.g. syntax, morphology and orthography), pronunciation (in writing or audio files), synonyms, antonyms, hyperonyms, collocations, phrases, example sentences, language usage and translation strategies, depending on the identified functions.

The linguistic approach is applicable to a wide range of issues and functions, and only a few can be mentioned here. Reviewers may examine and discuss whether the lexicographical data in bilingual translation dictionaries support the translation function from a linguistic or translation strategic perspective. For example, translation dictionaries that do not indicate the gender of French or German equivalents do not provide sufficient translation help, and data on gender and morphology should be correct, usable and easy to understand. Finally, reviewers may examine and discuss whether translation dictionaries use a particular translation strategy consistently or not. These examples show that the linguistic approach is suitable for addressing lexicographical data and how they support identified communicative or cognitive functions.

5.3.4 The informative quality of reviews

Reviewers owe dictionary authors and readers of reviews a general duty of care and should not give readers wrong or misleading information about dictionaries. The main qualitative requirement is that reviews should give a fair presentation of dictionaries as described in Section 5.2.2. This means that reviewers must present fairly dictionary functions, dictionary data, data presentation and data access related to surface and underlying features so as to allow readers to make informed decisions about dictionaries and lexicography. In broad terms, a fair presentation should be based on four qualitative characteristics, and the first acts as a general threshold: the characteristic of materiality. Information, observations, comments, etc., are material if their omission distorts a fair presentation of the dictionary. For instance, it is only material to point out spelling mistakes and extra-lexicographical onsite advertisements if there are many of them and they diminish the value of the lexicographical help provided. A piece of information, an observation, a comment, etc., is thus material if it influences readers' decisions to use, buy or recommend a dictionary; applies its lexicographical principles in theory or in practice; or influences the reviewer's assessment of a review topic or the entire dictionary. The main reason is that statements, etc., made by reviewers that do not influence the decision-making of readers are not useful and may cause readers to lose track of the essential message, become confused and make bad decisions due to an overload of information.

The second characteristic in the hierarchy of informative quality is the characteristic of relevance. Information, observations, comments, etc., are relevant if they actually relate to the purpose of reviewing and can be used by its intended readers when they make decisions in the five general types of situation listed in Section 5.2.2. For example, Bogaards (2002: 112) reviews a business dictionary by testing the words in the wordlist against two business-related texts written more than 10 years earlier. There is nothing wrong in testing dictionaries in this way, but it does not seem relevant to use texts that are significantly older than the dictionary because business terminology develops continually. In general, statements, etc., made by reviewers are relevant if they can be used to make contemplative research (i.e. provide feedback and control) and to make transformative research (i.e. to propose new principles for dictionary making and research).

Information is only useful if readers can depend on it: information must be reliable. A review must not contain improbable, unrealistic or wrong statements that distort a fair presentation of the dictionary. The characteristic of reliability emphasises that reviews are serious texts and that statements must be substantiated so as to avoid pure value judgements and wrong assertions that can only be detected by consulting the dictionary reviewed. In other words, reliable information is verifiable (i.e. objective in the sense described in Section 5.3) and is representationally faithful in the sense that a review is a subset of a totality (i.e. the dictionary under review), and this subset must be a faithful representation of the whole dictionary in order to comply with the purpose of reviewing.

Finally, reviews must be neutral in the sense that they should contain all material and relevant aspects regardless whether they affect the reviewers' assessments positively or negatively. This means that any personal relationship between the reviewer and the dictionary, its author(s) and publishers must not lead to (excessively) negative or (excessively) positive evaluations of single aspects or the dictionary as a whole. However, it may be argued that this requirement of unbiased information is implied in the previous three assumptions. These four qualitative characteristics should be followed by reviewers exercising 'professional' judgement on a case-by-case basis, and it is the duty of any reviewer to give a comprehensive and fair description and evaluation of the dictionary concerned.

5.4 Looking to the future

As a basic feature of every review, dictionaries should be evaluated on the degree in which their data fulfil the intended function(s). This means comparing individual data types with the help dictionaries provide in the intended use situation in which specific types of potential users in specific types of extra-lexicographical situations exist. One challenge for reviewers will be that tomorrow's dictionaries will be designed in line with advances in communications technology and the general use of digital media with the result that dictionaries may look very different from what we know today. However, a lexicographical, functional approach to dictionary criticism should be able to cope with that challenge: It can be used to give a fair presentation of dictionaries and provide useful information that is material, relevant and reliable. This also emphasises the need for reviewers to have a clear picture of the object they analyse, describe and examine because we should expect new ways in which users search for help in communicative, cognitive and operative situations; that users can personalise dictionaries; that users can be involved in making dictionaries; and that lexicographers can offer users different ways of access to dictionary data.

5.5 Conclusion

This discussion shows that reviewers can give a fair presentation of dictionaries, thus providing readers with useful information, when reviewers adopt the lexicographical approach supported by the factual and linguistic approaches and relate the critical analysis to the surface and underlying features of dictionaries. Good dictionary reviews can be described as critical analyses and evaluations that examine and discuss which function(s) the dictionary under review has so that reviewers focus on the types of help the dictionary is intended to give to particular types of user in particular types of situation. Furthermore, reviews examine and discuss whether the data in the dictionary support the function(s) identified. Reviewers thus focus on whether the data satisfy the needs of the target group(s) and whether the data are presented so that users can easily access and process them to get the information they need. Finally, dictionary reviews examine and discuss whether the data are arranged and linked so that they combine with the function(s) to meet the needs of users. This involves an analysis of where the data are placed in the dictionary and whether they are presented and linked in such a way that user needs are satisfied.

These review characteristics allow reviewers to focus on the relationship and interplay between surface and underlying features and the three approaches to reviewing. This focus may help reviewers to ensure a high degree of trustworthiness in that their reviews contain useful information that is material, relevant and reliable. All this should result in dictionary criticism that gives a fair presentation of function(s), data, presentation of data and accessibility of data contained in dictionaries under review.

Related topics

Dictionaries and access; the concept of dictionary; dictionaries for text reception; dictionaries for text production; dictionaries for translation; dictionaries to assist teaching and learning.

Further reading

Bergenholtz, H. and R. H. Gouws. (2016). "On the Metalexicographic Genre of Dictionary Reviews, With Specific Reference to LexicoNordica and Lexikos". *Lexikos* 26: 60–81.
This paper discusses the scope of dictionary criticism, looks at some criteria for dictionary reviews and examines aspects of dictionary reviews in two academic journals in order to propose methods intended to enhance the quality of reviews and ensure a stronger theoretical approach to reviews as a genre.

Boogards, P. (1996). "Dictionaries for Learners of English". *International Journal of Lexicography* 9(4): 277–320.
This paper lists 12 questions that can be used as evaluation criteria or instructions to evaluate learner's dictionaries with regard to the findability and comprehensibility of lexicographical-linguistic data.

Fuertes-Olivera, P. A. and S. Tarp. (2014). *Theory and Practice of Specialised Online Dictionaries: Lexicography Versus Terminography*. Berlin and Boston: De Gruyter.
Chapter 8 of this book lists 10 criteria that can be used for evaluating specialised online dictionaries. These criteria are based on the tenets of the *function theory of lexicography* and whether or not existing technological possibilities are being used.

Svensén, B. (2009). *A Handbook of Lexicography: The Theory and Practice of Dictionary-Making*. Cambridge: Cambridge University Press.

Chapter 28 of this book provides a concise overview of different types of dictionary review, methods of criticism and demands on good dictionary reviews as well as ethical aspects of dictionary criticism.

References

Bergenholtz, H. and S. Tarp. (2010) "LSP Lexicography or Terminography? The Lexicographer's Point of View", in Pedro A. Fuertes-Olivera (ed.), *Specialised Dictionaries for Learners*. Berlin/Boston: de Gruyter, pp. 27–37.

Black, J., N. Hashimzade and G. D. Myles. (2012) *Dictionary of Economics*. 4th edition. Oxford: Oxford University Press.

Bogaards, P. (2002) "DAFA: An Innovative Learners' Dictionary of Business French", *International Journal of Lexicography* 15(1): 105–116.

Chan, A.Y.W. and Y. Loong. (1999) "Establishing Criteria for Evaluating a Learner's Dictionary", in R. Berry, B. Asker, H. Hyland and M. Lam (eds.), *Language Analysis, Description and Pedagogy*. Hong Kong: Hong Kong University of Science and Technology, pp. 298–307.

Chan, A.Y.W. and A. Taylor. (2001) "Evaluating Learner Dictionaries: What the Reviews Say", *International Journal of Lexicography* 14(3): 163–180.

Crystal, D. (2010) *The Cambridge Encyclopedia of Language*. Cambridge: Cambridge University Press.

Deuter, M., J. Bradbery and J. Turnbull (eds.) (2015) *Oxford Advanced Learner's Dictionary*, 9th edition. Oxford: Oxford University Press.

Durkin, P. (ed.) (2016) *The Oxford Handbook of Lexicography*. Oxford: Oxford University Press.

Fox, C. and R. Combley (eds.) (2014) *Longman Dictionary of Contemporary English*, 6th edition. Harlow: Pearson.

Gold, D. L. (1993) "P. A. Joubert. Bilingual Phrase Dictionary/Tweetalige Frasewoordeboek (E-A), 1st edition 1992", *Lexikos* 3: 303–313.

Grix, J. (2010) *The Foundations of Research*, 2nd edition. Basingstoke: Palgrave Macmillan.

Hands, P. (ed.) (2009) *Collins COBUILD Advanced Dictionary of English*. Boston, MA/Glasgow: Heinle Cengage Learning/Harper Collins.

Hashimzade, N., G. A. Myles and G. D. Myles. (2014) "Can Authority Be Sustained While Balancing Accessibility and Formality?", *Hermes – Journal of Language and Communication in Business* 52: 11–24.

Mason, J. (2002) *Qualitative Researching*, 2nd edition. London: Sage.

Nielsen, S. (2000) "Translation Strategies for Culture-Specific Textual Conventions in Bilingual Dictionaries", *Lexicographica: International Annual for Lexicography* 16: 152–168.

Nielsen, S. (2008) "The Effect of Lexicographical Information Costs on Dictionary Making and Use", *Lexikos* 18: 1–20.

Nielsen, S. (2009a) "Reviewing Printed and Electronic Dictionaries: A Theoretical and Practical Framework", in S. Nielsen and S. Tarp (eds.), *Lexicography in the 21st Century*. Amsterdam/Philadelphia: Benjamins, pp. 23–41.

Nielsen, S. (2009b) "The Evaluation of the Outside Matter in Dictionary Reviews", *Lexikos* 19: 207–224.

Nielsen, S. (2015a) "Bilingual Dictionaries for Communication in the Domain of Economics: Function-Based Translation Dictionaries", *Hermes – Journal of Language and Communication in Business* 54: 161–176.

Nielsen, S. (2015b) "Legal Terms in General Dictionaries of English: The Civil Procedure Mystery", *Lexikos* 25: 246–261.

Nygaard, L. P. (2015) *Writing for Scholars: A Practical Guide to Making Sense and Being Heard*. 2nd edition. London: Sage.

Pearsons, E. and W. Nichols. (2013) "Toward a Framework for Reviewing Online English Dictionaries", *Dictionaries: Journal of the Dictionary Society of North America* 34: 201–210.

Ripfel, M. (1989) *Wörterbuchkritik. Eine empirische Analyse von Wörterbuchrezensionen*. Tübingen: Niemeyer.

Steiner, R. J. (1979) "Guidelines for Reviewers of Bilingual Dictionaries", *Dictionaries: Journal of the Dictionary Society of North America* 1: 166–181.

Sterkenburg, P. van (ed.) (2003) *A Practical Guide to Lexicography*. Amsterdam/Philadelphia: Benjamins.

Swanepoel, P. (2008) "Towards a Framework for the Description and Evaluation of Dictionary Evaluation Criteria", *Lexikos* 18: 207–231.

Swanepoel, P. (2013) "Evaluation of Dictionaries", in R. H. Gouws, U. Heid, W. Schweickard and H. E. Wiegand (eds.), *Supplementary Volume Dictionaries: An International Encyclopedia of Lexicography – Recent Developments With Focus on Electronic and Computational Lexicography*. Berlin/New York: de Gruyter Mouton, pp. 587–596.

Tarp, S. and T.J.D. Bothma. (2013) "An Alternative Approach to Enlightenment Age Lexicography: The Universal Dictionary of Trade and Commerce", *Lexicographica: International Annual for Lexicography* 29: 222–284.

Part II

The interdisciplinary nature of lexicography

6

Lexicography and interdisciplinarity

Sandro Nielsen

6.1 Introduction

One of the trends in many types of activity is the increased cooperation between members of different knowledge domains and subject fields. Academics often refer to such types of cooperation as interdisciplinary work, and this trend may be seen as a wind of change blowing across the landscape of traditional disciplines. Cooperation between disciplines has been with us since ancient times, and Bruun et al. (2005: 22–23) explain that the use of the term *interdisciplinarity* in its modern sense can be traced back to the 1920s and especially began to gain ground during and after the Second World War, for instance, in physics and engineering. More recently, interdisciplinary activities have spread to many areas such as social sciences, life sciences, environmental studies, literature studies, educational studies, cultural studies and information science, to mention but a few. One result of this trend is that increased interdisciplinary cooperation challenges the hierarchical structure of well-defined disciplines adding to the complexity of activities and subject fields. Several factors indicate that this trend extends to lexicography.

In a very basic form dictionary making involves two distinct processes: the making of an information tool and the management of data to be included in the tool. This could be an author writing a manuscript and a publisher printing the manuscript in the form of a book. However, lexicography is more complex than that, and scholars have discussed specific aspects of interdisciplinary collaboration as exemplified by Hartmann (2005), who examines interdisciplinary collaboration between the fields of lexicography and linguistics. Other scholars look at types of cooperation from different perspectives, and Fuertes-Olivera and Tarp (2014: 193–240) discuss the need for collaboration across disciplines (such as lexicography, information technology and accounting) in different phases of designing and making specialised online dictionaries. Finally, the nature of lexicography is multi-faceted, which various lexicographical journals illustrate by announcing that they are "interdisciplinary as well as international" (*International Journal of Lexicography*) and they publish articles that "treat pure lexicography or the implications that related fields such as linguistics, general linguistics, computer science and management have for lexicography" (*Lexikos*). This chapter looks at the nature of interdisciplinarity in lexicography and how interdisciplinarity affects practical as well as theoretical lexicography. The discussion opens with a brief examination of the concept of interdisciplinarity (Section 6.2). Section 6.3 looks at core issues and topics: the involvement of actors from different disciplines in the project design phase; the way in which modern dictionaries draw on various types of domain knowledge in the production phase; the integration of domain-specific knowledge and cooperation in the post-production phase; and how theoretical lexicography is informed by theories and methods from other disciplines. Section 6.4 provides a brief glimpse of what the future may bring for lexicography and interdisciplinarity.

6.2 Historical perspective: the many faces of interdisciplinarity

Dictionary making and dictionary research can be carried out by a single individual or by teams of individuals depending on the specific tasks a hand. If they examine a particular phenomenon within lexicography, scholars may use principles and methods from a specific discipline, for instance, studying the inflection of irregular verbs using linguistic principles. However, in order to achieve relevance in lexicography, scholars usually need to relate their studies and findings to something outside the discipline (in this case the information tool containing data on irregular inflection and the tool's intended function). This means that the quest for better information tools leads lexicographers to look for assistance from different quarters, and it is possible to identify a number of general factors that illustrate the importance of interdisciplinarity in lexicography. First, lexicography is complex by nature due to its multi-faceted challenge of providing help to users in a wide range of extra-lexicographical situations (e.g. reading, writing and translating texts, making calculations and acquiring knowledge – within any subject field and knowledge domain). Lexicographers should have a proper understanding of these situations so that they can provide the correct responses to user needs. Second, theoretical and practical lexicography involves challenges and problems that are not restricted to one specific discipline (e.g. how to design and prepare databases, how to present lexicographical data and how to allow users to search for data in dictionaries). Third, lexicography can help develop information tools that may solve practical problems in general in an increasingly complex society (e.g. by providing help in educational contexts and by providing new theoretical and practical insights that can be exported to other disciplines). Finally, lexicography depends to a considerable extent on the development of new technologies (e.g. database technology and Internet technology for online dictionaries). The relevance of lexicography thus extends to many societal areas.

As the concept of interdisciplinarity has gained popularity, more and more scholars attempt to describe different types of cross-disciplinary collaboration from specific viewpoints. Some academics talk about broad and narrow interdisciplinarity depending on how conceptually distantly or closely related theories and methods are, and researchers may conduct instrumental, strategic or opportunistic interdisciplinarity depending on the non-academic goals of projects (Bruun et al. (2005: 29). Boden (1999), Bruun et al. (2005) and Klein (2010) provide detailed accounts of the nature of interdisciplinarity and distinguish between three general types of collaboration. *Multidisciplinarity* "juxtapose[s] disciplinary/professional perspectives, adding breath and available knowledge, information, and methods", so that participants from different disciplines work separately and provide separate results. On the other hand, *interdisciplinarity* "integrate[s] separate disciplinary data, methods, tools, concepts, and theories in order to create a holistic view or common understanding of a complex issue, question or problem" so that participants plan, analyse, produce and evaluate jointly (Bruun et al. 2005: 28). Finally, *transdisciplinarity* is more difficult to define, but the term often refers to "collaborative research and problem solving that cross both disciplinary boundaries and sectors of society" (Bruun et al. 2005: 31), implying that methods and principles are transferred from one discipline to another.

Literature on interdisciplinarity often focuses on the degree and type of integration involved, and such distinctions may be relevant in many situations. However, lexicographers seldom need to make detailed distinctions between the degree to which and manner in which disciplines interact. For the purposes of this discussion, the following general definition of interdisciplinarity in lexicography applies:

> Interdisciplinarity is the use of knowledge from two or more disciplines – whether or not this knowledge is possessed by one or more persons – with the goal of using this knowledge from several disciplines to solve complex challenges or problems that are lexicographically relevant.

Nevertheless, lexicographers may find that some contexts require more detailed and elaborate descriptions of interdisciplinarity along the lines presented in Klein (2010), for example, when they apply for research funding and write research reports, but such situations are extra-lexicographical activities.

The practical or research designs of lexicographical projects should factor in the complexity of lexicography even if such projects examine minute parts of the discipline. In the words of Popper (1963: 88): "We are not students of some subject matter, but students of problems. And problems may cut right across the borders of any subject matter or discipline." The challenge for lexicographers is to develop principles and methods relevant for, or to design and compile, lexicographical information tools that provide specific types of help to specific types of user in specific types of extra-lexicographical use situation and, as indicated by Popper, this requires the importation of knowledge and skills from a number of disciplines. Such interdisciplinary lexicography concerns the complexity of the subject matter (i.e. dictionaries and lexicography) as well as the complexity of the knowledge brought to projects by members of different disciplinary groups. If such collaboration is to be successful, it is imperative that the members of different disciplines develop a common discourse so that they all know exactly what their contributions involve and develop a bi-disciplinary discourse between lexicographers and members of each of the other disciplines in order to achieve the common goal. All this requires qualified management of resources.

6.3 Core issues and topics

All projects have a beginning and an end, and many lexicographers make sure that their projects are organised in systematic ways to increase the chances of successful endings. Bergenholtz (see Chapter 2 of this *Handbook*) argues that lexicographers should prepare clear plans for their projects whether or not the projects are single-person or multi-person projects. Add to this whether projects are theoretical or practical. A type of project management is highly recommendable in light of the complex, interdisciplinary nature of lexicography, and even interdisciplinary individuals will benefit from plans that ensure systematic work such as research, collection, analysis and presentation of data. Lexicographical projects that involve members from different disciplines should be guided by clear plans detailing what is to be done by whom and when, so that all participants have a clear picture of the project from the start. This and the following three sub-sections discuss selected issues of practical dictionary projects, but the issues are also relevant for theoretical projects, and it should be noted that the discussion also applies to lexicographical projects carried out by only one person with knowledge from several disciplines and subject fields.

The discipline of lexicography forms the foundation of lexicographical projects and its object of study: dictionaries. Because dictionaries are lexicographical tools intended to provide various types of help to various types of user in various types of use situation, lexicographers often need input from other disciplines to solve general and specific problems. This may result in language problems, especially because words and terms used in several disciplines but with different meanings often cause confusion. For example, linguists distinguish terminologically between polysemy and homonymy using linguistic principles, whereas some lexicographers argue that such a distinction may be valid but the two terms should be defined differently and according to principles that are directly relevant for lexicographical work (see e.g. Bergenholtz and Agerbo 2014: 27–35). Another problem is that members of different disciplines often use terms and concepts that are at the core of their disciplines and unfamiliar to other members of the project. Because dictionary projects are exercises in lexicography, lexicographers should be heads of projects, and one of the main tasks of such lexicographers-in-chief should be to make sure that everyone understands each other and, if necessary, mediate between participants.

A brief example illustrates the complexity of lexicographical projects and the need for clear plans for interdisciplinary cooperation. The planning of a dictionary like *Longman Dictionary of English Language and Culture* (Murphy 2005) will require a team composed of participants from at least the following disciplines: lexicography, linguistics, culture, English language varieties, history, law, literature, medicine, politics, arts, sports, education and information technology. The dictionary's list of acknowledgements shows that the project also involved a researcher, project manager, production manager, computational linguist, production editor, project and database administrator, technical support manager, network administrator, pronunciation editor and designer. All these participants must be able to work together in a coordinated way and communicate effectively across disciplinary boundaries to achieve their common goal.

6.3.1 Preliminary stages in lexicographical projects

In order to achieve their goal of producing a dictionary, lexicographers should carefully prepare the preliminary stage of the project. Fuertes-Olivera and Tarp (2014: 197) explain that this stage involves the following tasks: "(a) deciding on potential users in a specific context or situation, (b) detecting lexicographically relevant information needs among potential users, and (c) deciding to set up a lexicographical project in order to satisfy their needs." Lexicographers (and other team members) should complete these steps with due regard to the financial, human and other resources available to the project. Potential users of dictionaries vary considerably, but lexicographers should ensure that dictionaries target one or more specific types of user, for example, translators within the field of biotechnology, journalists in general, school children of different age groups and experts within particular subject fields. Lexicographers are likely to need input from experts from fields other than lexicography in order to determine the factual, language and use-specific competences and hence information needs of such target groups, bearing in mind that dictionaries cannot properly cater for the needs of all such groups at the same time.

User competences and information needs are directly linked to the extra-lexicographical use situations in which the need for information arises, and this may require assistance from other disciplines. For instance, knowledge of translation processes and strategies is needed in order to determine the information needs of student translators and specialised translators, and such knowledge may be imported from other disciplines. Similarly, dictionaries intended to help users write texts in a foreign language should be based on knowledge about text production, foreign languages, grammar, language use and pragmatics, which all fall outside the discipline of lexicography. Furthermore, dictionaries treating one or more subject fields should be based on lexicographically relevant knowledge provided by experts from the fields concerned, such as accountants, physicians, physicists and zoologists. Finally, databases operate as repositories for data to be put into offline and online dictionaries, and lexicographers should work closely with database experts to find proper designs for the storage of data. However, databases cannot be complete until lexicographers have identified the various types of data that can support dictionary functions. Databases are merely data repositories and not dictionaries, because the data they hold will be presented either in print or on screen, and print copies or user interfaces are the dictionaries. This means that lexicographers should have a clear vision of the interactions between database, user interface and dictionary search engine (alternatively databases and print copies), something that involves knowledge of information technology, web design and layout.

Despite the potentially large number of interdisciplinary contributions, non-lexicographical participants must not take charge of projects. Lexicographers-in-chief are in charge of projects and make all final decisions after having considered the input from other team members. The disciplinary specialisation involved in dictionary projects should be adapted according to project goals, and this may mean that disciplinary experts may see that knowledge borrowed across disciplines and used for lexicographical projects is applied in ways that differ from their intradisciplinary application. Nevertheless, practical or theoretical projects aim to provide principles or practices related to dictionaries as information tools that disseminate knowledge to users, and clear project designs are necessary before embarking on practical or theoretical activities.

6.3.2 Dictionary making calls for interdisciplinary work

When the design for the project is ready, lexicographers and other team members begin on the next stage, the compilation phase. This stage extends the preliminary stage into practical and theoretical new territory, because the collaboration between members of different disciplines will put different intradisciplinary principles, routines and techniques to the test. At the beginning of and during the compilation stage, team members and lexicographers-in-chief will have to make decisions concerning a number of important issues. Fuertes-Olivera and Tarp (2014: 198) sum up the types of decision as follows: "These are basically concerned with dictionary concepts, preparing the material needed for the dictionary project, writing the lexicographical instructions, assignment of specific tasks to every member of the team, and preparation for the book's publication."

Most, if not all, dictionary projects use electronic databases as repositories for data. The preparation of databases in which lexicographers and other team members can place data is one of the first practical tasks to be completed. Lexicographers-in-chief should prepare lists of data types to be placed in discrete fields in databases on the basis of input from other team members such as subject-field specialists, use-type specialists (e.g. translators, copywriters and educationalists) and IT specialists. In all these cases, lexicographers need to master a minimum of discipline-specific language, usually terms, and to have a good grasp of the extra-lexicographical situations in which users engage. Furthermore, lexicographers-in-chief should be able to communicate properly with database experts so that lexicographical experts stay in charge of the project and will not be outmanoeuvred by IT specialists, because even projects for online dictionaries are lexicographical projects. Lexicographers who master database-speak can clearly explain to database specialists which data fields need to be included, how these should be linked and which user search options are envisaged.

The selection of corpus data is one of the first tasks to be undertaken. The criteria for selection of texts depend on the subject field(s) concerned (e.g. accounting, insurance, law, philosophy, science and technology) and the dictionary function(s) (e.g. provide help to understand, write or translate texts, provide help to learn theories, principles and practices or provide help to acquire knowledge in certain situations). This means that the selection of corpus texts requires interdisciplinary knowledge about text types, genres, domain-specific topics and use-specific issues (e.g. translating of specialised texts), and such interdisciplinary knowledge may relate to more than one culture, language and subject field.

The selection of lemmas, or headwords, also requires assistance across disciplines. Lexicographers decide which lemmas to include in the database together with subject-field specialists and use-specific experts, usually based on electronic text corpora. Computer software may generate lists of potential lemmas automatically, but lexicographers and subject-field specialists must work together to make sure that all relevant lemmas are selected, whether they appear in the lists or not. Subject-field specialists can suggest terms that, for some reason or other, do not appear in the lists, for example because they do not occur in the text corpora or because the software cannot identify multi-word terms. Another problem concerns the selection of lemmas in specialised translation dictionaries, as the focus tends to be on domain-specific terminology. This means that lexicographers and subject-field specialists run the risk of excluding ordinary words and phrases that are important for communication within specific domains and may be difficult to translate. This should lead to the inclusion of non-technical words due to, for example, differences in syntax, culture, factual structures of subject fields and genre conventions in the two languages involved; such words should be selected after consultation with specialist translators, who possess knowledge about translating processes in theory and practice.

Preliminary lemma lists usually form a good basis for another task: writing lexicographical definitions of lemmas. Lexicographers often use the term *definition* in a sense that differs from that found in disciplines such as philosophy or logic and adapt the term to lexicographical situations and in this context, a lexicographical definition is the specific set of data that explains the meaning of a lemma and which is clearly addressed to the lemma. A better term for this may be lexicographical meaning explanations (see Wiegand 1992). In order to write useful meaning explanations, team members should cooperate in various ways depending on the intended function(s) and users of dictionaries. Subject-field specialists should write meaning explanations of terms and concepts within their fields of expertise and lexicographers should edit and revise the explanations so that they are appropriate for intended users, matching their language, factual and cultural competences. In connection with dictionaries intended for learning and acquisition of knowledge, subject-field specialists and lexicographers should consider extending meaning explanations so that they do not merely 'define' lemmas but also address lemma-specific functions and relations to other lemmas and show terminological hierarchies (see e.g. Nielsen 2011). It is important that lexicographical meaning explanations are written in a style that is carefully adapted to user competences and, at the same time, offer factually correct data that help users understand lemmas and acquire knowledge.

Translation dictionaries contain equivalents to lemmas, often in addition to meaning explanations. Lexicographers should join forces with subject-field specialists, terminologists and translators when deciding on equivalents for a number of reasons. First, subject-field specialists and terminologists often know the subject-specific terminology in their native and one or more other languages and may thus be able to suggest correct equivalents. Second, specialised translators and terminologists often know a wide range of terms in the native and foreign languages treated by translation dictionaries and can thus add to the knowledge of subject-field specialists, who are primarily experts within their own language community. Third, specialised translators are often in a better position to suggest equivalents and translations of non-technical terms and phrases than subject-field specialists and lexicographers. Interdisciplinary work like this should also ensure the offer of geographical language varieties as equivalents where appropriate, especially when the United Nations' world languages are target languages in translation dictionaries. Finally, subject-field specialists, translators and intercultural experts know where languages, subject-field structures and cultures differ between languages and geographical areas and can provide valuable data explaining important cultural, factual and language differences to users and project team members.

The correct meaning and use of words and terms depend on the contexts in which they appear. Monolingual dictionaries intended to provide help to write texts should include collocations and phrases selected by lexicographers, linguists and writing experts who know which syntactic, collocational and pragmatic restrictions affect the use of words and terms and which fixed expressions are relevant for the intended users. Translation dictionaries should include the same types of data in two or more languages and the above group of team members should be extended, so that it includes translators, linguists and writing experts with the relevant knowledge of all the languages concerned. In general, dictionaries with communicative functions should provide data on grammar peculiarities, grammar differences, factual differences, usage restrictions and usage differences depending on the number of languages involved and the competences of intended users. Lexicographers should consider including similar types of data in dictionaries with cognitive functions, because users may need help with these issues when acquiring knowledge about something in general or specific knowledge about a particular matter. Providing data about such discursive, factual and sociolinguistic contexts clearly require different types of disciplinary knowledge.

The advances made in lexicographically relevant electronic technology also affect the production of dictionaries, in particular the selection of data. Lexicographers import knowledge, practices and tools developed in other disciplines such as information and computer sciences in order to speed up the dictionary making process and at the same time get valid and reliable data. When they select lemmas, collocations, example sentences and equivalents, lexicographers use technical tools that perform statistical analyses that can be used to describe syntactic and lexical patterns such as collocations and word combinations, typically in the form of concordances. Similarly, lexicographers use software to analyse lexicographical corpora with a view to finding sense differentiation, analyses of meaning and valency descriptions. Lexicographers can use these tools directly as they are in specific dictionary projects, as adapted to specific projects, or as developed specifically for projects (Kilgarriff and Kosem 2012: 32–36). When the interdisciplinary data selection process has been completed, lexicographers must present data in appropriate ways, something lexicographers and other team members should consider as early as in the preliminary stage.

When they have selected data for dictionaries, lexicographers must decide how to present the data. Print dictionaries tend to present data in rather traditional ways, although lexicographers often introduce new solutions such as different types of illustrations, use of colours, signposts and other structural indicators. Online dictionaries tend to present data in three ways. First, they present data in the same way as print dictionaries, because the online dictionaries are mere electronic copies of print dictionaries. Second, online dictionaries present data in the same way as lexicographers see the data in their databases, because the dictionaries are identical to the databases. Third, online dictionaries present data as proper online texts using web design layout, because the dictionaries are proper online information tools that retrieve data from databases and present data on web interfaces in changed but pre-arranged order. Irrespective of medium, lexicographers should import web design and layout knowledge into the project so that data can be presented in ways that make them easy to decode by users, including audio-visual presentations. In addition, lexicographers who prepare online dictionaries should consider how they best can merge technical options with modern lexicographical principles and practices. The presentation of lexicographical data online is directly related to search options available to users, because a specific dictionary may offer several search options and should present different search results in the form of straight-to-the-point data that focus on a particular dictionary function. The presentation of data is thus linked to the way in which users retrieve data and related access routes, and this interrelationship requires knowledge of information search strategies, technical capabilities and options as well as web design.

To sum up, this discussion shows that lexicography and dictionaries are complex concepts and objects. Lexicographers should point out to project team members that lexicography concerns information tools that provide help to users about language, factual matters or procedures related to one or more subject fields (e.g. economics, law and physics – even in so-called general-language dictionaries). One advantage of a description like this is that the focus for all participants, irrespective of disciplinary affiliation, is to help someone disseminate knowledge that others may find useful, and this knowledge is not constrained to, for example, language and linguistics but involve knowledge from the disciplines participants come from.

6.3.3 Dictionaries as ongoing projects

Some dictionary projects are only partially finished when pre-determined numbers of data are reached according to the plans for the projects, for instance, when 10,000 lemmas and definitions have been written. At least two issues must be addressed: maintaining and updating databases, and maintaining and updating user interfaces (i.e. dictionaries). Existing database software will eventually become incompatible with new dictionary software or vice versa, and lexicographers should consider how this can be remedied. Apart from securing financial resources, lexicographers-in-chief should retain or find team members with the relevant knowledge about databases, web interfaces and other computational tools because these technologies are needed to keep projects alive, as existing software must be maintained and new software must be bought.

Human resources will be needed to keep track of developments in society. This means that new data will be added and existing data will be updated or deleted, as the case may be, and this applies to dictionary databases and lexicographical corpora alike. Again, knowledge from many disciplines is needed along the lines discussed in Sections 6.3.1 and 6.3.2. More specifically, post-compilation work may involve the correction of mistakes, the adaption of meanings as new meanings appear in usage, the change of meanings as rules and regulations change and the inclusion of new words and phrases that appear as a result of the general development of language, technology and society at large. Furthermore, new ways of searching for help in online dictionaries may be conceived, leading to changes in user interfaces and search engines, though such changes should not be made just because the options are technologically possible but because they support the search for help by specific types of user in specific types of situation. As discussed earlier, practical projects within the discipline of lexicography are interdisciplinary collaborations, but it should be appreciated that nothing is more practical than a good theoretical foundation.

6.3.4 Interdisciplinary assistance to lexicographical research

The theoretical branch of lexicography is important because its research, empirical bases and critical analyses open the way for new principles applicable to dictionary making. Researchers studying user behaviour and user needs often use methods from other disciplines, for example, surveys, interviews, protocols, audio-visual recordings and eye-tracking systems (see e.g. Dziemianko 2012; Müller-Spitzer, Koplenig and Töpel 2012; Lew, Grzelak and Leszkowicz 2013). Other lexicographers join forces with researchers from information science in order to develop principles that can describe user search patterns as well as lexicographically relevant needs for information (see e.g. Bergenholtz, Bothma and Gouws 2015). This type of collaboration is in line with the idea that dictionaries are information tools and lexicography concerns theoretical and practical issues relating to dictionaries, as Tarp (2012: 111) points out: "lexicography has a great deal to contribute to other theories dealing with punctual information tools and to information science in general and, in turn, it has a great deal to learn from them".

Interdisciplinarity in lexicography also extends to dictionary criticism and dictionary reviews. Dictionary criticism can be part of lexicographical projects where lexicographers examine existing dictionaries to discover and describe principles and practices that may be relevant to current projects, and dictionary criticism can be independent examinations and evaluations of existing dictionaries published as reviews in journals (see Chapter 5 of this *Handbook*). For instance, critical examinations and evaluations of dictionaries require knowledge about words, terms, things, facts and methods related to potentially many disciplines and subject fields. Even so-called general-language dictionaries contain lemmas that belong to specific subject fields such as medicine, engineering, sports, law, technology, zoology and business, and the lexicographical treatment of these areas directly affect the examination and evaluation.

6.4 Looking to the future

Some believe that dictionaries are inventories "of the words of a language" and that "lexicographers are, first and foremost, linguistic inventory clerks" (Hanks 2013: 503). If people generally believe that lexicography is essentially applied linguistics and dictionaries products of linguistic work, there is no need for authors of dictionaries of, for instance, economics, law, medicine and physics to consult lexicographers, because their dictionaries are not related to linguistics. However, future advances in lexicography may shift the traditional focus and regard dictionaries as information tools that members of any discipline and subject field can use to disseminate knowledge about specific aspects of their domain in communicative, cognitive, interpretive and operative situations. Lexicography will then be a discipline that concerns theories, principles and practices relating to research, production and criticism of information tools informed by input from members of several disciplines. A similar development of increased collaboration can be found among scholars of interdisciplinarity and shifts the focus from traditional disciplines to real-life phenomena: "The core premise of this trendline is that problems in the *Lebenswelt* – the life-world – need to frame research questions and practices, not the disciplines" (Klein 2010: 25). The interdisciplinarity observed in lexicography is thus in line with a general attempt to integrate knowledge in a systematic way, as current developments seem to suggest that this systematic integration of knowledge "does not follow automatically from a pregiven order of things" (Klein 2010: 24).

So what competences should lexicographers have? Bergenholtz (2013) has provided an answer to this question based on an ongoing dictionary project with specific reference to writing definitions in a general dictionary of Danish. The main conclusion is that linguists are not better suited as lexicographers than persons from other subject fields but have relevant knowledge about linguistic aspects. The main challenge is to find lexicographers or team members who are able to write meaning explanations that are clear and understandable by the intended users. This ability is not sufficient, however, because "excellent style is no substitute for substantive correctness; the result could still be lexicographical articles about molecular biology with serious mistakes" (Bergenholtz 2013: 5). The lexicographical team includes persons with knowledge from mathematics, lexicography, information science, linguistics, Arabic language and culture, Danish, Spanish, molecular biology, physics, legal science, economics, chemistry and English. The team members must be native speakers of Danish and have a sound knowledge of the world in general and at least one subject field. In addition, they must be able to write meaning explanations that are correct and easy to understand and be able to find correct and relevant data. Finally, team members must be able to identify other team members who possess the necessary knowledge in order to transfer the writing task to those other members when appropriate.

The time has gone when lexicography was regarded as a field that developed in ever-decreasing circles into a small sub-part of linguistics or lexicology. Developments show that lexicography is now expanding in ever-increasing circles into either an independent discipline or part of information science, to wit the growing interdisciplinarity and complexity of lexicography. This expansive trend is likely to continue in future.

6.5 Conclusion

A brief look at the dictionaries available now and in the past shows that lexicography is full of interdisciplinarity. Lexicography is not a sub-discipline of linguistics or lexicology, but rather a discipline in its own right with its own object of research, namely the dictionary. Lexicography concerns the development of theoretical and practical principles as well as the production of lexicographical tools, so several disciplines are involved in any dictionary project. First, IT specialists contribute to the development of databases and user interfaces and lexicographers must be able to communicate effectively with those specialists. Second, modern dictionaries use electronic corpora as sources so knowledge about corpus building and analysis is relevant. Third, almost all dictionaries contain words or terms from more than one discipline and subject field, whether they are general-language or specialised dictionaries, so domain-specific knowledge and cooperation with subject-field specialists are necessary in relation to both the internal structure of the subject field and the language used. Finally, dictionaries are information tools that are designed to fulfil the needs of users in specific types of use situations: communicative, cognitive, operative and interpretive. Therefore, knowledge about and cooperation with specialists of, for instance, translation, copyediting, knowledge management, operative skills and text production are necessary.

From a lexicographical point of view, it is important to have interdisciplinary networks involving several specialists so that they can contribute to dictionary projects as required;

for example, linguists provide linguistic data, subject-field specialists provide factual data and translation specialists provide translation-relevant data. The job of lexicographers-in-chief is to plan, design and implement the entire project with due regard to the interdisciplinary input that is necessary to bring the project to a successful conclusion. This cooperation may then lead to the development of new or revised theoretical principles. All this indicates that lexicography is not a one-dimensional discipline with an interface to one other discipline, but is a multidimensional discipline with many interfaces to many disciplines.

Related topics

Lexicography and applied linguistics; lexicography and corpus linguistics; lexicography and information science; lexicography and terminology; dictionaries and language policy; lexicography and natural language processing; dictionaries and culture; using the Web for lexicographic purposes.

Further reading

Bergenholtz, H. and J. Nielsen. (2013). "What Is a Lexicographical Database?", *Lexikos* 23: 77–87.
This paper explains how databases for dictionaries should be prepared, and the authors argue that the optimal database should be planned by lexicographers and database experts jointly. The authors also show specific examples of database fields for completed online dictionaries.

Nielsen, S. (2015). "Bilingual Dictionaries for Communication in the Domain of Economics: Function-Based Translation Dictionaries", *Hermes* 54: 161–176.
This article argues that dictionaries for translation of economic texts are about more than terms in that they include data about terms, grammatical properties, combinatorial potential, syntactic options, restrictions on language use, differences in the structure of the domains in the cultures involved, pragmatic issues and translation processes within the field of economics.

References

Bergenholtz, H. (2013) "The Role of Linguists in Planning and Making Dictionaries in the Modern Information Society", in D. Kwary, N. Wulan and L. Musyahda (eds.), *Lexicography and Dictionaries in the Information Age: Selected Papers from the 8th ASIALEX Conference*. Surabaya: Airlangga University Press, pp. 1–10.

Bergenholtz, H. and H. Agerbo. (2014) "There Is No Need for the Terms Polysemy and Homonymy in Lexicography", *Lexikos* 24: 27–35.

Bergenholtz, H., T.J.D. Bothma and R. H. Gouws. (2015) "Phases and Steps in the Access to Data in Information Tools", *Lexikos* 25: 1–30.

Boden, M. A. (1999) "What Is Interdisciplinarity?", in R. Cunningham (ed.), *Interdisciplinarity and the Organization of Knowledge in Europe*. Luxembourg: Office for Official Publications of the European Communities, pp. 13–24.

Bruun, H., J. Hukkinen, K. Huutoniemi and J. T. Klein. (2005) *Promoting Interdisciplinary Research: The Case of the Academy of Finland*. Helsinki: Academy of Finland.

Dziemianko, A. (2012) "On the Use(fullness) of Paper and Electronic Dictionaries", in S. Granger and M. Paqout (eds.), *Electronic Lexicography*. Oxford: Oxford University Press, pp. 319–342.

Fuertes-Olivera, P. A. and S. Tarp. (2014) *Theory and Practice of Specialised Online Dictionaries: Lexicography Versus Terminography*. Berlin and Boston: de Gruyter.

Hanks, P. (2013) "Lexicography from Earliest Times to the Present", in K. Allens (ed.), *The Oxford Handbook of the History of Linguistics*. Oxford: Oxford University Press, pp. 503–536.

Hartmann, R.R.K. (2005) "Lexicography and Its Interdisciplinary Contacts, With Special Reference to Linguistics and Onomasiology", *Lexikos* 15: 70–89.

Kilgarriff, A. and I. Kosem. (2012) "Corpus Tools for Lexicographers," in S. Granger and M. Paquot (eds.), *Electronic Lexicography*. Oxford: Oxford University Press, pp. 31–55.

Klein, J. T. (2010) "A Taxonomy of Interdisciplinarity", in R. Frodeman (ed.), *The Oxford Handbook of Interdisciplinarity*. Oxford: Oxford University Press, pp. 15–30.

Lew, R., M. Crzelak and M. Leszkowicz. (2013) "How Dictionary Users Choose Senses in Bilingual Dictionary Entries: An Eye-Tracking Study", *Lexikos* 23: 228–254.

Murphy, M. (ed.) (2005) *Longman Dictionary of English Language and Culture*. 3rd edition. Harlow: Pearson Education.

Müller-Spitzer, C., A. Koplenig and A. Töpel. (2012) "Online Dictionary Use: Key Findings From an Empirical Research Project", in S. Granger and M. Paqout (eds.), *Electronic Lexicography*. Oxford: Oxford University Press, pp. 425–457.

Nielsen, S. (2011) "Function– and User–Related Definitions in Online Dictionaries", in F. I. Kartashkova (ed.), *Ivanovo School of Lexicography: Traditions and Innovations: A Festschrift in Honour of Professor Olga Karpova*. Ivanovo: Ivanovo State University, pp. 197–219.

Popper, K. R. (1963) *Conjectures and Refutations: The Growth of Scientific Knowledge*. New York: Routledge and Kegan Paul.

Tarp, S. (2012) "Theoretical Challenges in the Transition from Lexicographical P-Works to E-Tools", in S. Granger and M. Paqout (eds.), *Electronic Lexicography*. Oxford: Oxford University Press, pp. 107–118.

Wiegand, H. E. (1992) "Elements of a Theory towards a So-called Lexicographical Definition", *Lexicographica* 8: 175–289.

7
Lexicography and applied linguistics

Pam Peters and Trinidad Fernández

7.1 Introduction: lexicography, applied linguistics and other disciplines

Lexicography and applied linguistics are broad fields with multiple disciplinary affiliations, which certainly overlap in the 20th and 21st centuries. Both are heterogeneous domains of intellectual activity through contact with other disciplines. It is therefore hardly surprising that their positioning in conventional disciplinary sets and hierarchies has been contested.

The prevailing view of lexicography from the seventeenth century through to the 1980s was of it being an area of composition about language on a par with grammar, except that it was about words rather than syntax. With the growth of linguistics in the twentieth century, some such as Kempcke (1982:44) also saw it under the superordinate of linguistics through its theoretical connections with lexicology: *Eine Wörterbuchtheorie kann nur Teil der Lexikologie sein* ("dictionary theory has to be part of lexicology"). Sinclair (1984:7) echoes this with the claim that the theory relevant to lexicography is to be found in linguistics (and information technology). However some early commentators also connected it directly with applied linguistics, for example, Urdang (1963: 594): "Lexicography, in practice is a form of applied linguistics". These different views are reconciled by Burkanov (1998), who finds different affiliations for lexicography as theory and as practice. He argues that lexicography is "a subject field whose theoretical aspect falls within the realm of theoretical linguistics, whereas its practice pertains to the sphere of applied linguistics".

But others prefer to put dictionary theory and practice within the bounds of lexicography itself. Bergenholtz and Gouws (2013:38) define theoretical lexicography/metalexicography as: "The development of theories about and the conceptualization of dictionaries, specifically with regard to the function, the structure and the contents of dictionaries"; and practical lexicography/ lexicographic practice as: "The planning and compilation of concrete dictionaries". Theoretical lexicography was earlier subdivided by Tarp (2008: 9–10) into three subtypes: "general and specific theories, integrated and non-integrated theories, and contemplative and transformative theories". The last pair he distinguished thus: "A purely contemplative approach only observes existing dictionaries and theoretical models . . .

A transformative approach is innovative, and . . . not only interpret[s] and explain[s] lexicographic practice but . . . transforms it." With these statements he suggests that innovations in dictionaries only come from within lexicography.

Such inward-focused definitions of lexicography were avoided from the start by the key English-language journal *International Journal of Lexicography*; witness the remarks of its first editor Ilson, in his Introduction to the first issue (1988):

> The journal is devoted to examining how people inform one another; and the problems facing the compilers and users of dictionaries and thesauruses are similar to those facing compilers and users of indexes, encyclopedias, atlases and other kinds of reference work.

He thus sites lexicography firmly among the reference sciences, and information sciences more generally. The "knowledge-orientated functions" of dictionaries are now set alongside the "communication functions" by theorists of lexicography (Fuertes-Olivera and Arribas-Baño 2008:7); and others have urged a wider interpretation of its scope (Fuertes-Olivera and Bergenholtz 2011).

Major rethinking of dictionaries, their content and structure has been catalysed by the different mediums in which they can now be published, new kinds of interactions with users and the purposes that they serve. Sinclair's early comment (1984) on the relevance of information technology was prescient in recognising the importance of computational science to lexicography and dictionary development. Developments in translation theory contribute to advances in bilingual dictionaries. Countless disciplinary fields and their knowledge structures contribute to the content of twenty-first-century specialised dictionaries, as now acknowledged (Fuertes-Olivera and Tarp 2014), although missing from formal definitions of the scope of lexicography like those noted earlier.

By contrast, the interdisciplinary nature of applied linguistics has always been well recognised. Beginning as a focus of pedagogy in the 1950s (Davies 2007), the American Association for Applied Linguistics states that it "addresses a broad range of language-related issues in order to improve the lives of individuals and coinditions in society." It continues by maintaining that this discipline

> draws on a wide range of theoretical and methodological approaches from various disciplines – from the humanities to the social and natural sciences – as it develops its own knowledge-base about language, its users and uses, and their underlying social and material conditions.
>
> (http://dissoilogoi2.blogspot.com.es/2011/11/what-is-applied-linguistics.html)

Many distinct disciplines are interconnected with applied linguistics, and the journal *Applied Linguistics*

> welcomes contributions in such areas of current enquiry as: bilingualism and multilingualism; computer-mediated communication; conversation analysis; corpus linguistics; critical discourse analysis; deaf linguistics; discourse analysis and pragmatics; first and additional language learning, teaching, and use; forensic linguistics; language assessment; language planning and policies; language for special purposes; lexicography; literacies; multimodal communication; rhetoric and stylistics; and translation.
>
> (www.oxfordjournals.org/our_journals/applij/about.html)

Thus the journal *Applied Linguistics* acknowledges the rich interdisciplinarity which feeds into it, including some of the disciplines already mentioned in connection with lexicography, such as computer-mediated communication, multimodal communication and corpus linguistics, as well as first and additional language learning, teaching and use. There is thus quite an overlap in the domains of intellectual inquiry that applied linguistics and lexicography draw on, and their shared interests and connections are evident there. Applied linguistics makes no claims to theoretical autonomy. It nevertheless aims to distil principles of language learning and communication that impact on the use of language in speaking and writing.

In what follows we discuss some of the lexicographic developments of the twentieth century, where applied linguistics can well be seen as input to lexicographic practice from which aspects of lexicographic theory are distilled. To provide two specific cases, English and Spanish learners' dictionaries will be discussed. (See Chapters 33 and 40 of this *Handbook* for a more detailed analysis of English and Spanish lexicography.)

7.2 Historical perspectives: professional, commercial and individual impacts on lexicography

7.2.1 Lexicography and communities of practice

For dictionary-makers, lexicography has long been a kind of professional practice. According to the *Oxford English Dictionary* (online), lexicography involves (i) "the writing or compilation of a lexicon or dictionary; and (ii) the art or practice of writing dictionaries", the latter quoted from Johnson (1755). The OED's entry for *lexicography* has not been updated since 1902, though Landau's title *The art and craft of lexicography* (2001) makes an elegant adjustment to the second part. Any revision of the OED's entry will need to update it with reference to changing dictionary practices and the vast expansion of the domain of lexicography during the twentieth century. Hartmann and James's (1998) list includes 29 subtypes without exhausting the range. Monolingual dictionaries of record that focus on the general language for native speakers, such as the OED and DRAE (*Diccionario de la Real Academia de la Lengua Española)* (ones which focus on the general language for native-speakers) no longer occupy centre stage for English and Spanish lexicography. The stage is actively shared with many specialised kinds of dictionary, which may be grouped into three domains as follows:

1 pedagogical lexicography, i.e. learners' dictionaries (*diccionarios de aprendizaje*) for L1 and L2 students of English and Spanish respectively
2 bilingual dictionaries for translators (translation dictionaries) (*diccionarios bilingües para traductores*)
3 specialised dictionaries (*diccionarios especializados*):
   (i) focusing on special areas of the general vocabulary, such as slang, or idioms and phraseologies
   (ii) or specialised vocabulary, i.e. terminology used in technical or specialised disciplinary fields (= terminography)

These three domains of modern lexicography constitute distinct areas of dictionary publishing, and different "communities of practice" (Wenger 1998), with multiple professional affiliations outside lexicography.

In the case of pedagogical lexicography, the community of practice involves applied linguists and language teachers, so as to optimise dictionary content for less/more advanced second-language learners, and serve their needs in terms of encoding and decoding, e.g. English or Spanish. Can language learners make the most of extended information about L2 in a monolingual dictionary (Rundell 1998)? For bilingual lexicography, the community of practice includes professional translators and interpreters (Tarp 2004a), as well as specialists in contrastive linguistics and semantics (Zgusta 1971; Svenssen 1993). For the specialised lexicography of technical and special vocabularies, the community of practice is with terminologists, scientists and specialists in the field (Temmerman 2000).

The communities of lexicographic practice are thus expanding circles of professionals, whose interdisciplinary expertise is drafted into individual types of dictionary. They have mobilised some of the most productive developments of dictionaries in the later twentieth century, so that there is now a plethora of dictionary types to choose between – for language teachers (Rundell 1988), for translators (Peters, Tent and Fernández 2006) and for trainers and students in professional specialisms (Peters and Fernández 2013).

7.2.2 Dictionary publishing and commercial considerations

Dictionary publishing is expensive because it relies on substantial lexical research for its content – and only the largest publishing houses have sufficient budget for it. Yet for any dictionary publisher, there's an incentive to maximise the value of its in-house dictionary raw material by reusing it in more than one publication, as could always be seen in successive editions of the same dictionary. The rise of digital publishing in the late twentieth century has made it easier for dictionary publishers to reuse the same core content, and to repurpose it for larger and smaller publications. Yet profitability tends to fall away after the first edition of a dictionary, because dictionary users and libraries are both aware that the second and subsequent editions produced within a decade of the previous edition may not be very different, despite the updating of some entries. Dictionary publishers who face shrinking profits naturally have less to invest in new lexical research, and so the previously published content may be maintained decades afterwards.

A major consequence is that dictionaries contain a high proportion of traditional material, in their definitional styles ("dictionaryese"), and in the semantic dissection of polysemous words into their different senses. To rethink those subdivisions, and perhaps reorder senses according to newer principles, involves an enormous investment in time and research, and new senses are often just added to the end of the sequence, rather than allowing for restructuring of the whole set. The registration of multi-word items, now recognised as crucial to the construction of Spanish and English, is still mostly relegated to the set of run-ons at the end of the entry, unless the dictionary makes a practice of "splitting" rather than "lumping" in its macrostructure. Part of the problem is that multi-word items are not easily classified into the traditional "part-of-speech" grammar which has dominated European dictionaries for centuries, and has so far been only lightly modified in millennial dictionaries in English. Commercial factors in monolingual dictionary publishing have contributed to conserving older dictionary content, entrenching its traditions as a genre.

Bilingual dictionaries in the twentieth century have also been subject to commercial pressures, in not acknowledging that their direction, whether it is say English-Spanish or Spanish-English, cannot be equally useful to both L2 encoders and L1 decoders because of their different language resources and lexicographical needs. The L2 encoder needs greatly enriched treatment of the target language in the microstructure of an English-Spanish dictionary, whereas the L2 decoder of English-Spanish needs a very large inventory of words from the source language in the macrostructure. There is scant formal recognition in bilingual dictionaries of this enormous difference in *directionality* of use, let alone the difficulty of serving both directionalities in the same word list. As indicated earlier, it entails adjustments to both macrostructure and microstructure of the bilingual dictionary to optimise its value for encoding or decoding. But commercialism dictates that the same bilingual dictionary is often recommended for both. The rise of pedagogical lexicography and (bilingualised) learners' dictionaries (see Section 7.3.2) is a professional response to this problem. The much greater scope available in the electronic medium removes some of the material constraints on meeting the directionality requirement of bilingual dictionaries (see Section 7.4). But the problems are perpetuated in pocket electronic dictionaries used by millions of L2 students, in which older bilingual print dictionaries are reproduced without modification.

7.2.3 Lexicographic innovations

The institutional and commercial constraints within dictionary publishing were nevertheless tackled during the twentieth century by two outstanding individuals in English and Spanish lexicography, whose work was grounded in decades of professional practice outside lexicography. We identify two such innovators – A. S. Hornby in English lexicography, and his contemporary María Moliner in Spanish – whose work in pedagogical lexicography has stimulated ongoing developments in mainstream lexicography of English and Spanish. They drew on their experience of working with language learners and information seekers, respectively, to create novel kinds of dictionary that attended to dictionary users' needs in ways not seen before.

Although AS Hornby made his name as a lexicographer, he always called himself "a simple teacher" (Rundell 1998: 254). His professional life began in teaching English to Japanese learners from 1924, and while in Japan he worked with ELT specialists at the Tokyo Institute for Research in English Teaching (IRET), most notably Harold Palmer. Hornby participated keenly in Palmer-led research at IRET, mapping English collocations and developing more analytical approaches to teaching verb complementation. This research was published in his *Idiomatic and Syntactic Dictionary* (= ISD 1942), and in the *Guide to Patterns and Usage in English* (1954), where he described patterns of noun and adjective complementation. At IRET Hornby also collaborated with West, and co-published the *General Service List* (1936) with him, Palmer and Faucett. He thus associated with the "vocabulary control" movement in language pedagogy and lexicography (Rundell 1998:255–6), though he applied the notion intuitively in his definitions (rather than by corpus-derived statistics, as did some later lexicographers (see Table 7.1). With his extensive experience in EFL teaching and research in English linguistics, Hornby was well prepared to launch into drafting material for the *Oxford Advanced Learner's Dictionary* (1st ed. 1948), which led the field for several decades (Rundell 1998). (See Chapters 11, 19 and 22 of this *Handbook*).

Moliner was a professional librarian who worked for many years in the Industrial Engineering School (Universidad Politécnica de Madrid). She was thus well versed in reference sciences through daily encounters with students, native speakers and second-language learners, and she evidently understood their needs in seeking specialised information and the language required to follow explanations. She understood the students' purposes in using technical language (encoding or decoding), and when their language knowledge was sufficient to shift from bilingual to monolingual dictionaries. Of her own dictionary she said

"It is . . . for the use of both native speakers of Spanish and learners of the language when they need to consult a monolingual dictionary and discard the bilingual". Her work thus anticipated many of the principles of modern language pedagogy, especially the need to use language clear and comprehensible to the reader. Her *Diccionario de Uso del Español*, first published in 1975, has since been taken up in numerous pedagogical units in search and retrieval, available through libraries and educational centres, and it remains "a bibliographic treasure" (Villanueva 2000).

The work of Hornby and Moliner was seminal for pedagogical lexicography in their respective countries, and for European lexicography more generally. They helped to crystallise new communities of practice for creating dictionaries for L2 learners, and to ensure that they were well connected with applied linguistics and reference sciences.

7.3 Core issues and topics

In order to discuss the interplay between pedagogical lexicography and applied linguistics in more detail, let us now analyse some features of Hornby's and Moliner's dictionaries that reflect it, and its further manifestations in the following generations of English and Spanish learners dictionaries. These publications clearly illustrate the value of applying linguistic knowledge to dictionary compilation, ensuring that dictionaries for learners consist of the language elements they most need and provide systematic material for them to become proficient users of the L2.

7.3.1 Hornby's Oxford Advanced Learner's Dictionary

The *Oxford Advanced Learner's Dictionary of Current English* (OALD 1st ed. 1948) marked a very substantial shift in English lexicography. Hornby recognised the fact that the unstated target reader of conventional monolingual English dictionaries was the native speaker, who could bring his or her full knowledge and intuitions about the language to bear on the dictionary text – and that such dictionaries did not meet second-language learners at their point of need (Rundell 1988, 1998). Hornby's strong background in teaching English as a foreign language, and his linguistic interests in the structure of English itself, are built into in the macrostructure and microstructure of OALD. It uses separate entries for homonymic nouns and verbs, so as to illustrate their different patterns of complementation, as well as common collocations. See for example the following excerpt (Figure 7.1):

> **doom**[1] /dum/ *n* **1** (usu *sing*) ruin; death; sth evil that is to come: *to go to one's ~; to send a man to his ~*. **2** (also **Doomsday** /'dumzdei/) the Day of Judgment; the end of the world: *from now till D~sday*, for ever.
> **doom**[2] /dum/ *vt* [VP14] ~ **sb** (***to sth/to do sth***), condemn (sb to some fate/to do sth): (esp in *pp*) *~ed to disappointment*; *~ed to die*; *poems ~ed to oblivion*, certain to be forgotten.

Figure 7.1 Dictionary entry in OALD (3rd ed. 1974)[1]

The microstructures of these parallel entries illustrate Hornby's use of simple paraphrases to define words for the language learner. As noted earlier, he didn't work with a controlled vocabulary, yet managed intuitively to avoid difficult vocabulary in his definitions. Unlike the contemporary *Concise Oxford Dictionary of Current English* (COD) (5th ed. 1964, 6th edition 1976), Hornby doesn't rely on sets of synonyms to project the meaning of the headword, but includes a definition to explain the word's meanings to non-native-speakers of English. Both OALD and COD refer in their titles to focusing on "current English", and accordingly OALD omits historical and archaic uses of *doom* to mean a "law", "decree", "sentence", "condemnation". These older senses are however foregrounded in the entry in COD (5th ed.), and retained in full in COD (6th ed.) – perhaps to provide "etymology-through-the-back-door" (Rundell 1998:132). OALD draws attention to the very common use of the past participle *doomed,* in several collocations, for example, "doomed to disappointment". Collocations like these are now recognised within construction grammar as crucial structures for language acquisition, for encoding as well as decoding (Tomasello 2003).

In the OALD entry for the verb *doom* (Figure 7.1), its syntax is identified as [VP14], one of the 25 verb patterns [VP14] which Hornby formulated in his earlier publication (ISD 1948), and used systematically in OALD to assist language learners in formulating English clauses correctly. All OALD verbs are cross-referenced to the full set of verb patterns laid out in the front matter for further reference. Hornby's work on the complementation of verbs was taken up by Quirk et al. in their *Comprehensive Grammar* (1st ed. 1972), and in later grammatical works by Levin (1993) in print and Fillmore's online FrameNet (1996) (see Chapter 24 of this *Handbook*), as well as by lexicographers Herbst and colleagues in their *Valency Dictionary of English* (2004).

OALD innovated also in providing pronunciations of all words in IPA (International Phonetic Alphabet) – unlike COD and other contemporary British native-speaker dictionaries, whose users are expected to know how to pronounce the words of their language. Pronunciation information is, of course, most helpful to language learners, especially when offered in phonetic code which is language neutral. OALD makes use of line drawings to support the verbal explanations of concepts that are difficult to define, for example, complex natural shapes or geometrical figures such as the cone and cylinder. OALD thus anticipates the much fuller use of graphic illustrations in learners' dictionaries in following decades.

7.3.2 Hornby's influence on later English learners' dictionaries and English lexicography at large

The innovations of OALD were taken further by other dictionary publishing houses in the 1990s, which saw publishers competing to produce helpful learners' dictionaries, in the so-called "big four" of 1995–56 (see Chapters 19 and 22 of this *Handbook*). Their directionality is clear: they are for L2 encoding and decoding, and best for intermediate to advanced learners, with large amounts of language detail for L2 students to read, especially in treating high-frequency function words (Coffey 2006). All are based on large corpora, from which word frequencies can be extracted for use in selecting words for the macrostructure, and in ordering of senses in microstructure. The corpora also provided countless examples of word usage and collocations in authentic contexts, which were more or less modified to fit the explanatory purpose.

All the dictionaries listed in Table 7.1 present unique kinds of innovations, taking pedagogical ideas from Hornby's OALD forward in different applications. Controlled vocabularies based on corpus frequencies were adopted for defining purposes, as a way of ensuring that definitions did not pose more difficulty than the headword. A totally new sentence style for definitions was introduced by CCLD (see Figure 7.2). Longer entries were subdivided semantically to provide more focused entry points for the language learners; different ways of indicating the grammar of verbs and nouns were adopted; more attention was given to

Table 7.1 English learners' dictionaries in the decade before and after 2000

	Year of publ'n	*Corpus, used for exx/ word frequencies*	*Control'd defining vocabulary*	*Graphics*	*Regional usage*	*Grammar*	*Prons*
Cambridge International Dictionary of English (CIDE)	1995	Cambridge Language Survey, yes/no	c.2000 words	b/w line drawings, inserts	Br, Am, Aus, Canad	Embedded: N[U,C],V[T], v aux; brief grammar summary	IPA: Br + Am
Collins Cobuild Learner's Dictionary (CCLD)	1996	Bank of English corpus: yes/yes	no	a few b/w line drawings in back matter	Br, Am	Detailed in side column, not embedded; full grammar section	IPA, incl. stress: Br + Am.
Longman Dictionary of Contemporary English 3rd ed (LDOCE3)	1995	Longman and British National corpus, yes/yes	c. 2000 words	colored pics as inserts; b/w drawings in text (lots)	Br v. Am spellings, meanings, colloc'ns	Embedded: N [U, C];V [T], phr vb; separate grammar section	IPA: Br + Am
Oxford Dictionary for Advanced Learners 5th ed. (OALD5)	1996	British National corpus) yes/no	c. 3500 words	b/w line drawings in main text; color maps	Br v Am spelling, meaning; Br/Am cultures*	Embedded: full grammar section; also phrasal verbs, colloca'ns	IPA: Br + Am
Macmillan English Dictionary for Advanced Learners (MEDAL)	2002	Bloomsbury corpus, yes/no	c. 2500 words + 7500 word "core vocab."	black/red font for core/non-core words; colored inserts	British or American editions	Embedded	CDROM Br + Am

collocations and idiomatic constructions; and graphics (black/white drawings as well as coloured ones) were used to illustrate word meanings. Variation between British and American English pronunciations are noted regularly in IPA symbols, as well as in spelling and some elements of meaning and collocation. The fifth dictionary in Table 7.1 (MEDAL) continues the innovative run of the "big four", with its extensive use of corpora, new features such as coloured typography to distinguish words of its "core vocabulary" from those with lower frequency, and using the CDROM for pronunciations.

Among the big four, it is the CCLD (1996) which presents some of the most remarkable lexicographic innovations. The use of corpora as input to learners' dictionaries was pioneered by Collins dictionaries from 1978, and is seen later in the exemplification of every sense of the word *doom* in CCLD. Its treatment of word grammar is also unusual – presenting full grammatical specifications for noun, verb and adjectival usage of the word in a separate column to the right, rather than relying on abbreviations embedded in the text. But the most innovative aspect of the CCLD entry is its approach to defining, intended to provide better access to word meanings and functions for the learner. Instead of the traditional phrasal definitions, CCLD uses full sentences with the headword used prominently in it. The elements of a traditional definition become part of the propositional content of the sentence while also illustrating the semantic field to which the word belongs. The sentence definitions are less lexically dense than the traditional phrasal ones, and thus more accessible, especially with CCLD's own *core vocabulary*, based on corpus-frequencies, to ensure that no word in the definitions is lower in frequency than the headword itself (Figure 7.2).

doom /du:m/ dooms, dooming, doomed.	♦◊◊◊◊
1 Doom is a terrible future state or event which you cannot prevent. . . .*his warnings of impending doom . . . I awoke with a terrible sense of doom and fear.*	N-UNCOUNT
2 If something **dooms** someone to an unpleasant fate or they **are doomed** to that fate, they are certain to suffer it. *That argument was the turning point for their marriage, and the one which doomed it to failure . . . If he lived, he would be doomed to spend the war as a prisoner.*	VERB V *n to n* *be* V-ed to-inf Also V *n* to-inf
♦ **doomed.** Someone or something that is **doomed** is certain to fail. . . . *a doomed attempt to rescue the children.*	ADJ
dooms•day /'du:mzdeɪ/. **1 Doomsday** is a day or time when you expect that something terrible will happen.	N-UNCOUNT
2 In the Christian religion, **Doomsday** is the last day of the world, on which God will judge everyone.	N-PROPER

Figure 7.2 Dictionary entry in CCLD

Sentence-style definitions are used consistently in CCLD, and occasionally by CIDE and OALD5. They help to capture word functions and speaker-hearer attitudes in a less formal way than is done in natural semantic metalanguage (Wierzbicka 1972). In CCLD the contents of the microstructure depends on how polysemous the word is. Those with three or four senses (including both noun and verb senses) are blocked together and run on, as shown earlier in Figure 7.2. Words with many senses (after the first three to six) are simply numbered in bold on separate lines in CCLD – whereas other learners' dictionaries provide separate paragraphs for the distinct senses, each with its semantic "guideword" (CIDE), or "signpost" (LDOCE3).

One further kind of innovation in L2 print dictionaries immediately after 2000 is the bilingualisation of the monolingual text so to support particular language-learner groups.

This feature can again be traced back to Hornby (Marello 1998), and both OALD5 and LDOCE3 have appeared in bilingualised Chinese editions (OALD in 2002, and LDOCE in 2004), with extensive bilingualisation of all definitions and example(s). These editions clearly identify their learners as Chinese native-speakers needing help with decoding and understanding the semantics of English words, but using the learners' L1 (Chinese) to help anchor their understanding. McArthur (2005) nevertheless suggests that with this level of bilingualisation, these dictionaries might be helpful for advanced English learners of Chinese as well – as the publishers would wish!

7.3.3 María Moliner's Diccionario de Uso del Español

Moliner's single lexicographical work was the *Diccionario de Uso del Español* (DUE), which she published 1975, after 15 years of working on it in her spare time. The fact that she was the sole author was continually criticised, yet she brought to her lexicography a strong sense of how language learners (L1 and L2) might acquire Spanish. Like many professional lexicographers, Moliner made use of the macrostructure of another dictionary her starting point, that is, the *Diccionario de la Real Academia de la Lengua Española* (DRAE). But she added many everyday words of Spanish not included in DRAE, especially those found in her reading of newspapers. In keeping with descriptive principles of lexicography, she noted regionalisms – words used in particular areas of Spain (Aragón, Asturias) or in the New World (e.g. Cuba). She also added foreign terms in common use (such as *cyber*) which the DRAE had not admitted – not waiting until they were in some danger of obsolescence. "In [DRAE], words are included when they are about to die", the dry comment of the contemporary Columbian writer García Márquez (1981).

Moliner's aim was not to supersede DRAE but to reconstruct it and improve it for the purposes of learning Spanish. She developed definitions in precise, modern Spanish, adapting the lofty, conservative language of DRAE to make the explanations accessible to language learners. The current senses of each word are ordered by their relative closeness to its stem, as shown below in the entries for *arraigar* and *arraigarse* (Figure 7.3). The first definition for *arraigar* foregrounds the word's formal and semantic association with the stem *raiz* "root" in an extended paraphrase, followed by a set of synonyms and antonyms that pick up shades of the core meaning. With the second and third definitions, the entry proceeds with definitions for special figurative senses of the word, and with the fourth, its specialised application in the domain of law.

> **arraigar.** ❶ Echar raíces los tallos, plantones o plantas recién plantados en un terreno, con lo que siguen viviendo y desarrollándose. (V.: "AGARRAR, *asir*, COGER, *encepar*, ENRAIZAR, PRENDER, *radicar, raigar* – ant.–, *tomar*. ➢ *Apreso*. ➢ *BROTAR. ➢ DESARRAIGAR".) ❷ (fig.). "Arraigarse". Hacerse *firme en alguien una costumbre, vicio, virtud, etc. ❸ (fig.; "en"). "Afincarse. Arraigarse. Radicarse". ***Establecerse de manera fija en un sitio, adquiriendo en él fincas o intereses de otra clase.** ❹ (*derecho). *Señalar o depositar una persona sometida a juicio ciertos bienes raíces o de otra clase para responder de las resultas.*
>
> **arraigarse.** ❶Echar raíces en un sitio. ❷ Es-tablecerse en un sitio. ❸ *Depositar garantía para las resultas de un juicio.*

Figure 7.3 Dictionary entries in DUE

The entry for *arraigar* (Figure 7.3) shows many of Moliner's key innovations. For instance, her extended use of definitions and clear specifications of core and figurative meanings promote understanding of the key word. In addition, she adds a bunch of synonyms which help build the learner's competence in both decoding and encoding Spanish. In each semantic group she used contrasting typefaces to indicate the synonym she considered to be more generally used, or more precise and expressive. Her entries thus combine the expansive onomasiology of the thesaurus with the sense-discriminating semasiology of the dictionary, anticipating the links between them which are now facilitated in electronic dictionaries.

Like Hornby, Moliner was alert to the presence of collocations in Spanish, which she refers to in numerous entries as "frequent links", "common/usual links" or "special affinities" for the headword: for example *risa* preceded by verbs such as *mondarse/troncharse (de)* ("to split one's sides/die of laughing"). Whether as fixed expressions/idioms, or less fixed "plurivalent" units (Alvar Ezquerra 1983), she sought to document the constructions which words commonly appear in as part of their usage.

Yet Moliner's title DUE with its emphasis on usage (*de uso*) proved controversial, partly because of her independent selection of entries for the macrostructure. Where there could be a choice of headwords, she used derivational richness as a criterion, so that learners would be introduced to clusters of words belonging to the same lemma or word family. For example, she preferred to list the verb *principiar* rather than its everyday counterpart *empezar* ("begin") as headword, because the former had more derivatives, such as *principio, principiante.* As it happens, *principiar* is now equally frequent, according to the *Gran Diccionario de Uso del Español Actual*/SGEL (2001). But Moliner saw her dictionary's purpose as "*guiar en el correcto y buen uso*" (Preface), rather than showing actual usage. Again this can be seen as her orientation to the needs of L2 language learners, rather than failing to differentiate between prescriptive and descriptive norms, as her critics commented.

7.3.4 Moliner's influence on Spanish learners' dictionaries and general lexicography in Spain

Moliner's DUE was updated and republished by others after her death, a second edition in two volumes in 1998, and a third in 2007. It too stimulated a suite of other *diccionarios de aprendizaje* (learners' dictionaries) from the 1990s, many of which took up and extended Moliner's innovations. One of these was to include words beginning with *ch* and *ll* within the letters C and L respectively (which the DRAE itself incorporated from 1994). The need to customise dictionary material for first and second-language learners was increasingly recognised, especially the challenge of providing for the encoding needs of second-language learners. Table 7.2 lists a set of monolingual Spanish *diccionarios de aprendizaje* published before and after the millennium, and differentiates them in terms of their content and notional users (see Tarp 2004b). Their directionality, as shown here, is as stated in the preface and/or as demonstrated in the scope of the macrostructure and in pedagogically significant material in the microstructure, for example, regular use of definitions, grammatical indications, pronunciations and constructional or illustrative material.

As Table 7.2 shows, this set of Spanish dictionaries takes on different areas and aspects of the Spanish language, with different kinds of language learners or users as their notional readers. Of those listed, an early edition of the first (SALAMANCA) was previously the one most widely used after DRAE and Moliner's DUE, according to Hernández (1989), at a time when there was a dearth of dictionaries designed for foreign learners. The linguistic

Table 7.2 Spanish dictionaries for learners before and after 2000

	Year publ'd	*Users, direct'lity*	*Level*	*Macrostructure includes:*	*Definitions/ grammar*	*Collocations/ examples*	*IPA prons*
Diccionario Salamanca de la Lengua Española	1996	L1/L2 decode; L2 encode	Students, teachers	**GL words, neologisms; Hispanic-Amer	yes (incl. pragmat. labels)	yes	yes
Diccionario del Español Actual (DEA)	1999	L1/L2 decode	Writers, translators, teachers, students	GL words, colloquial, youthspeak, regionalisms	yes	examples from up-to-date corpus	
Gran Diccionario de Uso del Español Actual (SGEL)	2001	L1 decode L2 encode	Students, teachers, profession'ls	GL words,	yes/clear grammar	yes/ exs for every def.	yes; + spelling notes
REDES: *Diccionario Combinatorio del Español Contemporáneo*	2004	L1 encode	advanced students, teachers, writers	GL collocations, based on semantics	synonym, antonym only	corpus-derived multiword combination	no
Diccionario Fraseológico Documentado del Español Actual (DFDEA)	2005	L1 encode	Educated users, teachers	GL collocations discourse formulae	No	multiword expressions from RAE corpus 1955–2004	no

features of the updated SALAMANCA (1996), indicated earlier, would address the needs of L2 learners in both decoding and encoding, with its pragmatic labels, and attention to pronunciations and collocations, anticipated by DUE.

The fourth and fifth dictionaries in Table 7.2 reflect and greatly expand Moliner's interest in collocations, making it the macrostructure of combinatorial and phraseological dictionaries, instead of focusing on individual words of Spanish, as in the first three. Although useful in advanced language education for L1s, these collocation-focused references are not so much learners' dictionaries as specialised language dictionaries (type 3 (i): see Section 7.2.1). The resources for creating such combinatorial dictionaries have been greatly enhanced with the creation of Spanish corpora both synchronic and diachronic, held by the Spanish Royal Academy (RAE), and other institutions.

Of the five dictionaries in Table 7.2, the third dictionary is the one most clearly designed for L2 learners, being systematic in its provision of multifaceted information about the forms and meanings of Spanish words. The entry for *arraigar* reproduced in Figure 7.4 illustrates the various features noted in Table 7.2 that support foreign language learning.

❷ ***a-rrai-gar*** [arraiɣár] **1.** ***intr REFL.(-se)*** Echar raíces las plantas recién colocadas en un lugar y desarrollarse: *Los tulipanes no han arraigado por falta de riego.* **2.** Adquirir una cosa firmeza o solidez, en sentido literal y, *esp*, FIG (referido a costumbres, hábitos, etc.): *Toda nueva moda aspira a arraigar en las costumbres. Esta idea obsesiva arraigó en él hace muchos años.* **3.** (Con *en*) Establecerse una persona en un lugar y fijar en él su residencia principal: *Después de recorrer varios países de Europa, se arraigó en Londres.* **4.** DER Depositar la persona que está sometida a un juicio una fianza económica para asegurar su responsabilidad en caso de que así lo decida el tribunal. **II.** *tr* **1.** Hacer que una cosa adquiera firmeza o solidez, en sentido literal o, tratándose de costumbres, hábitos, formas de actuar, etc., en sentido FIG: *Esa actitud hace arraigar prejuicios que más tarde serán casi imposibles de extirpar.* **2.** (Con *en*) Hacer que una persona se establezca en un lugar o viva o fije su residencia en él: *Esta acción política se encamina a arraigar a los habitantes en su lugar de origen.*

ORT Ante *e* la *g* cambia a *gu*: *Arraigué.*

SIN **I. 1.** Agarrar(se), prender(se).
2. Afincar(se), enraizars(se), establecer(se).
3. Afincarse.
II. 1. Enraizar, reafirmar.
ANT **II. 1.** Desarraigar.

Figure 7.4 Entry for **arraigar** in SGEL (*Gran Diccionario de Uso del Español Actual*)

Comparing this SGEL entry for *arraigar/arraigarse* with Moliner's (Figure 7.3), we see a generational shift in the accessibility of information within the comparable SGEL microstructure, although it embodies the same kinds of information that DUE provided. The grammatical coverage is more inclusive, foregrounding the reflexive use (*arraigarse)* as more common than the basic non-reflexive use. The synonyms/antonyms that were embedded in the DUE entry to support the definitional paraphrase are relocated to a list at the bottom of the entry. Information on pronunciation and orthography is also added there. Definitions are provided for all senses of the word, along with example sentences, to illustrate collocational patterns and authentic usage. SGEL (2001) thus provides strong support for learning all aspects of learning words, lexical structures of language – based on best principles and practice in language pedagogy.

By coincidence in 2001 (the same year as SGEL), the established *Real Academia de la Lengua Española* published an abridged version of its dictionary (DRAE), intended for all types of users, including foreign learners. DRAE had the advantage of being compiled on the basis of several large corpora owned by the Spanish Academy, of all the Spanish speaking countries of the last 25 years, covering Spanish usage in both the Old and New World, and including words from the American and the Philippine dialects. With this evidential base, it can identify general, foreign and technical words in frequent use, giving better coverage of the contemporary Spanish lexicon than ever before. However, teachers surveyed on their use of DRAE and Moliner's DUE (3rd ed. 2007) recognised that although DRAE was most appropriate for native speakers of Spanish, DUE still distinguished itself as contributing better to the learning of Spanish as a second language because of the information it provides on usage (García Sanz 2009). Importantly, DUE supports language learners in encoding as well as decoding, and is a good deal more descriptive than DRAE.

7.4 Looking to the future

This review of monolingual learners' dictionaries in English and Spanish published around the turn of the millennium shows the strong impact of applied linguistics in this rapidly expanding area of lexicography. The many innovations to be found in paper-based learners' dictionaries around 2000 are still being taken up in dictionary theory and practice, with lexicographers ready to embrace the opportunities of producing learners' dictionaries online. They begin with the digitisation of the pre-existing dictionary text on line (as was done on CD), but rapidly develop into interactive resources which can expand on particular language learners questions. For example, uncertainties about valencies/arguments of the verb in a foreign language can be addressed through an electronic feature which displays the *actants* (L'Homme 2010). The first decades of the twenty-first century offer new pedagogical potential and greatly enhanced scope for general lexicography in the electronic medium. Dictionary-makers are freed from the constraints of the print medium, with unlimited access to language resources to supplement/complement the online learners' dictionary.

With the unlimited information resources that can be linked up, the twenty-first century is a "Cambrian explosion" (Fuertes-Olivera 2016) for specialised dictionaries, apart from all the sophisticated technology in information processing and customised analyses which can be provided. In new three-way partnerships between discipline specialists, IT experts and lexicographers, the dictionary becomes a multifaceted information system. It still uses individual words as their point of entry, but relies much less on alphabetical ordering of their material, because it can be interconnected into ontological structures (e.g. hyponymic/meronymic) in the electronic medium, and thus make the most of both semasiological and onomasiological approaches to language.

The online medium offers much more to users in terms of adapting the information supplied to their particular needs – an interactive environment which responds to the parameters of individual searches, as with the pioneering online *Diccionario de Contabilidad Inglés-Español* (2010) (Spanish-English dictionary of accounting). The online medium supports all kinds of digital display: textual and graphic, audio and video, thus using multimodal resources for communicating with the language learner and enhancing the "user experience". It makes for stronger cognitive engagement with online learning systems, especially for those with limited language or reading abilities. The online medium now hosts the world's first dictionary of sign language: see the Australian AUSLAN website at *www.**auslan**.org.*

au/about/dictionary/. Multimodal termbanks are also an effective medium for displaying multidimensional information in specialised fields such as architecture and construction (Fernández and Faber 2011) and public health communication (Peters et al. 2015).

The impact of the online medium on general lexicography is also profound, because online users can be connected to the dictionary's own corpora of actual usage from around the Hispanic and Anglo-worlds. This underwrites the now generally accepted role of large unabridged dictionaries to be descriptive rather than prescriptive and would allow users to discover for themselves some of the variability in regional usage of words and collocations in these major world languages. It could thus at the same time limit the dictionary's heavy obligation to articulate all the finer detail of regional variation while facilitating users' access to it.

7.5 Conclusion

The influence of applied linguistics and language pedagogy on learners' dictionaries of both English and Spanish in the late twentieth century cannot be doubted, nor the many innovations prompted by contact language teachers and information specialists, and their colleagues in educational research and reference science. Most importantly they helped to shift the focus from the dictionary's substance to its utilisation by learners, and how to optimise its content to meet learners' needs. But this shift of emphasis from the product to the consumer now goes well beyond learners' dictionaries to lexicography at large, helping it to reposition itself effectively in the electronic age, and to optimise its use of the online medium.

The elevation of the user perspective in functional theories of lexicography shows how lexicographic principles are readily extrapolated from lexicographic practice. It is proof of its intrinsic vitality as a discipline as well as its ability to embrace insights and strategies from other disciplines. Fresh external inputs from twenty-first-century information technology, communication science and computational linguistics will again help to enlarge its scope and content. Lexicography will thus continue to evolve from its origins as the art and practice of writing about words – to a multifaceted discipline within the knowledge and reference sciences.

Related topics

Lexicography and corpus linguistics; dictionaries to assist teaching and learning; learners' dictionaries of English; English lexicography in the Internet era; Spanish lexicography in the Internet era.

Further reading

Fernández, T. and P. Faber. (2011). "The Representation of Multidimensionality in a Bilingualised English-Spanish Thesaurus for Learners in Architecture and Building Construction", *International Journal of Lexicography* 24(2): 198–225.

This paper shows how an online thesaurus can accommodate the multiple dimensions of meaning (form/function) in terms for physical objects in the built environment.

Fuertes-Olivera, P. A. (2016). "A Cambrian Explosion in Lexicography: Some Reflections for Designing and Constructing Specialised Online Dictionaries", *International Journal of Lexicography* 29(2): 226–247.

The author reflects on the innovative *Diccionarios de Contabilidad Inglés-Español*, and the need to balance access to unlimited data with selectivity for the user.

Peters, P. (2015). "Transcending Their Formats: Dictionaries, Encyclopedias and Atlases", *Humanities Australia* 6: 68–81.

This highlights the continuous evolution of dictionary formats in response to particular user needs, and lexicography's expanding scope and capacity in the digital medium.

Peters, P., A. Smith, Y. Funk and J. Boyages. (2015). "Language, Terminology and the Readability of Online Cancer Information", *Medical Humanities* 42(1): 36–41. doi:10.1136/medhum-2015–010766

This paper discusses the linguistic inaccessibility of medical language, and the capacity of online termbanks to offer multimedia terminography for public access/ L2 users.

Note

1 The first three editions of OALD (1948, 1963, 1974) were all edited by Hornby, so these excerpts from the 1974 edition may be taken as his dictionary style in its most mature form.

References

Dictionaries

CCLD = *Collins Cobuild Learners Dictionary* (1995). HarperCollins Publishers.

CIDE = *Cambridge International Dictionary of English* (1995) Cambridge University Press.

COD = *Concise Oxford Dictionary of Current English* (5th edition 1964, 6th edition 1976) Oxford University Press.

DEA = *Diccionario del Español Actual (*1999) ed. Manuel Seco, Olimpia Andrés and Gabino Ramos. Madrid: Aguilar-Santillana.

DFDEA = *Diccionario Fraseológico Documentado del Español* 2nd ed. (2005) ed. Manuel Seco, Olimpia Andrés and Gabino Ramos. Madrid: Aguilar-Santillana.

DRAE: *Diccionario de la Real Academia de la Lengua Española.* Madrid: Real Academia Española. Since 2014 DEL = *Diccionario de la Lengua Española.*

DUE = *Diccionario de Uso del Español* (1975) Madrid: Gredos.

Gran Diccionario de Uso del Español Actual (2001) ed. by Aquilino Sánchez et al. Madrid: SGEL.

Herbst, T. et al. (2004) *A Valency Dictionary of English: A Corpus-Based Analysis of the Complementation Patterns of English Verbs, Nouns, and Adjectives.* Berlin: Mouton de Gruyter.

ISD = Hornby, AS (1942) *Idiomatic and Syntactic Dictionary.* Oxford Tokyo.

LDOCE = *Longman Dictionary of Contemporary English.* 3rd edition (1995) Longman.

MEDAL = *Macmillan English Dictionary for Advanced Learners* (2002) Palgrave Macmillan.

OALD = *Oxford Advanced Learners Dictionary of Current English* 1st edition (1948), 2nd edition (1963), 3rd edition (1974), 5th edition (1996).

OED = *Oxford English Dictionary* (online) 2010, www.oed.com/.

REDES/*Diccionario Combinatorio del Español Contemporáneo* (2004) ed. by Ignacio Bosque. Madrid: EDICIONES SM.

SALAMANCA = *Diccionario Salamanca de la Lengua Española* (1996). Madrid: Santillana Educación.

SGEL = *Gran Diccionario de Uso del Español Actual.*

Other literature

Alvar Ezquerra, M. (1983) "Sobre María Moliner, *Diccionario de Uso del Español, Lexicología y Lexicografía*". *Guía Bibliográfica.* Salamanca: Almar, pp. 214–228.

Bergenholtz, H. and R. Gouws. (2013) "What Is Lexicography?", *Lexikos* 22: 31–42.

Burkhanov, I. (1998) *Lexicography: A Dictionary of Basic Terminology*. Wydawn: Wyższej Szkoły Pedagogicznej w Rzeszowie

Coffey, S. (2006) "High-frequency Grammatical Lexis in Advanced-level English Learners' Dictionaries: from Language Description to Pedagogical Usefulness", *International Journal of Lexicography* 19(2), pp. 157–173.

Davies, A. (2007) *An Introduction to Applied Linguistics: From Practice to Theory*. 2nd edition. Edinburgh: Edinburgh University Press.

Fernández, T. and P. Faber. (2011) "The Representation of Multidimensionality in a Bilingualised English-Spanish Thesaurus for Learners in Architecture and Building Construction", *International Journal of Lexicography* 24(2): 198–225.

Fuertes-Olivera, P. A. (ed.) (2010) *Specialised Dictionaries for Learners*. Berlin: de Gruyter.

Fuertes-Olivera, P. A. (2016) "A Cambrian Explosion in Lexicography: Some Reflections for Designing and Constructing Specialised Online Dictionaries", *International Journal of Lexicography* 29(2): 226–247.

Fuertes-Olivera, P. A. and A. Arribas Baño. (2008) *Pedagogical Specialised Lexicography. The Representation of Meaning in English and Spanish Business Dictionaries*. Amsterdam/Philadelphia: John Benjamins.

Fuertes-Olivera, P. A. and H. Bergenholtz (eds.) (2011) *e-Lexicography: The Internet, Digital Initiatives and Lexicography*. London/New York: Continuum.

Fuertes-Olivera, P. A., P. Gordo Gómez, M. Niño Amo, Á. Ríos Rodicio, A. Sastre Ruano, S. Tarp, Marisol Velasco Sacristán Nielsen, L. Mourier and H. Bergenholtz. (2010) *Diccionario de Contabilidad Inglés-Español*. Navarra: Thomson Reuters-Aranzadi.

Fuertes-Olivera, P. A. and S. Tarp. (2014) *Theory and Practice of Specialised Online Dictionaries: Lexicography versus Terminography*. Berlin: de Gruyter.

García Márquez, G. (1981) "La Mujer que Escribió un Diccionario", *El País, 10 de febrero de 1981*.http://elpais.com/diario/1981/02/10/opinion/350607617_850215.html (Last accessed: May, 2017).

García Sanz, E. (2009) *El diccionario: su utilidad en el proceso de enseñanza-aprendizaje de ELE. Una vuelta más de tuerca*. www.mecd.gob.es/dctm/redele/Material-RedEle/Biblioteca/2011_BV_12/2011_BV_12_2do_semestre/2011_BV_12_11Garc%C3%ADa_Sanz.pdf?documentId=0901e72b8101ef31 (Last accessed: 1 February 2017).

Hartmann R. and G. James. (1998) *Dictionary of Lexicography*. London/New York: Routledge.

Herbst, T., D. Heath, I. Roe and D. Götz (eds.) (2004) *A Valency Dictionary of English*. Berlin: Mouton de Gruyter.

Hernández, H. (1989) *Los diccionarios de orientación escolar*. Tubingen: Niemeyer.

Kempcke, G. (1982) "Lexikologie, lexikographische Theorie und lexikographische Praxis", in E. Agricola et al. (eds.) *Wortschatzforschung Heute*. Leipzig: VEB Verlag, pp. 42–61.

Levin, B. (1993) *English Verb Classes and Alternations*. Chicago: University of Chicago Press.

Landau, S. (2001) *The Art and Craft of Lexicography*. 2nd edition. Cambridge: Cambridge University Press.

L'Homme, M.-C. (2010) "Designing Terminological Dictionaries for Learners Based on Lexical Semantics", in P. Fuertes-Olivera (ed.), 141–153.

McArthur T. (2005) "The First English Learners Dictionary: The Chinese Dimension", *English Today* 81: 21(1): 60–64.

Marello, C. (1998) "Hornby's Bilingualised Dictionaries", *International Journal of Lexicography* 11(4): 292–314.

Peters, P. and T. Fernández. (2013) "The Lexical Needs of ESP Students in a Professional Field", *English for Specific Purposes* 32: 236–247.

Peters, P., J. Tent and T. Fernández. (2006) "Critical Lexicography", in C. Marello (ed.), *Proceedings of Euralex XII International Congress*. Turin. Alessandria, Edition dell'Orso, pp. 561–565.

Peters, P., A. Smith, Y. Funk and J. Boyages. (2015) "Language, Terminology and the Readability of Online Cancer Information", *Medical Humanities* 42(1): 36–41. doi:10.1136/medhum-2015–010766

Rundell, M. (1988) "Changing the Rules: Why the Monolingual Learner's Dictionary Should Move Away From the Native-Speaker Tradition", in M. Snell-Hornby (ed.) *Zurilex'86: Proceedings of Euralex International Congress,* Zurich: A. Francke Verlag, pp. 127–137.

Rundell, M. (1998) "Recent Trends in Pedagogical Lexicography", *International Journal of Lexicography* 18(4): 315–342.

Sinclair, J. (1984) "Lexicography as an Academic Subject", in R.R.K. Hartmann (ed.), *LEXeter '83 Proceedings [EURALEX 1st Congress]*. pp. 3–12.

Svenssen, B. (1993) *Practical Lexicography*. Oxford: Oxford University Press.

Tarp, S. (2004a) "How Can Dictionaries Assist Translators", in C. Sin-wai (ed.), *Translation and Bilingual Dictionaries*. Tübingen: Max Niemeyer Verlag, pp. 23–39.

Tarp, S. (2004b) "Basic Problems of Learner's Lexicography", *Lexikos* 14: 222–252.

Tarp, S. (2008) *Lexicography in the Borderland Between Knowledge and Non-knowledge: General Lexicographical Theory With Particular Focus on Learner's Lexicography*. Tübingen: Max Niemeyer.

Temmerman, R. (2000) *Towards New Ways of Terminology Description*. Amsterdam: John Benjamins.

Tomasello, M. (2003) *Constructing a Language: A Usage-Based Theory of Language Acquisition*. Cambridge, MA: Harvard University Press

Urdang, L. (1963) "Review of *Problems in Lexicography*", *Language* 39: 586–594.

Villanueva, A. (2000) "En el centenario de María Moliner", www.avempace.com/file_download/751/En+el+centenario+de+María Moliner.pdf (Accessed 1 February 2017)

Wenger, E. (1998) *Communities of Practice: Learning, Meaning, and Identity*. Cambridge: Cambridge University Press.

Wierzbicka, A. (1972) *Semantic Primitives*. Frankfurt: Athenäum.

Zgusta, L. (1971) "Equivalents and Explanations in Bilingual Dictionaries", in L. Zgusta (ed.), *Manual of Lexicography*. Series: Janua Linguarum Series Maior 39. Berlin, de Gruyter Mouton, pp. 536–548.

8

Lexicography and corpus linguistics

Gertrud Faaß

8.1 Introduction

As Firth (1957:11) has rightly stated with his famous sentence: "You shall know a word by the company it keeps", we need to look at the use of words before we attempt to describe them. A single human, or even a group of expert researchers, cannot be expected to know every use of every word or, more generally, of every linguistic phenomenon produced by all speakers of a language; we thus need to collect samples of language in use (and compile them in a way computationally that they can be studied by humans). It is moreover argued that such empiricism is an adequate practice aiming at widening the lexicographic (and linguistic) horizon, as Douglas Biber and Randi Reppen (2015:2) state: "corpus analyses have documented the existence of linguistic constructs that are not recognized by current linguistic theories".

Hanks (2012:64) states that there is one major task for a lexicographer when using appropriate corpora: "To select contexts that are maximally general (and therefore offer maximum predictive power about the word's meaning in future, unseen contexts), while at the same time preserving a sharp semantic focus". He furtherly defines "contexts" as having two meanings: (1) "context of utterance" (in the sense of interpreting texts utilising our world knowledge) and (2) "textual context". Current uses of corpora assist with (2) only, but, as Section 8.3 will show, in the near future, corpus linguistics may also support the lexicographer at least partially with defining (1).

Dictionary compilers have been using samples of language for centuries, like, for example, the Brothers Grimm collecting samples of the German language for their dictionary of the German language describing its development over a time span of four centuries (Grimm and Grimm 1854). In 1857, the compilation of the *Oxford English Dictionary* (OED) began – again on the basis of written samples – leading to the biggest collections of the use of the English vocabulary at that time (as warmly described by Simon Winchester in his book *The Professor and the Madman*). The step from collections of samples of word usage to be described in a dictionary from cardbox to electronic collections of running texts took place with the advent of computers. Lexicographers as a matter of fact have been using corpora since their rise in the 1960s, and the following sections will mention several dictionaries utilising corpora as their data basis.

The method of compilation of such resources is a crucial factor, and metadata are highly relevant when deciding which existing corpus is adequate for the purpose of finding certain phenomena. Lastly, finding appropriate software to access the corpus will determine whether the corpus data will assist the lexicographer in finding all of the senses of a lexeme, and supply him or her with the right usage examples.

This chapter thus explains past and present of corpus linguistics. Issues under consideration are representativeness, re-usability, corpus annotation and access to data. The utilisation of corpora for lexicography now and possible future uses form the second part, followed by a conclusion and references to related topics.

8.2 Core issues and topics

8.2.1 Basic requirements and properties of corpora

Geoffrey Leech, an icon in the world of corpus linguistics, long preferred the term "computer corpus", as he acknowledged non-digital forms of corpora, too (he also coined this author's favorite definition of a corpus as "a helluva lot of text stored on a computer" (Leech 1992:106)). We will however use the term "corpus" only, as nowadays, non-digitalized forms of text collections do not seem relevant anymore. The understanding of the term "corpus" in this chapter is based on Lemnitzer and Zinsmeister (2010:40), who define it as

> a collection of written or spoken utterances in one or more languages. The data of the corpus are digitalized, i.e. stored on computers and machine readable. The parts of the corpus, the texts and the utterance sequences, consist of the data itself and possibly of metadata, which describe these data, and of linguistic annotations that are assigned to them.[1]

This definition covers a number of perspectives on the term. First, a corpus may contain both written text and/or spoken utterances that were transcribed. It might be multilingual, which means that the corpus may contain text and utterance sequences of several languages. Often, such texts are parallel (strict translations of each other), like is the case with the EUROPARL[2] corpus containing speeches of members of the European parliament which are translated into all of the official EU languages (Koehn [2005]). Comparable corpora, on the other hand, contain different texts of different languages although describing similar issues.

The second property of a corpus is that it must be machine readable because computer programmes analysing corpora need to be able to identify the characters occurring in it. To avoid, for example, umlaut or other special characters to be unprocessable symbols for these programmes, we need consider its character encoding, too. When text is collected from the Internet, re-encoding is often one of the first tasks of a corpus compiler, because in order to be processable each corpus should consist of one character encoding only. Kilgarriff and Kosem (2012:32) mention ASCII, ISO 8859-1 (Latin-1) and UTF-8 and Big-5 (for Chinese) to be the most commonly occurring encodings.

The more data known about the sources of a corpus, the more useful it will be; and as it is quite an effort to compile a clean corpus usable for dictionary compilation or update, any compiler should seek to describe its contents as detailed as possible in order to make it re-usable for future, currently unknown purposes, too. Although data concerning the language(s) used, the year or even date when a text was written, when it was published, the author's name or the name of the copyright owner can often be retrieved automatically from headers of the. html files downloaded from the Internet. Modern natural language processing tools go a step further by identifying text types (to the knowledge of the author, Douglas and Finegan (1986) were the first developing algorithms for this task) and by finding additional metadata automatically from the data itself,[3] too. Provided such metadata, every corpus can be sorted into a typology of features like the one Lemnitzer and Zinsmeister have collected (from various sources, see footnote on Lemnitzer and Zinsmeister 2010:102). Such features include the following: functionality (purpose of the compilation), language(s), medium, size, annotation, persistence, variety of language (general versus special language) and, lastly, its availability.

When the metadata is known, it is necessary to store it in a machine-readable way, and there are international standards like Dublin Core[4] which in the past has been used quite frequently. Its elements are, *inter alia,* title, creator, subject, description, publisher, contributor, date (users of Dublin Core are to define which type of date is meant), format, source, etc. This data is to be stored in an XML format, and it might appear in an XHTML header of the data files, but may also be stored separately.

The European *Common Language Resources and Technology Infrastructure* (CLARIN) project network (Hinrichs and Krauwer 2014) has recently developed another standard which is called the "Component MetaData Infractructure" (CMDI) standard. CMDI can be used to describe many other resources, too, like the tools or workbenches utilised when compiling or pre-processing corpora, and thus delivers information with a much higher degree of fineness. CMDI files are machine readable and thus usable for electronic search engines like the Virtual Language Observatory[5] (VLO) provided by the CLARIN network of European researchers making their resources (*inter alia* corpora) available. In other words: Anyone belonging to the network of providers may submit CDMI-files describing their resources to CLARIN; the CLARIN tools then will integrate them into the VLO search engine, making the resource known and accessible for thousands of researchers all over the world. Such handling eases re-usability and the sustainability of these and other resources immensely.

Still, before compiling a corpus, we need to consider what kinds (or types) of texts and utterances should be contained by taking into account the purpose we are planning to utilize it for. Finding some samples for each of the senses of a word is necessary, but not enough, as it is also deemed relevant how often a linguistic phenomenon occurs in language use before the need arises to describe it in a dictionary. Renouf (1987:1) describes the aim (for the COBUILD corpus) as "the availability of sufficient and relevant textual evidence". McEnery and Hardie (2012:32) use the term "standard reference" because the compilation process should lead to a result "maximally representative of the language variety under consideration". This issue is however tricky as one cannot easily determine whether the number of samples collected is in any way representative for describing the phenomena in question. Any new corpus data collected may offer additional information not seen so far, and seeing this fact, data collection for dictionary compilation may never end. In the early days of digital corpora, a corpus containing a few million words was considered huge. Compilers hence were able to select the samples rather carefully in order to build so-called "balanced" corpora because they hoped those to be samples being as close to representative as possible for the language in question. The first widely known corpus, the BROWN corpus of American English (Kučera and Francis 1967), was later described by Sinclair (1996:3) as setting a standard concerning this issue because it was compiled from "written published sources" only where each genre had "roughly" the same share. Sinclair added however that any corpus moreover "should include samples from a broad range of material in order to attain some sort of representativeness" (Sinclair 1996:4). For instance, Renouf (1987:12–16) gives a detailed account of the types of written and orally produced (and transcribed) texts that were selected and categorized "according to their primary discourse function" for the COBUILD corpus. The range contains fiction and non-fiction texts of which the latter category includes *inter alia* surveys, procedural texts, newspapers, etc. The spoken part of the corpus contains "Face to Face Informal Conversation" (ibid:16) together with radio discussions and interviews. Sinclair's standards set with COBUILD were also implemented later in the British National Corpus[6] (BNC, Burnage and Dunlop 1992) but somehow seem to be forgotten nowadays as language samples for corpus compilation are usually crawled from the Internet and often immediately extracted automatically from the body of html files they are contained in[7] while ignoring existing metadata about those pages as described in their headers. Without further processing, as described earlier, such handling leads to completely undocumented primary data. In several projects, it seems that corpus compilers are of the opinion that collecting huge amounts of texts from the Internet alone would make a corpus at least near representative (and thus usable also for dictionary compilation). However, there are other voices, too: Mark Davis (2015:13) offers an overview of corpus' purposes for phenomena to be examined. Interestingly, he directly links the necessary size of corpora with these purposes (ibid:13–16) and with the confidence of getting a good overview from it (see Table 8.1). For instance, for purpose 5, the examination of high-frequency grammatical features, a small and well-annotated corpus is considered much more useful

Table 8.1 Types of phenomena

Types of phenomena	
Lexical	
1	Frequency and distribution of specific words or phrases
2	Lists of all common words in a language or genre
Morphology	
3	Processes involving word formation (e.g., nouns formed with suffixes like *ism or *ousness)
4	Contrasts in the use of grammatical alternatives, such as *HAVE* + *proven/proved*, or *sincerest/most sincere*
Grammar/syntax	
5	High-frequency grammatical features, like modals, passives, perfect or progressive aspect
6	Less frequent grammatical variation, such as choices with verb subcategorization (*John started to walk/walking*; *she'd like* (*for*) *him to stay overnight*)
Phraseological patterns	
7	Collocational preferences for specific words (e.g., *true feelings* or *naked eye*)
8	Constructions, e.g. [*V NP into V-ing*] (*they talked him into staying*) or [*V* POSS *way* PREP] (*he elbowed his way through the crowd*)
Semantics	
9	Collocates (generally) as a guide to meaning and usage (e.g. with *click* (n), *nibble* (v), or *serenely*)
10	Semantic prosody, e.g. the types of words preceding the verb *budge* or nouns following the verb *cause*.

Source: adapted from (Davis 2015: 13)

than a huge corpus collected from the Internet containing lots of "noise" (which is in the end another word for unusable data).

Lastly, when solely crawling our data from the Internet, we face another problem: compared to the amount of written resources available, only a few utterances are available online (some in the VLO mentioned earlier), that is, spoken language which is stored as machine-readable text. Some compilers thus still take into account this need for balanced corpora, that is, corpora containing the right proportions of all kinds of texts that are produced by speakers of the language. Mark Davis (2009) decided on equal divisions of "spoken, fiction, popular magazines, newspapers and academic texts" when compiling his *Corpus of Contemporary American English* as it is stated on the COCA website.[8] However, to the knowledge of the author, no corpora of similar size are available at the present for other languages. If corpus-based dictionaries should mirror not only written forms and variants of language, but also our everyday oral utterances, there is still a long way to go.

8.2.2 Annotation

Whereas metadata describe the resource as such, linguistic annotation describes corpus' contents. Typical such annotations are part-of-speech categories and lemmas (in the sense of base forms for inflected word forms) assigned to words contained in a corpus.

The activity of compiling a corpus does not only consist of collecting appropriate text types from a wide range of genres while linking metadata with it. The data needs to be enriched with the help of Natural Language Processing (NLP) tools generating linguistic annotations or "labels" that add information to the linguistic units contained (see Chapters 12 and 43 of this *Handbook*). The types of necessary annotations depend on the purpose of the corpus.

The smallest such units are named "tokens"; the process to identify them is usually called "tokenisation". For most languages, identifying tokens is the first necessary step before any annotation process can begin. A token may be a word, a multi-word unit, but also symbols and punctuation of any kind. Sequences of punctuations also play a role in current texts, like, for example, ":-)", representing an emoticon, the so-called "smiley".

Lexicographers (and other corpus researchers, too) are often interested to read full sentences when enquiring about words, hence, identifying sentence borders is often part of the tokenisation process. Grefenstette and Tapanainen (1994) have described in detail the problems a machine has to face when attempting to determine sentence borders because of the ambiguity of the period sign. And though their article may be in a way outdated, even the latest tokenisers sometimes identify the period finalizing the abbreviation "Dr." as a sentence border, so this problem has still not been solved completely.[9]

After the tokens (and sentence borders) have been determined, linguistic annotations can be added to each of them. First, a labelling software (usually called "pos-tagger" or "tagger") assigns parts of speech to each token in the corpus. This is necessary as most languages show a high degree of syncretism: the English word "save" may be an adjective, but also a verb, and to describe the word in a dictionary, we need to look at both forms separately. Taggers usually make use of heuristics based on their training data, some with a rule-based component included. To achieve a high precision, they hence need to be trained on similar textual material before being used. One should not train a tagger with newspaper text and then expect the same tagger to work perfectly well with texts conceptually spoken (as found in online forums). Huge corpora crawled from the Internet as described earlier may pose problems concerning this matter: we can only expect a satisfying tagging quality if the text types of the corpus are identified correctly and if the tagger is trained and applied for each of those text types separately. Therefore, the availability of metadata about these (parts of) corpora again plays an important role.

In morphologically rich languages, it is necessary to assign a base form for each word – the so-called "lemma" – in order to allow for searches showing all inflected forms. In German, for example, the lexical unit, or lemma *gehen* ([to] go/walk) appears as the word forms: *gehe, gehst, geht, gehen, ging, gegangen*. If the lexicographer is to find all of the lexical units' occurrences later in the corpus, its lemma *gehen* should be annotated to all of them. There are taggers assigning both lemmas and parts of speech in one go, which makes sense as, for example, the German word *sichere* (save) may be an inflected adjective form with the lemma *sicher* or an inflected verb form with the lemma *sichern*, like in examples (1) and (2). In a dictionary, these two parts of speech of "save" would need to be described separately, too.

(1)
Er sagte, diese neue Maßnahme sichere Arbeitsplätze.
He said that this new measure would save jobs.

(2)
Sind da noch sichere Arbeitsplätze?
Are there still any save jobs?

Such taggers, however, need a knowledge base, a so-called lexicon (see, for example, the tree-tagger by Helmut Schmidt (1994; 1995)) and cannot work solely on the basis of heuristics.

It is also necessary to identify grammatical (syntactic) structures of sentences so that the lexicographer will be enabled to find typical arguments of verbs or typical adjectives a noun occurs with. This process is called "parsing", and there are in principle two ways to do this: one identifies a hierarchy of constituents, the other determines dependencies of the words in a sentence, beginning with the verb. For both methods, parsers are available which usually make use of heuristics. However again, like with taggers, these parsers are to be trained on the text type that they were trained for. Coming back to example (1) earlier, the Stanford Parser,[10] which offers both methods of parsing, generates the constituent tree in (3a) and identifies dependencies in (3b):

(3a)
```
(ROOT
  (S
  (NP (PRP He))
  (VP (VBD said)
    (SBAR (IN that)
      (S
      (NP (DT this) (JJ new) (NN measure))
      (VP (MD would)
      (VP (VB save)
        (NP (NNS jobs)))))))
      (.. )))
```

(3b)

nsubj(said-2, He-1)
root(ROOT-0, said-2)
mark(save-7, that-3)
det(measure-5, this-4)
nsubj(save-7, measure-5)
aux(save-7, would-6)
ccomp(said-2, save-7)
dobj(save-7, jobs-8)

Using information provided in (3), it is possible to identify typical phrases that the words of interest are contained in (like, "this new measure") helping the lexicographer to identify frequent attributes for a noun, for example. This is also possible with (3b), but such an extraction requires more effort there. Data from (3b), on the other hand, allows the lexicographer to easily identify, for example, typical grammatical functions appearing with the verb (subjects, for example) and to check valency data in general.

8.2.3 Corpus encoding

Corpus encoding describes the ways that linguistic annotations can be assigned to the tokens. These might not be labelled as such, but can be stored separately by generating a copy of the original document where the running text is changed to a one-token-per-line format (while deleting all spaces). A rather simple way to annotate data is the use of tables (Table 8.2). This shows an excerpt of the freely available DICKENS corpus used with the Open Corpus WorkBench Software OCWB[11] (see also Section 8.2.4.1). This system allows searching at a high speed as corpora are encoded binary and provided with indices.

The parts of speech annotated in Table 8.2 are based on the so-called "Penn TreeBank tagset" which is often used for tagging English text (Taylor, Marcus and Santorini 2003). Structural annotations like phrases or sentences are found on the first level and marked by angle brackets and by positional annotations on the others. More positional annotations may be necessary; however, this depends on the planned usage of the corpus.

Other annotation tools first produce XML annotations in the corpus file itself, others, more recent ones, generate standoff markup XML by first assigning sequences of byte ranges of the given document to token IDs. Other separate annotation files (e.g. parts-of-speech

Table 8.2 A simple annotation method

<s>	*(sentence begin = structural annotation)*	
It	PP	it
was	VBD	be
all	PDT	all
the	DT	the
same	JJ	same
to	TO	to
him	PP	him
.	SENT	.
</s>	(sentence end = structural annotation)	

assignments) are then generated on that basis. For using standoff markup XML, several ISO standards are available of which all can be used to enrich the primary data significantly: Bosch et al. (2014) list *inter alia* ISO 24610–2 which is based on the XML encoding proposed by the Text Encoding Initiative[12] (TEI). Note that TEI and other XML standards make corpora interchangeable and are thus highly reusable, as publicly available NLP tools (see Chapter 12) are often trained to furtherly process such formats. Because XML formats are however difficult to read for humans, graphical user interfaces are necessary. Figure 8.1 shows an example header of a TEI file (Version P5).

```
<teiHeader>
  <fileDesc>
   <titleStmt>
    <title>
<!-- title of the resource -->
    </title>
   </titleStmt>
   <publicationStmt>
    <p>
<!-- Information about distribution of the resource -->
    </p>
   </publicationStmt>
  <sourceDesc>
 <p>
<!-- Information about source from which the resource
derives -->
 </p>
 </sourceDesc>
</fileDesc>
</teiHeader>
```

Figure 8.1 A typical TEI header[13]

For the linguistic annotation webservice "Weblicht" provided by the CLARIN-D (Germany) project, the so-called *Text Corpus Format* (TCF) Format is utilized. Example data is shown in Figure 8.2. Here, the sentences *Karin fliegt nach New York. Sie will dort Urlaub machen* ("Karin flies to New York, she wants to spend her holidays there") are first annotated with token IDs 0 to 11. Further down the xml file, the two sentences are described by the token IDs they contain and, lastly, parts of speech (pos) are assigned to those IDs. Such is a typical example of a standoff annotation. Note that for space reasons, some of the lines of the xml file have been deleted in Figure 8.2.

```
<?xml version="1.0" encoding="UTF-8"?>
<D-Spin xmlns="www.dspin.de/data" version="0.4">
 <MetaData xmlns="www.dspin.de/data/metadata">
  <source></source>
  <Services>
   <CMD xmlns:xsi="www.w3.org/2001/XMLSchema-instance"
xmlns="www.clarin.eu/cmd/" CMDVersion="1.1"
```

```
    xsi:schemaLocation="www.clarin.eu/cmd/ http://catalog.
clarin.eu/ds/ComponentRegistry/rest/registry/profiles/clarin.
eu:cr1:p_1320657629623/xsd">
    [. . .]
    <Components>
     <WebServiceToolChain>
       . . .
      <Toolchain>
       <ToolInChain>
        <Parameter name="version" value="0.4"></Parameter>
       </ToolInChain>
        . . .
     </WebServiceToolChain>
    </Components>
   </CMD>
  </Services>
 </MetaData>
 <TextCorpus xmlns="www.dspin.de/data/textcorpus" lang="de">
  <text>Karin fliegt nach New York. Sie will dort Urlaub
machen.</text>
  <tokens>
   <token ID="t_0">Karin</token>
   <token ID="t_1">fliegt</token>
   <token ID="t_2">nach</token>
[. . .]
   <token ID="t_10">machen</token>
   <token ID="t_11">.</token>
  </tokens>
  <sentences>
   <sentence ID="s_0" tokenIDs="t_0 t_1 t_2 t_3 t_4 t_5"></
sentence>
   <sentence ID="s_1" tokenIDs="t_6 t_7 t_8 t_9 t_10
t_11"></sentence>
  </sentences>
  <POStags tagset="stts">
   <tag ID="pt_0" tokenIDs="t_0">NE</tag>
   <tag ID="pt_1" tokenIDs="t_1">VVFIN</tag>
   <tag ID="pt_2" tokenIDs="t_2">APPR</tag>
[. . .]
   <tag ID="pt_10" tokenIDs="t_10">VVINF</tag>
   <tag ID="pt_11" tokenIDs="t_11">$.</tag>
  </POStags>
  [. . .]
 </TextCorpus>
</D-Spin>
```

Figure 8.2 An example TCF-File[14]

For the purposes of lexicography, several linguistic annotations are possible; however, the currently most important labels added to the tokens are still pos and lemma. Other possible labels and their automatic identification will be discussed in Section 8.2.4.1. (Chapter 12 will go into further detail concerning these issues.)

8.2.4 Corpus tools for lexicography

A section describing corpus tools can never describe all that are available or give a comprehensive overview. The author hence selected a few tools that are either easily available (most of them freely) or accessible online (see Chapters 12 and 43 of this *Handbook*). These might be useful for beginners in the utilization of corpora for lexicography.

8.2.4.1 Concordancing locally

The first instruments to make corpus data available for lexicography were the so-called "Key Word In Context" (KWIC) tools, showing non-annotated text where the search-word is in a central position. Such a typical concordancer still widely in use is ANTConc;[15] it can be installed locally and it utilizes files stored on the computer. The tool offers to sort the co-occurring words to the left and/or to the right of the search word in the text to give a better overview of the contexts the word appears in, and to generate word lists (so that the frequencies of all words can be examined). There are some word statistics provided, too, supporting the user to find typical collocations.

Such tools assist with identifying ambiguities: In South African English, for example, a "robot" may be a computer sensitive to its surrounding, but the word usually (that is in most general texts) describes a traffic light. Whereas only the former may be utilized to produce cars, for example, one stops at the latter – meaning that just by examining the surrounding words of the word in question, one will be able to distinguish its meaning in each of the sentences – which again proves Leech's sentence mentioned at the beginning of this chapter. A similar corpus query tool to be installed locally, however commercial and with more functionalities, is WordSmith.[16]

8.2.4.2 (Online) Corpus Query Tools

The Open CorpusWorkbench (OCWB, Evert and Hardie 2011) not only offers tools to encode corpora, but also includes the Corpus Query Processor (CQP). This command-line processor allows for querying corpora (with a rather intuitive "corpus query language") on all levels of their annotation. One can find all occurrences of "save" as an adjective just by processing the query [(lemma="save") and (pos="JJ")]. Additionally, sub-corpora can be excerpted from others, and several corpora can also be fused for combined searches. The tool also allows for a random sampling as no one can be expected to inspect thousands of corpus matches manually. Its web version (CQP-web) finds its use with corpora encoded in an XML format and a number of providers of online corpora make use of it, the British National Corpus[17] at Lancaster University being the most prominent. Another provider of online corpora is the Syddansk Universitet (SDU, Southern Denmark University) which offers the online tool *Corpus Eye*[18] for monolingual KWIC searches. This tool offers queries on a number of corpora in different languages, and several heuristics are also available. As the SDU corpora are all annotated *inter alia* with parts of speech, it also allows for queries on this and other annotation levels and annotation levels may also be combined in queries. *Corpus Eye* enables experienced corpus linguistics to make use of the Corpus Query Language (developed for the corpora of the Open Corpus WorkBench mentioned earlier), whereas inexperienced users may utilize the graphical user interface which allows for defining properties of tokens in the corpus on several levels of annotation, too. Such gadgets make it an ideal tool for beginners.

A more sophisticated online tool is *OPUS*[19] (Tiedemann 2012), offered by the Swedish Uppsala Universitet. Here, a lexicographer can query bi- and multilingual corpora for gaining knowledge on translations. As corpora of many different text types are offered (*inter alia* political speeches, newspapers, manuals, etc.), it is also possible to find language of specific purposes (LSP) data which might be useful when compiling an LSP-dictionary.

Specialized corpus tools are available that are capable of providing a number of preprocessing utilities too, in order to save time with formulating corpus queries. The "Sketch Engine" is a commercial tool which comes with a number of corpora in several languages (own corpora can also be added). It is described in a number of publications; one of the latest is by Kilgarriff and Kosem (2012). The tool – an online version[20] is available – offers a simple concordancer and, like the CQP processor earlier, random sampling, too. Users may also set filters excluding or including specific contextual words quite easily, whereas in CQP such has to be formulated explicitly with the queries. Like other corpus linguistic tools, frequency distribution lists and several statistical measures to calculate typical collocates of words are available, assisting the lexicographer to fulfill Hanks's (2012:65) demand to examine data in textual contexts.

A unique feature of the tool are its "word sketches", summarizing co-occurrences and grammatical functions appearing with a specific word of a specific part-of-speech. Figure 8.3 shows the word sketch of the verb "save".

All these features are designed to assist researchers with getting a better overview of the word in its typical environments to help with finding appropriate definitions. Users of such tools are moreover enabled to find or to make up good example sentences for their dictionary entries by, for example, selecting typical collocates, or, in case such is available, typical subjects, objects or other arguments for the word under examination.

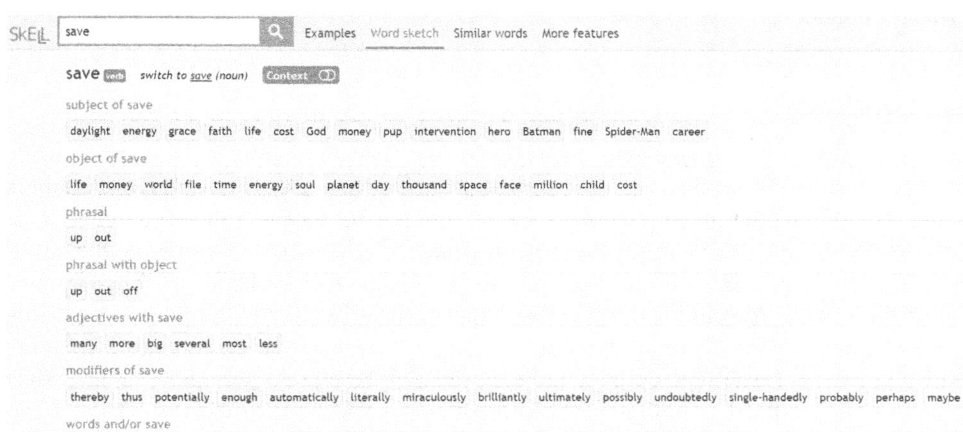

Figure 8.3 Screenshot of **save**[21]

8.2.4.3 Tools specifically designed for lexicographic use

As Heid (2008:143) rightly states and as shown earlier, there is actually no need for developing specific corpus query tools for lexicography as such. It is rather the metadata available for a specific corpus being the decisive factor for a corpus to be useful for lexicography or not. Tools to be used in "lexicographic workflows" (Heid 2008:144), however, may indeed be of assistance for lexicographers: As such tools can pre-process corpus data and compare it to the lexicographic data available, they will find words that are frequent in the corpus but have not been listed in the dictionary yet, or they may identify obsolete words. Pre-processing might also include the comparison of data about words, like, for example, parts of speech, typical contexts and typical multi-word units the word appears in. Evert et al. (2004) describe such a tool which was developed together with a dictionary publisher (see Chapters 12 and 43 of this *Handbook*).

8.3 Looking to the future: topics of related research fields

Hanks (2012:65–67) proposes to integrate knowledge and tools of other fields of research, like, *inter alia*, the Frame Semantics developed by Fillmore (1968).[22] Frame Semantics further develops case grammar, and one could briefly summarize it as a thorough definition of lexical items by means of describing the roles that they assign to other units occurring with them in (corpus) sentences. In its implementation *FrameNet*[23] (see Chapter 24 of this *Handbook*), similar items are summarized in frames, like the verb "save" which is part of the frame "Rescuing", together with the verb "rescue". Core roles (frame elements) that are assigned by "save" are named "Agent", "Patient/Asset" and "Harmful Situation/Harm"; non-core roles may be "Circumstances", "Degree", "Manner", "Time", "Place" and others. Such frame elements can be assigned and annotated to corpus data, and naturally they can describe lexical units in a much finer granulated way than grammatical functions. Additionally, *FrameNet* also describes hierarchical frame–frame relations which leads to an ontology of concepts. At the current point in time, these assignments are however still difficult to annotate automatically, though there often is a clear relation between these roles and their grammatical functions, or, in other words: semantics and syntax. Taking Italian as an example, Tonelli and Riccardi (2010) report on an automated way of annotation; still, there were manual corrections necessary before the corpus was fully annotated with the *FrameNet* data.

8.4 Conclusion

Corpus linguistics has come a long way since its first appearance, and lexicographers using corpora have often been the ones who pushed the matter forward. There are the three main issues of (1) compilation (or selection) of appropriate corpora, (2) the determination of metadata describing them and annotations enriching their contents and, lastly, (3) the development of tools assisting with queries and pre-processing data for lexicographic purposes. All of those have been influenced by the purposes of lexicography. Beginning with Key Word In Context (KWIC) tools and ending in highly specialized workbenches comparing existing dictionary data with corpora and vice versa, the use of corpora plays an important role for lexicography. In addition, we should not ignore that ways to select and store metadata, decisions on the annotations and tasks towards automated annotation procedures, may they be rule-based or statistical or hybrid, and the development of corpus tools assisting with queries and pre-processing are also relevant for other fields of linguistics, may it be grammar development or, especially nowadays, lexical semantics. Throughout the past years, research methods used in both lexical semantics and lexicography have begun to develop towards each other, each able to enrich the other field. In summary, corpora that are documented with proper metadata providing a rich and finely granulated, but still reliable morphological, syntactic and semantic annotation, will always be of importance to lexicography.

Related topics

Lexicography and applied linguistics; lexicography and information science; lexicography and natural language processing; terminological knowledge bases; FrameNet; using the Web for lexicographic purposes; domain ontologies; information retrieval for lexicographic purposes.

Further reading

Biber, D. and R. Reppen (eds.) (2015). *The Cambridge Handbook of English Corpus Linguistics*. Cambridge, UK: Cambridge University Press.
The *Cambridge Handbook of English Corpus Linguistics* is concerned with English as a language of study in the past and at present.

O'Keeffe, A. and M. McCarthy (eds.) (2010). *The Routledge Handbook of Corpus Linguistics*. London and New York: Routledge.
The *Routledge Handbook of Corpus Linguistics* describes the evolution of corpus linguistics, corpus analyses and the application of corpus linguistics for other fields of research, from social linguistics to language testing.

Supplementary Volume Dictionaries. An International Encyclopedia of Lexicography. Supplementary Volume: Recent Developments with Focus on Electronic and Computational Lexicography. (2013). Berlin, Boston: De Gruyter Mouton.
The series "Handbücher zur Sprach- und Kommunikationswissenschaft" by de Gruyter offers bilingual (usually German and English) overviews of a number of linguistic research fields, *inter alia* corpus linguistics and lexicography. Detailed information of what was described only superficially in this chapter can be found in the supplementary volume on lexicography and the two-volume handbook on corpus linguistics.

Notes

1 Translation by author. Original text: "Ein Korpus ist eine Sammlung schriftlicher oder gesprochener Äußerungen in einer oder mehreren Sprachen. Die Daten des Korpus sind digitalisiert, d.h. auf Rechnern gespeichert und maschinenlesbar. Die Bestandteile des Korpus, die Texte oder Äußerungsfolgen, bestehen aus den Daten selber sowie möglicherweise aus Metadaten, die diese Daten beschreiben, und aus linguistischen Annotationen, die diesen Daten zugeordnet sind."
2 www.statmt.org/europarl/ [accessed on 2016–03–03]
3 *eIdentity* is a project where topics of a text are extracted automatically, see www.ims.uni-stuttgart.de/forschung/demos/topic_classification_sandbox.html [accessed on 2016–05–01]
4 http://dublincore.org [accessed on 2016–03–03]. This standard is officially described in ISO/IEC 19788, part 2.
5 www.clarin.eu/content/virtual-language-observatory [accessed on 2016–06–11]
6 www.natcorp.ox.ac.uk/ [accessed on 2016–03–03]
7 See, for example the www.ttc-project.eu/ [accessed on 2016–03–03]
8 http://corpus.byu.edu/coca/ [accessed on 2016–06–26]

9 When testing tokenizers with WebLicht (an online corpus annotation tool available in the CLARIN network) with the sentence “They are reading 100.000 lines on 10.12.2014 not remembering that Dr. No won’t help them.”, the IMS tokenizer identified 2 sentences, the second beginning with “No”. [accessed on 2016–06–26]

10 http://nlp.stanford.edu:8080/parser/ [accessed on 2016–06–25]

11 http://cwb.sourceforge.net/ [accessed on 2016–06–11]

12 www.tei-c.org/index.xml [accessed on 2016–05–05]

13 See at www.tei-c.org/release/doc/tei-p5-doc/en/html/HD.html#HD1 [accessed 2016–06–07]

14 See at http://weblicht.sfs.uni-tuebingen.de/weblichtwiki/index.php/The_TCF_Format [accessed 2016–05–07]

15 AntConc (Version 3.4.4w) [Computer Software by Anthony, Laurence]. Tokyo, Japan: Waseda University. Available from www.laurenceanthony.net/ [accessed on 2016–06–11]

16 www.lexically.net/wordsmith/ [accessed on 2016–06–11]

17 www.natcorp.ox.ac.uk/ [accessed on 2016–06–11]

18 http://corp.hum.sdu.dk/ [accessed on 2016–06–11]

19 http://opus.lingfil.uu.se/ [accessed on 2016–06–11]

20 http://skell.sketchengine.co.uk/run.cgi/skell [accessed on 2016–11–26]

21 See at http://skell.sketchengine.co.uk/run.cgi/wordsketch?lpos=&query=save [accessed on 2016–06–26]

22 For more, up-to-date publications on FrameNet, see their bibliography at https://framenet.icsi.berkeley.edu/fndrupal/index.php?q=fnbibliography [accessed on 2016–06–26]

23 https://framenet.icsi.berkeley.edu/fndrupal/ [accessed on 2016–06–26]

References

Biber, D. and E. Finegan. (1986) “An Initial Typology of English Text Types”, In J. M. Aarts and W. Meijs (eds.), *Corpus Linguistics II:: New Studies in the Analysis and Exploitation of Computer Corpora*. Amsterdam: Editions Rodopi B.V., pp. 19–46.

Biber, D. and R. Reppen. (2015) “Introduction”, in D. Biber and R. Reppen (eds.), *The Cambridge handbook of English corpus linguistics:* CHECL. Cambridge: Cambridge University Press, pp. 1–8.

Bosch, S. u.a. (2014) “From <tiger2/> to ISOTiger – Community Driven Developments for Syntax Annotation in SynAF”, in V. Henrich et al. (ed.), *Proceedings of the Thirteenth International Workshop on Treebanks and Linguistic Theories (TLT13)*, pp. 258–264.

Burnage, G. and D. Dunlop. (1992) “Encoding the British National Corpus”, in J. Aarts, P. de Haan and N. Oostdijk (eds.), *English Language Corpora: Design, Analysis and English Language Corpora: Design, Analysis and Exploitation: Papers From the 13th International Conference on English Language Research on Computerized Corpora:* Nijmegen 1992, edited.

Davies, M. (2009) “The 385+ Million Word Corpus of Contemporary American English (1990–2008+): Design, Architecture, and Linguistic Insights”, *IJCL* 14(2): 159–190.

Davis, M. (2015) “Corpora: An Introduction”, in D. Biber and R. Reppen (eds.), *The Cambridge Handbook of English Corpus Linguistics:* CHECL. Cambridge: Cambridge University Press, pp. 11–31.

Evert, Stefan, u.a. (2004) “Supporting Corpus-Based Dictionary Updating”, in G. Williams and S. Vessier (eds.), *Proceedings of the 11th EURALEX International Congress: Université de Bretagne-Sud, Faculté des lettres et des sciences humaines*, Lorient: Université de Bretagne-Sud, Faculté des lettres et des sciences humaines, pp. 255–264.

Evert, S. and A. Hardie. (2011) “Twenty-First Century Corpus Workbench: Updating a Query Architecture for the New Millennium”, (online) *Proceedings of the Corpus Linguistics Conference*.

Fillmore, C. J. (1968) “The Case for Case”, in E. Bach and R. T. Harms (eds.), *Universals in Linguistic Theory*. New York: Holt, Rinehart, and Winston, pp. 1–88.

Firth, J. R. (1957) *Papers in Linguistics 1934–1951*. London: Oxford University Press.

Grefenstette, G. and P. Tapanainen. (1994) *What Is a Word, What Is a Sentence? Problems of Tokenization*. Rank Xerox Research Centre. www.delph-in.net/courses/07/nlp/Gre:Tap:94.pdf [Accessed 26 June 2016].

Grimm, J. and W. Grimm. (1854) *Deutsches Wörterbuch: Digitized by the "Kompetenzzentrum für elektronische Erschließungs- und Publikationsverfahren in den Geisteswissenschaften", Universität Trier*. Leipzig: S. Hirzel. http://woerterbuchnetz.de/DWB/ [accessed 2016–06–26].

Hanks, P. (2012) "Corpus Evidence and Electronic Lexicography", in S. Granger and M. Paquot (eds.), *Electronic Lexicography*. Oxford: Oxford University Press, pp. 57–82.

Heid, U. (2008) *Corpus Linguistics and Lexicography: Corpus Linguistics: An International Handbook: Volume 1*. Berlin: De Gruyter Mouton. (Handbücher zur Sprach- und Kommunikationswissenschaft, 29.1), pp. 131–153.

Hinrichs, E. and S. Krauwer. (2014) "The CLARIN Research Infrastructure: Resources and Tools for e-Humanities Scholars", in N. Calzolari et al. (eds.), *Proceedings of the Ninth International Conference on Language Resources and Evaluation*, The European Language Resources Association (ELRA) Reykjavik, Iceland, pp. 1525–1531.

Kilgarriff, A. and I. Kosem. (2012) "Corpus Tools for Lexicographers", in S. Granger and M. Paquot (eds.), *Electronic Lexicography*. Oxford: Oxford University Press, pp. 31–55.

Koehn, P. E. (2005) "A Parallel Corpus for Statistical Machine Translation", *Proceedings of The Tenth Machine Translation Summit*, 79–86. www.mt-archive.info/MTS-2005-TOC.htm [accessed 2016–04–05].

Kučera, H. and W. N. Francis. (1967) *Computational Analysis of Present Day American English*. Providence, RI: Brown University Press.

Leech, G. (1992) "Corpora and Theories of Linguistic Performance", in J. Svartvik (ed.), *Directions in Corpus Linguistics: Proceedings of Nobel Symposium 82 Stockholm, 4–8 August 1991*. Berlin, New York: Mouton de Gruyter. (Trends in Linguistics, Bd. Studies and Monographs 65Bd), pp. 105–122.

Lemnitzer, L. and H. Zinsmeister. (2010) *Korpuslinguistik. Eine Einführung*. 2. Aufl. Tübingen: narr. (narr studienbücher).

McEnery, T. and A. Hardie. (2012) *Corpus Linguistics: Method, Theory and Practice*. Cambridge, New York: Cambridge University Press. (Cambridge Textbooks in Linguistics).

Renouf, A. (1987) "Corpus Development", in J. M. Sinclair (ed.), *Looking Up: An Account of the COBUILD Project in Lexical Computing*. London and Glasgow: Collins ELT, pp. 1–22.

Schmidt, H. (1994) "Probabilistic Part-of-Speech Tagging Using Decision Trees", *Proceedings of the International Conference on New Methods in Language Processing*.

Schmidt, H. (1995) "Improvements in Part-of-Speech Tagging with an Application to German", *Proceedings of the ACL SIGDAT-Workshop*.

Sinclair, J. M. (1996) *Preliminary Recommendations on Corpus Typology: EAGLES Document EAG-TCWG-CTYP/P*. www.ilc.cnr.it/EAGLES/pub/eagles/corpora/corpustyp.ps.gz

Taylor, A., M. Marcus and B. Santorini. (2003) "The Penn Treebank: An Overview", in A. Abeillé (ed.), *Treebanks: Building and Using Parsed Corpora*. Dordrecht, Boston, MA: Kluwer Academic Publishers. (Text, speech, and language technology, Bd. v. 20Bd), pp. 5–22.

Tiedemann, J. (2012) "Parallel Data, Tools and Interfaces in OPUS", in N. Calzolari et al. (eds.), *Proceedings of the Eight International Conference on Language Resources and Evaluation*, European Language Resources Association (ELRA), Istanbul, Turkey, pp. 23–25.

Tonelli, S. and G. Riccardi. (2010) *Guidelines for Annotating the LUNA Corpus with Frame Information: Technical Report # DISI-10–017*. Trento, Italy. https://core.ac.uk/download/files/407/11830047.pdf [accessed 2016–06–26].

9

Lexicography and terminology

Lynne Bowker

9.1 Introduction

An oft-cited explanation of terminology[1] is that it refers to "the study of and field of activity concerned with the collection, description, processing and presentation of terms, i.e. lexical items belonging to specialized areas of usage of one or more languages" (Sager 1990: 2). Sager goes on to suggest that, in its objectives, terminology is akin to lexicography which combines the double aim of collecting information about the lexicon of a language with providing an information – and sometimes even an advisory – service to language users.

Many different opinions have been expressed about whether lexicography and terminology are two fully independent disciplines, whether terminology is equivalent to specialized lexicography, or whether their relationship lies somewhere in between (e.g. Humbley 1997; Alberts 2001; Bergenholtz and Tarp 2010; Kageura 2015). Furthering this debate is beyond the scope of this chapter; however, one thing that seems evident is that both lexicography and terminology are undeniably interdisciplinary in nature. Indeed, the section of this volume in which the present chapter appears is entitled 'The Interdisciplinary Nature of Lexicography', and its other chapters explore the relationship that lexicography has with disciplines such as applied linguistics, corpus linguistics, information science, language policy and natural language processing, among others. Terminology, too, has a long history of both drawing on and contributing to other disciplines, including lexicography, but also linguistics, translation, computer science, cognitive science and philosophy, to name just a few. Indeed, there are cases where both lexicography and terminology have drawn on the same theories or methods that have originated in other disciplines. Frame semantics, which is a theory of linguistic meaning, is one such example, and the prototype theory of categorization borrowed from cognitive science is another. A deeper exploration of the relationship between terminology and disciplines other than lexicography is beyond the scope of this chapter, but interested readers might like to refer to works such as Temmerman (2000) for an in-depth look at ways in which terminology and cognitive science interact, Pimentel (2015) for more information on the use of frame semantics in terminology, Bowker (2015) for a detailed investigation of the relationship between terminology and translation, or Bowker and Delsey (2016) for a comparative analysis of terminology and information science. In addition, the proceedings of well-established conference series such as *Terminology and Knowledge Engineering (TKE)* and *Terminologie et intelligence artificielle (TIA)* provide a wealth of material outlining collaborative efforts between researchers in these disciplines.

For now, let us return to the case of lexicography and terminology where, even if there is no consensus on the precise degree of relatedness between the two, we can observe that most people agree that there is a close affiliation between these disciplines. Indeed, they are sometimes referred to as sister disciplines, and, like any pair of siblings, they have a complex and multifaceted relationship. The goal of this chapter is to explore some of these facets to arrive at a better understanding of the interdisciplinary relationship between lexicography and terminology, and to consider some of the ways in which lexicographers and terminologists have been inspired by one another to better serve the needs of their respective – and sometimes shared – target users.

9.2 Historical perspective: lexicography versus terminology: an outdated binary view

Historically, lexicography and terminology have typically been presented in opposition to one another. More recently, there has been an increasing acceptance of the idea that the boundaries between them are actually somewhat fuzzy, and that there are shared areas of overlap. Nonetheless, as a starting point, it is useful to understand the main criteria that have conventionally been used to contrast lexicography with terminology, before going on to engage in a more nuanced examination of the evolution of the interdisciplinary relationship between the two. Table 9.1, which has been adapted from Kageura (2015: 57), summarizes the key characteristics that have traditionally been used to present lexicography and terminology in binary opposition.

As presented in Table 9.1, lexicography and terminology would indeed seem to represent distinct and largely independent practices. However, although we can recognize these

Table 9.1 Characteristics typically used to contrast lexicography and terminology

	Lexicography	*Terminology*
Practitioner	lexicographer	terminologist
Object of investigation	words	terms
Domain	general language	language of a specialized domain
Orientation	mainly descriptive	mainly normative/prescriptive
Approach	semasiological (from word to meaning)	onomasiological (from concept to term)
Product	dictionary	glossary or term bank/termbase
Organization	alphabetical	thematic or systematic
Main information provided	words, meanings, examples, usage information, a range of linguistic information (e.g. part of speech, pronunciation)	concept system and conceptual relations, preferred term, definition
Intended users	lay people	public sector (for language planning), domain experts, scientific/technical writers, translators (for bi- or multilingual resources)

differences at a general – if perhaps somewhat idealized – level, individual practices in both lexicography and terminology are rarely characterized by these generalized features. On the ground, practice is considerably messier than neat and tidy textbook examples or categorizations would suggest. This is in part because the overriding goal of many lexicography and terminology projects is to create a product that is useful for their target audiences, whose needs may criss-cross the conventionally recognized boundaries of these two disciplines. As summed up by Bergenholtz and Tarp (2010: 36), "at the end of the day it is unimportant for the user whether the compilers call themselves terminographers or lexicographers. What is important is the ease and certainty with which the user can find reliable information to fulfil his/her needs." This theme of addressing user needs is an important one that will be revisited at various points in this chapter; responding to user needs has been one of the principal drivers in furthering the interdisciplinary relationship between lexicography and terminology.

9.3 Core issues and topics: lexicography and terminology: a rapprochement?

Although it may be convenient to present lexicography and terminology as two clearly delineated disciplines, the reality of the situation is that the boundaries between them are somewhat fuzzy. In 1990, Juan C. Sager noted

> The justification of considering it [terminology] as a separate activity from lexicography lies in the different nature of the data traditionally assembled, the different background of the people involved in this work, and to some extent in the different methods used.
>
> (Sager 1990: 3)

If we consider these three aspects – practitioners, methods and data – then it would seem that, over the past quarter century, lexicography and terminology have both evolved and appear to be growing closer, rather than becoming more separate. Meanwhile, the evolution of these three aspects in both disciplines has been influenced by two overarching factors: the desire to better respond to users' needs on the one hand, and technology on the other.

Nearly three decades ago, Francis Knowles (1988: 335) argued for a closer alignment between the work of lexicographers and terminologists, and he predicted that technology would act as a catalyst in this regard: "lexicographers and terminographers need to discover each other and to cross-fertilise each other's work. The auguries for such a rapprochement and marriage of lexicography and terminography are very good: the computer would seem to be an ideal match-maker!" Indeed, it seems that Knowles's prediction has come true to a large extent as computer-based tools and their associated methods have contributed to a closer alignment of the working techniques of lexicographers and terminologists as both of these groups seek to better respond to their target users. This close link between technology and the ability to address user needs has been confirmed more recently by John Humbley (2002: 95), who observes: "Dictionaries, and more particularly specialist dictionaries, are ever increasingly being adapted to correspond more closely to users' needs. This has been made possible by advances in information technology, which open up new possibilities."

In the following sections, we will examine how both lexicography and terminology have evolved with regard to practitioners, tools and techniques, and data, placing a particular focus on interdisciplinarity and areas of shared or similar practices between the two. In this short chapter, our intent is not to be exhaustive, but rather to explore some areas of rapprochement between lexicography and terminology and to support these observations with a selection of illustrative examples.

9.3.1 Expanding the community of practice

In the case of both lexicography and terminology, there are relatively few dedicated training programs to prepare practitioners to work in these disciplines. Given that lexicography is commonly viewed as a branch of applied linguistics, many lexicographers have a background in language or linguistics. Meanwhile, with regard to terminology, many practicing terminologists are actually trained in translation because terminology is widely, though not exclusively, carried out in a bi- or multilingual context; the vast majority of translator training programs include at least one course on terminology (Warburton 2015: 364).

The tradition has long been to entrust the development of lexicographical and terminological resources to language specialists; however, both disciplines are currently undergoing a similar shift that has been spurred on by technology, and in particular by widespread access to the Internet: they are actively expanding their conventional communities of practice to include a larger pool of non-language experts. In other words, they are crowdsourcing, which is typically understood to refer to the practice of obtaining needed services, ideas or content by soliciting contributions from a large group of people – and especially from the online community – rather than from traditional employees or suppliers.

Though it has been greatly facilitated by the Internet in recent years, crowdsourcing of a sort has a much longer history within the field of lexicography. For example, the *Oxford English Dictionary (OED)* has operated a Reading Programme since the mid-1800s. This program recruits voluntary readers who provide the *OED* editors with quotations that illustrate how words are used. From humble beginnings, when there were approximately 500 participants who provided quotations on slips of paper, the Reading Programme has grown to the point where, thanks to the reach of the Internet, it now collects approximately 200,000 new quotations per year, which are stored in a full-text database (*OED* website: Reading Programme). More recently, the *OED* has launched a new crowdsourced endeavour known as the *OED Appeals*. The *OED Appeals* is a major new online initiative involving the public in tracing the history of English words. Using a dedicated community space on the *OED* website, editors are soliciting help in unearthing new information about the history and usage of English, including the earliest examples of particular words. The website enables the public to post evidence online in direct response to *OED* editors, fostering a collective effort to record the English language and find the true roots of its vocabulary. Note that although anyone can submit evidence to the *OED*, their team of lexicographers examine all submitted suggestions and documents very carefully to make sure that they are genuinely acceptable. For instance, the *OED* editor provided the following report on the results of a 2014 appeal for evidence pertaining to lexical items related to World War I:

> Evidence submitted from the WWI-related *Appeals* has now been incorporated in the latest *OED* update. Nine of the twelve requests yielded results which helped us to update the corresponding *OED* entries, including *shell shock, conchie, demob, jusqu'auboutiste,* and *Zepps in a cloud.* The *Appeals* pages have now been updated with results. Two words, *camouflage* and *skive*, which were previously thought to have entered English during the period of the First World War, have now been traced back to the nineteenth century.
>
> (*OED* website: Appeals)

Another recent example of crowdsourcing in lexicography is the Macmillan *Open Dictionary*, which is a crowdsourced dictionary where members of the general public are invited to suggest new words and expressions, which are vetted by lexicographers to determine if there is independent evidence showing the suggested word in use. The *Open Dictionary* began in 2009 and now contains over 4000 entries, approximately half of which have been 'promoted' to become full entries in the *Macmillan English Dictionary* (Macmillan website: *Open Dictionary*).

Like lexicography, terminology work has also historically relied on a sort of crowdsourcing, albeit in a very restricted way. In terminology work, the linguistic skills of a terminologist must be combined with subject matter expertise. Although this combination of linguistic and subject matter knowledge is crucial, terminologists have often found it challenging to gain access to subject matter experts. Adopting or adapting a more contemporary and technology-enabled crowdsourcing model – such as using a 'closed crowd', whose membership is limited to vetted members – can facilitate access to subject experts and result in higher quality products. Some types of terminological activities that can be outsourced to a crowd include suggesting or validating candidate terms, or voting on a preferred term from among a group of synonyms. One such example of crowdsourcing in a terminology context is the Microsoft Terminology Community Forum (MTCF), which is described by DePalma and Kelly (2011: 389–390) as an initiative that benefits end users and helps to improve the company's products. The MTCF enables community members to develop, discuss and approve new terminology for Microsoft products. It also allows product groups and individual localization teams to obtain user feedback on legacy and new terminology. The forum organizers can open the MTCF portal to the general public or limit it to a subject-matter expert community on an invitation-only basis. Participants can provide feedback on a range of terminology-related issues, such as outdated terms, unclear definitions or preferred foreign-language equivalents. By leveraging the expertise of subject matter experts and customers and giving them a voice, product uptake can be increased and user satisfaction improved.

Another example of crowdsourcing in terminology is the open and free version of TermWiki, a web-based platform that allows any user to create, store, share and discover term records and glossaries. The site emphasizes collaboration, with a forum, a question/answer module, messaging features that encourage user interaction and discussion pages on each term. Although the open version of TermWiki presents a vast and interesting collection of layperson-generated term records on a wide range of subjects, it is unclear the extent to which professional terminologists actually consult or make use of this collection. However, TermWiki also offers private, professional versions that could be used internally within an organization by a 'closed crowd' in a manner similar to that of the MTCF described above.

In summary, although the crowdsourcing models that have been implemented differ slightly, with lexicography tending to embrace a more fully open model, and terminology favouring more of a 'closed crowd' option or a hybrid open/closed combination, both disciplines are increasingly moving toward a situation whereby non-language experts are being involved more fully in the production of resources – a shift that has been greatly facilitated by information technology.

9.3.2 Corpus is king

Computer technology has also been a driving force behind what can be considered as the greatest methodological revolution witnessed to date in both lexicography and terminology:

the adoption of a corpus-based approach. Again, we must acknowledge that both disciplines have always been corpus-based to some degree if we consider a corpus to be simply a body of text to be consulted as a source of linguistic (and extra-linguistic) information. However, once again we see that computer technology has greatly expanded the possibilities associated with corpus construction and analysis. Nowadays, the practice of using electronic corpora and associated corpus analysis tools has become so widespread and so firmly established that one can scarcely imagine undertaking a credible lexicographic or a terminological project that does not have a corpus-based approach at its centre.

The first large-scale general-language electronic corpora, such as the Brown Corpus and the Lancaster-Oslo/Bergen (LOB) Corpus, appeared in the 1960s (Kučera and Francis 1967; Johansson 1980). These early corpora were designed, built and exploited by linguists looking to undertake empirical investigations of syntactic and lexical phenomena. However, it did not take long for the potential of corpora to be recognized by lexicographers, and the 1980s saw the appearance of a second generation of electronic corpora, represented by the Birmingham Collection of English Texts (BCET) (Renouf 1987) and the Longman/Lancaster English Language Corpus (LLELC) (Summers 1993), whose size massively surpassed that of the first generation. The use of these corpora to produce dictionaries such as the *Collins COBUILD English Language Dictionary* and the *Longman Dictionary of Contemporary English* (*LDOCE*) set a new standard for lexicography, where the use of corpora has continued to grow ever since (see Chapters 8, 12, 42 and 43 of this *Handbook*).

If lexicographers were early adopters of corpus-based approaches, terminologists lagged behind somewhat in capitalizing on electronic corpora as a source of information, in large part because gaining access to specialized documentation in electronic form was more difficult than acquiring general language materials. Nevertheless, the success of lexicographers in designing and exploiting corpora as part of their efforts to provide richer and more helpful resources to their users provided a great impetus to terminologists. Bowker (1996) and Meyer and Mackintosh (1996) summarize some of the early efforts made by terminologists to incorporate corpus-based practices, exploring how these were inspired by lexicography and the challenges faced by terminologists in adapting the lexicographic methods to their own needs. Nowadays, as access to a wide range of documentation in machine-readable form has become significantly easier, corpus-based work has become the norm in terminology also.

Initially, different sets of corpus analysis tools were conceived to meet the needs of lexicographers and of terminologists. However, more recently, it has been recognized that practitioners in these two disciplines may actually benefit from having access to both sets of tools. An excellent example of a tool suite that was initially developed with lexicographers in mind, but which has since been expanded to include functions that address terminology-related needs, is the Sketch Engine. As noted by Kilgarriff et al. (2014), the first Sketch Engine users were lexicographers, back in 1998, and lexicography continues to be a core use for the Sketch Engine to this day. Consequently, although the Sketch Engine contained corpus resources and functionality that were relevant for terminologists (e.g. concordancer, collocation generator, frequency analyzer), it did not have any tools or resources that were specialized for them. Since 2013, however, terminologists have been an important target of the Sketch Engine team's development efforts, and there are now a number of tools designed specifically for terminology-related needs, such as a specialized corpus construction tool (WebBootCaT) and a term extractor. Using WebBootCaT, a user can specify a specialized topic (e.g. by providing seed words) and relevant texts will be downloaded from the Internet and cleaned to form a specialized corpus. The term extractor works by comparing the contents of the specialized corpus against a much larger general reference corpus (e.g. British National Corpus, Web as Corpus (WaC)) and calculating the degree of 'keyness' (i.e., a measure of the frequency of disproportionate occurrence). Moreover, in recognition of the fact that terminology work often takes place in a bi- or multilingual context, the Sketch Engine has also incorporated functionality that supports parallel concordancing and bilingual word sketch generation.

The development of a single tool suite containing tools to support both lexicographic and terminological activities can be seen as evidence of the rapprochement of these two disciplines and of the fact that a single language professional may increasingly be expected to perform tasks of both a lexicographic and terminological nature. As we will see in an upcoming section, hybrid resources that contain both general language words and specialized terms are becoming more common, and a tool suite that supports both types of linguistic research will be valuable in such endeavours.

9.3.3 Blending perspectives

The adoption of corpus-based methods has brought about another change, which may be seen as a further sign of the rapprochement between lexicography and terminology. Lexicographers tend to work in a semasiological fashion, starting from the analysis of words and then looking for the senses or meanings. In contrast, terminologists have conventionally adopted an onomasiological or concept-based perspective in their work where concepts are delimited first, through an analysis of the concept system. Only then can terms be identified to denote those concepts. In other words, terminology work begins with an analysis of concepts and then terms are assigned as designations of these concepts. However, the introduction and widespread adoption of corpora has had a significant impact on the approach used by terminologists. Because the entry point into a corpus is via a lexical item or designator, and because automatic term extractors extract lists of candidate terms, rather than concepts, terminologists are now increasingly incorporating semasiological techniques into their working methods. In fact, as far back as the turn of the millennium, Sager (2001: 765) observed "terminology compilation is therefore becoming increasingly text-oriented and less governed by the desire to construct separate concept systems". This observation that terminologists are beginning to work in a progressively more semasiological fashion by taking text as the starting point for identifying terms has also been made by other terminology researchers (e.g. Temmerman 2000: 230; Warburton 2015: 374).

Another way that technology has prompted terminologists to integrate a more semasiological perspective into their work is by encouraging them to record different forms of a term on a term record. The conventional instruction given to terminologists is that only the canonical form of a term – which designates a concept – should be recorded. However, now that terminology collections are being integrated with other types of tools (e.g. word processors, translation memory systems), users want the option of 'one-click insertion' which would allow them to paste the term directly into their document without having to edit it. Therefore, a growing number of term records now contain different forms of a given term (e.g. conjugated forms, plural form, forms demonstrating gender or number agreements) to better address users' needs.

For their part, lexicographers have also taken a step towards blending a semasiological approach with an onomasiologal one, although this example of a rapprochement owes less to technology than it does to user requests. Earlier in this chapter, we cited Bergenholtz and Tarp (2010: 36), who remind us that users are not concerned with the disciplinary conventions of lexicography or terminology. Rather, they simply want products that meet their needs. Traditionally, the semasiological approach adopted by lexicographers has resulted in an alphabetical ordering of the dictionary entries according to headwords, which means that synonyms are therefore treated in separate entries. In contrast, the onomasiological approach more commonly used by terminologists means that entries are concept based, and synonyms therefore appear in the same entry because they refer to a single concept. One lexicographic product that has attempted to blend these two approaches to some extent is the second edition of the combined *Oxford Dictionary and Thesaurus* (2007). In this product, the dictionary and thesaurus texts are integrated so that the thesaurus entry for a word follows the dictionary entry directly. This decision was based on market research into user preferences, and it aims to make the dictionary accessible, clear and easy to use.

Meanwhile, the JuriDiCo – a bilingual lexical resource on legal terminology – also presents a macrostructure that reflects an attempt to describe the linguistic as well as the extra-linguistic information related to the entries. Users are allowed to search either onomasiologically, by introducing the knowledge that they already have about a concept (search by frames), or semasiologically, by introducing a term so as to learn about its characteristics (search by term) (Pimentel 2015: 444).

9.3.4 Blending the object of study

As noted earlier, traditionally, dictionaries dealt with general language, whereas terminology resources treated the lexicon of one or more specialized subject fields. However, there is a growing recognition that an increasing number of users of language resources actually require support for both general and specialized language. As noted by Warburton (2015: 362), "in many communicative contexts, one cannot easily distinguish between general language (LGP) and special language (LSP)". Given this fluidity, users of language resources have suggested that they would prefer to be able consult a single resource – or at least a coordinated set of resources – rather than moving between a number of unrelated resources. For instance, Rundell (2007) reports that a major survey conducted among close to 2000 users of the first edition of the *Macmillan English Dictionary* (2002) revealed that a growing number of users need and expect their dictionary to explain the specialist terms they encounter on a regular basis. Therefore, when compiling the second edition of the *Macmillan English Dictionary* (2007), the lexicographic team made an effort to create a sort of 'hybrid' resource that combines general and specialized lexicographic information.

> As well as adding lot of general new vocabulary, we also – in response to our user-survey – made the dictionary more useful for professional and academic users by adding hundreds of specialist terms. These come from a range of subject-fields, especially business and finance, science, information technology, medicine, and the arts. People studying to be doctors or nurses, for example, can now look up terms like *ventricle*, *lymphocyte*, *carcinoma*, and *synovial fluid*. Similar technical vocabulary is now included for many other fields as well. Take cinema, for example; if you've ever looked at the credits at the end of a movie and wondered what a best boy is, what job the gaffer does on a film set, or what is meant by a director's cut, you can find the answers in *MED*. In another innovation, we applied 'labels' to indicate when a word or meaning belongs to a particular subject-field. The terms mentioned above have the labels MEDICAL or CINEMA.
>
> (Rundell 2007)

In terminology, too, there has been a movement towards developing resources that cover elements of both general and specialized language. Warburton (2015: 360) points out that whereas terminology work used to be carried out almost exclusively in the public and academic spheres, it has recently become the object of increased interest on the part of private companies who have a growing need to manage their terminology. However, the terminology needs in a commercial environment are not the same as those in the public or academic sectors. For instance, Warburton (2015: 365) suggests that "the conventional definition, whereby a term is a designation of a concept in a subject field, is too restrictive for commercial environments". She goes on to note that using the conventional notion of what constitutes a term as a basis for selecting terms for a company term base is likely to result in a significant number of terms being overlooked that are actually needed to support commercial content production. Therefore, if terminologists are to make products that are truly useful for this growing segment of corporate users, they must continue to broaden the content of their term bases to include all lexical items of interest to these users, regardless of whether or not they meet the conventional definition of a term.

As mentioned previously, a considerable amount of terminology work is undertaken by and for translators, and this group is likely to be less concerned about the respective ideologies of lexicographers and terminologists and more concerned about ensuring that the resource in question will be a useful tool for translation purposes. According to Désilets et al. (2009), who undertook a study of how translators use tools and resources to solve translation problems, the translators who participated in their study encountered difficulties with general and with specialized language in almost equal proportions. Therefore, translators are likely to want to preserve the results of their general language research for future reference, and so they may include a record in the term base even if the object of that record does not correspond to a specialized concept or meet the strict criteria for termhood. Similarly, Warburton (2015: 383) proposes that translation difficulty should become a criterion for selecting items for inclusion in a term base in a commercial environment, noting that "translation difficulty has various manifestations. If the meaning is unclear, the translator will have to expend effort to clarify it. What companies want to avoid is the situation where multiple translators are expending this same effort". In addition, for a translator who uses a term base that is integrated with other tools, such as a translation memory system and word processor, it can be advantageous to include not only terms but also frequently occurring general language expressions. In this way, the pre-translation feature of the tool can automatically integrate these expressions into the target language text and thus save the translator time and effort (Bowker 2015).

Finally, in addition to individual resources containing hybrid content, it is becoming increasingly common to find language portals that bring together a wealth of resources and tools and make them accessible from a single website. One example is the Language Portal of Canada, managed by the government of Canada, which co-locates a vast array of general and specialized lexicographic resources, alongside other language tools, such as guides for general and specialized writing.

9.3.5 Increased focus on usage

Historically, both lexicography and terminology tended to place more emphasis on comprehension than on production. The shift to a corpus-based approach made it easier for both disciplines to provide users' with a greater range of usage-oriented data, such as collocations, phraseology, more reliable frequency data and a wider choice of authentic examples. These have already been widely discussed and documented in the literature, and so we mention them here only in passing.

It is worth observing, however, that terminology in particular has opened up to a more descriptive approach overall. Traditionally normative and prescriptive by design – particularly when it is being carried out for language planning or academic purposes – terminology work now incorporates a greater descriptive component, particularly when aimed at users in the commercial sector. Rather than being frowned upon, terminological variation is now increasingly recognized as being well motivated in some cases, and in need of being documented (Warburton 2015: 364). In admitting a more descriptive approach where warranted, terminology is coming closer to the point of view already prevalent in lexicography.

Similarly, the ability to study usage more easily has led terminologists to provide more information about elements of specialized language other than nouns. Traditionally, terminology tended to focus on objects and their designations, but now more attention is being paid to other parts of speech as well. JuriDiCo is an example of a specialized lexical resource which focuses on descriptions of specialized verbs (Pimentel 2015).

9.4 Conclusion

Earlier in this chapter, it was observed that, over a quarter century ago, Sager (1990: 3) suggested that lexicography and terminology could be viewed as separate activities largely because of differences in the practitioners involved, the methods used, and the nature of the data collected. It was also noted that a desire to better serve users, along with new possibilities opened up by technology, have contributed to an evolution in the working practices found in both lexicography and terminology. Throughout this chapter, we have seen that, although some differences remain, the two disciplines nonetheless appear to be converging with regard to many aspects of their practices.

For instance, we saw that both lexicographers and terminologists have sought to involve users more actively in the production of dictionaries and terminological resources through technology-enabled crowdsourcing. Similarly, both lexicographical and terminological investigations are now both firmly centred on corpus-based analysis, which lends itself to a semasiological approach. As a result, the principles and methods of terminology compilation now have an increasing commonality with those used in lexicography as terminologists move away from an onomasiological starting point for their research and towards a semasiological one. Tools used for the analysis of corpora have also shown signs of bringing lexicographers and terminologists closer together. The tools of the trade used by the two groups were first introduced as separate packages; however, a more recent trend has witnessed the combining of lexicographic and terminological corpus-based tools into a single tool suite (e.g. Sketch Engine). This combined tool offering reflects the growing need for language professionals to be able to respond to users' desires to have resources at their disposal, which can support both their general language and specialized language needs.

Both lexicographers and terminologists have indeed taken up this challenge to produce resources that meet user needs. For instance, in response to user requests, the second edition of the *Macmillan English Dictionary* (2007) now incorporates a range of specialist terms along with its general language offering. Meanwhile, term bases for private corporations, as well as those developed for use by translators, now regularly include general language expressions alongside specialized terms. Such a combination allows translators to capitalize on the pre-translation feature built into many Translation Environment Tools (TEnTs). Meanwhile in a corporate environment, it ensures that the term base supports a broader range of a company's linguistic needs.

Although by no means an exhaustive list, the examples discussed in this chapter paint a picture of an evolution both in lexicography and in terminology which has resulted in a higher degree of interdisciplinarity between them than previously existed. Although Table 9.1 near the start of this chapter summarized the binary way in which lexicography and terminology have conventionally been presented, we have modified and updated its contents to create Table 9.2, which presents a more contemporary view of these two disciplines, drawing attention to areas of convergence and interdisciplinarity.

As illustrated in Table 9.2, both lexicography and terminology are becoming increasingly interdisciplinary, and the two share many common perspectives. Many of the target users for lexicographic and terminological resources actually need to work with both general and specialized language, so it makes sense for lexicographers and terminologists to be informed about trends and developments in each other's disciplines and to work more closely to design and build resources that will better serve the needs of a wide range of users. Although we have

Table 9.2 Evolution and convergence of characteristics associated with lexicography and terminology

	Lexicography	*Terminology*
Practitioner	mainly lexicographers, but with greater involvement from the general public (via crowdsourcing)	mainly terminologists, but with greater involvement from the general public and subject matter experts (via open and closed crowdsourcing)
Object of study	mainly words, but also some terms	mainly terms, but also some general language words or expressions
Domain	mainly general language, but also some specialized language	mainly the language of a specialized domain, but also some general language
Point of view	mainly descriptive	mainly normative/prescriptive in the public and academic sectors, but incorporating more descriptive elements in commercial settings
Approach	mainly semasiological	increasingly semasiological, but retaining some onomasiological elements where useful
Organization	mainly alphabetical, but sometimes incorporating thematic elements	mainly thematic, but allowing alphabetic searching
Main information provided	words, meanings, examples, usage information (e.g. collocations, frequency, phraseology), a range of linguistic information (e.g. part of speech, pronunciation)	preferred term, variants, context and usage information (e.g. collocations, frequency, phraseology), meaning, conceptual relations
Intended users	lay people, professional and academic audiences	public sector (for language planning), domain experts, scientific/technical writers, translators (for bi- or multilingual resources), commercial enterprises

not yet witnessed the 'marriage' between lexicography and terminology that was predicted by Knowles (1988), it is heartening to see that the two have at least become closer friends. Let's hope that the relationship continues to blossom and that lexicographers and terminologists continue to work together to tackle new challenges and embrace new opportunities.

Related topics

Specialized dictionaries; dictionaries for translation; lexicography and corpus linguistics; domain ontologies; the Accounting Dictionaries; the Alicante Dictionaries.

Further reading

Bowker, L. (2011). "Off the Record and on the Fly: Examining the Impact of Corpora on Terminographic Practice in the Context of Translation", in A. Kruger, K. Wallmach and J. Munday (eds.), *Corpus-Based Translation Studies: Research and Applications*. London/New York: Continuum, pp. 211–236.

This chapter examines the effects that the adoption of corpus-based techniques has had on terminology work practices, including both the process and products of terminology research.

Karsch, B. I. (2015). "Terminology Work and Crowdsourcing: Coming to Terms With the Crowd", in H. J. Kockaert and F. Steurs (eds.), *Handbook of Terminology, Vol. 1*. Amsterdam/Philadelphia: John Benjamins Publishing Company, pp. 291–303.

This chapter explores the opportunities that crowdsourcing strategies can present when they are applied appropriately to terminology tasks, and explains how terminologists and terminology project managers can make effective use of crowdsourcing. It also addresses a number of technological challenges associated with platforms for terminology crowdsourcing.

Kilgarriff, A. (2013). "Terminology Finding, Parallel Corpora and Bilingual Word Sketches in the Sketch Engine", in *Proceedings of ASLIB 35th Translating and the Computer Conference*, London. www.mt-archive.info/10/Aslib-2013-Kilgarriff.pdf

The Sketch Engine has been known as a leading tool for lexicography for more than a decade. Over that period, it has built up corpus resources and functionality which are relevant for terminologists, but not specialized for them. This paper reports on recent efforts to incorporate tools designed specifically for terminologists, thus expanding the reach of the Sketch Engine to include both lexicography and terminology.

Note

1 As pointed out by Humbley (1997: 14) "terminologists, perhaps perversely and certainly inconsequentially, often use terminology in several different meanings [. . .] The extent to which terminologists use *terminology* for *terminography* does indeed suggest that the distinction is not always pertinent, perhaps because terminology implies terminographical work to a greater extent than lexicology implies lexicographical work." For ease of comprehension and consistency within this chapter, we will use 'terminology' unless citing a work in which 'terminography' appears.

References

Alberts, M. (2001) "Lexicography Versus Terminography", *Lexikos* 11: 71–84.

Bergenholtz, H. and S. Tarp. (2010) "LSP Lexicography or Terminography? The Lexicographer's Point of View", in P. A. Fuertes-Olivera (ed.), *Specialised Dictionaries for Learners*. Berlin/New York: De Gruyter, pp. 27–37.

Bowker, L. (1996) "A Corpus-Based Approach to Terminography", *Terminology* 3(2): 27–52.

Bowker, L. (2015) "Terminology and Translation", in H. J. Kockaert and F. Steurs (eds.), *Handbook of Terminology, Vol. 1*. Amsterdam/Philadelphia: John Benjamins Publishing Company, pp. 304–323.

Bowker, L. and T. Delsey. (2016) "Information Science, Terminology and Translation Studies: Adaptation, Collaboration, Integration", in Y. Gambier and L. van Doorslaer (eds.), *Border Crossings: Translation Studies and Other Disciplines*. Amsterdam/Philadelphia: John Benjamins Publishing Company, pp. 73–95.

DePalma, D. A. and N. Kelly. (2011) "Project Management for Crowdsourced Translation: How User-Translated Content Projects Work in Real Life', in K. J. Dunne and E. S. Dunne (eds.), *Translation and Localization Project Management: The Art of the Possible*. Amsterdam/Philadelphia: John Benjamins Publishing Company, pp. 379–407.

Désilets, A., C. Melançon, G. Patenaude and L. Brunette. (2009) "How Translators Use Tools and Resources to Resolve Translation Problems: An Ethnographic Study", in *Proceedings of the Workshop Beyond Translation Memories: New Tools for Translators*, MT-Summit XII (Ottawa, Canada, August 26–30).

Government of Canada. "Language Portal of Canada". www.noslangues-ourlanguages.gc.ca/index-eng.php.

Humbley, J. (1997) "Is Terminology Specialised Lexicography? The Experience of French-Speaking Countries", *Hermes, Journal of Linguistics* 18: 13–31.

Humbley, J. (2002) "Nouveaux dictionnaires, nouveaux rapports avec les utilisateurs", *Meta* 47(1): 95–104.

Johansson, S. (1980) "The LOB Corpus of British English Texts: Presentation and Comments", *Association of Literary and Linguistic Computing Journal* 1(1): 25–36.

Kageura, K. (2015) "Terminology and Lexicography", in H. J. Kockaert and F. Steurs (eds.), *Handbook of Terminology, Vol. 1*. Amsterdam/Philadelphia: John Benjamins Publishing Company, 45–59.

Kilgarriff, A., V. Baisa, J. Bušta, M. Jakubíček, V. Kovář, J. Michelfeit, P. Rychlý and V. Suchomel. (2014) "The Sketch Engine: Ten Years On", *Lexicography* 1(1): 7–36.

Knowles, F. E. (1988) "Lexicography and Terminography: A Rapprochement?", in M. Snell-Hornby (ed.), *ZüriLEX '86 Proceedings*: *Papers Read at the EURALEX International Congress, University of Zurich, 9–14 September 1986*. Tübingen: Francke, pp. 329–337.

Kučera, H. and W. N. Francis. (1967) *Computational Analysis of Present-Day American English*. Providence, RI: Brown University Press.

Macmillan English Dictionary. "Open Dictionary", www.macmillandictionary.com/us/open-dictionary/

Meyer, I. and K. Mackintosh. (1996) "The Corpus From a Terminographer's Viewpoint", *International Journal of Corpus Linguistics* 1(2): 257–285.

Oxford English Dictionary. "Appeals", http://public.oed.com/the-oed-appeals/about-the-oed-appeals/

Oxford English Dictionary. "Reading Programme", http://public.oed.com/history-of-the-oed/reading-programme/

Pimentel, J. (2015) "Using Frame Semantics to Build a Bilingual Lexical Resource on Legal Terminology", in H. J. Kockaert and F. Steurs (eds.), *Handbook of Terminology, Vol. 1*. Amsterdam/Philadelphia: John Benjamins Publishing Company, pp. 427–450.

Renouf, A. (1987) "Corpus Development", in J.M. Sinclair (ed.), *Looking Up*. London: Collins, pp. 1–40.

Rundell, M. (2007) "Macmillan English Dictionary – How It Was Created". www.macmillandictionaries.com/features/how-dictionaries-are-written/med/.

Sager, J. C. (1990) *A Practical Course in Terminology Processing*. Amsterdam/Philadelphia: John Benjamins Publishing Company.

Sager, J. C. (2001) "Terminology Compilation: Consequences and Aspects of Automation", in S. E. Wright and G. Budin (eds.), *Handbook of Terminology Management, Vol. 2*. Amsterdam/Philadelphia: John Benjamins Publishing Company, pp. 761–771.

Summers, D. (1993) "Longman/Lancaster English Language Corpus: Criteria and Design", *International Journal of Lexicography* 6(3): 181–208.

Temmerman, R. (2000) *Towards New Ways of Terminology Description: The Sociocognitive Approach.* Amsterdam/Philadelphia: John Benjamins Publishing Company.
TermWiki: en.termwiki.com
Warburton, K. (2015) "Managing Terminology in Commercial Environments", in H. J. Kockaert and F. Steurs (eds.), *Handbook of Terminology, Vol. 1*. Amsterdam/Philadelphia: John Benjamins Publishing Company, pp. 361–392.

10

Dictionaries and language policy

Dion Nkomo

10.1 Introduction

The references listed at the end of this contribution, especially those recommended for further reading, indicate that the topic of dictionaries and language policy is not new. Earlier publications (Noyes 1943; Litto 1963; Haugen 1985) suggest that the relationship between dictionaries and language policy might be as old as lexicography. Publications dealing with African contexts (Bergenholtz and Gouws 2006; Gouws 2005, 2007; Gouws and Potgieter 2010; Hadebe 2007; Ndinga-Koumba-Binza 2005; Tarp and Gouws 2008) indicate a symbiotic relationship which presents lexicography and language planning as part–whole, if not twin processes, in language development. A two-pronged argument is therefore made: (1) lexicography has been largely influenced by language policy, regardless of whether such policies are in place or prospective, overt or covert; and (2) lexicography has significantly influenced language policy in terms of status and functions of specific languages.

Wiegand (1984) argues that lexicography is neither linguistics nor applied linguistics, indicating that certain types of dictionaries need extra-linguistic theoretical and methodological procedures. Tarp (2008) is even more affirmative as he regards lexicography an independent discipline. As Hartmann (2005) shows, linguistics is just one of the disciplines from which lexicography draws in its interdisciplinary vocation. Based on this premise, a more nuanced understanding of dictionaries as utility products needs to prevail in any critical engagement with dictionaries, including their relationship with language policy.

Language policy may be difficult to fully conceptualise without evoking language planning. The terms *language policy* and *language planning* are sometimes used interchangeably, although the latter seems to mainly refer to practice and field of study (Cluver 1993; Haugen 1959). This makes language policy a product or object of language planning. Fettes (1997: 14) suggests *Language Policy and Planning* as the name for the field, which to him is a discipline in its own right, despite its origins in sociolinguistics (Kaplan and Baldauf 1997) or linguistics generally.

Definitions of both *Language Policy* and *Language Planning* (Bamgbose 1991; Cluver 1993; Spolsky 2005) place emphasis on the following:

- Governments, government-authorised agencies or other such authoritative bodies as language planners or policy-makers.
- Language policy as an authoritative document or pronouncement with respect to language usage.
- Language planning as problem-solving.

These issues have been singled out for restricting the concepts of language policy and planning. First, recognising only governments or their agencies as language planners excludes lexicographers whose works have had language policy motivations and implications. Among other components, definitions of *corpus planning* refer to dictionary-making as an important component. Cooper (1989) acknowledges the enormous language planning contributions of language academies and lexicographers. Second, Bamgbose (1991) notes that either overt or covert, language policy is always present. For the present topic, even undeclared or hidden policies may influence lexicography. Third, whereas problem-solving is commonly expressed as the ultimate motivation for language policy, Cooper (1989) underlines language regulation a major goal. Dictionaries also perform language regulation, with long-term repercussions for language policy.

10.2 Historical perspectives

Although it is tempting to suggest that the relationship between dictionaries and language policy may be as old as lexicography, it is easier to trace it back to the transformation of European vernaculars into modern national languages during the Renaissance period when language became a major rallying point in the emerging nation states. As part of the rebirth processes, patriotic elites aspired for their vernaculars to supplant Latin, which dominated all prestigious domains. The new languages had to be recorded and regulated in order to provide a firm basis for language use. Vogl (2012) regards this as the emergence of a "standard language culture". Mugglestone (2015: 28) acknowledges the convictions about the influential role of lexicography in the language standardisation process.

During that period, bilingual dictionaries pairing Latin with the respective vernaculars existed to facilitate access to the language that was knowledge incarnate. Latin was the gateway to knowledge that dictionaries such as William Bathe's (1611) *Ianua Linguarum* (The Gate of Tongues) and Amos Komensky's (1631) *Ianua Linguarum Reserata* (The Gate of Tongues Unlocked) had to unlock "so that unskilful persons could gain access to knowledge" (Gouws and Potgieter 2010: 236). Campaigns for shifting onto vernaculars set the right tone for language planning-oriented lexicography.

The establishment and work of language academies in Europe was historic for both lexicography and language policy/planning. Together with grammars, dictionaries would be pivotal in codification of prospective national languages. Mugglestone (2015: 27) writes:

> Language academies . . . easily integrated lexicography into intended processes of standardisation and linguistic reform. Dictionary-making on this model was a means by which language would not merely be codified but also corrected and refined.

Language planning-oriented lexicography effectively began with the founding of the *Accademia della Crusca*, formally constituted in 1583 by a group protesting the stringent rules of the original academy, the *Accademia fiorentina*, which had successfully set the stage for developing the Tuscan dialect into standard Italian (Sherberg 2003). The protestant group, which named itself '*brigata dei crusconi*' (brigade of coarse bran) was, however, aggrieved by the *Accademia fiorentina*'s rejection of vulgar poetry (*Accademia della Crusca* 2011) from the Italian linguistic, literary and cultural heritage. This group espoused a more flexible approach. Ironically, their organisation became quite normative under the leadership of Lionardo Salviati, as captured by its name which translates into "The Academy of the bran", that is, referring to the sifting process of separating chaff from the bran (*Accademia della Crusca* 2011). Nevertheless, the academy would become the vanguard of the development of Italian into a modern language.

Lexicography became an integral component of the work of the *Accademia della Crusca*. Work on the *Vocabolario degli Accademici* (henceforth the *Vocabolario*) commenced in 1590, and became "fundamental in the difficult path towards the establishment of Italian as a national language" (*Accademia della Crusca* 2011). The academy's normative approach prevailed as the project endeavoured "to demonstrate and preserve the beauty of the Florentine language in the 14th century" (*Accademia della Crusca* 2011). Consequently, the lexicographers prioritised fourteenth-century authors when establishing the dictionary basis, only resorting to contemporary writings as sources for current usage. The *Vocabolario* was published in 1612, becoming the first dictionary to affirm Italian as a standard language and the symbol of good Italian that inspired lexicographers in other languages.

Despite the pioneering status of the *Accademia della Crusca*, it is the *Académie française* of France, established in 1635, that has become a classic example of the interface between dictionaries and language policy. The *Académie française* became the pre-eminent authoritative body on the French language which became the "world's diplomatic and cultural language" (Litto 1963: 134). Even today, Deumert and Vandenbussche (2003: 8) note the "on-going purification efforts of the *Académie française*", which remains responsible for regulating French vocabulary, grammar, spelling and usage. From the outset, its purist approach comprised a strict stance against Anglicisms and Latinisms. Likewise, the *Dictionnaire de l'Académie française*, which has been at the core of implementing the language policy, is still considered the official dictionary in France (*Wikipedia online*). Its different editions are available from the Classiques Garnier Numérique online database.

Apart from language academies, some individual lexicographers distinguished themselves by expressing language policy ideals in their dictionaries. In English, several patriots such as Richard Mulcaster, a schoolmaster by profession, expressed concerns about the limited functional reach of English and a strong conviction that an English academy and dictionary in the model of the *Vocabolario* and the *Dictionnaire de l'Académie française* would address the concerns (Crystal 1997: 73; Mugglestone 2015: 28; Noyes 1943). The idea of the academy did not materialise, but it was ultimately Samuel Johnson who wielded the responsibility by compiling *A Dictionary of the English Language*. This was by no means the first English dictionary, but it was a very special one (Litto 1963; Gouws and Potgieter 2010). Johnson articulated the idea of the dictionary unequivocally in the *Plan of a Dictionary of the English Language* presented to the Earl of Chesterfield:

> This, my Lord, is my idea of an English dictionary; a dictionary by which the pronunciation of our language may be fixed, and its attainment facilitated; by which its purity may be preserved, its use ascertained, and its duration lengthened.
>
> (Johnson 1755: 32)

The state and status of English did not inspire Johnson's pride, confidence and optimism as an English patriot prior to his work. He recalls in the preface of his dictionary that:

> When I took the first survey of my undertaking, I found our speech copious without order, and energetick without rules: wherever I turned my view, there was perplexity to be disentangled, and confusion to be regulated; choice was to be made out of boundless variety, without any established principle of selection; adulterations were to be detected, without the sufferages of any writers of classical reputation or acknowledged authority.
>
> (Crystal 2005: 21)

This compared unfavourably to French, in which Johnson marvelled the speakers' accuracy of "stating sounds their letters", and Italian, whose guidance regarding spelling he found exemplary (Mugglestone 2015: 31). Therefore, much more than a harmless drudge, as he defined the lexicographer in his dictionary, Johnson clearly conceived his role from the conceptualisation of his dictionary as that of a "linguistic legislator" (Mugglestone 2015: 31) with national responsibility. His dictionary remains influential as the basis for the *Oxford English Dictionary* (OED), including Johnson's authoritarianism such as his ridiculing, "rubbishing" and ultimate dismissal of certain words and senses of meaning from the first volume (Mugglestone 2005).

Another special mention regarding language policy-oriented lexicography is Noah Webster, author of *An American Dictionary of English* (Webster 1828). Webster occupies an important place in American history not only for his dictionary but his overall contribution to nationalist reforms. Generally, he sought to forge national solidarity through language, school and government as key national institutions (Litto 1963: 135). Regarding language, he occupied himself with idiosyncratic features of American usage of English, including spelling, pronunciation and vocabulary. Litto (1963: 139) lists the benefits that Webster envisaged from his linguistic reform work, as outlined in a letter that he wrote in 1736:

1 It will render the acquisition of the language easy for both natives and foreigners.
2 All the trouble of learning to spell will be saved. When no character has more sounds than one, every man, woman, and child who knows his alphabet can spell words, even by the sound without ever seeing them.
3 Pronunciation must necessarily be uniform.
4 The orthography of the language will be fixed.
5 The necessity of encouraging printing in this country and of manufacturing all our own books, is a political advantage, obvious and immense.
6 A national language is a national tie, and what country wants it more than America?

Accordingly, he used his dictionary as a platform of fostering some of his main ideas about language with a bigger picture in mind. English, as used in prestigious literary works held in high esteem in England and defined in Samuel Johnson's dictionary, struck Webster as inadequate in expressing American experience and dream. He was convinced that America needed a system of her own, "in language as well as government" (Litto 1963: 139). *An American Dictionary of English* was meant to pay particular attention to spelling, pronunciation and vocabulary usage prevalent in America. By redefining English from America, Webster sought to establish America's national language, thereby weaning the nation from England.

In Africa, colonialism was accompanied by European linguistic imperialism, according to Phillipson (1992), in the form of language policies that favoured European languages. This generally restricted African languages to the home, the church and elementary education. They were not part of the civilisation that colonialism purported to usher, making their development for modern roles less of an investment priority. Bergenholtz and Gouws (2006) cite funding discrepancies favouring Afrikaans, and to some extent, English lexicography in apartheid South Africa. It was missionaries who generally became the major role-players in African lexicography as they valued African languages for evangelical activities. Early dictionaries set initial standards for African languages, although developing the languages and supporting local speech communities was not their objective. The promotion of African languages and multilingualism after the independence of some African countries established a new language policy framework with implications for lexicography in ways that are parallel to the lexicographic activities of the European language academies and the works of prominent lexicographers discussed above.

10.3 Core issues and topics

Within the historical framework outlined in the previous section, the interface between lexicography and language policy seems to be characterised by mutual influences and impacts. Language policy motivations of regulating and influencing language usage and development have been pivotal in the conceptualisation and compilation of many dictionaries in different societies. Such motivations have had implications for the decisions made by lexicographers in terms of lexicographic methods and approaches. Conversely, many dictionaries have had far-reaching implications on the affirmation of existing language policies or formulation of new policies. This has been due to the lexicographic methods and choices adopted by lexicographers during the lexicographic process, raising pertinent issues at both macro- and micro-levels.

10.3.1 Macro-level issues

According to Tarp and Gouws (2008: 234), "only very few contributions dealing theoretically with the complex relation between language policy at a macro level and the conception of lexicographic works can be found in the existing literature". Within the historical framework outlined earlier, the question of how language policy has influenced lexicography by enabling or restricting the production of certain types of dictionaries in different languages will be addressed. At the same time, it will be shown how lexicography, in a reversal role, has influenced language policy by entrenching a particular policy or heralding reforms that lead to languages to assume or change statuses.

History shows that the production of dictionaries in general, or certain types of dictionaries in some cases, is influenced by current or prospective functional roles of languages and their level of development. In other words, language policies may provide necessary conditions for the production of certain dictionaries. More prestigious languages in terms of status and functions tend to have a variety of dictionaries supporting the various functions served by particular languages. On the other hand, certain dictionary types or dictionaries in general may not be a priority within particular language policy frameworks, leading to dictionaries being sparse or absent in certain languages. Dictionaries are thus products of language policies or policy-making processes. However, on the flipside, lexicography may play a crucial role in the redress of linguistic inequalities within language policies by contributing towards the development of previously marginalised languages for more prestigious functions. That way, dictionaries also become relevant tools for the conferment of language status.

Writing on the history of English lexicography, Landau (2001: 37) observes that "[t]the earliest word reference books for English-speaking people were bilingual glossaries that provided English equivalents for Latin or French words". A similar trend is reported regarding the history of Scandinavian languages (Haugen 1959; Malmgren and Sköldberg 2013), reflecting the erstwhile policies within which Latin dominated as Europe's *lingua franca* outlined above. Gallardo (1980: 61) considers bilingual dictionaries as the best one can find in non-standardised languages, emphasising that they may not even exist. Before a certain level of rigour and sophistication of mother-tongue scholarship, it is only through bilingual lexicography that lexicographers can viably codify and describe languages, which they do in the function of more established languages. The linguistic hierarchy prevalent in bilingual dictionaries also prevails in language policies, while standardised languages whose "lexicon can be organized in monolingual dictionaries" (Gallardo 1980: 61) serve more prestigious functions.

Similarly, the dominance of bilingual dictionaries in Africa is linked to language policies which favoured European languages at the expense of indigenous languages. Bilingual dictionaries in African languages were compiled to assist foreigners like missionaries and colonial administrators in their interactions with local speech communities (Awak 1990; Busane 1990; Gouws 2005; 2007; Mavoungou 2013). The subtitle of Weale's (1903) *Matebele and Makalaka Vocabulary: Intended for the use of Prospectors and Farmers in Mashonaland*, a Zimbabwean dictionary with two sections each pairing English with Shona and Ndebele, is self-telling. Mother-tongue speakers of Shona and Ndebele did not feature in the user profile of this dictionary. As merely mine and farm labourers who were incompetent in English, the language of lexicographical description, they could not benefit from the dictionary. Another example is a bilingual isiXhosa-English dictionary entitled *A Kafir-English Dictionary*. This dictionary was first published in 1899 by Albert Kropf, a German missionary who, having successfully learnt the language, albeit with struggles associated with paucity of reference works, endeavoured to provide a reference tool for fellow Europeans coming to work among amaXhosa in South Africa (Kropf 1915). Similar examples also exist in Francophone Africa such as Gabon where bilingual dictionaries pairing French, the country's official language, with indigenous Gabonese languages had a clear bias towards French (Mavoungou 2013). Accordingly, although acknowledging their role in the standardisation of African languages and their use as platforms for future dictionaries, Gouws (2005; 2007) classifies such dictionaries as externally motivated.

The emergence of the monolingual general-purpose dictionary in different communities, be it a comprehensive historical one or standard-size one, has always signalled new language policy directions. Monolingual lexicography was fundamental in the pursuit of linguistic and cultural affirmation through the extension of European vernaculars into formal spheres of life previously reserved for Latin. This would become the case in America where Noah Webster regarded unreformed English a British colonial relic and in Africa where English, French and other European languages are hegemonic. Monolingual lexicography typically becomes a corrective procedure, with the dictionary becoming a symbol of political and cultural independence, issues that are pertinent in language policies. Béjoint (2000: 138) writes:

> The emblematic power of the general-purpose dictionary is so strong, so real in a way, that the dictionary is felt necessary to any nation that wants to be recognized as an independent entity.

It is on this account that the production of comprehensive multivolume monolingual dictionaries in South Africa's official languages became the line function of NLUs (National Lexicographic Units) upon their establishment under the guidance of the Pan-South African Language Board (PanSALB). Lexicography was conceived as part of language planning as it was the case in England, France, Italy, etc.

Apart from the prestigious monolingual general-purpose dictionaries, languages that have been bestowed with a prestigious status in terms of language policy require other types of dictionaries to support new functions. South Africa's language policy does not only promote indigenous languages for their own sake but to foster multilingualism among the citizenry. It is desirable that South Africans are competent in more than one language and also that the different official languages can be used effectively in different functional domains for purposes of social transformation and national cohesion. The role of the education sector is crucial in this endeavour, as indicated by the Language-in-Education Policy which provides for the study of languages as Home Languages, First-Additional Languages and Second-Additional Languages, as well as their use as languages of teaching alongside English and Afrikaans. For the purposes of language learning, bilingual school dictionaries such as the *Longman Foundation Phase Dictionaries*, the *Oxford First Bilingual Dictionaries* and *Oxford Bilingual School Dictionaries* have been produced by commercial publishers. A number of bilingual or multilingual specialised dictionaries have also become available on the South African dictionary market to support the use of different languages as languages of teaching and learning in the aftermath of the post-apartheid multilingual policy.

10.3.2 Microlevel issues

What has been shown at a macro-level is how dictionaries are broadly conceived within the framework of language policy and the impact that particular dictionaries may have on specific languages and language policy in general. When it comes to the micro level, the concern is on lexicographic decisions regarding specific aspects of a language such as pronunciation, spelling, vocabulary, terminology, etc. in the context of a specific lexicographic project. These are typically matters of language variation which metalexicographers have engaged with under the topics of prescription, description and proscription (Bergenholtz 2003). The implications of such decisions are also important, and while lexicographers grapple with these issues in relation to specific dictionary projects, the implications may extend to the macro level in the long term.

Lemma selection normally contends with competition between orthographical variants, synonyms, indigenous coinages versus loanwords, formal versus informal forms such as slang, offensive words, etc. Choices may also have to be made regarding pronunciation, meaning, usage, etc. Authoritative language bodies, as is the case in South Africa where each official language has a national language body working under PanSALB, and language academies discussed earlier, preside on these matters as standardising agents. In prescriptive lexicography, the lexicographer may include in the dictionary only those forms that have been endorsed as standard by the relevant authority (Bergenholtz 2003), thereby making the dictionary an extension of language policy. In this regard, the French and Italian dictionaries produced by the respective academies are classic examples given that academies wielded language policy responsibilities. On the other hand, the lexicographer may include forms that he or she approves even in opposition not only to empirical evidence of language usage but also the relevant authorities. Samuel Johnson's intention of fixing and purifying English spelling, pronunciation and vocabulary (usage from low-class members of the English community, obsolete words and French borrowings) makes him an epitome of prescriptive lexicography. Without an academy to refer to, he was the language law unto himself.

Prescription has been criticised essentially for presenting linguistic judgements and tastes of the minority elite, that is, lexicographers and language policy authorities, as standards of appropriate usage (Trench 1860). However, Bergenholtz (2003), Gouws and Potgieter (2010) and Tarp and Gouws (2008), among others, engage with it from the view of dictionaries as utility products. Bergenholtz (2003) identifies and illustrates different forms of prescription, together with their implications for dictionary functions (Tarp and Gouws 2008). Those forms will not be discussed here. Instead, insight into an opposite approach, descriptive lexicography, will be given in order to put perspective into a brief critical engagement of how dictionaries have interacted with language policy at a micro-level.

Unlike prescription which purports to give dictionary users access only to good language, description entails providing "a comprehensive account of actual language use by presenting a variety of forms, whether orthographic, morphological or pronunciation variants, or, for example, words representing dialectal, sociolectal or chronolectal variants" (Tarp and Gouws 2008: 237). This implies going beyond the standards or recommendations of relevant authorities that regulate language usage. At its extreme (see Bergenholtz 2003; Tarp and Gouws 2008 for different forms of description), it amounts to the ideas that question the nobility of language planning in general (Rubin and Jernudd 1971). It is the approach Richard Chenevix Trench seems to advocate when he writes:

> A Dictionary . . . is an inventory of the language . . . It is no task of the maker of it to select the *good* words of the language. If he fancies that it is so and begins to pick and choose, to leave this and to take that, he will at once go astray. The business which he has undertaken is to collect and arrange all words, whether good or bad . . . He is an historian of it, not a critic.
>
> (Trench 1860: 5–6)

Specifically, he makes reference to the French and Italian academies, which he criticises for setting the precedence especially for Johnson. Despite being imposed as the official dictionary because of the powerful position of the academy in France, the *Dictionnaire de l'Académie française* has been criticised for containing "shocking words" (Béjoint 2000: 125). For Trench, by sanctioning words and their usage, prescriptive lexicography represents linguistic dictatorship. He prefers a situation in which language speakers decide how to use language, having been presented with its full spectrum in a dictionary (Trench 1860: 8).

However, the rhetorical question "Does Johnson's prescriptive approach still have a role to play in modern-day dictionaries?" (Gouws and Potgieter 2010) suggests that modern lexicography should be guided by dictionary functions rather than the approaches. The Faroe Islands case discussed by Tarp and Gouws (2008: 240–242) illustrates an uncritically extreme case of projecting language policy in dictionaries to the detriment of lexicography, resulting in some users resorting to a bilingual Danish-Faroese dictionary from Denmark. This would be a case of "strong prescription" (Bergenholtz and Gouws 2006: 75). On the other hand, the descriptive approach is also not without problems. Gouws and Potgieter (2010: 236) remind us that "the typical dictionary user regards . . . the dictionary, as an authoritative source of data from which they want to retrieve the information needed to solve those specific problems that prompted the consultation process". A free-for-all descriptive approach is not only burdensome, but may also be unhelpful to some users, especially for text production purposes for which they need definite answers on what to use in a particular context.

Having illustrated different forms, extents and implications of both prescription and description as lexicographic approaches, Bergenholtz (2003) introduces proscription (see Tarp and Gouws 2008). Gouws and Potgieter (2010: 239) describe it as "the best of both worlds of prescription and description" since it informs the user about language usage, be it good or bad, before advising on forms recommended by either the lexicographer or relevant language regulator. Depending on the different forms of proscription (Bergenholtz 2003), users may benefit immensely not only in terms of broad information regarding language use and variation but also in connection with text reception and text production. This means that in producing the dictionary, the lexicographer would have critically utilised evidence from linguistic research on language usage and language policy recommendations to the benefit of the user.

Besides implications for the satisfaction of user needs, micro-level issues associated with prescription, description or proscription may also have implications for specific languages in terms of their development and ultimately their position within language policy even at national level and international levels. The cases of English, both in England and America, French in France and the rest of the French-speaking world, Italian, Afrikaans in South Africa and African languages indicate how lexicography has become a factor in their development and status. The Afrikaans case is even more interesting. Gouws (2007) outlines the antagonistic agendas of two pioneer Afrikaans lexicographers, Changuin who was determined to preserve Dutch and Mansvelt who intended to foster the position of Afrikaans as a developing language. Although Changuin's prescriptive approach upheld the standards of Dutch, Afrikaans would have not flourished without Mansvelt's intervention. Similarly, although Gouws (2007: 319) regrets the purist approach of successive lexicographers who excluded natural borrowings from English in favour of artificial forms, the approach might have fostered the independent identity of Afrikaans and fast-tracked its development, making it more prestigious than isiXhosa, an African language with a longer literary tradition.

10.4 Looking to the future

The role of language in national and international affairs, as well as the ideology towards it, which constitute the most important premises for language planning, mean that the relationship between dictionaries and language policy will remain a relevant topic. However, at a macro-level, the topic will remain more pronounced in linguistic communities like those of Africa where language planning remains an outstanding matter on the decolonisation agenda. African countries are still dealing with the marginalisation of indigenous languages and dominance of ex-colonial languages. Also, some indigenous languages have been promoted arbitrarily at the expense of others. On the contrary, languages in developed countries have become fully standardised and now operate efficiently as national and official languages. The production of dictionaries that will contribute to the establishment of a standard language culture and general intellectualisation of indigenous languages remains a priority in Africa; however, developed communities need to update, revise or compile rival dictionaries for existing ones. Besides that, possibilities for language policy-oriented lexicography may come in the form of bilingual dictionaries which facilitate language learning across languages. Bilingual lexicography is more likely to increase in languages like Mandarin, which has become attractive for second-language learning in the wake of the rapid growth of the Chinese economy.

Although African lexicography now has a history of more than a century, it is only recent that it started transitioning from externally motivated to internally motivated processes (see Chapter 30 of this *Handbook*). Language policies prioritising multilingualism in general and the promotion of African languages in particular have provided conditions for such a necessary transition. The South African context has been inspiring in that the ambitious internally motivated lexicographic processes evolved with legislative, financial and infrastructural commitment at government level. Universities began to offer academic courses in lexicography, with the Programme for Lexicography at Stellenbosch University attracting students even from other African countries. Sooner, it was felt that the academic needs for African lexicography were not being sufficiently addressed in the existing associations dedicated to language issues, leading to the establishment of African Association for Lexicography (AFRILEX) in 1995. Coupled with developments in Gabon, from where a collaboration was forged with Stellenbosch University for training purposes, and Zimbabwe, where mother-tongue lexicography was thriving, this led to the celebration of the period from the 1990s as the golden age of African lexicography (Gouws 2007; Chabata and Nkomo 2010).

The NLUs in South Africa have been in operation for at least fifteen years now. Indigenous languages, namely isiXhosa and isiZulu, now have medium-sized monolingual dictionaries while all the others have at least one small bilingual dictionary pairing each language with English. These are milestones but frustration, fear and scepticism has overtaken the optimism of the past two decades. Alberts (2011) feels that the NLUs have misdirected their efforts by engaging in smaller projects instead of focusing on their line function. Gouws (2007) is equally concerned, although he understands how those challenges are consequences of previous marginalisation. He fears that the opportunity to produce the prestigious dictionaries provided by the post-apartheid language policy environment might be missed, as bilingual lexicography might further entrench the already dominant English. However, this should not be seen as the failure of lexicography per se but generally a language policy implementation problem for South Africa. PanSALB has been embroiled in administrative challenges which have crippled the NLUs especially from a financial point of view. With the comprehensive multi-volume monolingual dictionary being a target for each language from a language policy perspective, measures are urgently required at a policy level to rescue the situation.

With South Africa having been the leader regarding both language policy and lexicography, the glory of the golden age of lexicography on the continent is also waning. Zimbabwe's recent achievements were realised in the framework of a covert policy through a collaborative project with the University of Oslo and University of Gothenburg which came with financial and infrastructural support. Neither the University of Zimbabwe, which housed the project, nor the government made significant commitments for the sustainability of lexicographic practice on any of Zimbabwe's languages. Instead, what followed at language policy level was the listing of sixteen languages as "officially recognised" in the new constitution which was adopted in 2013. Future language policy-oriented lexicography in Zimbabwe will have to contend with all those languages, with even possibilities for bi- or multilingual dictionaries in which the newly recognised languages may be treated with the major languages, namely Ndebele, Shona and English. Such a procedure may be necessary for the teaching of the new officially recognised languages, given that most of their teachers would have learnt the major languages at school and teacher-training level. Furthermore, if multilingualism proves to be a genuine priority at government level, internally motivated dictionaries pairing English with either Ndebele or Shona, as well as Shona-Ndebele dictionaries, would become worthwhile.

At a macro-level, language-policy oriented lexicography in Africa may appear gloomy looking into the future based on the earlier reflections. However, the milestones achieved in terms of policy, the role of commercial publishers, developments in technology, lexicographic training and research make the future better than the past. Despite financial challenges which cripple effective language policy implementation, including lexicographic practice, all those factors may modestly influence language policy directions in a manner that may eventually give lead to another upsurge of lexicographic practice.

One major positive outcome of South Africa's enabling language policy network was the production of bilingual school dictionaries pairing indigenous languages with English by commercial publishers such as Oxford University Press and Maskew Miller Longman. Some of the dictionaries target learners at the elementary stages and others focus on higher grades. For its own series of elementary dictionaries, namely the Oxford First bilingual dictionaries, Oxford University Press has extended the scope to cater for neighbouring countries such as Botswana, Namibia and Zimbabwe. These efforts bear a positive impact for the development of a dictionary culture.

The Internet also offers opportunities that may be exploited in line with language policy or even to offset some language policy problems. The talking dictionaries project of the Living Tongues Institute for Endangered Languages is one such initiative.[1] Online talking dictionaries are part of the broader language documentation activities which have covered over 100 languages in Africa, India and South America. The project coordinators are buoyed by the possibilities offered by the Internet which allows them to produce inexpensive, interactive and organic dictionaries working with community members who are able to continuously upload data onto the dictionaries. In Zimbabwe, eight languages were covered, six of which are the new officially recognised languages which had been barely catered for before 2013 in terms of languages. However, in reality this may be acknowledged as more of prospects rather than achievements. The criteria used in lemma selection and provision of other data types seems arbitrary, as some of the dictionaries only have fewer than a thousand entries. The overall quality of the dictionaries and the practice leave a lot to desire from a lexicographic point of view. This shows that lexicographic training and planning remain critical even in an era when the Internet seems to offer expanded possibilities. In the case of Zimbabwe, the language policy injustices remain apparent from the distribution of lexicographic resources, and this may remain so for some time.

The level of development with respect to lexicographic traditions and metalexicographical research will also have different implications at micro-levels when it comes to lexicographic approaches that revolve around the relationship between dictionaries and language policies. Among other factors, this relationship will be affected in different contexts by developments in national and international affairs, as well as technology, including the use of corpora.

10.5 Conclusion

Given their engagement with language, dictionaries and language policies appear to influence each other in various ways. At a macro-level, the language policy environment tends to influence lexicographic practice, determining the availability of dictionaries and types. This becomes unfortunate as it may perpetuate the marginalisation of certain languages and deny their speakers tools that may solve various communication problems even within the restricted spaces of language use. It is on such an account that lexicographic practice may go contrary to language policy by making certain dictionaries that may contribute to language policy reform available. This requires resources and becomes a problem for developing countries. At a micro-level, the key issues revolve around prescription, description and proscription. Bergenholtz and Tarp (2006) stress the far-reaching implications of lexicographic decisions when it comes to choices in the context of variation, ranging from user access to data to political implications regarding the status and future of languages. In all this, the lexicographer needs to remain cognisant of the fundamental role of lexicography, which implies a critical engagement with language policy.

Related topics

Lexicography as an independent science; lexicography and interdisciplinarity; lexicography and applied linguistics; dictionaries to assist teaching and learning; African lexicography in the Internet era.

Further reading

Bergenholtz, H. and R. H. Gouws. (2006). "How to Do Language Policy with Dictionaries", *Lexikos* 16: 13–45.
This article discusses ways in which dictionaries participate in the implementation of language policy and highlight the implications of decisions made by lexicographers even beyond issues of access to lexicographic data.

Gouws, R. H. (2007). "On the Development of Bilingual Dictionaries in South Africa: Aspects of Dictionary Culture and Government Policy", *International Journal of Lexicography* 20(3): 313–327.
This article outlines a mutual influence between language policy and bilingual lexicography from apartheid to democratic South Africa, highlighting how early dictionaries influenced the standardisation of Afrikaans and how bilingual lexicography may respond to the country's democratic language policy.

Gouws, R. H. and L. Potgieter. (2010). "Does Johnson's Prescriptive Approach Still Have a Role to Play in Modern-Day Dictionaries?", *Lexikos* 20: 234–247.
This article investigates prescription, description and proscription in modern-day dictionaries and argues for a considered approach in order to satisfy the needs of users who regard dictionaries as prescriptive references.

Mugglestone, L. (2015). *Samuel Johnson and the Journey into Words*. Oxford: Oxford University Press.
This book deals with Johnson's ideas about language and dictionaries which influenced him in the conception of his Plan (1747) and the actual compilation of dictionary (1755). His ideas constitute the core of the nexus between dictionaries and language policy.

Note

1 see at Living Tongues Institute for Endangered Languages: *Talking Dictionaries*. http://talkingdictionary.swarthmore.edu/ [Accessed 27 June 2016]

References

Accademia della Crusca. (2011) www.accademiadellacrusca.it (Accessed 27 June 2016).
Alberts, M. (2011) "National Lexicography Units – Past, Present, Future", *Lexikos* 21: 23–52.

Awak, M. K. (1990) "Historical Background, With Special Reference to Western Africa", in R.R.K. Hartmann (ed.), *Lexicography in Africa*. Exeter: University of Exeter Press.

Bamgbose, A. (1991) *Language and the Nation: The Language Question in Sub-Saharan Africa*. Edinburgh: Edinburgh University Press.

Bathe, W. (1615) *Ianua Linguarum*. Salamanca: Salmanticae.

Béjoint, H. (2000) *Modern Lexicography*. Oxford: Oxford University Press.

Bergenholtz, H. (2003) "User-Oriented Understanding of Descriptive, Proscriptive and Prescriptive Lexicography", *Lexikos* 13: 65–80.

Bergenholtz, H. and R. H. Gouws. (2006) "How to Do Language Policy With Dictionaries", *Lexikos* 16: 13–45.

Bergenholtz, H. and S. Tarp. (2003) "Two Opposing Theories: On H. E. Wiegand's Recent Discovery of Lexicographic Functions", *Hermes. Journal of Linguistics* 31: 171–196.

Burke, P. (2004) *Languages and Communities in Early Modern Europe*. Cambridge: Cambridge University Press.

Busane. M. (1990) "Lexicography in Central Africa: The User Perspective, With Special Reference to Zaire", in R.R.K. Hartmann (ed.), *Lexicography in Africa*. Exeter: University of Exeter Press, pp. 19–35.

Chabata, E. and D. Nkomo. (2010) "The Utilisation of Outer Texts in the Practical Lexicography of African Languages", *Lexikos* 20: 73–91.

Cluver, V. (1993) *A Dictionary of Language Planning Terms*. Pretoria: University of South Africa.

Cooper, R. L. (1989) *Language Planning and Social Change*. Cambridge: Cambridge University Press.

Crystal, D. (1997) *English as a Global Language*. Cambridge/New York: Cambridge University Press.

Crystal, D. (2005) *Samuel Johnson: A Dictionary of the English Language: An Anthology*. London: Penguin.

Deumert, A. and W. Vandenbussche. (2003) "Standard Languages: Taxonomies and Histories", in A. Deumert and W. Vandenbussche (eds.), *Germanic Standardizations: Past to Present*. Amsterdam: John Benjamins, pp. 1–14.

Fettes, M. (1997) "Language Planning and Education", in R. Wodak and D. Corson (eds.), *Encyclopedia of Language and Education: Volume 1. Language Policy and Political Issues in Education*. Dordrecht/Boston, MA/London: Kluwer, pp. 13–22.

Gallardo, A. (1980) "Dictionaries and the Standardization Process", in L. Zgusta (ed.), *Theory and Method in Lexicography*. Columbia: Hornbeam Press, pp. 59–69.

Gouws, R. H. (2005) "Lexicography of Africa", in K. Brown (ed.), *Encyclopedia of Language and Linguistics*. 2nd edition. Oxford: Elsevier, pp. 95–101.

Gouws, R. H. (2007) "On the Development of Bilingual Dictionaries in South Africa: Aspects of Dictionary Culture and Government Policy", *International Journal of Lexicography* 20(3): 313–327.

Gouws, R. H. and L. Potgieter. (2010) "Does Johnson's Prescriptive Approach Still Have a Role to Play in Modern-Day Dictionaries?" *Lexikos* 20: 234–247.

Hadebe, S. (2007) "Language Planning and Monolingual Dictionaries: With Special Reference to Ndebele", *Lexikos* 17: 292–306.

Hartmann, R.R.K. (2005) "Lexicography and Its Interdisciplinary Contacts, with Special Reference to Linguistics and Onomasiology", *Lexikos* 15: 70–89.

Haugen, E. (1959) "Lexicography and Language Planning", in K. R. Jankowsky (ed.), *Scientific and Humanistic Dimensions of Language*. Amsterdam: John Benjamins, pp. 571–580.

Johnson, S. (1747) *The Plan of a Dictionary of the English Language*. Facsimile Edition 1970. Menston: The Scholar Press.

Johnson, S. (1755) *A Dictionary of the English Language*. London: J. and P. Knapton/T. T. Longman et al.

Kaplan, R. B. and R. B. Baldauf. (1997) *Language Planning: From Practice to Theory*. Clevedon: Multilingual Matters.

Komensky, A. (1631) *Ianua Linguarum Reserata*. Amstelodami: Apud Ludovicum Elzevirium.

Kropf, A. (1915) *A Kafir – English Dictionary*. 2nd edition. Alice: Lovedale.

Landau, S. I. (2001) *Dictionaries: The Art and Craft of Lexicography*. 2nd edition. New York/Cambridge: Cambridge University Press.

Litto, F. M. (1963) "Noah Webster's Theory of Linguistic Nationalism", *Acta Semiótica et Lingvistica* 5(1): 133–155.

Malmgren, S-G. and E. Sköldberg. (2013) "The Lexicography of Swedish and Other Scandinavian Languages", *International Journal of Lexicography* 26(2): 117–134.

Mavoungou, P. A. (2013) "Gabonese French Dictionaries: Survey and Perspectives", *Lexikos* 23: 255–272.

Mugglestone, L. (2005) *Lost for Words: The Hidden History of the Oxford English Dictionary*. London: Yale University Press.

Mugglestone, L. (2015) *Samuel Johnson and the Journey Into Words*. Oxford: Oxford University Press.

Ndinga-Koumba-Binza, H. (2005) "Considering a Lexicographic Plan for Gabon Within the Gabonese Language Landscape", *Lexikos* 15: 132–150.

Noyes, G. E. (1943) "The First English Dictionary, Cawdrey's *Table Alphabeticall*", *Modern Language Notes* 58(8): 600–605.

Phillipson, R. (1992) *Linguistic Imperialism*. London: Oxford University Press.

Rubin, J. and B. H. Jernudd (eds.) (1971) *Can Language Be Planned*? Honolulu: East West Center and University of Hawaii Press.

Sherberg, M. (2003) "The Accademia Fiorentina and the Question of the Language: The Policies of Theory in Ducal Florence", *Renaissance Quarterly* 56(1): 26–55.

Spolsky, B. (2004) *Language Policy*. Cambridge: Cambridge University Press.

Tarp, S. (2008) *Lexicography in the Borderland between Knowledge and Non knowledge: General Lexicographical Theory With Particular Focus on Learner's Lexicography*. Tübingen: Max Niemeyer.

Tarp, S. and R. H. Gouws. (2008) "A Lexicographic Approach to Language Policy and Recommendations for Future Dictionaries", *Lexikos* 18: 232–255.

Trench, R. C. (1860) "On Some Deficiencies in Our English Dictionaries", London. http://public.oed.com/history-of-the-oed/archived-documents/on-some-deficiencies/ (Accessed 1 February 2017).

Vogl, U. (2012) "Multilingualism in a Standard Language Culture", in M. Hunning, U. Vogl and O. Moliner (eds.), *Standard Languages and Multilingualism*. Amsterdam/Philadelphia: John Benjamins, pp. 1–42.

Webster, N. (1828) *American Dictionary of the English Language*. New Haven, CT: Foundation for American Christian Education.

Wealie, M. E. (1903) *Matebele and Malaka Vocabulary: Intended for the Use of Prospectors and Farmers in Mashonaland*. Cape Town: Murray and St. Leger.

Wiegand, H. E. (1984) "On the Structure and Contents of a General Theory of Lexicography", in R.R.K. Hartmann (ed.), *LEX'eter '83 Proceedings: Papers From the International Conference on Lexicography at Exeter, 9–12 September 1983*. Tübingen: Max Niemeyer, pp.13–30.

Wikipedia Online. Académie française https://en.wikipedia.org/wiki/Académie_française. (Accessed 27 June 2016).

11

Dictionaries and culture

Przemysław Łozowski

11.1 Introduction

If we follow the opinion that "when we use a word, we need to know both its meaning and its grammar" (*LDCE* 1987 (2nd ed.): F10), the question of the role and place of cultural information in a dictionary framework covers the meaning-related, or functional, as much as grammar-related, or formal, aspects of a given dictionary entry. Indeed, whether the plural of *fungus* is *funguses* or *fungi*, and, if it is the latter, whether it is pronounced with /g/ or /ʤ/, and whether or not one knows and uses *fungus* in one of its possible extended senses as "someone who is lazy and does nothing all day" (*urbandictionary.com*) – this is a matter of cultural considerations because it reflects the user's expected preferences, choices, values, ideologies, knowledge, experience, and mentality, which is all that we typically call *culture*. So, if your dictionary specifies only one plural form of the singular *fungus*, or it insists on only one of the two pronunciations of *fungi*, or conceals slang meanings of *fungus*, this shows what group of speakers the dictionary makers want you to identify with and what forms and meanings they consider to be (in)appropriate, (un)desirable, (dis)agreeable, or (non)standard, be it in terms of meaning or grammar.

For the economy of space, in this chapter we focus on substance (meaning), rather than form (grammar). Accordingly, it is in relation to functional considerations that we elaborate on two related problems, both having to do with the language–culture interface. One issue evolves around the question of *whether or not culture happens at all to be reflected in dictionaries*, which depends on what one takes both language (here: dictionary) and culture to be. As much as certain conceptions of language and certain kinds of dictionaries favour cultural parameters to be included in the overall dictionary microstructure, there are likewise conceptions of culture, especially those of an experiential and interpretative slant, that make it desirable for cultural information to find its way into the dictionary. The other issue is more practical and involves the question of *where it is in the dictionary microstructure that cultural data could be accommodated.* As far as the meaning of words is concerned, the three primary and potential lexicographic resources of cultural data are, respectively, the dictionary definition itself (with or without special (usage) notes), the illustrative/example sentences, and the so-called stylistic labels. Of these three, we will, again for the sake of limited space, deal with the first one, rather than the other two.

11.2 Core issues and topics

11.2.1 Definitions: with and/or without cultural information

Dictionary makers appear to do their best to include cultural information as well as to avoid possible undesired consequences. Take this preliminary example (1): the definitions of *white* and *black* as terms (nouns and adjectives) of racial identity, or, if you prefer, names of races, in selected online EFL (pedagogical) dictionaries (emphasis added).

(1) *OALD online*
white a member of a race or people who have **pale** skin
black a member of a race of people who have **dark** skin

Clearly, *white* and *black* are defined fairly symmetrically to each other as if all that mattered could be derived from the very contrast between one word and the other.[1] Indeed, the respective definitions reveal one distinction, of skin colour, which we probably take to be objective and uncontroversial.

However, in three other English as a Foreign Language (EFL) dictionaries we can identify a growing tendency towards going beyond the mere contrast between the semantic content of words alone and incorporating part of the experiential information speakers of English may (stereo)typically have in reference to the white–black racial distinction.

(2) *LDCE online*
white someone who belongs to the race of people with pale skin
black someone who belongs to the race of **people who originally came from Africa** and who have dark brown skin

(3) *MED online*
white (adj.) a white person belongs to a race of people with pale skin
black (adj.) belonging or relating to a race of people with dark skin, especially **people whose families were originally from Africa**

(4) *CALD online*
white (adj.) of a person who has skin that is pale in colour
black (adj.) relating or belonging to people with black or dark brown skin, especially **people who live in Africa or whose family originally came from Africa**

The definition of *black* is now only partially related to *white*, and this correspondence is maintained, similarly to *OALD online* in (1) earlier, in terms of the pale *vis-à-vis* dark/dark brown/black distinction. Next to the skin colour information, all the three definitions of *black* in (2–4) offer a further identification note that is either limited to the African origin of black people, as in *LDCE online* and *MED online*, or extended to cover additionally the present-day African geographical stand of black people, as in *CALD online*. Whatever the source and the reason of this remark on origin/habitation is, it makes the *white–black* pairs asymmetrical, with the definition of *white* somewhat of a default, or a standard, and the definition of *black* being marked in the sense that it has been written in relation to the *white* standard.

If, now, in comparison to the definition of *white*, the one of *black* seems to have racist overtones, this can be evidenced also with the choice of the defining vocabulary. Notice that in (3) and (4) *white* is given a personal/individual slant ('a person'), whereas *black* has a collective dimension ('people'). Having read the definitions as they stand in the dictionaries, we probably picture to ourselves a pale-skinned individual human being at one end and a dark-skinned human mass at the other end, which could suggest that whereas each of pale-skinned people is unique and unparalleled, the dark-skinned people can only be referred to in terms of an indiscriminate crowd, or a throng.

There is nothing in the lexical opposition between *black* and *white* alone as race terms to justify the origin/habitation note in *black* and a complete lack of something corresponding in *white*. Technically speaking, this origin note does not project from language relations themselves (here: the *white–black* lexical opposition), but must be inferred from culturally shaped real-world relations (here: the white–black racial opposition). The latter comes with lexicographers' experience, knowledge included, of the world, or, at least, with what they think their fellow language users take for granted and express in their language. In short, the definitions of *black* and *white* reflect, intentionally or not, how the English happen to conceptualize about the dark- and white-skinned races. The lesson that diligent EFL learners take here, having read the respective entries, is that the cards are stacked against those named *black*: the racial status of those termed as *white* is so self-evident that all that is included in the definition of the word has got to do with the colour of the skin, whereas the racial status of those termed as *black* needs a further qualification.

A reverse situation can be found in *CED online*:

(5) *CED online*
black a member of a human population having dark pigmentation of the skin
white a person, esp one of **European ancestry**, from a human population having light pigmentation of the skin

Similarly to the definitions in (2–4), there is a clear inclination to give a personal reading to *white* ('a person') and an impersonal reading to *black* ('a member'), yet this time it is the ancestry of those named *white* that is specified with no word on the ancestry of those named *black*.

Finally, we come a full circle in the definitions of *black* and *white* as race adjectives in *CABED online*:

(6) *CABED online*
black (adj.) a black person belongs to a race of people with dark skins, especially a race **from Africa**
white (adj.) a white person has a pale skin and belongs to a race which is of **European origin**

Unlike those in (2–5), the definitions in (6) are nearly as symmetrical as the two we find in *OALD online* and discuss at the beginning of this section (see (1) earlier). Yet there is a crucial difference: *black* and *white* are defined purely linguistically in *OALD online*, which is when one attempts to capture the mere contrast between the involved lexemes, whereas the *CABED* lexicographers allow for an extra-linguistic piece of information, which is when one tries to make the definition relevant experientially, cognitively, encyclopedically, or, most broadly, culturally. In other words, linguistically speaking, *black* and *white* as race names relate to *black* and *white* as colour terms, hence the skin-colour contrast reflected, but culturally speaking, *black* and *white* relate to the mental idealizations of the objects that are behind *black* and *white*, hence the ancestry contrast expressed, either symmetrically (6) or asymmetrically (2–5).

As we can see, various dictionaries employ various strategies to give and/or not to give expression to cultural considerations. Words happen to be defined in the dictionary as sets of related lexemes, not as independent units, which allows for these three basic possibilities:

(i) that none/neither of the related lexemes is given any cultural qualification (example 1),
(ii) that one of the related lexemes is provided with some cultural information (examples 2–5), and
(iii) that both/all of the related lexemes reflect cultural considerations (example 6).

However, one should not expect any easy and clear-cut generalizations as to which dictionaries favour cultural information and which do not. We should rather expect a fair amount of inconsistency, with cultural considerations coming to the fore whenever the word to be defined clashes with the assumed users' expectations. Here there is an example that within one and same dictionary of the EFL type, such as *OALD*, there can be much of a tension as to whether or not cultural qualification should be given to which of the related words. Take *black* and *white* again.

It is already in the first edition of the dictionary (1948) that we see the correlation between *black* and *negro*. Were it not for this reference, the nouns *black* and *white*, as race names, to be remembered, would appear perfectly symmetrical. The definition of *negro* itself is descriptive and encyclopedic in the sense that it specifies three highly selected physical attributes of the human race called *negro*:

(7) *OALD* (1948, 1st. ed.)
black a black man (a negro)
white a white man
negro, Negro a member of the dark African race, having woolly hair, thick lips and a flat nose

As *black* is correlated with *negro*, we do obtain, in effect, in a somewhat roundabout way, a cultural definition of *black*. Out of numerous physical characteristics of black people, only those are given that seem to impose themselves most as salient in a white person's perception of 'a black man'. In other words, it is from a white person's experiential perspective only that 'woolly hair, thick lips and a flat nose' make sense as attributes of black people, simply because this is not what white people typically think that they themselves are like.

The same asymmetry can be seen nearly three decades later in the third edition of *OALD* (1974). Although both *black* and *white* are recognized as race names, they are again given different cultural qualifications:

(8) *OALD* (1974, 3rd ed.)
white white man/woman European person
black Negro (formerly derog, but now widely used)
Negro member (or, outside Africa, descendant) of one of the black-skinned African peoples south of the Sahara

Whereas *white* features in the expression *white man/woman* that is defined as "European person", *black* is defined independently as "Negro" and annotated in this way: "formerly derog[atively], but now widely used". As we understand, the cultural import behind *black* might have been pejorative in the past, but by the mid-1970s the word had been ameliorated enough to become a synonym of *Negro*. The question is whether *Negro* itself can be considered a positive reference if it is given (in the same edition) the definition that specifically, if not meticulously, pinpoints black people as to their origin and habitation. It takes a job to tell why *black* should be defined through *Negro* with all the detailed encyclopaedic details of the latter, but one thing seems to be evident: in the third edition of *OALD*, *black* is an issue, hence its relatively extensive and indirect cultural specification, whereas *white* is not.[2] From a white person's perspective, that is.

Moreover, giving the "formerly derog" qualification to *negro*, the editors of the third edition of *OALD* (1974) admit indirectly that both *negro* and *black* should have been labelled pejoratively in the first edition of the dictionary (1948), which amounts to saying that the definitions of these two lexemes project, in fact, negative overtones. This means that the selected attributes ascribed to black people in the definition of *negro* and, then by analogy, extended to the definition of *black* (1st ed.) are all part of a white person's derogative assessment of black people. Again, *woolly hair*, *thick lips*, and a *flat nose* is not what objectively characterizes the black race, but this is what white people subjectively find in the black race as cognitively and experientially significant. A profound cultural lesson, indeed.

In the next edition of *OALD* (1989, 4th ed.), we have a further progression towards the amelioration of *black* and, hence, the disjunction between *black* and *Negro*:

(9) *OALD* (1989, 4th ed.)

white white-skinned person; Caucasian
black (formely derog, now the preferred word) person of a dark-skinned race; negro
Negro (sometimes offensive) member of the black-skinned race of mankind that originated in Africa

Although *negro* is given as a synonym of *black*, we understand the two have quite different cultural groundings, of acceptance in *black* and of rejection in *Negro*, respectively. This explicitly goes well with that the skin colour is 'dark' in *black* and 'black' in *Negro*, which leads to a conclusion that the Blacks are not black, but dark, or that for the Blacks to be black, they must be called *Negroes*. Despite the suggested synonymy relationship between *black* and *Negro*, one may have serious doubts whether we are talking about one and the same race of people. This may sound absurd in terms of objective truth, but cultural terms are never objective as they tend to be stained with human experience.

Another cultural note has to do with the *Caucasian-Africa* contrast. This distinction is completely unbalanced because *Caucasian* is a racial term that could be set against, should that be necessary, *Negroid*, or, for more specific references, *Congoid* and *Capoid*, whereas *Africa* is a geographical term that differentiates well with *Europe, America*, or *Asia*. Yet from a cultural point of view, the suggestion that the Whites come from the Caucasus region and the Blacks from Africa tells us a lot about what the lexicographers behind the fourth edition of *OALD* take for granted as culturally salient attributes of being a white-skinned person and being a dark- and/or black-skinned person. One day we may learn that the out-of-Africa origin of the whole humankind has been ultimately confirmed and no lexicographer will ever risk any origin/habitation remark as part of the dictionary definitions of *black, Negro*, or *white*. Yet, the *OALD* 1989 definitions of these words will forever stand for how white- and dark-skinned people happened to be conceptualized by a specific group of users, lexicographers included, for specific purposes at a specific point in time and space.

Half a century after the publication of the first edition of *OALD*, in the sixth edition of the dictionary (2000), we find the cultural information behind the nouns *black, white* and *Negro* that has not really changed ever since: *Negro* is labelled as "old-fashioned and often offensive", the definitions of *black* and *white* are symmetrically narrowed down to the pale/dark skin characteristic, and *black* is given a fully-fledged usage note that, in fact, is a piece of cultural navigation that discloses what values can be found behind which words:

(10) *OALD* (2000, 6th ed.)

black (n.) (. . .) *Black* is more common in the plural. It can sound offensive in the singular. Instead you can use the adjective ('a black man/woman'), or, in the US, African American.

black (adj.) *Black* is the word most widely used and generally accepted in Britain. In the US the currently accepted term is *African American.*

To round off, the cultural lesson we learn from the subsequent editions of *OALD* is that *black*, or rather its lexicographic definition, is still an issue because it relates to an uneasy black–white racial contrast in the world. Although *black* is no longer asymmetrically defined in relation to *white*, and has for good been disentangled from *Negro*, the *OALD* editors do find it relevant to provide a culturally oriented usage note in order to guide one's cultural behaviour or satisfy one's cognitive needs. This all, naturally, holds true providing that the dictionary reflects, deliberately or not, cognitive tensions of the users the dictionary represents as a speaking community and/or is aimed at as a reading audience.

11.2.2 Definitions: system based and/or culture based

Methodologically, then, if any of the related lexemes is given some special treatment in terms of its definition and/or stylistic label, this usually ticks that lexeme, or some of its senses, off as marked and vulnerable to cultural qualification. Then, by means of examining a given lexeme across different dictionaries or subsequent editions of one and the same dictionary, or comparing related lexemes, either within a single edition or across subsequent editions, a careful reader may deduce from the definitions analysed a lot about the cultural grounding of the lexeme(s) in question. This ascribes to the dictionary, or at least to the dictionary definition, yet another role, that could be termed as *cultural function*, or, as cognitive linguists would probably say, *conceptual function*:

> Language is part of a cognitive system which comprises perception, emotions, categorization, abstraction processes, and reasoning. (. . .) Thus the study of language, in a sense, becomes the study of *the way we express and exchange ideas and thoughts.* (. . .) Language not only enables communication, but also reflects *mankind's conceptual world.* (. . .) Linguistic categories not only enable us to communicate, but also impose a certain *way of understanding the world.*
>
> (Dirven and Verspoor 2004: ix and 1; emphasis added)

If we apply this general tenet to the dictionary, we must conclude that what we aim at in every single dictionary definition is a certain group of language users' shared understanding of their world experience that happens to be explicated for the sake of the same or any other group of language users. To follow Levisen and Waters (2015: 255) in this respect, no matter whether human groupings are "defined nationally, regionally, religiously, professionally, or subculturally", which determines the kind, the structure, and the purpose of a given dictionary, "the shared sociality of any group of people (. . .) is conceptual, imagined, and constructed". This makes the relationship between dictionaries and cultures as close as possible and brings us to Goodenough's influential conception of culture:

> A society's culture consists of whatever it is one has to *know* or *believe* in order to operate in a manner acceptable to its members. (. . .) Culture is not a material phenomenon; it does not consist of things, people, behaviour, or emotions. It is rather an organization of these things. It is the *forms of things that people have in mind*, their models for perceiving, relating, and otherwise interpreting them.
>
> (Goodenough 1964: 36–37; emphasis added)

As recently generalized by Ostermann (2015: 1) in her making the case for cognitve lexicography, "with language not being seen as an isolated faculty but as relating to the world", dictionaries in general and lexicographic definitions in specific may prove suitable for explaining "how humans perceive and conceptualise the world", or, to put it simply, for explicating culture(s).

A similar opinion is voiced on several occasions in the preceding and following chapters. Nielsen (see Chapter 5 of this *Handbook*) makes it clear that dictionaries are much more than mere vessels of linguistic categories because they have been developed to fulfil specific types of needs of specific types of users in specific types of situations in the real (extra-lexicographic) world. Similarly, Agerbo (see Chapter 4 of this *Handbook*) emphasizes the importance of investigating what the specific user type is interested in knowing in a specific extra-lexicographic user situation.

As we understand, it is plausible to assume that no matter what actual needs given users may have in specific contexts (e.g. naming objects with appropriate words, fixing the extension of words, getting to know a synonym, identifying a typical token/situation behind a word, categorizing objects with words, etc.), one over-arching need of all users in all situations is to understand fellow humans in their conceptualizing the world, or, to use Goodenough's phrase, "to know or believe in order to operate in a manner acceptable" to others. So, what we term here as cultural function of the dictionary is, in fact, reflecting not what words mean, but what users mean by the words they use, which amounts to identifying meanings as users' experiential need to externalize their ways of thinking. In other words, the language we speak is shaped by our experiential make-up, by what we specifically and actually are as humans. The whole point behind doing lexicography, specifically behind writing dictionary definitions, is no longer to describe the system of relations allegedly residing in the mind of some idealized speaker-hearer, but assume that words must be taken as symbols of human experience of the world: quite like national emblems (the Polish white-tailed eagle, the German red-footed black eagle, the British lion, the Swedish three crowns, the Irish gold harp), social and religious tokens and conventions (the wedding ring, the Christian cross, the Islamic crescent and star), or even omens (the black cat, the raven, the lightning), words are forms that have been given their meanings proportionately to the experience of those who find the given form-meaning correlation absolutely justified and necessary.

The net effect of this externalization is that every single word is an accumulative record of the subsequent layers of the self-awareness that the past and present generations of speakers did and do find relevant enough to self-express as their cultural experience. On this reading, the search of words, lexicographic examination included, amounts to a search of conceptualizations, or of symbols of human experience, or to a study of what humans symbolize in language when they verbalize what they think that they experience in the world.[3]

But can we really read dictionary definitions to the effect of identifying mentalities, attitudes, and values in/behind them so that we could get to know the conceptual world of a given group of speakers and their 'way of understanding the world'? This question brings us to the specific problem of meaning explanation/explication, or, more practically, of constructing lexicographic definitions, which, at least in part, is a theoretical linguistic (semantic) dilemma.

In order to limit theoretical issues to the absolute minimum, yet maintain the clarity of presentation and exemplification, let us assume that, in reality, two broad approaches to *presenting semantic content in dictionary entries* can be distinguished and maintained. One is *systemic* (also: intra-linguistic, denotative, defining, scientific, objective) and has to do with giving the central characteristics of a lexeme, each being a reflection of some systemic relation the lexeme contracts with the remaining relevant lexemes. The other one is *symbolic* (also: extra-linguistic, cultural, connotative, descriptive, axiological, naïve) and provides a description of the speaker's conceptualization behind the lexeme. The former shows what the lexeme means *beyond* the speaker's experience and *within* the system of a given language, whereas the latter places the lexeme *beyond* that system and *within* the speaker's experiential values.

This systemic-symbolic distinction is not meant to supersede any of the traditionally delimited types of dictionary definitions that are typically given in probably all introductory or comprehensive books on lexicography and related subjects, such as Béjoint (2000), Atkins and Rundell (2008), Svensén (2009), or Riemer (2010). That we reduce possible defining mechanisms, strategies, and principles to just two broad categories is believed to reflect, in the first place, the ongoing polarization between structurally and functionally oriented linguistic methodologies that embrace, respectively, either the inclusion or exclusion of the parameter of culture. At the simplest, we have two broad kinds of linguistics: *with* and *without* cultural considerations. The culture-friendly type would include typically (non-autonomous) function- and performance-oriented paradigms, whereas the culture-hostile type would favour mostly (autonomous) form- and competence-oriented ones.

In structuralism, one typically assumes that language is a system of arbitrary signs, each being a form–substance pairing organized by what minimally sets them apart from the other pairings they are related to. If so, writing a dictionary definition amounts to setting a word against all the other relevant words and this produces a system of relations, each being a part of the definition. In functionalism, by contrast, language is a set of motivated signs, each being a form–substance pairing organized by the cognitively motivated associations between language and experience, with language representing (standing for) and evoking experience. In order to write a dictionary definition, one sets a word against language users' awareness as expressed in language, which produces a certain mental (cultural) picture of the world.

For example, in reference to *bachelor* defined as 'man who has never been married', the purely systemic definition of *spinster* should simply read 'woman who has never been married'. Compare that with the following three definitions of *spinster*, all showing a gradual increase of cultural information along the from-systemic-to-symbolic cline:

(11) *CCED* 1987
1. a woman who has never been married, esp. an old or middle-aged woman

(12) *OALD* 1989, 4th ed.
2. woman who remains single after the usual age for marrying

(13) *LDCE* 1995, 3rd ed.
3. an unmarried woman, usually one who is no longer young and seems unlikely to marry

Each of these three definitions is marked with a growing amount of cultural overtones (here: pejoration, prejudice, sexism) in the sense that the selected defining vocabulary – *especially, old, middle-aged, usual age for marrying, no longer young, seems, unlikely* – are highly subjective, relative, and vague, which is precisely what human experience and its cultural manifestations are like. At the symbolic end, we find not a possible definition of the lexeme *spinster*, but a culturally loaded expression of the way people tend to think about spinsters. In the last resort, this, naturally, tells us more about the speakers of English than about their language, more about *the* English than about English, more about the English mentality than about the English word.

If we were now to go back to our preliminary *black/white* example, we could say that (1) is systemic, (2–5) and (7–9) are symbolic, and (6) seems to be a borderline case. The same three possibilities can also be found in selected definitions of *monk* and *nun*:

(14) OALD online
monk a member of a religious community of **men** typically living under vows of poverty, chastity, and obedience
nun a member of a religious community of **women**, typically one living under vows of poverty, chastity, and obedience

(15) *LDCE* (1995, 3rd ed.)
monk a member of an all-male religious group that lives **apart from** other people in a monastery
nun a member of an all-female religious group who live **together** in a convent

(16) MED online
monk a man who lives in a religious community **away from** other people; monks live in a building called a monastery
nun a woman who belongs to a religious community of women and who lives in a convent

(17) FD online
monk a man who is a member of a brotherhood living in a monastery and **devoted** to a discipline prescribed by his **order**
nun a woman who belongs to a religious **order** or congregation **devoted** to active service or meditation, living under vows of poverty, chastity, and obedience

Here, again, similarly to the *black/white* example in (1) earlier, the definitions in (14) are symmetrical with one binary (men/women) opposition expressed. On a close reading, however, one can notice a little crack in what otherwise appears a perfectly balanced systemic contrast: the presence/absence of the comma in front of *typically* makes the definition of *monk* more restrictive, or less inclusive, in comparison to the definition of *nun*. In other words, whereas *monk* must typically involve living under vows of poverty, chastity, and obedience, *nun* may, but does not have to. This provides a real-world piece of information already: there are various communities of nuns, of which the typical one is based on vows of poverty, chastity, and obedience.

Now, the way *monk* and *nun* are presented in the third edition of *LDCE* (15) is systemic in the first half of the two definitions and symbolic in the other half. For the first part of the two, *monk* and *nun* function within the autonomous linguistic system as mutually related elements, which is when the only consideration worth mentioning is the sex distinction. Frankly, a monk is a feminine version of a nun, and a nun is a masculine counterpart of a monk.

However, the remaining wording of the two definitions escape systemic oppositions and give two different experiential pictures of being a nun and being a monk, respectively. Whereas monks constitute a group that 'lives apart', nuns build up a group who 'live together', which invites making interesting inferences about how monks and nuns are conceptualized in the English culture and what experiential associations the two bring about. Specifically, the symbolic parts of the definitions of *monk* and *nun* reflect two different cultural images or, say, stereotypes: the one of a man as a lone wolf and the one of a woman, as, if we can risk it, a hen on the perch. Though objectively there is no difference between being a monk and being a nun except the sex distinction, as in (14), what appears significant culturally in (15) is that neither monks nor nuns lose their respective male *vis-à-vis* female characteristics as perceived and typically conceptualized in terms of gender roles. Simply, out there behind the walls of, respectively, monasteries and convents, there are two groups of religious people, monks and nuns, both by definition living away from other people. Yet this living away is emphasized only in reference to monks and watered away in reference to nuns (see (16) as well). It is not implausible to assume that the reason comes with the societal gendered expectations that women are social creatures, whereas men are solitary. This could be sexist, unfair, or undesirable, but it certainly is cultural even if this cultural import represents a very limited group of English users or is addressed to a highly specific audience (such as EFL learners, for example).

So it is in (17) where the definitions of *monk* and *nun* correspond to each other minimally, sharing just two defining words, *order* and *devoted.* Notice that *brotherhood* is not contrasted or matched with *sisterhood, monastery* with *convent*, *passive* with *active*, and the general term *discipline* correlates with a much more specific description of *vows of poverty, chastity, and obedience.* It may well be that these two definitions are badly constructed, hence the impression of a haphazard wording, but, again, we see in them what we think we see in monks and nuns as human objects of the world: nuns cannot live away from the world as much as monks do because nuns are expected of doing active service in/for the world. Should we need any stereotypical expression for this, here it is: social work is women's work. On the other hand, monks live apart from other people to a greater extent than nuns do because monks are expected to constrain themselves to their confined space called *brotherhood.*

11.3 Conclusion

In this chapter, we have focused on one language (English), one type of dictionary (monolingual pedagogical EFL dictionaries), and, presumably, one culture (say, the English culture that EFL dictionary makers find relevant for TEFL purposes). Naturally, the question of the dictionary-versus-culture interface can easily, and, admittedly, with more conspicuous results, be asked in a cross-linguistic perspective, which is when the same lexical items show convergent and/or divergent cultural qualifications in different languages or different varieties of the same language. Providing that lexicographers do reflect users' understanding of the world and, thus, allow for extra-linguistic considerations to be included in dictionary definitions, what we get in the latter is powerful enhancement of the mere semantic exposition of the word (as when one assumes that lexemes constitute a system) with the values that are inherently cognitive, symbolic, metaphorical, experiential, and subjective (as when one assumes that words are symbols).

In what precedes, the point is exclusively linguistic, not ideological, political, or prescriptive, and has much to do with the necessity of anchoring language analysis, advanced learner's dictionary making included, in the fact, as Mithun (2003: 572) concludes, that "languages are shaped in significant ways by the physiological, cognitive, and contextual circumstances surrounding their use". In other words, this is to appreciate what we hope can become a growing and irresistible tendency of giving dictionary definitions more and more room for, precisely, human agency, in order to open the closed, self-regulating and self-defining system of lexical oppositions in favour of experientially delimited and cognitively driven considerations. These include (i) giving expression to the users' cultural awareness, (ii) recording their relative cognitive tensions, and (iii) demystifying symbols of their experience. Next to the semantic definition of a word, a dictionary reader will then find a huge dose of the world knowledge as reflected in the language. Because it is human cultural experience that shapes language (and not the other way round), the knowledge one finds in the dictionary is what human experience can actually be – unbalanced, unstable, dynamic, vague, loaded with prejudice, and marked with asymmetry. This turns words into social labels that, as such, draw "on social stereotypes, moral attitudes, old connotations and future possibilities – in short, ideologies of various kinds" (Wong *et al.* 2002: 6). Indeed, human experience is so much stained with the subjectivity of the one who verbalizes it that any attempt at objectivizing that experience (e.g. in the form of an autonomous lexical system) can only prove futile and superfluous.

Related topics

Dictionaries and language policy; explaining meaning in lexicographic information tools; dictionaries for translation; dictionaries to assist teaching and learning; lexicography and terminology; learners' dictionaries of English.

Further reading

An introduction to cultural topics in dictionaries is Mugglestone (2011), esp. chapters 4 and 5. Béjoint (2001: ch. 2) shows that the potential cultural differences between the United States, Great Britain, and other English-speaking countries may determine the shape of dictionaries. Equally illustrative is Dollinger (2016), where selected (Austrian, German, and Canadian English) national dictionaries are set *vis-à-vis* the question of cultural identity. The most comprehensive account of the dictionary–culture interface is probably Béjoint (2010), esp. sections 6.1.1 and 6.1.2. That the role and place of cultural insights in dictionaries depend on theoretical linguistics positions can be found in Atkins and Rundell (2008: sections 8.3 and 10.5), Svensén (2009: ch. 16), Mugglestone (2016), and – in reference to bilingual dictionaries and culture-specific expressions – Adamska-Sałaciak (2016).

Notes

1 Technically speaking, this contrast holds between lexemes, not words, because what is listed in dictionaries are lexemes (in the form of headwords), a lexeme being a generalization, an abstraction, a base form for all morphological variants of one and the same unit abstracted from all its occurrences. Quite like a phoneme, then, a lexeme is void of a user's age, sex, gender, attitude, connotation, real-world association, or experience grounding, its primary meaning being the extra-contextual sense it shows in contrastive distinctions with the other lexemes it is related to. Nevertheless, in this contribution, we tend to use *lexemes* and *words* interchangeably, thus obliterating any technical distinction between them. Yet once we ascribe some cultural grounding to lexical units and attempt to identify cultural qualification in dictionary definitions, the preferred term should not be *lexeme*, but *word*.

2 Notice that the defining word for *white*, as in *white man/woman*, is *person*, and the defining word for *black*-via-*Negro* is *member*, which confirms our earlier observation that, at least in EFL dictionaries, whereas *white* tends to be given a personal reference, *black* is referred to quite impersonally. The same applies to (9): although both *black* and *white* are defined with the word *person*, *black* is synonymically identified with *negro* that is defined with the word *member*.

3 For more on the symbolic dimension of words in the context of the language–culture interface, see Łozowski (2012, 2013, 2015).

References

Dictionaries

——— online editions (all accessed in June 2016)

CABED online = COBUILD Advanced British English Dictionary.
www.collinsdictionary.com
CALD online = Cambridge Advanced Learner's Dictionary.
http://dictionary.cambridge.org/dictionary/english/
CED online = Collins English Dictionary.
www.collinsdictionary.com
FD online = The Free Dictionary by Farlex.
www.thefreedictionary.com
LDCE online = Longman Dictionary of Contemporary English.
www.ldoceonline.com
MED online = Macmillan English Dictionary.
www.macmillandictionaries.com
OALD online = Oxford Advanced Learner's Dictionary.
www.oxfordlearnersdictionaries.com

—— printed editions

CCED – *Collins COBUILD English Language Dictionary* (1987, 1st edition) London: Collins ELT.

LDCE – *Longman Dictionary of Contemporary English* (1995, 3rd edition) Harlow: Pearson-Longman.

OALD – *Oxford Advanced Learner's Dictionary* (1948, 1st edition; 1974, 3rd edition; 1989, 4th edition; 2000, 6th edition) Oxford: Oxford University Press.

Other literature

Adamska-Sałaciak, A. (2016) "Explaining Meaning in Bilingual Dictionaries", in P. Durkin (ed.), *The Oxford Handbook of Lexicography*. Oxford: Oxford University Press, pp. 144–162.

Atkins, S. and M. Rundell. (2008) *The Oxford Guide to Practical Lexicography*. Oxford: Oxford University Press.

Béjoint, H. (2000) *Modern Lexicography: An Introduction*. New York: Oxford University Press.

Béjoint, H. (2010) *The Lexicography of English*. Oxford: Oxford University Press.

Dirven, R. and M. Verspoor. (2004) *Cognitive Exploration of Language and Linguistics*, 2nd revised edition. Amsterdam/Philadelphia: John Benjamins Publishing Company.

Dollinger, S. (2016) "National Dictionaries and Cultural Identity: Insights From Austrian, German and Canadian English", in P. Durkin (ed.), *The Oxford Handbook of Lexicography*. Oxford: Oxford University Press, pp. 590–604.

Goodenough, W. H. (1964) "Cultural Anthropology and Linguistics", in D. Hymes (ed.), *Language in Culture and Society: A Reader in Linguistics and Anthropology*. New York: Harper & Row, pp. 36–39.

Levisen, C. and S. Waters. (2015) "*Lige*, a Danish 'Magic Word'? An Ethnopragmatic Analysis", *International Journal of Language and Culture* 2(2): 244–268.

Łozowski, P. (2012) "Experience behind Language: Panchronic Motivation Behind Polish Names of the Months", in E. Cyran, H. Kardela and B. Szymanek (eds.), *Sound, Structure and Sense: Studies in Memory of Edmund Gussmann*. Lublin: Wydawnictwo KUL, pp. 407–420.

Łozowski, P. (2013) "Language *vis-a-vis* Culture in Jerzy Bartmiński's Cognitive Ethnolinguistics", in A. Głaz, J. Danaher and P. Łozowski (eds.), *The Linguistic Worldview: Ethnolinguistics, Cognition and Culture*. London: Versita, pp. 332–351.

Łozowski, P. (2015) "Lexical Semantics with and without Sense Relations: Pig Terms in EFL Dictionaries. In L. Cao and L. Jin (eds.), *New Pilgrimage: Selected Papers From the IAUPE Beijing Conference in 2013*. Beijing: Tsinghua University Press, pp. 321–336.

Ostermann, C. (2015) *Cognitive Lexicography: A New Approach to Lexicography, Making Use of Cognitive Semantics* (Lexicographica. Series Maior. Vol. 149.) Berlin: de Gruyter.

Mithun, M. (2003) "Functional Perspectives on Syntactic Change", in J. Joseph and J. Janda (eds.), *The Handbook of Historical Linguistics* (Blackwell Handbooks in Linguistics 12.) Oxford: Blackwell Publishing Ltd, pp. 552–572.

Mugglestone, L. (2011) *Dictionaries: A Very Short Introduction*. Oxford: Oxford University Press.

Mugglestone, L. (2016) "Description and Prescription in Dictionaries", in P. Durkin (ed.), *The Oxford Handbook of Lexicography*. Oxford: Oxford University Press, pp. 546–560.

Riemer, N. (2010) *Introducing Semantics*. Cambridge: Cambridge University Press.

Svensén, B. (2009) *A Handbook of Lexicography*. Cambridge: Cambridge University Press.

Wong, A., S. J. Roberts and K. Campbell-Kibler. (2002) "Speaking Sex", in K. Campbell-Kibler, M. Podesva, S. J. Roberts and A. Wong (eds.), *Language and Sexuality: Contesting Meaning in Theory and Practice*. Stanford, CA: CSLI Publications, pp. 1–22.

12

Lexicography and natural language processing

Aleš Horák and Adam Rambousek

12.1 Introduction

The chapter introduces links between lexicography and natural language processing in both directions – first, how the lexicographic work benefits from techniques of natural language processing such as word sense disambiguation, semantic similarity measures, named entity recognition, relation extraction, or corpora good example search, and second, intensive exploitation of lexicographic data in language engineering technologies, in the form of general dictionaries or encyclopaedias as well as specialized lexicons, ontologies, or lexicographic databases.

During the last decades, the dictionary publishing process has changed dramatically with regard to how dictionary entry information is obtained. Originally, all instructions and data came from introspective knowledge of lexicographic experts, who carefully and tediously verified all pieces of information in authentic sources. Nowadays, most input for dictionary preparation originates in automatic computer analysis of very large text collections, called text corpora (see Chapters 8, 9, 42, and 43 of this *Handbook*). Of course, all such data still has to undergo a detailed review and amendments by human experts. The resulting dictionary entry is thus more specific, heavily interlinked with supplemental information and well founded with real-world evidence. The techniques of word sense disambiguation allow us to describe specific word meaning in typical usage contexts, and semantic similarity measures offer a numeric value expressing how much two words are interchangeable in certain contexts (thus stating a value of synonymy). Named entities denote parts of text (usually noun phrases), which refer to specific concepts, such as names (of persons, locations, organizations, and so on) or a certain amount of a measurable variable (time, temperature, weight, etc.). Automatic identification of all named entities in texts (with their respective types) together with relation extraction provides a firm basis of all kinds of encyclopaedic knowledge. Practical understanding of abstract data descriptions is enabled by numerous text corpus examples, gathered programmatically and carefully selected by the expert.

Vice versa, the techniques of automatic natural language processing often build upon information from dictionaries, ranging from digitized versions of printed books to specifically oriented electronic lexicons of complex language relations, such as semantic networks, verb frame lexicons or logical ontologies, and knowledge bases. Various kinds of computer lexicons are discussed in detail in the chapter and compared with regard to the respective language technologies.

12.2 Historical perspectives

Computer usage in dictionary writing dates back to the 1960s; however, at that time lexicographers still prepared the dictionary entries on paper, and computer specialists copied the texts into computer databases.

Longman Dictionary of Contemporary English, published in 1978, introduced the restricted vocabulary of words in definitions and use of computers to check if definitions really contained just the words from the list. Dictionary source and electronic edition data also included a special grammar coding system and systematic semantic classification used extensively in natural language processing research (Bouguraev and Briscoe 1987).

The *COBUILD* project, started in 1980, presented a new approach into computer utilization and built a large corpus of contemporary English. Relevant selections from the corpus were printed for the lexicographers. They still worked with paper, but the form of a dictionary entry was structured to correspond to the fields in computer databases (Sinclair 1987).

During the 1990s dictionary publishers started to buy or develop in-house specialized dictionary writing systems, and lexicographers were moving from papers to computers. Thanks to the development of computers and Internet connection, language resources are available online, and dictionary writing systems support the co-operation of geographically distant authors (Rundell 2012: 25).

The major revision project to publish a completely revised third edition of the Oxford English Dictionary started in 2000 with expected completion in 2037 (Brewer 2007). Unlike with printed versions, readers do not have to wait several years for each dictionary volume, but new material is published in the online version every three months (Simpson 2014).

Also many software tools are now being developed and used as support in the dictionary writing process, such as statistical language analysis, corpus querying, or candidates selection. Nevertheless, the main goal of the new lexicographic and language resource tools is not to completely automate the process of resource building, but to help authors with 'tedious' tasks and concentrate on interesting and challenging questions:

> various software tools devised in recent years to streamline corpus-analysis and dictionary-creation process have had the effect of releasing lexicographers from the more banal tasks . . . and the editorial management to produce more systematic, more internally-consistent, and simply better descriptions of language in shorter time.
>
> (Rundell 2012: 29)

12.3 Core issues and topics

In this section, we will first concentrate on selected topics of natural language processing (NLP) that are often advantageously used in lexicographic processes. The supportive tasks provide important data both for dictionary entry headword preparation (collocation extraction, named entity recognition, and word sense disambiguation), as well as interlinks between particular dictionary entries (semantic similarity, relation extraction).

In the second part of this section, an opposite point of view is introduced: how lexicographic resources support various tasks of natural language processing. Here we present a range of resources, including general dictionaries and encyclopaedias or ontologies and semantic networks.

12.3.1 Natural language processing techniques in lexicographic workflow

12.3.1.1 Collocations and named entities

Techniques for automatic recognition of named entities and collocations in large texts can create a basis for headword candidate lists for explanatory dictionaries and encyclopaedias. Collocations are phrases or, generally, multiword expressions that are formed by syntactic or semantic linguistic rules and often denote a specific sense of a lexical item. Examples of collocations include noun phrases (*high school, tropical fish*), terminological terms (*colour hue, trigonometrical subsidiary point)*, phrasal verbs and idiomatic phrases (*blow up, wear off, cry over spilt milk*), or names of entities such as persons, organizations, or places, which are specifically denoted as named entities and handled a little differently.

Standard collocations are usually identified with the use of an association measure; see e.g. Pecina (2009) or Pearce (2002) for an overview of particular methods. As an example, we may mention the measure of (pointwise) *mutual information*, or MI score (Figure 12.1). This measure is originally defined for identifying correlations between random events, which can be understood as a score of how much are two (or more) words related in common texts:

$$MI(w_1, w_2) = \frac{log_2 p(w_1, w_2)}{p(w_1)p(w_2)}$$

Figure 12.1 Calculation of MI score

Here *p(w)* denotes the probability of word "w" occurring in a text and *p(w1,w2)* corresponds to the probability of the two-word phrase "w_1 w_2". For completely independent words the MI score value is zero. The higher the MI score value is, the higher level of *collocability* the measured words express.

Named entities are words or phrases which serve as a name for something – the most common examples are persons (*Barack Obama, Mohandas Karamchand Gandhi*), organizations (*Google, Foreign and Commonwealth Office*), and place names (*Czech Republic, Long Island*), which all represent candidate encyclopaedic headwords. These types of entities are together denoted as ENAMEX ("entity name expression") since the first use in MUC-6 – Message Understanding Conference (Grishman and Sundheim 1996). The term of named entities is also used for expressions of measure and quantity and structured denotations (e.g. phone numbers or e-mail addresses), but these are usually not included in lexicographic processing.

The methods for the *named entity recognition* (*NER*) task can be generally divided into two categories: rule-based techniques and machine learning approaches. The rule-based techniques rely on hand-crafted rules and rule templates accompanied with large collections of names (called "gazetteers"), for example:

(1)

{Mr., Mrs., Ms., . . .} CapitalizedWord → person
CapitalizedWord(s) {company, Ltd., . . .} → organization
CapitalizedWord {Street, Avenue, . . .} → location

The precision of such techniques is high, but preparation of such rules is a tedious process, which cannot handle all examples. Prevailing approaches to the NER task are thus based on machine learning solutions – *supervised* or *semisupervised learning* (Nadeau and Sekine 2007). All these techniques need to be trained on annotated data of sufficient amount, with the semisupervised techniques aiming to reduce the number of examples needed by *bootstrapping*, that is, using a small set of annotated data and a large set of unannotated texts used for detecting other examples by context similarities (Kozareva 2006). The most successful supervised techniques reach a nearly human-level accuracy of above 90 percent based on variations of algorithms such as Conditional Random Fields (CRF) (Finkel et al 2005) or Support Vector Machines (SVM) (Asahara and Matsumoto 2003).

12.3.1.2 Word sense disambiguation

Every dictionary which works with common words and phrases has to cope with *word polysemy*, that is, the fact that many words have more than one meaning (*word sense*) when used in different contexts. An example from *WordNet* (Fellbaum 1998) for the word *fish* as a noun includes:

(2)

1 *fish* – any of various mostly cold-blooded aquatic vertebrates usually having scales and breathing through gills "*The shark is a large fish.*"
2 *fish* – the flesh of fish used as food "*In Japan most fish is eaten raw.*"
3 *Fish* (astrology) – a person who is born while the sun is in Pisces
4 *Pisces, Fish* – the twelfth sign of the zodiac

Being able to identify the correct word sense for a particular occurrence of a word, that is, to solve the task of *word sense disambiguation* (WSD), plays a key role in many NLP applications such as *machine translation, speech synthesis*, or *information retrieval* (e.g. Google web search; see Chapters 29, 42, and 43 of this *Handbook*). From the technical point of view, the WSD task is a classification problem – when given a *sense inventory*, that is, a list of all words and word senses, each word (or phrase) in text obtains a label of particular *word:sense pair* from the list (Navigli 2012). The word "*fish*" in the *shark* sentence earlier (example 2.1) would be labelled as *fish:1* and the Japan food in example 2.2 as *fish:2*. Current approaches use either machine learning techniques, for example, SVM (Mihalcea and Faruque 2004; Zhong and Ng 2010), to train classifiers based on contexts or particular word sense occurrences, or techniques that exploit graph-based knowledge databases using graph traversing algorithms such as Personalized PageRank (Agirre and Soroa 2009). The accuracy of the WSD algorithm is always tightly related to the *level of granularity* on the respective inventory. For fine-grained inventories, the best accuracy is between 60 and 70 percent, and with coarse-grained inventory (i.e. less strict distinctions of senses per word) the accuracy surpasses 80 percent.

From the lexicographic point of view, another task related to word senses is of interest – to identify different senses of a word *without* the need of a sense inventory, only by differentiating the word contexts. This task is called *word sense induction* (WSI), because an automatically constructed sense inventory can be seen as one of the results. Of course, such an automatically identified word sense list serves as a very good basis for dictionary data.

All approaches to the WSI task analyse words via their context information obtained from large corpora. Standard WSI techniques compare the contexts (or the contextual features) and identify *clusters*, that is, groups of similar entities (Pantel and Lin 2002). Finally, each such cluster corresponds to one *word:sense pair*. Recently, the WSI task is also faced using *vector-space models* (Mikolov, Chen et al. 2013) classifying distributional semantic similarities of words and assigning each word meaning a numerical vector representation with the fundamental property that two vectors being (mathematically) close means that the corresponding words (word meanings) are similar. These models expose many interesting features from the linguistic point of view, and their usage allows achieving the best results in tasks related to word sense similarity measures, which are presented in detail in the following section.

12.3.1.3 Semantic similarity measures

A key relationship between entries in many kinds of dictionaries is the *see-also* link, pointing to similar entries or entries with extra details. The actual nature of such links can be very versatile, but in many cases the related entries are *similar* in some respect.

Language processing techniques can identify those kinds of word similarities that are, in some way, expressed in texts. In the simplest case, the word similarity is derived merely from the similarity of their usage contexts. Sophisticated approaches *translate* the contexts to *lists of context features*. An example of such approach are the *word sketches* (Kilgarriff and Rundell 2003) available in the Sketch Engine corpus management system (Kilgarriff et al. 2004). Word sketches are obtained via analysing large tagged corpora (i.e. with word Part-Of-Speech tags) using shallow syntactic relation rules and building tables of several (tens of) word relations such as (being a) *modifier*, *object-of*, or *and/or* compound relation. Examples of such relations for the verb "*develop*" as computed from the British National Corpus (Burnard 2007) are (example 3):

(3)

develop freq = 23,388 (208.48 per million)

- *subject*: scientist, capitalism, researcher, . . .
- *object*: skill, technique, strategy, model, . . .
- *modifier*: rapidly, jointly, fully, . . .
- *and/or*: refine, market, implement, . . .

The whole word sketch of this verb consists of 24 different relation tables allowing thus to represent the verb context in a concise way. Similar words are then identified via a measure of similarity between their word sketches. Using the Sketch Engine automatic thesaurus feature to find words similar to "*develop*" presents us with, for example, *produce, create, provide*, or *establish*.

Specific approaches to word *relation extraction* employ searching word *patterns* in texts to find candidate members of a relation. The patterns can have a form of simple text patterns, such as *sub-class-of (X,Y): "such Y as X"*, or "*X and other Y*", which are either automatically expanded (Snow et al. 2004) or are based on advanced features obtained from syntactic analysis (Fundel et al. 2007) or from external knowledge sources (Mintz et al. 2009).

A new approach based on distributional semantics of words was introduced as an algorithm named Word2Vec by Mikolov, Chen et al. (2013a), where the authors use adapted structures of recurrent neural networks for building a translational model from words to "word embeddings", high-dimensional numerical vectors (internally representing values of "hidden" word features). If such a model is built from very large texts (100 billion words), the resulting vectors express not only word similarity (via simple mathematical measure of vector cosine distance), but are able to model other linguistic-semantic features of words using simple vector operations of addition and subtraction. For example, the relation between the words *man* and *woman* is modelled via subtracting the vector for *man* from the vector for *woman*: $\overrightarrow{(woman)}-\overrightarrow{(man)}$ (Mikolov, Yihand et al. 2013b). The result can then be added to other vectors to obtain a word in the same relation (Figure 12.2):

$$\overrightarrow{(king)}+\overrightarrow{(woman)}-\overrightarrow{(man)}=\overrightarrow{(queen)}$$

Figure 12.2 Word2Vec vector relations

The model is able to represent different kinds of relations such as the grammatical number (*king-kings→queen-queens*), verb tense and aspect (*fall-fell-fallen→draw-drew-drawn*), or comparison (*big-bigger→cold-colder*).

12.3.1.4 Corpora evidence – good example search

To get a better understanding of word meanings, lexicographers look for evidence of use in corpora, which also provide valuable statistical information. Nowadays, very large corpora for many languages are available (Jakubíček et al. 2013), allowing lexicographers to get a very good insight in language use. As summarized by Atkins and Rundell (2008: 61): "We don't actually know how much data we need in order to account for a given linguistic feature . . . What we do know is that the more data we have, the more we learn."

On the other hand, there is a danger in presenting the corpus data directly to the readers of the dictionary and a reason why corpus should mainly be used as background evidence by lexicographers and presented only to skilled users. The biggest corpora are usually acquired from the Web. And although the downloaded data are tidied up, they still contain texts from sources of varied quality, including texts with spelling errors or grammar errors. If such texts are presented directly to the readers in the final dictionary, readers may think it was written by the lexicographers. This point is mentioned for example by Asmussen (2013):

> [users] might consider a concordance as further examples on the use of a certain meaning of a word or expression, but may be confused by the fact that they are often incomplete, may illustrate different meaning of the word or expression to the one in question, and may even show spelling mistakes or uses generally considered substandard.
>
> (Asmussen 2013:1082)

Appropriate language technologies can greatly reduce the time of searching for good "real-world" example sentences (i.e. not introspective "artificial" combinations). The GDEX (Good Dictionary EXamples) tool (Kilgarriff et al. 2008) precomputes and scores thousands of corpus query results (*concordances*) and offers 20 best-scored examples for expert selection. The tool uses measurable qualities of concordances which allow to define the demanded good examples: sentence length (between 10 and 25 words), word frequencies (penalize low-frequency words), pronouns (penalize anaphoric expressions), prominent position of the queried collocation, etc. The tool results are being used in the dictionary preparation process in large publishing houses (Oxford University Press, Macmillan Publishers) as well as in online language learning tools such as SkELL (Sketch Engine for Language Learning (Brain and Suchomel 2014).

12.3.2 Exploitation of lexicographic resources in language engineering technologies

12.3.2.1 Lexicographic databases

A lexical database (or lexicographic database) is a structured resource that contains as much lexicographic information as possible regarding words and lexical units in a language. A lexical database is usually created by experts based on corpus evidence analysis. The database does not need to contain conclusions about the language; however, it should offer all relevant information (e.g. rich selection of example sentences, wide range of collocations, statistical information, etc.). A well-designed and well-built database may be reused for many kinds of dictionaries and serve as a resource for natural language processing applications. For example, Atkins and Rundell (2008) describe the lexical database as a founding resource for dictionary writing.

There are cases of lexical databases compiled by merging existing dictionary entries; for example, the German publisher Duden merged several separate dictionary resources into a combined lexical database called *Wissensnetz deutsche Sprache* (Alexa 2011).

Spohr (2011) proposes to expand the lexical database model to multiple layers (called *pluri-monofunctional lexical database*) and to use such a database to provide customized dictionary information for each user.

Many lexical databases are available for various languages. A selection of recently published or prominent resources is described in the following paragraphs:

- DANTE (Atkins et al. 2010) – an English lexical database, providing detailed information for more than 40,000 most common words of English. As an information resource for the database, 1.7-billion-word corpus was created. The GDEX tool (Kilgarriff et al. 2008 was used to heuristically detect the best example sentences from the corpus. The database is freely available for language research.
- OWID (Müller-Spitzer 2008) – a compilation of several electronic lexicographic resources created at the Institute of the German Language. The database consists of about 300,000 short entries and a detailed description for high-frequency words. All the resources are available online for free, together with non-dictionary resources (e.g. the bibliography of electronic lexicography).
- Pralex (Rangelova and Králík 2007) – a Czech lexical database created by the Institute of Czech Language (ICL) of the Academy of Sciences. The database was compiled using existing dictionaries by ICL, together with the data from the Czech National

Corpus (Kocek et al. 2000). The database contains 213,533 entries and is available for research; a small selection of entries is publicly available. The Pralex database was built using the application described in Horák and Rambousek (2013).

- Cornetto (Vosset et al. 2008) – a lexical semantic database of Dutch, combining a WordNet-like semantic network (from the Dutch wordnet) (Vossen 1998) with a complex lexical database (*Referentiebestand Nederlands* (Maks et al. 1999)). Existing resources were aligned together, expanded with new data, and mapped to the ontology. The Cornetto lexical database was created (and later published) using the tools described in Horák et al. (2008). The database is publicly available without the copyrighted parts from original resources.
- Aralex (Boudelaa and Marslen-Wilson 2010) – a lexical database for Modern Standard Arabic, which is the pan-Arabic variety of Arabic shared throughout the Arab world and used for formal communication. Part of the Aralex preparation was a compilation of annotated Arabic corpus (with 40 million words). The combined lexical database contains information about orthographic forms, stems, roots, word patterns, and much statistical information about words. Aralex is freely available online.

12.3.2.2 Ontologies and semantic networks

Electronic dictionaries and lexicographic databases are designed prevalently for being used by humans. Computer techniques are able to exploit such data, however, mostly in the form of analyzing them as common texts, which always means some percentage of unwanted errors. That is the reason why specialized electronic lexicons and databases for exact computer processing are devised with the most common forms denoted as *ontologies*. Ontologies can be generally divided to three levels (see Chapter 14 of this *Handbook*):

- *upper ontology* (top-level ontology, foundation ontology) – describing very general and abstract concepts that are shared across all knowledge domains,
- *middle-level ontology* – spanning multiple domains and serving as a bridge between upper ontology and individual domain ontologies (best known example is MILO) (Niles and Pease 2001),
- *domain ontology* – representing concepts in one specific domain.

Well-known examples of upper ontologies include Cyc (Lenat et al. 1990), a large commercial ontology developed by Cycorp with smaller subsets released as open source (OpenCyc) and for research (ResearchCyc), or Suggested Upper Merged Ontology (SUMO) (Pease et al. 2002) – the largest freely available and open source formal ontology, owned by IEEE.

Semantic networks as specific kind of ontologies are graph-like collections of words and phrases connected with several kinds of linguistic relations such as hypernymy/hyponymy, synonymy, antonymy, or meronymy/holonymy. WordNet (Fellbaum 1998) is the largest semantic network for the English language, created in the Cognitive Science Laboratory of Princeton University. Parts of WordNet structure are modelled on the evidence of psycholinguistic experiments concerning the theories of human semantic memory and knowledge retrieval. Words (only in lexical categories of nouns, verbs, adjectives, and adverbs) are grouped into sets of cognitive synonyms, called synsets. The current version of WordNet (3.1) contains 155,287 words organized in 117,659 synsets.

POS: noun
Synonyms: car :1, auto :1, automobile :1, machine :4, motorcar :1
Definition: 4-wheeled motor vehicle; usually propelled by an internal combustion engi
Usage: he needs a car to get to work
Domain: tourism
SUMO/MILO: TransportationDevice
-->> [hypernym] motor vehicle:1, automotive vehicle:1
-->> [eng_derivative] automobile:1
<<-- [hyponym] cab:3, hack:5, taxi:1, taxicab:1
<<-- [category_member] backseat:2
<<-- [hyponym] minicar:1
<<-- [hyponym] bus:4, jalopy:1, heap:3
<<-- [mero_part] sunroof:1, sunshine-roof:1
<<-- [category_member] hopped-up:1
<<-- [mero_part] car door:1
<<-- [mero_part] roof:2
<<-- [hyponym] hatchback:1
<<-- [hyponym] loaner:2
<<-- [mero_part] high gear:1, high:7
<<-- [mero_part] window:2
<<-- [mero_part] third gear:1, third:5
<<-- [hyponym] sedan:1
<<-- [hyponym] hardtop:1
<<-- [mero_part] car window:1
<<-- [hyponym] hot rod:1, hot-rod:1
<<-- [mero_part] luggage compartment:1, automobile trunk:1, trunk:4
<<-- [mero_part] stabilizer bar:1, anti-sway bar:1
<<-- [hyponym] jeep:1, landrover:1
<<-- [eng_derivative] automobile:1
<<-- [category_member] passenger:1, rider:4

Figure 12.3 WordNet synset for *car* (sense 1, as a hyponym of *motor vehicle*)

Each synset contains a brief definition (gloss), and most of the synsets are extended with example sentences (see Figure 12.3). All synsets are linked by semantic and lexical relations with hypernymy/hyponymy being the taxonomical relation for nouns, linking more general synsets to more specific synsets (e.g. *cat* is hyponym of *feline*). The hierarchy of verb synsets is expressed by the hypernymy/troponymy relation, representing increasingly specific manner of verb (e.g. *whisper* is a troponym of *talk*). The main relation for adjectives is antonymy, representing strong semantic relationship of "direct" antonyms.

WordNet has been utilized for many purposes in natural language processing, lexicography, or information science, including word sense disambiguation, automatic text generation, text classification, machine translation, or information retrieval.

WordNet inspired many related projects, like building semantic networks for various languages, extending the WordNet with more information, or linking WordNet data to other resources:

- BabelNet (Navigli and Ponzetto 2010) – large multilingual semantic network integrating WordNet and Wikipedia,
- BalkaNet (Christodoulakis 2004) – wordnets for Bulgarian, Czech, Greek, Romanian, Turkish, and Serbian,

- DBPedia (Auer et al. 2007) – extracting structured content from Wikipedia and linking to WordNet,
- EuroWordNet (Vossen 1998) – wordnets for Dutch, Italian, Spanish, German, French, Czech, and Estonian,
- eXtended WordNet (Mihalcea and Moldovan 2001) – enhancing WordNet glosses with syntactic parsing, semantic tagging, and transformation to logical forms,
- ImageNet (Deng et al. 2009) – image database organized according to the WordNet hierarchy.

12.3.2.3 Linked data

The term linked data refers to a methodology for publishing and interlinking lexicographic or structured data online. This methodology was proposed by Berners-Lee (2006), who outlined four rules the data are required to meet for easy sharing and interconnecting:

1 objects are identified by URI (Uniform Resource Identifier, e.g. *http://dbpedia.org/page/Brno*),
2 URI identifiers are HTTP links, where people or software tools can access the data,
3 useful information is provided at the given URI, using the appropriate standards like RDF (the previous URI example contains links to the same information in multiple formats, the RDF format is served at *http://dbpedia.org/data/Brno.rdf*),
4 other objects are referenced using their URIs to get more information (e.g. link from the *Brno.rdf* to *http://dbpedia.org/resource/South_Moravian_Region*).

Berners-Lee later added also the rating system for published data (Bizer et al. 2009) while expanding the term *Linked Data* to *Linked Open Data* – which means Linked Data that are released under an open licence. This rating system is aimed especially at government agencies to encourage them to publish valuable information. The importance of Linked Open Data is acknowledged, for example, by the European Union, funding projects like LOD2 (Auer 2014), a large integrating project to develop tools, standards, and management methods for Linked Open Data, or Open Data Portal (European Union 2016), a catalogue of data available for reuse. The rating system follows these principles (5 stars is the best):

- 1 star – the data are available on the Web in any format, with an open licence.
- 2 stars – the data are published in machine-readable structured format.
- 3 stars – the data use non-proprietary format.
- 4 stars – W3C open standards (RDF and SPARQL) are used to identify objects for linking.
- 5 stars – the data contain links to other resources to give context.

12.4 Looking to the future

12.4.1 User interface adaptation

Many research projects were carried out with regard to dictionary usability and the impact of dictionary design, structure, or content on different tasks required by different groups of users, for example, a difference in word comprehension by learners using either a learner's dictionary or a native speaker dictionary.

With the growing popularity and availability of electronic dictionaries, the focus of research is extending to comparison of usability and contribution to word comprehension between printed dictionaries and electronic dictionaries (for example, Dziemianko 2014; Koyama et al. 2004). Recently, the research area is even shifting to comparing several electronic dictionaries or different methods of dictionary access among themselves, for example research by Chen (2010) and Hill and Laufer (2003).

However, the important question of electronic lexicography is not whether the printed or electronic dictionaries are better, but how can modern electronic dictionaries help their users with the required tasks. Since the beginning of electronic dictionary spread, publishers were not limited by space as in the printed dictionary, and the electronic version of the dictionary is usually an extended version of the printed edition, for example, using full labels instead of abbreviations.

Descriptive labels help unskilled users of dictionaries to better navigate the dictionary and find information in an entry structure (Almind 2005). On the other hand, extending the amount of information (expanding and explaining labels, introducing more examples from corpora, etc.) may be too overwhelming for the users. The situation is even more distinct with the users moving from desktop computers to tablets and mobile phones, where limited space to display the dictionary information is present. Lew (2011) proposes to use different terms for the available size of dictionary data and the amount of information that can be displayed and defines a *presentation space*, that is, how much can be presented (displayed, visualized) at a given time to the dictionary user.

Current research in lexicography is aiming to design and develop tools to allow high level of customization by users, both in terms of dictionary presentation and data provided. Unfortunately, there is not only one set of settings for each user, but different preferred ways depending on a given task. This requirement is summed up for example by Tarp (2012: 115) as "in the real world, the individual needs of individual users may differ from each other and that the concrete data to meet these needs therefore may be slightly different from user to user and from user situation to user situation".

Adaptability of the data and presentation based on users' preferences is the task for electronic dictionaries. The first step in achieving this goal is giving users the possibility to select the "level" (e.g. by age, or proficiency with language) of dictionary they want to work with. This may reflect different editions of printed dictionaries, although it has been found that the distinction of dictionary level as drafted by lexicographers may not be consistent with users' notions. For example, De Schryver and Prinsloo (2011: 26) performed a study with three Dutch dictionaries and concluded that "the intended age group itself prefers the dictionary definitions compiled for the immediately lower age group".

Probably the best way to achieve the desired level of user customization is to employ a lexical database with a well-defined structure containing properly completed lexicographic data and develop the system that will select the right information and present them in a suitable way according to the user's current requirements. This approach is discussed for example by Müller-Spitzer and Möhrs (2008: 43) with regards to the OWID project ("the lexicographic contents are structured granularly and strictly content-based. This technology allows to define user-adapted views of the lexicographic data"), or in an enhanced form by Spohr (2011: 105) when describing the model of what he calls "pluri-monofunctional lexicographic tool, in the sense that it is capable of deriving multiple monofunctional dictionaries".

Currently, several available electronic dictionaries allow their users to select the amount of information and its presentation. The most widespread customization solution lets users choose from several pre-defined user profiles, usually a sort of "short" and "long" version of a dictionary entry. This type is used for example in *Macmillan Dictionary* (Rundell and Others 2002) or *Den Danske Ordbog* (Hjorth and Kristensen 2004). A similar approach is used by several electronic encyclopaedias, offering "simple" and "in-depth" versions of each entry, for example, in Swedish National Encyclopaedia (*Nationalencyclopedin* 2000). The same method is used in the *New Encyclopaedia of the Czech Language*, based on the DEB platform (Rambousek 2015).

Several dictionaries extended this concept to selection of profiles for different situations. For example the Danish phraseological dictionary (Bergenholtz et al 2007) offers a selection from the following categories: 1) *I am reading, but have a reception problem*, 2) *I am writing and want to use a particular expression*, 3) *I am writing and am looking for an expression with a particular meaning*, and 4) *I want to know everything about an expression*. The most flexible customization type is offered by *Oxford English Dictionary*, where users are able to configure which information they want to see (e.g. pronunciation or etymology) (Trap-Jensen 2010).

An adaptive dictionary interface may not only help users to better search for the data, but may also be beneficial for language learning and support language acquisition. Such a dictionary interface, named *RoLo* (Remind on Lookup), was proposed during research by Dang et al. (2013/2). Experimental dictionary interface highlights collocations or meanings that the users previously explored, thus making the search faster and supporting the acquisition of new words in a foreign language. On the other hand, the dictionary interface proposed in *RoLo* project focuses solely on a learner's dictionary and is not applicable generally.

12.4.2 Crowdsourcing

Following the success of *Wikipedia* in collaborative resource editing, many projects and applications emerged that make use of crowdsourcing. In linguistics and NLP research, crowdsourcing is usually used to manually annotate large data sets with semantic or syntactic information (Grác 2013), word sense disambiguation (Rumshisky 2011), or to evaluate the results of automatic tools (Nevěřilová 2014), but may even help to detect epidemic outbreaks (Munro et al. 2012).

The results of crowdsourcing experiments in NLP research were evaluated multiple times, concluding that combining annotation by several "unskilled" annotators may result in cheaper and faster annotation. Snow et al. (2008) evaluated annotation of five linguistic experiments by non-experts and concluded on the text analysis experiment that on average it requires only four non-expert annotations per example to achieve the equivalent ITA (Inter-Annotator Agreement) as a single expert annotator. Callison-Burch (2009) experimented with evaluation of machine translation using crowdsourcing and suggested that by combining the judgments of many non-experts, they are able to achieve the equivalent quality of experts.

In the field of lexicography, the most prominent crowdsourced resource is the *Wiktionary*, a sister project of *Wikipedia*. The goal of *Wiktionary* is to create a freely available "dictionary of all words in all languages" (Wikipedia 2016) edited by volunteers. Although the *Wiktionary* has started in 2002 and is constantly growing in size and number of languages covered, it has been studied and evaluated only in recent years. One of the first qualitative studies was accomplished by Fuertes-Olivera, who compared English and Spanish entries with expert-built lexicons, and he proposed that *Wiktionary* need to enforce "stricter editorial criteria in order to enhance their reliability and their users' confidence." (Fuertes-Olivera 2009: 130). A similar conclusion is suggested in Hanks (2012: 82):

> The hypertext structure [. . .] is eminently suitable as a model for the electronic dictionary of the future. What is needed is some way of ensuring that definitions are properly supported by links to corpus evidence.

Wiktionary is already an enormous structured resource for linguistic research – containing almost 2 million word sense definitions for words from 1,500 languages (497,247 word senses for English). It has already been used in several research projects, including extraction of lexical knowledge (Zesch et al. 2008a) or pronunciation (Schlippe et al. 2010), computation of semantic relatedness of words (Zesch et al. 2008b), or enhancing synonymy networks (Navarro et al. 2009).

12.5 Conclusion

Natural language processing covers a broad range of text and speech analysis, data and knowledge mining techniques, or statistical methods for classification and feature extraction. With the power of automatic processing of huge linguistic evidence in the form of very large corpora, these techniques offer valuable supportive data for lexicographic work, which can both help to concentrate lexicographers on expert decisions and offer an inexhaustible supply of linguistic evidence for every attribute of presented lexicographic results.

Related topics

Lexicography and corpus linguistics; using the Web for lexicographic purposes; information retrieval for lexicographic purposes; domain ontologies; Wordnik.

Further reading

Bergenholtz, H., S. Nielsen, and S. Tarp. (2009). *Lexicography at a Crossroads: Dictionaries and Encyclopedias Today, Lexicographical Tools Tomorrow*. Bern: Peter Lang.

This book aims to describe the state-of-the-art in lexicography at the beginning of the twenty-first century. Several chapters show how lexicography adapts to new information retrieval technologies and present the details on several ongoing lexicographic projects.

Mitkov, R. (2005). *The Oxford Handbook of Computational Linguistics*. Oxford: Oxford University Press.

The book describes major concepts, methods, and applications in computational linguistics. Part I looks at linguistic fundamentals; Part II describes current tasks, techniques, and tools in natural language processing; and Part III surveys language technology applications.

References

Agirre, E. and A. Soroa. (2009) Personalizing PageRank for Word Sense Disambiguation. In *Proceedings of the 12th Conference of the European Chapter of the Association for Computational*

Linguistics. EACL '09. Stroudsburg, PA, USA: Association for Computational Linguistics, pp. 33–41.

Alexa, M. (2011) "Modellierung eines semantischen Wissensnetzes für lexikographische Anwendungen am Beispiel der Duden-Ontologie", *Datenmodellierung für Internetwörterbücher Datenmodellierung für Internetwörterbücher*, p. 61.

Almind, R. (2005) "Designing Internet Dictionaries", *Hermes* 34: 37–54.

Asahara, M. and Y. Matsumoto. (2003) "Japanese Named Entity Extraction with Redundant Morphological Analysis", in *Proceedings of the 2003 Conference of the North American Chapter of the Association for Computational Linguistics on Human Language Technology – Volume 1*. NAACL '03. Stroudsburg, PA: Association for Computational Linguistics, pp. 8–15.

Asmussen, J. (2013) "Combined Products: Dictionary and Corpus," in R. H. Gouws, U. Heid, W. Schweickard and H. E. Wiegand (eds.), *Dictionaries: An International Encyclopedia of Lexicography. Supplementary Volume: Recent Developments With Special Focus on Computational Lexicography*. Berlin/New York: de Gruyter, pp. 1081–1090.

Atkins, B.T.S., A. Kilgarriff and M. Rundell. (2010) "Database of Analysed Texts of English (DANTE): The NEID Database Project", in *Proceedings of the XIV Euralex International Congress. Ljouwert: Afûk*. nl.ijs.si, Leeuwarden: Fryske Akademy; Afûk, pp. 549–556.

Atkins, B.T.S. and M. Rundell. (2008) *The Oxford Guide to Practical Lexicography*. Oxford: Oxford University Press.

Auer, S. (2014) "Introduction to LOD2 – Springer". http://link.springer.com/chapter/10.1007/978-3-319-09846-3_1 [Accessed 24 June 2016].

Auer, S., C. Bizer, G. Kobilarov, J. Lehmann, R. Cyganiak and Z. Ives. (2007) "DBpedia: A Nucleus for a Web of Open Data", in K. Aberer, K-S. Choi, N. Noy, D. Allemang, K-I. Lee, L. Nixon, J. Golbeck, P. Mika, D. Maynard, R. Mizoguchi, G. Schreiber and P. Cudré-Mauroux (eds.), *The Semantic Web*. Lecture Notes in Computer Science. Berlin Heidelberg: Springer, pp. 722–735.

Baisa, V. and V. Suchomel. (2014) "SkELL: Web Interface for English Language Learning", in A. Horák and P. Rychlý (eds.), *Eighth Workshop on Recent Advances in Slavonic Natural Language Processing*. Brno: Tribun EU, pp. 63–70.

Bergenholtz, H., V. Vrang, and R. Almind. (2007) "Ordbogen over faste vendinger". www.forskningsdatabasen.dk/en/catalog/2186115941 [Accessed 24 June 2016].

Berners-Lee, T. (2006) "Design Issues: Linked Data". www.w3.org/DesignIssues/LinkedData.html [Accessed 1 February 2017].

Bizer, C., T. Heath and T. Berners-Lee. (2009) "Linked Data – the Story So Far", in Ap. P. Sheth (ed.), *Semantic Services, Interoperability and Web Applications: Emerging Concepts*, Hershey, PA: Information Science Reference - Imprint of: IGI Publishing, pp. 205–227.

Boguraev, B. and T. Briscoe. (1987) "Large Lexicons for Natural Language Processing: Utilising the Grammar Coding System of LDOCE", *Computational Linguistics* 13(3–4), pp. 203–218.

Boudelaa, S. and W. D. Marslen-Wilson. (2010) "Aralex: A Lexical Database for Modern Standard Arabic", *Behavior Research Methods* 42(2), pp. 481–487.

Brewer, C. (2007) *Treasure-House of the Language: The Living OED*. New Haven, CT: Yale University Press.

Burnard, L. (ed.) (2007) *Reference Guide for the British National Corpus (XML Edition)*, Oxford: Oxford University Computing Services.

Callison-Burch, C. (2009) "Fast, Cheap, and Creative: Evaluating Translation Quality Using Amazon's Mechanical Turk", in *Proceedings of the 2009 Conference on Empirical Methods in Natural Language Processing: Volume 1 – Volume 1*. EMNLP '09. Stroudsburg, PA: Association for Computational Linguistics, pp. 286–295.

Chen, Y. (2010) "Dictionary Use and EFL Learning: A Contrastive Study of Pocket Electronic Dictionaries and Paper Dictionaries", *International Journal of Lexicography* 23(3): 275–306.

Christodoulakis, D. (2004) *Balkanet Final Report. University of Patras, DBLAB. No*, IST-2000-29388.

Dang, T.-D., G-D. Chen, G. Dang, Li, L.-Y. and N. Nurkhamid. (2013/2) "RoLo: A Dictionary Interface That Minimizes Extraneous Cognitive Load of Lookup and Supports Incidental and Incremental Learning of Vocabulary", *Computers and Education* 61: 251–260.

Deng, J., W. Dong, R. Socher, L. J. Li, K. Li and L. Fei-Fei. (2009) "ImageNet: A Large-Scale Hierarchical Image Database", in *Computer Vision and Pattern Recognition, 2009. CVPR 2009. IEEE Conference on.* ieeexplore.ieee.org, pp. 248–255.

De Schryver, G.-M. and D. J. Prinsloo. (2011) "Do Dictionaries Define on the Level of Their Target Users? A Case Study for Three Dutch Dictionaries", *International Journal of Lexicography* 24(1): 5–28.

Dziemianko, A. (2014) "On the Presentation and Placement of Collocations in Monolingual English Learners' Dictionaries: Insights Into Encoding and Retention", *International Journal of Lexicography* 27(3): 259–279.

European Union. (2016) "European Union Open Data Portal". http://data.europa.eu/euodp/en/data [Last accessed 1 February 2017].

Fellbaum, C. (ed.) (1998) *Wordnet: An Electronic Lexical Database*. Cambridge, MA: MIT Press.

Finkel, J. R., T. Grenager and C. Manning. (2005) "Incorporating Non-Local Information Into Information Extraction Systems by Gibbs Sampling", in K. Knight, H.Tou Ng and K. Oflazer (eds.), *Proceedings of the 43rd Annual Meeting on Association for Computational Linguistics*. ACL '05. Stroudsburg, PA: Association for Computational Linguistics, pp. 363–370.

Fuertes-Olivera, P. A. (2009) "The Function Theory of Lexicography and Electronic Dictionaries: WIKTIONARY as a Prototype of Collective Free Multiple-Language Internet Dictionary", in H. Bergenholtz, S. Nielsen and S. Tarp (eds.), *Lexicography at a Crossroads: Dictionaries and Encyclopedias Today, Lexicographical Tools Tomorrow*. Bern: Peter Lang, pp. 99–134.

Fundel, K., R. Küffner and R. Zimmer. (2007) "RelEx – Relation Extraction Using Dependency Parse Trees", *Bioinformatics* 23(3): 365–371.

Grác, M. (2013) *Rapid Development of Language Resources*. Ph.D. Masaryk University. http://is.muni.cz/th/50728/fi_d/thesis.pdf.

Grishman, R. and B. Sundheim. (1996) "Message Understanding Conference-6: A Brief History", in *COLING*. alta.asn.au, pp. 466–471.

Hanks, P. (2012) "Corpus Evidence and Electronic Lexicography", in S. Granger and M. Paquot (eds.), *Electronic Lexicography*. Oxford: Oxford University Press, pp. 57–82.

Hill, M. and B. Laufer. (2003) "Type of Task, Time-on-Task and Electronic Dictionaries in Incidental Vocabulary Acquisition", *IRAL, International Review of Applied Linguistics in Language Teaching: Revue internationale de linguistique appliquee enseignement des langues. Internationale Zeitschrift fur angewandte Linguistik in der Spracherziehung* 41(2): 87–106.

Hjorth, E. and K. Kristensen. (2004) *Den danske ordbog*, Danske Sprog-og Litteraturselskab.

Horák, A. and A. Rambousek. (2013) "PRALED – A New Kind of Lexicographic Workstation", in A. Przepiórkowski, M., Piasecki, K. Jassem and P. Fuglewicz (eds.), *Computational Linguistics*. Studies in Computational Intelligence. Springer Berlin Heidelberg, pp. 131–141.

Horák, A., P. Vossen and A. Rambousek. (2008) "A Distributed Database System for Developing Ontological and Lexical Resources in Harmony", in A. Gelbukh (ed.), *Computational Linguistics and Intelligent Text Processing*. Lecture Notes in Computer Science. International Conference on Intelligent Text Processing and Computational Linguistics. Springer Berlin Heidelberg, pp. 1–15.

Jakubíček, M., A. Kilgarriff, V. Kovář, P. Rychlý and V. Suchomel. (2013) "The TenTen Corpus Family", in *7th International Corpus Linguistics Conference CL*. sketchengine.co.uk, pp. 125–127.

Kilgarriff, A., M. Husák, K. McAdam, M. Rundell and P. Rychlý. (2008) "GDEX: Automatically Finding Good Dictionary Examples in a Corpus", in *Proceedings of the XIII EURALEX International Congress (Barcelona, 15–19 July 2008)*. dialnet.unirioja.es, pp. 425–432.

Kilgarriff, A., P. Rychly, P. Smrz and D. Tugwell. (2004) "The Sketch Engine", *Information Technology* 105: 116.

Kilgarriff, A. and M. Rundell. (2003) "Lexical Profiling Software and Its Lexicographic Applications: A Case Study", in *Proceedings of the Tenth EURALEX International Congress, EURALEX 2002: Copenhagen, Denmark, August 13–17, 2002*. dialnet.unirioja.es, pp. 807–818.

Kocek, J., M. Koprivová and V. Schmiedtová. (2000) "The Czech National Corpus", in *Proceedings of the Ninth EURALEX International Congress, EURALEX 2000: Stuttgart, Germany, August 8th–12th, 2000*, pp. 127–132.

Koyama, T. and O. Takeuchi. (2004) "How Look-Up Frequency Affects EFL Learning? An Empirical Study on the Uuse of Handheld-Electronic Dictionaries", in the CLaSIC 2004 Conference. http://kuir.jm.kansai-u.ac.jp/dspace/handle/10112/5189.

Kozareva, Z. (2006) "Bootstrapping Named Entity Recognition with Automatically Generated Gazetteer Lists", in S. Pado, J. Read and V. Seretan (eds.), *Proceedings of the Eleventh Conference of the European Chapter of the Association for Computational Linguistics: Student Research Workshop*. EACL '06. Stroudsburg, PA: Association for Computational Linguistics, pp. 15–21.

Lenat, D. B., R. V. Guha, K. Pittman, D. Pratt and M. Shepherd. (1990) "Cyc: Toward Programs with Common Sense", *Communications of the ACM* 33(8): 30–49.

Lew, R. (2011) "Space Restrictions in Paper and Electronic Dictionaries and Their Implications for the Design of Production Dictionaries". https://repozytorium.amu.edu.pl/handle/10593/799.

Maks, I., W. Martin and H. de Meerseman. (1999) *RBN Manual*. Amsterdam: Vrije Universiteit.

Mihalcea, R. and E. Faruque. (2004) "Senselearner: Minimally Supervised Word Sense Disambiguation for All Words in Open Text", in *Proceedings of ACL/SIGLEX Senseval*. aclweb.org, pp. 155–158.

Mihalcea, R. and D. I. Moldovan. (2001) "Extended Wordnet: Progress Report". http://digital.library.unt.edu/ark:/67531/metadc83309/.

Mikolov, T., K. Chen, G. Corrado and J. Dean. (2013) "Efficient Estimation of Word Representations in Vector Space", *arXiv [cs.CL]*. http://arxiv.org/abs/1301.3781.

Mikolov, T., W.-T. Yihand and G. Zweig. (2013) "Linguistic Regularities in Continuous Space Word Representations", in *HLT-NAACL*. aclweb.org, pp. 746–751.

Mintz, M., S. Bills, R. Snow and D. Jurafsky. (2009) "Distant Supervision for Relation Extraction without Labeled Data", in *Proceedings of the Joint Conference of the 47th Annual Meeting of the ACL and the 4th International Joint Conference on Natural Language Processing of the AFNLP: Volume 2 – Volume 2*. ACL '09. Stroudsburg, PA: Association for Computational Linguistics, pp. 1003–1011.

Müller-Spitzer, C. (2008) "The Lexicographic Portal of the IDS: Connecting Heterogeneous Lexicographic Resources by a Consistent Concept of Data Modelling", in *Proceedings of the XIII EURALEX International Congress (Barcelona, 15–19 July 2008)*. dialnet.unirioja.es, pp. 457–461.

Müller-Spitzer, C. and C. Möhrs. (2008) "First Ideas of User-Adapted Views of Lexicographic Data Exemplified on OWID and Elexiko", in *Proceedings of the Workshop on Cognitive Aspects of the Lexicon*. COGALEX '08. Stroudsburg, PA: Association for Computational Linguistics, pp. 39–46.

Munro, R., L. Gunasekara, S. Nevins, L. Polepeddi and E. Rosen. (2012) "Tracking Epidemics with Natural Language Processing and Crowdsourcing", in *2012 AAAI Spring Symposium Series*.

Nadeau, D. and S. Sekine. (2007) "A Survey of Named Entity Recognition and Classification", *Lingvisticae Investigationes* 30(1): 3–26.

Nationalencyklopedin. (2000) NE Nationalencyklopedin.

Navarro, E., F. Sajous, B. Gaume, L. Prévot, H. ShuKai, K. Tzu-Yi and H. Chu-Ren. (2009) "Wiktionary and NLP: Improving Synonymy Networks", in *Proceedings of the 2009 Workshop on The People's Web Meets NLP Collaboratively Constructed Semantic Resources – People's Web '09*. The 2009 Workshop. Morristown, NJ: Association for Computational Linguistics, pp. 19–27.

Navigli, R. (2012) "A Quick Tour of Word Sense Disambiguation, Induction and Related Approaches", in M. Bieliková, G. Friedrich, G Gottlob, S. Katzenbeisser and G. Turáneds. *SOFSEM 2012: Theory and Practice of Computer Science*. Lecture Notes in Computer Science. International Conference on Current Trends in Theory and Practice of Computer Science. Springer Berlin Heidelberg, pp. 115–129.

Navigli, R. and S. P. Ponzetto. (2010) "BabelNet: Building a Very Large Multilingual Semantic Network", in *Proceedings of the 48th Annual Meeting of the Association for Computational Linguistics*. ACL '10. Stroudsburg, PA: Association for Computational Linguistics, pp. 216–225.

Nevěřilová, Z. (2014) *Paraphrase and Textual Entailment Generation in Czech*. Ph.D. Masaryk University. https://is.muni.cz/th/3839/fi_d/.

Niles, I. and A. Pease. (2001) "Towards a Standard Upper Ontology", In *Proceedings of the International Conference on Formal Ontology in Information Systems – Volume 2001*. FOIS '01. New York: ACM, pp. 2–9.

Pantel, P. and D. Lin. (2002) "Discovering Word Senses From Text", in *Proceedings of the Eighth ACM SIGKDD International Conference on Knowledge Discovery and Data Mining*. KDD '02. New York: ACM, pp. 613–619.

Pearce, D. (2002) "A Comparative Evaluation of Collocation Extraction Techniques", in *LREC*. lrec-conf.org. www.lrec-conf.org/proceedings/lrec2002/pdf/169.pdf.

Pease, A., I. Niles. and J. Li. (2002) "The Suggested Upper Merged Ontology: A Large Ontology for the Semantic Web and Its Applications", in *Working notes of the AAAI-2002 Workshop on Ontologies and the Semantic Web*. aaai.org. www.aaai.org/Papers/Workshops/2002/WS-02-11/WS02-11-011.pdf.

Pecina, P. (2009) "Lexical Association Measures and Collocation Extraction", *Language Resources and Evaluation* 44(1–2): 137–158.

Rambousek, A. (2015) *Creation and Management of Structured Language Resources*. Ph.D. Masaryk University. http://is.muni.cz/th/60380/fi_d/dissertation.pdf.

Rangelova, A. and J. Králík. (2007) "Wider Framework of the Research Plan Creation of a Lexical Database of the Czech Language of the Beginning of the 21st Century", *Proceedings of the Computer Treatment of Slavic and East European Languages*: 209–217.

Rumshisky, A. (2011) "Crowdsourcing Word Sense Definition", in *Proceedings of the 5th Linguistic Annotation Workshop*. LAW V '11. Stroudsburg, PA: Association for Computational Linguistics, pp. 74–81.

Rundell, M. (2012) "The Road to Automated Lexicography: An Editor's Viewpoint", in S. Granger and M. Paquot (eds.), *Electronic Lexicography*. Oxford: Oxford University Press, pp. 15–30.

Rundell, M. et al. (2002) *Macmillan English Dictionary: For Advanced Learners*. London: Palgrave Macmillan.

Schlippe, T., S. Ochs and T. Schultz. (2010) "Wiktionary as a Source for Automatic Pronunciation Extraction", *Interspeech* (2010), 2290–2293.

Simpson, J. (2014) "What Would Dr Murray Have Made of the OED Online Today", *Slovenščina* 2(2): 2.

Sinclair, J. M. (1987) *Looking Up: An Account of the COBUILD Project in Lexical Computing and the Development of the Collins COBUILD English Language Dictionary*. London: Collins ELT.

Snow, R., B. O'Connor, D. Jurafsky and A. Y. Ng. (2008) "Cheap and Fast – But Is It Good? Evaluating Non-Expert Annotations for Natural Language Tasks", in *Proceedings of the Conference on Empirical Methods in Natural Language Processing – EMNLP '08*. The Conference. Morristown, NJ: Association for Computational Linguistics, p. 254.

Snow, R., D. Jurafsky and A. Y. Ng. (2004) "Learning Syntactic Patterns for Automatic Hypernym Discovery", *Advances in Neural Information Processing Systems 17*. Advances in Neural Information Processing Systems (NIPS 2004). ilpubs.stanford.edu. http://ilpubs.stanford.edu:8090/665 [Accessed 23 June 2016].

Spohr, D. (2011) "A Multi-Layer Architecture for Plurimonofunctional Dictionaries", in P. A. Fuertes-Olivera and H. Bergenholtz (eds.), *e-Lexicography: The Internet, Digital Initiatives and Lexicography*. London: Continuum, pp. 103–120.

Tarp, S. (2012) "Theoretical Challenges in the Transition From Lexicographical P-Works to E-Tools", in S. Granger and M. Paquot (eds.), *Electronic Lexicography*. Oxford: Oxford University Press, pp. 107–118.

Trap-Jensen, L. (2010) "One, Two, Many: Customization and User Profiles in Internet Dictionaries", in *Proceedings of the XIV Euralex International Congress*. euralex.org, pp. 1133–1143.
Vossen, P. (1998) *EuroWordNet: A Multilingual Database with Lexical Semantic Networks*. P. Vossen, ed. The Netherlands: Springer.
Vossen, P., I. Maks, R. Segers and H. van der Vliet. (2008) "Integrating Lexical Units, Synsets and Ontology in the Cornetto Database", in N. Calzolari (Conference Chair), K. Choukri, B. Maegaard, J. Mariani, J. Odijk, S. Piperidis, D. Tapias (eds.), *Proceedings of the Sixth International Conference on Language Resources and Evaluation (LREC'08)*. European Language Resources Association (ELRA). http://citeseerx.ist.psu.edu/viewdoc/download?doi=10.1.1.484.1045&rep=rep1&type=pdf Wiktionary. Available at: https://en.wiktionary.org/.
Zesch, T., C. Müller and I. Gurevych. (2008a) "Extracting Lexical Semantic Knowledge From Wikipedia and Wiktionary", in N. Calzolari (Conference Chair), K. Choukri, B. Maegaard, J. Mariani, J. Odijk, S. Piperidis, D. Tapias (eds.), *Proceedings of the Sixth International Conference on Language Resources and Evaluation (LREC'08)*, pp. 1646–1652.
Zesch, T., C. Müller and I. Gurevych. (2008b) "Using Wiktionary for Computing Semantic Relatedness", In *AAAI'08 Proceedings of the 23rd National Conference on Artificial Intelligence – Volume 2*. Menlo Park, CA: AAAI Press, pp. 861–866.
Zhong, Z. and H. T. Ng. (2010) "It Makes Sense: A Wide-Coverage Word Sense Disambiguation System for Free Text", in *Proceedings of the ACL 2010 System Demonstrations*. ACLDemos '10. Stroudsburg, PA: Association for Computational Linguistics, pp. 78–83.

13

Lexicography and information science

Theo J. D. Bothma

13.1 Introduction

The discipline of information science per definition deals with data, information and knowledge, and the interrelationships between these concepts. There are many definitions for these concepts, and it is not the purpose of this chapter to discuss different definitions. There are a number of sub-disciplines in information science, *inter alia* information and knowledge management, information organisation and retrieval, information behaviour and seeking, information ethics, law, philosophy, politics and economics, digital libraries and repositories, indigenous information systems and indigenous knowledge, the information and knowledge society, etc. Common to all these sub-disciplines is that, in all cases, the relationship between data/information/knowledge, humans and (information and communication) technology is studied. In some cases the emphasis is on the relationship between all three components, in others between only two components, for example between humans and information, or between technology and information. Humans typically refer to end users, that is, the people that eventually use the information for work, leisure, study and so forth. Technology currently refers mostly to information and communication technologies in the form of modern e-technologies, but information used to be and can still be organised and managed, etc., in paper-based and other formats. Each sub-discipline in information science has a number of different theories, and these are discussed in the literature in depth, and often quite acrimoniously with little consensus. A few examples are briefly discussed in Section 13.2.

Lexicography in essence also deals with data, information and knowledge (even though the definitions of these concepts may differ from those of information science), humans and technology and the interaction between these three components. The data may be essentially data about words and words in combination with other words (for example collocations, fixed expressions and so forth). Humans are typically end users, as is the case in information science, and the technology used may be 'old' technology (paper) or e-technology. There are a number of theories of lexicography and within these theories different approaches; this is discussed in more detail in this volume. Bothma, Gouws and Prinsloo (2016: 110) summarise this as follows:

> A modern general lexicographic theory should be anchored in three fundamental phases of the early development of lexicographic theory, see Gouws 2005, i.e. Zgusta's

approach with the linguistic contents of dictionaries at the core, Wiegand's focus on dictionary structures and Bergenholtz and Tarp's emphasis on lexicographic functions.

There are, however, those that are strongly of the opinion that there is no such thing as a theory of lexicography and that lexicography is only practice, specifically the practice of making dictionaries, for example Atkins and Rundell (2008: 4). See also Gouws 2015 and Chapter 1 in this book for a discussion on lexicographic theories, as well as Tarp 2012 for a brief discussion.

If an e-dictionary is developed within the framework of the *Function Theory*, the end user typically has a number of options to access the data, based on the types of information need defined in the theory. That is, the lexicographer has decided that, if the user needs information for a text reception information need, a predefined set of data will be displayed on screen, and if she or he has a text production information need, a different predefined set of data will be displayed. Many of the dictionaries produced at the Centre for Lexicography at Aarhus University (in future referred to by their standard abbreviation, Centlex) follow this paradigm; see, for example, Tarp 2008; Fuertes-Olivera et al. 2013; Fuertes-Olivera and Tarp 2014; Tarp 2015 and the references listed in these publications, as well as the Centlex dictionaries at Ordbogen.com.

From this very brief discussion, it is evident that there are a number of commonalities between information science and lexicography, and a number of researchers have pointed this out in the recent past. This could imply that information science can learn from lexicography at the level of theory and practice, and vice versa. Obviously, however, these commonalities are not evident in all sub-disciplines of information science and of lexicography. In both cases, the eventual use of the data by end users is the reason why the data are organised, in both cases the data are retrieved by end users and in both cases, especially currently, e-technologies, that is, modern information and communication technologies, play an important role in how the data are organised and how they are retrieved. Both disciplines have used computers since their popularisation in the 1980s to organise and retrieve data/information, in both cases moving from originally paper-based systems to digital systems, in both cases using database systems for organising the data and search algorithms for retrieving the data. In both cases, end users need to understand how the information source is organised and how to access data optimally; therefore, in both cases literacy about the resources is needed, called information literacy and dictionary literacy, respectively.

13.2 Historical perspective: a brief introduction to some topics and theories of information science

This section provides a high-level overview of some of the sub-disciplines and related theories of information science that could provide a wider context to this chapter.

Research in knowledge management started in the early 1990s. Many approaches to knowledge management exist. In this chapter, only the early seminal research of Nonaka and Takeuchi (1995) and Davenport and colleagues (for example, Davenport, De Long and Beers 1998) is mentioned, as well as the research by Snowden and others (for example, Snowden 2000; Snowden 2002; Kurz and Snowden 2003, extended in Snowden 2013). A vast research literature on knowledge management has appeared since the earliest research, and the reader is referred to Bolisani and Handzic (2015) for an overview of past and current research and predictions for the future.

Information retrieval has its own set of theories, one of the most recent being interactive information retrieval, as described in Ingwersen and Järvelin 2005 (see Chapters 9, 12 and 43 of this *Handbook* for an overview of the role information retrieval plays in lexicography). Information retrieval also deals with recall and precision, that is, the percentage of documents form a collection that is recalled and the percentage of these documents that are actually relevant to the original information need. This relates more to a mathematical/algorithmic approach to retrieval; the most important projects in this regard are the Trec and Clef projects.[1] The latter focuses mostly on multi-language/cross-language information retrieval.

Information-seeking behaviour has been studied in detail by numerous researchers, and a number of books provide good overviews of research, frameworks and models. This includes, but is not limited to, Case and Given 2016; Fisher, Erdelez and McKechnie (eds.) 2005; Ford 2015; Ingwersen and Järvelin 2005; Kuhlthau 2003; and Kuhlthau, Maniotes and Caspari 2015.

Relevance of retrieved results to the information need of the user is paramount in information science. Relevance theory and relevance studies started with the research of Tefko Saracevic in the 1960s, who recently, in a keynote at the *LIDA 2016 Conference* in Zadar, Croatia, stated that *relevance* is *the* basic notion in information science. Much research has been published on the topic. See, for example, the critical reviews by Saracevic 2015; Saracevic 2016; and also Cosijn 2003; Cosijn and Bothma 2005; and Cosijn and Ingwersen 2000.

Information organisation (often also known as knowledge organisation) deals primarily with the description of the so-called 'is-ness' and 'about-ness' of information objects, which results in the production of a surrogate of the information object on the basis of which retrieval was done before full-text retrieval became generally available. In the traditional library environment, the process that assigns the descriptions is called cataloguing and classification. Many different systems have been developed throughout the years, some of the most common being Resource Description and Access (RDA), Anglo-American Cataloguing Rules (AACR2), Dewey Decimal Classification (or System) (DDC), MARC 21 Format for Classification Data (MARC = MAchine Readable Cataloging) and Library of Congress Subject Headings (LCSH).[2]

In the Web and many other environments, a subset of elements was developed to describe information objects, namely the Dublin Core Metadata Initiative (DCMI).[3] The Dublin Core (DC) metadata set contains 15 elements,[4] which is too restricted to describe all information objects in sufficient detail. The Dublin Core set of elements is therefore often combined with other metadata schemas in in the Resource Description Framework (RDF).[5] There are many discipline-related metadata schemas.[6]

Providing a user with precisely the information she or he needs to solve an information need is an important principle in information science, even though most research in this environment has been done in computer science, and specifically in the sub-discipline of adaptive hypertext and hypermedia and profiling research (see Brusilovsky 1996; Brusilovsky and Maybury 2002; Brusilovksy and Millán 2007; and, for a brief summary of relevant details, Bothma 2011).

Interfaces to digital systems need to be evaluated to determine whether they fulfil their role to provide access to relevant information for end-users. Principles of human computer interaction (HCI) and usability studies are therefore very important in the design of any system. Extensive research on this has been undertaken by Jacob Nielsen (see, for example, Nielsen 1994; Nielsen and Budiu 2012; Nielsen and Loranger 2006), Ben Shneiderman and colleagues (see, for example, Shneiderman et al. 2016), Jenny Preece (see Preece and Sharp 2015) and many others.

Information literacy is the sub-discipline in information science that relates to teaching users the skills set of knowing about different information sources and how to find, retrieve, evaluate, analyse and use information. There are a number of frameworks/theories of information literacy, for example the Big Six,[7] the framework of the Association for College and Research Libraries (ACRL)[8] and the Australian and New Zealand Information Literacy Framework.[9] All these frameworks cover the same aspects, often only with different terms and different groupings of sub-topics. Information literacy is often linked to computer literacy, seen as related to media literacy, and included in a number of literacies under various umbrella terms, such as *digital literacies/skills* (see, for example, Van Dijk and Van Deursen 2014).

There are many further sub-disciplines of information science, which include (but is not limited to) information ethics, law, economics and politics, the information and knowledge society, as well as sub-disciplines that relate more to librarianship and library science (such as library management). These topics are not dealt with further, and therefore no details about research in these fields are provided.

Theory usually also links to practice – theories of information science are often reflections on how data, information and knowledge are managed, stored, retrieved, etc., in practice, trying to systematise practice, or abstract rules from practice that explain practice and that can be generalised to other situations.

13.3 Core issues and topics: linking information science theory and practice to lexicography

This section links the topics and theories mentioned in the preceding section with specifically the *Function Theory* of lexicography. It provides examples of how information science theories relate to lexicographic research (and more specifically e-lexicographic research), and vice versa. The following topics are addressed:

- User information needs and user information behaviour
- Access to data and information
- Relevance theory
- Information/dictionary literacy.

13.3.1 User information needs and user information behaviour

At Centlex, much research has been done by Henning Bergenholtz, Sven Tarp and their colleagues in formulating the *Function Theory* of lexicography and to compile especially mono-functional dictionaries within this theoretical framework (see Part 1 of this *Handbook* and references in Section 13.1). The theory focuses on end-user information needs in a specific situation, viz. communicative, cognitive, operative and interpretive situations:

1 Communicative situations where a need to solve a communication problem may occur.
2 Cognitive situations where a need for knowledge may occur.
3 Operative situations where a need for instructions on how to perform a physical or mental action may occur.
4 Interpretive situations where a need to interpret and understand a sign, signal, symbol etc. may occur.

(Bothma and Tarp 2012: 90)

The four situations are described briefly in Bothma and Tarp 2012: 90–92. It is, however, dealt with in considerable detail by Sven Tarp in his 2008 book (Tarp 2008). (See also Fuertes-Olivera and Tarp 2014, Tarp 2015 and in many other publications by Tarp, Bergenholtz and many others, and also in Part 1 and Chapters 6, 15, 16, 17, 27 and 28 of this *Handbook*; they all discuss the main tenets of the *Function Theory* and its applications when making specific dictionary projects).

Already in 2009, Tarp suggested that user needs may be further refined:

- [S]cientific lexicography would above all be interested in knowing in which situations – e.g. reception and production – these needs may occur. Then it would set itself the task of uncovering the needs users have in the last 20 percent of the look-ups, i.e. in one out of five consultations. And it would not stop here, but would try to go even deeper into the problem in order to discover the needs that only show up in one out of a hundred or one out of a thousand consultations. (Tarp 2009b: 292)
- [. . .] or, even more rarely, in order to conceive dictionaries capable of meeting all the users' needs in specific types of situations. (Tarp 2009b: 292)
- [. . .] dynamic articles [. . .] structured in different ways according to each type of search criteria. ' [. . .] articles that are especially adapted [. . .] ; [. . .] define their own profile [. . .] ; [. . .] one direction will probably be the 'individualization' of the lexical product, adapting to the concrete needs of a concrete user. (Tarp 2009a: 57, 59, 61)

From these quotations it is clear that Tarp envisaged further refinements to data presentation on demand. I have tried to show what technologies are currently available to make these ideas feasible (for example in Bothma 2011), both in terms of limiting data through filtering and profiling, as well as enabling the user to obtain more data for support in specific usage situations.

End-user information needs are not abstract, as explained in Bothma and Tarp 2012: 90:

> According to the function theory, the types of information needs relevant to lexicography should never be considered abstract needs, but specific and even concrete needs which are determined by the types of *potential users* of lexicography's practical works as well as the types of extra-lexicographical *situations* where lexicographically relevant information needs may occur, i.e. needs that may be satisfied by lexicographical tools. Of these *two determining factors*, the most important is the extra-lexicographical situation which also determines how many of the various lexicographically relevant characteristics of a potential type of user are relevant in each case. This also means that user needs should always be understood in their intimate relation to a specific type of situation and that they can never be defined only based upon the characteristics of a potential user however relevant these characteristics may be.

Bothma and Tarp (2012: 92) conclude that:

> [T]he function theory does not only study the processes taking place from the moment the user starts a consultation process to the moment where the needed information is retrieved from the lexicographical data, i.e. the intra-lexicographical consultation processes. It also studies the extra-lexicographical processes taking place immediately before and after the consultation process. The reason for this approach is double: on the

> one hand it is necessary to know in which situation the lexicographically relevant information needs occur in order to determine the nature of these needs, and on the other hand, it is absolutely necessary to evaluate the post-lexicographical process in order to establish an objective criterion for success or failure instead of the subjective one used by questionnaires and the like.[10]

The process described here is represented in Figure 13 (see also Bergenholtz and Bothma 2011).

The *Function Theory* describes the context in which the information need is experienced and the processes according to which the interactive information retrieval occurs in limited detail. This is specified in much more detail in some theories of information science, for example, Ingwersen 2001; Ingwersen 2007; Ingwersen and Järvelin 2004; Ingwersen and Järvelin 2005; and Järvelin and Ingwersen 2012. They define six context dimensions in interactive information retrieval (IIR), viz. intra-object structures (dimension 1 in Figure 13.2); inter-object structures (dimension 2); the session context dealing with features (evidence) of the interaction (or activity) (dimension 3); social, systemic, domain and work task contexts which can be either individual (dimension 4a) or collective (dimension 4b); techno-economic-politico-societal infrastructures (dimension 5); and the historic context operating across this stratification (dimension 6) (Ingwersen 2007). These context domains are represented diagrammatically in Figure 13.2.

Ingwersen (2007) explains the different context domains as follows:

1 intra-object contexts in the model – signs in context of sign structures or elements, constituting objects;
2 inter-object structures refer to social networking, hyperlinks or citations between objects, identifying the research framework component in question (the core of the nested set of contexts of the model);
3 the session context dealing with features (evidence) of the interaction (or activity) between two components or actors of the research framework – with the situation at hand as a central cognitive-emotional element. Session context is embedded in broader seeking and information behaviour. The situation at hand is constructed by the actor's perception of work and search tasks (interest), knowledge gap and potential sources, and so on (Ingwersen and Järvelin 2005: 278);
4 session interaction is placed in the context of social, systemic, domain and work task contexts – depending on the nature of the core component:
    4a individual conceptual and emotional (actor: searcher; author); systemic (engine; interface; information object); and domain properties immediately surrounding the core actor or component (work task; interest, preference, product).
    4b collective conceptual and emotional (actors: search teams; author groups); systemic (networks; meta-engines; information objects, information space); sociocultural and organizational structures in local settings.
5 techno-economic-politico-societal infrastructures influencing (not necessarily always in a remote way) all actors, components and interactive sessions.
6 the historic context operating across this stratification, i.e. that of all participating actors' experiences, forming their expectations. All IIR processes and activities are under influence of this temporal form of context.

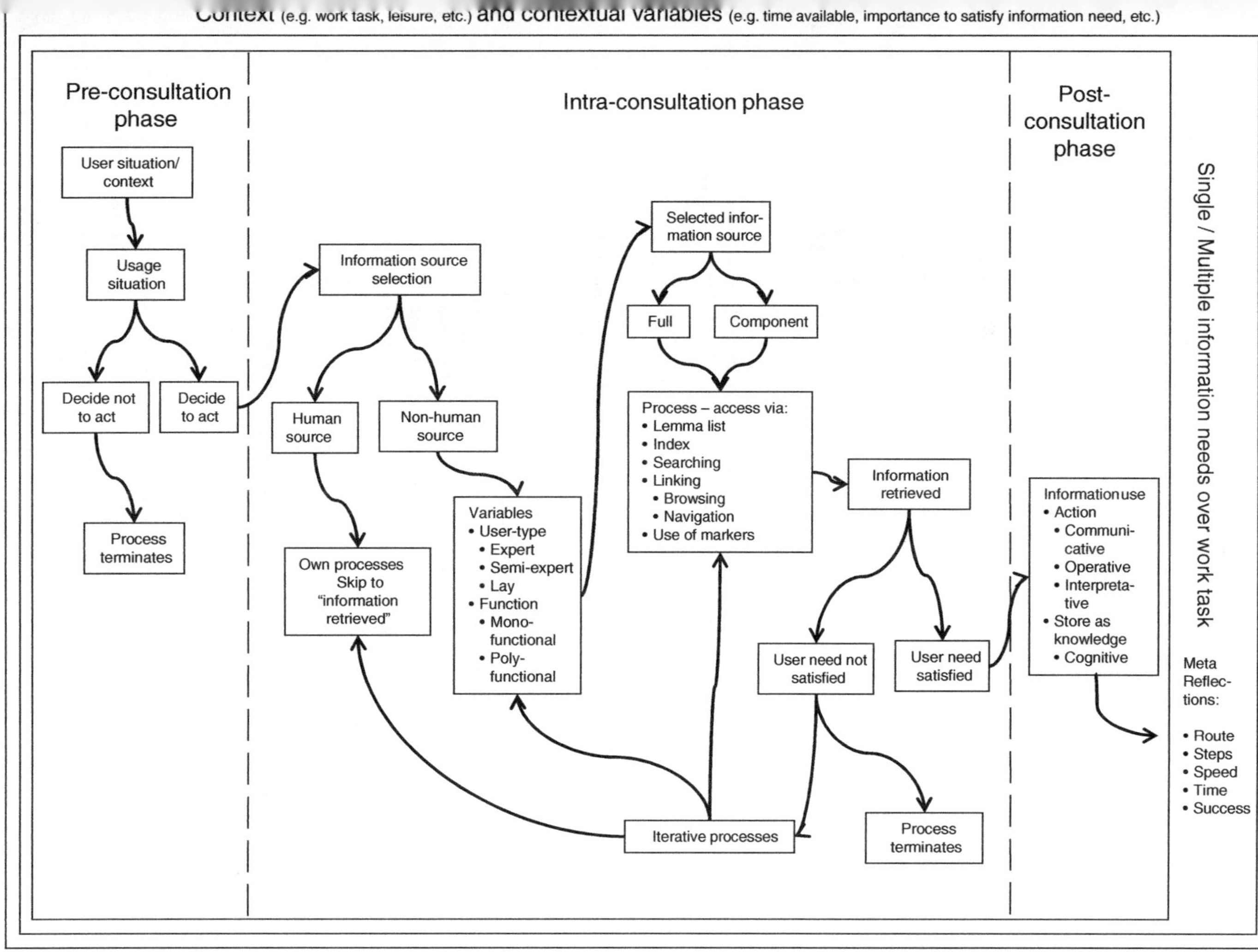

Figure 13.1 A schematic representation of the workflow in the access process
Source: (Bergenholtz, Bothma and Gouws 2015: 20)

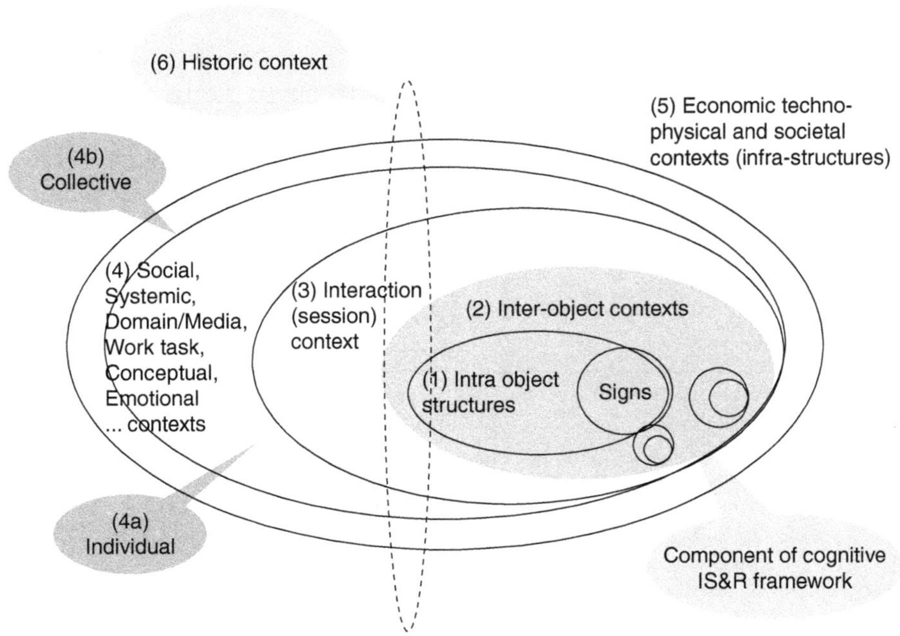

Figure 13.2 Nested general model of context stratification for interactive information retrieval
Source: (Ingwersen 2007, revised from Ingwersen and Järvelin 2004; Ingwersen and Järvelin 2005)

Even though these contexts are formulated in terms of interactive information retrieval, these contexts are equally relevant in terms of information needs, information use and information use behaviour.

The *Function Theory* is not in conflict with the context domains described earlier. To be satisfied, the information needs of the *Function Theory* require interaction of the user with information objects that have intra- and inter-object relationships. Equally, the user that has a specific information need operates in any given interaction with the information within an individual or collective/collaborative social or work task context with specific infrastructures and a specific historic context.

Lexicographic theory, and specifically the *Function Theory*, could be enriched by taking the preceding stratification into account and by describing the contexts in which the information needs occur in more detail, specifically at a theoretical level.

On the other hand, in information science, information needs are not sub-divided in terms of the four situations listed earlier. The end user's need for and use of the information is typically not the focus of the research, and the information need can be within a work task, for leisure purposes, for cognitive purposes and so forth. For information science, retrieving only sufficient information to satisfy the specific information need of a user is extremely important, to ensure that she or he does not suffer from information overload. Even though dictionaries based on the *Function Theory* filter data effectively to ensure that users are not presented with an overload of information and data, the problems persist in most e-dictionaries; see Gouws and Tarp (2016) for a detailed discussion and many examples.

Information science theory can be enhanced by describing the nature of the information needs of users in more detail, as is done in the *Function Theory*. All four current situations of the *Function Theory* can be identified in information retrieval in information science, even though such distinctions are not currently made in either theory or praxis. In the *Function Theory*, most research has been done on communicative situations and only limited attention is paid to detailed discussions on any possible subdivisions of cognitive situations. Cognitive and operative situations will most probably be dominant in information science. Information is retrieved to be studied and internalised in long-term memory for future use. Alternatively, information can be retrieved for a specific task, such as writing an assignment or for research purposes. In the latter case, the intention is not to memorise the information, but to use it in a given situation. The retrieved information can be a simple fact (for example, the date of a specific event, to be memorised) or a complex, theoretical essay or book (for example, on quantum theory, to be studied for an examination). If both these situations are classified as cognitive situations, how are they to be described in a function theory for information science? Similar situations can apply in lexicography, for example, to learn when the first occurrence of a word is in written English (a simple fact) or the origin of an idiom (for example, the cultural background in which it was originally used, how it developed over possibly centuries and in different languages, with meaning changes, etc.). In the preceding cases, it is undoubtedly a cognitive situation in each case, as the primary task is to learn. However, should the cognitive situation be further subdivided or described? Further research is required, and this probably applies to all situations, and probably requires an inter- and multidisciplinary approach.

13.3.2 Access to data and information

A number of technologies are commonly used in information science (and to a lesser extent in e-lexicography) to provide the end user with the required information. The following topics will be discussed in this section:

- Searching and navigation
- Filtering and profiling
- Adaptive hypertext and hypermedia
- Data markup.[11]

13.3.2.1 Searching and navigating

According to Bothma (2011: 81) searching can be defined as "the directed exploration of a defined information space with a defined objective in view and a defined search strategy". This is contrasted with navigating, which is "the exploration of a defined or undefined information space without using a defined strategy" (Bothma 2011: 81). Navigating consists of two sub-categories, viz. browsing (where the user has a defined objective but no defined strategy) and surfing (in which case the user may have no or a loosely defined objective, but serendipitously follows links that could potentially lead to relevant and/or interesting information). Both technologies are commented on next.

When a user conducts a search, she or he is required to define one or more search terms or phrases that are input into a search engine, by means of which the user searches for documents that match the search terms or phrases. A search can be conducted through a simple search interface (such as a standard Google search interface) or a complex search interface (such as the advanced search interface in Google Scholar). In the latter, the user can specify in which fields certain search terms should occur, for example in a keyword field, author field, or publication field, and even a range can be specified (such as a range of dates). In a complex search interface, Boolean operators (e.g. "and", "or" "not") can be used, combined with brackets to indicate precedence. Compare, for example, the different results that will be obtained through the following searches: ((apples and pears) or oranges)), compared to (apples and ((pears or oranges)). (Also see Bothma (2011) and Lew (2013) for detail on other search techniques, including the use of wildcards, truncation.)

Bibliographic and full-text databases of journals all usually have a simple and complex search interface, and support many more options to do a field-oriented search because of the structure of the database. Search engines also usually support wildcard searching (e.g. using a symbol to replace a letter to make provision for spelling variations). Matches can either be an exact match or best match, that is, the search term exactly or only closely matches the term in the source (Järvelin and Ingwersen 2012).

Typical support for searching in e-dictionaries is at the level of exact match and simple search, sometimes with an advanced search interface included. Advanced search interfaces can be of different complexity, as is evident from those in the *Elektroniese Woordeboek van die Afrikaanse Taal* (*E-WAT*) and the *Oxford English Dictionary* (*OED*): the *OED* supports much more specific search than does the *E-WAT*. As stated in Bothma (2011: 82–83),

> [t]he OED makes a distinction between searching the full entry or only quotations and supports inter alia Boolean operators indicating in which fields should be searched, proximity operators and a part of speech filter. The *E-WAT* supports only an "and" or "or" operator and phrase searching.

E-dictionaries should consider providing the user with the opportunity to specify the search in more detail, similar to what is done in bibliographic and full-text databases of journals. This would enable the user to access exactly the information required in a specific situation, or, as Tarp has stated, "to discover the needs that only show up in one out of a hundred or one out of a thousand consultations" (Tarp 2009b:292, quoted in more detail earlier). The importance of advanced search options was already observed by Almind (2005: 39) in his evaluation of e-dictionaries when he remarked that "[g]iving access to powerful search-functions is essential to a dictionary's success".

Navigation is, on the other hand, as stated in Bothma (2011: 83),

> [t]he most common way to move between discrete information entities on the web – a user can either browse or surf from Web page to Web page, trying to find either specific information or simply follow links that appear interesting. Links can be reference links to information outside the current website or cross-references to related material in the same website.

Clickable links occur in most e-dictionaries. In most cases, good usability conventions are followed to indicate clearly whether the link is a cross-reference to material in the current dictionary, or whether the link is to outside sources.

Any Internet search provides multiple search results, and the user then accesses the site or document of his or her choice by clicking on the link that is provided. This practice is common in e-dictionaries as well. Users therefore usually combine searching and browsing to satisfy an information need.

From the preceding it is evident that there are many similarities in the processes to provide access to information based on general information sources, on the one hand, and e-dictionaries, on the other hand. Compilers of e-dictionaries could nevertheless emulate information science in providing more complex search interfaces to enable users to refine their searches better. Usability studies should, however, be conducted to ensure that the complex interfaces are not so complex that users don't understand how to use them. Good design principles should therefore always be followed, and detailed usability studies should be conducted.

13.3.2.2 Profiling and filtering

User profiling can be used very effectively to filter information retrieved through a specific search. Therefore, two users with different profiles searching the same database with the same terms may retrieve different results. This can help to reduce information overload and provide the user with customized information tailored to his or her specific needs in a specific situation. The user should be able to change his or her profile, based on the specific information need at any given time. As explained in Bothma (2011: 84),

> [u]ser profiling can be accomplished through the user supplying the system with specific data, by the system tracking user behaviour and thereby automatically constructing a profile of the user or a combination of the two. User profiles can be transitory (e.g. applied to a single search only) or persistent (e.g. be stored on the system and be used for future retrieval actions).

A user profile can be constructed by the user himself or herself by filling in an online form, by the system through tracking the user's use of the system or through a combination of both. (For more detail, see Bothma 2011: 84–86).

User profiling is not commonly used in general information sources, but occurs regularly in commercial systems such as Amazon[12] and many others. To the best of my knowledge, user profiling has not been utilised in commercial e-dictionaries.

As explained in Bothma (2011: 86),

> [f]iltering can be user-controlled through the choices that the user indicates in the system or can be system-controlled. [. . .] User-controlled filtering can be based on a persistent user profile that the user has created through filling in data in a form, or it can be based on selections the user makes at the time of consultation.

Limited filtering of elements occurs in standard search engines, for example the possibility to specify the date, language or region of origin of the results in Bing,[13] as well as the option to limit the results to web documents, images, videos, maps, etc. Such filtering options are much more sophisticated in e-journal platforms such as EbscoHost[14] and ScienceDirect,[15] "where one can filter the results to specific databases and/or subject fields, date ranges, publication type (journals, books, reference works), language and so on" (Bothma 2011: 87).

Filters are not commonly used in e-dictionaries. In e-dictionaries based on the *Function Theory*, selecting a specific function is in essence the application of a sophisticated filter to the database. For example, in the *Ordbogen over faste vendinger*,[16] the data are filtered according to the specific information need. If the user wants to use a fixed expression to write a text, she or he selects the filter "*skrive en teks*", which provides him or her with the grammatical information, examples etc. necessary to satisfy the information need. In the advanced search option in the *OED*, it is possible to search according to specified fields in the database, and this is similar to the filtering found in database searches, described earlier.

Based on the user profile, the system could also automatically filter information presented to the user. No example of such filtering could be found in the e-dictionaries consulted.

Advanced filtering to present to the user the exact information she or he requires to satisfy a specific information need, as is often done in advanced information resources, is a functionality that could be explored for e-dictionaries.

13.3.2.3 Adaptive hypertext and hypermedia

Adaptive hypermedia can be subdivided into two categories, namely "adaptive presentation" and "adaptive navigation support" (Brusilovsky 1996: 100). Adaptive presentation again consists of either text or multimedia presentation. Adaptive navigation support "refers to a system's ability to manipulate links, viz. sort, hide or annotate links, and to provide direct guidance through linking, either text-based, multimedia-based or based on a navigational map" (Bothma 2011: 88). Adaptive presentation is the most common methodology used in adaptive hypermedia. It implies that the user can either expand (show) or hide (not show) data/information, based on his or her preferences, either managed through a profile or by the user at the time of reading. (For more detail and examples, see Bothma 2011: 88–90). The user is therefore able to change any level of information presented to him or her by the system, in terms of complexity, detail and many other parameters (obviously if the specific text contains data that complies with these criteria). Bothma (2011: 89–90) formulates this as follows (see also Bothma, Gouws and Prinsloo 2016):

> These characterizations of text-based information available to a user could be at the document level, page level, paragraph level or even smaller. This implies that a whole document can be aimed at the expert and another document on the same topic at a lay person. However, it is also possible that the granularity can be much finer grained. A single document can, therefore, be written in such a way that certain sections are aimed at the expert, others at the semi-expert and others at the lay person. The system should be able to present the correct level of information to the user, depending on his/her specified user profile in any given situation. Currently, the only way this can be done effectively is by means of marking up data in the document to indicate for which type of user the data is intended.

13.3.2.4 Data markup

Bothma (2011: 90) states that

> [b]y means of metadata, it is [. . .] possible to describe the properties of any data element, at the macro level of a full document, but also at a much finer granularity, even up to the individual paragraph, sentence or even smaller. An existing metadata schema can be used, or a combination of metadata schemas or even a totally new metadata schema can be created, based upon the characteristics of the user profile referred to earlier.

Complex markup of data in information sources (be that research publications and the Web in general) by means of metadata is not common. To the best of my knowledge, such complex metadata markup of data also does not occur in commercial e-dictionaries, and neither does the possibility of specifying (and changing) detailed user profiles and/or tracking user behaviour and adapting information presented to the user based on the profile.

Metadata, user profiling, filtering and adaptive hypermedia are closely linked. This is formulated as follows in Bothma (2011: 91):

> Proper metadata markup of data in an e-dictionary and sophisticated user profiling go hand-in-hand – the one is only useful as a complement of the other. It is, therefore, not useful to profile a user extensively if this cannot have an influence on the data which is presented to the user; conversely, it is not useful to mark data in the dictionary up extensively if these characteristics of a data element are not used to present information selectively to the user, depending on his/her information needs.

There is therefore much scope for research on all these aspects, for general information sources as well as for e-dictionaries. User acceptance of such methodologies should obviously also be researched, and various types of usability testing (including expert evaluations and user evaluations) should be done. Fruitful collaboration between information science and e-lexicography can be envisaged for such research. There are, therefore, many opportunities for collaborative research and experimental development work to see to what extent such features will make e-dictionaries more useful for users.

Bothma (2011: 91–93) furthermore discusses that extensive metadata markup is also required if an e-dictionary intends making use of external data sources as supplementary data for the dictionary, for example, to refer to examples of real-life usage of expressions in literature, newspapers and other corpora, by making use of open data sources. How e-dictionaries can be linked through proper markup to unprocessed and processed corpus data to provide added value on demand to users of e-dictionaries is discussed in, for example, Heid, Prinsloo and Bothma (2012) and Prinsloo et al. (2012). In addition to the links between e-dictionaries and e-corpora, e-texts can be dynamically linked to e-dictionaries, for example as occurs in Kindle e-books, as described in detail in Bothma and Prinsloo (2013). Links to additional support tools could be made to external resources or integrated into e-dictionaries to provide support on demand to users for solving information needs in complex grammatical structures. (See, for example, Prinsloo, Bothma and Heid (2014) and Prinsloo, Prinsloo and Prinsloo (2015).)

13.4 Looking to the future

Future cooperation between lexicography and information science could, in addition to the issues mentioned earlier, include research about a proper understanding of relevance theory and information/dictionary literacy. Both issues are analysed in the following paragraphs.

13.4.1 Relevance theory

As stated in Section 13.2, Tefko Saracevic regards *relevance* as *the* basic notion in information science. Relevance theory has been applied to e-lexicography as well, specifically in Bothma and Tarp (2012 and 2014). They (2012: 95–96) distinguish two basic classes of relevance, each defined as follows:

- objective relevance which is system-based (algorithmic or system relevance), and
- subjective relevance which is user-based and which can then be further subdivided into the following:
  - topical relevance,
  - cognitive relevance or pertinence,
  - situational relevance,
  - socio-cognitive relevance, and
  - affective relevance.

The different types and subtypes are described in a fair amount of detail in Bothma and Tarp (2012), and an illustrative example is provided; relevance theory is also applied to the lexicographical process. Further examples are provided in Bothma and Tarp (2014). These authors come to the conclusion that the comparison of relevance theory is important for lexicography and information science for the following:

> For information science the comparison is important because it is evident that, in information science, the theory of relevance stops at a crucial stage, viz. before the use of the information. It deals with retrieval issues and judgment of relevance of the retrieved information, but does not deal at all with the actual use of the information to solve problems or help in decision making. In addition, information science deals mainly or solely with cognitive information needs, and the different user situations as defined in the *Function Theory* are not distinguished. This research indicates that the theory of relevance in information science should be expanded to include the "post-lexicographical phase", i.e., the actual situation where the information is used, as well as a more finely grained situation assessment. This is an important theoretical consideration for information science and requires further research in information science.
>
> In lexicography, relevance theory as outlined and illustrated above, provides an elegant theory to understand relevance as a complex phenomenon that may have a profound influence on lexicographers' analysis of users' information needs. Users' information needs are paramount for lexicographers to decide what data are to be shown to the user in any given usage situation, as is evident from *Function Theory* (and even general lexicographic practice). Relevance theory implies that lexicographers have to make an even more in-depth study of the users of their products to enable them to understand exactly what may influence a user to use or not use a specific dictionary and to ensure that the lexicographic offering presents to the user only the required data to solve the user's information need in a given situation – no more and no less. If lexicographers understand that there are multiple relevances that may influence a user's judgment they may be able to design the underlying databases and filtering mechanisms in such a way that the end product provides the ideal solution for every user in every usage situation. This requires additional research in both metalexicography and lexicographical practice, especially at the level of database design and the design of filtering mechanisms.
>
> Research in relevance theory therefore enriches the theoretical underpinnings of both information science and lexicography, and has a practical implication for providing better information tools (lexicographic information tools as well as other information tools) to users of such tools.

Bothma and Tarp's analysis (2012, and 2014) has also allowed them to conclude that relevance theory and function theory, although developed separately in different theoretical and practical frameworks, have many similarities and fit very well into each other. Both theories, and disciplines, then, have much to learn from and contribute to each other.

13.4.2 Information/dictionary literacy

The skills set required to be information literate mentioned in Section 13.2 applies to dictionary literacy as well. A dictionary is a highly specialised information tool, and additional skills and knowledge are required to use a dictionary effectively. To use e-information tools and e-dictionaries a high level of computer literacy is a necessary prerequisite. Lew (2013: 17–22) identified and described 30 skills that are required to use dictionaries effectively, grouped together in four stages, viz. before the study commences, before the dictionary consultation commences, locating the entry information and interpreting the entry information. A number of these skills are identical to the skills identified for 'standard' information literacy; some, however, relate specifically to the specialised content of dictionaries. He (Lew 2013: 23–28) also discussed available search techniques that are required to access data in e-dictionaries quite comprehensively; these techniques correspond to techniques that are available in sophisticated e-resources. Standard information literacy teaching and practice should evidently be extended to make provision for specialised sources, such as e-dictionaries, and collaborative research should be conducted to ensure that this is included effectively in information literacy programmes. This also applies to other specialised information resources, such as maps and atlases, especially in the e-environment.

13.5 Conclusion

The topics discussed here, and a number of other publications, have strengthened my belief that information science and lexicography both have much to learn from each other and that the inter- and multidisciplinary research will lead to more innovative e-information tools.

Some of the innovations discussed earlier may not necessarily currently be commercially feasible. However, if researchers do not experiment with concepts and technologies that currently do not seem commercially realistic or feasible, innovation in e-information tools will be stifled. Such "blue sky research" could eventually lead to e-information tools that are not only incrementally better than those that are currently available, but provide different tools through disruptive innovation (Bergenholtz, Bothma and Gouws 2011).

All the research projects – and many others – therefore provide platforms to experiment with disruptive technologies, to develop prototypes and to see to what extent any of these technologies can add value for the user in providing access to information in terms of the user's specific information need in a given user situation. Such "blue sky research" is absolutely essential to ensure that not only better but different types of e-tools are developed. Users may help to improve e-dictionaries incrementally, but only fundamental research in metalexicography, user needs, database technologies and principles of information organisation, access and retrieval will result in different types of e-tools (Bergenholtz, Bothma and Gouws 2011). These topics emphasise the inter- and multidisciplinary nature of the research that needs to be done, at the intersections of information science and lexicography, in conjunction with other disciplines such as linguistics, natural language processing, computer science, human-computer interaction and interface design, and others.

The preceding discussions confirm the independence of lexicography as a discipline, but also the inter- and multidisciplinary nature of lexicography, as stated in Bothma, Gouws and Prinsloo (2016): "A new theory of lexicography is expanded by describing and taking cognisance of all innovative technological features enabled by the computer era, including data collection and processing and data representation and interface design, in order to respond to the different needs of the envisaged target users in an optimal way. This confirms that lexicographic theory needs more than a linguistic approach to ensure the best possible outcome." They conclude:

> The transition from printed to e-lexicography has ascertained the interdisciplinary nature of lexicography as an independent and multidisciplinary field. Different disciplines, e.g. human language technology, linguistics and information science, become increasingly important role players in the development of a lexicographic theory directed at the practice of dictionary compilation. A redefined theory of lexicography needs to reflect these contributions but should also display a comprehensive nature that gives a sound theoretical basis to the lexicographic practice that responds to the needs of diverse and wide-ranging potential target user groups.

Related topics

Lexicography as an independent science; lexicography and natural language processing; information retrieval for lexicographic purposes; terminological knowledge bases.

Further reading

The reader is referred to the fairly extensive list of references provided in Sections 13.2 and 13.3 of this chapter for further reading. The following, however, provide in-depth overviews of some of the information science-related topics addressed in this chapter:

Ingwersen and Järvelin (2005) and Järvelin and Ingwersen (2012) provide detailed discussions with extensive references on models of information retrieval.

Case and Given (2016) provide detailed discussions on research in information needs, seeking and use and theories used in information behaviour research, as well as related topics.

For research on interface design and usability, the reader is referred to Shneiderman et al. 2016, as well as the large number of short articles by Jakob Nielsen, Don Norman and a number of other usability experts on the website of the NielsenNormanGroup, www.nngroup.com/articles.

Van Dijk and Van Deursen (2014) is an excellent overview of the digital skills that are required for navigating the Internet successfully, aimed at both researchers and practitioners.

Notes

1 See respectively http://trec.nist.gov/ and www.clef-initiative.eu/.
2 For RDA, see www.rdatoolkit.org/; www.loc.gov/aba/rda/; www.oclc.org/rda/about.en.html; for AACR2, see www.aacr2.org/; for DDC, see www.oclc.org/dewey.en.html; for MARC, see www.loc.gov/marc/classification/; for LCSH, see www.loc.gov/aba/cataloging/subject/.
3 See http://dublincore.org/.
4 See http://dublincore.org/documents/dces/.
5 See www.w3.org/RDF/.

6 See, for example, www.dcc.ac.uk/drupal/resources/metadata-standards for an (incomplete) list of such standards.
7 See http://big6.com/.
8 See www.ala.org/acrl/standards/, specifically www.ala.org/acrl/standards/ilframework.
9 See https://akoaotearoa.ac.nz/community/ako-aotearoa-suggested-resources/resources/pages/australian-and-new-zealand-information-li, specifically http://archive.caul.edu.au/info-literacy/InfoLiteracy-Framework.pdf.
10 See Bothma and Tarp 2012: 92–93 for more detail on these phases.
11 These topics have been dealt with in some detail in Bothma (2011), and the papers cited there.
12 See www.amazon.com.
13 See www.bing.com.
14 See www.ebscohost.com.
15 See www.sciencedirect.com.
16 See www.ordbogen.com.

References

Almind, R. (2005) "Designing Internet Dictionaries", *Hermes, Journal of Linguistics* 34: 37–54.

Amato, G. and U. Straccia (1999) "User Profile Modeling and Applications to Digital Libraries", *Research and Advanced Technology for Digital Libraries* (Lecture Notes in Computer Science, Volume 1696): 184–197.

Anglo-American Cataloguing Rules (AACR2). [Online] Available www.aacr2.org/. Accessed July 2016.

Association for College and Research Libraries (ACRL). [Online] www.ala.org/acrl/standards/ and www.ala.org/acrl/standards/ilframework [Accessed July 2016].

Atkins, B.T.S. and M. Rundell (2008) *The Oxford Guide to Practical Lexicography*. Oxford: Oxford University Press.

Australian and New Zealand Information Literacy Framework. [Online] https://akoaotearoa.ac.nz/community/ako-aotearoa-suggested-resources/resources/pages/australian-and-new-zealand-information-li and http://archive.caul.edu.au/info-literacy/InfoLiteracyFramework.pdf. [Accessed July 2016].

Bergenholtz, H. and T.J.D. Bothma (2011) "Needs Adapted Data Presentation in E-Information Tools", *Lexikos* 21: 53–77.

Bergenholtz, H., T.J.D. Bothma and R. H. Gouws (2011) "A Model for Integrated Dictionaries of Fixed Expressions", in I. Kosem and K. Kosem (eds.), *Electronic Lexicography in the 21st Century: New Applications for New Users. Proceedings of eLex 2011, Bled, 10–12 November 2011*. Bled: Trojína, pp. 34–42.

Bergenholtz, H., T.J.D. Bothma and R. H. Gouws (2015) "Phases and Steps in the Access to Data in Information Tools". *Lexikos* 25: 1–30.

Big Six. [Online] http://big6.com/. [Accessed July 2016].

Bolisani, E. and M. Handzic (2015) *Advances in Knowledge Management: Celebrating Twenty Years of Research and Practice*. Heidelberg: Springer.

Bothma, T.J.D. (2011) "Filtering and Adapting Data and Information in the Online Environment in Response to User Needs", in P. A. Fuertes-Olivera and H. Bergenholtz (eds.), pp. 71–102.

Bothma, T.J.D. (2015) "Reflexiones sobre la interrelación entre lexicografía y ciencia de la información: una perspectiva personal" ("Reflections on the interrelationship between lexicography and information science: a personal perspective"), *Estudios de Lexicografía* 4: 21–30.

Bothma, T.J.D., R. H. Gouws and D. J. Prinsloo (2016) "The Role of e-Lexicography in the Confirmation of Lexicography as an Independent and Multidisciplinary Field", in *Proceedings of the XVII EURALEX International Congress: Lexicography and Linguistic Diversity, 6–10 September 2016*, pp. 111–118.

Bothma, T.J.D. and D. J. Prinsloo (2013) "Automated Dictionary Consultation for Text Reception: A Critical Evaluation of Lexicographic Guidance in Linked Kindle E-Dictionaries", *Lexicographica* 29: 165–198.

Bothma, T.J.D. and S. Tarp (2012) "Lexicography and the Relevance Criterion", *Lexikos* 22: 86–108.

Bothma, T.J.D. and S. Tarp (2014) "Why Relevance Theory Is Relevant for Lexicographers", *Lexicographica* 30: 350–378.

Brusilovksy, P. (1996) "Methods and Techniques of Adaptive Hypermedia", in P. Brusilovsky, A. Kobsa and J. Vassileva (eds.), *Adaptive Hypertext and Hypermedia*. Berlin: Springer Verlag, pp. 1–43.

Brusilovsky, P. and M. T. Maybury (2002) "From Adaptive Hypermedia to the Adaptive Web", *Communications of the ACM* 45(5): 30–33.

Brusilovksy, P. and E. Millán (2007) "User Models for Adaptive Hypermedia and Adaptive Educational Systems", in P. Brusilovsky, A. Kobsa and W. Nejdl (eds.), *The Adaptive Web: Methods and Strategies of Web Personalization*. Berlin: Springer Verlag, pp. 3–53.

Case, D. O. and L. M. Given (2016) *Looking for Information: A Survey of Research on Information Seeking, Needs, and Behaviour*. Bingley: Emerald.

Cosijn, E. (2003) *Relevance Judgements in Information Retrieval*. DPhil thesis. Pretoria: University of Pretoria.

Cosijn, E. and T.J.D. Bothma (2005) "Contexts of Relevance for Information Retrieval System Design", in F. Crestani and I. Ruthven (ed.), *Context: Nature, Impact, and Role: 5th International Conference on Conceptions of Library and Information Sciences, CoLIS 2005*. Glasgow, UK, June 4–8, 2005. Berlin/Heidelberg: Springer, pp. 47–58.

Cosijn, E. and P. Ingwersen (2000) "Dimensions of Relevance", *Information Processing and Management* 36: 533–550.

Davenport, T. H., D. W. De Long and M. C. Beers (1998) "Successful Knowledge Management Projects", *Sloan Management Review* 39(2): 43–57.

Dewey Decimal Classification (DDC). [Online] www.oclc.org/dewey.en.html. [Accessed July 2016].

Dublin Core Metadata Initiative (DCMI). [Online] http://dublincore.org/ and http://dublincore.org/documents/dces/. [Accessed July 2016].

Fisher, K. E., S. Erdelez and L. McKechnie (eds.) (2005) *Theories of Information Behaviour*. Medford: Information Today.

Ford, N. (2015) *Introduction to Information Behaviour*. London: Facet Publishing.

Fuertes-Olivera, P. A. and H. Bergenholtz (eds.) (2011) *e-Lexicography: The Internet, Digital Initiatives and Lexicography*. London and New York: Continuum.

Fuertes-Olivera, P. A. and S. Tarp (2014) *Theory and Practice of Specialised Online Dictionaries. Lexicography Versus Terminography* (Lexicographica Series Maior 146). Berlin and Boston: de Gruyter.

Fuertes-Olivera, P. A., H. Bergenholtz, P. Gordo Gómez, S. Nielsen, M. Niño Amo, A. Los Rios Rodicio, Á. S. Ruano and M. Velasco Sacristán (2013) "From Theory to Practice: The Selection of Spanish Lemmas in the *Accounting Dictionaries*", *Fachsprache* 2013(1–2): 23–41.

Gauch, S., M. Speretta, A. Chandramouli and A. Micarelli (2007) "User Profiles for Personalized Information Access", in P. Brusilovsky, A. Kobsa, and W. Nejdl (eds.), *The Adaptive Web: Methods and Strategies of Web Personalization*. Berlin: Springer, pp. 54–89.

Gouws, R. H. (2005) "Meilensteine auf dem historischen Weg der Metalexikographie", *Lexicographica* 21: 158–178.

Gouws, R. H. (2015) "Hacia una cultura lexicográfica de discusión crítica". ("Towards a Critical Lexicographic Discussion Culture"), *Estudios de Lexicografía* 4: 15–20.

Gouws, R. H. and S. Tarp (2016) "Information Overload and Data Overload in Lexicography", *International Journal of Lexicography* 26: 3, doi:10.1093/ijl/ecw030.

Heid, U., D. J. Prinsloo and T.J.D. Bothma (2012) "Dictionary and Corpus Data in a Common Portal: State of the Art and Requirements for the Future", *Lexicographica* 28: 269–291.

Ingwersen, P. (2001) "Cognitive Information Retrieval", *Annual Review of Information Science and Technology* 34: 3–51.

Ingwersen, P. (2007) "Context in Information Interaction – Revisited 2006", in T.J.D. Bothma and A. Kaniki (eds.), *ProLISSA 2006: Proceedings of the Fourth Biennial DISSAnet Conference*. Farm Inn, Pretoria, 2–3 November. Pretoria: Infuse, 13–23.

Ingwersen, P. and K. Järvelin (2004) "Context in Information Interaction", in T.J.D. Bothma and A. Kaniki (eds.), *Progress in Library and Information Science in Southern Africa (ProLISSA): Proceedings of the Third Biennal DISSAnet Conference*. Pretoria: Infuse, pp. 301–310.

Ingwersen P. and K. Järvelin (2005) *The Turn: Integration of Information Seeking and Retrieval in Context*. Dordrecht: Springer.

Järvelin, K. and P. Ingwersen (2012) "User-Oriented and Cognitive Models of Information Retrieval", in M. J. Bates (ed.), *Understanding Information Retrieval Systems: Management, Types and Standards*. Boca Raton, FL: CRC Press, pp. 47–64.

Kobsa, A. (2007) "Generic User Modeling Systems", in P. Brusilovsky, A. Kobsa and W. Nejdl (eds.), *The Adaptive Web: Methods and Strategies of Web Personalization*. Berlin: Springer, pp. 136–154.

Kuhlthau, C. C. (2003) *Seeking Meaning: A Process Approach to Library and Information Services*. 2nd edition. Santa Barbara, CA: Libraries Unlimited.

Kuhlthau, C. C., L. K. Maniotes and A. K. Caspari (2015) *Guided Inquiry: Learning in the 21st Century*. 2nd edition. Santa Barbara, CA: Libraries Unlimited.

Kurtz, C. F. and D. J. Snowden (2003) "The New Dynamics of Strategy: Sense-Making in a Complex and Complicated World", *IBM Systems Journal* 42(3): 462–483.

Lew, R. (2013) "Online Dictionary Skills", in I. Kosem, J. Kallas, P. Gantar, S. Krek, M. Langemets and M. Tuulik (eds.), *Electronic Lexicography in the 21st Century: Thinking Outside the Paper. Proceedings of the eLex 2013 Conference*, 17–19 October 2013, Tallinn, Estonia. Ljubljana/Tallinn: Trojina, Institute for Applied Slovene Studies/Eesti Keele Instituut, pp. 16–31.

Library of Congress Subject Headings (LCSH). [Online] www.loc.gov/aba/cataloging/subject/ [Accessed July 2016].

MARC 21 Format for Classification Data. [Online] http://www.loc.gov/marc/classification [Accessed July 2016].

Nielsen, J. (1994) *Usability Engineering*. Boston, MA: AP Professional.

Nielsen, J. and R. Budiu (2012) *Mobile Usability*. Berkeley, CA: New Riders.

Nielsen, J. and H. Loranger (2006) *Prioritizing Web Usability*. Berkeley: New Riders.

Nonaka, I and H. Takeuchi (1995) *The Knowledge Creating Company: How Japanese Companies Create the Dynamics of Innovation*. New York: Oxford University Press.

Preece, J. and H. Sharp (2015) *Interaction Design: Beyond Human-Computer Interaction*. 4th edition. Chichester: Wiley.

Prinsloo, D. J., T.J.D. Bothma and U. Heid (2014) "User Support in e-Dictionaries for Complex Grammatical Structures in the Bantu Languages", in A. Abel, C. Vettori and N. Ralli (eds.), *Proceedings of the XVI EURALEX International Congress: The User in Focus. 15–19 July 2014*. Bolzano/Bozen: EURAC Research. [Online] www.euralex.org/elx_proceedings/Euralex2014/euralex_2014_062_p_819.pdf. [Accessed July 2016].

Prinsloo, D. J., U. Heid, T.J.D. Bothma and G. Faaß (2012) "Interactive, Dynamic Electronic Dictionaries for Text Production", *Lexikos* 22: 290–320.

Prinsloo, D. J., D. Prinsloo, and J. Prinsloo (2015) "A Writing Tool for Sepedi", *E-Lex 2015*, Herstmonceux Castle, United Kingdom, 11–13 August 2015.

Resource Description and Access (RDA). [Online]. www.rdatoolkit.org/, www.loc.gov/aba/rda/ and www.oclc.org/rda/about.en.html. [Accessed July 2016].

Resource Description Framework (RDF). [Online]. www.w3.org/RDF/ and www.dcc.ac.uk/drupal/resources/metadata-standards. [Accessed July 2016].

Saracevic, T. (2015) "Why Is Relevance Still the Basic Notion in Information Science?", Keynote paper at *ISI 2015, International Symposium on Information Science*, 18–21 May 2015, Zadar, Croatia. [Online]https://comminfo.rutgers.edu/~tefko/Saracevic%20Why%20relevance%20-%20ISI2015.doc. [Accessed July 2016].

Saracevic, T. (2016) "Relevance: In Search of a Theoretical Foundation", in D. H. Sonnenwald (ed.), *Theory Development in Information Sciences*. Austin: University of Texas Press, p. 141.

Shneiderman, B., C. Plaisant, M. Cohen, S. Jacobs, N. Elmqvist and N. Diakopoulos (2016) *Designing the User Interface: Strategies for Effective Human-Computer Interaction*. 6th edition. London: Pearson.

Snowden, D. J. (2000) "Cynefin: A Sense of Time and Space, the Social Ecology of Knowledge Management", in C. Despres and D. Chauvel (2000) *Knowledge Horizons: The Present and the Promise of Knowledge Management*. Oxford: Butterworth Heinemann.

Snowden, D. J. (2002) "Complex Acts of Knowing – Paradox and Descriptive Self-Awareness", *Journal of Knowledge Management (Special Issue)* 6(2): 100–111.

Snowden, D. J. (2013) "Cynefin v45° complete", [Online] http://cognitive-edge.com/blog/cynefin-v45-complete/. [Accessed July 2016].

Tarp, S. (2008) *Lexicography in the Borderland between Knowledge and Non-Knowledge: General Lexicographical Theory With Particular Focus on Learner's Lexicography*. Tübingen: Niemeyer.

Tarp, S. (2009a) "Reflections on Data Access in Lexicographic Works", in S. Nielsen and S. Tarp (eds.), *Lexicography in the 21st Century: In Honour of Henning Bergenholtz*. Amsterdam/Philadelphia: John Benjamins, pp. 43–62.

Tarp, S. (2009b) "Reflections on Lexicographical User Research", *Lexikos* 19: 275–296.

Tarp, S. (2012) "Do We Need a (new) Theory of Lexicography?", *Lexikos* 22: 321–332.

Tarp, S. (2015) "Presentación del Centro de Lexicografía de Aarhus, Dinamarca" ("Presentation of the Center for Lexicography in Aarhus, Denmark"), *Estudios de Lexicografía* 4: 1–14.

Van Dijk, J.A.G.M. and A.J.A.M. van Deursen (2014) *Digital Skills, Unlocking the Information Society*. New York: Palgrave Macmillan.

14

Domain ontologies

Catherine Roussey, Nathalie Hernandez and Haïfa Zargayouna

14.1 Introduction

In computer science, ontologies were originally used in artificial intelligence in order to share knowledge among applications. Nowadays ontologies are used in many different fields of information systems. Our goal is to give an overview of the different types of ontologies and their use in these applications. First, we will present the concept in its historical context with the aim of summarising what most scholars agree on. Second, we will enumerate some core issues and topics focusing on the relationship of domain ontologies and information systems, especially systems that can be used for lexicographic purposes. For example, *WordNet* is a well-known lexical database that is used in information retrieval system. Other types of resources were developed by computer scientists in order to store more information (lexical, semantic, etc. . .) and reuse them in information system.

14.2 Historical perspective

14.2.1 What is an ontology in computer science?

The main cited definition of ontology is that of Grüber (1993:199) stating "[a]n ontology is an explicit specification of a conceptualization." This definition is very generic and can be applied to any conceptualisation used in information systems. Many researchers have therefore extended it.

According to Arp et al. (2015:1) an ontology is a "representational artifact, comprising a taxonomy as proper part whose representational units are intended to designate some combination of universals, defined classes and certain relations between them."

Several ontology definitions are analysed in Gómez-Pérez et al. (2004). For the authors, there is no real consensus on what an ontology should be. For example, the definition of Uschold and Jasper (1999:11–12) states "an ontology may take a variety of forms, but it will necessarily include a vocabulary of terms and some specification of their meaning." This includes definitions and indications of how concepts are inter-related, which collectively imposes a structure on the domain and constrains the possible interpretations of terms. Gómez-Pérez et al. (2004: 8) conclude that "ontologies aim to capture consensual knowledge in a generic way, and that they may be reused and shared across software applications and by groups of people."

All these definitions agree on:

1 Ontologies are computer science artefacts. Computer science deals only with representations of reality and not real objects.
2 Ontologies represent a conceptualisation.
3 The conceptualisations have to be shared between applications and their associated meanings have to be agreed on by a community of people.

14.2.2 A conceptualisation

According to the semiotic triangle (Ogden and Richards 1923), there are different entities in a conceptualisation. We propose in Figure 14.1 an illustration of the semiotic triangle based on the definitions given in Arp et al. (2015: 2–11).

Representation artefacts are any symbols (i.e. terms or icons) used for communication purposes. A communication event implies some cognitive processes in the human brain in order to understand the symbols and associate them with the corresponding entities in the real world. This association is called *represent* in Figure 14.1. Note that it is not a direct association as it depends on two other associations made by cognitive processes. A first cognitive process interprets symbols and links them to mental representations that can also be called thoughts or concepts. This association is called *denote* in Figure 14.1. Then a second cognitive process associates mental representations to entities of the world. This is called *refer* in Figure14.1.

The International Standard Organisation (ISO) (2000, 2015) also agrees on how symbols are associated with real objects via mental representations. Figure 14.2 presents the vision described in ISO 1087. The link between designations (term, symbol) and real objects is not represented because the interpretation of designation involves concepts.

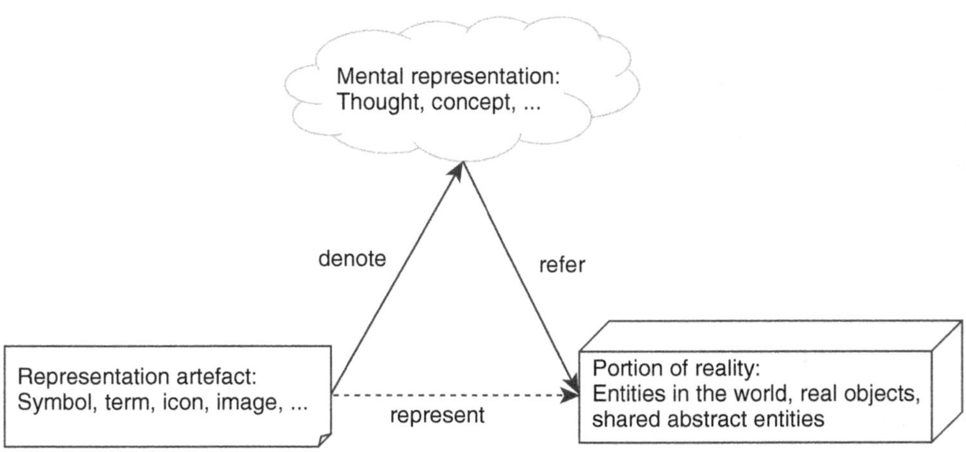

Figure 14.1 Semiotic triangle

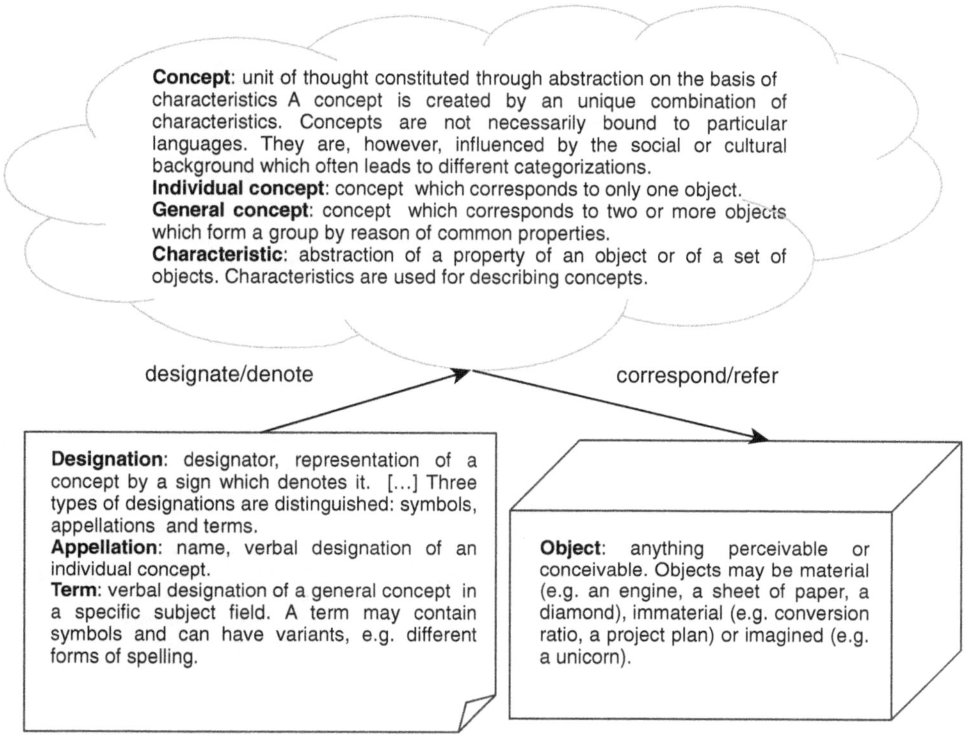

Figure 14.2 ISO definition for mental representations (ISO 1087)

It is important to note that computer science does not manage real objects but manages digital descriptions of real objects. All entities in computer science systems are representation artefacts. Two types of representation artefacts must be distinguished:

1 Schema entities like "person, document or organization" corresponding to representations of a set of objects that are referenced by general concepts.
2 Facts like "the person whose family name is Grüber has written a document untitled: A translation approach to portable ontology specifications" corresponding to digital descriptions of individual objects that are referenced by individual concepts.

Figure 14.3 (on page 220) presents these two types of representation artefacts. Computer scientists make this type of distinction because they design software at the schema level defining classes, their attributes and so on. Let's take an example from the FOAF ontology (Brickley and Miller 2014). The '*Person*' class has two attributes '*familyName*' and '*givenName*'. Then, at run time, each schema entity, like the '*Person*' class, is instantiated by a fact stating for example a '*familyName*' and a '*givenName*'. The '*family name*' attribute stores the string value "Grüber" and the '*givenName*' stores the string value "Thomas Robert". An instance is a prototype of the class that replicates all the class attributes and gives them a value.

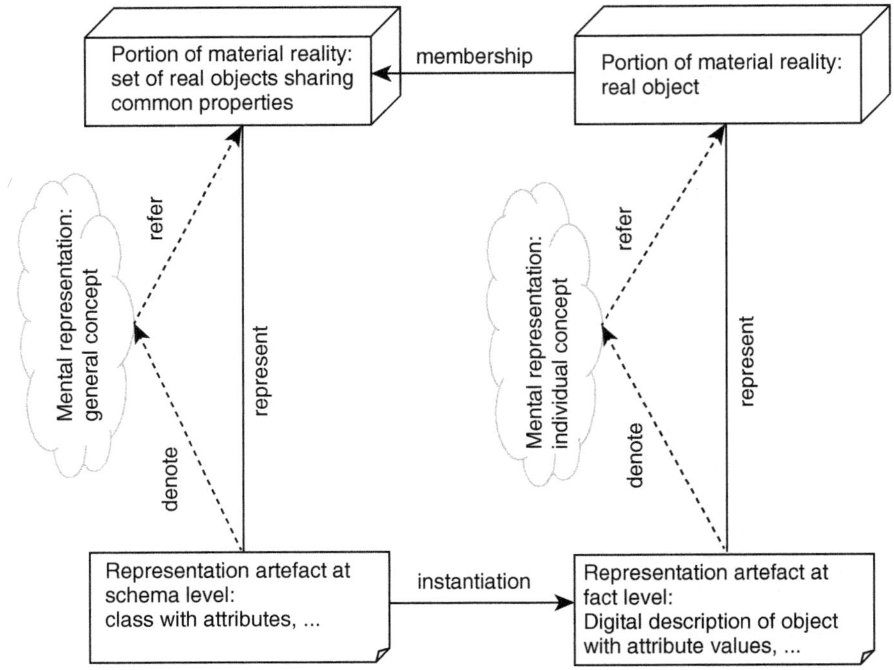

Figure 14.3 Representation artefacts in computer science

14.3 Core issues and topics

14.3.1 Domain ontology components

Ontologies are composed of different elements depending on the usage their designers have planned. In this section, we present these elements and the reasons for integrating them in an ontology. Figure 14.4 gives an overview on the different elements and the possible interactions between them through a Unified Modelling Language (UML) schema.

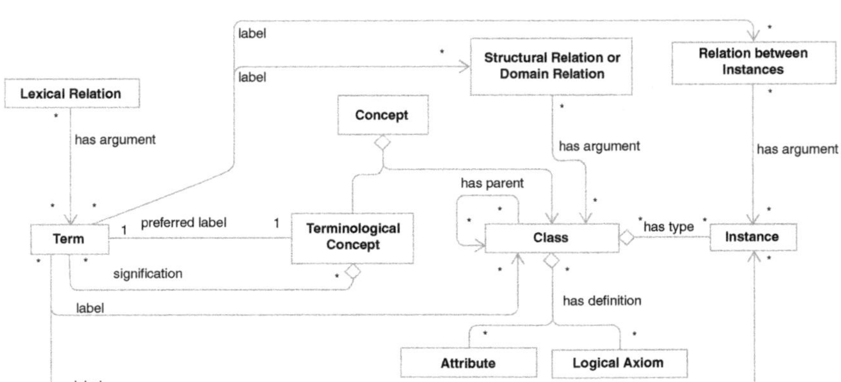

Figure 14.4 UML schema representing the different components of ontology

14.3.1.1 Term

A *term* corresponds to a word or a sequence of words (called *phrases*) to which a human can associate a meaning. A term can be chosen to play the role of a label associated to a concept (Aussenac-Gilles and Soergel 2005). A term has to have a stable and consensual signification in a specific domain, outside the context of a specific document. For example, we all share a common interpretation of the term *populated place* as a place with inhabitants and a geographic position. A term occurrence may have slight differences of interpretation depending on the context of a document (Biebow et al. 1999). For example, the occurrence of the term *populated place* in a document dealing with government laws will denote a more specific meaning about different types of human settlement.

14.3.1.2 Lexical relations

A lexical relation is a relation between terms such as synonymy, antonymy, hyponymy, hyperonymy or meronymy. The term is then contextualised by the relation it has to other terms. For example, the two terms *locality* and *populated place* will have the same meaning as they are defined as synonyms (see Chapter 21 of this *Handbook*).

14.3.1.3 Concept

A concept is defined as an element of thought (ISO 1087). Within the semiotic triangle (term, concept, object; see Figure 14.1), a concept is the mental construction that gives the meaning of the term which denotes the concept. The concept consists in a set of characteristics that we identify as common to a set of objects of the real or imaginary world (Daconta et al. 2003). For example, the concept denoted by the term *populated place* corresponds to any object that can be situated somewhere and that has inhabitants.

14.3.1.4 Terminological concept

A terminological concept represents the normalised meaning of a term through a definition in natural language. The definition states the necessary and sufficient conditions for the term to be associated to its correct denotation. For instance, Wikipedia defines *populated place* as "a place or area with clustered or scattered buildings and a permanent human population (city, settlement, town, or village) referenced with geographic coordinates."

14.3.1.5 Class and attribute

A class represents a concept in a computer science language. The FOAF ontology is defined in the Web Ontology Language (OWL). This ontology defines the classes '*Person*', '*Agent*', '*Document*', '*Organization*', and '*Project*'. A class is a partial and oriented representation of the concept. For example, the class '*PopulatedPlace*' can be associated with the attribute '*hasNumberOfInhabitant*' and the class '*Place*' with the attribute '*hasGPScoordinates*'. Note that other attributes like surface area could be chosen.

To sum up, a terminological concept is associated to a definition in natural language, whereas a class is associated to a set of attributes that characterise the concept expressed in a computer science language.

14.3.1.6 Relations between classes

Classes can also be defined according to their relations to each other. The hierarchical relation of specialisation/generalisation is one kind of these relations. Here, the representation states that any characteristic of the parent class is also true for the child class. For example, we can represent that '*PopulatedPlace*' is a specialisation of '*Place*', which means than any instance of populated place has a GPS coordinate.

Other relations can be defined according to usage. For example, two classes can be linked through a spatial inclusion relation enabling localisation. This kind of relation can define a hierarchy ('*Town*' is included in '*Country*'). Other non-hierarchical relations, associative relations, are also useful for making explicit domain knowledge. For example, the FOAF ontology expresses that the class '*Person*' is disjoint from the class '*Organization*' and '*Document*'.

14.3.1.7 Object or class instance

A class can also be defined by the set of its instances, i.e. the set of objects typed by this class. For example, we can define the class '*PopulatedPlace*' with a set of cities such as '*Paris*', '*London*', '*Madrid*'. In texts, the expressions designating the instances are mainly proper nouns also called named entities in information extraction processes (see Chapters 12 and 43 of this *Handbook*).

Instances can also be described according to their links to each other. For example, the instance 'Paris' which is a '*PopulatedPlace*' is linked by the '*hasGPScoordinates*' attribute to the value <N48 51.39827 E2 34.13445>. The FOAF ontology enables to associate to an instance of the class '*Person*' several instances of the class '*Document*' using the different attributes '*homepage*', '*workplaceHomepage*', '*schoolHomepage*', and '*publication*'.

14.3.1.8 Logical axioms

When reasoning is needed in order to infer new knowledge, logical axioms can be represented in a targeted knowledge representation language. Different kinds of axioms can be considered. For example, by using the *subsumption relation*, any instance of the child class is also an instance of the parent class. The instance 'Paris' is of the type '*PopulatedPlace*' and of the type '*Place*'.

A class can also be defined by expressing the necessary and sufficient conditions that instances must fulfil to be typed by the class. For example, the class '*Place*' may be defined by the constraint stating that having a unique GPS coordinate using the attribute *hasGPScoordinate* is a sufficient and necessary condition to be a '*Place*'. This axiom can be used to infer an instance of the class '*Place*'.

A relation can also handle conditions about its arguments. For example in FOAF ontology, the relation publication has conditions about its two arguments: the first one should be an instance of the class '*Person*'; the second one should be an instance of the class '*Document*'. Thus a reasoner will deduce automatically that any instance, which is the first argument of the relation publication, should be typed by the class '*Person*'.

The different kinds of axioms that can be considered depend on the knowledge representation language (and its underlying logic) used to express the ontology.

14.3.2 Domain ontologies: examples and usages

Ontologies are built for different purposes that strongly affect their types and components. To illustrate these different types of ontologies, we present some examples of ontologies based on their usage.

14.3.2.1 Ontologies to normalise the meaning of terms

The first goal of ontologies is to normalise the vocabulary used in communication purposes (i.e. ontologies state which term can be used and what its meaning is exactly). In this case, only the link of denotation between term and concept of the semiotic triangle is exploited (see Figure 14.1). Vocabulary normalisation has two aspects:

- decides which term is the preferred label to denote the concept and which terms are alternative labels that may denote the same concept but should not be used for communication purposes;
- provides a sufficient natural language definition so that someone reading this definition will have in mind the same concept.

Normalisation has to follow some rules:

- A term has to be the preferred label of only one concept.
- A concept should have one preferred label per language and only one. It may be associated with several alternative labels.

Rich lexical relations can be expressed between terms. This type of ontology can be a thesaurus, a taxonomy, a classification scheme, a network of words or a lexical database. *A thesaurus* is composed of terms, terminological concepts and lexical relations. It is widely used in document management applications for indexing documents and queries. The librarian chooses the descriptors of a document or of a query within the thesaurus. Thesauri normalise the terms in order to make them exploitable by an information retrieval system (see Chapters 12, 13 and 43 of this *Handbook*). Terms are considered either as descriptors or non-descriptors. Non-descriptor terms correspond to synonyms of descriptor terms but are not recommended to be used when indexing the document. Descriptors are linked to each other by a hierarchical relation and by associative relations without explicit meaning.

A lexical database is also composed of terms, terminological concepts and lexical relations. This kind of resource is close to a thesaurus as terms are grouped by synonyms linked to one another through relations and terminological concepts are associated to terms. A thesaurus and a lexical database have different objectives. The aim of a lexical database is to differentiate all the possible meanings of a term occurring in a document. A thesaurus aims to represent the most consensual meaning in the considered domain.

WordNet (Fellbaum 1998) is a well-known lexical database for English. Nouns, verbs, adjectives and adverbs are grouped in *synsets*, each of them expressing a distinct terminological concept. *Synsets* are linked by lexical relations such as synonymy, hyperonymy/hyponymy, meronymy, troponymy for the verbs and antonymy for adjectives.

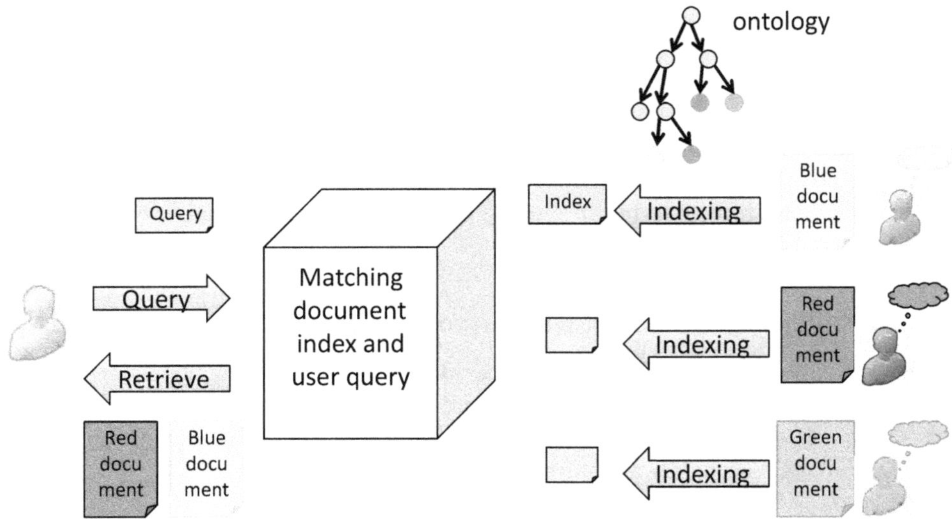

Figure 14.5 Architecture of information retrieval system
Source: (Roussey et al. 2010)

The ontologies described are used in information retrieval systems (IRS) to normalize the vocabulary used to index the content of documents and queries (see Chapters 12, 13, 21 and 43 of this *Handbook*). In information retrieval, a user sends a query to the system in order to retrieve relevant documents. Documents may be any information resource like a book, a photo, or a video. Figure 14.5 presents the architecture of IRS.

IRS represent the content of documents by at least a bag of terms called an index as shown in Figure 14.5. The user information need is expressed by a query, which is also a bag of terms. IRS compares the document indexes in order to select those that match the query index. The matching process is done by computing the similarity between document indexes and the query index. Then IRS orders the set of selected document indexes in order to present first the one that best matches the query index.

Ontologies in IRS make it possible to take into account synonyms and hierarchical relations in order to enhance the retrieval process. For example, one author, represented in Figure 14.5, employs the term *river* in the green document and another author employs the term *watercourse* in the red document to refer to the same concept. In an ontology the terms *river* and *watercourse* will be associated to the same terminological concept. *Watercourse* is defined as the preferred label of the terminological concept. Thus, in IRS, this term will be part of the green document index and the red document index. All queries that contain the term *watercourse* will find the green and the red document (Roussey et al. 2010). Ontologies can also help to enrich the initial user query with similar terms. This technique is called *query expansion* (Alonso and Contreras 2016).

IRS generally performs a disambiguation phase in order to select the most appropriate terminological concept to represent the document or query content and resolve lexical ambiguities implied by polysemic terms (Rais and Lachkar 2016). IRS can also take into account the network of concepts for computing a semantic similarity during the matching process (Varelas et al. 2005).

14.3.2.2 Ontologies to reference real objects

The previous described ontologies do not contain the reference links that associated a term to a real object. An ontology can also be used to organize data that describe these real objects and reference them. For example, consider that two researchers, Peter and Alice, want to analyse a new corpus of antiquarian books that they have just received. They decide to split the work in two and share their findings about these books. First, they have to share a common description of the book. For this, they decide to store its title, the author, the publisher, its state and its location inside the library (room, shelf). They want to provide a unique ID for each book. In order to be able to share these data and to keep the description up to date they decide to define a common data schema. A data schema specifies "the organisation of data in a manner that reflects an information structure" (ISO 11179). In this case the common schema is not an ontology because it is shared only between Peter and Alice, but if several people decide to define a data schema to share the data about book descriptions, this common schema becomes an ontology.

A common schema is also called a *lightweight ontology* and is composed of terms, classes, attributes and relations.

14.3.2.2.1 DATA EXCHANGE USING INTERCHANGE FORMATS

Interchange formats are used to exchange data between different information systems based on different technologies. An interchange format is the description of a common schema using a specific format such as XML (tree syntax), RDF (graph syntax) or CSV (table syntax).

Consider that based on their common schema, Peter and Alice decide to propose an XML schema to store the description of their books. Peter decides to store his data in a database. Alice prefers to store data in a CSV file. Peter's database will produce as output an XML document following the XML schema. Alice's CSV system will be able to import the XML document to keep her CSV file up-to-date (and vice versa).

An example of interchange formats that Peter and Alice may use to exchange their description of *book* could be the header of Text Encoding Initiative (TEI). TEI is a consortium that collectively develops and maintains a standard for the representation of texts in digital form. The TEI header stores information about the book title, the publisher and the source description. The TEI Guidelines define a schema in XML. Example 1 shows the TEI header about a Shakespeare work.

```
(1)
<teiHeader>
  <fileDesc>
    <titleStmt>
      <title>Shakespeare: the first folio (1623) in electronic
      form</title>
      <author>Shakespeare, William (1564-1616)</author>
    </titleStmt>
    <publicationStmt>
      <distributor>Oxford Text Archive</distributor>
      <address>
```

```
        <addrLine>13 Banbury Road, Oxford OX2 6NN, UK</
        addrLine>
      </address>
      <idno type="OTA">119</idno>
      <availability>
        <p>Freely available on a non-commercial basis.</p>
      </availability>
      <date when="1968">1968</date>
    </publicationStmt>
    <sourceDesc>
      <bibl>The first folio of Shakespeare, prepared by Charl-
      ton Hinman (The Norton Facsimile, 1968)</bibl>
    </sourceDesc>
  </fileDesc>
</teiHeader>
```

TEI Guidelines have been widely used by libraries, museums, publishers and individual scholars to present texts for online research, teaching and preservation. For storing bibliographic records, other schema promoted by the librarian community are available, like the Functional Requirements for Bibliographic Records (FRBR) or the Resource Description and Access (RDA).

14.3.2.2.2 DATA INTEGRATION AND MEDIATION

Consider now that Peter and Alice are two librarians that manage different corpora using their own database and that they want to build a common system to query both their bibliographic records. They have to face a data integration problem. Data integration and mediation come from the database domain. When several databases describe the same reality (the same set of real object, the same corpus), they may have different schema due to the fact that they develop different points of view of this reality. Computer scientists have developed some techniques to be able to query the different databases with a single query, whereas the user has the impression he is querying a homogeneous and centralised database.

First they have to define a new global schema that integrates all the data described by the schema of the source databases. This process is called *schema integration* (Fu 2016) and starts with mapping discovery. Mapping discovery takes two or more source schemas as input and produces a mapping between elements of the input schemas that correspond semantically to each other. The goal is to identify the common elements of the source data schemas. Schema integration constructs the global schema based on the output of the mapping discovery.

After the creation of the global schema, the computer scientist has to decide if the data from the sources will be copied into one database organised by the global schema. This solution is called *data integration*. Another solution is to keep the data in each source database. Then a data mediation system is built to enable the user to query all the sources with a single query based on the global schema. In data mediation the global schema is called an *ontology* (Reynaud and Giraldo 2003).

In data integration techniques, some Extraction Transformation Load (ETL) processes are defined that query a source database and load the data into the final database (Keith et al. 2005).

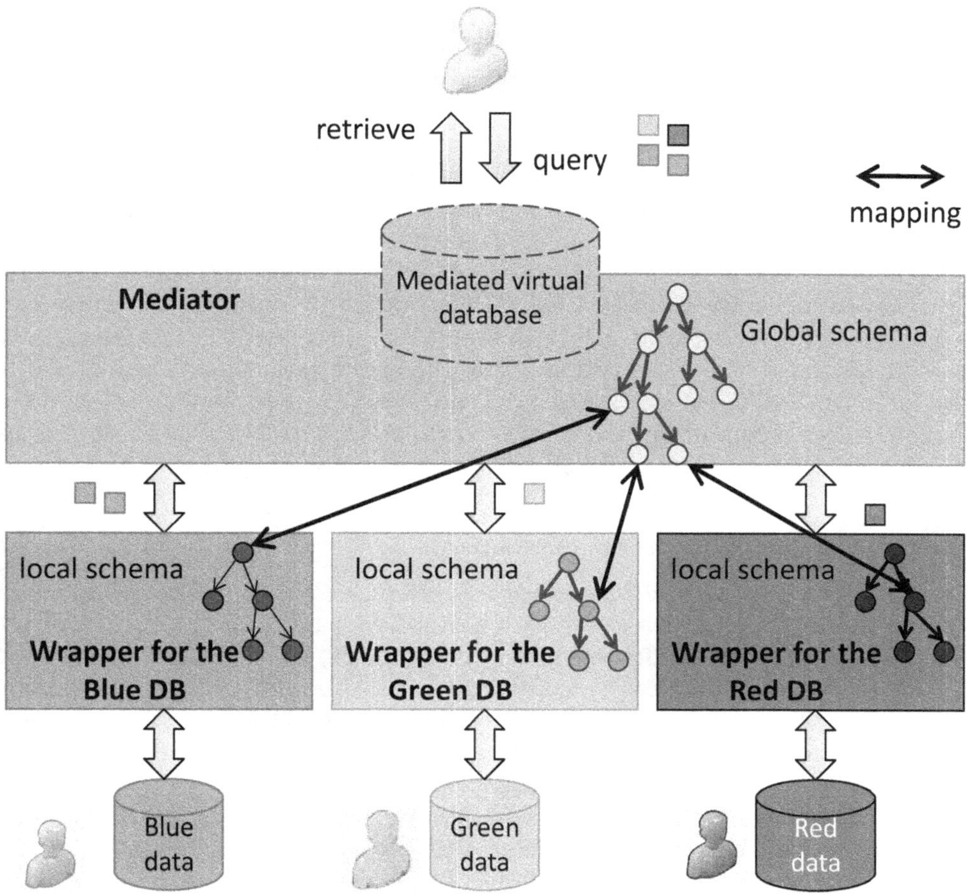

Figure 14.6 Architecture of mediation system
Source: (Roussey et al. 2010)

A mediation system implies several processes: selecting the data source that could answer part of the user query, translating the user query to queries interpretable by source schemas, retrieving the data from the source and merging all the results to build a global answer to the user query. In mediation technique, the queries applied to the source database are built thanks to logical mappings between the entity of the global schema and entity of the source schema (Figure 14.6). The logical mappings and the global schema are based on a single *axiomatised ontology* (Reynaud and Giraldo 2003).

14.3.2.2.3 LOD AND SEMANTIC WEB TECHNOLOGIES

Semantic Web technologies are a set of new technologies that makes it possible to publish data sets on the Web. Publishing data sets on the Web means first publishing their schema on the Web. Second, all data values may be also published on the Web according to these schemas. And finally data sets should be linked to each other. The link can represent, for example, that two different digital descriptions represent the same real object. All the data sets, published freely on the Web thanks to these technologies, composes the *Linked Open Data* (LOD) cloud. In Semantic Web technologies, a published schema is called an *ontology*. When the schema is very simple, it is called a *vocabulary*. For example, the Dublin Core published on the LOD a small vocabulary of metadata like author, publisher and so on.

Data providers share their data on the Web in order to enable unknown applications to discover them and reuse them. Their data schema is composed of several ontologies already published on the LOD in order to improve interoperability. For example, the French National Library, the BNF, published on the LOD part of its catalogue (Simon *et al.* 2013). Their schema reuses simple vocabulary like Dublin Core, FOAF and SKOS. The *Europeana* project, which has the same goal at the European level, has proposed its own schema called Europeana Data Model (EDM) based also on the vocabulary Dublin Core, FOAF and SKOS (Haslhofer and Isaac 2011). Because the two projects share the same vocabularies, it is easy to see the common parts of the two schemas and their differences. The same can be done on the data, which can help in finding bibliographic records referencing the same book.

14.3.2.3 Ontologies to perform inferences

Inference systems, also called *knowledge base systems*, are able to deduce new information from previous information. This type of system manages what computer scientists call *knowledge* (Kayser 1997). Information (data with meaning) becomes knowledge when it is the basis for an inference leading to new knowledge. A knowledge base system dissociates reasoning knowledge used to make inferences from domain knowledge – that is to say facts (information) on which inferences are applied. The same set of reasoning rules can be applied to different sets of factual knowledge.

In this case, ontologies are called *heavyweight ontologies*. They are composed of classes, attributes, relations, axioms, instances and relations between instances. This kind of ontology exploits the formalism available in the knowledge representation languages. They aim to produce inferences thanks to a reasoner (in description logics or with rules) (Hebeler et al. 2011). They are difficult to reuse as the inferences they produce are oriented for a specific application.

In the Semlib project that developed the Pundit tool (Grassi *et al.* 2013) such kinds of ontologies are used. Pundit is a semantic annotation tool allowing users to create structured data annotating the Web in various ways (comments, citations, bookmarks, etc.). All annotations are available on the Web as LOD. Imagine that Alice has published on the Web some transcriptions of an ancient philosopher's work. She can use Pundit to annotate those transcriptions with *DBpedia* entities (see Chapters 12, 13, and 43 of this *Handbook*). *DBpedia* is the data set extracted from the infobox of Wikipedia web pages. *DBpedia* is used as a normalized list of philosophers and provides unique ID for each of them and for each of their works. Alice can then specify, for example, the author of the document and the citations of other philosophers' works inside the document. Her annotations are open to others. Peter can do the same with his own transcription corpus of philosopher works. Based on Alice's and Peter's annotations, the system computes the influence between philosophers. The influence is computed through an inference mechanism, which states that the influence is proportional to the number of times the philosopher cites the works of another one.

More recently, *terminological knowledge bases* are emerging (see Chapter 21 of this *Handbook*). These resources are knowledge bases represented with lightweight or heavyweight ontologies in which the terminological concepts have a central role in the representation. The Lemon model defines the link between the terminological concept and the class (McCrae et al. 2012). This model has been used as a common interchange format for lexical resources on the Semantic Web and several lexical resources such as *WordNet*, *FrameNet*, *VerbNet*, English and German *Wiktionary*, and the English and German entries of *Omega-Wiki* are now available on the LOD constituting a new initiative, the *Linguistic Linked Open Data* (Eckle-Koher et al. 2015).

14.3.3 Building and reusing domain ontologies

In the previous section we illustrated how ontologies are used in different applications and the impact on their organization. Now we will present the main processes involved in ontology creation and reuse.

14.3.3.1 Ontology engineering methodologies

Ontology engineering and management are similar in many ways to software engineering and project management. Thus, the same techniques and guidelines are adapted and processed.

The main ontology engineering phases can be synthesised as follows: requirement analysis, ontology modelling and design, ontology development and ontology testing (see Figure 14.7).

Requirement analysis aims to identify the scope of the ontology and elicit the purpose of the domain ontology (Suárez-Figueroa et al. 2009). This phase has to determine the use of the ontology, which requirements it has to fulfil, its scope and its granularity. It also has to specify the role of end users and who will maintain the ontology. For example, competency questions help to specify the ontology requirements. It consists of defining the questions that the ontology should resolve and listing all the possible answers. The analysis results in an ontology requirements specification document.

Ontology modelling and design consists of knowledge acquisition and conceptualisation. The knowledge acquisition can be done from scratch by brainstorming and dialoguing with different stakeholders (users, domain experts and so on) but it is mostly performed by exploiting existing data such as document collections, interviews or existing structured

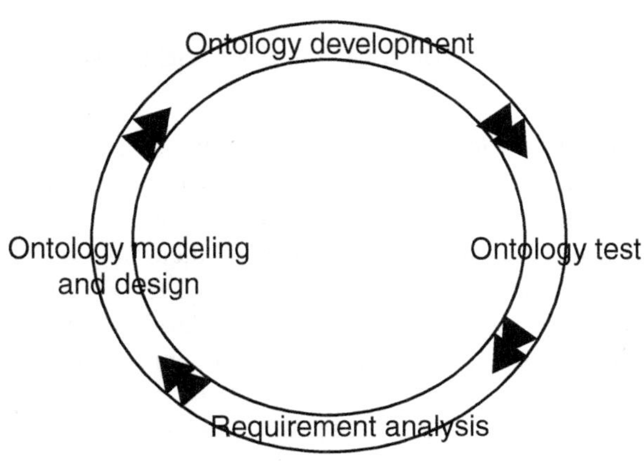

Figure 14.7 Main ontology engineering phases

resources as Unified Modeling Language (UML) diagrams (Pinet et al. 2009) or databases (Cerbah and Lammari 2012). The conceptualisation is split into several tasks. One major task is the building of the hierarchy of concepts which can be done as (i) a bottom-up approach by first determining the low level concepts and then generalising them, (ii) a top-down approach by first determining the top concepts and then specialising them or (iii) a middle-out approach which mixes the two approaches and first determines the core concepts and then generalises and specialises them (Gandon 2002).

Ontology development consists in implementing the conceptualisation in a computer science language. The output is an ontology: a computer science artefact.

Ontology testing consists of comparing the produced ontology to the requirements specifications. Evaluating the ontology quality is crucial and can be done with respect to different characteristics: syntactic, semantic, pragmatic and social (De Nicola et al. 2009). The test and evaluation phase help designers evolve the ontologies in order to comply with their usage.

Other phases, such as integration and maintenance, are important and should be done carefully. They are essential to making produced ontologies easy to reuse and share.

One of the most complete methodologies for ontology engineering is METHONTOLOGY (Gómez-Pérez et al. 2004), which proposes a set of activities to develop ontologies based on a life cycle and on prototype refinement. Recent methodologies propose integrating agility at each step. An example is the *Unified Process for Ontology Building* (UPON) which proposes an approach that takes advantage of the UP and the UML. The main objectives of UPON are reduction of time and costs in the production of large-scale domain ontologies (also providing useful guidelines for small ontologies); enhancement of the quality of the produced ontology by progressive validation of the intermediate results; creation of a methodological setting where the two kinds of expertise, knowledge engineer and domain engineer expertise, are explicitly identified and used at best; clear identification of the activities, with roles and responsibilities of the different experts; and production of intermediate results that can be readily available to the users of the ontology-based applications (e.g. semantic search) (De Nicola et al. 2009).

As one aim of ontologies is to be reused in several applications or data sets, a crucial step, once they have been evaluated, is also to make them available to others. The most common approach used to share ontologies consists of publishing them on the Web by following Semantic Web principles (Berners-Lee and Hendler 2001).

14.4 Looking to the future: tools for editing and reusing ontologies

Hundreds of thousands of ontologies are available today on the Web, and tools have been designed in order to help editing and finding them. Some of them, which will be mentioned next, may be of some use for lexicographers. In particular, we will refer to ontology editors and search engines, which may help lexicographers in their daily activities (e.g. complete dictionary articles, find suitable synonyms and antonyms, etc.).

The most popular ontology editor is *Protégé* (Musen 2013) which is a free, open-source platform that enables, among other functionalities, to import, visualise and reason on ontologies.

To find existing ontologies published in the Web, two kinds of approaches exist. Ontologies can either be looked for with an ontology search engine or directly within ontology libraries. An ontology search engine such as SWOOGLE (Finin et al. 1999) crawls the Web for ontologies that have been published. The ontologies that are found are then indexed by the search engine according to the terms that compose them, and users can retrieve them by using traditional keyword queries. Search engines are today less used as ontology libraries offer more functionalities. An *ontology library* is a "Web-based system that provides access to an extensible collection of ontologies with the primary purpose of enabling users to find and use one or several ontologies from this collection" (d'Aquin and Noy 2011: 97). More concretely the aim of these libraries is not to index all the ontologies that exist but to propose mechanisms to easily access and reuse ontologies that designers have deliberately submitted. Among domain libraries in biology, *BioPortal* (Noy et al. 2009) and *OBO Foundry* (Smith et al. 2007) libraries focus on community-based tools for ontology annotation and evaluation, which help users to share comments and reviews on ontologies. Other kind of libraries, focus on specific functionalities such as *OntoSearch2* (Thomas et al. 2007) that provides an efficient querying mechanism across hundreds of ontologies by proposing a keyword-based search mechanism dedicated to ontology specificities. The *Linked Open Vocabulary* (LOV) (Vandenbussche et al. 2015) is another platform whose aim is to facilitate the choice of ontologies to use when publishing data on the LOD. To do so, the LOV proposes different functionalities which benefit from the fact that the ontologies are used on the LOD. For example, ontology statistics, ontology assessment and ontology mapping are proposed according to the LOD data sets in which they are used.

14.5 Conclusion and perspectives

In this chapter, a general overview of what domain ontology is for computer scientists is given. Ontologies can be composed of different elements depending on the applications they are used in. Clues are given in order to help identify an ontology's role and usage in specific applications. Our overview also aims to describe ontology editors and search engines, which may be of some use for lexicographic purposes. For instance, the lexical database *WordNet* describes relations among words which can help lexicographers to spot, say, examples of synonymy, antonomy, hyperymy, meronymy and so on.

The future of lexical resources will be in the Linguistic Linked Open Data initiative (LLOD) (Chiarcos *et al.* 2012). This initiative aims to publish data for linguistics and natural language processing using the LOD principles. LLOD contains two groups of resources. The first one contains lexical semantic resources like machine-readable dictionaries, ontologies and terminologies. The second group is composed of annotated corpora. LLOD leads to enhance interoperability and scalability for any applications that integrate lexical resources. A recent example is "DBlexipedia: A nucleus for a multilingual lexical Semantic Web." *DBlexipedia* provides a multilingual lexicon for the *DBpedia* ontology by means of existing automatic methods for lexicon induction (Walter *et al.* 2015).

Related topics

Lexicography and natural language processing; FrameNet; towards an international directory of lexicography; information retrieval for lexicographic purposes.

Further reading

Cimiano, P., C. Unger and J. McCrae. (2014). *Ontology-Based Interpretation of Natural Language*. Morgan & Claypool Publishers. Synthesis Lectures on Human Language Technologies 7(2).

www.morganclaypool.com/doi/abs/10.2200/S00561ED1V01Y201401HLT024 [Last accessed: 2 February, 2017]

This book presents a synthesis on how ontologies are used in natural language technologies.

Maedche, A. (2012). *Ontology Learning for the Semantic Web*. Heidelberg: Springer (Springer Science & Business Media. Vol. 665)
This books presents on overview on approaches used in ontology construction.

Rudolph, S., G. Gottlob, I. Horrocks, F. van Harmelen. (2013). *Reasoning Web. Semantic Technologies for Intelligent Data Access*: Proceedings of the 9th international summer school 2013 Mannheim Germany July August 2013, LNCS 8067 Tutorial
This book contains the tutorials presented during a summer school of Semantic Web technologies. It presents the basis of Semantic Web technologies and their usage.

Suárez-Figueroa, M. C., A. Gómez-Pérez, E. Motta, and A. Gangemi (eds.) (2012). *Ontology Engineering in a Networked World.* Heidelberg: Springer. Springer Science & Business Media.
This book presents the last ontology engineering methods used for publishing data on the LOD cloud.

Wood, D., M. Zaidman, L. Ruth, and M. Hausenblas. (2013). *Linked Data.* Manning Publications Co. ISBN 9781617290398.
This book explains the principles of Linked Open Data.

References

Alonso, I. and D. Contreras. (2016) "Evaluation of Semantic Similarity Metrics Applied to the Automatic Retrieval of Medical Documents: An UMLS Approach", *Expert Systems With Applications* 44: 386–399. http://dx.doi.org/10.1016/j.eswa.2015.09.028. [Last accessed: 2 February, 2017]

Arp, R., B. Smith and A. D. Spear. (2015) *Building Ontologies With Basic Formal Ontology*. Cambridge, MA: MIT Press.

Aussenac-Gilles, N. and D. Soergel. (2005) "Text Analysis for Ontology and Terminology Engineering", *Applied Ontology* 1(1): 35–46.

Berners-Lee, T. and J. Hendler, (2001) "Publishing on the Semantic Web", *Nature* 410(6832): 1023–1024.

Biebow, B., S. Szulman and A. J. Clément. (1999) "TERMINAE: A Linguistics-Based Tool for the Building of a Domain Ontology", in D. Fensel and R. Studer (eds.), *Knowledge Acquisition, Modelling and Management. Lecture Notes in Computer Science*, vol. 1621. Heidelberg: Springer, pp. 49–66.

Brickley, D. and L. Miller. (2014) "FOAF Vocabulary Specification 0.99", http://xmlns.com/foaf/spec/#term_publications [Last accessed: 2 February 2017].

Cerbah, F. and N. Lammari. (2012) "Ontology Learning From Databases: Some Efficient Methods to Discover Semantic Patterns in Data", in J. Lehmann and J. Völker (eds.), *Perspectives of Ontology Learning*. Amsterdam: IOS Press, pp. 207–222.

Chiarcos, C., S. Hellmann and S. Nordhoff. (2012) "Linking Linguistic Resources: Examples From the Open Linguistics Working Group", in C. Chiarcos, S. Nordhoff and S. Hellmann (eds.), *Linked Data in Linguistics. Representing Language Data and Metadata*. Heidelberg: Springer, pp. 201–216.

Daconta, M. C., L. J. Obrst and K. T. Smith. (2003) *The Semantic Web: A Guide to the Future of XML, Web Services, and Knowledge Management*. New York: John Wiley & Sons.

d'Aquin, M. and N. F. Noy. (2011) "Where to Publish and Find Ontologies? A Survey of Ontology Libraries", *Web Semantics: Science, Services and Agents on the World Wide Web* 11(0): 96, 111, 2012. doi:10.1016/j.websem.2011.08.005.

DBlexipedia = http://dblexipedia.org/ [Last accessed 2 February 2017].

DBpedia = http://wiki.dbpedia.org [Last accessed 2 February 2017].

De Nicola, A., M. Missikoff and R. Navigli. (2009) "A Software Engineering Approach to Ontology Building", *Information Systems* 34(2): 258–275.

Eckle-Kohler, J., J. P. McCrae and C. Chiarcos. (2015) "Lemon Uby – A Large, Interlinked, Syntactically-Rich Lexical Resource for Ontologies", *Semantic Web* 6(4): 371–378.

Fellbaum, C. (1998) *WordNet. An Electronic Lexical Database*. Cambridge, MA: MIT Press.

Finin, T., L. Ding, R. Pan, A. Joshi, P. Kolari, A. Java and Y. Peng. (2005) "Swoogle: Searching for Knowledge on the Semantic Web", in *Proceedings of the National Conference on Artificial Intelligence*; AAAI 20(4): 1682.

Fu, G. (2016) "FCA Based Ontology Development for Data Integration", in *Information Processing and Management* 52(2): 765–782. http://dx.doi.org/10.1016/j.ipm.2016.02.003. [Last accessed 2 February 2017].

Gandon, F. (2002) "Ontology Engineering: A Survey and a Return on Experience." Internal report 4396, INRIA. 181 pages. https://hal.inria.fr/inria-00072192/document [Last accessed: 2 February 2017].

Gómez-Pérez, A., M. Fernández López and O. Corcho. (2004) *Ontological Engineering*. Heidelberg: Springer.

Grassi, M., C. Morbidoni, M. Nucci, S. Fonda and F. Di Donato. (2013) "Pundit: Creating, Exploring and Consuming Semantic Annotations", in *Proceedings of the 3rd International Workshop on Semantic Digital Archives, Ceur-ws.org* 1091: 65–72.

Grüber, T. R. (1993). "A Translation Approach to Portable Ontology Specifications." *Knowledge Acquisition* 5(2): 199–220. doi:10.1006/knac.1993.1008.

Haslhofer, B. and A. Isaac. (2011) "data.europeana.eu The Europeana Linked Open Data Pilot", in *Proceedings of International Conference on Dublin Core and Metadata Applications*, pp. 94–104.

Hebeler, J., M. Fisher, R. Blace, and A. Perez-Lopez. (2011) *Semantic Web Programming*. New York: John Wiley & Sons.

International Standard Organisation. (2000) *International Standard ISO 1087–1 Terminology Work – Vocabulary-Part 1: Theory and Application*. First edition 2000/10/15.

International Standard Organisation. (2015) *International Standard ISO/IEC 11179 Metadata Registry (MDR) Part 1 Framework*. Third edition 2015/12/15

Kayser, D. (1997) *La représentation des connaissances*'. Paris: Hermes.

Keith, S., O. Kaser and D. Lemire. (2005) "Analyzing Large Collections of Electronic Text Using OLAP". http://citeseerx.ist.psu.edu/viewdoc/download?doi=10.1.1.88.3087&rep=rep1&type=pdf [Last accessed: 2 February 2017].

McCrae, J., G. Aguado-de Cea, P. Buitelaar, P. Cimiano, T. Declerck, A. Gómez-Pérez, J. Gracia, L. Hollink, E. Montiel-Ponsoda, D. Spohrand T. Wunner. (2012) "Interchanging Lexical Resources on the Semantic Web", *Language Resources and Evaluation* 46: 701–710.

Musen, M. A. (2013) "Protégé Ontology Editor", *Encyclopedia of Systems Biology*: 1763–1765.

Noy, N. F., N. H. Shah, P. L. Whetzel, B. Dai, M. Dorf, N. Griffith, C. Jonquet, D. L. Rubin, M. A. Storey, C. G. Chute and M. A. Musen. (2009) "Bioportal: Ontologies and Integrated Data Resources at the Click of a Mouse", *Nucleic Acids Research*. New York: Springer.

Suárez-Figueroa, M. C., A. Gómez-Pérez and B. Villazón-Terrazas. (2009) "How to Write and Use the Ontology Requirements Specification Document", in *OTM Confederated International Conferences 'On the Move to Meaningful Internet Systems'*. Heidelberg: Springer, pp. 966–982.

Ogden, C. K. and I. A. Richards. (1923) *The Meaning of Meaning*. London: Kegan, Paul, Trench, Trubner.

Pinet, F., C. Roussey, T. Brun and F. Vigier. (2009) "The Use of UML as a Tool for the Formalisation of Standards and the Design of Ontologies in Agriculture", in P. J. Papajorgji and P. M. Pardalos (eds.) *Advances in Modeling Agricultural Systems*. Heidelberg: Springer, pp. 131–147.

Rais, M., and A. Lachkar. (2016) "Biomedical Word Sense Disambiguation Context-Based: Improvement of Sense Relate Method", in *Proceedings of International Conference on Information Technology for Organizations Development* (IT4OD 2016), March 30, 2016–April 1, 2016, Fez, Morocco, pp. 1–6.

Reynaud, C. and G. Giraldo. (2003) "An Application of the Mediator Approach to Services Over the Web", in *Special Track Data Integration in Engineering, Concurrent Engineering (CE'2003)-the Vision for the Future Generation in Research and Applications*, pp. 209–216.

Roussey, C., V. Soulignac, J. C. Champomier, V. Abt, and J. P. Chanet. (2010) "Ontologies in Agriculture". in *Dans International Conference on Agricultural Engineering (AGENG 2010), September 2010*, Clermont-Ferrand, France, edition Cemagref: 178. 2010.

Simon, A., R. Wenz, V. Michel and A. Di Mascio. (2013) "Publishing Bibliographic Records on the Web of Data: Opportunities for the BnF (French National Library)", in *Proceedings of 10th European Semantic Web Conference ESWC (ESWC 2013)*. DOI:10.1007/978-3-642-38288-8_38.

Smith, B., M. Ashburner, C. Rosse, J. Bard, W. Ceusters, W. Bug, L. J. Goldberg, K. Eilbeck, C. J. Mungall, A. Ireland, N. Leontis, P. Rocca-Serra, A. Ruttenberg, S.-A. Sansone, R. H. Scheuermann, P. L. Whetzel, N. Shah and S. Lewis. (2007) "The OBO Foundry: Coordinated Evolution of Ontologies to Support Biomedical Data Integration", *Nature Biotechnology* 25(11): 1251–1255.

Thomas, E., J. Z. Pan and D. Sleeman. (2007) "ONTOSEARCH2: Searching Ontologies Semantically", in *Proceedings of the OWLED 2007 Workshop on OWL: Experiences and Directions*. http://ceur-ws.org/Vol-258/paper26.pdf [Last accessed: 2 February 2017].

Uschold, M. and R. Jasper. (1999) "A Framework for Understanding and Classifying Ontology Applications", in *Proceedings of the IJCAI-99 Workshop on Ontologies and Problem-Solving Methods (KRR5)*, Stockholm, Sweden, 2 August 1999. Ceur-ws.org 18

Vandenbussche, P. Y., G. A. Atemezing, M. Poveda-Villalón and B. Vatant. (2015) "Linked Open Vocabularies (LOV): A Gateway to Reusable Semantic Vocabularies on the Web", *Semantic Web* (Preprint): 1–16. www.semantic-web-journal.net/system/files/swj974.pdf [Last accessed: 2 February, 2017].

Varelas, G., E. Voutsakis, P. Raftopoulou, E. G. Petrakis and E. E. Milios. (2005) "Semantic Similarity Methods in WordNet and Their Application to Information Retrieval on the Web", in *Proceedings of the 7th Annual ACM International Workshop on Web Information and Data Management, ACM: 10–16*. http://nike.psu.edu/widm05/p/p10-varelas.pdf [Last accessed: 2 February, 2017].

Walter, S., C. Unger and P. Cimiano. (2015) "DBlexipedia: A Nucleus for a Multilingual Lexical Semantic Web", in *Proceedings of 3th International Workshop on NLP and DBpedia, ISWC2015*. http://ceur-ws.org/Vol-1581/paper9.pdf [Last accessed: 2 February 2017].

Part III

Types of dictionaries

15
The concept of dictionary

Sven Tarp

15.1 Introduction

Few people involved in lexicography will deny that dictionaries are the *raison d'être* of their discipline. These artefacts have been produced in large numbers for more than 4,000 years. Apart from dictionaries, they have been referred to as glosses, glossaries, vocabularies, thesauri, lexicons, encyclopaedias, anthologies and resources, among various names. Many of these works have long ago been transformed into dust, and the rhythm of appearance and extinction is faster than ever before in today's digital world. Nobody knows the exact number of published dictionaries, but we are probably speaking of hundreds of thousands, if not millions, of different titles. These works have been compiled with very different technologies and presented on different media such as clay, papyrus, paper and various digital platforms, among them the Internet. They have been designed with a wide variety of purposes and have covered a large number of languages and areas of human knowledge.

Although trained to write definitions, many individual lexicographers tend to view this exceptionally rich discipline from the relatively limited perspective of their own personal experience in dictionary making, an experience which seldom comprises more than one or, at the most, two different categories of dictionary. Against this background, it is hardly surprising that there is no general agreement in the lexicographical community on how to define a dictionary.

In this contribution, we will first look at some of the definitions suggested by renowned scholars and contrast them with the existing empirical reality, that is, the various categories of dictionaries actually published. Then follows a discussion of the requirements to a general definition of the concept of dictionary, a definition which necessarily has to be inclusive in the sense that no category of dictionary should be ignored. Finally, the contribution will present such a definition and discuss its various implications.

15.2 Historical perspective

15.2.1 Transmitting knowledge

Before the advent of modern computer and information technologies, the hitherto most important technological revolution in lexicography was triggered by the invention of the printing press. This disruptive technology quickly made its way into lexicography with radical consequences for both the typography and format of the dictionary article as explained by Hanks (2010, 2013). In a longer perspective, it also implied that dictionaries reached a much bigger audience composed of new social strata with other types of need that could be solved by consulting dictionaries. The result was that the discipline branched out and completely new categories of dictionary saw the light, a development that accelerated in the period of European history known as the Enlightenment Era (see Tarp and Bothma 2013).

The first lexicographer not only took note of this development but also proved to have a profound and almost encyclopaedic understanding of dictionaries was Jean le Rond d'Alembert. In 1754, this Enlightenment philosopher and scientist published a long article titled *Dictionnaire* in the fourth volume of the great French *Encyclopédie* which he edited together with Denis Diderot. In this readworthy contribution he proposed, among other things, the following classification of contemporary dictionaries:

> It is possible to distinguish between three types of *dictionary*: language dictionaries, historical dictionaries, and science and art dictionaries. This subdivision could be presented from a more general point of view as *dictionaries* of words, *dictionaries* of facts and *dictionaries* of things. Nevertheless, we retain the first subdivision because we believe that it is more convenient and even more precise. In fact, a language *dictionary*, which would seem to be nothing other than a word *dictionary*, when well done must often be a *dictionary* of things and is thus a very philosophical work. [. . .] A science *dictionary* can, and must, only be a *dictionary* of facts, whenever the causes are unknown to us, that is, almost always. [. . .] Finally, a historical *dictionary*, assembled by a philosopher, will often be a *dictionary* of things. Produced by an ordinary writer, by a compiler of facts and dates, it will be but a *dictionary* of words. [. . .] Language *dictionary*. This is how we refer to a *dictionary* destined to explain the most common and ordinary words in a language. It is different from the historical *dictionary*, in that it excludes facts and the names of places and people, and is different from the science *dictionary*, in that it excludes little-known scientific terms and those familiar only to the knowledgeable.
>
> (d'Alembert 1754: 958)

Although different from modern terminology in some aspects, these exceptionally rich reflections corresponded to the eighteenth-century empirical reality which did not only comprise "dictionaries of words". Harris (1704), for instance, wrote in the preface to his *Lexicon Technicum*, which he also titled *Universal English Dictionary of Arts and Sciences*, that it did not only contain "bare Words but [also] Things"; and that "the Reader may not only find here an Explication of the Technical Words, or the Terms of Art made use of in all the Liberal Sciences, [. . .] but also those Arts themselves".

Similar ideas can be found in several other dictionaries from that period. Chambers' (1728) *Cyclopædia* was "intended as a course of ancient and modern learning" and therefore contained both "definitions of the terms, and accounts of the things signify'd thereby, in the several arts". In the same vein, Postlethwayt (1749: 2) wrote that his *Universal Dictionary of Trade and Commerce*, which was published in four editions in the following 25 years, would reduce foreign and domestic trade "to the form of a Dictionary, for alphabetical reference" in order to assist those who did not have a "satisfactory knowledge of Facts in complicated matters of a commercial nature".

According to Yeo (2003: 248), the first half of the eighteenth century "was a period in which the various branches of knowledge were laid out on paper in a manner supposedly accessible to people outside the formal university system". However, dictionaries of things, or of arts and sciences as they were more often called, are not a phenomenon limited to the eighteenth century, and neither are they exclusively dedicated to people outside the universities. In fact, the French economist and lexicographer Charles Ganilh (1826: xxvii) highlighted dictionaries as "the best means to disseminate sciences, speed up their progress, and make them quickly move to the highest stage they can reach". A similar example is Canga Argüelles, a former Spanish Minister of Public Finance, who in 1826–27 and 1833–34 published two dictionaries aimed at training senior civil servants in the Department of Public Finance, described by the author (1826: vii) as "a small library of Public Finance". According to three experts in economic history, "these two dictionaries contained the most worthwhile articles on economics written by a Spanish economist during the first half of the 19th century" (Astigarraga Zabalza and Almodovar 2001: 29).

Specialised dictionaries (i.e. dictionaries of arts and sciences) may be dedicated either to fellow experts or to laymen "outside the formal university system". An example of the latter is Johnson and Emerson's (1844) *American farmer's encyclopedia and dictionary of rural affairs* which was "adapted to the comprehension of unscientific readers", also referred to as "book-farmers":

> We are indeed much mistaken if the day has not arrived when the successes of the book-farmer shall cause his incredulous brother farmer of the old routine system, to cease his taunts and spend some of his leisure hours in searching into books containing modern information in regard to matters of husbandry.
>
> (Johnson and Emerson 1844: 5)

In an article on the popularisation of science in Great Britain, Layton (1965) stresses the historical importance of these and other specialised dictionaries:

> Whilst the extension of the popular science movement to the artisan and working classes had scarcely begun in the eighteenth century, the existence of scientific dictionaries helped to make possible the self-education of many scientists of humble origins, and directed the attention of men to a field of activity which was often neglected in an age when formal education was still predominantly classical.
>
> (Layton 1965: 222)

The tradition continued up to our time as can be seen, for instance, in the many specialised dictionaries dedicated to a variety of subject matters published by Oxford University Press, among other publishing houses. Speaking about economic dictionaries, Besomi (2011), an expert in the history of economics, sums up:

> These reference works played an important role in the popularization but also in the systematization of knowledge during the nineteenth century and the early twentieth century, and – judging from the continuing exponential increase in their publication – are still widely used in the support of teaching and, to a lesser extent, research.
>
> (Besomi 2011: 4)

All the dictionaries mentioned in this section have been designed with the overall purpose of *transmitting knowledge* of specific subject matters (e.g. husbandry, trade, or public finance) from an author who is necessarily a subject-field expert to fellow experts, semi-experts or laypeople. As mentioned, they have played, and still play, an important role in the development of society. It is thus surprising that they are largely ignored in most definitions of the concept of dictionary. A relatively rare exception is the Spanish scholar Martínez de Sousa who, in his *Diccionario de lexicografía práctica*, adds the following second sense to the definition of *diccionario*:

> Many sciences and techniques that could be expounded in the form of a treatise or a study are reduced to the form of a dictionary, a formula which is generally well received by the users.
>
> (Martínez de Souza 1995: 144)

15.2.2 Providing instructions and explaining non-linguistic signs

As we will discuss in the subsequent sections, dictionaries are reference works by excellence. It is therefore interesting to see how specialised dictionaries from the Enlightenment Era were frequently designed not only to transmit knowledge to their users, but also to give advice, suggestions, and instructions, that is, the sort of information which we would normally expect to find in manuals, how-to's, user guides, instruction books, etc.

The impressive subtitle of the 1767 edition of Chomel's *Dictionnaire oeconomique*, for instance, informs the readers that this dictionary also contains "an exact description of the plants", which can be used as food, to cultivate the land or embellish our gardens, as well as "instructions on how to prevent diseases and how to cure them". Similarly, in the fourth edition of his *Universal Dictionary of Trade and Commerce*, Postlethwayt (1774: iii) writes that the "work abounds with no small variety of suggestions and intimations for the advancement of numerous branches of the trade and commerce of these kingdoms".

There are many other dictionaries with similar purposes. In imperial China, for instance, some dictionaries, apart from explaining the words, also instructed their readers on how to address the emperor and even how to dress in such occasions. It is a matter of course that dictionaries with purposes of this kind should also be recognisable in a general definition of the concept of dictionary. The same holds true for dictionaries that are not designed to define or describe words, but to explain the meaning and use of non-linguistic signs, symbols, illustrations, etc., (i.e. dictionaries where the 'lemma' is not a linguistic sign or part of it). Any definition of the concept of dictionary that ignores lexicographical works with these and similar purposes can only be considered a partial definition that does not reflect the empirical reality in its totality.

15.2.3 D'Alembert versus Johnson

D'Alembert's (1754) classification of dictionaries was not specifically based on the criterion of purpose, but on that of content, that is, whether or not the dictionaries contained words, facts or things and how these phenomena were treated. There is, however, little doubt that it did not only take account of dictionaries designed to transmit knowledge as the ones discussed earlier but also of those conceived to assist their users in solving communication problems (i.e. another very common class of dictionary included in the concept of 'language dictionary').

With d'Alembert's (1754) rich reflections in mind, it is disappointing to see how Samuel Johnson (1755), in his *Dictionary of the English Language*, just one year later showed a much narrower approach to the discipline and defined a dictionary as a "book containing the words of any language in alphabetical order, with explanations of their meaning; a lexicon; a vocabulary; a word-book". This definition completely excludes a large part of the dictionaries mentioned by d'Alembert, among them the dictionaries of arts and sciences discussed earlier. The reason for this omission was not that Johnson was unaware of the existence of such dictionaries, but that he did not consider them to be useful as can be seen in the prologue which he wrote to the second edition of Rolt's *New Dictionary of Trade and Commerce*:

> It has lately been the practice of the learned to range knowledge by the alphabet, and publish dictionaries of every kind of literature. This practice has, perhaps, been carried too far by the force of fashion. Sciences, in themselves systematical and coherent, are not very properly broken into such fortuitous distributions. A dictionary of arithmetic or geometry can serve only to confound.
>
> (Johnson 1761)

15.2.4 Existing definitions

Since then, a kind of schism seems to reign in the lexicographical community with a number of scholars tacitly excluding all other classes of dictionary, except for "language dictionaries", from the concept of dictionary, at the same time as they consider lexicography to be a purely linguistic discipline. With reference to Trench (1858), Hanks (2013: 503) writes that a dictionary "is an inventory of the words of a language" and that "lexicographers are, first and foremost, linguistic inventory clerks". The statement is undoubtedly grounded in the empirical reality inasmuch as many dictionaries *are* "inventories of words" and many lexicographers rightfully can be regarded as "linguistic inventory clerks", but it is nevertheless incomplete as there are many other dictionaries and other lexicographers that cannot be characterised in this way.

Most modern definitions of the concept of dictionary are exclusive in the sense that they, if taken literally in all aspects, only cover a fraction of the dictionaries published until now. Landau (2001: 5), for instance, defines a dictionary as "a book that lists words in alphabetic order and describes their meanings". This short definition suffers from at least four problems:

1 When categorising a dictionary as a *book*, it excludes not only modern digital dictionaries but also dictionaries presented in the form of papyrus rolls and clay tablets.
2 When referring to *words*, it excludes dictionaries with lemmata consisting of parts of words (e.g. suffixes) or multi-word expressions (e.g. idioms), as well as non-linguistic signs.
3 When speaking about *alphabetic order*, it excludes dictionaries with other types of lemma arrangement as well as those which are not structured in the form of lists (i.e. most digital dictionaries).
4 When stating that dictionaries *describe meaning*, it excludes dictionaries that do not describe meaning (e.g. purely orthographical dictionaries).

Many of the same problems can be found in another, almost classical, definition where "alphabetic order" has been substituted with "systematic arrangement" and "words" with "linguistic forms", but where the other aspects are more or less identical:

> A dictionary is a systematically arranged list of socialized linguistic forms compiled from the speech-habits of a given speech community and commented on by the author in such a way that the qualified reader understands the meaning (. . .) of each separate form, and is informed of the relevant facts concerning the function of this form in its community.
>
> (Zgusta 1971: 197)

Instead of classifying dictionaries as books, various lexicographers such as Bergenholtz et al. 1997: 198), Burkhanov (1998: 64), and Hartmann and James (1998: 41) categorise them as *reference works* (or *reference resources* as they are called in the online *MacMillan English Dictionary*). These two terms, especially the latter, are much more precise as they represent a higher level of abstraction that does not exclude digital dictionaries, among others. In addition, they highlight an essential aspect of dictionaries, namely that they are *designed to be consulted* by their users.

Ten Haken (2009: 399) takes the discussion to an even higher level of abstraction and defines dictionaries as "*tools for solving problems*". Regretfully, he does not explore this highly interesting line of argumentation as he seemingly takes for granted that users consult dictionaries in order to get answers to "questions they have about vocabulary". This is undeniable, but it should not be forgotten that people also consult dictionaries with other purposes as discussed earlier. Among the lexicographers mentioned in this section, only Burkhanov seems to recognise the fact that dictionaries are much more than just "language dictionaries":

> The term 'dictionary' in a broad sense denotes the central category of lexicography, i.e. any reference work intended to provide *linguistic information*: pronunciation, spelling, lexical meaning, etymology, various aspects of usage including valence, etc., and/or *encyclopedic information*: biographical, geographical and historical, scientific concepts and taxonomies, and so on.
>
> (Burkhanov 1998: 64–65)

This definition appears to cover all three classes of dictionary included in d'Alembert's (1754) classification, that is, "dictionaries of words, dictionaries of facts and dictionaries of things". The same can partially be said about Bergenholtz (2012) who suggests the following definition of a dictionary:

> Lexicographic reference work containing dictionary articles related to individual topics or elements of language, and possibly several outer texts as well, which can be consulted if someone needs assistance with text reception, text production or translation or would simply like to know more about a word, part of a word or a combination of words.
>
> (Bergenholtz 2012: 30)

The first half of this definition is important because it does not only refer to "elements of language" but also to "individual topics" which also include 'facts' and 'things'. Unfortunately, this is contradicted by the second half of the definition which, apart from dictionaries with communicative purposes, only mentions dictionaries that are consulted in order to get knowledge of "a word, part of a word or a combination of words", but not the ones consulted in order to get knowledge of these topics. The author has subsequently added the last "detail" to the definition provided in a series of online dictionaries edited by him (see Bergenholtz 2016). As it is formulated earlier, the definition has many similarities to the one given in the *MacMillan English Dictionary* which speaks of dictionaries dealing "with a particular subject, providing the words, phrases, and terms used in that field, with information about their meaning and use", but not of dictionaries providing knowledge of this particular subject.

Generally it can be concluded that dictionaries of 'facts' and 'things', whatever their names, are left uncovered in most modern definitions of the concept of dictionary. Some lexicographers, like Landau (2001), go even further and explicitly disqualify these two classes of dictionary as dictionaries. Instead, they categorise them as encyclopaedias:

> A dictionary is a book that lists words in alphabetic order and describes their meanings. (. . .) An encyclopedia is a collection of articles about every branch of knowledge. Although the articles are usually arranged alphabetically, and though they often include definition, their descriptions go far beyond the information given in a dictionary. (. . .) The difference is sometimes stated, perhaps a bit too simply, by the apothegm, 'Dictionaries are about words, encyclopedias are about things.' This is true enough if we look at dictionaries and encyclopedias as a whole, but it admits of many exceptions if we try to apply it to every item in each type of work.
>
> (Landau 2001: 5–6)

Apart from ignoring the fact that many (most?) so-called encyclopaedias have been titled and published as dictionaries for more than 300 years, this argumentation gives rise to a whole series of new questions when a demarcation line between the various classes of dictionary has to be drawn:

1 What do descriptions "far beyond the information given in a dictionary" mean?
2 Where exactly is the demarcation line?
3 What principled difference is there between a thorough description of any "branch of knowledge" and a thorough description of any language?
4 Is knowledge of a language not a branch of knowledge?
5 What is the difference between semantic and encyclopaedic knowledge, if any?

In fact, the dismissal of some classes of dictionary only seems to create additional problems when defining the concept of dictionary and classifying these works. Many practical lexicographers, for example, Rundell (2016), try to solve this problem by treating *dictionary* as a polysemous word (or term) in their dictionaries. This may undoubtedly assist their users in understanding the word *dictionary* in specific contexts. However, instead of explaining the meaning elements common to all dictionaries, this approach rather underscores the differences between various classes of dictionary. It ignores the fact that if all the very different works indicated earlier, and many more together with them, can be grouped under the category of dictionaries (or similar names), then there must be *something common to all of them*. These uniting elements and aspects common to all types of dictionary should definitely be brought out and emphasised in a definition of the concept of dictionary. What is needed is therefore a completely different approach as the one discussed later.

15.3 Core issues and topics

As can be seen, the concept of dictionary may be defined according to various criteria. In this respect, three fundamental ones have been mentioned, or tacitly applied, in the previous discussion, namely *form*, *content* and *purpose*. These three criteria are compulsory for any definition aimed at covering the central aspects of dictionaries.

However, too many definitions found in the lexicographical literature are only based upon one or two of these criteria. They are therefore, at the best, partial definitions. Examples of this are the ones quoted earlier from Zgusta (1971), Burkhanov (1998) and Landau (2001). These definitions only refer to the dictionary form (book, wordlist, reference work, etc.) and content (e.g. meaning), but not to the purpose with which dictionaries are produced (i.e. which category of user need they are intended to satisfy). Besides, more often than not definitions are formulated at a too low level of abstraction, that is, they are too concrete, with the unavoidable result that various subtypes of dictionary are virtually excluded from the concept of dictionary, thus paving the way to confusion and misunderstandings.

A truly scientific definition covering the whole concept of dictionary must therefore take its point of departure in all three criteria. In addition, it should be formulated at such a high level of abstraction that no subset of dictionaries is left orphan, a requirement that does not exclude concrete exemplifications in order to make it more comprehensible.

15.3.1 Genuine purpose

Ten Haken (2009) characterises dictionaries as *tools*, whereas Wiegand (1987, 1998) defines them as *utility tools* (Gebrauchsgegenstände). A tool is a category formulated at a very high level of abstraction and, as such, it constitutes a hypernym of dictionary. What is important here is that a common characteristic of all tools is that they are produced in order to satisfy specific types of *human needs* (i.e. they have a *purpose*). Both authors also point out that the general purpose of dictionaries is to provide *information*. Ten Haken considers the information to be about vocabulary excluding in this way various categories of dictionary. By contrast, Wiegand (1987) takes the discussion to "the highest level of generalisation" where all dictionaries only have one genuine purpose which he defines as follows:

> The genuine purpose of a dictionary is that it can be used to acquire particular information about language or the non-linguistic world from lexicographical data belonging to certain data types.
>
> (Wiegand 1987: 200)

This short quotation is a good starting point for formulating a definition of a dictionary, but it also contains some problems. It refers to information about both "language", which is a broader concept than Ten Haken's "vocabulary", and "the non-linguistic world" whereby it seems to cover everything that exists. The question is nonetheless why the distinction between language and world is considered to be relevant here, instead of just referring to "information" which, without being qualified, would be equivalent to 'information about anything', which includes both language and world.

Another problem is the attributive adjective *particular* (bestimmt) which is not sufficiently precise. Dictionaries are not the only tools or works where people may get information, but contrary to other works, they are not designed to be read from one end to another. The specific category of information that can be retrieved from them can be defined as *punctual information* as opposed to *global information* which people can get in treatises, textbooks, scientific and popular journals, etc. In this respect, the opposition global-punctual should not be understood as an opposition between big and small, but between *the whole and the part* (see Bothma and Tarp (2012: 89).

15.3.2 Content

Different tools have different characteristics and therefore require different criteria to be defined. The fact that dictionaries are designed to provide information implies that the criteria of content and form are essential to their definition. Previously, we have seen how many definitions provided in the literature are too concrete in terms of content and thus exclusive. By contrast, in his definition of genuine purpose Wiegand (1987) just states that the user requires information from "lexicographical data". The term *data* represents a very high level of abstraction that does not exclude any specific type of content. And when it is qualified by the adjective *lexicographical* it specifies that the data have been selected and prepared lexicographically in one way or another, whereby it separates these data from the unelaborated raw data found in corpora and elsewhere.

It is important to note that Wiegand also distinguishes between data and information, two terms that are often mixed up. Dictionaries do not contain information but only lexicographical data (or items) from which the required information can be retrieved through a complex mental process, the success of which depends on the characteristics and capacity of each individual user (see Wiegand (2002) and Tarp (2007). This is why Ten Haken (2009: 399) asserts that "the solution of problems is not in the dictionary, but constructed by the user on the basis of information [read: data] found in the dictionary" and therefore emphasizes "the optimal presentation of information [read: data] as a central criterion of quality".

15.3.2 Form

As was seen, the dictionary form is frequently defined too narrowly as a book, a wordlist, etc. The term *reference resource* (or *work*), which has been proposed by various scholars, was therefore highlighted because it does not only embrace the 'traditional' book form but also clay tablets, papyrus rolls and the different types of digital dictionary (i.e. all the hitherto known forms of dictionaries).

Reference resource reflects much better that dictionaries are not designed to be read from one end to another but to be used in order to achieve punctual information. This also implies that dictionaries can be consulted and that the lexicographical data contained in them are accessible in one way or another. These reflections are valid both when dictionaries are designed to be consulted manually by their users (i.e. the traditional way of using them) and when they are conceived to be consulted automatically as in the case of a small but growing number of dictionaries that support and are integrated into other digital tools (e.g. the various spelling and grammar checkers). In this respect, dictionaries could also be called *consultation tools*.

15.3.3 Definition of dictionary

To sum up, the purpose of a dictionary, at the highest level of abstraction, is to assist its users in satisfying punctual information needs. The users retrieve the needed information from the lexicographically prepared data contained in the dictionary. A dictionary can therefore be classified as a reference resource or consultation tool. This resource or tool does not by itself solve its users' needs but rightly used it can assist them doing so.

It is necessary to place the consultation of dictionaries in a broader social context. The direct relation between a dictionary and a user is brought to an end (at least temporarily) when the latter has retrieved the required information from the lexicographical data contained in the former. However, this does not mean that the user's problem has been solved. The information need has been met, but the problem giving rise to it usually occurs extra-lexicographically in a specific context or situation. Thus, until the user has taken the obtained information back to this situation and solved the original problem, it cannot be claimed that the dictionary consultation in the broadest sense of the word is completely successful.

In this regard, the information needs that can be met by dictionaries and other lexicographical products are not abstract needs. On the contrary, the nature of these needs is, in the last instance, determined by the context where they occur and shaped by the characteristics of the person who experiences them (see Tarp 2008). All this has to be taken into consideration when planning dictionaries and preparing lexicographical data, and it should therefore also be reflected in a definition of the concept of dictionary. And the same should the increasingly important class of dictionary integrated into other digital tools which automatically come up with suggestions or even intervene directly in activities in which the users are engaged (e.g. by correcting texts in terms of orthography, grammar, etc.).

These reflections lead to the following definition of the concept of dictionary:

> *A dictionary is a utility tool, which is conceived for consultation with the genuine purpose of meeting punctual information needs experienced by specific types of potential user in specific types of extra-lexicographical context, and which is designed to assist its users by providing manual or automatic access to lexicographically prepared data, which can either be used directly by the users in order to retrieve the required information which they can subsequently use to solve specific problems in the context where the needs originally occurred, or by a digital tool in order to make automatic corrections in texts or translations produced by the users of this tool.*

This definition is formulated at a very high level of abstraction in order to embrace the elements and aspects that are common to all dictionaries. As mentioned earlier, this does not exclude exemplifications which may put flesh to the bones and make the definition easier to understand and handle. Besides, short definitions are as a rule not the most appropriate to describe a complex reality. The conclusion is that instead of short definitions of the concept of dictionary, it would be much better to have longer 'encyclopaedic' articles like the one written by d'Alembert (1754). After more than 4,000 years of existence, dictionaries represent a complex reality that deserves more than a few lines.

15.3.4 Classification of dictionaries

Dictionaries can be classified in different ways in accordance with the objective of the classification. The three fundamental criteria that can be used to classify dictionaries are the ones discussed earlier, namely *form*, *content* and *purpose*. As to form, they can be subdivided into clay tablet, papyrus roll, book and digital dictionaries; into dictionaries with alphabetical and systematic wordlists; into monolingual, bilingual and plurilingual ones; etc. The criterion of content is reflected, among others, in the long tradition of subdividing them into language and encyclopaedic dictionaries, although the demarcation line between the two classes may be difficult to establish.

Finally, and as discussed in the beginning of this contribution, dictionaries may have four fundamental purposes which can be called communicative, cognitive, operative and interpretive, respectively (see Fuertes-Olivera and Tarp 2014). Thus, based on the criterion of purpose, dictionaries can be subdivided into the following four main categories:

1 Dictionaries with communicative functions, that is, dictionaries designed to assist their users in solving problems related to written and oral communication (text reception, text production, translation and text revision).
2 Dictionaries with cognitive functions, that is, dictionaries designed to transmit knowledge to their users.
3 Dictionaries with operative functions, that is, dictionaries designed to assist their users in performing specific types of action.
4 Dictionaries with interpretive functions, that is, dictionaries designed to assist their users in interpreting non-linguistic signs.

Because of the fact that dictionaries are utility tools conceived with the genuine purpose of satisfying specific types of information need, and without rejecting any of the other classification criteria, it seems much more appropriate to classify them according to their purpose.

Related topics

Dictionaries for text reception; dictionaries for text production; dictionaries for translation; dictionaries to assist teaching and learning; electronic dictionaries; specialised dictionaries; domain ontologies; terminological knowledge bases; learners' dictionaries of English; the Accounting Dictionaries; the online dictionary of New Zealand sign language; Dictionary of Canadianisms on Historical Principles; the Onoelex dictionary; the Alicante Dictionaries; Wordnik.

Further reading

d'Alembert, J.L.R. (1754). "Dictionnaire," in D. Diderot and J.L.R. d'Alembert (eds.), *Encyclopédie, ou Dictionnaire raisonné des sciences, des arts et des metiers*. Tome IV. Paris: Briasson, pp. 958–969.
In this historical article from the big French encyclopaedia, the author presents a classification of all types of dictionary published in the Enlightenment Era as well as a number of reflections on the relationship between the various types of dictionary.

Bergenholtz, H. (2012). "What Is a Dictionary?", *Lexikos* 22: 22–30.
In this short article, Bergenholtz provides a critical review of a number of definitions which various scholars have given of the concept of dictionary. As a conclusion, he also proposes two alternative definitions of this concept.

Tarp, S. (2008). *Lexicography in the Borderland Between Knowledge and Non-Knowledge*. Tübingen: Niemeyer.
This book provides a comprehensive introduction to the function theory of lexicography upon which the earlier contribution is based. It contains a profound discussion of the relationship between dictionaries, users and information needs.

Ten Hacken, P. (2009). "What Is a Dictionary? A View From Chomskyan Linguistics", *International Journal of Lexicography* 22(4): 399–421.

In this article, which is based on Chomskyan linguistics, Ten Haken has a number of very interesting reflections on how users can make use of the lexicographical data found in dictionaries.

Wiegand, H. E. (1987). "Zur handlungstheoretischen Grundlegung der Wörterbenutzungsforschung", *Lexicographica* 3: 178–227.

This article contains important reflections on the genuine purpose and usage of dictionaries. These reflections have later been developed by the author in a number of books and articles.

References

d'Alembert, J.L.R. (1754) "Dictionnaire", in D. Diderot and J.L.R. d'Alembert (eds.), *Encyclopédie, ou Dictionnaire raisonné des sciences, des arts et des metiers*. Tome IV. Paris: Briasson, pp. 958–969.

Astigarraga, J., J. Zabalza and A. Almodovar (2001) "Dictionaries and Encyclopaedias on Political Economy in the Iberian Peninsula (18th, 19th and 20th Centuries)", *Storia del Pensiero Economico* 41: 25–63.

Bergenholtz, H. (2012) "What Is a Dictionary?", *Lexikos* 22: 22–30.

Bergenholtz, H. (ed.) (2016) *De Danske Netordbøger*. Odense: Ordbogen.com.

Bergenholtz, H., I. Cantell, R. V. Fjeld, D. Gundersen, J. H. Jónsson and B. Svensén (1997) *Nordisk leksikografisk ordbok*. Oslo: Universitetsforlaget.

Besomi, D. (ed.) (2011) *Crises and Cycles in Economic Dictionaries and Encyclopaedias*. London, New York: Routledge.

Bothma, T.J.D. and S. Tarp (2012) "Lexicography and the Relevance Criterion", *Lexikos* 22: 86–108.

Burkhanov, I. (1998) *Lexicography: A Dictionary of Basic Terminology*. Rzeszów: Wydawnictwo Wyzszej Zskoły Pedagogicznej.

Chambers, E. (1728) *Cyclopaedia, or an Universal Dictionary of Arts and Sciences*. London: James and John Knapton.

Fuertes-Olivera, P. A. and S. Tarp (2014) *Theory and Practice of Specialised Online Dictionaries: Lexicography Versus Terminography*. Berlin, Boston, MA: de Gruyter.

Ganilh, C. (1826) *Dictionnaire Analytique de L'Economie Politique*. Paris: Ladvocat.

Hanks, P. (2010) "Lexicography, Printing Technology, and the Spread of Renaissance Culture", in A. Dykstra and T. Schoonheim (eds.), *Proceedings of the XIV Euralex International Congress*. Leeuwarden: Fryske Akademy, pp. 988–1016.

Hanks, P. (2013) "Lexicography From Earliest Times to the Present", in K. Allens (ed.), *The Oxford Handbook of the History of Linguistics*. Oxford: Oxford University Press, pp. 503–536.

Harris, J. (1704) *Lexicon Technicum: Or, an Universal English Dictionary of Arts and Sciences: Explaining Not Only the Terms of Art, But the Arts Themselves*. London: Printed for D. Brown, J. Walthoe, J. Knapton, B. and S. Tooke, D. Midwinter, B. Cowse, T. Ward, E. Symon, E. Valentine, and J. Clark.

Hartmann, R.R.K. and J. Gregory (1998) *Dictionary of Lexicography*. London, New York: Routledge.

Johnson, C. W. and G. G. Emerson (1844) *The American Farmer's Encyclopedia and Dictionary of Rural Affairs*. 3rd edition. Philadelphia: Carey and Hart, 1744.

Johnson, S. (1755) *Dictionary of the English Language*. London: J. & P. Knapton.

Johnson, S. (1761) "Preface", in R. Rolt (ed.), *A New Dictionary of Trade and Commerce*. 2nd edition. London: Printed for G. Keith, S. Crowder, and H. Woodgate and S. Brooks.

Landau, S. (2001) *Dictionaries: The Art and Craft of Lexicography*. Cambridge: Cambridge University Press.

Layton, D. (1965) "Diction and Dictionaries in the Diffusion of Scientific Knowledge: An Aspect of the History of the Popularization of Science in Great Britain", *The British Journal for the History of Science* 2(3): 221–234.

Martínez de Sousa, J. (1995) *Diccionario de lexicografía práctica*. Barcelona: Biblograf.

Postlethwayt, M. (1749) *A Dissertation on the Plan, Use, and Importance, of the Universal Dictionary of Trade and Commerce*. London: John and Paul Knapton.

Postlethwayt, M. (1774) *The Universal Dictionary of Trade and Commerce*. 4th edition. London: Printed for W. Strahan, J. and F. Rivington, J. Hinton.

Rundell, M. (ed.) (2016) *MacMillan English Dictionary*. London: Palgrave Macmillan. [www.macmillandictionary.com]

Tarp, S. (2007) "Lexicography in the Information Age", *Lexikos* 17: 170–179.

Tarp, S. (2008) *Lexicography in the Borderland Between Knowledge and Non-Knowledge*. Tübingen: Niemeyer.

Tarp, S., and T.J.D. Bothma (2013) "An Alternative Approach to Enlightenment Age Lexicography: *The Universal Dictionary of Trade and Commerce*", *Lexicographica* 29: 222–284.

Ten Hacken, P. (2009) "What Is a Dictionary? A View From Chomskyan Linguistics", *International Journal of Lexicography* 22(4): 399–421.

Trench, R. C. (1858) *On Some Deficiencies in Our English Dictionaries*. London: The Philological Society.

Wiegand, H. E. (1987) "Zur handlungstheoretischen Grundlegung der Wörterbenutzungsforschung", *Lexicographica* 3: 178–227.

Wiegand, H. E. (1998) *Wörterbuchforschung. Untersuchungen zur Wörterbuchbenutzung, zur Theorie, Geschichte, Kritik und Automatisierung der Lexikographie*. 1. Teilband. Berlin, New York: Walter de Gruyter.

Wiegand, H. E. (2002) "Wissen in der Sprachlexikografie. Ein Plädoyer für einige immer noch notwendige Differenzierungen", in K. Ezawa, W. Kürschner, K. H. Rensch and M. Ringmacher (eds.), *Linguistik jenseits des Strukturalismus*. Tübingen: Gunter Narr Verlag, pp. 265–281.

Yeo, R. (2003) "Classifying the Sciences", in R. Porter (ed.), *The Cambridge History of Science. Volume 4. Eighteenth-Century Science*. Cambridge: Cambridge University Press, pp. 241–266.

Zgusta, L. (1971) *Manual of Lexicography*. The Hague: Mouton.

16

Dictionaries for text reception

Patrick Leroyer

16.1 Introduction

It is possible to distinguish between three basic approaches to the study of dictionaries for text reception, also known as 'decoding dictionaries': (a) as objects of study per se; (b) as expressions of a relationship between them and their usefulness for users; and (c) as to their planning and construction. Due to space constraints, this chapter will focus on (b) through a critical discussion of the concept of the dictionary for text reception and of the specific needs that specific users may have in specific text reception situations in the extra-lexicographical world. In the first sections of this chapter, we will address theoretical arguments needed to conceptualise dictionaries for text reception. This will be done in the framework of the function theory of lexicography (Tarp 2008; Fuertes Olivera and Tarp 2014), in which dictionaries are apprehended as utility tools for consultation. We will then address a number of lexicographic issues raised by specific text reception problems. Finally, we will briefly outline lexicographic challenges related to the growing number of computational applications for machine reception. The optimistic conclusion is that lexicography has not become outdated. High-quality lexicographic datasets are needed in systems designed to automate meaning extraction and enhance human reception.

16.2 Theoretical issue

16.2.1 Text reception patterns

Human text reception is a highly complex, cognitive activity which can be studied from various angles. It involves a number of related, scientific disciplines such as philosophy of language, language and cognition, neurolinguistics, linguistics, sociolinguistics, computational linguistics, and language acquisition. Albeit relevant to the scientific study of text reception, we will not refer to these disciplines, but address text reception solely within a lexicographic conceptual framework. When successful, lexicographic text reception can be understood as the user's faculty of rapidly processing lexicographic meaning elicitation data and thus retrieve needed meaning information in the frame of a rapid cognitive uptake, so as much meaning opacity or uncertainty as possible can be removed. It is therefore the 'ability' of the dictionary to provide effective access to such lexicographic data so information retrieval can be processed correctly that makes the dictionary trustworthy or not. Reception dictionaries are frequently used in educational environments, in the classroom and in various situations including special tasks. Among these is the use of the dictionary to check on reception, for example, in exercises in which students have to choose the correct synonym from a list of alternatives (Scholfield 1999: 13). The most frequent use, however, occurs under reading. It is targeted to the retrieval of information on the meaning of a single lexical item or a combination of these and involves the following steps (Bergenholtz, Bothma and Gouws 2015: 4):

1. Identifying a vocabulary problem impairing the reading process – a word or a phrase whose meaning is completely unknown or is opaque.
2. Deciding to solve the problem immediately.
3. Choosing a dictionary, either paper or e-dictionary, as a possible means to solve the problem rather than using other means, or in addition to other means:
    a) Finding the right entry for the word form or phrase in the paper dictionary
    b) Making the right search in the e-dictionary search field
4. Accessing the relevant data at their right position.
5. Processing the relevant data, so useful information can be retrieved and processed to solve the problem in part or in totality.
6. Resuming the reading process from its point of rupture.

16.2.2 Degrees of text reception

Text reception is subject to various degrees of reception. Unknown words may constitute integral, communicative obstacles to the reception of texts when meaning cannot be inferred or guessed at from the context. The dictionary then can be consulted to rapidly grasp meaning. But words and expressions can also be partial obstacles blocking a precise reception and interpretation of the text. According to Kühn (1989: 116–117) text reception dictionaries are used both in the case of comprehension problems, *Verstandigungsstörung*, and in the case of consolidation of interpretation, *Interpretationsverstärkung*. In the case of comprehension, the dictionary is a clarification tool for the reception of language data (word abbreviations, single words, multiword expressions, specialised words, idiomatic expressions, etc.), whereas the need for even better comprehension and interpretation consolidation can also lead to the wish to access knowledge on the history or ideology of the words, on how meaning has changed over time, etc. For this purpose, Kühn (1989:116) includes various types of specialised dictionaries as dictionaries of the history and evolution of the meaning of words and concepts, dictionaries of archaisms, buzzwords, etymology, etc., as well as 'Konversationslexika'(= encyclopaedic, popularising dictionaries):

> Man will etwas über die Geschichte des Wortgebrauchs wissen – meist dann, wenn man eine Äußerung besser oder genauer verstehen will.[1]

Etymological and historical word data are normally only useful to users who are curious about a word or an expression and wish to acquire knowledge of its history. However, it cannot be denied that a better, more accurate meaning elicitation of a specific word or expression in a reading situation can be needed for complete and unbiased understanding and can be achieved by the consultation of specialised dictionaries. This speaks in favor of dual data presentations, with short, basic explanations for elicitation of totally unknown meaning, and extended explanations in the case of incomplete or biased meaning interpretation. In any case, what is fundamental is that receptive problems should be solved quickly, as users usually do not want to be excessively disrupted by look-ups when performing a reading activity.

16.2.3 Text reception dictionaries at the cusp of text reception

Text reception dictionaries are used by native speakers as well as users of a foreign language to solve one-off, punctual[2] information needs when comprehension problems arise when reading texts in various contexts. Recent surveys of what kind of information users look for confirm that information that can be applied immediately to solve text reception problems is of utmost interest (Besharat 2014; Lew 2013; Müller-Spitzer 2014). This has been so for centuries, and medieval dictionaries were actually comprehension dictionaries (Rey and Morvan 2005: 48). Reception is also related to translation, which besides reception of the source text in the source language also includes transfer of the source text to the target text and production of the text in the target language. Text reception dictionaries are conventionally seen as collections of meaning descriptions on the text side, as well as sources of meaning comprehension on the reception side (Figure 16.1):

TEXT ← TEXT RECEPTION DICTIONARY → RECEPTION

Figure 16.1 Schematic representation of text reception dictionaries

Figure 16.1 shows that text reception dictionaries are subject to competing conceptualisations as their theoretical and practical study can be attracted by one or the opposite direction, whereas the natural focus should be on the relationship between the two. A great number of studies deal with meaning description (Atkins and Rundell 2008: 2; Béjoint 2000: 41; Fontenelle 2008; Lew and al. 2013; Ten Hacken 2015; Wiegand: 1992) while a growing number is being addressed to empirical studies of users and dictionary use in receptive situations (Dziemianko 2012; Hausmann 1977; Lew, Grzelak and Leszkowicz 2013; Lew 2013; Müller-Spitzer 2014; Nesi 2013; Scholfield 1999; Tono 2011). In function theory, (Tarp 2008), focus is on the relationship. This entails adaptation of descriptions and access to receivers and receptive situations. Hence, the main issue of the theoretical and practical development of text reception dictionaries is to identify the intended receivers and determine what their receptive needs are in the foreseen situations in order to effectively adapt the dictionary.

Dictionary consultation can be motivated by reading a text, translating a text, proofreading a text (revision and editing), or marking a text, and dictionaries needed in every single case can have different forms. According to Hausmann (1977), a distinction must be made between reception of the foreign language within the foreign language, when users have achieved advanced foreign language competence, or via the mother tongue, when such competence is still poor. Tarp (2008: 63 ff) has identified 10 specific combinations in which different kinds of dictionary design and directions – from mother tongue to foreign language, or the other way round, as well as from one foreign language to another – can make up the best lexicographic solution in every single case: reception of produced texts only, translation-related reception, and reception of a special kind in connection with proofreading of produced or translated texts, including marking and post-editing. Corresponding to these situations, various dictionary types can be used, alone or in combination: monolingual dictionaries in the mother tongue or in the foreign language, and for bilingual dictionaries, dictionaries based on the mother tongue and dictionaries based on the foreign language. For the latter, the receptive needs of beginners will be best catered by a bilingual dictionary providing an array of meaning elicitation data either in the form of meaning explanations in the mother tongue, equivalents or illustrations, or by a combination of these. For intermediate learners, both the monolingual dictionary of the foreign language and bilingual dictionaries can be used and can cater for reception needs. Choice of dictionary may also depend on teaching methodology used in class, within the foreign language or including a contrastive approach. Advanced learners have normally learnt to receive texts in the foreign language, and a monolingual learner's dictionary is therefore the best-suited type of dictionary. As both intermediate and advanced learners experience the same kinds of reception problems, there is no particularly need to develop special dictionary solutions for these two groups. Advanced learners will benefit from the use of general dictionaries designed for mother-tongue users. Learners of a second language need same dictionary types, but these should include a lot of cultural lemmas giving access to the understanding of the new culture which they have to accommodate, and meaning explanations should contain contrastive information to the original home culture. Learners of the mother tongue need specially adapted reception dictionaries. This is however not always the case. Leroyer, Binon and Verlinde (2009) show that French monolingual school dictionaries, although different in size according to school level, show little innovation and have all mixed functions. Big monolingual general purpose dictionaries are also strongly polyfunctional, and meaning elicitation data are normally part of intricate data presentation structures, as in the *Trésor de la langue française informatisé* (2016).

16.3 Core issues and topics

16.3.1 Definition

The *Nordic Dictionary of Lexicography* does mention the concept of 'text reception dictionary for understanding texts' (Bergenholtz and al 1997: 201) but fails to provide a definition, whereas several articles deal with meaning and 'definition dictionaries'. In line with Bergenholtz (2011: 30), who criticizes theoretical lexicography for not having had a significant effect on practical lexicography, it can be argued that text reception dictionaries suffer from a lexicographic paradox. Although needs for text reception are ranking high among users (Koplenig and Müller-Spitzer: 2014), there are no text reception dictionaries as such on the market, *viz* monofunctional dictionaries. As a general rule, dictionaries, regardless of their type, are polyfunctional. They include lexicographic data aimed at text reception alongside data aimed at the satisfaction of other types of information needs. To our knowledge, there is but one exception to this rule, the *Meaning Dictionary of Danish* (Bergenholtz et al. 2016a). Bergenholtz and Bergenholtz (2011: 187–188) argue that the dictionary is a tool, and that just like a good tool, in order to be effective, it has to be monofunctional to fulfill one genuine purpose at a time. This argument is refuted by those who claim that users do not really make a conscious choice prior to consultation, and that they often look for all kind of data types.

Only very few theories make provision for text reception dictionaries. One is the active-passive theory (Kroman, Riiber and Rosbach 1984) based on Scerba (1940). It makes a distinction between bilingual 'active' and 'passive' translation dictionaries depending on mother tongue, foreign language, and directionality. The theory is also used by Svensén (2009; 19) who for the bilingual dictionary counts with eight different dictionaries, and by Hartmann and James (1998: 106,) for whom text reception dictionaries are passive dictionaries when reading a foreign language or translating from it into the mother tongue. The idea is right, but the denomination 'passive' is unfortunate, as text reception is an active interpretation process.

As already stated, the theory followed in this chapter, is function theory. Text reception dictionaries can be defined by their purpose, which is to help their intended users solve problems caused by the reception of texts in their mother tongue or in a foreign language. Accordingly, they are to be conceptualized as lexicographic information tools that are specifically designed and constructed for helping their intended users to read and understand texts, mainly written, in various communication contexts. These may include non-specialized as well as specialized communication. In both cases, the issues at stake are the same. The meaning of a single word, a multiple word expression, or a chain of words happens to be unknown or unclear to the user, thus impairing or even blocking the communication process. Meaning has to be elicited in such a way so it can be understood and interpreted correctly in the given context. By successfully accessing and retrieving the needed and relevant information from the lexicographic data, the user can reestablish comprehension, go back to the text, and resume the reading process. Hence, the main quality of a good text reception dictionary relies on its ability to provide fast and easy access to the lexicographic data so that the needed and relevant information can be retrieved effortlessly, efficiently, and first and foremost quickly. In analogy with Aristotle (quoted by Abizadeh 2008: 36), it can be argued that the function of the dictionary for text reception is not to "create text reception" but to "promote text reception" as much as possible by providing access to specific datasets addressed to meaning elicitation. Text reception belongs, alongside with text production and translation, to communicative situations. At the highest level of abstraction, text reception is an interpretive situation, "when a person needs information to understand or interpret a specific phenomenon, sign, symbol, text, etc." (Fuertes-Olivera and Tarp 2014: 51) In line with Tarp (see Chapter 15), the text reception dictionary can then be defined in the following terms:

> *A text reception dictionary is a utility tool, which is conceived for consultation with the genuine purpose of meeting punctual information needs experienced by specific types of potential user in specific text reception situations, and which is designed to assist its users by providing manual or automatic access to lexicographically prepared data, which can either be used directly by the users in order to retrieve the required information which they can subsequently use to solve specific reception problems in the context where the needs originally occurred.*

The dictionary can be designed as an autonomous text reception–only dictionary or as a text reception–filtering dictionary, in which the user can choose the option to access meaning elicitation data only. The lexicographic data can also be part of a computational text reception system performing meaning extraction for enhanced information retrieval purposes. This use, however, does not correspond to the earlier definition of a dictionary, because human consultation is bypassed, and it might be better to speak of lexicographic resources for text reception.

16.3.2 Access

The challenge for lexicographers is to compile text reception dictionaries that can be accessed rapidly and easily, and in the case of meaning differentiation, to provide signposts, glosses, or other indicators associated with the lemmata in order to help users gain access to the meaning data they are looking for in the context of the text they are reading (and not stop at the first meaning explanation as is unfortunately often the case). Genuine e-dictionaries (i.e. dictionaries that are not copies of print dictionaries) have proved to be superior to print dictionaries and provide faster and easier access to the lexicographic data from which the needed information can be retrieved. They will normally provide more advanced search options and search functionalities, and more accessible data presentations, (Fuertes Olivera 2016; Müller-Spitzer 2014; Pastor and Alcina: 2013; Verlinde and Peeters: 2012).

16.3.2.1 Lemmatization

Text reception dictionaries should provide lemmata (meaning items) that can directly match encountered reception problems in texts. A descriptive approach must normally be chosen, with the lemmatization of all different variants (Fuertes Olivera and Tarp 2014: 80). Extensive lemmatization principles should be applied, including conjugated forms (Svensén 2009: 163–164), abbreviations, acronyms, proper names when necessary, and new words. Lexicographers should not wait for inclusion of new words (*neonyms*) and their variant forms until these words have "settled" in the language or achieved some acceptable frequency. No one can tell if they have really settled or may become obsolete in the near future. The problem is that text reception help is missing when mostly needed. New words appear every day, spread rapidly, and are a major cause of comprehension problems.

16.3.2.2 Sense ordering, polysemy, and homonymy

A distinction should be made between sense in vitro and sense *in vivo*. Words are polysemous in vitro, in dictionaries, but polysemy disappears in discourse in vivo, where the word is contextualized and the right reading is inferred by the reader. Polysemous units have a range of different meanings, whereas homonymic units differ in meaning, although it is in many cases difficult to differentiate. In the dictionary, the distinction is then between one article for polysemous units, or several articles in the case of homonymy. This affects the lexicographic treatment of these close-related units, because the lexicographer has to choose an appropriate data distribution structure which does not impair access. Polysemy is normally dealt with by the technique of sense ordering, in which related meanings are lumped together, whereas seemingly unrelated meanings (homonyms) are treated separately. Sense ordering is then a data presentation technique which in mono and bilingual dictionaries refers to the lexicographic practice of systematically arranging and presenting the various meanings of lemma (Lew 2009, 2013). Although used by lexicographers to achieve accurate semantic representation and hereby to provide access to the different meanings activated by dictionary consultations, the result of splitting lemmas into discrete senses may have the opposite effect and impair reception. The rationale of sense ordering is to facilitate and speed up data access by providing clearer guidance to the user in search of the relevant meaning. However, it implies that the user has to possess the necessary dictionary skills to fully realize and exploit the sense ordering principles. It also implies that the principles are effective and truly useful in the first place, and that they are used consistently throughout the dictionary articles. However, studies of English learners' dictionaries reveal that several principles are used simultaneously and that the splitting or lumping of meanings into discrete senses evolves over time in various editions (Scholfield: 1999).

There are three types of sense ordering: the historical or chronological principle; the statistical principle, ranking most frequent uses on top and less frequent at the bottom of the linear presentation of senses; and the logical principle, according to which the word can be analyzed and lumped into hierarchies according to categories of core meanings and derived meanings (general to specific, concrete to abstract, literal to metaphoric, etc.). Yet sense ordering can be said to be the output of the linguistic concepts of homonymy and polysemy, denoting lexical units that share the same form but have different content. In terms of Tarp (2009: 296 ff), the two concepts are neither relevant nor useful for lexicography, and differentiation should be dismissed as a linguistic issue, not a lexicographic one. It is even possible to go further in an e-dictionary, as argued by Bergenholtz and Agerbo (2014a), and simply do without polysemy. The solution then is to record and structure lexicographic data according to the one entry (or lemma) = one meaning lemmatization principle, and treat lemmas as separate meaning items.

16.3.3 Meaning elicitation

Although definitions are considered to make up the paramount data category for meaning elicitation, text reception dictionaries involve many other data categories and datasets that can be used in accordance with specific text reception situations: terminological definitions, lexicographic definitions, multimodal definitions, meaning explanations, examples, synonyms, equivalents, illustrations, etc. The term "definition" is also vastly debated, and various wordings are used. Svensén (2009) speaks of "meaning descriptions and explanations". Wiegand (1992) rejects the so-called "lexicographic definition" (at least for general language dictionaries), and prefers to speak about "meaning paraphrases" and "frame-based description patterns".

16.3.3.1 Definitions and meaning explanations

Some linguists reject the idea of defining anything. Béjoint (2000: 225) argues that any attempt to differentiate and describe word meanings in dictionaries is doomed to failure. The meaning of words in reference varies constantly because the referent varies with each new use of the word in different linguistic contexts, and words do not have meanings but meaning potentials. It is argued that the solution then is to develop semantic networks and word pattern dictionaries with collocations and valency patterns as keys to word meaning. Such solutions, however, are far from being user friendly. The huge attention paid in lexicography to meaning explanation is revealed by Zgusta (1971: 21) for whom "Lexical meaning stands in the center of the lexicographer's attention", whereby all practical decisions are directly or indirectly related to the way in which meaning is being dealt with. Subsuming lexicography to lexical semantics seems to be a narrow approach to lexicography in comparison with earlier lexicographic theory making. A broader approach, 200 years before that, comes from the French encyclopaedist d'Alembert, who in an article on *language dictionaries* (d'Alembert: 2016 [1751]: volume 4, 958) makes a modern distinction between dictionaries for reception (with "good definitions"), dictionaries for text production (with "outstanding syntax"), and dictionaries for knowledge purposes (with "the nature of words"), as specialized dictionaries can be defined "by the nature of the subjects they treat" (see Chapter 20 of this volume). Yet there is no general agreement on how definitions should be structured and written. Should the *definiendum* (the word being defined) be included in a full-sentence definition, or should such definitions be reserved to a limited number of cases? Some lexicographers recommend the use of controlled vocabulary to make access easier, whereas others prefer natural, full sentence definitions (Collins 2016). This format however is more adequate to illustrate the grammatical construction of the lemma. With the words of d'Alembert (2016, [1751: volume 4, 959]), "meaning explanations should be clear, accurate and as short as possible, because shortness fosters clarity. What makes explanations obscure is not shortness but a poor choice of ideas and lack of order between them". This wisdom has not changed and still holds today. Meaning explanation can also include some degree of encyclopaedic explanation, in the form of text or other formats of information, such as illustrations. In the discussion on definitions, some scholars (Gross 1989: 176–177) recommend that definitions in learner's dictionaries should include all arguments of the word to enhance comprehensibility. Other scholars (Nielsen 2011: 209) advocate for definitions to match the function – to provide help to understand words, texts, and concepts – and recommend definitions to be written in respect of user profiles (laypersons, semi-experts, or experts), and foremost to be comprehensible, so they are easy to understand at low comprehension-related information costs. For the purpose of reception, providing a simple answer to the question "what is it?" will normally suffice, so other elements such as function ("what does it do?") and relation ("how is it related to other concepts") can be left out. However, Agerbo (Chapter 4 of this volume) argues that more detailed explanations may be needed whenever factual and cultural elements are constitutive of understanding.

16.3.3.2 Examples

Meaning elicitation can be complemented by lexicographic examples, particularly in interlingual text reception. When carefully adapted, examples can reinforce meaning interpretation, and the role of examples in lexicography has been, and still is, a popular field of study. Harras (1989) formulates example guidelines depending on use situations. Today, the trend is to prefer "authentic" examples from a corpus, as these reflect genuine usage, and to reject made-up examples. However, authentic examples often contain noise (Gross: 1989), and the choice of examples depends on the functions of the dictionary. Made-up examples in learners' dictionaries make sense to achieve transparent meaning illustration.

16.3.3.3 Multimodal meaning elicitation

Following the idea that a picture is worth a thousand words, and taking advantage of the digital revolution in lexicography, illustrative, dynamic data can be added to – or even replace – conventional meaning elicitation. These can come in the form of sound files, graphs, charts, animations and videos, etc., and are referred to as multimodal data. When carefully selected, they can speed up consultation, although the general expectation that they always improve comprehension cannot be fulfilled (Lew 2010: 303). Xiqin Liu (2015: 210) advocates for multimodal corpora and multimodal definitions, and some of the examples found in Longman (2016) and Oxford Learners Dictionaries (2016) seem useful, whereas others using advanced, visual representations (floating 3D graphs of semantic networks) fail to do so. They prioritize access to lexical knowledge representation and are better suited for presentations in ontologies and knowledge bases. Such visual data presentations are rejected by Fuertes Olivera and Tarp (2014: 16) as cases of "lexicotainment", and multimodal meaning elicitation should therefore be used with caution.

16.3.4 Text reception issues

Certain lexical categories are known to pose challenges to access and meaning elicitation. This section addresses three of these: idiomatic items, cultural items, and specialized items.

16.3.4.1 Idiomatic items

Fixed expressions and particularly idioms have attracted much lexicographical attention. Their meaning cannot be deduced from the concatenation of individual meaning components, and they have a singular, non-transparent meaning that must be known to the user (Svensén 2009: 245–57). Also, due to their semantic singularity (meaning is use centered and relies heavily on use in context) and to their prolific, lexical creativity (idioms appear in many variations), idioms pose lexicographic challenges. Their treatment has been extensively discussed with a focus on the selection of variants and the lemmatization of meaning components providing access, a major issue in print dictionaries, which now profits from the flexible search options offered by advanced e-dictionaries (Fuertes-Olivera 2016; Leroyer 2011). Kilgariff (2012: 28–29) argues that lexicographers should identify all variants and subsume them to some core meaning, which is a challenge to language description, and the Danish dictionary of fixed expressions (Bergenholtz et al. 2016b) is criticized for ignoring this fact. This dictionary, however, provides access to meaning elicitation in an innovative manner. It only deals with idioms, all frequent variants are selected and have their own description, and all meaning components are lemmatized and made searchable. For receptive purposes, idioms should be treated separately rather than being subsumed to some core meanings.

16.3.4.2 Cultural items and cultural fields

The lexicographic discussion of cultural items and cultural fields as special obstacles to text reception has often been a philosophical discussion of what culture really is and whether it is inside or outside language. Galisson (1991) makes the case for an independent treatment of "lexicultural" items (food, religion, climatic elements). To this must be added the treatment of culture-dependent fields such as law (Sánchez 2010). For text reception purposes, there is no need to separate language and culture which should be treated as intertwined phenomena. Yet separation can be found in the cultural editions of LGP-dictionaries (Rey and Morvan: 2005), which make extensive use of cultural labels, notes, and synoptic articles, thus reinforcing the divorce between language and culture. In translation-related reception, contrastive information should be provided to help users in order to pick up the adapted equivalent. Simple dictionary solutions to the treatment of cultural items are proposed in Leroyer and Bergenholtz (2013). In the case of reception in the mother tongue, the users will be familiar with cultural phenomena shared by the members of their community, and no special treatment is needed to explain meaning. For items that are scarcely used and can be obstacles to comprehension, the solution is to provide extended explanation in the L1. For L2 users, explanations should be written in the L2 unless their proficiency in the L1 is on a par with L1 users. Bergenholtz et al. (1991) address these issues in dictionaries between German and

Malagasy, in which many articles deal with "exotic" cultural items, the solution being to provide longer explanations and resort to illustrations for further elicitation.

A special case is the reception of items experienced by tourists travelling abroad, who need special help to interpret items appearing on signs, boards, menus, etc. In the case of menus, help should provide access to experiential knowledge, for example, to short evaluations of how items on a menu taste like and not only explanations of what they are. Yet no dictionaries of text reception aimed at this category of potential users has been developed (Leroyer 2009). Cultural separation seems to have prevented lexicographic innovation, and travel dictionaries are miniature replica of general, bilingual dictionaries, whereas the so-called "phrase books" for travelers are designed for (unrealistic) production purposes only. Culture can also be responsible of the marked usage of usually "normal" items in texts. The solution will be to resort to style labelling (Haussmann 1989: 651) to signal such items. According to Ptaszynski (2010: 412), lexicographical practice is unfortunately governed by description concerns rather by principles for signaling potential reception problems. Cultural labelling should be limited to cases in which the cultural reading is not activated by the denotative reading. The treatment of culture proves that there are fuzzy boundaries between linguistic and cultural knowledge, and that no demarcation lines should be drawn by lexicographers.

16.3.4.3 Specialized items

In line with the debate on cultural items as being within or outside language, the reception of specialized items (called *terms* in terminography and treated as units of conceptual knowledge) and the way how this should be dealt with, is a much-debated lexicographic issue. Words used by experts are carriers of linguistic as well as encyclopaedic knowledge elements which both contribute to meaning. Some scholars (Rossenbeck 1994; Wiegand 1994) favour a separation of the two types of knowledge, leaving semantics to dictionaries and knowledge of the world to encyclopaedias, even though boundaries are fuzzy and there seems to be a continuum. Other scholars claim that meaning elements are intertwined and that it is impossible to distinguish between the two (Bergenholtz and Agerbo 2014b: 128; Bergenholtz and Kaufmann 1996), making a separation harmful. Rather, all meaning components should be clearly identified in a corpus and treated separately. Hence in terms of text reception what counts the most, as also suggested by Geeb (1998: 206), is not the question of separation or not, but the function of the dictionary, the user type and the usage situation and purpose which determine how access should be provided to relevant and needed means of meaning elicitation. The tricky part is to decide on what should be brought in and what should be left out. One should remember that the purpose is to provide means to meaning elicitation, not to provide means to knowledge acquisition. In dictionaries for learners of a specialized fields (Fuertes Olivera: 2010), it could be wise to provide two-steps explanations: a short one for basic reception problems (total ignorance of meaning) and an elaborate version for advanced reception problems (uncertain meaning interpretation). Also, a distinction should be made between experts, semi-experts and laypeople. Laypeople have normally no knowledge of the field and its basic theories. Semi-experts form a heterogeneous group and may include experts from related subject fields or highly educated specialists having a particular interest in the field, but who have not been educated in the field and do not work with it as professionals. Experts of the field are not relevant because they normally will not experience reception problems (Bergenholtz and Kaufmann 1997: 102) and will not consult any dictionary, unless problems occur in a foreign language. In this case, they simply need equivalents. For laypersons, the challenge is to provide meaning indications that are comprehensible and yet correct. Bergenholtz and Kaufmann (1997) analyze a number of definitions of the word "gen" in various dictionaries and find that these are incorrect. For semi-experts, the problem is that meaning indications are too long, and may contain irrelevant information or inaccuracies, although generally written by experts (Hashimzade and al. 2014: 16 ff). For reception, specialized dictionaries for semi-experts contain an insufficient number of entries, and meaning explanations have to balance between accessibility – conveying meaning elicitation in an accessible language – and authority, providing correct explanations. In the Spanish accounting dictionary (Fuertes Olivera et al. 2016), the search interface provides direct access to text reception datasets, and definitions are provided in English and Spanish because Spanish users, due to insufficient proficiency in English, need reception within their mother tongue. Whether intensional, that is, stating a generic concept and delimiting characteristics, or prototypical, that is, with fuzzy boundaries (Ten Hacken 2015: 7), explanations should be adapted to the degree of specialization of intended users. They should be updated whenever progress in science and technology modify meaning and may jeopardize understanding.

It should finally be noted that language description in specialized dictionaries is often guided in terms of preference for specific theoretical approaches to definitory formats, but omit to take functions into account. Faber, Araúz and Hernández (2010: 117) recommend frame semantics highlighting semantic roles, but leave out important meaning elements necessary for comprehension. In the DicoInfo (L'Homme et al. 2016), the authors use actantial definitions which are in pace with the linguistic theory, but are best suited for text production.

16.3.5 The reception of text reception dictionaries

User studies have become more accurate (Dziemianko 2012; Lew, Grzelak and Leszkowicz 2013; Lew 2013; Müller-Spitzer 2014; Nesi 2013; Scholfield 1999; Tono 2011) but still bring insufficient output (Nesi 2013: 64). Tarp (2009) remains quite skeptical about the overall usefulness of such studies even though one should expect that tests or tasks triggering consultation could rapidly provide valuable data, particularly for comparative studies of looking up conditions, comprehension scores, etc. However, this optimistic agenda doesn't hold true. Results mirror the conditions in use in experimental settings and do not match the conditions of real-life reading situations. The major flaw in research on dictionary use in receptive situations is that it deals with constructed reception. However, as the key asset of text reception dictionaries must be their capacity to meet and satisfy lexicographically relevant text reception needs in society in a vast array of social situations, there is still a *desideratum* for further experimental, quantitative, and qualitative research in text reception that can shed light on the conditions in which text reception needs can trigger the consultation of dictionaries and, if so, how these can be effectively catered by high-quality dictionaries in the foreseen use situations. Large-scale studies of the use of e-dictionaries in immediate 'did you find what you searched for' feedback systems could provide valuable quantitative data and exploit the meta-cognitive evaluations of the results by users.

16.4 Looking to the future of text reception dictionaries

The future is marked by three technological trends. First, the integration of reception dictionaries in the written medium. Second, automated reception of oral texts for instantaneous reception. And third, automated text reception for enhanced information search and retrieval. In all three cases, lexicography can deliver but is challenged. Too much weight can be put on the technology for the sake of the technology only.

Today's integration of the dictionaries in reading devices or online reading resources is growing rapidly. It makes the dictionary available whenever needed in the reading situation that has motivated consultation. Clicking on or tapping a word on screen and getting the explanation popping up is a lot easier than having to make a search somewhere else. But to perform better, meaning explanations should be given in accordance with the context, so users get access to disambiguated words, avoiding the problems described by Bothma and Prinsloo (2013). If not around the corner yet, true disambiguation is bound to become a lexicographic functionality in the future. The same *desideratum* can be formulated concerning the integration of text reception dictionary in specialized text resources. At present, glossaries are sometimes available on the webpages of institutional or business actors, but further integrative efforts are needed to offer readers (= clients, customers, citizens) the same degree of reading comfort, and facilitate communication and business in the modern information and knowledge society.

Oral text reception has been left out in this chapter, as dictionary use there is quite rare. This might change in the future, particularly in interlingual situations, where we will experience the growing use of more effective speech-to-speech translation technology running on laptops or mobile terminals. Three modules are needed: speech recognition, machine translation, and voice synthesis. Speech recognition input is converted into strings of words and needs high-quality lexicographic data, including grammatical data, as well as text corpora for language A. Also, for the translation of language A to B, the system needs quality corpora in the form of bilingual corpora or web corpora. Because lexicographers are experts in the preparation of lexicographic data and in the compiling of corpora, it can be expected that lexicographers will take an active part in the development of the technology.

As recently stated by the European Network in e-Lexicography (ENeL: 2016), there is a growing need for lexicographic datasets in computational text reception systems. Lexicographic datasets will run in a number of applications in information processing and information retrieval in knowledge and rule-based systems for text reception, including enhanced lexical resources for word meaning processing. These systems are already using lexicographic meaning datasets, particularly synsets, and include (non-exhaustive list) e-readers and e-learning programs, machine translation and translation memory, question answering systems, query expansion, word sense disambiguation, semantic web, thesauri, ontologies, terminologies and semantic parsing. All these need high-quality lexicographic datasets, either already existing or to be compiled in the future, which will have to be converted to a common resource description framework (RDF) so they can be interchanged across languages. The future of these technologies is not simply dependant on language descriptions but on the close relationship between systems and the information needs of their human receivers, *viz* their lexicographically relevant text reception needs in the extra-lexicographical world.

16.5 Conclusion

The title of this chapter refers to the plethora of dictionaries that can help users encountering comprehension problems when reading texts. They are used in a great number of intra- and interlingual text reception situations, including intercultural and interprofessional contexts. They should be designed in accordance with the information needs raised in these contexts and the profile of their users, but most of them are polyfunctional and one-size-fits-all data presentation is the rule rather than the exception. This chapter has also suggested that lexicographers do not agree on what is to be understood by meaning description, and the idea of describing "true" meaning is guided by the theoretical approaches that are supposed to work best. One could fear that dictionaries are incapable of describing meaning, which is impossible to catch in isolation without the pragmatic contextual conditions in which words are used. This problem will, to a certain extent, be solved in the future, but the fear seems to be the expression of language description concerns per se which are at the core of many studies denouncing dictionaries for not describing words properly, and proposing better, more accurate or even more "user-friendly" descriptions. At a high level of abstraction, text reception dictionaries are not about meaning description, but about access to meaning elicitation. Means of elicitation and types of access should be adapted to reception situations. Therefore, description is mostly a linguistic concern, whereas access and elicitation are lexicographic concerns. Naturally, lexicographers cannot do without descriptions and linguistic expertise (and in the case of specialized words, subject field expertise). Béjoint (2000: 237) foresees that "dictionaries will be improved" [and that] "the improvements will arise from research by linguists of all kinds". This is a partial view, as descriptions are only part of the lexicographic picture. Going back to the orientation model introduced at the beginning of this chapter, text reception dictionaries are embedded in their relationship between text and reception. It is therefore the responsibility of lexicographers to focus on the relationship, and transform "dictionaries for text reception" into true "text reception dictionaries", thus making function and dictionaries coincide.

Related topics

The concept of dictionary; dictionaries for text production; dictionaries for translation; dictionaries and access; dictionaries and culture; specialized dictionaries; explaining meaning in lexicographical information tools.

Further reading

Fuertes-Olivera, P. A. and S. Tarp. (2014). *Theory and Practice of Specialised Online Dictionaries*. Berlin: de Gruyter.
This book provides a comprehensive treatment of the theory and practice of specialized online dictionaries. It deals with the various methods that can be used in order to determine what the needs of the intended user group are, including text receptive needs.

Granger, S. and M. Paquot (eds.) (2012). *Electronic Lexicography*. Oxford: Oxford University Press.
This collective volume includes a section on the use of electronic dictionaries in contrast with print dictionaries. It brings valuable insights in the way e-dictionaries are used and can be improved for text-reception situations.

Müller-Spitzer, C. (ed.) (2014). *Using Online Dictionaries*. Berlin and Boston: de Gruyter.
This collective volume contains contributions on dictionary usage research, including text reception "in the extra-lexicographic situations in which a dictionary consultation is embedded" (Müller-Spitzer: 85).

Notes

1 My translation is: one wants to know something about the history of the use of a word – usually when one wants to get a better or more accurate understanding of an utterance.

2 It should be noted that the word 'punctual' here is not used in its usual sense, which in the Oxford Learner's Dictionaries Online (2016) is defined as "Happening or doing something at the agreed

or proper time". A very similar definition can be found in the four other big English dictionaries online: Cambridge English Dictionary (2016), Collins English Dictionary Online (2016), Longman Dictionary of Contemporary English (2016), and Macmillan Dictionary Online (2016). In function theory the concept of 'punctual information needs' refers to lexicographically relevant information needs that can be satisfied by a one-off dictionary consultation at a particular *point* in time.

References

Dictionaries

d'Alembert, J.-B.L.R. and D. Diderot (2016) *Encyclopédie ou Dictionnaire Raisonné des Sciences, des Arts et des Métiers* [1751]. Morrisey, R. and G. Roe (eds.) *Encyclopédie de Diderot et d'Alembert*. Chicago: University of Chicago. http://encyclopedie.uchicago.edu/ [Accessed 14 February 2016].

Bergenholtz, H., S. Rajaonarivo, R. Ramasomanana, B. Radanielina, J. Richter-Johanningmeier, E. Olszowski, V. Zeiss, H. Ranaivoson, N. Rasoarimanana, R. Ravololomboahangy and M. Razafiarivony (eds.) et al. (1991) *Madagassisch-deutsches Wörterbuch-Rakibolana Malagasy-Alema*. Antananarivo: Tsipika/Moers: Aragon.

Bergenholtz, H., L. Cantell, R. V. Fjeld, D. Gundersen, J. H. Jónsson and B. Svensén (1997) *Nordisk leksikografisk ordbok*. Oslo: Universitetsforlaget.

Bergenholtz, H., Halkjær Jensen, H. Agerbo, A. Bodilsen, S. Guldager, J. Nørgaard Poulsen, C. Kastorp, E. Nyborg, A. Toftgaard Madsen, K. Torp Mikkelsen, K. Ryttersgaard, J. Uldum Erlandse (eds.) (2016a) *Den Danske Betydningsordbog*. Aarhus Universitet, Centre for leksikografi. www.ordbogen.com/products/center-for-leksikografi/de-danske-netordboeger.php?product_id=59&business=1#Betydningsordbogen [Accessed 9 May 2016].

Bergenholtz, H., E. Bjærge, R. Almind and J. Nielsen. (eds.) (2016b) *Ordbogen over faste vendinger*. Aarhus Universitet, Centre for leksikografi. www.ordbogen.com/products/center-for-leksikografi/ordbogen-over-faste-vendinger.php?product_id=10 [Accessed 9 May 2016].

Cambridge English Dictionary Online (2016). Cambridge: Cambridge University Press. http://dictionary.cambridge.org/us/dictionary/english/ [Accessed 9 May 2016].

Collins English Dictionary Online (2016). Glasgow: Collins Learning, Harper Collins Publishers. www.collinsdictionary.com/dictionary/english [Accessed 9 May 2016].

ENeL (2016) *European Network of e-Lexicography*. www.elexicography.eu/working-groups/working-group-3/wg3-objectives/ [Accessed 9 May 2016].

Fuertes-Olivera, P. A., H. Bergenholtz, S. Nielsen, P. G. Gómez, L. Mourier, M. N. Amo, Á d. l. R. Rodicios, Á. S. Ruano, S. Tarp and M. V. Sacristán (2016) *The Spanish-English Accounting Dictionary, Diccionarios Inglés-Español de Contabilidad*. https://lemma.com/about/?id=spa-eng-acc [Accessed 29. February 2016].

L'Homme, M. C., M. Alipour, H. Sook Bae, J. Beaulieu, P. Bolle, A. Bouchard, G. Camirand, S. Caron, S. Iveth Carreño Cruz, V. Claveau, L-P. Dargis, M-C. Demers, L. Demers-Dion, P. Drouin, A-M. Gagné, C. Gagné, P. Hanscom, Z. Jia, A-L. Jousse, S. Klebetsanis, M-E. Laneville, A. Le Serrec, M. Lechelt, C. Lemay (2003–2004), E. Marshman, M-E. Paquette, J. Pimentel and C. Tellier (eds.) (2016) *DiCoInfo, le dictionnaire fondamental de l'informatique et de l'internet*. Montréal: Université de Montréal, Observatoire de Linguistique Sens-Texte. http://olst.ling.umontreal.ca/cgi-bin/dicoinfo/search.cgi [Accessed 4 May 2016].

Longman Dictionary of Contemporary English Online (2016). Pearson Education Limited. www.ldoceonline.com/dictionary [Accessed 12 January 2016].

Macmillan Dictionary Online (2016). Bedford/St Martins: Macmillan Education. www.macmillandictionary.com/ [Accessed 9 May 2016].

Oxford Learner's Dictionaries Online (2016). Oxford: Oxford University Press. www.oxfordlearnersdictionaries.com [Accessed 12 January 2016].

Rey. A. and D. Morvan (2005) *Dictionnaire culturel en langue française*. Paris: Dictionnaires Le Robert.

Trésor de la Langue Française informatisé (2016). Université de Lorraine: ATILF. http://atilf.atilf.fr/ [Accessed 2 May 2016].

Other literature

Abizadeh, A. (2008) "The Passions of the Wise: Phronēsis, Rhetoric, and Aristotle's Passionate Deliberation", in R. Kingston and L. Ferry (eds.), *Bringing the Passions Back In: The Emotions in Political Philosophy*, Vancouver, Toronto: UBC, p. 67.

Atkins, B.T.S. and M. Rundell (2008) *The Oxford Guide to Practical Lexicography*. Oxford: Oxford University Press.

Béjoint, H. (2000) *Modern Lexicography: An Introduction*. Oxford: Oxford University Press.

Bergenholtz, H. (2011) "Access to and Presentation of Needs-Adapted Data in Monofunctional Internet Dictionaries", in P. A. Fuertes Olivera and H. Bergenholtz, pp. 30–53.

Bergenholtz, H. and I. Bergenholtz (2011) "A Dictionary Is a Tool, a Good Dictionary Is a Monofunctional Tool", in P. A. Fuertes Olivera and H. Bergenholtz, pp. 181–207.

Bergenholtz, H. and H. Agerbo (2014a) "There Is No Need for the Terms Polysemy and Homonymy in Lexicography", *Lexikos* 24: 27–35.

Bergenholtz, H. and H. Agerbo (2014b) "Meaning Identification and Meaning Selection for General Language Mononolingual Dictionaries", *Hermes* 52: 125–139.

Bergenholtz, H., T. Bothma and R. Gouws (2015) "Phases and Steps in the Access to Data in Information Tools", *Lexikos* 25: 1–30.

Bergenholtz, H. and U. Kaufmann (1996) "Enzyklopädische Informationen in Wörterbüchern", in N. Weber (ed.), *Theorie der Semantik und Theorie der Lexikographie*, pp. 168–82. Tübingen: Niemeyer.

Bergenholtz, H. and U. Kaufmann (1997) "Terminography and Lexicography: A Critical Survey of Dictionaries From a Single Specialised Field", *Hermes* 18, 91–125.

Besharat, F. (2014) "Experts and Specialised Lexicography: Perspectives and Needs", *Terminàlia* 9: 12–21.

Bothma, T. and D. J. Prinsloo (2013) "Automated Dictionary Consultation for Text Reception: A Critical Evaluation of Lexicographic Guidance in Linked Kindle e-Dictionaries", *Lexicographica* 29: 165–198.

Dziemianko, A. (2012) "On the Use(Fullness) of Paper and Electronic Dictionaries", in S. Granger and M. Paquot (eds.), pp. 319–41.

Faber, P., P. L. Araúz and C. P. Hernández (2010) "A Wine Dictionary for Non-Drinkers: LSP Dictionary Functions", in M. I. Rodríguez (ed.), *Vino, lengua y traducción*, Volume 3. Valladolid: Universidad de Valladolid, 189–213.

Fontenelle, T. (2008) (ed.) *Practical Lexicography: A Reader*. Oxford: Oxford University Press.

Fuertes-Olivera, P. A. (ed.) (2010) *Specialised Dictionaries for Learners*. Lexicographica Series Maior 136. Berlin, New York: de Gruyter.

Fuertes-Olivera, P. A. (2013) "e-Lexicography: The Continuing Challenge of Applying New Technology to Dictionary Making", in H. Jackson (ed.), 323–40.

Fuertes-Olivera, P. A. (2016) "A Cambrian Explosion in Lexicography: Some Reflections for Designing and Constructing Specialised Online Dictionaries", *International Journal of Lexicography* 29(2): 226–47.

Fuertes-Olivera, P. A. and H. Bergenholtz (eds.) (2011) *E-Lexicography: The Internet, Digital Initiatives and Lexicography*. London: Continuum.

Fuertes-Olivera, P. A. and S. Tarp (2014) *Theory and Practice of Specialised Online Dictionaries*. Berlin: de Gruyter.

Galisson, R. (1991) *De la langue à la culture par les mots*. Paris: Clé International.

Geeb, F. (1998) "Semantische und enzyklopädische Informationen in Fachwörterbüchern. Eine Untersuchung zu fachinformativen Informationstypen mit besonderer Berücksichtigung wortgebundener Darstellungsformen", *Hermes* 20: 205–215.

Granger, S. and M. Paquot (eds.) (2012) *Electronic Lexicography*. Oxford: Oxford University Press.

Gross, G. (1989) "Le dictionnaire et l'enseignement de la langue maternelle", in HSK 5.1 (1989), 174–180.

Harras, G. (1989) "Zu einer Theorie des lexikographischen Beispiels", in: HSK 5.1 (1989), 607–14.

Hartmann, R.R.K. and G. James (1998) *Dictionary of Lexicography*. London: Routledge.

Hashimzade, N., G. A. Myles and G. D. Myles (2014) "Can Authority Be Sustained While Balancing Accessibility and Formality?", *Hermes* 52: 11–24.

Hausmann, F. J. (1977) *Einfürhung in die Benutzung der neufranzösischen Wörterbücher*. Tübingen: Niemeyer.

HSK 5.1 (1989) = F. J. Hausmann, O. Reichmann, H. E. Wiegand and L. Zgusta (eds.) (1989) *Wörterbücher, Dictionaries, Dictionnaires, Ein internationales Handbuch zur Lexikographie, An International Encyclopedia of Lexicography, Encyclopédie internationale de lexicographhie*, Erste Teilband, /First Volume/Tome Premier. Berlin, New York: de Gruyter.

Hausmann, F. J. (1989) "Die Markierung in einem allgemeinen einsprachigen Wörterbuch: eine Übersicht", in *HSK 5.1* (1989), 649–57.

Jackson, H. (ed.) (2013) *The Bloomsbury Companion to Lexicography*. London, New York: Bloomsbury.

Kilgariff, A. (2012) "Review of Pedro A. F. Olivera and H. Bergenholtz (eds.), e-Lexicography: The Internet, Digital Initiatives and Lexicography", *Kernermann Dictionary News* July 2012: 26–9.

Koplenig, A. and C. Müller-Spitzer. (2014) "Empirical Data on Contexts of Dictionary Use", in C. Müller-Spitzer (2014), 127–43.

Kromann, H. P., T. Riiber and P. Rosbach (1984) " 'Active' and 'Passive' Bilingual Dictionaries: The Scerba Concept Reconsidered", in R.R.K. Hartmann (ed.), *Papers From the International Conference on Lexicography*. Lexicographica Series Maior 1, 207–2015.

Kühn, P. (1989) "Typologie der wörterbücher nach benutzungmögligkeiten", in *HSK 5.1* (1989), 111–27.

Leroyer, P. (2009) "Lexicography Hits the Road. New Information Tools for Tourists", in H. Bergenholtz, S. Nielsen and S. Tarp (ed.) *Lexicography at a Crossroads: Dictionaries and Encyclopedias Today, Lexicographical Tools Tomorrow*. Bern, Berlin, Bruxelles, Frankfurt am Main, New York, Oxford, Wien: Peter Lang, pp. 285–310.

Leroyer, P. (2011) "Change of Paradigm: From Linguistics to Information Science and From Dictionaries to Information Tools", in P. A. Fuertes-Olivera and H. Bergenholtz (2011), 121–40.

Leroyer, P. and H. Bergenholtz (2013) "Métalexicographie culturelle, fonctions lexicographiques et finalité pragmatique", *Etudes de Linguistique Appliquée* 170(2): 153–78.

Leroyer, P., J. Binon and S. Verlinde (2009) "La lexicographie d'apprentissage française au tournant du troisième millénaire: le couple FLM/FLE(S) entre tradition et innovation", *Lexicographica* 25: 109–33.

Lew, R. (2009) "Toward Variable Function-Dependent Sense Ordering in Future Dictionaries", in H. Bergenholtz, S. Nielsen and S. Tarp (ed.), *Lexicography at a Crossroads: Dictionaries and Encyclopedias Today, Lexicographical Tools Tomorrow*. Bern, Berlin, Bruxelles, Frankfurt am Main, New York, Oxford, Wien: Peter Lang, pp. 237–64.

Lew, R. (2010) "Multimodal Lexicography: The Representation of Meaning in Electronic Dictionaries", *Lexikos* 20: 290–306.

Lew, R. (2013) "Identifying Ordering and Defining Senses", in H. Jackson (2013), 284–302.

Lew, R., M. Grzelak and M. Leszkowicz (2013) "How Dictionary Users Choose Senses in Bilingual Dictionary Entries: An Eye-Tracking Study", *Lexikos* 23: 228–54.

Müller-Spitzer, C. (ed.) (2014) *Using Online Dictionaries*. Lexicographica Series Maior 145. Berlin, Boston: De Gruyter.

Nesi, H. (2013) "Researching Users and Uses of Dictionaries", in H. Jackson (2013), 62–74.

Nielsen, S. (2011) "Function- and User-Related Definitions in Online Dictionaries", in F. I. Kartashkova (ed.), *Ivanovskaya lekskograficheskaya shkola: traditsii i innovatsii (Ivanonvo Shcool of*

Lexicography: Traditions and Innovations: A Festschrift in Honour of Professor Olga Karpova). Ivanovo State University, pp. 197–219.

Pastor, V. and A. Alcina (2013) "Researching the Use of Electronic Dictionaries", in H. Jackson (2013), 97–147.

Ptaszynski, M. (2010) "Theoretical Considerations for the Improvement of Usage Labelling in Dictionaries: A Combined Formal-Functional Approach", *International Journal of Lexicography* 23(4): 411–42.

Rossenbeck, K. (1994) "Enzyklopädische Informationen im zweisprachigen Fachwörterbuch", in B. Schaeder and H. Bergenholtz (eds.), *Fachlexikographie, Fachwissen und seine Repräsentation in Wörterbüchern*, pp. 133–59. Tübingen: Narr.

Sanchéz, A. (2010) "The Treatment of Cultural and/or Encyclopaedic Items in Specialised Dictionaries for Learners", in P. A. Fuertes-Olivera (ed.), 107–130.

Scerba, L. V. (1940) "Towards a General Theory of Lexicography", *International Journal of Lexicography* 8(4), 1995. Oxford: Oxford University Press: 315–350.

Scholfield, P. (1999) "Dictionary Use in Reception", *International Journal of Lexicography* 12(1): 13–34.

Svensén, B. (2009). *A Handbook of Lexicography: The Theory and Practice of Dictionary-Making*. Cambridge: Cambridge University Press.

Tarp, S. (2008) *Lexicography in the Borderland Between Knowledge and Non-Knowledge: General Lexicographical Theory With Particular Focus on Learner's Lexicography*. Tübingen: Niemeyer.

Tarp, S. (2009) "Reflections on Lexicographical User Research", *Lexikos* 19: 275–96.

Tarp, S. (2011) "Polysemy and Homonymy in a Lexicographic Perspective", *Zeitschrift für Anglistik und Amerikanistik*, 57(3): 289–305.

Tarp, S. (2013) "Lexicographic Functions", in R. Gouws, U. Heid, W. Scheickhard and H. E. Wiegand (eds.), *Dictionaries: An International Encyclopedia of Lexicography. Supplementary Volume. Recent Developments With Focus on Electronic and Computational Lexicography*. Berlin, Boston, MA: De Gruyter, pp. 460–468.

Ten Hakcen, P. (2015) "Terms and Specialised Vocabulary: Taming the Prototypes", in H. Kockaert and F. Steurs (eds.), *Handbook of Terminology*, Volume 1. Amsterdam/Philadelphia: John Benjamins, pp. 3–13.

Tono, Y. (2011) *Research on Dictionary Use in the Context of Foreign Language Learning: Focus on Reading Comprehension*. Tübingen: Niemeyer.

Trap-Jensen, L. (2013) "Researching Lexicographical Practice", in H. Jackson (2013), 35–47.

Verlinde, S. and G. Peeters (2012) "Data Access Revisited: The Interactive Language Tool-Box", in S. Granger and M. Paquot (eds.), pp. 147–62.

Wiegand, H. E. (1992) "Elements of a Theory towards a So-called Lexicographic Definition", *Lexicographica* 8: 175–289.

Wiegand, H. E. (1994) "Zur Unterscheidung von semantischen und enzyklopädischen Daten in Fachwörterbüchern", in B. Schaeder and H. Bergenholtz (eds.), *Fachlexikographie. Fachwissen und seine Repräsentation in Wörterbüchern*, pp. 103–32. Tübingen: Narr

Xiqin, L. (2015) "Multimodal Definition: The Multiplication of Meaning in Electronic Dictionaries", *Lexikos* 25: 210–32.

Zgusta, L. (1971) *Manual of Lexicography*. Janua Linguarum 39. The Hague: De Gruyter.

17

Dictionaries for text production

Pedro A. Fuertes-Olivera and Henning Bergenholtz

17.1 Introduction

It is possible to distinguish between three basic approaches to the study of dictionaries for text production: (a) as object of study per se; (b) as expressions of relationship between them and their usefulness for users; and (c) as to their planning and construction. This chapter adopts a different approach to the one exposed by Leroyer in the previous chapter (see Chapter 16). Instead of focusing *only* on a critical discussion of the same concept (e.g. "dictionary for text production"), we will *also* analyse existing dictionaries for text production and will offer a description of a dictionary for text production which we are making just now (in July 2016, this dictionary project has around 40,000 completed cards, around 25 percent of the foreseen cards). This chapter must be read in conjunction with Chapters 16 and 18 as most of the arguments discussed by Leroyer and Giacomini also apply in dictionaries for text production.

Tarp (Chapter 15 of this *Handbook*) claims that dictionaries should be defined in terms of their form, content and purpose. Regarding content, dictionaries contain lexicographical data, that is, data that have been selected and prepared lexicographically in one way or another. With reference to form, dictionaries are reference sources and consultation tools which are prepared to be consulted in order to achieve punctual information needs. Finally, dictionaries may have four fundamental purposes, which can be called communicative, cognitive, operative and interpretive.

This chapter addresses lexicographic issues related with dictionaries for communicative purposes, that is, dictionaries designed with a view to solving problems of text communication, typically problems related to text reception, text production, translation and text revision. All these possible problems arise in written and oral communication, for example, when users are writing a text (production), preparing an oral presentation (production), reading a text (reception), translating a text (written translation), making an interpretation (oral translation or interpretation) and/or correcting a text (revision). All these situations are extra-lexicographical as they can be approached by consulting many different tools – typically, dictionaries, textbooks, handbooks, scientific journals, the Internet – as well as human assessors. In addition, extra-lexicographic use situations must take into consideration the advent of new types of users. For instance, Google Translate (a new user type) translates automatically (a communicative situation) and uses machine dictionaries to support the translation task; also computers are being used in information centres of companies and institutions for answering telephone calls (a production situation). In these new use situations, users may be humans or machines; and machines are typically using *NLP dictionaries*, defined by IBM as a list of like terms or phrases that is used to label domain concepts (e.g. names, as a building block of text analysis).

Within this framework, this chapter will be *primarily* focused on dictionaries that are conceptualized as utility tools and conceived for human consultation with the genuine purpose of meeting punctual information needs experienced by specific types of potential human users in text production situations (i.e. human dictionaries for text production). It will also mention some reflections concerned with dictionaries for machines (see Part VI of this *Handbook* for a broader view on them). For reasons of space, we will restrict this chapter to three main issues: (a) a review of the main types of human dictionaries for text production (historical perspectives); (b) a description of the concept of production situation and examples of the same (core issues and topics); and (c) a look into the future, especially to present possible developments of human dictionaries for text production in the era of the Internet in which users can access lexicographic data both manually and automatically.

17.2 Historical perspective: reviewing human dictionaries for text production

From both theoretical and practical points of view, there are many different sub-situations and consequently many different types of dictionaries for text production. They are *typically* restricted dictionaries (i.e. dictionaries that cover a limited set of phenomena). These can be "areas outside general cultural knowledge and the corresponding Language for General Purposes (LGP)" (Fuertes-Olivera and Tarp 2014: 7), or particular language aspects such as synonyms and antonyms, pronunciation, idioms and phrases, collocations, dialect terms, neologisms and so on (Cowie 2009). For reasons of space, we will analyse two specific types of restricted dictionaries for text production: (a) dictionaries of synonyms and antonyms; and (b) dictionaries of collocations. Chapters 14, 20, 21 and 28 of this *Handbook* also comment on other types of restricted dictionaries for text production.

17.2.1 Synonym dictionaries

Synonym dictionaries – they typically cover synonyms, antonyms and related words – are a special kind of text production dictionary that aims to help the user to find another word and use it instead of the word he or she already knows. These dictionaries, which use a lexicographical concept of synonymy, defend that two words are synonyms if they are interchangeable in most contexts. This means that lexicographers are typically using a broad and operational definition of synonymy, similar to the distinction between full and partial equivalence (Bergenholtz and Gouws 2012).

There are four main sub-types of synonym dictionaries, that is, dictionaries that are using a broad concept of synonym, which typically results in lemmas with between 10 and 15 synonyms. Most synonym dictionaries are *cumulative synonym dictionaries* (i.e. synonyms are clustered and listed alphabetically after the lemma). They are ordered after a semantic principle but without any kind of meaning item, even when the lemma is polysemous. In such dictionaries, users have to determine the most suitable synonym by themselves. Example (1) shows a typical example of a cumulative synonym dictionary: the Spanish word **casa** in the synonym dictionary of *WordReference.com* is followed by three rows of synonyms without any meaning item identifying them, although synonyms in rows 1, 2 and 3 are not interchangeable in Spanish texts. In a word, users have to decide by themselves which synonym can be useful as the dictionary does not discriminate among rows of synonyms:

(1)[1]

casa

- domicilio, hogar, vivienda, morada, residencia, piso, habitación, lar
- familia, linaje, raza, estirpe, sangre, solar, blazon, prosapia
- empresa, sociedad, companía, firma, razón social

A second type is called *explicative* or *distinctive synonym dictionary*. Synonyms are listed alphabetically after a meaning item identifying each sense of the lemma. This means that there is only one meaning item if the lemma is monosemous but two or more meaning items if the lemma is polysemous. In addition, in such dictionaries, lemmas usually go with their word class and examples of each meaning. In example (2), taken from the online version of the *Merriam Webster Dictionary*, users have an ordered list of synonyms grouped by word class, meaning item, examples of the lemma, related words, antonyms and near antonyms:

(2)[2]

distinctive

adjective

1 being not of the same kind <she seems to alternate between two *distinctive* hairstyles>

Synonyms disparate, dissimilar, distant, distinct, different, distinguishable, diverse, nonidentical, other, unalike, unlike

Related Words divers, miscellaneous, mixed, several, sundry, variant, varied, various; (. . .)

Near Antonyms equal, selfsame; equivalent, tantamount; (. . .)

Antonyms alike, identical, indistinguishable, kin, kindred, like, parallel, same, similar

2 serving to identify as belonging to an individual or group <the *distinctive* odor of a barnyard>

Synonyms classic, diagnostic (*also* diagnostical), discriminating, distinct, characteristic, distinguishing, identifying, individual, peculiar, proper, symptomatic, typical

Related Words idiosyncratic; identifiable, pronounced, unmistakable; (. . .)

Antonyms atypical, nontypical, uncharacteristic, untypical

A third type has come to life in recent times. It is a variant of cumulative and distinctive synonym dictionaries: the cluster of synonyms is ordered after an example, which seems to work as a proxy of a meaning item. Example (3) shows an entry from the *Oxford Synonym Dictionary* for Spanish speakers. It lists a cluster of synonyms after the lemma **house** and a word class label in Spanish (*sustantivo* = noun), an example and a style marker (if needed). In other words, the example sentence offers the meaning of the lemma. It goes without saying that such dictionary type forces users to extract each meaning of the form and example sentence, which is not always an easy task to accomplish:

(3)[3]

house sustantivo

1 'the new state comprises 200 houses'
home, place of residence, homestead, lodging place, a roof over one's head
formal habitation, residence, dwelling, dwelling place, abode, domicile

2 'make yourself scarce before you wake the whole house'
household, family, family circle, ménage, clan, tribe
informal brood

The fourth type is the *semi-explicating* or *semi-distinctive synonym dictionary*. Such dictionaries contain meaning items preceding a list of alphabetically ordered synonyms when the lemma is polysemous, but only a list of alphabetically ordered synonyms when the lemma is monosemous. For instance, **cabecera de puente** offers a list of synonyms after the word class and meaning item, whereas **macaurel** only lists synonyms after its word class. Example (4) is taken from a dictionary project under construction (see Section 17.4 of this chapter; Fuertes-Olivera and Bergenholtz 2015):

(4)

cabecera de puente nombre

1 Definición

línea militar que se crea cuando un ejército armado llega a una costa y comienza a defender la playa hasta que el total de los hombres que componen ese ejército ha desembarcado y ya cuentan con los suficientes soldados para realizar un ataque

Sinónimo(s)

cabeza de puente
cabecera de playa
cabeza de playa

2 Definición

acción de preparar la llegada de una persona, una entidad, un grupo o un país a algún sitio, asociación, grupo político o social para formar parte de él e integrarse como miembro

Sinónimo(s)

desembarco
cabeza de playa
cabeza de Puente
cabecera de playa
(. . .)

macaurel nombre

Sinónimo(s)

tragavenado
mazacuata
Boa constrictor imperator
boa común

17.2.2 Collocation dictionaries

Dictionaries of collocations, or collocation dictionaries, are experiencing some important changes in connection with the development of new tendencies in the treatment of collocations. Following Hausmann (1989), Mittmann (2013: 500) argues that a large number of lexicographers follow a *significance-oriented approach*, that is, "collocations are prototypically combinations of two lexical words which stand in some kind of grammatical relationship to one another." Some other lexicographers take a different position and define collocations statistically. Neo-Firthians such as Moon (2007), for example, look at individual word forms in corpora and present collocations in terms of their frequent co-occurrence. Typically, "the collocates of any given word (the *node word*) are defined as being those words which occur with a higher than expected frequency within a span of four words to the left and right of it" (Mittmann 2013: 501). Both approaches can be observed in collocation dictionaries, most of which aim at assisting learners – pre-intermediate to advanced learners – for example, *Oxford Collocation Dictionary for Students of English* (online version as *Online OXFORD Collocation Dictionary)* and *Macmillan Collocation Dictionary for Learners of English.* These two are different in the approach taken and offer very different results. Example (5) is taken from the *Online Oxford Collocation Dictionary*. It offers more collocations than the *Macmillan Collocation Dictionary*. They are typically placed after a brief definition of the different senses of the lemma – base or node – which is grammatically identified by means of its word class. The collocations are preceded by abbreviations of word class, and sometimes followed by usage examples. The data sets used to identify them are well structured, as shown in example (5):

(5)[4]

balance *verb*
1 keep steady
ADV. **carefully, precariously**
PREP. **on** *He balanced the glasses carefully on the tray.*
2 compare two things; give them equal value
VERB + BALANCE **have to, need to/seek to, try to** *The plan seeks to balance two important objectives./* **manage to**
PREP. **against** *We have to balance the risks of the new strategy against the possible benefits./* **with** *She tries to balance the needs of her children with those of her employer.*

The *Macmillan Collocation Dictionary* is based on the statistical approach and offers fewer collocations than the *Online Oxford Collocation Dictionary*. In addition, the ordering of the data sets demands a lot of attention from users, who might be puzzled if they happen to look up these two dictionaries. For instance, collocations of "V+n" are only found in the *Macmillan Collocation Dictionary* (example 6) but not in the *Online Oxford Collocation Dictionary* (example 5), the first meaning of **balance** in the *Online Oxford Collocation Dictionary* (example 5) is not in the *Macmillan Collocation Dictionary* (example 6) and the extension of **balance** in the *Macmillan Collocation Dictionary* (example 6) is absent from the *Online Oxford Collocation Dictionary* (example 5):

(6)[5]

balance *V*
create a good balance between different things

- **V** + n balance different needs **demands, desires, needs, rights** *I struggle to balance the demands of my family* ***with*** *my job* □ *We are trying to balance the needs of the individual* ***against*** *the needs of the population.*

Δ balance money received and money spent **books, budget, checkbook** *Headteachers have been told that they must balance their budgets by next year.*

Examples (5) and (6) illustrate quite well the data sets typically found in learner's collocation dictionaries for text production. These follow the influence of the *Longman Language Activator*, which makes its case for defending the inclusion of lexicographical data such as these (xxiv–xxv):

1. Keywords, which are typically the bases of most collocations.
2. References, i.e. cross-references to other related keywords.
3. Menu, i.e. a lexicographical index enumerating all the words in the section corresponding to each of the meanings of the keyword.
4. Label, i.e. a lexicographical indication of style, regional variety (e.g. American or British English), and so on.
5. Definition, typically in the form of short definitions, which are crafted by using restricted vocabularies.
6. Pronunciation, typically using the International Phonetic Alphabet.
7. Arabic numbers, i.e. ways of enumerating the different meanings of the keyword in question.
8. Collocation information, i.e. an alphabetical list of collocates for each of the list of words in each of the sections of each keyword. They may go with a short explanation of the combination.
9. Examples of use for all the words and collocations.
10. Grammar information, usually by inserting grammar words such as preposition, conjunctions, and so on in a particular collocation.
11. Parts of speech, usually in the form of codes such as these (n C) or (V phrase) for indicating whether the word is a countable noun, a verb, etc. and its characteristics.

This review of synonym and collocations dictionaries allow us to draw three provisional conclusions: (a) although the concept of *production situation* is well established in lexicographical circles, there are different, sometime contradictory, ways of approaching it lexicographically; (b) there are different text production patterns, for example, experienced learners may need different production dictionaries than beginners, and so on; and (c) the coming of age of the Internet facilitates the design and making of different types of production dictionaries, each devised to assist users in one of the different production situations described so far.

17.3 Core issues and topics

17.3.1 Definition

We defend that dictionaries for text production must be constructed with the main aim of helping potential users to write, translate and/or speak. Our previous analysis has also shown that there is not a single production situation but many of them, although some of them may be more prototypical than others. We have also commented that users of dictionaries for text production may be humans and/or machines. Taken all our previous comments into consideration we define a dictionary for text production

> *as a utility tool which is conceived for consultation with the genuine purpose of meeting punctual information needs experienced by specific types of potential user in specific text production situation, and which is designed to assist its users by providing manual or automatic access to either lexicographically prepared data (for human users) or unprepared data (for machine) in order to retrieve the required information which they can subsequently use to solve specific production problems in the context where the needs originally occurred.*

From these definitions, three specific comments should be made (see Section 16.3 (Chapter 16) and Section 18.3 (Chapter 18) for an overview of functions and functionalities that may be similar in dictionaries for text production, dictionaries for text reception and dictionaries for translation. For reasons of space, we will limit the rest of the section to aspects totally or mostly connected with production situations).

17.3.2 Production situations

Simple communicative models typically contain three levels: a text level, a process level and a player level (Tarp 2008: 47). A three-level model such as this operates millions of times every single day, in which a player sends and/or receives a text. The player can be a sender or a receiver – a person or machine – producing or receiving a text, which can be codified by humans or machines by means of a language, that is, any system of communication (e.g. a human language or a programming language). By production situations, we refer to use situations in which a sender codifies a text by using a particular form of language. This model is present in three main production situations: (a) a human acting as sender codifies a text in his or her native language; (b) a human acting as sender codifies a text in a foreign language; and (c) a machine acting as sender codifies a text by using a programming language with the aim of crafting a message which will be understood by humans or machines.

This model is related to lexicography as understood in this volume, with several relevant production situations in which potential dictionary users may find themselves:

1. A human sender is producing a text in his or her native language.
2. A human sender is producing a text in a foreign language.
3. A machine is producing a text in one of the languages it has NLP dictionaries and production rules for.

17.3.2.1 Datasets in production situations for native speakers

In the first relevant production situation, the user is creating a text in his or her native language. Such production situation can be subdivided into myriad possibilities, two of them relevant in current lexicographical theory and practice: (a) to which extent does the user master his or her native language; and (b) to what extent does the user master the topic of the text he or she is producing. In such situation, the needs for the potential users determine the specific lexicographical data to be included in the dictionary article. These needs must be lexicographically relevant, and can be subdivided into two groups: primary user needs and secondary user needs (Tarp 2008: 56). Primary user needs are primarily connected with information categories such as "information about mother tongue", "general cultural information", "information about culture in specific language area" and "information about a specific subject or science" (Tarp 2008: 57). Secondary user needs mainly refer to "general education in lexicography", "general instruction in dictionary usage", "information about the specific dictionary" and "instruction in use of the specific dictionary" (Tarp 2008: 57).

Translating the previously mentioned two types of needs into human dictionaries for text production demands the inclusion of some specific data types, the exact number and categories of which will depend on the exact purpose of the dictionary as well as its form and content. For example, in online dictionaries for text production aiming at Spanish native speakers, data types such as the following should be taken into consideration at the conceptualisation phase. In other words, these data must be analysed with the aim of deciding which of them must be included in the specific dictionary for text production we aim to compile:

1 Texts such as user guides that explain how to use the dictionary (e.g. how to search for concepts in a thesaurus).
2 Lemmas of real and existing words, phrases, idioms, proverbs, etc. These must be written in a way that will allow potential users to understand them easily. For instance, we should lemmatize both *profesor* and *profesora* (male and female teacher respectively), instead of traditionally conceived lemmas such as *professor, ra* (*Diccionario de la Lengua Española* 2014), which are not intelligible for dictionary users who have not received previous instruction in dictionary usage and its typical meta-language.
3 Homonymy indices for signalling grammatical differences among lemma homography.
4 Polysemy indices for indicating different meanings of the same lemma.
5 Grammar data addressed to the lemma, basically inflections, syntactic patterns, valencies, spelling and grammar remarks and pronunciation of loan words.
6 Meaning explanations, usually by writing lexicographically relevant definitions (see Chapter 4 of this *Handbook*).
7 Synonyms and antonyms, that is, words or expressions that can be employed instead of the lemma, either because they refer to the same entity (synonym) or to an opposite one (antonym).
8 Word formations, that is, possible lemmas that have some kind of relation with the lemma, for example, *casa grande* in the dictionary article for **casa**. (A *casa grande* is a colloquial way of referring to the main building of a *cortijo* (En "country estate"). If needed, these word formations can be lemmatised easily.
9 Collocations, that is, chunks of words that do not form a complete sentence and help users to contextualize the meaning and form of the lemma.
10 Examples, that is, one or more complete sentences that help users to contextualize the meaning and form of the lemma.
11 Language specifications attached to lemmas, synonyms and antonyms, for example, "formal", "informal" for marking style variation in connection with the lemma or a particular meaning of the lemma.
12 Subject specifications attached to the lemma for indicating subject field, if any.
13 Lexicographical remarks, which can be lexical remarks (e.g. by indicating that a particular meaning has very negative connotations and is offensive, etc.), synonym or antonym remarks (e.g. by indicating that some of the synonyms or antonyms are only

used in Mexico), production remarks (e.g. by indicating that a particular meaning or a particular lemma are used in Latin America), etc.

14 Texts for improving users' writing skills. These typically consist of writing and grammar sections that include topics that are considered difficult for the intended user, such as accentuation rules, verb conjugations and word formation rules in Spanish dictionaries (for instance, Spanish adjectives can be converted into nouns by using them with definite or indefinite articles).

15 Hyperlinks to open data sources, for example, a link to a conjugator of Spanish verbs.[6]

16 Proscriptive remarks, that is, ways of indicating a preferred spelling, inflection, verb form, etc.

17 Cultural data, especially data signalling important differences among cultures and different types of native speakers, for example, popular names of trees and plants may refer to different realities in the Spanish-speaking world (around 500 million native speakers).

18 A systematic introduction, that is, a text catering for users who may need a general understanding, a more systematic presentation, or a comparative description of a subject field.

17.3.2.2 Datasets in production situations for foreigners

The second relevant production situation differs from the first one in that the sender is producing a text in a foreign language. As before, this use situation must be typically addressed by adapting the data types of the dictionary to the potential users' language level in a foreign language and their knowledge of the subject field(s) addressed by the dictionary. In such use situations, secondary user needs are basically the same than in the previous use situation. However, primary user needs are different, and consequently lexicographers have to adapt the data types to be included to the new primary user needs, typically to address lexicographically information issues such as these: "information about foreign language", "information about specialized language in foreign language", "comparative information about mother tongue and foreign language", "comparative information about specialized language in mother tongue and foreign language" and "comparative information about a subject in national and foreign culture" (Tarp 2008: 57).

Tarp (2008: 59) also indicates that such use situation can be subdivided into two main sub-situations: (a) "production of text in a foreign language *thinking via mother tongue*", and (b) "production of text in foreign language *thinking via the foreign language*" (italics in the original). The main difference between both possibilities is that we need a bilingual dictionary from the mother tongue into the foreign language in (a), whereas in (b) we need a dictionary based on the foreign language, whether it is monolingual or biscopal. For reasons of space, we will focus only on monolingual dictionaries for text production. These should contain all the data types already mentioned in Section 17.3.2.1 – these should be adapted if needed by offering simpler definitions – and make room for some more data types, especially these:

1 The pronunciation of all the lemmas.

2 Menus or indices of the dictionary article, especially when polysemy is abundant.

3 Hyperlinks to corpus data (e.g. concordances and paragraphs) with the aim of offering more possible collocations, examples and syntactic patterns of the lemma.

4 Cultural data, especially data signalling important differences among cultures and languages covered.
5 Dictionary meta-language referring to the data type (e.g. definition, collocation, example, pronunciation and so on).

17.3.2.3 Datasets in production situations for machines

Finally, the third production situation is totally new and connected to the digital world. Although this new situation will be dealt with in Part VI of this *Handbook* (see also Chapter 29 of this *Handbook*), it may be interesting for this chapter to indicate that machine dictionaries are being used in production use situations such as writing a text, writing and/or translating weather forecasts, answering routine telephone conversations and so on. Lenders (2013: 990) indicates in his history of computational lexicography that during the late 1970s and early 1980s some publishing houses and research institutions such as IBM commercialized their dictionaries for use in information processing systems, typically for research purposes. Since then, the number and titles of lexicographical projects related to electronic dictionaries for machine use has grown exponentially (see Gouws et al. 2013: 1091–1194 for a review). For the objectives of this chapter, we will only mention that electronic dictionaries for machine use are typically named "lexicons" or "ontologies" and are integral parts of different types of information systems such as spoken language systems, text processing and correction systems, information retrieval, information extraction and text mining systems, computer-assisted language learning systems, question answering and natural language database access systems, natural language generation systems and machine translation and machine-aided translation systems (see Chapters 13, 14, 21 and 29 of this *Handbook*).

Some of the "lexicons" or "ontologies" used in the previously mentioned information systems are polyfunctional printed dictionaries turned digital. In the last decade, however, we are witnessing a new generation of electronic dictionaries for machine use. Instead of lexicographically prepared data types, these typically contain lexicographically unprepared data which are converted into meaningful bits by developing knowledge-based management systems. Clark et al. (2012: 555–558), for example, present an overview of them, and indicate that methods for building knowledge structures from text collections are approached in two ways, which are known as data-driven and knowledge-driven approaches. To sum up, this new generation of electronic dictionaries for machine use contain large amounts of lexicographically unprepared data, which are converted into lexicographically relevant data by using data-driven or knowledge-driven algorithms. For instance, some researchers are constructing *mined dictionaries*, that is, dictionaries that are constructed automatically by mining the Web (Ye et al. 2012), typically by extracting data from Wikipedia and ordering them in a way that allow users to, say, observe language and/or conceptual similarities and differences among languages and subject domains. The data thus obtained could be used in different production situations, for instance IBM presents its "Natural Language Processing (NLP) Dictionary Server"[7] as a web-based system with two main functions: (a) to help create, edit, and manage sets of dictionaries for NLP applications and (b) provide a real-time service for using those NLP dictionaries created. In a word, IBM and other technology companies are developing machine dictionaries for being used in different production situation. These dictionaries contain lexicographically unprepared data that are made relevant by automatic means. Without doubt, this will influence the future of lexicography (see Chapter 29 and Part VI of this *Handbook*).

17.4 Looking to the future

The coming of age of the Internet is having a lot of impact on lexicography (cf. Fuertes-Olivera 2016; Fuertes-Olivera and Bergenholtz 2011; Granger and Paquot 2012; Jackson 2013; Tarp and Fuertes-Olivera 2016; and Part VI of this *Handbook* for a review). Regarding dictionaries for text production, we think that the Internet allows the constructions of *integrated information systems*, for example, sets of different monofunctional dictionaries that *must* be conceptualized and constructed at the same time. Nielsen and Almind (2011) and Bergenholtz and Skovgård Nielsen (2013), for instance, claim that databases and lexicographical databases are related, albeit representing different concepts: a database is a structured collection of values, whereas a lexicographical database is a storage system constructed to contain lexicographical data. Lexicographers can use them for constructing integrated information systems that consist of, say, three different components: a lexicographic database on which lexicographers work, storing as much data as possible (Fuertes-Olivera 2015); a graphical user interface or web homepage where users retrieve data in one way or another, depending on the innovations employed in a particular dictionary project; and, finally, a search engine which connects the database and the webpage.

These concepts underline the making of a current lexicographical project which consists of seven different dictionaries, four of which are dictionaries for text production (Fuertes-Olivera and Bergenholtz 2015; Tarp and Fuertes-Olivera 2016). This project consists of a lexicographical database, seven search engines and seven graphical user interfaces. Four of the seven interfaces and search engines offer users lexicographical data that is especially prepared for being used in several communication situations: (a) the grammar and spelling of the lemma; (b) synonyms and antonyms of the lemma; (c) concepts; and (d) data types being used by native speakers in prototypical production situations such as day-to-day interactions, writing of documents and so on.

17.4.1 The grammar and spelling dictionary

The grammar and spelling dictionary aims to help users in both text production and text correction situations. It uses a *minimizing search*, that is, the search finishes once the system explores one field of the database and finds what it was looking for. There are up to three possible searches: (a) it initially searches ==lemma, that is, it searches the lemma field and retrieves all the lemmas equal to the search string with its inflected forms; (b) if it does not find what it was looking for, it searches *lemma*, that is, it searches all the lemma fields and retrieves all the dictionary articles where the search string is part of the lemma; and (c) if it does not find what it was looking for, it continues with a fuzzy search, that is, it retrieves lemmas which are similar to the search string.

This dictionary offers up to nine lexicographical data: the lemma; the homonym number of the lemma (if needed); the word class and inflections of the lemma; alternative spellings and inflections (if needed); valencies of the lemma (if needed); grammar and spelling remarks (if needed); polysemy number (if needed); meaning item if the lemma is polysemous or if it goes with a grammar and spelling remark; cross-reference to a different lemma with a proscriptive remark (if needed); and hyperlinks to a conjugator of Spanish verbs (if needed) (see Sections 17.3.2.1 and 17.3.2.2).

17.4.2 The synonym and antonym dictionary

The synonym and antonym dictionary aims to help users in use production situations in which it offers words that can be used instead of the lemma. This dictionary only shows lemmas that have synonyms and/or antonyms. It also uses a *minimizing search* with up to six search possibilities: (a) it initially searches ==lemma, that is, it searches the lemma field and retrieves all the lemmas equal to the search string with its inflected forms; (b) if it does not find what it was looking for, it searches *lemma*, that is, it searches the lemma field and retrieves all the dictionary articles where the search string is part of the lemma; (c) if it does not find what it was looking for, it searches ==lemma in the synonym field, that is, it searches in the synonym field and retrieves all the dictionary articles in which the search string is a synonym; (d) if it does not find what it was looking for, it searches *lemma* in the synonym field, that is, it searches in the synonym field and retrieves all the dictionary articles in which the search string is part of a synonym; (e) if it does not find what it was looking for, it searches ==lemma in the antonym field, that is, it searches in the antonym field and retrieves all the dictionary articles in which the search string is an antonym; and (f) if it does not find what it was looking for, it searches *lemma* in the antonym field, that is, it searches in the antonym field and retrieves all the dictionary articles in which the search string is part of an antonym.

This dictionary offers up to 12 lexicographical data: the lemma; the homonym number of the lemma (if needed); the style marker attached to the lemma (if needed); the polysemy number of the lemma (if needed); the word class of the lemma; cross-reference to a different lemma (if needed); synonym(s); style marker attached to the synonym(s) (if needed); synonym and/or antonym remarks (if needed); antonym(s); style marker attached to the antonym(s); and the meaning item if the lemma is polysemous, that is, it is a semi-explicative synonym dictionary (see Sections 17.3.2.1 and 17.3.2.2).

17.4.3 The concept dictionary

The concept dictionary – they are usually called thesaurus or Word Finder dictionaries – uses a *maximizing search*, that is, it searches in two fields and does not terminate until it has searched all the data stored in these two fields: (a) the meaning field; and (b) the lexical remark field (see Section 17.3.2.1). The search uses Boolean operators and concepts, and the system retrieves all the dictionary articles that contain the concept or part of the concept searched for. For instance, the search string "veneno + serpiente" (En "poison" + "serpent") retrieves all the dictionary articles in which the concepts "poison" and "serpent" are present in whatever order. In other words, this dictionary is used when a person who is producing a text cannot remember or does not know the word he or she is looking for, but he or she knows its meaning or part of it. The Boolean operators serve the purpose of allowing users to search for the word they do not remember. Each dictionary article retrieved in this dictionary offers users all the lexicographical data of the next dictionary (see Section 17.4.4).

17.4.4 General production dictionary (text production dictionary for native speakers of Spanish)

Finally, there is a dictionary for text production aiming to help native speakers in prototypical production situations. It contains up to 21 different lexicographical data types (see Section 17.3.2.1). The dictionary uses a *minimizing search* with up to three possible searches:

(a) it initially searches ==lemma, that is, it searches the lemma field and retrieves all the lemmas equal to the search string with its inflected forms; (b) if it does not find what it was looking for, it searches *lemma*, that is, it searches all the lemma fields and retrieves all the dictionary articles where the search string is part of the lemma; and (c) if it does not find what it was looking for, it continues with a fuzzy search, that is, it retrieves lemmas which are similar to the search string.

As mentioned, this dictionary offers up to 21 data: the lemma; the homonym number of the lemma (if needed); the style marker attached to the lemma (if needed); the word class of the lemma; the inflections of the lemma; the valencies of the lemma (if needed); grammar and/or spelling remarks (if needed); the policy number of the lemma (if needed); cross-reference to a different lemma (if needed); proscriptive remarks (if needed); the meaning item of the lemma; lexical remarks for text production (if needed); collocations; examples; word-formations, that is, a set of related words that can be lemmatized (if needed); synonym(s) (if needed); style marker attached to the synonym(s) (if needed); antonym(s) (if needed); style marker attached to the antonym(s) (if needed); synonym and/or antonym remarks (if needed); and a hyperlink of a conjugator of Spanish verbs (if needed) (see Section 17.3.2.1). Figure 17.1 offers a screenshot of the lemma **acordarse del día que nació** (En "fuck off and die"). This is an informal idiomatic expression which illustrates most of the data sets included in this dictionary for text production. For instance, it explains that the Spanish verbs "acordarse" and "nació" change as they must agree in gender and number with the subject. We illustrate these changes by offering inflections and conjugations and by including the grammar valency of this idiomatic expression:

acordarse del día que nació *expresión*

Flexiones
me acuerdo del día que nací, me acordé del día que nací, me acordaba del día que nací, me acordaré del día que nací, me acordaría del día que nací, me acuerde del día que nací, acordándome del día que nací

Nota gramatical y/o ortográfica
La forma del verbo "nacer" concuerda en número y persona con la persona gramatical del sujeto: me acuerdo del día que nací, te acuerdas del día que naciste, se acuerda del día que nació, nos acordamos del día que nacimos, os acordáis del día que nacisteis, se acuerdan del día que nacieron.

Definición
expresión que indica que alguien está realmente enfadado, hastiado y cabreado por el comportamiento, actitud o hechos de otra persona, de modo que, en su pensamiento, le maldice, le condena y despotrica de ella; amenazar alguien a otra persona verbal o físicamente, por tenerle odio, rencor o aversión profunda

Colocacion(es)
que como siga por ese camino voy a enseñarle una lección que se va a acordar para siempre del día que nació
que esa chama me llega a decir algo que no me guste y se acordará del día que nació

que le hice acordarse del día que nació a punta de correazo
que no me voy corriendo, espero con un palo bien gordo al dueño y le hago acordarse del día que nació

Ejemplo(s)
Se acordará del día que nació, deseará nunca haber nacido, lamentará el día que se interesó en mi amigo.

Formación de palabras
acordarse
día
nacer

Sinónimos
acordarse de toda su familia
cagarse en todos sus muertos [informal]

Gramática Valencias:

Alguien se acuerda del día que nació

Figure 17.1 Screenshot of **acordarse del día que nació** in a general production dictionary for native speakers of Spanish

These four dictionaries are in line with the title of this chapter and the foundations of lexicography presented in Part I of this *Handbook*. The coming of age of the Internet will allow lexicographers to make new dictionary types and put them into practice, for example, by designing dictionaries that attempt to assist specifically in the different use situations in which potential users need lexicographic assistance in a quick and easy way.

17.5 Conclusion

This chapter has focused on human dictionaries for text production, that is, dictionaries typically used when a human sender is producing a text in his or her native language or in a foreign language. It has not only explained the main characteristics of production situation and examples of the same but also has reviewed the state of the art concerning two main dictionary types for text production: synonym and antonym dictionaries, and collocation dictionaries. Our review has shown that dictionaries for text production can be greatly improved. For instance, we have referred to a lexicographic project that target Spanish native speakers. This project contains up to 21 different lexicographic data. All these data may be typically needed in production situations.

Acknowledgments

Thanks are due to the Ministerio de Economía y Competitividad for financial support (Grant FFI2014-52462-P).

Related topics

The concept of dictionary; dictionaries for text reception; dictionaries for translation; dictionaries to assist teaching and learning; learners' dictionaries of English; Spanish lexicography in the Internet era.

Further reading

Fuertes-Olivera, P. A. (2016). "A Cambrian Explosion in Lexicography: Some Reflections for Designing and Constructing Specialised Online Dictionaries", *International Journal of Lexicography* 29 (2): 226–247.
The author reflects on lexicographic innovations, especially those being used for creating *dynamic dictionaries*, i.e. dictionaries that offer different data in different situations, all of which stem from the same lexicographic database.

Gouws, R. H., U. Heid, W. Schweickard and H. E. Wiegand (eds.) (2013). *Dictionaries, An International Encyclopedia of Lexicography*. Suppl.Vol. Berlin/Boston: de Gruyter Mouton.
Chapter XV of this encyclopaedia offers a typology of electronic dictionaries for machine use, especially for speech recognition, text processing and correcting, information retrieval, computer-assisted language learning, and machine translation.

Volume 31 of Lexicographica (2015).
The thematic part of this volume, directed by H.E. Wiegand, reflects on structures in general and specialized online dictionaries. Several articles – especially those written by Bergenholtz and Agerbo, Fuerets-Olivera, Klosa and Gouws, Nielsen and Tarp – offer new ideas on *dynamic dictionaries*.

Rundell, M. (1999). "Dictionary Use in Production", *International Journal of Lexicography* 12(1): 35–53.
This article analyses different aspects of paper dictionaries, monolingual and bilingual, in production situations. It focuses on the Anglo-Saxon tradition and concludes that monolingual English learners' dictionaries are very adequate options in such situations.

Tarp, S. and P. A. Fuertes-Olivera. (2016). "Advantages and Disadvantages in the Use of Internet as a Corpus: The Case of the Online Dictionaries of Spanish Valladolid-UVa", *Lexikos* 26: 273–295.
This article offers insights on the process of compilation of the Spanish dictionaries described in Section 17.4 of this chapter.

Notes

1 See at www.wordreference.com/sinonimos/casa
2 See at www.merriam-webster.com/thesaurus/distinctive
3 See at www.oxforddictionaries.com/es/definicion/ingles-tesauro/house
4 See at http://oxforddictionary.so8848.com/search?word=balance
5 Extracted from the *Macmillan Collocation Dictionary for Learners of English*
6 See for example www.spanishdict.com/conjugate/decir
7 See at www.youtube.com/watch?v=Fi0gAfAxzbw

References

Dictionaries

Diccionario de la lengua española. (2014) Real Academia Española de la Lengua. http://dle.rae.es/?id=DglqVCc [Accessed: 2 February 2017].

Macmillan Collocations Dictionary for Learners of English. (2010) London: Palgrave Macmillan.
Merriam Webster. www.merriam-webster.com/thesaurus/distinctive [Accessed: 2 February 2017].
Oxford Dictionaries: Synonyms. www.oxforddictionaries.com/thesaurus/house [Accessed: 2 February 2017].
WordReference. www.wordreference.com/es/ [Accessed: 2 February 2017].

Other literature

Bergenholtz, H. and R. H. Gouws (2012) "Synonymy and Synonyms in Lexicography", *Lexicographica* 28: 307–333.
Bergenholtz, H. and J. S. Nielsen (2013) "What Is a Lexicographical Database?", *Lexikos* 23: 77–87.
Clark, M., Y. Kim, U. Kruschwitz, D. Song, D. Albakour, S. Dignum, U. Cerviño Baresi, M. Fasli and A. D. Roeck (2012) "Automatically Structuring Domain Knowledge From Text: An Overview of Current Research", *Information Processing and Management* 48: 552–568.
Cowie, A. P. (ed.) (2009) *The Oxford History of English Lexicography. Volume II: Specialized Dictionaries.* Oxford: Oxford University Press.
Fuertes-Olivera, P. A. (2016) "A Cambrian Explosion in Lexicography: Some Reflections for Designing and Constructing Specialized Online Dictionaries. *International Journal of Lexicography* 29(2): 226–247.
Fuertes-Olivera, P. A. and H. Bergenholtz (eds.) (2011) *e-Lexicography: The Internet, Digital Initiatives and Lexicography.* London: Continuum.
Fuertes-Olivera, P. A. and H. Bergenholtz (2015) Los diccionarios en línea de español "Universidad de Valladolid". *Revista de Lexicografía* 4: 71–98.
Fuertes-Olivera, P. A. and S. Tarp (2014) *Theory and Practice of Specialised Online Dictionaries: Lexicography Versus Terminography.* Berlin, Boston: Walter de Gruyter.
Gouws, R. H., U. Heid, W. Schweickard and H. E. Wiegand (eds.) (2013) *Dictionaries: An International Encyclopedia of Lexicography. Supplementary Volume: Recent Developments with Focus on Electronic and Computational Lexicography.* Berlin/Boston: De Gruyter Mouton.
Granger, S. and M. Paquot (eds.) (2012) *Electronic Lexicography.* Oxford: Oxford University Press.
Hausmann, F. J. (1989) "Le Dictionnaire de collocations", in F. Hausmann, O. Reichmann, H. E. Wiegand and L. Zgusta (eds.), *Dictionaries. International Encyclopedia of Lexicography. First Volume.* Berlin: de Gruyer, pp 1010–1019.
Hausmann, F. J. (2013) "The Concept of Semiotaxis", in R. H. Gouws, et al. (eds.), pp. 496–499.
Jackson, H. (ed.) (2013) *The Bloomsbury Companion to Lexicography.* London: Bloomsbury Academics.
Lenders, W. (2013) "The Early History of Computational Lexicography: The 1950s and 1960s", in R. H. Gouws et al. (eds.), pp. 969–982.
Mittmann, B. (2013) "New Tendencies in the Treatment of Collocations", in R. H. Gouws et al. (eds.), pp. 500–509.
Moon, R. (2007) "Phraseology in General Monolingual Dictionaries", in H. Burger, D. Dobrovol'skij, P. Kühn and N. R. Norrick (eds.), *Phraseologie. Phraseology. Ein internationals Handbuch der zeitgenössischen Forschung: An International Handbook of Contemporary Research.* Volume 2. Berlin/New York: De Gruyter, pp. 909–918.
Nielsen, S. and R. Almind (2011) "From Data to Dictionary", in P. A. Fuertes-Olivera and H. Bergenholtz (eds.), pp. 141–167.
Tarp, S. (2008) *Lexicography in the Borderland Between Knowledge and Non-Knowledge: General Lexicographical Theory With Particular Focus on Learner's Lexicography.* Tübingen: Max Niemeyer Verlag.

Tarp, S. and P. A. Fuertes-Olivera (2016) "Advantages and Disadvantages in the Use of Internet as a Corpus: The Case of the Online Dictionaries of Spanish Valladolid-UVa", *Lexikos* 26: 273–295.

Ye, Z., J. Xiiangji, B. He and H. Lin (2012) "Mining a Multilingual Association Dictionary From Wikipedia for Cross-Language Information Retrieval", *Journal of the American Society for Information Science and Technology* 63(12): 2474–2487.

18

Dictionaries for translation

Laura Giacomini

18.1 Introduction

As in Chapters 16 and 17, it is possible to distinguish between three basic approaches to the study of dictionaries for translation: (a) as object of study per se; (b) as expressions of relationship between them and their usefulness for users; and (c) as to their planning and construction. The focus of this chapter is on a critical discussion of the very concept of a dictionary for translation (in the following: DfT), as well as of the specific needs of translators as an unexpectedly heterogeneous user group. The complexity of the translation process and the related variables (e.g. translation direction and native language) raise a challenging question: Does a DfT exist as an autonomous, multifunctional lexicographic tool, or are translators better served by a combination of resources, the choice of which can be tailored to the needs of each translation situation? For reasons of space, I will not discuss topics and issues that have already been discussed in Chapters 16 and 17, that is, topics and issues concerned with communicative situations and functions.

After a preliminary discussion on the theoretical background of DfTs, Section 18.2 analyses macrostructural and microstructural properties of last-generation bilingual dictionaries that are specifically designed to serve translation purposes, pointing out the differences between traditional and innovative approaches. Section 18.3 concentrates on future work in lexicography for translation and provides an answer to the general question regarding resources for translators, and Section 18.4 draws some conclusions on the topics explored in the chapter.

18.2 Core issues and topics

18.2.1 Dictionaries for translation in the theoretical discussion: searching for a distinct identity

What is a dictionary for translation? The answer to this question should be obvious: it is, of course, a dictionary designed to serve translation purposes, a tool that provides means for translating texts from an interlingual perspective. Yet the awareness that dictionaries for translation are specific lexicographic products seems to be a rather recent achievement. According to Zgusta (1971: 294), bilingual dictionaries and translation dictionaries are the same object, and the purpose of this object is "to co-ordinate with the lexical units of one language those units of another language which are equivalent in their lexical meaning." This point of view has long been taken for granted in most metalexicographic literature, among others in the field of dictionary typology, in which dictionaries for translation are tacitly identified with bilingual (or multilingual) dictionaries. In the same year as the well-known Hausmann's typology, Kühn (1989) provided a functional classification in which dictionaries are sorted according to the usage aim, and translation dictionaries are explicitly mentioned as those dictionaries which meet translation purposes. This evidences the fact that, intuitively, translation has been perceived as a kind of function, exactly like text reception and text production, but function, in comparison to criteria such as the orientation towards certain lemma types, information types, varieties or users, has not been generally considered cardinal for typologising lexicographic resources. In publications on metalexicography, periodic attempts have been made towards the interpretation of function as a relevant topic (see the significant input given by Wiegand with the concept of genuine purpose as described in Tarp 2008: 91).

This tendency has also been displayed over the course of time by comprehensive handbooks such as the influential *Dictionaries. An International Encyclopedia of Lexicography HSK 5.1–3* (1989–1991). Its third volume includes several contributions on the theory and practice of general and specialised bilingual or multilingual lexicography; however, translation is not dealt with as a specific topic. The more recent *Oxford Handbook of Lexicography* (Durkin 2016) contains a chapter on bilingual dictionaries that points out the different functions a bilingual dictionary can have, among which is translation. In this way, it at least takes into account late developments in lexicographic theory, in which concrete users' needs become central to metalexicographic description (see Bergenholtz et al. 1997).

The function theory of lexicography (see Tarp 2008), prompting a change in metalexicographic perspective, shifts the focus of attention away from the conception of dictionary type as determining the function of a dictionary. With the emerging awareness that function as "the satisfaction of the specific types of the lexicographically relevant need that may arise in a specific type of potential user in a specific type of extralexicographical situation" (Tarp 2008: 81) plays a key role in the description of lexicographic resources, greater attention has been paid to the possibility of compiling dictionaries with a distinct translational function. In view of these considerations, the designation *dictionary for translation* itself seems to the author of this chapter to be more appropriate than *translation dictionary*, which is the established term in lexicographic studies, for expressing the predominance of the functional aspect over the typological issue.

Over the last twenty years, the aim of publications dealing with dictionaries for translation, primarily concerning general and specialised bilingual lexicography, has been the identification of structural properties, the specification of compilation criteria and the assessment of effectiveness of this kind of dictionary (Fuertes-Olivera and Nielsen 2012, Fuertes-Olivera and Tarp 2014, Gouws 2002, Louw 1999, Tarp 2013, Vermeer 1989, among others). Another perspective on bilingual DfTs concerns their actual implementation, from the corpus-based data extraction and the building of a lexicographic database up to the compilation of the digital tool. DfTs have been considered more and more in light of the functional approach.

Despite the fact that most lexicographic literature has considered DfTs as bilingual dictionaries by definition, and that the vast majority of publications on this topic concerns bilingual dictionaries for translation, attention should be drawn to the fact that, taking into account translation support as a function of a dictionary, a monolingual dictionary, if performing this function, is also to be seen as a DfT (Tarp 2013: 26–27). Awareness of this, however, has not yet exerted a concrete influence over dictionary making, and last-generation dictionaries expressly designed to serve translation purposes are, as a matter of fact, bilingual. These bilingual resources will now be examined in Section 18.2.2.

18.2.2 Bilingual DfTs, translator(s) and the translation process

All bilingual dictionaries are designed for assisting translation, if by *translation* we mean not only the explicit transfer process from a source language to a target language but also partial or, better, implicit realisations (i.e. comprehending a text in L2, or producing a text in L2). However, this does not mean that bilingual dictionaries are intended to have translators as their main target group. Bergenholtz et al. (1997: 221) reminds us of the distinction which should be made between active/passive translation dictionaries, on the one hand, and bilingual production/reception dictionaries on the other hand.

The term *translation* is commonly used to cover a heterogeneous range of activity profiles and, accordingly, different lexicographic needs. Leaving aside laypersons approaching translation as non-experts (e.g. language learners, language teachers, among others), the two best definable user categories falling under the label *translator-as-dictionary-user* are definitely translation students and translation professionals. These categories, at different levels, master practical knowledge and possess a theoretical background in the field of translation, so that the activity scenarios in which they are usually involved can be delineated with no great effort. A difference has therefore to be made between generic bilingual dictionaries, which serve generic translation needs, and dictionaries for translation in the narrower sense. This chapter will consider DfTs as bilingual dictionaries that particularly address a restricted subset of users, namely students and professionals in the field of translation.

Depending on the specific situation, both students and professionals resort to various reference tools: lexicographic and encyclopaedic resources, corpora/the web as corpus. Consultation is strictly related to factors such as the complexity of the translation task, the user's L2/L1 language competence, his previous knowledge of a topic or his level of expertise in a specialised field. The purpose of consultation is primarily of a communicative nature (e.g. looking up a word in order to find the best possible equivalent for a particular context). This also involves using reference tools for competence control whenever a potential translation equivalent needs to be tested against other available candidates or has to be checked from a morphosyntactic, semantic or pragmatic point of view.

Whereas translation students are required to improve their linguistic and cultural transfer skills by getting involved in passive and active translation activities and other translation-oriented exercises (e.g. cooperative translation, sight translation, proofreading tasks), professionals are usually required to translate into their native language. The concept of a native language will here be intended in a broad sense to include translators who possess a nearly native competence of a working language.

The translation direction affects, of course, the user's needs towards a reference resource, in particular towards a bilingual dictionary. In fact, the process of translation should be supported by such a dictionary in all of its stages. From a theoretical perspective, these stages include reception of a source text, transfer of linguistic and cultural elements from the source to the target language, and production of a target text (see Gerzymisch-Arbogast 2005). Although the process is structurally the same during active and passive translation, the microstructural information needed when translating into the foreign language vs. the native language partly differs. For instance, when translating into L2, a coherent system of semantic disambiguators is crucial for the choice of the appropriate translation equivalents. Active translation also requires the availability of phraseological units and semantically related items such as synonyms and antonyms. On the contrary, translation into L1 necessarily requires detailed semantic coverage of lemmata and all types of their phraseological combinations in the form of equivalents. Also, microstructural items concerning phonetic/phonological, morphosyntactic and pragmatic/cultural information require different treatment depending on the translation direction and are determinant for L2 items (see the "Further reading" section on this topic).

18.2.3 Macrostructural aspects of bilingual DfTs

As pointed out by Fontenelle (2016: 45), among communicative usage situations is translation. Given a bilingual dictionary with the lemma list subdivided into sections A>B and B>A, the following key dictionary features can be combined to obtain a specific dictionary profile: (a) translation competence; (b) directionality and functionality; (c) general language or specialised language; and (d) medium. Next, I will refer to each of them in more detail.

18.2.3.1 Translation competence

Assuming that the target user of a DfT is a translation student or a professional (see Section 18.2.2), an obvious consequence is that DfTs should take into account the translation skills (i.e. linguistic and cultural knowledge in L1 and L2) of each group and comply with their particular lexicographic needs. For instance, if users have achieved a high linguistic competence (CEFR reference level C2 in L2) they will require a lesser amount of certain kinds of lexicographic information and, as explained later on, in the case of general language, their needs will be best satisfied by the combination of a bilingual and a monolingual dictionary.

18.2.3.2 Directionality and functionality

Each of the two sections of the dictionary can support either active translation (reception in L1 and production in L2) or passive translation (reception in L2 and production in L1). Directionality of a dictionary (see Hausmann and Werner 1991) is related to the way in which these translation functions are distributed in its two sections (*functionality*) and establishes if a dictionary serves the needs of one (*monodirectional*) or both language communities (*bidirectional*). In summary, the combination of functionality and directionality features can be described as follows (Figure 18.1).

	section A>B:	section B>A:	functionality/directionality:
1	active (>L2)	passive (>L1)	bifunctional/monodirectional (A)
2	passive (>L1)	active (>L2)	bifunctional/monodirectional (B)
3	active (>L2)	active (>L2)	monofunctional/bidirectional (A and B)
4	passive (>L1)	passive (>L1)	monofunctional/bidirectional (A and B)

Figure 18.1 Translation directionality and functionality

Existing bilingual resources, especially in printed form, which are specifically meant to support translation in a narrower sense usually do not include microstructural items which are exclusively relevant for active or for passive translation, but the two types are merged in order to maximise the reach of the product (see Fontenelle 2016). Publisher's notes and introductory outer texts will highlight translation as belonging to the scope of these dictionaries. However, they will not pin down an exact translation direction.

18.2.3.3 General language or specialised language

A DfT can be either a general dictionary or a special dictionary dealing with a specialised field. Accordingly it will be used to support translation of text or parts of texts containing language for general purpose (LGP) or language for specific purpose (LSP) lexical items. For the purpose of this chapter, a specialised language dictionary is the dictionary that covers areas outside general cultural knowledge and the corresponding language for general purposes. (See Cowie (2009) and Durkin (2016) for a different concept of specialised dictionary, one which includes "slang dictionaries", "etymological dictionaries", "spelling dictionaries", "grammar dictionaries" and so on.)

18.2.3.4 Medium

A DfT can be either a print or an e-dictionary. Printed dictionaries are still largely used both in the professional and educational/academic environment. However, the advantages of electronic DfTs, first of all time-saving access to information and manageability, are becoming more and more popular among translators. Nowadays, offline and online dictionaries in the form of desktop, web and mobile applications have become an integral part of the several reference tools translation professionals rely on, and are often efficiently combined with other translation-related software such as CAT-tools. Other than paper resources, e-dictionaries can potentially include all possible functionality and directionality profiles, and provide users with tailored microstructural results according to their competence-related and situation-related needs, as will be later pointed out in Section 18.2.4. Dissimilarly from the translation competence and directionality, the choice of the lexicographic medium is not a translation-related aspect, but, in any case, an aspect that can directly influence the practice of translation by making it more or less productive. Macrostructures of DfTs, like of any other dictionary, can be of a different nature depending, for instance, on the organisational system, which can be form-determined vs. non-form determined (e.g. systematic) or display different levels of external access structures (see Wiegand and Gouws 2013). Taking into consideration medium-related restrictions and adaptations, macrostructures of e-dictionaries turn out to be of particular interest in the case of non-retrodigitized resources, that is, resources that are not digital versions of paper dictionaries but purely digital (see Giacomini 2015).

The combination of different features originates different macrostructures that serve translators belonging to a certain community during concrete extralexicographic situations. Directionality establishes the so-called *language of focus* (Tarp 2008: 83) of a dictionary, that is the language which will be at the centre of lexicographic description as being the one the translator usually has as his native language. This, of course, strongly depends on editorial and publishing choices, which take into account, for instance, if the two language communities have the same relevance in terms of a target public and, in particular, if a dictionary will be published in both countries.

18.2.4 Microstructures of bilingual DfTs

This section concentrates on existing DfTs to show how microstructures have been implemented to comply with specific macrostructural choices and, in particular, how directionality has actually been developed. A question resulting from this is: Which are the minimum requirements the microstructure of a DfT should satisfy to effectively support translation? Various models will now be presented according to the following features: focus on LGP/LSP, medium and directionality. The distinction between LGP and LSP dictionaries has been chosen as the main categorisation principle, because it exerts a considerable influence on the surface macrostructure and unveils more than other criteria (e.g. the printed vs. electronic medium) homogeneous macrostructural tendencies. This section provides examples for each model and covers bilingual dictionaries, especially with German (DE), English (EN) and Italian (IT) as their languages of focus. These examples do not claim to be exhaustive, but rather aim to give an overview of the most widespread microstructural patterns in contemporary translation-oriented lexicography.

One important consideration to be made at this point is that the following models concern the ideal target community and the ideal usage situation lexicographers have in mind while compiling a dictionary. However, this does not prevent concrete usage in non-ideal circumstances: a bidirectional DfT which supports active translation, for instance, can be used during passive translation as well, whereas a monodirectional DfT can definitely be consulted by both language communities.

18.2.4.1 Trends of LGP printed DfTs: active bidirectionality

Contemporary LGP printed DfTs show a marked predisposition towards bidirectionality, whereas monodirectionality is to be found predominantly in older publications. Bidirectional DfTs aim to address two language communities, providing both with the same necessary lexicographic means to passively or actively translate texts, and are usually one-volume books that rarely contain fewer than 160,000 to 170,000 lemmas. From a formal point of view (e.g. dimensions, number of lemmas), they display the same characteristics as their monodirectional counterparts.

A representative instance of the bidirectional profile is *il nuovo dizionario di Tedesco* by Luisa Giacoma and Susanne Kolb (2014), an IT-DE/DE-IT general language dictionary which mentions translation among the supported usage situations. Short excerpts from the articles of *braccio* (example 1) and *Arm* (example 2) (both meaning 'arm' in their main sense) show that this dictionary addresses native speakers of both communities and exhibits a dominant active functionality.

(1)

bràccio m

1 <pl: -cia f> {+ PERSONA} Arm m: prendere qu per un braccio, jdn am/beim Arm nehmen; med Oberarm m

2 f<pl> fig (*mano d'opera*): braccia, Arbeitskräfte f pl: braccia strappate all'agricoltura, der Landwirtschaft entzogene Arbeitskräfte

3 *metrol* Elle f (. . .)

(2)

Ạrm <-(e)s, -e> m
1 *anat* braccio m
2 (*Fangarm*) {+ KRAKE, POLYP} tentacolo m
3 (*Zugriff*) {+ GERECHTIGKEIT, GESETZ} braccio m; {+ MAFIA} tentacolo m: jds Arm reicht weit, qu ha le braccia lunghe, qu arriva dappertutto; der Arm des Gesetzes reicht weit/[ist lang], il braccio della legge arriva dappertutto
4 (*Flussarm*) braccio m, diramazione f, ramo m (. . .)

The semantic commentary is highly developed and consists of coherently provided items that distinguish the meanings of the polysemous lemma: meaning discriminators (e.g. *Fangarm*, *Zugriff*, *Flussarm*, in parentheses), diaphasic labels (e.g. *metrol*, *anat*) indicating a specialised field and collocates (e.g. {+ GERECHTIGKEIT, GESETZ}). The unique role of collocates as metalexicographic elements is to further differentiate between already distinguished meanings. Moreover, each article contains a separate functional segment dedicated to alphabetically sorted phraseological units with mixed information both for passive and active translation. Information is specular in the two sections.

Passive translation requires comparatively less information than active translation, but this kind of information, mostly of a morphosyntactic and pragmatic nature, can be quite easily integrated into an "active" dictionary with no great space consumption. The usual functionality of general language bidirectional DfTs is the active one, exactly because of the good balance it can achieve between data economicity and audience reach. Other bilingual DfTs with the same structure are the well-known series of comprehensive dictionaries distributed by major publishers (see, among others, Oxford, Collins, Pons, Langenscheidt, Sansoni).

LGP monodirectional DfTs in print form are usually published in one country and intended to address a single language community. If compared to the modern bidirectional publications, they have quite a traditional structure, with one section dedicated to active and the other to passive translation. An example of a monodirectional resource is the IT-DE/DE-IT *Dizionario Garzanti di Tedesco* (1995) for Italian native speakers. The active section IT>DE offers morphosyntactic information about German equivalents as well as meaning discriminators and pragmatic labels distinguishing different senses of the lemma. The passive section DE>IT, on the contrary, is characterised by phonetic information about the lemma and translation equivalents with no further specification.

18.2.4.2 Trends of LSP printed DfTs: passive bidirectionality; monodirectionality

In comparison to LGP printed DfTs, LSP ones are published under various formats ranging from one-volume and multivolume comprehensive dictionaries to concise and pocket dictionaries, chiefly depending on terminology extension of a certain specialised field. In general, LSP dictionaries designed for translation purposes seem to follow more stringent rules concerning target users' communities and usage situations. For this reason, they tend to favour other directionality distributions. LSP lexicographic coverage serves very specific purposes: it is generally not intended for a broad non-expert public but rather a comparatively small community of subject-field experts and specialised translators. Accordingly, the number of users who will need lexicographic support for active translation should be relatively low. The two directionality profiles that frequently emerge in this lexicographic category are the bidirectional for passive translation and the monodirectional.

A bidirectional passive DfT is the German-English *Spektrum Wörterbuch der Biologie/ Dictionary of Biology* (2015). In both sections this dictionary occasionally provides broad meaning discriminators; however, its overall design is characterised by cumulative listings of translation equivalents. Moreover, morphosyntactic information is only given in the case of terms belonging to more than one part of speech. These aspects are exemplified in the following articles (example 3):

(3)

envelope/hull Hülle (*auch:* Viren/Bakterien); (water: jacket) Wasserhülle
Hülle/Involukrum ***bot*** envelope, hull, involucre

The same DfT profile can be found in other specialised dictionaries, for instance in *Pons Fachwörterbuch der Kfz-Technik* (Schmitt 1992), a DE-EN/EN-DE dictionary of automotive engineering which has become a classic in this field and language combination. A slightly different way of providing data for passive translation purposes in both translation directions is exemplified by the DE-EN/EN-DE *Taschenwörterbuch der Kraftfahrzeugtechnik* (Blaha 2009), a pocket dictionary of automotive engineering, which, like the previous ones, addresses users of both language communities and clearly supports passive translation, providing restricted information for active translation. This dictionary, however, does not contain meaning discriminators and opts for a complex set of pragmatic labels (English in both sections), referring to subfields of the main topic (e.g. Automotive, Traffic Control), automobile systems (e.g. Brake, Transmission, Engine), company-specific terminology (i.e. names of companies) and diatopic variants (e.g. GB, US) (example 4):

(4)

Break *m* (Citroen/Peugeot) (Automot)/station wagon (US), estate car (GB), estate *n* (GB), Break (Citroen/Peugeot)

Besides the bidirectional model, LSP printed DfTs can also have a monodirectional structure and, accordingly, specifically address a single group of native speakers. In this case, both passive and active translation are promoted, and the two sections no longer display specular metalanguage items. The *Wörterbuch der exakten Naturwissenschaften und der Technik/ Dictionary of Exact Science and Technology* (Kučera 2002–2005) is intended to serve German speakers who translate from and into English, as indicated by example (5):

(5)

Ausbreitung *f* (einer Tierart) (Biol, Umwelt)/dispersion n ‖ ~ (des Schalles, des Lichts, von Erdbebenwellen) (Phys)/propagation* *n* ‖ ~ (in neue Gebiete) (Umwelt)/ spread* *n*, spreading *n* ‖ ~ (der Schadstoffe in der Luft) (Umwelt)/transmission *n* ‖ ~ in der Ionosphäre (Radio)/ionospheric propagation

dispersion *n*/Dispersion *f* (bei Glasfasern die zeitliche Verbreiterung des optischen Eingangsimpulses bei der Signalübertragung (. . .)) ‖ ~/Dispergierung *f* (von Pigment- oder Füllstoffpulvern) (. . .) ‖ ~/(Ecol)/Individuenverteilung *f*, Dispersion *f* (. . .)

The active section DE>EN shows extensive employment of meaning discriminators and pragmatic labels, whereas the passive section EN>DE adds explanatory contexts of morphologically similar terms in the German language (see *Dispersion* vs. *Dispergierung*). The two presented profiles are the most common to be found in LSP printed DfTs and do not display relevant differences in distribution in older and newer publications.

18.2.4.3 Trends of LGP electronic DfTs: printed legacy and digital novelties

For the most part, electronic DfTs of general language are still digital versions of printed dictionaries and not purely digital resources. From the point of view of the translation purpose, these retrodigitised dictionaries can be largely described along the same descriptive parameters as their printed counterparts, because their microstructure coincides with the printed lexicographic entries. A restricted number of medium-specific features usually complements these dictionaries at a macrostructural and mediostructural level and confers a few advantages (e.g. faster and more precise queries, efficiency of data accessibility) over printed dictionaries. These features can be summarised as follows:

1 The macrostructure generally mirrors the printed version and is usually of a complex and fully developed nature: in addition to the term inventory, it is made up of different macrostructural components which provide users with "information about the use of the dictionary, its overall organisation, and the arrangement of lemmata" (Nielsen 1994: 80–84). However, external access can take place through medium-specific elements, such as directly via alphabetical lists of entries and/or indirectly via a search interface which can allow for simple and complex queries. The latter possibility, in particular, has a considerable influence on the search for equivalents in both passive and active translation, because it usually allows the user to refine a search, for instance with the help of filters.

2 The mediostructure is usually more developed than in printed dictionaries and is implemented through cross-references in the form of hyperlinks. The level of development and complexity can vary from one resource to another, whereby at the highest level hyperlinks are provided for each lexical unit inside a lexicographic entry and cross-reference these units to the corresponding lemmas.

An example of an LGP resource designed for the digital medium is the *Grande dizionario elettronico italiano-neerlandese* by Vincenzo Lo Cascio. The present online version represents the latest development of a resource which has been expressly adapted to the digital medium. The dictionary has a composite structure which offers various kinds of data visualisation. The microstructure in the lemma view reveals the presence of bidirectionality for active translation, with both sections displaying the following data types, as can be seen in the excerpt of the article *arrivare* ("to arrive") (example 6):

(6)

arrivare [ar-ri-và-re]
V IN ES
1. *prep. a, in* {raggiungere} la destinazione, giungere a piedi o con un mezzo in un dato luogo; anche di cose recapitate

- komen
- aankomen
- arriveren

Esempi
a che pagina sei arrivato? > tot welke bladzijde ben je gekomen? (. . .)

Fraseologie

- arrivare a casa > thuiskomen
- arrivare a una conclusione/a una decisione *[raggiungere una decisione conclusiva]* > tot een besluit/conclusie komen (. . .)

2. {a un *punto* nello spazio} a un certo limite

- bereiken
- komen

Esempi

fin dove arriva lo sguardo > zover het oog reikt (. . .)

Equivalents are not introduced by traditional meaning discriminators in parentheses but by functional segments that take the form of more or less detailed definitions. The digital medium clearly increases availability of examples and phraseological coverage, thus presenting an excellent choice in terms of translation equivalents. In the lexical combinatory view, the bilingual dictionary merges with a collocation dictionary to supply a vast amount of collocational data for each sense of the lemma. In this case, collocations replace examples and phraseology in the previous microstructure.

From a macrostructural perspective, the translation process is supported by a simple query, an advanced query and a meaning-based search. External access to data takes place indirectly via the search interfaces and the alphabetical index. The mediostructure is characterised by an extensive cross-referencing network in which each lexeme is linked to the respective entry, allowing for faster consultation of lexicographic data. This overall system, the primary function of which is to enhance internal access to data, does not replace specific cross-references of morphologic, semantic and pragmatic nature.

This example evidences, on the one hand, that translation can substantially benefit from the presence of e-lexicographic resources, which can make available large amounts of corpus-based data in context, combine different lexicographic typologies and offer not only quick access to information, but, most of all, "dynamic articles with dynamic data" (Fuertes-Olivera and Tarp 2014: 16). On the other hand, the example makes clear that these goals are still far away and present e-lexicography is still massively following print-oriented assumptions and structures. Future implementation of translation-related functionalities, for instance the selection of viewed macrostructural data according to translation requirements, will be discussed later in Section 18.3.

18.2.4.4 Trends of LSP electronic DfTs: the gradual shift towards dynamic monofunctionality

This category is undoubtedly the one which has revealed the most innovative potential in recent decades, even though, as pointed out by Fuertes-Olivera and Tarp (2014: 15), "specialised lexicography has still a long way to go until it takes full advantage of the new technologies and techniques available." The looked-for structural and data dynamism has partly been obtained only by a few dictionaries, and among resources designed for translation purposes the number of these dictionaries is even more restricted. This section presents a set of heterogeneous resources (dictionaries, glossaries, term-bases) that, to a different extent, move away from the retrodigitisation practice.

A large part of the LSP e-lexicographic resources translators make use of are, indeed, multilingual terminology databases, mostly published by an institutional, academic or corporate source. Well-known examples include *IATE* (Inter-active Terminology for Europe) and *UNTERM* (United Nations Multilingual Terminology Database), covering a wide range of subject fields, and more field-specific resources such as *IFADTERM* (Glossary of the Fund for Agricultural Development available through the FAO Term Portal) or *Electropedia* (the IEC's Online Electrotechnical Vocabulary). These databases primarily address translators working for international/supranational institutions and organisations who need to translate official texts. From a macrostructural perspective, they usually display a primarily systematic (i.e. subject-group-oriented) or systematic (i.e. purely conceptual) organisation (Giacomini 2015: 108), which means access to terms and term descriptions are informed by a conceptual orientation. In order to benefit the translation process by providing users with a coherent network relating concepts, terms and equivalents, the conceptual macrostructural orientation needs to be supported by a coherent mediostructure, which unfortunately is still missing in the mentioned terminology databases. A considerable difference between the databases can be noticed in the availability and sorting of macrostructural items, whereas microstructural views appear static, do not allow for item-specific or function-specific restrictions and generally have a traditional printed-like design, as shown by the following excerpt from the entries of *aqualculture* in *IFADTERM* (example 7):

(7)
aquaculture EN LAW; FISHERIES FAOTERM

Definition
The farming of aquatic organisms including fish, molluscs, crustaceans and aquatic plants with some sort of intervention in the rearing process to enhance production (. . .)

Definition source
FAO Fisheries and Aquaculture Department, FAO, 2014.

Related terms
seefish (sic) culture; mariculture

Remarks
For statistical purposes, aquatic organisms which are harvested by an individual or corporate body which has owned them throughout their rearing period contribute to aquaculture.

Remarks source
FAO/FIDI (1989): Aquaculture production (1984–1986). (. . .)

IFADTERM has multilevel entries consisting of language-independent data (domain, related domains), language-dependent data (definition) and terminological data (term, related terms) for each language. Terminological data are generally restricted to denominations in the various languages. There are no morphosyntactic and pragmatic indications, usage examples, or systematic cross-references (e.g. between *aquaculture* to *aquaculture farm* or *aquaculture animal*). Terminological databases of this type are multidirectional and support users in passive translation tasks. Nevertheless, in comparison to other similar resources, *IATE* has reinforced the upper level by cross-referencing a domain to specific classes of other domains (narrower/broader, antonyms, related etc.).

A restricted number of translation-oriented resources has a non-form-determined organisational structure, i.e. does not rest upon an underlying conceptual system but concentrates in a detailed way on the terminological level. For instance, this is the case of the multilingual dictionaries *DiColnfo* (information technology terms), *DiCoEnviro* (environmental terms) and *Juridico* (law terms) developed by OLST (University of Montréal, Canada) and designed under the tenets of both Théorie Sens-Texte and Frames Semantics. The entry *account*$_1$ in *DiColnfo* discloses a microstructure, assisting active translation by means of frames-like semantic items, as well as the presence of contexts and phraseological combinations (example 8):

(8)

account 1, n *Statut* : *0*
an account: ~ used by ***user 1*** (Agent) + to act on ***computer 1*** (Destination), ***network 1*** (Destination) +
Définition : Space allocated to a ***user*** (Agent) + and associated with a set of parameters that gives this ***user*** (Agent) access the resources of a ***computer*** (Destination) or a ***network*** (Destination)

Synonyme(s) : user account
Contexte(s)
Liens lexicaux
français : *compte* $_1$

A larger group of LSP electronic DfTs is of academic origin and has a mixed organisational system, merging systematic and non-systematic features. Representative instances are the multilingual *Information System for Legal Terminology Bistro* with DE and IT local variants (EURAC Bolzano, Italy), the multilingual terminological knowledge base of environmental terms *EcoLexicon* (University of Granada, Spain) and the *Accounting Dictionaries/Diccionarios de Contabilidad* (Aarhus University, Denmark, and University of Valladolid, Spain) (see Chapter 28 of this *Handbook*).

EcoLexicon offers no traditional microstructure in the form of an article with functional segments, but search results are viewed in a multifunctional GUI where single data types can be selected by the user: a definition, synonymic terms in the same language and equivalent terms in other languages, term information (term, language, term type, context, part of speech), corpus concordances, resources, conceptual categories, phraseology, a tree mode representing the search term and its semantic relations to other terms. The limited amount of linguistic information concerning terms makes this resource a good tool for passive translation but an insufficient aid for active translation.

Besides language-independent and language-specific information (domain, corpus-based definitions and contexts), *Bistro Information System for Legal Terminology* supports active translation in both directions by providing equivalents and grammatical information for both the lemma and fuzzy matches, that is, multiword expressions such as compounds or collocations that include the lemma and coincide with other terms in the database (*Prozessvollmacht*, *Vollmachtgeber*, *Auftrag unter Erteilung einer Vollmacht*, etc.), as shown in the following excerpt from the article of *Vollmacht* ("procuration") (example 9):

(9)

Fachgebiet	diritto civile/Zivilrecht
Deutsch	**Vollmacht**

Grammatik	f.
Sprachgebrauch	AT, STAA
Termstatus	Entscheidung TerKom
Definition AT	Rechtliches Dürfen im Innenverhältnis: Der Ermächtigte muß nicht tätig werden, er darf aber auf Rechnung des Ermächtigenden handeln. Quelle: KOZI I 92:168
Kontext	Die Vollmacht kann nur auf einen namentlich bezeichneten Vertreter ausgestellt werden. (...) Quelle: CC BL 92, Art. 2372, Abs. 3

Vollmacht $_{N\text{-}f}$	delega $_{N\text{-}f}$ (atto di delega)	civil law
	procura $_{N\text{-}f}$	civil law
Prozessvollmacht $_{N\text{-}f}$	procura alle liti $_{N\text{-}f}$	civil proced. law

Macrostructural and microstructural choices result in a series of efficient linguistic tools for translation, although the overall design is, even in this case, static and not customizable.

The *Accounting Dictionaries* (see Chapter 28) have been designed and compiled with a conscious effort to produce a dynamic resource for translation between Danish, English and Spanish for three user groups: translators and language staff, accounting (semi) experts and students and interested laypersons. The *Accounting Dictionaries* suit both active and passive translation purposes for each of the covered languages. All elaboration phases (pre-compilation, compilation, post-compilation), conducted in an interdisciplinary environment made up of lexicographers, accounting and IT experts (Fuertes-Olivera and Tarp 2014), aim at building a resource in which the purpose of structural and data dynamism is to provide specific support in specific usage situations by means of monofunctional modules the user can choose. Monofunctionality, in this sense, is no longer a limitation, as was the case, for instance, in printed dictionaries, but rather the obvious and most positive result of lexicographic dynamism. The innovative trait of this dictionary bundle is its consistent application of the new technologies on which e-dictionaries can rely, and which enable both the orientation towards specific user needs and the dynamic selection and presentation of usage-specific information.

18.3 Looking to the future

The overview of microstructures of bilingual DfTs presented in Section 18.2.4 has highlighted important aspects and clear tendencies. Most DfTs presented are not described in their prefaces, introductions or other outer texts as resources exclusively designed for translation purposes in a narrow sense, but rather address a wide variety of target users including teachers and language learners. This is especially the case of general language dictionaries, whereas specialised dictionaries are more often intended to serve translators' and experts' needs. Today's DfTs are still far from being an autonomous product category and, in general, *translation* is simply one of the various functions of quite heterogeneous resources.

A strong tendency can be generally noticed towards bidirectionality. Moreover, LGP bidirectional resources display mixed functionalities, with active functionality being prevalent over the passive. LSP DfTs show a shift from pure cumulative microstructures to increasingly descriptive microstructures, an aspect that, in turn, promotes compilation of lexicographic data with active functionality. More innovative resources which seek to take full advantage of new technologies and lexicographic studies move towards monofunctionality as the opportunity to select definite functions according to specific usage needs.

What does the future hold for translation-oriented lexicography and dictionaries for translation? Recent advances in lexicographic theory, especially those concerning the critical role of lexicographic functions and the importance of usage situations, have marked the birth of a new awareness of translators' lexicographic needs. As a result, the following developments are to be expected in the near future:

1 LSP e-lexicography will most likely continue to lead the way towards innovation in the development and implementation of dynamic solutions in lexicography for translation, not only because of its obvious proximity to translation practice, but also due to the restricted and more manageable nature of the lexicon of any specialised field. These aspects make the testing or application of new approaches more feasible in comparison to general language.
2 Increasing availability of digital technologies will promote readiness of translators to use e-lexicographic resources and their propensity to look for dictionaries offering tailored monofunctional solutions.
3 In the practice of professional translation, translators do not rely on a single resource typology but combine multiple resources in order to cover the functions that specific usage situations and problems demand: bilingual and monolingual dictionaries, LGP and LSP dictionaries, special dictionaries (e.g. collocation dictionary), thesauri, corpora of parallel texts, etc. On the one hand, as already said, these resources are, at least in part, not designed for translation purposes. On the other hand, simultaneous consultation turns out to be a time-consuming activity and does not always result in efficient assistance in translation. For these reasons, future work should move in the direction of comprehensive translation-oriented platforms hosting dictionaries, corpora and linguistic analysis tools to support translators in a more immediate and effective way. Efforts in this direction are still rare and not expressly translation-related, although promising. One needs to only mention *Antidote 9*, a powerful set of software and monolingual reference tools for text production in French consisting of a collection of dictionaries (which include, among other items, corpus co-occurrences), a grammar checker and interactive grammar guides.

18.4 Conclusion

Starting with an overview of the main theoretical approaches to lexicography for translation, this chapter has revealed how, up to recent times with the emergence of the new function theory, DfTs have been identified, by definition, with bilingual dictionaries. This perspective is wrong in two ways: it does not distinguish between functions of bilingual dictionaries (active/passive translation, text production/reception) and it does not account for the fact that a dictionary *for* translation is not necessarily a bilingual dictionary. Still, bilingual DfTs have been at the centre of the description in this chapter because of their present preponderance on the market. Innovative approaches, primarily towards dynamic monofunctionality, have been highlighted mostly in LSP lexicography, in which greater attention is paid towards specific usage needs of translators. Macrostructural and microstructural analysis of selected examples has pointed out particular tendencies depending on the represented language (LGP or LSP) and the medium (printed or digital form). In general, the study of various groups of dictionaries brings to light the urgent need to give a distinct identity to dictionaries for translation. At the same time, it seems to confirm the viability of a clear and systematic translation-oriented approach in lexicography, which should encourage lexicographers to follow new paths towards the elaboration of novel structural concepts with the help of state-of-the-art technologies, and translators to ask for more specific, high-quality resources.

Related topics

Dictionaries for text reception; dictionaries for text production; electronic dictionaries; specialised dictionaries; the Accounting Dictionaries; the Alicante Dictionaries.

Further reading

Fuertes-Olivera, P. and S. Tarp. (2014). *Theory and Practice of Specialised Online Dictionaries*. Lexicographica Series Maior. Berlin/Boston: de Gruyter.
This book is a comprehensive study of online LSP dictionaries, which focuses on theoretical aspects and medium-related problems and offers a detailed view of the compilation phases.

Giacomini, L. (2015). "Macrostructural Properties and Access Structures of LSP e-Dictionaries for Translation", in *Lexicographica 2015/31*. Berlin/Boston: de Gruyter, pp. 90–117.
This article introduces an evaluation framework for macrostructures of LSP e-dictionaries according to the organisational system, the available elements and the kind of term selection.

Tarp, S. (2013). "How Can Dictionaries Assist Translators?", in C. Sin-wai (ed.), *Translation and Bilingual Dictionaries*. Lexicographica Series Maior. Berlin/Boston: de Gruyter.
This article critically analyses the role of dictionaries as reference resources in translation and primarily discusses the concept of a translation dictionary by referring to its different possible functions.

References

Accounting Dictionaries. Fuertes-Olivera et al.; Nielsen, S. et al. ordbogen.com (see complete list of references in Chapter 28).

Antidote 9. Druide informatique inc. www.antidote.info/antidote.

Bergenholtz, H., I. Cantell, R. Vatvedt Fjeld, D. Gundersen, J. H. Jonsson and B. Svensén (eds.) (1997) *Nordisk leksikografisk ordbok*. Oslo: Universitetsforlaget.

Bistro Information System for Legal Terminology. Eurac Bolzano http://bistro.eurac.edu

Blaha, H. F. (2009) *Taschenwörterbuch der Kraftfahrzeugtechnik*. Wiesbaden: Oscar Brandstetter Verlag.

Cowie, A. P. (2009) *The Oxford History of English Lexicography*. Oxford: Oxford University Press.

DiCoInfo Le dictionnaire fondamental de l'informatique et de l'Internet. Observatoire de linguistique Sens-Texte. University of Montréal. olst.ling.umontreal.ca/cgi-bin/dicoinfo. Last accessed: May 2017

Dizionario Garzanti di Tedesco (1995). Milano: Garzanti.

Durkin, P. (ed.) (2016) *The Oxford Handbook of Lexicography*. Oxford: Oxford University Press.

Faber, P. et al. *EcoLexicon. Terminological Knowledge Base on the Environment*. University of Granada. www.ecolexicon.ugr.es. Last accessed: May 2017

Fontenelle, T. (2016) "Bilingual Dictionaries: History and Development; Current Issues", in P. Durkin (ed.), pp. 44–61.

Fuertes-Olivera, P. and S. Nielsen. (2012) "Online Dictionaries for Assisting Translators of LSP Texts: The *Accounting Dictionaries*", *International Journal of Lexicography* 25(2): 191–215.

Fuertes-Olivera, P. and S. Tarp. (2014) *Theory and Practice of Specialised Online Dictionaries*. Lexicographica Series Maior. Berlin/Boston: de Gruyter.

Gerzymisch-Arbogast, H. (2005) "Introducing Multidimensional Translation", in *MuTra 2005 – Challenges of Multidimensional Translation: Conference Proceedings*: 1–15.

Giacoma, L. and S. Kolb. (2014) *Il Nuovo Dizionario di Tedesco*. Bologna: Zanichelli.

Giacomini, L. (2015) "Macrostructural Properties and Access Structures of LSP e-Dictionaries for Translation", *Lexicographica* 31: 90–117.

Gouws, R. H. (2002) "Equivalent Relations, Context and Cotext in Bilingual Dictionaries", *Hermes. Journal of Linguistics* 28: 195–209.

Grande dizionario elettronico italiano-neerlandese. Lo Cascio, V. www.locasciodictionary.com

Hausmann, F. J. (1989) "Wörterbuchtypologie", in R.F.J. Hausmann, O. Reichmann, H. E. Wiegand and L. Zgusta (eds.), *Dictionaries: An International Encyclopedia of Lexicography*, Volume 1. Berlin/Boston/New York: de Gruyter, pp. 968–981.

Hausmann, F. J. and R. O. Werner. (1991) "Spezifische Bauteile und Strukturen zweisprachiger Wörterbücher: eine Übersicht", in F. J. Hausmann, O. Reichmann, H. E. Wiegand and L. Zgusta (eds.), *Dictionaries: An International Encyclopedia of Lexicography*. Volume 3. Berlin/Boston/New York: de Gruyter, pp. 2729–2769.

IATE Inter-active Terminology for Europe. iate.europa.eu

IFADTERM Glossary of the Fund for Agricultural Development. www.fao.org/faoterm/collection/ifadterm

Kučera, A. (2002–2005) *Wörterbuch der exakten Naturwissenschaften und der Technik/Dictionary of Exact Science and Technology*. 2nd edition. Wiesbaden: Oscar Brandstetter Verlag.

Kühn, P. (1989) "Typologie der Wörterbücher nach Benutzungsmöglichkeiten", In F. J. Hausmann, O. Reichmannn, H. E. Wiegand and L. Zgusta (eds.), *Dictionaries: An International Encyclopedia of Lexicography*, Volume 1. Berlin/Boston/New York: de Gruyter, pp. 111–127.

Louw, P. A. (1999) "Access Structures in a Standard Translation Dictionary", *Lexikos* 9: 108–118.

Nielsen, S. (1994) *The Bilingual LSP Dictionary. Principles and Practice for Legal Language*. Tübingen: Gunter Narr Verlag.

Schmitt, P. A. (1992) *Fachwörterbuch der Kfz-Technik*. Stuttgart: Pons.

Tarp, S. (2013) "How Can Dictionaries Assist Translators?", in C. Sin-wai (ed.), *Translation and Bilingual Dictionaries*. Berlin/Boston: de Gruyter, pp. 23–38.

Tarp, S. (2008) *Lexicography in the Borderland Between Knowledge and Non-Knowledge*. Tübingen: Max Niemeyer Verlag.

Vermeer, H. (1989) "Wörterbücher als Hilfsmittel für unterschiedliche Typen der Translation", in R.F.J. Hausmann, O. Reichmann, H. E. Wiegand and L. Zgusta (eds.), *Dictionaries: An International Encyclopedia of Lexicography*. Volume 1. Berlin/Boston/New York: de Gruyter, pp. 171–174.

Wiegand, H. E. and R. Gouws. (2013) "Macrostructures in Printed Dictionaries", in R. Gouws, U. Heid, W. Schweickard and E. H. Wiegand (eds.), *Dictionaries: An International Encyclopedia of Lexicography. Supplementary Volume* HSK 5.4. Berlin/Boston, MA/New York: de Gruyter, pp. 73–110.

Wörterbuch der Biologie/ Dictionary of Biology (2015). Heidelberg/Berlin: Spektrum Akademischer Verlag.

Zgusta, L. (1971) *Manual of Lexicography*. The Hague: Mouton.

19

Dictionaries to assist teaching and learning

Reinhard Heuberger

19.1 Introduction

The monolingual English learners' dictionary for intermediate and advanced users has enjoyed a long and successful history. A. S. Hornby's *Idiomatic and Syntactic English Dictionary* (*ISED*) of 1942 is usually regarded as the first milestone in this highly innovative branch of lexicography, which keeps producing new editions of learners' dictionaries on a regular, almost yearly, basis. The lucrative market has long been dominated by the British publishers Oxford University Press, Pearson Longman, Collins COBUILD, Cambridge University Press and Macmillan ELT, with Merriam-Webster as the most recent and only American competitor.

This article examines the peculiarities of monolingual learners' dictionaries (MLDs), both in print and electronic form. Section 19.2 provides a short overview of the development of the monolingual English learners' dictionary, with a focus on the history of print editions. In Section 19.3, the salient features of MLDs together with selected core issues in learner lexicography are discussed and a few special types of learners' dictionaries touched upon. Section 19.4 turns to future trends in the field, which is increasingly dominated by electronic applications.

19.2 Historical perspectives

For more than three decades following the publication of *ISED* (1942), A. S. Hornby's dictionary faced little competition on the EFL market. *ISED* was originally produced by the Tokyo-based publisher Kaitakusha, as Hornby was working as a teacher of English in Japan. It was only after World War II that Oxford University Press became interested in *ISED*, republishing it as *A Learner's Dictionary of Current English* in 1948, and changing the title to *The Advanced Learner's Dictionary of Current English* (*ALD1*) in 1952. As Hornby's original title suggests, the dictionary was meant to be suitable not only for receptive but also for productive (hence "idiomatic and syntactic") purposes. *ALD1* relied on the International Phonetic Alphabet (IPA) to indicate RP pronunciations, an approach that later became the standard in EFL lexicography. Its successor *ALD2* was published in 1963, and the third edition in 1974 – then for the first time called *Oxford Advanced Learner's Dictionary* (*OALD3*).

The first serious competitor to Oxford's learners' dictionaries was not published until 1978 – the year in which Hornby died. This new dictionary, Paul Proctor's *Longman Dictionary of Contemporary English* (*LDOCE1*), was highly innovative at the time. It was claimed that all headwords were defined by a limited vocabulary of only 2,000 words, though the actual figure was clearly higher (see Heuberger 2016a: 27). *LDOCE1* is also remembered for its systematic attempt to organize grammatical codes and categories, which was further refined in later editions (see Fontenelle 2009: 414ff).

It would take almost another decade for the third major learners' dictionary to be published, John Sinclair's *Collins Cobuild English Language Dictionary* (*COBUILD1* 1987). *COBUILD1* was the first corpus-based dictionary of English, an approach that is firmly established in EFL lexicography today (see Section 19.3.1.8). *COBUILD1* is also famous for introducing full-sentence definitions and its use of the so-called extra-column, a slim marginal column to the right of the entry. It was supposed to reduce non-discursive elements in the main text by listing grammatical labels, synonyms and antonyms, etc. (see Moon 2009: 453).

The year 1995 was one of the most prolific in the history of monolingual English learners' dictionaries. Apart from the publication of *OALD5*, *LDOCE3* and *COBUILD2*, it saw the appearance of a fourth competitor, the *Cambridge International Dictionary of English*[1] (*CIDE1*). Several features that are standard practice today were first introduced in this generation of learners' dictionaries: frequency information, guide words (or "sign posts", as Longman called them) to facilitate the location of individual word meanings within the microstructure, explicit grammatical information rather than obscure pattern codes, etc. For the first time, all MLDs on the market were corpus-based, a feature that publishers strongly advertised. In hindsight, 1995 was extremely fruitful for learner lexicography, but it also marked the beginning of a convergence (see Yamada 2010: 150).

Later editions introduced further refinements, including more thorough treatment of collocations and neologisms, layout changes (more use of colours), accompanying optical data carriers and increases in size. But the key features of today's print MLDs can essentially be traced back to the 1995 generation of learners' dictionaries. This does not mean that the evolution of MLDs has come to an end (see Bogaards 2010: 25) – and there is arguably still need for refinement in several respects. But this potential especially concerns the electronic medium, as will be discussed in Section 19.3.2.1.

After the turn of the millenium, two further well-known publishers entered the EFL market. In 2002, the *Macmillan English Dictionary for Advanced Learners* (*MEDAL1*) was published, followed by its second edition in 2007. One year later, the first American learners' dictionary was issued, *Merriam-Webster's Advanced Learner's English Dictionary* (*MWALED1* 2008). It had a special focus on American vocabulary and usage but otherwise added hardly any new elements to EFL lexicography (Bogaards 2010: 25). The latter criticism also applies to the two aforementioned Macmillan[2] dictionaries, which successfully adopted various features that had proven useful in previous learners' dictionaries (Bogaards 2010: 21).

Today, foreign learners of English can choose from the following current editions of MLDs: *OALD9* (2016), *LDOCE6* (2014), *COBUILD8* (2014), *CALD4* (2013), *MEDAL2* (2007) and *MWALED1* (2008). All of these have their individual strengths and weaknesses, and it largely depends on the skills and preferences of the user as to which edition serves his or her needs best. For instance, learners who want detailed grammatical information have traditionally been well served with a *COBUILD* dictionary. Longman, by contrast, has focused on an easy-to-understand coding system, spelling out grammatical patterns in full since *LDOCE3* (1995). To name the "best" dictionary on the market is thus a highly individual choice.

19.3 Core issues and topics

Section 19.3.1 provides an outline of the salient features of current learners' dictionaries, also discussing a few debated issues within learner lexicography. Section 19.3.2 is dedicated to special types of learners' dictionaries.

19.3.1 Main features of learners' dictionaries

Learners' dictionaries show various unique features and have – also due to their sales and innovativeness – become a firmly established and distinct genre within English lexicography. Perhaps most strikingly, MLDs use a limited and simplified vocabulary for definitions, known as "defining vocabulary". Learners' dictionaries provide detailed information on grammar and usage, which also makes them useful for language production. Example sentences and collocations are included in vast numbers, whereas etymological information is usually excluded. These and other peculiarities of learners' dictionaries are discussed in greater detail next.

19.3.1.1 Defining vocabularies and definitions

First introduced in *LDOCE1* in 1978, defining vocabularies have become a standard feature in today's MLDs. The term refers to the method of constructing definitions from a relatively restricted set of terms – usually up to 3,500 words – that are preselected for that purpose. The rationale is, of course, to ensure that the definitions are easily understood by learners – even at the expense of precision (Moon 2016: 125). The following comparison between an MLD and a native speaker dictionary illustrates the effects of a defining vocabulary policy (examples 1 and 2):

(1)

tear, tears Tears are the drops of salty liquid that come out of your eyes when you are crying. (*COBUILD2*)

(2)

tears the clear salty solution secreted by the lacrimal glands that lubricates and cleanses the surface of the eyeball and inner surface of the eyelids. (*Collins English Dictionary Online*)

Definitions intended for native speakers like in *Collins English Dictionary Online* are likely to overtax even advanced learners, who may be sent from one unknown term to another. The careful employment of defining vocabularies can spare the learner this sort of frustration. At least in theory, learners who are familiar with the meanings of the terms in the defining vocabulary list can expect to understand all definitions in the dictionary. When definitions are impossible without additional terms, these are indicated as cross-references. Defining vocabularies also have some drawbacks (see Heuberger 2016a: 30), but their overall usefulness is indisputable for most scholars.

The compilation of appropriate definitions is a challenging task for various reasons (arguably not facilitated by the restrictions imposed by a defining vocabulary policy). MLDs assume little about the learners' linguistic background except for a certain proficiency with English (see Moon 2016: 124). The learners' native language may be closely related to English (e.g. German), partially cognate (French), or even entirely different structurally and conceptually (Chinese). Unlike bilingual dictionaries, MLDs can hardly address semantic asymmetries between English and other languages explicitly (see Moon 2016: 124). This is a difficult starting point for the lexicographers.

Definitions are, also because of their importance, one of the most hotly debated areas in MLDs, and perhaps the one most in need of refinement. Many definitions both fail to help the user and to please the critic. There are a few lexicographic shortcomings that seem to affect learners' dictionaries more than those for native speakers. Dictionaries for the latter target audience often present a more apposite description of the headwords, partly due to the greater length of their entries. Heuberger's (2000: 19ff) systematic analysis of definitions of selected lexical fields in MLDs revealed five recurring shortcomings: irrelevance, ideology, inaccuracy, insufficiency and incoherence. A more thorough discussion of these problems is beyond the scope of this chapter. Suffice it to say that most of them could be avoided by adhering to a clearer defining policy, using componential analysis to identify the distinctive features of lexemes and defining related terms together (see Heuberger 2016a: 33).[3]

19.3.1.2 Verbal and visual illustration

Example sentences and pictures fulfil similar functions in MLDs and are useful for receptive and productive purposes. Both of them support definitions and help to clarify the meanings of headwords,[4] and they can also be used as a starting point for language production. As a side effect, they help to counteract "the dry effect of an entire book of abstract analyses of words as words" (Kipfer 1984: 78).

Both example sentences and pictorial illustrations have been discussed rather controversially within learner lexicography. In particular, the selection of example sentences was strongly debated for many years until all publishers finally decided on a similar approach. The basic question was whether example sentences should be invented or authentic. Invented examples can include lexical and grammatical details suited to help learners, and difficult terms can be removed. Authentic examples, on the other hand, show how a word is actually used, which makes them more natural and reliable. A. S. Hornby (*OALD*) was a confirmed advocate of the first position, whereas John Sinclair (*COBUILD*) strongly spoke out in favour of authentic examples. All current MLDs use a combination of these two policies; authentic (i.e. corpus-based) examples are used as a starting point, but they are usually edited to remove difficult terms and include typical structures and collocations.

Interestingly, none of the publishers has applied the defining vocabulary policy to example sentences. Bogaards states that those examples mainly intended to support definitions (rather than syntactic patterns) ought to be kept simple (1996: 298). Instead, lexicographers' intuition decides whether a less frequent term should remain within the example, and it seems unavoidable that unsuitable terms occasionally slip through (see Heuberger 2000: 54).

The less fervid debate regarding pictorial illustrations mainly concerns the potential of photographs as compared to drawings. At first glance, photographs may seem superior because they are more realistic (see Hupka 1989: 708) – similar to corpus-based examples. However, as Svensén (1993: 169) points out, realistic is not the same as typical.

A photograph of a car only represents one particular vehicle and not "a composite distillation of elements regarded as typical of all [cars]" (Landau 1993: 112). Besides, photographs often include "visual noise" (Svensén 1993: 169), that is, features that are irrelevant for a particular context and potentially distracting. This is not the case with drawings, where every line is usually motivated and only those surroundings are incorporated that contribute to the information content of the picture. However, the most important reason to rate drawings higher than photographs is that they are understood more quickly and easily (Hupka 1989: 708). Studies have – and this may seem surprising – also shown that black and white drawings are usually recognised equally well as coloured ones (Hupka 1989: 709). The areas in which the use of colours seems essential are few, but full-colour illustrations admittedly make the dictionary more attractive.

Illustrations are also extremely versatile in their range of application.[5] They are, for instance, helpful in grouping and disambiguating words that belong to the same lexical field (e.g. insects). They can depict the parts and components of concrete objects and contrast the various meanings of polysemous and homonymous terms. *LDOCE3* (1995) shows that there is seemingly no word class or type of word that cannot be illustrated effectively, e.g. prepositions (p. 1179) or different types of walk (p. 1438). Figure 19.1 (originally full-page and full-colour) from the same dictionary, for instance, illustrates various sounds efficiently.

A comparison of current MLDs shows that the dictionaries usually illustrate completely different terms. This impression is confirmed by Klosa, who notes that the question of "how many and which illustrations belong in the dictionary has not yet been definitively answered" (2016: 530). Pictures should be used more systematically for terms which are likely to cause confusion for the learner, be it due to their complexity or ambiguity. Clearly, the aesthetic value of pictorial illustrations should not be placed ahead of their lexicographic relevance.

19.3.1.3 Grammar and usage

MLDs provide far more grammatical and usage information than dictionaries for native speakers. In addition to grammatical aspects of word classes (e.g. plurality, transitivity, reflexivity), they indicate syntactic patterns and irregular inflections, to mention just a few relevant areas. The coding systems of learners' dictionaries have been improved – and simplified – significantly during the past few decades (cf. Yamada 2013: 198). Earlier editions included opaque codes that were not suggestive of the syntactic patterns they were supposed to illustrate, meaning that occasional users were likely to struggle with the notations. Several current MLDs spell out grammatical information in full, a user-friendly approach first introduced in the 1995 edition of *LDOCE*. Rundell (2006: 741) aptly summarises this development as follows: "More recently, the emphasis has shifted toward a simpler, surface-grammar model which – while sacrificing some of the delicacy of earlier systems – assumes very little grammatical knowledge on the part of users". The following example from *LDOCE Online* illustrates this approach, indicating a common pattern of the verb 'want' as "want somebody to do something" (Figure 19.2).

Notes on usage (sometimes called "usage notes") were first included in *LDOCE1* and are also employed to provide grammatical information. Additionally, they focus on subtle differences in meaning of related words and often deal with pragmatic aspects.[6] Like pictorial illustrations, they are included rather irregularly and sporadically, a given set of words usually only being discussed in one of the MLDs currently available.

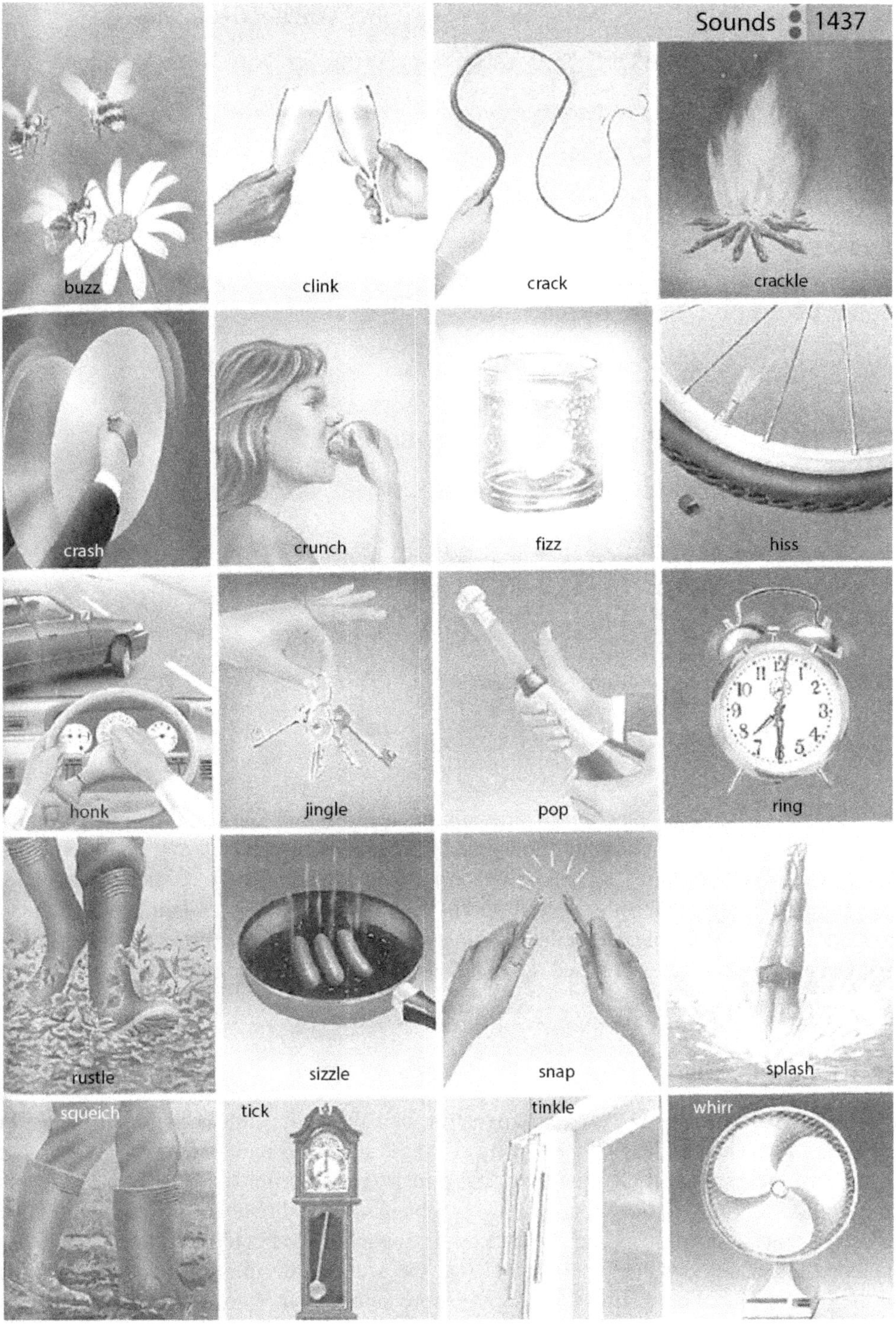

Figure 19.1 Collective picture entitled 'sounds' in *LDOCE3*

2 NEED **[transitive]** used to say that you need something or to ask someone firmly to do something for you

Do you still want these magazines, or can I throw them out?

want something done

I want that letter typed today.

want somebody to do something

I want you to find out what they're planning.

make you want to cry/throw up etc (=give you a strong feeling that you must do something)

It always makes me want to sneeze.

What do you want with a tool kit (=what do you need it for)?

want doing British English *informal* (=need to be done)

The carpet really wants cleaning.

Figure 19.2 Grammar codes for the term 'want' in *LDOCE Online*

Labels also have the function of providing usage information, for example, information on currency and temporality ("obsolete"), frequency of use ("rare"), regional variation ("American"), technical or specialised terminology ("chemistry"), restricted or socially unacceptable usage ("taboo"), style ("formal") and status ("non-standard") (see Landau 1993: 175). The criticism stated in connection with usage notes also applies to labels; their main weakness is that they are used rather inconsistently (i.e. not for all headwords to which they are applicable).

19.3.1.4 Collocations

Collocations differ greatly between languages, and they constitute a major difficulty in mastering a foreign language. In English, we "face" problems and "interpret" dreams; but in modern Hebrew as in German, we "stand in front of" problems and "solve" dreams (Crystal 1997: 105). Collocations are also problematic for dictionary makers, who need to select suitable candidates and decide how and where to indicate them. They are either included under the so-called "collocator" (i.e. the semantically more dependent element) or the "collocational base" (the semantically more autonomous word) – but usually, due to space restrictions, not within both entries. Example sentences, definitions and usage notes are primarily used as a vehicle for indicating collocations, which may, however, also be listed separately, for instance within self-contained boxes (as in *COBUILD6* and *LDOCE5*). All current MLDs have their individual approaches to this feature, sometimes showing inconsistencies in the treatment of collocations. Walker (2009: 298) emphasises in this context that lexicographers' awareness of the nature of collocations should be raised:

> In fact, it can be argued that some of these limitations may result from a lack of clarity concerning what exactly constitutes a collocation, and a lack of understanding of the linguistic features and processes which influence the process by which collocations are formed.

19.3.1.5 Pronunciation

In contrast to many dictionaries for native speakers, learners' dictionaries indicate phonetic transcriptions by means of the International Phonetic Alphabet (IPA). This tradition dates back to *ALD1* and is well justified, as most foreign learners of English become familiar with the IPA in the course of their language studies anyway. Phonetic transcription in the current generation of learners' dictionaries is largely homogeneous. All MLDs additionally indicate American English pronunciations (with the exception of *MEDAL2*), and *MWALED1*, unsurprisingly, focuses on this variety.

19.3.1.6 Accessibility

Learners' dictionaries are intended for both receptive and productive purposes. This versatility is problematic, as dictionaries for language production should ideally be arranged semantically,[7] whereas all current MLDs are organised alphabetically. In compensation, cross-references allow the learner to find unknown terms starting from familiar ones, and information categories such as definitions, examples and illustrations can indirectly fulfil this function as well. Despite these tools, the translation of complex texts with only an MLD at hand remains a time-consuming and laborious task, often with unsatisfactory results.

As the access structure of MLDs is an extensive topic, only one feature designed to facilitate the location of senses of polysemous terms will be mentioned. The introduction of "signposts" and "guide words" in the 1995 generation of learners' dictionaries (i.e. *LDOCE3* and *CIDE1*) has proven to be a seminal innovation simplifying the retrieval of individual word senses.[8] The entry for "key" in *CALD Online* illustrates how guide words (usually synonyms, short definitions, hypernoyms, etc.) are employed (Figure 19.3).

19.3.1.7 Front and back matter

Learners tend to believe that one dictionary is very much like another (Kirkpatrick 1989: 754), and as a result, the front matter of MLDs is seldom read (Herbst 1996: 339). This misconception entails that learners' dictionaries may not be used to their full potential, especially with regard to innovative features. In response to these user habits, more recent MLDs have drastically shortened the length of their guides compared to previous editions and now rely on annotated sample pages (sometimes called "visual keys") in combination with succinct verbal descriptions.

The information included in the back matter of learners' dictionaries is also often neglected by users (see Jackson 1994: 38). Dictionary makers continue to provide this section, usually including (some of) the following tools: lists of irregular verbs, the defining vocabulary list, short articles on how to compose essays, letters and emails, geographical names, English prefixes and suffixes, numbers, weights and guidance on punctuation.

key *noun* [C] **(MUSICAL NOTES)**

a set of musical notes based on one particular note:

The song changes key halfway through.

the key of C minor

+ Thesaurus: synonyms and related words

key *noun* [C] **(SYMBOLS)**

a list of the symbols used in a map or book with explanations of what they mean

+ Thesaurus: synonyms and related words

key *noun* [C] **(ANSWERS)**

A2 **a list of the answers to the questions in an exercise or test:**

See the key to test 3 on page 176.

+ Thesaurus: synonyms and related words

Figure 19.3 Guide words for the term 'key' in *CALD Online*

19.3.1.8 The role of corpora

The extensive use of corpora and special corpus tools in the dictionary compilation process is certainly a major reason why MLDs have improved substantially in the past three decades (see Bowker 2010: 155ff). However, learner lexicography has not only benefited from corpus linguistics but has also given back to it. Initially, collecting data for a corpus was an expensive and labour-intensive task. It was, fittingly, in the profitable area of learners' dictionaries that the first lexicographic corpus was developed (see Rundell 2012: 18). As mentioned earlier, *COBUILD1* (1987) was the first MLD to rely heavily on a corpus, the Birmingham Collection of English Texts (BCET, then 7.3 million words). During the 1990s, the corpus revolution fully took off in EFL lexicography. All four new editions of learners' dictionaries that were published in 1995 (*OALD5*, *LDOCE3*, *COBUILD2* and *CIDE1*) strongly emphasized the use of corpora in their blurbs.

Until the turn of the millennium, corpora were mainly employed by lexicographers to obtain authentic example sentences and typical collocations. Newly developed software tools allow dictionary makers to do much more. So-called "word sketches" provide the lexicographer with a succinct summary of the most significant patterns of a word's lexical and grammatical co-occurrences. First used for the *Macmillan English Dictionary* (*MEDAL1* 2002), they have become the preferred starting point for lexicographers who want to analyse complex headwords (Kilgarriff and Kosem 2012: 44). These software tools can automatically choose sentences that are likely to be good dictionary examples.[9] According to

Kilgarriff (2013: 91), the tools enable lexicographers to find a suitable example in the top 5 suggestions, rather than, on average, within the top 20 to 30.

Some learners' dictionaries are not only corpus based but include self-contained corpora as CD-ROM or DVD supplements. The first MLD to provide direct corpus access was *COBUILD5* (2006). It included a 5-million-word sample from the Bank of English and allowed learners to search for both single lexemes and phrases within a concordance search. The potential of such dictionary-cum-corpus tools can hardly be overstated. Even for less frequent terms, learners are usually provided with a sizeable number of examples that serve as syntactic models for correct usage or as the basis for lexical analysis. These corpora are expected to play an important role in the learning process, as they may foster learners' interest in the language and its structures.

19.3.1.9 Information on word frequency

Frequency information is a rather recent and innovative feature of MLDs, simultaneously introduced in *LDOCE3* and *COBUILD2* in 1995. Language learners can infer from frequency data whether a term is worth remembering at a certain stage of learning, and teachers or authors of textbooks can judge whether the knowledge of a word can reasonably be taken for granted. However, more than 20 years after its introduction, this feature is still in its infancy. Not all current learners' dictionaries give frequency information, and if they do, it is usually provided for a few thousand words only. MLDs aiming at *advanced* learners should indicate these data at least for the 10,000 most common words of the language, ideally differentiating between written and spoken English as well as between different parts of speech.[10] Collins is currently the only publisher to cover an even wider frequency range in *COBUILD Online*. Remarkably, the dictionary provides frequency information not only for present-day English, but additionally gives a chart for the usage development of every headword within the past 300 years (Figure 19.4).

There is no doubt that the ever-increasing size of corpora, as well as highly sophisticated corpus tools, will allow for yet more extensive and reliable frequency data in future editions of MLDs. Frequency information is thus a prime example of the immense potential of corpus use in learner lexicography.

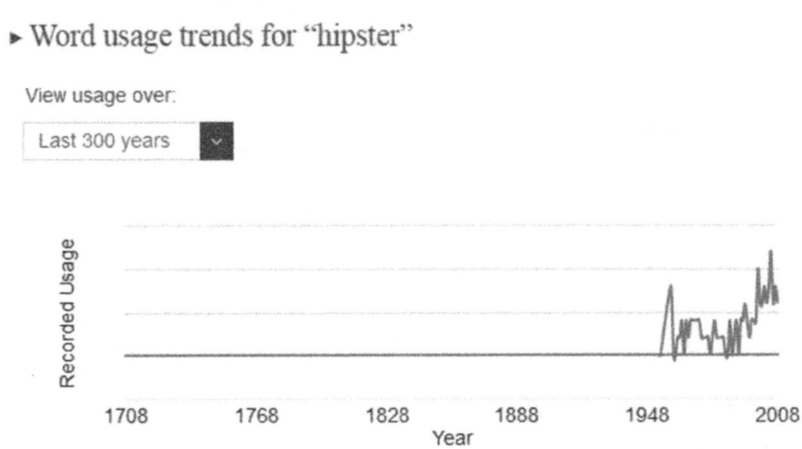

Figure 19.4 Word usage trends for the term **hipster** in *COBUILD Online*

19.3.1.10 Etymological information

Battenburg (1991: 60) claims that "no lexicographer or researcher focusing on MLDs would argue that ESL and EFL students need to know [. . .] that the adjective 'rich' comes from the Anglo-Saxon 'rice' which is a cognate of the Latin 'rex'". Even though this assertion is not as undisputed as Battenburg suggests, it is in line with the policies of most current publishers of learners' dictionaries. A key argument against etymologies is that language learners do not need to know *why* words have come to be used in certain ways, but rather *how* they are used today (Battenburg 1991: 17). Svensén warns that etymological information may not only be of little help but even prove harmful to the learner, as it can give incorrect ideas as to the present meaning of words (1993: 189). By excluding etymologies, however, "the entries in a dictionary appear to have been granted their present shapes by divine right, without relation to any other language and without relation to the past" (Landau 1993: 103). Etymologies may enable the learner to understand and remember the structure of words better, and this sort of knowledge is also likely to be helpful when encountering unfamiliar lexemes. Despite the many arguments for an inclusion of etymological information, *OALD Online* is currently the only learners' dictionary to do so (Figure 19.5):

> – Word Origin
>
> Old English *hūs* (noun), *hūsian* (verb), of Germanic origin; related to Dutch *huis*, German *Haus* (nouns), and Dutch *huizen*, German *hausen* (verbs).

Figure 19.5 Etymological information ("word origin") for the term **house** in *OALD Online*

I would argue that at least a basic treatment of etymologies ought to be considered for MLDs. Clearly, it should not be a lengthy paragraph tracing the various origins of a lexeme and its changes throughout history, but rather some facts on historical linguistic forms including origin. Especially the electronic medium, where space restrictions play only a minor role, is an ideal platform for this information category. Learners who feel that they do not benefit from etymologies should be able to customize the software so that this feature is not displayed, as is the case with OALD Online.

19.3.2 Special types of learners' dictionaries

A number of special types of learners' dictionaries can only be mentioned briefly here for reasons of space. Theses dictionaries differ from standard MLDs in both format and lexicographic structure: Electronic learners' dictionaries have become widely used in the past few years and offer unique possibilities. Less common but also very useful are "bilingualised learners' dictionaries", which currently only exist for a small number of languages. Finally, there are increasingly more learners' dictionaries for specific purposes entering the market.

19.3.2.1 Electronic learners' dictionaries

To date, no large-scale electronic MLD in its own right (i.e. originally conceived for the electronic medium) has been created. All current electronic learners' dictionaries are essentially conversions of print dictionaries. Thus, there are only minor differences between print and electronic learners' dictionaries in terms of entry texts; the main differences concern features enabled by technology. The six major publishers of print MLDs also provide free online versions of their reference works, and some print dictionaries continue to be sold in combination with optical data carriers (CDs or DVDs). There is also a trend for publishers to offer mobile dictionary apps for smartphones or tablets, first introduced by *COBUILD7* in 2012.

Amongst the most prominent features of electronic learners' dictionaries is arguably the provision of audio (and sometimes video) material, allowing for a more natural and vivid description of the language. Recorded pronunciations are usually provided for both British and American English. Other features are (visual) thesauruses, vocabulary builders, language games and exercises. As mentioned in Section 19.3.1.8, electronic dictionaries on CDs and DVDs sometimes include self-contained corpora. Unfortunately, online learners' dictionaries by and large fail to do so to this day.[11] A great advantage of electronic MLDs is that sophisticated retrieval systems can reduce access times considerably,[12] also enabling complex filter searches. Equally, they allow for customisation with regard to typeface and layout and can be linked with other software such as word processing tools. Learners' dictionaries have finally found their ideal platform in the electronic medium, though it will take a few more years or even decades to take full advantage of its opportunities. For a more thorough treatment of electronic learners' dictionaries, see Miller (Chapter 22 of this volume).

19.3.2.2 Bilingualised learners' dictionaries

The entry structure of bilingualised English learners' dictionaries (BLDs) resembles that of MLDs in that definitions and examples are given in English. In addition, they provide a translation for every sense into the learner's L1. Thus, BLDs need to be compiled for every foreign language and have a restricted market. In several studies, bilingualised learners' dictionaries have proven effective, especially for less advanced users (see Laufer and Hadar 1997: 192ff). The electronic medium[13] lends itself particularly well to the realisation of BLDs, as users of computerised reference works can search for both the English term and its L1 equivalent, starting from either language. A well-compiled bilingualised learners' dictionary in electronic form can in theory combine the best features of monolingual and bilingual dictionaries without sacrificing any of their individual strengths. However, the fact that they cannot be sold worldwide is presumably a major reason why BLDs continue to be a niche product. They are, for example, very popular with Chinese learners, whereas languages such as German still await the publication of the first BLD.

19.3.2.3 Other specialised learners' dictionaries

The need for specialised dictionaries is constantly growing, as is the market for them (see Fuertes-Olivera 2010: 24). The various types of specialised learners' dictionaries currently available are thoroughly described by Fuertes-Olivera (2010). Among the reference works surveyed are monolingual, translation and bilingual dictionaries, both in print and online. A more thorough discussion of these dictionaries would be beyond the scope of this paper, and readers interested in this topic are referred to the aforementioned volume.

Similarly, the situation of monolingual learners' dictionaries in languages other than English can only be touched upon here. The majority of MLDs are for learners of English

(Moon 2016: 124), but they have also been compiled for Chinese, Dutch, German, Spanish and French. Some of these dictionaries are available in electronic form (e.g. *DAFLES*, an online dictionary for foreign learners of French).[14] MLDs for languages other than English have received little attention from lexicographers, with most research and reviews focusing on the leading MLDs by British publishers, which arguably represent the state of the art in the field.

19.4 Looking to the future

Despite the many prophecies of their doom, print learners' dictionaries will continue to be published in the years and decades to come. At the same time, electronic learners' dictionaries will keep increasing in importance and market share, and they certainly have a much greater scope for development. Changes will most likely affect the well-established format of the MLD: Rundell (2010: 171f.) predicts that learners' dictionaries will have to adapt more flexibly to the needs and demands of their users – a development referred to as *customization*. Electronic learners' dictionaries could, for instance, be customized with regard to layout, individual access to corpora, collocation banks and translation systems. Future MLDs might be programmed to match users' changing learning needs (e.g. by calibrating the level of L1 support). *User input*, which already plays a central role for popular online platforms such as *Wiktionary*, *Urban Dictionary* and *LEO*, is also likely to become more relevant for learner lexicography (e.g. in the form of dictionary-related online forums where learners help each other).[15]

19.5 Conclusion

Today, foreign learners of English have a tremendous choice of MLDs at their disposal. The abundance of dictionaries on the market does not, however, mean that there is no scope for improvement – especially with regard to the electronic medium. Compared to the lexicographic tradition of print MLDs, electronic learners' dictionaries are still in their infancy. The online dictionaries available are basically one-to-one conversions of print dictionaries, with little or no additional textual data. This has been the case for a while now, and the underlying problem is most likely a financial one. Whereas print MLDs have always been lucrative for publishers, electronic learners' dictionaries are generally offered free of charge – financed by advertisements or, indirectly, via book sales. It seems that none of the major publishers is currently willing or able to spend the money necessary for an in-depth revision of their online reference works, even though a different business model might prove rewarding for both dictionary makers and users: If a thoroughly revised and expanded online MLD offered considerably more features than existing Internet dictionaries, a significant – yet unquantifiable – number of users would be willing to pay for this extra functionality.[16] This is, in my opinion, the most desirable development within learner lexicography from today's viewpoint: an MLD newly designed for the electronic medium and fully using the advantages the platform can offer.

Related topics

Lexicography and corpus linguistics; electronic dictionaries; dictionary criticism; lexicography and applied linguistics; learners' dictionaries of English; English lexicography in the Internet era; Wordnik.

Further reading

Cowie, A. P. (2002). *English Dictionaries for Foreign Learners: A History*. Oxford: Oxford University Press.
Cowie's book is the most detailed account of the history of (print) learners' dictionaries, describing their development until the turn of the millenium.

Durkin, P. (2016). *The Oxford Handbook of Lexicography*. Oxford: Oxford University Press.
Durkin's seminal 700-page edition provides an up-to-date collection of articles on a great many aspects of lexicography, not limited to Anglophone research.

Jackson, H. (2002). *Lexicography. An Introduction*. London and New York: Routledge.
Jackson gives an excellent and accessible overview of various aspects of dictionary making and research.

Notes

1 From the second edition onwards, Cambridge changed the title to *Cambridge Advanced Learner's Dictionary* (*CALD*).
2 The editor of the *MEDAL* dictionaries, Michael Rundell, announced in November 2012 that Macmillan would no longer publish learners' dictionaries in print form, focusing on online dictionaries instead (Ostermann 2015: 16).
3 For a more thorough treatment of general principles and methods of defining, including a historical perspective, see Hanks (2016); the peculiarities of definitions in learners' dictionaries have been discussed by Moon (2016).
4 Exemplification and illustration constitute two of the five basic explanatory techniques in dictionaries, the other three being definition, translation and discussion (Ilson 1987: 1993).
5 See Klosa (2016) for an up-to-date account of the function of illustrations in dictionaries, including a typology.
6 For a recent discussion of pragmatic information in learners' dictionaries, see Yang (2007).
7 Compare the arrangement in the *Longman Language Activator*, a dictionary designed especially for production.
8 Nesi and Tan (2011: 90) have recently evaluated this feature largely positively.
9 The Sketch Engine is nowadays the leading tool for lexicographic corpus analysis. It provides a function called "GDEX" (Good Dictionary Examples), which automatically sorts example sentences according to how likely they are to be suitable candidates. Examples with infrequent words, proper nouns, unusual sentence or word length are ranked lower, whereas sentences including typical collocates of the expression are ranked higher (cf. Heuberger 2016b).
10 Cambridge has taken a different approach in *CALD Online*. Rather than using figures or graphs to indicate frequency information, the dictionary uses the symbols A1–C2 to show which words and phrases learners should know at each level, very much in line with the Common European Framework of Reference for Languages.
11 An exception is the special purpose dictionary *LEAD* (Louvain English for Academic Purposes Dictionaries), an online reference tool aimed at non-native speaker students and researchers who want to write academic English.
12 Interestingly, as studies have shown, the short time needed to retrieve information may prove detrimental to its retention (cf. Dziemianko 2010: 258).
13 *COBUILD Online* offers translations for selected languages at the end of each dictionary entry (headword translations rather than sense translations). *CALD Online* also provides a translation tool.
14 See at www.kuleuven.ac.be/dafles.
15 For instance, Macmillan invites learners who access *MEDAL Online* to contribute words for the crowdsourced *Open Dictionary*, cf. www.macmillandictionary.com/open-dictionary/submit.html.
16 Music streaming services such as Spotify illustrate this point. Many users pay a monthly rate in order to remove advertisements, improve audio quality and to download music for offline listening. Online MLDs might, similarly, be offered in a basic version that comes free of charge, as well

as an advanced version with extended functionality (via paid subscription). Oxford has taken a first step in this direction, offering some extra features in its "Premium" version of *OALD Online* (GBP 9.99 for one year's access).

References

Dictionaries

The Advanced Learner's Dictionary of Current English. 2nd edition (1963). Eds. A. S. Hornby, E. V. Gatenby, and H. Wakefield. London: Oxford University Press. [= *ALD2*]

Cambridge Advanced Learner's Dictionary. 2nd edition (2005). Ed. E. Walter. Cambridge: Cambridge University Press. [= *CALD2*]

Cambridge Advanced Learner's Dictionary. 4th edition (2013). Ed. Colin McIntosh.Cambridge: Cambridge University Press. [= *CALD4*]

Cambridge Advanced Learner's Dictionary Online (accessed April 2016). http://dictionary.cambridge.org/. [= *CALD Online*]

Cambridge International Dictionary of English. 1st edition (1995). Ed. Paul Procter. Cambridge: Cambridge University Press. [= *CIDE1*]

Collins Cobuild Advanced Dictionary. 6th edition (2009). Ed. J. Sinclair, London and Glasgow: HarperCollins. [= *COBUILD6*]

Collins Cobuild Advanced Dictionary of English. 7th edition (2012). Ed. J. Sinclair, London and Glasgow: HarperCollins. [= *COBUILD7*]

Collins Cobuild Advanced Learner's Dictionary. 8th edition (2014). Ed. J. Sinclair, London and Glasgow: HarperCollins. [= *COBUILD8*]

Collins Cobuild Advanced Learner's Dictionary Online. www.collinsdictionary.com/dictionary/english-cobuild-learners [Accessed April 2016]. [= *COBUILD Online*]

Collins Cobuild Advanced Learner's English Dictionary. 5th edition (2006). Ed. J. Sinclair, London and Glasgow: HarperCollins. [= *COBUILD5*]

Collins Cobuild English Dictionary. 2nd edition (1995). Ed. P. Hanks. London: HarperCollins. [= *COBUILD2*]

Collins Cobuild English Language Dictionary. 1st edition (1987). Eds. J. Sinclair, and P. Hanks. London and Glasgow: HarperCollins. [= *COBUILD1*]

Collins English Dictionary Online. www.collinsdictionary.com/dictionary/english [Accessed April 2016]. [= *CED Online*]

Dictionnaire d'Apprentissage du Francais Langue Étrangère ou Seconde. www.kuleuven.ac.be/dafles [Accessed October 2016]. [= *DAFLES*]

Idiomatic and Syntactic English Dictionary (1942). Eds. A. S. Hornby, E. V. Gatenby, and H. Wakefield. Tokyo: Kaitakusha. (Photographically reprinted and published as *A Learner's Dictionary of Current English* by Oxford University Press, 1948; in 1952, retitled *The Advanced Learner's Dictionary of Current English* (*ALD1*).) [= *ISED*]

Longman Dictionary of Contemporary English. 1st edition (1978). Ed. Paul Proctor. Harlow: Longman. [= *LDOCE1*]

Longman Dictionary of Contemporary English. 3rd edition (1995). Ed. Della Summers. Harlow: Longman. [= *LDOCE3*]

Longman Dictionary of Contemporary English. 5th edition (2009). Ed. M. Mayor. Harlow: Pearson Longman. [= *LDOCE5*]

Longman Dictionary of Contemporary English for Advanced Learners. 6th edition (2014). Harlow: Pearson Longman. [= *LDOCE6*]

Longman Dictionary of Contemporary English for Advanced Learners Online. www.ldoceonline.com/ [Accessed April 2016]. [= *LDOCE Online*]

Longman Language Activator. 2nd edition (2002). Ed. Della Summers. Harlow: Pearson Education. [= *LLA2*]

Louvain English for Academic Purposes Dictionary. Eds. S. Granger and M. Paquot. www.uclouvain.be/en-322619.html [Accessed April 2016]. [= *LEAD*]

Macmillan English Dictionary for Advanced Learners. 1st edition (2002). Ed. M. Rundell. Oxford: Macmillan Education. [= *MEDAL1*]

Macmillan English Dictionary for Advanced Learners. 2nd edition (2007). Ed. M. Rundell. Oxford: Macmillan Education. [= *MEDAL2*]

Macmillan English Dictionary for Advanced Learners Online. www.macmillandictionary.com/ [Accessed April 2016]. [= *MEDAL Online*]

Merriam-Webster's Advanced Learner's English Dictionary. 1st edition (2008). Ed. S. J. Perrault. Springfield, MA: Merriam-Webster. [= *MWALED1*]

Merriam-Webster's Advanced Learner's English Dictionary Online. www.learnersdictionary.com/ [Accessed April 2016]. [= *MWALED Online*]

Oxford Advanced Learner's Dictionary of Current English. 3rd edition (1974). Eds. A. S. Hornby, A. P. Cowie, and J. Windsor Lewis. London: Oxford University Press. [= *OALD3*]

Oxford Advanced Learner's Dictionary of Current English. 5th edition (1995). Ed. J. Crowther. Oxford: Oxford University Press. [= *OALD5*]

Oxford Advanced Learner's Dictionary of Current English. 9th edition (2015). Oxford: Oxford University Press. [= *OALD9*]

Oxford Advanced Learner's Dictionary Online (accessed April 2016). www.oxfordadvancedlearners-dictionary.com/. [= *OALD Online*]

Other literature

Battenburg, J. (1991) *English Monolingual Learners' Dictionaries: A User-Oriented Study*. Tübingen: Max Niemeyer Verlag.

Bogaards, P. (1996) "Dictionaries for Learners of English", *International Journal of Lexicography* 9(4): 277–320.

Bogaards, P. (2010) "The Evolution of Learners' Dictionaries and *Merriam Webster's Advanced Learner's Dictionary*", in I. J. Kernemann and P. Bogaards (eds.), *English Learners' Dictionaries at the DSNA 2009*. Tel Aviv: K Dictionaries, pp. 11–28.

Bowker, L. (2010) "The Contribution of Corpus Linguistics to the Development of Specialised Dictionaries for Learners", in P. A. Fuertes-Olivera (ed.), pp. 155–168.

Cowie, A. P. (2002). *English Dictionaries for Foreign Learners: A History*. Oxford: Oxford University Press.

Crystal, David (1997). *The Cambridge Encyclopedia of Language*. Cambridge: Cambridge University Press.

Durkin, Philip (ed.) (2016). *The Oxford Handbook of Lexicography*. Oxford: Oxford University Press.

Dziemianko, A. (2010) "Paper or Electronic? The Role of Dictionary Form in Language Reception, Production and the Retention of Meaning and Collocations", *International Journal of Lexicography* 23(3): 257–273.

Fontenelle, T. (2009) "Linguistic Research and Learners' Dictionaries: The *Longman Dictionary of Contemporary English*", in A. P. Cowie (ed.), *The Oxford History of English Lexicography. Volume II: Specialized Dictionaries*. Oxford: Clarendon Press, pp. 412–435.

Fuertes-Olivera, P. A. (ed.) (2010). *Specialised Dictionaries for Learners*. Berlin/New York: de Gruyter.

Hanks, P. (2016) "Definition", in P. Durkin (ed.), pp. 94–122.

Herbst, T. (1996) "On the Way to the Perfect Learners' Dictionary: A First Comparison of *OALD5*, *LDOCE3*, *COBUILD2* and *CIDE*", *International Journal of Lexicography* 9(4): 321–356.

Heuberger, R. (2000) *Monolingual Dictionaries for Foreign Learners of English: A Constructive Evaluation of the State-of-the-Art Reference Works in Book Form and on CD-ROM*. Wien: Braumüller.

Heuberger, R. (2016a) "Learners' Dictionaries: History and Development; Current Issues", in P. Durkin (ed.), pp. 25–43.

Heuberger, R. (2016b) "Corpora as Game Changers: The Growing Impact of Corpus Tools for Dictionary Makers and Users", *English Today* 32(2): 24–30.

Hupka, W. (1989) "Die Bebilderung und sonstige Formen der Veranschaulichung im allgemeinen einsprachigen Wörterbuch", in F. J. Hausmann, O. Reichmann, H. E. Wiegand and L. Zgusta (eds.), *Wörterbücher, Dictionaries, Dictionnaires: Ein internationales Handbuch zur Lexikographie*. Berlin/New York: Walter de Gruyter, pp. 704–725.

Ilson, R. (1987) "Towards a Taxonomy of Dictionary Definitions", in R. Ilson (ed.), *A Spectrum of Lexicography: Papers From AILA Brussels 1984*. Amsterdam/Philadelphia: John Benjamins Publishing Company, pp. 61–74.

Jackson, H. (1994) *Words and Their Meaning*. London/New York: Longman.

Jackson, H. (2002) *Lexicography. An Introduction*. London/New York: Routledge.

Kilgarriff, A. (2013) "Using Corpora as Data Sources for Dictionaries", in H. Jackson (ed.), *The Bloomsbury Companion to Lexicography*. London: Bloomsbury, pp. 77–96.

Kilgarriff, A. and I. Kosem (2012) "Corpus Tools for Lexicographers", in S. Granger and M. Paquot (eds.), *Electronic Lexicography*. Oxford. Oxford University Press, pp. 31–55.

Kirkpatrick, B. (1989) "User's Guides in Dictionaries", in F. J. Hausmann, O. Reichmann, H. E. Wiegand, and L. Zgusta (eds.), *Wörterbücher, Dictionaries, Dictionnaires: Ein internationales Handbuch zur Lexikographie*. Berlin/New York: Walter de Gruyter, pp. 754–760.

Kipfer, B. A. (1984) *Workbook on Lexicography: A Course for Dictionary Users With a Glossary of English Lexicographical Terms*. Exeter: University of Exeter Press.

Klosa, A. (2016) "Illustrations in Dictionaries; Encyclopaedic and Cultural Information in Dictionaries", in P. Durkin (ed.), pp. 515–531.

Landau, S. I. (1993) *Dictionaries: The Art and Craft of Lexicography*. Cambridge: Cambridge University Press.

Laufer, B. and L. Hadar (1997) "Assessing the Effectiveness of Monolingual, Bilingual and 'Bilingualised' Dictionaries in the Comprehension and Production of New Words", *The Modern Language Journal* 81: 189–197.

Moon, R. (2009) "The Cobuild Project", in A. P. Cowie (ed.), *The Oxford History of English Lexicography. Volume II: Specialized Dictionaries*. Oxford: Clarendon Press, pp. 436–457.

Moon, R. (2016) "Explaining Meaning in Learners' Dictionaries", in P. Durkin (ed.), pp. 123–143.

Nesi, H. and K. Hua Tan (2011) "The Effect of Menus and Signposting on the Speed and Accuracy of Sense Selection", *International Journal of Lexicography* 24(1): 79–96.

Ostermann, C. (2015) *Cognitive Lexicography: A New Approach to Lexicography Making Use of Cognitive Semantics*. Berlin/Boston, MA: Walter de Gruyter.

Rundell, M. (2006) "Learners' Dictionaries", in K. Brown (ed.), *Elsevier Encyclopedia of Language and Linguistics*. Oxford: Elsevier, pp. 739–743.

Rundell, M. (2010) "What Future for the Learner's Dictionary?", in I. J. Kernemann and P. Bogaards (eds.), *English Learners' Dictionaries at the DSNA 2009*. Tel Aviv: K Dictionaries, pp. 169–175.

Rundell, M. (2012) "The Road to Automated Lexicography: An Editor's Viewpoint', in S. Granger and M. Paquot (eds.), *Electronic Lexicography*. Oxford: Oxford University Press, pp. 15–30.

Svensén, B. (1993) *Practical Lexicography*. Oxford and New York: Oxford University Press.

Walker, C. (2009) "The Treatment of Collocation by Learners' Dictionaries, Collocational Dictionaries and Dictionaries of Business English", *International Journal of Lexicography* 22(3): 281–299.

Yamada, S. (2010) "EFL Dictionary Evolution: Innovations and Drawbacks", in I. J. Kernemann and P. Bogaards (eds.), *English Learners' Dictionaries at the DSNA 2009*. Tel Aviv: K Dictionaries, pp. 147–168.

Yamada, S. (2013) "Monolingual Learners' Dictionaries – Where Now?", in H. Jackson (ed.), *The Bloomsbury Companion to Lexicography*. London: Bloomsbury, pp. 188–212.

Yang, W. X. (2007) "On Pragmatic Information in Learners' Dictionaries, With Particular Reference to LDOCE4", *International Journal of Lexicography* 20(2): 147–173.

20
Specialised dictionaries

John Humbley

20.1 Introduction and definitions

Specialised dictionaries are defined here by the specialised nature of the subjects they treat, focusing on particular subject fields, professional practices or even leisure activities such as sports[1] with the aim of helping the user to acquire specialised knowledge, read specialised texts or engage in specialised translation. They can usefully be thought of as LSP (language for special purposes) dictionaries or special-purpose dictionaries (Nielsen 1994:1), although the definition of LSP can be questioned as being too broad (Sager, Dungworth, McDonald 1980: 3) or subject to national variations (Humbley 2007). Dictionaries dealing with specific language issues (pronunciation, proverbs, etc.) are not dealt with here, and no advice is offered on writing a specialised dictionary. The survey is confined to Western European languages. It is not possible, furthermore, to find any clear cut-off between dictionaries and encyclopaedias, although prototypically dictionaries aim at the language of specialised fields, whereas encyclopaedias focus on the extra-linguistic. Fuertes-Olivera and Tarp (2014:7) define the category as "dictionaries, encyclopaedias, lexica, glossaries, vocabularies and other information tools outside general cultural knowledge". Indeed, as Dancette and Réthoré (1997: 230) claim, linguistic and encyclopaedic methods complement one another in the making of the specialised dictionary. Term bases are subsumed in this chapter: they were derived from the automation of cardboard term records kept by specialised translators, thus bypassing the printed book stage, unlike general language lexicography.

The distinction between specialised lexicography and terminology, or terminography, as it is sometimes known, can also be considered prototypical, and Kageura (2015: 57) lists seven contrastive characteristics, all of which are differences of degree rather than nature. Indeed, most of the researchers who have written on the subject (Antia 2005, Bergenholtz and Kaufmann 1997, Kageura 2015) base their distinction on general language lexicography rather than specialised lexicography. Costa (2013) considers the two approaches as complementary, corresponding to two different social needs, the first prioritizing concept analysis and how concepts are reflected by language, the second specialised language use.

There are, as is suggested earlier, two distinct although increasingly overlapping academic traditions concerning specialised dictionaries: that of a terminological orientation, starting with Eugen Wüster (1931), prioritizing concept analysis, and the functional lexicographical orientation, which has its origin in general language metalexicography and can be traced back to Wiegand (1998, 2001) and more recently Bergenholtz and Tarp (1995). In broad terms it can be said that the first approach is conceptually oriented and involves term extraction, manual or increasingly automatic, and how the results of term extraction are analysed and structured; relatively less emphasis had been put on how this information is presented to the user in paper or electronic form. The second approach can be characterized as user orientated by definition, the functions being those the user needs.

20.2 Historical perspectives

Although the study of specialised dictionaries has only emerged recently, they have been produced in large numbers and in different language communities for perhaps thousands of years, though they only took the form in which we know them today in seventeenth- and eighteenth-century Europe (Zanola 2010, 2014). Predecessors of the modern specialised dictionary can be found in the thirty-volume Arabic medical encyclopaedias *Al-Tasrif* in particular, but in Europe and in France in particular, special lexicography emerged either as part of general language dictionaries (*Dictionnaire universelle*, 1690, by Furetière, being the prototype) or in separate dictionaries covering all specialities, such as the *Dictionnaire des termes des arts et des sciences*, by Thomas Corneille in 1694. Pharmacy and medicine were among the first specialities to have their own dictionaries, with the *Dictionnaire pharmaceutique* by de Meuve appearing in 1677. The beginning of the eighteenth century saw the publication of many specialised dictionaries, such as Liger for agriculture (1703), Brossard for music (1703) and Bruslons for commerce (1723–1730) (Zanola 2014:93). P. J. Macquer's (1766) *Dictionnaire de Chimie* is the first dictionary of chemistry in French, translated into several languages, including Danish (Bergenholtz and Tarp 1995:290). These dictionaries reflected the fast expanding vocabulary of science and technology of their times. Technology, a concept which really only emerged in the early nineteenth century, was already treated in such dictionaries as Henri-Gabriel Duchesne's, *Dictionnaire de l'Industrie*, 1776. The culmination of work on the language of science and what would later be called technology came in the form of Denis Diderot and d'Alembert's *Encyclopédie (1751–1772)*, modelled on Chambers's *Cyclopaedia* (1728), to be followed by the *Encyclopédie méthodique*, published by Panckoucke between 1782 and 1832, where each volume, generally entrusted to a leading expert in the field, was dedicated to a particular speciality. They prefigure the modern LSP dictionary inasmuch as their aim was very clearly to present the scientific or technical concepts as clearly as possible, though this did not exclude speculation on the language used and suggestions as to usage. They contain material selected according to set criteria and are arranged in alphabetical order. They were generally monolingual, although many were subsequently translated into other languages. The bilingual and multilingual specialist dictionary was generally a product of the nineteenth century. One of the most remarkable of the detailed multilingual works was the marine dictionary by Captain Paasch, which went in successive editions from three languages (Paasch 1885) to five (Paasch 1937).

It can be claimed that these specialised dictionaries of the past contributed to making Western European languages into languages of science and technology. Their modern counterparts continue to play an important role in language planning, as exemplified by those produced by the Office québécois de la langue française to accompany the promotion of French in Québec and to make French the effective language of the workplace.

20.3 Core issues and topics

The theory of specialised dictionaries was elaborated first in the terminology tradition: Wüster (1971) in his posthumous handbook states that his aim is terminological lexicography. The first study specifically termed special lexicography was probably Bergenholtz and Tarp (1995), that is much later than studies in general lexicography, which was the main focus of the emerging field of metalexicography (Haussmann 1989). The De Gruyter series *Lexicography* (Haussmann et al. 1989–1991), for example, contains almost no chapters specifically devoted to specialised lexicography. This can be explained in part at least by the importance taken by terminology in the 1970s and 1980s. Approaches to special language lexicography tend to be disparate: the main lines of thought are presented: various forms of functional analysis – in particular on how user needs are defined and met – on the one hand, and terminology as specialised lexicography on the other.

The seven characteristics which Kageura (2015) gives to contrast terminography and lexicography are not all relevant here, as the latter is implicitly general language lexicography, but certain features are worth commenting on. The first is that terminology is concerned with terms, whereas lexicography deals with words. Terms can be understood as the expression of concepts inside a field or conceptual system. Following this logic, it is supposed that the terminological dictionary will help the user to understand how these elements function as a whole. To this extent, the other features listed by Kageura can be explained. Thus terminologies are more often normative or prescriptive, as they tend towards a certain rigidity in expressing concepts (Kageura 2015: 49), their nomenclature is overwhelmingly made up of lexical units of more than one word (complex terms), thereby reflecting the conceptual structure by being motivated. Thus, extremely precise, multi-unit terms may not need to be defined in a dictionary, because the meaning can be construed from its elements. This was used as early as the nineteenth century, for example in Paasch's dictionary (Paasch 1885, Van Campenhoudt 2003).

From an empirical point of view, specialised dictionaries vary immensely, so analysis will focus on the most important defining criteria.

20.3.1 Degree of specialisation

The degree of specialisation of a dictionary depends on its target. LSP dictionaries can be aimed at total laypersons, educated laypersons or experts, as Mikkelsen (1991: 100) schematises it, though questioning whether experts need dictionaries at all. Particular types of "non-specialists" may be specifically catered for students, laypeople, and patients (see Delavigne 2008a, 2008b for the last mentioned). There will be differences, for example, between the selection and presentation of information in a dictionary of vulcanology, for example, aimed at laypeople reading about the subject simply to enrich their general knowledge, and a dictionary of information technology consulted by the frustrated computer newbie who has a practical problem to solve. General lexicography, in English in particular, has devoted much attention to learners' dictionaries. Some of these already contain some specialised, generally scientific, vocabulary, which could be expanded to meet some of the user's specialised needs (Williams 2011). It should be remembered that for special language dictionaries, the learner can be both a non-native speaker and a beginner in the specialised field. Fuertes-Olivera and Arribas-Baño (2008) were the first to devote a book to the subject, illustrating how learning business English for Spanish speakers could be enhanced by appropriate lexicological tools. Pioneers in the electronic era have been Binon et al. (2007)

with their learners' dictionary of business French or DAFA[2] going back to the 1980s. More recent works include *DiCoInfo, Dictionnaire fondamental de l'informatique et de l'Internet* (L'Homme 2009, 2014 on the tool itself and Alipour et al. 2015 on how the database was turned into a learners' dictionary), which carefully defines its target audience (in fact quite narrowly as students in translation, still a sizable population in Quebec), and uses situations and functions deduced from this. A number of simplifications were then undertaken: data categories and layout simplified for users who do not have a linguistic background, enhanced multimedia and different technologies incorporated.

20.3.2 Range of specialisation

A dictionary may cover a single field or a range of related subfields. Thus, a sports dictionary may cover all sports, or simply one single sport (basketball, rugby, etc.), or even a particular aspect of a sport. Dictionaries may cover the whole of a specialised field (broadly or narrowly), or only part of it, based on other criteria (for example the specialised terms of a book or a thesis). Bergenholtz and Tarp (1995: 58) speak of maximizing dictionaries for those which aim at a high degree of exhaustivity within a particular subject area, while minimizing dictionaries contain only a selection of terms in the field, according to various criteria.

Term banks (also known as term bases) can be regarded as specialised dictionaries, which may in turn have an extremely broad range of specialisation (*Termium*, *Grand dictionnaire terminologique*, *IATE*), or a narrow one (Dancette 2013).

20.3.3 Number of languages used

Specialised dictionaries can be monolingual, bilingual or multilingual. Monolingual dictionaries have no explicit translation function, though they can be used for translation. Bilingual dictionaries, intended for translation, can be unidirectional (going from language A to language B, but not vice versa) or bidirectional (A to B and B to A), although bidirectional dictionaries usually provide more information in one direction than the other. For bilingual dictionaries, and to a lesser extent multilingual dictionaries, the language functions are more numerous, and closer akin to those of a general language dictionary. These include understanding specialised texts in the target language, writing in the target language and translating into the target language. These are sometimes termed passive and active functions, though receptive and productive or decoding and encoding may be more appropriate. Nielsen (1994: 46) distinguishes four such functions: from Language 1 to Language 2 for Language 1 and Language 2 speakers, and from Language 2 to Language 1 for both sets of speakers. In practice, this tends to be simplified, since if one language is English, native English speakers will not use the productive resources for the other language. In addition, specialised paper dictionaries tend to limit the full presentation to Language 1 to Language 2, and use indices at the end of the volume to provide equivalents on the opposite direction (Van Campenhoudt 2003 :3).

The explication language may be either the *lingua franca*, or in the minority language, on the assumption that majority language users will not need the resource. Thus, in its Danish edition, Kaufmann and Bergenholtz's (1998) genetic engineering dictionary has explanations in Danish, as it is reckoned that only Danish-language users will need them, whereas the English-Spanish dictionary has explanations in English. When the learners are all from the same language background, bilingualised dictionaries may be used: that is, dictionaries in which the headword and the rest of the article is in the target language, but this is provided with an equivalent in the learner's own language (Kaalep and Mikk 2008: 371).

Multilingual dictionaries comprise three or more languages and have traditionally been used for specialised subjects. Bergenholtz and Tarp (1995: 55) distinguish three types: dictionaries going from one language to two or more other languages, but not from these languages back to the first; dictionaries going from one language to two or more other languages and back again; and three or more source languages, going in either direction. Other distinctions may also be made: multilingual dictionaries are often simply lists of equivalences, without definitions or other contextual information, generally necessitating an index to serve all the pairs of languages. As Bowker (2003:159) warns, the greater the number of languages concerned, the less information is included for each equivalent. A variant on this type will include one definition per term, but in only one language. In former times, such multilingual dictionaries were common-place (see *Elseviers dictionaries*, which would typically have six languages but the definition only in English), but these have been largely superseded by term banks.

20.3.4 Type of specialisation

The field covered in the dictionary can be culture dependent (for example, law) or culture independent (e.g. physics) (Bergenholtz and Tarp 1995: 53, 60–63). This is of crucial importance in bilingual dictionaries. For example, an English-Spanish dictionary of law will have difficulty in providing equivalents for the legal concept of *class action.* This fairly broad concept has a generally accepted definition in American English, where the corresponding practice has a long history. In Spain the concept has been adapted into Spanish law, but on a much more restrictive basis. The scope of a class action is therefore limited in Spain as compared to the United States, and the conditions that need to be met much more stringent. In addition, however, the Spanish legislator has not given any particular name to the legal device, using the generic *defensa de los intereses colectivos* in legislative texts. Spanish lawyers therefore tend to refer to the concept as *acción de clase*, thereby recalling the American model, whereas the press focuses on the process, and uses *demanda colectiva.* A bilingual English-Spanish law dictionary would need to indicate these three terms as partial synonyms, indicating in the usage note in which context they are used, and to mark these as peculiar to Spain, because many other Spanish-speaking countries have their own quasi-equivalents of *class action.*

20.3.5 Macrostructure and microstructure

As in general lexicography for printed dictionaries, the macrostructure is the organisation of articles (usually known as entries) in the dictionary, and the microstructure is the organisation of information within the various entries. Of relevance too for the general economy of the dictionary is the front and back material, as is said of paper dictionaries. Front material includes an introduction (Fuertes-Olivera 2009), which often indicates how the dictionary is to be used and what the criteria for inclusion are. Bergenholtz and Kaufmann (1997) have underlined the need for didactic introductions to specialised dictionaries to initiate the non-specialist user into the basics of the subject matter. For example, their gene technology dictionary (Kaufmann and Bergenholtz et al. 1998) contains forty closely printed pages of introduction to the subject matter. Back material typically include bibliographies, indices and appendices. In electronic dictionaries, these sources of information are usually available through hyperlinks.

20.3.5.1 Macrostructure

Paper dictionaries have a fixed order of presentation of articles: the lemmata (also known as headwords) are either arranged alphabetically or thematically. Thematically arranged dictionaries were favoured by the terminological approach, because they suggested the way the subject field was organised: onomasiological or systematic in presentation, that is, they are arranged thematically, according to a conceptual system, rather than alphabetically (see van Sterkenburg (2003) for a history of onomasiological dictionaries). Onomasiological dictionaries are used for general language (thesauri, synonym dictionaries) but also for special dictionaries, notably pictorial dictionaries. Specialised dictionaries, often including only a limited number of illustrations, may be presented thematically, as is Wüster's *Machine Tool* dictionary (1968), which may be more appropriate for advanced lay users, but difficult to handle for beginners (Mikkelsen 1991: 101). As Bowker (2003: 158) observes, systematic ordering is typical of culture-independent fields such as botany or zoology, where a systematic presentation of the concepts of the field has long been characteristic. Even if alphabetical order is adopted, specialised dictionaries will be based on a conceptual structure, whether this is made explicit or not, harking back to Diderot's "tree of knowledge".

In the case of thematic paper dictionaries, an alphabetical index is required to permit access for those unfamiliar with the conceptual cartography of the domain. Structural considerations also determine the criteria of inclusion in a particular dictionary with regard to the scope and the level of depth or detail the dictionary will include. In the case of electronic dictionaries, other search facilities are proposed, showing results in an order that the user can determine and other supporting features. Access to the conceptual structure may be afforded by hyperlinks.

The choice of lemmata for a dictionary depends on several factors, depending on the functions it is supposed to fulfil. Thus, a dictionary will provide more specialised terms if it is aimed at a readership of advanced users and fewer if it is aimed at beginners in the subject field. Once the terms have been chosen, it has to be decided how they will be presented in the dictionary, either split up or lumped together (see Chapters 16 and 28 in this volume). General language dictionaries tend to the latter, whereas specialised dictionaries, especially those of a terminological nature, tend to the former. This means that there will be separate entries for what might be considered phraseologisms in a general language dictionary. Thus there will be separate entries for *printer*, *daisy-wheel printer*, *inkjet printer*. This is because each item is considered to be a separate concept, defined in relation to other related concepts.

20.3.5.2 Microstructure

Dictionaries vary on the number and type of fields included in the microstructure, depending on number of languages, and other criteria. Bilingual dictionaries will always include an equivalent, monolingual dictionaries will include a definition or some other description of the meaning of the lemma. The microstructure of terminological dictionaries is derived from the cardboard term record (Dubuc 1997:10), which explains some of the differences with general language lexicography. Taking the big term banks such as *Termium*, *Grand Dictionnaire terminologique* and *IATE* as a yardstick, the following fields are included for each entry, though not necessarily filled in: domain, headword, equivalent(s), definition, context, usage labels, validity, dates, sources and notes. Other fields commonly found in both paper and electronic dictionaries are illustrations.

20.3.5.2.1 DOMAIN OR SUBJECT LABELS

The indication of what field or domain a particular term is used in is a vital piece of information. Indeed, a term is only a term within a precise subject field. For all-purpose specialised dictionaries, such as the large term bases, the architecture of the domain structure is that of the whole database, whereas Terminological Knowledge Bases are confined to a single area (see Chapter 21 in this volume). In broadly based dictionaries, these are generally set out in the same way as documentary classification systems. Wüster (1968 [2.16]) used the Universal Decimal Classification (UDC) for his machine-tool dictionary. In this case, the domain indication is represented by an index number. Domains provide essential information in wide-ranging specialised dictionaries, but are also used in much more specialised works as well, where they indicate subfields. For example in Routledge's *French Dictionary of Business, Commerce and Finance*, each headword (as well as compounds and phrasal units found within the entry) has at least one subfield label – e.g. *multidevise* BANQUE, ECON FIN, meaning that the term is found in the subfields of banking, economy and finance, covered by the dictionary. The *Robert des sports* indicates the subfield just before the definition; thus the verb *dribbler* has one general definition without any subfield indicated, then further specific definitions or examples, each labelled for the sport under consideration (*Fb-Rb; basket; handb, Hockey*).

20.3.5.2.2 DEFINITION

In general language lexicography, monolingual dictionaries contain definitions, whereas bilingual or multilingual dictionaries as a rule do not. In special language dictionaries, especially those of a terminological orientation, definitions are included. This is consistent with the conceptual nature of LSP dictionaries. The presence and the quality of the definitions are an important factor in determining the reliability of the dictionary. In bilingual dictionaries, the definition is usually given in both languages, but in multilingual dictionaries it is more usual to limit to one pivot language. The type of definition to be used in specialised dictionaries has also been a topic of discussion. Terminographers recommend the *intensional definition*, that is, the definition incorporating necessary and sufficient conditions (Bessé 1994). This form of definition comes from logic, and is defined in ISO 1087–1/2000, as opposed to the *extensional definition*, that is, the description of a concept enumerating all the subordinate concepts corresponding to a criterion of subdivision. The extensional definition was not considered appropriate though recently Nilsson (2015) claims that it is justified in certain circumstances, such as legal definitions, where it is necessary to spell out all the members of a particular category. Other types of less formal definitions more typically found in general language dictionaries, such as the *prototypical definition*, are increasingly accepted in specialised dictionaries. Ten Hacken (2015: 7) suggests that prototypical definitions are sufficient for most specialised dictionaries, and that intensional definitions should only be used to avoid potential conflict or when specific scientific claims are made (see Chapter 4 in this volume for a different approach to definition in specialised lexicography).

In the terminological tradition, the definition serves exclusively to distinguish the term from other closely related terms (Vézina et al. 2009). Other relevant information is generally included in a separate, encyclopaedic field. This information may be just as useful for the lay reader who has little idea of how the subject field is structured conceptually, to fully grasp the concept. On the other hand, it is good practice for terms which are all specifics of the same generic (otherwise known in the lexicographic tradition as *hyperonyms* which share the same *hyponym*) to cast their definitions in the same structure. Thus, in the field of the insurance of the person, various forms of life insurance should be defined in the same way (example 1):

(1)

- *Term insurance: life insurance which pays benefits on the death of the insured within a specified period*
- *Whole of life insurance: life insurance which pays benefits on the death of the insured, whenever this occurs*
- *Pure endowment insurance: life insurance which provides benefits at the end of a specified period, provided the insured is still alive*

In example (1) we have three types of life insurance; *life insurance* is the generic term or hyperonym: *term insurance, whole of life insurance* and *pure endowment insurance* are specific types of life insurance or hyperonyms. The definitions are crafted in the same way so the user can easily identify what the differences between these sorts of life insurance are (and the list is not exhaustive). This method of definition can then be extended to different sorts of term insurance, whole of life insurance, etc.

Not all specialised dictionaries include fully fledged definitions, and it can be argued that some subject fields would not allow non-specialists to grasp the terms and therefore settle for "encyclopaedic notes" as in Kaufmann, Bergenholtz et al (1998).

20.3.5.2.3 EQUIVALENCES

The only obligatory field in the microstructure of a bilingual or multilingual dictionary – and in some cases the only field – is the equivalent.[3] Contrary to general language dictionaries, however, bilingual and multilingual specialised dictionaries often include both equivalent and definition, with the latter having the function of placing the headword in its conceptual context, thus helping pick up the right equivalent in the translation-related receptive task.

The choice of equivalents is often problematical in culture-bound areas (Van der Velde et al. 2012), but it should not be assumed that this poses no particular problem in non–culture-bound domains, such as chemistry or physics (Pimentel: 2013). Although this may be true of the natural sciences, it is far from being the case in most areas of technology. This is because terms, just like words, can have several meanings. In principle, polysemy is limited in LSPs because only one subject area is taken into consideration, but it often happens, through historical evolution and use of terms from other areas, that the same linguistic expression can represent more than one specialised concept. Even in the very narrow and relatively standardized field of mechanical construction, for example, the two English terms (and associated concepts) of *key* and *cotter* both correspond to one French term (and thus a single concept) of *clavette* (Arntz 1993:6). It is also possible that different language communities focus on different aspects of a concept: thus *serrations on a shaft* are characterized as *spikes* by English-speaking engineers, whereas their French colleagues focus on the interstices (*stries*) (Wüster 1968 [8.84]). The maritime dictionary has many examples of different conceptual systems: thus for *watch* in English, French equivalents are *veille* ('not sleeping'), *quart* ('on duty') and *bordée* ('crew on duty') (Van Campenhoudt 1996). This means that the English entry is divided into three, each with a distinct definition.

20.3.5.2.4 CONTEXTS

General language dictionaries often contain illustrative contexts in which the headword is featured. These may be authentic quotations or examples made up by the lexicographer. Similarly, special language dictionaries may also include one or several illustrative contexts, though these are more frequently taken from specialised documents of the field. An ISO standard (ISO 1087:1990, 6.1.5.7.), which defines a context as "A text or part of a text in which a term occurs" illustrates contexts in terminology work.[4] These include illustrating how the term is used in actual discourse, thereby supplementing the metalinguistic and encyclopaedic information found elsewhere in the entry. They may also give information which complements the formal definition or may indicate features which are useful for the understanding of the term. The principle of knowledge-rich contexts, developed for terminology extraction and analysis, are ideal illustrations for inclusion in dictionaries. Ingrid Meyer (2001: 281) first defined these as contexts which include at least one attribute or one relationship which help to identify characteristics useful for term analysis. Marshman (2014:226) has recently noted how useful these contexts are for one important category of user, that is, the trainee translator, by providing "in context" knowledge about the term within the speciality. The "terminology resource" proposed to meet this need is a database, similar to such tools as *DiCoInfo* and *DiCoEnviro*, which incorporates a text base and an analysis of the knowledge rich contexts, which categorize the relationships, which include the traditional generic–specific and part–whole, but also extend to cause–effect and entity–function, the markers of which can often be counterintuitive.

20.3.5.2.5 USAGE LABELS

This field is most often found in prescriptive dictionaries, either those editing by standardization boards (such as ISO or their national equivalents) or language planning authorities (e.g. Office québécois de la langue française). Its purpose is to inform the reader about the status of the term, which may be recommended or, on the contrary, deprecated. Usage markers can also indicate the degree of specialisation of a term: is it used only by specialists or only by a lay public? They may also give indication of the geographical specificities: in an automobile or railway dictionary in English, there will be considerable differences of this nature, even in such relatively unified languages such as Dutch, where Van der Veld et al (2012) report considerable differences between Belgium and the Netherlands in accounting terms. These differences will have an impact on the macrostructure in bilingual and multilingual dictionaries, as their equivalences will be different. They may also give an indication as to whether a term is still current, not yet current or no longer current.

20.3.5.2.6 SOURCES

There may be one field to indicate the origin of information in a dictionary article, but best practice requires any part of the entry to be fully sourced. Thus all fields may be concerned. The form used for the headword may be that recommended by a particular technical standard (ISO, BS, DIN, etc.; Wüster 1968); the definition may be taken without modification from a particular source (this is of vital importance for standardised terms or legal terms);

the contexts should similarly be referenced, as part of their function is to attest the usage of experts.

20.3.5.2.7 SYNONYMS OR VARIANTS

The treatment of synonyms in terminology has evolved since Wüster's time, when one of the goals of terminology was held to be the elimination of synonyms. However, Wüster (1968) included these in his prototype dictionary, following the headword (i.e. the approved term), Laterly, terminologists have been encouraged to recognize synonyms and provide the user of the dictionary with information about differences in usage.

20.3.5.2.8 NOTES

Notes can include all information not already provided in one of the specific fields, and its content will thus depend on what fields have been provided. The additional information may concern the concept dealt with in the entry, providing more encyclopaedic information, or may concern the term itself, from a metalinguistic point of view – for example explaining the origin of the term or its changes in meaning, or an epilinguistic point of view, giving an opinion on the term itself as a word. *See also* indicates to the reader where further information on the headword may be found, thereby providing the means of navigating round the dictionary and taking the form of hyperlinks in electronic dictionaries. These cross-references are important in distributing the data in accessible forms according to function, the so-called mediostructure (Oliveira and Peters 2009).

20.3.5.2.9 ILLUSTRATIONS AND OTHER GRAPHIC DEVICES

Illustrations and other graphic devices are typical of many sorts of LSP texts (Kocourek 1991:10–11), so it is only natural that specialised dictionaries make intensive use of them. Ushered in by Diderot's *Encyclopédie*, the use of illustrations became an integral part of many specialised dictionaries and encyclopaedias (eleven of its twenty-eight volumes were wholly devoted to illustrations). Dictionaries of chemistry include chemical formulae, dictionaries of mechanics diagrams showing how machinery functions, etc. Captain Paasch's (1894) dictionary in its second edition comprises 109 pages of illustration, which clarify equivalences, often differently in individual pairs of languages. In the third edition, 3750 elements of a ship were illustrated for 11,700 concepts (Van Campenhoudt 1997: 86).

20.3.6 Language information included

Traditionally, special language dictionaries exclusively contained information on the topic covered with little or no attention paid to language use. Many of the fields found in a general language dictionary were therefore largely missing in a special language dictionary, though not systematically. For example, the *Oxford Dictionary of Nursing* from its first edition (McFerran and Martin 1990) has included an indication of the pronunciation of certain terms, medical terms posing problems of pronunciation to both native and non-native users. With the emergence of the concept of language for special purposes (LSP), however, it became obvious that specialities have their own usages, and that these can and indeed should be mirrored in dictionaries. This was recognized in dictionaries to be used for translation services, in particular in bilingual countries such as Canada, where the need for highly specialised dictionaries containing information on the phraseology of a particular subject field made itself felt (RINT 1993). Many of these dictionaries were made by terminology services, such as that of the Canadian federal government, but some were elaborated to accompany non-native students embarking on specialised course, and thus represent specialised learner's dictionaries. Phraseology is also important in culture-based domains, such as law (Buendia Castro and Faber 2015).

20.3.7 *Medium: paper or electronic*

As for general language dictionaries, the use of electronic form makes systematic or alphabetical presentation irrelevant for the user. Furthermore, because many terms are made up of more than one word, users find it easier to search than in paper format (Kaalep and Mikk 2008: 388). One of the most commonly used electronic special language dictionary is the term bank. Bergenholtz (2009) warns, however, that the mere fact of using the electronic format is not enough to facilitate easy access: it took longer in his experiment to access factual information in the term bank (*IATE*) than in a paper dictionary when indeed the information searched for was present. Marshman (2014: 245) regrets that more use has not been made by the big term banks of the possibilities that electronic format offers, including "customizable displays, multimedia content, dynamic representation of the information, hyperlinks and other intuitive methods of navigation". Køhler Simonsen (2014) encourages experiments using mobile phones as a medium for specialised dictionaries and reports on one made for medical doctors, although he reckons that the ease of access is less than optimal because of interference from the outside world.

20.3.8 *Authorship*

Traditionally, specialised dictionaries were made by subject specialists. Eugen Wüster was an engineer who trained himself in lexicography, which he adapted for LSP. Today, most term banks are maintained by professional terminologists (i.e. linguists trained in term management). In spite of the change in specialisation, these can still be considered "top-down" dictionaries. "Bottom-up" lexicography is best illustrated by the collaborative encyclopaedia, *Wikipedia*, which has quickly become what is probably the world's most used specialised dictionaries, as just one of its functions. Some individual lexicographers intend to use crowdsourcing to update and expand their dictionaries, such as the *Kicktionary* (Schmidt 131). Some university online terminology databases are at least partly created by students or trainee translators, offering thematic terminology to a broader audience, which includes students (see Kübler and Pecman (2012) for the earth sciences).

20.3.9 *Degree of autonomy of an LSP dictionary*

Fuertes-Olivera and Tarp (2014:7) note that LSP dictionaries can take the form of "lexica, glossaries, vocabularies" thereby underlining that they are not necessarily stand-alone books or electronic packages. The glossaries found at the end of textbooks or theses can also be claimed to be varieties of LSP dictionaries, but ones which have been infrequently studied. These "dependent" dictionaries usually have as their criteria of selection the terms contained in the main work (book, treaties, thesis or other) which need explaining. These generally short works have the advantage of accompanying the texts where the specialised terms occur, and are frequently written by subject-field specialists. In the case of theses, the terms defined are those resulting from the candidate's research and may represent the most up-to-date account of cutting-edge neology. The drawback of this type of dictionary is that the contents are rarely incorporated into larger term banks where they would reach a broader audience (but see Holzem 1999). Verlinde, Leroyer and Binon (2010) predict that electronic dictionaries – specialised ones in particular – will be more and more frequently incorporated into an interactive environment, in particular in learning situations.

20.4 Looking to the future

Some corpus linguists predict that consulting corpora are replacing dictionaries at least for some functions, in particular in language-learning contexts (see Chambers 2007). Buyse and Verlinde (2013) found the translation-memory tool *Linguee* to be more efficient in writing tests than traditional dictionaries (see also Alonso Jiménez 2013), and suggest that lexical information be placed in other tools than dictionaries. Indeed, the key word could be claimed to be collaboration: dictionaries, and functions of dictionaries, incorporated into other tools, or into a toolbox, as Verlinde et al. (2010) suggest.

Collaborative specialised dictionaries have not experienced the same revolution as encyclopaedias, where the bottom-up, multilingual *Wikipedia* has been a game-changer, driving traditional, top-down authored encyclopaedias to the wall. We argue that *Wikipedia* has taken on some of the roles of specialised dictionaries, in particularly in areas not previously touched by dictionaries or terminologies, in particular in the sphere of popular culture, not considered worthy of inclusion in traditional works. *Wikipedia*'s great strength is indeed in its scope, covering a very large number of domains in many languages, most of which dispose of few if any traditional dictionaries. Thanks to links to different language versions of *Wikipedia*, it offers unrivalled availability of resource. It can be used as a bilingual specialised dictionary with considerable authenticity, since each language version is usually elaborated directly in the language concerned. In-house dictionaries are defined by their readership, which is limited to a specific institution (private or public, commercial or not-for-profit). The specialisation is thus that of the institution itself. Corporate or in-house terminology has been theorized by de Vecchi (2004) under the name of *pragmatermilogy* and developed in dictionary form by Leroyer and Møller (2006) and Leroyer (2007), who mention specifications for databases to be used by the institutions. Some in-house dictionaries have been created at the instigation of the institution itself, such as the European Court of Human Rights (Humbley, et al. 1999), where the bulk of the terminology presented comes from the written production of the institution itself (in this case to treaties, agreements, decisions), and indeed is intended to refer back to these documents by a system of hyperlinks.

20.5 Conclusion

Today, the paper encyclopaedia clearly belongs to the past. It will probably not be long until the paper specialised dictionary is also consigned to history. The forms that the electronic dictionary may take will be many and varied, doubtlessly even more so than the paper predecessor. Many of the functions previously played by the specialised dictionary may well migrate to other environments: *Wikipedia*, translation memory and simply the use of hyperlinks to access knowledge where it is available.

The trend to incorporate dictionaries or dictionary functions into other applications or tools affects specialised as well as general lexicography. As Tarp (2008: 127) suggests, dictionaries may function as "how-to's", books giving instructions on how to do specific things such as how to operate machines. Whatever the form taken, it can be assumed that many of the building blocks which can be assembled according to need from a centralized platform will be simply developments of terms, equivalents, language and conceptual relations, which were already present in more rigid forms in the specialised paper dictionary.

Related topics

Lexicography and terminology; domain ontologies; terminological knowledge bases; Accounting Dictionaries; FrameNet; the Oenolex wine dictionary; the Alicante Dictionaries; user participation in the era of the Internet.

Further reading

Bergenholtz, H. and S. Tarp (1995). *Manual of Specialised Lexicography*, Amsterdam/Philadelphia, John Benjamins Publishing Co.
This is the international version of the handbook that established specialised lexicography as an autonomous discipline and against which subsequent studies position themselves.

Fuertes-Olivera, P. A. and A. Arribas-Baño (2008). *Pedagogical Specialised Lexicography*. Amsterdam/Philadelphia: John Benjamins.
This monography is exclusively devoted to specialised dictionaries for learners, though limited to the business sector and the English-Spanish language pair.

Kockaert, H. and F. Steurs (eds.) (2015). *Handbook of Terminology (HOT), volume 1*. Amsterdam, Philadelphia: John Benjamins Publishing Company.
Many of the chapters in this first of a series of five volumes concern the lexicological dimension of terminology.

Three journals can also be recommended:

Terminology: International Journal of Theoretical and Applied Issues in Specialized Communication: www.jbe-platform.com/content/journals/15699994

Fachsprache: International Journal of Specialized Communication:
www.fachsprache.net/upload/Fachsprache_3-4_2009_gesamt.pdf

Hermes Journal of Language and Communication in Business:
http://bcom.au.dk/research/publications/journals/hermes/

Nielsen, S. (1994). *The Bilingual LSP Dictionary: Principles and Practice for Legal language*. Tübingen: Gunter Narr. (Forum für Fachsprachen-Forschung 24).
This pioneering book provides the foundation for understanding the principles of bilingual lexicography in the context of a culture-determined field.

Notes

1 Gasiglia (2012) refers to *mass specialised lexicon*, ("lexique spécialisé de masse"), used for certain popular yet specialised activities, such as sports, which are conveyed to a very broad section of the public by written and spoken press. Sager, Dunghill and McDonald (1980:3) already recognized this: "The fact that humbler occupations like nursing, book-keeping and cooking and even hobbies also involve special areas of human interest and therefore require and indeed have their own special language is much less often acknowledged".
2 www.projetdafa.net/
3 Translators distinguish between equivalents and translations. Only messages can be translated. Equivalents are words or terms that can virtually be used. Van Campenhoudt (2003:2) describes the equivalent as the best synonym in the foreign language.

4 • defining context, including features which help to distinguish the term from semantically related concepts;
- explanatory context, including information which helps the non-specialist to understand the term;
- associative context, including concepts semantically connected to the term;
- linguistic context, illustrating the behaviour of the term in discourse;
- metalinguistic context, in which the author of the text quotes and possibly analyses the term.

References

Websites

DiColnfo, Le dictionnaire fondamental de l'informatique et de l'Internet: http://olst.ling.umontreal.ca/cgi-bin/dicoinfo/search.cgi
Elsevier Dictionaries: www.nhbs.com/series/48180/elsevier-dictionaries
Kicktionary: the multilingual electronic dictionary of football language www.kicktionary.de/
Linguee: www.linguee.com
Office québécois de la langue française: www.oqlf.gouv.qc.ca/
Paasch – Marine dictionary: www.termisti.org/chronique52.pdf

Other literature

Alipour, M., B. Robichaud, B. and M. C. L'Homme (2015) "Towards an Electronic Specialised Dictionary for Learners", in I. Kosem, M. Jakubiček, J. Kallas, and S. Krek (eds.), *Electronic Lexicography in the 21st Century: Linking Lexical Data in the Digital Age: Proceedings of the eLex 2015 Conference, 11–13 August 2015, Herstmonceux Castle, United Kingdom.* Ljubljana/Brighton: Trojina, Institute for Applied Slovene Studies/Lexical Computing Ltd., pp. 51–69.
Alonso Jiménez, E. (2013) "Linguee y las nuevas formas de traducir", *Skopos* 2: 5–28.
Arntz, R. (1993) "Terminological Equivalence and Translation", in H. Sonneveld and K. Leunig (eds.), *Terminology: Applications in Interdisciplinary Communication.* Amsterdam/Philadelphia: John Benjamin, pp. 5–19.
Antia, B. E. (2005) "Lexicography Versus Terminography: Some Practical Reasons for Distinction", *TermNet: International Network for Terminology.* www.termnet.org/english/projects/TermTrain_Presentations.php.
Bergenholtz, H. (2009) "Schneller und sicherer Datenzugriff in gedruckten und elektronischen Fachwörterbüchern und Lexika", *Revue française de linguistique appliquée* XIV/2: 93–97.
Bergenholtz, H. and U. Kaufmann (1997) "Terminography and Lexicography: A Critical Survey of Dictionaries From a Single Specialised Field", *Hermes* 18: 91–125.
Bergenholtz, H. and S. Tarp (1995) *Manual of Specialised Lexicography.* Amsterdam/Philadelphia: John Benjamins Publishing Co.
Bessé, B. de (1994) "Contribution à la définition de la terminologie", in P. Martel and J. Maurais (eds.), *Langues et sociétés en contact: Mélanges offerts à Jean-Claude Corbeil.* Tübingen: Max Niemeyer, pp. 135–138.
Binon, J., S. Verlinde and J. Van Dyck (2007) *Dictionnaire d'apprentissage du français des affaires: dictionnaire de compréhension et de production de la langue des affaires.* Paris: Didier.
Bowker, L. (2003) "Specialised Lexicography and Specialised Dictionaries", in P. van Sterkenburg (ed.), *A Practical Guide to Lexicography.* Amsterdam: John Benjamins, pp. 154–164.
Buendia Castro, M. and P. Faber (2015) "Phraseological Units in English-Spanish Legal Dictionaries: A Comparative Study", *Fachsprache* 37/3–4: 161–175.
Buyse, C. and S. Verlinde (2013) "The Effect of Free on Line Data Driven Lexicographic Instruments on Language Learning", *Procedia – Social and Behavioral Sciences* 95: 507–412. www.fnrs.be/SITE2/Donnees/as400data/rap2013/cng2013.htm

Chambers, A. (2007) "Popularising Corpus Consultation by Language Learners and Teachers", in E. Hildalgo, L. Quereda and J. Santana (eds.) *Corpora in the Foreign Language Classroom: Selected Papers From the Sixth International Conference on Teaching and Language Corpora*. Amsterdam and New York: Rodopi, pp. 3–16.

Costa, R. (2013) "Terminology and Specialised Lexicography: Two Complementary Domains", *Lexicographica* 29: 29–42.

Dancette, J. (2013) *Dictionnaire analytique de la mondialisation et du travail – Analytical Dictionary of Globalisation and Labour – Diccionario analítico de la mundialización y del trabajo*. Montréal: Centre de recherche universitaire sur la mondialisation et de travail. http://damt-dico.rhcloud.com/ http://damt-dico.rhcloud.com/index

Dancette, J. and C. Réthoré (1997) "Le Dictionnaire bilingue (anglais-français) de la distribution: entre dictionnaire de langue et encylopédie", *Meta* 42(2): 229–243.

Delavigne, V. (2008a) "Les mots des patients atteints de cancer: Socioterminologie et pratique professionnelle en santé", *Les langues de spécialité en question: perspectives d'étude et applications* 2007, Paris: 18–32. hal-00920651v1

Delavigne, V. (2008b) "Construire un dictionnaire d'oncologie pour les patients: aspects méthodologiques", *Corpus et dictionnaires de langues de spécialité*, PUG: 153–173. hal-00920650v1.

Dubuc, R. (1997) *Terminology: A Practical Approach*, adapted by E. Kennedy. Quebec: Linguatech.

Fuertes-Olivera, P. A. (2009) "Systematic Introductions in Specialised Dictionaries: Some Proposals in Relation to Accounting Dictionaries", in S. Nielsen and S.Tarp (eds.), *Lexicography in the 21st Century: In Honour of Henning Bergenholtz*. Amsterdam/Philadelphia: John Benjamins, pp. 161–178.

Fuertes-Olivera, P. A. and A. Arribas-Baño (2008) *Pedagogical Specialised Lexicography*. Amsterdam/Philadelphia: John Benjamins.

Fuertes-Olivera, P. A. and S. Tarp (2014) "*Theory and Practice of Specialised Online Dictionaries: Lexicography Versus Terminography*, Berlin, Boston: de Gruyter, and review by Pilar Léon-Arauaz and Pamela Faber (2015)", *Terminology* 21/1: 126–136.

Gasiglia, N. (2012) "Exploiter les énoncés de corpus thématiques à haut rendement pour décrire des prédicats verbaux de lexiques spécialisés de masse", *Lexicographica* 28 ('Corpora and lexicography'): 207–232.

Hausmann, F. J. (1989) "Wörterbuchtypologie", in Hausmann et al., pp. 968–981.

Hausmann, F. J., O. Reichmann, H. E. Wiegand and L. Zgusta (eds.) (1989–1991) *Wörterbücher, Dictionaries, Dictionnaires: An International Encyclopedia of Lexicography*. Berlin, New York: Walter de Gruyter (= *Handbücher zur Sprach- und Kommunikationswissenschaft, Band 5.1., 5.2; 5.3*)

Hermans, A. (1997) *Les dictionnaires spécialisés et l'analyse de la valeur; Actes du colloque organisé en avril 1995 par le Centre de terminologie de Bruxelles* (Institut libre Marie Haps, Louvain La Neuve, Peeters Bibliothèque des cahiers de l'Institut de linguistique de Louvain, n° 87)

Holzem, M. (1999) *Terminologie et documentation: pour une meilleure circulation des savoirs*. Paris : ADBS éditions.

Humbley, J. (2007) "Réflexions autour de la définition du champ de l'anglistique de spécialité: le cas de l'Europe du Nord", *Asp* 2007: 53–70.

Humbley, J., D. Bourigault and C. Chodkiewicz (1999) "Some Techniques and Tools for Tailor-Made Terminologies", in P. Sandrini (ed.), *TKE'99 Terminology and Knowledge Engineering*, Vienna: Termnet, pp. 378–390.

Kaalep, H-J., and J. Mikk (2008) "Creating Specialised Dictionaries for Foreign Language Learners: A Case Study", *International Journal of Lexicography* 21(4): 369–394.

Kageura, K. (2015) "Terminology and Lexicography", in J. Kockaert and F. Steurs (eds.), *Handbook of Terminology*. Volume 1. Amsterdam/Philadelphia: John Benjamins, pp. 45–59.

Kaufmann, U. and H. Bergenholtz in cooperation with B. Stummann, S. Tarp, L. de la Rosa Marabet, N. de la Serra Torres and G. la Serna Miranda (1998) *Encyclopedic Dictionary of Gene Technology, vol. 1, English (With Spanish equivalents)*, 385 p. Volume 2, Spanish (With English equivalents). Toronto: Lugus Libros.

Kockaert, H. and F. Steurs (eds.) (2015) *Handbook of Terminology* (*HOT*). Volume 1, Amsterdam, Philadelphia: John Benjamins.

Kocourek, R. ([1982] 1991) *La langue française de la technique et de la science. Vers une linguistique de la langue savante*, Wiesbaden: Otto Brandstetter Verlag.

Køhler Simonsen, H. (2014) "Mobile Lexicography: A Survey of the Mobile User Situation", in A. Abel, C. Vettori and N. Ralli (eds.), *Proceedings of the XVI EURALEX International Congress: The User in Focus. 15–19 July 2014, Bolzano/Bozen*, pp. 249–261. www.euralex.org/elx_proceedings/Euralex2014/euralex_2014_017_p_249.pdf

Kübler, N. and M. Pecman (2012) "The ARTES Bilingual LSP Dictionary: From Collocation to Higher Order Phraseology", in S. Granger and M. Paquot (eds.), *Electronic lexicography*. Oxford: Oxford University Press, pp. 187–207.

Leroyer, P. (2007) "Bringing Corporate Dictionary Design Into Accord With Corporate Image: From Words to Messages and Back Again", in H. Gotlieb and J. Mogensen (eds.), *Dictionaries, Lexicographical Options and User Needs*. Amsterdam: Benjamins, pp. 109–117.

Leroyer, P. and H. Bergenholtz (2013) "Métalexicographie culturelle, fonctions lexicographiques et finalité pragmatique", in M. Murano and G. Tallarico (eds.), *Special issue of Les dictionnaires bilingues et l'interculturel, Etudes de linguistique appliquée/ELA* 170, pp. 139–152.

Leroyer, P. and B. Møller (2006) "Intégration du genre dans le dictionnaire d'entreprise: le cas des *case stories*", in M. Gotti and D. Giannoni (eds.), *New Trends in Specialised Disccourse Analysis*. Bern: Peter Lang, pp. 91–108.

L'Homme, M.-C. (2009) *DiCoInfo: Le Dictionnaire fondamental de l'informatique et de l'Internet*. Montréal: Université de Montréal.

L'Homme, M.-C. (2014) *Manuel de DiCoInfo*. http://olst.ling.umontreal.ca/dicoinfo/manuel-DiCoInfo.pdf.

Marshman, E. (2014) "Enriching Terminology Resources With Knowledge-Rich Contexts: A Case Study", *Terminology* 20(2): 225–249.

McFerran, T. and E. Martin (1990) *Oxford Dictionary of Nursing*. 3rd edition. Oxford: Oxford University Press.

Meyer, I. (2001) "Extracting Knowledge-Rich Contexts for Terrminography: A Conceptual and Methodological Framework", in D. Bourigault, C. Jacquemin, and M. C. L'Homme (eds.), *Recent Advances in Computational Terminology*. Amsterdam: John Benjamin, pp. 279–302.

Mikkelsen, H. K. (1991) "Towards the Ideal Special Language Translation Dictionary", *Hermes* 6: 91–109.

Nielsen, S. (1994) *The Bilingual LSP Dictionary: Principles and Practice for Legal language*. Tübingen: Gunter Narr.

Nielsen, S. (2011) "Function- and User-related Definitions in Online Dictionaries", in F. I. Kartashkove (ed.), *Ivanovo School of Lexicography: Traditions and Innovations. A Festschrif in Honour of Professor Olga Karpova*. Ivanovo: Ivanovo State University, pp. 197–219.

Nilsson, H. (2015) "Enumerations Count: Extensional and Partitive Definitions", in J. Kockaert and F. Steurs (eds.), *Handbook of Terminology*, vol. 1. Amsterdam/Philadelphia: John Benjamins Publishing Company, pp. 82–100.

Oliveira, C. and P. Peters (2009) "Ontologies in the Mediostructure of LSP e-Dictionaries", *eLEX* 2009: 169–171 www.ucllouvain.be/cps/ucl/doc/cecl/documents/eLEX_book_abstracts_FINAL_New.pdf#page=183

Paasch, H. (1885, 1937) *De la quille à la pomme de mât. Dictionnaire de marine*. Antwerp. https://archive.org/details/DeLaQuilleALaPommeDeMat.

Pimentel, J. (2013) "Methodological Bases for Assigning Terminological Equivalents: A Contribution", *Terminology* 19(2): 237–257.

RINT (1993) *Phraséologie et terminologie*

Petiot, G. (1982) *Robert des sports*, Les usuels de Robert 1982

Routledge (1996) *French dictionary of Business, Commerce and Finance*

Sager, J. C, D. Dungworth and P. F. McDonald (1980) *English Special Languages: Principles and Practice in Science and Technology*. Wiesbaden: Oscar Brandstetter Verlag.

Schmidt, T. (2008) "The Kicktionary: Combining Corpus Linguistics and Lexical Semantics for a Multilingual Football Dictionary", in E. Lavric, G. Pisek, A. Skinner and W. Stadler (eds.), *The Linguistics of Football*. Tübingen: Gunter Narr Verlag, pp. 11–23.

Schmidt, T. (2014) "Kicktionary", in A. Burkhardt and P. Schlobinski (eds.), *Flickflack, Foul und Tsukahara: Der Sport und seine Sprache*. Mannheim, Dudenverlag, pp. 117–131.

Sterkenburg, P. van (2003) "Onomasiological Specifications and a Concise History of Onomasiological Dictionaries", in van Sterkenburg (ed.), *A Practical Guide to Lexicography*. Amsterdam: Benjamin, pp. 127–153.

Tarp, S. (2008) "The Third Leg of Two-Legged Lexicography", *Hermes* 40: 117–131.

Ten Hacken, P. (2015) "Terms and Specialised Vocabulary: Taming the Prototypes", in J. Kockaert and F. Steurs (eds.), *Handbook of Terminology*. Volume 1. Amsterdam/Philadelphia : John Benjamins Publishing Company, pp. 3–13.

Van Campenhoudt, M. (1996) "Réseau notionnel, intelligence artificielle et équivalence en terminologie multilingue: essai de modélisation", in A. Clas, P. Thoiron and H. Béjoint (eds.) *Lexicomatique et dictionnairiques, IVes journées scientifiques du réseau thématique Lexicologie, terminologie, traduction, Université Lumière (Lyon II), 28–30 septembre 1995*, Montréal, AUPELF-UREF and Beyrouth, F.M.A., pp. 281–306. www.termisti.org/marcweb.htm.

Van Campenhoudt, M. (1997) "Evaluation des terminographies multilingues: le dictionnaire nautique du capitaine Paasch au dictionnaire aéronautique de l'ingénieur Schlomann", in A. Hermans (ed.), 75–115.

Van Campenhoudt, M. (2003) "L'évolution des dictionnaires du domaine de la maritime au XIXè siècle: aux sources de *De la quille à la pomme de mât*", *Chronique d'histoire maritime*, revue de la Société française d'histoire maritime, septembre 2003, n° 52 : 83–97. www.termisti.org/chronique52.pdf.

Van der Velde, W., M. Van Campenhoudt, N. Lemaire and P. Muraille (2012) "Problèmes d'équivalence notionnelle: le découpage des phases d'une mission d'audit interne en français et en néerlandais", *Actes de la Journée d'études du Cratil (ISIT, Paris), Terminologies – La terminologie face au défi de la traduction et de l'interculturel* (1er avril 2011), in *Le bulletin du CRATIL*, septembre 2012, n° 9, pp. 152–133. www.termisti.org/cratil_termisti.pdf.

Vecchi, Dardo de (2004) "La terminologie dans la communication de l'entreprise: bases d'une pragmaterminologie", in C. Cortès (ed.), *Cahiers du CIEL 2004*, pp. 71–83. www.eila.univ-paris-diderot.fr/_media/recherche/clillac/ciel/cahiers/2004/cahierciel2004.pdf#page=71

Verlinde, S., P. Leroyer and J. Binon (2010) "Search and You Will Find", *International Journal of Lexicography* 23(1): 1–17.

Vézina, R., X. Darras, J. Bédard and M. Lapointe-Giguère (2009) *La rédaction de définitions terminologiques*. Montréal: Office québécois de la langue française. www.oqlf.gouv.qc.ca/ressources/bibliotheque/terminologie/redaction_def_terminologiques_2009.pdf.

Wiegand, H. E. (1998) *Wörterbuchforschung. Untersuchungen zur Wörterbuch-benutzung, zur Theorie, Geschichte, Kritik und Automatisierung der Lexikographie*.1. Teilband. Berlin/New York: de Gruyter.

Wiegand, H. E. (2001) "Was eigentlich sind Wörterbuchfunktionen? Kritische Anmerkungen zur neueren und neuesten Wörterbuchforschung", *Lexicographica* 17: 217–248.

Williams, G. (2011) "The Learner's Dictionary and the Sciences: Mismatch or No Match?", in Kübler (ed.), *Corpora, Language, Teaching, and Resources: From Theory to Practice*. Bern: Peter Lang, pp. 323–340.

Wüster, E. (1931): *Internationale Sprachnormung in der Technik, besonders in der Elektrotechnik*. Berlin: VDJ.

Wüster, E. (1968) *The Machine Tool: An Interlingual Dictionary of Basic Concepts*. London: Technical Press.

Wüster, E. (1971) "Begriffs- und Themaklassifikationen: Unterschiede in ihrem Wesen und in ihrer Anwendung", *Nachrichten für Dokumentation* 22 (3), pp. 98–104, and (4), pp. 143–150.

Zanola, M. T. (2010) "Histoire des sciences et des techniques, histoire des dictionnaires", *Les Cahiers du dictionnaire* 2 : 45–48.

Zanola, M. T. (2014) *Arts et métiers au XVIIIe siècle: études de terminologie diachronique*; preface by A. Rey; postface by B/Madinier, Paris: L'Harmattan.

21
Terminological knowledge bases

Anne Condamines

21.1 Introduction

This chapter addresses issues concerning terminological knowledge bases (TKBs). A TKB was initially defined at the crossroads of terminology and knowledge engineering as a knowledge base taking into account the twofold nature of a term: conceptual and linguistic. In fact, at the beginning, issues concerning TKBs mainly concerned the way knowledge engineering could help terminologists to structure specialised knowledge. The main aim was to build knowledge representation models that were usable by tools. On the one hand, this step was of great importance for the improvement of terminology studies, particularly because terminologists had to analyse the link between terms and specialised discourses. But, on the other hand, the necessity of representing knowledge under a network model sometimes appeared to be too restrictive and too far remote from discourse, and this point generated dissatisfaction. Nevertheless, an unforeseen result of studies developed with the aim of building TKBs from texts was that tool-assisted methods were designed for exploring specialised texts systematically. First, this chapter presents the origins and the aim of terminological knowledge bases. Second, it details the tool-assisted linguistic methods for building TKBs from texts. Finally, it shows how similar methods may be applied to meet other needs in which terms and relations are not the result of linguistic analyses but rather the point of departure for the study of specialized texts. Note that the viewpoint adopted in this chapter is mainly that of a linguist.

21.2 Historical perspectives

In the case of terminological knowledge bases, a historical perspective is very important because this concept symbolizes the confluence between at least two disciplines: terminology and knowledge engineering. The name itself reflects this dual heritage. The first occurrence of this name was in articles produced by I. Meyer and her team in the Cogniterm project (Meyer et al. 1992), but other teams, at almost the same time, were developing similar projects and methods to build them (in Surrey, (Ahmad 1993); in Toulouse, (Condamines and Amsili 1993)). In all cases, the teams involved in the project were composed of linguists/terminologists and computer scientists, a clear sign that the concept presented an interest for both communities. In the following two sections, the respective interests of the two communities in this concept are presented.

21.2.1 Knowledge engineering point of view

In the 1990s and even before, some authors noted the possible convergence between terminology and artificial intelligence (Parent 1989). For example Wijnands (1993: 168) wrote: "Terminology and artificial intelligence face the same problem". For knowledge engineering, three elements motivated the encounter with terminology:

1 *Taking into account the linguistic nature of computerized representations*: When knowledge has to be represented, knowledge engineering models always use linguistic forms to designate the represented objects. This way of labelling representations is very important because these models are built to give access to textual data; thus, they have to use the same character strings as the ones used in texts. The problem is that these labels are not only character strings, they are also words, which implies meaningful elements. They allow the switch between the formal representations and the texts. For most knowledge engineers, it appeared crucial to take this twofold aspect of linguistic labels into account.

2 *Integrating terminological data into existing models of representation*: The most widely used model of knowledge representation in the 1990s, and even now, is the one using conceptual networks in which both nodes and links are labelled by linguistic forms. In such models, the node labels may easily correspond to terms and the link labels to conceptual relations. This mode of representation influenced terminologists and led them to develop methods to build terminological networks from texts, but also to focus only on contexts assumed to be useful for building a relational representation (see Section 21.4).

3 *Exploring textual data rather than just soliciting experts*: For several years, knowledge acquisition was done by interviewing experts about their own knowledge. This method was rather unsatisfactory, however, for two main reasons. Experts were not always prepared to contribute to this process either for lack of time or because they did not understand how to collaborate with knowledge engineers. In addition, it appeared that domain experts had some difficulty describing their own knowledge, and sometimes their description did not correspond to their practices. The use of expert texts was considered as a good solution to tackle these difficulties.

21.2.2 Terminological point of view

From a terminological viewpoint, four elements contributed to the junction with knowledge engineering.

1 *Need for the management of technical documentation* (Condamines 1995): Since the 1980s, the e-management of massive amounts of documentation had become a great challenge within firms. For example, in the Airbus Company, it was estimated that the documentation concerning a plane would fill the plane. So a large number of projects were developed in order to assist in processing the documentation. In most of these projects, terminology played a crucial role.

2 *Inadequacy of existing terminological resources*: With these new needs emerging within firms, most of the terminologies developed by official bodies appeared to be inadequate because they were too far from real uses. Moreover, most engineers did not even know that there were terminological standards built by official bodies. For terminologies to be usable in documentation management within firms, it became necessary to build them based on real usage.
3 *Development of corpus linguistics methods*: At the end of the 1980s and the beginning of the 1990s, several projects to build general corpora were carried out, especially for English. One of their main aims was to design methods to help dictionary definitions. One of the most important projects was the design of the *Cobuild* dictionary, using a large corpus. Sinclair anchored the process and inspired generations of lexicographers (Sinclair 1991). At the same time, studies were carried out on definitions in discourse (Flowerdew 1992). The main bases of e-lexicology were then defined and usable for building terminologies from texts. See Chapter 8 in this volume.
4 *Development of natural language processing tools*: During the 1990s, natural language processing perspectives evolved. The main point became not only to implement formalisms assumed to be relevant for describing the functioning of language, but rather to help a user to use the texts. Concordancers were designed and made available to linguists, but also tools dedicated to the exploration of specialized corpora such as candidate-terms extractors or candidate-relations extractors (see later and Chapter 12 this volume).

The 1990s and 2000s were also marked by the fact that a large number of researchers criticized the General Theory of Terminology, developed by an Austrian engineer, Eugen Wüster, during the 1930s. In order to limit the difficulties inherent to language functioning, he proposed to standardize terminology, considering that specialized languages were very different from general language because they were used in highly constrained situations. He thought that it was easy to standardise the terminology in such controlled situations (Wüster 1974). With such a point of view, it was necessary to keep terminology away from linguistics and to consider terms as just labels of concepts which became the main elements to be studied (Wüster 1979).

Unfortunately, even if they have some specific characteristics, specialised texts are not so different from general ones and it is impossible to control all the possible variations of terms.

New theories such as socioterminology (Gaudin 1990), sociocognitive terminology (Temmerman 2000) or the communicative theory of terminology (Cabré 1999) were proposed to describe terms according to their functioning in real situations. All these approaches can be subsumed under the term of "textual terminology" (Pearson 1998).

So both from an applicative and a theoretical point of view – knowledge engineering and terminology – all the parameters were converging towards the definition of a new concept developed to take into account the methods and needs common to both knowledge engineering and textual terminology, namely the *terminological knowledge base*.

21.3 Core issues and topics

Even if many projects have developed different models of TKBs, some characteristics are always present in the definition of a terminological knowledge base.

21.3.1 Distinction between terms and concepts

Whatever the model, in a TKB, there are always two levels for representing knowledge. The first one may be considered as the conceptual level, that supports the network representation; the second one is the linguistic level, in charge of the lexicalization of the conceptual level in each language or language community considered. From a linguistic point of view, this representation can be criticised because it assumes that there is a unique knowledge representation, common to all languages. In the wake of Sapir and Whorf's work, it is difficult to accept such a point of view because, as they claimed, language shapes our behaviour and not the opposite. Nevertheless, this linguistic relativism should be qualified, for two reasons. First, TKBs are concerned by a limited domain and, in most cases, by a limited application. Within this domain and this application, one may consider that there is no crucial variation in knowledge representation among languages, even if it is a strong hypothesis. Second, this representation is very useful in order to deal with phenomena such as synonymy (two terms/ one concept) or polysemy (one term/two linked concepts) and even inter-linguistic equivalence (one concept/terms in different languages). Finally, the representation is controlled both by the uses within the corpus and by the aim of the TKB design.

21.3.2 Knowledge representation in a network form

Probably the most important characteristic of a TKB, at least for terminologists, is the fact that knowledge is represented in the form of conceptual relations. In previous terminological databases, definitions appeared in a discursive form. The challenge with TKBs was to replace most of these discursive forms by a reticular one, that is to say, first, to de-contextualise the terms and, second, to retain only the contexts that can be used to code knowledge in a network form. This form is not always adequate and may lead to a loss of knowledge. However, as for the separation between concepts and terms, this representational choice may have advantages. The most important one is that terminological data become manageable by tools and then tools can be used to verify the terminological data: consistency, completeness and so on. For example if a father (*hypernym*) appears as having only one son (*hyponym*), which seems impossible from a linguistic point of view, the user may be alerted and then try to identify at least one *co-hyponym* (a brother) within the corpus or by consulting an expert.

21.3.3 Corpus as a source of knowledge

TKBs are always built by using a corpus as a source of knowledge. As a result, the first step in the study consists in building a corpus that is well adapted not only to the domain but also, most of the time, to the application concerned by the resource. Then, as for general corpora, the specialised corpus becomes the object to be studied and must be as representative as possible.

From a linguistic point of view, the emergence of the TKB concept led to two kinds of studies, the first concerning the characterisation of the specificities of terms and how to spot them within a corpus, the second concerning the description of relationships and how they are expressed within corpora.

Of course, studies on these two issues already existed. The definition of terms had been addressed especially in lexicology or in translation. In the theory of sublanguages, the functioning of terms was very often described in comparison with the general lexicon by using the notion of "deviant mode" (Lehrberger 1986).

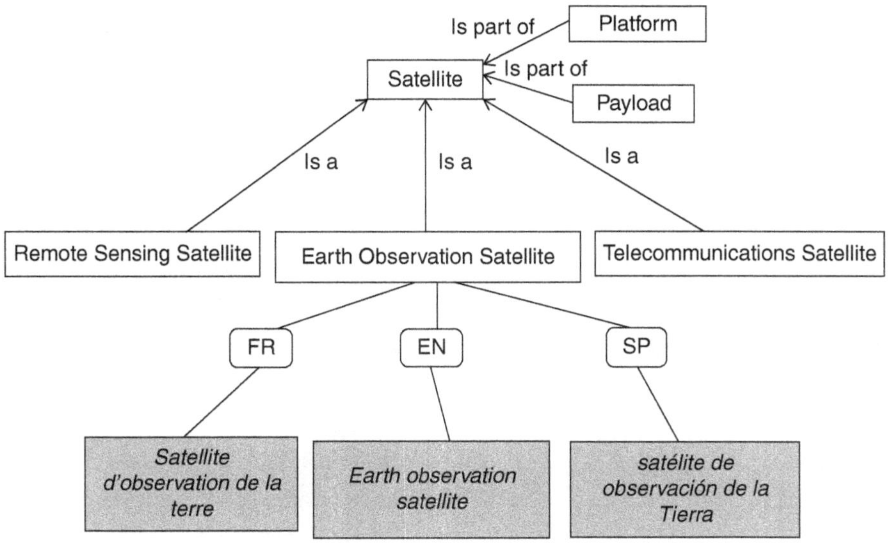

Figure 21.1 An excerpt of a terminological knowledge base

Conceptual (or semantic) relationships and the way they are expressed in languages had also been studied by semanticists, lexicologists and even philosophers (for example, Green et al. 2002; Winston et al. 1987; Cruse 2002).

However, the need to propose systematic descriptions for specialised languages, usable by tools, strengthened the research and opened up new perspectives.

Figure 21.1 presents an excerpt of a terminological knowledge base.

21.3.4 Tools and methods

Since the 1990s, many tools have been developed in order to assist the extraction of terms and relations from texts. In most cases, researchers speak about "candidate-terms extraction" rather than "terms extraction" to highlight the fact that the results must be validated by terminologists and/or domain experts. From a linguistic point of view, three assumptions about how terms function underlie the design of these tools.

The first assumption is that terms are mainly nominal groups. Several studies have shown that, in existing terminologies, around 70 percent of terms are nominal groups. Tools applying this characteristic use a tagged corpus and seek all the strings of characters corresponding to nominal structures, for example: adjective noun (*incandescent lava*), noun preposition noun (*eruption of magma*), noun preposition adjective noun (*mantle of molten rock*), noun preposition determiner noun preposition determiner noun (*collapse of the summit of a volcano*), etc.

The second assumption is that, in a specialised corpus, the most recurrent character strings are likely to correspond to terms. When implemented, this statistical method makes it possible to spot not only nominal compounds but all the recurrent forms: verbs (*to extrude*), adjectives (*eruptive*), etc.

The third assumption is that terms can be extracted by comparing the number of occurrences of a character string in a specialized corpus with the number of occurrences of the same character string in a general corpus. The point is that if a character string (or a sequence of character strings) appears significantly more often in a specialised corpus than in a general one, this string of characters may correspond to a term. With such a method, terms that also correspond to general words may be proposed as results. Such cases are not rare because many terms are used in general corpora (see for example, *telecommunication satellite, haemoglobin, oceanographer,* etc.).

Most of the time, tools implement two of these assumptions. For example, Termostat (Drouin 2003) combines statistical and comparative approaches, whereas TerMine (Frantzi et al. 2000) combines statistical and linguistic approaches.

21.3.5 The notion of "knowledge-rich contexts"

The term "knowledge-rich context" was proposed by Meyer in the context of building TKBs. It was defined as "a context indicating at least one item of domain knowledge that could be useful for conceptual analysis" (Meyer 2001: 281).

From a corpus linguistics perspective, knowledge-rich contexts can be described as all the linguistic elements that can be used in order to identify a conceptual relationship. Depending on the authors, these linguistic elements have different names, for example, *formulae* (Lyons 1977), *diagnostic frames* (Cruse 1986), and *hinges* (Pearson 1996). From a linguistic point of view, these patterns correspond mainly to local grammars (Gross 1997) that may be designed (and then used in a tool) in order to describe relationships (Barnbrook and Sinclair 2001). More precisely, local grammars aim to spot triplets such as [T1-relationship-T2], for example, [branch is-a-part-of tree]. Indeed, such triplets are searched in order to build a network by combining them. For example, the two triplets [leaf is-a-part-of branch] [branch is-a-part-of tree] make it possible to start the design of a network.

Here are some examples of relational patterns and the triplets spotted.

(1)
[NP1 especially NP2] (hypernym between NP1 and NP2):
Furthermore, compared to the minorities especially blacks, the majority population generally has a higher likelihood of living in a nuclear family within a stable community.

(2)
[NP1, the most adjective NP2] (hypernym between NP2 and NP1
Breakfast is the most important meal of the day.

(3)
[NP1 be composed of NP2] (meronymy between NP1 and NP2)
The vasculature of human skin is composed of the nutritional capillaries and the thermoregulatory blood vessels.

Several studies have described relational patterns (Auger and Barrière 2008). Concerning the productivity of such relational patterns, variations have been identified among corpora, in particular according to the textual genre, which has been described as crucial in the functioning of patterns of conceptual relations patterns (Condamines 2002; Marshman et al. 2008). The role of textual genre is important both for the presence *vs* absence of patterns but also for the way polysemic patterns may be interpreted. For example, *to provoke* may have the meaning of *to cause*. But this meaning mainly occurs in scientific or technical texts where the verb appears mostly with inanimate arguments as in (4):

(4)
Higher lengths and lower diameters can provoke excessive voltage fall.

In general texts, where animate arguments are frequent, it is probably the case that the main use is equivalent *to excite* as in (5):

(5)
The child provokes the animal.

Several studies have described step by step how to use these patterns to build a conceptual network (Condamines and Rebeyrolle 2001; L'homme and Marshman 2006).

However, the design of triplets [term-relationship-term] using texts is far from easy. In Aussenac-Gilles and Condamines (2012), several difficulties of this process are presented:

1 *One of the terms-concepts is missing:* This is the case for example when an anaphoric pronoun is used instead of the term itself. It may be very difficult to identify the correct antecedent.
2 *T1 and T2 do not belong to the same grammatical category:* This is the case for example with nouns and verbs. It is not possible to link them in a terminology. Nevertheless, this situation can be found in discourse as in (6):

(6)
The numbering of cables consists in identifying and numbering each cable for an electrical cabinet.

3 *Pattern and T2 are present in the same word:* This phenomenon is seldom described. Some words composed of a base and an affix may contain both a term and a relational pattern (the affix) (example 7):

(7)
The willow has been uprooted.
One can deduce that, generally, *roots* are parts of a *willow* and, consequently, that a *willow* is probably a tree. The *up* prefix can be considered as a part-of-all pat*tern. Then uprooted is a term and it also contains a relational pattern (up) and* another term (*root*).

4 *Polysemy of patterns:* It is well known that some patterns can be polysemic. See, for example, *to provoke* in (4) and (5).
5 *Implicit relationship:* Sometimes, the pattern cannot be interpreted directly but must be deduced. This can be the case with nominal anaphora. It is well known that, in some cases, there is a hypernymic relation between a head noun within a nominal anaphor and its antecedent. For example in:

(8)
A cat entered, the animal had shiny fur.
There is a hypernymic relation between *animal* and *cat*. This relation is not posed by the sentence but is assumed to be known. Nevertheless, some textual genres foster this type of relation (Condamines 2005).

6 *Indirect interpretation* (Condamines 2000): In some cases, the relation must be deduced because the utterance does not directly express it. In (9),

(9)
Chez les colobinés, le nez fait saillie sur la lèvre supérieure.
[In colobines, the nose juts out over the upper lip.]

Here, there is a meronymic relation between *nose* and *colobines*. The knowledge about this element is presupposed and not posed by the sentence. In other cases, the same pattern may correspond to another relation or not correspond to any relation at all:

(10)
Chez les colobinés, la nourriture . . .
[Among colobines, food . . .]

7 *Multiple binary relations:* From some utterances, it is impossible to build triplets corresponding to the meaning because depending on the discourse, the relationships are interdependent as in (11):

(11)
Each subdivision transmits to CIGT a form related to a complete site

This sentence corresponds to the syntaxico-semantic structure: NP1 *(person) communicates* NP2 *(information) to* NP3 *(person,* in which all the arguments are linked. It is impossible to represent this sentence by a binary-relation or even by several binary-relations.

21.3.6 Distributional contexts

In fact, few results are obtained using relational patterns, even in didactic texts. An alternative is to use a distributional approach. This approach originated within two schools of linguistics. The first one, based on a behaviourist and mathematical approach, was developed by Bloomfield and then Harris. The second one, based on a sociolinguistic point of view, was developed by Firth. Both are based on the same idea: if you do not know the meaning of a word, you can guess it by examining the contexts in which it appears. Hence, if you identify several contexts (or rather, categories of contexts), you may decide that the word in question has more than one meaning:

> "You shall know a word by the company it keeps."
>
> (Firth 1957: 11)

> "Difference in meaning correlates with differences of distribution."
>
> (Harris 1954:156)

With distributional approaches, it is often necessary to use different contexts, containing what can be called "cues", rather than transparent patterns, in order to build a conceptual relation or a lexical relation such as synonymy or polysemy.

While the relational pattern approach can be considered as top-down because the patterns are described for a language and then projected into the discourse, the distributional approach can be considered as bottom-up because the interpretation is mainly built directly from the textual contexts. Examples (12) and (13) are extracted from a corpus on volcanology. For French readers, the meaning of *are extruded* is not clear in (12). However, as (13) contains some elements close to (12), that is, *from the vents* as origin argument and *magma*, which can be considered as pertaining to the same paradigm as *lavas* in (12), this orients the interpretation towards a synonymy (or at least a semantic proximity) between *extruded* and *ejected.*

(12)
Lavas and ash of lavas and ash of granitic composition are extruded from vents

(13)
Gas-rich magma is ejected from the vent to produce a bomb

From a linguistic point of view, what we can retain from this brief description of TKBs is that this new concept boosted research in textual terminology and, especially, in the systematic exploration of specialised texts.

21.4 Looking to the future

At the moment, three observations concerning TKBs can be made. First of all, TKBs are still built, even if less frequently, and always with the same main characteristics: distinction between terms and concepts, knowledge representation in a network form and role of texts as knowledge source. This is the case for example with *Ecolexicon*, built in Granada by Faber's team (Faber and Buendia-Castro 2014).

Second, the original "symbiotic relationship" between terminology and knowledge engineering, evoked by Skuce and Meyer (Skuce and Meyer 1991), no longer applies. Now, the most widely used term within knowledge engineering to refer to a network representation is *ontology* (see Chapter 14 this volume). One difference with TKBs is that concepts and linguistic forms are not identified separately. However, the main difference likely resides in the methods used in knowledge engineering to build networks, which are now rarely symbolic (linguistic). Most often, machine learning methods are applied on very large corpora (very often, the entire Web) in order to spot new patterns and new triplets. The initial machine learning method, proposed by Hearst (Hearst 1992), used triplets linked by a known relation (*hypernym*) and learned new patterns from texts, using the recurrent linguistic forms appearing between the couple of terms. The hypothesis was that these recurrent forms could correspond to patterns of conceptual relations. Then, new triplets were detected by these patterns and, in their turn, projected on the corpus. This recursive method was used and improved in different projects (Agichtein and Gravano 2000; Buitelaar and Ciminao 2008). In more fine-grained analyses, belonging to what is named "distributional semantics", the syntactic links between the terms are used, which leads to more precise results from a linguistic point of view (Lenci 2008). But with machine-learning methods, interpretation of the relationships is not as fundamental as in TKBs. This is due to the fact that the main aim of the learning is not to build a precise representation of the knowledge but, rather, to detect enough regularities to assume that some couples of terms have a constant and relevant relationship. In these cases, the most important application is to improve information retrieval. So, the objectives of linguists and those of knowledge engineers moved apart. Nevertheless, some meeting points still exist that strengthen the collaboration between the two communities. This is the case of the two conferences "Terminology and Artificial Intelligence" and "Terminology and Knowledge Engineering" that are held every two years.

But from a purely linguistic point of view and as a result of the studies carried out in order to build TKBs, two main perspectives emerge. The first one concerns the improvement of the methods for studying terms in discourse systematically, and the second deals with the use of the terms and their contexts for other objectives than building conceptual networks.

21.4.1 Terms in discourse

The aim of building conceptual networks from texts as systematically as possible has enabled the improvement of terminological analysis methods using the results of natural language processing tools.

This issue has brought lexicology and terminology closer, because, with a fine-grained textual analysis, it is impossible to consider terms as just concept labels (as in the Wüsterian perspective); rather, they have to be considered as words (or word groups) used in specialized corpora.

With such a point of view, many of the analyses conducted for the general lexicon can be adapted for terminology. One of the main consequences of considering terms as words is to re-contextualize them and study them within discourses. Hence, there is no reason to take only nouns into account. On the contrary, other parts of speech and especially verbs, which are generally considered as sentence pivots, can be seen to play an important role. In the building of a TKB, verbs are mainly used in relational patterns (as in (4) and (11)), that is, only for their capacity to link terms. However, verbs may also be terms and, moreover, they may be used to describe specialised nouns in discourse (L'Homme 2002). This idea underlies the FrameNet project, which is adapted to terminology description (see Chapter 24 this volume). The FrameNet project derives from frame semantic theory (Fillmore et al. 2003) in which verbs play the role of pivot around which arguments are organised. Some projects try to adapt this approach in specialised domains in order to take into account not only paradigmatic relations (as in traditional TKBs) but also syntagmatic ones (Faber 2015). This is an obvious way to bring terms and the discourses that use them closer together.

But more than anything, what appears most specific to terms in use is, on the one hand, the situation in which the texts (in the broad sense including speaking situations) are produced and, on the other, the aim of the study (either theoretical or applied). One of the unforeseen consequences of the development of methods for building TKBs was that, depending on the needs, TKBs may be different in a given domain. The role of the application then becomes crucial in constructing the TKB. Moreover, methods aimed at building conceptual networks may be adapted for other types of studies. So what appeared is that computer-assisted methods defined for building conceptual networks may be adapted to other aims, as shown in the following section. Two main methods have been described in Section 21.3: one based on patterns (a top-down method) and the other based on distributional contexts (a bottom-up method). The same two approaches can be adapted for other aims, as discussed in Section 21.4.2.

21.4.2 Terms as a key for entering the texts

There are many needs for which these two approaches may be used. However, whereas in TKBs the aim is to build a relational network, with other needs, the network (or even just the terms) becomes the starting point of the study. In most cases, needs are linked to the variation of terms (presence or not, frequency variation, variation in meaning), and the study requires detecting the variations and explaining them by situational elements.

To a certain extent, terms may be used as pivots of contexts whose study may lead to results that are relevant for new needs. The adaptation of the methods concerns different aspects:

a. The corpus to be analysed. The corpus must be built in accordance with the aim of the study. In most cases, the corpus is organized in sub-corpora according to the situational element of variation to be compared (time, place, communities, etc.). The sub-corpora are then compared and the linguistic variations are linked with situational variations. So the structuration of the corpus plays a crucial role in the study.
b. The distributional contexts. The choice and the interpretation of the relevant contexts of the terms are linked to the aim of the study.
c. The top-down contexts. They are also defined (pre-defined) depending on the aim.

Here are two examples of studies using the two different contexts for two very different needs (Condamines et al. 2012).

a. *Detecting variations in terms' contexts in order to control knowledge evolution*: Generally, one considers that the meaning of terms evolves slowly and that a dictionary remains valid over a number of years. But this is not always the case. In some domains, knowledge evolution may be very rapid, but not only because experts make discoveries in a short time but also because external elements (social pressure) affect the evolution of knowledge. What can be very problematic is that speakers may be unaware of this evolution. We encountered this situation in some CNES (*Centre National d'Etudes Spatiales*) projects. In order to propose a method to detect knowledge evolution via the study of terms, A. Picton, in her PhD thesis, used the two kinds of contexts occurring with candidate-terms (Picton 2009). With the top-down approach, she used linguistic patterns such as: *nouveau* (new), *autrefois* (formerly), *est apparu* (appeared), which are directly linked to the idea of novelty and occur in utterances containing terms (or candidate-terms). In such cases, we can consider that speakers are more or less aware of the phenomenon. With bottom-up contexts (distributional ones), speakers are probably much less aware of the variation among corpora. For example, it may concern the nature of verbs of which a term is an argument (see, for example, the case of 11). Once identified, these variations are submitted to the domain experts who decide if they could be problematic or not.
b. *Detecting variations in terms' contexts in order to help to stabilize a neo-discipline*: We encountered this case with a project concerning exobiology, the study of life beyond the earth's atmosphere. Four disciplines are involved in the characterisation of this neo-discipline: astronomy, biology, chemistry and geology. Within the context of a project funded by the CNRS (*Centre National de la Recherche Scientifique*) we built a corpus organized in four sub-corpora and we detected the terms that were present in at least two of them. The items that came top of the list were *atmosphère, eau, temperature, planète, acide, vie*. Then we analysed their contexts. With top-down patterns, we detected terms for which speakers are aware of the variation in meaning. We used patterns such as: "as said in . . . ", "it is not the same meaning in . . .". As for evolution over time, we also examined distributional contexts and we spotted variations according to disciplines. Note that in this study, distributional variation was not a problem, unlike in

the previous study. If experts are made aware of it, it can be very fruitful and help them to better define new concepts in the neo-discipline (Condamines 2014).

In these two examples, the terms constitute the base of the study, and the different contexts in which they appear are interpreted from a specific perspective, contributing to help experts in the situations they face. In both cases, the study used NLP tools (candidate-terms extractors, statistical tools, concordancers or Perl programs). The method was similar but the results, for domain experts and for linguists, were different. In the first case, seventeen types of linguistic phenomena (variations linked to the evolution over time) were identified (Picton 2009). In the second case, twelve types of phenomena were identified.

21.5 Conclusion

In the 1990s, TKBs represented the convergence between terminology and knowledge engineering. Three elements characterised this new concept: terminological knowledge representation under a conceptual network, the use of corpora as knowledge sources and the development of tools and methods to systematically spot terms and conceptual relations in corpora. Twenty-five years later, the representational model is still used in both terminology and knowledge engineering, and the corpus is still the departure point of study for both disciplines. But the methods and the aims of the two disciplines have evolved. Now the aim of knowledge engineering is mainly to build ontologies from texts using large corpora. From a linguistic point of view, although TKBs continue to be built (and, especially, conceptual networks), new needs emerged which the systematic study of terms and their contexts can satisfactorily meet. Two kinds of contexts may then be used. The first belong to a top-down approach: linguistic patterns linked to the need are defined a priori and searched in co-occurrence with a (candidate-)term in the corpus. The second ones, belonging to a bottom-up approach, consist in choosing and interpreting the contexts of (candidate-)terms depending on the final aim. Whereas the main initial aim of TKBs was to analyse texts in order to define terms, new aims lead mainly to using terms in order to approach texts. In both cases, the tool-assisted methods are very similar, and in both cases, the main issue, from a linguistic point of view, concerns the study of the semantic link between terms and texts.

Related topics

Lexicography and corpus linguistics; lexicography and terminology; domain ontologies; specialised dictionaries; using the Web for lexicographic purposes.

Further reading

Bowker, L. and J. Pearson. (2003). *Working With Specialized Language – A Practical Guide to Using Corpora*. London: Routledge.
This book is a good introduction for beginners to the study of specialised corpora. It looks at issues such as corpus design, compilation and processing or corpus-based applications in LSP.

Ibekwe-San Juan, F., A. Condamines, and T. Cabré Castellví. (2007). *Application-Driven Terminology Engineering*. Amsterdam/Philadephia: John Benjamins.
The fundamental role of the application in the design of a terminology is the core issue of this book. It presents various types of applications, seen either as the end use of the terminology (information

retrieval, information extraction, competitive intelligence) or as an intermediate step serving the previous ones (dictionaries, the lexicon, taxonomies – namely terminological ressources).

Khurshid, A. and M. Rogers. (2007). *Evidence-Based LSP: Translation Text and Terminology*. Bern, Berlin, Bruxelles, Frankfurt am Main, New York, Oxford, Wien: Peter Lang.
This book presents different studies in LSP, observing language in use through the use of corpora. Part four focuses especially on "Terminology and Knowledge Management". Many domains are taken into account and several applications are described in order to show the different aspects of knowledge management.

Proceedings of Computerm (Computational Terminology) workshop associated to Coling (Computational Linguistics).
The workshop has existed since 1998. The proceedings are online. The workshop brings together natural language processing researchers and linguists/terminologists around issues such as term extraction, conceptual relations extraction, text mining, or summarization.

Temmerman, R. and M. Van Campenhoudt. (2014). *Dynamics and Terminology: An Interdisciplinary Perspective on Monolingual and Multilingual Culture-Bound Communication*. Amsterdam/ Philadephia: John Benjamins.
This book presents different views on the dynamicity within terminology. Different languages, different disciplines (linguistics, sociology, psychology, ethnology and even language philosophy), different domains and different types of needs are taken into account in this rich panorama.

References

Agichtein, E. and L. Gravano. (2000) "Snowball: Extracting Relations From Large Plain Text Collections", *Proceedings, 5th ACM Conference on Digital Libraries*. San Antonio, Texas, pp. 85–94.

Ahmad, K. (1993) "Terminology and Knowledge Acquisition: A Text Based Approach", in K. D. Schmitz (ed.), *Proceeding, Terminology and Knowledge Engineering (TKE 2013)*. Frankfurt: Indeks Verlag, pp. 56–70.

Auger, A. and C. Barrière (eds.) (2008) "Pattern Based Approaches to Semantic Relation Extraction: A State-of-the-Art", *Terminology* 14(1): 1–19.

Aussenac-Gilles, N. and A. Condamines. (2012) "Variation and Semantic Relation Interpretation: Linguistic and Processing Issues", in *Proceedings, Terminology and Knowledge Engineering Conference (TKE 2012)*. Spain: Madrid, pp. 106–122.

Barnbrook, G. and J. Sinclair. (2001) "Specialised Corpus, Local and Functional Grammars", in M. Ghadessy, A. Henry and R. L. Roseberry (eds.), *Studies in Corpus Linguistics*. Amsterdam/ Philadephia: John Benjamins, pp. 237–275.

Buitelaar, P. and P. Cimiano. (2008) *Ontology Learning and Population: Bridging the Gap Between Text and Knowledge*. Amsterdam: IOS Press.

Cabré, M.-T. (1999) *Terminology: Theory, Methods and Application*. Amsterdam/Philadelphia: John Benjamins.

Condamines, A. (1995) "Terminology: New Needs, New Perspectives", *Terminology* 2(2): 219–238.

Condamines, A. (2000) "*Chez* dans un corpus de sciences naturelles: un marqueur de méronymie?", *Cahiers de Lexicologie* 77(2): 165–187.

Condamines, A. (2002) "Corpus Analysis and Conceptual Relation Patterns", *Terminology* 8(1): 141–162.

Condamines, A. (2005) "Anaphore nominale infidèle et hyperonymie: le rôle du genre textuel", *Revue de Sémantique et Pragmatique* 18: 23–42.

Condamines, A. (2014) "How Can Linguistics Help to Structure a Multidisciplinary Neo-Domain Such as Exobiology", in *Bioweb of Conferences*. http://dx.doi.org/10.1051/bioconf/20140206001.

Condamines A. and P. Amsili. (1993) "Terminology between Language and Knowledge: An Example of Terminological Knowledge Base", in K.-D. Schmitz (ed.), *Terminology and Knowledge Engineering* (*TKE 199)*, Frankfurt: Indeks Verlag: 316–323.

Condamines, A., N. Dehaut and A. Picton. (2012) "Rôle du temps et de la pluridisciplinarité dans la néologie sémantique en contexte scientifique. Études outillées en corpus", in C. Gérard and J. Kabatek (eds.), *Les Cahiers de Lexicologie* n°101, *Néologie sémantique et analyse de corpus*, Paris: Garnier Classiques, pp. 161–184.

Condamines, A. and J. Rebeyrolle. (2001) "Searching for and Identifying Conceptual Relationships via a Corpus-Based Approach to a Terminological Knowledge Base (CTKB): Method and Results", in D. Bourigault, M. C. L'Homme and C. Jacquemin (eds), *Recent Advances in Computational Terminology*, Amsterdam/Philadelphia: John Benjamins, pp. 127–148.

Cruse, D. A. (1986) *Lexical Semantics*. Cambridge: Cambridge University Press.

Cruse, D. A. (2002) "Hyponymy and Its Varieties", in R. Green, C. A. Bean and S. H. Myaeng (eds.), *The Semantics of Relationships: An Interdisciplinary Perspective*. Dordrecht/Boston/London: Kluwer Academic Publishers, pp. 3–21.

Drouin, P. (2003) "Term Extraction Using Non-Technical Corpora as a Point of Leverage", *Terminology* 9(1): 99–117.

Faber, P. (2015) "Frames as a Framework for Terminology", in H. J. Kockaert and F. Steurs (eds.), *Handbook of Terminology*. Amsterdam/Philadelphia: John Benjamins, pp. 14–33.

Faber, P. and M. Buendía Castro. (2014) "EcoLexicon", in C. V. Andrea Abel and N. Ralli (eds.), *Proceedings of the XVI EURALEX International Congress*. Bolzano: Euralex, pp. 601–607.

Fillmore, C. J., C. Johnson and M. R. Petruck. (2003) "Background to FrameNet", *International Journal of Lexicography* 16(3): 235–250.

Flowerdew, J. (1992) "Definitions in Science Lectures", *Applied Linguistics* 13(2), Oxford University Press: 203–221.

Frantzi, K., S. Ananiadou and H. Mima. (2000) "Automatic Recognition of Multi-Word Terms", *International Journal of Digital Libraries* 3(2): 117–132.

Firth, J. R. (1957) *Papers in Linguistics 1934–1951*. Oxford: Oxford University Press. (first edition: 1957).

Gaudin, F. (1990) "Socioterminology and Expert Discourses", *Proceedings, Terminology and Knowledge Engineering (TKE 1990)* 1: 631–641.

Green, R., C. A. Bean, and S.-H. Myaeng (eds.) (2002) *The Semantics of Relationships*. Dordrecht/Boston, MA/London: Kluwer Academic Publishers.

Gross, M. (1997) "The Construction of Local Grammars", in E. Roche and Y. Schabes (eds.), *Finite-State Language Processing*. Cambridge, MA: MIT Press, pp. 329–354.

Harris, Z. (1954) "Distributional Structure", *Word* 10(23): 146–162.

Hearst, M. A. (1992) "Automatic Acquisition of Hyponyms from Large Text Corpora", in *Proceedings, 14th International Conference on Computational Linguistics*, Nantes, France, pp. 539–545.

Lenci, A. (ed.) (2008) "From Context to Meaning: Distributional Models of the Lexicon in Linguistics and Cognitive Science", *Italian Journal of Linguistics*, 20(1): 1–31.

Lehrberger, J. (1986) "Sublanguage Analysis", in R. Grishman and R. Kittredge (eds.), *Analyzing Language in Restricted Domains*. Hillsdale, NJ, London: Lawrence Erlbaum Associates Publishers, pp. 19–38.

L'Homme, M.-Cl. (2002) "What Can Verbs and Adjectives Tell Us About Terms?", *Proceedings of the 6th International Conference on, "Terminology and Knowledge Engineering" (TKE 2002)*: 65–70.

L'Homme, M.-C. and E. Marshman. (2006) "Terminological Relationships and Corpus-Based Methods for Discovering Them: An Assessment for Terminographers", in L. Bowker (ed.), *Lexicography, Terminology, and Translation: Text-Based Studies in Honour of Ingrid Meye*r. Ottawa: University of Ottawa Press, pp. 67–80.

Lyons, J. (1977) *Semantics: Volume 1*. Cambridge: Cambridge University Press.

Marshman E., M.-C. L'Homme and V. Surtees. (2008) "Portability of Cause-Effect Relation Markers Across Specialized Domains and Text Genres: A Comparative Evaluation", *Corpora* 3(2), pp. 141–172.

Meyer, I. (2001) "Extracting Knowledge-Rich Contexts for Terminography: A Conceptual and Methodological Framework", in D. Bourigault, M. C. L'Homme and C. Jacquemin (eds.), *Recent Advances in Computational Terminology*. Amsterdam/Philadelphia: John Benjamins, pp. 279–302.

Meyer, I., L. Bowker and K. Eck. (1992) "Cogniterm: An Experiment in Building a Terminological Knowledge Base", in *Proceedings, 5th EURALEX International Congress on Lexicography*. Tampere, Finland: 159–172.

Parent, R. (1989) "Recherche d'une synergie entre développement linguistique informatisé et systèmes experts: importance de la terminologie", *Meta* 34–3: 611–614.

Pearson, J. (1996) "The Expression of Definitions in Specialised Texts: A Corpus-Based Analysis", in J.J.M. Gellerstam, S.-G. Malmgren, K. Norén, L. Rogström and C. Röjder Papmehl (eds.), *Proceedings, Seventh EURALEX International Congress on Lexicography*, Part II. Göteborg, Sweden: Göteborg University, Department of Swedish, pp. 817–824.

Pearson J. (1998) *Terms in Context*. Amsterdam /Philadelphia: John Benjamins.

Picton, A. (2009) *Diachronie en langue de spécialité: Définition d'une méthode linguistique outillée pour repérer l'évolution des connaissances en corpus. Un exemple appliqué au domaine spatial.* PhD Dissertation, Université Toulouse Le Mirail, France.

Sinclair, J. (1991) *Corpus, Concordance, Collocation: Describing English Language*. Oxford: Oxford University Press.

Skuce, D. and I. Meyer. (1991) "Terminology and Knowledge Engineering: Exploring a Symbiotic Relationship", *Proceedings 6th International Workshop on Knowledge Acquisition for Knowledge-Based Systems* (Banff): 29/1–29/21.

Temmerman, R. (2000) *Towards New Ways of Terminology Description: The Sociocognitive Approach.* Amsterdam/Philadelphia: John Benjamins.

Wijnands, P. (1993) "Terminology versus Artificial Intelligence", in H. B. Sonneveld and K. L. Loening (eds.), *Terminology, Applications in Interdisciplinary Communication.* Amsterdam/Philadelphia: John Benjamins, pp. 165–179.

Winston, M. E., R. Chaffin and D. Hermann. (1987) "A Taxonomy of Part-Whole Relations", *Cognitive Science* 11(4): 417–444.

Wüster, E. (1974) "General Terminology Theory – Fine Line Between Linguistics, Logic, Ontology, Information Science and Business Sciences", *Linguistics* 119: 61–106.

Wüster, E. (1979) *Introduction to the General Theory of Terminology and Terminological Lexicography.* Wien: Springer.

Part IV
Innovative dictionaries

22 Learners' dictionaries of English

Julia Miller

22.1 Introduction

Learners of English need dictionaries for both decoding (understanding, production) and encoding (writing and speaking, reception) in English (see Chapters 16, 17, 18 and 19 of this *Handbook*). In the past, most teachers relied on bilingual dictionaries and grammar books to help learners achieve these goals. However, the method of English language teaching (ELT) (whether as a foreign, second or additional language) has changed in many countries in recent decades. Where most students once learned English through a grammar translation method, translating English texts into and out of their first language with the aid of a bilingual dictionary, the communicative approach to ELT has required that learners work as much as possible in the target language of English. For this reason, bilingual dictionaries are now often discouraged by teachers, and learners are encouraged to use dictionaries written entirely in English. A dictionary for a native speaker of English, however, may be too complicated for a learner, as it will commonly include words in its definitions that the learner does not understand. For example, the *Oxford English Dictionary* defines a *spade* as

> A tool for digging, paring, or cutting ground, turf, etc., now usually consisting of a flattish rectangular iron blade socketed on a wooden handle which has a grip or cross-piece at the upper end, the whole being adapted for grasping with both hands while the blade is pressed into the ground with the foot.

A number of these words (*paring*, *turf*, *socketed*, *grip*, *cross-piece*) would be problematic for many learners of English. Compare this with the *Oxford Advanced Learner's Dictionary* (*OALD*) definition of *spade*: "a garden tool with a broad metal blade and a long handle, used for digging." *OALD* uses a limited defining vocabulary of 3000 words (*OALD* 2010: R43), each of which is also defined in the dictionary. This means that the learner is not confronted with a definition that obscures their understanding of the term they are searching for. The user can also see that *spade* is a countable noun; hear its audio pronunciation; read an example sentence (*Turn the soil over with a spade*); see a comparison word (*shovel*) and related entries (*gardening*); and view a set of pictures including a spade in a set of gardening tools.

A dictionary with features such as this, known as a monolingual English learner's dictionary (MELD), is in many ways more suitable than a bilingual dictionary for those who do not speak English as a first language, provided they have at least enough knowledge of English to navigate an English dictionary entry. MELDs are thus particularly suited to advanced learners.

Online MELDs provide even greater possibilities. One study of advanced learners found that 75 percent preferred online to paper dictionaries, with users valuing audio pronunciation and videos (Miller, Kwary and Setiawan 2017). Such information can be more readily provided online, due to the greater flexibility in terms of space. Searching is also easier; if a user is unsure of a word's spelling, they can type an approximation of a word in the search box and be presented with several potential entries. (See Chapters 19, 33 and 41 of this *Handbook* for different perspectives on the innovative role of these dictionaries).

This chapter analyses the main features of online MELDs and examines their advantages, disadvantages and possibilities for innovation.

22.2 Historical perspective

The first MELD for advanced learners was Hornby, Gatenby and Wakefield's 1942 *Idiomatic and Syntactic English Dictionary*, later published by Oxford University Press in 1948 as the *Advanced Learner's Dictionary of Current English*. Other publishing companies followed, and MELDs were developed for speakers at different levels (elementary, intermediate, advanced). (For a table outlining the development of MELDs in more detail, see Stark 1999.) There are now six major MELDs, often referred to as the Big Six: *Cambridge Advanced Learner's Dictionary* (*CALD*), *Collins COBUILD* (*COBUILD*), *Longman Dictionary of Contemporary English* (*LDOCE*), *Macmillan English Dictionary* (*MED*), *Merriam Webster Learner's Dictionary* (*MWLD*) and *Oxford Advanced Learner's Dictionary* (*OALD*). Most of these dictionaries existed first in hard copy alone, before incorporating CDs. All six of these MELDs are now freely available online. In fact, at the time of writing, one major publisher (Macmillan) is now publishing its learner's dictionary only online, with no further paper copies.

Targeting a particular group of users meant that paper dictionaries were very focussed on different proficiency levels, because learners would traditionally carry their paper copy MELD with them to classes or exams, and there is a limit to the size that is practicable for transportation. The use of the Internet means that publishers can now combine dictionaries for users of different language levels on one website, and even include other types of work, such as idioms dictionaries and thesauri. On the one hand, this is an advantage to the user, who is no longer restricted to headwords aimed at a particular level of English ability. On the other hand, lower-level users may be daunted by the large amount of information available. However, because producing a MELD is a complicated process, involving many features at each entry, the number of headwords in a MELD is still restricted, and it is debatable whether publishers will expand the number of their entries greatly.

The transition from printed to online dictionaries has implications for publishers, users and teachers. Although the cost to publishers when producing an online dictionary may be no less than the cost of producing a print dictionary, the areas of expenditure are different. For example, money may be saved on printing costs and binding, but computer coding and the demand for freely available resources create different expenses. Users also need to develop different searching skills and be more discerning when choosing an online dictionary, because popularity and greater freedom of access do not always equate to reliability (Lew 2013). Many language teachers do not teach dictionary skills, and among those who do many may lag behind their students in keeping up with digital advances (Lew 2013). The change from a paper to an online medium is thus not as straightforward as it might first appear.

22.3 Core issues and topics

To meet learners' decoding and encoding needs, printed and online MELDs provide not only word definitions and spelling, but also pronunciation (usually UK/US), example sentences, usage information (e.g. currency, register), word frequency, grammatical information (e.g. noun countability), common learner errors and illustrations. Online MELDs make this range of possibilities even greater, with exercises, blogs, the potential to draw on several databases (e.g. for idioms and thesauri), links to 'nearby words', topics and words of the day, crowdsourced entries, greater facility in adding new words and, occasionally, etymology. The major online MELDs vary in their approach, but each includes most of the following features.

22.3.1 Definitions

MELDs limit the number of words used in their definitions, so that learners are not faced with incompressible explanations. The concept of a limited defining vocabulary was first developed by West and Endicott in their 1935 *New Method English Dictionary*, which used 1490 words to define 23,898 entries (Cowie 1999: 24). *LDOCE* was the next major MELD to use this method, in 1978 (Atkins and Rundell 2008: 112). Now, all the major MELDs except *COBUILD* (Xu 2012) have such a vocabulary. Most defining vocabularies range from 2000 to 3000 words and are corpus based. For example, *OALD* uses words from the British National Corpus and the Oxford Corpus Collection, spread over a range of text types, as well as consulting "a panel of over seventy experts in the fields of teaching and language study" (*OALD* online). However, the number of words declared may not be the same as the number of words actually used (Cowie 1999: 110), as the stated number refers only to the lemma (e.g. *find*) and does not account for variations (e.g. *finds, found*).

The very fact of being limited, however, means that a defining vocabulary may not be sophisticated enough to define more specialised terms. For example, *LDOCE* defines a porcupine *quill* as "one of the long pointed things that grow on the back of a porcupine". This is accurate, but *things* sounds vague. *MED* has "a long thin sharp object like a stick that grows from the body of porcupines", but the word *stick* does not give the impression of tapering, which is an important feature of a quill. *OALD* has "one of the long sharp stiff spines", but the word *spine* is itself problematic, given its usual reference to vertebrae. *COBUILD* has "long sharp points", but *CALD* is the most accurate, with "long sharp pointed hairs", although *hairs* does not convey the stiffness of quills. A defining vocabulary, therefore, is a praiseworthy aim but does not always work in practice. To avoid such limitations, some MELDs use words in addition to the defining vocabulary, shown in a different font, and encourage the user to look up these extra words. This practice is made even easier in online MELDs, with the use of hyperlinks (see Chapters 4 and 11 of this *Handbook*).

22.3.2 Spelling variations

The spelling in a MELD is usually given with both British and American English variations (e.g. *centre/center*). However, because all the major MELDs except *MWLD* are based on British English, the full information for the entry is usually given at the British English spelling, with a cross-reference from the American English spelling. For example, the entry for *center* in *CALD* has only "US spelling for centre", with a hyperlink or cross-reference to the British English spelling for the definition. *MWLD* does the same in reverse, with the information under the American English spelling and a hyperlink from the British English spelling. Such cross-referencing is easier for the user of an online MELD, who can click on a hyperlink rather than having to turn pages in a heavy paper volume, but there seems to be no reason why the complete entry should not appear at each spelling, because storage space is no longer an issue (Lew 2011b). This appears to be an instance of a paper dictionary's limitations impinging needlessly on an online version.

22.3.3 Pronunciation

All of the Big Six except *LDOCE* include International Phonetic Association symbols for pronunciation in the online and written versions of the dictionaries. Whereas native speakers of English are often not familiar with these symbols, learners of English as an additional language encounter them frequently in language classes and find them easier to interpret. There is no doubt, though, that audio files are more helpful (Miller, Kwary and Setiawan 2017). Three of the Big Six (*CALD*, *LDOCE* and *OALD*) provide both British and American English audio pronunciation; the others give only British English (*COBUILD*, *MED*) or American English (*MWLD*). Both men's and women's voices are used, but none of these dictionaries gives spoken pronunciation in any other accent, leaving a large gap for learners of other varieties of English, in Australia, New Zealand or South Africa, for example. This is a serious omission, as learners want and need to hear different accents (Miller, Kwary and Setiawan 2017).

22.3.4 Examples

MELDs usually have one or more example sentences for each entry, normally taken from corpora of actual usage. Although Hornby (1965 in Cowie 1999: 134) argued for the use of lexicographer-generated sentences as being more suited to learners' needs, Sinclair (1987) claimed that authentic corpus examples are more effective, and corpus examples are now the norm. Nevertheless, it may be hard to find a suitable corpus example, as example sentences ideally add to the understanding of a word rather than simply using it in a sentence, and it is better to omit an example if it adds nothing to the reader's comprehension. For example, *platypus* has no accompanying example sentence in the major MELDs. However, in the small online *Australian Cultural Dictionary*, intended for learners in Australia, the example "Watch carefully for platypus anywhere along the creek" makes it clear to the user that platypus are hard to spot and that they are found in creeks. This sentence also indicates the irregular plural form of the headword; the Australian word *creek* demonstrates a regional equivalent of the word *river*; and the preposition *along* illustrates a collocation. Example sentences are therefore vital for indicating cultural, grammatical and collocational information.

Because the major MELDs are freely available online, users can look up a word and compare it across dictionaries to find the most frequent collocations, which are often highlighted. Unfortunately, however, there is sometimes a lack of consistency across the major MELDs, which may confuse learners. In their example sentences for the headword *essay*, for example, referring to a piece of writing by a student or a published author, *CALD* gives only the preposition *on*; *COBUILD* has *about* for student work and *on* for published work; *LDOCE* has *on/about* for student work and only *on* for published work; *MED* has *on/about* for both student and published work; *MWLD* has *on* for the student example and *on/about* for the published example; and *OALD* has only *on* for both student and published writing. As if that were not confusing enough, the learner is then presented with a third definition of *essay* in three of the MELDs (i.e. "an attempt to do something"), and this meaning takes the preposition *in* (e.g. "his first essay in politics was a complete disaster", *OALD*). Students must therefore not only read the entries carefully to distinguish the meanings and their collocations, but also decide which is the correct collocation when faced with such a variety of choice. A larger number of examples at each entry would help learners to distinguish between the different uses of homonyms.

22.3.5 Usage

MELDs label words to indicate their currency, register (formal/informal), status (slang, taboo) and language variety. However, they vary in the amount of information they provide and in their use of labels. For example, the phrase *spanking new* is labelled as "old-fashioned" and "informal" in *CALD*, but only as "informal" in *COBUILD* and *MWLD*. *MED* gives no label, and *LDOCE* and *OALD* have only the adjective *spanking* (e.g. *spanking pace*), labelled as "old-fashioned". Does "old-fashioned" mean that the word is no longer used, or that it is used by older speakers? This overlap and lack of consistency in the use of labels may be confusing for users. Do they risk sounding archaic themselves, if they refer to a *spanking new dictionary*? Or do they restrict their vocabulary unnecessarily by avoiding the word? Is the phrase *spanking new* still in use, but in an ironic sense, as one might use if imitating the language of a 1910 *Boys' Own* paper? More clarity is needed for labels to be efficacious. Even then, however, users do not necessarily read information about labels and other dictionary features (Béjoint 1981), and this information may be hard to find in an online dictionary. To date, no research seems to have been conducted on learners' use of such matter in online MELDs.

22.3.6 Word frequency

An indication of frequency of use is helpful for learners, as it shows which words they are most likely to encounter and which words would help them join in a conversation with a native speaker. For example, *affect* (verb) has a four out of five star rating in *COBUILD* online, indicating that the word is "very common" and "one of the 4000 mostly commonly used words in the Collins dictionary". There is also a graph under the word entry indicating usage in a given year, but the lack of a vertical axis label makes the graph hard to interpret. *MED* online has a simpler three star system and highlights common words in red, with the explanation "90% of the time, speakers of English use just 7,500 words in speech and writing. These words appear in red, and are graded with stars". *MWLD* online contains 3000 "core English vocabulary" words, listed individually and by topic. It also has a "most popular" section, where learners can see the 25 words looked up most frequently in the last 24 hours, seven days or "all time". The three words at the top of the "all time" column at the time of writing are *evidence*, *humble* and *research*, though in fact *research* appears in all the columns, suggesting that the dictionary is used frequently for the purposes of academic English. *Humble* is an unusual word to include in a popular words list, and indications of its use would be helpful. Frequency data can be gathered and updated more frequently in an online dictionary, and linked to accompanying blog or comment entries, providing the user with target words for enriching their vocabulary.

22.3.7 Grammatical information

The Big Six all contain grammatical information in their entries. At the minimum, they indicate the word's part of speech, whether a verb is transitive or intransitive, and whether a noun is countable or uncountable. (Countability information is essential for learners when deciding whether to use a definite or indefinite article.) They also indicate irregular plural forms (*child/children*; *thesis/theses*). *COBUILD* was the only dictionary to include an indication of a verb's possible ergativity (e.g. *I opened the door/The door was opened/The door opened*), but dropped this useful information in its later print versions and has not reinstated it in the online version. This may reflect debate over how much students use grammatical information in dictionaries (Bogaards 2001), with some evidence that learners do not use this information frequently (Harvey and Yuill 1997), perhaps because they are not used to searching for grammatical information in a dictionary. Most paper MELDs also include a separate section on English grammar, with lists of irregular verbs, word families and common errors, but these are not apparent (or, at least, freely available) in their online versions. Further research into learners' use of grammatical information could help to inform publishers' decisions as to how much to include.

22.3 8 Common learner errors

Some MELDs include common learner mistakes or "Which word?" boxes. For instance, *OALD* and *CALD* online both give notes about the difference between *effect* and *affect*. No research is yet available on whether learners use these features or how helpful they find them.

22.3.9 Illustrations

The cost of colour illustrations in a printed book traditionally restricted the number of pictures in the hard-copy MELDs. Some had no pictures, whereas others (e.g. *CALD*) would include coloured pictures in a separate section, and occasional black-and-white illustrations with a word's entry. Because storage space and printing costs are not an issue for online dictionaries (Lew 2011b), MELDs are no longer faced with this restriction. However, most online MELDs still do not routinely include pictures. For instance, a picture of a kangaroo appears at the entry only in *LDOCE*, *MWLD* and *OALD*. Some dictionaries also use pictures to expand learners' vocabulary. For instance, *LDOCE* has "daily pictures", where the user can click on a picture and see related dictionary entries. *LDOCE* also has a "Dictionary pictures of the day" section, and *MWLD* has a "Name that thing" visual quiz. Because learners value illustrations (Kwary and Miller 2013), this is an area that online MELDs should investigate. Although the cost of commercial photographs is high, these could be supplemented by user contributions, thereby extending the learning community and giving learners a greater sense of involvement in the dictionary making process.

22.3.10 Exercises

Although online MELDs have the possibility of creating exercises, or linking exercises from their associated grammar books, they do not appear to have followed this option in their free versions. Some provide quizzes, but none posts online exercises with answers. This may be due to the publishers' understandable unwillingness to make all their materials freely available. One MELD (*MWLD*), however, has a feature whereby users can pose questions, such as "Why is the plural of *fish* still *fish* and not *fishes*?" These are answered in a comprehensive post that invites comments and discussion, thus involving the learner in a knowledge-building community.

22.3.11 Blogs

Reader participation is also invited through the use of blogs in four MELDs (*CALD*, *COBUILD*, *MED* and *OALD*). The language of the blogs does not appear to be governed by the dictionaries' defining vocabularies, however, so many posts may be complicated for learners to understand. For instance, words such as *relativism*, *brook no argument* or *touchy-feely* (found in the *MED* blog on 3 May 2016) are not commonly part of a learner's vocabulary, although it could be argued that reading a word in a blog will prompt a user to extend their knowledge by seeing an unfamiliar word in different contexts, provided enough words in the blog are understandable. Readers can 'like' posts or add comments, but the uptake of these features is very small.

22.3.12 Idioms

The field of phraseology includes much debate over what exactly an idiom is, but for the purposes of this chapter an idiom will be taken as a figurative, opaque expression containing more than one word. One example is *a wolf in sheep's clothing*, where the figurative meaning (a deceptive person masquerading as someone innocent) is not the same as the literal meaning. MELDs label such expressions in different ways, with some calling them *idioms*, some *phrases* and some *sayings*. Each publisher has its own separate dictionary of idioms, and some online MELDs combine their idioms dictionaries with their learner's dictionaries to give greater coverage. One problem for a MELD is which word of an idiom to list as its headword, and the Big Six show great diversity. *CALD* lists *a wolf in sheep's clothing* at *wolf* and *clothing*; *COBUILD* does not include it; *LDOCE* has it under *wolf* and *sheep*; *MED* lists it at *wolf*, *sheep* and *clothing*; *MWLD* has it at *wolf* with a cross-reference from *clothing* and *sheep*; and *OALD* lists it only under *wolf*. At times, idioms are given their own entry line, under another headword; at other times, they appear almost incidentally as part of an example sentence. For example, *an albatross around someone's neck* has its own entry under *albatross* only in *LDOCE* and *MED*, and appears only in example sentences in *CALD*, *COBUILD*, *MWLD* and *OALD*. The online search function has made it easier to find idioms, however, with hyperlinks between entries and the possibility of typing the whole phrase into a dictionary's search box. The possibilities of such functions need to be explored further.

22.3.13 Thesauri

Print dictionaries are usually separate from print thesauri. The online medium, however, enables both to be searched simultaneously. Synonyms and related words can be presented in a word cloud (*CALD*), a thesaurus section (*COBUILD*), a mind map (*MED*) or a related entry (*OALD*). The advantage of the combined online dictionary and thesaurus is that the reader can see the related word in context, with a definition, and is therefore less likely to use the wrong synonym.

22.3.14 "Nearby words"

One problem with an online dictionary is that it does not permit the reader's eye to wander over a page and linger on other entries. Some MELDs (*CALD*, *LDOCE*, *OALD* and *COBUILD*) try to overcome this problem with links to "nearby words" for the user to "browse" (*COBUILD*). For example, at the entry for *affect*, *COBUILD* lists the "nearby words" *affable*, *affair*, *affectation* and *affected* in a widget on the right. Research is needed to see what use learners make of this feature.

22.3.15 Topics

One way for dictionaries to overcome the limitations of the single entry per page view is to include vocabulary sets of words relating to a topic. For instance, the topic "animals" in *OALD* online includes a section on "animal homes", with a box containing 30 dwellings associated with different types of animals, each with a hyperlink to the relevant dictionary entry.

22.3.16 Words of the day

Several MELDs (*LDOCE*, *MED*, *MWLD*, *OALD*) include a "word of the day", encouraging readers to learn new vocabulary. However, no explanation is given as to how these words are chosen or who is using the words. Such information would help learners to know where they might encounter the word and when or where it would be appropriate for them to use it, and could be linked to data on word frequency.

22.3.17 Crowdsourcing

MED invites readers to contribute words and phrases to its crowdsourced "open dictionary". If a term is accepted, the user's name is included in the open dictionary entry. Roughly half of these suggestions are promoted to the regular online dictionary. Such features make users part of a lexicographic community and could be used by language teachers to stimulate interest in vocabulary building.

22.3.18 Latest additions/new words

Many MELDs (*CALD*, *COBUILD*, *MED* and *OALD*) highlight latest additions or new words. This information provides an insight into emerging language but does not help a learner to know when to use the words, or indeed, if it is appropriate to use them in different contexts. Again, connections between such a section and words of the day or word frequency would be beneficial.

22.3.19 Etymology

Most learner's dictionaries do not indicate the origin of a word, but *OALD* features a "word origin" box at the bottom of the entry, and *COBUILD* has an "etymology corner". Research on paper dictionaries (Szczepaniak and Lew 2011) indicates that most learners are not interested in etymology, and it is therefore not included in hard copy MELDs, which have no space to spare. An online dictionary does not face the same constraints as a paper dictionary, however, and future research could be conducted to see if some learners do enjoy reading this information.

22.4 Looking to the future

22.4.1 Research on online MELDs

The advent of e-lexicography has allowed for a major rethink in the conceptualisation of the dictionary. Formerly seen as a subdomain of linguistics, lexicography has developed as a theoretical domain since Wiegand (1984) emphasised lexicography as a discipline in its own right and Bergenholtz and Tarp proposed a function theory of lexicography based on users' needs (Tarp 2008). Despite the emergence of lexicography as a separate field, with its own theories and constructs, the possibilities of online presentation have nevertheless not yet been fully explored. There has been a tendency for publishers merely to post electronic versions of paper dictionaries online, without considering the advantages and disadvantages of the new medium (Fuertes-Olivera and Bergenholtz 2011:1). Presentation space, for example, is no longer at a premium in an online dictionary (Lew 2011b); conversely, the focus on a single entry per online page means that users cannot browse adjacent entries easily. Developments in dictionary compilation should therefore encompass both paper and online modes (Gouws 2011).

Different studies have been conducted on learners' needs and use of MELDs. For example, Tono (2011) used eye-tracking to examine how users search within a dictionary entry. Research has also been conducted on the type of words users look up (Bogaards 1998) and the use of MELDs to teach a specific area of English grammar (Miller 2006). (For a précis of many studies on the use of MELDs, see Nesi (2014).)

One thing most learners value is a dictionary that reflects the variety of English used in the country where they are living. However, MELDs generally do not provide enough cultural information (Tseng 2003: 217). This is a major problem, as the Big Six largely address British or US English, with only small concessions to words used in other English speaking countries. The word *football* is one example (Algeo 1995). *Football* is defined in its British and American versions in all the Big Six, but only *MED* addresses Australian Rules football, and only *OALD* mentions Canadian football. Labels such as "Australian English" indicate whether a word is used in a certain country, while unmarked words are assumed to be in use everywhere. This is not always the case, however, as some words may be standard in the UK but not necessarily in other English speaking countries (Benson 2001: 118). For example, the word *bluebottle* refers to a large blue fly in all the British English MELDs. An international student in Australia would not be unduly worried, therefore, by a sign at the beach warning about bluebottles; after all, there are a lot of flies in Australia. In Australia, however, *bluebottle* is another word for *Portuguese man o'war*, a stinging jellyfish. The "standard" meaning of the word obviously does not apply in Australia. Moreover, a label such as "American English" implies that a word is only used in that variety. However, such a word may be used in many other varieties of English too. For example, *zucchini* is labelled "American English" in most MELDs, as an alternative to the English word *courgette*, but *zucchini* is also standard in Australian English. A learner using a MELD would assume, however, that *zucchini* is only used in the United States and that *courgette* is the word used everywhere else. Since dictionaries provide insights into the culture associated with a language, the choice of entries is vital for learners (Dalgish 1995) and should reflect a wider cultural perspective and a greater understanding of users' needs.

Although studies have addressed learners' needs, little research has been conducted on teachers' attitudes to student dictionary use. This is an important area, as one study of 55 teachers of English as an additional language in Australia (Miller 2008) revealed that many were not familiar with the features of a reputable MELD, or of how a MELD could help their students. One teacher in the study, for example, criticised MELDs as "too basic . . . and sometimes dodgy in their definitions", and another regarded them as "a backup to be used after trying other ways to discover what it is you need to learn about a language" (Miller 2008: 15). Over half the teachers in the study were unaware that dictionaries could be used for teaching about grammar, idioms or collocations. The study was conducted before MELDs became freely available online, but anecdotal evidence suggests that attitudes have not changed, and that dictionary skills are not taught, or even regarded as important, in most Western language schools.

Most studies to date have focussed on the use of paper learner's dictionaries rather than online versions. It is therefore time to conduct research on teachers' and users' attitudes to, and use of, online MELDs.

22.4.2 Advantages and disadvantages of online MELDs

One advantage of online MELDs is their use of multiple data banks. For example, *CALD* draws on both its learner's dictionary and its idioms dictionary, enabling users to search for idioms on its dictionary website without going to a separate print volume. It also combines dictionaries for learners of different levels, meaning that an intermediate-level learner is not restricted to what a publisher deems to be intermediate-level vocabulary, but instead has access to the full databank of words. The downside of this is that learners of different levels can be swamped by information. For example, when typing in a search word, most online MELDs present a list of entries to choose from or give a list of similar words in a column at the side, meaning that the user may be faced with an overwhelming choice. As with any dictionary, entries should be tailored to what users need and want (Gouws 2011: 21), but this is hard to control in a comprehensive online dictionary.

A second advantage of online MELDs is the possibility for the user to jump quickly between entries by clicking on a hyperlink. This is particularly useful for multiword expressions, which may be listed at one or more of the component words with links between them. Users can also enter a whole phrase in a search box. For example, the idiom *cry wolf* can be found at both *cry* and *wolf* in a MELD, with hyperlinks between the entries; alternatively, if the learner knows that the words constitute a phrase, they can enter *cry wolf* in the search box and go straight to the idiom. This solves the problem in hard copy MELDs of having to identify the headword for an idiom and being referred to a definition elsewhere in the dictionary, involving multiple lookups.

A further advantage of an online MELD is its potential to foster an online community of learners. Various features (blogs, "ask the editor", "add a word") involve learners in the dictionary making process, in the spirit of the early *Oxford English Dictionary*, which invited readers to contribute example sentences. Such involvement adds to a learner's sense of English as a means of communication and helps them to feel that they are part of an academic community.

Online MELDs are not without problems, however. Some of these are the same as those found in a print MELD, such as an understanding of the target age group. Although anyone may refer to a MELD, the largest market comprises learners of high school or university age (Nesi 2000), usually studying at a language school or university. Entries need to match the needs of this group, and usage labels should indicate whether a word is appropriate for them to use in a modern day setting (Zgusta 2006: 135), as different age groups may use different terms. For instance, young native speakers of English in different countries tend to use the same expressions as each other, rather than using terms used by older speakers in their own country (Miller 2011). The online medium presents the possibility of greater learner involvement in tracking norms of use such as this, but such an opportunity has yet to be explored.

Another problem with putting MELDs entirely online is their use in exam situations. Many universities in English speaking countries allow international students to use a MELD during their examinations. Hard copy MELDs are carefully inspected for hidden material that could help the student with their answers, and online resources are banned during the exam. If a MELD is not available in a hard copy, the student will not have access to the resource when they need it most.

Another issue for both learners and publishers is the multiplicity of free online resources. Learners are mainly unaware of the reliability of competing online dictionaries and will often opt for the most popular website if no charge is associated with its use. This means that they may be confused by definitions in a source such as *Urban Dictionary*, not realising that it is "satirical [and] crowdsourced" (Urbandictionary.com), or may rely on sites such as Google Translate or Youdao. Publishers are faced with making their online dictionaries free to use, in order to compete with such sources, and thus may need to rely on advertising on their webpages. Such advertising, however, is often indiscriminate, and has the effect of making the page look unacademic, with advertisements for slimming products and holidays jostling for space around the definitions and words of the day. In a lecture on dictionary use, for example, my students' attention to the dictionary website on the lecture screen was amusingly diverted by graphics promising to help them achieve a flatter stomach. This prompted discussion of what constitutes an academic resource and the explanation that even some reliable sources may include advertising if it makes the resource freely available, but it was rather a distracting element in the lecture.

22.5 Conclusion

This chapter has analysed the main features of online MELDs, which are at the forefront of a new business model based on free access and user participation. Some of these features are innovative, but there is still great potential for the new online medium to extend what has previously been possible. Research is now needed to see how effective any new approaches might be.

Several features of the online medium remain to be explored. Videos, for example, are a possibility on the Internet. Whereas some researchers (e.g. Chun and Plass 1996 in Lew 2011a) caution against their use, others (Miller, Kwary and Setiawan 2017) have found that learners do welcome video illustrations. Lew and Doroszewska (2009 in Lew 2011a) have found that animated graphics do not help vocabulary retention, but the same may not be true for vocabulary decoding. Videos could usefully be included to demonstrate movement, for example, on the basis that if a picture is worth a thousand words then a moving picture would be worth even more, and seeing a kangaroo jumping in a video would give an insight into its distinctive movement that is impossible to describe in words. Videos, or at least audio files, could also be used to demonstrate different sounds. *MED* online already does this for certain musical instruments (e.g. *guitar*), bird sounds (e.g. *kookaburra*) and the weather (e.g. *rain*). However, these audio files would be more meaningful if attached to a moving image. One drawback is that links to existing Internet files are unstable, and so a dictionary would need to produce its own video files. This would of course be time-consuming, but could be done gradually, perhaps with the use of crowdsourced contributions.

Although there is a lack of teacher awareness generally with regard to the richness of a MELD in language instruction, online MELDs make it possible to be innovative in teaching dictionary use. If a class takes place in a room where Internet access is possible, the teacher can explain different features of a MELD and have students try out each of these features in turn. There is always the risk that students will use the occasion to surf the Web instead of doing what the teacher suggests, but free student response systems (such as Socrative) allow the students to post their answers to questions in class online, and the teacher can check that everyone has responded. Possible lessons include familiarising students with the parts of a dictionary entry to gain a fuller understanding of a word, prompting them to search for irregular plurals, encouraging them to compare entries in different dictionaries, getting them to search for collocations and giving them a short online quiz about areas such as noun countability.

The world of online MELDs thus presents limitless opportunities but requires a new way of thinking. Instead of regarding online MELDs as Internet versions of paper-based originals, it would be better to start with a completely fresh slate (as it were) and think of what the user needs and expects in a digital world. Online MELDs are catching up with the online market slowly, but the market is moving on quickly. In 10 years' time, the way we access and use the Internet may have changed completely. Is pedagogical lexicography ready for the challenge?

Related topics

Lexicography and applied linguistics; dictionaries to assist teaching and learning; dictionaries for text production; dictionaries for text reception; English lexicography in the Internet era; revising the Dictionary on Canadianisms on Historical Principles; Wordnik.

Further reading

Cowie, A. P. (1999). *English Dictionaries for Foreign Learners: A History*. Oxford: Clarendon Press.
Cowie's book is a classic, giving a complete history of the genesis, development and design of English learner's dictionaries.

Lew, R. (2011a). "Online Dictionaries of English", in P. A. Fuertes-Olivera and H. Bergenholtz (eds.), *e-Lexicography: The Internet, Digital Initiatives and Lexicography*. London: Continuum International Publishing Group, pp. 230–250.
Lew's chapter gives an overview of different types of online English dictionary, evaluating their advantages and disadvantages.

Nesi, H. (2014). "Dictionary Use by English Language Learners", *Language Teaching*, 47(1): 38–55.
Nesi's article presents a comprehensive timeline of empirical studies on dictionary use.

References

Algeo, J. (1995) "British and American Biases in English Dictionaries", in B. B. Kachru and H. Kahane (eds.), *Cultures, Ideologies and the Dictionary*. Tübingen: Max Niemeyer Verlag, pp. 205–212.

Atkins, B.T.S. and M. Rundell. (2008) *The Oxford Guide to Practical Lexicography*. Oxford: Oxford University Press.

Béjoint, H. (1981) "The Foreign Student's Use of Monolingual English Dictionaries: A Study of Language Needs and Reference Skills", *Applied Linguistics* 2(3): 207–222.

Benson, P. (2001) *Ethnocentrism and the English Dictionary*. London: Routledge.

Bogaards, P. (1998) "What Type of Words Do Language Learners Look Up?" in B.T.S. Atkins (ed.), *Using Dictionaries: Studies of Dictionary Use by Language Learners and Translators*. Tübingen: Max Niemeyer Verlag, pp. 151–158.

Bogaards, P. (2001) "The Use of Grammatical Information in Learners' Dictionaries", *International Journal of Lexicography* 14(2): 97–121.

CALD. (2013) *Cambridge Advanced Learner's Dictionary*. [online] Cambridge: Cambridge University Press. http://dictionary.cambridge.org/ [Accessed 15 February 2016].

Chun, D. and J. L. Plass. (1996) "Effects of Multimedia Annotation on Vocabulary Acquisition", *Modern Language Journal* 80(2): 183–198.

COBUILD. (2016) *COBUILD*. [online] Glasgow: HarperCollins Publishers. www.collinsdictionary.com/dictionary/english-*COBUILD*-learners [Accessed 26 May 2016].

Cowie, A. P. (1999) *English Dictionaries for Foreign Learners: A History*. Oxford: Clarendon Press.

Dalgish, G. M. (1995) "Learners' Dictionaries: Keeping the Learner in Mind", in B. B. Kachru and H. Kahane (eds.), *Cultures, Ideologies and the Dictionary*. Tübingen: Max Niemeyer Verlag, 329–338.

Fuertes-Olivera, P. A. and H. Bergenholtz. (eds.) (2011) *e-Lexicography: The Internet, Digital Initiatives and Lexicography*. London: Continuum.

Gouws, R. H. (2011) "Learning, Unlearning and Innovation in the Planning of Electronic Dictionaries", in P. A. Fuertes-Olivera and H. Bergenholtz (eds.), pp. 17–29.

Harvey, K. and D. Yuill. (1997) "A Study of the Use of a Monolingual Pedagogical Dictionary by Learners of English Engaged in Writing", *Applied Linguistics* 18(3): 253–278.

Hornby, A. S. (1965) "Some Problems of Lexicography", *English Language Teaching* 19(3): 104–110.

Hornby, A. S., E. V. Gatenby and H. Wakefield. (1942) *Idiomatic and Syntactic English Dictionary*. Tokyo: Kaitakusha.

Kwary, D. and J. Miller. (2013) "A Model for an Online Australian English Cultural Dictionary Database", *Terminology* 19(2): 258–276.

Lew, R. (2011a) "Online Dictionaries of English", in P. A. Fuertes-Olivera and H. Bergenholtz (eds.), pp. 230–250.

Lew, R. (2011b) "Space Restrictions in Paper and Electronic Dictionaries and Their Implications for the Design of Production Dictionaries", in P. Bański and B. Wójtowicz (eds.), *Issues in Modern Lexicography*. München: Lincom Europa. http://works.bepress.com/robert_lew/1/ [Accessed 19 October 2016].

Lew, R. (2013) "Online Dictionary Skills", in *Electronic Lexicography in the 21st Century: Thinking Outside the Paper. Proceedings of the eLex Conference 17–19 October 2013*. http://eki.ee/elex2013/proceedings/eLex2013_02_Lew.pdf [Accessed 19 October 2016].

Lew, R. and J. Doroszewska. (2009) "Electronic Dictionaries with Animated Pictures: Lookup Preferences and Word Retention", *International Journal of Lexicography* 22(3): 239–257.

LDOCE. (2013) *Longman Dictionary of Contemporary English*. [online] Harlow: Longman. www.ldoceonline.com/ [Accessed 26 May 2016].

MED. (2016) *Macmillan English Dictionary*. [online] London: Macmillan. www.macmillandictionary.com [Accessed 26 May 2016].

MWLD. (2016) *Merriam-Webster Learner's Dictionary*. [online] Merriam-Webster, Incorporated. www.learnersdictionary.com [Accessed 26 May 2016].

Miller, J. (2006) "An Investigation into the Effect of English Learners' Dictionaries on International Students' Acquisition of the English Article System, Specifically in the Area of Countability", *International Education Journal* 7(4): 435–445.

Miller, J. (2008) "Teachers and Dictionaries in Australia: Is There a Need to Train the Trainers?", *TESOL in Context* 17(2): 11–19.

Miller, J. (2011) "Never Judge a Wolf by Its Cover: An Investigation Into the Relevance of Phrasemes Included in Advanced Learners' Dictionaries for Learners of English as an Additional Language in Australia", unpublished PhD thesis, Adelaide: Flinders University.

Miller, J., D. Kwary and A. Setiawan. (2017) "Kangaroos, Koalas and Kiwis: The Challenges of Creating an Online Australian Cultural Dictionary for EAL learners", *Lexikos* 27.

Nesi, H. (2000) *The Use and Abuse of EFL Dictionaries*. Tübingen: Max Niemeyer Verlag.

Nesi, H. (2014) "Dictionary Use by English Language Learners", *Language Teaching* 47(1): 38–55.

OALD. (2016) *Oxford Advanced Learner's Dictionary*. [online] Oxford: Oxford University Press. www.oxfordlearnersdictionaries.com [Accessed 26 May 2016].

Oxford Advanced Learner's Dictionary. 8th edition (2010) Oxford: Oxford University Press.

Szczepaniak, R. and R. Lew. (2011) "The Role of Imagery in Dictionaries of Idioms", *Applied Linguistics* 32(3): 323–347.

Sinclair, J. (ed.) (1987) *Collins Cobuild English Language Dictionary*. London and Glasgow: Collins.

Stark, M. (1999) *Encyclopaedic Learner's Dictionaries: A Study of Their Design Features From the User Perspective*. Tübingen: Max Niemeyer Verlag.

Tarp, S. (2008) *Lexicography in the Borderland Between Knowledge and Non-Knowledge*. Tübingen: Max Niemeyer Verlag.

Tono, Y. (2011) "Application of Eye-Tracking in EFL Learners' Dictionary Look-Up Process Research", *International Journal of Lexicography* 24(1): 124–153.

Tseng, T.H.T. (2003) "The Cultural Component in an Ideal Monolingual English Learner's Dictionary", in L. Ming, H. Hue Feng and Z. J. Zhuang (eds.), *Aspects of English Language Teaching and Research*. Suzhou, P. R. China: Suzhou University Press, pp. 215–226.

Wiegand, H. E. (1984) "On the Structure and Contents of a General Theory of Lexicography", in R.R.K. Hartmann (ed.), *Lexeter '83 Proceedings*. Tübingen: Max Niemeyer Verlag, pp. 13–30.

Xu, H. (2012) "A Critique of the Controlled Defining Vocabulary in *Longman Dictionary of Contemporary English*", *Lexikos* 22: 367–381.

Zgusta, L. (2006) *Lexicography Then and Now*. Tübingen: Max Niemeyer Verlag.

23

Revising the *Dictionary of Canadianisms on Historical Principles*

World Englishes and linguistic variation in real time

Stefan Dollinger

23.1 Introduction[1]

The *Dictionary of Canadianisms on Historical Principles* (DCHP-1, Avis et al. 1967) was published to considerable acclaim in 1967 by a Canadian editorial team and a Canadian publishing house, W.J. Gage Ltd. DCHP-1's benchmarks appear somewhat modest by today's standards: 927 pages long, it contains 10,000 headwords, 13,400 meanings, about 30,000 quotations and was published as a beautifully made one-volume hardcover for the then-hefty price of $25 (about $180 in 2016 money). When Raven I. McDavid (1970:289), then one of the best English-language dialectologists, wrote that DCHP-1 would see "unlike most other historical dictionaries [. . .] frequent and adequate revision", he could not know that half a century would pass before a second edition would see the light of day.

The present contribution aims to situate the second edition (DCHP-2, Dollinger and Fee 2017.) historically and present its features and functionality. Guided by five principles (see Section 23.3), DCHP-2 has given new roles to undergraduates, which includes entry drafting. Important milestones were the digitization of the first edition, which is now available in open access (DCHP-1 Online, Dollinger, Brinton and Fee 2013), the creation of an online database of historical Canadian English (the Bank of Canadian English) and a web-based editing tool (Dictionary Editing Tool) (Dollinger 2010). DCHP-2 will, like DCHP-1 Online, be available to anyone on the Web free of charge.

This chapter begins with a historical contextualization of DCHP-1. This cultural-historical perspective is followed by a lexicographical characterization of the main features and functionality of DCHP-2 (Section 24.3), with a focus on entry structure, the applied typology of Canadianisms and, in the context of historical lexicography, innovative visualization techniques of frequency data. A section on future issues looks ahead to what issues a third edition would have to address (Section 24.4), before a conclusion harks back to the early days of project planning, in 2005 and 2006, to see how much of the original plans could be accomplished (Section 24.5).

23.2 Historical perspective

DCHP is in Görlach's classification (1990) an "exclusive historical dictionary", which means that it includes only terms and meanings considered to be Canadianisms. Avis (1967: xiii) defined a Canadianism as

> a word, expression, or meaning which is native to Canada or which is distinctively characteristic of Canadian usage though not necessarily exclusive to Canada.
> (Avis 1967, qtd in Dollinger, Brinton and Fee 2013)

Based on Avis' definition, DCHP-2 set out to produce

> a revision that remedies at least the biggest gaps of *DCHP*-1; a revision that corrects (and possibly purges) misconceived and outdated entries, a revision that updates the work for the twenty-first century [. . .] in today's information age. As such, it has great potential to reach beyond the core circle of users of *DCHP*-1 such as lexicographers, diachronic linguists and historians.
> (Dollinger 2006: section 24.1)

The update for the twenty-first century has been fully implemented. Of the other goals, the correction of errors was accomplished to some degree, as was the filling of gaps: given that documenting words from the late 20th and early 21st centuries was the biggest desideratum, the task was satisfactorily achieved, while gaps in the historical coverage were only addressed within the limited funds at our disposal, for example, *adhesion* "addition to treaty", *button blanket* "festive West Coast First Nations blanket" or *gem jar* "Mason jar" (dating back to 1893). Overall, perhaps 5 percent of the revision content are such fully revised terms.

Historically DCHP-2 is best understood in the context of DCHP-1 and the Canadian lexicographical tradition. DCHP-1's first editor, Charles J. Lovell (1958: 23), stated that the dictionary "should not attempt to deal with the complete vocabulary of English-speaking Canadians", but deal with the linguistic influences of the British, American, French and Aboriginal peoples on English in Canada. Lovell, an American and former assistant to Mitford M. Mathews' *Dictionary of Americanisms* (1951), whose personal collection formed the core of DCHP-1's quotation file, was the driving force behind DCHP-1, and it is safe to say that without Lovell the project would not have been commenced at such point in time (see Lovell 1955: 3). After Lovell's untimely death after only two years of part-time work on the project, Walter S. Avis took over and saw, with his team (Charles Crate, Paddy Drysdale, Douglas Leechman and M. H. Scargill) the project to completion. DCHP-1's focus requires a comparative perspective with other World Englishes, making DCHP a profoundly contrastive dictionary: in order to establish that a term, meaning or distribution is Canadian, a cross-comparison with many other varieties is necessary.

DCHP-1 was described in the publisher's foreword as a "contribution to Centennial thinking" (Wees 1967) on the occasion of the celebrations commemorating the first century of the modern Canadian state, which began with Confederation in 1867. In order to meet that goal, publication of the work was pushed ahead from the planned publication date of 1970–72 to 1967 making "hectic days" even "more hectic" (Avis 1969: 3). This move emphasized the national importance of the foundational work of a "lexicography of CanE [that] was almost non-existent before W. S. Avis" (Görlach 1990: 1484) and C. J. Lovell, to be sure (see Considine 2003 for pre-Avis Canadian English lexicography). Moving the publication date forward inevitably forced some compromises onto the project. The resulting dictionary was, as a prominent Canadian linguist reviewer put it, a collection of "important linguistic evidence for the claim of a Canadian identity" (Alexander 1967: A13), and there was widespread agreement of the book's pioneering status as the first "systematic record of the special features of Canadian English" (ibid).

As the discussion of Canadian identity became a national obsession in the years following Confederation, DCHP-1 was poised to contribute to the debate. Canadianists embraced the work; for example, one important figure described DCHP-1 as bearing "lively and scholarly witness to that most elusive of Centennial projects, the Canadian identity" (Moore 1967: 55).

23.2.1 Praise

DCHP-1 was embraced not only by historians and cultural theorists, but also by more unlikely reader groups such as the news reporters at the *Toronto Telegram*, who were "much impressed by this work" (Currell 1967). Other writers went even further: Dresser (1968), who is the most exuberant of them all, declared DCHP-1 as "[p]erhaps the most significant contribution to Canadian letters in the past 300 years". Superlatives, both of a public and private dimension, were not rare in the early days following publication. Gage Love, the president of publishing house W.J. Gage Ltd., which specialized in Canadian content, considered DCHP-1 "his greatest legacy by far, and one of his proudest achievements" (David Love qtd in Ray 2003: R9). From these quotes one can glean a sense of the cultural importance of the work; however, by the late 1970s, enthusiasm had waned. When Scargill (1977) used the data from DCHP-1 to write a cultural narrative as evidence for cultural identity, the resulting book not only disappointed scholarly – McDavid (1980: 47) attested instances of "professional irresponsibility" – but also in terms of public impact.

DCHP-1, today, is all but forgotten in the public eye: a search for "Dictionary of Canadianisms" in *The Globe and Mail* in 2016 returned a mere 11 hits over a period of half a century. Sales figures of the 1980s and 1990s were negligible, whereas a thousand or more copies of newly printed paperback copies lay in a warehouse as of 1991 with no sales catalogue listing (David Friend: personal conversation 2007). By the turn of the millennium DCHP-1 was all but forgotten. Nonetheless, DCHP-1 provided much of the historical, methodical and theoretical grounding for the subsequent study of Canadian lexis, as it served as the flagship dictionary for the most successful Canadian dictionary series to date, *The Dictionary of Canadian English Series* (Gage Ltd. Toronto), whose beginnings date back to 1959 (Gregg 1993: 35).

23.2.2 Contribution and missing critique

What is often overlooked by the focus on Canadian national identity is that DCHP-1 contributed to the study of World Englishes at a time when that academic field had not yet solidified. DCHP-1 and Cassidy and Le Page's *Dictionary of Jamaican English* (Cassidy and Le Page 1980), both published in 1967, were the first scholarly historical dictionaries of a non-dominant variety of English (i.e. of neither British nor American English). Even competitors held the dictionary in high esteem: Random House president Jess Stein referred to the DCHP-1 in a congratulatory letter as a "a real landmark in English lexicography" (1 Dec. 1967), and Sidney Landau, then editor-in-chief of Funk & Wagnalls dictionaries wrote "now that we have it [DCHP-1] I cannot imagine how we managed to get along so long without it" (29 Nov. 1967) (University of Victoria Archives, Centre for Lexicography Fond, 90–66, files 1–15/16). Such praise extends to more recent practicing lexicographers, such as Katherine Barber (2010: 142), who consider DCHP-2 a "truly wonderful work of scholarship".

Nonetheless, in 1969, two years after publication, editor-in-chief Walter S. Avis readily admitted that the dictionary was "neither complete nor perfect. But it does exist – which is something" (1969: 1). The national significance of DCHP-1 pushed the linguistic and lexicographic questions into the background. For example, Lovell stressed the importance of comparative work early on: "the importance of cross-checking in dictionaries", he wrote in the year he became editor-in-chief, "cannot be too highly stressed" (1958: 31). Although this checking was carried out on the paper slips for many terms, such evidence is absent from the first edition. In an insightful overview article, Görlach (1990: 1484) identified the lack of comparisons with other dictionaries as one of the problems of DCHP-1. He also suggested that considering the absence or presence of terms in other national dictionaries would have provided useful evidence on the distinctiveness of particular terms. For a second edition, Görlach (ibid) recommended the integration of linguistic survey results, such as the Survey of Canadian English (Scargill and Warkentyne 1972) and comparisons with the *Dictionary of American Regional English* (Cassidy and Hall 1985–2013) and the *Dictionary of Newfoundland English* (Story et al. [1982] 1999). It is noteworthy that such detailed critique, from a German scholar writing two decades after the fact, was not to be found in Canada, the United States or the UK for that matter.

The original editorial team never published a revision or addendum of DCHP-1. Rather, a more affordable abridgement without any new information was released in 1973. Avis and Scargill, however, continued to collect quotations until their respective deaths in 1979 and 1997. Avis's data has been incorporated into DCHP-2 (thanks to the Strathy Language Unit, Queen's University). The 1990s saw increased commercial interest in synchronic lexicography, an interest that manifested itself in a Canadian "dictionary war" between the *Gage Canadian Dictionary*, the market leader, and the new publications of the *ITP Nelson Dictionary of English* (1997) and the *Canadian Oxford Dictionary* (1998, rev. 2004) (Dollinger and Gaylie 2015). This extremely active period for Canadian lexicography restored interest in a new historical dictionary; at this point, no Canadian publisher was prepared for the sudden demise of the print dictionary caused by the rise of dictionary software on personal computers and online dictionaries on the Web.

In January 2005, the Canadian English in the Global Context conference in Toronto in honour of J. K. Chambers offered a new springboard for historical lexicography of Canadian English with a panel discussion on a new edition of DCHP-1 (see Barber and Considine 2010). Work on a revision began in March 2006 with the appointment of the author as editor-in-chief by Terry Pratt and David Friend of Nelson Ltd., the successor company of Gage Ltd. Nelson provided some support until 2009, at which point the language reference unit *de facto* closed as a consequence of a changing dictionary market. From that point on, DCHP-2 became a purely academic project with no publishing affiliation or support. The Canadian language reference market was shaken hard at that time: in October 2008, Oxford University Press decided not to revise the *Canadian Oxford Dictionary* and to lay off its staff, despite the sales records that the dictionary managed to achieve.

23.3 Core issues and topics

Work on DCHP-2 is based on five principles. A key aspect has been the integration of diachronic data from the quotation file with synchronic studies of Canadian English where possible (#1: diachrony and synchrony). The second goal was to cater to a wide readership, both scholarly and popular, leading to the adoption of open access publication (#2: accessibility and user friendliness). The third principle was to present the evidence supporting all decisions to include items as Canadianisms, something that the limitations of print publication prevented in the major Canadian desk dictionaries (Gage, ITP Nelson and COD) (#3: presentation of data beyond the quotation paragraph), together with a clear rationale for a classification of a term or meaning as Canadian in an accessible account, the "Word Story", which gives important context, relevant linguistic information and, where possible, details on the historical development and trajectory of the term or meaning that go beyond the information shown in the quotation paragraph (#4: a readable and encyclopaedically enriched etymological account). Fifth and finally, linguistic variation has been treated seriously, with a focus on geographical variation (#5 focus on variation).

23.3.1 Structure of an entry

These principles are reflected in the entry structure. Entries are organized by a headword's meanings. Figure 23.1 shows the first meaning of the term *all-dressed*, which is an adjective referring to the standard (free) toppings for fast foods such as pizza. The second meaning, referring to a flavour of potato chips (*all-dressed chips*), is not shown for space constraints, and has an identical structure as meaning 1. An entry begins, above the horizontal line, with the headword (lemma) and is followed by the source language or donor variety where applicable.

The meaning number is next, 1, and names the first meaning, its quotations and information. The number is followed by the part of speech, here *adj*. DCHP-2 provides the most frequent meaning first, as in a synchronic dictionary rather than a historical one, emphasizing the nature of the second edition, which focuses on twentieth-century terms. This is followed by a short definition. The two definitions are quoted next (example 1):

(1)

1 *adj*. all the standard, free garnishes and condiments for some foods such as pizzas, hamburgers, or hot dogs.

2 *adj*. a flavour of potato chip, usually in the compound ***all-dressed chips***.

Each meaning is assigned to one of seven types (see Section 23.3.2) and in some cases more than one. The type is followed by a "Word Story", which expresses the rationale for the type assignment. The Word Story links all information, referring to frequency charts when available (see Section 23.3.3) and often contextualizing select quotations from the quotation block or, in this case, material from the linguistic literature. For *all-dressed*, meaning 1, the Type Assignment and Word Story are as shown in Figure 23.1, with the latter shown below (example 2):

(2)

Type: 1. Origin – Internationally, the term is still almost uniquely used in Canada (see Chart 1), but shows an interesting regional distribution within Canada. The term is a literal translation of a French term (*toute garnie*) and is most frequent in Quebec English, Eastern Ontario and Saskatechewan (the latter of which is a bit of a mystery) (Boberg 2005: 38; 43). The term is most frequently used in the province of Quebec (92 percent of the time when referring to pizza), particularly in Montreal (96 percent with pizza). Canada outside Quebec only uses *all-dressed* with pizza a mere 8 percent of the time (see Boberg 2012:500), employing instead terms such as "deluxe" (parts

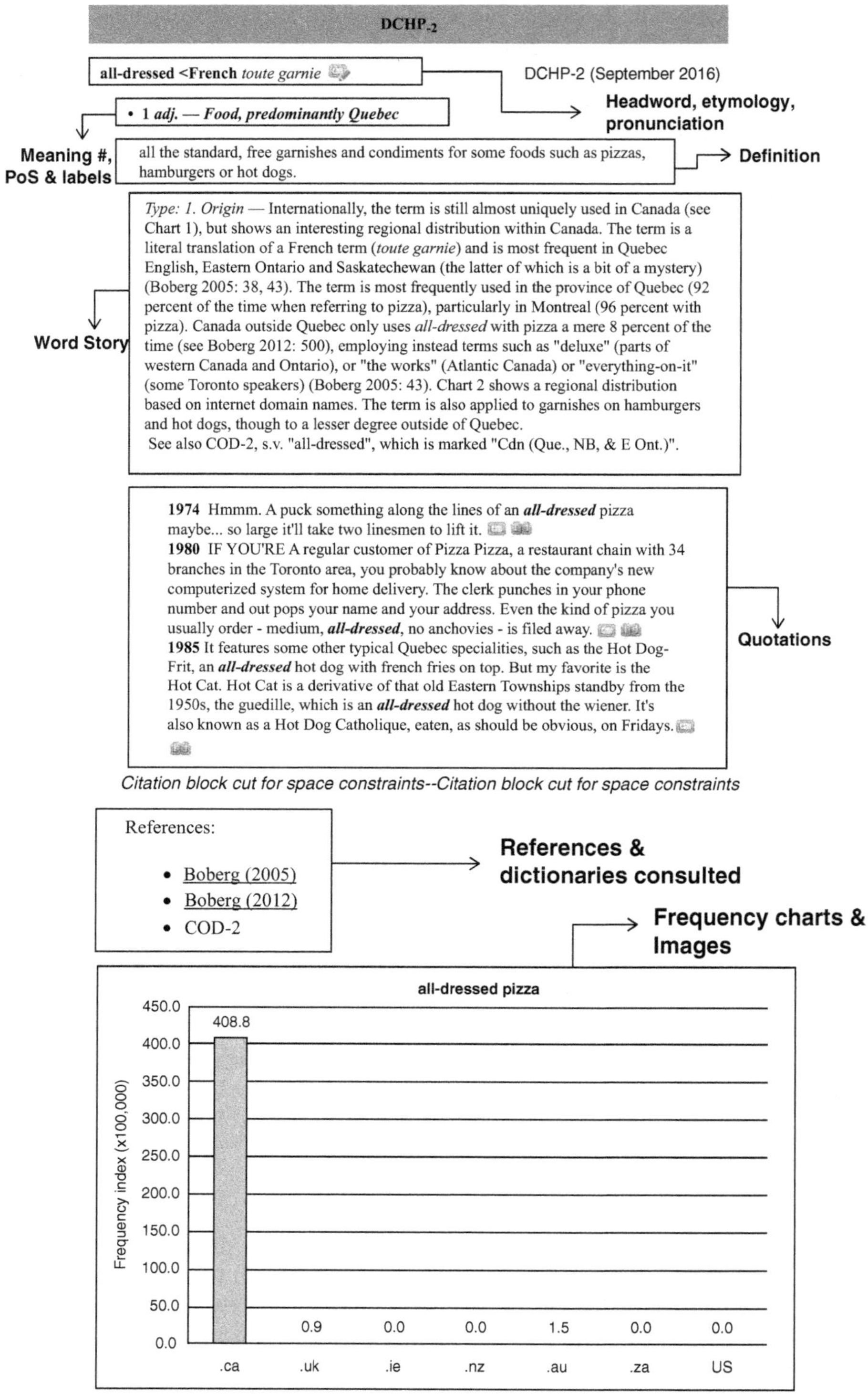

Figure 23.1 Structure of an entry at the example of *all-dressed*, meaning 1 (meaning 2 omitted for space constraints)

of western Canada and Ontario), "the works" (Atlantic Canada) or "everything-on-it" (some Toronto speakers) (Boberg 2005: 43). Chart 2 shows a regional distribution based on Internet domain names. The term is also applied to garnishes on hamburgers and hot dogs, though to a lesser degree outside of Quebec.
See also COD-2, s.v. "all-dressed", which is marked "Cdn (Que., NB, and E Ont.)".

For meaning 2, referring to potato chips, the situation is a bit different, as shown below (example 3). This meaning is attested from 1990 onwards and is classified as Type 3 – Semantic Change in Canadian English (see 23.3.2):

(3)
Type: 3. Semantic Change – In contrast to meaning 1, this term is in use nationally and in contrast to other locations (see Chart 3). As the 1990 quotation suggests, the motivation behind the flavour was to combine the all-dressed pizza flavour with chips.

The length of the quotations is rather generous as it was aimed at providing rather more than less context, so much so that traditional lexicographical principles of brevity stand in contrast to the online scenario where page limitations do not apply. The 1990 quotation from the *Ottawa Citizen*, referred to in the Word Story, reads as follows:

> Unless he or she has pretty persuasive excuses for not being capable of it, a middle-years kid is expected to be able to: ride a bike; skip a rope; be good at swimming-pool cannonballs, running, ad hoc wrestling and Nintendo; blow gum bubbles; know the plot premises of at least 17 afterschool and Saturday-morning cartoon shows; have a minimum of four different smartass comebacks that can be made out loud in the schoolyard or (quietly, in a mutter) to teachers and parents; know the lyrics to a couple of gross and disgusting songs; and be capable of consuming vast quantities of all-dressed-pizza-flavored potato chips, soda-pop Skittles and Slimer ghost gum.
>
> (*Ottawa Citizen*, 1 Oct. 1990: C1)

Quotations longer than the traditionally only sentence-long quotations in historical dictionaries are required for many linguistic purposes. An automated highlighting function is integrated into the search tool and allows the easy location of the term even in longer quotations.

The quotation block follows the Word Story or a Fist Note, the latter of which can be inserted to highlight a salient aspect of the meaning. While not shown in *all-dressed*, the Fist Note adds information that would help the general reader to contextualize the definition. Under *adhesion*, defined as "an agreement between an Aboriginal group and the federal government to join an existing treaty agreed to by another Aboriginal group or groups", the following Fist Note is offered (example 4):

(4)
☞ Treaties are only signed with the Crown, the federal government, yet provincial governments often play a role in the negotiations.

As some of the quotations refer to provincial governments, such clarification seemed in order. Fist Notes disambiguate potentially problematic issues without creating long, unwieldy definitions. For information pertaining to all meanings, another Fist Note can be inserted above the horizontal line following the headword.

Cross-references, which are hyperlinked (not shown in *all-dressed*), are found below the definition and possible Fist Note. *Skidoo*, for instance, is linked to the head words *bombardier*[2] from DCHP-2 and *motor toboggan* and *snowmobile* from DCHP-1 legacy data. DCHP-1 entries, such as the last two headwords, are visually separated by labels and yellow backgrounds from the new content, which appears on white background.

Finally, the quotation block follows, set apart by brown shading from the rest of the entry. As can be expected, the earliest quotation is always listed, here for meaning 1 from 1974, and quotations, insofar as possible, go up to the years 2015 or 2016. Clicking on the book symbol after each quotation provides the reference source in the right-hand margin (not shown in Figure 23.1). For the 1974 quotation it is the following (example 5):

(5)

ID	100423
Author	Boulton, Rick
Title	The Ottawa Citizen
Page	20
Periodical Date	20 Apr. 1974
Year Published	1974
URL	http://news.google.com/newspapers?id=tLoyAAAAIBAJ&sjid=xOwFAAAAIBAJ&pg=3876, 2454279&dq=all-dressed-pizza&hl=en
Place	Ottawa, ON

We include the full URL for any digital sources for further consultation, though some of our databases require a subscription.

The quotation block is followed by the literature references. Here is referenced one dictionary, COD-2, which is the second edition of the *Canadian Oxford Dictionary* (Barber 2004) and two variationist studies by Boberg (2005, 2012), whose reference details are displayed in the right-hand margin in the same manner as the quotations.

The reference list may include audio-visual references, such as YouTube videos, for example, for (ice) hockey shots, to illustrate the specifics of a *slap shot* or a *wrist shot*. Although videos are always linked from external sites, images are provided on our own server and are shown just above the first frequency chart; in the case of *all-dressed*, meaning 2, we include a photo of a package of chips of the all-dressed flavour (not shown in Figure 23.1).

23.3.2 Six-tiered typology plus a "Non-Canadian" class

One of the biggest desiderata in Canadian English lexicography to date has been a lack of tangible contrastive evidence for claims about the Canadian status of a given term or meaning. Although all desk dictionaries were hampered by methodological and space constraints, the point is best illustrated with a look at some of COD-2's terms labelled "Cdn" (Barber 2004). Some examples reveal cases of very narrow definitions, such as *VAdm* "Vice Admiral, a naval officer ranking below admiral and above rear admiral", extremely localized contexts, such as *nose* "the northeast portion of the Grand Banks of Newfoundland", *principal* "a lawyer who supervises an articling student", or *wreckhouse winds* "extremely strong winds which blow across Cape Ray from the Long Range Mountains in Newfoundland". In other cases, such as *gold* "an especially good seat in a hockey arena etc.", *tent ring* "a ring of stones for holding down a tent etc., indicating a past campsite", *UFFI* "urea formaldehyde foam insulation" or *farmer's sausage* "type of raw pork sausage", the lack of rationale for the terms' assessment as Canadian casts doubts as to their status. COD-2 might be accused of using opaque criteria in order to boost their Canadianism count (Dollinger and Gaylie 2015): why is *gold* Canadian? Why *farmer's sausage*? If such questions arise from a labelling practice, it causes more problems than it solves. COD-2 has taken this practice to the extreme, while similar cases are also found in Gage-5, for instance.

In order to improve this situation, a six-tiered typology of Canadianisms is offered in DCHP-2, together with a category of "non-Canadian" (Dollinger 2015a):

- **Type 1 – Origin:** terms or meanings created in what is now Canada
- **Type 2 – Preservation:** terms or meanings once widespread in many Englishes but now preserved mainly in Canadian English
- **Type 3 – Semantic Change:** terms that have undergone semantic change in Canadian English (i.e. terms that have acquired new meanings in Canada)
- **Type 4 – Culturally Significant:** terms or meanings widely regarded as important to national identity or history
- **Type 5 – Frequency:** terms or meanings that are more frequent in Canadian English than in the other major national varieties
- **Type 6 – Memorial:** terms or meanings that are the flip-side of cultural salience: terms or meanings that derive from negative events in Canada's past
- **Non-Canadian:** terms or meanings that have been labelled 'Canadian' in other sources or that we originally suspected to be Canadian

Type 1 (Origin) includes terms such as *all-dressed*, *garburator* "in-sink organic waste disposal", *frosh week* "orientation week at university", *humidex* "subjective heat index depending on humidity" or *parkade* "parking garage". Preservations (Type 2) include *drinking box* (vs. drink box, the more modern form without – *ing* (see Dollinger 2015b: 181–183), *dunch* "soggy bread" (a Newfoundland regionalism), *invigilate* "to supervise students during an exam" from British English, or *pencil crayon* "coloured pencil". Semantic change in Canadian English (Type 3) includes *to acclaim* "elected by virtue of being the sole candidate"; *toque* "beanie, woolen hat", which in British English referred to other kinds of hats; or *Canuck* "Canadian", which was formerly a racist term of abuse derived from Hawaiian *kanaka* "Hawaiian, or dark-skinned person". Culturally salient terms (Type 4) include terms relating to universal health care, e.g. *health care card*, ice hockey terms, e.g. *backhander* "shot with the back of the hockey stick" or *goalie mask* "protective mask", and others, such as *Native Canadian*, which is now used more frequently outside of Canada.

Type 5 (Frequency) includes terms that occur most often in Canada based on the normalized Internet searches we provide for most terms (see Dollinger 2016a for the methodology). These include, for example, *advanced green* "traffic signal allowing oncoming traffic to turn left", *cube van* "type of truck", *ginger group* "more radical part of group", *to table something* "bring forward, rather than to postpone [as in US English]", as in *to table legislation*, or *goalie pads* "protective shin pads for hockey goalie". This merger of comparative corpus linguistics methods with lexicography is perhaps the most important methodological innovation of DCHP-2. What was the introduction of maps in DARE with the geographical depiction of all occurrences of a term in the United States, might be the introduction of the comparative frequency charts in DCHP-2.

Type 6, finally, was the last addition to the typology scheme and is the flip side of Cultural Salience (Type 4): whereas the latter is something Canadians take pride in, *Memorial* terms refer to negative entities in Canada's history, for example, *residential school* "schools that abused aboriginal people, schools for cultural genocide"; terms of abuse, for example, *chink* "Chinese", *wop* "Italian"; or terms now obsolete, for example, *Eskimo* "Inuit people", or racist, for example, *iron chink* "fish-gutting machine, named for the predominant role of Chinese labourers in gutting fish before the machine's invention". In other words, terms or meanings that were once widespread and form part of Canada's negative heritage today.

The seventh category highlights terms that were thought to be Canadian, either in previous works or by the editorial team, but which have now been assigned to the category Non-Canadian. Please note that the label Non-Canadian merely means that a term has no special Canadian dimension, although it may be widely used and understood by speakers of Canadian English. This category is an integral part of a contrastive dictionary, because without it, future lexicographers will be forced to repeat unnecessary labour. This category includes terms such as *ASA* "acetylsalicylic acid" (labelled Canadian in COD-2), *candyfloss* "sugar spun cotton candy" (COD-2), *friendship cake* "type of cake with shared ingredients" (ITP Nelson), or *icing sugar* (COD-2 "Cdn, Brit., Austral. and NZ"). Terms the editors suspected to be Canadian but turned out not to be include *to write* (an exam) – vs. to take an exam, etc., which has higher frequencies elsewhere – and *clawback* "funds taken back", which is most frequent in the United States. Non-Canadianisms are set on a red background with a label on the top-right, as is shown in Figure 23.2 for the expression *Bob's your uncle* "all is good, all is clear".

23.3.3 Visualization of evidence

The Word Story, which gives the evidence for inclusion and assignment of one or more typology classes, is supported with visual charts of two kinds: frequency charts that use normalized site-restricted web searches based on a measure called the 'Frequency Index' on the one hand (see Dollinger 2016a), and charts of semantically analysed terms in the corpus linguistics tradition (e.g. percentages of meaning 1 vs. meaning 2), on the other hand.

The Frequency Index charts can be either international – comparing Canadian with U.S. with UK and other data (top left pane in Figure 23.3 for *all-dressed pizza*) – or regional within Canada (top right pane in Figure 23.3) – comparing frequencies among Canada's 13 provinces and territories. (It was not possible to provide information for areas that are linguistically defined rather than geographically). The two charts show that with more than 400 index points[2] *all-dressed pizza* is most frequent in the .ca domain, followed after a considerable gap by .uk with a mere 0.9 index points. Within Canada, however, the province of Quebec stands out with 13.1 index points, followed by Newfoundland with 4.6 and Saskatchewan with 2.4, allowing the confirmation of studies based on written questionnaires (Boberg 2005: 38) that *all-dressed* has a regional Quebec dimension within Canada and is more infrequent elsewhere. For *all-dressed chips*, the second meaning of the entry, the middle left pane shows that this term is almost exclusive to the .ca domain.

The case is very different for the expression *Bob's your uncle*, shown already in Figure 23.2. Here the claim of Canadian-ness by COD-2 is refuted on frequency grounds

Bob's your uncle DCHP-2 (July 2016)

Non-Canadianism

• *expression — slang, informal*

denoting completion of a task, ease of completion, or satisfaction.

The phrase Bob's your uncle is likely a preservation from British English, possibly Cockney English, yet one that is not used in distinct ways in Canada. According to internet searches the expression is used in many former British colonies (see Chart 1). The term is used in ways characteristic of informal speech in Inner Circle varieties more generally (Inner Circle as defined by Kachru (1985), the countries that have predominantly first language speakers of English, usually the UK, Canada, the US, Australia, New Zealand). Many theories exist as to the origin of the phrase, a popular one being that it refers to the appointment of Arthur Balfour to the position of Chief Secretary of Ireland by his uncle Robert Cecil (see, e.g. the 1997 quotation). The origins, however, remain unknown. OED-3 lists the earliest citation for Bob's your uncle from Partridge's 1937 slang dictionary (see OED-3, s.v. "Bob (n7, 3.) - Bob's your uncle").
See also COD-2, s.v. "Bob", which is marked "Cdn & Brit.".

☞ Used in many Inner Circle varieties of English. Not meeting any of the requirements of Canadianness in DCHP-2 (see Dollinger 2015c).

1970 I'm beginning to get the idea, and to start to whistle when the attacking team makes a sloppy kick out of bounds. After all, you've heard of 10-goal polo players? I am now a one-goal spectator. I plan to be insufferable in the Rams' press box all season. "But, really, if you want to see a kicker, I mean, bash on, you should see the goalie England have." A pass pattern may find me stifling a yawn. "Oh, yes, good and all that. But, now, you should see Bobby Charlton, after all." I may even get a Manchester United pocket patch. And ***Bob's your uncle.***

Figure 23.2 Example of a non-Canadian expression, *Bob's your uncle*

by the middle right pane in Figure 23.3, which shows that South Africa (.za), New Zealand (.nz) and Ireland (.ie) show much higher frequencies than Canada (.ca), which is roughly on par with the US domains (a compound measure for the U.S. domains .gov, .edu, .us and .mil). The methodological details are discussed in Dollinger (2016a), where it is shown that "cleaner" web-scaled resources of 12 billion words or more (e.g. Sketch-Engine) are still not large enough to allow for comparisons of open class lexical items across varieties of English.

Besides the two kinds of frequency charts, there is a third type of chart in use. The bottom row of Figure 23.3 shows a percentage comparison, based on 100 semantically analysed sentences in each of the years 1990, 2000 and 2013 for the verb *to table*. In both figures, the columns on the left show the percentage of the meaning "bring forward", as in *The proposal*

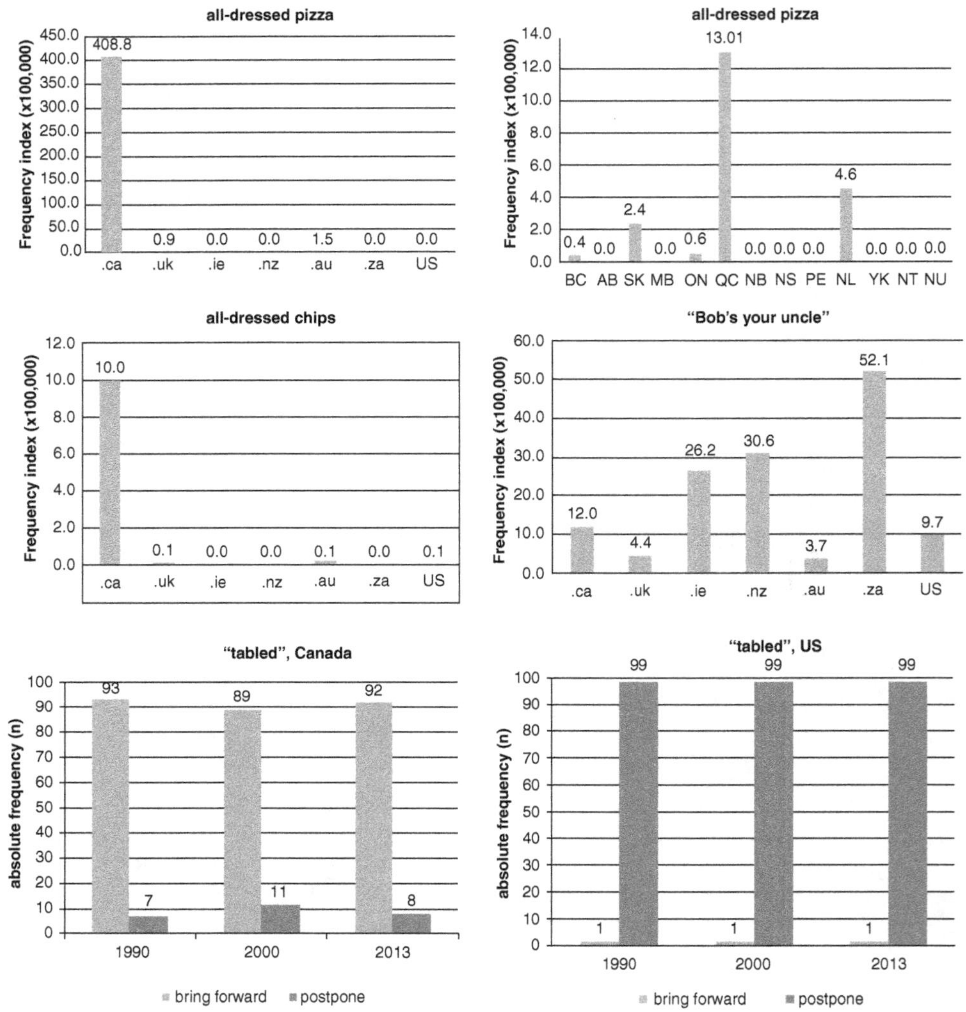

Figure 23.3 Frequency charts (top four) and percentile charts (bottom two)

was tabled for immediate discussion, and on the right of the meaning "postpone, delay", as in, *The issue was tabled until the next meeting*. The data shows consistently over the three periods, that the prevalent meaning in Canada in about 90 percent of unambiguous terms is "to bring forward, raise for discussion", whereas the American meaning, in 99 out of 100, is "to postpone". Such differences and variation require the consistent analysis of comparable samples, and it is hoped that this distinction, which has been undocumented, together with others will prove useful to the readers of DCHP-2.

23.4 Looking to the future

The frequency charts may be considered the major methodological innovation of DCHP-2 because of their linking of variationist approaches with historical lexicography (see Dollinger and Brinton 2008: 57–59). The quantitative techniques and, in the case of frequency charts, the big data approach via open web searches means that there is a lot more to discover about CanE lexis and semantics than meets the eye. The first chief editor of the DCHP-1, Charles J. Lovell surmised that the label of Canadianism in the sense of "origin alone" "would limit our field to but a few hundred words" (1955: 4). Although this category provides interesting examples: e.g. *parkade*, *Canadian tuxedo* "denim trousers paired with a denim jacket" or *loonie* "one-dollar coin", these terms may not be the biggest or even the most important part of the lexicon. What is increasingly becoming clear is that smaller, yet consistent semantic differences may be among the most important lexical distinctions (see, e.g. the case of *take up #9* "going over the answers of a test", which is an Ontarian innovation that has not entered the United States, Dollinger 2016b). If this component is indeed as important as it seems, linguists need to take a closer look at lexical meanings, semantic fields and meanings in use, which is more challenging than form-based approaches, which, in contrast to meanings, can be easily searched. Improvements on that side would be an area for innovation for any new edition, a DCHP-3, so to speak, and it is here that advances in semantic web technologies might come to the rescue, as a Web 2.0 morphs into a semantically tagged version of the Web.

Although regional variation is one of the main foci in DCHP-2, it was unfortunately impossible to go beyond the provincial and territorial levels for most terms. Here, the technology of geo-tagging in combination with Twitter feeds (e.g. Huang et al. 2016) or other social media services would offer the most promising avenue for innovation. But there are also theoretically more challenging problems: for instance, Avis's suggestion of the introduction of a cross-border label of North American, as "hosts of terms cannot be claimed by one country or the other with any degree of confidence whatever" (1967: n. p.). Obviously, in DCHP-2 we chose another path, including only terms with a claim to the North American label that could be considered *culturally significant* or as *memorial* in Canada. In that sense, we avoided the difficult question of how to characterize a North Americanism (Dollinger and von Schneidemesser 2011: 118).

As with OED-3, a primary task of DCHP-2 was to move the dictionary to an online format, a move that allowed space to present much more information and evidence to the reader. To produce a DCHP-3 would require a great deal more work to revise and update all 10,000 entries in DCHP-1 as well as to track and add more new Canadianisms. Unfortunately, given the emphasis of scholarly funding agencies on theoretical or methodological innovation, DCHP-2 was never seen as producing a complete revision of DCHP-1. This work was deemed less important than introducing innovative features and adding newer terms and new kinds of evidence to the standard historical dictionary.

23.5 Conclusion

Landau (2001: 347) writes that the scheduling of "dictionaries is notoriously inaccurate, most dramatically in the preparation of scholarly dictionaries". In more than one way, there is always reason for celebration when a historical dictionary is finished. Or begun for that matter. Lovell was the right man with the right knowledge to kick start DCHP-1. Lovell saw historical lexicography as the "neglected stepchild of the arts" (1956: 24), reaching the conclusion that in order to obtain funding one would need to have to show quite a bit of work already; a prediction that proved him right and that was repeated in DCHP-2.

DCHP-1 was celebrated, perhaps 'hyped', and quickly forgotten. With its demise the expertise for how to produce such works in Canada went also missing in a discipline of linguistics that had largely disassociated itself from such practical projects. John Considine's assessment, predating the start of the DCHP-2 project by three years, is telling:

> There is an important respect in which Canada is, at the beginning of the twenty-first century, lagging behind Australia and South Africa in the documentation of its own variety of English, just as it was at the beginning of the twentieth.
>
> (Considine 2003: 265)

What is hoped is that DCHP-2's publication in the format that is most appreciated by the born-digital generation, with free and unlimited access, will make up ground in contrast to its sister varieties and would place the discussion about Canadianisms on an empirically and theoretically sounder footing. There clearly is an interest in the lexis of Canadian English, yet the tools were "lagging behind", to use Considine's words, if they were available at all. There are added benefits as well, as the data behind DCHP-2 represents the biggest and most precise lexical resource on Canadian English, certainly from an historical angle (see Dollinger forthcoming).

The goal from 2006 was to finish a second edition within seven years, in 2013. Since our first three-year grant proposal procured only 14 percent, c. $36,000, of the funds sought (in line with Lovell's predictions for DCHP-1), the 2017 publication date, coinciding with Canada's 150th anniversary celebrations and half a century after DCHP-1, can be seen as on target in the larger context. It is hoped that the finished product reflects to some degree the very sensible ideas and words of warning from 2005 (see Considine 2010a: 146) that "what matters is what has been achieved in the real world with real money". Money we did spend, I am proud to say, exclusively in Canada, but that money was slow to come forth. Katherine Barber, editor of the *Canadian Oxford Dictionary* surmised in 2005 that revising DCHP-1 is, if done "right, an enormous project" (2010: 144). I hope that we got it right to some degree.

Related topics

Lexicography and corpus linguistics; lexicography and information science; dictionaries and language policy; dictionaries and culture; electronic dictionaries; FrameNet; using the Web for lexicographic purposes; information retrieval for lexicographic purposes; English lexicography in the Internet era.

Further reading

Dollinger, S. (2015a). "How to Write a Historical Dictionary: A Sketch of The Dictionary of Canadianisms on Historical Principles, Second Edition", *Ozwords* 24(2): 1–3 and 6 (October 2015). www.academia.edu/18967380/ (14 Oct. 2016).

This article is a concise and accessible introduction to DCHP-2 for a general readership, offering a different viewpoint and more examples.

Dollinger, S. (2016a). "Googleology as Smart Lexicography: Big Messy Data for Better Regional Labels", *Dictionaries: Journal of the Dictionary Society of North America* 37(2): 60–98.

This paper introduces the methodology behind the frequency charts in DCHP-2. It shows that the unfiltered Web, when used with caution and fail-safes, offers information that even the largest web-scaled resources cannot provide.

Dollinger, S. and L. von Schneidemesser. (2011). "Canadianism, Americanism, North Americanism? A Comparison of DARE and DCHP", *American Speech* 86(2): 115–151.

This article problematizes issues relating to American and Canadian lexicography and the concept of North Americanism based on a comparison from fascicle T in both DCHP and the Dictionary of American Regional English. It introduces a method using Facebook to identify the regional dimension of terms.

Notes

1 A thank-you to DCHP-2's associate editor, Prof. Margery Fee, for most useful and detailed feedback on an earlier version of this chapter and to Joseph Farquharson for a detailed reading of the chapter in an academia.edu session discussion.
2 Index points are the normalized measure that allows cross-comparisons across Internet domains of different sizes (Dollinger 2016a).

References

Alexander, H. (1967) "Words to Call Our Own [Review of DCHP-1]", *The Globe and Mail*, 30 December 1967: A13.

Avis, W. S. (1967) "Introduction", in Dollinger, Brinton and Fee (2013), www.dchp.ca/DCHP-1/pages/frontmatter#introduction.

Avis, W. S. (1969) "Problems in Editing *A Dictionary of Canadianisms on Historical Principles*". Paper presented in Section 13, *Modern Languages Association*, December 28, 1969, Denver, CO. Typescript University of Queen's Archives, Avis Fonds.

Avis, W. S., C. Crate, P. Drysdale, D. Leechman and M. H. Scargill and J. Charles (eds.) (1967) *A Dictionary of Canadianisms on Historical Principles*. Toronto: Gage. See Dollinger, Brinton and Fee (2013)

Barber, K. (2004) *Canadian Oxford Dictionary*. Don Mills, ON: Oxford University Press.

Barber, K. (2010), see Barber and Considine (2010).

Barber, K. and J. Considine (2010) "Revising the Dictionary of Canadianisms: Views From 2005", in Considine (2010b) (ed.), pp. 141–149.

Boberg, C. (2005) "The North American Regional Vocabulary Survey: New Variables and Methods in the Study of North American English", *American Speech* 80(1): 22–60.

Boberg, C. (2012) "English as a Minority Language in Quebec", *World Englishes* 31 (4), pp. 493–502.

Cassidy, F. G. and R. Le Page (eds.) (1980) *Dictionary of Jamaican English*. 2nd edition. Cambridge: Cambridge University Press.

Considine, J. (2003) "Dictionaries of Canadian English", *Lexikos* 13: 250–270.

Considine, J. (2010a) See Considine (2010b), pp. 144–49.

Considine, J. (ed.) (2010b) *Current Projects in Historical Lexicography*. Newcastle: Cambridge Scholars.

Clarke, S. (ed.) (1993) *Focus on Canada*. Amsterdam: Benjamins.

Craigie, W., and J. R. Hulbert (eds.) (1968 [1938–44]). *A Dictionary of American English on Historical Principles*. 4 Volumes. Chicago: University of Chicago Press.

Currell, H. (1967) "Letter to P.D. Drysdale, W. J. Gage. Apr. 18, 1967", University of Victoria Archives. Centre for Lexicography Fond.

Dollinger, S. (2006) "Towards a Fully Revised and Extended Edition of the *Dictionary of Canadianisms on Historical Principles* (DCHP-2): Background, Challenges, Prospects", *Historical Sociolinguistics/Sociohistorical Linguistics* 6. www.academia.edu/4591720/.

Dollinger, S. (2010) "Software From the Bank of Canadian English as an Open Source Tool for the Dialectologist: ling.surf and Its Features", in M. Markus, C. Upton and R. Heuberger (eds.), *Joseph Wright's English Dialect Dictionary and Beyond: Studies in Late Modern English Dialectology*. Berne: Lang, pp. 249–261.

Dollinger, S. (2015a) "How to Write a Historical Dictionary: A Sketch of *The Dictionary of Canadianisms on Historical Principles*, Second Edition", *Ozwords* 24(2): 1–3 and 6 (October 2015).

Dollinger, S. (2015b) *The Written Questionnaire in Social Dialectology: History, Theory, Practice.* [IMPACT 40]. Amsterdam: Benjamins.

Dollinger, S. (2016a) "Googleology as Smart Lexicography: Big Messy Data for Better Regional Labels". *Dictionaries* 37(2): 60–98.

Dollinger, S. (2016b) "TAKE UP #9 as a Semantic Isogloss on the Canada-US Border", *World Englishes* (Early View) http://onlinelibrary.wiley.com.ezproxy.ub.gu.se/doi/10.1111/weng.12212/full.

Dollinger, S. (forthcoming) "Canadian English Lexis and Semantics: An Assessment in Contrastive, Real-time Perspective, 1683–2016", in M. Kytö and L. Siebers (eds.), *Early North American Englishes*, Amsterdam/Philadelphia: Benjamins.

Dollinger, S. and L. Brinton. (2008) "Canadian English Lexis: Historical and Variationist Perspectives", *Anglistik: International Journal of English Studies* 19(2): 43–64.

Dollinger, S. and A. Gaylie. (2015) "Canadianisms in Canadian Desk Dictionaries: Scope, Accuracy, Desiderata", paper presented at DSNA-20 and SHEL-9 Conference, Vancouver, 5 June 2015.

Dollinger, S. and L. von Schneidemesser (2011) "Canadianism, Americanism, North American? A Comparison of DARE and DCHP", *American Speech* 86 (2), pp. 115–151.

Dollinger, S. (ed.-in-chief), L. J. Brinton and M. Fee (eds.) (2013) *DCHP-1 Online: A Dictionary of Canadianisms on Historical Principles Online*. Based on W. S. Avis et al. (1967). Online dictionary, http://dchp.ca/dchp1. Vancouver: University of British Columbia.

Dollinger, S. (chief editor) and M. Fee (associate editor). (2017). *DCHP-2: The Dictionary of Canadianisms on Historical Principles, Second Edition.* With the assistance of Baillie Ford, Alexandra Gaylie and Gabrielle Lim. Online dictionary. Vancouver and Gothenburg: University of British Columbia and University of Gothenburg. www.dchp.ca/dchp2

Dresser, N. (1968) "Centennial Reader", *Voxair*, Winnipeg, MB, January 2: n.p.

Gregg, R. J. (1993) "Canadian English Lexicography", in S. Clarke (ed.), pp. 27–44.

Görlach, M. (1990) "The Dictionaries of Transplanted Varieties of Languages: English", in Hausmann et al. (eds.). Vol. II: pp. 1475–99.

Hausmann, F. J., O. Reichmann, H. E. Wiegand and L. Zgusta (eds.) (1989–1991). *Wörterbücher: Dictionaries: Dictionnaires: An International Encyclopedia of Lexicography*. 3 Volumes. Berlin: de Gruyter.

Huang, Y., D. Guo, A. Kasakoff and J. Grieve (2016) "Understanding U.S. Regional Linguistic Variation with Twitter Data Analysis", *Computers, Environment and Urban Systems* 59: 244–255.

Landau, S. (2001) *The Art and Craft of Lexicography*. 2nd edition. Cambridge: Cambridge University Press.

Lovell, C. J. (1955) "Whys and Hows of Collecting for the Dictionary of Canadian English: Part I: Scope and Source Material", *Journal of the Canadian Linguistic Association* 1(2, Oct.): 3–8.

Lovell, C. J. (1958) "A Sampling of Materials for a Dictionary of Canadian English Based on Historical Principles", *Canadian Journal of Linguistics* 4(/1), pp. 7–33.

McDavid, R. I. (1980) "[Reviews of] Scargill, M. H. (1977) A Short History of Canadian English. Victoria, B.C. and McConnell, Ruth E. (1979) Our Own Voice: Canadian English and How It Is Studied. Toronto", *Journal of English Linguistics* 14(March): 45–58.

McDavid, R. I. (1970) "Canadian English", *American Speech* 46(3–4): 287–289.

Mathews, M. M. (ed.) (1951) *Dictionary of Americanisms*. Chicago: University of Chicago Press.

Moore, M. (1967) "How We Talk Canadian", *Saturday Night*. November 1967: 54–55.

Ray, R. (2003) "Obituary of Gage Love 1917–2003: Making the World a Better Place", *The Globe and Mail*, 30 October 2003: R9.

Scargill, M. H. (1977) *A Short History of Canadian English*. Victoria: Sono Nis.

Scargill, M. H. (1967) "Preface", in Dollinger et al. (2013), www.dchp.ca/DCHP-1/pages/frontmatter#preface.

Scargill, M. H. and H. J. Warkentyne (1972) "The Survey of Canadian English: A Report", *The English Quarterly: A Publication of the* Canadian Council of Teachers of English 5(3, Fall): 47–104.

Story, G. M., K. William and J.D.A. Widdowson (eds.) (1999) *Dictionary of Newfoundland English*. Online edition. www.heritage.nf.ca/dictionary/ (Accessed 21 January 2016).

Wees, W. R. (1967) "Foreword in Dollinger et al. (2013)". www.dchp.ca/DCHP-1/pages/frontmatter#foreword.

24
FrameNet

Josef Ruppenhofer, Hans C. Boas and Collin F. Baker

24.1 Introduction

FrameNet is a research project that seeks to instantiate the principles of Frame Semantics as proposed by Charles J. Fillmore (1977, 1985) in the analysis of the English lexicon. The main idea is that the meanings of words are best characterized in terms of experience-based schematizations of events and objects in the speaker's world. Such schematizations relate to particular types of events and the participants and circumstances involved in them. The schematizations are referred to in Frame Semantics as "semantic frames". Individual word senses are called "lexical units" (LUs). When a lexical unit belongs to a given frame, the LU is said to "evoke" that frame. Typically, senses of several distinct lemmas evoke a common schematization, that is, groups of word senses evoke the same frame. The roles associated with an event are referred to as "frame elements" (FEs). One and the same system of analysis applies to events, relations, states, and objects; the frame-evoking expressions may be single items or multi-word expressions, and they may belong to any syntactic category (Fillmore, Johnson and Petruck 2003).

For example, in (1) the adjective *different* (the "target" LU) is said to evoke the Similarity frame, which is also evoked, among others, by further adjectives such as *alike* and *disparate*; verbs such as *differ* and *resemble*; nouns such as *similarity* and *distinction*; and the prepositions *like* and *unlike*, as well as multi-words such as *spitting image.n* and *take after.v*.

(1)
The qualities that make a poet are not **different** in kind from what other men have.

The Similarity frame is characterized by relationships holding between different FEs, such as *Entity1* and *Entity2* (which may instead be jointly presented as *Entities)*. The frame has to do with the degree to which two or more distinct entities, whether concrete or abstract, are similar to or different from each other, along some implicit or explicit *Dimension*. The *Degree* of similarity or difference may or may not be specified explicitly.

In addition to assembling frame descriptions and lists of frame-evoking LUs, frame semanticists are also concerned with documenting the syntactic realizations of *Frame Elements* (Atkins, Fillmore and Johnson 2003, Fillmore 2007).

24.2 Historical perspective

The FrameNet project is the result of the application of the insights of Charles Fillmore's theory of Frame Semantics, which he and his colleagues developed during the 1980s and 1990s (Fillmore 1982, 1985; Fillmore and Atkins 1992). Frame Semantics grew out of Fillmore's earlier work on Case Grammar (Fillmore 1968), which proposed a list of semantic roles aimed at identifying grammatically relevant facets of a verb's meaning in terms of a set of basic labels such as Agentive, Instrumental, Dative, Factitive, Locative, etc., which served to identify the role played by each of the verb's arguments in the event it denotes. The collection of sets of different semantic roles came to be known as case frames, which specify a verb's semantic valency. One of the major ideas behind these semantic roles was that they are ordered in a hierarchy depending on their realization in terms of grammatical function. This hierarchy puts the semantic role Agentive at the top, followed by Instrumental, Objective, and other semantic roles. Following the initial success of Fillmore's proposals, several problems emerged regarding the status of semantic roles, including issues with the definition and granularity of semantic roles, problems reflecting cross-role generalizations, and problems of one-to-one correspondence (for an overview, see Levin and Rappaport Hovav 2005). As a result, during the 1970s, Fillmore moved away from his initial proposal that semantic roles are primary, and should be limited to a small set of roles (see, e.g., Fillmore 1975, 1976, 1977, 1978, 1979). The goal of this move was to develop a more elaborated model of the semantics of understanding, in contrast to a truth-conditional semantics, the prevalent approach to linguistic semantics at the time. More specifically, Fillmore suggested that so-called semantic frames should be regarded as primary for the description and analysis of meaning (and its syntactic relevance), and that semantic roles should be defined in terms of their semantic frames. The early 1980s saw the first fully developed version of Frame Semantics, which was articulated as a model based on the full and rich understanding required for the production of a text as well as the understanding of a text (Fillmore 1982) (for details, see Ziem 2008, Busse 2012, and Boas (2017)). Subsequently, Fillmore and Atkins's (1992) paper on the semantics of *risk* can be regarded as the blueprint for the architecture of FrameNet, which started in 1997 at the International Computer Science Institute in Berkeley, California, with funding from the National Science Foundation.

24.3 Core issues and topics: the FrameNet database

The core activity of FrameNet is the compilation of a lexicographic database, which currently (as of June, 2016) holds more than 1,223 frame descriptions together with lexical entries for more than 13,500 LUs and more than 202,000 manually annotated examples. The FrameNet database is made available free of charge for any purpose, and is used by hundreds of research groups worldwide.[1]

24.3.1 Lexical data

The lexicographic process starts with FN (FrameNet) staff members proposing a frame description, including what sorts of FEs the frame needs and what LUs might evoke it. At this stage, lexicographers rely both on their intuitions and on carefully constructed queries of electronic corpora. The basic criterion for delineating the boundaries of a frame is that all LUs should evoke the same type of event[2] and share the same inventory and configuration of FEs. In other words, the FEs should have the same semantic types, be of the same relative importance (which roughly equates to the traditional argument-adjunct distinction), and take the same pragmatic perspective (e.g. in active-form clauses, the verbs in the frame should take the same FE as their subject). For further discussion of these points, see Petruck et al. (2004).

24.3.2 Annotation of data

In the next step, example sentences are retrieved from electronic corpora for each target LU; trained annotators then use the FrameNet Desktop software to manually annotate roughly 10 to 20 sentences per LU. As the annotators apply labels showing which parts of the sentence fill which FE role, labels for their phrase types (PTs) and their grammatical functions (GFs) *vis-à-vis* the target word are added automatically. (The GF and PT labels can be manually corrected if necessary.) Annotations for three sentences are given in example 2:

(2)

a. [Customs officers AGENTS] **substituted** [the drugs OLD] [with another substance NEW] [as the consignment arrived TIME] . . .
b. [this measure NEW] was **substituted** [for birth weight OLD] [in the regression equation PLACE] [CNI AGENT]
c. [He AGENT] **substituted** [lower price labels NEW] [for those on the goods OLD].

The goal is to arrive at an annotation set capturing every possible combination of FE, GF, and PT. For instance, for the verb *substitute* in the frame **Replacing**, the annotations in (2a) and (2b) capture different mappings of the FEs OLD and NEW to grammatical functions due to a difference in voice, whereas (2a) and (2c) illustrate the possibility to express either of the FEs OLD and NEW as an object in an active-form clause, with the other being expressed as a PP. When the annotation is completed, the valence of each LU is automatically summarized by abstracting over the annotated examples. Finally, the lexical entry is "produced" as a report from the FrameNet database. It contains a brief definition of the LU together with the frame it evokes and valence tables that exhaustively document every attested combinatorial possibility of FEs and their syntactic realizations. Depending on the LU, it may also contain information such as the semantic type of the LU and a list of annotated support or controller verbs, etc. For an in-depth description of the FN workflow, see Fillmore et al. (2003), Ruppenhofer et al. (2010), and Fillmore and Baker (2010). Baker, Fillmore and Cronin (2003) provide a technical description of the FN database.

Since 2004, FN staff have also been annotating continuous texts, thereby creating lexical entries and a continuous corpus of annotated sentences. This full-text annotation differs from FN's lexicographic research in several ways:

1 Typically, between 2 and 10 LUs are annotated per sentence, in as many different frames. By contrast, in the lexicographic work, only one LU per sentence is annotated.
2 With full texts, annotators must label whatever the text contains, regardless of syntactic complexity, ambiguity, rhetorical infelicity, etc., whereas lexicographers can choose the clearest and simplest examples of a given LU to annotate
3 Full-text annotation drives the discovery of new frames, that is, if there are no existing frames they have to be created "on the fly".

24.3.3 Frame-to-frame relations

Over time, the number of semantic frames has grown to more than 1,000. To show that frames are not simply isolated entities, FN has developed an elaborate system of frame-to-frame relations producing a network of frames in which some frames are instances of others, some are components of others, etc. The most commonly found relations include those representing generalizations (INHERITANCE, USING, PERSPECTIVE ON), complex events (SUBFRAME, PRECEDES), and "systematic" relations (CAUSATIVE OF, INCHOATIVE OF); an additional relation, called "SEE ALSO" serves as a cross-reference between frames (see Fillmore and Baker (2010) and Ruppenhofer et al. (2010) for more details on frame-to-frame relations).

24.3.4 Access to FrameNet

Although machine-readable data releases representing snapshots of the evolving FrameNet database are regularly made available for download for computational use,[3] human users mainly access FrameNet by browsing the FrameNet website.[4] The top-level page of FN's website presents several ways to access the data, which is updated daily.

The information in FN can be accessed from two major perspectives: beginning with a concept (frame) to be encoded ("onomasiologically") and looking for lemmas that express it, or beginning with a form (lemma) to be decoded ("semasiologically"), that is, finding the concepts (frames) that it evokes. The first perspective is realized by the Frame Index, which leads to a page with an alphabetized list of frames in a navigation pane on the left and a larger panel on the right in which descriptions of chosen frames are displayed. The frame descriptions contain, in order:

1 a definition;
2 a list of FEs, grouped according to grammatical prominence, with each item including a definition and one or more examples;
3 a list of frame-to-frame relations; and
4 a table of LUs that evoke the frame.

The FEs used in the example sentences of the frame and FE definitions are identified by colours. In the frame-to-frame relations section, hyperlinks provide access to related frames. Similarly, in the table of associated LUs, each item comes with two links: one to the Annotation Report for that LU and the other to the Lexical Entry Report.

The Annotation Report consists of a listing of the FEs for the associated frame and then a display of annotated instances of the LU, sub-divided into sets ("sub-corpora") according to the syntactic patterns used to extract them. These patterns usually select for particular syntactic complementation types. For example, for the noun *oath* in the Commitment frame, there are sub-corpora named *VPto* and *Sthat* which are supposed to contain the uses with infinitival and finite-clause complements, respectively.

The Lexical Entry Report contains two types of summary: First, it gives a list of the individual FEs and the ways in which they are realized in the annotated instances. Figure 24.1 shows the syntactic realizations found with the verb *give* in the **Giving** frame for the three core frame elements Donor, Theme and Recipient. Note that the notion of "realization" used by FrameNet extends to cases in which the Frame Element is not realized explicitly at all but instead "null instantiated". This can happen through the idiosyncratic licensing of a lexical unit or the licensing of a syntactic construction.

Frame Element	Number Annotated	Realization (s)
Donor	(51)	CNI.--(12) DNI.--(2) NP.Ext (36) PP[by].Dep (1)
Recipient	(51)	PP[to] .Dep (16) DNL.--(5) INI.--(2) NP.Ext (4) NP.Obj (21) NP.Dep (3)
Theme	(50)	NP.Ext (2) NP.Obj (26) NP.Dep (20) PP[of].Dep (1) INI.-- (1)

Figure 24.1 Partial syntactic realization table for *give* in the frame **Giving**

FrameNet distinguishes three types of missing elements, abbreviates DNI, INI, and CNI. DNI ("definite null instantiation") marks FEs that are unrealized but which have to be recoverable from the context. An example is the FE RECIPIENT in a sentence such as *The prize was given by an international committee.* Figure 24.1 shows that there are five cases of DNI for the FE RECIPIENT among the annotated instances for *give.* INI ("indefinite null instantiation") covers FEs that are merely existentially bound, an example of which is the FE THEME in *Sure, I gave to the Red Cross last year – everybody did.* CNI ("constructional null instantiation") marks all omissions licensed by a syntactic construction. A typical case is the omission of agentive FEs in the imperative construction, as in *give a generous gift to Goodwill today.*

The Lexical Entry report also contains another summary table that shows all the attested combinations in which **groups** of FEs were co-realized. Some of the attestations found with *substitute* in the **Replacing** frame are shown in Figure 24.2.

The last row in the Valence Pattern Table (Figure 24.2) shows that there is exactly one sentence in the FN database with the pattern AGENT as CNI, NEW as External (Subject), OLD in a PP*for*, PURPOSE in an infinitive phrase, and TIME in a PP*after*, which is the sentence *After verification for the effect of the typesetting code combinations, they were substituted for more computer-recognizable codes to simplify further processing.* Both of these tables contain hyperlinked counts for the number of annotated instances exemplifying the FE (or valence pattern), which can be displayed by following the links. The two associated reports for a given lexical unit are also interlinked.

The decoding point of view is represented by the alphabetized "Lexical Unit Index". Users can simply browse this index or use a search box to retrieve LUs. There is no direct representation of lemmas per se; the different LUs (senses) connected to a given lemma simply follow each other. Unlike on the semantic side, where one can easily follow links from frame to related frame, on the form side there are no direct links between the LUs associated with the same lemma, or between LUs belonging to morphologically related lemmas. The

6 TOTAL	Agent	New	Old	Place	
(2)	CNI —	NP Ext	PPLfor] Dep	PP[in] Dep	
(1)	NP Ext	NP Obj	PP[for] Dep	AVP Dep	
(1)	NP Ext	NP Obj	PPtfor] Dep	PP[in] Dep	
(1)	NP Ext	NP Obj	PPLfor] Dep	PPLon] Dep	
(1)	NP Ext	PP[with] Dep	NP Obj	AVP Dep	
2 TOTAL	Agent	New	Old	Purpose	
(1)	CNI --	NP Ext	PPLfor] Dep	VPto Dep	
(1)	NP Ext	NP Obj	DN1 —	VPto Dep	
1 TOTAL	Agent	New	Old	Purpose	Time
(1)	CNI --	NP Ext	PPLfor] Dep	VPto Dep	PP [after] Dep

Figure 24.2 Partial valence pattern table for *substitute* in the **Replacing** frame

entry for each LU provides information on the work-flow status of the item and three links: one to the Frame description, one to the Annotation Report, and one to the Lexical Entry Report (as described earlier).

A third type of access is based on the fact that FrameNet performs some annotation of running texts, which are listed on the Full-Text annotation index. The Full-Text Annotation Report pairs a display of a document's running text with a display of the annotations of specific user-selectable items from the text. Although the annotation instances in full-text documents are also integrated into the Annotation and Lexical Entry Reports for the relevant lexical units, they can be viewed in their document context only via the Full-Text Annotation Report.

A fourth kind of data access focuses on the frame relations in the lexical part of the database. Although these relations are also listed in the Frame reports, the FrameGrapher visualization tool (*https://framenet.icsi.berkeley.edu/fndrupal/FrameGrapher*) is uniquely suited to interactively exploring the topology of relations that exist in a set of related frames. For example, users can choose a focal frame on which the display is to be centred and a group of frame relation types they are interested in. In order to manage the size and layout of the resulting display, users can specify the number of levels of the (sub-)hierarchy and the number of leaf nodes to be displayed. Clicking on one of the frames in the graph displays a re-centred graph with a new focal frame; clicking on the head of the arrow representing a frame-frame relation will create an expanded graph, where the frame element-to-frame element relations that go along with the chosen frame-to-frame relationship are displayed in detail (see Fillmore and Baker 2010: 332–333 for details).

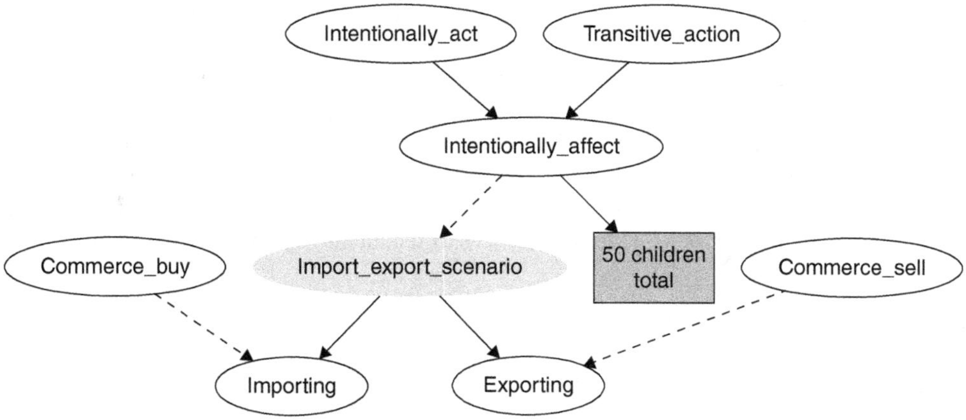

Figure 24.3 FrameGrapher display for import-export–related frames

Figure 24.3 shows a set of frames related to the idea of Importing and Exporting as portrayed in the FrameGrapher. The dashed (green) arrows indicate USING relations, the thick (red) arrows indicate INHERITANCE relations, and the thin (pink) arrows show RESPECTIVE ON relations. Thus, **Importing** and **Exporting** are different perspectives on the same event, the buyer's and the seller's respectively. The **Import export scenario** "uses" the frame **Intentionally affect**, a high-level frame with many children.

Finally, a multi- and cross-lingual view on FrameNet data is provided by the FrameSQL search tool (http://sato.fm.senshu-u.ac.jp/frameSQL/fn2_15/notes) which is developed and maintained independently by Prof. Hiroaki Sato of Senshu University, Japan. In addition to the English-language FrameNet, FrameSQL can search the frame semantic annotations of FrameNet's German, Japanese, and Spanish sister projects. Moreover, the tool integrates information from all four resources. As a result, users can see the information from the different sources aligned seamlessly, as if they were a single database. Hyperlinks among the databases and accompanying search capabilities facilitate comparison between the semantic structures of corresponding frames or lexical units across the languages (see Sato 2008).

Independently of the FN website, human users may also access the first three kinds of information (Frame, LU-specific Lexical Entry and Annotation Reports, and Full-text annotation reports) in the FN data release.[5] The download consists of a set of static interlinked XML files that are browser-viewable by means of accompanying XSL/Javascript scripts, although the FrameGrapher and FrameSQL tools are not included.

24.3.5 Efforts to generate or enhance FrameNet resources through crowdsourcing

Hong and Baker (2011) investigated frame disambiguation by non-expert annotators. The task of frame element assignment remained outside the purview of their experiments. The authors experimented with various approaches for frame assignment, the most promising being one in which sentences containing the lemma of interest were grouped by frame. This approach yielded accuracy scores between 73 percent and 92 percent. Chang et al. (2015) extended the grouping approach of Hong und Baker (2011) to additional lemmas, and they also incorporate a mechanism that gives the annotators feedback on their work.

The latter resulted in an increase of average frame assignment accuracy from 78 percent to 92 percent.

Fossati et al. (2013) also crowdsourced frame semantic annotation, including the labelling of frame elements. The reported accuracy for frame disambiguation is 90 percent and that for FE labelling 68.7 percent. (The FE figure is low because it is calculated over all FEs, not merely the ones where the assumed frame was correct.) However, Fossati et al. use simplified definitions instead of the original FrameNet definitions which are often difficult to understand for laypersons due to occurrences of technical/linguistic terminology.

24.3.6 FrameNet and multilinguality

24.3.6.1 Lexicographic sister projects in other languages

The frames created by the Berkeley FrameNet for the lexicon for English have also been "recycled" for other languages. The first efforts in this direction applied frame-semantic insights to the systematic analysis of the lexicons of languages other than English (Heid 1996, Fontenelle 1997). Subsequent research demonstrated in greater detail how semantic frames derived on the basis of English data could be employed for the creation of FrameNets for other languages (Fillmore and Atkins 2000, Boas 2005, Petruck and Boas 2003). The results of this research inspired the creation of FrameNets for other languages, most notably Spanish (Subirats and Petruck 2003; Subirats 2009), Japanese (Ohara et al. 2003, Ohara 2009), German (Burchardt et al. 2009), Brazilian Portuguese (Salomão *et al.* 2013), Chinese (Liu 2011), Swedish (Borin et al. 2010), and French (Candito et al. 2014). Although the technical resources and workflows of the non-English FrameNets differ from each other, they all produce FN-style entries similar to the English original discussed earlier, including detailed information about how the semantics of a given frame are realized syntactically by different LUs evoking that frame in that language. This information allows researchers to systematically conduct contrastive and comparative research on topics in lexical semantics such as polysemy (Fillmore and Atkins 2000, Willems 2012), typological differences in profiling properties (Ohara 2009, Petruck 2009), and the interface between the lexicon and syntax (Hasegawa et al. 2010, Bouveret 2012). The multilingual data contained in the FrameNets for various languages is also relevant for cross-linguistic research on argument structure constructions, as shown by Boas (2003), Leino (2010), and Timyam and Bergen (2010), among others.

24.3.6.2 Uses in foreign language education

FrameNet data has also proven to be useful for foreign language education. To this end, an effort has been underway at the University of Texas at Austin to create an online learner's dictionary for German. The goal is to create simplified FrameNet-style lexical entries for all of the ca. 2,000 LUs in the first-year online German textbook *Deutsch im Blick* (http://coerll.utexas.edu/dib/). The basic idea is to use existing English FrameNet frames for the description of those German words that beginning and intermediate learners of German have to learn during the course of their language studies. To achieve this goal, the Berkeley English FrameNet database was downloaded and installed on local servers at UT Austin and subsequently stripped of all English-specific information, leaving only the frames and the frame-to-frame relations intact. Then, a team of Germanic linguists at UT Austin went through the vocabulary lists of the textbook used for the first year of German instruction at UT in order to identify sets of relevant words evoking the same semantic frame. Using a variety of online corpora, the team of linguists extracted simple German example sentences and annotated them with frame-semantic information. Based on this information, the team then created user-friendly lexical entries to be stored in the stripped FrameNet database on local servers. The result is a set of simple to use contrastive German-English entries with notes on contrastive differences between German and English, culture-specific information, collocational information, and information about basic grammar usage. Finally, a team of web designers created an easy to use website for presenting the resulting information to learners of German. The prototype of the German Frame-based Online Lexicon (G-FOL; http://coerll.utexas.edu/frames/) currently contains nine frames with contrastive lexical entries for about 350 LUs. For details see Boas and Dux (2013) and Boas et al. (2016).

24.3.7 NLP applications

24.3.7.1 Automatic semantic role labelling

FrameNet has had a considerable impact on the field of computational linguistics. Above all, it has paved the way for the task of automatic semantic role labelling (ASRL) introduced by the seminal work of Gildea and Jurafsky (2002). Several evaluations for automatic role labelling systems have since taken place under the umbrella of the SemEval (http://aclweb.org/aclwiki/index.php?title=SemEval_Portal) series of evaluation campaigns (2004, 2007, 2010).

Because the largest amount of FrameNet data is available for English, research on ASRL systems was pioneered and is most advanced for that language, as embodied by the SEMAFOR system (Das et al. 2014). Typically, ASRL systems are language specific. This is true for SEMAFOR but also, for instance, for the Shalmaneser system, which is trained separately for German and for English (Erk and Padó 2006). Still, often such language-specific systems involve some cross-lingual transfer of knowledge from one language (typically English) to another in order to enlarge the amount of data for training the system in the target language. In a departure from this transfer approach, an attempt has recently been made to build an any-language semantic parser that uses a single model for all languages (Johannsen et al. 2015).

24.3.7.2 Applications of core inference

Usually, ASRL is not an end in itself. Instead it is one of several processing steps in a pipeline that makes available to downstream processing some foundational information on "who did what to whom". Subsequent steps then involve some kind of task-specific inferencing. The most basic inferencing makes use of information on 1) alternative ways in which FEs may be realized, 2) co-frame membership of lexical units, and 3) frame-to-frame relations. Together these types of information provide a sort of syntactic-semantic normalization of textual information that allows for the recognition of (near-)paraphrases, that is, of something like mutual entailment. Such paraphrases may involve simple syntactic variants such as active–passive or involve the more challenging recognition that two propositions involving converse predicates located in different frames such as *buy* and *sell* may be equivalent, given the frame relations and a particular filling of their FE roles. Shen and Lapata (2007) used an ASRL system in this spirit to match questions with potential answer passages in the context of the Question Answering task. However, Question Answering itself may be seen as merely one of several specific applications of an abstract textual entailment recognition task, others being Information Retrieval, Information Extraction, and Text Summarization. Burchardt (2008) used FrameNet in his thesis on entailment recognition. Ruppenhofer and Pinkal (2011) experimented with merging frames with particular types of frame relations for the purpose of improved entailment recognition.

24.3.7.3 Applications of extended inference

Beyond the use of FrameNet for recognizing mutual entailment, research has begun to explore ways in which the resource can be used for several types of extended inference. We discuss these in what follows.

- **Overloading of semantic with opinion roles**: In recent years, FrameNet-based semantic role labelling has been used for additional inference purposes in the context of sentiment analysis. However, these new applications involve the enriching of FrameNet's current information. For instance, Bethard et al. (2004) and Kim and Hovy (2006) used frame ASRL as a basis to assign so-called opinion roles to those sentence constituents that represent the Source or Holder of an *opinion* and its Target (or: Topic). Basically, this involves mapping frame roles to opinion roles, where appropriate, as in example 3:

  (3)
  (FFF) [Mayor Quimby JUDGE] **criticized** [the townspeople EVALUEE] [in his annual speech MEDIUM].
  (FFF') [Mayor Quimby SOURCE] **criticized** [the townspeople TARGET] in his annual speech.

  The mappings used in the earlier cited works were created (and re-created) by specific researchers working on the sentiment analysis task. They are not currently part of FrameNet itself. Ruppenhofer and Rehbein (2012) and Ruppenhofer (2013) propose integrating this information into FrameNet, arguing that, more generally, the sentiment analysis task should be fundamentally based on semantic role labelling. They propose associating so-called opinion frames with regular frames or (groups of) LUs and mapping the roles of these two types of frames onto each other. An advantage of such an explicit representation is that multiple co-present opinions can be accurately represented. For instance, whereas the SPEAKER in the **Bragging** frame speaks positively about the TOPIC or communicates a MESSAGE with propositional content that they evaluate positively, the external reporter of the situation evoked by the frame evaluates the SPEAKER and/or the TOPIC/MESSAGE negatively.

- **Scale-related inferences**: A basic type of inference that is currently not supported by explicit information is the one that has to do with values on a scale. Knowing that *good* < *great* is needed, for instance, for the task of understanding certain dialog acts. In the exchange *A: Was it good?* B: *It was great*. B's statement can only be interpreted as an affirmative response if it is known that *good* < *great*. But in FN there is no information that directly states or lets one infer the relative ranking of the degrees of positivity conveyed by the two predicates. Of course, this same knowledge is also of great interest for sentiment analysis, where the degree of positive or negative valence expressed is an important aspect of understanding expressions of opinion.

Further, as pointed out by Fillmore and Baker (2010), the lack of information on the various types of oppositions means that FrameNet is not straightforwardly usable for paraphrase generation involving negation. Consider that in the **Compliance** frame, for example, compliance and noncompliance are binary notions, ordinarily excluding any middle ground: an act which is *compliant* with a law is *not in violation* of the law. However, when antonyms are merely contrary, as in the **Expensiveness** frame, weaker inferences are possible. For instance, if something is *cheap*, it is *not expensive*; if it is *expensive* it is *not cheap*. But the opposite inferences are not possible. Thus, something that is *not expensive*, is not necessarily *cheap*. At the moment, the differences in conceptual structure between the frames for **Compliance** and **Expensiveness** are not spelled out.

- **Event evaluativity inferences**: Reschke and Anand (2011) proposed considering the "entailments" of verbs and the attitude towards participants as the basis for calculating an external reporter's attitude towards the events. For instance, an event that results in a state of possession is evaluated positively, if both the THEME and the RECIPIENT are evaluated positively, or if both are viewed negatively (i.e. *Schadenfreude*). The event is evaluated negatively, whenever the two participants have *different* evaluations. Reasoning like this has been shown to be useful for modelling speakers' understanding of attitudes conveyed in text. Anand and Reschke manually looked for FrameNet frames that might contain verbs bearing relevant entailments. Although for the possession entailment, some relevant frames can be retrieved by automatically exploring FrameNet's hierarchy, not all of them can. The reason is that the relevant frames need not have possession as an actual entailment. Frames in which possession post-states occur embedded under some modality are also of interest for reasoning about event evaluation. For instance, the **Offering** frame is related to **Giving** merely by the Using relationship, but the evaluative reasoning applies as if the modalized future situation were actualized, as in the **Giving** frame. If *Peter offers John the job of director*, and the speaker approves both of John and the job of director, then they should also evaluate the offering event as a whole positively. The Using relation is, however, generally too weak to be a basis for inference. Thus, a fully automatic way of extracting frames with possession entailments would miss this. Expanding FrameNet's representational capabilities to explicitly model the modalized possession would be desirable in the longer run. In the interim, an alternative approach would be to associate information about Anand and Reschke's reasoning schemes with frames and LUs, similar to what Ruppenhofer and Rehbein (2012) proposed for the fixed sentiment associated with opinion roles, and what Ruppenhofer and Brandes (2016) did for GermaNet synsets.

24.4 Looking to the future

In terms of its analytical scope, FrameNet is moving towards capturing the semantics of grammar. This means dealing both with general and abstract grammatical phenomena (negation, tense, aspect) as well as with phraseology (constructions and syntactic idioms). This expansion will enable the integration of lexical meanings and grammatical meanings and facilitate a more complete account of text understanding. Efforts to build constructional resources tied to frame semantics are underway for English (Fillmore et al. 2012), Swedish (Lyngfelt et al. 2012; Gruzitis et al. 2015), Japanese (Ohara 2015), and Portuguese.[6] Throughout the FrameNet project, research on Construction Grammar has continued and has been presupposed in decisions about how to represent frames. Likewise, Fillmore regarded LUs as minimal lexical constructions, and posited that many non-lexical constructions also evoke semantic frames, which serve as a partial representation of their semantics.

There are also plans for increased cooperation and coordination among the FrameNets for different languages, including (1) the creation of a database connecting the work on all of the languages, with alignments at both frame and LU levels; (2) efforts to expand existing FrameNets by semi-automatic cross-linguistic projection; and (3) closer collaboration among existing FrameNets and systematic assistance for fledgling FrameNets in new languages. This project will also move beyond the current XML distribution of the FrameNet data, making the data available in ways that are more compatible with the needs of NLP research.

24.5 Conclusion

FrameNet is a rich, yet still evolving lexical resource that seeks to apply the theory of Frame Semantics to the analysis of the English lexicon. FrameNet has attracted interest from diverse research communities, ranging from theoretical linguistics to natural language processing applications. In its original domain of lexicography, FrameNet has inspired many sister projects in other languages and is seeing new specialized uses, such as foreign language instruction. In the field of natural language processing FrameNet is used as a resource in a great number of applications, notably semantic role labelling. In addition, many efforts have been and are being undertaken to (semi-)automatically expand frame semantic resources or construct them from scratch. Such efforts, on the one hand, underscore the keen interest in using frame semantic annotations and lexicon resources, but on the other reflect the challenges and limitations of pursuing large coverage only through the manual work of linguistic experts. The next phase of frame semantic development will therefore seek to speed up the progress of frame semantic resources by combining the work of human experts with that of laypeople while also attempting to better leverage the growing analytical powers of automatic systems.

Related topics

Lexicography and applied linguistics; lexicography and natural language processing; electronic dictionaries; user participation in the era of the Internet; information retrieval for lexicographic purposes; Wordnik; English lexicography in the Internet era.

Further reading

Boas, H. C. (ed.) (2009). *Multilingual FrameNets: Methods and Applications*. Berlin/New York: Mouton de Gruyter.

This edited volume consists of 11 chapters describing and explaining how the Berkeley FrameNet frames for English are employed to build FrameNets for other languages such as Spanish, Japanese, and German.

Fillmore, C. J. and C. F. Baker. (2010). "A Frames Approach to Semantic Analysis", in B. Heine and H. Narrog (eds.), *The Oxford Handbook of Linguistic Analysis*. Oxford: Oxford University Press, pp. 313–340.

This chapter provides a detailed overview of the FrameNet project, including its workflow, database, the structure of lexical entries, and theoretical considerations.

Fillmore, C. J., R. Lee-Goldman and R. Rhomieux. (2012). "The FrameNet Constructicon", in H. C. Boas and I. Sag (eds.), *Sign-Based Construction Grammar*. Stanford: CSLI Publications, pp. 309–372.

This chapter discusses the expansion of the FrameNet lexical database and methodology to include entries for grammatical constructions using the same format.

Ruppenhofer, J., M. Ellsworth, M. Petruck, C. Johnson, and J. Scheffczyk. (2010). *FrameNet II: Extended Theory and Practice*. http://framenet.icsi.berkeley.edu.

This technical report provides details about the policies and workflow of the FrameNet project, including frame creation, annotation of corpus examples, and creation of lexical entries in the FrameNet database.

Notes

1 See https://framenet.icsi.berkeley.edu/fndrupal/framenet_users for a list of users.
2 We discuss frames here in terms of "events" and their "participants", which are the clearest case, but semantic frames can also represent relations (such as the Similarity frame discussed in Section 24.1), states (e.g. the Dead_or_alive frame), and entities (e.g. the Clothing frame), all of which have related entities and properties which are treated as frame elements.
3 For information on the architecture and physical implementation of the FrameNet database, see Baker, Fillmore and Cronin 2003.
4 See at http://framenet.icsi.berkeley.edu
5 For information on FrameNet's machine-readable data distribution in XML format, please consult the FrameNet website and the Release Notes in the data distribution.
6 See at www.ufjf.br/framenetbr-eng/projects/frames-and-constructions (2016/6/22).

References

Atkins, B.T.S., C. J. Fillmore and C. R. Johnson (2003) "Lexicographic Relevance: Selecting Information From Corpus Evidence", *International Journal of Lexicography* 16(3): 251–280.

Baker, C. F., C. J. Fillmore and B. Cronin (2003) "The Structure of the FrameNet Database", *International Journal of Lexicography* 16(3): 281–296.

Bethard, S., H. Yu, A. Thornton, V. Hatzivassiloglou and D. Jurafsky (2004) "Automatic Extraction of Opinion Propositions and Their Holders", in *Proceedings of the AAAI Spring Symposium on Exploring Attitude and Affect in Text: Theories and Applications*, pp. 20–27.

Boas, H. C. (2003) *A Constructional Approach to Resultatives*. Stanford, CA: CSLI Publications.

Boas, H. C. (2005) "Semantic Frames as Interlingual Representations for Multilingual Lexical Databases", *International Journal of Lexicography* 18(4): 445–478.

Boas, H. C. (2017) "Computational Resources: FrameNet and Constructicon", in B. Dancygier (ed.), *The Cambridge Handbook of Cognitive Linguistics*. Cambridge: Cambridge University Press, pp. 549–573.

Boas, H. C., and R. Dux (2013) "Semantic Frames for Foreign Language Education: Towards a German Frame-Based Dictionary", *Veredas* 17(1): 82–100.

Boas, H. C., R. Dux and A. Ziem (2016) "Frames and Constructions in an Online Learner's Dictionary of German", in S. De Knop and G. Guilquin (eds.), *Constructional Approaches to Language Pedagogy*. Berlin: Mouton de Gruyter, pp. 303–326.

Borin, L., D. Dannélls, M. Forsberg, M. T. Gronostaj and D. Kokkinakis (2010) "The Past Meets the Present in the Swedish FrameNet++", Extended version of EURALEX 2010 presentation. https://svn.spraakdata.gu.se/sb/fnplusplus/pub/SweFN_Euralex_extended.pdf.

Bouveret, M. (2012) "GIVE Frames and Constructions in French", in M. Bouveret and D. Legallois (eds.), *Constructions in French*. Amsterdam/Philadelphia: Benjamins, pp. 99–126.

Burchardt, A. (2008) *Modeling Textual Entailment With Role-semantic Information*, PhD thesis, Universität des Saarlandes.

Burchardt, A., K. Erk, A. Frank, A. Kowalski, S. Padó and M. Pinkal (2009) "Using FrameNet for the Semantic Analysis of German: Annotation, Representation, and Automation", in H. C. Boas (ed.), *Multilingual FrameNets: Methods and Applications*. Berlin/New York: Mouton de Gruyter, pp. 209–244.

Busse, D. (2012) *Frame-Semantik: Ein Kompendium*. Berlin/New York: Mouton de Gruyter.

Candito, M., P. Amsili, L. Barque, F. Benamara, G. de Chalendar, M. Djemaa, P. Haas, R. Huyghe, Y. Mathieu, P. Muller, B. Sagot and L. Vieu (2014) "Developing a French FrameNet: Methodology and First Results", *Proceedings of LREC 2014*, pp. 1372–1379.

Chang, N., P. Paritosh, D. Huynh and C. F. Baker (2015) "Scaling Semantic Frame Annotation", in *Proceedings of The 9th Linguistic Annotation Workshop*, pp. 1–10.

Das, D., D. Chen, A.F.T. Martins, N. Schneider and N. A. Smith (2014) "Frame-Semantic Parsing", *Computational Linguistics* 40(1): 9–56.

Erk, K. and S. Pado (2006) "Shalmaneser – A Flexible Toolbox for Semantic Role Assignment", in *Proceedings of LREC 2006*, pp. 527–532.

Fillmore, C. J. (1968) "The Case for Case", in E. Bach and R. Harms (eds.), *Universals in Linguistic Theory*. New York: Rinehart & Winston, pp. 1–90.

Fillmore, C. J. (1975) "An Alternative to Checklist Theories of Meaning", in *Proceedings of the First Annual Meeting of the Berkeley Linguistic Society (BLS)*, pp. 123–131.

Fillmore, C. J. (1976) "Frame Semantics and the Nature of Language", *Annals of the New York Academy of Sciences: Conference on the Origin and Development of Language and Speech*, 280, pp. 20–32.

Fillmore, C. J. (1977) "Scenes-and-Frames Semantics", in A. Zampolli (ed.), *Fundamental Studies in Computer Science*. Dordrecht: North Holland Publishing, pp. 55–88.

Fillmore, C. J. (1978) "On the Organization of Semantic Information in the Lexicon", *Papers From the Parasession on the Lexicon, Chicago Linguistic Society*, pp. 148–173.

Fillmore, C. J. (1979) "Innocence: A Second Idealization for Linguistics", in *Proceedings of the Fifth Annual Meeting of the Berkeley Linguistic Society (BLS)*, pp. 63–76.

Fillmore, C. J. (1982) "Frame Semantics", in Linguistic Society of Korea (ed.), *Linguistics in the Morning Calm*. Seoul: Hanshin, pp. 111–38.

Fillmore, C. J. (1985) "Frames and the Semantics of Understanding", *Quaderni di Semantica* 6: 222–254.

Fillmore, C. J. (2007) "Valency Issues in FrameNet", in T. Herbst and K. Götz-Vetteler (eds.), *Valency: Theoretical, Descriptive, and Cognitive Issues*. Berlin/New York: Mouton de Gruyter, pp. 129–160.

Fillmore, C. J. and B.T.S. Atkins (1992) "Toward a Frame-Based Lexicon: The Semantics of RISK and Its Neighbors", in A. Lehrer and E. Kittay (eds.), *Frames, Fields and Contrasts: New Essays in Semantic and Lexical Organization*. Hillsdale: Erlbaum, pp. 75–102.

Fillmore, C. J. and B.T.S. Atkins (2000) "Describing Polysemy: The Case of Crawl", in Y. Ravin and C. Leacock (eds.), *Polysemy: Linguistic and Computational Approaches*. Oxford: Oxford University Press, pp. 91–110.

Fillmore, C. J. and C. F. Baker (2010) "A Frames Approach to Semantic Analysis", in B. Heine and H. Narrog (eds.), *The Oxford Handbook of Linguistic Analysis*. Oxford: Oxford University Press, pp. 313–340.

Fillmore, C. J., C. Johnson and M. Petruck (2003) "Background to FrameNet", *International Journal of Lexicography* 16: 235–251.

Fillmore, C. J., R. Lee-Goldman and R. Rhomieux (2012) "The FrameNet Constructicon", in H. C. Boas and I. Sag (eds.), *Sign-Based Construction Grammar*. Stanford, CA: CSLI Publications, pp. 309–372.

Fontenelle, T. (1997) "Using a Bilingual Dictionary to Create Semantic Networks", *International Journal of Lexicography* 10(4): 275–303.

Fossati, M., C. Giuliano and S. Tonelli (2013) "Outsourcing FrameNet to the Crowd", in *Proceedings of the 51st Annual Meeting of the Association for Computational Linguistics (Volume 2: Short Papers)*, pp. 742–747.

Gildea, D. and D. Jurafsky (2002) "Automatic Labeling of Semantic Roles", *Computational Linguistics* 28(3): 245–288.

Gruzitis, N., D. Dannélls, B. Lyngfelt and A. Ranta (2015). "Formalising the Swedish Constructicon in Grammatical Framework", in *Proceedings of ACL-IJCNLP 2015*, pp. 49–56.

Hasegawa, Y., R. Lee-Goldman, K. Ohara, S. Fuji and C. Fillmore (2010) "On Expressing Measurement and Comparison in English and Japanese", in H. C. Boas (ed.), *Contrastive Studies in Construction Grammar*. Amsterdam/Philadelphia: Benjamins, pp. 169–200.

Heid, U. (1996) "Creating a Multilingual Data Collection for Bilingual Lexicography From Parallel Monolingual Lexicons", in *Proceedings of the VIIth EURALEX International Congress*, pp. 573–559.

Hong, J. and C. F. Baker (2011) "How Good Is the Crowd at 'Real' WSD?", in *Proceedings of the 5th Linguistic Annotation Workshop*, pp. 30–37.

Johannsen, A., H. Martinez Alonso and A. Søgaard (2015) "Any-Language Frame-Semantic Parsing", in *Proceedings of the 2015 Conference on Empirical Methods in Natural Language Processing*, pp. 2062–2066.

Kim, S.-M. and E. Hovy (2006) "Extracting Opinions, Opinion Holders, and Topics Expressed in Online News Media Text", *Proceedings of the Workshop on Sentiment and Subjectivity in Text*, pp. 1–8.

Kipper, K., A. Korhonen, N. Ryant, and M. Palmer (2008) "A Large-Scale Classification of English Verbs", *Language Resources and Evaluation Journal* 42(1): 21–40.

Leino, J. (2010) "Results, Cases, and Constructions: Argument Structure Constructions in English and Finnish", in H. C. Boas (ed.), *Contrastive Studies in Construction Grammar*. Amsterdam/Philadelphia: Benjamins, pp. 103–136.

Levin, B. and M. Rappaport-Hovav (2005) *Argument Realization*. Cambridge: Cambridge University Press.

Liu, K. (2011) "Research on Chinese FrameNet Construction and Application Technologies" *Journal of Chinese Information Processing* 25(6): 46–52.

Lyngfelt, B., L. Borin, M. Forsberg, J. Prentice, R. Rydstedt, E. Sköldberg and S. Tingsell. (2012) "Adding a Constructicon to the Swedish Resource Network of Språkbanken", *Proceedings of KONVENS 2012*, pp. 452–461.

Ohara, K. (2009) "Frame-Based Contrastive Lexical Semantics in Japanese FrameNet: The Case of Risk and Kakeru", in H. C. Boas (Ed.), *Multilingual FrameNets: Methods and Applications*. Berlin/New York: Mouton de Gruyter, pp. 163–182.

Ohara, K. (2015) "Constructicon Building as a Practical Implementation of Construction Grammar and Frame Semantics: Japanese FrameNet", Poster at the 13th International Cognitive Linguistics Conference (ICLC 13) Northumbria University at Newcastle. www.northumbria.ac.uk/media/6836834/poster-abstracts-9-july.pdf.

Ohara, K. H., S. Fujii, H. Saito, S. Ishizaki, T. Ohori and R. Suzuki (2003) "The Japanese FrameNet Project: A Preliminary Report", in *Proceedings of Pacific Association for Computational Linguistics (PACLING'03)*, pp. 249–254.

Petruck, M. (2009) "Typological Considerations in Constructing a Hebrew FrameNet", in H. C. Boas (Ed.), *Multilingual FrameNets: Methods and Applications*. Berlin/New York: Mouton de Gruyter, pp. 183–208.

Petruck, M. and H. C. Boas (2003) "All in a Day's Week", *Proceedings of CIL 17*. CD-ROM. Prague: Matfyzpress.

Petruck, M., C. J. Fillmore, C. F. Baker, M. Ellsworth and J. Ruppenhofer (2004) "Reframing FrameNet Data", in *Proceedings of The 11th EURALEX International Congress*, pp. 405–416.

Ruppenhofer, J. (2013) "Anchoring Sentiment Analysis in Frame Semantics", *Veredas* 17(1): 66–81.

Ruppenhofer, J. and J. Brandes (2016) "Effect Functors for Opinion Inference", in *Proceedings of the Tenth International Conference on Language Resources and Evaluation (LREC 2016)*, pp. 2879–2887.

Ruppenhofer, J., M. Ellsworth, M. Petruck, C. Johnson and J. Scheffczyk (2010) *FrameNet II: Extended Theory and Practice*. http://framenet.icsi.berkeley.edu.

Ruppenhofer, J. and M. Pinkal (2011) "Folding FrameNet – Unfolding Its Potential?", *International Journal of Computational Linguistics and Applications* 2(1–2): 25–40.
Ruppenhofer, J. and I. Rehbein (2012) "Semantic Frames as an Anchor Representation for Sentiment Analysis", in *Proceedings of the 3rd Workshop in Computational Approaches to Subjectivity and Sentiment Analysis*, pp. 104–109.
Salomão, M., T. Timponi Torrent and T. Fernandes Sampaio (2013) "A linguística de corpus encontra a linguística computacional: Notícias do projeto FrameNet Brasil", *Cadernos de Estudos Linguísticos* 55(1): 7–34.
Sato, H. (2008) "New Functions of FrameSQL for Multilingual FrameNets", in *Proceedings of the Sixth International Language Resources and Evaluation (LREC'08)*, pp. 758–762.
Shen, D. and M. Lapata (2007) "Using Semantic Roles to Improve Question Answering", in *Proceedings of the Conference on Empirical Methods in Natural Language Processing and on Computational Natural Language Learning*, pp. 12–21.
Subirats, C. (2009) "Spanish FrameNet: A Frame-Semantic Analysis of the Spanish Lexicon", in H. C. Boas (ed.), *Multilingual FrameNets: Methods and Applications*. Berlin/New York: Mouton de Gruyter, pp. 135–162.
Subirats, C. and M. Petruck. (2003) Surprise: Spanish FrameNet! *Proceedings of CIL 17*, CD-ROM, Matfyzpress, Prague.
Timyam, N. and B. Bergen. (2010) "A Contrastive Study of the Caused-Motion and Ditransitive Construction in English and Thai: Semantic and Pragmatic Constraints", in H. C. Boas (eds.), *Contrastive Studies in Construction Grammar*. Amsterdam/Philadelphia: Benjamins, pp. 137–168.
Willems, D. (2012) "Verb Typology: Between Construction and Lexicon", in M. Bouveret and D. Legallois (eds.), *Constructions in French*. Amstedam/Philadelphia: Benjamins, pp. 23–48.
Ziem, A. (2008) *Frames und sprachliches Wissen*. Berlin/New York: Mouton de Gruyter.

25

The Online Dictionary of New Zealand Sign Language

A case study of contemporary sign lexicography

Rachel McKee and David McKee

25.1 Introduction

Signed languages evolve wherever communities of Deaf people form. Ethnologue (2016) lists 141 named signed languages and notes the existence of many more that are not listed; some are considered threatened. National sign languages commonly developed in the context of residential schools for the Deaf (from the eighteenth century onwards) which brought together Deaf children from amongst hearing populations and formed the basis for adult communities. Isolated villages in which hereditary deafness is prevalent are also contexts for the emergence and transmission of smaller-scale signed languages (Meir, Sandler, Padden and Aranoff 2010). Sign languages in different countries have familial relationships that do not always mirror the distribution of spoken languages; for instance, British, New Zealand and Australian Sign Languages are mutually intelligible, yet unrelated to American Sign Language which is used in an English-speaking continent (McKee and Kennedy 2000). However, in some countries sign language varieties do correspond with spoken language boundaries; for example, Deaf communities in Dutch- and French-speaking states of Belgium use differentiated sign language varieties (van Mulders 2004). Historical relationships between signed languages are often traceable to specific trans-national influences in the establishment of Deaf schools or foreign-led development projects which introduce a sign language from another nation. Documentation of signed languages has burgeoned since the late 1960s, inspired in particular by Stokoe et al.'s seminal work on the 1965 dictionary of American Sign Language which analysed signs in phonological terms, leading to further linguistic description of signed languages.

Words and grammar in a signed language are produced on the hands in combination with movements of the face, head and body. Although signed languages exist in contact with spoken languages, their visual-gestural production modality leads to more grammatical similarity between signed languages in disparate countries than with their surrounding spoken languages (Emmorey 2002). Signed languages do not have a conventional orthography and have a relatively short history of linguistic description, which presents practical challenges for making dictionaries. Nevertheless, techniques and concepts in sign language lexicography have progressed from collections of captioned illustrations – effectively bilingual wordlists (Johnston 2003) – to descriptive dictionaries that reflect linguistic analysis of their formational structure, to contemporary multimedia electronic dictionaries and to current work on corpus-based lexicography.

The case of the Online Dictionary of New Zealand Sign Language (ODNZSL) (McKee et al 2011) is presented here as an example of a contemporary user-facing dictionary that is based on linguistic research and leverages the advantages of a digital, online medium. Discussion of the ODNZSL is preceded by a brief overview of the aims and historical development of NZSL dictionaries, and common issues in signed lexicons are discussed in relation to making the ODNZSL.

25.2 Historical perspective

25.2.1 Aims and impacts of sign language dictionaries

In most countries, making a sign language dictionary has been the foundation of raising critical awareness of the linguistic status and cultural identity of a Deaf community (Padden 1980; Lucas 2003; Haualand and Allen 2009). Typical aims are captured in the introduction to the print Dictionary of New Zealand Sign Language (DNZSL):

> The dictionary is a record of lexicalized signs of a unique, systematic and fully functional human language in use in the New Zealand Deaf community. It is hoped that the work will help increase recognition and acceptance of NZSL and encourage both deaf and hearing people to learn to use this language.
>
> (Kennedy et al 1997, p. xi)

In practical terms, documentation is a first step to supporting teaching and learning of a sign language (acquisition planning), and in particular, the training of interpreters, which increases Deaf people's access to society and their capacity to advocate for their rights and needs. A dictionary distinguishes the identity of a sign language from the local spoken language and from other national or regional sign language varieties.

Dictionary projects are often initiated by educational authorities aiming to standardise a lexicon for national use by teachers, Deaf students and parents. In the Netherlands, for example, a standardisation project was described as an effective collaboration between linguists, Deaf communities and education stakeholders (Schermer 2012). However, top-down standardising projects can be controversial (Adam 2015), as in the recent development of "pan-Arabic sign language" dictionaries in a region that has multiple signed languages identified with Deaf communities of various countries (Al-Fityani and Padden 2010). This attempt at imposed lexical unification was decried by the World Federation of the Deaf (2009) as "a violation of the linguistic human rights of Deaf people in the region and an unwanted interference with linguistic diversity. Language planning decisions regarding Sign Languages should always remain with the linguistic community, in this case Deaf people". Less controversial planning efforts, although not unproblematic, are collaborative projects to develop lexicons of technical signs with the aim of improving Deaf people's access to specialised domains that are mediated by interpreting, for example, the British Sign Language Glossaries of Curriculum Terms (Scottish Sensory Centre) or the Medical Signbank (Napier et al 2015). In addition to practical lexicography skills, critical factors in the impact of sign language dictionary projects are effective partnership with the sign language community, a sociolinguistic understanding of current and historical context of use and appreciation of the relationships between various stakeholders (sponsors, editors, informants, user groups).

In New Zealand, as elsewhere, the activity and outputs of dictionary making have advanced language recognition. NZSL was made an official language (NZSL Act 2006) 21 years after the first dictionary was made (Levitt 1985) and 9 years after a second, larger dictionary appeared (Kennedy et al 1997). Although advocacy, policy, teaching and research all contributed to status change for NZSL (McKee 2007), the publication of dictionaries was fundamental to authorizing the Deaf community's claims for language recognition.

25.2.2 Development of the NZSL Dictionary

Two print NZSL dictionaries preceding the Online Dictionary of NZSL illustrate the recent development of sign language lexicography. The first NZSL dictionary (Levitt 1985) was a by-product of the first training of sign language interpreters in New Zealand by an American interpreter (Levitt) contracted by the Deaf Association to train interpreters. At that time, NZSL was just starting to be described (Collins-Ahlgren 1989), and no teaching resources existed. In the absence of fluent bilinguals or materials, second language acquisition relied upon Deaf visitors coming to class who interacted with trainees daily for four months. During these class sessions, their signed narratives were video-recorded and subsequently analysed and compiled in a dictionary by Levitt and a team of community volunteers. Deaf people involved in the project expressed a preference for photographic illustrations of signs, perhaps because they could not envisage signs disembodied from their known users. The 1200 entries in the 1985 dictionary, including variants, are alphabetically ordered by English headword. Each sign is accompanied by a gloss and a description of how to produce it. Front matter includes a short history of NZSL, myths about signed languages, a guide to symbols in entries, an explanation of inflecting verbs and classifier constructions, and numbers. This content reflects the editor's familiarity with contemporaneous research on features of ASL (American Sign Language) lexicon, for which he saw parallels in NZSL. Many of the sign models in the book are older-generation signers and their backgrounds are noted, making the document a valuable historical record of early signs that have since been replaced by modern variants. The transformative impact of the project is expressed in Levitt's introduction: "For many people who assisted in the preparation of this book, it constituted a surprising act of courage to display publicly and proudly a language which has been suppressed for its entire existence" (ibid, p. ix). The dictionary was a first step in taking the language outside the private domains of the Deaf community.

The next print dictionary (Kennedy et al 1997; hereafter DNZSL) was a collaboration between the national Deaf Association and Victoria University of Wellington. The project was led by Professor Graeme Kennedy, an applied linguist and lexicographer who had become acquainted with sign language research by supervising a seminal PhD thesis describing NZSL (Collins-Ahlgren 1989). The methodology of the DNZSL underlies the structure of the current ODNZSL, and is outlined briefly below.

The DNZSL was completed in six years and contains 4500 entries. Content selection was based on a 'concept net' of universal semantic domains, and a list of words salient to New Zealand life and to Deaf culture. Deaf groups were recorded conversing about suggested topics, and responding to lexical elicitation prompts. From over 80 hours of recordings, sign types were identified and re-filmed as citation forms, which were then validated by representative Deaf groups in three regions who attested whether the sign was known in their region, if another variant existed, and what the sign meant in context. Validated signs were coded using the Hamburg Notation System ('HamNoSys'; Prillwitz et al 1989), which allows transcription of the phonological parameters of a sign, originally identified by Stokoe (1960) as handshape, place of articulation, movement and orientation of the palm. The set of HamNoSys symbols represents all permutations of these parameters and allows the formational features of any sign to be coded in a linear string, in the order of handshape, orientation, location (place of articulation) and movement (as seen in Figure 25.1, which shows the entry microstructure in the DNZSL). Each sign was drawn according to the citation video, and movement symbols added. A description of formation, usage, secondary glosses and a sign ID number were added to create records for each entry (Kennedy et al. 1997, p. xi).

The DNZSL was among a pioneering generation of dictionaries appearing in the 1990s[1] that departed from the tradition of alphabetically ordering entries by their translations and instead made signs the headwords, sorted into sections by handshape and location identity. In the DNZSL, automated sorting by HamNoSys coding in each record made this macrostructure possible; however, contrastive handshapes and allophone groupings had to be determined. Entries are grouped into 27 handshape categories, each of which includes up to eight variants or allophones (as shown at the top of Figure 25.1). A pictorial index of the handshape categories enables a user to identify in which section a given sign should be found. Within each handshape section, signs are sequenced by place of articulation, in descending order from the top of the head downwards in the signing space. Searchability by the formational features of signs is required for bi-directional access, allowing a user to search by the appearance of a sign if an English translation is not known. However, this visual analytic mode of dictionary use is not familiar to dictionary users and can be challenging to use with precision. An English index allows alternative searching for signs via English equivalents. Front matter

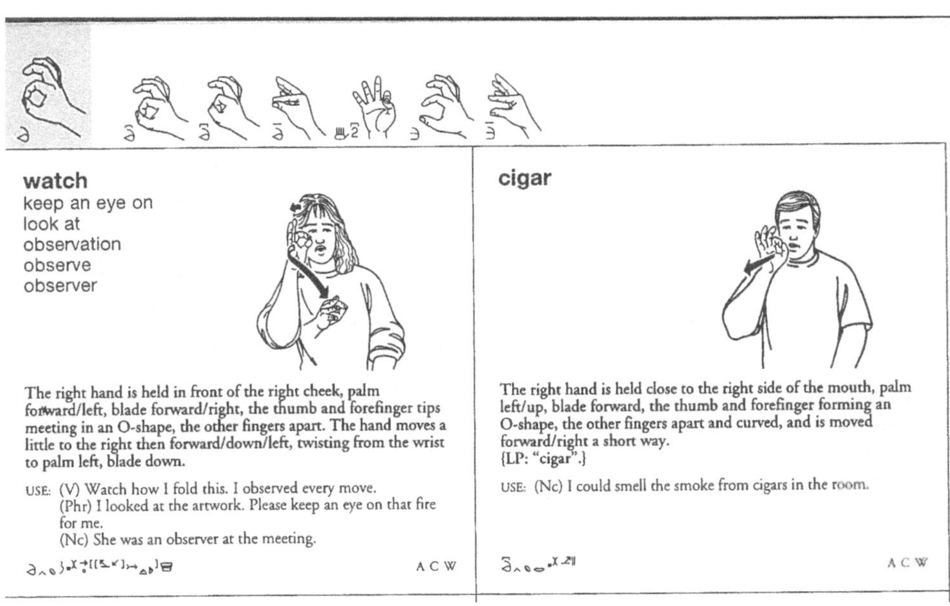

Figure 25.1 Entry structure in DNZSL, 1997

includes 30 pages that introduce the social-historical context of NZSL, characteristics of the lexicon, sign notation and a guide to entry structure and symbols (see Figure 25.1).

25.2.3 Making the Online Dictionary of NZSL (ODNZSL)

Capacity for bi-directional searching, linguistically enriched entry information, dynamic rendering of signs through video and a more interactive user interface has been advanced in recent online dictionaries of Finnish Sign Language (Kuurojen Liittory 2003), Flemish Sign Language (Van Herreweeghe et al. 2004), Danish Sign Language (Center for Tegnsprog 2008) and Swedish Sign Language (Institutionen för Lingvistik 2009). An online format was the logical progression for a twenty-first-century NZSL dictionary. The ODNZSL project was the initiative of the Deaf Studies Research Unit at Victoria University, funded by a government grant of NZD$750,000 for a three-year project (approx. €470,000 at current exchange rate).[2] The editorial team comprised a managing editor, two consulting editors, a database manager and two research assistants, all working on the project part-time. A technical editor (database programmer), illustrator, translators and web designers were also contracted.

Effective dictionary design proceeds from a realistic understanding of the purposes and capacities of users (Atkins and Rundell 2008). The ODNZSL project team knew that the dictionary should be accessible to both L1 and L2 users of NZSL and that the largest use would be as a translation dictionary for L2 users seeking NZSL equivalents for words, but it should also serve general documentary purposes. Nevertheless, user needs were formally investigated by a written survey of potential users in the following categories: teachers of Deaf children, adult learners of NZSL, Deaf NZSL teachers, Deaf community, interpreters, Deaf and hearing students in schools and parents/families of Deaf children/adults (mainly non-Deaf). Three hundred and one survey responses informed decisions about how to meet the expectations of most user groups.

Moving to an online format required re-design at all levels: the micro-structure and content of entries, the macro-structure of dictionary organisation and access, and the mega-structure of all elements in the dictionary (Hausman and Wiegand 1989). The first step was to migrate the 1997 DNZSL data records to an online database designed by the technical editor, known as Freelex,[3] an open-source application that enables multi-user, online workflow, editing of data fields within records, quality assurance (QA) management, corpus search and reports on user activity and record history. Following migration to Freelex, all records were checked and revised as needed. Entries were tagged for variation information (e.g., use by region, age) where known, and grammatical features. New records were added, including variants, neologisms and borrowings collected in the 20 years since the 1997 dictionary. Candidate signs to be added were validated by community groups in three regions. Although ODNZSL was intended as a general dictionary, Deaf Education Centres were invited to submit signs relating to school curriculum subjects that they had already documented, for potential inclusion in the dictionary. Many of the items submitted were nonce translations for English terms that had only locally recognisable meaning, and some were neologisms for concepts that could in fact be translated by semantic extension of signs already in the dictionary (possibly overlooked due to ineffective translation skills). Approximately half of the suggested school signs thus did not pass validation in a process of cross-school and adult community consultation, but approximately 100 were added. During revision of the database, some entries from the previous dictionary failed QA for various reasons and are not displayed in the current ODNZSL. The number of entries displayed in ODNZSL is 4376, with a further 2187 undisplayed records in the database. This number is still growing.

The next phase was to film citation forms of headwords and usage examples for each sign, as discussed in more detail later in this article. Headwords and usage examples (between one and four examples per entry) were filmed in 25 days, over 18 months. In total 11,000 clips were recorded, edited, quality assured, archived on a server and linked as assets to records in the database. Each usage example was translated into English, to appear beside the video. Below the translation is a literal gloss of signs in the NZSL sentence; to allow cross-referencing, each of these glosses was tagged with its database ID number to create a hyperlink to the entry for that sign. The hyperlinked gloss feature was modelled on the Danish Sign Language Dictionary (Centre for Tegnsprog 2008). Figure 25.2 shows the structure of an entry in ODNZSL.

A web design company worked closely with the project team to create a user interface and to integrate this with the database search engine. Ideas about features and functions of the website were drawn from recent online sign language dictionaries, in particular, the Danish and Finnish dictionaries. In the testing phase, a range of users trialled a set of search tasks in the website and provided feedback on problems that were resolved prior to launch.

The mega-structure of ODNZSL contains tabs that provide textual information about how to use the dictionary, history and grammatical aspects of NZSL, systems of numbers, fingerspelling, classifiers and links to relevant organisations and learning resources. Like other electronic sign language dictionaries, NZSL is not used as a meta-language within entries (Kristoffersen and Troelsgård 2012), but the 'front matter' tabs contain NZSL translation in am embedded video window, making the dictionary more accessible to Deaf NZSL users. A 'News' tab imparts updates to users and offers a Facebook link, which has been

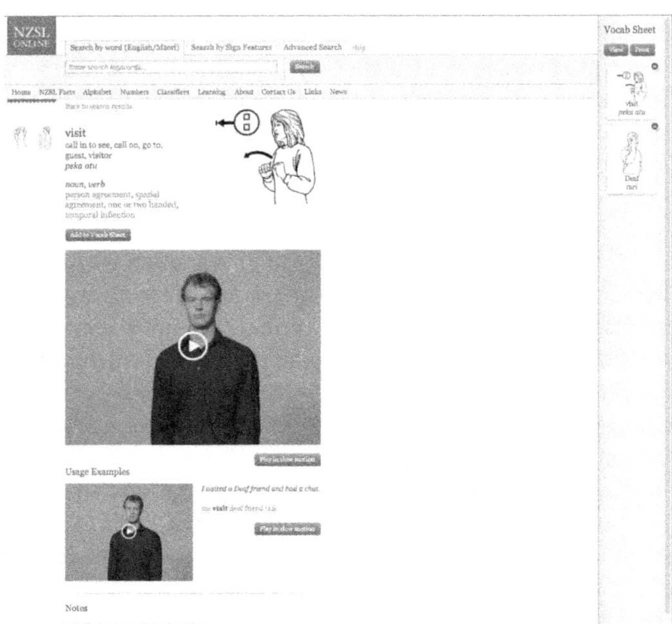

Figure 25.2 Example of ODNZSL entry display

effective in disseminating awareness of the dictionary and uptake of a free mobile app of the dictionary in a reduced format.

25.3 Core issues and topics

25.3.1 Ordering and searching entries

An online database and interface greatly reduce problems of how to order signs as headwords and enables searching for signs in more than one way. Entries in the ODNZSL can be searched via English equivalents, via Māori words, by handshape and location features of a sign, by topic domains or by usage status (archaic, neologism, rare, informal and obscene). Addressing users' receptive needs requires being able to identify the visual form of a sign. Fortunately, the immense task of coding of handshape and location features of each sign had been completed for all records in the 1997 dictionary database, which is the basis for 'search by sign features' in the ODNZSL (Figure 25.3).

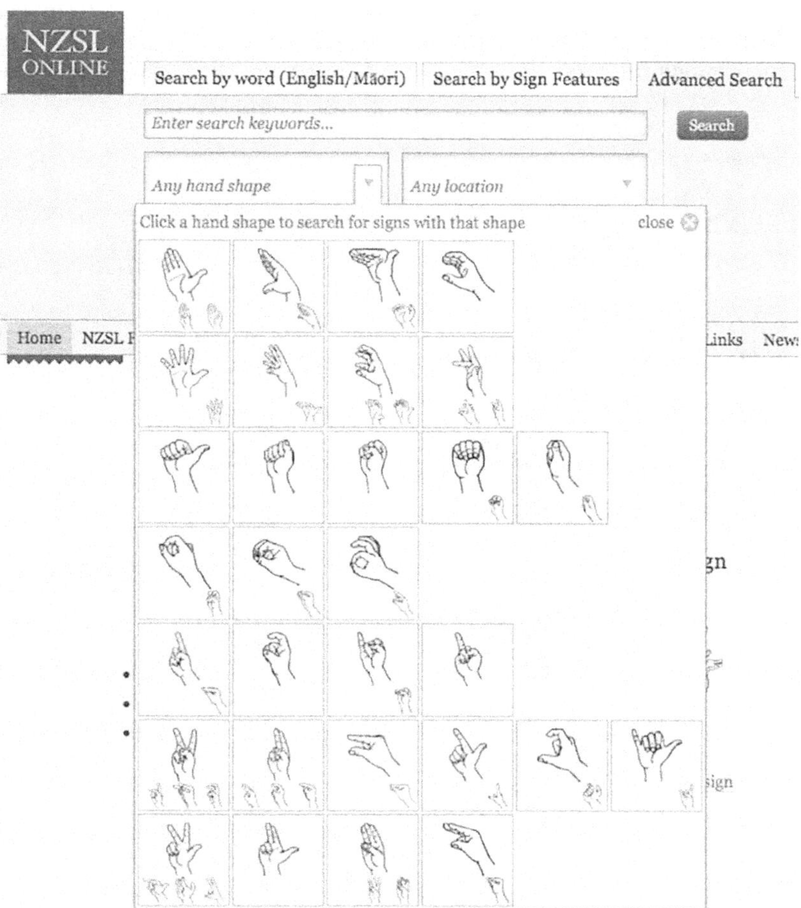

Figure 25.3 Handshape search menu

Selecting phonological features of handshape and location as the parameters for a search is more unaccustomed and analytically demanding for users than searching by English word. Handshape and location features thus needed to be grouped in a logical manner to simplify selection of salient features. We closely examined the sign feature search menus of the Danish and Finnish online sign language dictionaries to refine our inventory of NZSL handshapes and locations. To determine the final content of these selection menus (see Figures 25.3 and 25.4), adult NZSL learners were given a pilot task to test how accurately they could identify salient handshapes and locations to find a given set of target signs. Results indicated that they could make quite accurate choices, and highlighted problematic options which informed the final inventory: that is, which handshapes to display at the top/category level, which as sub-handshapes and which were redundant or ambiguous distinctions.

A search by any method yields a results list, each displaying an illustration, playable videoclip, a main gloss hyperlinked to the entry and secondary translations. Results are ordered by frequency of the variant when there is more than one sign for the same sense. Otherwise, sign results are ordered alphabetically by their translations, which is not the most relevant logic, but a better solution has not yet been implemented.

An 'add to vocab sheet' button in each entry allows users to select, caption and print customized sheets of sign illustrations, which is valuable for learning and teaching purposes. Other online learning resources are linked from a 'Learning' tab.

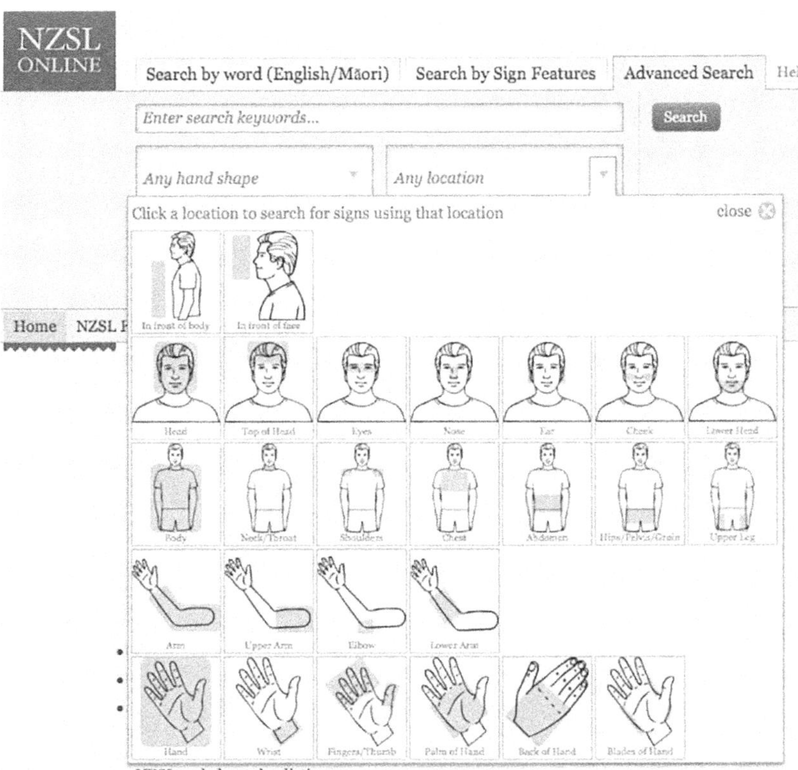

Figure 25.4 Location search menu

25.3.2 Evidence-based content: frequency and usage examples

The availability of electronic corpora has revolutionalised sources of usage evidence for dictionaries of major spoken languages (Atkins and Rundell 2008). Most sign language dictionaries, however, have lacked any usage information, let alone attested examples of use or frequency information (Johnston 2003; Wilcox 2003; Zwitserlood 2010). The chief constraint on corpus-informed dictionaries of signed languages has been the difficulty of developing machine-searchable corpora for visual languages without a conventional written form.[4] Rapid advances have been made recently in sign language corpus development with the advent of tools that enable annotation of time-linked video files. ELAN, (EUDICO Linguistic Annotator), originally developed for research on gesture, has become a widely used corpus-building tool that allows users to create and search multi-tier annotations for video data (Johnston and Schembri 2005). Nevertheless, annotating a spoken corpus involves transcribing and tagging known words and particles, whereas basic transcription of a signed corpus requires first identifying and determining a written code for each sign type and token, even before further annotation (Kristoffersen and Troelsgård 2012). Transcription of signs via a written gloss and/or a phonetic notation system is a time intensive analytic process that poses dilemmas such as the determination of lexemes, lemmas and phrasal units (Johnston and Schembri 1999; Fenlon et al 2015).

Although the ODNZSL does not provide user access to a corpus, it utilised one as the main source of frequency and usage information. Following the 1997 DNZSL project, the general editor created a first glossed corpus of NZSL in order to analyse lexical frequency to guide compilation of a concise dictionary and teaching curricula (McKee and Kennedy 2006). The Wellington Corpus of NZSL is based on more than 50 hours of videotaped NZSL discourse, involving 80 Deaf people in discourse events, including conversations, narratives, speeches, meetings and discussions on more than 30 topics, including school, education, sport, work, health and politics. Over one year, videotapes were transcribed into English glosses, creating a text file of 100,000 running signs, comprising 7222 types (McKee and Kennedy 2006). At the time it was the largest transcribed corpus of sign language, but by modern standards its format is primitive in that the transcript is detached from the video source texts and it lacks further annotation of linguistic features. Although the 1997 dictionary database served as a reference for glossing signs, there is some inconsistency of type labels. (See Johnston 2008, 2012 on the importance of consistent ID glosses for analysing lexical frequency in signed corpora.) However, the text form of the corpus allowed the use of a concordance tool, Wordsmith, to analyse lexical distribution (as reported in McKee and Kennedy 2006). Analysis revealed that only 15 frequent signs (in the top 500) were missing from the 1997 DNZSL, confirming that its coverage was quite representative. The subsequent Concise DNZSL (Kennedy et al 2002) contained the most frequent 2000 signs in the corpus.

Between 2005 and 2008, the corpus was extended by a further 14,000 tokens from data recorded in a sociolinguistic variation project, which was transcribed using ELAN and was more richly annotated. Text files from the two projects were combined to form a glossed corpus linked to the ODNZSL editorial database from which types and concordances can be searched.

Atkins and Rundell (2008) acknowledge that, "Corpus creation is a pragmatic exercise, with compromise at all phases – design, data collection, and encoding" (2008:56). Although this corpus of 114,000 tokens is compromised by its smallness (relative to spoken language corpus standards), imperfect sampling and transcription flaws, it nevertheless represents data from a wide range of speakers using authentic language on many topics, and thus provided valuable usage information about the lexicon. Corpus evidence informed our consideration of questions such as:

- Is the sign FIGHT used metaphorically as well as literally?
- Does the sign AFFAIR have a nominal or only a verbal sense?
- Which variants of HOT collocate with human vs. non-human subjects?

In the editing process, the corpus informed decisions about sense, word class, collocation and so on provided the basis for example sentences, as explained next.

25.3.3 Creating example sentences

Examples indicating grammatical usage in the 1997 and 2002 print NZSL dictionaries are presented in English, which is some distance from illustrating actual contexts of use in NZSL. An electronic medium allows the inclusion of filmed examples that are more authentic and informative with regard to both form and context. To create usage examples for ODNZSL, the corpus was searched for tokens of each headword, and up to three utterances were selected as potential examples. Few utterances could be used verbatim, as per Atkins and Rundell's (2008) advice that the vast majority of examples in a learners' dictionary must be modified from raw data in order to be accessible and maximally informative. We adopted Atkins and Rundell's guiding principles that examples should be:

(i) *Natural and Typical*: the word is shown in its most usual context, syntax and collocation; not idiosyncratic usage.
(ii) *Informative*: the sentence gives informative context (helps understand the sense of the word).
(iii) *Intelligible*: the sentence contains no words that are more difficult than the headword; clear structure; succinct. To aid intelligibility, extraneous clauses or contexts that did not clarify typical sense or grammatical use were removed.

As a general rule, each headword in an example sentence had to appear in an uninflected form, whereas it might have been inflected in the corpus data. Examples also had to be de-contextualised enough to stand alone as an intelligible utterance, which is not always the character of discourse among interlocutors who share a real-world context. Citations that required implicit knowledge of the conversational context were discarded or re-worked.

With learners in mind, we tried to ensure that signs within examples were high-frequency and in the dictionary to allow cross-referencing. The imperative for clarity, and the fact that each example would have to be performed to camera and later translated into English, led us to avoid certain structures of signed languages, including the following: (a) 'constructed action', a quotative device that enacts reported speech or action (which is convoluted to translate in writing); and (b) 'classifier constructions' that depict objects and actions specific to the discourse context, which are wordy to translate, and not possible to cross-reference to dictionary entries since they are not part of the conventional lexicon. We made some exceptions to the guidelines: for instance, it is unnatural to illustrate an imperative sign such as "Stop-it!", or a response, "Oh-I-see", without embedding it in constructed dialogue (i.e. directed to an imaginary addressee). In some cases, examples were modified during filming, if it became apparent that a sentence was too complex, or lacked sense out of context.

The goal of deriving all usage examples from corpus data was not achieved, as also reported for the Danish Sign Language dictionary (Kristoffersen 2010). Almost 50 percent of headwords were not found in our corpus due to its size or glossing limitations. Approximately 30 percent of examples were devised by a native signer in the editorial team. In the end, the usage examples reflect "pragmatic compromise" (Atkins and Rundell 2008), being corpus informed, but modified to achieve accessibility for users and performability and translatability in their production.

A benefit of corpus-based examples in the ODNZSL is a glimpse of the Deaf cultural frames that underpin the lexicon in use. Fillmore (2003: 284) explains frames as the "background set of beliefs, practices, institutions, or ready-made conceptualizations available to the speakers of the language as the necessary underpinnings of the way they speak". The way signs are used in Deaf discourse invoke frames that are particular to their cultural experiences. For instance, the usage example for *family* is, MY FAMILY ALL HEARING ME ONE DEAF ("My family are all hearing. I'm the only Deaf person"). This statement illustrates a frequent collocation between the signs 'one/only' and 'Deaf', and is commonly uttered in Deaf life narratives; it invokes mutually understood implications about the ensuing obstacles to family relationships, language acquisition and social identity. Similarly, the example for the sign *oral/speaking* conveys a distinctly Deaf perspective; the example is glossed as, HE ORAL SPEAK GOOD CAN HE ("He can speak well"). Although the translation is understandable on face value, the example makes implicit reference to social categorisation of Deaf individuals into those who can and choose to communicate through speech and identify more with the hearing world, in contrast to those who prefer to sign and to identify as NZSL users. Culturally rich examples such as these add a valuable element to dictionary content. We agree with Fillmore's (2003) argument that dictionaries could usefully go further in making explicit the background frames that underpin native use of lexical items, especially for non-native users wanting to understand why a word exists and why a speaker would choose to use it in a context (2003: 269) – in effect, providing ethnographic reference. Augmenting dictionary entries with a link to such commentary, where relevant, is feasible in an online format and is an interesting prospect for future development.

25.3.4 What qualifies as a conventional lexeme?

Johnston and Schembri (1999) observe that it is difficult to judge the lexicon size of most signed languages via existing dictionaries because they usually include inflected forms and phonological variants of signs, and list homonym signs by senses without noting relationships between these forms. In the absence of lemmatised sources, they estimate that most signed languages have a small established lexicon, of perhaps "a few thousand" unique signs. Some reasons for this are that signed languages have not been historically used in specialised domains that foster elaborated vocabularies (Johnston 2002), and signers can fingerspell "non-native" vocabulary from a spoken language to supplement the sign lexicon (Brentari and Padden 2001). However, another important reason is the multimodal character of signs which allows a sign to be modified by manual, facial and spatial means, rather than lexically, to express adverbial meanings such as manner, degree, temporal aspect. Due to these productive properties, determining which signs qualify as dictionary entries, and what constitutes a citation form, are vexing theoretical and practical issues for sign lexicographers (Brennan 2001; Brien and Turner 1994; Fenlon, Cormier and Schembri 2015; Johnston and Schembri 1999; Johnston 2012).

A key distinction is made between fully lexicalised (frozen) signs, which have a conventional and consistent form–meaning pairing, and partly lexicalised (productive) signs which are conventional in most parameters, but can be used to create novel form–meaning pairings in particular contexts (Johnston and Schembri 1999). Fully lexicalised signs are more straightforward candidates for dictionary entries. Johnston (2012) describes two main categories (and further subcategories) of partly lexicalised signs that are prevalent in signed languages: (i) 'pointing signs' that make deictic reference to person (pronouns), location, determiners, possession and visible referents (such as body parts or objects) in which the particular direction and referential meaning of pointing are contextually determined; and (ii) 'depicting signs' (also known as classifier constructions and polycomponential signs; Supalla 1982; Emmorey 2003), which combine conventional handshapes with movement and spatial arrangement in novel ways to mimetically or metaphorically represent the appearance, arrangement, handling and actions of animate and inanimate entities.

Lexicographers agree that the productive use of depicting signs challenge the construct of 'word' or lexeme (Johnston and Schembri 1999; Brennan 2001). However, most sign language dictionaries include pointing and depicting signs that are used frequently enough with regular form-meaning association to serve as lexemes. For instance, Figure 25.5 shows a sign in the ODNZSL translated as *overtake*; its form comprises four meaningful components: two pro-forms representing vehicles, the movement path of the overtaking vehicle and the agency of the overtaking driver represented by the signer's head tilt and expression. Although this form has a consistent form and predictable meaning, its productive depicting potential can be "re-activated" (Brennan 2001) by varying the production of path and manner elements to describe details of a specific event (e.g. overtaking recklessly, cautiously, on a bend, on a hill, etc.).

A depicting sign that is not lexicalised for most signers (i.e. lacks a specified form–meaning association out of context) might be considered lexicalised by some signers who use it regularly in a particular context (Johnston and Schembri 1999: 133). For example, the NZSL sign, JURY (Figure 25.6) depicts a number of upright entities (people, in this case) facing forward in an orderly row. Only in the context of legal talk is this understood to mean 'jury', whereas in other everyday contexts, it could depict any orderly line of upright entities, such as a row of spectators at a race, a row of candles or fence posts. The fact that slightly different forms of "multiple upright entities" (translated as jury) are shown in the 1997 and 2011 dictionaries (Figure 26.6) suggest that it retains a more productive than fully lexicalised character.

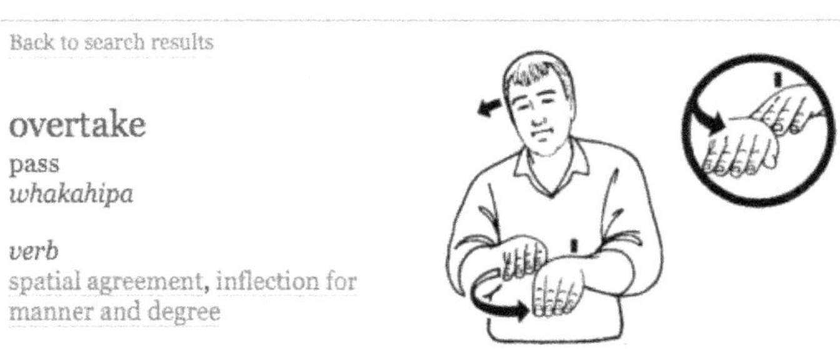

Figure 25.5 Lexicalised depicting sign: OVERTAKE[5]

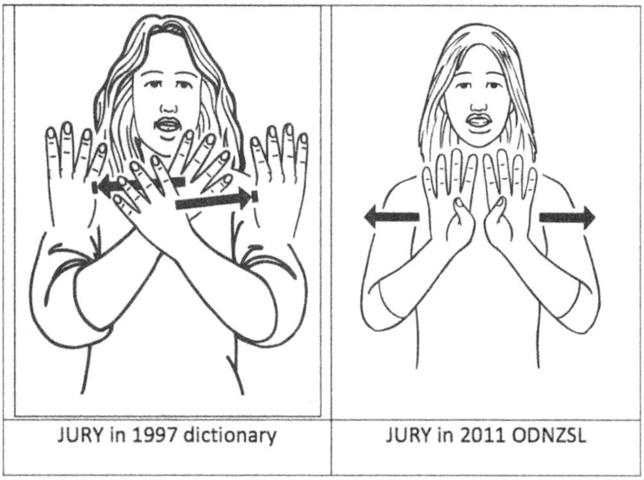

Figure 25.6 Semi-lexicalised sign: JURY[6]

25.3.5 Ambiguity in lemmas and citation forms

Determining lemma and citation form of signs is a complex problem in signed languages, for numerous reasons to do with ambiguity in inflected and variant forms, as discussed in detail by Fenlon et al (2015). Few sign dictionaries are lemmatised, and the ODNZSL is no exception. Although principled identification of lemmas is important for a lexical database being used as a reference for corpus annotation, it is less critical in the presentation of a translation-focused dictionary. Many regularly inflected sign forms (particularly verbs) acquire semi-lexicalised status through frequency of use and thus warrant inclusion in a translation dictionary, in which indicating semantic equivalence between languages is an important goal (Johnston and Schembri 1999; Fenlon et al 2015). For instance, Figure 25.7 shows three entries in ODNZSL that are modified forms of the verb 'RIGHT' (to be correct).

During filming, native sign models often struggled to produce citation forms (especially verbs and adjectives) that were devoid of inflections for manner, degree or directionality; the un-naturalness of doing so suggests that although these features are, technically optional, in natural usage they seem closely fused with the semantics and form of particular signs. Arbitrating on citation form for each performed item in a dictionary is somewhat like the orthography decisions required in dictionaries of oral languages (see Axelrod et al 2003). As Axelrod et al observe, native speaker perspective in this process is vital, but does not guarantee consensus on 'accurate' or 'neutral' forms for a dictionary.

25.3.6 Sociolinguistic variation: recording lexical variation and change

Signed languages have considerable lexical and phonological variation, both socially patterned and idiosyncratic (Lucas 2003). Natural variation has often been sidelined in sign language dictionaries, especially those made by non-linguists with standardizing aims (Johnston 2003; Lucas 2003; Schermer 2012). Lexical variation and change are not problematic for native sign language users; however, it can be challenging for dictionary makers to capture, and sometimes

Right (correct) – 'root', citation form, two handed.	*That's /you're right* - reduced to one hand; spatially inflected to indicate a notional object	*Oh yes, that's right/ I remember now* - reduced to one hand; reduplicated; spatially inflected; head tilt expressing inchoative aspect of 'realising'

Figure 25.7 Conventionally inflected forms of RIGHT

for both L1 and L2 users to accept in documented form. Age and regional lexical variation is prevalent in NZSL, (McKee and McKee 2011), and this is reflected in ODNZSL. Wilcox (2003) notes the role of dictionaries as archives of language change. The NZSL dictionaries document diachronic and synchronic variation in the lexicon. Some signs used only by older or previous generations are tagged as rare or archaic. Variants recorded in the ODNZSL reflect both external and internal processes of change; external influences include foreign vocabulary introduced through the Deaf education system, through lexical borrowing by Deaf individuals travelling abroad and immigrants to the NZSL community. These origins are noted in entries where they are known. Internal change is prompted by innovation and by natural phonological and morphological processes. Figure 25.8, for example, shows four variants of the DIE/DEAD, of which (1) and (2) are 'original' or early signs now used by older generations and (3) and (4) have been borrowed into NZSL from overseas and are now in general use.

25.3.7 Polysemy and mouthing

Polysemous and homophonous signs call for decisions about the representation of form-sense relationships in a dictionary that take into account both linguistic awareness and translation

DIE, DEAD (1) *Early (older) NZSL*	DIE, DEAD, KILL (2) *Early (older) NZSL*	DIE, DEAD (3) *BSL/Auslan origin*	DIE, DEAD (4) *ASL origin*

Figure 25.8 Variants of DIE/DEAD in ODNZSL

needs of users. In the ODNZSL, homophonous signs that have the same form but unrelated senses – for example, LIVE[7] and TRUE[8] – have separate entries in ODNZSL. This departs from the principle of organising written dictionaries by contrasting forms, thereby entering a headword once, with all senses (related and unrelated) listed later. Because the predominant use of the ODNZSL is searching for semantic equivalence by an English word, and considering that the online medium allows unlimited space for entries and that visual overcrowding of one entry with extensive information is undesirable for users, we chose to display different senses of homophones separately. Currently, related forms (both homophonous and polysemous) in separate entries are not cross-referenced, which is a flaw to be addressed.

NZSL contains many polysemous signs that express a range of meanings; for example the entry for BAD[9] gives 13 English translations: *at fault, awful, badly, harmful, immoral, incorrect, make a mistake, mistake, mistaken, not right, poor quality, severe, unpleasant*, thus covering a wide range of 'negative' senses with one sign. In many signed languages, the meaning of such signs in context is disambiguated by the simultaneous, silent mouthing of spoken words (Boyes-Braem and Sutton-Spence 2001). Linguists debate whether mouthing is integral to the lexicon or a form of code mixing (Bank, Crasborn and van Hout 2011; Boyes-Braem and Sutton-Spence 2001; Ebbinghaus and Hessman 1996), but regardless, video representation in a dictionary requires decisions about whether to include mouthing at all, and if so, which of the likely mouthings. Kristoffersen and Niemala (2008) outline a rationale for addressing this question in the online Danish Sign Language Dictionary, explaining that if associated mouth patterns are treated as a stable formational element of a sign, the result would be multiple entries for one sign form paired with alternate mouthings. For example, a sign with the prototypical meaning 'house' might have seven entries paired with seven dwelling-related Danish words that are regularly mouthed with this sign. On the other hand, if mouthing is treated at the level of meaning (i.e. not part of sign form, but contributing to sense), the result would be one entry for a polysemous sign that lists translations frequently expressed by mouth patterns. The Danish dictionary favoured the latter approach, as did the ODNZSL editors; that is, one sign that is typically used with several mouthings generally has a single entry.[10] An example is BOY (Figure 25.9), which lists related senses that can be specified by mouthing and/or semantic context. However, as not all secondary translations in every entry are necessarily typical mouthings, this is not an ideal solution for informing users how signs are potentially combined with mouthing.

Video clips of citation signs required a decision as to which, if any, mouthing should accompany the sign. Our compromise was to film a polysemous citation form with no mouthing (although this is atypical use in NZSL) and to show contextually appropriate mouthing in the usage examples. For instance, the entry LEARN/SCHOOL (secondary translations – exam, lesson, schooling)[12] has a citation video with no mouthing, but the two usage examples contain natural mouthing of 'learn' and 'school', respectively.

Another semantic equivalence challenge within ODNZSL was the addition of Māori glosses based on the main English translation, with direct reference to the NZSL sense as needed. Secondary translation was problematic where the semantic range of NZSL, English and Māori words diverged. For instance, 'grey' in NZSL takes different forms for the generic colour, sky and hair, whereas Māori words differentiate the colour of sky, a dog, human hair and the plumage of specific birds, without a truly generic colour term. The sense of a citation form (main gloss) and that of the usage example often prompted different translations in Māori; for example, in Māori, 'build' can be expressed by different verbs according to the type of object being built, so the Māori main gloss is not always the best match for a specific usage example in an entry. Ambiguous word class of many signs (noun/verb), and polysemous signs complicated

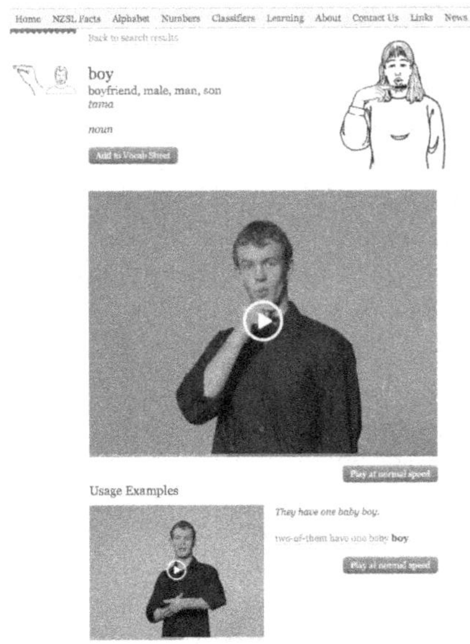

Figure 25.9 Polysemous sign: BOY[11]

Māori translation. In Figure 25.9, for example, the Māori gloss is equivalent to the main gloss, 'boy', and one secondary gloss, 'son', but not to the additional senses. Overall, Māori glosses in the dictionary are the best approximation within the constraints, but precise equivalence across three languages is acknowledged to be compromised in many cases, since translation requires contextual information.

25.4 Looking to the future

Strengthening the empirical basis of sign language dictionaries with corpus evidence is the new wave in sign language lexicography. Sign language corpora and lexical databases are being developed with increasing sophistication, although the scale is small in comparison to spoken languages, due to the time-consuming nature of transcription and annotation, and constraints on the supply of skilled annotators.[13] Some major corpus projects are now advancing practical and theoretical approaches to corpus-based lexicography; for example, the iLex database of German Sign Language (DGS) (University of Hamburg, n.d.), the Auslan corpus project (Johnston, n.d.) and the British Sign Language Corpus project (www.bslcorpusproject.org). The primary focus of these is to create an annotated corpus as the basis of a lemmatised lexical database, which in turn supports ongoing corpus development that will increasingly inform user-facing dictionaries, possibly for differentiated uses. Interrogation of signed corpora can be expected to enrich sign language dictionaries with attested evidence about frequency, sense, grammatical usage and collocation of signs.

The development of automated signing avatars and animated characters to model signs anonymously is another contemporary innovation likely to be exploited further in sign language dictionaries (e.g. Chiriac et al 2015).

Advances in technology and linguistic insight are not the only relevant drivers of future developments. Evaluating usability and user needs has been neglected, and is important to the improvement of sign language dictionaries. To address this gap, Vale (2015) undertook a user study of the ODNZSL, collecting 'back end' data about user behaviour from website log files, as well as 'front-end' qualitative data on observed user behaviour. Findings reveal how users search in the dictionary; for example, mainly for high-frequency vocabulary, very rarely by sign or advanced features and commonly by entering Google-type enquiries into the word search box, such as 'zoo animals', translation requests such as 'my name is', or inflected word forms such as 'ate'. Vale reports that most ODNZSL users had no prior experience with any kind of electronic dictionary, meaning that usage strategies are not intuitive, even when dictionary design has prioritised user ease. Vale highlights the need to strike a balance between the information available and user ability to navigate and process it; whereas the pre-ODNZSL user survey indicated that information about sign variation and grammar was desired, the study showed that many users ignored or were overwhelmed by hyperlinked information about grammar, or choices of variants. Vale's study also suggested practical improvements, such as displaying and playing videos directly in the search results page, rather than clicking through to an entry, which was subsequently implemented.

Few sign language dictionaries contain information in the target language beyond video content demonstrating signs and usage examples (Kristoffersen and Troelsgård 2012). Although translation of textual information (about the dictionary and about the language) displayed in a video window is one way to add this (as in ODNZSL), a bigger step towards a monolingual dictionary would be the addition of definitions in sign language. Implementation of this requires research based on corpus data and native speaker consultation about senses and principles for forming folk definitions, as well as consideration of their potential benefit and usability for dictionary users (see Vale 2017).

25.5 Conclusion

The ODNZSL has been described as a case study to exemplify some challenges and innovations in online sign language dictionaries. National dictionaries such as this are expected to address descriptive, pedagogical and status-raising purposes. The ODNZSL and comparable online sign dictionaries leverage decades of descriptive work by previous sign linguists, practical lexicographers and the affordances of electronic technology and the Internet. The advent of video content, online data storage and relational search capabilities and interactive user interfaces combine to offer dictionary makers and users richer and more dynamic resources than in previous eras when the representation of sign languages was confined to one dimension, between the covers of a book.

Corpus-based approaches to empirical investigation of sign language lexicons are currently being refined and promise to enrich the content of future dictionaries. Investigation of user needs and behaviour will also be important in guiding the design of databases and dictionaries that meet differentiated aims of language description, language learning and specialised vocabulary resources.

In terms of social impacts, open access to the ODNZSL and shareable content ensures that all potential users have equal access to it as a resource and are free to use it creatively to promote knowledge of NZSL more widely. Availability of the dictionary and links to related resources expand opportunities for sign language acquisition, especially for families and educators of Deaf children who are not connected to a Deaf community. The dictionary's presence on the Internet and personal mobile devices contribute to normalising NZSL and a signing community in the linguistic landscape.

Related topics

Dictionaries and access; lexicography and corpus linguistics; dictionaries and culture; electronic dictionaries; English lexicography in the Internet era; explaining meaning in lexicographic information tools; specialized dictionaries.

Further reading

Fenlon, J., K. Cormier and A. Schembri. (2015). "Building BSL SignBank: The Lemma Dilemma Revisited", *International Journal of Lexicography* 28(2): 169–206.
Following up on issues raised by Johnston and Schembri (1999), this article explores principles and practices for determining which idiosyncratic and systematically modified variants group together to form a lexeme or a lemma, based on their work on a corpus and lexical database of British Sign Language.

Johnston, T. and A. Schembri. (1999). "On Defining Lexeme in a Signed Language", *Sign Language and Linguistics* 2(2): 115–185.
Starting from the premise that conventional dictionaries list lemmas (uninflected forms) as headwords, Johnston and Schembri consider why the same principle is not easily applied to sign language dictionaries. They distinguish categories of lexical units in signed languages that have different kinds of form–meaning relationships – some more frozen and conventional, and others more productive and contextualised. They examine arguments for the status of different types of signs as potential lexemes in a dictionary. This is an important overview of the properties of signed lexicons and implications for lexicography.

Zwitserlood, I., J. H. Kristoffersen and T. Troelsgård. (2013). "Issues in Sign Language Lexicography", in H. Jackson (ed.), *The Bloomsbury Companion to Lexicography*. London: Bloomsbury, pp. 259–283.
This is a comprehensive historical overview of sign lexicography, surveying linguistic issues in content selection, and technical considerations in the organisation, rendering and searching of content. Illustrations from various electronic sign language dictionaries make it a useful resource for readers with practical involvement in a dictionary project.

Notes

1 A sign-based approach was used, for example, in dictionaries made in Australia (Johnston, 1989), Thailand (Suwanarat et al, 1990), Britain (Brien, 1992), and Italy (Radutsky, 1992).
2 The ODNZSL project was funded by the New Zealand Tertiary Education Commission's 'Encouraging and Supporting Innovation' Fund.
3 Freelex is Open Source lexicography software by Dave Moskovitz. Contact: http://dave.moskovitz.co.nz/
4 Several systems have been created to capture the phonetic or lexical form of signs, but their use is limited to linguists and educators who adopt them for pedagogical purposes. They are not widely known by signers. See Zwiterslood (2010) for a summary of sign writing systems.
5 http://nzsl.vuw.ac.nz/signs/514
6 http://nzsl.vuw.ac.nz/signs/1415
7 http://nzsl.vuw.ac.nz/signs/565
8 http://nzsl.vuw.ac.nz/signs/440
9 http://nzsl.vuw.ac.nz/signs/4581
10 Boyes-Braem (2001) reports the opposite decision for a lexical database of Swiss-German Sign Language: identical manual signs with contrasting mouthings are separate entries. In the iLex lexical database of German Sign Language (DGS), the manual sign is treated as the type and combinations of the manual form with different German mouthings are treated as sub-types (lexemes). (Reiner Konrad, 2012 Sign Corpus Linguistics Summer School, University of Hamburg, unpublished lecture notes.)

11 http://nzsl.vuw.ac.nz/signs/2184
12 http://nzsl.vuw.ac.nz/signs/5724
13 An overview of recent developments in sign language corpus work is found in Crasborn, O., Hanke, T., Thoutenhoofd, E.D., Zwitserlood, I. and Efthimiou, E. (2008). Also see the work of the Sign Linguistics Corpora Network hosted at Radboud University, Nijmegen: www.ru.nl/slcn/

References

Adam, R. (2015) "Standardization of Sign Languages", *Sign Language Studies 15*(4): 432–445.

Al-Fityani, K. and C. Padden (2010) "Sign Language Geography in the Arab World", in D. Brentari (ed.), *Sign Languages: A Cambridge Survey*. New York: Cambridge University Press, pp. 433–450.

Atkins, B.T.S. and M. Rundell (2008) *The Oxford Guide to Practical Lexicography*. Oxford: Oxford University Press.

Axelrod, M., J. Gómez de Garcia and J. Lachler (2003) "The Role of Literacy and Collaboration in Documenting Native American Languages: A Report From the Jicarilla Apache Dictionary Project", *Sign Language Studies* 3(3): 296–321.

Bank, R., O. Crasborn, and R. van Hout (2011) "Variation in Mouth Actions With Manual Signs in Sign Language of the Netherlands (NGT)", *Sign Language and Linguistics 14*(2): 248–270.

Boyes-Braem, P. (2001) "A Multimedia Bilingual Database for the Lexicon of Swiss German Sign Language", in *Sign Language and Linguistics, 4:1/2. Special Volume: Sign Transcription and Database Storage of Sign Information*, pp. 133–144.

Boyes-Braem, P. and R. Sutton-Spence (eds.) (2001) *The Hands Are the Head of the Mouth: The Mouth as Articulator in Sign Languages*. Seedorf and Hamburg: Signum-Verlag.

Brennan, M. (2001) "Encoding and Capturing Productive Morphology", *Sign Language and Linguistics, 4:1/2. Special Volume: Sign Transcription and Database Storage of Sign Information:* 47–62.

Brentari, D., and C. A. Padden (2001) "Native and Foreign Vocabulary in American Sign Language: A Lexicon With Multiple Origins", in D. Brentari (ed.), *Foreign Vocabulary in Sign Languages: A Cross-linguistic Investigation of Word Formation*. Mahwah, NJ: Lawrence Erlbaum Associates, pp. 87–120.

Brien, D. (ed.) (1992) *Dictionary of British Sign Language/English*. London: Faber and Faber.

Brien, D. and G. Turner (1994) "Lemmas, Dilemmas and Lexicographical Anisomorphism: Presenting Meanings in the First BSL-English Dictionary", in I. Ahlgren, B. Bergman and M. Brennan (eds.), *Perspectives on Sign Language Usage: Papers From the Fifth International Symposium on Sign Language Research*. Durham: The International Sign Linguistics Association (ISLA), pp. 391–407.

Center for Tegnsprog (2008) *Ordbog Over Dansk Tegnsprog*. The Danish Sign Language Dictionary. www.tegnsprog.dk/

Chiriac, I., L. Stoicu-Tivadar and E. Podoleanu (2015) "Romanian Sign Language e-Health Application for Deaf People with Animated Avatar Technology", *The International Scientific Conference ELearning and Software for Education* 1: 510–517.

Collins-Ahlgren, M. (1989) *Aspects of New Zealand Sign Language*. Unpublished doctoral thesis, Victoria University of Wellington, New Zealand.

Crasborn, O., T. Hanke, E. D. Thoutenhoofd, I. Zwitserlood and E. Efthimiou (eds.) (2008) "Construction and Exploitation of Sign Language Corpora", *Proceedings of the 3rd Workshop on the Representation and Processing of Sign Languages*. Paris: ELRA. www.lrec-conf.org/proceedings/lrec2008/workshops/W25_Proceedings.pdf.

Ebbinghaus, H. and J. Hessman (1996) "Signs and Words: Accounting for Spoken Elements in German Sign Language", in W. Edmonson and R. Wilbur (eds.), *International Review of Sign Linguistics*. Volume 1. Mahwah, NJ: Lawrence Erlbaum Associates, pp. 23–54.

Emmorey, K. (2002) *Language, Cognition, and the Brain: Insights From Sign Language Research*. Mahwah, NJ: Lawrence Erlbaum Associates.

Emmorey, K. (ed.) (2003) *Perspectives on Classifier Constructions in Sign Languages*. Mahwah, NJ: Lawrence Erlbaum Associates.

Ethnologue 19th Edition (2016) *Sign Language*. www.ethnologue.com/subgroups/sign-language.

Fenlon, J., K. Cormier and A. Schembri. (2015) "Building BSL SignBank: The Lemma Dilemma Revisited", *International Journal of Lexicography* 28(2): 169–206.

Fillmore, C. J. (2003) "Double-Decker Definitions: The Role of Frames in Meaning Explanations", *Sign Language Studies* 3(3): 263–295.

Haualand, H. and C. Allen (2009) *Deaf People and Human Rights*. Helsinki: World Federation of the Deaf.

Hausman, F. J. and H. E. Wiegand (1989) "Component Parts and Structures of General Monolingual Dictionaries: A Survey", in F. J. Hausman, I. Reichmann, H. E. Wiegand, and L. Zgusta (eds.), *Wörterbücher: Ein internationales Handbuch zur Lexicographie*, pp. 328–360. Handbücher zur Sprachund Kommunikationswissenschaft 5.1. Berlin: de Gruyter.

Institutionen for Lingvistik (2009) *Svenskt teckenspraksIexikon* (Swedish Sign Language Dictionary) www.ling.su.se/teckenspraksIexikon.

Johnston, T. n.d. *Auslan Corpus*. Endangered languages archive. http://elar.soas.ac.uk/deposit/0001.

Johnson, T. (1989) *Auslan Dictionary: A Dictionary of the Sign Language of the Australian Deaf Community*. Deafness Resources, Australia Limited.

Johnston, T. (2002) "The Representation of English Using Auslan: Implications for Deaf Bilingualism and English Literacy", *Australian Journal of Education of the Deaf* 8: 23–37.

Johnston, T. (2003) "Language Standardisation and Signed Language Dictionaries", *Sign Language Studies* 3(4): 431–468.

Johnston, T. (2008) "Corpus Linguistics and Signed Languages: No Lemmata, No Corpus", in O. Crasborn, T. Hanke, E. D. Thoutenhoofd, I. Zwitserlood and E. Efthimiou (eds.) (2008) *Construction and Exploitation of Sign Language Corpora: Proceedings of the 3rd Workshop on the Representation and Processing of Sign Languages*. Paris: ELRA, pp. 82–87. Online: www.lrecconf.org/proceedings/lrec2008/workshops/W25_Proceedings.pdf.

Johnston, T. (2012) "Lexical Frequency in Sign Languages", *Journal of Deaf Studies and Deaf Education* 17(2): 163–193.

Johnston, T. and A. Schembri (1999) "On Defining Lexeme in a Signed Language", *Sign Language and Linguistics* 2(2): 115–185.

Johnston, T. and A. Schembri (2005) "The Use of ELAN Annotation Software in the Auslan Archive/Corpus Project", presentation at the Ethnographic E-reserach Annotation Conference, University of Melbourne.

Kennedy, G., R. Arnold, P. Dugdale, S. Fahey and D. Moskovitz (eds.) (1997) *A Dictionary of New Zealand Sign Language*. Wellington: Auckland University Press and Bridget Williams Books.

Kennedy, G., D. McKee, R. Arnold, P. Dugdale, S. Fahey and D. Moskovitz (eds.) (2002) *Concise Dictionary of New Zealand Sign Language*. Wellington: Bridget Williams Books.

Kristoffersen, J. H. (2010) "From Utterance to Example Sentence: A Lexicographic Approach to Exploitation of Corpus", poster presented at *Sign Linguistics Corpora Network (SLCN) Workshop 4: Exploitation*. Deaf Centre, Friedrichstraße 12, 10969, Berlin. December 3–4, 2010. Retrieved electronically July 31, 2012, from: www.ru.nl/slcn/workshops/4_exploitation/workshop-posters/

Kristoffersen, J. H. and J. B. Niemalä (2008) "How to Describe Mouth Patterns in the Danish Sign Language Dictionary", in R. M. de Quadros (ed.), *Sign Languages: Spinning and Unraveling the Past, Present and Future. TISLR9, Forty Five Papers and Three Posters From the 9th. Theoretical Issues in Sign Language Research Conference*, Florianopolis, Brazil, December 2006. Editora Arara Azul. Petrópolis/RJ. Brazil. www.editora-arara-azul.com.br/EstudosSurdos.php.

Kristoffersen, J. H. and T. Troelsgård (2012) "The Electronic Lexicographical Treatment of Sign Languages: The Danish Sign Language Dictionary", in S. Granger and M. Paquot (eds.), *Electronic Lexicography*. First edition.. Oxford: Oxford University Press, pp. 293–318.

Kuurojen Liittory (2003) *Suvi Suomalaisen viittomakielen verkosanakirja*. (Finnish Sign Language Dictionary) http://suvi.viittomat.net.
Levitt, D. (1985) *Introduction to New Zealand Sign Language*. Auckland: National Foundation for the Deaf.
Lucas, C. (2003) "The Role of Variation in Lexicography", *Sign Language Studies* 3(3): 322–340.
McKee, D., and G. Kennedy (2000) "Lexical Comparison of Signs From American, Australian, British and New Zealand Sign Languages", in K. Emmorey and H. Lane (eds.), *The Signs of Language Revisited: An Anthology to Honor Ursula Bellugi and Edward Klima*. Mahwah, NJ: Erlbaum, pp. 49–76.
McKee, D. and G. Kennedy (2006) "The Distribution of Signs in New Zealand Sign Language", *Sign Language Studies* 6(4): 372–390.
McKee D., R. McKee, S. Pivac Alexander, M. Vale and L. Pivac (eds.) (2011) *Online Dictionary of New Zealand Sign Language*. http://nzsl.vuw.ac.nz/.
McKee, R. (2007) "The Eyes Have It! Our Third Official Language – New Zealand Sign Language", *Journal of New Zealand Studies* 4–5: 129–148.
McKee, R., and D. McKee (2011) "Old Signs, New Signs, Whose Signs? Sociolinguistic Variation in the NZSL Lexicon", *Sign Language Studies* 11(4): 485–527. doi:10.1353/sls.2011.0012.
Meir, I., W. Sandler, C. Padden, and M. Aronoff (2010) "Emerging Sign Languages", in M. Marschark and P. Spencer (eds.), *Oxford Handbook of Deaf Studies, Language, and Education*, Volume 2. Oxford: Oxford University Press, pp. 267–280.
Napier, J., G. Major, L. Ferrara, and T. Johnston (2015) "Medical Signbank as a Model for Sign Language Planning? A Review of Community Engagement", *Current Issues in Language Planning* 16(3): 279–295.
Padden, C. (1980) "The Deaf Community and the Culture of Deaf People", in C. Baker and R. Battison (eds.), *Sign Language and the Deaf Community: Essays in Honor of William Stokoe*.Washington, DC: National Association of the Deaf, pp. 89–103.
Prillwitz, S., R. Leven, H. Zienert, T. Hanke and J. Henning (1989) *HamNoSys Version 2.0. Hamburg Notation System for Sign Languages: An Introductory Guide*. Hamburg: Signum.
Radutzky, E. (ed.) (1992) *Dizionario Bilingue Elementare della Lingua Italiana dei Signi*. Rome: Edizioni Kappa.
Schermer, T. (2012) "Sign Language Planning in the Netherlands Between 1980 and 2010", *Sign Language Studies* 12(4): 467–493.
Scottish Sensory Centre, University of Edinburgh. n.d. *British Sign Language Glossaries of Curriculum Terms*. www.ssc.education.ed.ac.uk/BSL/list.html
Stokoe, W. C. (1960) *Sign Language Structure: An Outline of the Visual Communication Systems of the American Deaf*. Buffalo, NY: Dept. of Anthropology and Linguistics, University of Buffalo.
Stokoe, W. C., D. C. Casterline and C. G. Croneberg (1965) *A Dictionary of American Sign Language on Linguistic Principles*. First edition. Washington, DC: Gallaudet College Press.
Supalla, T. (1982) *Structure and Acquisition of Verbs of Motion and Location in American Sign Language*. Unpublished doctoral dissertation, University of California, San Diego.
Suwanarat, M., A. Ratanasint, V. Rungsrithong, L. Anderson and O. Wrigley (1990) *The Thai Sign Language Dictionary. Revised and Expanded Edition*. Bangkok: The National Association of the Deaf in Thailand.
University of Hamburg n.d. *iLex – A Tool for Sign Language Lexicography and Corpus Analysis*. www.sign-lang.uni-hamburg.de/ilex/
Vale, M. (2015) "A Study of the Users of an Online Sign Language Dictionary", in I. Kosem, M. Jakubíček, J. Kallas, and S. Krek (eds.), *Electronic Lexicography in the 21st Century: Linking Lexical Data in the Digital Age. Proceedings of the eLex 2015 Conference, 11–13 August 2015, Herstmonceux Castle, United Kingdom*. Ljubljana / Brighton: Trojina, Institute for Applied Slovene Studies / Lexical Computing Ltd, pp. 281–303.
Vale, M. (2017) *Folk Definitions as a Model for Sign Language Dictionary Definitions: A User-Focused Case Study of the Online Dictionary of New Zealand Sign Language*. Unpublished PhD thesis. Victoria University of Wellington.

Van Herreweghe, M., S. Slembrouck and M. Vermeerbergen (2004) *Digitaal Vlaamse Gebarentaal-Nederlands/ Nederlands-Vlaamse Gebarentaal woordenboek.* http://gebaren.ugent.be/.

Van Mulders, K. (2004) "Information", in *Digitaal Vlaamse Gebarentaal-Nederlands/ Nederlands-Vlaamse Gebarentaal woordenboek.* http://gearen.ugent.be/information.php.

Wilcox, S. (2003) "The Multimedia Dictionary of American Sign Language: Learning Lessons About Language, Technology and Business", *Sign Language Studies* 3(4): 379–392.

World Federation of the Deaf (2009) *WFD Statement: WFD Calls for the Unification Process of Sign Languages in the Arab Region to Cease Immediately.* www.wfdeaf.org/wp-content/uploads/2011/04/Statement-on-the-Unification-of-Arab-Sign-Languages-FINAL-091.pdf.

Zwitserlood, I. (2010) "Sign Language Lexicography in the Early 21st Century and a Recently Published Dictionary of Sign Language of The Netherlands", *International Journal of Lexicography* 23(4): 443–476.

26
The *Alicante Dictionaries*

José Mateo

26.1 Introduction

We, the members of IPA[1], understand specialised lexicography as an independent science that deals with terminological analysis and dictionary making. It aims to meet the needs of specific types of users who have specific problems that arise in situation-specific uses and contexts. Consequently, we consider specialised lexicography the theory and design of specialised dictionaries meant to facilitate target users a quick and easy access to explicit linguistic data. Our works are intended to help users reach the specific type of information that will satisfy their specific needs (lexicographically relevant) required by their specific social and professional contexts.

From this perspective, the linguistic criteria used in our dictionary design and writing is determined by their initial purpose and by their users' specific lexicographical needs. Hence, the making of specialised dictionaries (e.g. the *Alicante Dictionaries* presented in this chapter) takes into consideration three different but inclusive angles:

1 the nature of specialised discourses;
2 the practical characteristics of information tools;
3 the interdisciplinary nature of dictionary making with incorporations and contributions from other specific fields: information and technology sciences, economics, law, tourism, etc. (see Section 2 of this *Handbook*).

Moreover, four specific premises are observed when compiling a new dictionary of the *Alicante* set (see References):

1 the kind of information it will include, typically facts and language specific to a particular domain. In such situations, it is convenient, for example, to get a helping hand from professionals and experts in the specialised fields of knowledge addressed. In my particular case, I will mention that in the process of elaborating the *Stock Market* and *Banking dictionaries*, I was advised by financial experts and professionals who supported or argued the adequacy of my Spanish-equivalent translations of specific English

terms, both in linguistic and functional terms. Consequently, the selection of lemmas and their target language meanings depended fundamentally on their specialised significance and actual use, that is, on the real needs of their final users. This inherent characteristic of specialised dictionaries implies that they can only be designed and written once the lexicographer has attained a sufficient knowledge of the language and concepts of the domain approached. However, this idea, which is apparently so obvious, has been the subject of academic dispute (see, for example, the critical reviews of L'Homme (2015) and León Araúz and Faber (2015) to Fuertes-Olivera and Tarp's work (2014) on the theory and practice of specialised dictionaries);
2 the needs of its potential users;
3 the organization and presentation of its lexicographical information; and
4 easy access as dictionaries are tools for punctual consultation that must meet users' needs in a quick and clear way.

Within this theoretical framework, the group of linguists, lexicographers and translators at the University of Alicante (Spain) that integrate IPA have been working in the design and compilation of a number of dictionaries referred as the *Alicante Dictionaries* (see References), which will be the object of study of this chapter. All of them are printed specialised bilingual (English-Spanish/Spanish-English) dictionaries, and have been conceived following similar lexicographical and methodological criteria.

26.2 Historical perspective

The design and making of the *Alicante Dictionaries* commenced in 1993, when Enrique Alcaraz and Brian Hughes – both Professors of English at the University of Alicante – published their first bilingual specialised dictionary: *Diccionario de Términos Jurídicos (Inglés-español, Spanish-English)* which soon became a milestone in Spanish specialised lexicography and the prelude of a comprehensive series of fourteen dictionaries published to date and authored by different components of the IPA Research Group plus a seminal book on professional and academic languages (Alcaraz Varó, Mateo Martínez and Yus Ramos 2007). These dictionaries were devised according to a functional approach to specialised lexicography and covered a multidisciplinary scope.

The functional formulation that underlies these dictionaries aims at adapting their entries to different groups of potential users, irrespective of their proficiency level on the subject addressed (Andersen and Fuertes-Olivera 2009; Béjoint 2010; Bergenholtz and Tarp 1995; Fuertes-Olivera and Tarp 2008, 2014; Mateo 2014a and b). This implies the use of lexicographic strategies intended to facilitate lemmas understanding and their semantic scope by means of examples, explanations and synonyms and the need to select and discriminate among the huge amount of compound lexical units that multiply in specialised texts and documents. This last aspect is crucial in paper dictionaries where the economy of space is an inescapable premise.

For adopting a functional approach it is necessary to identify and understand the characteristics and needs of our potential users before we start drafting a specialised dictionary. This is currently done by establishing a basic typology of potential users and use situations based on questions such as these:

1 What is the users' mother language?
2 How proficient are they in both their mother and the foreign language?

3 What is their cultural level?
4 What is their cultural level related to the foreign language?
5 What is their level in both their mother and the foreign language specialised discourse?
6 What is their level in the discipline considered?
7 What is their level in the discipline considered in both their culture and in the foreign language?

The background knowledge provided by answering questions such as these helps to define the guidelines that are going to be used in the making of new specialised dictionaries. Tasks related to specific knowledge acquisition and its application to concrete lexicographical works, are the essence of the specialised dictionaries developed by IPA members along these years. In this regard, we have typically taken into consideration four stages when planning and writing a specialised dictionary: the *cognitive*, the *communicative*, the *interpretive* and the *operational*. They involve approaching:

1 the writers' prelinguistic intentional phase where authors select the specialised terms that, in their opinion, will satisfy the target readers' lexical needs;
2 the communicative or 'interactive' author/readers relationship, that is, the methodology used to stimulate the appropriate readers' inferential mechanisms;
3 the readers' correct interpretive response necessary to make the author-reader communication process efficient; and,
4 the technical and operational processes used by dictionary authors and aimed at integrating the three preceding stages in a coherent and effective way.

Of these four stages, perhaps the *communicative* and the *operational* stages have been the most studied as they refer to the four fundamental and practical issues present in any bilingual lexicographical work: *term and text production*, *reception*, *translation* and *revision and proofreading* in both the mother and the foreign languages (see chapters 16, 17, and 18 of this *Handbook*). These stages describe the specific linguistic and communicative situations where lexicographical problems can be solved with the use of dictionaries.

The *Alicante* specialised dictionaries are devised keeping in mind a broad group of users that include not only experts in the field and specialised translators, but also semi-expert and even lay users occasionally interested in the terms included and in their native/foreign language equivalents. As they are paper dictionaries and due to their lack of space, we often have to renounce to certain specific requirements as for example, when translators with a high professional competence require more lexicographical information to meet very specific professional needs arising from their specialisation.

26.3 Core issues and topics

26.3.1 General overview

The *Alicante* specialised dictionaries consist of thirteen specialised dictionaries covering areas such as business, economics, stock markets, human rights, pharmaceutical sciences and so on (see References). In their prefaces they detail their functional approach and their likely readers: professionals in the field, academics and students, lexicographers and translators with different levels of expertise (expert, semi-expert and lay). Their contents are organised according to the basic principles of *relevance, clarity* and *economy* which aim at adjusting their lexicographic information to their users' different levels of specialisation. These three principles work holistically as shown, say, in meaning descriptions of most terms (see Chapter 4 of this *Handbook*). We know that meanings multiply the words available to define them and consequently speakers recycle them to cope with those new senses. This characteristic is notable in the case of specific terms. Very rarely, new words are coined to describe new concepts, ideas, objects or procedures. Reusing existing ones with new or loosely related meanings seems to be more efficient. Let us consider the term *short*[2]. In our common lexicon, *short* relates to *reduced, small, inadequate, poor,* etc. However, in "Stock market trading" it describes a "debit or exposed position" as in the example: *The short sale of stock is a bet that the price of that stock will decline.*

Due to their wide range of users, meaning searches in our dictionaries are facilitated by cognitive and lexicographical explanations or by the aid of linguistic recourses such as synonyms, homonyms, hyperonyms, etc. This makes these dictionaries very innovative: they discarded the practice of providing only lemmas and equivalents, which is so typical and common in specialised bilingual dictionaries, most of which usually result in unwanted outcomes, for example, expert users are often left in doubt regarding their language uses, whereas semi-expert and laypeople are often unable to understand its specialised meaning. In order to alleviate these shortcomings, whenever we deem it necessary, instructive or useful, we illustrate entries with brief explanations, provide appropriate examples or supply related terms. Furthermore, in order to dispel additional doubts and in the likely case the same term has several specialised meanings, a numbered list of them is provided, as shown in Figure 26.1.

These explanations, illustrations and references in highly specialised entries have the clear instructional purpose to facilitate users' comprehensive tasks and are especially intended to clarify the meanings of certain bleary terms due to their novelty or complexity (example 1):

(1)

bracket *n*: GRAL/SUS nivel; define el grado de compromiso, alto – *major bracket* – o bajo – *minor bracket* –, que adquiere el suscriptor de una emisión nueva.[3]

In many cases, an example to *illustrate* the meaning of a given term in context is added. These *illustrations* are always preceded by the symbol ◊ (example 2):

(2)

high-tech stock (VAL valores tecnológicos; títulos pertenecientes a empresas de alta tecnología ◊ *High-tech stock prices have plunged dramatically*).

Given its elusive nature, a specialised meaning can be captured better when other semantically related words are provided. As the use of *complementary terms* and *cross-references* can help ease these meaning shortcomings, other related terms at the end of most entries, preceded by V. (véase) or S. (see), are offered (example 3):

(3)

current/earnings/flat/running yield (BENEF rendimiento corriente; rédito actual; V. *return, nominal yield, yield to/at maturity, expected dividend yield*).

A more specific problem originates in the inclusion and translation of English neologisms (neonyms) and colloquialisms into Spanish. In these cases, we have always tried to find a

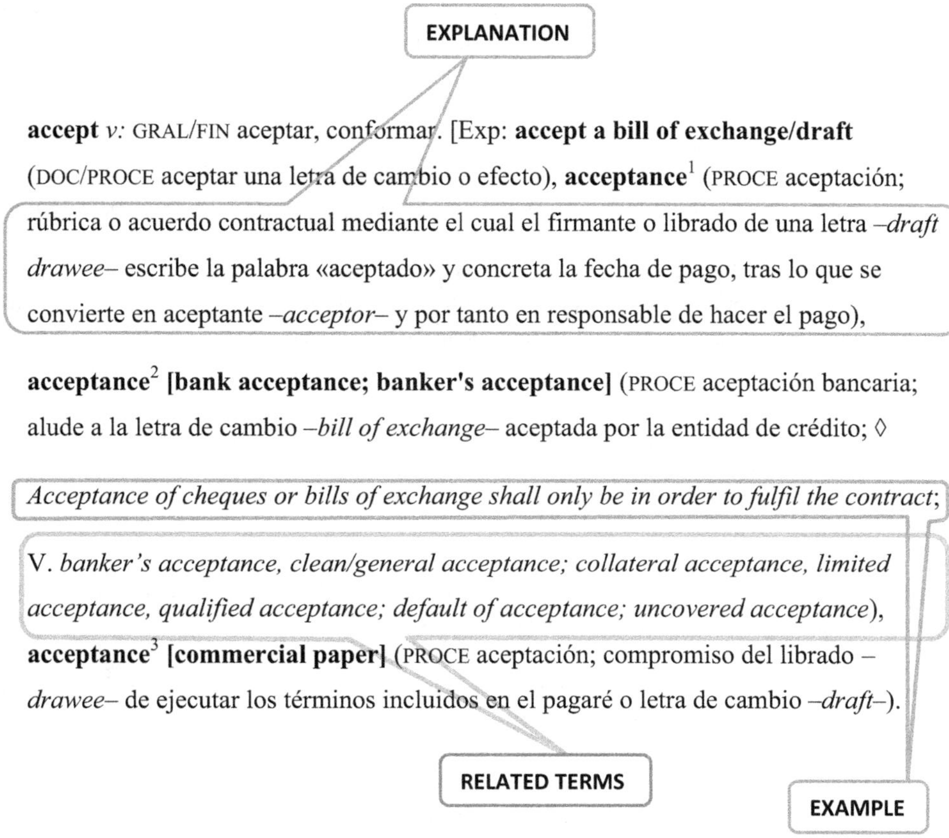

Figure 26.1 Typical dictionary article in the *Alicante Dictionaries*

translation in the source language. In the case of business and finance, for example, it is common practice in Spanish to borrow or calque English neonyms due to their novelty and the need to be used overnight (Mateo 2007; 2014b). Sometimes an explanation in Spanish is offered but rarely a suitable translation. This strategy would look reasonable with inexistent products or mechanisms in Spanish but, unfortunately, this is not always the case. Terms such as *cash flow, leasing* or *warrants* are increasingly used in their English form (pronunciation problems included) rather than their Spanish equivalents: *flujo de caja, arrendamiento financiero, certificados de compra*. This widespread practice, not only in Spanish but also in most other languages, might be alleviated by adopting eclectic solutions such as translating the new term while keeping the English one in italics when its use has consolidated: *swaption* (PROD "opciones sobre permutas financieras" o *swaps*).

In the specific case of business and financial terms, the definition and translation of newly coined specialised terms is especially tricky because they usually describe or name unknown commercial and financial practices in other cultures and languages. In these cases, a sensible procedure might be to seek a target language translation which contained the underlying idea after consulting manuals, experts, etc., and thus avoid literal and straightforward loans. Our role as lexicographers has always been to encourage the consolidation of equivalent solutions in our target working language before foreign calques succeed.

The issue gets more complex in the case of colloquialisms. The stock market language in English, for example, is full of colloquial twists that reflect the professional jargon used by agents and brokers (example 4):

(4)

Ankle biter: a stock with low market capitalization.
Killer bees: an individual or firm that helps a company fend off a takeover attempt.

Most of these English colloquial twists are metaphors, and they reveal a commendable effort to help lay users to understand the difficulties of certain financial concepts. English-speaking financial experts resort to different techniques to reach semi expert and lay financial addressees:

1 Popular and colloquial registers: *yo-yo stocks, bear hug, plain vanilla, turkey.*
2 Humoristic expressions: *Belt and suspenders, Hara-Kiri swap, James bonds.*
3 Metaphoric structures: *Back of the napkin business model, Pac-Man defense, Tulipmania.*

In order to include these technical colloquialisms in our dictionaries and adapt them to our target language (Spanish), different strategies are used:

1 A technical translation plus an explanation without any colloquial connotation: *golden hello*, for instance, is rendered "incentivo de enganche", and explained with the wording "prima que paga una sociedad intermediadora para contratar a un empleado de una firma rival".
2 A technical translation with a colloquialism in inverted commas which may have not been coined in Spanish yet but which may help understand the original meaning, plus an explanation: *bed-and-breakfast deal*, for example is translated as "operación 'cama y desayuno'", which is also explained saying that this "sugiere la venta de un valor por la noche para recomprarlo a la mañana siguiente y compensar con la plusvalía obtenida las posibles minusvalías".
3 Finally, a translation with an equivalent colloquialism in Spanish, although this is not a frequent case: *big bucks* is rendered "pasta gansa" and "pastón" and *buy a pup* is translated "dar gato por liebre".

This strategy signals another innovation of these dictionaries: we have applied the *economy* criterion systematically. This is fundamental in paper dictionaries due to physical space constrains which limit the selection of compound lexical units contained in specialised documents and texts. The initial job, selecting and organizing the terminological database, implies thorough and complex tasks. Among the likely term candidates, some have emerged and consolidated as lexical units, whereas many others had a fleeting existence or were created by a particular author to cover certain explanatory needs but with little chance to succeed or settle as specialised terms. Consequently, in many cases, they are not worth being included in our dictionaries.

To sum up, our dictionary entries contain parallel correspondences of both the lemma that heads the entry and its resulting combinations according to their cognitive, linguistic and pragmatic constituents. They include real examples of their use extracted from the main corpus and from other available electronic or paper corpora. They also combine diverse cognitive, linguistic and pragmatic information. With regard to the cognitive data, lemmas will include a brief definition explaining their conceptual content intended to illustrate those conflicting cognitive differences that might trigger different inferential responses. Cognitive results will be put in context (in square brackets [. . .]) with references to related entries, and to their thematic subdomains (Economics, Finance, Accounting, and so on). As for the linguistic data, lemmas will be specified grammatically. And with regard to their pragmatic information, the use of notes indicating geographical variants (GB, US), diachronic variation (obsolete, neologism) and register (expert, semi expert or colloquial) will favour users' comprehension. Finally, they provide more than one target language equivalent when possible or when required by the lemma alone or combined (example 5):

(5)

deferred bond (lemma)

bono de interés diferido (equivalents)
bono de cupón cero
título diferido

26.3.2 Methodological issues

Basically, the methodologies applied to create and develop a specialised dictionary could be summarised in the three following procedures: a) *manual*, b) *automated* and c) *mixed*. The manual methodology reflects pre-computer times when specialised lexicographers undertook the long and arduous task of collecting thousands of terminology records by hand that should be organised and categorised and which, some years later, would hopefully see the light in the form of dictionaries. No wonder that with this system the number of specialised dictionaries was clearly sparse and inadequate.

The automated methodology started with the wake of new information and communication technologies in the last decade of the twentieth century. It is based on the use of computers and digital technologies. Today, computers provide the tools that facilitate most of the repetitive tasks lexicographers must perform and simultaneously speed up data search and retrieval processes. In this context, computing has acquired a capital role in preliminary dictionary organization, corpus design, database construction and exploitation and subsequently in lexicographical management and edition phases. Computerised lexicographic work has allowed, among other things:

1 the possibility of working with representative digitised text corpora;
2 an easy and quick access to information through the use of storage and information retrieval (SIR) systems; and
3 the access, use and exploitation of lexicographical and knowledge databases.

Basically, the different automated stages we use in the process of making the *Alicante Dictionaries* are stages 3 and 4 (Figure 26.2) (Vargas 2005):

Figure 26.2 also shows a thorough and systematic procedure that allows lexicographers to work either alone or integrated in teams. It also defines in an orderly manner the successive stages from the moment a dictionary is devised until it is finally published. From a technical perspective, the fundamental stages are logically *corpus design, building and exploitation* (3) and *lexicographical management* (4).

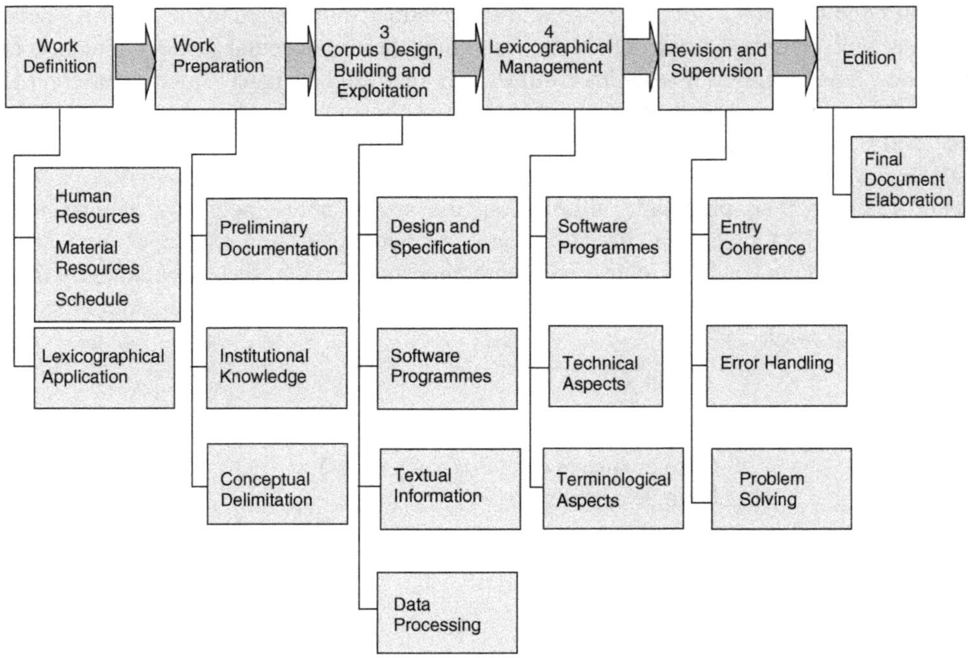

Figure 26.2 Stages contemplated in the making of the *Alicante Dictionaries*

The design of a specialised corpus implies to know in advance the target users of the dictionary. Appropriate tools for extracting corpus data are also needed: dedicated software to facilitate processing tasks, databases to retrieve and organise text information or register textual attributes and concordance applications. The methodology used by IPA lexicographers to build a specialised corpus is highly technical and requires mastery of a number of applications, some commercial, others developed by members of the group like *Gescorpus*.[4] The procedure can be summarised in Figure 26.3 where texts are processed with specific software, converted into a .txt file format and revised and treated with *Gescorpus* to obtain term listings (Vargas 2008:15).

Once extracted and analyzed, the term 'candidates' are managed computationally to become the electronic registers that will conform the specialised database. Today a wide range of dedicated computer software is available for the management of terminological databases, such as *SDL Multiterm*, *TermStar*, *SDLX* or *DVX (Déjà Vu)*. These terminology databases are integrated into computer-aided translation systems, also known as translation memories.

The mixed methodology combines "manual" work with the use of computer tools. It basically takes advantage of the existing digitised glossaries and corpora to make up a specialised basic corpus which is completed with the addition of new lemmas drawn from other referential works and dictionaries, paper or electronic documents (Internet, magazines, brochures, reports, minutes, etc.) and oral documents (surveys, interviews with experts, radio and TV) related to the specific field approached. This job implies both the use of word processors, databases, scanners and fast Internet connections and manual chores with paper documents (dictionaries, glossaries, books and specialised magazines, brochures and business records and the like).

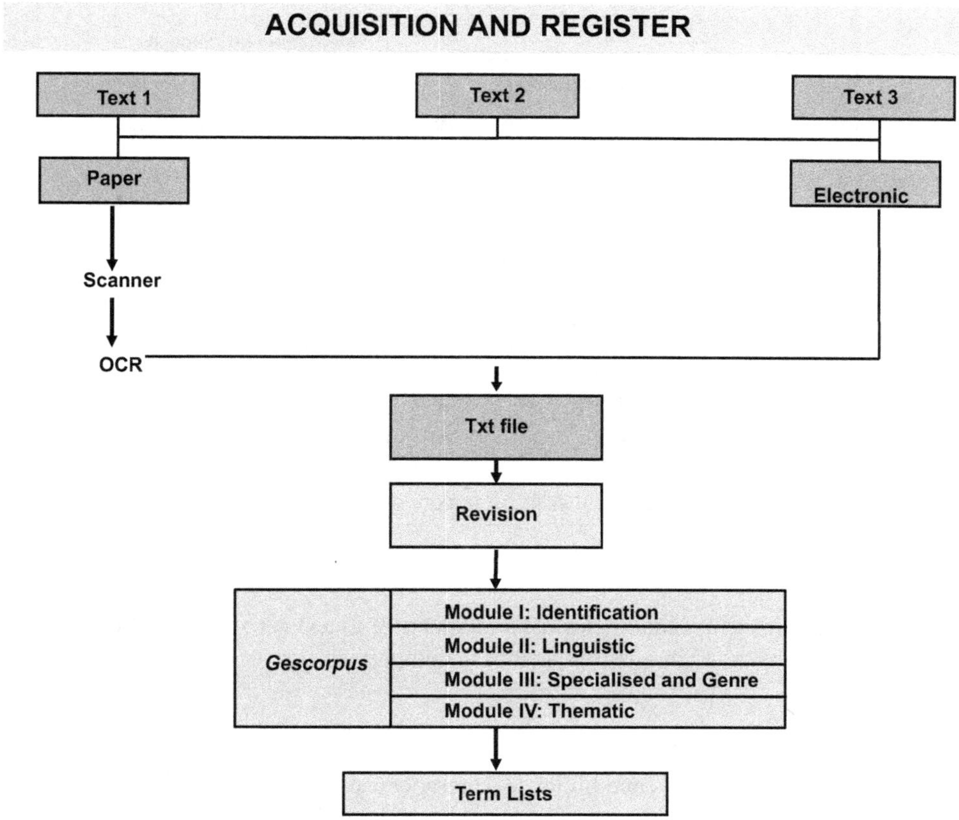

Figure 26.3 Working with *Gescorpus*

This mixed methodology is also adequate to produce new editions of existing specialised dictionaries if we do not have an advanced mastery of corpora management and organisation tools or if the work is to be done alone.

These three methodologies are commonly applied in the *Alicante Dictionaries*. Their use demonstrates that these dictionaries are open to new ideas and methodologies without putting old ones back, just for the sake of being old. This is especially relevant regarding lemma selection and description of specialised meanings and uses. Because specialised discourse is very technical and restricted, it is not easy to undertake this task unless the lexicographer has a qualified knowledge base on the matter addressed. This is a fundamental premise not only to guarantee the quality and relevance of its content but also to facilitate the tasks of selecting, organizing, explaining and translating the terms the specialists will need, the translators will search or the occasional users will look up in their pages.

It seems clear that modern specialised lexicographers should be endowed with some talents and master different basic technical abilities (Fuertes-Olivera and Tarp 2011). For example, in the specific case of Economics and Business, the essential training skills specialised lexicographers should have are summarised next (Mateo 2014a) (Figure 26.4). A quick glance at this figure reveals that we need both traditional methods (e.g. good knowledge of

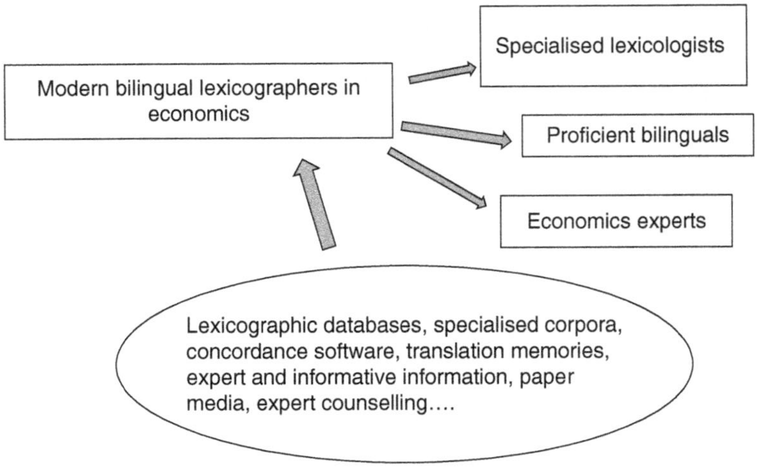

Figure 26.4 Required knowledge and skills for making business/economics dictionaries

the subject domain) and technological developments (e.g. text corpora, translation memories and so on) to make high-quality specialised dictionaries.

26.3.3 Selecting the empirical basis

After establishing boundaries and limits, lexicographers establish their empirical basis (i.e. sources for their lexicographic data). Four main empirical bases are used in the *Alicante Dictionaries*. First, existing specialised dictionaries and corpora are of primary importance and constitute our most important empirical basis.

We consider that Corpus Linguistics is essential in the compilation and organization of those specific terms that are to be included in any lexicographical work (see Chapters 8, 12, 45 and 46 of this *Handbook*). It provides useful and valuable tools that allow lexicographers to achieve more complete and accurate descriptive levels than ever before. There is no doubt that the quality of any lexicographical work is directly related to the quality of the texts that integrate the specialised corpus base (Bowker 1996; Rondeau 1984; Picht and Draskau 1985). Consequently, the quality and representativeness of the texts that conform any specialised corpus will be ultimately a more important factor than the amount of texts it includes (Meyer and Mackintosh 1996).

In the process of managing specialised corpora, it is important that the results of the lexicographical queries on the specialised field addressed are labelled morphologically. This will allow the extraction of possible terminological combinations after questioning their morpho-syntactic pattern system. For example, in order to process a financial corpus, the original texts and samples will be transformed in such a way that when accessed later, we may extract as much relevant information as possible. In that respect, corpora usually go through several analytical processes, depending on the degree of labeling detail we want to achieve. The simplest is the morphological or categorical process. In subsequent stages, the corpus obtained will be tagged using deeper cognitive, semantic and pragmatic information. The specialised corpus obtained will be treated following six major steps, all of which are used during the process of compilation of the *Alicante Dictionaries*:

1 *Segmentation* (technically called *tokenization*) or division of text strings between spaces.
2 *Lemmatization* or segmentation of texts into strings of characters and numbers between spaces.
3 *Morphological and categorical analysis* or process of allocating lemmas appropriate grammatical and morphological categories.
4 *Morphosyntactic and semantic disambiguation labeling*, basically a process of contextualisation as a result of the information gathered in point 3. Lemmas, which are normally ambiguous about their morphosyntactic category when taken in isolation, cease to be so within an appropriate context.
5 *Cognitive processes and pragmatic uses*. These are introspective processes that require full information about the intentional-inferential processes triggered by lemmas when used in context and which manifest in pragmatic and communicative professional settings.
6 *Exploitation* of the different findings obtained in the previous stages with the use of concordance programs.

The handling, storage and retrieval of terminological data are usually carried out with the use of terminology databases (TDBs). They are, concisely, tools or software packages specifically designed to manage lexicographical data. Managing implies that users can perform collection, storage, manipulation and retrieval of terminological data tasks. In a broad sense, a TDB is a system devised for storing and managing specialised lexical units that are treated according to specific criteria and specific users with the aim of compiling specific lexicography.

Our work with corpus data stored in terminological databases has allowed us to delimit the subject areas users will move across. These areas or professional fields are subdivided into further subfields which describe complementary domains whose boundaries frequently overlap. Although language is a continuum of intertwined meanings, from an operational perspective, dictionary users must be helped to choose the exact meanings they look for. For example, in the stock market terms dictionary seventeen different subject areas and twenty-five in the banking terms one were used – but could have certainly been more. Figure 26.5 illustrates the use of subject areas in the *Alicante Dictionaries*.

The subject areas which are placed immediately after lemmas and their grammar attributes (noun, verb, adjective, etc.) stand out with a clear typography in small caps that draw immediate attention and allow users to find the necessary contextual reference to obtain the intended word meaning. Figure 26.5 shows that five subject areas were introduced for **actual**: a general one in **actual**[1] and **actual**[2] but with different meanings and four specialised ones: **actual**[3]/ **actuals**[1,2,3], applied to accountancy, finance, financial markets, products and money.

Second, books, magazines, newspapers, letters, brochures, etc., are very valuable as they depict a living and updated use of today's technical language. With the use of appropriate computer tools, it is possible to detect, scan, isolate and organise new terms or uses.

Third, the Internet is more and more being used as a valuable empirical basis. Innumerable glossaries, some better than others, and the possibility to access thousands of highly technical websites, many of them constantly updated, conform a great source of specialised

actual[1] *a:* GRAL real, auténtico, verdadero, visible, físico, original; V. *effective, current, present*. [Exp: **actual**[2] (GRAL efectivo, físico; V. *physical, solid, tangible*), **actual**[3] (BOLSA precio efectivo de un valor, como elipsis de *actual price* o *cash*). [next follows a list of 24 compounds with ***actual*** and their corresponding equivalent forms and explanations in Spanish before reaching the plural form, **actuals**, which acquires different meanings]; **actuals**[1] (CONT cifras reales –no las estimadas– de un negocio; V. *ball-park figure; approximation, estimate*), **actuals**[2] (FINAN instrumentos financieros de contado; V. *spot, forward*), **actuals**[3] (MERC FINAN/PROD/DINER dactivos/productos físicos; mercaderías; mercancías, artículos de consumo, bienes; existencias, disponibilidades de fondos; acciones [and finish with a thorough explanation of how these "acciones" (shares) are used in this context. This explanation is intended for semi expert and lay dictionary users].

Subject area

Figure 26.5 Labels illustrating "subject areas" in the *Alicante Dictionaries*

lexicography. The search for a particular entry will let us know which terms are still in force, which are no longer used and which name innovative developments. Surely, the Internet is also full of inaccuracies and errors, but if we apply stringent parameters in our search, we shall obtain the results we expect.

Finally, we also use surveys, interviews with experts, radio and television data. These allow us to carry out some fieldwork about frequency of use, and other important data, typically for spotting gaps that must be included especially when they reflect the linguistic and cultural habits of the peoples who speak them. In this respect, we try to reconcile different linguistic uses which reflect pragmatic, cultural or use contrasts. In the case of English, these differences manifest mainly in the American and British varieties. For some specialised lexicon, for example, law, we adopted a certain British preference for obvious cultural proximity reasons, whereas, on the other hand, in our economics and finance dictionaries, we chose mainly the American usage as being the most widespread variety of English in today's global economy.

Our work with specialised lexical combinations (collocations or collocatives) illustrates the different uses of the previously mentioned empirical bases. The most common type of collocation in English specialised dictionaries is the compound made by a verb, adjective or noun that combines with the root term. These compounds have a conventional nature, that is, they have been agreed within a certain epistemological community. Thus, in legal discourse, for example, we can say *open/institute/bring proceedings*, but not *start proceedings*.

26.3.4 General practical considerations

Practice is obviously related to the conceptualisation phase briefly referred to in the previous paragraphs. This phase is broad and meticulous as it expands from the lexicographical criteria to be followed in the selection of lemmas to all the additional information that should be included or the support technologies (databases, corpora, etc.) that will be used. In the past, a key principle many lexicographers followed was to include the largest number of possible entries within the constraints imposed by the paper dictionary format. In this regard, we decided to use a principle of relevance, that is, to choose those terms that could better reflect the specific situations specialised use demanded and adapt them to the different groups of target readers. This user-oriented approach also entailed not considering those entrenched notions that were deemed fixed or immovable, such as the distinction between language dictionaries and encyclopaedias, based on a supposedly philosophical or linguistic distinction between the two (Zgusta 1971; Landau 2001).

Our experience of past years confirms that the greater the users' specialization, the bigger their need for lexicographical information. This kind of axiom has been thoroughly observed in the process of making our specialised dictionaries according to three central elements: *data, potential users' needs* and *lexicographical information organization and presentation.* In that respect, we have, for example, considered it important to include the lemma's grammatical category to reassure users this is the term they are looking for. There is little point in having excellent lexicographical data if they are not suitably organised and easily accessible. These three elements are part of the very nature of lexicography and are present in our dictionaries, understood as the information tools they are. This emphasis on fast and effective access to specialised lexical data speeds up professional users' efficiency and shortens the timespan spent in dictionary consultation. For example, when translators work with professional texts, the result will depend not only on their level of mastery in the fields addressed but also in their ability to manage these specific discourses in both languages (source and target). Specialised dictionaries are invaluable tools for this endeavour as they provide linguistic and/or conceptual information in practically any field of knowledge or expertise area.

26.4 Looking to the future

In the case of Spanish, although at first we used the European variety only, we soon realised that English specialised terms had often been translated differently in Mexico or Argentine; therefore, we considered including these translations in our dictionaries. However, this circumstance gave us some problems. Latin America is a vast continent with many and important differences in their Spanish technical varieties. We found that countries close to the United States were more prone to use English calques and borrowings as was the case with Mexico, Central American and the Caribbean countries, whereas large countries like Venezuela, Colombia, Argentina or Chile had their own local versions of the same term. Finally, we decided to add the most neutral and most used Latin American equivalents and make our dictionaries *panhispanic*, as shown in Figure 26.6, which illustrates comments attached to terms in inverted commas. These comments indicate whether the term is used in European Spanish or in Latin American Spanish (Figure 26.6).

Figure 26.6 clearly shows the need to follow the example of the Spanish *Diccionario Panhispánico de Dudas* or the *DRAE – Diccionario de la Real Academia Española* which included 19,000 Americanisms in its 23rd edition. In that respect, we have started the process of adapting our existing specialised dictionaries to this global world and expanding our subsequent editions by incorporating as much lexical information as possible from Latin American sources. We consider it a necessary and worthwhile effort from a lexicographic, economic and strategic perspective.

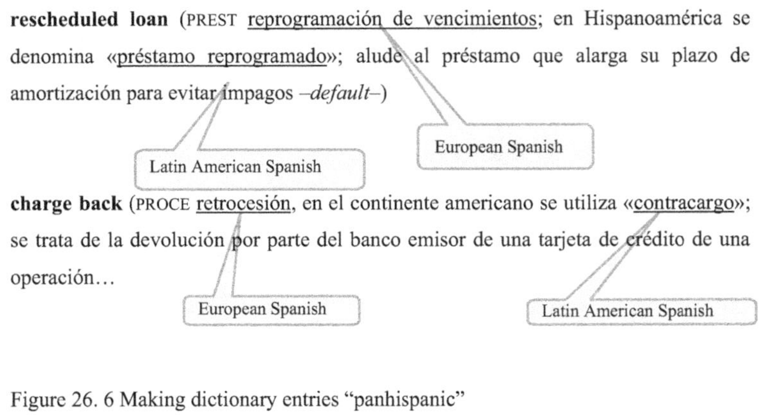

Figure 26.6 Making dictionary entries "panhispanic"

26.5 Conclusion

We at IPA reckon that today specialised dictionaries on paper face uneven competition from electronic ones (Dziemianko 2010; Jesensek 2013). In this age of speed when everything is instantly reproduced and accessed, paper dictionaries need years to be published or updated. Logically, printed lexicographical works should be abandoned and replaced by more accessible electronic versions. However, in our opinion, online specialised bilingual dictionaries today are not in all cases as good and stable as they should be. Publishing houses are still reluctant to allocate the necessary resources in electronic specialised lexicography. They require a constant update which demands full- or part-time staff and, more importantly, a large client base willing to pay for this service. As far as we know, this service is not being offered today with the exception of a few and limited websites. Consequently, expert users still have to rely on the existing paper dictionaries for specialised lexicographic information and this seems to be the tendency in the near future.

Related topics

The concept of dictionary; specialised dictionaries; The *Oenelex dictionary*; the *Accounting Dictionaries*; Spanish lexicography in the Internet era; dictionaries for translation.

Further reading

Alcaraz Varó, E., J. Mateo Martínez and F. Yus Ramos (eds.) (2007). *Las lenguas profesionales y académicas*. Barcelona: Ariel.

This book includes a series of relevant contributions to the wide universe of professional and academic languages and describes the linguistic, discursive and lexicographic peculiarities of a wide range of specialised discourses (economics, law, medical, tourism, technology and advertising) of interest for professionals and students alike.

Béjoint, H. (2010). *The Lexicography of English*. Oxford: Oxford University Press.

This work offers a comparative account of British and American approaches to lexicography and a good introduction to dictionary making and use. The author finds looking up words in dictionaries a fascinating task full of unexpected results.

Fuertes-Olivera, P. and S. Tarp. (2011). "Lexicography for the Third Millennium: Cognitive-Oriented Specialized Dictionaries for Learners", *Ibérica* 21: 141–162.

This paper approaches the current situation of lexicography in general, and of dictionary making in particular, advocating more expertise and a solid academic background in specialised lexicographers. The authors consider it necessary to reconsider traditional lexicographic approaches and adapt them to new needs and theoretical demands.

Jesensek, V. (2013). *Specialised Lexicography: Print and Digital, Specialised Dictionaries, Databases*. Berlin: Mouton de Gruyter.

This volume offers a kind of state-of-the-art approach to modern specialised lexicography from four perspectives: its formal, methodological and socio-functional structure; the role of computers in dictionary making; specialised dictionaries assessment; and their application to education and translation.

Notes

1 Inglés Profesional y Académico (Academic and Professional English). It is a research group sited at the University of Alicante whose work focusses in academic and professional English, including lexicographical research and specialised dictionary compilation.

2 The examples used in this chapter relate to economy, commerce and finance as these are the specialised fields I have mainly approached in my dictionaries. However, the lexicographic methodology employed applies to all the specialised dictionaries published by IPA lexicographers.

3 bracket *n*: GRAL/SUS nivel; it defines the degree of commitment, high *-major bracket-* or low *-minor bracket-* acquired by underwriters for new issues.

4 *Gescorpus* is a Relational Database Manager System (RDBMS) in Access. It was developed by Dr. Chelo Vargas Sierra (2005; 2008), a member of the IPA group and coauthor of two specialised dictionaries.

References

a) The Alicante specialised dictionaries ordered by year of publication

Alcaraz, E., B. Hugues and M. A. Campos ([1993] 2012) *Diccionario de Términos Jurídicos/ A Dictionary of Legal Terms. Inglés-Español/Spanish-English.* Barcelona: Ariel.

Alcaraz, E., B. Hugues. and J. Mateo Martínez ([1996] 2012) *Diccionario de Términos Económicos, Financieros y Comerciales/ A Dictionary of Economic, Financial and Commercial Terms. Inglés-Español/Spanish-English.* Barcelona: Ariel.

Alcaraz, E., B. Hugues and M. Á. Campos (1999) *Diccionario de Términos de Marketing, Publicidad y Medios de Comunicación. Inglés-Español/Spanish-English.* Barcelona: Ariel.

Alcaraz, E., B. Hugues, M. Á. Campos, V. M. Pina and M. A. Alesón Carbonell (2000) *Diccionario de Términos de Turismo y Ocio: Inglés-Español/Spanish-English.* Barcelona: Ariel.

Mateo Martínez, J. (2003) *Diccionario de Términos de la Bolsa. Inglés-Español/Spanish-English.* Barcelona: Ariel.

Castro Calvín, J. (2003) *Diccionario de Términos de Seguros: Inglés-Español/Spanish-English.* Barcelona: Ariel.

Campos, M. A. (2003) *Diccionario de la Propiedad Inmobiliaria: Inglés-Español/Spanish-English.* Barcelona: Ariel.

Alcaraz, E., B. Hughes, J. Mateo Martínez, C. Vargas Sierra and G. Gonzáles-Jover Adelina (2005) *Diccionario de Términos de la Piedra Natural e Industrias Afines.* Inglés-Español/Spanish-English. Barcelona: Ariel.

Alcaraz, E., B. Hughes, J. Mateo Martínez, Ch. Vargas Sierra, and G. González-Jover Adelina (2006) *Diccionario de Términos del Calzado e Industrias Afines: Inglés-Español/Spanish-English.* Barcelona: Ariel.

Alcaraz, E., A. Domínguez-Gil and R. Martínez (2007) *Diccionario Terminológico de las Ciencias Farmacéuticas/A Terminological Dictionary of the Pharmaceutical Sciencies. Inglés-Español/ Spanish-English.* Barcelona: Ariel.

Campos, M. A. (2008) *Diccionario de Términos de los Derechos Humanos/A Dictionary of Human Rights.* Inglés-Español/Spanish-English. Barcelona: Ariel.

Mateo Martínez, J. (2009) *Diccionario de Términos de la Banca. Inglés-Español/Spanish-English.* Barcelona: Ariel.

Castro Calvín, J. (2009) *Diccionario de Fiscalidad Internacional y Aduanas: Inglés-Español/Spanish-English.* Barcelona: Ariel.

b) Other Dictionaries

Diccionario de la Real Academia Española. 23rd edition. Madrid: Espasa Calpe.

Diccionario panhispánico de dudas. 2nd edition. Madrid: Santillana.

Other literature

Alcaraz Varó, E., J. Mateo Martínez, and F. Yus Ramos (eds.) (2007) *Las lenguas profesionales y académicas.* Barcelona: Ariel.

Andersen, B. and P. Fuertes-Olivera (2009) "The Application of Functional Theory to the Classification of English Monolingual Business Dictionaries", *Lexicographica* 25: 213–239.

Béjoint, H. (2010) *The Lexicography of English.* Oxford: Oxford University Press.

Bergenholtz, H. and S. Tarp (eds.) (1995) *Manual of Specialised Lexicography.* Amsterdam/Philadelphia: John Benjamins.

Bowker, L. (1996) "Towards a Corpus-based Approach to Terminography", *Terminology* 3 (1): 27–52.

Bowker, L. (2006) *Lexicography, Terminology, and Translation.* Ottawa: Ottawa University Press.

Dziemianko, A. (2010) "Paper or Electronic? The Role of Dictionary Form in Language Reception, Production and the Retention of Meaning and Collocations", *International Journal of Lexicography* 23(3): 257–273.

Fuertes-Olivera, P. and S. Tarp (2008) "La teoría functional de la lexicografía y sus consecuencias para los diccionarios de economía del español", *Revista de Lexicografía* 14: 89–109.

Fuertes-Olivera, P. and S. Tarp (2011) "Lexicography for the Third Millennium: Cognitive-Oriented Specialized Dictionaries for Learners", *Ibérica* 21: 141–162.

Fuertes-Olivera, P. and S. Tarp (2014) *Theory and Practice of Specialised Online Dictionaries: Lexicography Versus Terminography.* Berlin and Boston, MA: De Gruyter.

Jesensek, V. (2013) *Specialised Lexicography: Print and Digital, Specialised Dictionaries, Databases.* Berlin: Mouton de Gruyter

Landau, S. (2001) *Dictionaries: The Art and Craft of Lexicography.* Cambridge: Cambridge University Press.

L'Homme, M.-C. (2015) "Pedro Fuertes-Olivera, and Sven Tarp. (2014) *Theory and Practice of Specialised Online Dictionaries. Lexicography versus Terminography*, Lexicographica Series Maior, Berlin/Boston, MA: De Gruyter. ISBN: 978-3-11-034883-5", *International Journal of Lexicography* 28(1): 124–130.

León-Araúz, P. and P. Faber (2015) "Review of Fuertes-Olivera, Pedro A., and Sven Tarp. (2014) *Theory and Practice of Specialised Online Dictionaries. Lexicography versus Terminography.* Berlin/ Boston, MA: De Gruyter. ISBN: 9783110348835", *Terminology* 21(1): 126–136.

Mateo, J. (2007) "El lenguaje de las ciencias económicas", in E. Alcaraz Varó, J. Mateo Martínez and F. Yus Ramos (eds.), *Las lenguas profesionales y académicas.* Barcelona: Ariel, pp. 191–203.

Mateo, J. (2014a) "Lexicographical and Translation Issues in the Inclusion of English Financial Neonyms in Spanish Bilingual Dictionaries of Economics on Paper", *Hermes – Journal of Language and Communication in Business* 52(1): 41–58.

Mateo, J. (2014b) "Neonyms for a Crisis: Cognitive, Terminological and Socio-Pragmatic Aspects in the Translation of New Financial Terms Into Spanish", *Babel* 60(4): 405–424.

Meyer, I. and K. Mackintosh (1996) "The Corpus From a Terminographer's Viewpoint", *International Journal of Corpus Linguistics* 1(2): 257–285.

Picht, H. and J. Draskau (1985) *Terminology: An Introduction*. Guildford: The University of Surrey.

Rondeau, G. (1984) *Introduction à la terminologie*. Montreal: Gaëtan Morin.

Vargas Sierra, C. (2005) *Aproximación terminográfica al lenguaje de la piedra natural. Propuesta de sistematización para la elaboración de un diccionario traductológico*. Tesis doctoral. Alicante: Universidad de Alicante.

Vargas Sierra, C. (2008) "La sistematización terminográfica: una propuesta metodológica para la elaboración de diccionarios traductológicos", *Actas del X Simposio Iberoamericano de Terminología*, Montevideo, Uruguay, 7–10 de noviembre de 2006. http://www.uv.es/cometval/wikibase/cas/Articulos/Vargas_2005_Diccionario_terminologico.pdf

Zgusta, L. (1971) *Manual of Lexicography*. Paris: Mouton.

27 The Oenolex wine dictionary

Patrick Leroyer

27.1 Introduction

The general purpose of this chapter is to illustrate how modern specialised e-lexicography focusing on user needs and use situations can innovate both in theory and in practice. The specific purpose is to present an innovative specialised French monolingual dictionary of wine tasting and wine knowledge communication. Called Oenolex (Leroyer et al. 2016), this online dictionary is constructed on the tenets of the function theory of lexicography (Fuertes-Olivera 2012, 2013; Fuertes-Olivera and Tarp 2014) and is unique in the light of a number of lexicographic parameters when compared to conventional wine dictionaries. These parameters include a strong focus on interdisciplinary dictionary management, original data generation and acquisition, and corpus compilation and processing, including lexicographic use of an oral corpus (the corpus being fully integrated and accessible, and thus at the heart of the dictionary), automated knowledge extraction processes, enhanced search functionalities, and cutting edge database and Internet technology. Moreover, what makes Oenolex unique is its strongly embedded user orientation and genuine purpose, as all lexicographic issues have been managed with a view to satisfy punctual,[1] lexicographically relevant information needs that have been identified and stipulated by the intended users themselves. In this chapter, we will very briefly introduce the relationship between wine and dictionaries and other lexicographic information tools on wine and will outline the genesis of Oenolex. We will then expand on the processes and innovative parameters that have been used in its construction and include a few examples of articles to illustrate its search and display functionalities. In the conclusion, we will address future perspectives concerning the development of the dictionary, and we will raise some implications for further research and innovation in specialised e-lexicography.

27.2 Historical perspective

27.2.1 Wine and lexicographic information tools of wine

Originated in ancient times, wine clearly belongs today to the world's cultural heritage (Unesco 2016). It has also turned into a huge business and a beloved object of consumption among millions of modern consumers worldwide. Thus, the needs for information on wine have grown correspondingly and so has the lexicography of wine, which is prolific and multifaceted. The focus of such lexicographic tools can be either on the language used – and to be used – to talk about wine, describe it and evaluate its qualities, or on the knowledge of the multiple specialised fields that make up the whole concept of wine, including history, geography, oenology and biochemistry, viticulture, winemaking processes, marketing, classification and legislation, food and wine agreement, etc. Print dictionaries (Coutier 2007) and lexicographically structured wine guides editions (Guide Hachette des Vins 2016) are immensely popular on the book market but are being rapidly replaced by online dictionaries (South African Trilingual Wine Dictionary 2016), encyclopaedic portals (Wikipedia 2016), and smartphone applications (Drync Wine 2016) giving access to practical information on millions of wines. Hundreds, even perhaps thousands, of wine glossaries in many languages are also available on the Internet and are accessible with a simple click of the mouse. Common to most of these lexicographical information tools seems to be their focus on the subject field rather than on the user needs perspective. It seems that the presentation of data representing communication about wine or knowledge of wine per se (Lerat 2011) tends to become the sole aim of the resource, and it is often unclear what the genuine purpose of the tool is or should be, although commercial interests often seem to play an important role. An exception to this lack of lexicographic clarity is provided by the online South African Trilingual Wine Industry Dictionary (Van der Merwe 2008), in which background, functions, and intended target users are clearly stated. Prior to any dictionary project, central questions as the followings should as a rule always be answered:

1 What are the social situations in which needs for information can appear, and to which extent can these needs be satisfied through the consultation of lexicographic information tools?
2 Who are the intended users and what is their profile?
3 What are their specific information needs, and how should a dictionary be designed in order to satisfy these needs?
4 What should be the functions of the tool? Should it help them to communicate about wine, to acquire knowledge of wine or of wine communication, to interpret non-verbal codes such as the information provided by wine labels, or to carry out wine-related mental and physical operations, such as wine tasting?

All these questions have governed the genesis of Oenolex.

27.2.2 The genesis of Oenolex

27.2.2.1 The specific information needs of the Bourgogne wine industry

The Bourgogne wine industry in France faces a number of information challenges and information gaps directly connected to the vocabulary of wine tasting and its discourse.[2] First, the industry is confronted with insufficient knowledge and experience of wine tasting and knowledge asymmetry with its key stakeholders, the consumers. Non-expert consumers are unable to fully identify, acknowledge, and accurately verbalise the organoleptic qualities of Bougogne wines. This entails a business problem, as the industry is closely dependent on quality recognition in order to legitimate its high price setting and top-of-the-range branding.

Second, there appears to be a high degree of register and discourse variation in various professional contexts. Teachers at the wine school, oenologists at wine fairs, or producers presenting their wines in their cellar do not employ the same wording and discourse strategies. Communication aims are different and feature didactic, scientific, PR, and marketing, as well as direct sales strategies. Third, there is no clear discursive consensus, as geographic disparity is a source of language variation. French Bourgogne stretches out in quite different *terroirs* from north to south, each with their own singularities in wine growing and making. Fourth, the emergence of new, dynamic wine concepts such as "minerality" and "mineral" makes meaning constructions unstable and subject to variable interpretations. Finally, multifaceted, polysemic concepts such as *Climats de Bourgogne*, of which the names appear individually on wine labels of the best bottles of the region, challenge meaning explanations and pose communication difficulties. The *Climats* have been recently added by the UNESCO to the World Heritage List and refer not only to "precisely delimited vineyard parcels", but also to the cultural landscape of production units including villages and towns. All together, these information challenges and gaps and their correlated information needs convinced us that the optimal solution would be to build up a corpus of professional, discursive interactions centred on wine tasting situations and events in order to generate and acquire the lexicographic data representing the various knowledge registers and ultimately to provide means to solve challenges and fill up the gaps.

27.2.2.2 Accessing various types of wine tasting knowledge

Wine tasting, which very briefly can be defined as the "activity of analysing the organoleptic qualities of one or several wines" (Coutier 2007) basically involves five types of knowledge constructions:

- declarative, encyclopaedic knowledge of wine estate localisation, history, reputation, 'terroir', grape varieties, year, wine-making process, etc., as well as oenologic knowledge of sensorial mechanisms;
- schematic knowledge, making it possible to relate the organoloptic profile of the specific wine being tasted to the established profiles of the wines as recognised by the professional community;
- operative knowledge of the activity of wine tasting, including pouring, holding and manipulating the glass, visualising, smelling, swirling, sipping, spitting, etc.;
- experiential, sensorial knowledge. This type of knowledge can normally only be achieved by training of the senses – vision, olfaction, and taste. The dictionary cannot provide data or means to access this type of personal knowledge and can only contribute indirectly by giving access to a better comprehension of sensorial descriptors and their use by others;
- evaluative knowledge, which is the abstract knowledge of the cognitive processes involved in quality assessment and rating, and which is expressed through cognitive verbs such as, to name just a few, *assert*, *compare*, *contrast*, *criticise*, *appraise*, *evaluate*, *rate*, *interpret*, *judge*, *justify*, *grade*.

These types of knowledge needs are all catered for in Oenolex through carefully prepared lexicographic data and datasets providing access to very specific knowledge of the sensorial lexical resources instantiated in authentic wine tasting discourse during dynamic interactions. These include knowledge of wine tasting descriptors, knowledge of specific wines profiles and knowledge of specific wine tasting sessions. All lexicographic data are interlinked. The most important data category in Oenolex is the category of lexicographic examples. These are carefully selected sequences of speech interactions highlighting the main information strategies used by the industry when going into dialogue and interacting with its publics. In this sense, Oenolex can be regarded as a fully contextual, discursive dictionary of professional, specialised wine communication.

27.2.2.3 Purpose and form of Oenolex

Initiated by the end of 2013, the Oenolex dictionary was originally commissioned by the BIVB – the Bourgogne Wine Board (BIVB 2016) – as a *nuancier lexicographique* (i.e. an enhanced glossary of the wine tasting vocabulary used by and in the profession). This special glossary should not only include the vocabulary actually used by wine professionals, namely producers, teachers, and marketing and PR people of the Bourgogne wine industry, but also the vocabulary used by consumers when tasting wine in company with professionals of the industry. Therefore, the lexicographic team decided at an early stage, in agreement with the BIVB, to develop a lexicographic information tool aimed at the communicatively and cognitively oriented information needs of two categories of users engaged in teaching and learning wine tasting in various situations, including wine promotion, the focus being on user group 1:

- User group 1: Expert users = wine experts teaching wine tasting at the Bourgogne wine school and wine producers or wine retailers planning and delivering promotional communication of their Bourgogne wines
- User group 2: Non-expert users, namely students attending wine tasting courses at the Bourgogne wine school)

External funding of the project was provided by the Bourgogne Wine Board and by the French Bourgogne region. The two universities involved, University of Bougogne and Aarhus University, both contributed internal funding to cover additional staff expenses in relation to the development of the dictionary concept, including terminological work, data acquisition, data transcription and cleaning, processing and extraction of speech data with the Audacity and Sonal software, and development of the MySQL database and server configuration, as well as all coordination of dictionary management between the two universities. It should be noted that part of return on investment comes from the publication of a number of contributions to international journals and books (Gautier and Hohota 2014; Gautier and Leroyer in press; Gautier, Hohota, Maazaoui, Chevalier and Leroyer (2015); Leroyer 2013a, 2013b, 2015, in press; Leroyer and Gautier 2015; Leroyer and Høy 2014; Leroyer, Maazaoui and Gautier 2015) on which the present chapter is also largely based.

The genuine purpose of Oenolex is to provide its intended expert users rich access to multimodal detailed knowledge of communication between the industry and its publics in real wine tasting situations. This knowledge is useful to the industry in order to support its communication strategies on the market – educating, qualifying, and persuading its publics of the high quality of the wines – and thus gaining further sympathy and legitimacy in the business. In addition, the industry can obtain inside knowledge of the main issues guiding the framing of its communicative and argumentative efforts in connection with market communication and public relations. In short, by providing knowledge of wine vocabulary and how it is actually used in various professional contexts, Oenolex can be used as a special source of information in connection with the following business activities:

1 business documentation
2 business communication, particularly marketing communication and public relations
3 development of vocational training in connection with wine schools

The 1.0 beta version of Oenolex was delivered by the lexicographic team to the BIVB at the beginning of 2016, which has the exclusive rights to access and use the tool. This is only the first step as discussions have been engaged on the optimisation of the tool in order to ensure its ongoing development, updating, and extension with new functionalites. Presently, Oenolex contains the following main lexicographic features:

1 Three types of dictionary articles: 1) wine terms, 2) AOC wine articles (= the single AOC – AOC being short for *Appellation d'origine contrôlée* – "controlled designation of origin" – which is the French official certification granted to geographical indications for wines), and 3) wine tasting sessions.
2 All data are linked together – wine terms are linked to corresponding AOCs making use of these terms, which in turn are linked to corresponding wine tasting sessions.
3 Two search modes – AOC search or TERM search – with advanced search options in both search modes.

The digital environment of the dictionary platform is presently made up of the following hard and software configuration:

1 Language: Java v8, XML, and XSL(T)
2 Integrated Development Environment: NetBeans v8.0.2 platform
3 Frameworks: Java Server Faces v2.2, Prime Faces v5.x
4 Operating system: Linux Debian 7 (Wheezy) 64 bits
5 Server: Apache Tomcat 8.x
6 Relational Database Management System: MySQL 5.x, including database editor

27.3 Core issues and topics: the construction of Oenolex

27.3.1 Corpus, data generation, acquisition, and processing

Oenolex makes use of both written and oral data sources. On the one hand, Oenolex makes use of a text corpus of promotional and pedagogical online wine records and wine tasting guides authored and provided by the commissioner. On the other hand, Oenolex exploits, in close cooperation with the BIVB and other actors of the profession (wine growers and makers, fair organisers), an oral corpus of wine tasting interactions specially recorded for the purpose. One reason for using oral corpora lies in the fact that the major part of professional interactions in wine tasting takes place in oral production situations. Another reason lies in the dynamic nature and fuzziness of wine tasting terminology and wine tasting descriptors. Recent research (see Gautier and Hohota 2014) shows that the terminology of wine tasting is subject to a high degree of variation, as terms and expressions are co-constructed in and by the discourse of wine during wine tasting sessions.

Lexicographical corpora for dictionary making are normally used as an empirical base of the dictionary because they provide highly valuable lexical material, patterns, attestations of use, etc. Yet in Oenolex, the corpus is not simply the empirical base of the dictionary. It is lexicographically structured so that it can be accessed by the user, and Oenolex demonstrates how oral corpora can become a functional, user-oriented asset for specialised dictionary projects, particularly in domains in which terminology is subject to a high degree of variation and unstability. The oral data has been generated through recordings of authentic professional interactions in which consumers, visitors of wine estates or wine fairs, and students at the wine school interact with the French wine experts. Following data acquisition, the data has been transcribed, processed, tagged, and analysed using a number of innovative data processing technologies in accordance with data standardisation recommendations. Automatic extraction based on the recognition of knowledge-rich contexts, a technique based on the recognition of conceptual knowledge around terms and initiated by Meyer (2001), has then been used to extract lemmas, collocations and examples. Finally, cutting-edge MySQL database programming has been applied to the whole data management system.

The corpus includes 12 recordings from a variety of speech interactions. Depending on context, the length of individual recordings varies from less than 10 minutes for the shortest to three hours for the longest one. Despite length variation, there is no significant skewing in the data as all discourse types are extremely stereotyped. The recordings all deal with a number of specific AOCs from Bourgogne (Côte de Beaune, Côte de Nuits, Côte chalonnaise, Mâconnais). The data have been generated in various interactive situations in which tasting wine is the common denominator: teaching of wine tasting in wine school, wine presentations, and tasting at wine fairs and wine domains. We have selected two categories of wine discourse production, a didactic discourse containing pedagogical features and a marketing discourse containing business rhetoric features. The marketing discourse includes a direct marketing discourse in sales situations and a promotional marketing discourse (= image promotion of the region) at wine fairs. Table 27.1 contains an overview of the corpus and recordings:

Table 27.1 Overview of corpus and recordings

Situation	*Number of recordings*	*Length*
Didactic	4	4hrs 33min. 20 sec.
Direct marketing	3	2hrs 9min. 5sec.
Promotional marketing	5	1hr 33min. 19sec.
Total	12	**8hrs 15min. 44sec.**

Prior to data generation, the interviewers received training in sound recording techniques and used a digital recorder. The data were then formatted in conformity with the technical research standards recommended by the guides for Digital Humanities in France (Huma-Num 2016). Audio recordings were produced using uncompressed 24-bit/96 kHz WAV format. We have used the Audacity (2016) audio software to delete segments irrelevant to lexicographic data acquisition. We have also tried to preserve the features of authentic, spontaneous discourse, including variation of speech intensity and pauses, and have refrained from applying noise reduction, clipping, or signal amplification. In line with the lexicographic concept, we have chosen to make use of an orthographic transcription methodology for the acquisition of the generated data in order to preserve the integrality of speech productions. We have used the Sonal software (2015) to process audio flows and align transcriptions. This software is specially designed to manage audio and video files and their matching transcriptions and provides a number of valuable functionalities including transcription formatting, alignment, annotating, tagging, quality balancing, and import of transcriptions from other programs. The Sonal software includes easy-to-use specific tools for linguistic analysis (POS tagging, frequency lists, concordances, sorting out). It is also possible to isolate and select single sequences in order to perform clean transcriptions. Once done, we used the synchronisation module to align transcription and recorded speech data. The corpus has been tagged using pre-defined thematic tags for the encoding of thematic content sequences such as 'process', 'definition', 'appellation', 'technique', 'wine presentation', 'definition', 'question', 'wine-food agreement', 'sensoriality', etc. These have then been used for the extraction of examples along with a range of formal segmentation and discourse strategic identification markers such as conventional segmentation expressions (*au premier nez/au deuxième nez*), negatives (*pas, pas que*), locatives (*on est sur. . .*), etc.

27.3.2 Multi-layered datasets and database

As Oenolex is constructed as a professional dictionary of wine tasting of Bourgogne wines exclusively, it is designed so that its user and commissioner, the BIVB, can systematically record, store, and retrieve specific data associated with the tasting of their wines in various tasting sessions. The database includes the following tables and datasets:

1 a pragmatic register (table) of wine tasting sessions with detailed records of tasted AOC, date and place of tasting, identification of participants involved (experts and non-experts) and evaluations assigned by these, including visual, olfactive, gustative, and general evaluations;
2 a multimodal (sound, text and images) encyclopaedic register (table) with detailed factual and evaluative records of every unique AOC that has been tasted: full name of AOC, AOC category, grape variety, climate and locality, village, year, producer, region, wine making process, visual, olfactive, gustative, and general evaluations;
3 a multimodal (sound, text and images) terminological register (table) of all wine tasting terms and expressions used by the BIVB during wine tasting sessions and presentations containing lemma records, grammatical and phraseological data, definitions, collocations, speech examples linked to the corpus, and source ID of examples and external links.

Besides these three registers, the database also stores the underlying digitalised and lexicographically structured corpus of recordings of wine tasting sessions. Wine tasting sessions are split up into sequences determined by the identification of the unique AOC being tasted and by the phases of the wine tasting procedure (= macro-sequencing). Lemmas, various discourse markers, and knowledge-rich contexts are used for the extraction of lexicographic examples (= micro-sequencing). The three registers and the corpus are all linked together through a network of relations between datasets and data fields which makes it possible to make targeted searches on:

1 wine tasting terms and expressions as they are actually used in situated contexts by different wine actors
2 circumstances under which these terms and expressions have been actually used in interaction: which terms and expressions have been assigned to which wines, by whom, in what circumstances, where, and when?

The design of the MySQL database as a mash-up of multimodal pragmatic, discursive, encyclopaedic, and lexical data is primarily oriented towards the satisfaction of knowledge oriented information needs and situations in which the users – the experts of the BIVB – use the dictionary because they need to acquire knowledge on the discourse of wine tasting in authentic situations and how this discourse acts upon the terminology of wine tasting, how it is created, communicated, understood (or misunderstood), develops, etc. The discourse of wine tasting features salient didactic elements and promotional elements that can be used by the BIVB to design new courses or develop new promotional campaigns.

27.3.3 Wine tasting lemmas and their definitions

Lemmas are extracted from the corpus of wine tasting evaluations and represent all the descriptive and evaluative characteristics assigned to the wines by both experts and non-experts. Other terminological units which are not related to wine tasting proper (e.g. chemical terms or viticultural terms) are excluded from lemma selection. Lemma records include the following data fields: lemma, grammatical information on lemma, definition, source of definition, collocations, examples, and source of examples as well as three specific BIVB data fields: oenological note, encyclopaedic note, and illustration.

Definitions are short and crafted according to well-established lexicographic definition standards, making use of *genus proximum and differentia specifica* (= sufficient and necessary conditions). In line with Faber (2010), but for other reasons than purely terminological, they rely on the conceptual features used by the BIVB in their reference documents such as wine tasting guides and protocols. An example of a definition is provided below for the lemma animal (example 1):

(1)

animal famille d'arômes faisant référence aux senteurs qui sont liées aux animaux telles que la fourrure, le cuir, le musc ou l'ambre, et qui peuvent être identifiés lors du nez et/ou de la rétro-olfaction

[= animal fragrance family referring to smells connected to animals such as smells of fur, leather, musk or amber, and that can be identified in olfaction and retro-olfaction phases]

The wine tasting vocabulary articles also contain philological definitions that are directly taken from the *Dictionnaire de la langue du vin* (Coutier 2007) as Oenolex has gained permission to use the data. These philologically oriented definitions serve as a complementary meaning resource, whereby professional users can directly compare their own in-house meaning explanations with the linguistic format used by Coutier.

27.3.4 Extraction of good wine tasting examples

The purpose of good lexicographic example sentences is to illustrate the correct meaning (for text reception) and use (for text production) of the lemma in context and thus reinforce the information provided by dictionary articles (meaning explanations, restrictions of use, collocations, etc.). The formal requirements for the quality of good lexicographic examples include, among other things, such factors as length (not too short, not too long), not too specific or too vague, free of corpus noise, typos, slang, and sensitive content (Michelfeit 2015). In Oenolex, examples do not have to comply entirely with these requirements as they share the fuzziness and natural variation of authentic interactions in (oral) professional discourse (Gunnarsson 2009). Following this, it should be noted that examples are actually assigned the status of main information units in the dictionary and are not subordinated to the lemmas in the same way as in conventional dictionaries. The dedicated function of lemmas is here to provide access to the structured examples of wine tasting interactions in which the lemmas are involved.

As we look for didactic quality, the selection of examples includes sequences in which the purpose of the teacher/student interaction is to redefine a term and to correct mistakes or misunderstandings. Examples are also retrieved from operative instructions sequences in which the teacher explains in a dialogical form how to proceed with the wine tasting. In both corpora, sequences are largely pre-established, as they follow the chronological and sequential phases of wine tasting, namely presentation of the wine, visual aspects, nose, taste, general impressions, and concluding remarks. This sequencing feature helped us delimit the corpus and assign the data to the relevant data fields of the wine tasting register in the database (visual, olfactive, gustative, general impression, as shown in Table 27.3). Frequent, stereotyped contributions (such as "au premier nez on est sur . . ." [at first nose we are on. . .], "au deuxième nez on évolue. . ." [at second nose we move to. . .]) helped us select collocations. Questions and riddles such as "Le vert indique la jeunesse ou l'origine?" [Does green indicate youth or origin?] have also been good indicators of important pedagogical moves and candidates to the selection of good examples. Hence, extraction of examples has been ruled by the recognition of "knowledge-rich contexts" used in terminographic applications (Meyer: 2001). In the extracted example that follows, the lemmatised descriptor **citron** is negated and illustrates a widespread didactic strategy in which the teacher anticipates erroneous interpretations and confusion from the students and states which descriptors should be used instead and which should be avoided. The teacher seems to perform a normalisation of wine description independently of what students might interpret, the ultimate purpose being here to (re)assert and establish the quality profile of the wine. Examples of this type in which knowledge is confronted to non-knowledge so to speak can be obtained by the extraction of the multiple tokens of **"ne pas"**- and **"pas que"**-marked negative contexts (example 2):

(2)

> [*Au premier nez, on est sur* des fruits plus mûrs, on n'est **pas** sur le côté **citron**, agrume, mais sur le côté prune. *Au deuxième nez,* on évolue sur des arômes un peu miellés, on déduit même une sucrosité. Quand vous l'aérez, il est assez frais, c'est **pas** compoté, cuit, il y a même aussi un côté floral, il n'y a **pas que** le fruit. *On est sur* des fruits plus mûrs, peut-être la pêche, la prune.]

To sum up, the semi-automatic extraction of examples we used relies on a three-level text- and data-oriented system: (i) thematic content descriptors to identify context relevant sequences; (ii) interaction descriptors to link the data with the two poles of specialised knowledge and non-knowledge; and (iii) linguistic markers ranging from discourse structuring elements to mere chunks (i.e. the special use of *être sur* in wine tasting discourse).

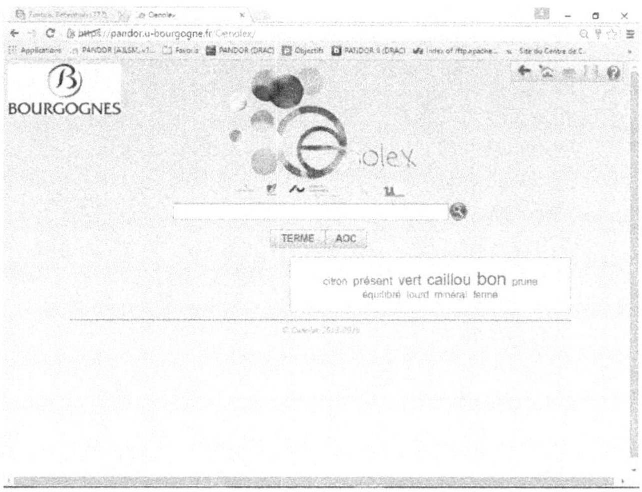

Figure 27.1 The Oenolex search interface

27.3.5 Search interface, search modes, and display of articles

The Oenolex user interface provides two basic search modes to its users. Both are activated by separate function buttons: the AOC search mode (= the 'AOC' button on user interface) and the wine tasting term search mode (= the 'TERME' button on user interface) (Figure 27.1).

The search field itself has a type ahead functionality which greatly speeds up data entry. In the underlying database structure, every single AOC is related to the specific terms that have been used to describe it, as well as to the specific wine tasting sessions under which the terms have been used. It is also possible for the user to refine his or her search (in order to show less information) and adapt the display of results by filtering out the data according to the following search options: region, wine process, AOC category (grand cru, premier cru, village, regional) as far as the AOC search is concerned, place of wine tasting session (wine schools, wine auction, wine fair, etc.), date of wine tasting session, and types of wine tasters present under wine tasting (wine teacher, oenologist, producer, etc.) as far as the TERME search is concerned.

The presentation of search results includes five different displays of articles, two for the display of terms and three for the display of AOCs. Besides, as shown in the illustration of the search interface (Figure 27.1), word clouds can be generated by the system to illustrate the frequency of wine tasting terms used to describe and evaluate any specific AOC indexed in the system.

27.3.6 AOC article with links to corresponding wine tasting sessions of the AOC

AOC articles include all data related to the unique AOC, as well as a list of all wine tasting sessions in which the specific AOC has been tasted (see Table 27.2). In this case, this specific article also contains an embedded video illustrating the actual 'climat' (not shown here in Table 27.2).

Table 27.2 AOC article with access to corresponding wine tasting session

AOC	*Chablis, 1er Cru, Fourchaume, Domaine Christophe SEBASTIEN, 2011*
Catégorie	Premier Cru
Cépage	Chardonnay
Climat & lieu-dit	Fourchaume
Commune	Maligny
Millésime	2011
Producteur	Domaine Christophe SEBASTIEN
Région viticole	Chablis
Vinification	blanc
2013–12–07 École des Vins de Bourgogne	

Table 27.3 Wine tasting article

AOC	*Chablis, 1er Cru, Fourchaume, Domaine Christophe SEBASTIEN, 2011*
Date	12 décembre 2013
Lieu	École des Vins de Bourgogne, 6 Rue du 16ème Chasseurs, 21200 Beaune
Évaluation visuelle expert	
Évaluation olfactive expert	Arômes persillés, des champignons. Commence à s'ouvrir. Au premier nez . . . on est sur des notes florales, sur le végétal et sur le minéral.
Évaluation olfactive non-expert	Le vin est encore fermé.
Évaluation gustative expert	En bouche, vous aller sentir acidité et sucrosité. En bouche, il y a aussi une certaine minéralité, ça sent un peu le côté caillou.
Évaluation générale expert	Un vin qui peut être gardé une dizaine d'années sans problème . . .
Liens	

27.3.7 Wine tasting article with links to corresponding term articles

Clicking on a place or date of a specific wine session from the list (in the example in Table 27.2, the list only contains one item) will display the corresponding wine tasting article of the AOC (see Table 27.3), in which all lemmatised wine tasting terms (*persillé*, *champignon*, *végétal*, etc.) are hyperlinked. Clicking on one of these opens the corresponding term article. Links are also provided to the corpus, to sound and video files, and to selected, external web page resources in line with Fuertes Olivera (2012) who recommends the use of the Internet as a lexicographical (re)source.

27.3.8 Term article with links to AOC articles

Term articles (see Table 27.4) contain all the fields already mentioned: term definition, grammatical information, collocations, examples, and type of source from which the term has been extracted (corpus). Below the term article are listed all the AOCs in which the term, here *pamplemousse*, has been used. Clicking on an item of the AOC list opens the corresponding AOC article at the position of the lemma in its context.

Table 27.4 Term article

Terme	*Pamplemousse*
Grammaire	nom masculin
Définition	arôme catégorisé dans la famille d'arômes "fruits frais, agrumes", faisant référence aux senteurs du pamplemousse, identifié lors du nez et/ou de la rétro-olfaction
Collocation	être sur le pamplemousse
Exemple	Donc, on était sur des fruits à chair blanche et le côté un petit peu citronné, mandarine, un petit peu **pamplemousse**, ce genre de choses.
Source	transcription du 7 novembre 2013, École des vins de Bourgogne, Beaune
AOC list:	
- Bourgogne Chitry, Chitry, 2010, Domaine Olivier MORIN	
- Mercurey blanc, Chardonnay, St. Martin-sous-Montaigu, 2012	

27.3.9 Cooperative work phases and interdisciplinary management

As stated by Fuertes Olivera (2013), applying new technology in e-lexicography constitutes a continuing challenge which also raises the question of participation of various experts and of end-users in the construction of the dictionary. Klosa (2013) has designed a work process model for the construction of e-dictionaries describing the various work phases and their content, from preparation of the dictionary to afterlife upon publication. Based on this model, we propose a slightly modified model (see Figure 27.2). Based on our experience so far in the construction of Oenolex, we are also in a position to formulate some general recommendations. The model shows the active involvement of users and experts in all phases of the workflows, and specifies the conditions of their involvement, viz to what degree experts or users should be involved or not.

In phase 1, preparation of the concept, experts should always be involved in decision making regarding the specific design of the lexicographic concept. In Oenolex, the BIVB is the commissioner and has subsequently taken part in all decision making in cooperation with the lexicographic team.

In phase 2, acquisition, both end users and experts can be involved depending on the genuine purpose of the dictionary. In Oenolex both groups have worked together because the data is generated in cooperation with experts, and include a written expert corpus of specialised documents as well as an oral, mixed corpus of recordings of specialised interactions between experts and non-experts. Thus, in Oenolex, data acquisition is the direct continuation of the preparation phase.

Phase 3, computerisation, normally does not require the participation of either end users of the dictionary or experts of the subject field, as the lexicographic team will generally manage this part of the work flow according to the database and corpus technology used by the lexicographic team, see for instance Nielsen and Almind (2011). In Oenolex, an IT expert has been working on all technical aspects concerning the construction of the database and the server solution.

In phase 4, processing, experts will rarely be needed. In Oenolex, research assistants have worked on the cleaning, tagging, and extraction of audio sequences and examples, and on the validation of the lexicographic quality of the data.

In phase 5, analysis, experts are always needed, as only experts can craft definitions of terms with the necessary lexicographic authority (see Hashimzade and al. 2014). In Oenolex,

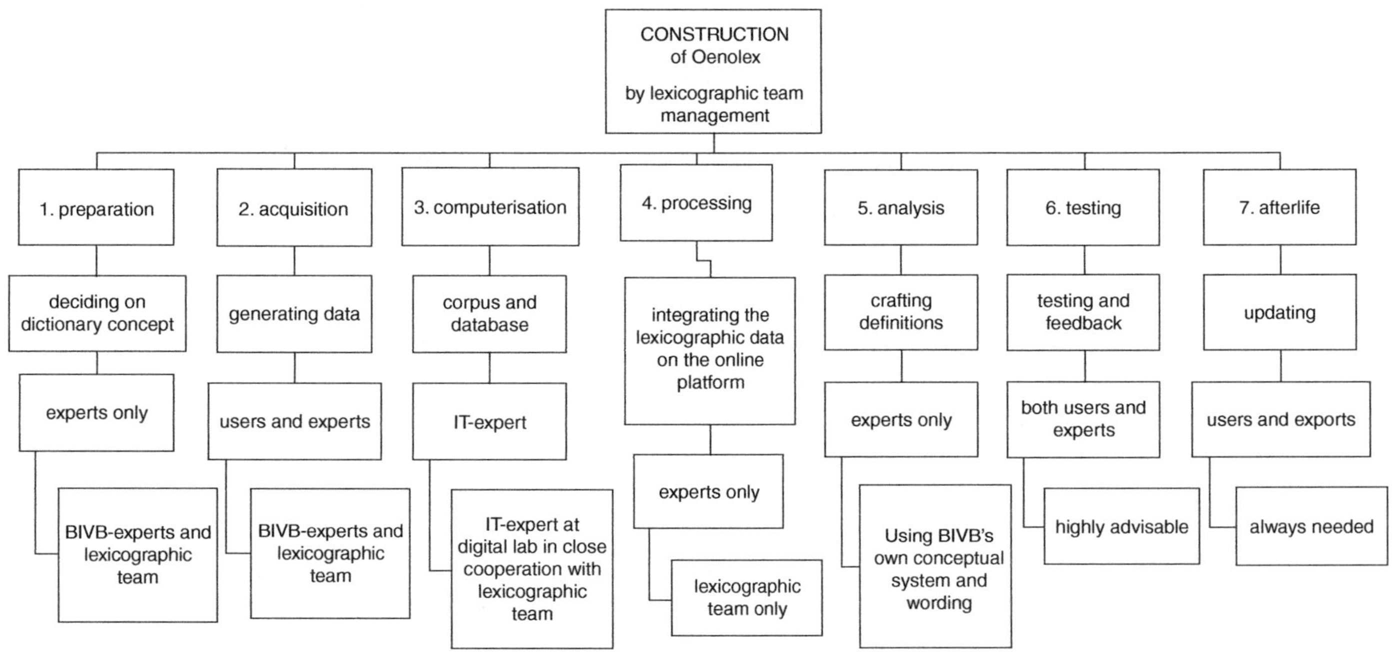

Figure 27.2 Work phases of Oenolex and cooperative work

Source: adapted from (Klosa 2013)

definitions and meaning explanations are all directly crafted in accordance with the conceptual system and the wording used in BIVB's own documents from which they are imported.

In phase 6, testing prior to release, the involvement of both users and experts is highly advisable. Only by then can their involvement in previous phases be assessed by the lexicographic team in the ongoing construction process of the dictionary; only by then can the lexicographic team make the necessary changes or adaptations in the work processes. It is therefore expected that the lexicographic team will have to make changes and adaptations after the release and the first use period of the 1.0 alpha version.

In phase 7, afterlife, both users and experts are always needed because the construction of the online dictionary is a recurrent, continuous loop process, much in the same way as in phase 6. User surveys and usability studies can also provide valuable feedback on the user-friendliness of Oenolex, so users will definitely be needed in the future developments and updating of the dictionary.

27.4 Looking to the future

The Oenolex dictionary of wine tasting paves the way for further lexicographic developments. First of all new vocabulary items can and will be continuously added as well as new instances of AOCs; new wine tasting data will also be continuously added, including new, planned recordings of wine tasting interactions in other settings (e.g. wine presentations and wine comments between sommeliers and customers in wine bars, online wine tasting surveys, etc.). Finally, the BIVB intends to develop an international version of the tool. So far, wine tasting vocabulary items and wine tasting expressions have been translated using conventional, multilingual lexicographic sources, and translations are not always reliable. Hence, it appears quite natural that translations in the future will be made on the basis of authentic, aligned wine tasting interactions, as these will do a far better, more genuine job. This implies a close cooperation with business partners of the BIVB on its main export markets in order to generate new wine tasting data of the wines that have already been tasted and evaluated in their homeland.

27.5 Conclusion

The Oenolex dictionary shows how specialised corpora in lexicography can be integrated and become true functional components of the lexicographic tool. Our experience so far clearly confirms that oral corpora can become a valuable asset in specialised, professional dictionary projects dealing with dynamic fields of knowledge, because oral interactions, although not as dialogic as expected, play an important role in the (de-) and (re)construction of knowledge of the profession. Our experience also clearly confirms that the corpus should not simply be treated as the empirical base of the dictionary, but can be turned into a fully fledged functional component of the dictionary and be put at the heart of the dictionary, so to speak. This necessitates a specific lexicographic structuring of the database linking lexicographic articles and examples from the corpus closely together, and consequently the programming of the user search interface accordingly. Hence, corpus and dictionary are not to be seen as separate entities, but as the two complementary sides of a modern 'linked data' information system which can be logically and effectively integrated.

However, one lexicographic aim that the Oenolex dictionary did not achieve as planned was the inclusion of the vocabulary used by non-expert consumers to describe wines, which was one of the central desiderata from the part of the BIVB. It appears that consumers are reticent to communicate their evaluation of wines when being asked to state their impressions in the presence of professionals. We will therefore have to develop new methods of data generation and acquisition, such as the use of electronic wine tasting forms to be filled online, in order to fill up this information gap.

Finally, working with Oenolex has taught us that the lexicographic management team should cooperate with a panel of experts almost all the way and not only, as commonly accepted today by specialised lexicographers, to check on and validate definitions of specialised items from the lemma list that have been selected by the lexicographer. Oenolex is a clear example of direct, cooperative lexicography. In today's world, professional words in professional discourses can no longer be separated from things and from actions and events in the world, and professional, expert knowledge is therefore needed in almost all phases of the lexicographic workflows. In other words, specialised lexicography is a truly cooperative and interdisciplinary discipline taking advantage of mixed methods of its own to adapt, in every single case, the treatment and the presentation of the lexicographic material to the genuine information needs of its intended users in the foreseen use situations. Oenolex clearly indicates that specialised e-lexicography in the future will be increasingly working together with information science, and will eventually develop the capacity to integrate a growing number of information retrieval systems largely based on the lexical and knowledge resources prepared by lexicographers.

Related topics

The concept of dictionary; dictionary management; dictionaries and access; lexicography and interdisciplinarity; lexicography and corpus linguistics; lexicography and information science; lexicography and terminology; electronic dictionaries; specialised dictionaries.

Further reading

Paradis, C. and M. Eeg-Olofsson (2013) "Describing Sensory Experience: The Genre of Wine Reviews", *Metaphor and Symbol* 28(1): 22–40.

This study deals with the language of sensory perceptions in reviews and identifies two types of descriptions of wines (use of words for properties and use of imagery and similes). The authors argue for a monosemic view of descriptors of wine and for metaphoric mappings across domains.

Van der Merwe, M. and P. A. Fuertes-Olivera (2014). "The Influence of the User Needs Paradigm in Specialised Lexicography: Some Reflections in Connection With Two South African Wine Dictionaries", *Ibérica* 27: 77–96.

This article convincingly makes the case for the effectiveness of function theory in general and of a user-oriented labelling system, in particular, in the compiling of multifield wine dictionaries.

Notes

1 It should be noted that the word 'punctual' here is not used in its usual sense, which in the Oxford Learner's Dictionaries Online (2016) is defined as "Happening or doing something at the agreed or proper time". In function theory the concept of 'punctual information needs' refers to lexicographically relevant information needs that can be satisfied by a one-off dictionary consultation at a particular *point* in time.

2 Needless to say, these information challenges and gaps also seem to go for other wine-producing regions in France and other countries.

References

Wine dictionaries, wine websites and applications, and software resources

Audacity (2016) Enregistreur et éditeur audio. www.audacity.fr [Accessed 2 May 2016].

BIVB (2016) *Bureau Interprofessionnel des vins de Bourgogne*. www.bourgogne-wines.com/who-are-we/the-bivb-the-voice-of-the-bourgogne-wine-trade,2329,9293.html? [Accessed 2 May 2016].

Coutier, M. (2007) *Le dictionnaire de la langue du vin*. Paris: Éditions du CNRS.

Drync Wine Free and Pro (2016) Find and Manage Wine Online or on Your Mobile. www. drync.com/ [Accessed 2 May 2016].

Guide Hachette des Vins (2016) Paris: Hachette pratique. www.hachette-vins.com/le-guide-hachette-des-vins/ [Accessed 2 May 2016].

Huma-num (2016) *Guide des bonnes pratiques numériques*. www.huma.num.fr/ressources/guides [Accessed 10 May 2016].

Leroyer, P. (2016) *Oenolex* Housed at https://pandor.u-bourgogne.fr/Oenolex/ [Accesed 20 June 2016].

Oxford Learner's Dictionaries Online (2016) Oxford: Oxford University Press. www.oxfordlearners dictionaries.com [Accessed 12 January 2016].

Sonal® (2016) Logiciel de retranscription et de dépouillement d'enquêtes par entretien. www. sonal-info.com [Accessed 15 June 2016].

South African Trilingual Wine Dictionary (2016). Sawis Winetech. www.sawis.co.za/dictionary/ [Accessed 3 May 2016].

Unesco (2016) *Chaire Unesco: Culture et traditions du vin*. http://chaireunesco-vinetculture.u-bourgogne.fr/ressources-chaire/annales/seminaires.html [Accessed 15 May 2016].

Wikipedia (2016) Le portail de la vigne et du vin. https://fr.wikipedia.org/wiki/Portail:Vigne_et_vin [Accessed 10 May 2016].

Other literature

Faber, P., P. L. Araúz and C. P. Hernández (2010) "A Wine Dictionary for NonDrinkers: LSP Dictionary Functions", in M. I. Rodríguez (ed.), *Vino, lengua y traducción*, Volume 3. Valladolid: Universidad de Valladolid, Secretariado de Publicaciones e Intercambio Científico, pp. 189–213.

Fuertes-Olivera, P. A. (2012) "Lexicography and the Internet as a (Re-)Source", *Lexicographica* 28: 49–70.

Fuertes-Olivera, P. A. (2013) "e-lexicography: The Continuing Challenge of Applying New Technology to Dictionary Making", in H. Jackson (ed.), *The Bloomsbury Companion to Lexicography*. London/New Delhi/New York/Sydney: Bloomsbury Academic, pp. 324–340.

Fuertes-Olivera, P. A. and S. Tarp (2014) *Theory and Practice of Specialised Online Dictionaries. Lexicography versus Terminography*. Berlin: De Gruyter.

Gautier, L. and V. Hohota (2014) "Construire et exploiter un corpus oral de situations de dégustation: l'exemple d'Oenolex Bourgogne", *Studia Universitatis Babes-Bolyai-Studia Philologia* LIX/41: 57–73.

Gautier, L., V. Hohota, H. Maazaoui, F. Chevalier and P. Leroyer (2015) "Faire déguster et parler de son vin pour le faire aimer et le vendre: quelques stratégies dans des interactions producteur-client", in *Vino Varietas*, Actes du colloque international de Toulouse 2015.

Gautier, L. and P. Leroyer (in press) "Construction, communication, représentation et réappropriation des discours vitivinicoles dans un 'nuancier' lexicographique en ligne", in C. Condei, L. Gautier and C. Teodorescu (eds.), *Situations professionnelles, discours et interactions en traduction spécialisée*. Berlin: Frank und Timme, GmbH Verlag für wissenschaftliche Literatur.

Gunnarsson, B. L. (2009) *Professional Discourse*. London: Continuum.

Hashimzade, N., G. A. Myles and G. D. Myles (2014) "Can Authority Be Sustained While Balancing Accessibility and Formality?", *Hermes* 52: 11–24.

Klosa, A. (2013) "The Lexicographical Process (With Special Focus on Online Dictionaries)", in R. H. Gouws, U. Heid, W. Schweickard and H. E. Wiegand (eds.), *Dictionaries: An International Encyclopedia of Lexicography. Supplement Volume: Recent Developments With Focus on Electronic and Computational Lexicography*. Berlin, Boston: de Gruyter, Handbücher zur Sprach- und Kommunikationswissenschaft 5.4, pp. 517–24.

Lerat, P. (2011) "Dénominations spécialisées, connaissances professionnelles et connaissances linguistiques en terminologie. Le cas du vin", in M. Ibáñez Rodríguez and M. T. Sánchez Nieto (eds.), *El lenguaje de la vid y el vino y su traducción*. Valladolid: Universidad de Valladolid, pp. 201–224.

Leroyer, P. (2013a) "New Proposals for the Design of Integrated Online Wine Industry Dictionaries", *Lexikos* 23: 209–27.

Leroyer, P. (2013b) "Putting Words on Wine: OENOLEX Bourgogne, New Directions in Wine Lexicography", in D. A. Kwary, N. Wulan and L. Musyahda (eds.), *Lexicography and Dictionaries in the Information Age* (Selected papers from the 8th ASIALEX International Conference). Airlangga: Airlangga University Press, 228–35.

Leroyer, P. (2015) "Turning the Corpus Into a Functional Component of the Dictionary: The Case of the Oenolex Wine Dictionary", *Procedia – Social and Behavioral Sciences*, 198: 257–265.

Leroyer, P. (in press) "La lexicographie du vin: état des lieux théorique et monofonctionnalité modulaire", in I. Rousseau-Jacob and L. Gautier (eds.), *Figures et images dans le discours sur le vin en Europe*. Peter Lang.

Leroyer, P. and L. Gautier (2015) "Le corpus oral au cœur de la lexicographie professionnelle du vin", *Estudios de Lexicografía* 4: 99–110.

Leroyer, P. and A. Høy (2014) "Vinsmagningsordbogen 'Oenolex Bourgogne'. En milepæl i pragmatisk fagleksikografi", in R. V. Fjeld and M. Hovdenak (eds.), *Nordiska Studier i lexikografi* 12, rapport fra konferansen om leksikografi i Norden. Oslo: Nordisk Forening for Leksikografi, pp. 287–303.

Leroyer, P., H. L. Gautier and H. Maazaoui (2015) "Extracting (Good) Discourse Examples From an Oral Specialised Corpus of Wine Tasting Interactions", ENeL-working papers, Hersmontceux 2015. https://hal.inria.fr/halshs-01213436/document [Accessed 6 February 2017].

Meyer, I. (2001) "Extracting Knowledge-Rich Contexts for Terminography", in D. Bourigault, C. Jacquemin and M.-C. L'Homme (eds.), *Recent Advances in Computational Terminology*. Philadelphia, Amsterdam: Benjamins, pp. 279–302.

Michelfeit, J. (2015) *GDEX in Sketch Engine*. ENeL 12 February 2015, WG3, Vienna, www.elexicography.eu/working-groups/working-group-3/wg3-workshops/automatic-extraction-of-good-dictionary-examples/ [Accessed 10 May 2016].

Nielsen, S. and R. Almind (2011). "From data to dictionary", in P. Fuertes Olivera and H. Bergenholtz (eds.), *e-Lexicography: The Internet, Digital Initiatives and Lexicography*. London, New Dehli, New York, Sidney: Continuum, pp. 141–67.

Van der Merwe, M. (2008) "Wine and Words: A Trilingual Wine Dictionary for South Africa", *Lexikos* 18: 337–348.

Van der Merwe, M. and P. A. Fuertes-Olivera (2014) "The Influence of the User Needs Paradigm in Specialised Lexicography: Some Reflections in Connection With Two South African Wine Dictionaries", *Ibérica* 27: 77–96.

28

The *Accounting Dictionaries*

Pedro A. Fuertes-Olivera and Marta Niño Amo

28.1 Introduction

The *Accounting Dictionaries* are the result of a joint project involving teams from Centre for Lexicography, Aarhus University in Denmark and International Centre for Lexicography, University of Valladolid (Spain). Each team consists of lexicographers, translators and accounting experts. The dictionaries are based on established principles of specialized lexicography integrating information technology and techniques with focus on providing help that can satisfy the needs for information when people are engaged in specific types of user situations (Bergenholtz and Tarp 2003; Fuertes-Olivera and Tarp 2014). There are at present three printed polyfunctional dictionaries and twenty-six online monofunctional accounting dictionaries, each linked to the same database containing data in Danish, English and Spanish (see References). This chapter will only focus on the online set of these dictionaries.

These online dictionaries represent a complex system of specific lexicographic and technological options available for creating interaction between database and dictionary. The database contains carefully selected types of data placed in discrete data fields and linked to each other in a specified way and to a specified extent. Users consult a dictionary, or user interface, through the homepage, and the dictionary sends their query to the database through a search engine that looks for matches in the database. Once found, the data are sent to the dictionary and presented to users in a predetermined way (Nielsen and Almind 2011). This setup allows users to access the data in the database in a number of ways that are designed to provide data giving help to users in different but specific types of user situations (Bergenholtz 2012; Nielsen and Fuertes-Olivera 2013; Fuertes-Olivera and Tarp 2014).

The present contribution aims to situate the *Accounting Dictionaries* historically (Section 28.2) and present its features and functionalities (Section 28.3). It will also look into the future, which may be dominated by the influence these dictionaries may have in the design and compilation of online dictionaries (Section 28.4). A final conclusion will summarise the main topics discussed (Section 28.5).

28.2 Historical perspectives

Nielsen and Fuertes-Olivera (2013) indicate that the conceptualization of the *Accounting Dictionaries* started in 2001 at the Danish Centre for Lexicography. Lexicographers Henning Bergenholtz and Sandro Nielsen as well as IT expert Richard Almind started preparing the lexicographic basis for the compilation of a bilingual accounting dictionary covering the languages Danish and English. The planned dictionary was intended to be a practical tool designed to help Danish enterprises meet the increasing need to present their financial reporting in linguistically and terminologically correct English. From the start, the dictionary was designed as an electronic dictionary to be freely accessible on the Internet.

At the turn of the century, lexicography was slowly changing its focus though conventional wisdom was still oriented towards linguistic and text-linguistic approaches to dictionary making and research. The lexicographers at the Danish centre felt that this focus on documentation, description and analysis based on a linguistic tradition was unsatisfactory; it did not provide the necessary help to establish a sound theoretical foundation embracing the types of problem involved in making the planned dictionary.

The challenge was not to make a bilingual dictionary that would be a repository of various types of data representing linguistic concepts and principles documenting the lexicon of accounting. The real problem was to make an online bilingual accounting dictionary that provided help to specific type(s) of user to solve specific types of problems, for example, when translating accounting texts from Danish into English or producing accounting texts directly in English. In other words, lexicographers at the Centre for Lexicography were in the process of putting into practice the tenets of the so-called *function theory of lexicography*, which was in full-swing at this Danish research centre at that time (Bergenholtz and Tarp 2003; Fuertes-Olivera and Tarp 2014; Tarp 2008; see Chapters 1 and 15 of this *Handbook*).

The adoption of the function theory of lexicography meant that the primary and most important goal of this lexicographic project was to develop an information tool that would provide help to solve specific types of problems encountered by specific types of users in several use situations. This approach resulted in a new way of approaching the conceptualizing phase of this project, that is, the time devoted to designing the lexicographic database, selecting the lexicographic fields for recording lexicographic data, deciding on lexicographic sources and staff and agreeing on a working methodology and time framework for finishing the project. Instead of resorting to user studies (see Chapter 44 of this *Handbook*), the Danish lexicographers carried out an analysis of users' needs, data types and access routes in a holistic way. This means that the Danish lexicographers not only analysed potential users' needs but also how to find the lexicographic data and treat it for offering users quick and easy consultation solutions. They agreed on compiling a dictionary of around 6,000 Danish and English accounting lemmas in around two years' time. Their analysis was totally based on introspection, that is, they decided users' needs, data types for meeting them and access routes for finding them by resorting to their experience as lexicographers, teachers, translators and researchers as well as publications in several fields of study (e.g. in the area of translation as these dictionaries primarily target translators of accounting texts).

Compared to the method of surveying dictionary users, the methodology used proved very useful and fruitful. First, these dictionaries lemmatise words and terms belonging to several parts of speech, typically nouns, adjectives, verbs, adverbs, prepositions and abbreviations (single and multi-word units). Second, lemmas are explained by means of definitions and inflectional paradigms, equivalents, collocations and phrases as well as example sentences and different types of lexicographic notes. Third, the compilation process was on time, and the Danish lexicographers could publish a polyfuncional online dictionary of around 6,000 lemmas in 2003, then freely accessible.

By 2008, four events occurred that were very important for the development of these dictionaries. First, a Danish company working in the industry of language technologies joined the project. Its presence allowed lexicographers to have at their disposal state-of-the-art technologies and IT specialists, for example, cloud computing facilities, easy access to log files, brand new databases and other lexicographic innovations (Fuertes-Olivera 2016).

Second the technology and human resources of the Danish company allowed lexicographers to convert the original polyfunctional dictionary into fifteen monolingual ones (see Nielsen et al. 2012a to n in the reference list under Dictionaries). This conversion proved that user interfaces, search engines and lexicographic databases are different concepts. This idea has resulted in the view espoused by proponents of the function theory of lexicography that online dictionaries consist of at least three components (Bergenholtz 2011): a database, a user interface, and a search system. The database is only a storage system that contains specially selected data that have been structured in a way that facilitates search and retrieval. The interface is a website that is used by users for retrieving lexicographic data. The search system is an engine equipped with search buttons, each offering different search possibilities. There may be as many search buttons as needed, for example, a search button for retrieving data for being used in a translation situation, a different button for retrieving data for being used in a reception situation, and so on (see Figures 28.1 and 28.2).

The previously mentioned three-component structure has a number of practical and theoretical implications:

1. The database can be the source of several dictionaries as the search engine allows users to make structured searches in structured data through a specific set of online dictionaries.
2. Online dictionaries contain no *macrostructures* in the traditional text-linguistic sense of the word (i.e. a lexicographical structure that arranges lemmata in a specific order so that they can easily be found).
3. The *Accounting Dictionaries* allow users to access data in the database and present the search results on the computer screen no matter where its data were actually located in the database.
4. The macrostructure has been replaced by a "data presentation structure" that arranges the data retrieved from the database according to type, and presents these data in a predetermined order depending on user needs as identified by the type of help sought (see also Nielsen and Almind 2011: 147–151).

Third, the new fifteen monolingual *Accounting Dictionaries* started to be sold in Scandinavia. In other words, the original polifunctional dictionary that could be accessed free of charge was converted into a surcharge service. The selling was and continues to be a success. This has three main implications. First, selling these dictionaries in Scandinavia proves that there is a market for high-quality information tools. Second, they are being sold as services and not as products, that is, servers work around the clock, and subscribers can communicate easily with lexicographers and can use a "help" system and be sure that the dictionaries contain up-to-date lexicographic data. This is especially relevant in specialised lexicography, where there are many information tools that are always presented as projects (i.e. dictionaries in the making). Third, in the era of the Internet, the interdisciplinarity of lexicography is more evident than ever (see Part 2 of the *Handbook*). We not only need experts from different fields but also IT experts and companies that know how to prepare online services for being sold or accessed by millions of Internet users.

Finally, a new language, Spanish, was included and added to the original project. The inclusion of Spanish was initiated with the translation of the English accounting terms and facts into Spanish. In 2008, these amounted to around 6,500 dictionary articles, which were translated into Spanish in nine months and published as a printed dictionary in 2010 (Fuertes-Olivera et al. 2010). This is the methodology used for translating the original English dictionary into a bilingual English-Spanish one:

1 A Spanish lexicographer explained the definition of the English terms to the accounting experts of the project. These allowed them to identify the Spanish equivalent quite easily in around 95 percent of the situations. The found equivalent was inserted into the "equivalent" field of the accounting database (see Section 28.3).
2 A Spanish lexicographer attached Spanish grammar and inflections to the Spanish equivalents. These data were stored in the grammar fields of the lexicographic database.
3 Two Spanish translators of English specialised texts translated the collocations and examples that contextualise each English headword (around 20,000 English collocations and 2,000 English examples at that time).
4 A Spanish lexicographer and an accounting expert searched for the unfound equivalents (around 5 percent of the English words and terms). In addition, they included translations and/or adaptations of English synonyms and antonyms (where necessary), contrastive notes (where necessary), and internal and external cross-references, that is, links to other dictionary articles or to external webpages, typically the homepage of the Instituto de Contabilidad y Auditoría de Cuentas (ICAC), which is the Spanish official institution in charge of accounting standards, rules and procedures in Spain.
5 A Spanish lexicographer and an accounting expert coined the Spanish equivalents of the English terms that had not been previously identified; sometimes, this coinage consisted in accepting equivalents found in other dictionaries or in Internet homepages, or verbatim translations of English accounting words and terms (Fuertes-Olivera 2011).
6 A Spanish lexicographer and an accounting expert translated into Spanish all the original English definitions. They also adapted the English definitions to the characteristics of Spanish accounting rules, standards and traditions.
7 A Spanish native speaker trained in Spanish grammar proofread all the Spanish data present in the layout "English-Spanish" of the accounting database. Her role was to check errors, mistakes and so on.

By December 2009, IT experts based in the Centre for Lexicography (Aarhus University) converted the data into a polyfunctional online dictionary (no longer in operation), and a printed one (Fuertes-Olivera et al. 2010). In 2012, the aforementioned Danish company also decided to join this part of the project. It initially transformed the stored data into several Spanish and English *Accounting Dictionaries*, which are currently freely accessible at http://lemma.com. In 2016 there were twelve different Spanish and English monolingual *Accounting Dictionaries* (see this chapter's references). We are in the process of including them into an information package, which will consist of several English and Spanish dictionaries (see Chapter 17 of this *Handbook*). The Danish company is planning to sell this information package in different markets by 2019.

28.3 Core issues and topics

28.3.1 Users and users' needs

The *Accounting Dictionaries* existing in May 2016 primarily aim at three intended Danish and Spanish user groups: (1) translators and language staff; (2) accounting experts and semi-experts; and (3) students and laypersons interested in Danish, English and Spanish accounting matters. For each of them we have assumed the following characteristics:

1 Translators and language staff generally have a relatively high level of general linguistic competence, a low to medium competence level in accounting language, a low to medium level of factual competence within accounting, a high level of translation competence and a medium to high level of competence in writing, editing and revising general texts in their native language as well as foreign language.
2 Accounting experts and semi-experts generally have a high level of factual competence, a medium level of general linguistic competence, a high to medium level in accounting language and a medium to low level in writing, editing and revising general texts in their native language as well as foreign language.
3 Students and interested persons generally have a high to medium level of linguistic competence, a low competence level in accounting language and facts and a medium to low level in translation, writing, editing and revising general texts in their native language as well as foreign language.

28.3.2 Data selection

These characteristics prompted lexicographers to select data by using the *principle of relevance* (Fuertes-Olivera and Nielsen 2011; Bothma and Tarp 2012). In this context, *relevance* means the quality of being directly connected with accounting, the dictionary function, the different use situations in which the dictionary will be used and the levels of competence of intended users. For instance, collocations are selected because they are important when translating accounting texts and because they are difficult to translate between the languages concerned; and examples are selected because they show how larger units of accounting texts can be translated and produced. Similarly, grammatical data help users to write, edit and revise specialized texts in their native or foreign language. Furthermore, English is the *lingua franca* of accounting, and the accounting community use three variants: the English adopted by the International Financial Reporting Standards, American English and British English (labelled in the dictionaries with the language codes IAS/IFRS, US and UK, respectively). This labelling of terms, collocations and phrases allows users to choose the correct terminological variant and to use the appropriate language variant consistently. The principle of relevance thus ensures that the data selected are actually connected with the dictionary functions, and that the data are presented in a way that satisfies users' needs.

28.3.3 Data types

The profiling of intended users and the study of the use situations led to the selection of a range of data types, which are shown in Table 28.1 together with their rationale, that is, why they were chosen at the conceptualisation phase (see Fuertes-Olivera and Tarp 2014: 199–200).

Table 28.1 Data types in the lexicographic accounting database and its rationale

Data Type	*Rationale*
Lemma	Self-evident: all dictionaries describe lemmas
Homonymy index (superscript in the dictionary)	Included when homographs have different inflectional paradigms or are countable or uncountable, respectively. It assists all user types in all situations: it restricts the meaning of lemmas.
Polysemy index (Arabic numerals in the dictionary)	Included when homographs have different definitions. It assists all user types in all situations. It restricts the meanings of the same lemma.
Language code to lemma	Included for indicating language and language variant of the lemma. It assists all user types in all situations.
Grammatical data addressed to lemma	It offers inflections, countability, and active and passive forms of verbs. It assists all user types in two communicative situations: production and translation. It offers linguistic profiles of lemmas
Equivalent	One Danish, English or Spanish equivalent in several dictionary combinations: Danish-English (Danish lemma; Danish definition; English equivalent); English-Danish (English lemma; English definition; Danish equivalent); English-Spanish (English lemma; English definition; Spanish definition; Spanish equivalent); Spanish-English (Spanish lemma; Spanish definition; English equivalent). It assists all user types in communicative situations.
Language code to equivalent	Included for indicating language and language variant of the equivalent. It assists all user types in communicative situations.
Grammatical data addressed to equivalent	It offers inflections, countability, and active and passive forms of verbs. It assists all user types in two communicative situations: production and translation. It offers linguistic profiles of equivalents.
Definition of lemma	It explains the meaning(s) of lemmas. Always one definition per sense. Definitions are crafted in the language of lemma. There is one exception: in the English-Spanish dictionary, definitions are in English and Spanish. It assists all user types in all situations.
Collocations	They are short and long phrases but not full sentences. They are crafted in the language of the lemma. They *mainly* assist users in two communicative situations: production and translation. In addition, the Spanish dictionary also includes collocations that assist users in cognitive situations (this is a useful method for dealing with culture-bound subject fields).
Translation of collocations	In some dictionary combinations collocations are translated: English collocations are translated into Danish and Spanish, and Danish and Spanish collocations are translated into English. They assist all user types in two communicative situations: production and translation.
Language code to translation of collocations	Included for indicating language and language variants of the lemma and equivalent. It assists all user types in two communicative situations: production and translation.
Examples	They are full sentences showing lemmas in use. They assist all user types in cognitive situations and two communicative situations: production and translation.
Translation of examples	They are full sentences showing equivalents in use. They are in some dictionary combinations: English examples are translated into Danish and Spanish, and Danish and Spanish examples are translated into English. They assist all user types in cognitive situations and two communicative situations: production and translation.

Table 28.1 (continued)

Data Type	*Rationale*
Synonyms and antonyms addressed to lemmas or equivalents	They assist all user types in two communicative situations: production and translation.
Language code to synonyms and antonyms	Included for indicating language and language variant of the synonym and antonym. It assists all user types in two communicative situations: production and translation.
Source	Hyperlinks to external texts. It mainly assists experts in cognitive situations. It can also assist translators and semi-experts in two communicative situations: production and translation.
Lexicographic notes	Usage, and/or contrastive notes that are addressed to lemma or equivalent, especially for indicating factual differences between lemma and/or equivalent, particular usages, cultural details, etc. They mainly assist all user types in cognitive situations.
Grammar notes attached to lemma and/or equivalent	They indicate language profiles of some lemmas and/or equivalents. They mainly assist users in two communicative situations: production and translation.
Proscriptive notes	They are used for recommending lemmas. They mainly assist all user types in communicative situations.
Cross-references	Hyperlinks to internal texts. They assist all user types in cognitive situations and two communicative situations: translation and production.

Table 28.1 shows that each data type may have one or more specific goal(s) within the general framework of the user's needs, functions and resources agreed on at the start of the project. In the following, we will comment on several aspects of the data types, specifically the methodology used for selecting them and their main function(s).

28.3.4 Empirical basis and data selection process

The selection of lexicographic data is a continuous process in e-lexicography (Fuertes-Olivera and Bergenholtz 2011). For instance, in the Spanish part of the *Accounting Dictionaries*, the Spanish lexicographers and accounting experts selected lemmas and equivalents and crafted definitions working side by side. The process started by delimiting the subject field, which in the case of accounting comprises decisions concerned with "macroaccounting", typically the treatment of *national accounts*, and "microaccounting", which deals with internal reporting, i.e. management accounting, and external reporting or financial accounting.

There are four main data sources for selecting lemmas, equivalents and crafting definitions. The first source consists of *institutionalized accounting texts*, that is, texts that do not deal with specific companies, problems, situations, etc., but with general aspects of accounting, as these are treated in standards, codes, legislative texts, manuals and handbooks which deal with the accounting rules and standards that operate all over the world. For instance, 645 Spanish IAS/IFRS (i.e. International Accounting Standards and International Financial Reporting Standards) terms are lemmatised in the Spanish *Accounting Dictionaries*. These terms are defined by official bodies and committees and do not have cultural connotations. To sum up, data extracted from institutionalised accounting texts usually refer to the same accounting concepts all over the world. Their equivalents can be easily found out in parallel and comparable texts (e.g. the English International Financial Reporting Standards and their translations into Spanish and Danish).

The second source comes from *private accounting texts*, that is, they deal with specific accounting problems, situations and practices (e.g. the financial reports, financial statements and audit reports of a specific Spanish company). With these texts we can easily find out accounting concepts that are used by all the companies of the same sector or industrial activity. In other words, representativeness in accounting is not associated with frequency but with *relevance*, as indicated in Section 28.3.2.

Private texts also contain culture specific elements (i.e. elements that describe accounting traditions). Only experts in accounting can easily spot and illustrate these elements, especially similarities and differences between variants, accounting treatments, etc. For instance, the Spanish accounting concept *amortización* corresponds to two English lemmas: *amortisation* and *depreciation*, which refer to two different English concepts. Due to English influence, Spanish accountants are also using *depreciación* as synonym of *amortización*, a situation that was not originally used in Spanish accounting. Hence, we decided to include *depreciación* and *amortización* as Spanish lemmas and indicate that they are treated as synonyms in Spanish although they are conceptually different in English. Definitions extracted from private accounting texts may contain differences which refer to cultural traditions and specificities of English, Spanish or Danish accounting.

An in-house corpus of around 3 million words was also used for selecting lemmas and different accounting data. This corpus contains basically research and popularised texts, for example, texts extracted from accounting journals such as *Partida Doble* and accounting articles published in dailies, bank leaflets, prospectuses and similar sources. Corpus data typically resulted in either *semi-terms*, that is, terms that are used in several subject fields with different meanings, or *words*, general words that may also have a specific meaning in accounting. For instance, the lemma *accumulate*, that is, "to increase or grow over a period of time because of periodical additions" (definition in the *Accounting Dictionaries*) is lemmatised because it forms lexical profiles with key accounting terms such as *cost*, *cash*, *financial instruments*, etc. We found some important differences in the grammar of semi-terms and general words in English, Spanish and Danish accounting. For instance, English accounting prefers plural *costs*, whereas Spanish accounting prefers singular *coste* or *costo*.

Finally, another source of lexicographic data is the compilation process. This means that during the process of compiling dictionaries the lexicographic team comes across synonyms, antonyms and new or changed terms. This process is highly productive and easy to implement when working with experts in the field. They easily remember synonyms, antonyms and other related terms when a definition is crafted. For instance, the Spanish institutionalised term *sistema institucional de protección* (abbreviated as *SIP*) was transformed by Spanish newspapers in *fusión fría*, a colloquial term introduced in 2010 in Spanish public discourse referring to fake mergers of Spanish saving banks. Our experts easily found that both terms referred to the same concept, and consequently were added to the Spanish part of the *Accounting Dictionaries*.

28.3.5 Explaining and contextualising meaning

Explanation of meaning is a key lexicographic activity whose purpose is to offer potential users data types that facilitate the understanding of each term (see Chapter 4 of this *Handbook*). This activity is basically concerned with crafting definitions and attaching equivalents, where necessary. These data types are in the accounting database (see Table 28.1), and its inclusion was decided once the user profile in several usage situations was agreed on. Lexicographers and subject experts did perform this activity jointly. The subject expert describes/explains the concept; the lexicographer decides on the definitional style and writes the definition. In the *Accounting Dictionaries* definitions are crafted as complete sentences, usually relating the *definiendum* to the *definiens* using a word or phrase expressing a clear relationship of identity between them, for example, "is". There are some exceptions to this definition type (e.g. function words such as *less* and *cum*), but these exceptions are irrelevant in the dictionaries (for instance, there are only thirty-one function words in the Spanish *Accounting Dictionaries*).

In terms of user needs, the definitions can be divided into two main types: (a) around 50 percent of the definitions are *general* definitions, that is, they are valid for assisting all potential users of the dictionary; and (b) around 50 percent of definitions are *special definitions*, that is, they have been subjected to lexicographic treatment with the aim of assisting specific types of potential users. For instance, definitions of culture specific terms are different in English, Spanish and Danish, as examples (1) and (2) show. They correspond to the concept of *building society*, which is only used in English accounting but not in Spanish accounting:

(1)

building society
Building societies in the UK are financial institutions whose objectives include accepting deposits for saving, granting mortgage loans as well as unsecured loans to the depositors for the purchase, construction or improvement of owner-occupied dwellings as well as offering various financial services.

(2)

Las sociedades de crédito hipotecario o inmobiliario son instituciones financieras que funcionan en el Reino Unido como cooperativa o mutua constructora. Sus objetivos incluyen el depósito de cuentas viviendas, la concesión de préstamos hipotecarios con avales y sin avales utilizados para la compra, construcción, o mejora de viviendas así como la oferta de varios tipos de servicios financieros.

After selecting lemmas, equivalents and crafting definitions, the next important step is the contextualization of meaning, that is, the inclusion of chunks of texts (e.g. example sentences) and/or lexicographic notes that show how a particular term is used in real texts. There are three main types of relevant contexts in the *Accounting Dictionaries*: the discursive context, the factual context and the sociolinguistic context. The discursive context is the language context of the term, typically the collocational context in which the term occurs. In the *Accounting Dictionaries*, the inclusion of some collocations and examples *primarily* aim to assist in communicative situations by including data types in Danish, English and Spanish (and translations among these languages, where relevant) that present the discursive context of lemma and equivalent.

The factual context is the inclusion of facts, figures, procedures and culture data that *primarily* aim to assist users in cognitive situations. In the *Accounting Dictionaries*, most examples and some collocations contain accounting data that contextualise the factual meaning of the lemma and equivalent (where relevant).

The sociolinguistic context is the language code(s) attached to lemmas, equivalents, synonyms, antonyms, collocations and examples, where relevant. These refer to a particular language or to a language variant. In the *Accounting Dictionaries*, two types of codes are mainly used: (a) language codes such as "DK", "UK", "US" and "E" for identifying the languages of the particular lemma and/or equivalent: Danish (DK), British English (UK), American English (US) or Spanish (E) lemmas; and (b) dialect codes such as "IAS/IFRS" for referring to international accounting variants.

In May 2016, the accounting database contained around 30,000 collocations and 3,000 examples in each language, many of which are translated to the other languages covered in the dictionary by the joint work of lexicographers, experts in accounting and experienced translators. This makes these dictionaries much appreciated and fulfils one of its most important genuine purposes: to assist users in a translation situation. Collocations and examples are typically extracted by performing Google searches, that is, by using the Web as a corpus (Fuertes-Olivera 2012; Tarp and Fuertes-Olivera 2016; see Chapter 42 of this *Handbook*). We believe that using the Web as a lexicographic corpus makes sense provided the adoption of "safe practices", that is, all the data taken from Google searches are analysed by the corresponding expert working in the dictionary project, who, in the end, decides on their inclusion or rejection. For instance, we used Google searches for completing the profile of the Spanish lemma *señal*: Googling "señal" retrieves almost 69 million hits. Such a number demonstrates that *señal* is polysemous: it is used in general Spanish, information technology, medicine, accounting, etc. In order to obtain its language profile in accounting, we used the accounting definition crafted by our accounting expert as a restriction element of the several Google searches undertaken: (a) we searched "señal" + "arras" (En *pledge*) + "contabilidad" (Eng *accounting*) retrieving hits such as "contrato de arras"; (b) we then searched "contrato de arras" + "señal" + "contabilidad" and obtained 11,000 hits; (c) an analysis of first 500 hits showed that "contrato de arras", "señal" and "contabilidad" coincided with "entrega a cuenta" (En *downpayment*); (d) this prompted us to search "señal" + "contabilidad" + "downpayment", obtaining around 400 hits. Its analysis allowed us to complete several data types:

1 the English equivalent of *señal* is *pledge*;
2 the language profile of *señal* in accounting is <la señal, una señal>, that is, it is always singular;
3 the accounting definition of *señal* must indicate that this term is a kind of downpayment, which is used in mortgage agreements with the aim of making a reservation of property.

28.3.6 Access routes

The access routes chosen by users determine which types of data will be presented in the dictionary. For instance, Spanish users can select four monolingual dictionaries, four English-Spanish dictionaries and four Spanish-English dictionaries. An example of this is the data retrieved when clicking on the search button "Traducción" (En Translation) or "Traducción de frases y expresiones" (En Translating phrases and sentences). Figures 28.1 and 28.2 show what the user retrieves when searching *cost accounting* with the search button "Traducción" and "Taducción de frases y expresiones". The main difference between them is that "Traducción" shows specific dictionary articles, whereas "Traducción de Frases y Expresiones" shows translations of the search string. The first button is mainly reserved for interested laypersons and semi-experts, whereas the second button is of much help for experienced translators, who can easily and quickly check (different) translations of the same search string:

Traducción

cost accounting

Definition

- La contabilidad de costes es la parte de la disciplina contable realizada y utilizada en el ámbito interno de la empresa, a los efectos de la toma de decisiones de gestión, ya que sirve para determinar el coste de un producto, el punto de equilibrio, y distintos márgenes económicos, como puede ser el margen comercial.
- Cost accounting is that part of the cost management system that measures costs for the purpose of management decisions and financial reporting. Cost accounting involves budgeting, breaking down of costs and revenues by product and location as well as analysing variances, profitability and use of funds.
  contabilidad de costes <una contabilidad de costes; la contabilidad de costes, las contabilidades de costes>

Synonyms

- *contabilidad interna*
- *contabilidad de gestión*

Collocations

- The application of cost accounting principles la aplicación de principios de una contabilidad de costes
- managerial cost accounting concepts la contabilidad de costes en la empresa

Figure 28.1 Definition of *cost accounting* in the English-Spanish *Accounting Dictionary* "Traducción"

The description of the main features and functionalities of the *Accounting Dictionaries* explain the innovative characteristics of these dictionaries, especially when they are compared with traditionally conceived specialized ones. In particular, we highlight the following:

1 They offer many lexicographic data, up to twenty-six as shown in Table 28.1. Most specialized dictionaries offer around five or six lexicographic data.
2 They aim to help particular user types in specific extra-lexicographic situations.
3 They are designed, compiled and updated in a specified time period (i.e. they are not projects in the making).
4 They adjust to the principle of "less is more", which is very necessary for avoiding the Google effect which typically results in information overload. Hence, users have up to twenty-six online dictionaries, each retrieving the data needed in particular situations.
5 The use of the Web as a corpus facilitates the making of the dictionary.
6 They illustrate the way ahead in specialized online lexicography: experts, lexicographers and IT experts must work side by side to make high-quality specialized online dictionaries.
7 The active participation of a technology company not only facilitates the use of brand-new lexicographic technologies and innovations but also proves that there may be a market for high-quality specialised online dictionaries.

Frases y Expresiones

cost accounting

Definition

- La contabilidad de costes es la parte de la disciplina contable realizada y utilizada en el ámbito interno de la empresa, a los efectos de la toma de decisiones de gestión, ya que sirve para determinar el coste de un producto, el punto de equilibrio, y distintos márgenes económicos, como puede ser el margen comercial.
- Cost accounting is that part of the cost management system that measures costs for the purpose of management decisions and financial reporting. Cost accounting involves budgeting, breaking down of costs and revenues by product and location as well as analysing variances, profitability and use of funds.

  contabilidad de costes <una contabilidad de costes; la contabilidad de costes, las contabilidades de costes>

Collocations

- the application of cost accounting principles la aplicación de los principios de una contabilidad de costes
- managerial cost accounting concepts la contabilidad de costes en la empresa

cost accounting system

Definition

- Un sistema de contabilidad de costes es un conjunto de técnicas utilizadas para identificar la influencia que las decisiones de la dirección tienen sobre los costes. El objetivo de un sistema de gestión de costes es ofrecer información sobre los costes que pueda usarse en la toma de decisioens estratégicas así como en las valoraciones del valor de las existencias y los costes de los bienes fabricados para las personas interesadas externas (stakeholders).
- Cost accounting systems support all other cost management systems and include techniques to analyse and measure the cost of a product, service, customer or other cost object. A cost accounting system must measure costs to meet the cost management system purposes.

  sistema de contabilidad de costes <un sistema de contabilidad de costes, el sistema de contabilidad de costes, unos sistemas de contabilidad de costes, los sistemas de contabilidad de costes>

Collocations

- implement a cost accounting system implementar un nuevo sistema de contabilidad de costes
- a centralised cost accounting system un sistema de contabilidad de costes integrado
- deficiencies in the cost accounting system deficiencias en el sistema de contabilidad de costes

Figure 28.2 Screenshot of *cost accounting* in the English-Spanish *Accounting Dictionary* "Traducción de Frases y Expresiones" (excerpts)

28.4 Looking to the future

The *Accounting Dictionaries* illustrate six trends that may be influencing the future of lexicography in the coming years. First, designing and making online dictionaries is clearly an interdisciplinary activity. Lexicographers, IT experts and subject-field experts must work side by side when designing, making and updating a particular dictionary (see Part 2 and Chapters 27 and 29 of this *Handbook*). Lexicographers must observe potential users in specific situations, detect lexicographically relevant information needs among them and select the lexicographic team which will start (and finish) the lexicographic project which should meet the observed information needs. IT specialists must design the lexicographic database, user interface and search routes for favouring the consultation time and process. Finally, experts in the field must be sure that there are viable data sources for completing the dictionary articles of the intended project.

Second, IT companies are totally necessary since online dictionaries should not be sold as products but as services (see Chapter 2 of this *Handbook*). Selling a service implies that the dictionary must be updated on a regular basis (i.e. there are no editions), that there are call centres and similar systems for aiding potential customers, that the lexicographic team and the users are in permanent contact and that servers and similar technologies are always on and working properly.

Third, instead of designing polyfunctional dictionaries, users demand several monofunctional dictionaries, that is, tools with lexicographic data adapted to a specific use situation. This trend is connected with individualization or article modelling, which can be defined *as the lexicographic process aiming to allow individual users to select the data he or she may need in a particular context.*

Fourth, a possible way for achieving individualization is using an idiosyncratic online system composed of, at least, a single lexicographic database and several search buttons, each linked to different user interfaces or online dictionaries. For instance, the *Accounting Dictionaries* use a single lexicographic database with seven different layouts (i.e. screens) where lexicographers work. In Layout 1 lexicographers record monolingual English data; in Layout 2 lexicographers record monolingual Danish data; in Layout 3 lexicographers record monolingual Spanish data; in Layout 4 lexicographers relate English and Danish data, for example, they record the Danish equivalent of the English lemmas and the translation of English collocations into Danish; in Layout 5 lexicographers relate English and Spanish data, for example, they record the Spanish equivalent of the English lemmas and the translation of English collocations into Spanish; in Layout 6 lexicographers relate Danish and English data, for example, they record the English equivalent of the Danish lemmas and the translation of Danish collocations into English; in Layout 7 lexicographers relate Spanish and English data, for example, they record the English equivalent of the Spanish lemmas and the translation of Spanish collocations into English. To the best of our knowledge, commercially available dictionary writing systems do not allow this flexibility and cannot therefore be used for constructing dictionary systems aiming at offering monofunctional solutions.

Fifth, cloud computing is totally necessary for making online dictionaries such as the *Accounting Dictionaries*. Cloud computing allows lexicographers living in different countries to work on them on a daily basis, communicate easily among them, store the vast amount of data that they should record and update them regularly and easily (see also Chapter 29 of this *Handbook*).

Finally, instead of dictionary portals consisting of many dictionaries (i.e. the aggregation of dictionaries), there should be integrated information tools, that is, sets of different monofunctional dictionaries that *must* be conceptualised and constructed under the same lexicographic principles, with the aim of favouring individualisation as previously indicated. For instance, one of the Spanish *Accounting Dictionaries* offers the possibility of a "user-generated exploratory search route", that is, it is a search button that allows users who are uncertain of their search to explore the data stored in particular fields by generating different types of searches (Fuertes-Olivera and Leroyer 2014). Users construct search strings that contain Boolean operators and concepts. The more precise the concept is the better the results obtained. For instance, a user unsure of the possible relationship between accounting concepts such as *cost, charge* and *capital* can construct the search string "+ coste + carga – capital" and will obtain clickable hits with which, say, the user can start different searches (Figure 28.3).

Figure 28.3 Definition of a "user-generated exploratory search route" in the *Accounting Dictionaries*

28.5 Conclusion

Innovative dictionaries are in the forefront of lexicographic knowledge and practice. The *Accounting Dictionaries* are treated as a case study of innovative dictionaries for several reasons. First, they clearly illustrate that the making of high-quality online dictionaries cannot be carried out without the active and continuous participation of lexicographers, IT specialists, domain experts and IT companies. Second, they offer up to twenty-six different data, which is clearly much more than existing specialized printed dictionaries. For instance, the *Accounting Dictionary. Diccionario de Contabilidad* (Nora Sánchéz 2003) offers the following entry for the English lemma *cost accounting* (see the difference between example (3) and Figure 28.1). Both example (3) and Figure 28.1 refer to the lemma *cost accounting*:

(3)

cost accounting contabilidad analítica,
contabilidad de costos * *Sp.* contabilidad de costes.

Third, users can select the data displayed according to their specific use situations and needs (see Figures 28.1 and 28.2). Fourth, users can even search for concepts (see Figure 28.3). Finally, they are part of integrated online information tools that will be the future of commercially oriented dictionaries, that is, dictionaries created, maintained and updated for making a profit and not as a kind of academic exercise for writing articles and presenting papers on lexicographic matters. In other words, the *Accounting Dictionaries* show that the practice of commercial lexicographic products in the era of the Internet demands a change of paradigm. Instead of approaching the design and construction of dictionaries as language products, we must consider them information services, which demands asking several questions, for example:

1 What is an information tool?
2 Which characteristics must an information tool have for qualifying as information service?
3 Which human resources, facilities and technologies are needed for selling information services?
4 Who can be interested in paying for information services?

Acknowledgments

Thanks are due to the Ministerio de Economía y Competitividad for financial support (Grant FFI2014–52462-P).

Related topics

Explaining meaning in lexicographic information tools; the concept of dictionary; dictionary for text reception; dictionary for text production; dictionary for translation; specialized dictionaries; domain ontologies; terminological knowledge bases; the Oenolex wine dictionary.

Further reading

Fuertes-Olivera, P. A. (2016). "A Cambrian Explosion in Lexicography: Some Reflections for Designing and Constructing Specialised Online Dictionaries", *International Journal of Lexicography* 29(2): 226–247.
This article explains the design and construction of online dictionaries with a focus on different Internet technologies and working methodologies.

Fuertes-Olivera, P. A. and H. Bergenholtz (eds.) (2011). *e-Lexicography: The Internet, Digital Initiatives and Lexicography*. London: Continuum.
In this book, various authors discuss the transition from the printed to the digital media and show how new technologies are transforming lexicography. It also contains many comments on the relationship between lexicography and information science.

Fuertes-Olivera, P. A. and S. Tarp. (2014). *Theory and Practice of Online Specialised Dictionaries. Lexicography Versus Terminography*. Berlin/Boston: De Gruyter.
This book is an update of the Function Theory of Lexicography, which illustrates its current situation and how it was applied in the design, compilation and updating of the *Accounting Dictionaries*.

References

Dictionaries

Fuertes-Olivera, P. A., H. Bergenholtz, S. Nielsen, P. Gordo Gómez, L. Mourier, M. Niño Amo, Á. Ríos Rodicio, Á. Sastre Ruano, S. Tarp and M. Velasco Sacristán (2012) *Diccionario Inglés-Español de Contabilidad: Recepción*. Database and Design: Richard Almind and Jesper Skovgård Nielsen. Odense: Lemma.com.

Fuertes-Olivera, P. A., H. Bergenholtz, S. Nielsen, P. Gordo Gómez, L. Mourier, M. Niño Amo, Á. Ríos Rodicio, Á. Sastre Ruano, S. Tarp, M. Velasco Sacristán (2012) *Diccionario Inglés-Español de Contabilidad: Traducción*. Base de Database and Design: Richard Almind and Jesper Skovgård Nielsen. Odense: Lemma.com.

Fuertes-Olivera, P. A., H. Bergenholtz, S. Nielsen, P. Gordo Gómez, L. Mourier, M. Niño Amo, Á. Ríos Rodicio, Á. Sastre Ruano, S. Tarp, M. Velasco Sacristán (2012) *Diccionario Inglés-Español de Contabilidad: Conocimiento*. Database and Design: Richard Almind and Jesper Skovgård Nielsen. Odense: *Lemma.com*.

Fuertes-Olivera, P. A., H. Bergenholtz, S. Nielsen, P. Gordo Gómez, L. Mourier, M. Niño Amo, Á. Ríos Rodicio, Á. Sastre Ruano, S. Tarp and M. Velasco Sacristán (2012) *Diccionario Inglés-Español de Contabilidad: Traducción de Frases y Expresiones*. Database and Design: Richard Almind and Jesper Skovgård Nielsen. Odense: *Lemma.com*.

Fuertes-Olivera, P. A., H. Bergenholtz, S. Nielsen, P. Gordo Gómez, M. Niño Amo, Á. Ríos Rodicio, Á. Sastre Ruano, S. Tarp and M. Velasco Sacristán (2013) *Diccionario Español de Contabilidad: Recepción*. Database and Design: Richard Almind and Jesper Skovgård Nielsen. Hamburg: *Lemma.com*.

Fuertes-Olivera, P. A., H. Bergenholtz, S. Nielsen, P. Gordo Gómez, M. Niño Amo, Á. Ríos Rodicio, Á. Sastre Ruano, S. Tarp and M. Velasco Sacristán (2013) *Diccionario Español de Contabilidad: Producción*. Database and Design: Richard Almind and Jesper Skovgård Nielsen. Hamburg: *Lemma.com*.

Fuertes-Olivera, P. A., H. Bergenholtz, S. Nielsen, P. Gordo Gómez, M. Niño Amo, Á. Ríos Rodicio, Á. Sastre Ruano, S. Tarp and M. Velasco Sacristán (2013) *Diccionario Español de Contabilidad: Encontrar un Término*. Database and Design: Richard Almind and Jesper Skovgård Nielsen. Hamburg: *Lemma.com*.

Fuertes-Olivera, P. A., H. Bergenholtz, S. Nielsen, P. Gordo Gómez, M. Niño Amo, Á. Ríos Rodicio, Á. Sastre Ruano, S. Tarp and M. Velasco Sacristán (2013) *Diccionario Español de Contabilidad. Conocimiento*. Database and Design: Richard Almind and Jesper Skovgård Nielsen. Hamburg: *Lemma.com*.

Fuertes-Olivera, P. A., H. Bergenholtz, S. Nielsen, P. Gordo Gómez, L. Mourier, M. Niño Amo, Á. Ríos Rodicio, Á. Sastre Ruano, S. Tarp and M. Velasco Sacristán (2014) *Diccionario Español-Inglés de Contabilidad: Recepción*. Database and Design: Richard Almind and Jesper Skovgård Nielsen. Hamburg: *Lemma.com*.

Fuertes-Olivera, P. A., H. Bergenholtz, S. Nielsen, P. Gordo Gómez, L. Mourier, M. Niño Amo, Á. Ríos Rodicio, Á. Sastre Ruano, S. Tarp and M. Velasco Sacristán (2014) *Diccionario Español-Inglés de Contabilidad: Traducción*. Database and Design: Richard Almind and Jesper Skovgård Nielsen. Hamburg: *Lemma.com*.

Fuertes-Olivera, P. A., H. Bergenholtz, S. Nielsen, P. Gordo Gómez, L. Mourier, M. Niño Amo, Á. Ríos Rodicio, Á. Sastre Ruano, S. Tarp and M. Velasco Sacristán (2014) *Diccionario Español-Inglés de Contabilidad: Conocimiento*. Database and Design: Richard Almind and Jesper Skovgård Nielsen. Hamburg: *Lemma.com*.

Fuertes-Olivera, P. A., H. Bergenholtz, S. Nielsen, P. Gordo Gómez, L. Mourier, M. Niño Amo, Á. Ríos Rodicio, Á. Sastre Ruano, S. Tarp and M. Velasco Sacristán (2014) *Diccionario Español-Inglés de Contabilidad: Traducción de Frases y Expresiones*. Database and Design: Richard Almind and Jesper Skovgård Nielsen. Hamburg: *Lemma.com*.

Fuertes Olivera, P. A., P. Gordo Gómez, M. N. Amo, A. Ríos Rodicio, A. Sastre Ruano, S. Tarp, M. Velasco Sacristán, S. Nielsen, L. Mourier, H. Bergenholtz (2010) *Diccionario de Contabilidad Inglés-Español*. Navarra: Thomson Reuters-Aranzadi.

Nielsen, S., L. Mourier, and H. Bergenholtz (2004) *Regnskabsordbogen dansk-engelsk*. Copenhagen: Thomson.

Nielsen, S., L. Mourier and H. Bergenholtz (2007) *Regnskabsordbogen engelsk-dansk*. Copenhagen: Thomson.

Nielsen, S., L. Mourier and H. Bergenholtz (2012a) *Den Dansk-Engelske Regnskabsordbog: Oversættelse*. Odense: Ordbogen.com.

Nielsen, S., L. Mourier and H. Bergenholtz (2012b) *Den Dansk-Engelske Regnskabsordbog: Oversættelse af ordforbindelse*. Odense: Ordbogen.com.

Nielsen, S., L. Mourier and H. Bergenholtz (2012c) *Den Danske Regnskabsordbog: Tekstproduktion*. Odense: Ordbogen.com.

Nielsen, S., L. Mourier and H. Bergenholtz (2012d) *Den Danske Regnskabsordbog: Hvad hedder dette regnskabsudtryk?* Odense: Ordbogen.com.

Nielsen, S., L. Mourier and H. Bergenholtz (2012e) *Den Danske Regnskabsordbog: Viden*. Odense: Ordbogen.com.

Nielsen, S., L. Mourier and H. Bergenholtz (2012f) *Den Danske Regnskabsordbog: Betydning*. Odense: Ordbogen.com.

Nielsen, S., L. Mourier and H. Bergenholtz (2012g) *Den Engelsk-Danske Regnskabsordbog: Viden*. Odense: Ordbogen.com.

Nielsen, S., L. Mourier and H. Bergenholtz (2012h) *Den Engelsk-Danske Regnskabsordbog: Betydning*. Odense: Ordbogen.com.

Nielsen, S., L. Mourier and H. Bergenholtz (2012i) *Den Engelsk-Danske Regnskabsordbog: Oversættelse*. Odense: Ordbogen.com.

Nielsen, S., L. Mourier and H. Bergenholtz (2012j) *Den Engelsk-Danske Regnskabsordbog: Oversættelse af ordforbindelser*. Odense: Ordbogen.com.

Nielsen, S., L. Mourier and H. Bergenholtz (2012k) *Den Engelske Regnskabsordbog: Viden*. Odense: Ordbogen.com.

Nielsen, S., L. Mourier and H. Bergenholtz (2012l) *Den Engelske Regnskabsordbog: Tekstproduktion*. Odense: Ordbogen.com.

Nielsen, S., L. Mourier and H. Bergenholtz (2012m) *Den Engelske Regnskabsordbog: Betydning*. Odense: Ordbogen.com.

Nielsen, S., L. Mourier and H. Bergenholtz (2012n) *Den Engelske Regnskabsordbog: Hvad hedder dette regnskabsudtryk?* Odense: Ordbogen.com.

Sánchez, N. (2003) *Accounting Dictionary. Diccionario de Contabilidad: English–Spanish/Spanish–English*. Hoboken, NJ: John Wiley & Sons.

Other literature

Bergenholtz, H. (2011) "Access to and Presentation of Needs-Adapted Data in Monofunctional Dictionaries", in P. A. Fuertes-Olivera and H. Bergenholtz (eds.), pp. 30–53.

Bergenholtz, H. (2012) "Concepts for Monofunctional Accounting Dictionaries", *Terminology* 18 (2): 243–263.

Bergenholtz, H. and S. Tarp (2003) "Two Opposing Theories: On H.E. Wiegand's Recent Discovery of Lexicographic Functions", *Hermes. Journal of Linguistics* 31: 171–196.

Bothma, T.J.D. and S. Tarp (2012) "Lexicography and the Relevance Criterion", *Lexikos* 22: 86–108.

Fuertes-Olivera, P. A. (2011) "Equivalent Selection in Specialized e-Lexicography: A Case Study With Spanish Accounting Terms", *Lexikos* 21: 95–119.

Fuertes-Olivera, P. A. (2012) "Lexicography and the Internet as a (Re-) Source", *Lexicographica* 28(1): 49–70.

Fuertes-Olivera, P. A. (2016) "A Cambrian Explosion in Lexicography: Some Reflections for Designing and Constructing Specialised Online Dictionaries", *International Journal of Lexicography* 29(2): 226–247.

Fuertes-Olivera, P. A. and H. Bergenholtz (eds.) (2011) *e-Lexicography: The Internet, Digital Initiatives and Lexicography*. London: Continuum.

Fuertes-Olivera, P. A. and S. Nielsen (2011) "The Dynamics of Terms in Accounting: What the Construction of the *Accounting Dictionaries* Reveals About Metaphorical Terms in Culture-Bound Subject Fields", *Terminology* 17(1): 157–180.

Fuertes-Olivera, P. A. and P. Leroyer (2014) "User-generated Exploratory Search Routes: ECONTRAR UN TÉRMINO in the *Accounting Dictionaries*", in J. Ruppenhoffer and G. Faaß (eds.), *Proceedings of the 12th Edition of the Konvens Conference*. Hildesheim: University of Hildesheim, pp. 86–95.

Fuertes-Olivera, P. A. and S. Tarp (2014) *Theory and Practice of Specialised Online Dictionaries: Lexicography Versus Terminography*. Berlin, Boston: Walter de Gruyter.

Nielsen, S. and R. Almind (2011) "From Data to Dictionary", in P. A. Fuertes-Olivera and H. Bergenholtz (eds.), pp. 141–167.

Nielsen, S. and P.A. Fuertes-Olivera (2013) "Development in Lexicography: From Polyfunctional to Monofunctional Accounting Dictionaries", Lexikos 23: 323–347.

Tarp, S. (2008) *Lexicography in the Borderland Between Knowledge and Non-Knowledge*. Tübingen: Niemeyer.

Tarp, S. and P. A. Fuertes-Olivera (2016) "Advantages and Disadvantages in the Use of Internet as a Corpus: The Case of the Online Dictionaries of Spanish Valladolid-UVa", *Lexikos* 26: 273–295.

29
Wordnik

Erin McKean

29.1 Introduction

Wordnik is an online-only dictionary of English, whose mission is to collect and share all the words of English. Instead of employing a staff of lexicographers and editors, or a organizing a community of wiki-style contributors to create definitions, *Wordnik* uses data-mining and machine-learning techniques to find example sentences that serve as brief explanations of a word's meaning in context, as shown in example (1), a sentence example explaining the meaning of *pretotype*:

(1)
A pretotype is a partially mocked-up of the intended product or service that can be built in minutes, hours or days instead of weeks, months or years.

In addition to these defining examples (sometimes called 'free-range definitions' or FRDs) and other example sentences showing usage, *Wordnik* includes traditional dictionary definitions from *The Century Dictionary*, *The American Heritage Dictionary of the English Language*, *The GNU International Dictionary of English*, *Wordnet*, and (English) *Wiktionary*. Other sections of each word page include related terms (synonyms, antonyms, rhymes, etc., as well as words that have similar distributional patterns and words whose dictionary definitions include the word being looked up); Creative Commons–licensed images sourced from Flickr; recent tweets including the word; audio pronunciations from *American Heritage* and *Macmillan Dictionaries*, as well as some sourced from users; and comments and tags submitted by users.

In addition to lexical information, *Wordnik* includes nearly 50,000 user-created word lists.

Wordnik also makes available an API (application programming interface) to more than 20,000 registered developers. This API provides dictionary definitions, example sentences, related words, and limited corpus information to users to embed in their own software and services.

The *Wordnik* website is free and ad-supported, although logged-in users do not see advertising. The *Wordnik* API is free for limited use, with developers who need higher call limits, batch data calls, or support paying fees for their use. *Wordnik* is a nonprofit corporation registered in Delaware and has filed for public charity status.

Wordnik's stated mission is to collect all the words of English and share them with everyone, everywhere.

29.2 Historical perspective

The seed for *Wordnik* was planted at the 2007 TED[1] conference in Monterey, California, where founder Erin McKean discussed the limitations of print dictionaries.[2] McKean saw a mismatch between the kinds of words typically included in print dictionaries and the kinds of words sought out by educated monolingual English speakers. Print dictionaries tend to exclude words that are very rare, very new, or very restricted in their range of use, and those are typically the words that are most likely to drive users to the dictionary in search of meanings (Müller-Spitzer, Wolfer and Koplenig 2015).

At that conference McKean was introduced to venture capitalist Roger McNamee, who encouraged McKean to think about starting a new dictionary project with his backing. Discussions continued for nearly a year, with *Wordnik* incorporating as a venture-backed startup in February 2008. McKean asked Grant Barrett and Orion Montoya to join her as co-founders, and they quickly hired a small technical team to create an alpha project (i.e. the underlying concepts of the online dictionary envisaged).

The alpha project's goal was to test the hypothesis that there were many unique wordforms in English that were not included in standard dictionaries. The team assembled headword lists from standard dictionaries of American English as a baseline, and then gathered a corpus to analyze, largely from Project Gutenberg texts. Development work began in March, and by September the team had a functioning website that had example sentences for more than 4 million unique English wordforms.

Simultaneously, the team was preparing a fully digitized and XML-tagged version of the out-of-copyright *Century Dictionary* (1914), which had previously only been available as scanned pages. The text was keyboarded and tagged in India, at a cost of over US$100,000. Other digital dictionaries were obtained and converted to a common tagset. Francis March's *Thesaurus Dictionary* was also digitized and tagged.

After the internal launch of the alpha, a closed beta, that is, a version of the site with full working versions of features, but made available only to a few users, was made available to a small group of testers and users, and the team worked to incorporate feedback. Although the original plan was to prioritize FRDs over traditional dictionary definitions in the design and layout of the word pages, feedback from the early users made it clear that they were not quite ready for that radical a change from printed dictionaries.

On the strength of the alpha, the team began fundraising to further development, raising more capital and adding several new investors to the board. The interim technical team lead, Stan James, was replaced by Tony Tam as VP of Engineering, and the bulk of the team relocated from Chicago and New York to the San Francisco Bay Area in early 2009.

The beta version was made publicly available in June of 2009. That fall, *Wordnik* acquired *Wordie*, a similar site run by John McGrath, and McGrath joined the *Wordnik* team. The *Wordie* site focused on wordlist creation and user commentary, which balanced out the data-heavy focus of *Wordnik*. The majority of the active *Wordie* user base transferred their activity to the new combined site, and McGrath took over as lead developer for the front end.

For most of 2009 and 2010, the team focused on acquiring more text from more sources (Mary Mark Ockerbloom was hired to be the corpus librarian identifying good texts and helping to maintain balance in the corpus). The team wrote custom adapters for many publications' RSS feeds, and agreements were made with Dow Jones and the Internet Archive, among others, to ingest text directly. By January of 2011, the corpus measured 12 billion words, with 11 million unique wordforms.

December of 2010 also saw *Wordnik* launch its public API, and a month later the API was seeing more than 100,000 calls per day.

Simultaneously, *Wordnik* partnered with Andrews McMeel to produce four small word books derived from *Wordnik* data.

Concurrently *Wordnik* was exploring several different business models. The site was ad-free and registration was free; API use was also free. The investors advised focusing on creating services for large corporations, so pilots were created to provide glossary services for a large online financial publisher, as well as dictionary definition plug-ins for search engines. New management joined the team and launched several other pilot programs, including topical recommendations for a large microblogging site.

In early 2012 the company launched a WordPress plugin to provide related content for blog posts, leveraging the NLP expertise of the Wordnik team and the Wordnik corpus data (see Chapters 8, 12, 13, 41, and 42 of this *Handbook*). By the end of 2012 *Wordnik* renamed the corporation as Reverb, and focused on creating an iOS newsreader[3] (also called Reverb) to provide relevant articles around topics, which was launched in 2013.

The *Wordnik* dictionary site and API service remained largely static for most of 2012 as the company sought new avenues of business. In mid-2013 the site was migrated to use a new front-end framework (Node/Express.js), and the functionality was simplified.

By early 2014 it was clear that the *Wordnik* site and API would never generate a venture-style return, and discussions were begun with the investors about how to support the project on an ongoing basis. Erin McKean suggested spinning off the *Wordnik* site and API to a new nonprofit entity, and the investors agreed. The new entity was incorporated in October 2014, with McKean taking over as the sole employee of the new corporation.

On January 1, 2015, *Wordnik* had launched its first public support program, Adopt a Word. By making a small donation (US$50 at first, and then US$25) a supporter could adopt a word on the *Wordnik* site, attaching their name and link in a prominent box on the word's page. The adoption also entitled the adopter to an adoption certificate and a set of *Wordnik* stickers. By early 2017, nearly 1000 words had been adopted.

In 2015, *Wordnik* also launched a Kickstarter[4] to update the identification and extraction pipeline for finding new words and new FRDs. It raised more than US$50,000 for the project. The new pipeline was completed summer of 2016, but compatibility issues with the *Wordnik* website have delayed display of the new examples and full integration, which is planned to launch by summer of 2017.

29.3 Core issues and topics

As the editor explains in the introduction to this *Handbook*, innovation is typically viewed as the application of better solutions to those traditionally considered and used. The creation of *Wordnik* responds to this idea as illustrated in Sections 29.1 and 29.2. In both sections I have indicated that the idea underlying the compilation of *Wordnik* did not result from applying standard lexicographic practices, for example, by compiling a corpus and extracting frequent patterns nor by making use of findings from user studies

(Atkins and Rundell 2008). Instead, the creation of *Wordnik* was based on the assumption that existing dictionaries tend to leave out of their word lists the terms that most users are especially interested in. In addition, *Wordnik* made use of state-of-the-art technologies (e.g. machine learning) for making dictionary content cheaper in terms of money spent and human resources used. These ideas, as well as the business model initially developed and then modified, are manifestations of the importance of innovation in lexicography. Innovation does not fall from trees, but it is intimately connected with adopting a theoretical basis (see Section 29.3.1), making use of specific technical details (Section 29.3.2), methodologies (Section 29.3.3), and support (Section 29.3.4), especially those connected with collaborative work in the era of the Internet (see Chapters 33, 42, 43, and 45 of this *Handbook*).

29.3.1 Theoretical basis

The idea that a word's meaning can be revealed by presenting it in sufficient context is by no means original to *Wordnik*, but is a tenet of modern English lexicography (Atkins and Rundell 2008) and many more lexicographic traditions (Fuertes-Olivera and Tarp 2014; see Part 5 of this *Handbook*).

Early dictionaries were often bereft of examples or context, consisting of little more than glosses. For instance, the definitions in Cawdrey's *A Table Alphabeticall* (1604) are mostly short lists of near-synonyms (example 2):

(2)

ABLUTION, a Purging or Wathing.
ABSORBENT, drinking or sucking up.
TO ABSTAIN, to keep from or forbear.
ABSTRUSE, obscure, dark, hard to be understood.

Later dictionaries began including, and even featuring, examples. Samuel Johnson admitted in the preface to his *Dictionary of the English Language* (1755) that "The solution of all difficulties, and the supply of all defects, must be sought in the examples," and Dean Trench, in his call-to-arms to the Philological Society (1860),[5] declared that the quotations selected by the lexicographer should "yield as much information as they can be made to yield."

Although examples were the foundation that supported the definitions constructed by the lexicographer, they were decidedly secondary to those definitions. Zgusta (1971:265) footnotes that "even if a quotation has the form of a definition, the lexicographer should try to extract his own form of it."

And the definitions 'extracted' by the lexicographer were very different in style from the citations ranged alongside them. As examples became more representative of present-day English (even, in some cases, controversially so, as with the inclusion of examples by the famous madam Polly Adler in Merriam-Webster's third *New International Dictionary*), the definitions became less so.

Patrick Hanks (1987:119–121) has an excellent exposition of how the literary construction we now call a dictionary definition came to be. Writing in *Looking Up: An Account of the COBUILD Project in Lexical Computing*, he blames (and it should be blamed) the mathematical philosophers for their focus on substitutability – the idea that a definition should be able to stand in the place of the word being defined – and for the notion that a definition should be a set of necessary and sufficient conditions for identifying "all and only all the objects or events correctly referred to by the word or expression under discussion." These logical prejudices had linguistic consequences, in that the format and conventions of dictionary definitions became further and further removed from the natural ways that words were defined by laypeople.

These 'natural' definitions (sometimes called 'folk definitions') were relegated to children's dictionaries, as example (3) shows:

(3)
drill A drill is a tool or machine for making holes
Example 3. Definition of **drill** in *My First Picture Dictionary*

In 1987, however, COBUILD (the *Collins COBUILD English Language Dictionary*) introduced a full-sentence defining style for adults (albeit adult learners of English). A typical COBUILD full-sentence definition uses the second person, and tries to give some indication of the usualness of an action, for example, by using 'if" instead of 'when' to indicate that a particular action is not an activity undertaken by everyone (example 4):

(4)
slim
If you are **slimming**, you are trying to make yourself thinner and lighter by eating less food
Example 4. Definition of **slim** in The *Collins COBUILD Dictionary*

Some lexicographers have criticized this style: Henri Béjoint (1994:72) said some of the new definitions were "long, inelegant, and sometimes even ambiguous." Michael Rundell (2006) also points out that full-sentence definitions tend to be long, and, further, that long sentences can lead to problems of comprehension, anaphora resolution, and (in traditional print dictionaries) fewer headwords being defined.

Although studies are inconclusive as to whether performance of linguistic tasks is better with full-sentence definitions, users of dictionaries have been found to prefer the full-sentence style (Tickoo 1989, Cumming et al 1994, Dziemianko 2006). Fuertes-Olivera and Arribas-Baño (2008: 47–70), for example, have analyzed meaning items in Business dictionaries (see Chapter 4 of this Handbook), some of which use 'definitions' whereas some others prefer 'examples' or 'equivalents' for explaining the meaning of the lemma. Their study allows them to conclude that existing definition typologies are not very relevant and that new dictionaries tend to rest more on sentence definitions than on other definition types. Following this view, *Wordnik* has adopted the practice of resting on full-sentence definitions assuming that there are tens of thousands of full-sentence definitions that exist naturally in the world, and that it is now both practical and economical to find them.

29.3.2 Technical details

The *Wordnik* site is powered by the Wordnik API, which draws data from several large MongoDB databases. User account data is stored in a separate MySQL database. The current site is written in Node.js, using the Express framework, and the current API is Java and Scala, although it is being transitioned to Node. The website and API servers are hosted on Amazon Web Services; the MongoDB instances are managed by mLab. Other third-party services used by *Wordnik* include Loggly, MailChimp, Sendgrid, and StatusPage. The source code for the site is hosted at Github.

The sentence extraction is done using a series of AWS Lambda functions. That code has been open-sourced under the MIT License[6] and is available at https://github.com/wordnik/serapis.

"Missing" words (words looked up but that do not have traditional dictionary definitions) are saved in an Amazon S3 bucket. This triggers a lambda function to call the Bing API to retrieve web pages that include the missing word. The resulting document is parsed to find all the sentences that include the missing word, and those sentences are rated according to how likely they are to be definitional. (Using a model trained on previously discovered FRDs.) The newly extracted and rated sentences are then stored as JSON documents in Amazon S3 and loaded into Elasticsearch. The new API for retrieving example sentences will be backed by Elasticsearch.

Wordnik expects to make more use of 'serverless' Lambda functions in the future to reduce operational overhead and more closely tie operations costs with usage.

29.3.3 Collaborative lexicography in action

Wordnik's lexicographic methodology is an example of collaborative lexicography, which is often presented as a new paradigm for compiling lexicons (Fuertes-Olivera 2009; Meyer and Gurevych 2012) (see also Chapters 33, 35, and 45 of this *Handbook*). This paradigm is a bottom-up approach, which "encourages lexicon readers to contribute to the writing of lexicon entries" (Meyer and Gurevych 2012: 259). *Wordnik* has a small but active community of users who participate in adding data to the site. Most of the active users maintain one or more word lists, usually on specific themes, such as the following:

- "5 letter animals": a list of words for animals that are five letters long;
- "There's No Place Like Nowhere": a list of terms for remote places, including 'East Jesus' and 'boonies';
- "Collectively": a list of words whose definitions include the word 'collectively'.

In addition, there are tens of thousands of users' lists, and several users have manually created lists that are thousands of words long. Several very active users maintain lists of new words they have discovered, beginning a new list each year. These lists are frequently mined and referenced during the annual American Dialect Society "Word of the Year" meeting and vote.

Wordnik allows users to do more than adding new words. It also allows them to code automatic programs that add words to lists, which have resulted in lists containing tens of thousands of words. These lists tend to search social media for phrases such as "I love the word X" or "I hate the word X" adding the target word to the list. The site currently does not have an efficient mechanism for searching or sorting lists, although creating one is on the roadmap.

Wordnik allows comments to be left on words, and these comments tend to fall into a few different categories. The most helpful comments are those that provide citations (with links); others often propose definitions (this is very common when the commenter has coined the word being commented upon). Occasionally, a user will leave a comment asking for clarification of a word's meaning, range of use, or pronunciation; more rarely a user will leave a comment complaining that the word they have looked up has no useful data, or criticizing the examples provided. For instance, one user (username 'qms') has commented on each day's 'word of the day' with an original limerick, going back several years.

Wordnik also allows for users to leave tags on words, although this feature is underutilized. Some of the more popular tags include 'neologism', 'misspelling', and 'onomatopoeia'. One user has been tagging words with their consonant-vowel pattern (e.g. 'spoon' is tagged 'ccvvc').

Earlier in the life of the site users were able to record their own audio pronunciations for words. This was not a high-traffic feature and it was discontinued in 2013.

29.3.4 Community behaviour and support and public response

Wordnik also allows researchers to rate its social impact. Until now, online questionnaries, eye tracking and log files have been mostly used to rate users' responses to a particular dictionary (see Chapter 44 of this *Handbook*). *Wordnik* was an early adopter of social media, and maintains an active social media presence, with more than 20,000 Twitter followers and nearly 9,000 Facebook 'likes'. A word-of-the-day email goes out to more than 6,000 recipients, and *Wordnik* also produces a monthly email for a small group of word-game enthusiasts.

The primary way that users can support *Wordnik* is through adopting a word. Users can also show their support by purchasing Wordnik-branded merchandise through the Threadless website.[7] It also offer patrons the ability to sponsor an entire letter of the alphabet. For instance, every word in the letter 'S' was sponsored by Ruth Ann Harnisch in 2015–2016.

A core group of volunteers receives weekly emails detailing *Wordnik*'s progress and provides suggestions and help on both an organizational and technical level.

Public response to *Wordnik* has been largely positive. Despite not being advertised as an educational resource (and explicitly stating that *Wordnik* is not intended for children under 13), many teachers use *Wordnik* in the classroom, and several educational technology companies (notably Magoosh) use *Wordnik*'s APIs to power their own tools and resources.

Professional namers are also a significant part of *Wordnik*'s most active users, and to recognize this, *Wordnik* produced a series of blog posts interviewing professional namers.[8]

Wordnik has been favorably mentioned in mainstream publications such as *The Economist*[9] and the *New York Times*[10] as well as web mainstays such as BoingBoing[11] and MetaFilter.[12]

In sum, users not only add words with their definitions but also include different types of lexicographic tags, something that traditionally conceived dictionaries hesitate to implement, as these are typically based on a top-down methodology which rests on the concept of 'authority', that is, someone's opinion on language issues must be taken for granted (see Chapters 10, 11, and 32 of this *Handbook*). And last but not least, *Wordnik* is making use of current social networks for expanding its social presence and revenues. Hence, it clearly offers a new approach for copying with the disruption suffered by dictionary editors and publishing houses, whose typical business models are no longer viable.

29.4 Looking to the future

Because of *Wordnik*'s limited staff and resources, our primary goal is simply to continue to exist. Given the extremely long timespan to completion of dictionaries produced by traditional dictionary publishers, the lack of attractive for-profit business models in the space discouraging competitors, and the scope of the problem (every English word!) we believe that it may take decades to fully exploit the potential of *Wordnik*.

In the short(er) term, our goals fall into three buckets: technical, content, and community:

- Technical
  - In order to keep the website functioning and add more paid customers to our API, significant API updates are in the works.
  - To help keep the site running as long as possible, we are re-engineering and re-architecting our server setup to be more cost-effective.
  - We also plan to update the design of the *Wordnik* website to be more mobile friendly and to continue to make security and speed improvements.

    We are also planning to make lists more searchable and discoverable and to add subscription functionality so that users can be notified when lists are expanded or changed.
- Content
  - As part of our API update we are adding new data sources to the API, including the fifth edition of the *American Heritage Dictionary of the English Language* and two American Heritage dictionaries for schoolchildren. We are working on new parses of *WordNet* and (English) *Wiktionary*; we are also planning an expansion of our thesaurus content.
- Community
  - Although we don't believe the wiki model is the most useful for communicating word meanings, we do think that *Wordnik* could create more opportunity for user contributions on the site, including upvoting and downvoting of example sentences, more metadata on user comments (e.g. marking a comment as a usage comment), and user flagging of problematic terms (vulgar, offensive, slurs) and typographical errors, among other contributions.

The biggest challenge ahead for *Wordnik* – aside from the existential one of keeping the servers running – is to add curatorial and editorial tools on top of the pure data-mining, in order to help verify and vet the information being presented to users. *Wordnik* has never considered editors superfluous, just unscaleable. As the amount of data available to scan and process increase, a tricky balance must be struck between comprehensiveness of results and confidence in their appropriateness. Luckily, new advances in machine learning makes it easier to create simple models that take into account features such as site of origin, surrounding text, traffic patterns, and user engagement in order to provide the linguistic counterpart to a 'confidence metric' in definitional sentences.

The problem that *Wordnik* was created to solve – filling the gap between the creation of a word and its inclusion in a traditional dictionary – shows no signs of going away, or even abating. Although traditional publishers have opened up their sites to community input, for example, Merriam's Open Dictionary[13] or Macmillan's identically named site,[14] these efforts have not addressed the scale of the problem of under-described English words. For instance, Macmillan's Open Dictionary has had 4,000 words added since 2009; Merriam does not publish the number of words added via their site.

29.5 Conclusion

Wordnik is innovative for several reasons, some of which have been analysed in this chapter and are summarized here:

- *Wordnik* uses existing lexicographic data for creating its traditional dictionary articles. These data are either copyright-free or acquired by *Wordnik*.

- *Wordnik* was initially a commercially oriented lexicographic project. Since then, it has adapted its business model to market conditions and innovations. It was initially financed by seed capital but is now under the aegis of a non-profit organization and raises operational funds from advertisements, individuals, and institutions whose contributions come in many forms and sizes. For instance, some users adopt a word and pay some money in exchange for having their names posted on their word's main page.
- *Wordnik* defends the necessity of having a lexicographic theory underlying the conception of any dictionary. In particular, *Wordnik* was created on the basis of two related hypotheses: (a) *Wordnik* must collect and share all the words of English, especially as it was assumed at the inception of the project that most existing dictionaries did not describe the words people tended to look up; and (b) *Wordnik* must describe each meaning of each English word in context.
- *Wordnik* augments the traditional lexicographic data available, especially online lexicographic data without copyright restrictions, with new, more accessible data extracted by using data-mining and machine-learning techniques. In other words, *Wordnik* uses innovations and technologies, from many fields, which clearly demonstrates the intimate relationship of lexicography to fields such as natural language processing, information science, corpus linguistics, and the like (see Part 2 of this *Handbook*). This is very important as we do not expect that the speakers of English around the world will ever become less inventive (or, in the case of borrowings from other languages, less acquisitive) and that *Wordnik*'s goal of including data for every word of English will remain always just out of reach.
- *Wordnik* is in the forefront of technological developments. Its different technical systems typically run on open source software. In addition, it offers data extracted from social networks, thus illustrating trends, tendencies, likes, and dislikes.
- *Wordnik* illustrates the role collaborative lexicography is already playing. It is a working project that shows how lexicographic projects can advance thanks to users' contributions, both lexicographically and financially.

Related topics

Lexicography and corpus linguistics; electronic dictionaries; English lexicography in the Internet era; lexicography and natural language processing; user participation in the Internet era; using the Web for lexicographic purposes.

Further reading

De Nart, D. and D. Tasso (2013). "A Keyphrase Generation Technique Based upon Keyphrase Extraction and Reasoning on Loosely Structured Ontologies", *Proceedings of the CEUR Workshop* 1109: 49–60.

Wordnik, as well as *Wikipedia* and the *Urban Dictionary*, are used for developing Information Retrieval and Personalization systems.

Fuertes-Olivera, P. A. (2016). "A Cambrian Explosion in Lexicography: Some Reflections for Designing and Constructing Specialised Online Dictionaries", *International Journal of Lexicography* 29(2): 226–247.

This article explains the design and construction of online dictionaries with a focus on different Internet technologies and working methodologies.

Granger, S. and M. Paquot (eds.) (2012). *Electronic Lexicography*. Oxford: Oxford University Press. This edited volume contains some chapters on the topic of English lexicography in the Internet era.

Merz, E. X. (2013). "Composing with All Sound Using the Freesound and Wordnik APIs". 9th Conference on "Artificial Intelligence and Interactive Digital Entertainment" Volume WS-13–22, pages 83–90.
This conference paper shows the use of the Wordnik API for creating algorithmic art. In other words, it shows potential uses of lexicographic data that have not been considered lexicographically relevant so far.

Van Dijk, J.A.G.M. and A.J.A.M. Van Deursen (2014). *Digital Skills: Unlocking the Information Society*. New York: Palgrave Macmillan.
This is an excellent overview of the digital skills that are required for navigating the Internet successfully, aimed at both researchers and practitioners.

Notes

1 TED stands for Technology, Entertainment, Design. It is a "non-profit organization which posts talks online for free distribution, under the slogan 'ideas worth sharing.' TED was founded in February as a conference, which has been held annually since 1990." (Wikipedia)
2 See at www.ted.com/talks/erin_mckean_redefines_the_dictionary
3 iOS newsreader is a RSS Feed Reader for Apple systems, i.e. an aggregator of web content such as newspaper articles, blogs and Tweets.
4 Kickstarter is an American public-benefit corporation that supports crowdfunding. Its stated mission is to help bring creative projects to life.
5 This paper was originally presented to the Philological Society in November 1857. The 1860 edition also contains Herbert Coleridge's response to Trench's critiques.
6 See at https://opensource.org/licenses/MIT
7 See at https://wordnik.threadless.com
8 See at http://blog.wordnik.com/category/naming
9 See at www.economist.com/blogs/johnson/2010/07/word_lists
10 See at www.nytimes.com/2015/10/04/technology/scouring-the-web-to-make-new-words-lookupable.html
11 See at https://boingboing.net/2015/09/19/kickstarting-1000000-new-ent.html
12 See at www.metafilter.com/82656/Not-just-another-dictionary
13 See http://nws.merriam-webster.com/opendictionary/
14 www.macmillandictionary.com/open-dictionary/

References

Dictionaries

English Wiktionary. https://en.wiktionary.org/wiki/English
Johnson, S. (1755) *A Dictionary of the English Language*. London: Consortium.
Macmillan Dictionary. www.macmillandictionary.com/open-dictionary/
My First Picture Dictionary. (2000) Scott Foresman & Co.
Sinclair, J. (ed.) (1987) *Collins COBUILD English Language Dictionary*. London Macmillan Dictionary. www.macmillandictionary.com/open-dictionary/&Glasgow: Collins ELT.
The American Heritage Dictionary of the English Language. https://ahdictionary.com
The Century Online Dictionary. www.global-language.com/CENTURY/
The *GNU Collaborative International Dictionary of English*. http://gcide.gnu.org.ua
Wordnik. www.wordnik.com
WordNet. https://wordnet.princeton.edu

Other Literature

Atkins, B.T.S. and M. Rundell (2008) *The Oxford Guide to Practical Lexicography*. Oxford: Oxford University Press.

Béjoint, H. (1994) *Modern Lexicography: An Introduction*. Oxford: Oxford University Press.

Cumming, G., S. Cropp and R. Sussex (1994) "On-Line Lexical Resources for Language Learners: Assessment of Some Approaches to Word Definition", *System* 22/3: 369–77.

Dziemianko, A. (2006) "A New Type of Folk-Inspired Definition in English Monolingual Learners' Dictionaries and Its Usefulness for Conveying Syntactic Information", *International Journal of Lexicography* 19(3): 225–242.

Fuertes-Olivera, P. A. (2009) "The Function Theory of Lexicography and Electronic Dictionaries: WIKTIONARY as a Prototype of Collective Multiple-Language Internet Dictionary", in H. Bergenholtz, S. Nielsen and S. Tarp (eds.), *Lexicography at a Crossroads: Dictionaries and Encyclopedias Today, Lexicographical Tools Tomorrow*. Bern: Peter Lang, pp. 99–134.

Fuertes-Olivera, P. A. and A. Arribas-Baño (2008) *Pedagogical Specialised Lexicography: The Representation of Meaning in Business and Spanish Business Dictionaries*. Amsterdam/Philadelphia: John Benjamins.

Fuertes-Olivera, P. A. and S. Tarp (2014) *Theory and Practice of Specialised Online Dictionaries: Lexicography Versus Terminography*. Berlin and Boston: De Gruyter.

Hanks, P. (1987) "Definitions and Explanations", in J. M. Sinclair (ed.), *Looking Up: An Account of the COBUILD Project in Lexical Computing*. London and Glasgow: Collins ELT.

Meyer, C. M. and I. Gurevych (2012) "Wiktionary: 'A New Rival for Expert-Built Lexicons? Exploring the Possibilities of Collaborative Lexicography", in S. Granger and M. Paquot (eds.) *Electronic Lexicography*. Oxford: Oxford University Press, pp. 259–291.

Müller-Spitzer, C., S. Wolfer, and A. Koplenig (2015) "Observing Online Dictionary Users: Studies Using Wiktionary Log Files", *International Journal of Lexicography* 28(1): 1–26.

Rundell, M. (2006) "More Than One Way to Skin a Cat: Why Full-Sentence Definitions Have Not Been Universally Adopted", in E. Corino, C. Marello and C. Onesti (eds.), *Proceedings of the 12th EURALEX International Congress*. Edizioni dell'Orso, pp. 323–337.

Tickoo, M. L. (ed.) (1989) *Learners' Dictionaries: State of the Art*. Singapore: SEAMEO Regional Language Centre.

Trench, R. C. (1860) *On Some Deficiencies in Our English Dictionaries*. London: John W. Parker and Son.

Zgusta, L. (1971) *Manual of Lexicography*. Berlin: Walter de Gruyter.

Part V

World languages, lexicography and the Internet

30

African lexicography in the Internet era

Danie Prinsloo, Jacobus Prinsloo and Daniel Prinsloo

30.1 Introduction

It is frequently echoed in the literature that the era of the Internet as far as electronic dictionaries are concerned was met with great enthusiasm. The Internet was expected to revolutionise dictionary compilation in the electronic age. To date this has not occurred yet. Many lexicographers express disappointment in respect to the pace of development of electronic dictionaries and non utilization or under utilization of innovative technology. In reality, they are voicing their concern because electronic dictionaries tend only to be old paper dictionaries 'on computer'.

A prominent expectation for the Bantu language family, which represent a large portion of African languages, was that the electronic dictionary should solve lexicographic problems pertaining to lemma identification for conjunctively written languages which cannot be solved in paper dictionaries. Due to the sub-classification of nouns into different classes, a complex concordial and pronominal system exist in these languages which is problematic to the learner for text production purposes.

The aim of this chapter is to reflect on the current state of the art in online African language dictionaries. It will be shown that a wide spectrum of achievement exists ranging from mere word lists with or without translations, very small dictionaries with limited treatment, technically fully functional dictionaries but with empty alphabetical stretches, to dictionaries of high lexicographic achievement employing innovative electronic technology. Specific attention will be given to the *presentation* of the data in online dictionaries for these languages.

This chapter is written against the background of African languages being lesser resourced languages.

The lack of a strong dictionary culture and human languages technologies contribute to the problems. The aim of this chapter is not to attempt a comprehensive overview of African language dictionaries or an attempt to calculate the number of such dictionaries, for example, as done by De Schryver (2003), but rather to reflect on the quality of current online dictionaries for the African languages.

30.2 Historical perspectives

The Internet was expected to revolutionise dictionary compilation in the electronic age. However, the first miscalculation was in terms of time. Meijs (1992: 152, as reported by Nesi 1999: 65) predicts "the imminent demise of the dictionary as a book . . . in a decade or so, online dictionaries on disk or CD-ROM will no doubt be the norm rather than the exception".

Compilers and publishers also did not realise that it was an entirely new concept requiring new designs. Atkins (1996: 515–516) states:

> dictionaries of the present . . . may even come to you on a CD-ROM rather than in book form, but underneath these superficial modernizations lurks the same old dictionary. . . . It is up to us to take up the real challenge of the computer age, by asking not how the computer can help us to produce old-style dictionaries better, but how it can help us to create something new.

Bolinger (1990: 144) says that hard-copy dictionaries have reached their capacity and that "any really dramatic advance would burst the covers".

Gouws (1990:55) says that the majority of African language dictionaries are the products of limited efforts not reflecting a high standard of lexicographical achievement. The magnitude of the new era was underestimated and financial factors play a major role, i.e. it was very expensive to build new dictionaries from scratch. Theoretical lexicographers also point out that adaptation of lexicographic theory is required for e-dictionaries. Bothma et al. (2016) argue in favour of an extended theory of lexicography for the fast-growing e-lexicography practice that should still be rooted in the three fundamental phases of lexicographic theory, that is, linguistic contents, dictionary structures, and functions with the user in focus. It should incorporate innovative technological features of the computer era.

Different stages in the development of Internet dictionaries could be distinguished. First, for many languages of the world paper dictionaries were compiled which could be described as of low lexicographic achievement. Then a stage was reached where paper dictionaries reached a level of real lexicographic achievement, cf. for example the so-called "big five" dictionaries by Macmillan, Longman, Cambridge, Collins, and Oxford where so much useful information were crammed into the dictionary that the risk was real that they would burst their covers or the pages becoming so thin that the user would virtually also read the reverse side of a page when consulting a dictionary (see Chapters 19 and 22 of this *Handbook*). At the dawning of the Internet era dictionaries also tried to get the best of both worlds by putting a CD ROM dictionary in the back pocket of the dictionary (e.g. Macmillan, Oxford, etc.). This was followed by an era characterised by efforts to put dictionaries online, that is, merely presenting the content of the paper dictionary online, sugar-coated by additional search functions and, for example, clickable icons for pronunciation guidance. Until recently publishers were hesitant to make the quantum leap from paper dictionaries to online dictionaries. Macmillan announced this leap in 2012:

> From next year, Macmillan Education's range of monolingual dictionaries for English learners will no longer appear as physical books, and will only be available online. . . . editor-in-chief Michael Rundell now believes the online medium is 'ideal' for dictionaries.
>
> 'The traditional book format is very limiting for any kind of reference work,' he said. 'Books are out of date as soon as they're printed, and the space constraints they impose

> often compromise our goals of clarity and completeness. There is so much more we can do for our users in digital media.[1]

For Internet dictionaries for the African languages the requirements for online dictionaries of high lexicographic achievement were no different, in fact there are specific additional challenges where the paper dictionary failed to satisfy the lexicographic needs of the users. A good example in this regard is problematic lemma identification, which could be resolved in the electronic dictionary and will be discussed in more detail later. For African languages, however, the development from paper dictionary to Internet dictionary was more traumatic because the Internet era dawned on the African languages at a time when the compilation of paper dictionaries of high lexicographic standards had not been achieved. Prinsloo (2015) sketches a rather grim picture for electronic dictionary development, arguing that the challenges to Internet dictionaries for these languages grow faster than the success rate of quality enhancement. In simple terms this means that the same pressure, that is, to produce electronic dictionaries, came at a time when most dictionaries for African languages did not even achieve the level of being sophisticated paper dictionaries, compared to the 'big five' for example.

30.3 Core issues and topics

When conducting a survey of online dictionaries for African languages, certain observations are prominent. Such online dictionaries are often described as a work in progress inviting user feedback and even user participation in the compilation of the dictionary, typically stated as 'help us to build this dictionary', crowdsourcing, feedback, etc. It is also apparent that treatment of the lemma is often limited to what is merely mechanically extracted from the database without any intelligent human intervention. In many cases the initiative, compilers and funding come from outside the African continent. The dictionaries often try to be more than a dictionary which leads to less quality attention to the dictionary itself.

30.3.1 African languages and lesser resourced languages

Languages can be regarded as lesser resourced on the basis of a combination of criteria. For many of these languages the number of speakers are limited, politically oppressed or marginalised, spoken by under-developed communities, and lacking a standardised orthography, financial resources, text and speech corpora, an established dictionary culture, etc. What is required in terms of Gouws and Prinsloo (2005) is improvement of the quality of dictionaries on the one hand and a dictionary culture and dictionary using skills on the other.

Atkins (1998:3) after having studied the South African situation, remarks as follows:

> the speakers of African languages have not in their formative years had access to dictionaries of the richness and complexity of those currently available for European languages. They have not had the chance to internalize the structure and objectives of a good dictionary, monolingual, bilingual or trilingual.

30.3.2 Quantity of online African language dictionaries

There seems to be an urge to go for quantity of languages covered rather than quality or comprehensiveness. Similarly, *Dicts.info* also lists a large number of clickable dictionaries, many of which are also of less resourced languages.[2]

More than a decade ago De Schryver (2003:2) found that there were already nearly 200 Internet dictionaries for nearly 120 different African languages. Most of them are very poor lexicographically. They are often mere word lists with basic translation(s) of each lemma and, in such cases, basic grammar information attached to the lemma. They do not answer the expectation of being dictionaries with true electronic features, appealing and effective screen presentation, and the ultimate: online dictionaries solving lexicographic problems that could not be satisfactorily solved in the paper dictionary.

30.3.3 Online dictionaries that are merely scanned images of paper dictionary pages

A number of African language dictionaries are available online in the form of scanned pages of the dictionary. It is not possible to search for words. It boils down to paging through the dictionary on screen as one would page through the paper dictionary. Examples in this regard include the *Wolof Dictionary* by Sierra Dem, Peace Corps, 1995 in PDF format which contains 76 pages.[3]

30.3.4 Electronic dictionaries identical to the paper dictionary

These dictionaries are also merely paper dictionaries but presented in electronic format, e.g. word processor files (e.g. MSWord, Text, etc.). Various degrees of search functionality is available ranging from very basic word searches to more sophisticated ones. Consider as an example the mono-lingual dictionary *Pukuntšutlhaloši ya Sesotho sa Leboa ka Inthanete* of the Sesotho sa Leboa National Lexicography Unit in South Africa (Example 1).[4]

(1)

sepela *(lediri)* **LEHLALOŠETŠAGOTEE** tsamaya

1 go iša maoto pele ka go a latelanya mo a dirago gore mmele o tloge mo o bego o le gona; ye ke tiragalo ye bohlokwa mo bophelong ka ge sephedi se kgona go ya mo se ratago : ***Bana ba sepela le mo mebileng ba rekiša dilo tša mehuta ye ka moka***

2 go tloga lefelong le itšeng go ya go le lengwe, e ka ba ka maoto goba ka go šomiša mokgwa wo mongwe wa senamelwa go swana le sefatanaga, bjalobjalo : ***Bošegong bjoo a sepela ka go itlheka a gopotše ga rangwane wa gagwe***

tsamaya *(lediri)* **BONA** sepela

For *sepela* 'to walk' the dictionary gives information on the part of speech, a synonym, two senses of the word, examples of usage, and cross-references as an added feature in the electronic dictionary. The lexicographic quality is good but not much is seen of electronic features.

30.3.5 Translated word lists for African languages

The majority of Internet dictionaries for the African languages can be described as word lists put online. Such dictionaries would typically consist of a word list containing a limited number of lemmas with or without translation equivalents, as example 2 shows:[5]

(2)

baka HH n 5 open space (between things)
bako LL n 5 cave
bala LH n 5 rodent: Lobengula gerbille
bala LL n 6 pole
balaga HHL n 5 beam
balanganda LLLL n 5 old type muzzle loader
– dambikulula L v neutralize magic
– dambitshela L v send (misfortunes) to a person by magic
– davhuka L v spring from
– davhuwa H v rise quickly
– dededza H v help a child to take first steps

In this Tshivenda dictionary (example 2) only basic treatment of the lemma is given, that is, tonal indication, part of speech, and translation equivalent(s). It contains 8,900 lemmas and forms part of the Comparative Bantu Online Dictionary (cBOLD) project[6] where published and unpublished dictionaries of selected Bantu languages were entered into the database. This is a joint effort by compilers from the United States, France, Belgium, the Netherlands, Cameroon, Tanzania, and other countries, organised into the Bantu Working Group (BWG). The project's primary goal as far as dictionaries were concerned is formulated as to "input extensive (annotated) dictionaries and wordlists of Bantu languages". It contains around 80 languages.

A popular way of presentation in many of the online dictionaries is by means of clickable alphabetical guidance letters or blocks. For instance, the presentation screen of a Yoruba English dictionary is like this (Figure 30.1):[7]

A B D E Ç F G GB H I J K L M N O Ô P R S ß T U W Y

Figure 30.1 Presentation screen of a Yoruba-English dictionary

30.3.6 Low lexicographic quality of online dictionaries

With the exception of a few dictionaries of high lexicographic quality for African languages as will be discussed in Section 30.7, the same claim for online dictionaries can be made as what Gouws (1990:55) claimed for paper dictionaries for African languages almost two decades ago, i.e. that they are the products of limited effort.

The nature of these presumed shortcomings will be briefly discussed in this paragraph. As a point of departure and as a benchmark of high lexicographic achievement, consider the open online *Macmillan Dictionary*.[8] A search for *table* in this dictionary returns, in addition to the lemma *table*, almost 20 clickable multi-word lemmas containing the word *table* under the heading 'Related words'. For the single-word lemma *table*, pronunciation guidance is offered in the form of a clickable audio icon, a phonetic transcription as well as word forms, i.e. singular and plural. Paraphrase of meaning (definitions) of three main senses and four sub-senses and eight examples of usage are given. For each of these senses and sub-senses synonyms and related words are offered, each with a clickable option to explore the thesaurus. All words in the definitions and example phrases are clickable, and

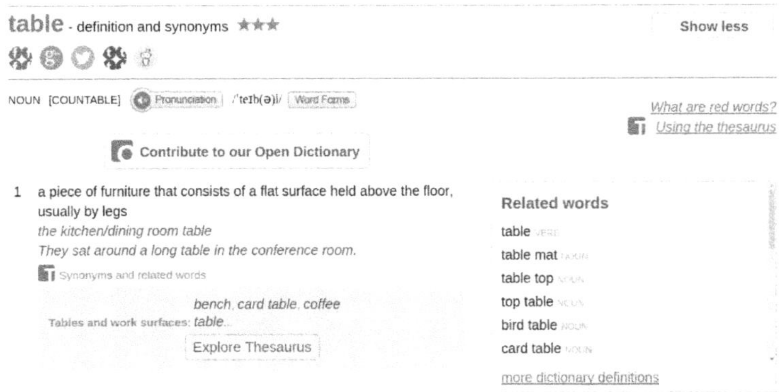

Figure 30.2 *Table* in the free online *Macmillan Dictionary* (extracts)

the user is taken directly to the full entry of such a word. For example, if the user clicks on *room* in the definition of *table*, (s)he is directly taken to the full article for *room*. An option to see more, or less, information is also given. In short: a wealth of information presented in an attractive, practical, and systematic way, utilising electronic features enabled by computer technology (Figure 30.2).

The major shortcomings in online dictionaries for African languages manifest in terms of dictionary content, dictionary design, or both. Consider the *Bilingo Multilingual South African Dictionary*[9] as an example where the dictionary's design and screen layout is quite appealing but the dictionary itself is poor in content (Figure 30.3).

The opening screen presents a clickable block-set for the letters of the alphabet with 'A' already highlighted, displaying the first ten articles in the dictionary in the category A. A running header entitled 'did you know' gives general information about Sepedi. Interesting clickable topics which can be very helpful for text and speech production by users such as how to express the date and time in all 11 languages, asking for directions, medical expressions, etc. are given. If the user types, for example, *walk* in the search box, no fewer than 37 entries are found for all 11 official languages of South Africa, with the number of hits per language indicated in Figure 30.3 under the header 'filter results by language below':

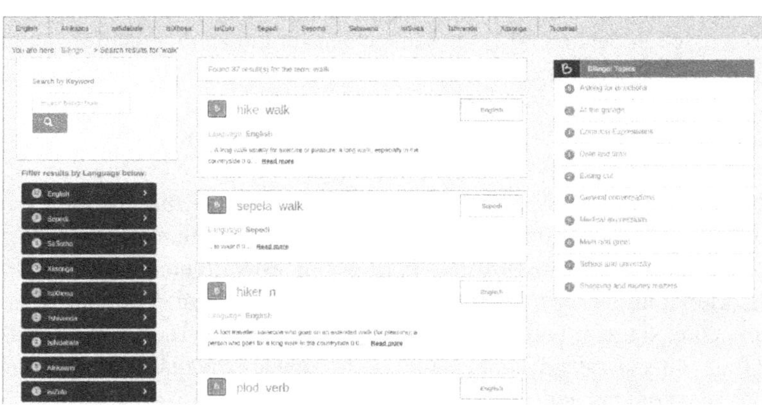

Figure 30.3 *Walk* in the Bilingo online dictionary (extracts)

Thus taken at face value the layout and magnitude of information is impressive. However, a closer look at this dictionary reveals a number of fundamental shortcomings and mistakes. The spelling of the names of two of the languages is incorrect, that is, *SeSotho and *IsiSwati, and reference to these languages are not in line with the strategy followed for the other languages (i.e. to give the spelling of the name of the languages in the language itself). It should have been Sesotho and Siswati.

In Figure 30.3 the 37 articles are presented in a layout of 10 blocks per screen with the name of the language given in the top right corner in each of these blocks, as well as repeated as a second entry after the lemma and translation. In the case of *walk*, the Sepedi translation equivalent is given first, followed by the lemma which was looked up, instead of giving the lemma first and then the translation(s). This is the first indication that it merely reflects a database entry and not a dictionary entry in the sense of *treatment* of the lemma *walk*. If the user clicks on 'read more' an effort towards pronunciation guidance is attempted (example 3):

(3)
Sepela Sounds like: *se-pe-la* (English: walk)

The value of the method of guidance through 'sounds like' is questionable. By merely breaking the word down into its three syllables does not help much in terms of pronunciation guidance. The user will still not know if she or he pronounced the word correctly. In an online dictionary this was a golden opportunity to provide a clickable pronunciation icon for audible guidance as for *table* in Figure 30.2. No further treatment – examples of usage, part of speech information, etc. – is given, but at least the basic translation equivalents provided are correct: *walk* is translated as *sepela* in Sepedi, *khamba* in isiNdebele, *tsamaya* in Setswana, etc. From here on, however, the presumed mere extracts from the database gradually go astray. One of the results for *walk* for Sepedi returns *wheelchair* (example 4):

(4)
setulo sa go thwetha wheelchair
. . . chair with wheels used by people who are unable to walk

Maybe one could still argue that there is a relation between *walk* and *wheelchair*, but a search for *walk* which returns *lesea*, 'baby', is inappropriate. Once again, this is probably the result of using a database entry as is: 'a very young child, especially one that cannot yet *walk* or talk; infant; very young child' as given in the treatment for Sesotho.[10]

Multilingual linking also only works for English, that is, English words linked to the other languages – a search for the Sepedi word *sepela* only returns links to English.

The number of lemmas presented per alphabetical stretch is also very limited. It is unlikely that the user would find most of the words (s)he is looking for. The stretch A only contains approximately 50 words, B 190, D 80, E 40, M 440, etc. Even common words such as *talk* and *speak* are not included in *Dicts.info*.[11] The dictionary simply returns the message, for example, *'talk' not found in this dictionary*. The word *man* can be looked up, but the dictionary does not contain *woman*. Furthermore, the Setswana word for speak is *bua*. Looking up *bua*, returns example 5:

(5)
bua ka go ngalo sarcastically
bua ka kgobololo roughly
bua le, o bua nae address

The dictionary thus misses the core translation of *bua*, i.e. 'talk'/'speak'.

Looking up *walk* returns: *walk kgato*. No guidance is given in terms of part of speech. In this case an attempt is made to translate the noun – 'a walk' – but *kgato* is the translation equivalent of *step*. The verb *walk* translated as *tsamaya* is missing in this case. The same is true for looking up *cook*: only the nominal meaning is given, that is, *moapei* 'a cook', and not the verb *apea* '(to) cook'. If animal is looked up in the English to Zulu dictionary of *Dicts.info*, the result is *animal isilwane, isilwane*. It is not clear why *isilwane* is listed twice in the translation equivalent paradigm.

A lookup for *body* returns example 6:

(6)
body Umzimba
bodyguard umlindi

These translations are both correct, but *umzimba* should not be written with a capital letter.

A lookup for "art" returns example 7:

(7)
art wena uyinkosi
artefact into eyenziwe ngokufanisa
arterial nezimpambosi
arthritis hatilayitisi
artichoke uhlobo lwesithombo esitshalwayo ukuba sidliwe
article atikili, inhlamvu
articulate umunci ocacile
articulation lapho kuhlangana khona amathambo
artifice okuqanjiweyo, umsebenzi wobuciko
artificial -enziweyo-nje ngokufanisa, -okuzenzisa
artificiality ukuzenzisa
artificially ngokulingisa, ngokuzenzisa
artillery izinkunzimalanga zezibhamu kanye nezinhlamvu zazo, ombayimbayi
artilleryman umdubulingombayimbayi
artistic -nobungcweti kobucilikisha
artistry ubungcweti bokunomfiya, ubuciko

These 16 articles are unrelated to the search, and the translation equivalent for *art* given as *wena uyinkosi* meaning 'you are a king' is inappropriate. The isiZulu word for *art* is *ubuciko*. Thus incorrect information is given which can mislead the user to produce incorrect speech and text.

Freedict.com offers the language pair English to 'African'. There is no language called 'African'; they mean Afrikaans (one of the official languages of South Africa). As for the majority of online dictionaries for African languages, this dictionary reflects what could be called 'impoverished dictionary articles'. Looking up the English word *table* returns 'African' *tafel*.[12] Missing out on Afrikaans *tabel*, that is, *table*, as a 'presentation of information in rows and columns' is a shortcoming.

Some of these entries also reflect very bad lexicography. Searching for the randomly selected Afrikaans lemma *koop* 'buy' in *Freelang.net* returns two entries: *Goed koop kak* (English: cheap piece of crap) and *koop* (English: buy, purchase).[13]

Koop should have been presented as the first entry. *Goed koop kak* should not be displayed as a search result for *koop* because *goedkoop* 'cheap' is not a translation equivalent of 'buy'. It is probably simply retrieved from the database because it contains the word 'koop'. To make things worse, the word sequence *Goed koop kak* is wrongly spelt: *Goed koop* should be one word and not start with a capital letter. *Kak* is a *vulgar* word and should have been labelled as such and definitely not used in an example phrase to illustrate the meaning of *koop*! This is bad lexicography.

30.3.7 Dictionaries of achievement

Good online dictionaries do exist for African languages. Consider as a first example the On-line Bargery's website which contains a Hausa-English sictionary of 39,000 words and an English-Hausa Vocabulary containing 4,600 words.[14] Looking up *gaba* returns a detailed article exceeding 2,000 words containing many different senses and sub-sense, grammatical information, parts of speech, etc. Consider the following extract from the article of *gaba* (Figure 30.4)[15]:

gaba.
I. [ga"ba/+].
1. {n.m.; no pl.}.
(a) (i) *The physical front of a p.* (ii) *The height of a p. as mneasured by the arms stretched out horizontally.* (iii) ya/ cika mini g., *it (the work) is more than I can properly cope with; his rank, &c., had such an awe-inspiring effect on me that I was afraid to ask him what I had come to ask.*
(b) *A fathom.* e.g. rijiyan nan g. uku ce, *this well is three fathoms deep.*
(c) *The middle part of a block (kantu) of salt.*
2. {n.m; pl. gabbuna"}. *The forepart of an animal.*
3. Idioms: kowa ya/ kama gabansa, *every one went his own way.* sa'an da ya ji maganan nan gabansa ya/ fa/'di, *when he heard this message (news), he was alarmed, his heart failed him, went down into his boots.* [ga"ba/+ 'da+ya/+], *simultaneously.* [ba/> shi+ da" ga"ba/+ ya" wu+k'a+r fa/>wa/+], *he has no sense, is like a butcher's knife.* hatsi ya/ yi gaban doki, *the corn is about threc [sic] feet high.* (Cf. garu 3; ja I.1(j).)
4. 'dan gaba. Vide alphahetically.
5. na/ tafi gabana ga'di; ya/ tafi gabansa ga'di. Vide gabaga'di.
6. {prep.}. *Towards.* gaba ina ya ke? ya/ yi gaba arewa, *whereabouts is he? he has gone northwards.*
II. [ga"ba+].
1. {adv.}. . . .
2. {prep.}. (= gaban.) . . .
3. {n.f.; no pl.}. . . .

Figure 30.4 Dictionary article for *gaba* in a Hausa-English dictionary (extract)

The user has a choice of search options when looking up a lemma, i.e. full match; partial match: word initial; partial match: initial/middle/final; and context matches.

As a second example of a good online dictionary for African languages, consider the *Kinyarwanda dictionary*.[16] It is stated that this dictionary is designed to be simple to use. The user can search for an English word or a Kinyarwanda word. If (s)he types a word into the search box it will show a list of suggestions, and the layout of the article in terms of data types is explained in detail in the 'Using the dictionary' section as follows in Figure 30.5.

Results

Each entry in the dictionary looks something like this:

ikirahure (**ibi-**)/ikirâhurê/ > n 7 8 (also ikirahuri) *glass* tumbler, from Sw. **bilauri**

1 2 3 4 5 6 7 8 9 10

1 **Prefix**: the prefix part of the entry. For nouns this will be the singular form prefix (assuming there is one) and for verbs it will be the infinitive form prefix.
2 **Stem**: the stem part of the entry.
3 **Modifier**: for nouns this is the plural prefix, and for verbs this is the past tense stem ending.
4 **Pronunciation**: shows how the word should be pronounced using the amasaku.
5 **Audio button**: some words have an **audio recording** which can be played by clicking this.
6 **Word class**: the abbreviated form of the word class. The statistics page gives a list of all the word classes used in the dictionary.
7 **Noun classes**: this is the class of the noun in it's [sic] singular and plural forms. For other word classes this may be the class of noun which it agrees with.
8 **Variant spellings**: other accepted spellings of this word.
9 **English meanings**: the English words with equivalent meaning
10 **Root word**: the word that this word is derived from.

Advanced searching

You can use * character as a wildcard to search for part of a word. For example: searching for **ikinya*** will return all entries that begin with "ikinya", and searching for ***gura** will return all entries that end with "gura".

You can also use parameters to refine your searches. For example **wclass:n has:audio** will return only nouns that have audio. For a complete list of parameters see here.[17]

Figure 30.5 Using the Kinyarwanda dictionary (adaptation of screen)

The navigation language can be set to be Language: English (search) or *Ururimi: Ikinyarwanda (shakisha)*. Nominal prefixes are indicated in a different colour. Part of speech and noun class information are given (e.g. n 9 with plural 10). Searching for only part of a word is enabled and explained by means of examples in the FAQ section (example 8):

(8)[18]

How do I search for part of a word?

You can use the * character as a wildcard, for example:

ama* will match all words beginning with 'ama'

*gura will match all words ending with 'gura'

kinya will match all words containing 'kinya'

In the FAQ section the compilers are also honest about, and sensitive to, the omissions of words from the dictionary:

> **Why doesn't this dictionary contain. . . ?**
> There are many reasons why you might not be able to find the word you are looking for. Firstly, the dictionary might be missing the word. We try to spot missing words by looking at the logs of what people have searched for, and then add them if appropriate. Secondly you might be searching for a conjugated form of a verb rather than the general form. Try stripping off prefixes and suffixes, e.g. *ndagukunda* which means 'I love you'.[19]

As a final example of an online African language dictionary of achievement, consider the isiZulu to English dictionary.[20] *IsiZulu.net* offers bidirectional lookups of either English or isiZulu words. (For a critical discussion of *isiZulu.net* see Prinsloo 2011.) It also offers automatic morphological decomposition, conjugation and phonetic spelling of Zulu words, translation of simple Zulu and English phrases, spell checking, and grammar and pronunciation basics.[21]

In order to look up the word *isichazamazwi* 'dictionary' the user only has to type the first four letters 'isic' to find *isichazamazwi* on a clickable list.

One of the difficulties that especially learners of African languages experience, especially for languages such as isiZulu which have a conjunctive way of writing, is to identify the stem of a word in order to look it up. So, for example, Van Wyk (1995: 90) says that to look up *impala* 'impala', *impilo* 'health', or *intombi* 'girl' in a paper dictionary for isiZulu, the user has to have advanced knowledge of the language to know that the stems for lookup are, respectively, *-mpala*, *-philo*, and *-thombi*.

Apart from rendering electronic features available in the computer era, the electronic dictionary can supersede the paper dictionaries if this problem of stem identification can be resolved, that is, that the user can look up the entire word, or a substantial part of the word, and the software reroutes him or her to the correct noun or verb. In *isiZulu.net* all of these nouns can successfully be looked up by typing in the full word. Ideally the user should be able to find any word with its affixes in an electronic dictionary.

If the user wants to look up the meaning of *babehamba* 'they were going' in a paper dictionary of isiZulu (s)he has to be able to identify the stem *-hamba* to look it up and will have to 'add' the past tense to the meaning of *hamba* 'go'. In *isiZulu.net*, the stem *-hamba* and *babelhamba* are treated as lemmas (example 9):

(9)[22]
– **hamba** **v/i.** ['ha:mba] . . .
go; walk [no direction implied]
travel
ride [on vehicle]
depart; leave
continue; go on; move on; proceed
work; function; operate; perform
~ **kahle!**
go well!; goodbye!

babehamba ['ɓa:ɓɛhamba] ← *babe + hamba*
Remote Past Continuous [←hamba (v/i.)]
SC: babe- (cl. 2, cl. 2a)
they were going

30.4 Looking to the future

Whether lexicographers believe it or not, the future existence of paper dictionaries and online dictionaries is seriously challenged by the information era. The amount of information available on the Internet which is easily accessible through search engines such as Google is simply mind-boggling. Online dictionaries have an uphill struggle to remain the preferred access point for lexicographic information retrieval. If users should find it more rewarding to go directly to Google for the meaning of a word, its use in contexts, etc., they will no longer feel the need to consult a dictionary.

Compilers of online dictionaries should therefore first get their house in order in terms of the compilation of electronic dictionaries of a high lexicographic standard, rich in content that render correct and trustworthy lexicographic information.

Second, they should employ more true electronic features enabled by the computer era.

Third, they should focus much attention on the design and layout of presentation on screen.

In the fourth instance they should develop more support tools for user guidance for the many instances of complicated structures in the African languages. Such support tools should include linking the dictionary with corpus data supporting the user in his or her needs for cognitive information as well as text and speech reception and production.

The view that electronic dictionaries 'can do more' if various dictionary support tools are incorporated is growing in strength. Most of the support tools and linking are rooted in processed corpus data. Such tools range from language checking tools such as spelling checkers, grammar checkers, and word-by-word pronunciation guidance, to interactive user support tools for communicative (text production or reception) or cognitive (language learning) purposes. Good examples of the compilation of such interactive text production support tools for African languages include the *Sepedihelper*,[23] decision trees and structured paths (Bothma et al. 2013), and linking dictionaries to processed and unprocessed corpus data (Prinsloo et al. 2013). The tools make use of different kinds of devices for presenting lexicographical data to users: these range from more or less sophisticated selection menus and dialogue-like stepwise interactive guidance over classical information-on-demand approaches. Incorporating such features in e-dictionaries would imply that e-dictionaries can fulfil a much wider range of information needs and provide much more support, on demand, to users than is currently the case.

The Sepedihelper (Figure 30.6) assists the user in text production of sentences in all of the eight verbal moods, present future and past tenses, positive or negative, intransitive, transitive, double transitive valencies, and for all types of subject and object nouns and their pronouns.

In addition, user studies need to be conducted and, based upon the feedback, the dictionaries should be updated accordingly.

Finally, although the financial, organisational, computational, and lexicographic input from foreign experts is highly appreciated, African compilers should increasingly take command of their destiny to compile good future online dictionaries.

30.5 Conclusion

In terms of lexicographic quality, online African language dictionaries reflect the full spectrum ranging from mere translated words lists that can hardly be called dictionaries, via

Figure 30.6 The Sepedihelper support tool for e-dictionary consultation

haphazard lemma selections with impoverished dictionary articles marred by many mistakes and shortcomings, to dictionaries of high lexicographic standard.

The current situation and perspective on future dictionaries is appropriately worded by Michael Rundell in his keynote address at Euralex (2012). He says:

> The current situation is messy, with a great deal of interesting but uncoordinated activity, and plenty of trial and error. For the moment, there are a lot more questions than answers. And the situation continues to change rapidly, as technologies from the wider field of Internet search increasingly impact on what we do. Thus there are new areas whose theories and applications we need to pay attention to. But the model which has served us so far still looks serviceable: the basic principles of focussing on the user and being faithful to the language data; seeking guidance from relevant linguistic and computational theory; and drawing on good-quality user research to identify what works. . . . we no longer have control over the behaviour of users seeking information on the Web or wishing to make their own contribution to it.
>
> Rundell (2012:83)

Related topics

Explaining meaning in lexicographic information tools; dictionary criticism; lexicography and corpus linguistics; learners' dictionaries of English; dictionaries and language policy.

Further reading

De Schryver, G.-M. (2003). "Online Dictionaries on the Internet: An Overview for the African Languages", *Lexikos* 13: 1–20.

A comprehensive overview of online dictionaries for the African languages at the time with focus on the key characteristics of these dictionaries.

De Schryver, G.-M. (2003). "Lexicographers' Dreams in the Electronic-Dictionary Age", *International Journal of Lexicography* 16(2): 143–199.
A state-of-the-art article on electronic dictionaries analysing the major achievements and future prospects of electronic dictionaries, various electronic dictionary typologies, discussion on pros and cons of paper versus electronic products, etc.

Prinsloo, D. J., T.J.D. Bothma and U. Heid. (2014). "User Support in e-Dictionaries for Complex Grammatical Structures in the Bantu Languages", *Proceedings of the 16th Euralex International Congress*. 15–19 July 2014. Bolzano. Italy.
This paper discusses direct user guidance as a mechanism in an e-dictionary to provide user support for complex grammatical structures in the Bantu languages.

Prinsloo, D. J. (2011). "A Critical Analysis of the Lemmatisation of Nouns and Verbs in IsiZulu", *Lexikos* 21: 169–193.
This article is a critical evaluation of lemmatisation strategies for nouns and verbs in isiZulu with specific attention to the problem of stem identification.

Prinsloo, D. J., U. Heid, T. Bothma and G. Faaß. (2012). "Devices for Information Presentation in Electronic Dictionaries", *Lexikos* 22: 290–320. (ISI).
This article sketches the principles of an interactive and dynamic electronic dictionary aimed at text production and text reception guiding users in innovative ways, especially with respect to difficult, complicated or confusing issues where users need more detailed support than currently available in e-dictionaries, enabling them to make valid and correct choices. Guidance through a decision tree-like device is suggested.

Acknowledgments

This research is conducted within the SeLA project (Scientific e-Lexicography for Africa), supported in part by (1) a grant from the German Ministry for Education and Research, administered by the DAAD and (2) the National Research Foundation of South Africa (grant-specific unique reference number (UID) 8576). The Grantholder acknowledges that the opinions, findings and conclusions or recommendations expressed in any publication generated by the NRF-supported research are those of the author, and that the NRF accepts no liability whatsoever in this regard.

Notes

1 See at www.theguardian.com/books/2012/nov/07/macmillan-dictionary-digital-final-print
2 They are available at http://dicts.info/dictlist1.php
3 It is available at www.africanculture.dk/gambia/ftp/wollof.pdf. See Afrikaans, Albanian, Arabic, Armenian, Azeri, Basque, Bengali, Bosnian, Brazilian Portuguese, Breton Bulgarian, Byelorussian, Catalan, Cebuano, Cornish, Croatian, Czech, Danish, Dutch, English Esperanto, Estonian, Faroese, Fijian, Finnish, French, Frisian, Galician, Georgian, German Greek, Guarani, Gujarati, Haitian Creole, Hawaiian, Hebrew, Hiligaynon, Hindi, Hmong, Hungarian Chinese, Icelandic, Indonesian, Interlingua, Inuit, Inuktitut, Irish, Italian, Japanese, Japanese Romaji, Kabyle, Kazakh, Kinyarwanda, Kiribati, Korean, Kurdish, Latin, Latvian, Lithuanian Macedonian, Malagasy, Malay, Malayalam, Maltese, Manx, Maori, Mapudungun, Marathi, Masai Mongolian, Nepali, Norwegian Bokmal, Norwegian Nynorsk, Pali, Papiamento, Persian, Polish Portuguese, Punjabi, Quechua, Rapanui, Romanian, Russian, Sanskrit, Scottish Gaelic, Serbian, Sesotho, Setswana, Sinhala, Slovak, Slovenian, Somali, Spanish, Sranan, Swahili, Swedish Tagalog, Tamil, Tatar, Telugu, Thai, Tok Pisin, Tongan, Turkish, Turkmen, Urdu, Valencian, Vietnamese Walloon, Welsh, Xhosa, Zulu

4 It is available at http://africanlanguages.com/psl/
5 Venda.Murphy1997.txt available at www.cbold.ish-lyon.cnrs.fr/
6 It is available at www.cbold.ish-lyon.cnrs.fr/
7 It is available at www.yorubadictionary.com/Yoruba_English/yoruba_p.htm. Similar "screen presentations" are used by the Sesotho online dictionary (http://bukantswe.sesotho.org) and the *Bilingo Multilingual South African Dictionary* (www.bilingo.co.za/english-dictionary-2/).
8 It is available at www.macmillandictionary.com/
9 It is available at www.bilingo.co.za
10 See www.bilingo.co.za/?s=walk&post_types=bilingo_sesotho
11 It is available at http://dicts.info/dictlist1.php
12 It is available at http://freedict.com/onldict/afr.html
13 It is available at www.freelang.net/online/afrikaans.php?lg=gb
14 It is available at http://maguzawa.dyndns.ws/
15 See at http://maguzawa.dyndns.ws/frame.html
16 It is available at http://kinyarwanda.net/
17 It is available at http://kinyarwanda.net/page.php?name=howtouse
18 It is available at http://kinyarwanda.net/page.php?name=faq
19 See at http://kinyarwanda.net/page.php?name=faq
20 It is available at https://isizulu.net/
21 See at Welcome to *isiZulu.net*: https://isizulu.net/
22 See at https://isizulu.net/. For a critical discussion of *isiZulu.net* see Prinsloo (2011).
23 It is available at www.sepedihelper.co.za

References

Online dictionaries [All accessed on April 5, 2007]

Bilingo Multilingual South African Dictionary: www.bilingo.co.za
Bukantswe: http://bukantswe.sesotho.org/
cBold: Venda.Murphy1997.txt: www.cbold.ish-lyon.cnrs.fr/
Dicts.info: http://dicts.info/dictlist1.php
Freedict.com: http://freedict.com/onldict/afr.html
Freelang.net: www.freelang.net/online/afrikaans.php?lg=gb
Hausa Dictionary: http://maguzawa.dyndns.ws/frame.html
isiZulu.net: https://isizulu.net/
Kinyarwanda Dictionary: http://kinyarwanda.net/
Macmillan online dictionary: www.macmillandictionary.com/
Pukuntšutlhaloši ya Sesotho sa Leboa ka Inthanete: http://africanlanguages.com/psl/.
Webster's Online Dictionary: www.websters-online-dictionary.org/.
Wolof Dictionary, Sierra Dem, Peace Corps. (1995) www.africanculture.dk/gambia/ftp/wollof.pdf
Yoruba – English dictionary: www.yorubadictionary.com/Yoruba_English/yoruba_p.htm

Other literature

Atkins, B.T.S. (1996) "Bilingual Dictionaries: Past, Present and Future", in M. Gellerstam J. Järborg, S-G. Malmgren, K. Norén, L. Rogström, and C. Röjder Papmehl (eds.), *Euralex '96 Proceedings: Papers Submitted to the Seventh EURALEX International Congress on Lexicography in Göteborg*. Sweden: Göteborg: Göteborg University, pp. 515–546.

Atkins, B.T.S. (1998) "Some Discussion Points Arising From Afrilex-Salex'98", Unpublished course evaluation document, University of Pretoria.

Bolinger, D. (1990) "Review of the Oxford Advanced Learner's Dictionary of Current English", *International Journal of Lexicography* 3(2): 133–145.

Bothma, T.J.D., R. H. Gouws and D. J. Prinsloo (2016) "The Role of e-Lexicography in the Confirmation of Lexicography as an Independent and Multidisciplinary Field", in *Proceedings of the 17th Euralex Conference*, 6–10 September 2016, Tbilisi, Georgia.

Bothma, T.J.D., U. Heid and D. J. Prinsloo (2013) "Implementing Decision Support for Text Production in e-Dictionaries", *eLex 2013. Electronic Lexicography in the 21st Century: Thinking Outside the Paper*. Institute of the Estonian Language and Trojina, Institute for Applied Slovene Studies. 17–19 October 2013. Tallinn, Estonia.

De Schryver, G.-M. (2003) "Online Dictionaries on the Internet: An Overview for the African Languages", *Lexikos* 13: 1–20. http://tshwanedje.com/publications/OBDs.pdf

De Schryver, G.-M. (2003) "Lexicographers' Dreams in the Electronic-Dictionary Age", *International Journal of Lexicography* 16/2: 143–199. http://tshwanedje.com/publications/dreams.pdf.

Gouws, R. H. (1990) "Information Categories in Dictionaries, With Special Reference to Southern Africa", in R.R.K. Hartmann (ed.), *Lexicography in Africa, Progress Reports From the Dictionary Research Centre Workshop at Exeter, 24–25 March 1989*. (Exeter Linguistic Studies 15.) Exeter: University of Exeter Press, pp. 52–65.

Gouws, R. H. and D. J. Prinsloo (2005) *Principles and Practice of South African Lexicography*. Stellenbosch: SUN Press.

Meijs, W. (1992) "Computers and Dictionaries", in C. Butler (ed.), *Computers and Written Texts*. Oxford: Blackwell, pp. 141–165.

Nesi, H. (1999) "A User's Guide to Electronic Dictionaries for Language Learners", *International Journal of Lexicography* 12(1): 55–66.

Prinsloo, D. J. (2011) "A Critical Analysis of the Lemmatisation of Nouns and Verbs in IsiZulu", *Lexikos* 21: 169–193. http://lexikos.journals.ac.za/pub/article/view/42.

Prinsloo, D. J. (2015) "African Language Lexicography: Yesterday, Today and Tomorrow", Unpublished paper presented at Stellenlex 30 March 2015: *Methods in lexicography*. University of Stellenbosch.

Prinsloo, D. J., T.J.D. Bothma and U. Heid (2014) "User Support in e-Dictionaries for Complex Grammatical Structures in the Bantu Languages", *Proceedings of the 16th Euralex International Congress*. 15–19 July 2014. Bolzano. Italy. www.euralex.org/publications/

Prinsloo, D. J., U. Heid and T. Bothma (2013) "Linking e-Dictionaries to Advanced Processed Corpus Data", *eLex 2013. Electronic Lexicography in the 21st Century: Thinking Outside the Paper*. Institute of the Estonian Language and Trojina, Institute for Applied Slovene Studies. Tallinn, Estonia.

Prinsloo, D. J., U. Heid, T. Bothma and G. Faaß (2012) "Devices for Information Presentation in Electronic Dictionaries", *Lexikos* 22: 290–320. (ISI). http://lexikos.journals.ac.za/pub.

Rundell, M. (2012) "'It Works in Practice But Will It Work in Theory?' The Uneasy Relationship Between Lexicography and Matters Theoretical", in R. V. Fjeld and J. M. Torjusen (eds.), *Proceedings of the 15th EURALEX International Congress*. 7–11 August 2012. Oslo: Department of Linguistics and Scandinavian Studies, University of Oslo, pp. 47–92.

Sepedihelper: http://sepedihelper.co.za/

Van Wyk, E. B. (1995) "Linguistic Assumptions and Lexicographical Traditions in the African Languages", *Lexikos* 5: 82–96.

31
Arabic lexicography in the Internet era

Karlheinz Mörth

31.1 Introduction

The purpose of this chapter is to give a brief overview of developments in the field of Arabic lexicography in the light of the deep technological transformations scholarship has undergone in the last decades. The focus of interest is on the impact of the ubiquitous presence of the Internet and digital applications on Arabic lexicography, on the impact of the new methods, new media and new tools which have fundamentally changed the way dictionaries are being produced, published and used. In view of the vastness of the material and the complexity of the field, the following paragraphs are perforce limited to selected examples.

31.2 Historical perspectives

Arabic scholars produced dictionaries as early as the eighth century CE and developed a very sophisticated culture of dictionary writing in the centuries thereafter. The *Kitāb al-ʿayn*[1] 'The Book of the Letter ʿAyn' written by Al-Xalīl Ibn Aḥmad al-Farāhīdī is generally regarded as the first Arabic dictionary. Although the fast expansion of the sphere of Arabic influence brought the Arabs in close contact with peoples speaking other languages during the first centuries of Islam, Arabic was so predominant in that period that it took almost four centuries until the earliest dictionaries into languages other than Arabic were compiled (Haywood 1991b: 3086). The first one we know of is az-Zamaxšarī's *Muqaddimat al-adab* 'Introduction to Literature', an Arabic-Persian collection of words and sentences dating from the twelfth century. During the 'Golden Age' of Islam, Arabic lexicographers produced many outstanding dictionaries which have stayed in use until today.

Descriptions of the modern era of Arabic lexicography generally start with Buṭrus al-Bustānī's *Muḥīṭ al-Muḥīṭ* (published in Beirut in 1870) (Benzehra 2013: 881; Hassanein 2008: 39). Since then, countless new dictionaries were produced in the Arab world and beyond, many of which have remained eclectic reflexes of their medieval predecessors (Hassanein 2008 43).

31.3 Core issues and topics

31.3.1 Linguistic particularities

Looking at the linguistic situation in the Arab World, two particular features of the Arabic language have to be taken into consideration: the highly conservative nature of the written language and the existence of quite divergent forms of spoken varieties. The coexistence of two distinct written forms, namely Classical Arabic (CA) and Modern Standard Arabic (MSA), has characterised the linguistic landscape until this day. CA, the basic structure of which has by and large remained unchanged until the present day, is generally regarded by Arabic philologers as the norm against which everything else has to be measured. By contrast, MSA is seen by many as a modernised version of CA that has emerged hand in hand with *an-Nahḍa* 'the awakening', a cultural renaissance that started in the late nineteenth century.

Closely related to this is the socio-linguistic situation of the Arab countries for which the American linguist Ferguson coined the term *diglossia*[2] by which he understood a "relatively stable language situation in which, in addition to the primary dialects of the language . . . there is a very divergent, highly codified (often grammatically more complex) superposed variety, the vehicle of a large and respected body of written literature" (Ferguson 1959: 336). In everyday life, all Arabs make use of a linguistic variety that is remarkably different from both CA and also MSA with regard to phonology, morphology and syntax. So-called 'colloquial' Arabic, which is seldom written and by many Arabic traditionalists regarded as a degraded form of language, is highly diverse and represents many local groups which historically constitute the current end-points of hundreds of years of development about which we actually do not know very much. The level of mutual intelligibility between varieties may vary from region to region.

For the most part of its history, a derivative of the Aramaic script was used to write the Arabic language. It is important to note that the alphabetical macrostructure of Arabic dictionaries was quite varied during the first centuries of its evolution. In al-Xalīl's very early dictionary (see Section 31.2), lexical items were arranged according to the place of articulation of the root consonants[3] of a particular lexical items (Seidensticker 2008: 31). In later times, varying systems were applied to arrange the roots, in many cases the alphabet being the ordering principle, in others the rhyme (Hoogland 2008: 20). Modern dictionaries usually have mixed systems, the headwords being arranged by root and alphabetical order. In the microstructure of dictionary entries, word class often plays a role, with verbs usually being listed before other word classes (Haywood 1991a: 2446).

31.3.2 Digital foundations

In recent years, our world has undergone deep and far-reaching transformations brought about by new technologies and media. Burgeoning digital tools and data have also started to fundamentally reshape the lexicographer's inventory of tools and the way lexical information is being communicated. This also holds true for Arabic lexicography.

31.3.2.1 Language technology

Today, lexicographers make use of digital tools, data, methods and standards which have evolved in parallel with developments in related specialised disciplines (such as corpus linguistics, computational linguistics and text technology) and play a role in all stages of the lexicographic workflow: data acquisition, processing and publication. In up-to-date lexicography, it has become common practise to compile dictionaries on the basis of digital corpora. Digital corpora have thus become an essential part of the modern lexicographical tool inventory.

31.3.2.2 Digital corpora

Incorporating references to literary sources into dictionary entries has a long tradition in Arabic lexicography going back to the very early times. In a sense, this can be interpreted as the very first precursors of corpus-based approaches, albeit modern concepts of representability did not exactly apply then. Good dictionaries used to be compiled on the basis of corpora long before the advent of digital tools (see Wehr 1985: XV). However, what printed corpora could not deliver was reliable statistical information on large amounts of data. Today, professional lexicographic endeavours draw on data gathered from digital corpora, structured collections of machine-readable text put together for particular research questions. During the past decades, various kinds of corpora were developed as particular dictionaries required particular corpora such as historical, diachronic, reference, monitor, balanced, comparable, multi-media, learners', parallel, speech etc.[4]

The situation with respect to digital Arabic corpora has improved considerably since the turn of the twenty-first century.[5] While then next to nothing was available the number of digitally encoded Arabic language corpora has been on the rise ever since, and fortunately more and more digital resources have become publicly available (Zaghouani 2014). The following list of corpora is by no means meant to be exhaustive and merely gives some historically outstanding examples.

Tim Buckwalter is generally regarded as the first one to create digital Arabic corpora. He started back in 1986 and has been working on Arabic NLP tools until the present day. The most notable result of his corpus-related activities was the *Frequency Dictionary of Arabic: Core Vocabulary for Learners* (2011), the first ever Arabic frequency dictionary based on a digital corpus.[6] The main challenge in compiling this dictionary was the analysis of the corpus of 30 million words, a "balanced" corpus compiled from written sources, such as newswire reports, newspaper editorials, scientific publications and works of modern literature. Ten percent of this corpus was made up of spontaneous speech data. Buckwalter has also maintained a website with some digital tables of frequency counts on Internet data from 1999, 2000 and 2002.[7]

Another rather early attempt at building a digital corpus for lexicographic purposes dates back as far as 1990. The so-called *Leuven Corpus* was built by Mark van Mol from the Catholic University Leuven in Belgium and was intended to support the creation of an Arabic-Dutch learner's dictionary (Van Mol et al. 2001). He collected 3 million words from radio and television news broadcasts from Algeria, Egypt and Saudi Arabia, interviews, speeches, plays, 50 handbooks for learning Arabic which were used in primary schools in nine countries as well as written material from the Internet derived from magazines and newspapers (Van Mol 2000).

The *Nijmegen Corpus* was created between 1994 and 1997. It was created in support of Hoogland's bilingual dictionaries (see Section 31.4.1) and made up of a number of novels and non-fiction articles from magazines which were made searchable by means of OCR. This material was enhanced by a complete volume of the London-based newspaper *Al*

Hayat, one of the first newspapers offering its archives in electronic format and containing some 3 million words.[8]

The institution holding the largest amount of Arabic data globally is the Linguistic Data Consortium (LDC), a group of universities, companies and government research laboratories which collects and distributes digital language resources such as text and speech corpora, dictionaries and others. The earliest appearance of Arabic in the LDC Catalogue[9] was in 2001 with the *Arabic Newswire*, a corpus containing approximately 76 million tokens.

Another large project is based at the *Bibliotheca Alexandrina* (Egypt): The *International Corpus of Arabic* (ICA) which was conceived and designed by a group around Sameh Alansary[10] and started in 2006. The corpus was supposed to eventually hold 100 million words from a wide range of sources representing a wide cross-section of regional variety in Modern Standard Arabic (Alansary et al. 2007).

In recent years, ease of availability has made data from the Internet an often used source on which to build digital corpora. The currently largest available web corpus is *arTenTen*, a corpus containing 7.4 billion words. It was crawled from the Internet in January 2012 and is one of the many corpora that were built in connection with *Sketch Engine* (SkE), a commercial corpus manager and analysis software developed by *Lexical Computing Limited* since 2003. Over many years SkE has become a standard application in many lexicographic endeavours.

In the past, digital CA data was often exchanged privately on CDs or flash sticks. In many instances, the quality of this data was quite good, presumably the result of typing rather than OCRing. However, its use for serious research was problematic as information regarding sources, provenance, modes of production, etc., was unavailable. Today, several websites offer access to such data. The largest of these, with thousands of Arabic texts, is the *al-Maktaba aš-šāmila* 'The Universal Library'.[11] Another very popular one is *al-Miškāt*[12] '(niche for a) lamp'. CA data can also been found in the *King Saud University Corpus of Classical Arabic* (KSUCCA), a long-term project of Saudi Arabia's most prestigious university. It has been available on the Internet since 2012. Particularly remarkable is the fact that the data of this project can be freely downloaded from their website.[13]

Whereas large amounts of data have become available for CA and MSA, the situation still looks rather bleak with respect to the many spoken varieties of Arabic. Interestingly, the few existing resources all document varieties in the western part of the Arabic world. The French *CorpAfroAs* project was an integrated pilot project that created transcribed and sound-indexed spoken data.[14] The involved varieties were Moroccan, Libyan and Juba-Arabic. The project set a positive example providing extensive documentation and offering free access to the data (Mettouchi et al. 2010).

A large collection of non-standard data was brought together in the *Tunisian Arabic Corpus*, a comparatively large collection of approximately 2000 Tunisian Arabic texts mainly collected from the Internet.[15] The corpus was created by two researchers based in the United States, all the data are presented in Arabic script (McNeil et al. 2012).

So far, we know of only one project making a digital dictionary of a spoken Arabic variety on the basis of a digital corpus: the project *Lexical Dynamics in the Greater Tunis Area: a Corpus Based Approach (TUNICO)* which was conducted between 2014 and 2016 as a joint project of the Austrian Academy of Sciences and the University of Vienna. The project was aimed at the creation of two digital language resources: a corpus of spoken Tunis Arabic and a micro-diachronic dictionary based on a combination of the new corpus data, interviews and previously published resources (Procházka and Mörth 2015).

31.3.2.3 Standards for Arabic lexical data

An important methodological issue of modern-day lexicography are digital encoding standards for lexical data. The significance of the matter becomes apparent wherever data are to be exchanged, to be shared, to be worked on in a collaborative manner or to be further developed. Lexical data has often been stored in relational databases, which usually constitute rather static environments. Over the past two decades, many different XML-based systems have become widely used in encoding lexical data. In spite of a general consensus with respect to a need to harmonise systems, we have seen a constant proliferation of schemas.

The *Guidelines of the Text Encoding Initiative* (TEI) are an important *de facto* standard in the field. They provide a specialised dictionary module (TEI Consortium 2016: 275–313) and have been used in numerous digitisation projects. The lexicography working group of the *Vienna Corpus of Arabic Varieties* (see Section 31.3.4.2) has been working on a specialised TEI schema for their dictionary projects. The intention was to create a reusable, well-documented schema for born-digital lexicographical data (Budin et al. 2012). Their work was accompanied by the development of a digital lexicographic XML editor offering special functionalities geared towards TEI (ibid).

LMF (Lexical Markup Framework; ISO-24613:2008) is the most recent ISO standard for lexical data which also has an XML serialisation. It has also played a role in many lexicographic projects. The lexicographic editing system used for the *Arabic-Dutch/Dutch-Arabic dictionaries* (see 31.4.1) was based on LMF (Maks et al. 2008), and experimental Tunisian and Moroccan projects applied LMF as a versatile means of encoding. A working group at the Tunisian *Multimedia, Information Systems and Advanced Computing Laboratory (MIRACL)* in Sfax worked on modelling lexical knowledge by means of LMF (Salmon-Alt et al. 2005; Haddar *et al.* 2012; Khemakhem et al. 2013; Lhioui et al. 2014). However, LMF has also been used for processing Arabic elsewhere (Attia et al. 2010).

In the recent past, Semantic Web technologies have also started to play a role in modelling the components of lexicographic information systems. RDF (Resource Description Framework), OWL (Web Ontology Language) and SKOS (Simple Knowledge Organization System) have been used to structure Arabic lexical data and to make it ready for semantic web applications, working towards distributed architectures by exposing, sharing and connecting lexical knowledge as Linked (Open) Data (Declerck et al. 2014, 2015) (see Chapters 8, 12, 14, and 43 of this *Handbook*).

31.3.2.4 Saving the past: facsimiles and PDFs

Unlike the advanced technologies referred to in the previous section much of what is available today is considerably less sophisticated. A widespread phenomenon of the past decades are libraries consisting in facsimiles of printed books. Large-scale digitisation programmes of major libraries (especially in the United States) produced and made available millions of digital books in the public domain. Large stretches of the historical canon of Arabic lexicography can be found in these collections. The central clearing house for such data is the website of the *Internet Archive*.[16] The Archive provides data in a number of formats, starting with digital images (of differing quality and in differing formats: GIF, JPEG, TIFF) through to various textual formats (TXT, ePUB, DJVU), the latter ones – in most cases – the result of automatic OCR (Optical Character Recognition) processing.

Many of these dictionaries are also available as PDF documents (Portable Document Format is an ISO standard; ISO 32000–1:2008) containing digital images of the printed originals. Although OCR has made good progress over the years, the results of purely automatic conversions of dictionaries are largely unusable, especially in scenarios where several languages are involved. To create meaningful digital text, time-consuming and costly human intervention is needed which usually cannot be achieved in wholesale digitisation programmes. Notwithstanding the shortcomings, these PDFs have come to be widely used in academia, in teaching as well as in research. The Archive also offers a comfortable book viewer on its website which makes using the dictionaries less cumbersome than in unedited PDF files without proper navigational mechanisms. Whereas well-done print dictionaries are often equipped with thumb indexes that guide users to the initial pages of a particular letter, in many of these digital dictionaries the right jump-in-points can only be guessed by sifting back and forth.

Among the many medieval dictionaries to be found on the Internet Archive's website, there are facsimilised versions of editions of some of the most important historical dictionaries that have come down to us, such as az-Zamaxšarī's *Muqaddimat al-Adab* (see 31.2), az-Zabīdī's (d. 1790) *Tāj al-ʿArūs* lit. 'Crown of the Bride' and al-Fīrūzābādī's *al-Qāmūs al-Muḥīṭ* lit. 'The Comprehensive Lexicon' (1760–1774). Early instances of European lexicography are Jacob Golius' *Lexicon Arabico-Latinum* (published in Leiden in 1653), Georg Wilhelm Friedrich Freytag's dictionary of the same title (Halle 1830–37) and Edward William Lane's *Arabic-English Lexicon* (1863–93).

A particular case in point is Hans Wehr's *Arabisches Wörterbuch für die Schriftsprache der Gegenwart 'Arabic Dictionary for the Contemporary Written Language'*. This initially Arabic-German dictionary was published for the first time in 1952 and appeared in five major editions, the last one in 1985. At the time of publication, the dictionary was the most complete bilingual MSA dictionary. Wehr made use of both the Arabic script and Latin transcriptions. The dictionary also contains some colloquialisms, many phraseologisms, multi-word expressions and illustrative examples. What added considerably to this dictionary's impact, was J. Milton Cowan's English third edition (1961) which since has been an important translation tool for generations of English-speaking students, teachers and scholars in many countries. Both Cowan's edition[17] and the fifth edition in German[18] are available from the Archive.org website.

31.3.2.5 Digital lexical data

Linguistic research is more and more based on digital data and increasing numbers of researchers pursue data-based or data-driven approaches in their work. Although considerable amounts of data have become available for CA, the situation for MSA is more unfavourable. Researchers can extract data from corpora or from digitised historical dictionaries, readily available structured data is hard to come by, let alone in standardised formats.

A longstanding project which deserves special mention as an excellent example of a reliable data provider and supporter of digital research is the Perseus Project, a digital library started by Tufts University in 1987 with the aim of collecting materials for the study of ancient Greek. Meanwhile Perseus Digital Library[19] has grown to become the central hub on the Internet for digitally working classicists working on Greek and/or Latin. Perseus also takes an interest in other languages now. Next to resources documenting nineteenth-century American English, collections dating from the English Renaissance and the Old Norse period, Perseus also contains two Arabic dictionaries which in accordance with the Perseus Open Source policy are completely free and available under creative commons licences. Both are encoded in TEI (P4; cf. 3.2.3). The first one is Edward William Lane's

Arabic-English Lexicon, the second one an otherwise almost forgotten *Advanced Learner's Arabic-English Dictionary* (Librairie du Liban 1889) by Anthony Salmoné.

Another digital lexical resource is *Arabic WordNet*,[20] an advanced digital language resource which has been described as a combination of dictionary and thesaurus (Miller et al. 1993). WordNets have so far been created for many languages. They organise the words of a language into sets of synonyms, so-called synsets, and usually contain formalised relations between the contained lexical units (see Chapter 12 of this *Handbook*).

31.3.3 A plethora of online dictionaries

The 'era of the Internet' has seen the emergence of new media used for the publication of digital dictionaries. Dictionaries were merchandised as computer programs to be installed on computers. Dictionaries on floppy discs were followed by applications on CDs and DVDs. Well into the third decade of the 'era of the Internet' these media have started to disappear. Fully integrated electronic dictionaries in the form of small computers or mobile phones have also started to give way to mobile apps on phones that basically offer the same functionality.

Today, the primary channel of publication is the Internet, and the number of online Arabic dictionaries has soared rapidly over the past few years. Many websites offering online access to dictionaries pursue commercial interests capitalising on easily available data in order to generate revenues through commercials. A list of such sites would be exceedingly long and of little use as addresses often change, the provenance of data is in most cases not clear and the quality of information – at best – dubious.

31.3.3.1 Publishing houses

With many internationally working publishers it has become common practice to accompany their print products with digital versions. For many years, CDs were sold together with print dictionaries. Meanwhile, customers rather expect digital products to be available on the Internet. A good example of a company relying on this publication channel in tandem with their print products is *Librairie du Liban Publishers* (LDLP). For a long time, LDLP has been the most successful publisher of dictionaries in the east of the Arab world. It entertains local branches in Lebanon, Jordan, Sudan, UAE and Egypt. Since 2011, they have been running a website with a large number of dictionaries on offer.[21] Eighty dictionaries are freely available on their website – users do not even have to register. There are mono-, bi- and trilingual dictionaries, mostly language pairs with Arabic, English or French. The interface offers both random access to dictionaries (allowing to browse through the entries) and a search interface allowing to concurrently query all the available dictionaries. Next to the many special language dictionaries on the list, there is, by way of example, also Wagdi Rizk Ghali's *Longman Dictionary of Modern English*, basically an English-English dictionary with Arabic translations.

Some of the major international publishing houses also offer access to online Arabic dictionaries. The *Cambridge English-Arabic Dictionary* is a dictionary for Arabic-speaking learners of English.[22] Access to the dictionary requires a password, but is free. Another free offer is Larousse's *French-Arabic Dictionary*[23] which is like the previous one intended for Arabic-speakers learning the foreign language. The dictionary has many usage examples, and all of the lemmas and examples are furnished with sound. It is also available as a mobile app. The *Oxford Dictionaries* Arabic site[24] accompanies the *Oxford Arabic Dictionary* (see

Section 31.4.1) and provides some additional material such as lists of popular words, general information on Arabic, the Arabic alphabet, etc. Meanwhile *Pons Online Dictionary* has also added an Arabic dictionary to their online products. A quite original feature is the text-to-speech functionality which has been implemented through software provided by *Linguatec Language Technologies*.[25]

31.3.3.2 Online historical dictionaries

We have outlined before that large parts of the historical literary canon (the Arabic concept of *adab* 'literature' also includes dictionaries) have already been digitised in some form (see Section 31.3.2.4). Over the past years, a number of websites have sprung into existence offering interfaces to this kind of data. One of the most popular sites providing access to Arabic historical dictionaries is *al-Bāḥiṯ al-ʿarabī* 'the Arabic Searcher'[26] which exposes five historical monolingual dictionaries:

- *Maqāyīs al-luġa*, 'Measures of the Language' by Ibn Fāris (d. 1004)
- *aṣ-Ṣiḥāḥ fi l-luġa*, 'The Correct Ones in the Language' by al-Jawharī (d. 1002 or 1008)
- *al-ʿUbāb az-zāḫir wa-lubāb al-fāḫir*, 'The Abounding Torrents and the Glorious Gist' by al-Ḥasan Ibn Muḥammad as-Saġānī (d. 1252), unfinished
- *Lisān al-ʿArab*, 'The Tongue of the Arabs' by Ibn Manẓūr, completed in 1290
- *al-Qāmūs al-Muḥīṭ*, 'The Comprehensive Dictionary' by al-Fīrūzābādī (1329–1414)

Some historical dictionaries are also available as digital full texts. In the course of inquiries for this overview, complete versions of Ibn Manẓūr's *Lisān al-ʿarab* and the widely used *al-Muʿjam al-wasīṭ* (published in 1960–61 by the Academy of the Arabic Language in Cairo) could be found on the Internet, not only as PDFs but also in the form of complete Word documents.

There are also websites with mixed approaches combining facsimiles with indices to navigate in them. A very good example of such a web application is the interface to Lane's 8-Volume Arabic Lexicon of 1863 of the *Tyndale Archive of Biblical Studies*.[27]

Another website offering numerous historical and some contemporary dictionaries as facsimiles is *Mawrid Reader: Arabic Dictionary Interface*.[28] This site was obviously developed by a single enthusiast who gives his name as Abdurahman Erik Taal Dua-ware. The website allows to search in the dictionaries through roots.

31.3.3.3 Websites and portals with bi- and multilingual interfaces

Internet dictionary portals have been on the rise for quite some time (see Chapter 46 of this *Handbook*). Some of these also have Arabic in their programmes:

- Bab.la – Online dictionary for 28 languages[29]
- Glosbe – the multilingual online dictionary[30]
- TheFreeDictionary[31]
- WordReference.com

A dedicated Arabic site is *Al-Maʿānī* 'the Senses' or 'the Meanings'. This multilingual dictionary site offers Arabic-English, Arabic-French, Arabic-Portuguese, Arabic-Spanish,

Arabic-Turkish and Arabic-Persian dictionary interfaces.[32] The website also holds some 50 PDFs of special language dictionaries, some of them dating back to the 1970s and 1980s.[33]

Dictionary portals with Arabic can be found in many countries and languages. A Dutch website is *Woordenboek.eu – 65+ talen* '65+ languages'.[34] Such websites are, of course, particularly important in countries with a predominantly Islamic population such as Indonesia (e.g. *e-alQamus*[35] or *Kamus Online Bahasa Arab*[36]) or Iran (e.g. *Abādis*[37]).

Using such sites entails a host of problems: metadata are almost always missing, data are often poorly structured or completely unstructured, there is no way of persistently referring to them as sites come and go and with most sites it is impossible to quantify the data involved.

31.4 Looking to the future: recent advances in Arabic lexicography

We will conclude this section focussing on two types of dictionaries: bilingual MSA dictionaries and bilingual dictionaries of local varieties of spoken Arabic. This is motivated by the substantial progress recently made in these fields. A great number of monolingual dictionaries were produced over the past decades. However, the preference of CA over modern forms of Arabic, the inclusion of large amounts of obsolete lexemes, remarkable lexical gaps and the absence of empirical evidence based on contemporary language have remained major stumbling blocks in creating modern dictionaries (see Ghazali et al. 2001). Monolingual Arabic dictionaries have thus often remained a rehash of what can be found in medieval dictionaries (see Section 31.3.3.2).

31.4.1 Bilingual dictionaries

The number of bilingual dictionaries published during the past two decades is very large. However, only a few can stand up to scientific examination. Julio Cortés's *Diccionario de árabe culto moderno: árabe-español* 'Dictionary of Modern Standard Arabic: Arabic-Spanish' (1996)[38] and Federico Corriente and Ferrando's *Diccionario Arabe-Español* (1998) represent the Spanish school of lexicography and were still produced by traditional lexicographical means (see Chapter 40 of this *Handbook*).

A real breakthrough in Arabic lexicography and a product of up-to-date, well-documented lexicographic work were the *Woordenboek Arabisch-Nederlands/Nederlands-Arabisch 'Arabic – Dutch/Dutch-Arabic Dictionaries'* by Hoogland, Versteegh and Woidich (2003). The project was part of a major initiative of the ministry of education of the Netherlands and Flanders in the 1990s aiming at improving the lexicographic situation with respect to the Dutch language. They promoted projects producing bilingual lexical resources, Dutch being either the source or the target language (Martin 2007). As a whole, the initiative which resulted in the production of over a dozen dictionaries had a strong technological background aiming at the development of multifunctional electronic lexical databases. The two volumes were compiled between 1998 and 2002 at the Radboud University of Nijmegen and were intended for both Arabic and Dutch speakers, for readers as well as translators. They therefore provided grammatical information for source as well as target language. The number of Arabic lemmas is indicated as 24,500. In the selection of the headwords, the authors looked primarily at media texts, modern literature and the basic vocabularies of various technical fields. The two dictionaries can be seen as the first Arabic dictionaries that were compiled making use of a scholarly compiled digital corpus (see Section 31.3.1.2).

Hoogland's dictionary made a significant impact on the field in terms of methodology and lexical contents. It serves as a good example of the beneficial effects data sharing can have on lexicographical work. Hoogland's Arabic lemma list was used as the basis for the new *Oxford Arabic Dictionary* which was edited by Tressy Arts and published in 2014. This latter one was the first bilingual Arabic dictionary that was produced on the basis of a sizeable digital corpus which was also tagged with tools already available at the time. To search and access the corpus, the team made use of Sketch Engine (see Section 31.3.2.2; Arts 2014). The Oxford team expanded Hoogland's lemma list, mostly by comparing their data with corpus data. However, 'old-fashioned' handwork, that is, critical reading of texts, was also mentioned as a method (ibid). Having cleaned out some 400 entries that were deemed obsolete they raised the number of Arabic entries from 24,682 to 26,316 (ibid).

31.4.2 Dialect dictionaries

Dictionaries dedicated to local spoken varieties (see Section 31.2) are a comparatively recent phenomenon. Whereas many of the earlier dictionaries were made for travellers and merchants in need of basic communication skills, over time linguistic research has resulted in more comprehensive and well-founded dictionaries. It is impossible to give an exhaustive list of relevant publications. Some varieties are covered better than others – almost all dictionaries were compiled without digital technology. A number of the older products are available as PDFs: Hinds and Badawi's *Dictionary of Egyptian Arabic* (1986) can be found at the Archive.org and Alfred-Louis de Prémare's monumental 12-volume *Dictionnaire Arabe-Français* (1993–1999) of Moroccan Arabic can be downloaded from the publisher's (l'Harmattan) website.[39]

Born-digital material is still scarce. Some smaller dictionaries are available in the *Vienna Corpus of Arabic Varieties*[40] (VICAV), an ongoing project which started quite some time ago. Although the initial intention behind VICAV was to build corpora, its objective has evolved into creating a collection of various digital language resources documenting varieties of spoken Arabic, including a series of digital bilingual dictionaries. These have been created with three main purposes in mind: (a) providing support for spoken Arabic classes, (b) to create a virtual research environment for comparative lexical studies and (c) to promote technological developments for digital lexical data. The available lexical resources are all small in size (none of them contains more than 8,000 entries) but constitute databases with structured lexicographic information (Mörth et al. 2014). The varieties covered so far are Cairo, Damascus and Tunis. The *Digital Dictionary of Damascene Arabic*, compiled by Carmen Berlinches Ramos and Stephan Procházka was based on all the vocabulary of Procházka's textbook of Syrian Arabic (2014/15) and is just being enhanced with audio recordings of lemmas and inflected forms. The largest dictionary in the series is the TUNICO dictionary (see Section 31.3.2.2) which was compiled on the basis of the Viennese TUNICO corpus. In addition, it also incorporates lexical material extracted from various printed sources published in the middle of the twentieth century and earlier. Together with several other smaller dictionaries in the collection, including an MSA-German dictionary, a mid-term goal of this undertaking is the creation of an integrated lexicographic system, a *Comparative Dictionary of Arabic Varieties*, which will allow researchers to query across a number of dictionaries and to obtain integrated results (Mörth et al. 2015). All these dictionaries have English translation equivalents (some also additional translations into German, French or Spanish). They are all built on the same technology and their encoding is based on a shared schema.

Another recent project is the *Moroccan Dialect Electronic Dictionary* which is being carried out by the Ibtikarat research group of the LARIE laboratory at the Mohammadia School of Engineers of the Mohammed Vth University in Rabat (Morocco).[41] As they are working on a tool to be used in machine translation (Tachicart 2014), the resulting dictionary will be very different from what variational linguists might expect.

In spite of the low status of colloquial Arabic in most of the Arab countries, it is considered by some as an interesting curiosity. A website with user-generated content is *Muʿjam*[42] which offers data from 18 regions, the region with by far most data being Saudi Arabia, an otherwise linguistically still poorly documented area. However, the data are presented in Arabic script only which detracts considerably from its usefulness for serious linguistic research.

31.5 Conclusion

Notwithstanding a certain degree of conservativism, retrospection and reluctance to engage with innovative approaches, Arabic lexicography has made great strides in the past decades. However, in view of its historical achievements and its current international status (Arabic is one of the United Nations' six official languages and the fifth most spoken language in the world) several important desiderata still remain to be fulfilled. On top of this wish list, there is a comprehensive and up-to-date monolingual information system for MSA based on digital corpora and modern lexicographical methods. In spite of a highly fragmented scholarly landscape, considerable socio-political challenges and missing adequate material resources (both in the Arabic world as well as in other areas), the situation regarding digital language technology – tools as well as data – has definitely changed over the past few years, and Arabic must no longer be regarded as a technologically under-resourced language.

Related topics

Lexicography and corpus linguistics; lexicography and information science; lexicography and natural language processing; dictionaries for text reception; electronic dictionaries; using the Web for lexicographic purposes; dictionary portals.

Further reading

Baalbaki, R. (2014). *The Arabic Lexicographical Tradition. From the 2nd/8th to the 12th/18th Century*. Leiden/Boston: Brill.

This is the most extensive treatise on the history of pre-modern Arabic lexicography.

Benzehra, R. (2013). "Arabic Lexicography", in R. H. Gows, U. Heid, W. Schweickard and H. E. Wiegand (eds.), *Dictionaries: An International Encyclopedia of Lexicography, 5.4. Supplementary Volume: Recent Developments With Focus on Electronic and Computational Lexicography*. Berlin/Boston: de Gruyter, pp. 872–884.

A very informative, insightful overview with a focus on recent developments.

Buckwalter, T. and D. B. Parkinson. (2013). "Modern Lexicography", in J. Owens (ed.), *The Oxford Handbook of Arabic Linguistics*. Oxford: Oxford University Press, pp. 539–560. DOI: 10.1093/oxfordhb/9780199764136.013.0024

This handbook chapter offers a concise, readable and comprehensive account of Arabic lexicography in the twentieth century.

Notes

1 Arabic names are transcribed according to the widely accepted system used in the EALL (Versteegh *et al.* 2006–2009).
2 We cannot discuss the term and concept here. In some regions there are even more than two varieties coexisting in functional complementarity which has been described as a polyglossic situation (with respect to Tunis see Lawson *et al.* 2000; with respect to Morocco see Ennaji 2015).
3 In Arabic, groups of mostly three or four consonants are used in combination with patterns for inflection and derivation. The consonants carrying a word's basic semantic information are called roots.
4 A special form of digital corpora are treebanks, corpora with syntactic annotations. These have played a minor role in lexicography and will therefore be ignored in the following paragraphs.
5 For a historical breakdown (until 2010) with some basic information see www.comp.leeds.ac.uk/eric/latifa/arabic_corpora.htm.
6 The history of Arabic frequency dictionaries goes back as far as 1940 when Moshe Brill published *The Basic Word List of the Arabic Daily Newspaper* based on a printed corpus from Egypt and Palestine (Haywood 1960: 137). In the years thereafter several other wordcounts of Arabic texts were published (see Buckwalter *et al.* 2011, p. 2sq.).
7 www.qamus.org/wordlist.htm
8 www.let.kun.nl/WBA
9 https://catalog.ldc.upenn.edu/byyear
10 Controlled access to this corpus is offered through this website: www.bibalex.org/ica/en.
11 https://islaamiclibrary.wordpress.com/2009/03/01/thecomprehensivelibrary
12 www.almeshkat.net
13 http://ksucorpus.ksu.edu.sa
14 http://corpafroas.tge-adonis.fr
15 www.tunisiya.org
16 https://archive.org; All in all, the *Internet Archive and Open Library* contains more than 10 million digital versions of books and texts. In May 2016, the Archive's Community Arabic Texts contained 81,797 items (https://archive.org/details/opensource_Arabic).
17 https://archive.org/details/Dict_Wehr.pdf
18 https://archive.org/details/26387126HansWehrArabischesWorterbuch
19 www.perseus.tufts.edu/hopper
20 https://sourceforge.net/projects/awnbrowser
21 www.ldlp-dictionary.com/home/dictionary
22 http://dictionary.cambridge.org/dictionary/english-arabic
23 www.larousse.fr/dictionnaires/francais-arabe
24 www.oxforddictionaries.com/arabic
25 www.linguatec.de
26 www.baheth.net
27 www.tyndalearchive.com/TABS/Lane/index.htm
28 http://ejtaal.net
29 http://bab.la
30 https://glosbe.com
31 http://thefreedictionary.com
32 www.almaany.com
33 www.almaany.com/dicpdf.php
34 www.woordenboek.eu
35 http://alqamus.moe.edu.my/ealqamus/v4/index.aspx
36 http://kamus.javakedaton.com/indonesia-arab.php
37 http://dictionary.abadis.ir
38 https://archive.org/details/DiccionarioArabe-espanolAvanzado-p1 and DiccionarioArabe-espanol Avanzado-p2
39 www.editions-harmattan.fr
40 www.acdh.oeaw.ac.at/vicav
41 http://sibawayh.emi.ac.ma/web/i
42 http://en.mo3jam.com/

References

Dictionaries

Arts, T. (ed.) (2014) *Oxford Arabic Dictionary: Qāmūs Uksfūrd al-ʿArabī*. Oxford: Oxford University Press.

Buckwalter, T. and D. Parkinson (2011) *A Frequency Dictionary of Arabic: Core Vocabulary for Learners*. London/New York: Routledge.

Corriente, F. and I. Ferrando (1998) *Diccionario avanzado árabe-español*. Barcelona: Herder.

Cortés, J. (1996) *Diccionario de árabe culto moderno: árabe-español*. Madrid: Gredos.

Freytag, G.W.F. (1830–1837) *Lexicon arabico-latinum praesertim ex Djeuharii Firuzabadiique et aliorum Arabum operibus, adhibitis Golii quoque et aliorum libris confectum*, 4 vols, Halle.

Hoogland, J., K. Versteegh and M. Woidich (2003) *Woordenboek Arabisch-Nederlands and Woordenboek Nederlands Arabisch*, Amsterdam: Bulaaq.

Prémare, A. (1993–1999) *Dictionnaire arabe-français: Langue et culture marocaines*. 12 volumes. Paris: l'Harmattan.

Van Mol, M. and K. Bergman (2001) *Leerwoordenboek Arabisch*. Amsterdam: Bulaaq.

Wehr, H. (1961) *A Dictionary of Modern Written Arabic: Arabic-English*, J. Milton Cowan, ed. 3rd edition. New York: Spoken Language Services, Inc.

Wehr, H. (1985) *Arabisches Wörterbuch für die Schriftsprache der Gegenwart*. 5th edition. Wiesbaden: Otto Harrassowitz.

Other literature

All the Internet references were last accessed in June 2016.

Alansary, S., M. Nagi and N. Adly (2007) "Building an International Corpus of Arabic (ICA): Progress of Compilation Stage", in *7th International Conference on Language Engineering, Cairo, Egypt*. www.bibalex.org/unl/Attachements/Paper/Building%20an%20International%20Corpus%20of%20Arabic%20(ICA).pdf.

Arts, T. (2014) "The Making of a Large English-Arabic/Arabic-English Dictionary: The Oxford Arabic Dictionary", in A. Abel, C. Vettori and N. Ralli (eds.), *Proceedings of the XVI EURALEX International Congress: The User in Focus*, Bolzano: EURAC Research, pp. 109–124.

Attia, M., L. Tounsi. and J. Genabith (2010) "Automatic Lexical Resource Acquisition for Constructing an LMF-Compatible Lexicon of Modern Standard Arabic", *The NCLT Seminar Series*, Dublin, Ireland. http://attiaspace.com/Publications/Corpus-Driven_Lexicon_of_MSA.pdf.

Benzehra, R. (2013) "Arabic Lexicography", in R. H. Gows, U. Heid, W. Schweickard and H. E. Wiegand (eds.), *Dictionaries: An International Encyclopedia of Lexicography, 5.4. Supplementary Volume: Recent Developments With Focus on Electronic and Computational Lexicography*. Berlin/ Boston, MA: de Gruyter, pp. 872–884.

Budin, G., S. Majewski and K. Moerth (2012) "Creating Lexical Resources in TEI P5", *Journal of the Text Encoding Initiative (jTEI)* 3. doi:10.4000/jtei.522

Declerck, T., K. Mörth and E. Wandl-Vogt (2014) "A SKOS-Based Schema for TEI Encoded Dictionaries at ICLTT", in *LREC 2014, Ninth International Conference on Language Resources and Evaluation*, Reykjavik: European Language Resources Association (ELRA). www.lrec-conf.org/ proceedings/lrec2014/pdf/1163_Paper.pdf.

Declerck, T., E. Wandl-Vogt and K. Mörth (2015) "Towards a Pan European Lexicography by Means of Linked (Open) Data", in I. Kosem, M. Jakubicek, J. Kallas and S. Krek (eds.), *Proceedings of eLex 2015*. Ljubljana: Trojina Institute for Applied Slovene Studies/Lexical Computing, pp. 342–355.

Ennaji, M. (2015) "Teaching and Learning Arabic as a Foreign Language", in G. Grigore and G. Biţună (eds.), *Arabic Varieties: Far and Wide. Proceedings of the 11th International Conference of AIDA*. Bucharest: Bucharest University Press, pp. 217–222.

Ferguson, C. (1959) "Diglossia", *Word* 15: 325–340.

Ghazali, S. and A. Braham (2001) "Dictionary Definitions and Corpus-Based Evidence in Modern Standard Arabic", *Arabic NLP Workshop at ACL/EACL*, Toulouse. www.researchgate.net/publication/2373612_Dictionary_Definitions_and_Corpus-Based_Evidence_in_Modern_Standard_Arabic.

Haddar, K., H. Fehri and L. Romary (2012) "A Prototype for Projecting HPSG Syntactic Lexica Towards LMF", *Journal of Language Technology and Computational Linguistics, Gesellschaft für Sprachtechnologie und Computerlinguistik e.V. (GSCL)* 27(1): 21–46. https://hal.archives-ouvertes.fr/hal-00719954v2.

Hassanein, A. T. (2008) "Lexicography: Monolingual Dictionaries", in K. Versteegh (ed.), *Encyclopedia of Arabic Language and Linguistics III*. Leiden/Boston, MA: Brill, pp. 37–45.

Haywood, J. A. (1960) *Arabic Lexicography: Its History and Its Place in the General History of Lexicography*. Leiden: Brill.

Haywood, J. A. (1991a) "Arabic Lexicography", in F. J. Hausmann, O. Reichmann, H. E. Wiegand and L. Zgusta (eds.), *Dictionaries: An International Encyclopedia of Lexicography* 5.3. Berlin/New York: de Gruyter, pp. 2438–2448.

Haywood, J. A. (1991b) "Bilingual Lexicography with Arabic", in F. J. Hausmann, O. Reichmann, H. E. Wiegand and L. Zgusta (eds.), *Dictionaries: An International Encyclopedia of Lexicography* 5.3. Berlin/New York: de Gruyter, 3086–3096.

Hoogland, J. (2008) "Lexicography: Bilingual Dictionaries", in K. Versteegh (ed.), *Encyclopedia of Arabic Language and Linguistics III*. Leiden/Boston, MA: Brill, pp. 21–30.

Khemakhem, A., B. Gargouri, K. Haddar and A. Ben Hamadou (2013) "LMF in Arabic", in G. Francopoulo (ed.), *LMF. Lexical Markup Framework*. London/Hoboken: Wiley, pp. 83–98.

Lawson, S. and I. Sachdev (2000) "Code Switching in Tunisia: Attitudinal and Behavioral Dimensions", *Journal of Pragmatics* 32(9): 1343–1361.

Lhioui, M., K. Haddar and L. Romary (2014) "Towards Modelling Arabic Lexicons Compliant LMF in OWL-DL", in *Terminology and Knowledge Engineering*. Berlin. https://hal.archives-ouvertes.fr/hal-01005854.

McNeil, K. and M. Faiza (2012) "Corpus of Tunisian Arabic: Design and Progress". www.tunisiya.org/media/TunisianArabicCorpusSummary.pdf.

Maks, I., C. Tiberius and R. Veenendaal (2008) "Standardising Bilingual Lexical Resources According to the Lexicon Markup Framework", *LREC* 2008. www.lrec-conf.org/proceedings/lrec2008/pdf/439_paper.pdf.

Martin, W. (2007) "Government Policy and the Planning and Production of Bilingual Dictionaries: The "Dutch" Approach as a Case in Point", *International Journal of Lexicography* 20(3): 221–238.

Mettouchi, A. and C. Chanard (2010) "From Fieldwork to Annotated Corpora: The CorpAfroAs Project", *Faits de Langue-Les Cahiers* n°2: 255–265. http://corpafroas.tge-adonis.fr/fichiers/Mettouchi_Chanard.pdf.

Miller, G. A., R. Beckwith, C. Fellbaum, D. Gross and K. Miller (1993) "Introduction to WordNet: An On-line Lexical Database". http://wordnetcode.princeton.edu/5papers.pdf.

Mörth, K., S. Procházka and I. Dallaji (2014) "Laying the Foundations for a Diachronic Dictionary of Tunis Arabic: A First Glance at an Evolving New Language Resource", in A. Abel, C. Vettori and N. Ralli (eds.), *Proceedings of the XVI EURALEX International Congress: The User in Focus*. Bolzano: EURAC Research, pp. 377–387.

Mörth, K., D. Schopper and O. Siam (2015) "Towards a Diatopic Dictionary of Spoken Arabic Varieties: Challenges in Compiling the VICAV Dictionaries", in G. Grigore and G. Biţună (eds.), *Arabic Varieties: Far and Wide. Proceedings of the 11th International Conference of AIDA*. Bucharest: Bucharest University Press, pp. 395–404.

Procházka, S., R. Aldoukhi and A. Telič (2014–2015) *Lehrbuch des Syrisch-Arabischen: Praxisnaher Einstieg in den Dialekt von Damaskus*. Wiesbaden: Harrassowitz.

Procházka, S. and K. Mörth (2015) "The Vienna Corpus of Arabic Varieties: Building a Digital Research Environment for Arabic Dialects", in M. Al-Hamad, R. Ahmed and H. Aloui (eds.), *Lisan*

Al-Arab: Studies in Contemporary Arabic Dialects, Proceedings of the 10th International Conference of AIDA, Qatar University 2013. Vienna, LIT: Verlag, pp. 176–183.

Salmon-Alt, S., A. Akrout and L. Romary (2005) "Proposals for a Normalized Representation of Standard Arabic Full Form Lexica", *International Conference on Machine Intelligence*. https://hal.archives-ouvertes.fr/halshs-00004541.

Seidensticker, T. (2008) "Lexicography: Classical Arabic", in K. Versteegh (ed.), *Encyclopedia of Arabic Language and Linguistics III*, Leiden/Boston: Brill, pp. 30–37.

Tachicart, R., K. Bouzoubaa and H. Jaafar (2014) "Building a Moroccan Dialect Electronic Dictionary (MDED)". http://sibawayh.emi.ac.ma/web/i/sites/default/files/TachikartEtAl%20CITALA2014.pdf.

TEI Consortium (2016) *TEI P5: Guidelines for Electronic Text Encoding and Interchange*, Version 3.0.0. www.tei-c.org/release/doc/tei-p5-doc/en/Guidelines.pdf.

Van Mol, M. (2000) "The Development of a New Learner's Dictionary for Modern Standard Arabic: The Linguistic Corpus Approach", *Proceedings of the Ninth EURALEX International Congress*, EURALEX 2000, 831–836.

Versteegh, K. (ed.) (2006–2009) *Encyclopedia of Arabic Language and Linguistics (EALL)*. 4 volumes. Leiden/Boston, MA: Brill.

Zaghouani, W. (2014) "Critical Survey of the Freely Available Arabic Corpora", *Workshop on Free/Open-Source Arabic Corpora and Corpora Processing Tools (LREC 2014)*: 1–8. www.lrec-conf.org/proceedings/lrec2014/workshops/LREC2014Workshop-OSACT%20Proceedings.pdf.

32

Chinese lexicography in the Internet era

Heming Yong and Jing Peng

32.1 Introduction

The Chinese lexicographical culture has its deep roots in the socio-cultural settings which called forth reading primers written for school children in the Western Zhou Dynasty (1046 BC to 771 BC). *The Ready Guide* (Eyra《尔雅》), which was written between the Qin and Han dynasties (221 BC to AD 25), is generally recognized as the earliest Chinese dictionary in its real sense.

There are four major types of Chinese character formation: pictographic (象形法), self-explanatory (指事法), ideographic (会意法), and pictophonetic (形声法). In addition, there are mutually explanatory formation (转注法) and phonetic loaning (假借法) (Yong and Peng 2008:16–21). That theory of "six-category Chinese characters" was proposed by ancient Chinese philologists and used as one of the most fundamental concepts for Chinese dictionary design and compilation, from ancient reading primers to glossaries and word-books, and then to character and word dictionaries in terms of compilation style and structural configuration.

The analysis of the theory of "six-category Chinese characters" reveals its influence on macrostructural and microstructural configuration. Starting from the Sui Dynasty, inquiries into lexicographic issues became substantial. In *Presenting a Memorial for Ancient and Contemporary Characters*, Jiang Shi (江式) held that characters and language serve the function of "when it is announced in the Palace, it would be passed among different trades in the world; when it is written down and printed in ten thousand copies, all things would be clearly identified." In discussing lexical coverage, Lu Deming (陆德明) held that "embracing both the ancient and the contemporary" should be a general principle for dictionaries of every kind. He also pointed out that the pronunciation for a character in a dictionary should be "put in the first place" so as to "help its user to compare in use." A dictionary "should add phonetic notation, define the character, trace its origin, and analyse and explain the difficult points or confusions." Lu Deming believed that the citations should be "taken from both the ancient and contemporary literature" and the compilers should "extract out the fundamental and essential elements." The citations for each character should be "plain but not crude, abundant but not chaotic."

This chapter offers a panoramic view of Chinese lexicography over the past three millennia. For several reasons it is quite different from the rest of chapters in Part V in terms of contents and structure. The fact that the Internet is not much used in Chinese lexicography and that both lexicographic theory and practice in China have followed a very different path to other traditions, especially from Western ones, has forced us to write a chapter focusing more on the history of Chinese lexicography than on its future developments in the era of the Internet.

32.2 Historical perspectives

32.2.1 Chinese character dictionaries: their development and innovation

Prior to the Western Han Dynasty, the prototypes of different dictionary genres had already taken shape, and the general styles and formats of dictionary making had begun to develop. Over the 1700 years between the Wei and the Qing Dynasty, new driving forces brought forth dictionary types never seen before, and lexicographic theories were extended and innovated. Chinese dictionaries, particularly character dictionaries, became well distinguished in type, scale, contents, functions, styles and formats, methodology, theorization, and technological sophistication.

32.2.1.1 Chinese character dictionaries in the Wei to the Southern and Northern Dynasties

Following the wake of dictionary compilation in the Han Dynasty, character dictionary making continued to develop with vigour and vitality in the Wei and the Jin Dynasty, represented by *The Exegesis of Ancient and Contemporary Characters* (《古今字诂》) by Zhang Yi (张揖) and *The Jade Chapters* (《玉篇》) by Gu Yewang (顾野王).

Between the Wei and the Southern and Northern Dynasties, the official script of the Han Dynasty was fading out of use. Scripts like running hand (行书) and regular script (楷书) were in wider circulation and adopted in formal writing. This transition resulted in chaos in spelling characters and caused serious problems to those who tried to learn and study the Classics and to the government who issued orders and decrees. Naturally, it became urgent to check and proofread the texts, to codify and standardize Chinese characters and their writing, and to print the Classic works and produce standard model textbooks that could be taken as a yardstick for the printing industry and as the final resort when disputes arose. The compilation of character dictionaries over this period was to codify character variants, hence the emergence of 'character model' dictionaries, which is the equivalent to the spelling dictionary in Europe. Typical works included *The Character Models* (《字样》) by Yan Shigu (颜师古) and *The Collection of Characters from Five Classics* (《五经文字》) by Zhang Shen (张参). This new type of dictionary played a key role in character codification and standardization.

32.2.1.2 Chinese character dictionaries in the Sui to the Yuan Dynasty

Over the period of the Sui to the Yuan Dynasty, new accomplishments were made, marked by a considerable number of character books and dictionaries in the Sui and the Tang Dynasty, such as *The Guiyuan Collection of Characters* (《桂苑珠丛》) by Zhuge Ying (诸葛颖) in the Sui Dynasty and *The Magnificent Character Dictionary* (《字海》) by Wu Zetian (武则天) in the Tang Dynasty. They are no longer in existence.

The simultaneous use and currency of different scripts gave rise to variations of existing characters, the appearance of new characters, and characters of different styles, which made it necessary to discriminate between ancient and contemporary characters in their forms, meanings and writing styles. A number of character dictionaries were compiled between the Song and the Yuan Dynasty to collate the styles of characters and to trace the evolutional changes of characters in form, meaning, and pronunciation, such as *The Pei Xi Dictionary* (《佩觿》) by Guo Zhongshu (郭忠恕) and *The Exegesis of Six-category Characters* (《六书故》) by Dai Tong (戴侗) in the Yuan Dynasty. As a result of the extensive influence of Dai Tong's dictionary, a series of six-category dictionaries appeared, such as *The General Exegesis of Six-Category Chinese Characters* (《六书统》) and *The Learned Exegesis of Six-Category Chinese Characters* (《六书通》).

32.2.1.3 Chinese character dictionaries in the Ming to the Qing Dynasty

When Chinese history stepped into the Ming Dynasty, the Chinese traditional culture was declining and was undergoing a transition towards modern culture. The transitional Ming and Qing cultures were characterized by cultural autocracy and the extremely cruel literacy inquisition on the one hand, and the promotion of practical learning and western learning and the sum-up of achievements in traditional Chinese civilization and the liberal academic studies on the other hand. In the Ming and Qing dynasties, a great deal of manpower and material resources were officially utilized for the compilation of magnificent lexicographical works, like *The Yongle Compendium* (《永乐大典》 1404) and *The Imperial Collection of Four Branches of Literature* (《四库全书》 1782). Congruous with the Chinese tradition of compiling books and dictionaries in times of prosperity, those dictionaries were splendid in size, adequate in content, and consistent in compilation style and format.

The compilers of character dictionaries in the Ming and the Qing Dynasty not only adopted the merits of the preceding wordbooks and dictionaries but also managed to innovate in styles and formats. *The Comprehensive Dictionary of Chinese Characters* (《字汇》) by Mei Yingzuo (梅膺祚) and *The Rectified Dictionary of Chinese Characters* (《正字通》) by Zhang Zilie (张自烈) were two important works in the early stage. The latter remedied the flaws and corrected the mistakes in the former. Over the period of the late Ming and early Qing Dynasties, the practical value of Classic works was advocated, with great emphasis given to textual researches and exegetic studies. In the 49th year of the Kangxi reign, Emperor Kangxi issued the order for the compilation of a Mandarin dictionary of the Chinese language, called *The Imperial Dictionary of Kangxi* (《康熙字典》 1711–1716). Several other remarkable compilations were completed as a result of the Shuowen studies, which was in its prime time in the Qing Dynasty, namely, *The Annotated Explanatory Dictionary of Chinese Characters* (《说文解字注》) by DuanYucai and *An Explanatory Book of Phonetic Sounds* (《说文通训定声》) by Zhu Junsheng. The period of the Ming and the Qing Dynasty integrated and crystallized the achievements in the history of Chinese civilization. The character dictionaries of this period not only represent a conclusion for previous philological studies but also exert direct impacts on the development of later character dictionaries.

32.2.2 Chinese word dictionaries: their development and innovation

From the Wei to the Yuan Dynasty, dramatic political, social, economic, and cultural changes took place. Since the Han Dynasty, the upper class in the Chinese society was under the predominant influence of the Confucian ideology, which had gradually become a powerful source and channel for advocating the 'truth' and seeking the 'meaning'. Scholars began to interpret, expound, and add explanatory notes to the Confucian classics to seek the 'meaning' beyond them. The lower class, on the other hand, was increasingly influenced by the gradual eastward penetration of Buddhism, and dictionaries were needed to facilitate the appreciation and interpretation of the sounds and meanings of Buddhist scriptures. Some important events during that period, such as the creation and implementation of the imperial examination system for civil servants, the establishment of academies of classic learning, the prosperous printing industry and the organized book collections, the spread of Western learning, and the promotion of government establishments, were directly relevant to the evolution of Chinese lexicographic culture and had profound and far-reaching impacts upon the history of the Chinese nation and of Chinese lexicography.

32.2.2.1 Chinese word dictionaries during the Wei to the Yuan Dynasty

Over the period of the Wei to the Yuan Dynasty, Chinese dictionary compilation continued to focus on the exegetic explanations of Confucian classics as the Confucian classics and their studies were still the focus of the Chinese academics. A new focus was the exegesis of Buddhist scriptures. Two major word dictionary strains dominated that period: dictionaries for interpreting Confucian classics and dictionaries for interpreting Buddhist scriptures. The first strain included *The Rectified Interpretation of Five Classics* (《五经正义》) and *The Broad Ready Guide* (《广雅》). *The Rectified Interpretation of Five Classics* surveyed and summarized the achievements accomplished in the period of the Han to the Jin (晋) Dynasty, and *The Broad Ready Guide*, a derivative from *The Ready Guide*, well preserved the exegetic studies of the Zhou, Qin, and Han Dynasties and was the most important exegetic dictionary since *The Ready Guide*. In the Song and Yuan Dynasty, similar Erya word dictionaries were compiled, such as Liu Bozhuang's (刘伯庄) *The Extended Ready Guide* (《续尔雅》) and Niu Zhong's (牛衷) *The Essentials of Augmented Ready Guide* (《埤雅广要》).

In order to study and spread the scriptures of Buddhism, a series of dictionaries were compiled for specific Buddhist scriptures, such as *Sounds and Meanings of the Saddharma-pundarika-sutra* (《妙法莲华经音义》) by Kui Ji (窥基, also known as 大乘基), *Sounds and Meanings of the Avatamsaka Sutra* (《华严经音义》) by Hui Yuan (慧苑), and *Sounds and Meanings of Mahaparinibbana-sutta* (《大般涅槃经音义》) by Yun Gong (云公) or for a set of scriptures, such as the two versions of *Sounds and Meanings of all the Buddhist Scriptures* by Xuan Ying and by Hui Lin (慧琳), respectively, and *The Extended Sounds and Meanings of all the Buddhist Scriptures* (《续一切经音义》) by Xi Lin (希麟).

32.2.2.2 Chinese word dictionaries in the Ming to the Qing Dynasty

Chinese dictionary compilation over the Ming and the Qing Dynasty served as a link between past achievements and future developments and integrated all major previous accomplishments. Eventually, the word dictionaries in the Ming and the Qing Dynasty were mainly the product of inheriting, extending, and innovating previous works, hence dictionaries for exegetic interpretations represented by Ruan Yuan's (阮元) *The Exegetic Interpretations of Ancient Classics* (《经籍纂诂》); the Erya dictionary type (dictionaries following the pattern of *The Ready Guide*), such as *The General Ready Guide* (《通雅》) by Fang Yizhi (方以智) in the Ming Dynasty and *The Distinctive Ready Guide* (《别雅》) by Wu Yujin (吴

玉摺) in the Qing Dynasty, which were superior for their more standardized formats, more innovative styles, and more comprehensive functions; and dialect dictionaries (dictionaries following the pattern of *The Dictionary of Dialectal Words*).

The major dialect works in the Ming Dynasty included *The Rectified Dictionary of Dialectal Words* (《方言据》) by Yue Yuansheng (岳元声) and *A Categoric Dictionary of Dialectal Words* (《方言类聚》) by Chen Yujiao (陈与郊). The more flourishing dialect dictionary compilation in the Qing Dynasty was proved by the appearance of three dictionary kinds: (a) dictionaries for elucidating and emendating *The Dictionary of Dialectal Words*, such as *The Rectification of the Dictionary of Dialectal Words* (《方言疏证》) by Dai Zhen (戴震); (b) dictionaries for supplementing and extending *The Dictionary of Dialectal Words*, such as *Supplements and Rectifications to the Augmented Dictionary of Dialectal Words* (《续方言补正》) by Cheng Jisheng (程际盛); (c) newly compiled dictionaries that collected dialectal words in famous works and those expounding regional dialects, such as *The Dictionary of Textual Researches on the Wu-Xia Dialect* (《吴下方言考》) by Hu Wenying (胡文英).

32.2.2.3 Innovative features and theoretical breakthroughs

The word dictionaries between the Wei and the Yuan Dynasty displayed some innovative features. In macrostructure, the entries were arranged according to their formation and structure and their phonological and semantic systems. Phonetic notation was chiefly provided by means of *fanqie*, which was invented toward the end of the Han Dynasty and was quickly adopted and became the dominant means of pronunciation notation. It indicates the pronunciation of a character by using two other characters, with the first having the same consonant as the given character and the second having the same vowel and tone. The focus of definition shifted from the original meaning to the multi-fold meanings, with more attention given to etymological investigation. Where controversial issues appeared, different opinions were collected and presented together for 'sense sorting' and 'set explanation'. An extremely wide-ranging scope of citation was opened up, including Confucian and Taoist works; books concerning history, philosophy, and Buddhism; and from other sources.

A theoretical breakthrough was achieved in *The Dictionary of Characters from Classics and Scriptures with Phonetic Discrimination* (《群经音辨》) by Jia Changchao (贾昌朝) in the Song Dynasty, who, for the first time in history, dealt with the transformation of parts of speech and of lexical meanings and the ways in which the change of character categories brought about the change in parts of speech and in lexical meanings. Innovation is also observed in the compilation of function word dictionaries and regional dialect dictionaries. Since Yang Xiong's monumental work, no substantial work of a similar kind appeared until the Ming and the Qing Dynasty, when the compilation of dialect dictionaries regained its momentum and sprinted into a rapid development in both quality and quantity.

In the word dictionaries of the Ming and the Qing Dynasty, compilation standards were basically established and conventionalized and both micro- and macrostructural configuration gradually became unified. On the macrostructural level, the arrangement of headwords and dictionary layout was founded on a more scientific and user-friendly basis, and ease of retrieval of information was greatly enhanced. The traditional method of transcribing pronunciation via *fanqie* and direct notation was ameliorated so that the level, rising, falling, and entering tones were used for phonetic notation if no corresponding character could be found for its direct phonetic notation. The clarity and hierarchy of meaning explanation showed the improvement in defining techniques, and explanations in terms of phonetic sounds related sounds more closely to meanings. The hierarchical meaning explanations set the precedent for sense division and differentiation in later dictionaries. As far as the back matter was concerned, it was not until the Ming and the Qing Dynasty that indexes were designed and appeared as part of the outside matter of the dictionary, which set the precedent for later compilation and ensured easier access to dictionary information, thus bringing the mega configuration of Chinese dictionaries one step further to maturity and leaving behind huge and profound impacts upon later lexicographers.

The word dictionaries mentioned earlier have turned out to extend well beyond their function as reference tools. They preserved precious cultural, historical, and linguistic data of extraordinary value. They conducted textual verification and provided later generations with abundant linguistic materials covering a wide range of fields. Some of them had become classic works by themselves. They served not only as references for studying and reading classics but also as beacons for researchers of later generations, and not surprisingly, some academic disciplines have stemmed from exploring those dictionaries. The word dictionaries in the Ming and the Qing Dynasty act as not only a summarization of the studies in ancient classics but also an invaluable reference work for future generations to read and understand ancient classics.

32.2.3 Chinese bilingual dictionaries: their origin and development

A careful examination of the origin and development of Chinese bilingual lexicography reveals that three main evolutional threads went through its history, namely the translation of religious scriptures and preaching of Buddhism and Christianity, the cultural and business interactions with its neighbours and countries on the Silk Road, and the collection of annotations of words and terms in history books and historical records. Its evolution from the earliest roots to the Qing Dynasty can be divided into the Buddhist period, the ethnic minority language period, the missionary period, and the government-led compilation period.

32.2.3.1 The Buddhist period

Chinese bilingual lexicography originated from preaching Buddhism, which was introduced into China in the late Western Han Dynasty (206 BC–AD 7). During the Tang Dynasty (618–907) Chinese monks made pilgrimages to India to study Buddhism and Sanskrit. They also started to write books about Sanskrit and compile glossaries of Buddhist scriptures. None of them can, in a strict sense, be considered Sanskrit-Chinese bilingual dictionaries, although they led to a significant improvement upon the quality of later sutra translation and paved the way for the advent of the earliest Chinese bilingual glossaries and dictionaries.

In translating Buddhist sutras, Chinese monks accumulated Buddhist terms and transliterated them with Chinese characters, which were later gathered to become glossaries. The earliest extant glossary of this kind – *Sounds and Meanings of all the Buddhist Sacred Books* (《一切经音义》) – was compiled by Dao Hui (道慧), a Chinese monk of the Northern Chi Dynasty (550–562). It preceded the first Western Sanskrit-English dictionary by Horace Hayman Wilson (1786–1860) by more than one thousand years (Collison 1982:127). There was a boom in the compilation of such glossaries in the Tang Dynasty, which saw the birth of such important works as Xuan Ying's (玄应) augmented version of *Sounds and Meanings of all the Buddhist Sacred Books* (also translated as *Sounds and Meanings of the Whole Canon*; Watters 1889: 52–3, 382); Hui Lin's (慧琳) *Sounds and Meanings of all the Buddhist Sacred Books*; Li Yan's (利言) *A Miscellaneous Collection of Sanskrit Terms* (《梵语

杂名》); and Yi Jing's (义净) *The One Thousand Sanskrit Character Glossary* (《梵语千字文》), a Sanskrit-Chinese vocabulary, which can be reckoned as the archetype of Chinese bilingual dictionaries.

Another contribution of far-reaching significance made by Buddhist monks was the introduction of the idea of consonants and vowels, a thirty-six character scheme of initial consonants, and the popularization of *fanqie* to indicate the pronunciation of a Chinese character (Chien and Creamer 1986).

32.2.3.2 The minority language period

The Buddhist sutra translation was beginning to decline with Buddhism dwindling in the Later Tang Dynasty. A typical feature in this transition was the increased intercourses and strengthened ties between the Han nationality and its neighbouring minority nationalities and other nationalities in the Eastern world. As a result of cultural penetration and exchange, dictionary compilation was an obvious necessity and a useful tool for enhancing such cultural promotion and development. The earliest extant Chinese-Japanese dictionary was compiled in 830 and was modelled after *The Jade Chapters*, which was compiled by GuYewang in the Southern and Northern Dynasties (420–589). In the eleventh century the first Chinese-Japanese encyclopaedic dictionary, the work of Minamoto no Shitago, made its appearance. *The Kagakushu*, another Chinese-Japanese dictionary, was already in wide use during the fifteenth and sixteenth centuries (Collison 1982: 51). Again, in the eleventh century, an anonymous Chinese-Vietnamese encyclopaedic work was produced with the title of *A Chinese-Foreign Language Vocabulary*. Another anonymous dictionary of a similar sort entitled *The Chinese-Vietnamese Guide to the Sound and Meaning* was in circulation in Vietnam around the sixteenth century (Dinh-Hoa Nguyen 1995). During the Song Dynasty, Sun Mu (孙穆) produced the earliest Chinese-Korean dictionary, which was entitled *A Miscellaneous Collection of Things and Events* (《鸡林类事》). The fact that half of the words in this collection were derived from Chinese bears witness to the profound and extensive influence of the Chinese language upon the Korean language and culture, and indeed all Oriental languages and cultures.

The interactions between the Han Nationality and minority groups gave rise to combinations of Chinese with Tangut, such as Yuan Hao's (元昊) *A Tangut-Chinese Ready Guide* (《番尔雅》), and Gulemaocai's (骨勒茂才) *A Timely Gem Dictionary Tangut-Chinese* (《番汉合时掌中珠》), the earliest extant Chinese and Tangut dictionary; with Tibetan, such as *The Tibetan-Chinese Bilingual Glossary* (《西番译语》); and with Mongolian, such as Chen Yuanjing's (陈元靓) *Explanations of the Mongolian Language* (《蒙古译语》, also known as 《至元译语》), a collection of Mongolian words and terms with Chinese explanations, which was included in *The Broad Records of Things and Events* (《事林广记》).

Other bilingual combinations include Mahmud Kashkarii's *The Complete Turkish Dictionary* (《突厥语大词典》) between 1072 and 1076, Tuoketuo's (脱脱, 1314–1355) Liao-Chinese vocabulary *Explanations of the Terms in the History of the Liao Language* (《辽国语解》), and the Nuchen and Chinese vocabulary *Explanations of the Terms in the History of the Jin Dynasty* (《金国语解》).

32.2.3.3 The missionary period

The missionary period, lasting from the late sixteenth century to the early twentieth century, is particularly marked by the appearance of Chinese and English combinations by missionaries, but they are preceded in time by combinations of Chinese with Latin, French, and Portuguese. Among the first missionaries to arrive in China was Matteo Ricci, an Italian Jesuit missionary. He compiled *Dizionario Portoghese-Cinese* (《葡汉词典》), the first Western language-Chinese dictionary, in collaboration with Michele Ruggieri. In the seventeenth century, the Polish Jesuit Michael Boym compiled a Chinese-Latin dictionary and a Chinese-French dictionary, which were printed in 1667 and 1670 respectively in the popular magazine *China Illustrata*. These two works, more of a vocabulary than of a dictionary, may be the first of their kind (Chien and Creamer 1986) published in the Western world. Another Jesuit, the Frenchman Nicolas Trigault, published *An Audio and Visual Guide for Foreign Scholars* (西儒耳目资) in Hangzhou, China, in 1625 "to help the Chinese learn Latin" (Chien and Creamer 1986). In 1813, M. de Guignes completed his *Dictionnaire Chinois, Francais et Latin* (《汉法拉辞典》 1813), probably the first combination of Chinese with both French and Latin.

Missionary compilations of Chinese bilingual dictionaries are most notable for Chinese-English and English-Chinese dictionaries. The first combination of Chinese with English, Robert Morrison's *A Dictionary of the Chinese Language* (《华英词典》) – (五车韵府), occurred between 1815 and 1822, followed by William Lobscheid's *A Chinese and English Dictionary* and George C. Stent's *A Chinese and English Vocabulary in the Pekinese Dialect* (Shanghai: China Inland Mission and American Presbyterian Mission Press). Three years later, Samuel Wells Williams' *A Syllabic Dictionary of the Chinese Language*, came out. In the last few years of the nineteenth century Herbert A. Giles' *A Chinese-English Dictionary* (《华英词典》 1892) and P. Poletti's *A Chinese and English Dictionary* (华英词典 1896) were completed and published.

Chinese missionary compilation had its roots in the early nineteenth century, flourished in the late nineteenth century, and extended with a great deal of remaining momentum into the twentieth century, with revisions and augmentations of previous works and creation of new works, represented by Adam Grainger's *Western Mandarin, or the Spoken Language of Western China; with Syllabic and English Indexes* (《西蜀方言》 1900). It ended with the publication of Mathews's *Chinese-English Dictionary* (1931). However, they were followed by another vigorous and endless stream of dictionaries compiled by Chinese authors in China and overseas and published in Chinese-English and English-Chinese editions. Moreover, there also appeared a great number of bilingual combinations of Chinese with Russian, German, Spanish, Italian, and other modern European languages and bilingual combinations of Chinese with languages spoken in Thailand, Malaysia, Indonesia, and so on. Multilingual combinations of Chinese with the previously mentioned languages also made their appearance, for instance, Paolo Desderi's *Piccolo dizionariocinese, italiano, francese, inglese*, (1933).

32.2.3.4 The government-led compilation period

In the early Ming Dynasty (1368–1644), foreign affairs establishments were set up to promote socio-economic exchanges and train personnel in international communication. The miscellaneous bilingual glossaries and vocabularies, which were listed under the general heading of *Chinese-Foreign Language Bilingual Glossaries* (《华夷译语》), were mostly under the charge of those organizations and were compiled by scholar officials serving the government.

Government-led compilations were especially remarkable for combinations of Chinese with Manchu in the Qing Dynasty, such as Shen Qiliang's (沈启亮) *A Comprehensive*

Dictionary of the Great Qing Dynasty (《大清全书》) and Fu Dali (傅达礼) et al.'s *The Dictionary of the Manchu Language* (《清文鉴》). They laid a solid foundation for official compilations of Manchu dictionaries and their combination with Chinese, Mongolian, Tibetan, and other ethnic minority languages and ushered in a brand-new era of Manchu dictionary compilation. In the late Qing Dynasty, John Fryer (1839–1928) compiled specialized bilingual vocabularies, like *Vocabulary of Terms Relating to the Steam Engine* (《汽机中西名目表》 1890), a natural result of the transmission of Western learning and standardization of technical terms. They signified the beginning of modern Chinese science terminology and furnished experience for the compilation of bilingual dictionaries of science and technology.

32.2.4 Special and encyclopaedic dictionaries: their origin and development

Both special and encyclopaedic dictionaries can be traced to the period of Three Kingdoms. *The Dictionary of Initial Consonants* (《声类》) by Li Deng (李登) and *The Imperial Survey* (《皇览》) by Confucian scholars could be considered their respective prototypes. In this section, special dictionaries are divided into special-subject/field (or, more commonly, specialized) dictionaries, which cover the technical terms of specific fields (such as law, medicine, etc.), and special-aspect dictionaries, which cover a certain part of the lexicon of language (such as verbs, prepositions, etc.) or a certain aspect of language use (such as spelling, pronunciation, idioms, rhymes, etc.).The special-aspect dictionaries to be discussed here mainly include rhyme dictionaries, dictionaries of function words, and dictionaries of quotations, idioms, and proverbs. Encyclopaedic dictionaries to be discussed here are mainly classified dictionaries, the forerunner of modern encyclopaedias.

32.2.4.1 *Representative special-subject dictionaries*

The compilation of special-subject dictionaries originated from the research in Chinese herbal medicine prior to the Tang Dynasty. Between 650 and 655, under the order of Emperor Gaozong, Li Ji (李勣) and Yu Zhining (于志宁) revised *An Annotated Collection of Materia Medica* (《本草经集注》). Medical dictionaries in the Tang Dynasty included *One Thousand Golden Medical Prescriptions* (《千金方》) by Sun Simiao (孙思邈) and *The Waitai Collection of Secret Prescriptions* (《外台秘要》) by Wang Tao (王焘). In the Song and the Yuan Dynasty appeared dictionaries of ancient articles, vessels, coins, and botanic terms – *Archaeological Diagrams* (《考古图》) by Lü Dalin (吕大临), *Records of Ancient Coins* (《泉志》) by Hong Zun (洪遵), and *The Botanic Compendium* (《全芳备祖》) by Chen Jingyi (陈景沂).

Special-subject dictionaries in the Ming and the Qing Dynasty were more wide-ranging, covering ancient currency, botany, geography, medicine, agriculture, handicraft industry, technology, chemistry, and physics. The major works include Li Zuoxian's (李佐贤) *A Dictionary of Ancient Currencies* (《古泉汇》), Li Shizhen's *The Compendium of Materia Medica* (《本草纲目》 1552–1578), XuGuangqi's (徐光启) *The Compendium of Agriculture* (《农政全书》 1619–1639), and Song Yingxing's (宋应星) *The Book of Nature's Engineering* (《天工开物》 1634–1637). They are broad in coverage, excellent in quality, and bulky in size. Their influence and value have extended well into the present day.

32.2.4.2 *Representative special-aspect dictionaries: rhyme dictionaries, dictionaries of function words, and dictionaries of lexical expressions*

Rhyme dictionaries: In the special-aspect dictionary family, rhyme dictionaries enjoy the longest history with a span of nearly 2,000 years. They had their roots in the phonological studies in the Wei Dynasty, when the first rhyme dictionary came into being, and continued to develop with vigour until the middle of the eighteenth century. They had highly practical value and phonological implications. Dictionaries of lexical expressions began to emerge in the Tang Dynasty, and dictionaries of function words did not appear until the Qing Dynasty, but with admirable academic value and linguistic sophistication.

Over the period of the Wei, Jin, and Southern and Northern Dynasties, the influx of foreign cultures, especially the introduction of Buddhism, brought forth innovations in the style and format of dictionary compilation and stimulated the emergence of rhyme dictionaries, which were principally used to guide the composition of poetry, prose, drama, and opera. They originated in the Wei Dynasty, got well established in the Sui and the Tang Dynasty, prospered in the Song and the Yuan Dynasty, and started to decline in the Qing Dynasty.

The pioneer of this unique Chinese dictionary family is *The Dictionary of Initial Consonants* in the Three Kingdoms Period, followed by *The Collection of Rhymes* by Lü Jing (吕静) in the Jin (晋) Dynasty, *The Dictionary of Chinese Rhymes* by Lu Fayan (陆法言) in the Sui Dynasty, *The Tang Dictionary of Rhymes* (《唐韵》) by Sun Mian (孙愐), and *The Rhyme Dictionary* (《集韵》) by Ding Du (丁度) et al. in the Tang Dynasty. More rhyme dictionaries were compiled to meet the needs of playwrights between the Song and the Yuan Dynasty, like *The Comprehensive Five-Sound Rhyme Dictionary* (《五音集韵》) by Han Daozhao (韩道昭), etc.

The compilation of rhyme dictionaries continued to develop in the Ming Dynasty, but began to fade out of the lexicographical scene by the mid-eighteenth century. The innovative format and style of rhyme dictionaries in the Wei and the Yuan Dynasty formed not only a paradigm for the compilation of later generations of rhyme dictionaries but also the theoretical sources and motivation for new reforms and innovations in their development.

Dictionaries of function words: Rhyme dictionaries were theoretically based on Chinese phonology and the discovery of the four-tone system. The foundation for dictionaries of function words was more in-depth and thorough philological studies. The Qing Dynasty witnessed a vigorous stream of function word dictionaries, which reached a fairly sophisticated level of compilation and were noticeable for their immense size and enviable quality. Representative works include *The Interpretative Dictionary of Function Words* (《助字辨略》) by Liu Qi (刘淇) and *The Dictionary of Function Words in Lections and Biographies* (《经传释词》) by Wang Yinzhi (王引之). They display systematic classifications of function words, a variety of interpretive methods, extensional sense relations, and the tracing of their origins.

Dictionaries of lexical expressions: Compared with Chinese character and word dictionaries, dictionaries of lexical expressions were a rather late arrival and did not come out until the early Yuan Dynasty, when Yin Shifu (阴时夫) compiled *The Gem Dictionary of Rhymes* (《韵府群玉》). The first such dictionary in the Ming Dynasty was *Wuju Rhyme Dictionary* (《五车韵瑞》) by Ling Zhilong (凌稚隆). Their style and format were, on the whole, standard and consistent. They proved to have served writing purposes quite well.

32.2.5 *Classified dictionaries*

Classified dictionaries (类书), reference books with entries arranged in the form of a dictionary according to thematic subjects, with materials taken from various sources, are the predecessors of Chinese encyclopaedias and modern encyclopaedic dictionaries. They started with *The Imperial Survey* of the Wei Dynasty. No other similar works, however, appeared until the Sui Dynasty, when Du Gongzhan (杜公瞻) compiled *The Pearl Collection* (《编珠》), the earliest classified dictionary presently available, with the first peak of compilation arriving in the Tang Dynasty and a second in the Ming and Qing Dynasty.

Representative works between the Sui and Yuan Dynasty include Yu Shinan (虞世南) et al.'s *The Beitang Collection of Copied Books* (《北堂书钞》); the earliest classified dictionary presently available in its original version; OuyangXun's (欧阳洵) *The Classified Collection of Art and Literary Works* (《艺文类聚》); and Yan Zhenqing's (颜真卿) *The Sources of Rhyme Ocean* (《韵海镜源》), the earliest classified dictionary whose entries were arranged in the rhyme order. The Song Dynasty witnessed the appearance of Li Fang (李昉) et al.'s two large-scale classified dictionaries, *The Imperial Records of the Taiping Reign* (《太平广记》) and *The Imperial Digest of the Taiping Reign* (《太平御览》), Shen Kuo's (沈括) *The Mengxi Collection of Written Dialogues* (《梦溪笔谈》), etc. Political stability and economic prosperity in the Ming and the Qing Dynasty brought forth another peak in the compilation of classified dictionaries, including Xie Jin's (解缙) *The Yongle Compendium* (《永乐大典》), Chen Menglei (陈梦雷) and Jiang Tingxi's (蒋廷锡) *The Compendium of Ancient and Contemporary Books* (《古今图书集成》), etc.

Special and classified dictionaries were compiled for the purpose of revealing the laws and scientific principles of the nature and the world; summarizing and crystallizing what natural sciences and social sciences achieved in specific stages; exploring the social, cultural, economic, and technological history; collating the non-existing ancient classic works as a result of their categorized accumulation of data; and, of course, acting as important reference tools for studying ancient Chinese and world civilization.

32.3 Core issues and topics

The following paragraphs review Chinese lexicography in the twentieth century. It covers five main types of Chinese dictionaries as well as their main innovations and transformations: (a) philological dictionaries, (b) bilingual dictionaries, (c) special and encyclopaedic dictionaries, (d) learners' dictionaries, and (e) electronic dictionaries. They are the result of linguistic accomplishments and technological attainments. They represent the state of the art of Chinese lexicography both in theory and practice.

32.3.1 *Chinese philological dictionaries: their innovation and transformation*

Twentieth-century Chinese philological dictionary making underwent a transition and transformation from a traditional paradigm to a modern one, that is, from a tradition characterized by three major dictionary genres – character dictionaries, exegetic dictionaries, and rhyming dictionaries (see Section 32.2), to a new enterprise influenced and guided by modern linguistic theories, co-varying with the pulse of the Chinese national and cultural development and the progress of science and technology in China.

Representative philological dictionaries established themselves as innovative models and ushered in the flourishing of three main strains of philological dictionary varieties – general dictionaries, dialect dictionaries, and minority language dictionaries. The first strain include Lu Erkui's (陆尔奎) Ci Yuan (《辞源》1915); Shu Xincheng (舒新城) et al.'s CiHai (《辞海》1936); *The Contemporary Chinese Dictionary*（《现代汉语词典》1978）by The Dictionary Compilation Division of The Chinese Academy of Social Sciences; Xu Zhongshu's (徐中舒) *The Great Chinese Character Dictionary*（《汉语大字典》1986–1990); and Luo Zhufeng's (罗竹风) *The Great Chinese Word Dictionary* (《汉语大词典》1986–1994).

Within the vast Chinese territories exist many Chinese dialects, and extensive dialect research has been conducted with the introduction of new methodology and the application of modern technology. Dialect dictionaries constituted the second strain of Chinese philological dictionaries, represented by Zhang Binglin's (章炳麟) *The New Dictionary of Dialectal Words* (《新方言》1911) and Li Rong (李荣) et al.'s *The Great Dialect Dictionary of Modern Chinese* (《现代汉语方言大词典》1993–1998). They are grand in scale, broad in coverage, and admirable in scholarship. In addition, a series of dialect dictionaries for particular regions were compiled, embracing almost all major dialects and dialect regions in China.

The third strain of philological dictionaries is minority language dictionaries. They have increased in number and strengthened from scarcity to plenty in content, reflecting the social, cultural, and linguistic transformations of 55 national minorities in China and over a hundred languages in use. Minority language dictionaries prior to 1949 were limited in type and number and restrained to only a few major ethnic groups, such as the Mongolian, Tibetan, Manchurian, Uygurian, Korean, and Naxi language. The 1980 launch of the project of Dictionary Series for National Minority Languages in China by The Institute of Ethnology & Anthropology of the Chinese Academy of Social Sciences turned over a new leaf in the compilation of minority language dictionaries. Generally, minority language dictionaries are small in size, though a few are much larger, such as *The Dictionary of the Mongolian Language* (《蒙古语辞典》 1998) compiled by the Language Institute of the Inner Mongolian Academy of Social Sciences and Mongolian Department of Inner Mongolian Normal University.

The prodigious progress of Chinese philological dictionary making in the second half of the twentieth century, especially after 1978, is chiefly the result of special attention and support from the central government, the underpinnings of linguistic studies and lexicographical research, and the training of teams of dictionary compilation and research.

32.3.2 Chinese bilingual dictionaries: their amelioration and prosperity

The making of bilingual dictionaries functions as a barometer that measures the international exchanges and political relationships between countries. The first half of the twentieth century was a time for Chinese bilingual dictionaries to pattern after Western dictionaries and gain gradual independence from foreign sources, represented by Yan Huiyun's (颜惠云) *A New English-Chinese Dictionary* (《英华大辞典》1908–1910), Zhao Liyan (赵立言) et al.'s *The Comprehensive Japanese-Chinese Dictionary* (《综合日华大辞典》1936), Cheng Yaochen's (程耀辰) *The Great Chinese-Russian Business Dictionary* (《华俄合璧商务大字典》1917), and Ma Junwu's (马君武) *The German-Chinese Character Dictionary* (《德华字典》1904).

Bilingual dictionaries developed in an uneven fashion throughout the century. It was not until the last two decades that the golden time came. Their compilation, publication, and research flourished; their numbers increased radically; and many new types were compiled. The most outstanding ones include Zheng Yili (郑易里) and Cao Chengxiu's (曹成修) *A New English-Chinese Dictionary* (《英华大词典》 1950), Ge Chuangui (葛传椝) et al.'s *The New English-Chinese Dictionary* (《新英汉词典》 1975), Liu Zerong's (刘泽荣) *The Comprehensive Russian-Chinese Dictionary* (《俄汉大辞典》 1960), Lu Gusun's (陆谷孙) *The English-Chinese Dictionary (Unabridged)* (《英汉大词典》 1989–1991), Wu Guanghua's (吴光华) *A Modern Comprehensive English-Chinese Dictionary* (《现代英汉综合大辞典》 1990), Liang Shiqiu's (梁实秋) *The Far East English-Chinese Dictionary* (《远东英汉大词典》 1977), etc. Bilingual dictionary compilation and research have become the dominant and persistent driving force for the development of Chinese lexicography.

32.3.3 Special and encyclopaedic dictionaries: their status and trends

Special dictionaries began to appear around the sixth century, when Jia Sixie (贾思勰) wrote the first specialized dictionary – *Important Arts for the People's Welfare* (《齐民要术》), but their rapid development took place only in the mid- and late twentieth century. Only 70 varieties were published between 1900 and 1949, but 710 appeared between 1979 and 1988, and the number increased steadily year by year, 84 in 1980, 122 in 1981, 206 in 1982, and 266 in 1983, marking a dramatic increase in number, variety, influence, standards, and other aspects. More new types emerged, enabling a relatively integrated system of special dictionaries to take shape.

Specialized dictionaries: The social and academic environment was not ripe and right for the compilation of large specialized dictionaries before 1949, but large specialized dictionaries were published in succession after 1949, such as Yu Guangyuan's (于光远) *The Comprehensive Dictionary of Economy* (《经济大辞典》 1983–1992). The majority of them are medium sized. As far as languages are concerned, most of them were monolingual, and bilingual ones were mainly foreign language-Chinese. They cover almost all major areas of Chinese and world civilization.

Special-aspect dictionaries: Special-aspect dictionaries account for a good proportion of special dictionaries. In the first half of the twentieth century, both their number and variety increased substantially, covering such aspects as pronunciation, idiom, function words, colloquialism, and proverbs and quotations. Typical works include Wang Kaiyu's (王恺予) *The Great Poetry and Rhythm Dictionary* (《诗韵大辞典》 1937), Lü Shuxiang's (吕叔湘) *A Dictionary of Function Words of Classical Chinese* (《文言虚字》 1944), etc.

In the second half, particularly in the last two decades, special-aspect dictionaries were greater in number, better in quality, and richer in variety. Their coverage expanded to include ancient characters and words, newly coined words, hard words, synonyms, antonyms, two-part allegorical sayings, allusions, grammar, usage, and collocation. The major dictionaries include Jiang Lihong's (蒋礼鸿) *A General Interpretive Dictionary of Variant Characters in Dunhuang Literature* (《敦煌变文字义通释》 1959), *A Comprehensive Dictionary of English Prepositions* (《英语介词多用词典》 1997), etc. Chinese linguistics broke away from the confinements of exegetical studies and traditional philology with outstanding achievements, which provided strong theoretical underpinnings for the compilation of such dictionaries.

Encyclopaedic dictionaries: In terms of the scope of lexical selection and the number of disciplines involved, encyclopaedic dictionaries can be divided into philological, general, and special-field types. Encyclopaedic dictionaries in the first half of the twentieth century are generally medium-sized with 10,000 entries or under. From 1949 to 1976, the development of Chinese encyclopaedic dictionaries was severely hindered. The last two decades, however, were the prime time of development, thanks to the stability of the Chinese society and the rapid progress in culture, economy, and science and technology. A great variety of encyclopaedic dictionaries were compiled, with in-depth content, broad discipline coverage, and high academic value. New varieties were developed, namely comprehensive, specialized, bilingual and bilingualized types, and types for specific target users and regional subjects. Representative works include Yu Guangyuan (于光远) et al.'s *A Chinese Encyclopaedic Dictionary* (《中国百科大辞典》 1990), Qi Yuchun (戚雨村) et al.'s *The Linguistics Encyclopaedic Dictionary* (《语言学百科词典》 1993), etc.

The development of special and encyclopaedic dictionaries in the last two decades manifested a strong tendency of serialization, structural systematization, electronic presentation, and information optimization. Such a tendency has extended into the twenty-first century and will be maintained and strengthened in the time to come.

32.3.4 Learners' dictionaries: their origin, status, and trends

Modern learners' dictionaries originated in Britain in the 1930s, and Chinese learners' dictionaries emerged with the publication of Lu Erkui and Fang Yi's (方毅) *The Students' Dictionary* (《学生词典》 1915). During the inception period (1900–1949) the New Culture Movement was surging all over the country, and classical Chinese was gradually replaced by Modern Chinese. Chinese learners' overwhelming enthusiasm for literacy education motivated their compilation. Representative works included Wu Yanheng's (吴研蘅) *The New Style Students Dictionary* (《新式学生词典》 1917), Gu Foying's (顾佛影) *The New Character Dictionary for Students with Standard National Pronunciation* (《标准国音学生新字典》 1937), etc. They were followed by a period of depression during the Great Cultural Revolution. However, the Beijing Languages Institute published, for the first time, a learners' dictionary intended for foreigners in 1976 – *The Little Dictionary of the Chinese Language* (《汉语小词典》). Between 1977 and 1999, the number and varieties increased. The most influential learners' dictionaries were Peking University's *The Character Dictionary for Elementary Learners* (《小学生字典》 1981), Sun Quanzhou's (孙全洲) *The Modern Chinese Learners Dictionary* (《现代汉语学习词典》 1995), the first extroversive Chinese learners' dictionary compiled on the basis of a unified code system and a pragmatic framework, and so on.

Almost simultaneously, compilers started to pay attention to introducing through translating and re-editing learners' dictionaries from abroad and tried to compile English-Chinese learners' dictionaries, like Zhan Wenhu's (詹文浒) *A Four-Use English-Chinese Dictionary: Definition, Composition, Grammar and Synonym Discrimination* (《英汉求解・作文・文法・辨义四用词典》 1936). Due to natural disasters, economic deterioration, international containment, and the Great Cultural Revolution, only five learners' dictionaries, English-Chinese, were produced from the 1950s to the 1970s. They were small or medium-sized, chiefly made for secondary school students and English beginners.

There came an upsurge of learning from Western countries from 1979, and English-Chinese learners' dictionaries were recovering and moving onto their normal track of development. Chinese compilers began to pay increasing attention to independent compilation, and the dictionaries compiled were chiefly an integrative product of independent development and Western experiences. There came in the last 10 years the golden time for the development of English-Chinese learners' dictionaries. The total number of

English-Chinese learners' dictionaries exceeded, for the first time in the history, other types intended for general users. The representative works included Li Siguo's (李思国)*The New Multipurpose English-Chinese Dictionary* (《全新多用英汉词典》1992) and Zhou Guozhen's (周国珍) *The English-Chinese Dictionary with Detailed Explanations* (《英汉详注词典》1997).

Apart from those previously mentioned, there appeared a small number of monolingual and bilingual learners' dictionaries in ethnic minority languages, such as Tibetan, Mongolian, and Korean, etc., and learners' dictionaries of foreign languages other than English and Chinese, such as Japanese-Chinese, French-Chinese, and Russian-Chinese. Even so, there remained a great deal for Chinese lexicographers to achieve in this regard.

32.3.5 Electronic dictionaries: their origin, status, and trends

In a sense, the twentieth century is a century for learners' dictionaries, but its last two decades are characterized by electronic dictionaries. Combining modern science and technology with the art and craft of lexicography, electronic dictionaries, a by-product of computer technology, have developed into an indispensable dictionary genre and have become a new facilitator to present-day lexicography. Three main sub-types dominate the Chinase lexicographic landscape: (a) machine-readable dictionaries, (b) chip electronic dictionaries, and (c) CD electronic dictionaries.

Machine-readable dictionaries: These were produced as early as in the 1940s in America. China started the development and research of the Chinese machine-readable dictionary in the 1970s. In the mid-1980s, substantial achievements were made, especially in syntactic analysis and sentence comprehension. From the mid-1990s, various machine-readable dictionaries were successfully developed for special uses, for instance for in-depth semantic and syntax processing, such as *A Machine Readable Predicate Verb Dictionary of Contemporary Chinese* (《现代汉语述语动词机器词典》) by Tsinghua University in collaboration with the Chinese Studies Center of Renmin University of China.

Chip electronic dictionaries: In December 1989, the first electronic dictionary of the Chinese language, *Instant-Dict EC-1000*, was market tested, and it was mass produced in August 1990. That initiated the rapid expansion of palm electronic dictionaries in China. Palm electronic dictionaries became popular for their ease of use. Popular products include *the Instant-Dict* (快译通), *Wenquxing* (文曲星), *Noah* (诺亚舟), etc. Most of them came into use in the last decade.

CD electronic dictionaries: In the late twentieth century, Chinese electronic dictionaries underwent the stages of emergence, simulation, exploration, and rapid expansion. Early electronic dictionaries were mainly CD versions. In January 1997, China Encyclopedia Press started collaborating with Zeon Corporation in Taiwan to publish *The Encyclopaedia of China on CD-ROM*, one of the earliest dictionaries on CD-ROM in China. In 1999, a CD version was developed for *The Great Chinese Word Dictionary*, indicating that monolingual dictionary making had entered into the epoch of digitalization, including such CD special dictionaries as *The Chinese Pharmacopoeia* 《中国药典》 and *The Chinese Scenic Spot Poetry Dictionary* (《中国名胜诗词大辞典》). However, the majority of achievements failed to be marketed and commercialized. There were limitations in interface and content, but their impacts upon later research projects were significant. The extensive use of computer technology, the potential value and prospects, and the interdisciplinary researches have instilled fresh power into the research, development, and production of electronic dictionaries, opening up even more promising prospects.

32.4 Looking to the future

Although Chinese lexicography boasts a history of around 2,200 years, the twentieth century was the most active, influential, and heterogeneous in both theoretical and practical aspects. In the early part of the century, lexicographical studies, under the influence of modern linguistics, started to extend beyond the domain of philology. In the middle and late parts, the achievements in linguistics and other relevant studies were extensively applied to dictionary making and research. Lexicographical studies have come to be recognized as an independent branch of learning. The practice of dictionary making is based more on theoretical researches than merely on experience gained in dictionary compilation. Dictionary making is more of a theory-driven and technology-based process. Within this new landscape, the future of Chinese lexicography will be dominated by three main endeavours: (a) new theoretical explorations, (b) new theoretical accomplishments, and (c) new lexicographic activities.

32.4.1 New theoretical explorations

At the turn of the twentieth century, Western learning was spreading to the East, which activated people's desire to pursue scientific knowledge; the overthrow of feudal imperialism and the upsurging of the New Culture Movement brought in fresh ideas to the ideological world and cultural circles. Lexicographical studies and dictionary making were closely interwoven with the socio-cultural environment of the time. After 1949, a new philological policy was adopted to popularize Mandarin, to introduce Pinyin, and to promote the use of simplified Chinese characters. Dictionary making became a necessary and effective means to implement this new policy. A great variety of normative dictionaries were compiled and published according to the plans made by the central government and the publishing administration, which motivated the compilers to carry out more in-depth theoretical researches. In 1979, the Shanghai Lexicographic Press launched *Lexicographical Studies*, a journal exclusively devoted to lexicographical issues. Its publication signified the independent status of lexicography in China as a branch of learning.

Starting in 1979, China experienced radical social transformation. The compilation and publication of dictionaries enjoyed unprecedented prosperity. Lexicographical researches were carried out in greater depth and in a more systematic fashion. The features of the dictionary were explored more thoroughly. Various new types of dictionaries emerged in close succession. Dictionary compilation became more closely linked to other disciplines and the scope of dictionary research was broadened. Lexicography gained its academic status as an independent discipline and formed its basic theories, methodologies, principles, and theoretical frameworks. We think that the future of Chinese lexicography will be very much dominated by promoting the independent status of lexicography as well as acknowledging its interdisciplinarity. This will be more visible in the development of new online dictionaries, whose development has already started, although with very hard beginnings, but will definitely speed up in the near future.

32.4.2 New theoretical accomplishments

Numerous dictionaries were compiled in the past century, with a great variety and an almost complete set of types. The publication of *Lexicographical Studies*, together with a good number of research papers and monographs, made lexicographical researches more systematic and more specialized. Representative works include *On Dictionaries* (《词典论》, Huang Jianhua 1987) and *Modern Lexicography* (《当代词典学》, Zhang Yihua and Yong Heming 2007) in the area of general lexicography and *Bilingual Lexicography: An Introduction* (《双语词典学导论》, Huang Jianhua et al. 1998) in the area of bilingual lexicography. In addition, a considerable number of papers were devoted to dictionary typology, the standardization of lexicographical terminology, dictionary criticism, and other areas.

32.4.3 Lexicographic activities

The innovation and development of dictionary making in quantity, type, quality, and influence promoted and benefited from the prosperity of academic activities for lexicography, involving academic teams, academic associations and societies, publication organizations, journals and periodicals, academic conferences, and global interactions. The academic teams are fundamental for promoting the development of lexicography and fall into two major categories: dictionary publishers and researchers. In the middle and late part of the century, the lexicographer teams expanded to include university teachers and were better organized.

With the growth of lexicographical teams and the frequent communication among them, lexicographers started in the early 1980s to feel the need to establish specialized academic organizations for lexicography. In 1982, Shanghai Association for Lexicography, the first local association for lexicography in China, was established, followed by some other provincial associations, such as Shaanxi (1985), Fujian (1989), and Anhui (1991). In 1992, The Chinese Association for Lexicography (Chinalex), a national lexicographic organization, was launched in Beijing, with its specialized committees and its academic journal, *Lexicographical Studies*, the first journal devoted exclusively to lexicographical studies. Meanwhile, lexicographical presses were set up, and specialized units for lexicographical research and dictionary research centres were founded in quite a few universities, research institutes, and publishing houses. They combined to play an important role in organizing lexicographers and holding academic conferences either periodically or one time only. Training programs on different levels and in different forms were launched on a regular basis, and international lexicographical exchanges provided a platform for the exchange of academic views and discussion of lexicographical issues.

Looking beyond into the twenty-first century, Chinese lexicographers face a lot of challenges. The scope of lexicographical studies needs to be further broadened, comprehensive studies to be carried out across disciplines, the systematicity and integrity of lexicography as an independent discipline to be further promoted, the application of theoretical researches to dictionary making to be facilitated, the findings in linguistics and other neighbouring disciplines to be integrated into lexicography, the interaction of lexicography with its neighbouring disciplines to be strengthened, new corpuses and Internet technologies to be developed and applied to dictionary researches and making, new channels to be opened for international exchanges, and the association of theoretical research and dictionary making inside China with those outside China to be accelerated and innovative changes to be introduced in lexicographical studies in China.

The beginning of the twenty-first century has turned out to be extremely fruitful in lexicographical explorations, marked by such important works as ZhaoYanchun's (赵彦春) *Explorations in Cognitive Lexicography* (《认知词典学探索》 2003) and Tian Bing's (田兵) *Sense Differentiation and Description: A Cognitive Semantic Study on Polysemous Words* (《意义分辨与描写：多义词的认知语义研究》 2004) in the field of cognitive lexicography, Heming Yong's (雍和明) *Lexicography from a Communicative Perspective* (《交际词典学》 2003) and Heming Yong and Jing Peng's (彭敬) *Bilingual Lexicography from a Communicative Perspective* (2007) in the field of communicative lexicography, and Heming Yong and Jing Peng's *Chinese Lexicography A History from 1046 BC to AD 1911* (2008) and Heming Yong et al.'s *Chinese Dictionaries: Three Millennia* (《中国辞典3000年》 2010) in the field of diachronic lexicography. More significant achievements are in prospect, and more theoretical breakthroughs are already under way.

Acknowledgements

Our special thanks go to Professor Henri Béjoint for going through this piece of writing and providing a lot of interesting suggestions and comments concerning its revision.

Related topics

Lexicography and applied linguistics; lexicography as an independent science; lexicography and interdisciplinarity; the concept of dictionary.

Further reading

Yong, H., and J. Peng. (2008). *Chinese Lexicography: A History From 1046 BC to AD 1911*. Oxford: Oxford University Press.
This book provides a systematic presentation of Chinese lexicography from its earliest beginnings to the end of the Qing Dynasty (1911).

Yong, H. and L. Zhenyue. (2010). *Chinese Dictionaries: Three Millennia*. Shanghai: Shanghai Foreign Language Education Press.
This book provides a synoptic history of dictionary making in China before the Qing Dynasty (1911) and a more concentrated description of dictionary making in the twentieth century.

Zou, F. (2001). *Explorations in Lexicography*. Wuhan: Hubei People's Press.
This book provides an in-depth theoretical description of the development of Chinese dictionary making over the past 2,000 years or so.

References

Major dictionaries

A Categoric Dictionary of Dialectal Words (《方言类聚》) published in the Ming Dynasty (1368–1662). Ed. by Chen Yujiao.

A Chinese and English Vocabulary in the Pekinese Dialect. (1923) Ed. by George C. Stent. Shanghai: China Inland Mission and American Presbyterian Mission Press.

A Chinese Encyclopaedic Dictionary (《中国百科大辞典》). (1990) Ed. by Yu Guangyuan et al. Beijing: Huaxia Press.

A Chinese-English Dictionary (《华英词典》). (1892. Ed. by Herbert A. Giles.

A Chinese-English Dictionary. (1931) Ed. by R.H. Mathews. Shanghai: China Inland Mission Press. (Also known as Mathews' Chinese-English Dictionary.

A Comprehensive Dictionary of English Prepositions (《英语介词多用词典》). (1997) Ed. by Yong Heming. Tianjin: Tianjin People's Publishing House. Revised and renamed *A Contemporary Dictionary of English Prepositions* 2010.

A Comprehensive Dictionary of the Great Qing Dynasty (《大清全书》) published in the Qing Dynasty (1636–1912). Ed. by Shen Qiliang.

A Dictionary of Ancient Currencies (《古泉汇》) published in the Qing Dynasty (1636–1912). Ed. by Li Zuoxian.

A Dictionary of Function Words of Classical Chinese (《文言虚字》). (1944) Ed. by Lü Shuxiang. Shanghai: Kaiming Book Company.

A Dictionary of the Chinese Language (《华英词典》 – 五车韵府). (1815–1822) Ed. by Robert Morrison. Macao: The Honorable East India Company's Press.

A Four-Use English-Chinese Dictionary: Definition, Composition, Grammar and Synonym Discrimination (《英汉求解・作文・文法・辨义四用词典》). (1936) Ed. by Zhan Wenhu. Beijing: The World Book Company.

A General Interpretive Dictionary of Variant Characters in Dunhuang Literature (《敦煌变文字义通释》). (1959) Ed. by Jiang Lihong. Shanghai: Shanghai Historical Literature Press.

A Modern Comprehensive English-Chinese Dictionary (《现代英汉综合大辞典》). (1990) Ed. by Wu Guanghua. Shanghai: Shanghai Scientific Literature Press.

A New English-Chinese Dictionary (《英华大词典》). (1950) Ed. by Zheng Yili and Cao Chengxiu. Shanghai: The Commercial Press.

A New English-Chinese Dictionary (《英华大辞典》). (1908–1910). Ed. by Yan Huiyun. Shanghai: The Commercial Press.

A Timely Gem Dictionary Tangut-Chinese (《番汉合时掌中珠》). (1190) Ed. by Gulemaocai

An Audio and Visual Guide for Foreign Scholars (西儒耳目资). (1625) Ed. by Nicolas Trigault. Hangzhou, China.

An Explanatory Book of Phonetic Sounds (《说文通训定声》) published in the Qing Dynasty (1636–1912). Ed by Zhu Junsheng.

Ci Hai (《辞海》). (1936) Ed. by Shu Xincheng et al. Beijing: China Book Company.

Ci Yuan (《辞源》). (1915) Ed. by Lu Erkui. Shanghai: The Commercial Press.

Dictionnaire Chinois, Francais et Latin (《汉法拉辞典》). (1813) Ed. by M. de. Guignes: De L'Imprimerie Imperiale.

Dizionario Portoghese-Cinese (《葡汉词典》). (c.1583) Ed. by Matteo Ricci and Michele Ruggieri.

Explanations of the Mongolian Language (《蒙古译语》, also known as 《至元译语》) published in the Qing Dynasty (1636–1912). Ed. by Chen Yuanjing.

One Thousand Golden Medical Prescriptions (《千金方》) published in the Tang Dynasty (618–907). Ed. by Sun Simiao.

Piccolo dizionariocinese, italiano, francese, inglese. (1933) Ed. by Paolo Desderi. Torino: Rosenberg & Sellier.

Sounds and Meanings of all the Buddhist Sacred Books (《一切经音义》) published in the Tang Dynasty (618–907). Ed. by Hui Lin.

Sounds and Meanings of Mahaparinibbana-sutta (《大般涅槃经音义》) published in the Tang Dynasty (618–907). Ed. by Yun Gong.

Sounds and Meanings of the Avatamsaka Sutra (《华严经音义》) published in the Tang Dynasty (618–907). Translated by Hui Yuan.

Sounds and Meanings of the Saddharmapundarika-sutra (《妙法莲华经音义》) (also known as 大乘基) published in the Tang Dynasty (618–907). Ed. by Kui Ji.

The Annotated Explanatory Dictionary of Chinese Characters (《说文解字注》). (1815) Ed. by Duan Yucai.

The Beitang Collection of Copied Books (《北堂书钞》) published in the Sui Dynasty (581–618). Ed. by Yu Shinan et al.

The Book of Nature's Engineering (《天工开物》) published in the Ming Dynasty (1368–1662). Ed. by Song Yingxing.

The Character Models (《字样》). c. 637. Ed. by Yan Shigu.

The Classified Collection of Art and Literary Works (《艺文类聚》) published in the Tang Dynasty (618–907). Ed. by Ouyang Xun.

The Collection of Characters from Five Classics (《五经文字》). (776) Ed. by Zhang Shen.

The Compendium of Agriculture (《农政全书》). (1619–1639) Ed. by Xu Guangqi.

The Compendium of Ancient and Contemporary Books (《古今图书集成》) published in the Qing Dynasty (1636–1912). Ed. by Chen Menglei and Jiang Tingxi.

The Compendium of Materia Medica (《本草纲目》). (1552–1578) Ed. by Li Shizhen.

The Complete Turkish Dictionary (《突厥语大词典》) between 1072 and 1076. Ed. by Mahmud Kashkarii.

The Comprehensive Dictionary of Chinese Characters (《字汇》) published in the Ming Dynasty (1368–1662). Ed. by Mei Yingzuo.

The Comprehensive Five-Sound Rhyme Dictionary (《五音集韵》) published in the Jin Dynasty (266–420). Ed. by Han Daozhao.

The Comprehensive Japanese-Chinese Dictionary (《综合日华大辞典》). (1936) Ed. by Zhao Liyan et al. Shanghai: Kaihua Book Company.

The Comprehensive Russian-Chinese Dictionary (《俄汉大辞典》). (1960). Ed. by Liu Zerong. Beijing: The Commercial Press.

The Dictionary Compilation Division of The Chinese Academy of Social Sciences. *The Contemporary Chinese Dictionary* (《现代汉语词典》). (1978). Beijing: The Commercial Press.

The Dictionary of Characters from Classics and Scriptures with Phonetic Discrimination (《群经音辨》) published in the Song Dynasty (960–1279). Ed. by Jia Changchao.

The Dictionary of Function Words in Lections and Biographies (《经传释词》) published in the Qing Dynasty (1636–1912). Ed. by Wang Yinzhi.

The Dictionary of Initial Consonants (《声类》) published in the Three Kingdoms (220–280). Ed. by Li Deng.

The Dictionary of Textual Researches on the Wu-Xia Dialect (《吴下方言考》). (1783) Ed. by Hu Wenying. Beijing: China Book Company.

The Dictionary of the Manchu Language (《清文鉴》) published in the Qing Dynasty (1636–1912). Ed. by Fu Dali et al.

The Distinctive Ready Guide (《别雅》) published in the Qing Dynasty (1636–1912). Ed. by Wu Yujin.

The English-Chinese Dictionary (Unabridged) (《英汉大词典》). (1989–1991) Ed. by Lu Gusun. Shanghai: Shanghai Yiwen Press.

The Essentials of Augmented Ready Guide (《埤雅广要》) published in the Ming Dynasty (1368–1662). Ed. by Niu Zhong.

The Exegesis of Ancient and Contemporary Characters (《古今字诂》) published in the Eastern Han Dynasty (25–220). Ed. by Zhang Yi.

The Exegesis of Six-category Characters (《六书故》) published in the Yuan Dynasty (1271–1368). Ed. by Dai Tong.

The Exegetic Interpretations of Ancient Classics (《经籍纂诂》) published in the Qing Dynasty (1636–1912). Ed. by Ruan Yuan.

The Far East English-Chinese Dictionary (《远东英汉大词典》). (1977) Ed. by Liang Shiqiu.Taiwan: Far East Book Company.

The Gem Dictionary of Rhymes (《韵府群玉》) published in the early Yuan Dynasty (1271–1368). Ed. by Yin Shifu.

The General Exegesis of Six-category Chinese Characters (《六书统》) published in the Yuan Dynasty (1271–1368). Ed. by Yang Huan.

The General Ready Guide (《通雅》) published in the Ming Dynasty (1368–1662). Ed. by Fang Yizhi.

The Great Chinese Character Dictionary (《汉语大字典》). (1986–1990) Ed. by Xu Zhongshu. Wuhan and Chengdu: Hubei Lexicographical Press and Sichuan Lexicographical Press.

The Great Chinese Word Dictionary (《汉语大词典). (1986–1994) Ed. by Luo Zhufeng. Beijing: The Great Chinese Dictionary Press.

The Great Chinese-Russian Business Dictionary (《华俄合璧商务大字典》). (1917) Ed. by Cheng Yaochen.

The Great Dialect Dictionary of Modern Chinese (《现代汉语方言大词典》). (1993–1998) Ed. by Li Rong et al.Nanjing: Jiangsu Education Press.
The Great Poetry and Rhythm Dictionary (《诗韵大辞典》). (1937) Ed. by Wang Kaiyu. Shanghai: Education Book Company.
The Guiyuan Collection of Characters (《桂苑珠丛》) published in the Sui Dynasty (581–618). Ed. by Zhuge Ying.
The Imperial Collection of Four Branches of Literature (《四库全书》). (1782) Ed. by Ji Yun et al.
The Imperial Dictionary of Kangxi (《康熙字典》). (1716) Ed. by Zhang Yushu, Chen Tingjing, et al.
The Imperial Digest of the Taiping Reign (《太平御览》) published in the Song Dynasty (960–1279). Ed. by Li Fang et al.
The Imperial Records of the Taiping Reign (《太平广记》) published in the Song Dynasty (960–1279). Ed. by Li Fang et al.
The Interpretative Dictionary of Function Words (《助字辨略》) published in the Qing Dynasty (1636–1912). Ed. by Liu Qi.
The Jade Chapters (《玉篇》). (543) Ed. by Gu Yewang.
The Learned Exegesis of Six-category Chinese Characters (《六书通》). (1720) Ed. by Min Qiji.
The Linguistics Encyclopaedic Dictionary (《语言学百科词典》). (1993) Ed. by Qi Yuchun. Shanghai: Shanghai Lexicographical Press.
The Magnificent Character Dictionary (《字海》) published in the Tang Dynasty (618–907). Ed. by Wu Zetian.
The Mengxi Collection of Written Dialogues (《梦溪笔谈》) published in the Northern Song Dynasty (960–1127). Ed. by Shen Kuo.
The Modern Chinese Learners Dictionary (《现代汉语学习词典》). (1995) Ed. by Sun Quanzhou. Beijing: The Commercial Press.
The New Character Dictionary for Students with Standard National Pronunciation (《标准国音学生新字典》). (1937) Ed. by Gu Foying. Shanghai: Shanghai Sanmin Book Company.
The New Dictionary of Dialectal Words (《新方言》). (1911) Ed. by Zhang Binglin. Hangzhou: Zhejiang Library.
The New English-Chinese Dictionary (《新英汉词典》). (1975) Ed. by Ge Chuangui et al. Shanghai: Shanghai Yiwen Press.
The One Thousand Sanskrit Character Glossary (《梵语千字文》) published in the Tang Dynasty (618–907). Ed. by Yi Jing.
The Pearl Collection (《编珠》) published in the Sui Dynasty (581–618). Ed. by Du Gongzhan.
The Pei Xi Dictionary (《佩觿》) published in the Five Dynasties and Ten Kingdoms (907–960). Ed. by Guo Zhongshu.
The Ready Guide (《尔雅》) between the Qin and Han Dynasty (221 BC to AD 25). Anonymous author.
The Rectification of the Dictionary of Dialectal Words (《方言疏证》) published in the Qing Dynasty (1636–1912). Ed. by Dai Zhen.
The Rectified Dictionary of Chinese Characters (《正字通》) published in the Ming Dynasty (1368–1662). Ed. by Zhang Zilie.
The Rectified Dictionary of Dialectal Words (《方言据》) published in the Ming Dynasty (1368–1662). Ed. by Yue Yuansheng.
The Rhyme Dictionary (《集韵》) published in the Tang Dynasty (618–907). Ed. by Ding Du et al.
The Sources of Rhyme Ocean (《韵海镜源》) published in the Tang Dynasty (618–907). Ed. by Yan Zhenqing.
The Tang Dictionary of Rhymes (《唐韵》) published in the Tang Dynasty (618–907). Ed. by Sun Mian.
The Waitai Collection of Secret Prescriptions (《外台秘要》) published in the Tang Dynasty (618–907). Ed. by Wang Tao.
The Yongle Compendium (《永乐大典》). (1404) Ed. by Xie Jin et al.

Western Mandarin, or the Spoken Language of Western China; With Syllabic and English Indexes (《西蜀方言》). (1900) Ed. by Adam Grainger. Shanghai: American Presbyterian Mission Press.
Wuju Rhyme Dictionary (《五车韵瑞》) published in the Ming Dynasty (1368–1662). Ed. by Ling Zhilong.

Other literature

Bei, Z. (2005) *A New Introduction to Exegetic Studies*. Shanghai: Shanghai Lexicographical Press.
Béjoint, H. (2000) *Modern Lexicography: An Introduction*. Oxford: Oxford University Press.
Chien, D. and C. T. Creamer (1986) "A Brief History of Chinese Bilingual Lexicography", in Hartmann (ed.), *The History of Lexicography*, papers from The Dictionary Research Centre Seminar at Exeter, March 1986. Amsterdam: John Benjamins Publishing Company, pp. 35–45.
Collison, R. L. (1982) *A History of Foreign-Language Dictionaries*. London: Andre Deutsch Limited.
Cowie, A. P. (ed.) (2008) *The Oxford History of English Lexicography*. Oxford: Oxford University Press.
Dinh-Hoa, N. (1995) "On Chi-nam Ngoc-am Giai-nghia: An Early Chinese-Vietnamese Dictionary", in B. B. Kachru and H. Kahane (eds.), *Culture, Ideologies, and the Dictionary: Studies in Honor of LadislavZgusta*. Tubingen: Max Niemeyer VerlagGmb. H. & Co. KG, pp. 187–195.
Dunn, R. (1977) *Chinese-English and English-Chinese Dictionaries in the Library of Congress: An Annotated Bibliography*. Washington, DC: Library of Congress.
Green, J. (1996) *Chasing the Sun*. London: Jonathan Cape.
Hartmann, R.R.K. (ed.) (1986) *The History of Lexicography*, papers from The Dictionary Research Centre Seminar at Exeter, March 1986. Amsterdam: John Benjamins Publishing Company.
Landau, S. I. (2001) *Dictionaries: The Art and Craft of Lexicography*, 2nd edition. Cambridge: Cambridge University Press.
Watters, T. (1889) *Essays on the Chinese Language*. Shanghai: Presbyterian Mission Press.
Yong, H. (2004) "Thoughts on the Studies of Chinese Dictionary History", *Lexicographical Studies* 2: 14–21. Shanghai: Shanghai Lexicographical Press.
Yong, H. and L. Zhenyue (2010) *Chinese Dictionaries: Three Millennia*. Shanghai: Shanghai Foreign Language Education Press.
Yong, H. and J. Peng (2008) *Chinese Lexicography: A History From 1046 BC to AD 1911*. Oxford: Oxford University Press.
Zou, F. (2001) *Explorations in Lexicography*. Wuhan: Hubei People's Press.

33

English lexicography in the Internet era

Howard Jackson

33.1 Introduction

It almost goes without saying that the Internet has exercised a profound influence on lexicography in general, and on English lexicography in particular. Not only have publishers put their dictionaries, in all their variety, online, but the Internet has also affected how dictionary making itself is carried out. The World Wide Web represents a vast sea of data that lexicographers can search for evidence of word usage, or indeed for new words and new uses of words. The Oxford University Press dictionaries department, for example, has compiled the over 2-billion-word Oxford English Corpus from the Internet for this purpose.[1]

Consulting a dictionary online is not the same experience as consulting a print dictionary. Although most online dictionaries had a previous life in print, they should be viewed as works in their own right, because the design and presentation differ significantly from those of print dictionaries (Almind 2005). The most significant issue is that of accessibility: how the user gets to the information that satisfies their need as efficiently and effectively as possible. Granger (2012: 3) has identified six significant innovations or developments (Eide 2014) that take online lexicography beyond the print medium: corpus integration, more and better data, efficiency of access, customisation, hybridisation, and user input. These issues, along with others, will be discussed further in Section 33.3 of this chapter.

In this digital age, if someone needs a piece of information, the first port of call is most likely to be the Internet (Béjoint 2016), and the information seeker will not be concerned about where the information is to be found. Online dictionaries need to find their place among the plethora of information sources that constitute the World Wide Web. In general they are free to access, they are potentially more up to date, and there is no restriction on space (Harley 2000). What, then, is the likely future of English dictionaries, now that the Internet is most people's one-stop source of information? We will consider this in Section 33.4.

33.2 Historical perspectives

In 1993 the World Wide Web became free to anyone and thus a potential platform for electronic dictionaries (Nesi 2016). According to Carr (1997), the Yahoo! search engine in 1997 listed 91 "cyberdictionaries", though he noted that the list omitted "some notable e-dictionaries" (Carr 1997: 213). Li (1998, 2005) estimates that by 1998 there were in excess of 400 English online dictionaries. In 1997 OneLook indexed 188 dictionaries; by 2005 this had increased to 992 (Nesi 2008), and in February 2016 the number stood at 1061[2]. In the early 2000s, when the advent of broadband technology made Internet access faster and more reliable, many more dictionaries were digitised and put online. For example, the Lexicons of Early Modern English website has over 200 digitised and searchable early modern English dictionaries.[3] These numbers give some indication of the expansion in online English lexicography since the Internet became publicly available.

The second edition of the mighty *Oxford English Dictionary*, whose 1989 print edition ran to twenty volumes, went online in 2000[4]; it is now being thoroughly revised and expanded, with no prospect of a third edition appearing in print. On 5 November 2012, the Macmillan Dictionary Blog[5] announced that the *Macmillan Dictionary for learners of English*[6] would from then on be available only online. This announcement has, however, not been followed by similar declarations from other dictionary publishers. Apart from the OED and Macmillan, the only other Internet-only English dictionaries are the crowdsourced ones like *Wiktionary*.[7]

All the major dictionary publishers, of both dictionaries for native speakers and those for learners, now have an online presence of varying sophistication. In the UK, this includes the following: Oxford, with their flagship *Oxford Dictionary of English*[8] and their *Oxford Advanced Learner's Dictionary*[9]; Collins, with their flagship *Collins English Dictionary* and the *COBUILD Dictionary* for learners[10]; Chambers, though not with their flagship *The Chambers Dictionary*, which is available only in print, but with the smaller *Chambers 21st Century Dictionary*[11]; Longman, with their *Longman Dictionary of Contemporary English* for learners[12]; Cambridge, with their *Cambridge Advanced Learner's Dictionary*[13]; and Macmillan, with the *Macmillan Dictionary* for learners[14]. In the United States, this includes the following: Merriam-Webster, with a native-speaker dictionary[15] and a learner's dictionary[16]; and Houghton-Mifflin, with *The American Heritage Dictionary*[17]. Many UK publishers have also produced American English versions of their dictionaries: Oxford and Collins, for example, offer an American English look-up on their websites, and some of the learner's dictionaries have an American English counterpart, for example, *Oxford Advanced American Dictionary*[18] and *Longman Dictionary of American English.*[19]

Additionally, many historical dictionaries and dictionaries of older periods of English have been digitised and made available online. The Lexicons of Early Modern English website was mentioned earlier. Joseph Wright's six-volume *English Dialect Dictionary* (1898–1905) has been digitised at the University of Innsbruck[20]. The *Middle English Dictionary*, covering the period 1100 to 1500, appeared in print in 2001 and is now available online.[21] And the *Dictionary of Old English* is in process of compilation and online publication[22]; at the time of writing letters A to H have been published. Noah Webster's 1828 edition of *The American Dictionary of the English Language* is available online,[23] as is *The Century Dictionary* of 1914[24], considered by some to be the greatest American dictionary of English. And then, the Internet is home to a number of specialist dictionaries, such as *The Historical Gazetteer of England's Place Names,*[25] the *Dictionary of American Regional English,*[26] and the *Online Etymological Dictionary*[27] (see Chapters 19 and 22 of this *Handbook* for a more detailed analysis of English learners' dictionaries; see also Chapter 29 of this *Handbook* on *Wordnik*).

33.3 Core issues and topics

33.3.1 Corpora in English lexicography online

According to L'Homme and Cormier (2014: 332), "the use of corpora and the improvement of tools to process them have had a profound impact on lexicography". Most, if not all, publishers of dictionaries of English use a corpus, that is, a searchable collection of texts stored electronically, either to inform ongoing development and revision of exisiting dictionaries (corpus-based lexicography) or as the basic raw data from which the dictionary is compiled (corpus-driven lexicography). *Collins English Dictionary* would be an example of the first type, and the *Macmillan Dictionary* an example of the second. It was noted earlier (in Section 33.1) that Oxford Dictionaries have compiled a 2-billion-word-plus corpus, largely from the World Wide Web, to inform their ongoing lexicographical developments. An even larger Internet-derived corpus of English is the 23-billion-word enTenTen corpus.[28] Publishers generally have access to corpora composed of hundreds of millions of words, usually taken from a wide variety of text genres and spoken discourse from across the English-speaking world. In fact, the problem that corpora and the Internet pose for lexicographers is a superabundance of data that is so vast that it is difficult to manage and process (Coleman 2016). The answer has been to develop tools to automatically analyse the raw data of language and so provide the lexicographer with data that are more manageable. Such a tool is Sketch Engine[29] (Kilgarriff 2013, Kilgarriff and Kosem 2012), which analyses the uses of a word in a corpus and produces a lexical profile for the lexicographer to utilise in writing a dictionary entry for that word. The Sketch Engine was used, for example, in the compilation of the *Macmillan Dictionary*.[30]

Apart from their utilisation in the process of compiling dictionaries, it has been suggested that an online dictionary should be linked to a corpus so that users have access to the same raw data that the lexicographers exploited (de Schryver 2003). Although not giving access to a complete corpus, which could be rather daunting for many online dictionary users, some online dictionaries offer the possibility of viewing additional corpus examples. The *Cambridge Dictionary Online*, for example, allows the user to click a 'More examples' bar to reveal further examples for a word, though this facility is not available for all words; more examples are available for 'spread' but not for 'elevation', for the verb 'refuse' but not for the noun 'refuse'. Oxford Dictionaries Online, on the other hand, provides a clickable 'example sentences' or 'more example sentences' bar for each sense of each word, and users of the *OED Online* can choose to either hide or reveal the quotations that support the definition of each word sense.

33.3.2 Online dictionary typologies

To some extent the typology of print dictionaries applies to online dictionaries as well: historical vs. synchronic, monolingual vs. bilingual, native speaker vs. learner, general purpose vs. specialist (see Jackson 2002: 23–24). But other sets of distinctions are exclusive to online dictionaries. The first is the distinction between 'replicated' and 'functional' dictionaries, to use Fuertes-Olivera's (2013) terms: replicated online dictionaries are those where the print dictionary has been transferred more or less wholesale to the electronic medium. Most online dictionaries, including learner's dictionaries (Heuberger 2016; see also Chapters 19 and 22 of this *Handbook*), are still like this, though often with an alternative layout (e.g. each sense on a new line, as space is no longer an issue), or with the addition of one or two features, such as audio pronunciation (see Section 33.3.5 below) or full-text searching (see Section 33.3.3). Functional online dictionaries, on the other hand, are built for the electronic medium and take account both of the possibilities of the electronic medium and of how the user will access the information that they are seeking (see Section 33.3.6). Among English online dictionaries, the *OED Online* has probably exploited the electronic medium to the greatest extent; but there is as yet no fully functional online dictionary that gives the user just what they need to answer the specific query that led to them consulting the dictionary (see Section 33.4.1).

Further distinctions relevant to online dictionary typology are those between institutional vs. collective, free vs. paid, individual vs. aggregate (Lew 2011; L'Homme and Cormier 2014). Institutional dictionaries are those produced by publishing houses, universities, or language academies, whereas collective online dictionaries are crowdsourced, with or without much editorial control. Collective dictionaries, such as *Wiktionary*[31] or *Urban Dictionary*,[32] are an Internet phenomenon. Most online dictionaries are free to access, though a few, notably the *OED Online*, are accessible by subscription only. Lew (2011) notes another type, which he calls 'freemium', where the basic content is available for free, but additional features or content are accessible only on the payment of a subscription: *Oxford Dictionaries Online* is like this and subscribers also enjoy an advert-free display; so is the *Longman Dictionary of Contemporary English* online, where audio pronunciation, for example, is provided free only for words beginning with the letters 'd' and 's' (you have to buy the CD to get full access). Individual online dictionaries, such as those provided by most dictionary publishers, are single dictionaries; some websites, though, provide access on look-up to entries in multiple dictionaries. OneLook,[33] for example, claims to index 1,061 dictionaries; Wordnik[34] and YourDictionary[35] provide information not only from dictionary sources but also from other online reference materials, such as thesauruses and encyclopaedias. Aggregate sites like these are in danger of presenting the user with too much information (Harley 2000), which the user may find difficult to sift through for the nugget they require.

33.3.3 Search capabilities

Potentially, dictionaries in the electronic format should offer a wider range of search possibilities than their print counterparts. To some extent this is the case. All online dictionaries have a search box, into which the user types the item they wish to look up. Provided it is spelled correctly, the user is taken instantly to the relevant entry; users are "liberated from the alphabetical straitjacket" (de Schryver 2003: 157). If the item is spelled incorrectly or the dictionary does not contain the item, the dictionary may offer suggestions (e.g. *Merriam-Webester*, *Macmillan*). Some online dictionaries (e.g. *Collins English Dictionary*, *Merriam-Webster*) offer "focus-in typing" (de Schryver 2003: 178), where, as you type, a list of possibilities is displayed, enabling you to click on an item before you have completed typing it. One search type that is greatly facilitated by electronic searching is that for phrasemes (Miller 2013); idioms and other fixed phrases are often hard to find in print dictionaries, because it is not always intuitively obvious under which word they will have been listed: do you look for 'hit the nail on the head', for example, under 'hit', 'nail', or 'head'? Type the expression into an online dictionary search box, and it will find it instantly, provided it has been entered in the dictionary.

Pastor and Alcina (2013: 103) note that "offline dictionaries provide more search techniques than online dictionaries." Dictionaries on CD often allow searches in the content of dictionary entries, not just in the headword list; online dictionaries are usually restricted to the latter. The *OED Online*, however, allows 'advanced searches' in a number of information types in the dictionary, including subject, language of origin, region, date of entry, and part of speech. The electronic format also enables onomasiological searches (Nesi 2016), that is searches according to meaning rather than form. A number of the online learner's dictionaries (including *Oxford*, *Longman*, *Macmillan*) have a 'thesaurus' or 'topic' feature, in which words are grouped according to subject matter or semantic field, and independent investigation of these fields is possible. The *OED Online* is now integrated with the *Historical Thesaurus of English*.[36] Also facilitated by the electronic medium is cross-referencing; a cross-reference within an entry is now only a click away (Lew 2010); and some online dictionaries (e.g. *Oxford Dictionaries*, *Macmillan*) allow the user to click on a word within a definition to be taken to the entry for that word.

33.3.4 Presentation

The structure and presentation of articles in printed dictionaries are constrained by limitations on space and the need to keep the dictionary to a reasonable size and cost. Some dictionaries, notably those for learners, have dispensed with the traditional tightly packed entry and have, for example, used a new line for each sense of a headword or dispensed with abbreviation. Without the same space constraints, electronic dictionaries have the potential to "move away from a static to a dynamic data display" (Gouws 2014: 164). Online dictionaries are more or less adventurous in their presentation of dictionary information. Most have abandoned the single paragraph entry of print dictionaries and at least use a new line for each sense. Many make generous use of the space available; in this respect the *American Heritage Dictionary*, still close to the tradition, can be compared with *Oxford Dictionaries* online, which spreads its entries down the page and with bigger font sizes than the *American Heritage*. The issue now becomes one of screen size and the need to scroll through multiple screens to view the whole entry or to find the sense that is being searched for; and with people now accessing the Internet with small-screen devices (smart phones or tablets), this is a pressing issue (L'Homme and Cormier 2014).

A related issue is that of deciding how much data should be presented in response to a look-up and in what order (Lew 2012, Lew and de Schryver 2014). Gouws (2014) argues for assigning different types of data to different blocks of text or "search zones" with a "multi-layered structure". The dictionary that currently comes closest to meeting these requirements is the *OED Online*, which has an 'Outline' option and a 'Full entry' option, as well as options to display truncated 'Forms' and 'Etymology' and to hide quotations under each sense. Some dictionaries have pop-up boxes for additional information: the *Oxford Advanced Learner's Dictionary* has them for 'Verb Forms' and for 'Word Origin', and *Macmillan Dictionary* has one for 'Word Forms'. The *Longman Dictionary Online* has a pop-up 'Menu' for longer entries (e.g. 'wait') that lists the senses and fixed expressions, enabling the user to navigate directly to the sense they are looking for.

One other presentation issue that has been discussed is the use of colour in electronic dictionaries (Dziemianko 2015, Pastor and Alcina 2010). Colour can be used to highlight specific information or to draw attention to particular information categories. Print learner's dictionaries had begun to employ colour in their presentation, but in the electronic medium it is more versatile and cost free. The number of different colours that are used and the elements of entries that are presented in colour vary enormously among the online English dictionaries: The *American Heritage Dictionary* has the headword in blue, but everything else in black; *Collins English Dictionary* has the headword and labels in blue; *Macmillan*

Dictionary has the 7,500 most frequent headwords in red and examples in blue; and *Longman Dictionaries Online* has headwords and subwords in blue and sense numbers in red. There is some evidence that judicious use of colour enhances learning (Dziemianko 2015), but the jury is still out on the effectiveness of the use of colour in online dictionaries.

33.3.5 Graphics, audio, and video

Audio, "the first novelty to be added" (de Schryver 2003: 167), has now invaded most online English dictionaries. In all dictionaries where audio is used, the pronunciation of the headword can be played, either in an American accent (*Merriam-Webster*) or in a British accent (*Macmillan*), or sometimes in both (*Oxford Learner's*, *Cambridge*). The *Collins COBUILD Online Dictionary* provides additionally the pronunciation of the inflectional forms of a headword. The *Macmillan Dictionary* has extended the use of audio to provide "recordings of non-linguistic sounds" (Lew 2010: 297), including the sounds of musical instruments (clarinet), animal and bird calls (cuckoo), sounds made by humans (whisper), as well as other sounds (clang). However, audio is limited to the pronunciation of single lexemes (de Schryver 2003); none of the major online English dictionaries offers audio for example sentences, where it would often be useful for learners to hear a word pronounced in context. Audio has potential for further development, perhaps even to voice-activated access (Nielsen 2013) and audio presentation of search results for visually impaired users.

Illustrations, either line drawings or photographs, can be found in a number of online English dictionaries, predominantly in learners' dictionaries, but not exclusively; the *American Heritage Dictionary*, for example, has a number of illustrations, although *Collins English Dictionary* does not. Pictorial illustrations are usually limited to concrete nouns, for which they can "provide an additional meaning indicator" (Lew 2010: 297). An extension of graphical illustrations would be to provide video footage for action verbs (e.g. 'gallop', 'saunter'); no major online English dictionary has done this as yet. Lew (2010: 303) suggests that video clips could "convey useful information on the pragmatic and situational context of linguistic communication." This is, perhaps, for the future and for when the "effectiveness of multimedia in dictionaries" has been established more securely (Lew 2012: 360).

33.3.6 Accessibility

How the user gets to the information that will answer their look-up query in the most efficient and effective way possible, that is, accessibility, is the most crucial issue for dictionaries generally and for online dictionaries in particular. Gouws (2014: 158) says that "accessibility is a critical factor of article structure", and for Granger (2012: 6) "improved accessiblity . . . remains a key challenge." Print learners' dictionaries provide menus or guide words for long entries to help users locate the sense that is relevant to their query; and this has been replicated with a drop-down menu in the *Longman Dictionary Online*. Viewing a long entry in an online dictionary may involve scrolling through multiple pages. In addition, the pages may contain numerous advertisements, creating a lot of "noise" (Dziemianko 2012) that the user needs to negotiate. The 'noise' brings in the revenue and so ensures free access, but it can be distracting for the user (Nesi 2016: 587) and compromise accessibility. Advertisements can be particularly distracting when they are placed not just at the top or sides of a lexical entry but within the entry itself, as in *Cambridge Dictionaries Online*.

The presence of "extraneous material on web pages" (Lew and de Schryver 2014: 347) may be one factor inhibiting access; another may be the sheer volume of lexical information that is presented (Harley 2000). This may become more of a problem depending on the screen size of the device with which the Internet is being accessed (Simonsen 2015). How does the user navigate through this jungle to find the specific piece of information that will answer their query? The online medium has the potential to incorporate features that will guide the user to their desired destination. The use of "partial entries" for "stepwise access'"(Lew 2011: 10), like the 'Quick Search Results' for lexemes with multiple entries in *OED Online*, may help; the user then chooses which of the partial entries to expand. Hiding less salient information, such as the quotations in *OED Online*, creates a less cluttered entry, as would the use of drop-down menus (Lew 2011) for specific information fields, frequently used on web pages but not yet widely for online dictionaries. Another answer is to develop features that will adapt to the needs of each particular user, so that they see only the information that they require to answer the look-up (see Sections 33.3.8 and 33.4.2).

33.3.7 Customization

One way to improve the user-friendliness and accessibility of online dictionaries is by customization (Heuberger 2016), that is, "customising the various dictionaries to suit individual needs" (de Schryver 2003: 163). De Schryver (2003) suggests that there are two types of dictionary consultation: browsing and look-up. In a customised dictionary, a user could switch on those information categories that they need, as is possible to some extent in the *OED Online*. Customization is "a process which allows the dictionary to be adapted to users' needs" (Granger 2012: 6). Granger (2012) cites Gamper and Knapp (2002), who distinguish between "adaptable" and "adaptive" customization, the former being manually controlled by the user (e.g. by switching on desired information categories) and the latter being built into the online dictionary, so that it adapts automatically to the user and the look-up. Such "complete customization" is not yet achievable according to Caruso (2013); it is dependent on the organisation of data storage and the development of appropriate electronic tools. The potential is there for online dictionaries to be customizable in this sense, and it is indeed the goal of "functional online dictionaries" (Fuertes-Olivera 2013).

An optimal online dictionary would present a user only with information that is relevant to them, to their look-up query, and to the task that has prompted the look-up (Lew and de Schryver 2014). The Internet environment should enable lexicographers to meet the variety of individual users' needs from a single lexical database by developing tools to select and present only those types of information that will satisfy the query that the user has made (Fuertes-Olivera 2013). The user may need to set parameters relevant to their status and stage of learning, as well as the tasks in which they are engaged (reading, writing, translation, vocabulary learning), or the online dictionary may develop a profile of the user based on their look-up practices, much as commercial websites anticipate our purchasing habits. None of the major online English dictionaries has pursued this path as yet; the *OED Online* probably incorporates the most customization, although it is manually invoked by the user. Some other online dictionaries have limited customization, to the extent that certain categories of supplementary information can be accessed by clicking on a button or bar, for example, 'Word forms and 'Word origin' in the *Oxford Learner's Dictionary* or 'Word Forms' and 'Synonyms and related words' in the *Macmillan Dictionary*.

33.4 Looking to the future

According to Brewer (2013: 353), "the future of historical dictionaries . . . is undeniably digital." What is true for historical dictionaries is true for dictionaries generally. Béjoint (2016) predicts the eventual demise of the dictionary for general users in print form, to be replaced by online resources, although he has doubts whether online versions can truly replace print dictionaries in all their functions (Béjoint 2010, 2016). Some of the advantages of online dictionaries are that they can be updated regularly (Lew and de Schryver 2014) and new words can be "identified and analyzed computationally" (Nesi 2016: 583), they are free to access, they are available wherever a portable electronic device is to be found, and they are not limited by alphabetical ordering. Indeed, some scholars see online lexicography as reinvigorating onomasiological, or meaning-based, dictionaries (Kay and Alexander 2016, Murphy 2016). The print dictionary may not be dead yet; apart from Macmillan, publishers currently maintain both a print and an online presence, although online is favoured for historical dictionaries, both for earlier dictionaries (e.g. *Webster's* 1828, Wright's *English Dialect Dictionary*) and for dictionaries dealing with the history of English (*OED*).

For most people, the Internet is the first port of call for finding information. Consequently, online dictionaries may come to be viewed as "services" rather than as "products" (Eide 2014: 181), services that are continuously improving to serve the needs of their users. Dictionaries will no longer be "a (partial) record of the vocabulary of a language" (Jackson 2002: 22) or "represent the language in the same way as a paper dictionary does" (Béjoint 2016: 23). They will, instead, be user focused and adaptable, perhaps integrated with other information sources, and even compiled from the contributions of users. We now explore some of these topics.

33.4.1 The user at the centre

One of the issues with dictionaries generally is information overload. This is a particular problem with dictionary sites like OneLook that aggregate several online dictionaries. Print dictionaries cannot avoid information overload and, to a large extent, merely mitigate it by sensible presentation. Online dictionaries, on the other hand, have the capabilities for overcoming this problem (Tarp 2015); they could "tailor the entries according to the users' needs" (Caruso 2014: 371). The presentation of information can take account of the function of the look-up and the profile of the user (Gouws 2014). Lexicographic data can be organised and presented in more user-friendly ways.

Although research on the users and uses of print dictionaries has a long history (Nesi 2013), little has so far been undertaken on online dictionaries (Lew 2015). One study, however, has been widely reported (Müller-Spitzer et al. 2011, Müller-Spitzer 2014, Lew 2015), though it was conducted with a sample largely made up of language professionals, which may account for the results. The sample tended to value traditional dictionary features (clarity, reliability) over those more characteristic of online dictionaries (multimedia, adaptability). When innovative features of online dictionaries were explained in more detail to participants, however, a greater appreciation of their potential was forthcoming. Some alternative layouts were tested, for example (Lew 2015:241), and the "tabbed view" was rated highest, that is, where a user clicks on a tab to view an information category, as opposed to the "panel view", where information is presented in different panes.

The function theory of lexicography (Fuertes-Olivera 2013, Nielsen 2013) argues strongly that the user and their needs must be central to the design of electronic dictionaries and how they present lexicographical information, so that the user receives only the information that they need to satisfy their query. Online presentation of dictionary information needs to adapt to the individual user and the specific look-up that is being made.

33.4.2 Adaptability

There are two ways in which dictionary information can be adapted or customized to the individual user. In the first method, the user sets up their personal user profile (Gouws 2014), for example, that they are a learner of English with a particular level of competence, and they are using the dictionary as an aid to writing texts in English. The online dictionary then presents information appropriate to the competence level of the user and to enable the information to be usable in the writing task. In the second method, the online dictionary makes use of "adaptive hypermedia systems" (de Schryver 2003: 189) or "a user-adaptive interface" (Koplenig 2011: 147) to automatically adapt to the user and their look-up needs, just as commercial websites anticipate the buying preferences of their users and tailor the presentation of their wares accordingly.

Both these methods may be combined to allow "the personalization of information presented to the user by means of filtering and adaptive technologies based on the user's profile" (Fuertes-Olivera 2013: 331). Both the user profile and the adaptive electronic tool work together to customize the presentation of lexicographical information. Arguably, most dictionary users and especially Internet dictionary users want to get to the desired information as quickly and efficiently as possible to satisfy a particular information need for a specific task. What may be missed is the serendipitous discovery that arises from either browsing or perusing a whole entry; users who value this feature will remain with their print dictionaries. After all, online dictionaries generally do not allow the kind of browsing that is possible with a print version.

33.4.3 Hybridisation

According to Rundell (2012: 29), "the dictionary is morphing from . . . autonomous 'product' to something more like a 'service', often embedded in other resources" (quoted in Caruso 2013: 597). It is the linking with "other resources" that occasions the term 'hybridisation'. Indeed it is such "resource integration" that Trap-Jensen (2013: 46) sees as the likely way forward for dictionaries, which face "the risk of drowning in the profusion of other resources with which they compete for user attention." Nesi (2008: 28) maintains that "electronic dictionaries are inclined to hybridization", and other scholars (de Schryver 2003, Hawke 2016) note the possibilities that websites have for linking to other resources on the Internet.

Hybridisation is already happening on the Internet. A number of dictionaries have links to other dictionaries, usually from the same publisher. For example, *Collins Dictionary Online* enables you to look up a word in its flagship dictionary, in the *COBUILD Learner's Dictionary*, and in several bilingual dictionaries, as well as to switch between them. If you look up a word (e.g. 'clarinet') in *Merriam-Webster Online*, there is a link to the corresponding article in the *Encyclopædia Britannica Online*, where such an article exists. The *Reverso Dictionary*[37], using *Collins English Dictionary* for its dictionary information, provides a number of links to other information sources, including *Wikipedia*, Google, an image bank, and a news website, as well as having an inbuilt grammar, conjugator, and spell checker. Many online dictionaries remain standalone publications, and it will be interesting to see how long they can continue as such.

33.4.4 Collaborative lexicography

Involving the public in the compilation of a dictionary has a long history, especially for a dictionary like the *Oxford English Dictionary*, whose editors recruited 'readers' from across the English-speaking world to participate in the dictionary's reading programme and send in to the editor slips of paper with quotations illustrating the meanings of words taken from their reading. The *OED* still receives communications from the general public and itself issues appeals to the public for help in finding antedatings for words being revised.[38] A number of general-purpose online dictionaries invite and make provision for their users to submit items for inclusion in the dictionary, for example *Merriam-Webster*, *American Heritage Dictionary*, *Collins English Dictionary*, and *Macmillan Dictionary*. The editorial control remains with the lexicographers employed by the dictionary publisher; they decide whether to include the submitted item and what content will be given for it. The user cannot directly edit the dictionary content, and the reliability and integrity of the dictionary are maintained. The collaborative nature of the lexicography is limited; the professional lexicographers continue to be responsible for the content of the dictionary.

A truly collaborative lexicography is found in online dictionaries like *Wiktionary*, the English version of which[39] began in December 2002, as a lexical offshoot of the online encyclopaedia *Wikipedia*[40] (Mayer and Gurevych 2012). Initially, *Wiktionary* imported the entries from the out-of-copyright 1913 edition of *Webster's New International Dictionary*; the entries have subsequently been revised and updated, though this task is not yet complete. Any person can sign up to edit *Wiktionary* entries or create new ones, as long as they follow the fairly strict guidelines on article structure and content that have been laid down by the administrators. Another well-known online crowdsourced dictionary is the *Urban Dictionary*, which accepts entries for English slang words and expressions (Cotter and Damaso 2007).

Opinions are mixed on whether crowdsourced dictionaries like *Wiktionary* and *Urban Dictionary* are a positive development in the lexicographical landscape (see Chapter 29 of this *Handbook*). Cibej et al (2015: 71) consider that crowdsourcing could be used "to great effect", and Moon (2016: 142) sees it as "lexicographical democratization". Others are less sure. Granger (2012: 7) worries that "accuracy is no longer guaranteed", and Hanks (2010: 592) reckons that "Wiktionary is full of second-hand, derivative entries, often wrongly defined or with erroneous examples." Coleman (2016: 335–6) notes that "the Internet has opened up slang lexicography to anyone who wants to become involved in it", but is of the opinion that "online slang dictionaries are often more interested in optimizing their advertising revenue than in improving the quality of their entries". As with so much else on the Internet, "bottom-up lexicography" (Nesi 2008: 26) is probably like the curate's egg, good in parts.

33.5 Conclusion

What is happening to English lexicography in the Internet era? It seems probable that "print-based dictionaries will disappear as content migrates to e-dictionaries" (Nesi 2016: 584), so that "the days of most authoritative, monolingual print dictionaries may be numbered" (Nesi 2016: 589), a view shared by Béjoint (2016). One result of the migration of dictionaries to the Internet is that "the traditional dividing line between dictionaries and other kinds of resources is more and more difficult to draw" (L'Homme and Cormier 2014: 335). Moreover, people tend to resort to Google for answers to all their information queries, and "this tendency presents a real threat to more specialized reference tools, including dictionaries" (Lew 2011: 15). The *Macmillan Dictionary*, whose chief editor is Michael Rundell, saw the writing on the wall in 2012; the *OED Third Edition* will exist only online; and all major dictionary publishers have online versions of their dictionaries, which are accessible at no cost to the user. A Google search for a term or expression may index a dictionary, but it may not be near the top of the list and the dictionary indexed may not be the most reliable. Dictionary publishers face a challenge to educate and persuade the Internet-using public to use a reliable dictionary when looking up a word or expression, rather than do a general Google search. For dictionaries aimed at learners of English, that may be easier than for native-speaker dictionaries.

Some scholars view the wholesale move to the Internet as not in the best interests of lexicography. In the context of historical dictionary projects, Considine (2016: 175) finds "the move to online-only publication . . . disturbing", arguing that long entries in particular are harder to consult online than on the printed page and that online dictionaries require "more active maintenance". As well as expressing doubts about crowdsourced online dictionaries, Hanks (2010: 596) asks whether the Internet is "as secure and durable a medium as the printed page". Certainly, for historians of the language, the ability to compare successive editions of a dictionary will be severely jeopardised. We are not yet at an online-only scenario for English lexicography, and it may be many years before that comes about; Béjoint (2010: 375) is of the opinion that it may take longer than we think.

Related topics

Dictionary and access; revising the *Dictionary of Canadianisms on Historical Principles*; dictionaries to assist teaching and learning; electronic dictionaries; FrameNet; information retrieval for lexicographic purposes; learners' dictionaries of English.

Further reading

For an overview of dictionary-making in English, Henri Béjoint's *The Lexicography of English* (2010) is the place to start. Although it has only a quite brief section on electronic dictionaries, including online ones, this is an impressive account of the history of dictionary making in English, together with an assessment of the state of English lexicography at the beginning of the twenty-first century.

Specifically on electronic dictionaries, including those on the Internet, Hilary Nesi's articles provide an insightful and comprehensive account. These include her 2008 "Dictionaries in electronic form" and her 2016 article in the Oxford Handbook, "The demands of users and the publishing world: printed or online, free or paid for?"

Robert Lew's 2011 article "Online dictionaries of English" specifically addresses the topic of this chapter. It is contained in Fuertes-Olivera and Bergenholtz's 2011 *E-lexicography: The Internet, Digital Initiatives and Lexicography*, which presents the case for the function theory of lexicography.

Granger and Paquot's edited volume (2012), entitled *Electronic Lexicography*, contains a variety of chapters on the topic, but not all of them relate to English lexicography. The same is true of Gouws et al (2013) with their supplementary volume to the *International Encyclopedia of Lexicography*, which concentrates on electronic lexicography. And a recent edition of the *International Journal of Lexicography*, Volume 27/4 (2014), edited by Marie-Claude L'Homme and Monique Cormier, is devoted to "Dictionaries and the digital revolution".

Notes

1 www.oxforddictionaries.com/words/about-the-oxford-english-corpus
2 http://onelook.com/
3 http://leme.library.utoronto.ca/public/intro.cfm

4 http://public.oed.com/about/
5 www.macmillandictionaryblog.com/
6 www.macmillandictionary.com/
7 www.wiktionary.org/
8 www.oxforddictionaries.com/
9 www.oxfordlearnersdictionaries.com/
10 www.collinsdictionary.com/
11 www.chambers.co.uk/
12 www.ldoceonline.com/
13 http://dictionary.cambridge.org/dictionary/english/
14 www.macmillandictionary.com/
15 www.merriam-webster.com/
16 www.learnersdictionary.com/
17 www.ahdictionary.com/
18 www.oxfordlearnersdictionaries.com/definition/american_english/
19 http://longmandictionariesusa.com/
20 www.uibk.ac.at/anglistik/projects/edd-online/
21 http://quod.lib.umich.edu/m/med/
22 http://doe.utoronto.ca/pages/index.html
23 http://webstersdictionary1828.com/
24 www.global-language.com/century/
25 http://placenames.org.uk/
26 www.daredictionary.com/
27 www.etymonline.com/
28 www.sketchengine.co.uk/ententen-corpus/
29 www.sketchengine.co.uk/
30 www.macmillandictionaries.com/features/from-corpus-to-dictionary/
31 www.wiktionary.org/
32 www.urbandictionary.com/
33 http://onelook.com/
34 www.wordnik.com/
35 www.yourdictionary.com/
36 http://public.oed.com/historical-thesaurus-of-the-oed/
37 http://dictionary.reverso.net/
38 http://public.oed.com/appeals
39 https://en.wiktionary.org/wiki/Wiktionary:Main_Page
40 https://en.wikipedia.org/wiki/Main_Page

References

Almind, R. (2005) "Designing Internet Dictionaries", *Hermes* 34: 37–54.

Béjoint, H. (2010) *The Lexicography of English*. Oxford: Oxford University Press.

Béjoint, H. (2016) "Dictionaries for General Users: History and Development; Current Issues", in P. Durkin (ed.), pp. 7–24.

Brewer, C. (2013) "The Future of Historical Dictionaries, With Special Reference to the Online OED and Thesaurus", in H. Jackson (ed.), pp. 341–354.

Carr, M. (1997) "Internet Dictionaries and Lexicography", *International Journal of Lexicography* 10(3): 209–230.

Caruso, V. (2013) "From e-Lexicography to Electronic Lexicography: A Joint Review", *Lexikos* 23: 585–610.

Caruso, V. (2014) "Key Issues in Fuertes-Olivera and Tarp's *Theory and Practice of Specialised Online Dictionaries*", *Lexikos* 24: 362–377.

Čibej, J., D. Fišer and I. Kosem (2015) "The Role of Crowdsourcing in Lexicography", in I. Kosem, M. Jakubíček, J. Kallas and S. Krek (eds.), pp. 70–83.

Coleman, J. (2016) "Slang Dictionaries", in P. Durkin (ed.), pp. 325–337.

Considine, J. (2016) "Historical Dictionaries: History and Development; Current Issues", in P. Durkin (ed.), pp. 163–175.

Cormier, M. C. & M-C. L'Homme (2014) *Dictionaries and the Digital Revolution*, Special Issue of *International Journal of Lexicography*, 27/4.

Cotter, C. and J. Damaso (2007) "Online Dictionaries as Emergent Archives of Contemporary Usage and Collaborative Codification", *Queen Mary's Occasional Papers Advancing Linguistics No. 9*, Queen Mary College, University of London.

de Schryver, G.-M. (2003) "Lexicographers' Dreams in the Electronic-Dictionary Age", *International Journal of Lexicography* 16(2): 143–199.

Durkin, P. (ed.) (2016) *The Oxford Handbook of Lexicography*. Oxford: Oxford University Press.

Dziemianko, A. (2012) "Why One and Two Do Not Make Three: Dictionary Form Revisited", *Lexikos* 22: 195–216.

Dziemianko, A. (2015) "Colours in Online Dictionaries: A Case of Functional Labels", *International Journal of Lexicography* 28(1): 27–61.

Eide, Ø. (2014) "Review of Granger and Paquot (eds.) (2012)", *International Journal of Lexicography* 27(2): 180–191.

Fuertes-Olivera, P. A. (2013) "e-Lexicography: The Continuing Challenge of Applying New Technology to Dictionary-Making", in H. Jackson (ed.), pp. 323–340.

Fuertes-Olivera, P. A. and H. Bergenholtz (eds.) (2011) *e-Lexicography: The Internet, Digital Initiatives and Lexicography*. London and New York: Continuum.

Gamper, J. and J. Knapp (2002) "A Review of Intelligent CALL Systems", *Computer Assisted Language Learning* 10(4): 329–342.

Gouws, R. H. (2014) "Article Structures: Moving From Printed to e-Dictionaries", *Lexikos* 24: 155–177.

Gouws, R. H., U. Heid, W. Schweickard and H. E. Wiegand (eds.) (2013) *Dictionaries: An International Encyclopedia of Lexicography. Supplementary Volume: Recent Developments With Focus on Electronic and Computational Lexicography*. Berlin: de Gruyter Mouton.

Granger, S. (2012) "Electronic Lexicography: From Challenge to Opportunity", in S. Granger and M. Paquot (eds.), pp. 1–11.

Granger, S. and M. Paquot (eds.) (2012) *Electronic Lexicography*. Oxford: Oxford University Press.

Hanks, P. (2010) "Compiling a Monolingual Dictionary for Native Speakers", *Lexikos* 20: 580–598.

Harley, A. (2000) "Cambridge Dictionaries online", in *Proceedings of the Ninth EuraLex International Congress*, pp. 85–88.

Hawke, A. (2016) "Quotation Evidence and Definitions", in P. Durkin (ed.), pp. 176–202.

Heuberger, R. (2016) "Learners' Dictionaries: History and Development; Current Issues", in P. Durkin (ed.), pp. 25–43.

Jackson, H. (2002) *Lexicography, an Introduction*. London: Routledge.

Jackson, H. (ed.) (2013) *The Bloomsbury Companion to Lexicography*. London and New York: Bloomsbury.

Kay, C. and M. Alexander (2016) "Diachronic and Synchronic Thesauruses", in P. Durkin (ed.), pp. 367–380.

Kilgarriff, A. (2013) "Using Corpora as Data Sources for Dictionaries", in H. Jackson (ed.), pp. 77–96.

Kilgarriff, A. and I. Kosem (2012) "Corpus Tools for Lexicographers", in S. Granger and M. Paquot (eds.), pp. 31–55.

Koplenig, A. (2011) "Understanding How Users Evaluate Innovative Features of Online Dictionaries – An Experimental Approach", in *Proceedings of e-Lex 2011*, pp. 147–150.

Kosem, I., M. Jakubíček, J. Kallas, S. Krek (eds.) (2015) *Electronic Lexicography in the 21st Century: Linking Lexical Data in the Digital Age: Proceedings of the eLex 2015 Conference, 11–13 August 2015, Herstmonceux Castle, United Kingdom*. Ljubljana/Brighton: Trojina, Institute for Applied Slovene Studies/Lexical Computing Ltd.

Lew, R. (2010) "Multimodal Lexicography: The Representation of Meaning in Electronic Dictionaries", *Lexikos* 20: 290–306.

Lew, R. (2011) "Online Dictionaries of English", in P. A. Fuertes-Olivera and H. Bergenholtz (eds.), pp. 230–250. https://repozytorium.amu.edu.pl/jspui/handle/10593/742 [Accessed 14 September 2015].
Lew, R. (2012) "How Can We Make Electronic Dictionaries More Effective?", in S. Granger and M. Paquot (eds.), pp. 343–361.
Lew, R. (2015) "Research Into the Use of Online Dictionaries", *International Journal of Lexicography* 28(2): 232–253.
Lew, R. and G.-M. de Schryver (2014) "Dictionary Users in the Digital Revolution", *International Journal of Lexicography* 27(4): 341–359.
L'Homme, M-C. and M. C. Cormier (2014) "Dictionaries and the Digital Revolution: A Focus on Users and Lexical Databases", *International Journal of Lexicography* 27(4): 331–340.
Li, L. (1998) "Cyberdictionaries", *English Today* 14(2): 21–24.
Li, L. (2005) "The Growing Prosperity of On-Line Dictionaries", *English Today* 21(3): 16–21.
Meyer, C. M. and I. Gurevych (2012) "Wiktionary: A New Rival for Expert-Built Lexicons? Exploring the Possibilities of Collaborative Lexicography", in S. Granger and M. Paquot (eds.), pp. 259–291.
Miller, J. (2013) "*Birds of a Feather* Don't Always *Flock Together*: User Problems in Identifying Headwords in English Learner's Dictionaries", *Lexikos* 23: 273–285.
Moon, R. (2016) "Explaining Meaning in Learners' Dictionaries", in P. Durkin (ed.), pp. 123–143.
Müller-Spitzer, C. (ed.) (2014) *Using Online Dictionaries: Lexicographica Series Maior 145*. Berlin: Walter de Gruyter.
Müller-Spitzer, C., A. Koplenig and A. Töpel (2011) "What Makes a Good Online Dictionary? – Empirical Insights From an Interdisciplinary Research Project", in *Proceedings of e-Lex 2011*, pp. 203–208.
Murphy, M. L. (2016) "Meaning Relations in Dictionaries: Hyponymy, Meronymy, Synonymy, Antonymy, and Contrast", in P. Durkin (ed.), pp. 439–456.
Nesi, H. (2008) "Dictionaries in Electronic Form", in A. P. Cowie (ed.), *The Oxford History of English Lexicography*. Oxford: Oxford University Press, pp. 458–478.
Nesi, H. (2013) "Researching Users and Uses of Dictionaries", in H. Jackson (ed.), pp. 62–74.
Nesi, H. (2016) "The Demands of Users and the Publishing World: Printed or Online, Free or Paid for?", in P. Durkin (ed.), pp. 579–589.
Nielsen, S. (2013) "The Future of Dictionaries, Dictionaries of the Future", in H. Jackson (ed.), pp. 355–372.
Pastor, V. and A. Alcina (2010) "Search Techniques in Electronic Dictionaries: A Classification for Translators", *International Journal of Lexicography* 23(3): 307–354.
Pastor, V. and A. Alcina (2013) "Researching the Use of Electronic Dictionaries", in H. Jackson (ed.), pp. 97–147.
Rundell, M. (2012) "The Road to Automated Lexicography: An Editor's Viewpoint", in S. Granger and M. Paquot (eds.), pp. 15–30.
Simonsen, H. K. (2015) "Mobile Lexicography – Let's Do It Right This Time!", in I. Kosem, M. Jakubíček, J. Kallas, S. Krek (eds.), pp. 84–104.
Tarp, S. (2015) "Detecting User Needs for New Online Dictionary Projects: Business as Usual, User Research, or . . .?", in C. Tiberius and C. Müller-Spitzer (eds.), *Research Into Dictionary Use, Wörterbuchbenutzungsforschung. 5. Arbeitsbericht des wissenschaftlichen Netzwerks "Internetlexikografie"*. OPAL, 2/2015, 17–27. Available at: http://pub.ids-mannheim.de/laufend/opal/titel5.html.
Trap-Jensen, L. (2013) "Researching Lexicographical Practice", in H. Jackson (ed.), pp. 35–47.

34

French lexicography in the Internet era

Paul Achille Mavoungou

34.1 Introduction

Today French is geographically spread in a significant number of continents and countries. The geographic dispersal of French has brought the language into daily contact with new usage in Europe (Switzerland, Belgium, Luxembourg), in North America (Canada, overseas territories, Louisiana), in Africa (Senegal, Ivory Coast, Republic of Congo, etc.), in Asia (Vietnam, Cambodia, Indochina) and in the Middle East (mainly in Lebanon).

This chapter will first attempt to give a comprehensive overview of the various existing French Internet dictionaries. Second, basic structures of these dictionaries will be investigated, especially access and mediostructures.

When I was asked to write this chapter, and given the geographic dispersal of the French language, I wondered whether just French Internet dictionaries produced in Europe (especially in France, Belgium, Sweden) or in Quebec were available.

Based on the terminology proposed by De Schryver (2003b: 5–6) and with the help of search engines such as Google, I have looked for French Internet dictionaries. Following the investigation a substantial number of such dictionaries are available. Among them one may find online dictionaries, that is, dictionaries stored in databases over the Internet; pop-up dictionaries, that is, dictionaries with which, once one has downloaded a small piece of software, one can move the mouse over words online, upon which the relevant articles pop up in dedicated screens; and PC dictionaries, that is, dictionaries for which a piece of software *cum* one or more lexica are downloaded from the Internet, to be used as offline PC dictionaries. I have also taken into account the following products, namely machine translation systems running between French and other languages of the world, online corpora assembled with dictionary compilation in mind and dictionaries in Portable Document Format (PDF). The distribution of the number of Internet French dictionaries per continents or countries is also something interesting to learn. There are also other Internet products, namely French foreign language websites, that can be found *en masse* on the Internet. Only a very few of them will be included in this study, especially the ones offering to prospective learners lexicographic reference works to sustain the learning process.

34.2 Historical perpsectives

According to Forget (1999: 7) the face of French electronic dictionaries started to change in the 1980s with the publication of the first French CD-based dictionary, namely: *Le Grand Robert électronique* (henceforth *LGRE*) for the overwhelming price of $1500 (Canadian dollars). The release of *LGRE* in 1989 has paved the way for other electronic French products: *Larousse multimédia encyclopédique*, *Dictionnaire Hachette multimédia*, etc., that were much cheaper than *LGRE* when it was first published. The appearance on the market of the very first electronic French dictionaries has also led to the publication in the late 1990s of scientific articles reflecting on them: Courtois and Silberztein (1990), Dugas (1990), Courtois (1990) and Silberztein (1993, 1997), to list but a few. During the last 20 years, a significant number of CD-based French dictionaries in particular have appeared on the market. These dictionaries together with online dictionaries, machine translation systems running between French and other languages of the world, online corpora assembled with dictionary compilation in mind, and French foreign language websites will be discussed next.

34.3 Core issues and topics

Following De Schryver's (2003a, 2003b) proposal, the analysis undertaken in this section covers so-called *electronic dictionaries* (ED), *online dictionaries* or *Internet dictionaries*, *offline PC dictionaries* and *CD-based dictionaries* as well as *machine translation systems*. In particular, my analysis will focus on Fuertes-Olivera's (2010: 195) questions regarding author, access and target users:

- Who has compiled the dictionary?
- Is it free or accessible through subscription?
- For whom has the dictionary been compiled?

These questions, which are based on De Schryver's (2003a: 150–151) question "Who accesses what where?" were answered with the aim of offering a broad typology of electronic dictionaries: *institutional Internet reference works* and *collective free multiple-language Internet reference works* (see Chapter 41 of this *Handbook* for a more refined typology of electronic dictionaries).

According to Fuertes-Olivera (2010: 196), *institutional Internet reference works* are "dictionaries compiled by lexicographers working in an identifiable institution and can be further subdivided into free or restricted Internet dictionaries according to whether they can be accessed by paying a subscription fee or not". On the other hand, *collective free multiple-language Internet reference works* (also referred to as *free institutional Internet reference*) are usually compiled by "amateur lexicographers" either as part of promotional campaigns or as a way of helping co-staff or possible customers to understand texts.

The distinction between *institutional Internet reference works* and *collective free multiple-language Internet reference works* presented earlier will be taken into consideration in the survey of existing French lexicographic Internet reference works later. Due to space constraints, my analysis will covers aspects such as authority, quality, ease of consultation and so on. These are studied in three main types of electronic information tools: (a) online dictionaries, PDF dictionaries and PC dictionaries; (b) machine translation systems; and

(c) online corpora and French foreign language websites. These works contain an array of very different, although related, systems. My analysis will focus on electronic dictionaries.

34.3.1 Online dictionaries, dictionaries in PDF format and PC dictionaries

Sparked by technological advancements, electronic dictionaries have developed rapidly in the last three decades. From the first French CD-based dictionary (*LGRE*), it can be said that today, French dictionaries on CD typically come in the back pocket of their hard-copy counterparts, namely: *Bibliorom Larousse*, *Dictionnaire Collins anglais-français/français-anglais*, *Dictionnaire Hachette multimédia*, *Dictionnaire Hachette-Oxford*, *Dictionnaire Larousse de la langue anglaise*, *Dictionnaire Larousse de la langue française*, *Grand dictionnaire Larousse français-anglais anglais-français*, *Harrap's Shorter anglais-français/français-anglais*, *Larousse Multimédia Encyclopédique*, *Le Petit Larousse Illustré* and *Nouveau Petit Robert électronique*.

Among these lexicographic products there are French monolingual and bilingual dictionaries. Monolingual reference works encompass well-known works such as *Le Trésor de la Langue Française Informatisé* (*TLFi*), *Bibliorom Larousse* (*BL*), *Dictionnaire Larousse de la langue française* (*DLF*), *Larousse Multimédia Encyclopédique* (LME), *Le Petit Larousse Illustré* (*PLI*), *Nouveau Petit Robert Électronique* (*NPRE*) and *Dictionnaire Hachette Multimédia* (*DHM*). Bilingual dictionaries come in many types and sizes, being relevant for this chapter prototypical bilingual dictionaries such as *Dictionnaire Collins anglais-français/français-anglais* (*DC*), *Dictionnaire Hachette-Oxford* (*DHO*), *Dictionnaire Larousse de la langue anglaise* (*DLA*), *Grand dictionnaire Larousse français-anglais anglais-français* (*GDL*) and *Harrap's Shorter anglais-français/français-anglais* (*HS*). Later, I will comment on the main characteristics of these monolingual and bilingual (also known as translation) dictionaries. My comments on their characteristics follow Forget (1999) and Bernet (2007), whose works on French electronic dictionaries are of the utmost importance in French lexicographic circles.

Both the previously mentioned monolingual and bilingual dictionaries are basically institutional Internet reference works. They are compiled by trained lexicographers (usually academics) working for publishing houses and/or academic institutions. As far as monolingual reference works are concerned, the package formed by *Le Trésor de la Langue Française Informatisé* (TLFi), *Bibliorom Larousse* (BL), *Dictionnaire Larousse de la langue française* (DLF), *Larousse Multimédia Encyclopédique* (LME) and *Le Petit Larousse Illustré* (PLI) is worth mentioning. All these lexicographical reference works can be viewed on the homepage of the Larousse publishing house.[1] The *Bibliorom Larousse* (BL) is a free app store for Windows. This reference lexicographic work falls within the category of pop-up dictionaries or PC dictionaries, that is, dictionaries for which a piece of software *cum* one or more lexica are downloaded from the Internet, to be used as offline PC dictionaries.[2]

The *Dictionnaire Larousse de la langue française* (DLF) is a free accessible dictionary whose home page constitutes a special outer access structure and *data exposure structure* (Gouws 2002).[3] This dictionary contains the following:

a. 135,000 definitions
b. 6,000 articles
c. 92,000 synonyms
d. 34,000 expressions
e. 15,000 homonyms

As was the case for the *Dictionnaire Larousse de la langue française* (*DLF*), the lexicographic reference work entitled *Le Petit Larousse Illustré* (PLI) (1905 edition) is also using the same marketing strategy in order to announce the contents of the e-book: (a) 44,819 lemmata and (b) 2,343 illustrations. This is the electronic version of the paper dictionary (the 1905 edition),[4] and its computer preparation took place at the University of Cergy-Pontoise under the supervision of Jean Pruvost.[5]

The last lexicographical reference work within the Larousse family is a kind of dictionary aggregator identified as *Lexilogos*.[6] This offers several types of French dictionaries, namely: ancient French, LSP terminologies, synonyms, antonyms, homonyms, proper names, citations and proverbs, rare words, etc.

Different situations occur for the *Nouveau Petit Robert Électronique* (NPRE), which is only accessible through subscription,[7] the *Dictionnaire Hachette Multimédia* (DHM), which can be accessed by either purchasing the CD-ROM or downloading it free of charge,[8] and the *Dictionnaire Larousse de la langue française* (DLF), which can also be accessed free of charge.[9]

Among French electronic monolingual dictionaries, *Le Trésor de la Langue Française Informatisé* is known around the world.[10] This is the electronic version of the work entitled *Le trésor de la langue française: dictionnaire de la langue du XIXe et du XXe siècle (1789–1960)* (*TLF*) which is a 16-volume dictionary of nineteenth- and twentieth-century French published by the *Centre de Recherche pour un Trésor de la Langue Française* from 1971 to 1994. The electronic edition, *Le Trésor de la langue française informatisé* (*TLFi*) was created by *Analyse et Traitement Informatique de la Langue Française* [Analysis and computer processing of the French language] or ATILF, a joint research unit associated with the CNRS and the University of Lorraine. The data processing phase of TLF [The Treasury of the French Language] within CNRS started in 1990 at the *Institut National de la Langue Française* (INLF). In 2001, INLF became *Analyse et Traitement Informatique de la Langue Française* (ATILF). The preparation of the Treasury of the French Language computerized (TLFi), which started in 1990, took almost 15 years to be completed. Once completed the lexicographic reference work was first accessible on the Web free of charge. At the end of 2004 and the beginning of 2005, the first CDs of TLFi appeared on the market. Today, the *Trésor de la langue française informatisé* (*TLFi*) is available on CD and on the Web (the CD can be ordered online through the home page of CNRS). The online dictionary was first available on the website of InaLF-Nancy and thereafter on the website of the *Centre National de Ressources Textuelles et Lexicales* (CNRTL). Bernet (2007: 85–86) has made some reservations with regard to the difference between the CD-ROM dictionary and its paper counterpart. As a matter of fact, TLFi is presented as the electronic version of TLF. In other words, TLFi should encompass the 16-volume dictionary of 19th and 20th centuries plus its supplement. The truth is that the paper version of the supplement of TLF was never published. It should be stressed that work on a supplement to the TLF that began in 1992 at the INaLF-Nancy is still to be published, although information in its home page does say the opposite.[11] Statistics on TLFi are also a bone of contention. With its 100,000 words and their history, 270,000 definitions and 430,000 examples, TLFi is indeed a huge container of knowledge. These figures extracted from TLFi's website should be taken with caution given Bernet's reservations (2007):

> The articles of TLF, like those of any dictionary, consist of a number of "text objects" whose nature and organization are familiar to the reader. These elementary objects range from the headword to the examples through the structure of the article, grammatical

> constructions, several types of indicators, definitions, etc. Some have been mentioned above, as "main lemmata", "syntagms or phrases" or "defined phrases". One wonders about their exact number. Only the main section of the dictionary, which describes the meaning of attested words in the nineteenth and twentieth centuries, has been the object of a full markup.[12]

The comparison of monolingual French dictionaries such as *Larousse Multimédia Encyclopédique* (*LME*), *Dictionnaire Hachette Multimédia* (*DHM*) and *Nouveau Petit Robert Électronique* (NPRE) allows me to comment on the main characteristics of the type of electronic dictionaries commented on in this sub-section.

First, with regard to presentation, *NPRE* is far better than *LME* and *DHM* for several reasons: (a) *NPRE* allows the prospective user to move, change and adjust the size of the windows; (b) *NPRE* is making provision for the potential user to modify the colour of the characters, their font size and to visualise different types of information. *LME* and *DHM* do not offer the same flexibility, although *DHM* allows its user to adjust the size of the windows by clicking on one of two buttons, 'Minimize' and 'Maximize'; and (c) *NPRE* offers six visualisation modes (Forget 1999: 32):

1 the plan of the article (main senses)
2 the history of the word (etymology and date)
3 analogical cross-references (synonyms, antonyms, homonyms)
4 usage examples
5 citations
6 homonyms

Second, with regard to their content, *LME* and *DHM* greatly differ from *NPRE*: (a) *LME* and *DHM* are encyclopaedic dictionaries, whereas the *NPRE* is a linguistic dictionary; (b) *LME* and *DHM* are naturally making use of multimedia aspects such as short films, audio and video files and illustrations (fixed or animated), whereas *NPRE* makes a limited use of these functionalities. Only 9,000 lemmas and 100 citations include audible data (Forget 1999: 35). Forget (1999: 16), however, has shown that *NPRE* provides users with transcriptions of the lemmata, whereas *LME* does not make use of phonetics; (c) *DHM* is only presenting phonetic transcriptions for some of its macrostructural elements. Phonetic charts are presented in *NPRE*, whereas they are totally absent in *LME* and *DHM*. Like the majority of languages in the world, due to its geographical distribution, French has a number of dialects marked by differences in pronunciation, grammar and vocabulary that can with difficulty be served by a single dictionary. That is the reason why pronunciation should be audible in an Internet dictionary.

Moreover, the content of the three dictionaries does not differ much from their paper counterparts. *LME* is the sole analysed dictionary that is updated every three months.[13] Once updated, the modified or added entries will appear in blue colour in the index, whereas modified entries from previous updates will appear in green colour (Forget 1999: 35–36). From this analysis and with regard to Internet requirements, it can be said that the display by *LME* of formal features such as colour is a good lexicographical practice. Furthermore, updating the dictionary and informing users on the process followed is essential. As a matter of fact, prospective users can access 'recently added terms', 'modified words', etc.

Third, with regard to accessibility, *NPRE* is more user-friendly than *LME* and *DHM*: (a) the navigation bars and menus of *NPRE* are truly complete and easy to interpret, whereas navigation bars of *LME* and *DHM* are very rudimentary and opaque; (b) *DHM* does not even have menu bars; and (c) as far as navigation is concerned, *NPRE* is the only one making use of hypertexts. It should be mentioned, however, that in the three dictionaries, the user is allowed to click on any item in the entries in order to get to another entry.

It was earlier mentioned that due to its geographical distribution French has a number of dialects marked by differences in pronunciation, grammar and vocabulary that can with difficulty be served by a single dictionary. French dictionaries produced outside France have also gone online. They are both *institutional Internet reference works* and *collective free multiple-language Internet reference works*. Within the first category one may find works published by national or international organizations such as the work entitled *Le Grand Dictionnaire Terminologique* (GDT) published by the *Office québécois de la langue française*.[14] A query-form entitled RECHERCHE is awaiting the prospective user, and once he/she has entered a search term, the terminological dictionary will get him/her to the desired French lemma in almost all domains (music, clothing, transport, zootechnics, etc.) together with its English translation equivalent in particular.

Users can also access a useful list of 14 French Quebec online dictionaries and corpora such as *BDLP* or the work entitled *Traduction du français au français*.[15] *BDLP* is a lexicographical panfrancophone database. It is an international project which aim is to contribute to the building of French Treasury vocabularies.[16] The project was launched by Professor Bernard Quemada in the 1980s. So far *BDLP* is underway in 20 countries and regions (Acadia, Algeria, West Indies, Belgium, Burundi, Cameroon, Central African Republic, Congo-Brazzaville, Ivory Coast, France, Louisiana, Madagascar, Morocco, Mauritius, New Caledonia, Quebec, Reunion Island, Sweden and Chad). The building of *BDLP* will serve as a supplement to the Treasury of the French Language computerised (TLFi) that is being compiled at ATILF. The *BDLP* project is sponsored by the *Agence Universitaire de la Francophonie* (AUF).

The work entitled *Traduction du français au français* falls within the category of *free multiple-language Internet reference works*. It is a linguistic guide the aim of which is to translate from Quebec French to the French language as it is spoken in France.[17] The work targets people from Quebec travelling to Europe as well as French people visiting Quebec. All the lemmata have hypertext links with usage notes, as examples (1) and (2) show:

(1)[18]

Abrier (ou abriller): Se coucher sous les couvertures, se mettre à l'abri

(2)[19]

J'aime pas ça quand tu me désabrilles !

Le verbe ***abrier***, ou ***abriller***, est disparu de l'usage en France, mais il a survécu au Québec. *Abrier*, *abriller ou rabrier* signifie recouvrir quelqu'un pour le protéger du froid. Au Québec, on *s'abrille* pour la nuit, c'est-à-dire qu'on se couche sous les draps ou sous la couverture.

"Deux petites minutes, *j'abrille* le petit, et je te rejoins au salon."

"Je me suis *rabrillé* durant la nuit, il faisait trop froid."

"Quand j'étais petit, j'aimais ça quand ma mère venait m'*abriller* durant la nuit."

Comme on peut *abrier*, on peut aussi ***désabriller***.

" Je n'ai pas réussi à dormir, tu m'as *désabrillé* toute la nuit " est synonyme donc de "Je n'ai pas réussi à dormir, tu n'arrêtais pas de tirer la couverture pour toi toute la nuit."

Les autres sens d'abrier

On peut aussi *s'abrier, ou s'abriller*, sous un auvent pour se protéger de la pluie. Il existe plusieurs variantes de ce verbe bien québécois.

J'aime pas ça quand tu me désabrilles ! (continued)

> Finalement, on peut *abrier* des objets, par exemple sous une bâche. Dans ce cas, *abrier* est synonyme de couvrir, recouvrir.
> " J'ai *abrié* ma moto pour l'hiver "
> " Même si nous sommes au mois de juin, je vais *abriller* mes rosiers pour éviter qu'ils ne gèlent durant la nuit. "
> *Abrier* peut aussi être synonyme de défendre, cacher ou excuser. Par exemple, on peut *abrier* la vérité pour la dissimuler, mais cet usage est plus rare.

These articles show that *Traduction du français au français* is a differential dictionary. The lexicon of French as it is spoken in Quebec differs enough from standard French. That is why lexical particularities of Quebec French have to be explained to dictionary users.

A comparison of several bilingual dictionaries (especially *DC*, *DHO*, *GDL* and *HS*) also shows differences among them. First, with regard to navigation, Forget (1999: 10–11) has listed four elements in order to evaluate bilingual French electronic dictionaries, namely:

- Historical: This function displays a list of preciously looked-up entries and allows the user to go back to one of them without having to retype the headword.
- Generalized hypertext: This technique allows the user to click on any word of a given text in order to get to a dictionary entry.
- Hypertext links: In electronic dictionaries, these are activated connections by a mouse click and give access to a dictionary article or miscellaneous information. Hypertext links are marked with an underline or a different colour.
- With regard to switching from one language to another without the request of the user: This is a command that allows the user to move from one part of the dictionary to another without requesting it. For example, if the user double-clicks on a French word under the entry of an English word in the English-French section, the dictionary automatically displays the entry for this French word in the French-English section.

The main differences among them are that *DC* does not have hypertexts, and *DHO* as well as *HS* do not allow the switch from one language to another without the user requesting it (Forget 1999: 37).

Second, with regard to the presentation, Forget (1999: 10–11) has analysed bilingual dictionaries of the French language focusing on the visualisation of different types of information. That is the function that allows, in some electronic dictionaries, to change viewing modes. For example, the user can choose to view only meaning indications and translation equivalents, without examples or expressions. As far as this point is concerned, *DC* is the best bilingual dictionary. Furthermore, *HS* does not allow changes to be made at the level of the language interface or at the font level. It is surprising that a bilingual dictionary does not allow its users to modify the language interface. The only bilingual dictionary that allows the visualisation of different types of information is *GDL*. Indeed, the user can choose to consult the article under its abbreviated form (without examples and expressions), or he or she may consider the full presentation of the article (with examples and expressions).

Third and as was the case with monolingual French dictionaries, the content of bilingual French dictionaries does not differ much from their paper counterparts, although some differences are noteworthy: (a) *HS* does not display conjugation tables for French verbs (Forget 1999: 38), and (b) *GDL* uses cultural notes or explanations for culture-bound lexical items. These cultural notes give an explanation of certain terms by placing them in their cultural context in the source language. For example, for the entry *mai* the menu CULTURAL NOTE displays an explanation of the events of May 1968 (example 3):

(3)
The events of May 1968 came about when student protests, coupled with widespread industrial unrest, culminated in a general strike and rioting. De Gaulle's government survived the crisis, but the issues raised made the events a turning point in French social history.

Finally, in the field of translation dictionaries and in addition to CD-based and handheld devices, researchers have begun to show interest in online dictionaries, pairing French and other languages than English, German or Spanish, for example. The work entitled *Le dictionnaire yiddish-français* by Yitskhok Niborski and Bernard Vaisbrot has Yiddish as its source language and French as its target language. The work can only be accessed by paying a subscription fee. Yitskhok Niborski and Bernard Vaisbrot claim that with its 37,000 words and phrases, this book is, of all bilingual Yiddish dictionaries published to date, one that covers the widest and most varied field.[20] It contains an updated vocabulary as well as rare words, acronyms, abbreviations and terms used in some areas. It was recognised by the most reputable linguists as a leading reference book.

34.3.2 Machine translation systems

SYSTRAN[21] and REVERSO[22] are two well-known machine translation systems that are much used by French speakers. SYSTRAN offers an array of online services, e.g. online dictionaries as well as on-demand translation services of Web pages, written texts or Microsoft Office files. With SYSTRAN, one can translate from and to English, French, Italian, German, Portuguese, Spanish, Dutch, Greek, Chinese, Japanese, Korean, Russian, Polish, Arabic and Swedish. SYSTRAN is based on a monolingual general French dictionary (*Larousse*) as well as 20 LSP French dictionaries. It provides users with a basic query system, which can be selected from the research menu option by entering the search query (Figure 34.1).

Entering the lemma 'alors' in thé query place, for instance, recovers macrostructural elements such as running head (in bold type). This is followed by other macrostructural elements, especially by its phonetic transcription (in blue colour), part of speech indicator (in green colour) and microstructural elements such as paraphrases of meaning/meaning translations and usage examples. All these data are presented in a micro-architecture format in the sense of Wiegand (1996: 36) (Figure 34.2).

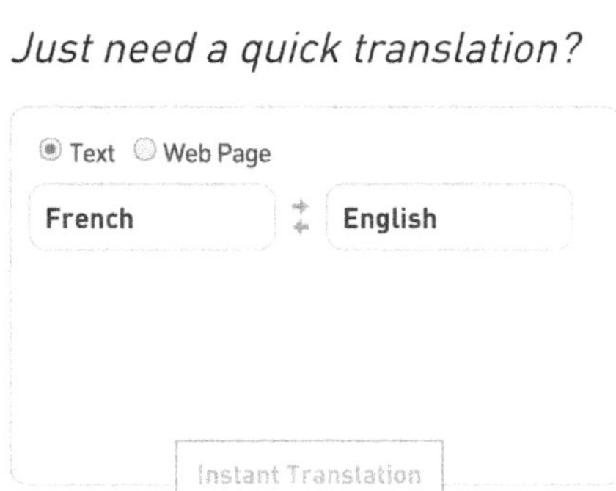

Figure 34.1 SYSTRAN's query form

At the end of the article, in a search zone labelled 'SYTRANS Dictionary', the machine translation system provides the user with a sum up of data, namely the lemma (*alors*), the part of speech indicator (*adv*) as well the different translations of the lemma (*then, so, well*). This search area can provide rapid access to the macrostructure as well as the microstructure and therefore forms part of both the rapid outer and inner access structures. Given the fact that in the printed version of Larousse, one finds no recap, this method combining elements of the rapid outer and inner access structures is truly innovative (see Chapter 3 of this *Handbook*).

French to English
Lø Larousse
1. alors [alɔr] *adv*
◊ [à ce momento-là] **then**
le cinema d'alors était encore muet : **films were still silent in those days**
le Premier ministre d'alors refusa de signer les accords: **the then Prime Minister refused to sign the agreement**
jusqu'alors : **until then**
◊ [en conséquence] **so**
il s'est mis à pleuvoir, alors nous sommes rentrés: **It started to rain, so we came back in**
◊ [dans ce cas] **then, so, in that case**
je prêfère reconcer tout de suite, alors! : **in that case I'd just as son give up straight away!**
Mais alors, ça change tout! : **but that changes everything!**
◊ [emploi expressif] *Other expressions*
il va se mettre en colère, et alors? : **so what if he gets angry?**
et alors, qu'est.ce qui s'est passé? : **so what happened then?**
alors, tu viens oui ou non? : **so are you coming or not?, are you coming or not, then?**
(. . .)
2. alors que *conj expression*
◊ [au momento où] **while, when**
l'orage 'eclata alors que nous 'etions encore loin de la maison : **the storm broke while, when we were still a long way from the house**
◊ [bien que, même si] **even though**
elle est sortie alors c'était interdit : **she went out, even though she wasn't supposed to**
(. . .)
◊ [tandis que] **while**
il part en vacances alors que je reste iic tout l'êtê : **he's going on holiday while I stay here all**
summer

S *SYSTRAN DICTIONARY*
1. **alors** *adv*
◊ **then**
◊ **so**
◊ **well**

Figure 34.2 The lemma *alors* in SYSTRAN

As far as REVERSO is concerned, it includes translation software, a dictionary, a spelling checker, conjugator and grammar tools. By selecting and clicking on a field, a search menu option appears and a search term can be entered. As far as the search zone 'Traduction Contexte' (context translation) is concerned, a list of language pairs appears for the user to choose the direction of the translation. By choosing 'Dictionnaire en ligne' (online dictionary), the search will take the user to a window displaying different options (translation, definition and synonyms) in different languages. After entering the desired lemma, a click on the desired language will then take the user to the correct article. By choosing 'traduction' (translation) on the opening screen, the search will take the user to a window in which he or she will be allowed to type or to paste the word or the text to be translated. The user will then just type a word in the text field and the translation will appear in seconds.

34.3.3 Online corpora and French foreign language websites

One can find on the Internet a great deal of corpora as well as descriptions of individual corpus projects for the French language. Nowadays, there are also various websites for learning French at a beginner's level. The number of these websites is vast and seems to increase daily in cyberspace. Only a very few of them will be included in this study, especially the ones offering to prospective learners lexicographic reference works to sustain the learning process. Both corpora assembled with dictionary compilation in mind as well as French Foreign Language websites are giving access to learning packages.

The website of the *Centre National des Ressources Textuelles et Lexicographiques*[23] is offering online French corpora, French dictionaries and lexica as well as translation software and tools. This is indeed a valuable tool for dictionary making, especially because lexicographers can make use of a free concordancer.[24] More free online resources are found in Wagner's blog,[25] in which information on corpora such as SACODEYL, FLEURON and CFPP2000 is offered. Most of these corpora contain audio and/or video with transcripts of authentic and spontaneous spoken French. SACODEYL stands for system-aided compilation: an open distribution of European youth language. It is actually available in seven EU languages (English, French, German, Italian, Spanish, Romanian and Lithuanian) and was designed specifically for teaching purposes. Very much in the same way, the *Français Langue Etrangère: Ressources et Outils Numériques* (FLEURON) is a collection of audio and video resources that cover aspects of student life in France. Captions and a glossary are also provided. The *Corpus de Français Parlé Parisien des années 2000* (CFPP2000) contains several interviews of Parisians within the past decade. Audio files and transcripts are available for download. The last element of the package is the *Corpus de Français Parlé au Québec* (CFPQ). This is a multimodal corpus that also includes information on non-verbal aspects of communication (such as gestures, facial movements, etc.). It also dates from the 2000s; however, only PDFs of the transcripts are available.

Français en ligne, *Easypronunciation* and the *Projet FILIPÉ* are three other interesting examples of French websites for free online teaching/learning. The information contained in these site can be useful for lexicographers, as they can find resources there such as dictionaries, lexica and grammar,[26] links to authentic documents with examples of pronunciation and phonetic transcriptions[27] and cultural data.[28]

Within this category, Verlinde's *Interactive Language Toolbox*[29] (Verlinde and Binon 2009; Verlinde and Peeters 2012) merits our attention. It is a sequel of the *Base lexicale du français*, which aims at offering a more user-friendly type of dictionary by simplifying both data treatment and access structure. For the purpose of this chapter, Verlinde's work is relevant: it signals the way ahead in e-lexicography: different products are combined and accessed at the same time, typically for helping users such as translators or students to cope with the niceties of foreign languages (see Chapter 17 of this *Handbook*).

34.4 Looking to the future

Internet dictionaries (online dictionaries, pop-up dictionaries, PC dictionaries, etc.) are valuable in many respects. The most innovative aspect of Internet dictionaries is probably the retrieval system. Compared to paper dictionaries characterised by slow retrieval, the increasing popularity of Internet dictionaries can be attributed to their relative ease of use which makes the consultation process less time consuming. However, the retrieval system also represents the biggest challenge of Internet dictionaries. In the domain of translation studies, Forget (1999: iv-v) has shown that

> CD-ROM dictionaries [in particular] have definite advantages over their paper counterparts: flexible consultation, easy handling, speedy navigation, powerful and varied search capabilities, and useful text management options. Nevertheless, they have some considerable drawbacks, especially regarding technical aspects. In conclusion, it is safe to say that CD-ROM dictionaries have the potential to increase translators' productivity as long as translators know how to take full advantage of the dictionaries' capabilities.

34.5 Conclusion

The earlier discussion covered the various available French Internet dictionaries. I focused on online dictionaries, machine translation systems running between French and other languages of the world, online corpora assembled with dictionary compilation in mind and dictionaries in PDF format, as well as various websites for learning French. Nearly all major traditional dictionaries of the French language, being monolingual (*TLFi*, *BL*, *DLF*, *LME* and *PLI*) or bilingual (*DC*, *DHO*, *DLA*, *GDL*, and *HS*), have provided online versions of their paper counterparts. Most French ED are based on a paper dictionary. In other words, they are digital versions of printed lexicographical reference works. However, an Internet dictionary should be a proper reference work in its own right (Fuertes-Olivera 2010: 204). One can also find on the Internet a great deal of corpora assembled with dictionary compilation in mind as well as descriptions of individual corpus projects for the French language (being a source language or a target language).

Together with the multi-functions provided by online dictionaries, dictionary users can learn more about the latest versions and new words as editors can update entry information every few months. Today, French Internet dictionaries have gained in popularity and accessibility. However, there is still room for improvements, especially in terms of Internet requirements: "updating the dictionary and informing users on the process followed; incorporating hypertextuality and proper digitalization; and constructing them as integrated products with links to Internet searches, and other language resources" (Fuertes-Olivera 2010: 209).

Related topics

Dictionaries and access; dictionaries for translation; the concept of dictionaries.

Further reading

Allen, T., R. Morrissey and G. Roe. (2011). "Re-Imagining French Lexicography: The Dictionnaire vivant de la langue française", *Dictionaries: Journal of the Dictionary Society of North America* 32: 129–143.

The paper describes a lexicographical endeavour developed by the University of Chicago's ARTFL Project (American and French Research on the Treasury of the French Language). DVLF is an innovative experimental approach to dictionary compilation that aims to offer an interactive and community-oriented alternative to traditional methods of French lexicography.

Fuertes-Olivera, P. A. (ed.) (2010). *Specialised Dictionaries for Learners*. Lexicographica. Series Maior. Berlin/New York: Walter de Gruyter, 237p.

The main purpose of this book is to fulfil the need for a general lexicographical theory with a particular interest on learner's lexicography. The book analyses at least four basic lexicographic categories, namely: learners, the learner's situation, learner's needs and dictionary assistance.

Martin, W., W. Meijs, M. Moerland, P. Elsemiek, P. Van Sterkenburg and P. Vossen. (eds.), *EURALEX 1994 Proceedings*. The Netherlands: EURALEX, 628p.

The book is made of papers submitted to the 6th EURALEX International Congress on Lexicography that was held in Amsterdam, The Netherlands. In the different contributions, particular attention is paid to word meaning, word combination issues and historical and learner's dictionaries.

Van Sterkenburg, P. (ed.) (2003). *A Practical Guide to Lexicography (Terminology and Lexicography Research and Practice 6)*. Amsterdam/Philadelphia: John Benjamins Publishing Company, 459p.

Electronic dictionaries, corpus analysis and database management form the central themes of the book. Various aspects of monolingual and translation dictionaries, such as types of definition, meaning, sense relations and stylistics are also investigated throughout.

Notes

1 See at www.larousse.fr/dictionnaires
2 See at http://microsoft-reference-bibliorom-larousse.software.informer.com/2.0/
3 See at www.larousse.fr/dictionnaires/francais
4 See at http://dictionnaire1905.u-cergy.fr
5 The computer work was done by researchers from the *Lexiques, Dictionnaires, Informatique* (LDI) research unit (Hélène Manuélian, Audrey Bruscand, Nicole Cholewka and Anne-Marie Hetzel). LDI started from the old *Centre de recherches métalexicographiques et dictionnaires francophones* (METADIF).
6 See at www.lexilogos.com/francais_langue_dictionnaires.htm
7 See at www.lerobert.com/espace-numerique/enligne.html
8 See at http://logiciel.quetelecharger.com/dictionnaire-hachette-multimedia-gratuit.html
9 See at www.larousse.fr/dictionnaires/francais
10 See at www.tresor-de-la-langue-francaise-informatise.fr
11 The homepage of this dictionary claims that "Le TLF est un dictionnaire des XIXe et XXe siècles en 16 volumes et 1 supplément. Le TLFi est la version informatisée du TLF". As indicated, this message is wrong. See at www.atilf.fr/spip.php?rubrique77 (last accessed: May, 26, 2016).
12 My translation of the original text in French: "Les articles du TLF, comme ceux de tout dictionnaire, sont constitués d'un certain nombre d'"objets textuels" dont la nature et l'organisation sont familières au lecteur. Ces objets élémentaires vont de l'entrée aux exemples en passant par la structure de l'article, les constructions grammaticales, plusieurs types d'indicateurs, les définitions, etc. Certains ont été évoqués plus haut, comme les " entrées principales ", les " syntagmes " ou les " syntagmes définis ". On s'interroge sur leur nombre exact[1]. La principale rubrique du dictionnaire, qui décrit les différents sens des mots attestés aux XIXe et XXe siècles, a fait, seule, l'objet d'un balisage réputé complet".
13 The update is made via the Website of Liris Interactive. See at www.larousse.fr/dictionnaires/francais/iris/44237
14 See at http://granddictionnaire.com

15 see at www.ats-group.net/dictionnaires/dictionnaire-francais-quebecois.html
16 See at www.bdlp.org/default.asp
17 See at www.dufrancaisaufrancais.com/lexique/
18 See at www.dufrancaisaufrancais.com/lexique/
19 See at www.dufrancaisaufrancais.com/jaime-pas-ca-quand-tu-me-desabrilles
20 See at http://yiddishweb.com/dictionnaire-yiddish-francais-en-ligne/
21 See at www.systransoft.com/lp/dictionnaire-francais/
22 See at www.reverso.net/text_translation.aspx?lang=FR
23 See at www.cnrtl.fr/lexicographie/
24 See at http://lextutor.ca/conc/fr/
25 See at http://ielanguages.com/blog/
26 See at francaisenligne@free.fr
27 See at http://easypronunciation.com/fr/french-phonetic-transcription-converter
28 See at www.e-filipe.org/liens-fle.php
29 See at https://ilt.kuleuven.be/inlato/

References

Online dictionaries (tools and resources, including lexicographic projects) [All accessed on June 30, 2016]

Analyse et Traitement Informatique de la Langue Française: www.atilf.fr/spip.php?rubrique77
Base de Données Lexicographiques Panfrancophone (BDLP): www.bdlp.org/default.asp
Centre National de Ressources Textuelles et Lexicographiques: www.cnrtl.fr/lexicographie/
Dictionnaire des synonymes français: http://synonymes.memodata.com/
Dictionnaire français-yiddish: http://yiddishweb.com/dictionnaire-yiddish-francais-en-ligne/
Dictionnaire Larousse: www.larousse.fr/dictionnaires/francais/iris/44237
Dictionnaire Larousse: www.larousse.fr/dictionnaires/francais
Dictionnaire Larousse: http://microsoft-reference-bibliorom-larousse.software.informer.com/2.0/
Dictionnaire-français-québécois: www.ats-group.net/dictionnaires/dictionnaire-francais-quebecois.html
Ielanguages: http://ielanguages.com/blog/
Interactive Language Toolbox: www.kuleuven.ac.be/dafles
LDI (Université de Cergy-Pontoise): www.u-cergy.fr/fr/laboratoires/labo-ldi.html
Le corpus CFPP 2000: http://cfpp2000.univ-paris3.fr/
Lexilogos: www.lexilogos.com/francais_langue_dictionnaires.htm
Lextutor: http://lextutor.ca/conc/fr/
Reverso: www.reverso.net/text_translation.aspx?lang=FR
Systransoft: www.systransoft.com/lp/dictionnaire-francais/
Traduction du français au français: www.dufrancaisaufrancais.com/lexique/
Trésor de la Langue Française informatisé (TLFi): www.tresor-de-la-langue-francaise-informatise.fr/

Dictionaries

DC = *Dictionnaire Collins anglais-français / français-anglais* (1996) Paris/London: Harper Collins Publishers Ltd./Novell Inc.
DHM = *Dictionnaire Hachette Multimédia* (1999) Paris: Hachette Livre/ISG Productions.
DHO = *Dictionnaire Hachette-Oxford* (1994–1996) Oxford/Paris: Oxford University Press/Hachette Livre/AND Technology Ltd.
GDL = *Grand dictionnaire Larousse français-anglais/anglais-français* (1996) Paris: Larousse / INSO Corporation.
HS = *Harraps Shorter anglais-français/français-anglais* (1997) Paris/London: Folio Corporation/ Larousse plc.

LDEL = *Longman Dictionary of English Language* (1948) Harlow: Longman.
LME = *Larousse Multimédia Encyclopédique* (1997) Paris: Larousse/LiRiS Interactive.
NPRE = *Nouveau Petit Robert électronique* (1996) Paris: Dictionnaires Le Robert/VAN DIJK.
NSOED = *New Shorter Oxford English Dictionary* (1996) Oxford: Oxford University Press I AND Electronic Publishg B.V.

Other literature

Bernard, P., J. Dendien, J. Lecomte and J-M. Pierrel. (2002) "Les ressources de l'ATILF pour l'analyse lexicale et textuelle: TLFi, Frantext et logiciel Stella", JADT 2002, 6es Journées internationales d'analyse statistique des données textuelles, 13–15 mars 2002, Rennes.
Bernet, C. (2007) "Le TLFi ou les infortunes de la lexicographie électronique", *Mots. Les langages du politique* [En ligne], 84 | 2007, mis en ligne le 01 juillet 2009, consulté le 10 avril 2016. http://mots.revues.org/1052; DOI: 10.4000/mots.1052
Courtois, B. (1990) "Dictionnaire électronique du LADL pour les mots simples du français", DELAS V06/2, LADL-CNRS, Université Paris 7: Paris. (Technical Report)
Courtois, B. and M. Silberztein (eds.) (1990) *Dictionnaires électroniques du français. Langue Française* 87. Paris: Larousse.
De Schryver, G.-M. (2003a) "Lexicographers' Dreams in the Electronic-Dictionary Age", *International Journal of Lexicography* 16(2): 143–199.
De Schryver, G.-M. (2003b) "Online Dictionaries on the Internet: An Overview for the African Languages", *Lexikos* 13: 1–20.
Dugas, A. (1990) "'La création lexicale et les dictionnaires électroniques', in B. Courtois and M. Silberztein (eds.), pp. 3–4.
Forget, N. (1999) "Les dictionnaires électroniques dans l'optique de la traduction", Unpublished Master thesis. Ottawa: University of Ottawa.
Fuertes-Olivera, P. A. (2010) "'Lexicography for the Third Millennium: Free Institutional Internet Terminological Dictionaries for Learners", in P. A. Fuertes-Olivera (ed.) *Specialised Dictionaries for Learners*. Berlin/New York: Walter de Gruyter, pp. 193–209.
Gouws, R. H. (2002) "Using a Frame Structure to Accommodate Cultural Data", in D. J. Emejulu (ed.), *Eléments de Lexicographie Gabonaise*. Tome II. New York: Jimacs-Hillman, pp. 54–69.
Selva, T., S. Verlinde and J. Binon (2002) "Le DAFLES, un nouveau dictionnaire électronique pour apprenants du français", in *Proceedings of the Tenth International Euralex Congress*. CST: Copenhague, pp. 199–208.
Silberztein, M. (1993) *Dictionnaires électroniques et analyse automatique de textes. Le système INTEX*. Paris: Masson.
Silberztein, M. (1997) *Manuel de référence du logiciel INTEX 3.4*, Université Paris 7-LADL, Paris.
Verlinde, S. and J. Binon (2009) "Pedagogical Lexicography Revisited", in H. Bergenholtz, S. Nielsen and S. Tarp (eds.), *Lexicography at a Crossroad. Dictionaries and Encyclopedias Today, Lexicographic Tools Tomorrow*. Bern: Peter Lang, pp. 69–89.
Verlinde, S. and G. Peeters (2012) "Data Access Revisited: The Interactive Language Toolbox", in S. Granger and M. Paquot (eds.), *Electronic Lexicography*. Oxford: Oxford University Press, pp.147–162.
Wiegand, H. E. (1996) "Textual Condensation in Printed Dictionaries. A Theoretical Draft", *Lexikos* 6, pp. 133–158.

35

German lexicography in the Internet era

Petra Storjohann

35.1 Introduction

Since the mid-1990s, innovations such as corpora, information technology, new media, the Web 2.0 and usage-based linguistic theory have broken new ground and changed the nature of German lexicography almost beyond recognition. Printing traditions have disappeared and new products of variable quality and with different objectives have emerged, dramatically changing the lexicographic landscape and the role of lexicographers. Today, German dictionaries vary considerably not only in structure and design but also with regard to their purposes and compilation methods. Whereas some retrieve linguistic information electronically, others link existing resources to lexical data systems. There are also user-generated dictionaries or lexical resources produced through the participation of volunteers. Only a small number of reference works adopt complementary approaches and combine corpus data with linguistic theory and lexicographic experience.

In this chapter, we will touch upon some of the issues involved in German lexicography in the era of the Internet. For obvious reasons, the main area of discussion will be electronic dictionaries. A more detailed account of traditional German print dictionaries is offered by Wiegand (1990), and Mann (2013) discusses multi-volume and specialised reference works in detail. This chapter examines general-purpose monolingual Internet dictionaries and German online portals. First, an overview of German reference works will summarise the different dictionary types that have been developed since the dawn of the digital age. As there is a strict division between commercial products, user-generated products and dictionaries written at academic institutions, each will be given special attention. These include retro-digitised editions of print dictionaries, newly developed corpus-assisted Internet dictionaries, computer-automated lexical databases, lexicographic information tools and user-generated dictionaries. We will explore their advantages and disadvantages by delineating their concepts, practices, methods and forms of presentation.

This chapter will then reflect on current topics in German lexicography. Particular attention will be given to user studies since they have been instrumental in revealing the discrepancies between the users' need for reliable information and the current trend for compiling dictionaries outside the realms of professional lexicography. A critical stance will be taken towards the practice of creating dictionaries using an information-science approach, in which the exploitation of corpus data are excluded from lexicographic analysis and interpretation. It will be argued that dictionaries benefit from complementary approaches with a strong commitment to data-driven procedures and introspective competence in order to facilitate entries with reliable information about language in use.

In this context, having surveyed some of the pros and cons of new strands of dictionary creation, we will ask what future direction German lexicography might take. With Web 2.0 technology posing enormous challenges to this discipline, we need to ask why it has failed to connect with the user and with linguistic theory for so long. As a result, some lexicographic initiatives have started to constitute a professional lexicographic research discipline. Given the unpredictability of information technology (IT) advances (see Chapter 13 of this *Handbook*), the chapter will conclude with the most urgent priorities and feasible options which might inspire professional lexicography to envisage products fit for reliable and exciting consultation experiences and with substantial linguistic explanatory power.

35.2 Historical perspectives

Germany has a long and rich lexicographic tradition covering a wide spectrum of dictionaries, such as dialect dictionaries, reference books for historical varieties, neologism or loanword dictionaries, etymological dictionaries, spelling dictionaries, learners' dictionaries and general-purpose reference works. Today, these are available in different formats, with electronic editions inarguably taking precedence over print volumes.

Over the last two decades, German lexicographers have been faced with five major challenges. First, new opportunities emerged through the availability of digital media such as CDs and the Internet in the mid-1990s. Second, the growing numbers of corpora, intermediary software and editing systems changed the dictionary-writing process at the end of the 1990s. Third, the launch of Web 2.0 formed a new generation of Internet users and quickly turned CDs into ageing technology approximately 10 years ago. The Internet developed into an interactive platform where digital natives changed from passive consumers to interactive users supplying content collectively. Fourth, with the introduction of the Apple iPad, the era of mobile computing started in 2010. And finally, new linguistic paradigms emerged, altering our perception of linguistic patterns and structures in authentic communication.

Importantly, these aspects have had considerable implications for German dictionaries; they turned working routines from individual interpretation to corpus-guided analysis. They also transformed dictionaries from print to digital formats, from privately owned, paid-for books to free online resources. Even more than that, they transformed them from passive consultation books to interactive systems and from human-oriented to computer-oriented instruments. The structure of dictionaries has been transformed from linear to adaptable poly-accessible architectures, and entries now focus on patterns and constructions, use and function rather than capturing isolated words and structures.

35.2.1 The advent of corpora, data processing and hypertextuality

With corpora available and information technology developing rapidly, German lexicography has shifted from intuition-guided to corpus-based documentation of language. The first pioneering data-based project *Brisante Wörter* (controversial words), carried out at the Institut für Deutsche Sprache (IDS) in the late 1980s, empirically grounded its investigations in the *Handbuchkorpus*, a collection of texts accessible through a corpus system called *Refer*

(1983–1991, see Brückner 1989), using a BS2000 operating system (see Haß and Klosa 2015). German corpora have been built by publishing houses such as Duden (*Dudenkorpus*) or Wahrig (*Das Wahrig Textkorpus*). These have not been made publically accessible. Simultaneously, corpora have also been compiled at the Berlin-Brandenburgische Akademie der Wissenschaften (*Kernkorpus 20./21. Jahrhundert*, *Deutsches Textarchiv*) and at the University of Leipzig (*Leipzig Corpora Collection*). Both of these can be used for word searches but individual texts cannot be selected for specific purposes. The development of computer technology accelerated and smaller electronic German corpora became freely available in 1992 through *Cosmas I*, collected by the IDS. By the end of 2015, it hosted the largest collection of electronic German texts (*Deutsches Referenzkorpus DeReKo*), encompassing more than 28 billion words from different genres, authors, regions and years. Today, these are freely accessible through *Cosmas II* and users can individually compose their data sets.

Corpora were originally seen as electronic archives replacing citation catalogues. They were used for finding good example sentences and served as validation tools for linguistic assumptions. Overall, employing query software, performing data-driven analyses and interpreting large amounts of semi-processed data did not emerge as a general practice in German projects until 2000. Since then, the benefits of corpus-based dictionary-making have been wide-ranging. With more material available, linguistic descriptions have become more objective, so lexicographic documentation is closer to communication in real language use. It became easy to quantify phenomena and to obtain copious examples from authentic material. Lexicographers started to access context through pre-analysed clusters of statistically relevant patterns, performed systematic collocation studies, detected typical constructions and obtained lemmatised frequency lists.

At the time, the overall impression was that the new tools would significantly speed up any compilation process. For data-mining projects that did not aim to identify semantic categories or detect rare linguistic phenomena, purely computer-generated lexical resources could indeed be created at breath-taking speed. However, for those projects which carefully interpreted and sorted their semi-processed data, the handling of massive pre-structured data meant an immense increase in editorial time (Klosa 2007). By and large, corpora and the Internet have brought profound changes to the field of lexicography in terms of production and reception of dictionaries. The choice of data and corpus methods has triggered different descriptions of natural discourse and has had an effect on authenticity, typicality and reliability of linguistic information. Furthermore, the new hypertext facilities have been closely connected with German dictionaries since the late 1990s, transforming the presentation of lexical information.

At first, producing electronic dictionaries simply meant digitising the data in traditional reference books without making any fundamental changes to their structures. Once the potential of hypertext structures was recognised, the possibilities of extended dictionary space, new designs and linking options were also appreciated. In the past two decades, dictionary portals and lexical information systems have been created, connecting different resources via a common user interface. Today, most electronic dictionaries can be attributed to one of three distinct categories, with hardly any overlap between them:

- Commercial lexicography has been established by publishing houses such as Duden, Langenscheidt, Wahrig and PONS. They are well-known trademarks in terms of general and learners' dictionaries.
- There are academic dictionary projects founded at academies of science or research institutes. This non-profit, publically less known lexicographic subfield links dictionary

creation with linguistic theory and metalexicographic principles and has developed multi-purpose as well as specialised dictionaries.
- Fully IT-oriented lexical systems or community-based dictionaries are popular, and free resources have been built by non- or semi-professional dictionary-makers.

These subfields have manifested themselves to varying degrees, producing different lexical e-tools, online reproductions of print dictionaries, newly developed functional online dictionaries, lexical resources or networks. They differ with respect to working practices, design and presentation as well as quantity and quality of information. (For a classification of German Internet dictionaries, see Storrer 2010.)

35.2.2 Developments in commercial lexicography

Commercial lexicography has contributed enormously to the widespread circulation of German dictionaries. Most commonly known are traditional reference books by Duden which, as Haß (2001) points out, are generally perceived as linguistic judges by the public. Products from publishing houses cover the market of general and learners' monolingual and bilingual dictionaries. Numerous established publishers are, nevertheless, abandoning their print medium, as they struggle to sell their products. As a consequence, between 2000 and 2010, many editing departments were closed or drastically reduced. Recent print dictionaries are often concise reference books produced for learners of German as a second language (e.g. *Langenscheidt* 2010 and *Pons* 2011). No printed multi-volume dictionaries have been published since 1999. Large monolingual reference works are e-dictionaries today, such as *Duden-GWDS* in 10 volumes, the largest of its kind. It was first published on CD in 2000, with revised editions following in 2005 and 2011. In its introduction, it states that it is a documentation of contemporary German in all its complexity, based on several billion records from the Duden archive (citation slips), the Duden corpora and the Internet. As the label struggled to exert its supremacy, *Duden Online* was launched in 2011. Table 35.1 summarises some general commercial products that are freely available online today.

Table 35.1 General-purpose monolingual products in commercial lexicography

Product	*Contents*	*Data/method*	*URL*
Wahrig	collection of dictionaries of loan words, synonyms, etymology and spelling	fully digitised data	www.wissen.de/lexikonsuche/lexicon/all
Duden-online	monolingual general dictionary with information on meaning, synonyms, grammar, pronunciation, etymology	computer-generated and digitised data	www.duden.de
PONS Online-Wörterbuch	collection of dictionaries: spelling, loan words, German as a second language and bilingual dictionaries	computer-generated and digitised data	www.pons.eu
canoonet - Deutsche Wörterbücher und Grammatik	lexical system with information on spelling, grammar, morphology and synonyms/antonyms with external links to other sources	computer-generated data	www.canoo.net/

Over the past few decades, several online products have been developed, most of which are automated extensions of existing editions increasingly lacking editorial criteria. Most commonly, we find conventional entries with information on spelling, meaning, examples, idiomatic expressions and synonyms. Generated frequencies, computer-retrieved morphology/grammar (e.g. declension patterns) and collocational contexts have been added to familiar information, further equipped with audio files and simple search options. Corpora have only been utilised to semi or fully automate specific information, but they have not been explored to detect new meanings, new patterns or language change. Consequently, large parts of *Duden-Online* is a "faster horse" (Tarp 2011: 58), a mere copy of the *Duden-GWDS* (1999). Definitions can be outdated, as for example is the case for *Mobilität* (*mobility*); see Figure 35.1. This lexical item has appeared frequently in public discourse in the past two decades, resulting in the expansion of its usage which is not captured here.

Professional editorial expertise has been consistently withdrawn as commercial lexicography competes for attention with all kinds of free online resources such as Microsoft spellchecker/thesaurus, Google, language forums or *Wiktionary*. In order to guarantee open access, their online resources rely on advertising revenue, and this makes users more likely to scroll and search for relevant information within an entry that is partially broken up.

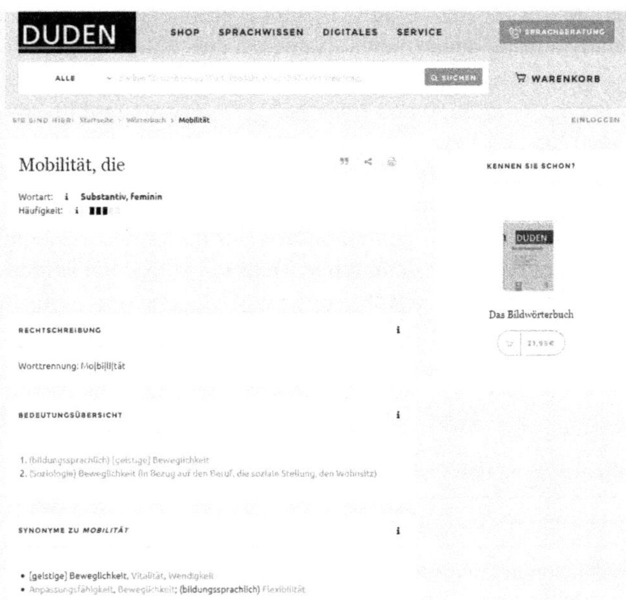

Figure 35.1 Entry *Mobilität* (*mobility*) in *Duden Online*

35.2.3 Developments in academic lexicography

Academic lexicography is an established discipline in scientific academies (Akademien der Wissenschaften), universities and some research institutes such as the IDS. It is a non-profit branch of lexicography, where a spectrum of products, both of a general monolingual and specialised nature, has been developed, such as dialectal or historical dictionaries and reference works dedicated to specialised terminology. It has given considerable impetus to German lexicography by implementing new linguistic insights, applying new corpus-guided methods, developing innovative presentations and incorporating meta-lexicographic research. Some major limitations of academic initiatives are that they often tend to be dedicated to specific vocabularies, there is no long-term commitment to larger general-purpose dictionaries and it has become difficult to reach the wider public (Haß 2001: 57). Nonetheless, in the past two decades, academic lexicography has brought the construction of corpus-based Internet dictionaries to light. Among these are a retro-digitised dictionary, a fully computer-extracted reference work, a lexical data system combining various electronic sources and a corpus-assisted dictionary in which data has been examined and interpreted lexicographically. Table 35.2 summarises some general academic German Internet dictionaries.

Serving as examples, two general monolingual dictionaries of contemporary standard German will be expounded upon, namely *elexiko* and *Digitales Wörterbuch der Deutschen Sprache (DWDS)*. These differ in aim, data methodology, structure and presentation.

35.2.3.1 *elexiko*

The first human-oriented, corpus-guided Internet dictionary of contemporary German is *elexiko*, with its first entries published in 2004. On the one hand, it took advantage of large corpora and query software, and on the other hand it accommodated new empirical theories which had redefined the perception of meaning, patterns and usage of items in authentic communicative situations. It is markedly different from other dictionaries, as it is the only German dictionary that was written from scratch on the basis of a large corpus (see

Table 35.2 Lexicographic products created in academic lexicography

Product	*Contents*	*Data/method*	*URL*
elexiko- *Online Wörterbuch zur deutschen Gegenwartssprache*	comprehensive human-oriented monolingual dictionary with information on spelling, grammar, collocations, construction and synonyms/antonyms	computer-generated data + linguistic interpretation	www.elexiko.de, www.owid.de
OWID – *Online Wortschatz-Informationssystem Deutsch*	dictionary portal with corpus-based dictionaries of new words, discourse terms, proverbs, communication verbs and elexiko	computer-generated data + linguistic interpretation	www.owid.de
Wörterbuch-Netz	dictionary portal with historical and dialectal dictionaries including DWB	fully digitised data	http://woerter buchnetz.de/
DWDS – *Das Digitale Wörterbuch der deutschen Sprache*	lexical data system with dictionaries (e.g. WDG), corpus, tools and a knowledge base (GermaNet)	computer-generated data digitised data +	www.dwds.de/
Wortschatzlexikon	fully IT-based lexical resource including digitised DORNSEIFF (2004)	computer-generated data	http://wortschatz.uni-leipzig.de/ http://corpora.uni-leipzig.de/

Chapters 8, 12 and 43 of this *Handbook*). As such, it was designed for hypertext presentation comprising 300,000 entries. Corpus-linguistic methods and paradigms, as well as metalexicographic ideas, were adopted in the development of its structure and design, defining its contents and testing its methods (Haß 2005). This project was the first serious attempt at e-lexicography with a flexible and modular data modelling architecture which, among other things, offered secure data consistency and an impressive amount of information on meaning, usage and grammar, encompassing pragmatic and discursive details and focussing on typical patterns (see Figure 35.2).

This dictionary is the first testimony that both empirical evidence and the medium of the Internet radically changed the depth of information and the appearance of a dictionary (see Part 6 of this *Handbook*). Overall, it broke with the past in terms of dictionary style, structure, methods of analysis, editing processes, design and presentation and by changing from descriptions of features to descriptions of usage patterns (Storjohann 2005; Haß and Klosa 2015).

elexiko is part of OWID (*Online Wortschatz Informationssystem Deutsch*), a platform which integrates multiple dictionaries via a common interface, with a joint lemma list and single search option. Although it was originally intended as a comprehensive lexical guide, *elexiko* remains a prototype. Its merits include a unique and meticulous documentation of lexicographic concept, theory, practice and experience.[1]

Figure 35.2 Entry *Mobilität* (*mobility*) in *elexiko*

35.2.3.2 *Digitales Wörterbuch der Deutschen Sprache (DWDS)*

DWDS is a computer-oriented integrated lexical resource comprising a number of discrete entities (panels), each of which offers different information or sources. There is a retro-digitised version of the six-volume *Wörterbuch der Deutschen Sprache* (*WDG*) written between 1961 and 1977, with its entries largely unmodified, and an electronic version of the *Deutsches Wörterbuch von Jacob und Wilhelm Grimm* (*DWB*). It also includes an etymological dictionary (*Pfeifer*), a user-created thesaurus (*OpenThesaurus*) and access to GermaNet, a lexical-semantic knowledge base. Alternatively, it is possible to search corpus material with corresponding search tools. Overall, its aim is to augment traditional lexicographic information by adding different specialised sources and extending it through extensive cross-references. All resources have interface customisation, which can be hidden by selection (see Figure 35.3).

The *DWDS* is not a corpus-based dictionary where the information in each panel is based on material from a single source. Although the uninitiated user might be under the impression that what they are seeing is comprehensive information about the meaning and usage of a search word, as it is composed as a single entry, in fact the information in each panel is based on different sources and collected using different methods for different purposes. An entry is thus not a coherent, consistent lexicographic entity. Consider the example of *Mobilität*: the collocations extracted from the DWDS-corpus are not compatible with the restricted meaning definition of the *WDG* entry (Figure 35.3). The reliability of each piece of information can only be considered in isolation and not in correspondence with or with reference to another, provided that users understand the internal structure of each entry and the different source material of each panel. Nevertheless, an advantage of this multifunctional lexical reference instrument lies in its ability to meet different individual user needs through the availability of different resources under one roof (Heid 2010: 567). Clearly, the *WDG* is outdated, with many lemmas missing and many meaning descriptions being largely incomplete. As revisions to some parts of the dictionaries are being carried out between 2013 and 2018, this reference work might become a more reliable and contemporary guide.[2]

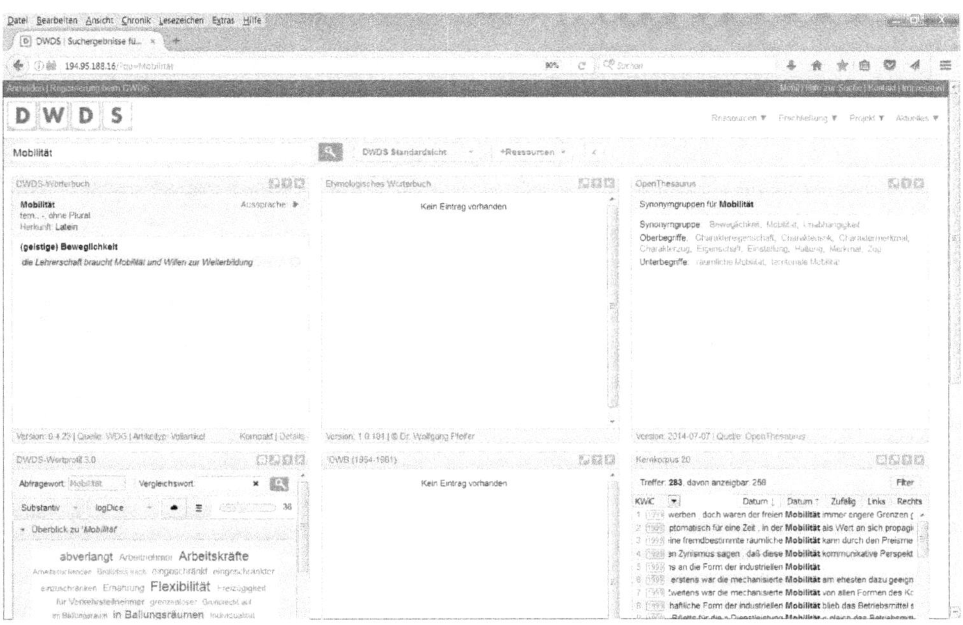

Figure 35.3 Entry *Mobilität* (*mobility*) in *DWDS*

35.2.4 Developments of Internet sources: Google, Wikipedia and Wiktionary

A number of lexical resources have been developed outside professional lexicography. Search engines (e.g. Google), crowd-sourced encyclopaedias such as *Wikipedia* and dictionaries such as *Wiktionary – Das Freie Wörterbuch* (launched in 2004) and *TheFreeDictionary* (launched in 2009) have shaped the German lexicographic landscape in the last decade by offering free, quick consultation routines, which overload users with vast amounts of data filtered according to criteria unknown to ordinary users (see Chapter 29 of this *Handbook*). Google is employed as a regular spell checker (Klosa 2014), and *Wiktionary* is a popular, ever-expanding collaborative online repository entirely created by contributors through Wiki-technology. *Wiktionary* also augments general information with specialised sources by adding external links to other data including *Wikipedia*, *DWDS* and *Canoonet* (Table 35.3).

Wiktionary contains more than 450,000 entries, and its advantage is the capacity to keep pace with language change and lexical innovation. However, a number of very frequent words cannot be found (e.g. *Mobilität*). In some ways, its structure and presentation replicate familiar dictionary traditions (see Figure 35.4). One major deficit is that the origin of

Table 35.3 User-generated monolingual lexicography

Product	*Contents*	*Data/method*	*URL*
Wiktionary – Das freie Wörterbuch	dictionary	intuition-based + digitised data	www.wiktionary.de
TheFreeDictionary.com	dictionary	intuition-based + digitised data	http://de.thefreedictionary.com

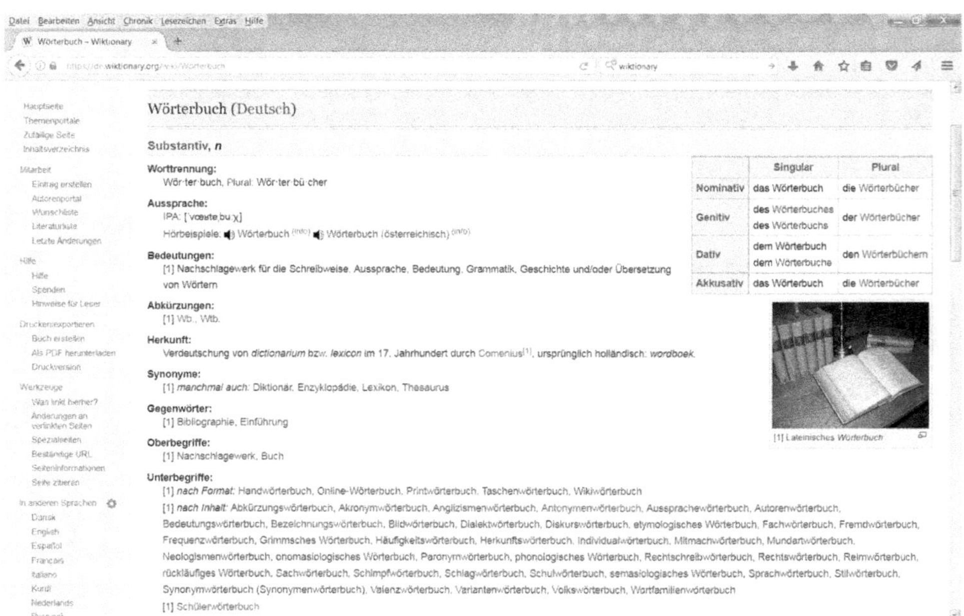

Figure 35.4 Entry *Wörterbuch* (*dictionary*) in *Wiktionary*

source material cannot be traced and the excessive use of hyperlinks appears to function as a navigation guide. The description style is conventional and prescriptive in nature, using cryptic abbreviations and circular meaning definitions. User-generated wiktionaries are not quality controlled by lexicographers, and a number of linguistic discrepancies become apparent because copying data and using intuition have their limits compared to the empirical underpinning gained with relevant corpus records.

Similarly, a vast quantity of information is also found in *TheFreeDictionary*, which contains user-generated entries as well as material obtained through copyright from different dictionaries (e.g. *KDictionaries*, *Collins German Dictionary*, *OpenThesaurus*). Certainly, the abundance of collaborative collective entries needs to be put into perspective. Critical examinations of *Wiktionary* entries inevitably give rise to questions of authenticity and reliability of the dictionary information, which are of utmost importance to users (see Section 35.3.1). Steube (2014) reveals that amateur lexicographers are not aware of the lexicographic profession and often write entries without consulting any data sources. No studies have as yet been conducted to investigate the extent to which users search in *Wikipedia/ Wiktionary* instead of consulting a dictionary, nor do we know whether users are satisfied with the avalanche of results and whether they correctly interpret the findings.

35.3 Core issues and topics

Within the German context, computational methods, corpus data, software and XML-based technology have changed lexicography into a practical corpus-based, computational and theoretical research discipline, but they have not necessarily brought a vast number of new, qualitatively reliable, user-friendly or adaptive e-dictionaries. Although for a time the focus was on the creation of larger integrated lexical systems or portals, attention has shifted towards research into the user, new genre and text types for linguistic analysis, exhaustive exploitation of hypertextuality and setting up lexicography as a modern professional discipline.

35.3.1 The user and the dictionary

Users have actively contributed to the creation of free monolingual online resources (see 35.2.4). Crowdsourced assistance is also found in bilingual open-source projects with editorial teams such as *Leo* or *Beolingus*, and web-based services have also recently started to play a role in commercial lexicography. Cooperation between editorial teams and users is implemented through social media via blog functions and feedback requests, where lexicographers interact with users, answer questions and discuss new proposals. Those conducting academic projects have been more reluctant to adopt these methods. In spite of this, catering for users' needs and improving usability have become central metalexicographic tasks for academic projects, and this has led dictionary-makers to base their work on the needs of dictionary-users more effectively (Klosa 2014: 32). Between 2009 and 2011, two major usage studies, with over 1,000 participants, were conducted at the IDS (Müller-Spitzer ed. 2014), which investigated general aspects of e-lexicography and the Internet dictionary *elexiko* in particular (see 35.2.3.1). One specific aim was to improve the usability of *elexiko* (Klosa, Koplenig and Töpel 2014) by analysing preferences of terms, order of presentation, navigation structures, expectations and degree of satisfaction of dictionary consultations.[3] The insight gained revealed significant differences in individual preferences depending on social background. For example, whereas linguists often preferred order by frequency, non-experts preferred to receive information in alphabetical order. Overall, it turned out that the concepts of e-dictionary interfaces and navigation structures needed further improvement. Users have developed consultation habits which are associated with familiar products and they are very used to traditional dictionaries, which is why they struggle with new types of content and innovative presentation. Search options and information boxes are often confusing. Often, not a lot of explicit help is provided, and users become distracted when too many windows open. Participants can be puzzled when presentations differ from classic constellations of documentation and when innovative features are introduced.

Today, we are able to survey personal preferences and track search strategies and routines, as well as consultation and navigation practices, systematically. We can now examine the amount of time users spend on a piece of information via log files, and we can track their eye-movements while they are consulting a reference guide (Müller-Spitzer, Wolfer and Koplenig 2015). These enable us to learn about user interests, focus of attention, level of interest and browsing habits. As findings from other user and usability studies attest (Bank 2010; Heid and Zimmermann 2012), German lexicography needs an empirically based user sociology (Bergenholtz and Johnsen 2013) using complementary approaches and methods. Systematic quantitative data analyses are currently being carried out with the aim of observing dictionary users through the study of log files as a major method of investigation. It uncovers the behaviour of users in a natural setting and consultation situation. Log file analyses reveal, for example, frequent searches, frequent misspellings and searches for non-existent words. Combined approaches, such as established empirical research methods, complement log file research in order to provide insights into users' profiles. Alternatively, it is possible to learn about users by studying blogs and platforms where linguistic topics are discussed by interested users who collaboratively collect information and discuss language-related issues (Storrer 2013). It is only through the study of user groups that we know what tailor-made, adaptive and intelligent dictionaries require and under which circumstances information on demand should be presented. The knowledge acquired from these studies then needs to be effectively integrated into a new digital dictionary in order to create accessible, user-friendly devices.

35.3.2 New data

Although German corpus-assisted Internet dictionaries are exclusively based on written corpora, the availability of web corpora, collections of e-mails, blogs, chats and spoken language are changing the nature of linguistic data. Linguistic variety as expressed through different corpora and new source material illustrates a wider spectrum of contemporary German than was known before. It ranges from formal written to informal spoken contexts and from everyday manifestations to technical terms, from standard to dialectal choices and from official letters to web-based chats. Their investigation will open the door to a variety of phenomena with genre-specific characteristics which have not been examined lexicographically before. As a result, some projects have started including a richer stratification of data representing collective authentic German in use, including web-sourced text collections or speech. With respect to German, spoken corpora are now accessible through the *Datenbank Gesprochenes Deutsch* (*DGD*). This material will serve as a basis for a future dictionary of contemporary German exclusively accounting for spoken idiosyncrasies (*Lexik des Gesprochenen Deutsch* in prep. at the IDS). Spoken language and text-type-specific analysis will, for example, also play an important role in the dictionary *Paronyme Dynamisch im Kontrast* (due to be published in *OWID* in 2017), which investigates easily confusable words in written, spoken and academic communication.

35.3.3 *Exploiting the benefits of the Internet*

Lexicographic content is being documented in information lists, tables, clouds, groups etc. Multi-media elements such as audio/video files, photos and games and the potential for regular updating enhance descriptions. Information on usage and lexical structures is presented through the use of colours and new organisational structures, such as panels and pop-up windows. But, taking possible e-lexicographic features today, numerous usage options are possible, for example, fault-tolerant searches, searches for components of definitions or grammatical categories, chronological stratification and much more. Nonetheless, in the case of most German Internet dictionaries, the potential of Internet publication is limited to hyperlinking and the merging of resources into portals. Hypertext dictionaries can break up conventional sequential ordering of information. A granular XML architecture allows for different data structures and therefore flexible access routes, adaptable presentations and complex searches. As digital data systems can represent their content in a structure that is not dependent on its presentation, it is possible to generate adaptable displays. Different lexicographic products could be created based on one XML-data set relating its presentation for example to different user groups. Tailor-made user-adaptivity is technologically feasible but will only become a realistic option once we know more about the users. Content can be arranged dynamically, changing linguistic focus to "allow users to recreate and re-represent their own dictionary data" (Fuertes-Olivera 2013: 330).

The introduction of portable devices has renewed discussions around the advantage of Internet reference guides. New innovative forms of presentation or design have been drawn to our attention. These concern adaptive hypermedia and the dynamic touch-screen options of mobile operating systems. For dictionaries which made use of the unlimited space of the Internet, deep depth entries now pose problems of screen visibility on smart phones, PDAs and other mobile devices. Care has to be taken not to overload entries as only a certain amount of information can be presented on a small screen at any given time. In light of this, options for dynamic content generation are in place, where entries are customised for tablet use and specific pieces of information can be displayed flexibly making it possible, for example, to change from interactive illustrations to narrative descriptions (see Chapters 17, 27 and 28 of this *Handbook*).

Furthermore, the demand for the development of more user-oriented products also triggered a new discussion revolving around the possibilities of a fruitful integration of e-dictionaries into new text remediation tools or interactive language toolboxes. These are web-based responsive writing aids designed to assist in the production of texts. As an intelligent tool, it is dynamic and adapts itself to new situations of use, that is, it learns from the user's profile, activities and consultation behaviour. Errors are identified, incorrect usage can be automatically detected, and assistance is at hand for the necessary correction process. E-dictionaries are not fully replaced but might become integrated components of smart remediation devices. The limits of individual dictionaries dissolve; different types of dictionaries disappear and merge into larger lexical systems or "containers" (Rundell 2013).

35.3.4 *Teaching and research initiatives*

An important step for keeping track of the rapidly changing IT world is the establishment of a professional discipline and community. In 2009, the creation of a unique international module at the master's level called *Europäischer Masterstudiengang für Lexikographie*[4] by the University of Erlangen-Nuremberg and a number of affiliated institutions was a significant contribution towards lexicography as a scholarly field. It provides interdisciplinary preparatory training including information science components. Another response to recent developments is the constitution of the Academic Network of Internet Lexicography (supported by the Deutsche Forschungsgemeinschaft [DFG]), initiated by Annette Klosa, former editor-in-chief of *elexiko*. As part of this network, researchers have debated the future of lexicography, covering relevant computer-technological and data modelling subjects and discussing user- as well as Internet-specific questions of design and presentation. Between 2011 and 2013, it hosted workshops and symposiums, thereby bringing together international scholars from lexicography and related fields and sparking academic debates. Both initiatives have contributed to equipping future lexicographers with the necessary knowledge and to recognising dictionary-making as an academic endeavour where new standards for training are required for a professional future.

35.4 Looking to the future

Dictionaries have been and will be utility tools for solving communication problems. Even though they are in a transitional phase and their future format might be unrecognisable (Klein 2014), they will keep serving as linguistic assistants. They might be able to adapt to the different consultation needs, backgrounds and interests of users. Undoubtedly, the focus of future German lexicography is on digital dictionaries. As Rundell (2013: 5) states, "for younger people living in developed economies, the print dictionary is already history". This accords with the user study (Müller-Spitzer ed. 2014), which revealed that only 8.5 percent of the participants mainly used print dictionaries, 40.9 percent worked with print and digital dictionaries and the majority, 47.4 percent, mainly referred to online dictionaries. But lexicography in general is exposed to a fast-changing environment that is not determined by lexicographers alone. The most decisive factors, among others, are the importance of users and usability, convincing quality and reliability, exploiting new technology, incorporating new lexicological models and creating space for new ideas. Lexicographers need to develop better imaginations in order to fully exploit the possibilities of the Internet, and they should not hesitate to experiment with new working methods and powerful software. Individual products require different approaches to data and editing practices in order to become reliable, rich and easy to use. And no less important is the need to prepare lexicography for "institutional, research oriented, intellectual and social challenges" (Fuertes-Olivera 2013: 337). All these criteria are inextricably linked. How well we adapt to new environments, whether we equip ourselves adequately for new requirements and how well we are able to transform products will determine whether we can pave the lexicographic future successfully.

35.4.1 Quality and reliability

Future lexicographers should be committed to quality. In the user study of German online dictionaries (Müller-Spitzer ed. 2014), the question of what makes a good online dictionary was addressed. Reliability was ranked highest, followed by clarity of presentation, up-to-date content, speed and permanent accessibility. The study also showed that 45.4 percent of participants wanted to find information on real communication situations, and 34.4 percent claimed they wanted data interpreted by language experts. Users want lexicographic results to be derived from scrutinising large and representative language material (i.e. corpus data) interpreted by linguists. They want to rely neither solely on the intuition of lexicographers nor on computer-driven information. These findings confirm only "appealing, relevant, high-quality content is what really draws users to the site and encourages them to come back" (Rundell 2013: 7). Certainly, the criterion of quality necessarily includes questions of comfortable usability and incentives to attract users.

35.4.2 Lexicography, corpora and information science

Reliable reference sources cannot be created without representative linguistic material, cutting-edge software and semi-automated editing processes in which lexicographers and computers interact. Intelligent systems which pre-analyse and select data and position the data in a dictionary database and where lexicographers simply validate and adjust the choices made by the software need to be put into practice (Rundell and Kilgarriff 2011). This does not mean giving up editorial judgement and awareness, but it is necessary to co-operate with computational linguistics and text technology to optimise query systems and corpus annotation tools in order to create an environment of collaborative partnership of human and computerised processes. A new generation of a German corpus system is currently being developed for the vast collection of German corpora at the IDS. *KorAP* (Korpusanalyseplattform) will be capable of multidimensional analysis with more complex but straightforward lexical search routines by including more metadata. The technical possibilities of web technology and hypertextuality will also have an impact on lexicographic data presentation. This remains a central task of e-lexicography and should therefore receive more attention (see Section 35.3.3). Contemporary German e-dictionaries are all too often nothing but linked data. But presentation needs to be open to variation. Provided lexicography links more closely with information science, dynamic, tailor-made e-dictionaries suitable for a variety of mobile devices can be created.

35.4.3 Theory and practice

The emergence of new semantic models, particularly cognitive and psycholinguistic frameworks, has prompted linguists to develop a range of immensely fruitful new approaches. As such, English reference works have successfully incorporated constructionists' approaches, for example, in *Collins Cobuild Grammar Patterns 1/2* (Francis et al 1996, 1998), or the *Pattern Dictionary of English Verbs*. By and large, German dictionary-making has not been fully linked with new strands of lexicology and has not been capable of treating linguistic material under the new tenets of semantic theories. For some time now, linguistic research has shown that language is a social practice functioning on linguistic and metalinguistic knowledge and based on diverse experience. It is stored in the mental lexicon as a highly complex cognitive entity where different networks are activated according to situation and use. German e-lexicography will have to contribute to breaking down these findings appropriately to users without overloading them with details. Cognitive models need to be utilised in the writing of entries, for example by organising information in a dynamic non-sequential fashion (Ostermann 2015).

35.4.4 Possibilities for the future

The art of contemporary dictionary writing has "reached a crossroads where it is difficult to develop further without a thorough rethink" (Bergenholtz et al 2009: 8). Lexicographers are not only competing with free online dictionaries but also with experts in information science. Future dictionaries might be more than just hypermedial gadgets and devices providing information on demand. Pioneering companies have started realising visionary ideas by developing existing educational, interactive journeys in virtual reality. Learning and understanding a language will be implemented in future revolutionary hands-on technology, where users navigate themselves through the virtual space of a mental lexicon in 3D. A future in which dictionary users travel through simulation language labs studying the structure of the mental lexicon by opening different doors to different language worlds, all of which are connected, is fast approaching. It is necessary to start responding to such visionary and transformative dimensions or this will be accomplished outside the lexicographer's realm. Effectively, this means that, as Gouws (2011: 18) stresses, "the planning of new dictionaries should not be dominated by tradition, but innovation and intelligent boldness should constitute the guiding principles".

35.5 Conclusion

The Internet has established itself as the platform for lexical reference resources and information systems. In the future, German dictionaries will differ from what we know now in function, format, accessibility, adaptability, working methods and depth of information. The German dictionary of the future will be a multifunctional technological tool designed for different consultation tasks and oriented towards acquiring diverse linguistic knowledge and information on language use (Engelberg 2014: 244). It will occupy a place between corpora and search engines, and it will be impossible to distinguish between language resource, dictionary, encyclopaedia, lexical database, learning software, writing aids, spell checker and translation tools. As such, the lexicographer of the future will have to take on a new role and working practice, where corpus-linguistic methods, IT equipment and smart systems form fundamental elements of daily work. The advances of new methods and tools will change lexicographic processing and editing routines and will determine the quality and quantity of linguistic research.

Even when lexicographers manage to successfully adapt to the new IT requirements, external factors will still have an impact on the development of dictionaries. Lexicography needs to engage in raising the consciousness of the public and making people aware that not only are dictionaries a piece of cultural reflection on language but they also have important functions in teaching language structures and conveying linguistic knowledge. This implies that students at all levels need to be educated about reflective dictionary consultation, dictionary functions and cultural value. And last but not least, it also takes political willingness to recognise the potential of lexicographic enterprises and to support linguistic and metalexicographic studies through continuous funding. Only then can digital lexicography fully develop from challenge to opportunity (Granger 2012).

Related topics

Dictionary usage research in the Internet era; explaining meaning in lexicographic information tools; lexicography and information science; electronic dictionaries; lexicography and corpus linguistics.

Further reading

Klosa, A. (ed.) (2011). *ELEXIKO: Erfahrungsberichte aus der lexikographischen Praxis eines Internetwörterbuchs*. Tübingen: Narr.

This book is a comprehensive account of the lexicographic issues experienced while developing an Internet dictionary and conducting various corpus-linguistic analyses.

Mann, M. (2013). "German II: Synchronic Lexicography", in R. H. Gouws, U. Heid, W. Schweickard and H. E. Wiegand (eds.), *Dictionaries: An International Encyclopedia of Lexicography*. Suppl. Berlin/Boston: de Gruyter, pp. 742–816.
This handbook article summarises current developments in German lexicography, illustrating different general and specialised print and e-dictionaries.

Müller-Spitzer, C. (ed.) (2014). *Using Online Dictionaries*. Berlin/Boston: de Gruyter.
This collection of articles reveals insights into the methods and results of comprehensive user surveys concerned with German online dictionaries.

Ostermann, C. (2015). *Cognitive Lexicography. A New Approach to Lexicography Making Use of Cognitive Semantics*. Berlin/Boston: de Gruyter.
This volume advances the view that linguistic theory should be implemented in lexicographic practice and proposes specific cognitive approaches to the lexicographic treatment of meaning descriptions.

Notes

1 See at http://www1.ids-mannheim.de/lexik/elexiko/publikationen.html.
2 For details, see www.dwds.de/ressourcen/woerterbuecher/#part_21
3 For details, see www.benutzungsforschung.de
4 For details, see www.emlex.phil.uni-erlangen.de/

References

Dictionaries, tools and resources

Beolingus: http://dict.tu-chemnitz.de/?lang=de

Strauß, G., U. Haß and G. Harras (1989) *Brisante Wörter von Agitation bis Zeitgeist: Ein Lexikon zum öffentlichen Sprachgebrauch*. Berlin/New York: de Gruyter.

Canoonet: Deutsche Wörterbücher und Grammatik: www.canoo.net/

Collins German Dictionary: www.collinsdictionary.com/dictionary/english-german

Cosmas I: http://www1.ids-mannheim.de/kl/projekte/cosmas_i.html

Cosmas II: https://cosmas2.ids-mannheim.de/cosmas2-web/

DGD: http://www1.ids-mannheim.de/prag/muendlichekorpora.html

DeReKo: Deutsches Referenzkorpus: http://www1.ids-mannheim.de/kl/projekte/korpora/

Deutsches Paronymwörterbuch – Ein Online-Wörterbuch zum Gebrauch verwechselbarer Ausdrücke: http://www1.ids-mannheim.de/lexik/paronymwoerterbuch.html

Dornseiff – Der deutsche Wortschatz nach Sachgruppen (2004) Ed. U. Quasthoff, 8. ed., Berlin/New York: de Gruyter.

Duden-GWDS – Das große Wörterbuch der deutschen Sprache, 10 Bände (1999) 3rd edition and on CD-ROM (2000) Mannheim: Bibliographisches Institut.

Duden-Online: www.duden.de

DWB – Deutsches Wörterbuch von Jacob Grimm und Wilhelm Grimm. 16 Bde. in 32 Teilbänden von 1854–1961, Leipzig: Hirzel. (http://woerterbuchnetz.de/)

DWDS – Das Digitale Wörterbuch der deutschen Sprache: www.dwds.de/

elexiko – Online-Wörterbuch zur deutschen Gegenwartssprache: www.elexiko.de

Etymologisches Wörterbuch des Deutschen (1993) Ed. W. Pfeifer. 2nd edition. Berlin: Akademie.

Collins Cobuild Grammar Patterns 1: Verbs (1996) Eds. G. Francis, S. Hunston, E. Manning. London: Harper Collins.

Collins Cobuild Grammar Patterns 2: Nouns and Adjectives (1998) Eds. G. Francis, S. Hunston, E. Manning. London: Harper Collins.

GermanNet: www.sfs.uni-tuebingen.de/GermaNet/
KDictionaries online: http://kdictionaries-online.com/
Korpusanalyseplattform (KorAP): http://www1.ids-mannheim.de/direktion/kl/projekte/korap.html
Langenscheidt Großwörterbuch Deutsch als Fremdsprache (2010) Eds. D. Götz, G. Haensch and H. Wellmann. Berlin: Langenscheidt.
Leo Wörterbücher: https://dict.leo.org/ende/index_de.html
OpenThesaurus – Synonyme und Assoziationen: www.openthesaurus.de/
OWID – Online-Wortschatz-Informationssystem Deutsch: www.owid.de
Pattern Dictionary of English Verbs: www.pdev.org.uk
Pons – Großwörterbuch Deutsch als Fremdsprache (2011) Stuttgart: PONS GmbH. Online edition: http://de.pons.com/
TheFreeDictionary: http://de.thefreedictionary.com/
Wahrig: www.wissen.de/lexika
WDG – Wörterbuch der deutschen Gegenwartssprache (1967–1977) Eds. R. Klappenbach and W. Steinitz, 6 volumes. Berlin: Akademie-Verlag.
Wiktionary, das freie Wörterbuch: www.wiktionary.de
Wortschatzlexikon: http://wortschatz.uni-leipzig.de/
Wörterbuchnetz: http://woerterbuchnetz.de/

Other literature

Bank, C. (2010) *Die Usability von Onlinewörterbüchern und elektronischen Sprachportalen*, MA Thesis, University of Hildesheim.
Bergenholtz, H. and M. Johnson. (2013) "User Research in the Field of Electronic Dictionaries: Method, First Results, Proposals", in R. H. Gouws, U. Heid, W. Schweickard and H. E. Wiegand (eds.), pp. 556–568.
Bergenholtz, H., S. Nielsen and S. Tarp. (2009) "Introduction", in H. Bergenholtz, S. Nielsen and S. Tarp (eds.), *Lexicography at a Crossroads: Dictionaries and Encyclopedias Today, Lexicographical Tools Tomorrow*. Bern: Peter Lang, pp. 7–16.
Brückner, T. (1989) *Refer. Benutzerhandbuch*. Mannheim: Institut für Deutsche Sprache.
Engelberg, S. (2014) "Gegenwart und Zukunft der Abteilung Lexik am IDS: Plädoyer für eine Lexikographie der Sprachdynamik", in Institut für Deutsche Sprache (ed.), *Ansichten und Einsichten: 50 Jahre Institut für Deutsche Sprache*. Mannheim: Institut für Deutsche Sprache, pp. 243–253.
Fuertes-Olivera, P. A. (2013) "e-Lexicography: The Continuing Challenge of Applying New Technology to Dictionary-Making", in H. Jackson (ed.), *The Bloomsbury Companion to Lexicography*. London: Bloomsbury, pp. 323–340.
Fuertes-Olivera, P. A. and H. Bergenholtz (eds.) (2011) *e-Lexicography: The Internet, Digital Initiatives and Lexicography*. London: Continuum.
Gouws, R. H. (2011) "Learning, Unlearning and Innovation in the Planning of Electronic Dictionaries", in P. A. Fuertes-Olivera and H. Bergenholtz (eds.), pp. 17–29.
Gouws, R., U. Heid, W. Schweickard and H. E. Wiegand (eds.) (2013) *Dictionaries: An International Encyclopedia of Lexicography. Supplementary Volume: Recent Developments with Focus on Electronic and Computational Lexicography*. Berlin/Boston: de Gruyter.
Granger, S. (2012) "Electronic Lexicography: From Challenge to Opportunity", in S. Granger and M. Paquot (eds.), *Electronic Lexicography*. Oxford: Oxford University Press, pp. 1–11.
Haß, U. (2001) *Deutsche Wörterbücher*. Berlin/New York: de Gruyter.
Haß, U. (ed.) (2005) *elexiko – Grundfragen der elektronischen Lexikographie. elexiko – das Online-Informationssystem zum deutschen Wortschatz*. Berlin/New York: de Gruyter.
Haß, U. and A. Klosa. (2015) "elexiko – Geschichte und Zukunft", *Sprachreport* 3: 10–20.
Heid, U. (2010) "Computergestützte Lexikographie und Terminologie", in K. U. Carstensen, Chr. Ebert, C. Ebert, S. Jekat, R. Klabunde and H. Langer (eds.), *Computerlinguistik und Sprachtechnologie*. 3rd edition. Heidelberg: Spektrum, pp. 566–575.

Heid, U. and J. T. Zimmermann. (2012) "Usability Testing as a Tool for e-Dictionary Design: Collocations as a Case in Point", in *Proceedings of EURALEX 2012*, www.euralex.org/elx_proceedings/Euralex2012/pp661-671%20Heid%20and%20Zimmermann.pdf.
Klein, W. (2014) "Das Wörterbuch der Zukunft ist kein Wörterbuch", in L. M. Eichinger (ed.), *Sprachwissenschaft im Fokus: Positionsbestimmungen und Perspektiven*. Berlin/Boston: de Gruyter, pp. 277–296.
Klosa, A. (2007) "Korpusgestützte Lexikographie: besser, schneller, umfangreicher?", in W. Kallmeyer and G. Zifonun (eds.), *Sprachkorpora – Datenmengen und Erkenntnisfortschritt*. Berlin/New York: de Gruyter, pp. 105–122.
Klosa, A. (2014) "Gibt es eine Zukunft für Wörterbücher?", *Sprachreport* 4: 28–37.
Klosa, A., A. Koplenig and A. Töpel. (2014) "Benutzerwünsche und -meinungen zu dem monolingualen deutschen Onlinewörterbuch elexiko", in C. Müller-Spitzer (ed.), pp. 281–384.
Mann, M. (2013) "German II: Synchronic Lexicography", in R. H. Gouws, U. Heid, W. Schweickard and H. E. Wiegand (eds.), pp. 742–816.
Müller-Spitzer, C. (ed.) (2014) *Using Online Dictionaries*. Berlin/Boston: de Gruyter.
Müller-Spitzer, C., S. Wolfer and A. Koplenig. (2015) "Observing Online Dictionary Users: Studies Using Wiktionary Log Files", *International Journal of Lexicography* 28(1): 1–26.
Ostermann, C. (2015) *Cognitive Lexicography: A New Approach to Lexicography Making Use of Cognitive Semantics*. Berlin/Boston: de Gruyter.
Rundell, M. (2013) "Redefining the Dictionary: From Print to Digital", *Kernermann Dictionary News* 21: 5–7. http://kdictionaries.com/kdn/kdn21.pdf.
Rundell, M. and A. Kilgarriff. (2011) "Automating the Creation of Dictionaries: Where Will It All End?", in F. Meunier, S. De Cock, G. Gilquin and M. Paquot (eds.), *A Taste for Corpora*. Amsterdam/Philadelphia: John Benjamins, pp. 257–281.
Steube, J. (2014) "Wörterbücher und lexikografisches Wissen von Amateurlexikografen im Internet", in M. Mann (ed.), *Digitale Lexikographie. Ein- und mehrsprachige elektronische Wörterbücher mit Deutsch: aktuelle Entwicklungen und Analysen*. Hildesheim: Olms, pp. 201–228.
Storjohann, P. (2005) "A Corpus-Based Monolingual German Dictionary", *Hermes* 34: 55–82.
Storrer, A. (2010) "Deutsche Internet-Wörterbücher: Ein Überblick", *Lexicographica* 26: 155–164.
Storrer, A. (2013) "Representing Dictionaries in Hypertextual Form", in R. H. Gouws, U. Heid, W. Schweickard and H. E. Wiegand (eds.), pp. 1244–1253.
Tarp, S. (2011) "Lexicographical and Other e-Tools for Consultation Purposes: Towards the Individualization of Needs and Satisfaction", in P. A. Fuertes-Olivera and H. Bergenholtz (eds.), pp. 54–70.
Wiegand, H. E. (1990) "Die deutsche Lexikografie der Gegenwart", in F. J. Hausmann, O. Reichmann, H. E. Wiegand and L. Zgusta (eds.), *Wörterbücher. Ein internationales Handbuch zur Lexikographie*. Volume 2. Berlin/New York: de Gruyter, pp. 2100–2246.

36

Hindi lexicography in the Internet era

Parman Singh and Arimardan Kumar Tripathi

36.1 Introduction

Keeping in view the status of 'e-lexicography' at the global level it is possible to say that Hindi e-lexicography has just taken the first step with regard to the great deal of e-lexicographical research and issues that have become relevant for the future. The status of Hindi lexicography has to be considered with respect to the past achievements within the social, cultural, and educational context of India before independence and the works done after it. In the present chapter we take a look at the development of Hindi lexicography before and after independence. In the next section, we present the technical and lexical development for the use of Hindi in computers in the post-independence era. This will be followed by a brief account of the publication of e-dictionaries and the development of the e-lexicographical tradition. Keeping in view the current status of e-lexicography databases and development of information science, we explore in the next section the core issues and the topics that require dedicated research as well as the resources for expansion and consolidation of Hindi e-lexicography. In the final section, we will explore the possibilities that the future holds for expansion of electronic dictionaries and e-lexicographical research in future. We conclude that a great deal of work and dedicated research is required for Hindi e-lexicography to make a mark and its relevance in India as well as at the global level.

36.2 Historical perspectives

36.2.1 Hindi lexicography: the past

The development of Hindi lexicography was based on the rich Sanskrit lexicographical tradition. The scholars of foreign nationalities initiated the modern lexicographical works in Hindi or Hindustani, and Urdu. In the seventeenth century, European scholars started preparing bilingual dictionaries for Indian languages modelled on modern European dictionaries (Miranda 2006: 614). They not only developed Hindi lexicography, but also they established printing press wherever they went for trade and religion, and produced literature as well as dictionaries applying modern techniques.

The Europeans introduced the western tradition of lexicography in the region. This initiated lexicography as an academic and scientific activity in its modern sense (Yugeshwar 1971: 28–29). They applied the modern techniques of lexicography for the Hindi language. The dictionaries compiled by the Indians also started utilizing the modern techniques. The introduction of the Western tradition in the field of Hindi lexicography and the scope, objectives, and methodology of Hindi lexicography have undergone a basic change and accordingly different types of lexicographical products have come into existence.

Sir Randolph Quirk's (1986: 3) remark is important at this stage. He writes,

> There is one thing that can be said with confidence: lexicographers have not laboured in ignorance of the work of their colleagues, competitors and predecessors. Not even the writer of a humble medieval glossary sat down without the work of predecessors in front of him.

The observation is not only true for the medieval glossary of English but also for the Sanskrit and Hindi lexicographers as well. Even Amar Singh at the beginning of his *Amarkosha* referred to the dictionaries and the lexicographers of the prior period. Directly or indirectly he acknowledged their contributions to the field of dictionary making which helped and provided insight for his composition. Making improvements in the coverage, method, material, presentation, etc., he composed *Amarkosha* (*Namalinganusashana*), a brilliant dictionary of Sanskrit. The same is also true with regard to Hindi lexicography.

It is necessary to take account of the development of Hindi language along with the initial attempts at Hindi lexicography. In the process of development the works were produced either in the Sanskrit-dominated style or Urdu-dominated style of Hindi. Gradually the two styles separated, and different traditions of language and literature development started to take shape in fiction and other works. Modern Hindi and its literary tradition evolved towards the end of the eighteenth century. Fort William College was founded on 10 July 1800 at Calcutta by the British East India Company. The principal of this college, John Gilchrist, wrote a grammar of Hindi and compiled a dictionary of Hindi to teach and train the British East India Company employees the Hindi language. This *lingua franca* had not been considered refined and elegant enough to be used in literature by Indian writers and therefore the lexicographical works were also ignored. However, in the nineteenth century genuine efforts were being made to use Khari Boli Hindi as the literary medium. Four writers (Insha Allah Khan, Lallulal, Sadal Mishra, and Sadasukh Lal) experimented in Hindi producing translations and literature in Khari Boli Hindi. They did it at the behest of John Gilchrist at the beginning of the nineteenth century in Fort William College. It was only with the work of Bhartendu Harishchandra (09 Sep 1850–07 Jan 1885) that Hindi established a strong literary tradition and began to take a separate course. The development of Hindi and Urdu in terms of two traditions is important in the context of conflict between Hindi and Urdu in the pre-independence period. Though Hindi and Urdu shared a grammatical structure, the conflict between Hindi and Urdu provided the basis for separate lexicographical traditions.

Prior to the compilation of *Hindi Shabd Sagar* several monolingual and bilingual dictionaries were published by foreigners as well as by Indians. Foreigners followed the Western tradition of lexicography, whereas the dictionaries compiled by Indians were under the impression of Sanskrit lexicographical tradition. Some of the remarkable dictionaries of this period are *Dictionary of Hindi Language* (1829) by Rev. M.T. Adam, *Shabdkosh* (1873) by Munshi Radha Lal, *Bhagwan Shabd Sagar* (1891) by Bhagwan Das, *Sridhar Bhasha Kosh*

(1894) by Pandit Badri Narayan Mishra, *Gauri Nagari Kosh* (1901) by Gauri Dutt, *Hindi Shabdarth Parijat* (1914) by Dvarika Prasad Chaturvedi, etc. (Singh 2013).

During this period no standard criterion was established regarding the headwords for Hindi dictionaries. Therefore, the Hindi dictionaries collected words ranging from the beginning of the Hindi language up to the contemporary time. Because of the lack of norms, the Hindi dictionaries exploited all kinds of lexical resources. As a result, we find in them lexical entries of different strata of the Hindi language and stylistic usage as well. At the one end 'tatsam' words from high-flown Sanskrit style were drawn and at the other end words from regionally marked local dialects were also included. Similarly, frequent words of foreign origin as well as words from a mixed variety of the Hindi language were also considered. No attempt was made to put any tag for their differentiation. Dictionary naming, up to some extent, followed the pattern of Sanskrit tradition. Some of the Hindi dictionaries are named after the name of their author. They show that partial alphabetization was present in Hindi dictionaries. One of the serious limitations of these dictionaries is their unsystematic order of appending words over and above the pages. One also notices a lack of system for explicating the meaning of a given lexical entry. Some of the lacking features in the published Hindi dictionaries are revealed through the projection for a good dictionary in the preface of the *Bhagwan Shabd Sagar* of Bhagwan Das. Some of them are: the paucity of contemporary spoken words of Hindi, collection of frequently borrowed words, and complete alphabetization.

In the nineteenth century Hindi language really felt the paucity of a comprehensive dictionary like *Hindi Shabd Sagar*. In other words, it was considered necessary to show the strength as well as to document the Hindi language in a single voluminous compilation. The inclusion of as many data as possible, which is a feature of western lexicography, also serves for language documentation and preservation.

At the end of nineteenth century, a great institution, Kashi Nagari Pracharini Sabha (1893)[1], was established for the promotion and documentation of the Hindi language and Devanagari script. The founding members of this institution resolved to publish a comprehensive and standard Hindi dictionary. Their research team collected plenty of Hindi words, varying from the verses of Old Hindi to the new words of prosaic Hindi. For the word collection, the team utilized various (published, unpublished) lexical resources. The labour of those scholars took shape in the form of *Hindi Shabd Sagar* (literally 'ocean of Hindi words').

The first edition of *Hindi Shabd Sagar* was finished in four parts. The first part of this dictionary was completed after eight years in 1916, second in 1920, third in 1925, and finally the last part was finished in 1928. The first edition of *Hindi Shabd Sagar* was published in eight volumes and described the meaning of 93,115 headwords (Das et al 1965: 7 Intro. to the first edition). Its second, revised and updated, edition was published from 1965 to 1975 in 11 volumes.

Hindi Shabd Sagar is the biggest dictionary of the Hindi language on the basis of domain and the number of entries. *Hindi Shabd Sagar* is the first voluminous dictionary among modern Indian languages. It is also the best one regarding traditionally-conceived lexicography, as it contains more words as well as meaning items, etymology and usage notes. Editors of this dictionary explored and utilized whatever Hindi literature was available to them as a lexical resource, and they used the literature to authenticate the words and their meanings.

If this dictionary is evaluated and compared with the published dictionaries, it is only comparable to the world famous English dictionary *Webster's Dictionary* for its encyclopaedic information. With reference to Hindi lexicography, the importance of *Hindi Shabd Sagar* can be equated with the importance of Dr. Johnson's *Dictionary for English Lexicography* and the importance of *Amarakosa* for Sanskrit lexicography. *Hindi Shabd Sagar* is a work of appreciation for its all-inclusiveness and the arrangement of the entries. Not even a single monolingual Hindi dictionary is compiled even today which can challenge the authority and quality of *Hindi Shabd Sagar*.

True to the fact, the publication of *Hindi Shabd Sagar* revolutionized the work of dictionary making in Indian languages. Actually, this dictionary established itself as a trendsetter in the field of Hindi lexicography. The importance of this dictionary is not confined to its modern techniques, but it is also recognized as a source for different dictionaries based on pragmatism.

After the publication of *Hindi Shabd Sagar* and its concise edition, there was no hesitation in the compilation of several dictionaries of Hindi based on *Hindi Shabd Sagar* were compiled. This does not mean that no original work has been published after this dictionary. There are some original dictionaries published after *Hindi Shabd Sagar*. They have applied new lexicographical methods. Some of the important monolingual Hindi dictionaries are *Pramanik Hindi Kosh* (1949) by Ramchandra Verma, *Bhargava Adarsh Hindi Shabdkosh* (1950) by Ram Chandra Pathak, *Brihat Hindi Kosh* (1950) by Kalika Prasad, Rajballabh Sahay and Mukundi Lal Shrivastava, *Manak Hindi Kosh* (1962) by Ram Chandra Verma et al. etc. (Singh 2013).

The most important feature of a dictionary is its word stock. Hindi lexicographers have increased the word stocks of dictionaries by adding those words which were never used in Hindi (Bahri 1980:48). The inclusion of such vocables to increase the volume of dictionaries only actually misleads the users and becomes useless.

> Most of the lexicographers are linguistically ill-equipped and unqualified. The planning, in most cases, is done by the publisher who simply knows that any compilation bearing his name and place would sell well in his region. Dictionary-makers are usually not in touch with modern trends in lexicography.
>
> (Bahri 1980: 49)

After independence Hindi became the official language of the Union in Devanagari script. Hindi and the regional languages started to replace English as a medium of instruction and to be used for official work. To make a change over from English to Hindi there was a need to find equivalents for scientific and technical terms. In this regard the Commission for Scientific and Technical Terminology (CSTT)[2] was set up on 1 October 1961 by a resolution of the government of India. The resolution ignited the compilation of subject dictionaries and definitional dictionaries in Hindi and other Indian languages. The CSTT has prepared and printed glossaries for agriculture, medicine, law, sciences, administration, linguistics, etc. under the influence of IT revolution and struggling to provide all its paper published glossaries online. Some of them are available on its official website but in Portable Document File (PDF) format.

Another institution of national importance to promote and widen the use of Hindi, the Central Hindi Directorate (CHD), was established in 1960. One of the major focuses of this premier institution is the preparation of bilingual and multilingual dictionaries of Hindi and other scheduled languages. To date it has published four multilingual dictionaries and 11 trilingual dictionaries in which each dictionary contains approximately 20,000 Hindi words as main entries. These dictionaries were also published as language-based dictionaries in which the headwords are given in regional languages. The CHD also published many bilingual dictionaries.

The CHD has also worked for the standardization of Hindi spelling. In this regard it has published the booklet *Hindi Vartani ka manakikaran* (Standardization of Hindi Spelling) in 1968 after the detailed discussion with distinguished scholars, linguists, Hindi voluntary organizations, and officials from state government and different ministries. The standardization was mainly based on user and typing instruments. It was also decided to enhance the standardization of Hindi by generating Unicode for Devanagari script, thus keeping pace with the coming of age of Information Technology. In 1983 a modified and revised edition was published, namely *Devanagari lipi tatha Hindi vartani ka manakikaran* (Standardization of Hindi spelling and Devanagari script), which contains the standard forms of Hindi alphabets, spelling, punctuation marks, alphabetic order for dictionaries, enhanced Devanagari script, and divisions and sub-divisions of paragraphs.

36.2.2 Hindi lexicography: the present

We stated in the introduction that the development of Hindi lexicography has to be considered in the context of the social, cultural, and educational situation in India. Within this framework, Hindi e-lexicography is starting to develop. This process is slow and will need some more time to consolidate as a discipline. There can be several reasons for this slow development, but we are mentioning a few of them here. The computer processing in Indian languages is delayed because the development of computers and computational skill arrived relatively late in comparison to developed countries. It is also a historical fact that the development of the computer happened in English-speaking countries, as was the development of its environment (Tripathi and Singh 2009). Another significant reason pertains to technological development. In the initial stage of Hindi computing, efforts were made to develop True Type Font (TTF) with the help of computer engineers. However, TTF did not provide a satisfactory solution for the use of Hindi in terms of computational processes and on the Internet. Use of multiple fonts in a single document was the biggest problem, and a document composed with TTF is not readable by other computers that have different fonts installed. It was only in 2000 that the Department of Information Technology became a full member of the Unicode Consortium with voting rights as supported by the government of India. With the acceptance of Unicode system, the computational scenario changed, making possible computational processing in general and the development of information retrieval techniques in particular. Thus the development of language technology in Indian languages and the emergence of Hindi e-lexicography made its beginning with the establishment of the Technology Development for Indian Languages (TDIL) under the Department of Electronics (Government of India) in 1991. The Unicode system proves efficient in the development of lexicographical tasks such as database creation, storage, sorting, up-gradation, and other tasks.

The forthcoming section of this chapter is not intended to provide an exhaustive list of the Hindi online dictionaries, but to give a glimpse of the dictionaries which has marked its presence on the Internet to the users. If anyone googles the string 'Hindi dictionaries online' it will show about 1,210,000 results, which is a matter of pride for the lover of Hindi, but when the search is restricted with 'this exact word or phrase' it will show only about 709 results. Similarly, googling 'online Hindi glossary' returned about 756,000 hits. But restricting the search by typing 'this exact word or phrase' in the advanced search system resulted in just one hit, which is not an online Hindi glosary but a printed one.

Before discussing the available online dictionaries of Hindi, it would be useful to go through the typologies of dictionaries on this new media. Several scholars have made typologies of dictionaries to understand the nature and scope of electronic lexicography in general. Cerquiglini, as cited in De Schryver (2003: 143–144), distinguishes three phases of use of computers in lexicography:

1 Computer-assisted (paper) lexicography,
2 Transfer of existing paper dictionaries to an electronic medium (digitization), and
3 Electronic dictionaries in their own right, conceived afresh for the electronic environment.

Fuertes-Olivera and Bergenholtz (2011a:1) remark that "many, perhaps a large majority of e-dictionaries were not e-dictionaries in their own way, but were printed dictionaries made available on electronic platforms", which shows that there is a paucity of dictionaries which are conceived afresh for the electronic environment, which is also true for Hindi lexicography.

The categories suggested by Tarp (2011) are important in terms of the available Hindi electronic dictionaries on the Internet. Tarp has suggested the following four categories: copycats, faster horses, Model T Fords, and Rolls Royces. Keeping in view these categories, we can take an account of the development and the present status of Hindi e-lexicography.

The earlier works of Hindi lexicography fall under the first category: copycats. Copycats are those dictionaries which have either been photocopied or directly copied from a text file and then placed on an electronic platform, frequently as PDF files. This is a very common practice of providing access to Internet dictionaries, particularly when the electronic media was in its infancy. In Hindi several dictionaries fall under this category. The Commission for Scientific and Technical Terminology has prepared many dictionaries, and the definitional dictionaries are available on Internet in PDF format. The Central Hindi Directorate has compiled some trilingual dictionaries, including Indian and foreign languages, available as PDFs on the Internet. *Anukriti*[3] is a project of the Central Institute of Indian Languages in collaboration with the National Book Trust and Sahitya Academy, New Delhi. It prepares trilingual dictionaries containing English, Hindi, and a tribal language. It also offers different reference tools in PDF and XML format.

The development of lexicography started making use of new technological tools in terms of research. Hindi lexicography made use of new technologies to provide quicker access to the databases. Tarp's (2011) second category, 'faster horses', includes this aspect. At the initial stage some of the printed Hindi dictionaries were digitized and converted into searchable text. The U.S. Department of Education has undertaken an ambitious mission of providing the dictionaries of South Asia in digital format with the help of the University of Chicago. Under this project three renowned dictionaries of Hindi language are available on the Internet in searchable format: *Hindi Shabdasagar*,[4] *A Practical Hindi-English Dictionary*,[5] and *Learner's Hindi-English Dictionary*.[6]

There are some other dictionaries which were never published as printed dictionaries but are available on Internet and can qualify as 'faster horses'. Some of them are *Shabdkosh*,[7] *HinKhoj*,[8] *Hindi Wordnet*,[9] *Universal Word Hindi Lexicon*,[10] *Google Dictionary*,[11] *Khandbahale Hindi Dictionary*,[12] etc. Although these dictionaries have one or more criteria to qualify as electronic dictionaries, we will discuss some of the expected features of e-dictionaries in detail for the previously mentioned dictionaries of Hindi.

It has already been mentioned that these dictionaries are equipped with a search facility to cater to users' need for easy and accurate access of the desired information. To implement this, customizable searching is required. Initially it can be done with the use of filters. Most of the Hindi online dictionaries do not provide filters for searches. Like a corpus search, if you search the word or the phrase in the dictionary, it will display all the information wherever this matches in the database either in the headword or in definition/information. With the search your screen will be flooded with irrelevant data. Only a few dictionaries, like *Shabdkosh*, *HinKhoj*, *Dictionaries of South Asia*, etc., provides some kind of filters. *HinKhoj* has filters to search the desired words in definitions, similar words, and opposite words. In this dictionary (Hindi to English), it was strange to see that using the opposite word filter, no entry is found for '*achchaa*' (good) which is a very commonly used adjective in Hindi. And in addition, the words for the noun, verb, and particle forms are given as the similar words for the adjective form. *Dictionaries of South Asia* has five filtering options: Search entry words only, Words matching exactly, Words starting with, Words containing, and Words ending with. Although this dictionary claims that user can search the words by typing in Hindi and in Roman, when the Hindi words for dictionary 'shabdkosh' and 'kosh' were searched in *Hindi Shabdsagar* in Roman, no result was displayed.

Space limitations have always been one of the main constraints for compiling comprehensive dictionaries, but the Internet has lifted these limitations and led to the integration of more and better data, richer collocational coverage, an exponential increase of example sentences, integration of multimedia content (images, graphs, videos, sound files), and extended notes (usage notes, cultural notes, error notes, etc.) (Granger 2012:3). Hindi dictionaries which were earlier available in print form and are now available on this new media have more data than the other dictionaries available. Many Hindi dictionaries claim that they have lot of data, and they are increasing their databases daily with the help of users, but the quality and coverage of data are not appreciable. Some of the lacunae of the database of Hindi online dictionaries have already been discussed while discussing the search facilities. *Hindi Wordnet* database has 28,687 synsets and 63,800 unique words based on every possible terminology, *Hindi Lexicon* contains 136,110 words, and *Hindicube*[13] claims to have a database of 200,000 words and is still growing. *Hindi Online Tools*[14] claims to have 14,000 English words and 40,000 Hindi meanings, but when a very common word, 'mango', was searched in this dictionary, it displayed 27 words of English and Hindi but not the word 'mango'. Multimedia is another important feature of e-dictionaries which is least utilized in Hindi Internet dictionaries. Only some of the Hindi dictionaries like *Shabdkosh*, *HinKhoj*, and *Hindicube* have the audio pronunciation of words. *Shabdkosh* and *HinKhoj* have the audio and transcription/transliteration of words from both Hindi and English languages, whereas *Hindicube* has the audio files for English words. Apart from audio pronunciation, no other facilities of multimedia have been utilized in the available Hindi Internet dictionaries.

Subject dictionaries in Hindi have almost no presence on the Internet. Dr. Arimardan Kumar Tripathi in 2007 prepared a bilingual glossary (English-Hindi) of natural language processing (NLP) for the use of language technology researchers who are pursuing courses on language technology through the Hindi medium. To date it is a standalone English-Hindi glossary, but now he is trying his best to host it on the Internet for wider coverage and utility. Subject dictionaries developed by CSTT are not available online even in PDF, which is expected as the very basic medium of e-lexicography.

Recently the Central Government of India decided to digitize the textbooks and dictionaries available or published with government funding on a single platform. The MHRD minister launched a portal on 25 May 2016 aiming to build a searchable knowledge repository in and about all the languages in India in multimedia (text, audio, video, images) formats. It is named *Bharatavani*.[15] This project is being implemented by the Central Institute of Indian Languages, Mysuru, and it offers search and browse facilities for the many dictionaries/glossaries published by Central Hindi Directorate and CSTT. It also has developed a multilingual app which aims to provide knowledge in more than 120 Indian languages. This app sources its data from the dictionaries that are published on the Bharatavani portal. Although more than 40 text-based dictionaries are readily available for usage on the app, 100 more dictionaries are available on the portal in book format.

Apart from the previously mentioned dictionaries, there are some other websites for Hindi dictionaries which provide links either to free Hindi dictionaries or to search facilities for working with them. *Lexilogos Hindi Online Dictionary*[16] and *Lexicool Hindi English Dictionary*[17] have nothing to do with either lexicography or e-lexicography – they only provide the platform for a dictionary search. However, a project of *Wikimedia, Vikshnari*,[18] claims that it is a free dictionary which gives the right to edit to the users, and it also provides external links for various Hindi dictionaries and glossaries available on the Internet.

The last two categories of dictionaries suggested by Tarp (2011), that is, 'Model T Fords' and 'Rolls Royces', are the products of advanced e-lexicography, and these types of electronic dictionaries are not really available in Hindi. Tarp's suggestion aimed for a radical shift in the lexicographical paradigm in order to make the best of the electronic medium and present-day technology but complete customization is not yet achievable. This could only become a reality if the data display is completely dynamic and adaptable to every single consultation need of all the possible users in all the possible situations. This issue will be addressed next as it relates to Hindi dictionaries.

36.3 Core issues and topics

Several core issues and topics need more consideration before e-lexicography consolidates as an advanced and growing area of research and development. We cannot undertake an exhaustive treatment of the various issues as it would go beyond the limits of the present assignment. To begin with, we may point out that lexicography has been a major domain for research in language and linguistic studies. We consider the field of lexicography in India to be underrepresented, as most linguistics departments do not focus on lexicographical issues but on linguistic ones, especially on the linguistic analysis of topics such as language learning, the role of English as a lingua franca, and so on. It is very essential to make lexicography a challenging area of research in linguistic departments of various universities in India. Furthermore, some basic issues of e-lexicography need to be incorporated in the lexicographical studies. The students of lexicography in Indian universities need to be exposed to the growing and challenging area of e-lexicography and its significance as a discipline in the era of the Internet and globalization. It is also necessary to recognize that the computer studies and construction of databases pursued in various computer courses in information technology departments do not expose the students to the challenging area of e-lexicography as a promising area of research.

Another major issue for the growth of e-lexicography in India is to understand the latest developments from the field of e-lexicography and information science at the global level. The students and researchers of e-lexicography must acquire the growing amount of research in this discipline and learn from other situations about the technological aspects of e-lexicography. We understand that neither the linguistics departments nor the information technology departments have created a dialogue with the advanced e-lexicographical studies at the global level. We are not in a situation to make a categorical statement, but we understand that Hindi e-dictionaries have not taken into account various types of users, situations of use, types of user needs, and the types of data that would be necessary to satisfy these needs. Without taking into account an individualization of dictionary content and the development of interactive methods for satisfaction of user needs in online Hindi dictionaries, we cannot build a strong tradition for e-lexicography in India.

The dictionary as a tool has fulfilled a significant social and cultural need in society. It has played a catalytic role in the standardization of language. As we have pointed out, the government of India has played an active role by establishing the Indian Institute of Technology, National Institute of Technology, and Indian Institute of Information Technology to help the development of Indian languages in terms of computer processing and building the necessary databases for creating interactive information tools and information networks. This implies that the development of e-lexicography has not only language policy relevance but also it is an important aspect of political planning. The fulfilment of user needs for the development of e-lexicography requires long-term planning and a constructive and coordinated role of linguists, lexicographers, and information scientists.

Another major issue of research and planning is to consider the distinction between corpus and database. We have pointed out that various products based on corpus research and documentation have been undertaken with the approval and support of the government and researchers. We do not underrate or dispute the relevance of corpus research. However, we consider that the construction of databases for the growth of e-lexicography is fundamental. It is also an important issue for planning to undertake advanced e-lexicographical research. As we understand it, the focus of corpus research is on collection of representative data with respect to subjects, various genres, style, frequency, etc. The corpus is not conerned with the users' need as it is understood in e-lexicography. Furthermore, the construction of corpora is quite relevant for different linguistic analyses, especially for problems related to language standardization, machine translation, and so on. Databases, especially lexicographic databases, are also needed, but for a different research agenda. We need them to store relevant lexicographic data (e.g. data connected with specific user needs and user situations). These databases must be part of robust systems that are necessary for compiling new online dictionaries from scratch. We therefore consider that we need to develop robust databases for high-quality lexicographical studies and construction of advanced and dynamic dictionaries.

36.4 Looking to the future

The Central Hindi Directorate has compiled Hindi dictionaries with one of the 15 Indian languages as the second language. The exact number of words are not very high, but Hindi and other Indian language bilingual dictionaries can be important tools for further expansion of such dictionaries. It may be pointed out that some of these dictionaries have been placed on the Internet recently. We may expect that these dictionaries will be further expanded, accessed for different purposes, and adapted to different situations in the foreseeable expansion of Hindi e-lexicography. We may also mention that the electronic dictionaries available so far on the Internet do not involve many other languages than English. With the expansion of accessibility of Hindi e-dictionaries, we may expect that Hindi may develop e-lexicographical connections with other developed global languages like Spanish, French, German, Russian, etc. It therefore seems that the consolidation of Hindi e-lexicographical research and expansion would provide a wider network for information for other languages for different purposes as well as for the other goals.

We aim that the future e-lexicography of Hindi should consider the need of regular upgrades and revision of e-dictionaries. Bergenholtz (2011:52–53) has rightly concluded that if Internet dictionaries, in principle, are not being extended or changed every day, then Internet dictionaries will also degenerate, like printed dictionaries, relatively quickly into a less useful and less reliable tool. The updating should not be done only at the word or entry level but also at the pronunciation, semantic, and sociolinguistic level based on the corpora or recent use. However, some of the Hindi online dictionaries have given the rights to users to update, but sometimes junk material is also included, which hampers the quality of a dictionary.

With regard to access, Hulstijn and Atkins (1998) proposed the 'step-wise-access' for electronic dictionaries. The search filters may include single word match; multiword expression such as phrases, idioms, or phrasal verbs; search in a particular subject; search a subject in particular semantic domain; search in a particular grammatical category; and search in sociolinguistic tag (slang, taboo, formal, colloquial, etc.). We propose the development of search tools for Hindi e-lexicographical products along these lines in near future.

Multimedia is a less exploited aspect in Hindi dictionaries of the Internet era where space is no longer a constraint. To elaborate the headword, multimedia tools like graphics, audio, photos, video, and animation can be utilized. However, graphics (diagram, photographs, and tables) have been used in Hindi printed dictionaries, but the Internet has provided the opportunity to attach audio and video files (for example, different types of ringing; the sound of different musical instruments, animal noises, and bird calls; sounds made by humans, etc.) along with the lexemes.

It has been pointed out that *WordNet* is actually a lexical database rather than a dictionary in the strict sense of the word (Lew 2011). This distinction is not very important for the average user. However, this points out the direction in which Hindi electronic dictionaries may extend their research and databases. We do not know whether *WordNet* has been used as a resource for the extension of Hindi e-lexicography. In any case, for adaptation and expansion of Hindi electronic dictionaries, *WordNet* may provide a great deal of structured data.

Machine translation is an advanced area of research and planning. Only a few languages have machine-readable corpora for machine translation. In the Indian context some work has been done on machine translation with respect to certain languages. We know that Google provides the facility of machine translation from Indian languages like Hindi, Punjabi, Bengali, etc., to English and many other pairs of languages. Tripathi (2012:45–48) has given a detailed discussion about the Hindi machine translation tools developed in India. However, it is not certain whether machine translation is available between Indian languages as source and target languages. In any case we can consider that machine translation may expand in the future and become a very useful resource for data adaptable for Hindi e-lexicography.

We can visualize that Hindi e-lexicography would provide in the future the lexical information available to the users for different situations and different purposes. This requires the individualization of the lexical information in relation to the user needs. In this regard Verlinde (2011) and Lew (2011) have pointed out the importance of bottom-up lexicography and the development of relevant user interface to access the information for a given context in a user-friendly way. Verlinde (2011) has pointed out the direction for future dictionaries in which Hindi electronic dictionaries may move for expanding its research and databases for modelling interactive reading, translation, and writing assistance.

The latest development in e-lexicography has been clearly brought out in the volume edited by Pedro A. Fuertes-Olivera and Henning Bergenholtz (2011). In this volume an article by Leroyer (2011) is significant as it points out the direction for the change of paradigm in e-lexicography. He has pointed out the need for the design and development of functional tools to satisfy human information needs and problems. He highlights the importance of three interrelated sets of social, logical, and semantic parameters for understanding the significance of the dimensions of user, access, and data. This highlights the necessity of integrating the design of databases as understood in information science in the lexicographic process. This is essential for the significance of the individualization of a user's need and construction of robust databases. This further implies that the use of more comprehensive databanks can form the basis of different types of dictionaries as well as different dictionaries of the same type. If we take the emergence of the new paradigm of e-lexicography into account, we do not know whether Hindi e-lexicography can develop along these lines in the near future.

It might appear that we visualize a very high expansion of Hindi e-lexicography. However, we feel that in the context of modern expansion of databases and information sciences e-lexicography in any language cannot make a mark if it does not develop robust databases that are specific, expandable, accessible, and adaptable to different user needs and user situations.

36.5 Conclusion

Hindi in Devanagari script is the official language of the Republic of India. Census of India 2001 reported 422,048,642 speakers of Hindi in India. If we include those people who speak Hindi as a second or third language, Hindi will be the third-most widely spoken language of the world after English and Mandarin. A great deal of support for the use of Hindi in India by the government and various other organizations implies that Hindi has a bright future for further development. However, Hindi is not used as a medium of instruction in higher education, particularly in science and technology and other advanced areas of research. It is because of this constraint that the development of Hindi e-lexicography may be a slow process and may not move in the direction of the new paradigm as we have pointed out in the last section. However, we may expect that linguistic development on the one hand, and the dissemination of information sciences on the other, may provide the basis for the development of a new range of Hindi e-lexicographical works.

Related topics

African lexicography in the Internet era; lexicography and information science; lexicography as an independent science; user participation in the Internet era; electronic dictionaries.

Further reading

Singh, P. (2013). *Hindi Lexicography: Past, Present and Future*. Germany: Lambart Academic Publishing.

The research reported here presents a comprehensive historical account of Hindi lexicography. Along with the status of monolingual, bilingual, and subject dictionaries, it presents a contemporary view of Hindi lexicography with the use of the computer and heralds the era of electronic lexicography.

Tripathi, A. K. (2012). *Bhasha Ke Samkaleen Sandarbh*. Allahabad: Sahitya Sangam.
The book is about the contemporary technological development of Hindi language processing in India. The field of natural language processing, lexicography and databases, machine translation, information retrieval system, computational grammar, and the future of language technology with reference to Hindi in India is focused on in this book.

Notes

1 See at https://en.wikipedia.org/wiki/Nagari_Pracharini_Sabha
2 See at www.cstt.nic.in/index.asp
3 See at www.anukriti.net/tools1.asp
4 See at http://dsal.uchicago.edu/dictionaries/dasa-hindi/
5 See at http://dsal.uchicago.edu/dictionaries/caturvedi/
6 See at http://dsal.uchicago.edu/dictionaries/bahri/
7 See at www.shabdkosh.com/
8 See at http://dict.hinkhoj.com/
9 See at www.cfilt.iitb.ac.in/wordnet/webhwn/wn.php
10 See at www.cfilt.iitb.ac.in/~hdict/webinterface_user/dict_search_user.php
11 See at https://translate.google.co.in/?hl=en&tab=wT)
12 See at www.khandbahale.org/englishhindi.php
13 See at http://hindicube.com/dictionary.aspx
14 See at http://hindi.changathi.com/Dictionary.aspx
15 See at http://bharatavani.in/
16 See at www.lexilogos.com/english/hindi_dictionary.htm
17 See at www.lexicool.com/
18 See at https://hi.wiktionary.org/wiki/मुखपृष्ठ

References

Dictionaries

Adam, M. T. (1829) *Dictionary of Hindee Language*. Calcutta: Schoolbook Society Press.
Bahari, H. (1981) *Learners' Hindi-English Dictionary*. Delhi: Rajpal and Sons.
Chaturvedi, D. P. (1914) *Hindi Shabdarth Parijat*. Allahabad: Ramnarayan Lal.
Chaturvedi, M. and B. N. Tiwari (eds.) (1970) *A Practical Hindi-English Dictionary*. Delhi: National Publishing House.
Das, B. (1891) *Bhagwan Shabd Sagar*. Mahmoodabaad, Sitapur.
Das, S., K. Bhatt, R. Shukla, A. Singh, J. Varma, M. Bhagwandeen and R. Verma. (eds.) (1965) *Hindi Shabd Sagar-II Edition*. Varanasi, Nagari Prachirini Sabha.
Dutt, G. (1901) *Gauri Nagari Kosh*. Meerut: Devanagari Pracharini Sabha.
Johnson, S. (1755) *Dictionary of the English Language*. London.
Lal, M. R. (1873) *Shabdkosh*. Varanasi: Light Press.
Pathak, R. C. (1950) *Bhargava Adarsh Hindi Shabdkosh*. Varanasi: Bhargava Book Depot.
Prasad, K., R. Sahay and Mukundi Lal Shrivastava (eds.) (1950) *Brihat Hindi Kosh*. Varanasi: Gyan Mandal Limited.
Sinha, A. (1937) *Amar-Kosha*. Benaras City: Master Khelarilal & Sons, Sanskrit Book Depot.
Tripathi, S. (1938) *Sridhar Bhasha Kosh. 5th edition*. Lucknow: Navalkishor Press.
Verma, R., B. N. Kapoor, T. Jha, G. Pandey and J. Tripathi. (eds.) (1962) *Maanak Hindi Kosh*. Prayag, Hinidi Sahitya Sammelan.
Verma, R. (1949) *Pramanik Hindi Kosh*. Varanasi: Sahitya Ratnmala Office.
Webster, N. (1828) *American Dictionary of English Language*. Springfield: Merriam-Webster.

Other literature

Bahri, H. (1980) “Hindi Lexicography since Independence and Its Future”, in B. G. Mishra (ed.), *Lexicography in India*. Mysore: Central Institute of Indian Languages, pp. 41–54.

Bergenholtz, H. (2011) “Access to and Presentation of Needs-Adapted Data in Monofunctional Internet Dictionaries”, in P. A. Fuertes-Olivera and H. Bergenholtz (eds.), pp. 30–53.

Bergenholtz, H. and I. Bergenholz (2011) “A Dictionary Is a Tool, a Good Dictionary Is a Monofunctional Tool”, in P. A. Fuertes-Olivera and H. Bergenholtz (eds.), pp. 187–207.

Fuertes-Olivera, P. A., and H. Bergenholtz (eds.) (2011) *e-Lexicography: The Internet, Digital Initiatives and Lexicography*. London and New York: Continuum.

Fuertes-Olivera, P. A., and H. Bergenholtz (2011a) “Introduction: The Construction of Internet Dictionaries”, in P. A. Fuertes-Olivera and H. Bergenholtz (eds.), pp. 1–16.

Granger, S. (2012) “Introduction: Electronic Lexicography-From Challenge to Opportunity”, in S. Granger and M. Paquot (eds.), *Electronic Lexicography*. Oxford: Oxford University Press, pp. 1–11.

Hulstijin, J. H. and B.T.S. Atkins (1998) “Empirical Research on Dictionary Use in Foreign-Language Learning: Survey and Discussion”, in B.T.S. Atkins (ed.), *Using Dictionaries: Studies of Dictionary Use by Language Learners and Translators*. Tubingen, Niemeyer, pp. 7–19.

Leroyer, P. (2011) “Change of Paradigm: From Linguistics to Information Science and from Dictionaries to Lexicographic Information Tools”, in P. A. Fuertes-Olivera and H. Bergenholtz (eds.), pp. 121–140.

Lew, R. (2011) “Online Dictionaries of English”, in P. A. Fuertes-Olivera and H. Bergenholtz (eds.), pp. 230–250.

Miranda, R. (2006) “Indian Lexicography”, in K. Brown (ed.), *Encyclopedia of Language and Linguistics*. 2nd edition. Boston, MA: Elsevier, pp. 614–616.

Quirk, R. (1986) “Opening Remarks”, in R. Ilson (ed.), *Lexicography – An Emerging International Profession*. Manchester: Manchester University Press, pp. 1–6.

Singh, P. (2013). *Hindi Lexicography: Past, Present and Future*. Germany: Lambart Academic Publishing.

Tarp, S. (2011) “Lexicographical and Other e-Tools for Consultation Purposes: Towards the Individualization of Needs Satisfaction”, in P. A. Fuertes-Olivera and H. Bergenholtz (eds.), pp. 54–70.

Tripathi, A. K. and P. Singh (2009) “Computer, Database aur Koshkarita”, *Gaveshna* 93: 47–54.

Verlinde, S. (2011) “Modeling Interactive Reading, Translation and Writing Assistants”, in P. A. Fuertes-Olivera and H. Bergenholtz (eds.), pp. 275–286.

Yugeshwar (1971) *Hindi Kosh Vigyan Ka Udbhav Aur Vikas*. Varanasi: Bharatiya Vidya Prakashan.

37

Indonesian lexicography in the Internet era

Deny Arnos Kwary

37.1 Introduction

The Indonesian language, also called Bahasa Indonesia, lacks much of a presence on the Internet. The report made by the World Wide Web Technology Survey[1] shows that the percentage of websites using the Indonesian language is only 0.5 percent. On the other hand, the population of Indonesia is approximately 3.5 percent of the population of the world.[2] The comparison of those percentages (i.e. 0.5 percent against 3.5 percent) confirms that the Indonesian language is indeed underrepresented on the Internet.

The condition is even more severe for the Indonesian lexicography as there are very few Indonesian language dictionaries available on the World Wide Web. Several websites provide Indonesian monolingual dictionaries, but the dictionaries are actually only taken from a single source, that is, *Kamus Besar Bahasa Indonesia* (KBBI), which was created by Badan Pengembangan dan Pembinaan Bahasa (*the National Language Body*).[3] For bilingual dictionaries, particularly those covering Indonesian and English, there are some more sources, publishers and websites.

This chapter aims at describing and analysing the issues related to Indonesian lexicography in the era of the Internet. The Indonesian lexicography in this chapter refers to the lexicography of the Indonesian language, as the national language of the Republic of Indonesia. The discussion does not include the local languages which are used by Indonesian people. After this introductory section, the second section presents the historical perspectives on Indonesian lexicography, starting from the creation of the first word list until the launching of the online version of the fifth edition of the Indonesian comprehensive dictionary (*Kamus Besar Bahasa Indonesia – KBBI*). The third section analyses the core issues in the development of Indonesian lexicography, including the issues on dictionary awareness, standardization, corpora, and technology. The fourth section offers some perspectives and ideas for the development of Indonesian lexicography in the future. This section also contains the description of the new projects on Indonesian lexicography, that is, the fifth edition of *KBBI*, the *Indonesian Advanced Learner Dictionary*, the *Indonesian National Corpus*, and the *Oxford Indonesian Living Dictionary*. The last section of this paper is the conclusion of the discussions presented in the previous sections.

37.2 Historical perspectives

Because the Indonesian language originates from the Malay language, the discussion on the historical perspectives of Indonesian lexicography starts from the dictionaries that include Malay language. The lexicography work in Indonesia was started in the early fifteenth century with a Chinese-Malay word list. The wordlist contains 500 entries, but it is not clear who the author or the lexicographer is. In 1522, an Italian scholar and explorer called Antonio Pigafetta made an Italian-Malay word list which contains 426 entries (Collins 1998).

The Indonesian monolingual dictionary was started in the nineteenth century. The first Indonesian dictionary was entitled the *Kitab Pengetahuan Bahasa iaitu Kamus Loghat Melayu-Johor-Pahang-Riau-Lingga, penggal yang pertama* (A Book of Language Knowledge, that is a Dictionary of the Malay Dialect of Johor-Pahang-Riau-Lingga, part one) by Raja Ali Haji from Riau (a city in Sumatra island of Indonesia). The cover of this dictionary states that it was published in the Arabic year of 1345 Hijriah (which was the year 1928 A.D.) by Al-Ahmadiah Press, Singapore. However, this dictionary may have existed before its formal publication year, because the author actually lived in the first half of the nineteenth century (i.e. 1808–1873). Therefore, it can be assumed that the content of the dictionary was already in circulation during the nineteenth century. The year 1928 written on the cover of the dictionary could be due to the fact that the Indonesian language was first mentioned as the language of national unity in that year. On 28 October 1928, a group of Indonesian youth took an oath that made the Indonesian language as a national language.

The work on Indonesian monolingual dictionaries continued after Indonesia proclaimed its independence. Nevertheless, the lexicography work did not start immediately after Indonesia's independence in 1945, because there were still battles in some areas in Indonesia several years after the independence was proclaimed. The first comprehensive Indonesian dictionary is *Kamus Umum Bahasa Indonesia* (General Dictionary of Indonesian). It was published in 1957. The author was W.J.S. Poerwadarminta, who worked at the lexicography unit at the University of Indonesia. This dictionary became the main reference for the Indonesian language for more than thirty years (before it was replaced by KBBI in 1988).

In 1974, *Pusat Pengembangan dan Pembinaan Bahasa* (which changed its name into *Badan Pengembangan dan Pembinaan Bahasa* or *Badan Bahasa* for short, since 2010) was established, based on the presidential decree numbers 44 and 45. The first Indonesian monolingual dictionary made by *Badan Bahasa* is *Kamus Besar Bahasa Indonesia* (KBBI). The dictionary was launched on 28 October 1988 at the Fifth Indonesian National Language Congress. The driving force behind this dictionary is Anton M. Moeliono, a professor from the University of Indonesia and the head of *Badan Bahasa*. In its first edition, this dictionary contained 62,100 entries. This number is relatively small if compared with the number of entries in other big language dictionaries. However, it was already the most comprehensive Indonesian dictionary at that time. The second until the fourth editions also carry the name of the head of *Badan Bahasa* as the chief editor. The second edition of this dictionary appeared in 1993. The chief editor was Harimurti Kridalaksana, and the dictionary contained approximately 72,000 entries. The third edition, with approximately 78,000 entries, appeared in 1998, and the chief editor was Hasan Alwi (1998). The fourth edition, where the chief editor was Dendy Sugono, was published in 2008, and it contains approximately 90,000 entries. In the fifth edition, the dictionary mentions the head of *Badan Bahasa* as the Person-in-Charge of the dictionary, but the chief editor is the head of the language development department, whose team members are the lexicographers of the dictionary. This fifth edition was launched on 28 October 2016, and it contains approximately 110,000 entries.

37.3 Core issues and topics

The Indonesian lexicography is largely prescriptive in nature. This can be due to the fact that most Indonesian people are actually not native speakers of the Indonesian language. Indonesia is an archipelago and it comprises hundreds of ethnic groups. Each ethnic group has its own language or local language. These local languages are usually the native languages of the people. Alwi et al. (1998) state that the number of Indonesian L1 speakers is smaller than that of local languages, such as Javanese and Sundanese. Consequently, the government, under its unit called *Badan Bahasa*, creates regulations concerning the use of Indonesian language. The prescriptive approach is implemented to ensure that the Indonesian language, as the national language of Indonesia, is used widely and correctly all over Indonesia (see Chapter 10 of this *Handbook*).

With the prescriptive nature of the Indonesian language implementation, there is only one Indonesian language dictionary that becomes the reference for the people. Currently, the *KBBI* fourth edition (2008) is the main reference to check the standard spellings and definitions of Indonesian words. The big size of this dictionary (*KBBI* fourth edition is only available in printed form, while the online version of *KBBI* fifth edition has just been launched when this chapter is written) and the fact that it is prescriptive in nature are probably the reason for the low awareness of dictionary use in Indonesia. Very few people have the *KBBI* fourth edition. Based on the writer's experience in teaching linguistics in Indonesian universities, less than 10 percent of the lecturers have the *KBBI*, and the percentage is even a lot lower for the students.

Although the Internet era has started some time ago, the presence of Indonesian lexicography on the web is very scant. For the past few years, we can actually find several websites that provide *KBBI*, but they are all based on the third edition of KBBI, and most of them are somehow illegal, because they do not obtain formal permission from *Badan Bahasa* to publish the dictionary. The fourth edition of *KBBI* has been published in printed form since 2008. However, the official online version of this dictionary has just been launched on 26 July 2016.[4] That website still uses the extension .com, which does not show that it belongs to the government. This is because *Badan Bahasa* was not planning to keep that website for a long time. It was a kind of beta version or pilot project for the launch of the fifth edition of KBBI. The online version of the fifth edition of KBBI was launched on 28 October 2016, which was at the same time as the celebration of the Youth Pledge day and the language month in Indonesia. The website of the fifth edition of KBBI[5] uses the extension. go.id which signifies that it is a government unit. A further explanation of the fifth edition of KBBI is given in the next section.

Badan Bahasa and its provincial level units have produced 83 local language dictionaries and several Indonesian language dictionaries, but only a few of them are available online. In addition to *KBBI* fourth edition and fifth edition, there is only an online glossary.[6] This glossary is also the only dictionary that is available in a CD form, so it can be installed in a computer and accessed offline. The rest of the dictionaries are only available in printed form.

Given the fact that the main and sole reference for a general language dictionary is *KBBI*, Indonesian scholars and universities that have research interest in or units related to lexicography usually work on specialized dictionaries, bilingual dictionaries, and local language dictionaries. For example, Gadjah Mada University has three bilingual dictionaries.[7] The dictionaries are Indonesian-English, Indonesian-Dutch, and Indonesian-Javanese dictionaries.

With the wave of corpus linguistics approach entering Indonesian academic work in 2010s, the work towards the creation of Indonesian corpus has started to be heard in several seminars and conferences. The initial work was actually started over a decade earlier by Muhadjir and his colleagues from the University of Indonesia. They collected 52 editions of the Kompas newspaper, in which each edition corresponded to one day in each of the weeks in the year 1994. The size of the corpus was only 2,200,818 word tokens. The result of their study was published in the book entitled *Frekuensi Kosakata Bahasa Indonesia* in 1996.

The first big corpus of the Indonesian language, with approximately 100 million running words, was created by Kilgarriff et al. (2010). This corpus can be accessed from the Sketch Engine website.[8] A bigger Indonesian corpus is available in the Leipzig Corpora Collection.[9] This corpus initially contains approximately 100 million words (Quasthoff, and Goldhahn and Heyer 2013). The corpus was developed further until 2014 from the following sources:

- newspaper texts collected from the Internet between 2007 and 2014 (approximately 17.0 million sentences);
- texts from the Indonesian edition of Wikipedia as it appeared between 2007 and 2012 (approximately 0.7 million sentences);
- randomly selected Internet texts gathered between 2007 and 2013 (approximately 66.3 million sentences).

After data pre-processing (which includes taking out duplicate crawling of non-changing web pages), the underlying corpus contains approximately 1.2 billion running words (among these are about 6.6 million different word forms). A word form was included in the *Indonesian Frequency Dictionary* (IFD) if it occurred at least 5 times in the sources. This corpus is the basis of the publication called *Indonesian Frequency Dictionary* by Kwary, Goldhahn, and Quasthoff (2015). The word dictionary used in the title of this publication does not mean that it is a dictionary proper. The word dictionary in this case actually refers to a database of words.

The two big corpora mentioned earlier (i.e. those available at the Sketch Engine and Leipzig Corpora Collection) have been used as the basis to create the first high-frequency list of the Indonesian language (Kwary 2013). The first base list consists of 500 word families. This base list is embedded in a modified AntWordProfiler software, which was originally created by Laurence Anthony from Waseda University. The modified version that can be used to check the profile of an Indonesian text is called AWP-IWL (Indonesian Word List) and is available online.[10] This first base list, with only 500 word families, is smaller than a similar word list in the English language, i.e. the General Service List (West 1953), which consists of 2,000 word families. However, several analyses on general texts show that this first base list already covers more than 60 percent of the words in the general texts. Further, work on the creation of a second base list and an academic word list needs to be done, so that the vocabulary profile of Indonesian texts can be produced more comprehensively.

The work towards a corpus-based dictionary was started in Indonesia in 2012, when *Badan Bahasa* initiated the project on *Kamus Pemelajar Bahasa Indonesia* (KPBI – 'Indonesian Advanced Learner Dictionary'). This dictionary was compiled using a home-made small corpus compiled from the books used in the BIPA (*Bahasa Indonesia untuk Penutur Asing* ['Indonesian language for foreign speakers']) programs in Indonesia. In addition, the Indonesian corpus available in the Leipzig Corpora Collection[11] was also consulted during the dictionary making process. This first corpus-based dictionary of the Indonesian language is scheduled to be published in 2017.

Another important development in the lexicography work in Indonesia is the attention to the needs of the users. In the past, dictionaries were created based on the needs of the projects or the lexicographers. In recent decades, more and more Indonesian lexicographers have realized the need to adapt the dictionaries to the needs of the users. One example of a scientific discussion on dictionary user needs is in the PhD thesis presented by Dora Amalia at the University of Indonesia in 2014. She conducted research on *Definition formulation and verbal entry models in a monolingual Indonesian learner's dictionary* using the modern theory of lexicographical functions (Tarp 2008). Dora Amalia was then elected as the head of the development department (i.e. the department that develops lexicography products) at *Badan Bahasa* in the last quarter of 2015.

On 26–28 July 2016, the lexicography unit of *Badan Bahasa* held the first national seminar on lexicography. The seminar is attended by well-selected presenters and participants. On the last day of the seminar, everyone agreed that there should be a lexicography association in Indonesia to assist in the development of lexicography of Indonesian and local languages. Consequently, an association called PERKAMUSI (*Perkumpulan Pekamus Seluruh Indonesia* 'association of lexicographers from all over Indonesia') was created.

37.4 Looking to the future

With the establishment of the Indonesian lexicography association and the increase of the interest of *Badan Bahasa* in modern lexicography theory and practice, we can expect a bright future for lexicography work in Indonesia. The projects which were running when this chapter was written were the fifth edition of *KBBI*, the *Indonesian Advanced Learner Dictionary*, the *Indonesian National Corpus*, and the *Oxford Indonesian Living Dictionary*.

The fifth edition of *KBBI* (henceforth KBBI5) is the first edition of KBBI which was published online first before its printed form. The online version of this dictionary was launched on 28 October 2016, but its printed form has not been available. The printed version is scheduled to be launched early 2017. There are two access options to the website of KBBI5. For users who do not or have not registered to the website, the access option is very limited (see Figure 37.1).

Figure 37.1 Screenshot of KBBI5 for non-registered users

As shown in Figure 37.1, the search function for general access, that is, non-registered users, is very limited. The users can only search the entries from the headwords by typing the words in the text box. For more functionalities, the users need to register by clicking "Daftar Baru" on the upper-right area. The registration is free of charge, and the required data are only a name and an email address. Registered users can see more functionalities, as shown in Figure 37.2.

As we can see in Figure 37.2, there are various options to search for entries in the dictionary. In addition to searching using a headword, we can search by alphabets, type of words (*Jenis*), register (*Ragam*), word class (*Kelas Kata*), field of study (*Bidang*), and source of language (*Bahasa*). We can also see the latest search (*Pencarian Terbaru Anda*) and most popular entries (*Terpopuler*). These options, however, do not necessarily relate to the needs of the users, particularly if we focus on the receptive and productive needs of the dictionary users. Consequently, further development, based on a more solid lexicographical theory, is needed to improve the function of this newly launched online dictionary.

In addition to KBBI5, *Badan Bahasa* has also planned to publish *Kamus Pemelajar Bahasa Indonesia* (KPBI – 'Indonesian Advanced Learner Dictionary') which is based on a modern lexicography theory and a corpus. The corpus was created in 2012, but the size is very small, and it is only based on textbooks and learning materials used at institutions that offer BIPA (*Bahasa Indonesian bagi Penutur Asing* 'Indonesian language for foreigners') courses. This dictionary is planned to be published in 2017. The features of this dictionary

Figure 37.2 Screenshot of KBBI5 for registered users

largely follow the features found in English learner dictionaries and focus on the needs of the users. The primary users are non-Indonesian people who want to learn or are learning the Indonesian language.

As mentioned in the previous section, there are actually already two big corpora of the Indonesian language. However, the samples are rather skewed because they are only taken from websites. Therefore, they do not really reflect the general use of the Indonesian language. The work on corpus lexicography was started at *Badan Bahasa* in a very small scale in 2012. Realizing the important role of a corpus in lexicography, particularly in pedagogical lexicography, *Badan Bahasa* initiated a new and bigger corpus project in August 2016, and it is expected to be completed by 2018. This new corpus project called *Korpus Indonesia* is planned to contain approximately 100 million words from well-selected sources using purposive sampling technique. Following the ratio used in the *British National Corpus*, the Indonesian corpus will contain 10 percent of transcribed spoken text and 90 percent written text. In the first phase, in 2016, the corpus will be derived from academic written texts, i.e. theses, dissertations, and academic journal articles, taken from a number of disciplines to ensure that each discipline is included in the corpus. The size of this academic text corpus is approximately 5 million words. This corpus will be made available online, so that it can be accessed by anyone who wants to know or conduct research on the Indonesian language. The corpus will also be useful for lexicographers to make corpus-based dictionaries.

In addition to the two projects explained above, *Badan Bahasa* has also started delivering modern lexicography workshops all over Indonesia. There were two workshops held in 2016 in two different locations. One was held in Medan (Sumatra island), a city in the western area of Indonesia, and the workshop was attended by language enthusiasts, mostly linguists, from several cities in the western area of Indonesia. The other one was held in Makassar (Sulawesi island), a city in the eastern area of Indonesia, and the workshop was attended by language enthusiasts from several cities in the eastern area of Indonesia. *Badan Bahasa* is planning to hold more lexicographer workshops in the future, so we can expect more lexicography products produced by Indonesian lexicographers. Since the workshop includes the creation of online dictionaries, we can also expect that Indonesian lexicography will have a wider existence in the era of the Internet.

In 2016, the work on establishing the existence of Indonesian lexicography in the era of the Internet was also done by Oxford University Press of the University of Oxford with its Oxford Indonesian Living Dictionary, which is a part of the project called *Oxford Global Languages* (OGL). The OGL Project was launched in 2015 with the aim of building lexicographical resources for 100 of the world's languages, especially the languages which are both global and digitally under-represented. The project is expected to transform the experience of millions of people worldwide by making content in their language available in digital form, on websites, in apps, and in many different tools and services.[12]. The first two languages included in the project were isiZulu and Northern Sotho (see Chapter 30 of this *Handbook*). Then, in 2016, the Indonesian language was also included. It was launched in June 2016,[13] a project called Oxford Indonesian Living Dictionary, which means that the dictionary is updated over time and includes the participation of all people who know and have an interest in developing the existence of the Indonesian language in the World Wide Web. The dictionary started with a small number of entries, approximately 10,000 entries, but we can expect it to be a lot bigger in the next few years, because a large number of users add new entries, and it is managed well by Oxford University Press.

37.5 Conclusion

Readers of this chapter may be surprised by the lack of online lexicographic resources related to the Indonesian language. The author of this chapter, however, is more optimistic: public, personal, and institutional initiatives are working very hard with the aim of developing online lexicographic resources for the Indonesian people.

The Indonesian government is putting money and effort toward creating a national corpus which can be used to design and create modern online dictionaries similar to those already available for English, which is being used as a model for Indonesian lexicographic resources. Individual lexicographers are already very active in lexicographic conferences and workshops, especially those analysing which innovations and methodologies can also be used to, first, create online dictionaries and, second, improve their quality, for example, by accepting that today's lexicography is basically concerned with satisfying users' needs in different use situations. For instance, groups of lexicographers, experts in the domain and IT specialists are following Fuertes-Olivera and Tarp's (2014) methodology with the aim of producing specialised online dictionaries in around three or four years and at a reasonable cost. Finally, institutions such as the University of Oxford have launched altruistic initiatives which will clearly benefit lesser resource languages.

Within the previously mentioned positive framework, this author hopes that the development of dictionaries goes hand in hand with theoretical analyses, especially those that place more emphasis on e-lexicography: (a) the role of corpora in Indonesian lexicography; (b) the creation of online dictionary typologies; (c) a better understanding of search capabilities, especially those connected with the 'niceties' of the Indonesian language, which may impede the use of search engines and systems created for western languages; (d) an analysis of presentations and access, especially 'ad-hoc presentations' such as those discussed in Fuertes-Olivera and Tarp's (2014) description of the *Accounting Dictionaries* (see Chapter 28 of this *Handbook*); and (e) the inclusion of multimedia, for example, the inclusion of images in a reception dictionary. These and similar issues will dominate the future of Indonesian lexicography in the era of the Internet in the near future.

Related topics

African lexicography in the Internet era; dictionary management; dictionaries and access; lexicography and corpus linguistics; specialised dictionaries; English lexicography in the Internet era.

Notes

1 See at www.w3techs.com (retrieved on 11 August 2016)
2 See at www.worldometers.info (retrieved on 11 August 2016)
3 See at www.kamusbesar.com/ and http://kbbi.web.id
4 See at http://kbbi4.portalbahasa.com
5 See at http://kbbi.kemdikbud.go.id
6 See at http://badanbahasa.kemdikbud.go.id/glosarium
7 See at http://kamus.ugm.ac.id
8 See at www.sketchengine.co.uk
9 See at http://corpora.informatik.uni-leipzig.de
10 See at http://kwary.net/iwl.html
11 See at http://corpora.uni-leipzig.de
12 See at https://id.oxforddictionaries.com/explore/tentang
13 See at https://id.oxforddictionaries.com

Further reading

Amalia, D. (2014). *Formulasi pendefinisian dan model pengentrian verba dalam kamus pemelajar Bahasa Indonesia.* Unpublished PhD Thesis. Jakarta: Universitas Indonesia.
In this PhD thesis, the author implements the Function Theory of Lexicography in creating the concept for a monolingual Indonesian learner's dictionary. This publication has also become one of the main references for the lexicography work in Indonesia.

Fuertes-Olivera, P. A. and H. Bergenholtz (eds.) (2011). *e-Lexicography: The Internet, Digital Initiatives and Lexicography.* London: Continuum.
In this book, various authors discuss the transition from the printed to the digital media and show how new technologies are transforming lexicography. It also contains many comments on the relationship between lexicography and information science.

Fuertes-Olivera, P. A. and S. Tarp. (2014). *Theory and Practice of Specialised Online Dictionaries: Lexicography versus Terminography.* Berlin: de Gruyter.
In this volume, the authors update their Function Theory of Lexicography for high-quality specialized online dictionaries in the Web 2.0 environment.

Kwary, D. A. (2012). "Adaptive Hypermedia and User-Oriented Data for Online Dictionaries: A Case Study on an English Dictionary of Finance for Indonesian Students", *International Journal of Lexicography* 25(1): 30–49.
In this article, the author combines the Function Theory of Lexicography and the concept of adaptive hypermedia in making a proposal for a future bilingual dictionary, particularly the one involving the Indonesian language.

References

Alwi, H., S. Dardjowidjojo, H. Lapoliwa, and A. M. Moeliono. (1998). *Tata Bahasa Bahasa Indonesia.* 3rd edition. Jakarta: Balai Pustaka.

Amalia, D. (2014). *Formulasi pendefinisian dan model pengentrian verba dalam kamus pemelajar Bahasa Indonesia.* Unpublished PhD Thesis. Jakarta: Universitas Indonesia.

Collins, J. T. (1998). *Malay, World Language: A Short History.* Kuala Lumpur: Dewan Bahasa dan Pustaka.

Fuertes-Olivera, P. A. and H. Bergenholtz (eds.) (2011). *e-Lexicography: The Internet, Digital Initiatives and Lexicography.* London: Continuum.

Fuertes-Olivera, P. A. and S. Tarp. (2014). *Theory and Practice of Specialised Online Dictionaries: Lexicography Versus Terminography.* Berlin and Boston: Walter de Gruyter.

Kilgarriff, A., S. Reddy, J. Pomikálek and P.V.S. Avinesh. (2010). "A Corpus Factory for Many Languages", in *The Seventh International Conference on Language Resources and Evaluation (LREC).* Malta: ELRA, pp. 904–910.

Kwary, D. A. (2012). "Adaptive Hypermedia and User-Oriented Data for Online Dictionaries: A Case Study on an English Dictionary of Finance for Indonesian Students", *International Journal of Lexicography* 25(1): 30–49.

Kwary, D. (2013). "Creating and Testing the Indonesian High Frequency Word List", *Konferensi Linguistik Tahunan Atma Jaya* (KOLITA). Jakarta: Unika Atma Jaya.

Kwary, D. A., D. Goldhahn and U. Quasthoff. (2015). *Frequency Dictionary Indonesian – Kamus Frekuensi Bahasa Indonesia.* Leipzig: Leipziger Universitätsverlag.

Quasthoff, U., D. Goldhahn and G. Heyer. (2013). *Technical Report Series on Corpus Building.* Leipzig: University of Leipzig.

Tarp, S. (2008). *Lexicography in the Borderland Between Knowledge and Non-Knowledge: General Lexicographical Theory With Particular Focus on Learner's Lexicography.* Tübingen: Niemeyer.

West, M. (1953). *A General Service List of English Words.* London: Longman.

38

Portuguese lexicography in the Internet era

Teresa Lino

38.1 Introduction

This chapter focuses on the Portuguese dictionaries that have been produced in the past two decades. These dictionaries have resulted from the evolution of research in the field of lexicography, terminology, and dictionary making in the Portuguese context. A dictionary is both an important cultural object for the public in general and an essential working tool for translators and those who teach native, second, and foreign languages (see Chapters 11, 18, and 19 of this *Handbook*).

The Portuguese language has grown considerably mostly due to certain international institutions, such as CPLP (Community of Portuguese Language Countries), IILP (International Portuguese Language Institute), and the European Union's translation services. Portuguese is striving to obtain an international status in several institutions, such as the World Health Organization and the UN Security Council, among others.

Simultaneously, the new countries where Portuguese is the official language follow the European – or Portuguese – standard and represent a large number of speakers. On the other hand, there is a growing interest in the teaching/learning of Portuguese in several African and Asian countries, particularly in Mainland China and Macau (Wang 2016).

Due to this new status acquired by Portuguese, there is also a growing need for new monolingual and bilingual dictionaries. Therefore, we shall look into general and specialized or terminological dictionaries – not only paper-based but also digital and/or online products. These contemporary Portuguese dictionaries have been produced by institutions such as the Academia das Ciências de Lisboa [Sciences Academy of Lisbon], or in collaboration between public institutions and university research centres or publishing houses that are aware of the needs of the different audiences.

38.2 Historical perspectives

The history of lexicography in Portugal went through many stages similarly to what happened in other European countries. Those stages were influenced by several cultural and social movements: 1) the pre-lexicographic stage of Medieval bilingual glossaries; 2) the period between the 16th and the 17th centuries, when the printing press was created, a new type of book – the dictionary – emerged, the first *thesaurus* was written, and finally, at the end of the seventeenth century, academies were created in some countries and made the first dictionaries; 3) in the eighteenth century, the first monolingual dictionary for Portuguese was published; 4) the nineteenth century and the beginning of the twentieth century; and 5) the end of the twentieth century and beginning of the twenty-first century, when lexicography dived into the age of the Internet.

These stages often reflect an attitude towards language(s) and a reflection on language(s) itself: the dictionary has been a cultural object ever since it was created, and has strived to define the lexical corpus of a language with a descriptive, didactic, and sometimes normalizing perspective.

Thus, the pre-lexicographic stage saw the creation of bilingual glossaries in the Middle Ages. Building on the experience of those bilingual glossaries and vocabularies written in monastic schools – particularly in the Monastery of Alcobaça – Portuguese lexicography developed in the context of humanistic Renaissance.

The Portuguese lexicographic genealogy of the 16th and 17th centuries closely followed the works of the great lexicographers of the Renaissance, particularly those by Nebrija (1492), the dictionary by Ambrogio Calepino (1502), and the *Thesaurus Linguae Latinae by* Robert Estienne (1531). We would also like to stress the influence of the *Vocabolario della Crusca* (1691) and the *Dictionnaire de l'Académie Françoise* (1694) for French, Spanish, and Portuguese lexicography.

The bilingual dictionary *Dictionarium ex Lusitanico in Latinum Sermonem* published by the first Portuguese lexicographer, Jerónimo Cardoso, in 1592 (Cardoso 1551), marked the beginning of the inclusion of the lexical corpus of Portuguese in a dictionary, establishing the lexicon and spelling of the language, which had been formed throughout the Middle Ages. This work was followed by several other dictionaries: some of which were aimed at a scientific audience that included a large number of scientific terms (medicine, pharmacology, botany, navy, astronomy, among others). At the same time, academic dictionaries were emerging with a pedagogical and learning approach aimed at a school audience. These types of dictionaries accompanied teaching activities in the Renaissance, which had a strong concern for higher education studies and the extension of schooling to a larger number of social strata. In 1647, in the scope of lexicographic production that was being carried out by the Jesuits (University of Évora), Bento Pereira published the *Thesaurus of the Portuguese Language* (Pereira 1647), aimed at establishing the lexicon (Verdelho 2007).

After this period, there was another important stage in the second half of the eighteenth century. It was then that Portuguese monolingual lexicography took root with two major works: the *Diccionario da Língua Portugueza* by Morais Silva, published in 1789; and the *Dicionário da Real Academia das Ciências de Lisboa*, published in 1793.

The nineteenth century witnessed the publication of several dictionaries: *Diccionario Contemporaneo da Língua Portugueza* (1881) by Caldas Aulete, *Novo Dicionario da Lingua Portugueza* (1899) by Cândido de Figueiredo, and *Dicionario Geral e Analógico* (1948) by Artur Bivar.

In the twentieth century, Porto Editora, a publishing house, published the paper-based *Dicionário da Língua Portuguesa* in 1952 with subsequent new editions in the following years. And in 1994, that dictionary was published in a digital format (CD) for the first time.

In this period, another lexicographic product was presented: the *Dicionário do Português Básico* (1991) by Mário Vilela. This dictionary had around 3,060 entries, but its microstructure had a lexicographic definition that encompassed three perspectives: lexical, semantic, and grammatical. Sometimes the author resorted to images to help describing or suggesting with humour a real situation in a situational context.

At the beginning of the twenty-first century, institutional lexicography, represented by the Academia das Ciências de Lisboa, published the *Dicionário da Língua Portuguesa Contemporânea*, whose macrostructure is composed of 70,000 entries that cover the lexicon of the 19th and 20th centuries. It includes not only general lexicon, but also the most frequent popularized terms from various scientific and technical fields. This macrostructure also includes a significant number of recent neologisms including foreign words, many of them English words that originated in the sciences and technologies. We would like to highlight that this is a paper-based dictionary aimed at a very wide audience: the public in general, educators, translators, writers, journalists, secondary school pupils, university students, foreign language students, and second-language students. This dictionary is mostly descriptive but has a standardizing perspective and the ambition of being known as a reference for European Portuguese. However, its nomenclature includes Brazilian, African, and Asian words. It also includes word-formation elements (prefixes, suffixes, and other word parts). The microstructure of this dictionary is characterized by presenting a definition based on periphrasis or inclusion, and resorting to heteronyms or words that designate the genus or class; it is a definition that shows the polysemy of the entry by presenting its several meanings. However, some definitions have an encyclopaedic character. Frequently, there are examples and quotes from contemporary authors of the 19th and 20th centuries. These quotes were extracted from the *Corpus de Referência do Português Contemporâneo*. This dictionary does not have a digital version. However, the Academia das Ciências de Lisboa has recently started working on a new edition of this dictionary, which up until now has been a work of reference for the whole Portuguese-speaking world.

Following the publication of the *Dicionário da Língua Portuguesa Contemporânea* by the Academia das Ciências de Lisboa, in that same year of 2001, the *Dicionário Houaiss da Língua Portuguesa* (2001), originally a Brazilian Portuguese dictionary, was published after being adapted to the European standard, with over 200,000 entries. The aim of that work is to approximate the lexical component of both the European (Portuguese) and the Brazilian standards. This dictionary presents the date and source of each entry; it also intends to present lexical diversity from a comparative perspective. Therefore, this dictionary tries to appeal to a vast audience in the whole of the Portuguese-speaking world. However, it does not have a digital version for the European standard.

Following the signing of the spelling agreement established between the eight countries that composed the CPLP (Community of Portuguese Language Countries), two dictionary products appeared that, from the point of view of their nomenclature, complement the *Dicionário da Língua Portuguesa Contemporânea* by the Academia das Ciências de Lisboa and the *Dicionário Houaiss da Língua Portuguesa*. In 2009, Porto Editora published the *Vocabulário Ortográfico da Língua Portuguesa* by J. Malaca Casteleiro. The aim of this work is to contribute towards the creation of a spelling vocabulary for the European standard with a nomenclature of 180,000 lemmas; 5,000 Brazilian, African, and Asian words; 800 Galician lexical units; 12,500 anthroponyms; 8,500 toponyms; 2,000 foreign words; and 2,500 word-formation elements.

In 2012, the Academia das Ciências de Lisboa published the *Vocabulário Ortográfico Atualizado da Língua Portuguesa*, whose nomenclature counts 70,000 entries, a small part of which is comprised of integrated foreign words. Some English words present morphosyntactic adaptations that are sometimes debatable. This *Vocabulário* has a complement composed of around 300 foreign words that have mostly kept their original spelling.

More recently, in 2014, Lidel published the *Dicionário Global da Língua Portuguesa* by Jaime Coelho. This is a paper-based dictionary with a pedagogical perspective, whose target audience are foreign students that study Portuguese as a foreign language, Portuguese as a non-native language, and Portuguese as a second language. This dictionary has around 55,000 entries. Its microstructure is composed of the meanings of the entry that are accompanied by contexts that actualize the entry. This microstructure is completed by information on phonology, morphology, and syntax of European Portuguese.

38.3 Core issues and topics

Portuguese e-lexicography started in the last years of the twentieth century. This has produced two main developments, in line with what has happened in similar national lexicographies, e.g. Spanish and French lexicographies (see Chapters 34 and 40 of this *Handbook*). First, the concept of 'dictionary' has changed. Second, existing dictionary typologies are blurred. Both developments permeate the following paragraphs, which are concerned with two specific analysis: (a) reconceptualization of the dictionary, that is, a new definition of what a dictionary is; and (b) a description of some Portuguese general language dictionaries.

38.3.1 Reconceptualization of the dictionary

With the turn of the century, we truly saw a change in the concept of dictionary: Jean Pruvost (2000) speaks about the reconceptualization of the dictionary. The concept of dictionary has been changing over the centuries, but particularly more so in these past few years thanks to the new information and telematics technologies that have enabled hypertext search. Many dictionaries are now published only in a digital format or are accessed over the Internet and aimed at different audiences. There are machine-readable dictionaries, accessed via computers or mobile phones (*computational lexicons*, *phonological lexicons*).

The new information technologies in general, and hypertext searches in particular, allow for the creation of relationships within the dictionary itself. We can create conceptual, semantic, and/or morphological networks. We can associate text and image corpora with several functions. Thus, the users may obtain and build their own data and information set, which would be impossible in a traditional dictionary. The student may build a network of relationships that will facilitate the learning process.

Lexicography usually makes a distinction between *computer dictionary*, i.e. online dictionaries or e-dictionaries, and *electronic dictionary*. A computer dictionary is the digital version of a paper-based dictionary, whereas an electronic dictionary corresponds to a product that was created to be read by a computer in the scope of the automatic treatment of language.

However, the metamorphosis of the dictionary was not limited to the underlying technology: the dictionary is no longer conceived as a book with two columns. Its evolution has mostly depended on a shift in perspective. The dictionary now tries to maintain a dialogue with its users, adapting to the demands and necessities of a mostly young audience of professionals and translators, as well as those involved in the teaching/learning process.

Thus, the online dictionary is accessed via the technological resources of the Internet. Computer dictionaries intend to provide information that corresponds to the requests made by their users with the utmost clarity, flexibility, and efficiency. These dictionaries work on the basis of a constant dialogue with their users, opening up the path to interactive dictionaries.

38.3.2 General language dictionaries in the Internet era

Following this new concern of creating new models for new audiences, Porto Editora published an online dictionary – *Dicionário da Língua Portuguesa* – targeted at the general public, with around 80,000 entries. The digital stage was thus jumpstarted with new products such as *Infopedia.pt* (a database that contains educational and cultural content in Portuguese) and *Diciopédia* (a multimedia product launched in 1997 and updated every year), which are examples of the work developed by Porto Editora towards the creation of digital products.

The *Dicionário da Língua Portuguesa* (both the paper-based version and several types of digital formats) compiles a vast general vocabulary and is augmented with neologisms that are currently used, as well as popularized terms from information technologies and developing scientific and technical areas. Presently, this publishing house has evolved towards the new web technologies and presented 22 online dictionaries (a monolingual one and several bilingual ones) and 10 integrated dictionaries (a monolingual one and several bilingual ones) in an app available in the App Store, which constitute powerful working tools and an indispensable study aid for young people who can access it with their iPhone, iPod touch, and iPad.

The *Dicionário Priberam da Língua Portuguesa* (*DPLP*) is a contemporary Portuguese dictionary that contains over 110,000 lexical entries, including fixed expressions and phraseologies, whose nomenclature includes general vocabulary, as well as the most common terms from the main scientific and technical areas. This dictionary provides synonyms and antonyms for each meaning and it also allows for verbal conjugation. We can also look up information on the origin and pronunciation of some words. The *DPLP* allows for searches according to the European Portuguese standard or the Brazilian one, with or without the spelling changes introduced by the Spelling Agreement of 1990. The current version of DPLP was adapted to the new web technologies and reshaped to facilitate access from any type of device: desktop computer, tablet, or mobile phone.

Both these dictionaries have had a significant evolution in terms of updating their nomenclature, which has been supplemented with currently used neologisms, as well as new ones that have resulted from the popularization of terms used in the sciences and technologies. We would also like to stress that both Porto Editora and Priberam have tried to adopt the new web technologies, which implied the adaptation of the dictionary content.

38.4 Looking to the future

The future of Portuguese e-lexicography will be similar to the one already discussed in other chapters of this part of the *Handbook*. Topics such as the following will be in the forefront of lexicographic debates in Portuguese-speaking countries: (a) the role of corpora in Portuguese lexicography; (b) the creation of online dictionary typologies; (c) a better understanding of search capabilities, especially those connected with the 'niceties' of the Portuguese language, for example, significant pronunciation differences among language varieties; (d) an analysis of presentations and access, especially 'ad-hoc presentations' and the quest for individualization; and (e) the inclusion of multimedia, for example, the inclusion of images in a reception dictionary. These and similar issues are already being discussed in some research projects as those carried out at the Lexicology, Lexicography and Terminology Group of the Centro de Linguística da Universidade Nova de Lisboa, which is investing heavily in the development of specialized online dictionaries (see Chapters 9, 20, and 21 of this *Handbook*).

Research in the field of specialized lexicography within the previously mentioned research group has benefited in the past few years from the rapid evolution of methodologies and semantic models of description in the fields of lexicography, terminology, and text-oriented computing. We are witnessing today a new chain of work in specialized lexicography that has resulted from these new theoretical and methodological guidelines.

We would like to stress the importance of the set of semantic, lexical, and pragmatic criteria that have presided over the construction of specialized text *corpora*. They were set following a certain number of hypotheses related with the types and characteristics of specialized discourse, its target users and the characteristics of specialized communication. Both the concept of monolingual text corpus and the concepts of bilingual and multilingual corpora have come to enhance the theoretical and methodological reflection on specialized lexicography. These corpora are composed of several types of scientific texts: texts written by experts for experts, semi-popularized texts, introductory texts to a specialized language, and scientific popularized texts. These corpora are managed by hypertext software packages that allow us to work with several types of linguistic data: extracting terms and neologisms; studying polysemy, homonymy, and synonymy; selecting defining or functional contexts; extracting collocations and phraseologies; observing lexical and terminological variants; using lexical statistics; and observing socioterminology and cultural terminology phenomena. These data are completed by material collected from specialized lexicographic corpora and specialized oral corpora based on situations of communication between experts (Lino 2010).

These different stages of the lexicographic work serve as the basis of a terminological dictionary: this is conceived as a hypertext system that is open to several usages according to various reading types. The hypertext interface constitutes a network that permits access to different lexicographic data, providing the user with the suitable tools to organize their reading and interpretative paths.

In this textual macrosystem, the dictionary is a novel textual object that implies new information management skills and has introduced a renewed topic in terms of lexicographic organization and semantic models that allow for new cognitive and pragmatic usages. The redefinition of the concepts of the language-system and discourse have defined the boundaries of a set of linguistic processes that depend on the navigation of the lexical, semantic, and pragmatic components of language. The user may infer from these concepts and these processes several cognitive types of learning, building on the empirically discovered lexical constants.

In the scope of the 'dictionary object', we are developing two projects whose aim is to teach terminology and medical language. In the current Portuguese, Communitarian, and International contexts (particularly in institutions such as the UN, WHO, and UNESCO), medical language is a privileged domain (as a first, second, and foreign language). The online dictionary *Dicionário Terminológico de Medicina* (ongoing) (Lino 2004), aimed at general practitioners, medical students, and health professionals in general, has several components:

- Conceptual and linguistic components: a) its microstructure is devised taking into consideration its audience; b) the lexicographic definition is written and consensually harmonized by lecturers from the School of Medicine; the definition is never a faithful representation of all the conceptual traits of the concept; the concept exists and is delimited by the systems of relations that establishes with the other concepts in the domain.
- The component *Textos e Imagens* [Texts and Images] integrates a text base and an image base. The text base was extracted from the text corpus and is composed of different types of texts that use medical communication and show the usage of neologisms or terms. The hypertext network allows the user to choose a text in particular or to browse through the whole collection of texts.
- The component *Comunicação e Exercícios* [Communication and Exercises] presents collocations, phraseologies, pragmatems, and other morphosyntactic and semantic-pragmatic exercises.

We have also presented the *Modelo de E-Dicionário Português-Kimbundu*, a model for an e-dictionary of Portuguese-Kimbundu in the field of health, which is being developed by Ana Pita Grôz (2016). This is a bilingual dictionary that features two languages in contact: Portuguese and Kimbundu, one of the most important languages in Angola. We would like to stress that Portuguese is an official language in Angola, but is actually a foreign language to many of its speakers in the country. Figure 38.1 shows a screenshot that contains links to anatomy or physiology texts. Both the context and the text have a pedagogical function, contextualizing the term in the discourse. The text shall make learning the meaning of the term easier and might contribute to the scientific update of students or health professionals.

Entry	*Anatomy texts*
heart, m.n. ***muxima***, n.	Anatomy conceptual map Kimbundu language: characteristics Links to the text(s) in the text corpora

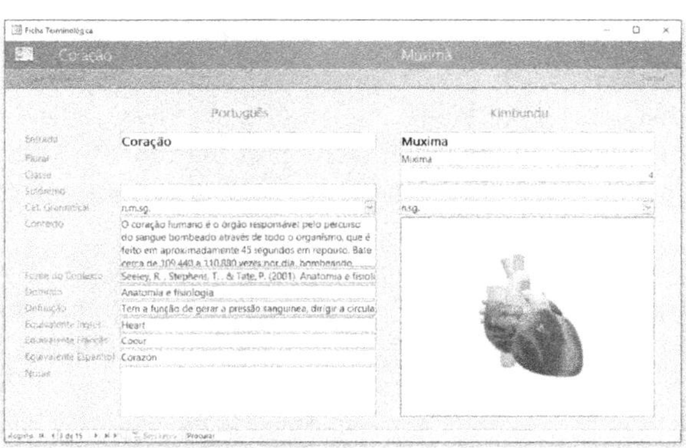

Figure 38.1 Screenshot of the *E-Dicionário Português-Kimbundu* (links to corpus texts)

Entry	*Anatomy texts*
Scapula, f.n. ***Dilonga dya Kisuxi,*** n. 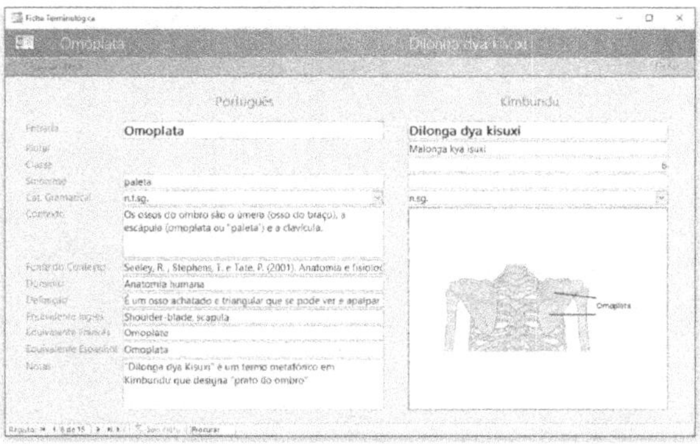	Anatomy conceptual map Kimbundu language: characteristics conceptual map of the skeletal system concepts, terms, and relationships (to be included)

Figure 38.2 Screenshot of the *E-Dicionário Português-Kimbundu* (conceptual map of the skeletal system)

The macrostructure of the dictionary contains several components: 1) a microstructure: the lexicographic definition, illustrated by an image; 2) the text database, composed of specialized texts of anatomy or physiology in Portuguese, but in the future we hope to include texts in Kimbundu despite the difficulties derived from the lack of standardized spelling; 3) conceptual maps of anatomy and physiology: these maps show concepts and terms and the relationships established between the terms; and 4) characteristics of Kimbundu: for example, rules to form the plural of nouns.

The next screenshot (Figure 38.2) shows another component of the dictionary that will make conceptual maps of anatomy or physiology available: the conceptual maps shall present a conceptual organization of concepts, terms, and the relationships established between concepts. These maps are today frequently used in anatomy university teaching, where the blackboard is no longer in use and has been replaced by new technologies. Digital conceptual maps present learning structures, conceptual networks that facilitate the learning process. In the future, we shall build conceptual maps for each of the languages.

The third screenshot (Figure 38.3) completes the pedagogical function of the dictionary. This component of the dictionary is dedicated to the teaching/learning of Kimbundu: the fundamental characteristics of the language are presented here to facilitate the task of those professionals that are not familiar with this Angolan language.

We would like to highlight that in many hospital or other health services, health professionals do not speak Kimbundu at all, which makes the communication between health professional/patient more difficult.

These dictionaries in which we are working shall be made available over the Internet via the site of the Centro de Linguística da Universidade Nova de Lisboa. These are dictionary products that may be used online to provide answers to queries or as a self-training and self-learning tool. They can also be used in libraries or in the classroom for collaborative learning purposes.

Entry	*Anatomy texts*
ovary, m.n. ***musanga,*** n.	Anatomy conceptual mapa Kimbundu language: characteristics

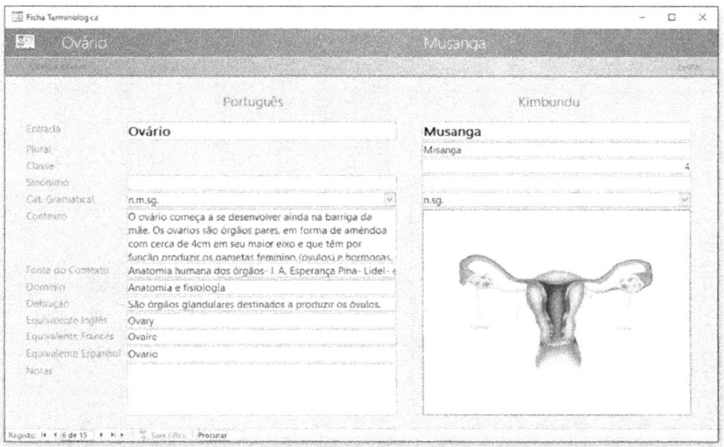

Classes nominais

Classes	Prefixo	Kimbundu	Português
1	Mu-	munjinu,	faringe
2	A-	anjinu,	faringes
3	Mu-	mulembu, musanga, mukonde	dedo, ovário, trompa
4	Mi-	milembu, misanga, mikonde	dedos, ovários, trompas
5	Di-	diju, dituba, divumu, dyele	dente, testículo, abdómen, mama
6	Ma-	maju, matuba, mavumu, mele	dentes, testículos, abdómenes, mamas
7	Ki-	kimbi, kivalelu, kisuxinu	cadáver, útero, bexiga
8	I-	imbi, ivalelu, isuxinu	cadáveres, úteros, bexigas
9	I-	ipumuna, inzeke	joelho, vesícula
10	Ji-	jipumuna, jinzeke	joelhos, vesículas

Figure 38.3 Screenshot of the *E-Dicionário Português-Kimbundu* (grammar data)

38.5 Conclusion

This chapter has focused on the Portuguese dictionaries that have been produced in the past two decades. These dictionaries have resulted from the evolution of research in the field of lexicography, terminology, and dictionary making in the Portuguese context. Three main conclusions can be drawn from our analysis. First, Portuguese dictionaries are subject to changes intimately related to their role as cultural objects and consultation tools. Second, the geostrategic importance of the Portuguese language in the word today – as different international institutions, for example, the Community of Portuguese Language Countries, the International Portuguese Language Institute, and the European Union's translation services can attest – has strongly encouraged universities and publishing houses to develop current language and specialized electronic dictionaries, thus meeting the needs of several types of users. Third, the coming of age of the Internet has influenced significantly the design and making of specialized dictionaries. Some of them, which are currently being developed at the Centro de Linguística da Universidade Nova de Lisboa, are presented in this chapter.

To conclude, lexicography in the age of the Internet has contributed to a new metamorphosis of the dictionary. New theoretical and methodological reflections have been made to answer the new demands not only of general lexicography, but also of specialized lexicography.

Related topics

Dictionaries and culture; electronic dictionaries; lexicography and corpus linguistics; specialised dictionaries; terminological knowledge bases; domain ontologies.

Further reading

Jesensek, V. (ed.) (2013). *Specialised Lexicography: Print and Digital, Specialised Dictionaries, Databases*. Berlin: Mouton de Gruyter.

This volume offers a kind of state-of-the-art approach to modern specialized lexicography from four perspectives: its formal, methodological, and socio-functional structure; the role of computers in dictionary making; specialized dictionaries assessment and their application to education; and translation.

Pruvost, J. (ed.) (2001). *Les dictionnaires de langue française. Dictionnaires d'apprentissage, dictionnaires spécialisés de la langue et dictionnaires de spécialité*. Paris: Honoré Champion.

This volume offers accurate analyses on monolingual lexicography, focusing on three types of dictionaries: first, learning dictionaries, whose aim is to help better understand language and its lexicon; second, specialized language dictionaries, which describe a particular aspect of language (e.g. etymology, analogy, etc.); and lastly, specialized dictionaries, whose object are human experience fields and scientific and technical fields and whose aim is very similar to that of terminology.

References

Academia das Ciências de Lisboa (1793) *Dicionário da Real Academia das Ciências de Lisboa*. Lisboa.

Academia das Ciências de Lisboa (2001) *Dicionário da Língua Portuguesa Contemporânea*. Lisboa: Verbo.

Academia das Ciências de Lisboa (2012) *Vocabulário Ortográfico Atualizado da Língua Portuguesa*. Lisboa: Imprensa Nacional Casa da Moeda.

Aulete, C. (1881) *Diccionario Contemporaneo da Língua Portugueza*. Lisboa: Imprensa Nacional.

Bivar, A. (1948) *Dicionario Geral e Analógico da língua portuguesa*. Porto: Edições Ouro vol. 1 1948, vol. 2 1958.

Calepino, A. (1502) *Thesaurus Linguae Latinae*. Reggio. Françoise

Cardoso, J. (1551) *Hieronymi Cardoso Dictionarium Juventuti studiosae admodum frugiferum*. Coimbra: João de Barreira; 2ª edição, 1562; 3ª edição, 1587.

Casteleiro, J. M. (2009) *Vocabulário Ortográfico da Língua* Portuguesa. Porto: Porto Editora.

Cardoso, J. (2014) *Dicionário Global da Língua Portuguesa*. Lisboa: Lidel.

Dicionário Priberam da Língua Portuguesa, on-line (2016) Lisboa: Priberam. www.priberam.pt/DLPO/ [Last accessed 20 September 2016].

Dictionnaire de l'Académie Françoise (1694) Paris. See at http://www.academie-francaise.fr/le-dictionnaire-les-neuf-prefaces/preface-de-la-premiere-edition-1694

Dicionário Houaiss da Língua Portuguesa (2001) Lisboa: Círculo dos Leitores, 6 volumes.

Diciopédia (1997) Porto: Porto Editora.

Estienne, R. (1531) *Thesaurus Linguae Latinae*. Paris.

Figueiredo, Cândido de. (1899) *Novo Dicionario da Lingua Portugueza*. Lisboa: Tavares Cardoso & Irmão.

Grôs, A. P. (2016) *Lexicografia Bilingue de Especialidade: E-dicionário Português-Kimbundu no Domínio da Saúde*, Phd Dissertation, Universidade Nova de Lisboa – FCSH.

Jesensek, V. (2013) *Specialised Lexicography: Print and Digital, Specialised Dictionaries, Databases*. Berlin: Mouton de Gruyter.

Lino, T. (ed.) (2004) "Vocabulaires de spécialité et lexicographie d'apprentissage en langues-cultures étrangères et maternelles", *Etudes de Linguistique Appliquée* 135: 261–262.

Lino, T. (2010) "Neologia, terminologia e lexicultura: a língua portuguesa em situação de contacto de línguas", *Revista de filologia e linguística portuguesa* 12(a): 187–201.

Pereira, B. (1647) *Thesouro da Língua Portugueza*. Lisboa: Oficina de Paulo Craesbecck.

Pruvost, J. (2000) *Dictionnaires et nouvelles technologies*. Paris: PUF.

Silva, M. (1789) *Diccionario da Língua Portugueza*. Lisboa: Ferreira.

Verdelho, T. (2007) *Dicionarística Portuguesa: Inventariação e estudo do património lexicográfico*. Aveiro: Universidade de Aveiro.

Vilela, M. (1991) *Dicionário do Português Básico*. Porto: ASA.

Vocabolario della Crusca (1691) See at: http://www.accademiadellacrusca.it/en/accademia/history/third-edition-vocabolario-1691

Wang, S. (2016) *Lexicultura na Lexicografia Bilingue de Chinês-Português*, Phd Dissertation, Universidade Nova de Lisboa – FCSH.

39

Russian lexicography in the Internet era

Olga M. Karpova

39.1 Introduction

This chapter describes the current situation of modern Russian lexicography within the context of global lexicographical developments and changes. It takes into consideration studies of different user groups' needs and demands, challenges of the new Internet technologies and growing intercultural dialogue in the global world. The main practices in dictionary making in today's Russian lexicography are given with special reference to current dictionary projects (printed, electronic and online) for general, special (slang, phraseological, author and other types of reference books) and learners' lexicography.

It also pays attention to recent changes influenced by socio-economic, linguistic and cultural factors along with changes in Russian dictionaries, which are abandoning 'authority' and relying more on 'usage', especially as many new lexicographic projects are corpus based.

The chapter reviews the main factors underpinning developments in Russian lexicography and focuses on several dictionary types, all of them accessible on the Internet. These dictionaries are in the forefront of Russian lexicography, which does not differ much from other national lexicographies.

39.2 Historical perspectives

39.2.1 Formation of Russian lexicography

Russian lexicography has rich historic roots and goes back to the thirteenth century. The milestones of Russian lexicography include the first *azbukovniks* or dictionaries of hard and difficult words from Old Church Slavonic, selected from the texts according to the compilers preference and organized in an alphabetical order (Sorokoletov 2001: 5–8).

Since the establishment of the Russian Academy of Sciences in 1783, which aimed at creating a reliable norm-based Russian dictionary, three main fundamental academic dictionaries appeared:

- *Slovar' Akademii Rossiiskoi* (Dictionary of Russian Academy; first edition): This big dictionary of the contemporary Russian language (in six volumes) was published in

1789–1794. It aimed at revealing the system of the Russian language which existed in two forms: Russian and Church Slavonic. For this reason the dictionary entries were presented also in two forms (i.e. Russian and Slavonic). The dictionary was revised in 1806–1822 and printed in a new alphabetical order, but it did not reflect peculiarities of the living language, which was rather typical of early academic dictionaries.

- *A Dictionary of Church Slavonic and Russian Languages* in four volumes (Sorokaletov 2001: 12: 12): It was launched in 1847. This time lexicographers introduced new labels into the entry line: grammar and phonetics, the positive features of the dictionary also being indication of word forms and orthographic variants of lexemes along with the homonymys and types of lexical meanings (Karpova 2005: 704–715).
- *Slovar' Akademii Rossiiskoi* (Dictionary of Russian Academy; third edition): The third edition of the academic dictionary was edited by Y. Grot. It appeared in 1895, and followed similar principles and practices to the previous editions of this dictionary.

After Grot's death, the dictionary started to change, as shown by modifications brought about in a new edition by famous Russian lexicographer A. Shakhmatov (Kozyrev and Chernyak 2014: 36). *Shakhmatov's era* is known as a climax in Russian academic lexicography, because the scholar considered reflection of living Russian as a main aim of the Russian dictionary. According to A. Shakhmatov's theory, a living language as a mixture of written and spoken languages must be the basis of the description of the national language. This reference work became a treasure trove of Russian living words and until today has been considered to be the milestone of Russian lexicography (Karpova 2005: 708).

In 1863 Vladimir Dal, a well-known Russian lexicographer, was the first to introduce the term *'tolkovij slovar'* in his *Tolkovij slovar' zhivogo velikorusskogo jazika* (Explanatory Dictionary of the Living Great Russian Language) which was republished many times in the future (Dal 1863–1866). The author managed to demonstrate in his dictionary the unique socio-cultural, linguo-cultural and historical-ethnical significance of the Russian language. As it was the first dictionary which explained all meanings of Russian words, including dialects or the so-called *narodnyi jazik* (the lexicographer was against putting borrowings from other languages into the macrostructure), its main purpose was to overcome the gap between written and spoken Russian language. The dictionary contained 200,000 keywords, 80,000 of which had never been registered in other dictionaries of Russian language. The dictionary obtained a high appreciation in Russia and abroad.

39.2.2 The Soviet era in Russian lexicography

The Soviet period in Russian lexicography was rather fruitful, and many reliable dictionaries appeared in this period of time which may be called *the milestones of Russian lexicography*. Among them:

- *Tolkovij slovar' russkogo jazika* (The Explanatory Dictionary of the Russian Language) edited by D.N. Ushakov in four volumes (Ushakov 1935–1940);
- *Slovar' russkogo jazika* (The Russian Language Dictionary) by S.I. Ozhegov (Ozhegov 1949);
- A famous Soviet academic dictionary *Slovar' sovremennogo russkogo literaturnogo jazika* (A Dictionary of Contemporary Russian Literary Language) in 17 volumes (The Russian Academic Dictionary1948–1965);
- The four-volume *Slovar' russkogo jazika* (Russian Dictionary) edited by A.P. Evgenjeva (Evgenjeva 1957–1961).

In general, about 9,000 dictionaries were issued in the USSR from 1918 to 1962 (Simchuk 2009: 37), and there appeared many fundamental theoretical works on Russian lexicography (Karpova 2005: 710).

L.V. Scherba's *"Opit obschei teorii leksikografii"* (Experience of General Theory of Lexicography) (Scherba 1974: 265–304) is known as the most internationally famous theoretical work, where an outstanding Russian linguist offered the first typology of Russian dictionaries based on six levels:

1 academic/informative dictionary;
2 encyclopaedic/general dictionary;
3 concordance/defining dictionary;
4 ordinary/ideological dictionary;
5 defining/translating dictionary;
6 nonhistorical/historical dictionary.

Scherba's typology became the burning theme of discussions throughout the years and is truly acknowledged as the most reliable typology of dictionaries of the twentieth century. The article was followed by other numerous scholarly papers and books by famous Russian linguists (see in detail: Ledeniova 2008; Miznikov and Krilova 2010; etc.).

The 1950s and 1960s gave rise to many types of specialized dictionaries, such as slang, phraseological, dialectal, author and many other reference works including not only linguistic, but also encyclopaedic dictionaries for general and special purposes (Shimchuk 2005). Moreover, intensive development of the Russian industry prompted creation of numerous LSP dictionaries of different subject fields: machine- and aircraft building, electricity and so on. At the same time this period is considered to be a time when Soviet terminology studies flourished and became famous throughout the world (Karpova and Averboukh 2008: 204).

39.3 Core issues and topics

Although the Internet and other electronic technologies are influencing Russian lexicography, it must be acknowledged that their influence is not broadly felt yet. Russian lexicographers are still discussing issues and topics brought about from abroad, mostly from English and German lexicographers who are leading this debate (see Chapters 33 and 35 of this *Handbook*). This section, then, will describe the state of the art of Russian lexicography by offering the reader information on some of its most acclaimed innovations as well as a review of some influential dictionary types, printed and online.

39.3.1 Linguistic changes in the Russian language

During *perestroika*, a period of changing socio-cultural, economic and political situations, Russian lexicographers had to modernize the whole strategy of the dictionary-making process, which was developing under the new situation in Russian society.

A lot of new words appeared, characterizing the new époque. Compilers of new dictionaries registered them. The 17-volume *Slovar' sovremennogo russkogo literaturnogo jazyka (Bol'shoj akademicheskij slovar')* (1948–1965) (A Dictionary of Contemporary Russian Literary Language) (Big Academic Dictionary), was one of this new generation of dictionaries that registered these new words.

In her article '*Antropotsentricheskaya leksikografiya: idei i praktika*' ('Anthropocentric Lexicography: Ideas and Practice'), famous Russian lexicographer Sklyarevskaja writes about vividly developing anthropocentric dictionaries, that is, usage-based dictionaries (Sklyarevskaja 2013: 95–104), which successfully co-existed along with famous academic dictionaries of Russian language (Karpova 2006: 1249–1254).

Sklyarevskaja produced the first dictionary of Russian language, *Tolkovyj slovar' russkogo jazyka nachala XXI veka. Jazikovije izmenenija* (The Russian Language Explanatory Dictionary of the Beginning of the 21st century. Linguistic Changes) after V. Dahl, opening a new page in Russian lexicography. She tried to reflect not only academic but also real uses of language, thus making use of corpora and incorporating slang words, borrowings, terms and the like (Sklyarevskaja 2002, 2014).

Her series of dictionaries of current Russian language became so popular among Russian users that Sklyarevskaja continued to publish further issues of the dictionary: *Tolkovyj slovar' russkogo jazyka nachala XXI veka. Aktual'naja leksika* (The Russian Language Explanatory Dictionary of the Beginning of the 21st century. Modern Lexis) (Sklyarevskaja 2008), adding new words and word combinations into the dictionary macrostructure. It should be said that her efforts answered needs and demands not only of Russian users, but also foreigners studying Russian as a foreign language.

This range of modern Russian dictionaries was followed by several new reference works: *Sovremennyj tolkovyj slovar' russkogo jazyka* in three volumes (The Modern Explanatory Dictionary of the Russian Language) (Efremova 2006); *Samij noveishij tolkovyi slovar' russkogo jazyka XXI veka* (The Newest Russian Language Dictionary of the 21st century) (Shagalova 2011); and other dictionaries. These reference works were aimed at describing new words which were accompanying the development of a new Russian society.

The post-*perestroika* time is considered in Russia to be the climax of the dictionary-making process. First of all, the introduction of new IT technologies into practical lexicography made it possible to intensify and enrich the lexicographic activities, which were actively influenced by extra-linguistic, socio-cultural and active processes in the development of the Russian language in the twenty-first century. The linguistic changes in modern Russian language obviously found reflection in new books by famous Russian linguists: M. Krongauz's *Russkij jazyk na grani nervnogo sriva* (The Russian Language on the Verge of a Nervous Breakdown) (Krongauz 2009); N. Yudina's *Russkij jazyk v XXI veke: krizis? evoljutsija? progress?* (The Russian Language in the 21st century: Crisis? Evolution? Progress?) (Yudina 2010); and other Russian scholars, where the new problems of the modern Russian language, caused by economic, cultural and political changes, were discussed for the first time in Russian linguistics.

These new features in Russian language found their reflection in a new range of *specialized dictionaries*: dictionaries of poets' and writers' (author) language; phraseological, etymological, dialectal; dictionaries of synonyms, homonyms, antonyms and paronyms; dictionaries of neologisms and archaisms; dictionaries of foreign words and expressions; dictionaries of abbreviations and acronyms; onomasticons; dictionaries of oral and written speech correctness; reverse dictionaries; grammatical; dictionaries of collocations and word-formation; and so on.

Thus, changes in contemporary speech practice and the noticeable downfall in speech culture in Russia demanded creation of new *orthological dictionaries*, for example, *Orfograficheskij slovar' russkogo jazyka (The Russian Language Spelling Dictionary)*, which are necessary to prevent people from making mistakes in spelling and communication, pronunciation, accent and word usage (Bukchina, Sazonova, Chel'tsova 2008). These reference books also offer users helpful information on recent borrowings as well as on new political, religious, economic, financial and other specialized vocabularies of Russian. See for example: *Grammaticheskij slovar' russkogo jazyka: Slovoizmenenije* (The Russian Language Grammar Book: Word-change; Zaliznjak 2008) and *Slovar' udarenij russkogo jazyka* (The Dictionary of Russian Language Accent; Reznichenko 2008). Orthological Russian dictionaries initiated by scholars from St. Petersburg University are published now by the famous publishing house *AST-PRESS KNIGA* and, as a rule, are easily accessed on the Internet.

One of the most popular groups of specialized reference works which appeared in this time is called *dictionaries of correct speech* and *speech etiquette*, for example, *Tolkovijslovar' russkogo rechevogo etiketa* (Explanatory Dictionary of Russian Speech Etiquette; Balakaj 2004), with the most famous being *Bol'shoi tolkovyj slovar' pravilnoi russkoi rechi* (Big Dictionary of Correct Russian Speech), compiled by an outstanding Russian lexicographer Skvortsov (2009).

A number of modern Russian dictionaries, along with linguistic data, provide the entry words with cultural background facts, taking into consideration basic Russian linguo-cultural and linguo-cognitive basis as the main element of the cultural space. Thus cultural aspect of Russian dictionaries became the focus of lexicographers' attention, and a special group of *cultural dictionaries* appeared on the Russian lexicographic scene, for example, *Konstanty: Slovar' russkoj kul'tury* (Constants: Dictionary of Russian Culture; Stepanov 2001); *Russkoe kul'turnoe prostranstvo: lingvokul'turologicheskij slovar'* (Russian Cultural Space: Cultural Dictionary; Brileva et al. 2004); *Rossija. Bol'shoj lingvostranovedcheskij slovar'* (Russia. Big Cultural Dictionary; Prokhorov 2007); *Kontseptosfera russkogo jazyka: kljuchevie kontsepty i ih reprezentatsii* (The Russian Language Sphere of Concepts: Key Concepts and Their Representations; Babenko 2010); and the like.

According to the compilers of the linguo-culturological dictionary *Russkoe kul'turnoe prostranstvo* (Russian Cultural Space; Brileva et al. 2004), the national cultural space should be treated as a form of culture existing in a man's mind, and reflected in the consciousness of its users. Moreover, the centre of this cultural space turns out to be the national cognitive basis treated in a certain way as structured knowledge, nationally marked and culturally determined ideas essentially necessary for all the representatives of the national-linguo-cultural community (Brileva et al. 2004: 10–11).

It should be noted that these linguistic and encyclopaedic reference works to a large extent found their users mainly among foreigners (studying Russian as a foreign language) and were also intended for immigrants who came to Russia after the collapse of the Soviet Union. The aim of these lexicographic enterprises was to involve the new users into the cultural background of the Russian language and have a great significance for users.

39.3.2 Russian lexicography in the new millennium

It is common knowledge that Russian lexicography gives preference to the lexicographical form of a *tolkovyi slovar'*, that is, an authority-based language dictionary. But recent developments in Western European lexicography, for example, the development of thesauri and frequency dictionaries, has also influenced Russian lexicography (Karpova 2010), as the publication of these works, both in print and online, shows: *Russkij assotsiativnyj slovar'* (Russian Associative Dictionary in 2 volumes; Karaulov et al. 2002), *Chastotnyi slovar' sovremennogo russkogo jazyka* (Frequency Dictionary of Modern Russian Language; Lashevskaya and Sharov 2009)[1] and *Slovar'-tezaurus russkih prilagatel'nyh, raspredelennyh po tematicheskim gruppam* (Thesaurus of Russian Adjectives Classified by Thematic Groups; Babenko 2011).

These lexicographic works represent the newest achievements in dictionary-making in Russia and often unite the features of different lexicographic forms to answer modern users' needs and demands who are eager to get necessary information as soon as possible in a convenient and comprehensive way.

The end of the twentieth century and the beginning of the twenty-first century are greatly influenced by intensive development of theoretical and applied research in the field of lexicography abroad (Apresjan 2000; Karpova 2010). Russian lexicographers are trying to apply the new theory and practice of e-lexicography to their fundamental theoretical works.

Importance of dictionary-making practice led to the creation of a new Russian state programme *Slovari XXI veka* (Dictionaries of the 21st century). It was launched in 2008 by the Russian Language Institute "V.V. Vinogradov" together with *AST-Press*, a publishing house. Its aim is to create a system of Russian dictionaries on traditional and innovative principles. The unique feature of the programme consists in presenting Russian as a living language registered in modern dictionaries, where the development and modern scene of Russian are fully reflected for the first time in Russian lexicography. The compilers are professional lexicographers taking into consideration achievements of other national lexicographies (e.g. English, German, French, etc.).

All dictionaries are online.[2] Each entry word is provided by comprehensive definitions and several informative labels. The range of Russian dictionaries starts from fundamental large norm-based dictionaries up to dictionaries for special purposes with important focus on learners' dictionaries for schoolchildren and teachers (see Section 39.3.3). Every dictionary is presented in printed form and then converted into electronic form to satisfy users' demands.

Apart from the state programme *Slovari XXI veka*, other new dictionaries by prominent Russian lexicographers appeared in printed and electronic format, such as Y. Apresyan's *Activnij slovar' russkogo jazyka* in two volumes (Russian Language Activator; Apresjan 2014), Kutnestov's *Bolshoi tolkovyi slovar' russkogoyazika* (Big Russian Language Dictionary 2000[3]), and T. Efremova's *Novij slovar' russkogo jazyka* (New Russian Language Dictionary 2000[4]), which are considered to be the most reliable up-to-date lexicographic enterprises of innovative anthropocentric character.

It should be stressed that all reliable modern dictionaries are corpus-based, for example, the *Oxford English Dictionary* has *British National Corpus* as a basis of the macrostructure, *Collins Dictionaries* the *Bank of English* and so on. As for Russian lexicography, the idea of creating a fund for designing a machine corpus of the Russian language (*mashinnyi fond Russkogo jazika*) was proclaimed in the 1960s, but due to the changing political system and financial difficulties its compilation was postponed to a later date. Only at the beginning of the twenty-first century did a national corpus of Russian language (NCRL) (*Natsionalnyj korpus russkogo jazika*)[5]come on to the Russian linguistic scene. Its creation is a great achievement and a step forward made by Russian scholars in the field of corpus lexicography.

This corpus is a comprehensive reference information system of written and conversational Russian, an electronic collection of texts in all the variety of genres, styles, territorial and social variants of usage, etc., having at its disposal 200 million words. It is aimed first and foremost at creating different types of Russian general-purpose and special-purpose dictionaries. Unlike simple collections of texts on the Internet, this corpus has additional information about the texts included by means of annotation which is the main feature of the corpus. Moreover, NCRL is of great academic and teaching value and contains four types of annotations: metatextual (information about the text), morphological, accentual and semantic (see Chapter 8 of this *Handbook*).

The NCRL embraces the period from the middle of the eighteenth century to the twenty-first century, representing the Russian language of both the past and the present in a wide range of sociolinguistic variants: literary, colloquial, vernacular and in part dialectal. Along with original works of fiction (prose, drama and poetry) the corpus registers many sources of written works, such as memoirs, essays, journalistic works, scientific and popular scientific literature, public speeches, letters, diaries, documents and so on. Being very well structured, the NCRL includes several subcorpora:

- The annotated corpus.
- The parallel corpora (with translation from Russian into English, German, Ukrainian, Belorussian, etc., and from these foreign languages into Russian).
- Mass media corpus (newspaper articles from 1990–2000).
- The dialectal corpus, including recordings of dialectal speech from various Russian regions.
- The poetical corpus.
- The educational corpus (adapted for the Russian school teaching programme).
- The corpus of spoken Russian.
- The accentological corpus (i.e. a corpus for studying word stress and stress variation, including the history of the Russian language stress development).
- Multimedia corpus (with Russian movies – 1930–2000).

This rich collection of sub-corpora makes it possible not only to carry out serious research of the Russian language but also to create new types of reference works which have never been compiled before. The NCRL is constantly discussed in numerous conferences, articles and practical works (see *Natsionalny korpus russkogo jazyka*).

39.3.3 Internet reference resources

Today Russian lexicographers are intensively working on creating different websites with a set of dictionaries for general and special purposes which are mostly demanded by modern Russian users who (according to user studies, Sklyarevskaya 2013: 96–98) prefer looking up terms in online dictionaries. The result of their recent efforts in Internet lexicography are the following websites of different Russian dictionaries which appeared in the twenty-first century, each having more than 100 dictionaries:

- *Sbornik elektronnih tolkovyh slovarei russkogo jazyka – Slovorus* (Collection of Russian Electronic Dictionaries)[6]
- *Spravochno-informatsionnyj portal Gramota.RU – russkiy jazyk dlia vseh* (Reference Portal Gramota.Ru – Russian Language for Everybody)[7]
- *Slovari russkogo jazyka* (Russian Language Dictionaries)[8]

An analysis of these reference sources reveals current trends in Russian lexicography. First, most existing printed dictionaries are being converted into online dictionaries. These include basic types of Russian general and special linguistic and encyclopaedic dictionaries for different user groups.

Second, the portals are differently structured, and their architecture is aimed at meeting different users' demands. Thus, some modern sites register only historic dictionaries of Russian language, for example, *Slovar'russkogo jazyka XVIII veka* (Russian Language Dictionary of the 18th century).[9] On the other hand, we can also find on the Internet the newest dictionaries of Russian, registering and describing current Russian language, for example, *Novyj obyasnitelnyj slovar' sinonimov russkogo jazyka* (New Explanatory Dictionary of the Russian Language Synonyms; Apresjan 1997) or *Slovar' trudnostei russkogo jazyka* (Dictionary of Russian Difficult Words; Rosental and Telenkov 2003)[10] which explain the modern Russian word usage in detail. Moreover, many fundamental theoretical works by Russian lexicographers are also found on the Internet (Ageenko 2010; Sherba 1974),[11] to name just a few.

Third, another noticeable feature of modern Russian lexicography is seen in many monographs and textbooks on Russian lexicography, which had been published of late in Moscow, St. Petersburg and other cities and universities (Dubichinsky 2008; Kozyrev, Chernjak 2004, 2014; Ledeniova 2008; Miznikov, Krilova 2010; Shimchuk 2009, etc.). Among them one should mention the new textbook *Russian Lexicography XXI v.*, which is mainly devoted to new IT technology in the future of Russian dictionary making (Bobunova 2013). These works discuss new discoveries in theoretical lexicography, which have been spurred by development of new technologies and the extension of numerous international contacts. These have extensively influenced modern dictionary making.

Finally, the coming of age of the Internet to Russian lexicography is quite visible in the creation of many types of specialized dictionaries, that is, dictionaries that cover a relatively restricted set of phenomena (Cowie 2009). Some of them are discussed next. For reasons of space, we will only focus on types of specialized dictionaries that are well known in the Russian lexicographic landscape. In addition, we will also discuss Russian learners' dictionaries, which have seen a renaissance in connection with new social mores (e.g. the increase of migration).

Although our review does not offer a detailed analysis of each dictionary type (such an analysis is out of reach in a handbook like this), it offers the reader a glimpse of the current state of e-lexicography in Russia. They are also witness to how lexicography and culture are interconnected and influence each other with the aim of bringing to the fore descriptions of new social, political and cultural life (see Chapter 11 of this *Handbook*).

39.3.3.1 Author dictionaries

By authors' dictionaries we refer to reference works devoted to explain the theoretical basis (Karaulov 2003; Shestakova 2011) and lexical treatment of famous Russian writers and poets. Some of them offer general perspectives and trends, for example, *Slovar' jazyka russkoi poezii XX veka* in five volumes (Dictionary of Russian Poetry of the 20th century (Grigorjev and Shestakova 2001, 2003, 2008, 2010); Sholokhov and Tsvetaeva, etc. (Shestakova 2011). Some others focus on a particular writer, for example, *Pushkin Dictionary*, which was first published in 1956–1961 in four volumes (Vinogradov 2000),[12] and *Dostoevsky's Dictionary*, which was first published in 2001 (Karaulov 2001).[13]

39.3.3.2 Phraseological dictionaries

Phraseological dictionaries describe chunks of words (i.e. phrases, idioms, proverbs and the like). They are very popular in Russian lexicography; especially famous are the following: *Bol'shoj frazeologicheskij slovar' russkogo jazyka. Znachenie. Upotreblenie. Kulturologicheskij kommentarij* (Big Phraseological Dictionary of the Russian Language. Meaning. Usage. Cultural Commentary; Telija 2008); *Slovar' frazeologicheskih sinonimov russkogo jazyka* (The Russian Language Dictionary of Phraseological Synonyms; Mokienko 2009); and *Leksiko-frazeologicheskij slovar' russkogo jazyka.* (Lexico-Phraseological Dictionary of the Russian Language; Zhukov 2010). These typically include theoretical analysis of 'phrases' being well known the works by Mokienko (2009), and Nikitina and Nicolaeva (2010). These are very convenient for students, researchers and other groups of users.

39.3.3.3 Dictionaries of foreign words and expressions

These dictionaries are needed to cope with the large amounts of borrowings and loans that are entering into the Russian language, especially since the 1980s, a period characterised by the opening of Russian society to the Western world. Among this type of dictionaries, the following works should be mentioned: *Slovar' abbreviator inojazychnogo proiskhozhdenija* (Baranova 2009) and *1000 novykh inostrannykh slov* (Krysin 2009).

39.3.3.4 Slang dictionaries

It is necessary to underline that Russian Internet *slang dictionaries* are rather numerous today and include three types of dictionaries registering general slang, youth slang and slang from various subject fields (*Slovari online*).[14] In Soviet times Russian and foreign users had no chance to see and study slang words, because the authoritative Russian lexicons were all norm-based. Nowadays, there are quite a few slang dictionaries. Some of them are general slang dictionaries (e.g. *Tolkovyj slovar' russkogo slenga* (Explanatory Dictionary of Russian Slang; Elistratov 2006); some others are special slang dictionaries, e.g. *Molodioznyi sleng. Tolkovyj slovar'* (Youth Slang Dictionary; Nikitina 2009); *Russkij zhargon. Istoriko-etimologicheskij slovar'* (Russian Slang. Historical-Etymological Dictionary; Mokienko and Grachev 2009). Access to these dictionaries is free, which seems to have prompted users to consult them in great numbers, especially by students of Russian who can access real informal language (i.e. the language that authoritative dictionaries do not usually record in Russia).

There are also dictionaries describing slang from different spheres of today's Russian life, see, for instance: *Slovar' modnykh slov. Jazykovaja kartina sovremennosti* (A Dictionary of Fashionable Words. Contemporary Language Scene; (Novikov 2011); *Slovar'- spravochnik po materialam pressi i literaturi 90-h godov XX veka* (New Words and Meanings with Special Reference to Mass Media of the 1900s) in three volumes. This dictionary is the most interesting dictionary of slang and foreign borrowings in Russian mass media.

39.3.3.5 Terminological dictionaries

Russian Internet sites today, for instance, *Yandex Slovari* (Yandex Dictionaries),[15] offer their users different groups of terminological or LSP dictionaries, that is:

- dictionaries of terms belonging to new subject areas;
- dictionaries of fundamental and natural sciences terms;
- learners' terminological dictionaries for students of non-philological faculties.

New subject areas, such as logistics, business and finance and so on, which have never been created earlier, appeared on Russian reference sites in the twenty-first century. Moreover, not only professional lexicographers but also volunteers started to offer the users their own lexicographic products. It is a common practice today for Russian specialists (scholars, engineers, etc.) in many subject fields to add their own glossaries of different LSP reference works, especially in bilingual Russian-English (or other foreign languages) lexicography, which they put on the Internet as open LSP dictionaries. This new feature of volunteer dictionary making is a new trend in Russian Internet lexicography (Karpova and Averboukh 2008: 204).

Development of new technologies in fundamental industries (for example, machine and automobile building) and correspondingly the appearance of new terms contributed to the creation of new terminological dictionaries, the majority being in Internet format. When describing the modern scene of Russian lexicography it is necessary to mention Russian learners' LSP dictionaries which are used in technical and scientific educational institutions.

39.3.3.6 Learners' dictionaries

Dictionaries for young learners have a long tradition and have been developed in Russia since the communist time (Kozyrev and Chernjak 2004). *Slovari dla shkolnikov* (dictionaries for schoolchildren) were always aimed at teaching Russian schoolchildren spelling, phonetics, correct speech, etc. Today modern learners' dictionaries are presented on many Internet sites. Moreover, a special site is created for Russian learners with a rich variety of Russian dictionaries – *Slovorus* (see endnote 6).

Today, Russian lexicographers are focused not only on beginners (schools) but also intermediate and advanced learners (Fiodorova 2006). Thus a new range of learners' dictionaries for high schools and universities was compiled by Ural lexicographers (in Ekaterinburg Univeristy), edited by Professor G.N. Babenko and titled *Tolkovye Slovari*, for lexicographic treatment of different parts of speech: nouns, verbs, proverbs, etc.

Among them the following dictionaries must be mentioned: *Bol'shoj tolkovyj slovar' russkih glagolov: Ideograficheskoe opisanie. Sinonimy. Antonimy* (Big Explanatory Dictionary of Russian Verbs: Ideographic Description. Synonyms. Antonyms; Babenko 2007); *Grammaticheskij slovar' russkogo jazyka: Slovoizmenenie* (The Russian Language Grammar Book: Word-Change) (Zaliznjak 2008); and *Bol'shoj tolkovy jslovar' russkih sushchestvitel'nyh: Ideograficheskoeo pisanie. Sinonimy. Antonimy* (Big Explanatory Dictionary of Russian Nouns: Ideographic Description. Synonyms. Antonyms) (Babenko 2008).

Another group of learners' dictionaries is being made available on the Internet for immigrants coming to Russia from former Soviet republics (Ukraine, Moldova, Tadjikistan, Uzbekistan, etc.), who must pass through a state examination in Russian and for this purpose need special learners' dictionaries. Thus, many Russian dictionaries became learner oriented and are offered on the Internet for different groups of learners.

39.4 Looking to the future

It is common knowledge that rich Internet reference resources attract more and more dictionary users, and Russian is no exception. In our view, the future will be dominated by the increase of online dictionaries, many of them traditionally conceived print dictionaries which are converted into digital form. These will appear on both the Internet and mobiles (i.e. 'apps-dictionaries').

These apps-dictionaries are currently being offered free of charge or for a moderate price in online stores, like App Store (Apple), Google Play (Android) and Windows Store (Windows), who develop and promote different reference apps, but the number of them is quite small.This number, however, seems to be increasing, and we can mention some of the most popular, which are gaining users every day:

- *Slovar' Ozhegova* (Ozhegov's Dictionary)[16]
- *Bol'shaja Sovetskaja entsiklopedija* (Big Soviet Encyclopaedia)[17]
- *Slovar' Dala* (Dal's Dictionary)[18]
- *Poslovitsy Dal'a* (Dal's Proverbs)[19]
- *Karmannyi slovar' 40 v 1* (Pocket Dictionary 40 in 1)[20]
- *Slovo dnia – Tolkovyi slovar'russkogo jazyka dla sovremennyh ludei* (The Word of the Day – Russian dictionary for modern people).[21]

39.5 Conclusion

Russian lexicography, as many other national lexicographies, cannot develop today independently. It is subjected to the influence of world lexicography, Western European in particular. Thus Russian lexicographers have mostly accepted and applied foreign theories and practices to Russian lexicography. Some recent tendencies, which have been analysed in this chapter, are the following:

- emphasis on users' needs, especially those arising in connection with new user profiles such as migrants into developed countries;
- application of new technologies into the dictionary-making process;
- developing a computer and Internet lexicography;
- applying volunteer lexicography practice in the dictionary-making process;
- studying users' perspective through sociology of dictionary users to satisfy modern users' needs and demands;
- appearance of new types of dictionaries and innovative dictionary architectures.

Along with common tendencies Russian lexicography developed its own approach to dictionary creation, taking into consideration changes in political, economic and social life in the new Russia, which has led to the reflection of these changes in new Russian dictionaries for general and special purposes. Moreover, new theoretical research in the field of lexicography put Russian lexicography into the range of up-to-date national lexicographies in the world.

Russian lexicography has gone through several historical periods, performing different important functions: (a) linguo-didactical and methodological (teaching native and foreign languages); (b) descriptive and codification (description and standardization of Russian language); (c) communicative (interlingual contact function); and (d) theoretical-methodological (research and description of basic language layers). These functions have contributed to the compilation of specific types of dictionaries, being each of them characteristic of each historical period.

Trying to keep up with international development of computer and Internet lexicography, Russian lexicographers very quickly created reliable electronic reference resources based on effective research works made by Russian scholars. The co-existence of printed, electronic and Internet dictionaries in the twenty-first century has helped to create a comprehensive portrait of a Russian dictionary user, where special attention is paid to school users who have at their disposal now a large variety of reliable learners' dictionaries of all levels.

Related topics

Dictionaries and culture; lexicography and applied linguistics; lexicography and corpus linguistics; explaining meaning in lexicographical information tools.

Further reading

Karpova, O. and F. Kartashkova. (2009). "Modern Trends in Lexicography with Special Reference to English and Russian Dictionaries", in O. Karpova and F. Kartashkova (eds.), *Lexicography and Terminology: A Worldwide Outlook*. Newcastle upon Tyne: Cambridge Scholars Publishing, pp. 41–55.
The paper analyses some of the problems posed by norm-based dictionaries for general purposes in Russian and English lexicography from different historic periods. The main focus is on Russian *tolkovie slovari* (explanatory dictionaries) published in the new millennium.

Kozyrev, V. A. and V. D. Chernjak. (2014). "Sovremennie orientatsii otechestvennoi leksikografii (Modern Orientations in Russian Lexicography)", *Voprosi leksikografii* (*Questions of Lexicography*), 1: 5–15. http://cyberleninka.ru/article/n/sovremennye-orientatsii-otechestvennoy-leksikografii
The article deals with the recently published Russian dictionaries with special reference to users' needs and demands. The authors analyse and classify 2,600 titles of reference books according to a new approach to modern Russian linguistic and encyclopaedic dictionaries in the époque of the Internet and new information technologies.

Mandrikova, G. M. (2011). "Osnovnie polozhenia antropotsentricheskoi leksikografii" (Basics of Antropocentric Lexicography), *Mir nauki, kultury i obrazovania* (*World of Science, Culture and Education*), 2: 8–12. http://cyberleninka.ru/article/n/osnovnye-polozheniya-antropotsentricheskoy-leksikografii
The author describes the basics of anthropocentric lexicography developing in modern Russian dictionaries, taking into consideration the new types of reference books appeared in recent years.

Shestakova, L. L. (2010). "Modern Scene of Russian Author Lexicography", in O. Karpova and F. Kartashkova (eds.), *New Trends in Lexicography: Ways of Registrating and Describing Lexis*. Newcastle upon Tyne: Cambridge Scholars Publishing, pp. 148–157.
The paper describes the main trends in modern Russian author lexicography. Dictionaries that appeared in the last two decades concerned with classical and modern Russian authors and poets are analysed.

Vvedenskaja, L. A. (2007). *Russkaja leksikografija* (*Russian Lexicography*). Rostov-on-Don: Feniks.
The book is concerned with new typologies of Russian dictionaries published in the twenty-first century. Special attention is given to the analysis of mega-, macro- and microstructure of specialized dictionaries with accent on slang, proper names, terms and other groups of entry words.

Notes

1 See at http://dict.ruslang.ru/freq.php
2 See at http://slovari21.ru.
3 See at www.gramota.ru/slovari/info/bts
4 See at www.efremova.info/
5 See at www.ruscorpora.ru/search-main.html

6 See athttp://slovorus.ru/
7 See at www.gramota.ru/biblio/magazines/gramota/slovari/28_102
8 See at http://povto.ru/books/slovari/slovari-russkogo-yazyka.htm
9 See at http://feb-web.ru/feb/sl18/default.asp
10 See at http://dazor.narod.ru/russkie/slovari/trudnostej/slovar-trudnostej_0001.htm
11 See at www.ruthenia.ru/apr/textes/sherba/sherba9.htm
12 See at http://slovari.ru/default.aspx?s=0&p=230
13 See at http://slovari.ru/default.aspx?s=0&p=227
14 See at http://slovonline.ru)
15 See at http://slovari.yandex.ru/
16 See at https://itunes.apple.com/us/app/slovar-ozegova/id511740037?mt=8
17 See at https://itunes.apple.com/us/app/dict-bse/id385945247?mt=8
18 See at https://itunes.apple.com/us/app/slovar-dala/id511743764?mt=8
19 https://itunes.apple.com/us/app/poslovicy-v.i.-dal/id686812094?mt=8
20 See at https://itunes.apple.com/us/app/karmannyj-slovar-40v1/id552337578?mt=8
21 See at https://itunes.apple.com/us/app/slovo-dna-tolkovyj-slovar/id594187735?mt=8

References

Dictionaries

Apresjan, Y. D. (2014) *Activnyj slovar' russkogo jazyka* (*Russian Language Activator*), 2 vols. Moscow: Jazyki Slavianskoi Kulturi.

Apresjan, J. D. (1997) *Novyj obyasnitelnyj slovar' sinonimov russkogo jazyka* (*New Explanatory Dictionary of the Russian Language Synonyms*), 1st edn. Moscow: Jazyki russkoj kultury.

Babenko, L. G. (ed.) (2007) *Bol'shoj tolkovyj slovar' russkih glagolov: Ideograficheskoe opisanie. Sinonimy. Antonimy* (*Big Explanatory Dictionary of Russian Verbs: Ideographic Description. Synonyms. Antonyms*). Moscow: AST-PRESS KNIGA.

Babenko, L. G. (ed.) (2008) *Bol'shoj tolkovyj slovar' russkikh sushchestvitel'nykh: Ideograficheskoe opisanie. Sinonimy. Antonimy* (*Big Explanatory Dictionary of Russian Nouns: Ideographic Description. Synonyms. Antonyms*). Moscow: AST-PRESS KNIGA.

Babenko, L. G. (ed.) (2010) *Kontseptosfera russkogo jazyka: kljuchevie kontsepty i ih reprezentatsii* (*The Russian Language Sphere of Concepts: Key Concepts and Their Representations*). Ekaterinburg: Ural University Press.

Babenko, L. G. (ed.). (2011) *Slovar'-tezaurus russkih prilagatel'nyh, raspredelennyh po tematicheskim gruppam* (*Thesaurus of Russian Adjectives Classified by Focus Groups*). Moscow: Prospekt.

Balakaj, A. G. (2004) *Tolkovij slovar' russkogo rechevogo etiketa* (*Explanatory Dictionary of Russian Speech Etiquette*). Moscow: AST.

Baranova, L. A. (2009) *Slovar' abbreviatur inojazychnogo proiskhozhdenija* (*Dictionary of Abbreviations of Foreign Origin*). Moscow: AST-PRESS KNIGA.

Brileva, I. S., N. P. Vol'skaya, Gudkov, I. V. Zakharenko, and V. V. Krasnykh (eds.) (2004) *Russkoe kul'turnoe prostranstvo: lingvokul'turologicheskij slovar'* (*Russian Cultural Space: Cultural Dictionary*). 1st edition. Moscow: Gnozis.

Bukchina, B. Z., I. K. Sazonova, and Chel'tsova (2008) *Orfograficheskij slovar' russkogo jazyka* (*The Russian Language Spelling Dictionary)*. Moscow: AST-PRESS.

Bukchina, B. Z. (2011) *Slitno? Razdel'no? Cherez defis?* (*One Word? Two Words? Hyphenated?*). Moscow: AST-PRESS KNIGA.

Efremova, T. F. (ed.) (2006) *Sovremennyj tolkovyj slovar' russkogo jazyka* (*The Modern Explanatory Dictionary of the Russian Language*). 3 volumes. Moscow: AST, Astrel'.

Elistratov, V. S. (2006) *Tolkovyj slovar' russkogo slenga (Explanatory Dictionary of Russian Slang*). Moscow: AST-PRESS KNIGA.

Evgenjeva, A. P. (1957–1961) *Slovar' russkogo jazika* (*Russian Dictionary*). Moscow: State Publishing House of Foreign and National Dictionaries.

Dahl', V. I. (1863–1866) *Tolkovyj slovar' zhivogo velikorusskogo jazyka* (*The Explanatory Dictionary of the Living Great Russian Language*), 4 volumes. St. Petersburg: M. O. Wolf.

Grigorjev, V. P. and L. L. Shestakova (eds.) (2001. 2003. 2008. 2010) *Slovar' jazyka russkoi poezii XXveka* (*Dictionary of Russian Poetry of the 20th Century*), 4 vols. Moscow: Jazyki slavyanskoi kulturi, Znak.

Karaulov, J. N., J. A. Sorokin, E. F. Tarasov, N. V. Ufimtseva, and G. A. Cherkasova (2002) *Russkij assotsiativnyj slovar'* (*Russian Associative Dictionary*), 2 vols. Moscow: AST-Astrel'.

Krysin, L. P. (2009) *1000 novykh inostrannykh slov* (*1000 New Foreign Words*). Moscow: AST-PRESS KNIGA.

Mokienko, V. M. and M. A. Grachev (2009) *Russkij zhargon. Istoriko-etimologicheskij slovar'* (*Russian Slang. Historical-Etymological Dictionary*). Moscow: AST-PRESS KNIGA.

Mokienko, V. M. (2009) *Slovar' frazeologicheskih sinonimov russkogo jazyka* (*The Russian Language Dictionary of Phraseological Synonyms*). Moscow: AST-PRESS KNIGA.

Novie slovaiznacheniya. Slovar'-spravochnik po materialam pressi i literaturi 90-h godov XX veka. (2014) (*New Words and Meanings With Special Reference to Mass Media of the 90-s XX c.*). 3 volumes. Moscow: Dmitri Bulanin Press.

Nikitina, T. G. (2009) *Molodioznyj sleng: Tolkovyj slovar'* (*Youth Slang Dictionary. Expanatory Dictionary*). Moscow: Astrel'.

Novikov, V. I. (2011) *Slovar' modnykh slov: Jazykovaja kartina sovremennosti* (*A Dictionary of Fashionable Words: Contemporary Language Scene*). Moscow: AST-PRESS KNIGA.

Ozhegov, S. I. (1949) *Slovar' russkogo jazika* (*The Russian Language Dictionary*), 1st edition. Moscow: Izdat.

Prokhorov, Y. E. (ed.) (2007) *Rossija. Bol'shoj lingvostranovedcheskij slovar'* (*Russia. Big Cultural Dictionary*). Moscow: AST-PRESS KNIGA.

Reznichenko, I. L. (2008) *Slovar' udarenij russkogo jazyka* (*The Dictionary of Russian Language Accent*). Moscow: AST-PRESS.

Shagalova, E. N. (2011) *Samyj noveishij tolkovyi slovar' russkogo jazyka XXI veka* (*The Newest Russian Language Dictionary of the XXI-st century*). Moscow: Astrel'.

Shimchuk, E. G. (2009) *Russkaja leksikografija* (*Russian Lexicography*). Moscow: Academia.

Skljarevskaja, G. N. (ed.) (2008) *Tolkovyj slovar' russkogo jazyka nachala XXI veka. Aktual'naja leksika (The Russian Language Explanatory Dictionary of the Beginning of the XXIst c. Modern Lexis*). Moscow: Eksmo.

Skljarevskaja, G. N. (ed.) (2002, 2014) *Tolkovyj slovar' russkogo jazyka nachala XXI veka. Jazikovije izmenenija* (*The Russian Language Explanatory Dictionary of the Beginning of the XXI-st Century. Linguistic Changes*). Moscow: Folio – Press.

Skvortsov, L. I. (2009) *Bolshoi tolkovyi slovar' pravilnoi russkoi rechi* (*Big Dictionary of Correct Russian Speech*). Moscow: Oniks, mir i obrazovanie.

Slovar' Akademii Rossijskoj (The Russian Academy Dictionary) (1789–1794) 6 volumes. St. Petersburg: Imperial Academy of Sciences.

Slovar' sovremennogo russkog oliteraturnogo jazika (Bol'shoj akademicheskij slovar') (1948–1965) *(A Dictionary of Contemporary Russian Literary Language) (Big Academic Dictionary)*, 17 volumes. Moscow and Leningrad: The USSR Academy of Sciences.

Stepanov, J. S. (2001) *Konstanty: Slovar' russkoj kul'tury* (*Constants: Dictionary of Russian Culture*). Moscow: Akademicheskiy proekt.

Telija, V. N. (2008) *Bol'shoj frazeologicheskij slovar' russkogo jazyka. Znachenie. Upotreblenie. Kulturologicheskij kommentarij* (*Big Phraseological Dictionary of the Russian Language. Meaning. Usage. Cultural Commentary*). Moscow: AST-PRESS.

Ushakov, D. N. (ed.) (1935–1940) *Tolkovij slovar' russkogo jazika* (*The Explanatory Dictionary of the Russian Language*). 4 volumes. Moscow: Stat Institute "Soviet Encyclopedia", Union of State Book and Journal Publishers, State Publishing House of Foreign and National Dictionaries.

Zaliznjak, A. A. (2008) *Grammaticheskij slovar' russkogo jazyka: Slovoizmenenie* (*The Russian Language Grammar Book: Word-Change*). Moscow: AST-PRESS KNIGA.

Zhukov, A. V. (2010) *Leksiko-frazeologicheskij slovar' russkogo jazyka* (*Lexico-Phraseological Dictionary of the Russian Language*). Moscow: AST-PRESS KNIGA.

Online dictionaries

Ageenko, F. L. (2010) *Slovar' sobstvennih imion russkogo jazyka* (*Dictionary of Russian Proper Names*). Moscow: Mir Ibrazovanie.Elektronnaya versija (Electronic version), 2011. http://gramota.ru/slovari/info/ag/

Arhiv russkoi russistiki (*Archive of Russian Language Theory*) www.ruthenia.ru/apr/textes/sherba/sherba9.htm

Efremova, T. F. (2000) *Novijslovar' russkogojazyka* (*New Russian Language Dictionary*). Moscow: Drofa.www.efremova.info/

Karaulov, Y. N. (ed.) (2001) *Slovar' jazyka Dostoevskogo. Leksicheskij stroi ideolekta (Dostoevsky's Dictionary: Ideolect's Lexis)*. Moscow: Azbukovnik.http://slovari.ru/default.aspx?s=0&p=227

Kuznetsov, S.A. (2000) *Bolshoi tolkovyi slovar' russkogo yazika* (*Big Russian Language Dictionary*). St. Petersburg: Norint. www.gramota.ru/slovari/info/bts

Lashevskaya, O. N. and S. A. Sharov (2009) *Chastotnyi slovar' sovremennogo russkogo jazyka* (*Frequency Dictionary of Modern Russian Language*). Moscow: Azbukovnik. http://dict.ruslang.ru/freq.php

Mokienko, V. M., T. G. Nikitina, and E. K. Nikolaeva (2010) *Bolshoi slovar' russkih poslovits* (*Big Dictionary of Russian Proverbs*). Moscow: ZAO "OLMA Media Group". https://books.google.ru/books?id=wwnu7Qh2Mq8C&printsec=frontcover&hl=ru&source=gbs_atb#v=onepage&q&f=false

Natsionalnyj korpus russkogo jazyka (*National Corpus of Russian Language*). www.ruscorpora.ru/search-main.html

Rosental, D. E. and M. A. Telenkov (2003) *Slovar' trudnostei russkogo jazyka* (*Dictionary of Russian Difficult Words*). 3rd edition. Moscow: Eiris Press. http://dazor.narod.ru/russkie/slovari/trudnostej/slovar-trudnostej_0001.htm

Slovari online (2010–2015) (*Russian Dictionaries On-line*). http://slovonline.ru

Sbornik elektronnih tolkovih slovarei russkogo jazyka – Slovorus (*Collection of Russian Electronic Dictionaries*). http://slovorus.ru/

Slovar' russkogo jazika XVIII veka (*Russian Language Dictionary of the 18th century*).
http://feb-web.ru/feb/sl18/default.asp.

Slovari russkogo jazyka (*Russian Language Dictionaries*). http://povto.ru/books/slovari/slovari-russkogo-yazyka.htm

Spravochno-informatsionnyi portal Gramota.RU – russkiy jazik dlia vseh (*Reference Portal Gramota.Ru – Russian Language for Everybody*).www.gramota.ru/biblio/magazines/gramota/slovari/28_102

Slovari XXI veka (*Dictionaries of the XXI-st century*). http://slovari21.ru

Vinogradov, V. V. (ed.) (2000) *Slovar' jazyka Pushkina* (*Pushkin's Dictionary*), 4 vols., 2nd edition. Moscow: Azbukovnik. http://slovari.ru/default.aspx?s=0&p=230

Yandex Slovari (Yandex Dictionaries). http://slovari.yandex.ru/

Apps-dictionaries

Slovar' Ozhegova (*Ozhegov's Dictionary*). https://itunes.apple.com/us/app/slovar-ozegova/id511740037?mt=8

Bol'shaja Sovetskaja entsiklopedija (*Big Soviet Encyclopedia*). https://itunes.apple.com/us/app/dict-bse/id385945247?mt=8

Slovar' Dala (*Dal's Dictionary*). https://itunes.apple.com/us/app/slovar-dala/id511743764?mt=8

Poslovitsy Dal'a (*Dal's Proverbs*). https://itunes.apple.com/us/app/poslovicy-v.i.-dal/id686812094?mt=8

Karmannyi slovar' 40 v 1 (*Pocket Dictionary 40 in 1*). https://itunes.apple.com/us/app/karmannyj-slovar-40v1/id552337578?mt=8

Slovodnia – Tolkovyi slovar' russkogo jazyka dla sovremennyh ludei (*The Word of the Day – Russian Dictionary for Modern People*). https://itunes.apple.com/us/app/slovo-dna-tolkovyj-slovar/id594187735?mt=8

Other literature

Apresjan, J. D. (2000) *Systematic Lexicography*. Oxford: Oxford University Press.

Bobunova, M. A. (2013) *Russkaja leksikografija XXI veka: uchebnoe posobie* (*Russian Lexicography of the XXI-st Century: Textbook*). Moscow: Flinta.

Cowie, A. P. (ed.) (2009) *The Oxford History of English Lexicography*. Two Volumes. Oxford: Oxford University Press.

Dubichinsky, V. V. (2008) *Leksikografija russkogo jazyka* (*Russian Lexicography*). Moscow: Nauka, Flinta.

Fiodorova, I. V. (2006) *Uchebnaya leksikographija. Teorijaipraktika* (*Learners' Lexicography. Theory and Practice*). Moscow: izdatelskij tsentr "Academia".

Karaulov, Y. N. (ed.) (2003) *Russkaya avtorskaya leksikografija XIX-XX vekov: Antologiya* (*Russian Author Lexicography of the XIX-XX-th Centuries: Antology*). Moscow: Azbukovnik.

Karpova, O. M. (2010) *Anglijskaja leksikografija. Uchebnoje posobie* (*English Lexicography. A Textbook*). Moscow: izdatelskij tsentr "Academia".

Karpova, O. M. (2005) "Russian Lexicography", in K. Brown (ed.), *Oxford Encyclopedia of Language and Linguistics*. Volume 10. Oxford: Elsevier, pp. 704–715.

Karpova, O. M. (2006) "Language Situation in Russia Today with Special Reference to New Russian Dictionaries", in E. Corino, C. Marello and C. Onesti (eds.), *Proceedings of the 12*th *EURALEX International Congress, Torino, Italia, September 6–9*. Torino: Edizionidell'Orso Alessandria, pp. 1249–1254.

Karpova, O. M. and K. Y. Averboukh (2008) "New Voices in Bilingual Russian Terminography with Special Reference to LSP Dictionaries", in E. Bernal and J. DeCesaris (eds.), *Proceedings of the XIII EURALEX International Congress* (Barcelona, 15–19 July 2008). Barcelona: Institut Universitari de Lingüística Aplicada. Universitat Pompeu Fabra, 989–996. See at: http://euralex.org/publications/new-voices-in-bilingual-russian-terminography-with-special-reference-to-lsp-dictionaries/

Kozyrev, V. A. and V. D. Chernjak (2004) *Russkaja leksikografija* (*Russian Lexicography*). Moscow: Drofa.

Kozyrev, V. A. and V. D. Chernjak (2014) *Leksikografija russkogo jazyka: vek nineshnij i vek minuvshij* (*Russian Lexicography: Past and Present*). St. Petersburg: izdatelstvo RGPU named after A.I. Gertsen.

Krongauz, M. (2009) *Russkiy jazyk na grani nervnogo sryva* (*The Russian Language on the Verge of a Nervous Breakdown*). Moscow, Znak.

Ledeniova, V. (2008) *Leksikografija sovremennogo Russkogo jazyka. Praktikum* (*Lexicography of Modern Ruissan Language. Practice*). Moscow: Visshaya skola.

Miznikov, S.A. and O.N. Krilova (eds.) (2010) *Sovremennaya russkaja leksikografija* (*Modern Russian Lexicography*). St. Petersburg: Nauka.

Natsionalnyj korpus russkogo jazyka: *2006–2008*. (2009) *Novyje resultaty i perspektivy. Sbornik statei* (*National Corpus of Russian Language: 2006–2008. New Results and Perspectives. Book of Articles*). St. Petersburg: Nestor-Istorija.

Scherba, L. V. (1974) *Opit obschei teorii leksikografii' (Experience of General Theory of Lexicography)*. Leningrad: Nauka, pp. 265–304. Electronic version: *Arhiv russkoi russistiki* (*Archive of Russian Language Theory*), www.ruthenia.ru/apr/textes/sherba/sherba9.htm Also in English (1995): *International Journal of Lexicography* 8(4): 315–350. Translated by D.M.T. Farina.

Shestakova, L. L. (2011) *Russkaja avtorskaja leksikografija. Teoria. Istoria. Sovremennost'* (*Russian Author lexicography. Theory. History. Modern State*). Moscow: Jaziki slavianskih kultur.

Shimchuk, E. G. (2009) *Russkaja leksikografija* (*Russian Lexicography*). Moscow: Academia.
Sklyarevskaya, G. N. (2013) "Antropotsentricheskaya leksikografiya: idei i praktika" ('Anthropocentric Lexicography: Ideas and Practice'), in J. D. Apresjan, I. V. Cherviankova, I. V. Kosmarskaja, A. Tosheva and N. Deleva (eds.), *Leksikografija. Jazyk. Rech'* (Lexicography. Language. Speech). Sofia: University publishing House named after St. Kliment Okhridsky, pp. 95–104.
Sorokoletov, F.P. (2001) *Istorija russkoj leksikografii* (*A History of Russian Lexicography*). St. Petersburg: Nauka.
Yudina, N. V. (2010) *Russkij jazyk v XXI veke: krizis? evoljutsija? progress?* (*The Russian Language in the XXI-st Century: Crisis? Evolution?Progress?*). Moscow: Gnozis.

40

Spanish lexicography in the Internet era*

Ignacio Bosque and María Auxiliadora Barrios Rodríguez

40.1 Introduction

Some years ago, the Nobel Prize winner Gabriel García Márquez wrote that he did not trust dictionaries, but he still liked to consult them every time he finished a text.[1] He used to do that – he declared – not in order to change some expression in his writing, but only to check whether or not his spontaneous and intuitive interpretations of words happened to coincide with the ones these works attempt to provide. The famous writer would have been surprised to know that, far from opposing the ordinary speaker's views on language, lexicographers strive to develop descriptions of the lexicon that match the linguistic knowledge of common speakers. They do not always succeed because the task of capturing all the nuances hidden in simple words is much more complex than we usually think. In this brief overview, we will schematically draw the main lines followed by current lexicographical studies in Spanish, and we will provide the bibliographical references necessary for the reader to complete our general picture. Perhaps García Márquez would have liked to know something about the enormous efforts lying behind the dictionaries he did not trust.

40.2 Historical perspectives: major works and main overviews

Spanish lexicography is a discipline with a long tradition, now widely established, which does not contradict the very fact that it must still face a number of challenges in the coming years. There are several bibliographic repertoires on Hispanic lexicography, arranged thematically. They include Fabbri (1979), Alvar Ezquerra (1983a), González Aranda (2002), Córdoba (2003), Fernández Gómez (2006), and Ahumada (2006, 2009).

Spanish lexicography also has good textbooks and handbooks, including Haensch et al. (1982), Porto Dapena (1980, 2002), Córdoba (2001), Medina (2003), Anglada (2005), Pérez Hernández (2005), and Martínez de Sousa (1995, 2009), in addition to the old treatise by Casares (1950). Almost all these works include overviews of the current state of art. One may add the overviews in Fontanillo (1984), Haensch (1982, 1990), Dodd (1995), Seco (1995), Marcos Marín (1998), Ahumada (2007), Herreras and De Hoyos (2011), Medina (2016), and García Platero (2016).

Current monographic journals on Spanish lexicography include *Revista de Lexicografía* (La Coruña University), and *Estudios de Lexicografía*, freely accessible online. The *Asociación Española de Estudios Lexicográficos* (Spanish Association of Lexicographical Studies) has already held seven international conferences, the last one in June 2016. Several university centres carry out intensive work in Spanish lexicography, including El Colegio de México (México D.F.), the University of Córdoba (Argentina), and the Universities of Coruña (*GLex*), Jaén, Málaga, and Pompeu Fabra (Spain), among others.

A large number of recent collective works on Spanish lexicography (mostly conference proceedings and other collections of articles) illustrate the remarkable vitality which characterizes the field today. For space reasons, we can only mention some of the compilations published in this century: Ruhstaller and Prado (2000), DeCesaris and Alsina (2001), Álvarez de Miranda and Polo (2002), Pérez Pascual and Campos (2002), Fuentes and Werner (1998), Martín Zorraquino and Aliaga (2003), Echenique and Sánchez Méndez (2003), Battaner and DeCesaris (2004), Bernal et al. (2006), Campos et al. (2007a), Nomdedeu and Sánchez (2008), Bastardín et al. (2009), Castillo and García Platero (2010), Calvo et al. (2010), Corbella et al. (2012), and Nomdedeu et al. (2012).

The history of Spanish lexicography (from the fifteenth to twentieth century) has also been the subject of close attention in recent years. For a brief overview we refer to Bajo (2000), the second part of Medina (2003), and Anglada (2005). There are several bibliographies on works which trace this historical development: Billick and Dworkin (1985), San Vicente (1995), Niederehe (1995a, b), and Esparza (2008). A number of monographs and collective works stand out among the many investigations on this topic. We can only mention a few of them: Alvar Ezquerra (1995, 1996, 2002), Azorín (1996–1997, 2000), Morales (2000), Ahumada (2000), Medina (2001), Campos and Pérez Pascual (2002), Corrales et al. (2004), Roldán (2006), Campos et al. (2007b), Carriscondo (2010), Álvarez de Miranda (2011), and Camacho (2014).

The influence that the dictionary of the *Real Academia Española* ('Royal Spanish Academy', henceforth, RAE) has had on Hispanic lexicographical tradition throughout its 23 editions has been very significant for nearly three centuries. Successive editions of the academic dictionary expanded and renewed the first dictionary by that institution (1726–1739), commonly referred to as *Diccionario de Autoridades* ('Dictionary of authorities'), because it contained examples from the most reputable writers. The academic dictionary is nowadays drawn up by RAE and ASALE ('Association of Academies of the Spanish Language'); in consequence, the old term *DRAE* (instead of *DLE*) is not recommended anymore.

One of the frequent criticisms about the *DLE* is that its pages contain a large number of old definitions and unused or obsolete words, often presented as "slightly used", and sometimes even as part of present-day vocabulary. The *DLE* has also been criticized for the highly ideological charge of some of its definitions. On one hand, the latter factor affects all dictionaries in one way or another, so it is no wonder that many words reflect cultural realities whose interpretation largely depends on social values, often changing within communities. On the other hand, it is well known that successive editions of the Royal Academy's dictionary kept unchanged a number of old, outdated definitions, instead of adapting them to new times, customs, and values. There is plenty on all these matters, including the following monographies and compilations: Forgas (1996, 2007), Sánchez García (2009), López Facal (2010), Rodríguez Barcia (2010, 2012), Nomdedeu (2011a), and Rodríguez Barcia and Ramallo (2015).

The joint work of RAE and ASALE has been very fruitful over the last two decades. In addition to two editions of *DLE*, they have published many dictionaries in recent years, including thesauri, didactic dictionaries, and dictionaries of essential vocabulary and linguistic doubts (somewhat similar to usage books in the British tradition). They have digitally renewed the *DLE* project (see Section 40.4), resumed work on the historical dictionary of Spanish (*NDHLE*, see Section 40.3.1), and have embarked on two new lexicographic projects: a phraseological dictionary and a dictionary of grammatical terminology for secondary school teachers. Most academic dictionaries and corpora are openly accessible in the Internet at the RAE's web page.[2]

The RAE's dictionaries have been carefully dissected, scrutinized, praised, and criticized in a large number of studies. The long list of existing monographs on them includes the following titles: Lapesa (1964), Salas (1964), Lázaro Carreter (1972, 1980), Mateu (1999), Abad (1998), Clavería (2003, 2016), Ruhstaller (2003), Rodríguez Marín (2003), Blecua (2006), Campos and Pérez Pascual (2006), Rodríguez Barcia (2008), Nomdedeu (2009 a,b), Sánchez García (2009), Portilla (2009), Freixas (2010), Rodríguez Ortiz and Garriga (2010), Lombardini (2011), Pascual Fernández (2013), and Jiménez Ríos (2013).

The study of the extent to which the prologues of dictionaries reveal the state of lexicography in each period of its history has some tradition in Spain. This issue is addressed at length in Alvar Ezquerra (1983b, 1985), Lombardini (2011), San Vicente and Lombardini (2012), and Camacho (2012).

Apart from the academic *DLE*, at least four other dictionaries may be considered true landmarks in the history of Spanish lexicography. They are very different in their conception and their objectives, but they all show considerable originality, as well as the result of a remarkable innovative spirit. In chronological order, these are R. J. Cuervo's *DCR*, M. Moliner's *DUE*, J. Corominas and J. A. Pascual's *DCECH*, and M. Seco's et al.'s *DEA*.

The *DCR* has no direct equivalent in other languages. It is a personal creation of R. J. Cuervo (1844–1911), who barely lived long enough to see a small part of his titanic work in print, despite having devoted more than 30 years to the same project. Cuervo aimed to compile a Spanish dictionary capable of describing all the words of some syntactic interest. He decided to do this by extracting the relevant grammatical patterns out of the texts in which they could be documented. The *DCR* has eight volumes, and only the first two were written by Cuervo himself. The authors of the other volumes respected his initial project and used Cuervo's archives, together with new material. The work was completed in 1995 and is now available on CD-ROM, which greatly alleviates the difficulties of the original typography. For other aspects of *DCR*, see Porto Dapena (1980), Cruz (1994), and Montes (1998), among other works.

The *DCECH*, by J. Corominas and J. A. Pascual, consists of six volumes. This is the second edition, greatly enlarged, of the etymological dictionary that Corominas published in the mid-1950s. The adjective *crítico* ('critical'), which appears in the title, implies that authors assess the etymologies proposed by other scholars and add their own analysis. This requires the management of a significant critical apparatus, and a rich set of textual sources.

The *DUE* is another personal creation, in this case by M. Moliner (1900–1981). Although she drew some of her definitions from the academic *DLE*, she simplified them considerably and added a large amount of grammatical information. She included a small number of morphology and syntax monographs, together with multiple lexical and conceptual associations: synonyms, idioms, collocations, and other related words. This is a dictionary of "use", as stated in its title; that is, a dictionary of common expressions employed in current Spanish. It has been repeatedly pointed out that *DUE* is one of the most useful existing tools for students of Spanish as a second language (on *DUE*'s influence on Spanish pedagogical lexicography see also Chapter 7 of this *Handbook*, especially Sections 7.3.3 and 7.3.4).

Successive editions of *DUE*, published by Gredos, contained many additions, but also structural changes that were controversial. The *DUE* is currently available on CD, but not online. This brief information can be expanded through Casas Gómez et al. (1998), Seco (2003), and Porto Dapena (2003), among other sources.

The *DEA*, devised and directed by Manuel Seco, is the most complete and modern of the existing dictionaries of contemporary Spanish, even if it is deliberately restricted to the European variety. The *DEA* is a dictionary of present-day Spanish in which all senses of all words are documented in texts covering a span of 40 years. *DEA* distinguishes senses from subsenses, so that a hierarchy of meanings is built up for each word. Traditional lexical marks are also updated, and syntactic contexts of lexical dependencies (*contornos* 'edge, contour' in Spanish) are clearly identified. All these are uncommon practices in the Hispanic grammatical tradition. On these and other aspects of *DEA*, we refer to Gelpí (2000a), García Pérez (2000), and Álvarez de Miranda (2011).

Lexicographical criticism has always been stronger in the Spanish-speaking intellectual world than initiatives to undertake new dictionaries aimed at overcoming the deficiencies of existing ones. The reason is not only the crude truism that judging is always easier than creating, but also the fact that – unlike England, France, and other countries with powerful publishing industries – projects addressed to undertake and subsidize comprehensive large-scale dictionaries have been scarce in Spain and other Spanish-speaking countries. Still, non-academic lexicography has produced very good dictionaries in the last 25 years, including *VOX* (expanded and updated as *LEMA* and *DUEAE*), *CLAVE*, *DSAL*, or *LAROUSSE* among others, almost all accessible online.[3]

In addition to specific studies on the five outstanding dictionaries mentioned above (*DLE*, *DCR*, *DCECH*, *DUE*, and *DEA*), a large number of monographic investigations focus on the analysis and the comparison of current dictionaries of Spanish, including Zimmerman (1985), Lara (1990), Ahumada (1992, 2006), Hernández (1998), Canellada (1988), Corrales (2000), Abad (2001), Salvador (2002), Fuentes et al. (2005–2006), and López Facal (2010).

40.3 Core issues and topics

So far, the coming of age of the Internet has not had an influence on Spanish lexicography as strong as the one it has certainly had on that of English or German (see Chapters 33 and 35 of this *Handbook*). But even so, a considerable number of new ongoing lexicographic projects start to reframe old issues in new formats, and begin to use current technical resources to set up new lexical programs. In this section we relate core issues and topics to specific dictionaries (both existing or in progress), most of them ascribed to well-known dictionary typologies. When needed, we will emphasize the main innovations introduced by the dictionaries analysed, whether Internet related or not. We will also add some lexical databases in the appropriate subsections, even if these are not dictionaries properly.

Like those compiled for other languages, dictionaries of Spanish can be grouped according to multiple criteria: the nature of the lexicon analysed, their addressees, their data sources, their macro and microstructure, etc. The most comprehensive classification of Spanish dictionaries is that of Haensch (2004a). Less detailed but quite useful typologies may be found in Malkiel (1959), Berson (1979), Gak (1991), Porto Dapena (2002: ch. 2), Lara (2005), and Anglada (2005: ch. 5). In the following a number of representative criteria will be chosen. Nevertheless, much of the existing literature on Spanish metalexicography cannot be mentioned, much less so discussed.

40.3.1 Etymological and historical dictionaries

NDHLE is the continuation of an old academic project aimed at describing the history of each Spanish word, as well as the sense changes it has undergone over the years. The project passed through two previous stages. A volume was published in 1933 of the first academic historical dictionary (*DHist*), and another one followed in 1936, shortly before the outbreak of the Spanish Civil War (see Chapter 23 of this *Handbook*). The *DHist* contained about 2000 entries. The project restarted in 1946 with a new design (*DHLE*) and a different working plan, and was carried out from 1990 to 1996. Almost 30,000 words (including graphical variants and cross references) were addressed in this second stage; but, even so, lexicographers only reached the start of the letter B. The *NDHLE*, started in 2006, is the continuation of these projects. 1,250 *NDHLE* entries have been made public so far. This dictionary contains important developments compared to its predecessors in the RAE, including the renewal of corpora and text sources, a digital editing platform, and the simple but crucial fact that the order of entries in the drafting process is not alphabetical, but conceptual. All academic historical dictionaries of Spanish are accessible online at RAE's web page.

We have already referred to *DCECH*. For a detailed analysis of etymological and historical dictionaries of Spanish, see Seco (1992), Fajardo (1999), Porto Dapena (2000), Álvarez de Miranda (2003), Pascual and García Pérez (2006), Campos (2007), Garcés (2008), Pérez Pascual (2008), and Campos and Pascual (2012), as well as vol. 3 (2015) of the journal *Estudios de Lexicografía*, accessible online.

40.3.2 Thesauri

The term *thesaurus* is generally used in two senses. In the first one, and albeit with slight nuances, it is an *analogic dictionary*, as in "*Webster's Thesaurus*". In the second one (the one used in the Hispanic tradition), *thesauri* are compilations of dictionaries carried out with some chronological or geographical basis. Gili Gaya's *TL* was interrupted early. *NTLLE*, by RAE, is accessible online. It not only contains all academic dictionaries previous to 2001, but also a dozen other non-academic ones published between the fifteenth and the nineteenth centuries. The more recent *NTLE*, by L. Nieto Jiménez and M. Alvar Ezquerra, is only available on paper. It consists of 11 volumes; each entry summarizes those in 40 dictionaries of the sixteenth and eighteenth centuries. The CD-ROM compiled by Álvarez de Miranda (1998) contains six old dictionaries. For other characteristics of existing thesauri on Spanish, we refer to Colón (1956), Alvar Ezquerra (2003), Alvar Ezquerra and Nieto (2006), and Vila (2014). On dialectal thesauri, see the following section.

40.3.3 Geographical variation: integral and differential dictionaries

Spanish is spoken in Spain, 20 American countries (21, if one includes the United States), and at least one African country (Equatorial Guinea). Although the degree of lexical and grammatical unity of the Spanish language is rather high – largely due to the work of the American republics after they achieved independence – a significant lexical variation in such a vast territory is entirely expected.

Considering geographical criteria, dictionaries can be *general*, if they cover all variants of Spanish wherever it is spoken, and *particular*, if they are limited to a country, some parts of it, or several countries. The latter are further divided into *integral* and *differential* (or *contrastive*) dictionaries. Integral dictionaries comprehensively collect all the lexicon known in the delimited area, whether or not it coincides with the one used in other areas. Differential or contrastive dictionaries only capture the lexicon characterizing the bounded area. Contrastive dictionaries can also become thesauri, as *TLHA* on the Andalusian lexicon, *TLEPR* on Puerto Rican Spanish, or *TLEC* on the Canary variety (see also *DHECan* on Canary Spanish on both descriptive and historical grounds).

Dictionaries of Spanish which present themselves as general are not too numerous: *DLE*, and – to a lesser extent – *DUEAE, DSAL, CLAVE*, besides a few others. Integral dictionaries are not very numerous either: *DEUM, DEM* (both on Mexican Spanish, directed by L. F. Lara), and *DIEA* on Argentinean Spanish, coordinated by F. Plager. On the contrary, differential dictionaries of Spanish exist for almost every American country (see Córdoba 2003 and Haensch 2004a for a complete list). R. Werner and G. Haensch, from the University of Augsburg, directed a comprehensive project of American contrastive dictionaries, specifically the varieties spoken in Colombia, Peru, Uruguay, Argentina, and Cuba. The existing differential dictionaries covering all American Spanish include *DDEA*, by M. Morínigo; *DH*, coordinated by R. Richards; and especially the recent *DA*, directed by H. López Morales.

The question whether or not the academic *DLE* is truly a general dictionary of Spanish has often been raised for at least three reasons: (i) there are no differential dictionaries of *españolismos* (words used in Spain, but not in the American Spanish-speaking countries); (ii) *DLE* sometimes omits the geographical mark "Spain" in entries that should include it; and (iii) *DLE* contains geographical marks for provinces or regions of Spain (Salamanca, Badajoz, etc.), but none for American provinces, regions, or even states (within a single country, such as Mexico). *RAE* and *ASALE* are currently developing a new dictionary of Spanish under a digital platform (24th edition of *DLE*) in which – so they have declared – all these problems will be satisfactorily solved. There is plenty of literature on these controversial issues. See Lara (1990, 2001, 2012), Lope Blanch (1995), Ávila (1998, 2003, 2003–2004), and Zimmerman (1980, 1986, 2003). For a general overview of American Spanish lexicography, we refer to Haensch (1987), Zimmermann and Wotjak (1994), Aleza (2000), Werner (2001), Fajardo (2010), Campos et al. (2006), and Matus (2007).

40.3.4 Dictionaries of lexical relations

Dictionaries of synonyms and antonyms are also traditional in Spanish lexicography. In fact, almost every important publishing house has published its own. Printed ones include J. Corripio's *GDS* and D. Ortega Cavero's *GSSAI*. The latter is an analogical dictionary as well. The most recent and comprehensive dictionary in this group is *DGSA*, directed by J. M. Blecua (see Chapter 17 of this *Handbook*). Synonyms and antonyms from these and other dictionaries are currently available from *WordReference*, *The Free Dictionary*, *Signum*, and other online platforms, to which one may add *BP* and *DS*, the latter from a university department.

Nowadays, interest in lexical relations goes beyond synonymy and antonymy. In fact, dictionaries start to systematically cover hyperonymy, hyponymy, or meronymy, wherever these relations are appropriate. Most databases including them are born associated to research projects led by psycholinguists. The best known and most used in computational applications are *WordNet*, *EuroWordNet*, the *Open Multilingual WordNet*, and *OpenThesaurus-es*. The Multilingual Central Repository (MCR) integrates the Spanish *WordNet* with wordnets in other languages, and includes domain labels and a top ontology of concept features, among other aspects. In the context of the web of data, *BabelNet* (which includes Spanish) emerges as a multilingual-encyclopaedic dictionary that also offers a semantic network of terms. *SENSEM*, a project from the GRIAL interuniversity research group, contains a bank of lexical and grammatical data (mostly on verbs) developed out of *EuroWordNet 3.0* for Spanish. In Bosque and Mairal (2012 a,b) another possible way of conceiving hyponymy, hyperonymy, and other relations of inclusion in the Spanish lexicon is suggested (see Chapter 12 of this *Handbook*).

A particular type of dictionary of lexical relations is often called *combinatory dictionary*. This concept is somewhat more comprehensive than that of *dictionary of collocations*, although they both share their basic content to a large extent. These dictionaries have some tradition in other languages, but it is only recently that they have been built for Spanish. They systematically describe syntagmatic associations or co-occurrences (from *law* to *enact, repeal, strike down, in force*, etc.), as opposed to paradigmatic ones, which characterize dictionaries of synonyms (from *law* to *rule, decree, norm*, etc.), or analogic dictionaries (from *law* to *justice, court, guilt, defendant*, etc.). In other languages, combinatorial dictionaries are rarely based on restrictive predicative-argument semantic relationships. This is the main feature of *REDES*, directed by I. Bosque. The *DCPEC*, coordinated by the same author, dispenses with this conceptual underpinning, but provides about 400,000 lexical combinations. On differences between these two combinatory dictionaries, see Barrios (2007) and Buendía Castro and Faber (2014). On *REDES*, see also DeCesaris and Battaner (2006).

The *DICE*, directed by M. Alonso Ramos, and framed within a simplified version of I. Melčuk's Meaning Text Theory, is an ongoing project. It currently offers 200 entries corresponding to emotion nouns, for which it provides more than 20,000 combinations, with plenty of exemplification. The *DICE* is accessible online. *REDES* and *DCPEC* are only available in printed format. Torner and Bernal (2017) contain 17 papers on the analysis of Spanish collocations and other restricted lexical combinations from different points of view.

As opposed to what is normal in several European countries, the concept *analogic dictionary* is not common in the Spanish lexicographic tradition. The terms used instead include *ideological dictionary, thematic dictionary*, and *dictionary of like-minded ideas* (Sp. *de ideas afines*). These dictionaries, which group words together according to conceptual associations, are generally considered *onomasiological* (i.e. coding or production dictionaries; see Chapters 17 and 18 of this *Handbook*), as opposed to so-called *semasiological* (i.e. decoding or deciphering dictionaries; see Chapter 16 of this *Handbook*), but the truth is that all dictionaries of lexical relations are production dictionaries as well. Both *DI*, by J. Casares, and *DILE*, directed by M. Alvar Ezquerra, are included as appendices of other dictionaries, whereas F. Corripio's *DIA* and R. del Moral's *DIALLE* are published as independent works, do not contain definitions, and display a higher number of associations and conceptual groupings.

DIALLE (2009) is the last and most complete of analogic dictionaries of Spanish. The online dictionary *IA* contains a great number of lexical associations (sometimes directly drawn from Corripio's *DIA* without the appropriate credit being given). Previous analogic dictionaries of Spanish include J. Ruiz León's, published in 1879, and E. Benot's, printed in 1897. Some projects of online analogic dictionaries exist (in various stages of development), such as *ZIRANO*. For a more complete picture of Spanish analogic dictionaries, see Soler (1999), Martínez Montoro (2006), and Moreno (2012).

40.3.5 Grammatical dictionaries: multi-purpose dictionaries

The term *grammatical dictionary* allows for various interpretations. In a broad sense, it applies to all dictionaries which collect syntactical or morphological information of any nature (including marks for transitive verbs, irregular plurals, etc.). The label can also be applied to phraseological and combinatory dictionaries. However, it is customary to reserve the term for dictionaries that systematically develop grammatical information that requires various types of lexical specifications, including regime (as in E. Slager's *DUPE* or the aforementioned *DCR*), verbal periphrases (as in *DPV*, directed by L. García Fernández, and *DCPV*, by M. Morera) and as well as particles and grammatical markers and connectors. Some dictionaries of this later group are concluded (as L. Santos's *DP* or C. Fuentes's *DCOE*), but others are still in process, as *DPDE*, directed by A. Briz (see Briz 2005). As regards morphological information in online platforms, see Santana et al. (2003).

The *DCR* is the only (concluded) dictionary of Spanish displaying information on the valence of predicates, although in a peculiar format. Entries also describe the particular options available for each set of constructions (including specification of complement clauses, verbal mood, etc.). The 24th edition of *DLE* is expected to update and enlarge this grammatical information. Other ongoing lexical projects in a digital format start to include all these specifications, often enriched with various semantic features. Most of them focus on the syntactic and semantic description of verbs: *BDS*, *ADESSE*, *DICEMTO*, or *SENSEM*. The *AnCora* project includes information on argument structure, as well as lexicons used for corpus annotation. Renau et al.'s *VERBARIO* is an adaptation of P. Hanks's *Corpus Pattern Analysis* to Spanish (see Alonso and Renau 2013 and Baisa et al. 2016 a,b). At the moment it provides detailed semantic restrictions for the arguments of 211 verbs.

The project *Spanish FrameNet*, led by C. Subirats, is also underway (see Chapter 24 of this *Handbook*). Its aim is to create a lexical database with syntactic and semantic information for verbs, adverbs, adjectives, prepositions, etc., derived from annotated sentences in order to represent the valence of these elements as realized in texts. Schemes associated with each lexical item are based on the theory of frames by C. Fillmore. For more information see Subirats (2005, 2009, 2012) and Batiukova (2009).

Some current digital dictionaries are actually online dictionary packages, sometimes called *multi-purpose dictionaries* or *multidictionaries* (Sp. *multidiccionarios*: Águila 2006, 2009). These dictionaries (e.g. *Lexicon*, *Woxikon*, *Wiktionary*, *BP*, etc.) often contain definitions, synonyms, antonyms, reverse order, and sometimes even a number of pieces of information concerning syllabic segmentation, etymology, frequency, derivative terms, set phrases, famous quotations, etc.

Numerous studies deal with the grammatical information in Spanish dictionaries and possible ways to improve it. Among many others, we will refer to Alvar Ezquerra (1997), Gutiérrez Cuadrado (1992), Bargalló (1999), and Bosque (2006). To these, one should add numerous articles on the concept of lexicographical *contour* (Sp. *contorno*), crucial to properly restrict definitions on syntactic and semantic grounds. Alonso (2002) and Serra (2006) provide excellent overviews of this issue (see also Chapter 17 of this *Handbook*).

40.3.6 Phraseological dictionaries

There is a large number of dictionaries of Spanish idiomatic expressions. The most complete is M. Seco et al.'s *DFDEA*. This is a comprehensive dictionary of European Spanish which exemplifies and documents more than 15,000 idiomatic expressions.

The *DFP* is an academic project in its initial phase. When completed, it will let us know what idiomatic expressions are general in the Hispanic world and which ones are limited to certain areas, a type of information still unknown. *DFDEA* is an integral phraseological dictionary, and so are *DFEM*, *DFE*, or *DELE*. On the contrary *DFHA*, on Argentine Spanish, is a differential dictionary, as well as *TLEPR* (on Puerto Rican Spanish, accessible online) or *DFED* on Dominican Spanish, among others. See also *DH*, coordinated by R. Richard, intended to cover all American countries. S. Fitch's *DCTDE* is presented as a general phraseological dictionary.

Most phraseological dictionaries do not group idioms on conceptual grounds. Somewhat paradoxically, they are provided by the already mentioned *DUE*, which is not a phraseological dictionary. Conceptual groups of idioms are also described in *DTFH* and *DIALLE*, as well as the various phraseological dictionaries for foreign learners published by I. Penadés in Arco/Libro. Slang dictionaries are not properly phraseological, because they contain numerous single-word expressions. The most recent ones include *GDA* and *DEDA*.

A number of research groups on Spanish phraseology regularly report their activities and online resources through web pages. These groups include *FRASYSTRAM* (Univ. of Alicante), *FRASESPAL* and *FRASEONET* (both at the Univ. of Santiago, Spain), and *PAREFRAS* and *FRASEMIA* (both at the Complutense University, Madrid). Similar groups exist at the Universities of Málaga and Murcia (Spain), as well as Córdoba (Argentina). Some projects also exist on the historical development of idioms, including *FRASLEDIA* (Univ. of Valencia). For a general overview of Spanish phraseology, see García Page (2008).

40.3.7 Didactic dictionaries

Didactic lexicography is one of the branches of this discipline that has aroused more interest in Spain in recent years, particularly as regards vocabulary learning in first- and second-language teaching. Traditionally, it was not uncommon to draw up word definitions for children by just cutting back or stripping standard definitions in major dictionaries, rather than building it completely from scratch according to the children's age and cognitive development.

The main traits that should characterize didactic school lexicography, and the various ways in which teachers can adapt them to improve their performance in the classroom, are discussed at length in a number of studies. Among monographs we will only mention Hernández (1989, 1991, 2001), Maldonado (1998, 2000, 2003), Martín García (1999), and Ávila Martín (2000). As for compilations of studies, we refer to Ayala (2001), Moya and Sosinski (2006), and Ruhstaller and Gordon (2010). One may also obtain a good overview through Martínez Marín (1992) and Sánchez Muñoz (2002–2003).

As applied to second-language teaching, didactic lexicography has seen a remarkable development in recent years. We can only mention some relevant collections of studies: García Platero and Castillo (2000), Castillo (2005), and Pérez Pascual et al. (2008). For general overviews of the features that these dictionaries have and/or should have, see Hernández (2001), Campanile et al. (2011), Nomdedeu (2009c, 2011b), Fuertes-Olivera (ed.) (2010), and Maldonado (2013). The proceedings of the *TISLID's* (= 'Technological Innovation for Specialized Linguistic Domains') workshops report a large number of new resources on Spanish as a second language.

As for the lexicographical works themselves, several publishing houses have published school dictionaries in recent years (SM, Santillana, Anaya, etc.). RAE published its own *Diccionario del estudiante* (*DE*), together with a simplified versión: *Diccionario práctico del estudiante* (*DPE*). Didactical dictionaries may be crossed with geographical variables. For example, SM built up an exclusive version for Latin America Spanish of its advanced school dictionary (*ADDE*). The Mexican Academy published *DEAML*, a didactic dictionary accessible online.

DAELE, directed by P. Battaner, is a very original lexicographic project. This is a monolingual dictionary targeted at advanced foreign students. At the moment only 363 verbal entries have been made public online. Definitions follow the original system devised by J. Sinclair for the *Collins Cobuild Dictionary*, which so far has never been applied to Spanish. Lexical entries also display grammatical, morphological, and orthographic information, as well as other contents relevant for foreign students (frequent errors, false friends, etc.). For more details, see Renau and Battaner (2011).

40.3.8 Bilingual dictionaries

Some existing online bilingual dictionaries are digital versions of printed ones. A very large number of the latter have been published, although – as Haensch (2004a) remarks – differences in quality among them are rather sharp. The *DLEA* is a Spanish-German/German-Spanish dictionary containing more than 200,000 entries. It stands out for its completeness and the richness of its grammatical information (Gouws et al. 2013). Sánchez Merino (2003) emphasizes the quality of *Sopena*'s bilingual dictionaries for French, Italian, and German; *Vox*'s dictionary for German; *Espasa*'s for Portuguese; *Larousse*'s for English and French; and *Oxford*'s for English. Bilingual dictionaries can also be phraseological, such as Carbonell's *DFCIS* for Spanish-Italian, and Sevilla and Cantera's *DTLF* for French-Spanish.

Online bilingual dictionaries have become almost indispensable tools for a large number of professionals nowadays. Particularly noteworthy is *CSD*. The *Reverso* dictionary is another product of the same company. It contains a program of automatic translation for short texts applied to the Lexibase corpus. *WordReference* is widely used as well. According to its creator, Michael Kellogg (personal communication), it is based on a first list of common words in a given language, out of which a corpus is constructed. Materials extracted from multiple monolingual and bilingual dictionaries are then associated to common patterns in this corpus which includes a deep analysis of these dictionaries, which are identified as "machine translation systems" (see also Chapter 34 of this *Handbook*). In the context of machine translation, projects such as the *Apertium* platform,[4] which includes bilingual dictionaries for multiple language pairs (recently converted to a Semantic Web–compliant format) are also noteworthy.

Most general overviews of Hispanic bilingual lexicography are not recent. We refer to Alvar Ezquerra (1981, 1993), Gelpí (2000b), Acero (2003), Haensch (2004b), and San Vicente (2007).

40.3.9 Terminological and specialized dictionaries

It is not possible to enumerate the existing Spanish terminological dictionaries (whether printed or online), because they have spread to multiple disciplines in recent years. These dictionaries contain encyclopaedic information, while still being lexicographical works. Interestingly, the technical information they provide does not always depend on the language in which it is offered. The topics for which these dictionaries exist include economics, architecture, agriculture, accounting, literature (with differentiated works for authors, literary terms, genres, etc.), music, cinema, sports, philosophy, law, linguistics, computer sciences, medicine, and many other domains.

Several dictionaries, both printed and online, may be found for some specific areas. As an example, on ecology and environmental issues one may use *ECOLEXICON* (online), which displays conceptual networks created within the frame-based terminology (Faber et al 2005, 2016), as well as *ECORESSOURCES*, on English, French, and Spanish. This information may be completed with other existing ecology dictionaries for French, Italian, and other European languages. Similarly, anyone consulting the recently published *DEJ* (on legal terminology), coordinated by S. Muñoz Machado, may complete the information found there with the one provided by various legal dictionaries in French, English, or German. Specialized dictionaries may be bilingual as well, as *DCIE* (on accounting), directed by P. Fuertes-Olivera (see Chapter 28 of this *Handbook*), *MLG* (on law), or *IATE*, published by the European Union, which addresses many different areas of the European Community administration. *TERMINESP* is a bank of terminological data promoted by AETER (standing for *Spanish Association of Terminology*).[5] On a projected bilingual (English-Spanish) dictionary of international trade, see García Llamas (2013). For a general overview of specialized dictionaries in Spanish, refer to Espinosa (1982), Mochón and Sorli (2001), Ahumada (2002), Gelpí (2004), Contreras (2008), Fuertes-Olivera and Bergenholtz (2011, 2015), and Fuertes-Olivera and Tarp (2014).

40.3.10 Illustrated dictionaries

Even though illustrated dictionaries are characterized by the inclusion of images, drawings, or figures, the true fact is that these are not always chosen to illustrate words that are difficult to understand through verbal descriptions. Barrios (2002) explains that the first illustrated dictionary published by RAE in 1927 was designed to collect American-Spanish lexicon, but ended up including illustrations almost accidentally. Similarly, in Vox's *DGILE*, directed by S. Gili Gaya, or in Sopena's *DIBSIS*, directed by L. Sanchez Landero, illustrations are not always chosen to supplement insufficient or imprecise verbal descriptions.

In contrast to this classic approach, all words are accompanied by particular illustrations in modern dictionaries of images, to the point that the image may replace the definition. This is the case of the current visual dictionaries, *IDI* (by SM), with bilingual versions; *SEÑÁLALO* (an adaptation of *POINTIT*). This dictionary is accessible on line, and so is *DBE*, by a Cuban university, which contains videos and images, as well as definitions. Larousse's *NDV* is a visual dictionary in Spanish, French, English, German, and Italian published on paper and online. Multilingual visual dictionaries include *AISA* (for Spanish, English, French, Chinese, Arabic, Berber, and Basque) and *DV* (by Ikonet), conceived as an illustrated encyclopaedia with comprehensive information on meronymy and hyponymy.

40.4 Looking to the future: open perspectives and final reflections

However long the preceding list of references might seem to be, it cannot encompass the totality of resources on the lexicon of Spanish and other Iberian languages currently available. For a more specific list of recent web resources, see the *IULA-UPF CLARIN Competence Center* web page,[6] the *IXA GROUP on Natural Language Processing*'s web page,[7] or the University of Alicante's *Dictionaries and glossaries* web page.[8] It is important to point out that a number of dictionaries and databases presented earlier (*NDHLE*, *DAELE*, *DICE*, *DPDE*, *ADESSE*, *SENSEM*, etc.) are still ongoing projects. The 24th edition of the *DLE*, barely started in a new digital environment, is also a new project. The 23rd (2014) on line edition (see footnote 2) offers some interesting features, such as access to verb conjugations, inverse order, immediate detection of idioms, etc. The 22nd (2001) edition was supplemented with a CD (=*DLE-CD*) with many more features (including independent access to specific grammatical, geographic, or sociolinguistic marks, as in any database).

New general dictionaries of the Spanish language conceived in digital format and based on renewed lexicographic approaches begin to emerge (see Chapter 17 of this *Handbook*). A good example is *DCLEA*, directed by A. Porto Dapena. Only 200 entries are available online at the moment. They contain a large amount of grammatical information (syntactic patterns, prepositional regime, mood selection, etc.), and – as in *DCR* or *DEA* – all word senses are illustrated through attested examples. The *DCLEA* also contains collocations and other lexical relations.

Most of the necessary changes that ought to take place in both standard user's routines and common lexicographer's habits are addressed at length in Fuertes-Olivera and Bergenholtz (2015). Some overviews of the perspectives on and possibilities for Spanish lexicography in the coming years, as well as the necessary challenges it must face, include Alvar Ezquerra (1992), Santana et al. (1996), Gelpí (2003, 2004), Martín Zorraquino and Aliaga (2003), Águila (2006), Rojo (2007), Batiukova (2009), Millán (2011), and Maldonado (2013).

We would like to point out three features of modern online dictionaries which – slowly, but progressively – begin to be incorporated into new, ongoing projects in Spanish lexicography. We will call them *lexical connectivity*, *personalization*, and *integration*.

By *lexical connectivity* we mean access to specific non-traditional lexical information, such as argument structure (or valency) for predicates, or lexical relations (synonymy, antonymy, meronymy, collocations, etc.). Facilities to access words included in definitions of other items are not standard yet. Notice that this would allow us to go from *niño* 'child' to *infancia* 'infancy', *potito* 'jarred baby food', or *canción de cuna* 'nursery rhyme', a possibility that most current dictionaries do not allow for in a systematic way (Barrios 2006). Current efforts in the interface between linguistics and knowledge engineering, especially in the context of the Semantic Web and the linked data paradigm, are already framing connectivity between lexical units as a central part in their approaches. The goal is not only to represent and link content but to do so in a machine-readable way able to allow for intelligent agents to exploit such content (Bosque-Gil et al. 2016 and references therein).

The second feature is *personalization*. The user of an online dictionary may or may not want to have more specific information on particular domains, including etymology, verbal conjugations, corpus data, geographical or historical information, pronunciation, phonetic transcription, or linguistic context. A modern online dictionary should allow the user to customize his or her preferences on these and other similar features. The 24th online edition of the *DLE* (hopefully out in the not too distant future) aims to provide most of them.

Finally, by *integration* we mean hypertextual access to other platforms, including online encyclopaedias, pictures, videos, and other graphic information from atlases of banks of images, monographs and handbooks on specialized topics, up-to-date bibliography, and scientific information on present-day research. We hope that new coming tools and mechanisms from approaches to the Web of Data will help us navigate such a stormy ocean without sinking, drifting, or losing direction.

40.5 Conclusion

In the preceding pages we have summarized the main achievements of the Spanish lexicographic tradition according to classic dictionary typologies. We have also schematically described recent and ongoing projects which attempt to develop some of these results in more modern formats, as well as other enterprises aimed at providing lexical resources which fall beyond the limits of printed lexicons. Finally, we have defended that e-lexicography must focus on pursuing three main objectives: *lexical connectivity, personalization*, and *integration*.

Related topics

Dictionaries for text production; dictionaries for text reception; dictionaries for translation; dictionaries to assist teaching and learning; the *Accounting Dictionaries*; the *Alicante Dictionaries*; the concept of dictionary.

Further reading

Anglada Boix, E. (2005). *Lexicografía española*. Barcelona: Universitat de Barcelona.
A good textbook for students. It contains many dictionary fragments useful for the classroom.

Bajo Pérez, E. (2000). *Los diccionarios. Introducción a la lexicografía del español*. Gijón: Trea.
A short overview of present-day and classical Spanish lexicography.

Martínez de Sousa, J. (2009). *Manual básico de lexicografía*. Gijón: Trea.
A good introduction for undergraduate students.

Medina Guerra, A. (ed.) (2003). *Lexicografía española*, Barcelona: Ariel.
A very complete book of readings on Spanish lexicography. It contains 14 chapters written by experienced specialists.

Notes

* We would like to thank Ricardo Mairal and Julia Bosque-Gil for providing us with some of the references mentioned here, as well as two anonymous reviewers for their detailed comments of a previous version of this chapter. Needless to say, all possible shortcomings are our own.

1 *El País*, May, 19, 1982.
2 See at www.rae.es
3 A list of current Spanish dictionaries with free online access may be seen at *Escritores.org*'s web page (under "Recursos"). For a more general list of Spanish dictionaries, see the web pages mentioned in Section 40.4. See also BNE (=Biblioteca Nacional de España)'s web page, section "Introducción a las obras de consulta. Guía de recursos bibliográficos". In any case, Haensch (2004a) still stands as the most complete list of Spanish dictionaries until that date.
4 See at www.apertium.org/index.spa.html?dir=spa-eng#translation
5 See at www.wikilengua.org/index.php/Wikilengua:Terminesp
6 See at www.clarin-es-lab.org/index-en.html
7 See at http://ixa.si.ehu.es/Ixa/Produktuak
8 See at https://dti.ua.es/en/resources/diccionaries-and-glosaries.html

References

Cited dictionaries and lexicographic projects

ADDE = *Avanzado. Diccionario Didáctico del Español para secundaria y preparatoria* (2002). Dir. by L. García and C. Maldonado. Edición para América Latina. Madrid: SM.

ADESSE = *Base de datos de verbos, alternancias de diátesis y esquemas sintáctico-semánticos del Español*. Universidad de Vigo. http://adesse.uvigo.es/data/

AISA = *Diccionario ilustrado para inmigrantes*. www.xarma.net/AISA2/index.html

AnCora = *AnCora*. Dir. by M. A. Martí. Universitat de Barcelona.

BabelNet = *A Multilingual Encyclopedic Dictionary*. http://babelnet.org/

BDS = *Base de datos sintácticos del español actual*. Universidad de Santiago de Compostela. www.bds.usc.es/

BP = *Buscapalabra*. Ignacio López. www.buscapalabra.com/

CLAVE = *Diccionario de uso del español actual* (2004) Dir. by C. Maldonado. Madrid: SM. http://clave.smdiccionarios.com/app.php

CSD = *Collins Spanish Dictionary* (2005) www.collinsdictionary.com/

DA = *Diccionario de americanismos* (2011) Dir. by H. López Morales. Real Academia Española. Lima: Santillana.

DAELE = *Diccionario de aprendizaje del español como lengua extranjera*. Dir. by P. Battaner. Barcelona: Universitat Pompeu Frabra. www.iula.upf.edu/rec/daele/

DBE = *Diccionario básico escolar* (2013) Santiago de Cuba: Centro de Lingüística Aplicada and Universidad del País Vasco. http://ixa2.si.ehu.es/dbe/index.html

DCECH = *Diccionario crítico etimológico castellano e hispánico* (1980–1994) Dir. by J. Corominas and J. A. Pascual. Madrid: Gredos.

DCIE = *Diccionario de contabilidad inglés-español* (2010) Fuertes-Olivera, P. et al. Navarra: Aranzadi.

DCLEA = *Diccionario 'Coruña' de la lengua española actual*. Dir. by A. Porto Dapena. Universidade da Coruña. www.udc.es/grupos/lexicografia/diccionario/

DCOE = *Diccionario de conectores y operadores del español* (2009) C. Fuentes. Madrid: Arco/Libros.

DCPEC = *Diccionario combinatorio* PRÁCTICO *del español contemporáneo* (2006) Dir. by I. Bosque. Madrid: S.M

DCPV = *Diccionario crítico de perífrasis verbales* (1991) M. Morera. Puerto del Rosario: Cabildo Insular de Fuerteventura.

DCR = *Diccionario de construcción y régimen de la lengua castellana* (1886–1994) R. J. Cuervo. Santafé de Bogotá: Instituto Caro y Cuervo / Barcelona: Herder. 8 vols.

DCTDE = *Diccionario de coloquialismos y términos dialectales del español* (2011) S. Fitch. Madrid: Arco/Libros.

DDEA = *Diccionario del español de América* (1993) M. Morínigo. Madrid: Anaya and Mario Muchnik.

DE = *Diccionario del estudiante* (2005) Real Academia Española. Madrid: Santillana.

DEA = *Diccionario del español actual* (1999) M. Seco, G. Ramos and O. Andrés. Madrid: Aguilar. 2nd ed., 2011.

DEAML = *Diccionario escolar de la AML*. Academia Mexicana de la lengua. www.academia.org.mx/universo:lema/obra:Diccionario-escolar-de-la-AML

DEDA = *Diccionario ejemplificado de argot* (2001) C. Ruiz. Barcelona: Península.

DEEH = *Diccionario etimológico español e hispánico* (1985) García de Diego, V. Madrid: Espasa Calpe.

DEJ = *Diccionario del español jurídico* (2016) Dir. by S. Muñoz Machado. Madrid: Real Academia Española. http://dej.rae.es/#/entry-id/E152500

DELE = *Diccionario de expresiones y locuciones del español* (2009) J. A. Martínez López and A. M. Jørgensen. Madrid: Ediciones de la Torre

DEM = L.F. *Diccionario del español de México* (2010) Dir. by. L. F. Lara. México: Colegio de México. http://dem.colmex.mx/

DEUM = *Diccionario del español usual en México* (1996) Dir. by. L.F. Lara. México: Colegio de México.

DFCIS = *Dizionario fraseologico completo Italiano Spagnolo* (2015) S. Carbonell. Milano: Hoepli.

DFDEA = *Diccionario fraseológico documentado del español actual* (2004) M. Seco, O. Andrés and G. Ramos. Madrid: Aguilar.

DFE = *Diccionario de fraseología española* (2007) J. Cantera and P. Gomis. Madrid: Abada.

DFED = *Diccionario fraseológico del español dominicano* (2016) B. R. Candelier et al. Santo Domingo: Academia Dominicana de la Lengua.

DFEM = *Diccionario fraseológico del español moderno* (1996) F. Varela and H. Kubarth. Madrid: Gredos.
DFHA = *Diccionario fraseológico del habla argentina* (2010) Dir. by. P.L. Barcia and G. Pauer. Buenos Aires: Planeta.
DFP = RAE and ASALE. *Diccionario fraseológico panhispánico*. In preparation.
DGILE = *Diccionario general ilustrado de la lengua española* (1976) Dir. by S. Gil y Gaya. Barcelona: Bibliograf.
DGSA = *Diccionario general de sinónimos y antónimos* (1999) Dir. by. J. M. Blecua. Barcelona: Vox.
DH = *Diccionario de hispanoamericanismos* (1997) Dir. by R. Richard. Madrid: Cátedra.
DHE = *Diccionario histórico del español de Canarias* (2013) C. Corrales and D. Corbella. Tenerife: Instituto de estudios canarios. http://web.frl.es/DHECan.html
DHist = *Diccionario histórico de la lengua española* (1933–1936) Real Academia Española. Madrid: Espasa-Calpe.
DHLE = *Diccionario histórico de la lengua española* (1960–1996) Real Academia Española. Madrid: RAE, 23 fascicles.
DI = *Diccionario ideológico de la lengua española* (1942) J. Casares. Barcelona: Gustavo Gili.
DIA = *Diccionario de ideas afines* (1996) F. Corripio. Barcelona: Herder.
DIALLE = *Diccionario ideológico. Atlas léxico de la lengua española* (2009) R. del Moral. Barcelona: Herder.
DIBSIS = *Diccionario ilustrado básico Sopena idiomático y sintáctico* (1973) L. Sánchez. Barcelona: Sopena.
DICE = *Diccionario de colocaciones del español*. Dir. by M. Alonso Ramos. Universidade da Coruña. www.dicesp.com/paginas
DICEMTO = *Proyecto lexicográfico electrónico multilingüe de verbos de movimiento*. Dir. by E. de Miguel. Madrid: Universidad Autónoma de Madrid. www.uam.es/gruposinv/upstairs/diccionario.html
DIEA = *Diccionario integral del español de la Argentina* (2008) Dir. by F. Plager. Buenos Aires: Tinta Fresca.
DILE = *Diccionario ideológico de la lengua española* (1995) Dir. by M. Alvar Ezquerra. Barcelona: Vox. Bibliograf.
DLE = *Diccionario de la Lengua Española* (2014) Real Academia Española y Asociación de Academias de la Lengua Española. Madrid: Espasa, 23rd edition. The 22nd ed. was published in 2001.
DLE-CD = *Diccionario de la lengua española (22nd ed)* (2001) Real Academia Española. CD-ROM edition. Madrid: Espasa.
DLEA = *Diccionario de las lenguas española y alemana* (1994) Slaby, R., J. R. Grossman and C. Illig. Barcelona: Herder.
DP = *Diccionario de partículas* (2003) L. Santos. Salamanca: Luso-Española.
DPDE = *Diccionario de partículas discursivas del español*. Dir. by A. Briz. Universidad de Valencia. www.dpde.es/
DPE = *Diccionario práctico del estudiante* (2005) Real Academia Española y Asociación de Academias de la Lengua Española. Madrid: Santillana.
DPV = *Diccionario de perífrasis verbales* (2006) Dir. by L. García et al. Madrid: Gredos.
DS = *Diccionario de sinónimos*. (2006) Oviedo: Universidad de Oviedo. http://www6.uniovi.es/dic/sinon.html
DSAL = *Diccionario Salamanca de la Lengua Española* (1996) Dir. by J. Gutiérrez Cuadrado. Salamanca: Universidad de Salamanca.
DTFH = *Diccionario temático de frases hechas* (2011) S. Rodríguez-Vida. Madrid: Octaedro.
DTLF = *Diccionario temático de locuciones francesas con su correspondencia española* (2004) J. Sevilla and J. Cantera. Madrid: Gredos.
DUE = *Diccionario de uso del español* (2007) M. Moliner. Madrid: Gredos, 3rd ed.
DUEAE = *Diccionario de uso del español de América y España* (2002) Dir. by P. Battaner. Barcelona: Vox.

DUPE = *Diccionario de uso de las preposiciones españolas* (2004) E. Slager. Madrid: Espasa.
DV = *Diccionario visual* (2016) Les Éditions Québec Amérique Inc. www.ikonet.com/es/
ECOLEXICON = *Base de conocimiento terminológica sobre el medio ambiente*. Dir. by P. Faber. Granada: Universidad de Granada. http://manila.ugr.es/es/index.htm
ECORESSOURCES = *Ressources terminologiques en environnement*. Dir. by M-C. L'Homme l'Homme. Montréal: Université de Montréal. http://termeco.info/EcoRessources/
GDA = *Gran diccionario de argot* (2000) D. Carbonell. Barcelona: Larousse.
GDS = *Gran diccionario de sinónimos* (1990) F. Corripio. Barcelona: Ediciones B.
GSSAI = *Thesaurus. Gran Sopena de sinónimos y asociación de ideas* (1996) D. Ortega. Barcelona: Sopena.
IA = *Ideas afines. Palabras, términos e ideas relacionadas. Generador de ideas*. www.ideasafines.com.ar/
IATE = *Interactive Terminology for Europe*. http://iate.europa.eu/brochure/index.html
IDI = *Imaginario. Diccionario en imágenes* (2007) Dir. by A. Moreno. Madrid: S.M.
LAROUSSE = *Gran diccionario de la lengua española* (1996) Barcelona: Larousse.
LEMA = *Lema. Diccionario de la Lengua Española* (2001) Dir. by P. Battaner. Barcelona: Vox.
MLG = *Multilingual Legal Glossary* (2009) Vancouver Community College.
NDHLE = *Nuevo diccionario histórico de la lengua española*. Real Academia Española. Dir. by J. A. Pascual. www.rae.es/recursos/diccionarios/nuevo-diccionario-historico
NDV = *Nuevo diccionario visual* (2012) C. Arahambaut. Madrid: Larousse.
NTLE = *Nuevo tesoro lexicográfico del español* (2007) Dir. by L. Nieto and M. Alvar Ezquerra Madrid: Arco/Libros, 11 vols.
NTLLE = *Nuevo tesoro lexicográfico de lengua española* (2001) Real Academia Española Madrid: Espasa. www.rae.es/recursos/diccionarios/diccionarios-anteriores-1726-1992/nuevo-tesoro-lexicografico
OPENTHESAURUS = *OpenThesaurus-es. Tesauro en español*. http://openoffice-es.sourceforge.net/thesaurus/
POINTIT = *Point it. Traveller's Language Kit* (2013) D. Graf. München: Dieter Graf.
REDES = *Redes. Diccionario combinatorio del español contemporáneo* (2004) Dir. by I. Bosque. Madrid: S.M.
SENSEM = *Sentence Semantics. Base de datos de semántica oracional*. Grial (Grup de Recerca Interuniversitari en Aplicacions Lingüístiques). Barcelona: Universitat Autònoma. http://lod.iula.upf.edu/resources/project_SenSem
SEÑÁLALO = *Diccionario de imágenes* (2001) D. Graf. Madrid: Ceapat.
TL = *Tesoro lexicográfico: 1492–1726* (1947) Dir. by S. Gili Gaya. Madrid: C.S.I.C.
TLEC = *Tesoro lexicográfico del español de Canarias* (1996) Real Academia Española and Gobierno de Canarias. Dir. by C. Corrales et. al.
TLEPR = *Tesoro lexicográfico del español de Puerto Rico* (2016) Academia Puertorriqueña de la Lengua. https://tesoro.pr/
TLHA = *Tesoro léxico de las hablas andaluzas* (2000) M. Alvar Ezquerra. Madrid: Arco/Libros.
VERBARIO = *Verbario. Semántica de los verbos en contexto* (2014) Dir. By I. Renau. www.verbario.com/
VOX = *Vox. Diccionario general de la lengua española* (1999) Dir. by M. Alvar Ezquerra. Barcelona: Bibliograf.
ZIRANO = *Zirano*. Dir. by M. Santolaria et al. www.zirano.com/

Other references

Abad, F. (1998) "Los diccionarios de la Academia (1780–1992)", in E. R.Trives and H. Provencio (eds.), *Estudios de lingüística textual*. Murcia: Universidad de Murcia, pp. 23–30.
Abad, F. (2001) *Cuestiones de lexicología y lexicografía*. Madrid: U.N.E.D.
Acero, I. (2003) "La lexicografía plurilingüe del español", in Medina (ed.), pp. 175–204.

Águila, G. (2006) "Las nuevas tecnologías al servicio de la lexicografía: los diccionarios electrónicos", in M. Villandre (ed.), *Actas del XXXV Simposio Internacional de la Sociedad Española de Lingüística*. León: Universidad de León, pp. 1–23.

Águila, G. (2009) *Los diccionarios electrónicos*. Madrid: Arco/Libros.

Ahumada, I. (ed.) (1992) *Diccionarios españoles: contenido y aplicaciones*. Jaén: Universidad de Jaén.

Ahumada, I. (ed.) (2000) *Cinco siglos de lexicografía del español*. Jaén: Universidad de Jaén.

Ahumada, I. (ed.) (2002) *Diccionarios y lenguas de especialidad*. Jaén: Universidad de Jaén.

Ahumada, I. (ed.) (2006) *Diccionario bibliográfico de la metalexicografía del español. Orígenes-2001*. Jaén: Universidad de Jaén.

Ahumada, I. (2007) "La metalexicografía del español: revisión y perspectivas", in San Vicente (ed.), pp. 18–29.

Ahumada, I. (ed.) (2009) *Diccionario bibliográfico de la metalexicografía del español*, 2001–2005. Jaén: Universidad de Jaén.

Ahumada, I. (ed.) (2015) *Diccionario bibliográfico de la metalexicografía del español*, 2006–2010. Jaén: Universidad de Jaén.

Aleza, M. (2000) "Nuevos enfoques metodológicos en la práctica lexicográfica hispanoamericana diferencial actual (sobre algunos diccionarios de los 90)", in M. Aleza and A. López (eds.) *Estudios de filología, historia y cultura hispánicas*. Valencia: Universidad de Valencia, pp. 27–48.

Alonso, M. (2002) "Colocaciones y contorno de la definición lexicográfica", *LEA* 24(1): 63–96.

Alonso, A. and I. Renau. (2013) "Corpus Pattern Analysis in Determining Specialised Uses of Verbal Lexical Units", *Terminàlia* 7: 26–33. http://publicacions.iec.cat/repository/pdf/00000194/00000099.pdf

Alvar Ezquerra, M. (1981) "Los diccionarios bilingües: su contenido", *Lingüística Española Actual* 3(1): 175–196.

Alvar Ezquerra, M. (1983a) *Lexicología y lexicografía. Guía bibliográfica*. Salamanca: Almar.

Alvar Ezquerra, M. (1983b) "Los prólogos del Diccionario académico: nomenclatura específica y microestructura", *Revista de Filología Española* 63(3): 205–222.

Alvar Ezquerra, M. (1985) "El diccionario de la Academia a través de sus prólogos: los planteamientos y el vocabulario general", *Philologica hispaniensia in honorem Manuel Alvar*, 2, *Lingüística*, Madrid: Gredos, pp. 33–44.

Alvar Ezquerra, M. (1992) "El futuro de los diccionarios del español", *Analecta Malacitana* 15(1–2): 103–108.

Alvar Ezquerra, M. (1993) *Lexicografía descriptiva*. Barcelona: Bibliograf.

Alvar Ezquerra, M. (1995) "Los diccionarios del español en su historia", *International Journal of Lexicography* 8(3): 173–201.

Alvar Ezquerra, M (ed.) (1996) *Estudios de historia de la lexicografía del español*. Málaga: Universidad de Málaga.

Alvar Ezquerra, M. (1997) "Algunos aspectos de la presencia gramatical en el diccionario", in J. Terrón and J. M. González (eds.), *IV Jornadas de metodología y didáctica de la lengua española*. Cáceres: Universidad de Extremadura, pp. 115–123.

Alvar Ezquerra, M. (2002) *De antiguos y nuevos diccionarios del español*. Madrid: Arco/Libros.

Alvar Ezquerra, M. (2003) "Estado actual del Nuevo Tesoro Lexicográfico del Español (s. XVI-1726): repertorios posteriores a 1600", in M. A. Martín Zorraquino and J. L. Aliaga (eds.), pp. 25–49.

Alvar Ezquerra, M. and L. Nieto. (2006) "La edición del Nuevo Tesoro Lexicográfico del Español (s. XIV-1726)", in E. Corino, C. Marello and C. Onesti (eds.), *Atti del XII Congresso Internazionale di Lessicografia*. Torino: Edizioni dell'Orso pp. 365–370.

Álvarez de Miranda, P. (ed.) (1998) *Lexicografía española peninsular. Diccionarios clásicos (I y II)*. Madrid: Fundación Histórica Tavera y Digibis.

Álvarez de Miranda, P. (2003) "Los diccionarios históricos", in M. A. Martín Zorraquino and J. L. Aliaga (eds.), pp. 51–70.

Álvarez de Miranda, P. (2011) *Los diccionarios del español moderno*. Gijón: Trea.

Álvarez de Miranda, P. and J. Polo (eds.) (2002) *Lengua y diccionarios. Estudios ofrecidos a Manuel Seco*. Madrid: Arco/Libros.

Anglada, E. (2005) *Lexicografía española*. Barcelona: Universitat de Barcelona.

Ávila, R. (1998) "Españolismos y mexicanismos: hacia un diccionario internacional de la lengua española", *Nueva Revista de Filología Hispánica* XLVI(2): 395–406.

Ávila, R. (2003) "Diccionarios locales, nacionales, internacionales", *Revista internacional de lingüística iberoamericana* 1: 51–66.

Ávila, R. (2003–2004) "El fin de los diccionarios diferenciales?: ¿el principio de los diccionarios integrales?", *Revista de lexicografía* 10: 7–20.

Ávila Martín, M. C. (2000): *El diccionario en el aula. Sobre los diccionarios escolares destinados a la enseñanza y aprendizaje del español como lengua materna*. Granada: Publicaciones de la Universidad.

Ayala, M. (ed.) (2001) *Diccionarios y enseñanza*. Alcalá de Henares: Universidad de Alcalá.

Azorín, D. (1996–1997) "La lexicografía española en el siglo XIX", *ELUA* 11: 111–122.

Azorín, D. (2000) *Los diccionarios del español en su perspectiva histórica*. Alicante: Universidad de Alicante.

Baisa, V., S. Sara Može and I. Renau. (2016a) "Linking Verb Pattern Dictionaries of English and Spanish", presented at the *5th Workshop on Linked Data in Linguistics: Managing, Building and Using Linked Language Resources*, Portorož Slovenia. www.lrec-conf.org/proceedings/lrec2016/workshops/LREC2016Workshop-LDL2016_Proceedings.pdf

Baisa, V., S. Sara Može and I. Renau. (2016b) "Multilingual CPA: Linking Verb Patterns Across Languages", in T. Margalitadze and G. Meladze (eds.), *Proceedings of the XVII EURALEX International Congress,* Tbilisi State University, pp. 410–417. See at: http://euralex.org/wp-content/themes/euralex/proceedings/Euralex%202016/euralex_2016_044_p410.pdf

Bajo, E. (2000) *Diccionarios: Introducción a la historia de la lexicografía del español*. Gijón: Trea.

Bargalló, M. (1999) "La información gramatical en los diccionarios didácticos monolingües del español", in M. N. Vila, Mª A. Calero, R. M. Mateu, M. Casanovas and J.L. Orduña (eds.), pp. 15–42.

Barrios, M. A. (2002) "La 15ª edición del DRAE y la 1ª del Diccionario Manual. Documentos del Archivo de Antonio Maura", *Presente y Futuro de la Lingüística en España. La sociedad de lingüística, 30 años después*. Madrid: Sociedad Española de Lingüística, pp. 338–344.

Barrios, M. A. (2006) "Macroestructura y microestructura de un diccionario explicativo y combinatorio: diferencias con respecto a un diccionario común", *Revista Española de Lingüística* 36: 349–377.

Barrios, M. A. (2007) "Diccionarios combinatorios del español: diferencias y semejanzas entre Redes y Práctico", *RedELE* 11: 1–14. http://www.mecd.gob.es/redele/revistaRedEle/2007/tercera.html

Bastardín Candón, T. and M. Rivas Zancarrón (eds.) (2009) *Estudios de historiografía lingüística*. Cádiz: Universidad de Cádiz.

Batiukova, O. (2009) "La teoría del léxico en los nuevos diccionarios", in E. de Miguel (ed.), *Panorama de la lexicología*. Barcelona: Ariel, pp. 487–519.

Battaner, P. and J. DeCesaris (eds.) (2004) *De lexicografía*. Girona: Documenta Universitaria.

Bernal, E., S. Torner and J. DeCesaris (eds.) (2006) *Palabra por palabra. Estudios ofrecidos a Paz Battaner*. Girona: Documenta Universitaria.

Berson, A. C. (1979) "A Basic List of Spanish Dictionaries", *The Incorporated Linguist* 18(1): 26-27.

Blecua, J. M. (2006) *Principios del Diccionario de Autoridades*. Madrid. Reception discourse at RAE.

Billick, D. J. and S. N. Dworkin. (1985) "An Annotated Bibliography of Glossaries, Vocabularies, Word Lists, and Concordances Based on or Appended to Medieval Spanish Texts", *La Corónica* 13(1): 104-129.

Bosque, I. (2006) "Una nota sobre la relevancia de la información sintáctica en el diccionario", in E. Bernal, S. Torner and J. Cesaris (eds.), pp. 47–53.

Bosque, I. and R. Mairal. (2012a) "Definiciones mínimas", in F. Rodríguez (ed.), *Estudios de lingüística española. Homenaje a Manuel Seco*. Alicante: Universidad de Alicante, pp. 183–210.

Bosque, I. and R. Mairal (2012b) "Hacia una organización conceptual del definiens. Capas nocionales del adverbio *arriba*", in D. Corbella, J. Dorta, A. Fajardo, L. Izquierdo, J. Medina and A. Nelsi (eds.), *Lexicografía hispánica del siglo XXI: nuevos proyectos y perspectivas*. Madrid: Arco/Libros, pp. 125–150.

Bosque-Gil. J., J. Gracia and A. Gómez-Pérez (2016) "Linked Data in Lexicography", *Kenerman Dictionary News* 24: 19–24. http://kdictionaries.com/kdn/kdn24.pdf.

Buendía Castro, M. and P. Faber (2014) "Collocation Dictionaries: A Comparative Analysis", *Monografías de Traducción e Interpretación* 6: 203–235.

Briz, A. (2005) "Diccionario de partículas discursivas del español (*DPDE*). Resultados de un proyecto de investigación". *Filología y Lingüística. Estudios ofrecidos a Antonio Quilis*. Madrid: CSIC, pp. 675–587.

Calvo, C., B. Lépinette, and J.-C. Anscombre (eds.) (2010) *Lexicografía en el ámbito hispánico*. Valencia: Universitat de València.

Camacho, J. (2012) "Evolución del contenido metalexicográfico en los prólogos al diccionario académico (1726–2001)", in A. Nomdedeu, E. Forgas and M. Bargalló (eds.), pp. 125–134.

Camacho, J. (2014) *Teoría de la lexicografía en diccionarios monolingües del español (orígenes-siglo XXI)*. Jaén: Universidad de Jaén.

Campanile, M., M. Cimmino, Y. D'Alessio, A. Di Lorenzo, M-T. Paone and R. Roca (2011) "Los diccionarios monolingües del español desde la perspectiva del estudiante de ELE", *RedELE* 21. www.redib.org/.

Campos, M. (2007) "Hacia la ordenación morfológica del NDHE: primer esbozo", *Verba* 34: 125–156.

Campos, M. and J. A. Pascual (2012) "Lexicografía, filología e informática: una alianza imprescindible: A propósito de la situación del NDHE", in AA.VV (ed.), *Lexicografía hispánica del siglo XXI. Nuevos proyectos y perspectivas. Homenaje al profesor Cristóbal Corrales Zumbado*. Madrid: Arco/Libros, pp. 151–170.

Campos, M. and J. I. Pérez Pascual (eds.) (2002) *De historia de la lexicografía*. Noia: Toxosoutos.

Campos, M. and J. I. Pérez Pascual (eds.) (2006) *El Diccionario de la Real Academia Española: Ayer y Hoy*. A Coruña: Universidade da Coruña.

Campos, M., F. Córdoba and J. I. Pérez Pascual (eds.) (2006) *América y el diccionario*. Coruña: Universidade da Coruña.

Campos, M., E. Conde Noguerol, J. I. Pérez Pascual and J. A. Porto Dapena (eds.) (2007a) *Reflexiones sobre el diccionario*. Coruña: Universidad de Coruña.

Campos, M., R. Cotelo García and J. I. Pérez Pascual (eds.) (2007b) *Historia de la lexicografía española*. Coruña, Universidad de Coruña.

Canellada, M. J. (1988) "Problemas de los diccionarios", *Nueva Revista de Filología Hispánica* 36(1): 123-130.

Carriscondo, F. M. (2010) *La épica del diccionario: hitos lexicográficos del XVIII*. Madrid: Calambur.

Casares, J. (1950) *Introducción a la lexicografía moderna*. Madrid: C.S.I.C.

Casas Gómez, M., I. Penadés and M. T. Díaz (eds.) (1998) *Estudios sobre el* Diccionario de uso del español *de María Moliner*. Cádiz: Universidad de Cádiz.

Castillo, M. A. (ed.) (2005) *Las gramáticas y los diccionarios en la enseñanza del español como segunda lengua: deseo y realidad*. Sevilla: Universidad de Sevilla.

Castillo, M. A., and J. García Platero (eds.) (2010) *La lexicografía en su dimensión teórica*. Málaga: Universidad de Málaga.

Clavería, G. (2003) "La Real Academia a finales del siglo XIX: el *Diccionario de la lengua castellana* de 1899 (13ª edición)", *BRAE* 83: 255–336.

Clavería, G. (2016) *De vacunar a dictaminar. La lexicografía académica decimonónica y el neologismo,* Madrid: Iberoamericana

Colón, G. (1956) "A propos du *Tesoro lexicográfico* de M. Gili Gaya", *ZRP* 72: 379–386.

Contreras, N. (2008) *El diccionario de lengua y el conocimiento especializado en la sociedad actual*. Jaén: Universidad de Jaén.

Corbella, D., J. Dorta, A. Fajardo, L. Izquierdo, J. Medina and A. Nelsi. (2012) *Lexicografía hispánica del siglo XXI. Nuevos proyectos y perspectivas*. Madrid: Arco/Libros.

Córdoba, F. (2001) *Introducción a la lexicografía española*. Olomouc: Univerzita Palackého.

Córdoba, F. (2003) *Bibliografía temática de la lexicografía*. Universidade da Coruña. Available on line. http://www.udc.es/grupos/lexicografia/bibliografia.htm (Last accessed: July 2017)

Corrales, C. (2000) " 'Tradición' y 'renovación' en el diccionario", in Oliver, J. M., C. J. Corrales, M. L. Izquierdo, D. García, D. Corbella, J. S. Gómez, M. Martínez, F. J. Cortés (eds.), *Cien años de investigación semántica: de Michel Bréal a la actualidad*. Madrid: Ediciones Clásicas, pp. 345–362.

Corrales, C., J. Dorta, A. Nelsi, D. Corbella and F-M Plaza Picón (eds.) (2004) *Nuevas aportaciones a la historiografía lingüística*. Madrid: Arco/Libros.

Cruz, E. (1994) "Diccionario de construcción y régimen de la lengua castellana: Historia y vicisitudes", *Thesaurus* 49: 563–576.

DeCesaris, J. and V. Alsina (eds.) (2001) *Estudis de lexicografia 1999-2000*. Barcelona: Universitat Pompeu Fabra.

DeCesaris, J. and P. Battaner (2006) "A New Kind of Dictionary: REDES, Diccionario combinatorio del español contemporáneo", in E. Corino, C. Marello and C. Onesti (eds.), *Proceedings of XII EURALEX Internacional Congreso*. Volume I. Turín: Edizioni dell'Orso, pp. 399–407.

Dodd, W. S. (1995) "A Survey of Spanish Lexicography", *International Journal of Lexicography* 8(3): 167–172.

Echenique, M. T. and J. Sánchez Méndez (eds.) (2003) *Lexicografía y lexicología en Europa*. Madrid: Gredos.

Esparza, M. A. (2008) *Bibliografía temática de historiografía lingüística española. Fuentes secundarias*. Hamburg: Helmut Buske.

Espinosa, M. L. (1982) *Annotated Bibliography of Technical and Specialized Dictionaries in Spanish-Spanish with Commentary*. New York: Whitson.

Fabbri, M. (1979) *A Bibliography of Hispanic Dictionaries: Catalan, Galician, Spanish in Latin American and the Philippines*. Imola: Galeati.

Faber, P., C. Márquez and M. Vega (2005) "Framing Terminology: A Process-Oriented Approach", *Meta: Journal des traducteurs* 50(4). CD-ROM.

Faber, P., P. León-Araúz and A. Reimerink (2016) "EcoLexicon: New Features and Challenges", in *GLOBALEX 2016. Lexicographic Resources for Human Language Technology*, pp. 73–80. Online Proceedings.

Fajardo, A. (1999) "Etimología y lexicografía: Problemas metodológicos", in M. Aleza (ed.), *Estudios de historia de la lengua española en América y España*. Valencia: Universidad de Valencia, pp. 155–162.

Fajardo, A. (2010) "La lexicografía del español de América. Parte primera: evolución, tipología y metodologías", in M. Aleza and J. M. Enguita (eds.), *La lengua española en América: normas y usos actuales*. Valencia: Universidad de Valencia, pp. 317–353. Available online.

Fernández Gómez, S. (2006) "Obras de referencia: enciclopedias, diccionarios, glosarios y otros recursos del idioma", in A. Maldonado Martínez and L. Rodríguez Yunta (eds.), *La información especializada en Internet*. Madrid: Cindoc, pp. 173–194.

Fontanillo, E. (1984) "Informe sobre la situación actual de la lexicografía en España", *Anthropos* 44(4): 43-47.

Forgas, E. (ed.) (1996) *Léxico y diccionarios*. Tarragona: Universitat Rovira i Virgili.

Forgas, E. (2007) "Diccionarios e ideología", *Interlingüística* 17: 2–16.

Freixas, M. (2010) *Planta y método del* Diccionario de autoridades. *Orígenes de la técnica lexicográfica de la Real Academia Española (1713–1739)*. Coruña: Universidad de Coruña.

Fuentes, M. T. and R. Werner (1998) *Lexicografías ibéricorrománicas: problemas, propuestas y proyectos*. Frankfurt am Mein: Vervuert.

Fuentes, M. T., J. García and J. Torres (2005–2006) "Algunos apuntes sobre la evaluación de diccionarios", *Revista de Lexicografía* 11: 69–80.

Fuertes-Olivera, P. A. (ed.) (2010) *Specialised Dictionaries for Learners*. Berlin/New York: De Gruyter.

Fuertes-Olivera, P. A. and H. Bergenholtz (eds.) (2011) *E-Lexicography: The Internet, Digital Initiatives and Lexicography*. London/New York: Continuum.

Fuertes-Olivera, P. A. and H. Bergenholtz (2015) "Los diccionarios en línea de español Universidad de Valladolid", *Estudios de lexicografía* 4: 71–98.

Fuertes-Olivera, P. A. and S. Tarp (2014) *Theory and Practice of Specialised Online Dictionaries: Lexicography Versus Terminography*. Berlin/Boston: De Gruyter.

Gak, V.-G. (1991) "Para una tipología de las tipologías de diccionarios", *Voz y letra* 2: 105–115.

Garcés, M. P. (ed.) (2008) *Diccionario histórico: nuevas perspectivas lingüísticas*. Madrid/Frankfurt: Iberoamericana.

García Llamas, B. I. (2013) "La lexicografía de internet y el diseño de diccionarios pedagógicos especializados: el diccionario de comercio internacional español-inglés", *Cuadernos de Investigación Filológica* 39: 7–26.

García Page, M. (2008) *Introducción a la fraseología española*. Barcelona: Anthropos.

García Pérez, R. (2000) "Los niveles de uso en el *Diccionario del Español Actual* de Manuel Seco", in. Borrego, J. Fernández, L. Santos, R. Senabre (eds.) *Cuestiones de actualidad en lengua española*. Salamanca: Universidad Salamanca, pp. 257–265.

García Platero, J. M. and M. A. Castillo (eds.) (2000) *Investigación lexicográfica para la enseñanza de lenguas*. Málaga: Universidad de Málaga.

García Platero, J. M. (2016) "Diccionarios", in J. Gutiérrez-Rexach (ed.), *Enciclopedia de Lingüística Hispánica*. Volume 2. London: Routledge, pp. 413–422.

Gelpí, C. (2000a) "El *Diccionario del Español Actual*: un diccionario nuevo", *Revista Bibliográfica de Geografía y Ciencias Sociales* 239. See at www.ub.edu/geocrit/b3w-239.htm

Gelpí, C. (2000b) "Los diccionarios bilingües: medidas de evaluación lexicográfica", in F. J. Ruiz de Mendoza (ed.), *Panorama actual de la lingüística aplicada*, vol. 2, pp. 1037–1044.

Gelpí C. (2003) "El estado actual de la lexicografía: los nuevos diccionarios", in A. Medina (ed.), pp. 307–328.

Gelpí C. (2004) "Diccionaris digitals especialitzats per la temàtica: estat actual i perspectives", *Scripta Nova* VIII(170). www.ub.edu/geocrit/sn/sn-170-69.htm

González Aranda, Y. (2002) *Lexicología y lexicografía del español: repertorio bibliográfico (1990–2002)*. Almería: Universidad de Almería.

Gouws, R. H., U. Heid, W. Schweickard and H. E. Wiegand (eds.) (2013) *Dictionaries: An International Encyclopedia of Lexicography. Supplementary Volume. Recent Developments with Focus on Electronic and Computational Lexicography*. Berlin/Boston: De Gruyter/Mouton.

Gutiérrez Cuadrado, J. (1992) "Gramática y diccionario", in *Actas del Congreso de la Lengua Española* (Sevilla, 1992). http://cvc.cervantes.es/obref/congresos/sevilla/unidad/ponenc_cuadrado.htm.

Haensch, G. (1982) "La lengua española y la lexicografía actual", *Lingüística Española Actual* IV(2): 239-252.

Haensch, G. (1987) "La lexicografía hispanoamericana entre la teoría y la práctica", in M. T. Vaquero and H. López Morales (eds.), *Actas del I Congreso Internacional sobre el español de América*. Puerto Rico: Academia Puertorriqueña de la Lengua Española, pp. 555–578.

Haensch, G. (1990) "Spanische Lexikographie", in F. J. Hausmann, O. Reichmann, H. E. Wiegand, and L. Zgusta (eds.) *An International Encyclopedia of Lexicography*, Volume 2. Berlin, New York: De Gruyter, pp. 1738-1767.

Haensch, G. (2004a) *Los diccionarios del español en el siglo XXI*. 2nd edition, enlarged by C. Omeñaca. Salamanca: Universidad de Salamanca. 1st edition, 1997.

Haensch, G. (2004b) "La lexicografía bilingüe en la actualidad y su valoración", *Revista de Lexicografía* 10: 133–138.

Haensch, G., L. Wolf, S. Ettinger, and R. Werner (1982) *La lexicografía: De la lingüística teórica a la lexicografía práctica*. Madrid: Gredos.

Hernández, H. (1989) *Los diccionarios de orientación escolar*. Tübingen: Max Niemeyer.

Hernández, H. (1991) "De la teoría lexicográfica al uso del diccionario. El diccionario en la aula", in S. Montesa and A. M. Garrido (eds.), *El español como lengua extranjera. De la teoría al aula.* Málaga: Universidad de Málaga, pp. 189–200.

Hernández, H. (1998) "La crítica lexicográfica: métodos y perspectivas", *Lingüística Española Actual* 20(1): 5–28.

Hernández, H. (2001) "El diccionario en la enseñanza de ELE. Diccionarios de español para extranjeros", en M. A. Martín Zorraquino (ed.) *¿Qué español enseñar? Norma y variación lingüística en la enseñanza del español a extranjeros.* Zaragoza: Universidad de Zaragoza, pp. 93–103.

Herreras, J. C. and J. C. de Hoyos (2011) *Lexicographie et métalexicographie en langue espagnole.* Valenciennes: Presses Universitaires de Valenciennes.

Jiménez Ríos, E. (2013) *La crítica lexicográfica y el* Diccionario de la Real Academia Española. A Coruña: Universidade da Coruña.

Lapesa, R. (1964) "Los diccionarios de la Academia", *Boletín de la Real Academia Española* XLIV: 425–430.

Lara, L. F. (1990) *Dimensiones de la lexicografía: a propósito del Diccionario del español de México.* México: El Colegio de México.

Lara, L. F. (2001) "Los diccionarios contemporáneos del español y la normatividad", in *Actas del II Congreso Internacional de la Lengua Española (Valladolid).* http://congresosdelalengua.es/valladolid/ponencias/

Lara, L. F. (2005) "El diccionario y sus disciplinas", in A. López and B. Gallardo (eds.), *Conocimiento y lenguaje.* Valencia: Universitat de València, pp. 437–450.

Lara, L. F. (2012) "[Reseña al] Diccionario de americanismos", *Panace@* XIII, 36. www.tremedica.org/panacea/IndiceGeneral/n36-plumero_LFLara.pdf.

Lázaro Carreter, F. (1972) *Crónica del Diccionario de Autoridades (1713–1740).* Discurso de ingreso en la Real Academia Española. Madrid.

Lázaro Carreter, F. (1980) "El primer diccionario de la Academia", in *Estudios de lingüística,* Barcelona: Grijalbo, pp. 83–148.

Lope Blanch, J. M. (1995) *"Americanismo frente a españolismo lingüísticos", Nueva Revista de Filología Hispánica* 43(2): 433–440.

López Facal, J. (2010) *La presunta autoridad de los diccionarios.* Madrid: CSIC.

Lombardini, H.-E. (2011) "La ideología en las tradiciones lexicográficas. La lexicografía académica española", in F. San Vicente et al. (eds.), pp. 305–328.

Maldonado, C. (1998) *El uso del diccionario en el aula.* Madrid: Arco Libros.

Maldonado, C. (2000) "Criterios para elegir un diccionario", in S. Ruhstaller and J. Prado (eds.), pp. 117–135.

Maldonado, C. (2003) "La lexicografía didáctica monolingüe en español", in M. A. Martín and J. L. Aliaga (eds.), pp. 129–150.

Maldonado, C. (2013) "La entrada léxica en el discurso lexicográfico digital", *Círculo de Lingüística Aplicada a la Comunicación* 56: 26–52.

Malkiel, Y. (1959) "Distinctive Features in Lexicography: A Typological Approach to Dictionaries Exemplified with Spanish (II)", *Romance Philology* 13(2): 111–115.

Marcos Marín, F. (1998) *Report on Spanish lexicography: New issues.* Madrid: Universidad Autónoma de Madrid. Available online.

Martín García, J. (1999) *El diccionario en la enseñanza del español.* Madrid: Arco/Libros.

Martín Zorraquino, M. A. and J. L. Aliaga (eds.) (2003) *La lexicografía hispánica ante el siglo XXI. Balance y perspectivas.* Zaragoza: Diputación de Zaragoza.

Martínez Marín, J. (1992) "Los diccionarios escolares del español: lo que son y lo que deberían ser", in I. Ahumada (ed.), *Lecciones del I Seminario de Lexicografía Hispánica.* Jaén: Casa Editora El Estudiante, pp. 53–70.

Martínez Montoro, J. (2006) "El 'Diccionario Ideológico' de Julio Casares. Análisis metalexicográfico", in J. Rodríguez and D. Moisés (eds.) *Diacronía, lengua española y lingüística.* Madrid: Síntesis, pp. 381–396.

Martínez de Sousa, J. (1995) *Diccionario de lexicografía práctica*. Barcelona: Bibliograf.

Martínez de Sousa, J. (2009) *Manual básico de lexicografía*. Gijón: Trea.

Mateu, R. (1999) "El DRAE: algunas consideraciones para un posible enfoque pragmático", in Vila et al. (eds.), pp. 203–222.

Matus, A. (2007) "El input en los diccionarios diferenciales: Instancias de planificación en el establecimiento de la nomenclatura", *Revista de Humanidades* 15–16: 7–16.

Medina, A. (ed.) (2001) *Estudios de lexicografía diacrónica del español*. Málaga: Universidad de Málaga.

Medina, A. (ed.) (2003) *Lexicografía española*. Barcelona: Ariel.

Medina, A. (2016) "Lexicografía", in J. Gutiérrez-Rexach (ed.), *Enciclopedia de Lingüística Hispánica*. Volume 1. London: Routledge, pp. 164–172.

Millán, J. A. (2011) "El diccionario oculto: Gloria y desaparición del diccionario en la era digital", *El País*, 2011–07–30. http://jamillan.com/librosybitios/gloriaydes.htm

Mochón, G. and A. Sorli (2001) "Tesauros, glosarios y diccionarios de biblioteconomía y documentación en Internet", *Revista Española de Documentación Científica* 24(3): 325-339.

Montes, J. J. (1998) "El *Diccionario de construcción y régimen* de Cuervo. Boceto histórico", *Thesaurus* 53(2): 314–324.

Morales, C. (2000) "La lexicografía del siglo XXI", in S. Ruhstaller and J. Prado (eds.), pp. 505–514.

Moreno, M. A. (2012) "El diccionario ideológico general del español", *Alfinge* 24: 129–154.

Moya, J. A. and M. Sosiński (eds.) (2006) *Lexicografía y enseñanza de la lengua española*. Granada: Universidad de Granada.

Niederehe, H.-J. (1995a) *Bibliografía cronológica de la lingüística, la gramática y la lexicografía del español (BICRES): desde los comienzos hasta el año 1600*. Amsterdam: John Benjamins.

Niederehe, H.-J. (1995b) *Bibliografía cronológica de la lingüística, la gramática y la lexicografía del español. Desde el año 1601 hasta el año 1700*. Amsterdam: John Benjamins.

Nomdedeu, A. (2009a) "Evolución del DRAE en la representación del léxico de especialidad", *Revista Española de Lingüística* 39(1): 141–166.

Nomdedeu, A. (2009b) "Los diccionarios de la Real Academia Española en el siglo XXI", *Annali dell'Università degli Studi di Napoli "L'Orientale"* LI(1): 159–179.

Nomdedeu, A. (2009c) "Diccionarios en Internet para el aula de ELE", *RedELE*, 15. www.mecd.gob.es/

Nomdedeu, A. (2011a) "La ideología y su reflejo en la lexicografía actual. Las voces malsonantes", in San Vicente, F., C. Garriga and H. Lombardini (eds.) *Ideolex: Estudios de Lexicografía e Ideología*. Monza: Polimetrica, pp. 172–187.

Nomdedeu, A. (2011b) "El uso del diccionario en el aula de E/LE: problemas y posibles soluciones", *Foro de profesores de E/LE* 7: 1–10. www.mecd.gob.es/.

Nomdedeu, A., E. Forgas and M. Bargalló (eds.) (2012) *Avances en Lexicografía Hispánica*. Tarragona: Publicacions URV.

Nomdedeu, A. and E. Sánchez. (eds.) (2008) *Perspectivas de la lexicografía del español en el siglo XXI*. Napoli: Universitá di Napoli.

Pascual, Fernández, M. L. (2013) *Diccionario de autoridades 2ª (ed.): técnica lexicográfica y lengua de la ciencia*. Barcelona: Universidad Autónoma de Barcelona.

Pascual, J. A. and R. García Pérez (2006) "La organización de los materiales de un diccionario histórico: las formas de interés filológico", in E. Bernal, S. Torner and J. DeCesaris (eds.), pp. 189–199.

Pérez Hernández, F. J. (2005) *Pensar y hacer el diccionario*. Venezuela: El Nacional.

Pérez Pascual, J. I. (2008) "Semántica y diccionario histórico", in M. P. Garcés (ed.), pp. 149–175.

Pérez Pascual, J. I. and M. Campos (eds.) (2002) *Cuestiones de lexicografía*. Lugo: Tris Tram.

Pérez Pascual, J. I., M. Campos and E. M. González (eds.) (2008) *La lexicografía bilingüe y didáctica: ayer y hoy*. A Coruña: Universidade da Coruña.

Portilla, L. P. (2009) "El *DRAE*, una tarea que no acaba sino para empezarla de nuevo", in M. Martos, A. Mendoza and I. Pinto (eds.), *Actas del III Congreso Internacional de Lexicología y Lexicografía*. Lima: Academia Peruana de la Lengua, pp. 559–580.

Porto Dapena, J. A. (1980) *Elementos de lexicografía*. Bogotá: Instituto Caro y Cuervo.

Porto Dapena, J. A. (2000) "Diccionarios históricos y etimológicos del español", in Ahumada (ed.), pp. 103–125.
Porto Dapena, J. A. (2002) *Manual de técnica lexicográfica.* Madrid: Arco/Libros.
Porto Dapena, J. A. (2003) "El *Diccionario* de María Moliner", in M. A. Martín Zorraquino and J. L. Aliaga (eds.), pp. 167–192.
Renau, I. and P. Battaner (2011) "The Spanish Learners Dictionary DAELE on the Panorama of the Spanish E-Lexicography", in I. Kosem, and K. Kosem (eds.) (2011) *Electronic Lexicography in the 21st Century: New Applications for New Users. Proceedings of eLex 2011.* http://elex2011.trojina.si/elex2011_proceedings.pdf., pp. 221–226.
Rodríguez Barcia, S. (2008) *La realidad relativa: Evolución ideológica en el trabajo lexicográfico de la Real Academia Española (1726–2006).* Vigo: Universidad de Vigo.
Rodríguez Barcia, S. (2010) "El componente ideológico en la historia de la lexicografía monolingüe española", in M. T. Encina, M. González, M. Gutiérrez, M. A. López, C- Martín, L. Romero, M. Torres and I. Vicente (eds.) *Ars Longa. Diez años de AJIHLE.* Buenos Aires: Voces del Sur, pp. 383–395.
Rodríguez Barcia, S. (2012) "El análisis ideológico del discurso lexicográfico: una propuesta metodológica aplicada a diccionarios monolingües del español", *Verba* 39: 135–159.
Rodríguez Barcia, S. and F. Ramallo (2015) "De masones, sodomitas, herejes y comunistas", *Estudios de Lingüística del Español* 36(3): 449–483.
Rodríguez Marín, R. (2003) "El Diccionario de la Real Academia en la actualidad", in M. Martín Zorraquino and J.L. Aliaga (eds.), pp. 193–208.
Rodríguez Ortiz, F. and C. Garriga (2010) "La teoría lexicográfica de la academia en los siglos XVIII y XIX a través de las Reglas", *Quaderns de Filologia: Estudis lingüístics XV*: 31–56.
Roldán, A. (ed.) (2006) *Caminos actuales de la Historiografía Lingüística.* Murcia: Universidad de Murcia.
Rojo, G. (2007) "Sobre la construcción de diccionarios basados en corpus", *Tradumàtica* 7: 1–7. http://webs2002.uab.es/tradumatica/revista/num7/articles/02/02.pdf.
Ruhstaller S. (2003) "Las obras lexicográficas de la Academia", in Medina (ed.), pp. 135–261.
Ruhstaller S. and M. D. Gordon (eds.) (2010) *Diccionario y aprendizaje del español.* Berna: Peter Lang.
Ruhstaller S. and J. Prado (eds.) (2000) *Tendencias en la investigación lexicográfica del español. El diccionario como objeto de estudio lingüístico y didáctico.* Huelva: Universidad de Huelva.
Salas, A. (1964) "Los diccionarios académicos y el estado actual de la lexicografía", *Boletín de Filología* XVI: 265-283.
Salvador, G. (2002) "La crítica de diccionarios", in P. Álvarez de Miranda y J. Polo (eds.), pp. 235–239.
San Vicente, F. (ed.) (1995) *Bibliografía de la lexicografía española del siglo XVII.* Abano Terme: Piovan Editore.
San Vicente, F. and H. Lombardini (2012) " 'Prólogos del *DRAE* (1780–2001): cánones formales y de contenido' ", in A. Nomdedeu, E. Forgas and M. Bargalló (eds.), pp. 479–494.
San Vicente, F. (ed.) (2007) *Perfiles para la historia y crítica de la lexicografía bilingüe del español,* Milano: Polimetrica.
Sánchez García, F. (2009) *El léxico religioso en los diccionarios de la Real Academia Española.* Barcelona: Universitat de Barcelona.
Sánchez Merino, A. (2002–2003) "Algunas consideraciones sobre diccionarios bilingües españoles", *Revista de Lexicografía* 9: 147–174.
Sánchez Muñoz, T. (2002–2003) "Los diccionarios escolares a comienzos del siglo XXI", *Revista de lexicografía* 9: 175–188.
Santana, O., Z. Hernández, G. Pérez, G. Rodríguez and F. Carreras (1996) "Diccionarios en soportes informáticos", *Cuadernos Cervantes de la lengua española* 2(11): 68–73. www.gedlc.ulpgc.es/art_ps/art25.pdf.
Santana, O., J. Pérez, F. Carreras, Z. J. Hernández, G. Rodríguez (2003) "The Spanish Morphology in Internet", in J. M. Cueva Lovelle., B. M. González Rodríguez., L. Joyanes Aguilar., J. E. Labra Gayo

and M. del Puerto Paule de Ruiz (eds.) (2003) *Web Engineering*. Berlín/N. York, Springer, pp. 507–510.

Seco, M. (1992) "Los diccionarios históricos", in Ahumada (ed.), pp. 91–107.

Seco, M. (1995) "Lexicografía del español en el fin del siglo", *Donaire* 4: 67–94.

Seco, M. (2003) "María Moliner o el diccionario", in M. A. Martín Zorraquino and J. L. Aliaga (eds.), pp. 275–277.

Serra, S. (2006) "El problema del contorno en lexicografía española", *Boletín de Filología* XLI: 197–240.

Soler, M. C. (1999) "Diccionario ideológico de Julio Casares", in *Métodos de información* 6(29–30): 28–31.

Subirats, C. (2005) "FrameNet español: Una red semántica de marcos conceptuales", in E. Serra and G. Wotjak (eds.) *Cognición y percepción lingüísticas*. Valencia: Universidad de Valencia, pp. 182–196.

Subirats, C. (2009) "FrameNet español: un análisis cognitivo del léxico del español", in A. Alcina, E. Valero and E. Rambla (eds.) *Terminología y sociedad del conocimiento*. Frankfurt: Peter Lang, pp. 309–320.

Subirats, C. (2012) "La integración de la semántica de marcos y la semántica de simulación: aplicaciones al procesamiento semántico automático del español", in M. L. Calero and M. A. Hermosilla (eds.), *Lenguaje, literatura y cognición*. Córdoba: Universidad de Córdoba, pp. 307–337.

Torner, S., and E. Bernal (eds.) (2017) *Collocations and Other Lexical Combinations in Spanish. Theoretical, Lexicographic and Applied Perspectives*. London and New York: Routledge.

Vila, M. N. (2014) "El *Tesoro Lexicográfico* de Samuel Gili Gaya. Contexto, recepción y destino de un diccionario inacabado", in M. Bargalló, M. P. Garcés and C. Garriga (eds.), *Llaneza: estudios dedicados al profesor Juan Gutiérrez Cuadrado*. A Coruña: Universidade da Coruña, pp. 371–394.

Vila, M. N., Mª A. Calero, R. M. Mateu, M. Casanovas and J.L. Orduña (eds.) (1999) *Así son los diccionarios*. Lleida: Universitat de Lleida.

Werner, R. (2001) "Áreas pendientes en la lexicografía del español americano", en *II Congreso internacional de la lengua española* (Valladolid). http://cvc.cervantes.es/

Zimmerman, K. (1980) "Algunas consideraciones sobre la problemática de los diccionarios del español de América", *Lingüística Española Actual* 2(2): 375–384.

Zimmerman, K. (1985) "La selección del material léxico para diccionarios descriptivos", *Philologica hispaniensia in honorem Manuel Alvar*, 2, *Lingüística*, Madrid: Gredos, pp. 227–254.

Zimmerman, K. (1986) "La situación actual de la lexicografía del español de América", *Revista de Filología Románica* 4: 281–293.

Zimmerman, K. (2003) "El fin de los diccionarios de americanismos. La situación de la lexicografía del español de América después de la publicación de los *Diccionarios contrastivos del español de América*", *RILI* 1(1): 71–83.

Zimmerman, K. and G. Wotjak (eds.) (1994) *Unidad y variación léxicas en el español de América*. Frankfurt: Vevuert.

Part VI

Looking to the future

lexicography in the Internet era

41

Electronic dictionaries

Anna Dziemianko

41.1 Introduction

According to De Schryver (2003: 146), electronic dictionaries targeted at humans are "collections of structured electronic data that can be accessed with multiple tools, enhanced with a wide range of functionalities, and used in various environments". Electronic dictionaries do not have to be used by humans only; they can also be read by machines, mainly computers. Machine-readable dictionaries (MRDs) have a great potential for being used in linguistic research. They are relied on in natural language processing, which benefits machine translation and has its applications in systems that automatically summarize texts or extract specific bits of information (Zaenen 2002: 240). It is however human-oriented electronic dictionaries that are the main focus of this chapter (see Chapter 12 of this *Handbook* for an in-depth analysis of lexicography and natural language processing).

De Schryver (2003: 146) proposes a three-step typology of electronic dictionaries based on answers to the question "Who accesses what, where?" The distinction between MRD and human-oriented electronic dictionaries is an answer to the question "Who accesses the dictionary?" In the case of the electronic medium, the question "What is accessed?" refers to robust machines and handheld devices. As for the last question "Where does one access the dictionary data?", a distinction needs to be drawn between electronic dictionaries on stand-alone computers and networked computers. The former include dictionaries accessed on robust machines (such as those stored on optical drives) and hand-held devices (like reading pens or portable electronic dictionaries). The latter involve dictionaries on the Internet or intranets. Taking into account compilers and cost, Fuertes-Olivera (2009) further divides Internet dictionaries into institutional and collective. Institutional dictionaries, as the name itself suggests, are compiled by institutions. They may be used free of charge, but they may also be fee based. Collective (also known as collaborative) dictionaries are created by users themselves (e.g., the *Urban Dictionary*). Usually, they are consulted for free. Lew (2011) notes that electronic dictionaries do not have to come singly; they can come in groups, for example, as portals or aggregators. Dictionary portals include hyperlinks to dictionaries, whereas aggregators offer other dictionary content already pasted on one website, as shown in Figures 41.1 and 41.2, respectively (see Chapter 46 of this *Handbook* on dictionary portals).

Béjoint (2010: 371) distinguishes three "sorts" of electronic dictionaries: on CD-ROM, online and pocket ones. The defining characteristic of all of them is that the content is displayed on a screen and is accessed by an electronic system. A similar classification is proposed by Klotz and Herbst (2016: 182), who distinguish between e-dictionaries on optical drives for laptops and desktops, e-dictionaries for handheld devices (preloaded or downloaded) and e-dictionaries available on the Internet. Yet, they rightly note that the merge of desktops and laptops with hand-held devices and the rise of convertibles implies that electronic dictionaries need to be scalable to adapt to many screen sizes.

Klotz and Herbst (2016: 181–182) draw a distinction between dictionary content, medium and format. Dictionary content is an abstract notion which refers to the lexical information included in a dictionary. The technical medium gives a shape to a dictionary and can be paper or electronic. The medium largely affects the presentation and retrieval of lexicographic data. Dictionary format denotes specific ways of presenting information,

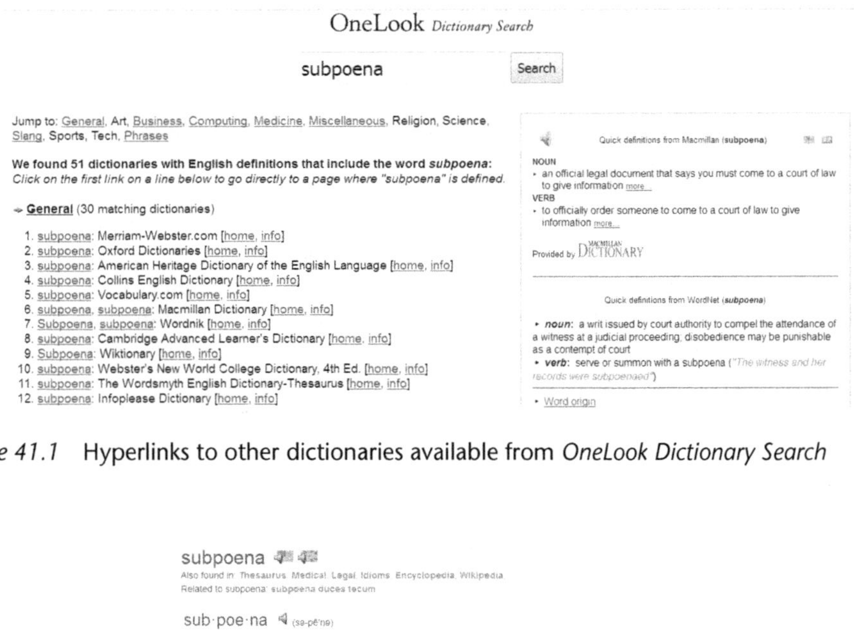

Figure 41.1 Hyperlinks to other dictionaries available from *OneLook Dictionary Search*

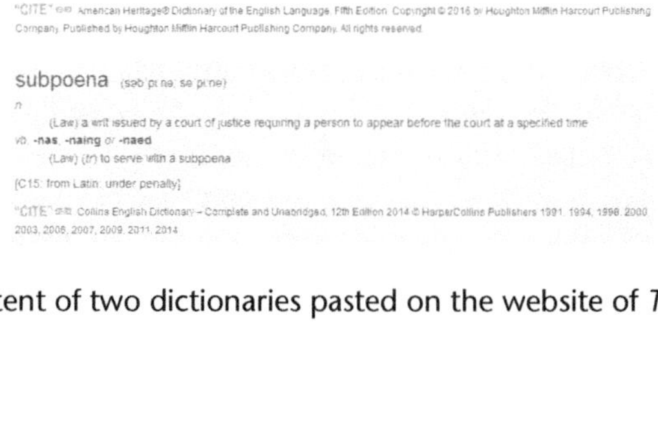

Figure 41.2 The content of two dictionaries pasted on the website of *The FreeDictionary.com*

like text, pictures, audio or video. Naturally, audio and video are possible only in the electronic medium, whereas text and pictures are allowed both in print and the electronic medium.

This chapter discusses the concept of electronic dictionaries for humans following mainly De Schryver's (2003) definition. It especially situates this type of dictionaries in their historical context, which goes from magnetic tape to the Internet (Section 41.2). It then comments on some of their main characteristics, focusing on access technologies and their impact on already observable lexicographic changes. These developments can affect the lexicographer, lexicography and lexicographic data (Section 41.3). Before the conclusion, this chapter makes some remarks on the future of electronic dictionaries. This future seems to be connected with new business models (see Chapter 29 of this *Handbook*) as well as users' real needs, automation and data personalization (Section 41.4).

41.2 Historical perspective

MRDs predate electronic dictionaries commercially available for the public. They have been consistently developed since the 1980s, although it is worth noting that the first dictionary (*Merriam-Webster Collegiate Dictionary*, 7th edition) available for research on magnetic tape was as early as the 1960s (Béjoint 2010: 376). It was, however, the *Longman Dictionary of Contemporary English* (1st edition, 1978) on tape that was more extensively used by researchers to automatically extract lexico-semantic information (Fontenelle 1997). More than merely "a typesetting tape", LDOCE1 was "the first truly computerized dictionary" (Cowie 1999: 120). The assignment of numerical markers to information categories made it a flexible editorial and research tool, open to further extensions and linguistic enrichment (Akkerman et al. 1988: 43, Cowie 1999: 120). The markers made it possible to extract all instances of a certain information category for proofreading, checking or the compilation of specialized dictionaries.

The advent of electronic dictionaries on CDs, whose content mirrored that of their paper counterparts, goes back to the 1980s. In Great Britain, the *Collins English Dictionary* (3rd edition, 1991) is most likely to be the first dictionary brought out in the electronic format, initially on floppy discs, and then on CD (in 1994) (Béjoint 2010: 373). The 1990s also saw the first dictionaries of English for foreign learners published on CDs. Yet, it is only the *Macmillan English Dictionary for Advanced Learners* (1st edition, 2002) that is said to be the first dictionary simultaneously produced on paper and on CD-ROM (Béjoint 2010: 373). The advent of the Internet also marked the gradual development of online dictionaries to the extent that now their number is almost infinite.

In 1993, CERN made an Internet site available for electronic dictionaries. Five years later, the number of English dictionaries on the Internet approximated 400 (Li 1998: 21). Apparently, in the last decade of the twentieth century, lexicographers were concentrated on assembling and trawling digital language data for research purposes. As Nesi (2015: 580) notes, the situation started to change at the beginning of the twenty-first century, with the increasing availability and decreasing cost of high-speed broadband Internet connections, which resulted in many print dictionaries being published online. Still, like in the case of CD-ROM dictionaries, the earliest online dictionaries were just copies of paper dictionaries, but they gradually took fuller advantage of the possibilities offered by the electronic medium. Tarp (2012b: 116–117) distinguishes four types of Internet dictionaries, depending on the extent to which they used new technologies (i.e., copycats, faster horses, model T Fords and Rolls Royces).

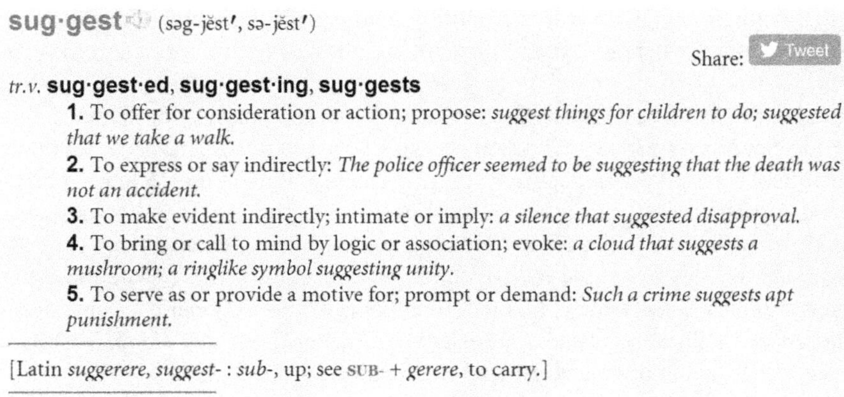

sug·gest (səg-jĕst′, sə-jĕst′)

Share: Tweet

tr.v. **sug·gest·ed, sug·gest·ing, sug·gests**

1. To offer for consideration or action; propose: *suggest things for children to do; suggested that we take a walk.*
2. To express or say indirectly: *The police officer seemed to be suggesting that the death was not an accident.*
3. To make evident indirectly; intimate or imply: *a silence that suggested disapproval.*
4. To bring or call to mind by logic or association; evoke: *a cloud that suggests a mushroom; a ringlike symbol suggesting unity.*
5. To serve as or provide a motive for; prompt or demand: *Such a crime suggests apt punishment.*

[Latin *suggerere, suggest-* : *sub-*, up; see SUB- + *gerere*, to carry.]

Figure 41.3 Non-adaptable, copycat content of *The American Heritage Dictionary*

Copycats are the most primitive online dictionaries, created by scanning or photographing existing printed dictionaries and putting up the files online. Faster horses, still modelled after paper dictionaries, are similar to copycats, in that they allow faster search by making only a restricted use of new technologies. Yet, such dictionaries are still static, non-customizable to user needs and contexts of dictionary consultation. They predate the compilation of dictionaries which exploit the potential of the electronic medium more fully, and not so long ago they were claimed to account for the vast majority of online dictionaries (Tarp 2012a: 258). Fuertes-Olivera (2013: 326) uses the term printed online dictionaries to refer to both these categories of retro-digitized versions of paper dictionaries (i.e., copycats and faster horses). An example of such a dictionary is shown in Figure 41.3. The main advantage of such a dictionary over a paper one is the search window to facilitate access to headwords.

The defining characteristics of Model T Fords are the adaptable, dynamic microstructure as well as interactive options to define user needs and contexts of dictionary use. User profiling, filtering and hypermedia feature prominently in such dictionaries. Thus, not only faster

Figure 41.4 Possibilities of adapting dictionary content in OED online

access to lexicographic data, but, above all, dictionary adaptability and content customization to the user profile and punctual needs at a given moment are at the heart of Model T Fords. Unfortunately, such dictionaries are in the minority (Tarp 2012a: 258). The possibility of personalizing search and adjusting it to specific needs is illustrated in Figure 41.4, which shows advanced search options in the *Oxford English Dictionary*. As can be seen, they include searching by subject, language of origin, region, usage, date of entry and part of speech, using Boolean operators as well as searching in entries, senses and quotations. Attractive as it is, these functionalities and level of user control might benefit those who are sophisticated enough to know which data fields they require.

Another possibility of adapting the microstructure can be found in the *Base Lexicale du Français*, where users determine the content of dictionary entries by specifying activity type or the non-linguistic context which triggers dictionary consultation. Then, relevant content, preselected in advance by lexicographers, is displayed (see Verline et al. 2010; Verlinde and Peeters 2012). It is also possible to give users very limited control over the content of the entry which they see. The *show more/show less* button in MEDO, for example, makes it possible to respectively, show and hide phonetic transcription, the menu of senses, some collocations, examples of usage or links to relevant thesaurus entries.

Electronic dictionaries which would deserve the name of Rolls Royces are, according to Tarp (2012a: 259), yet to be compiled. Compared to driverless cars, they would need to

> combine access to selected data in a prepared database with search on the Internet (and in existing corpora) in order to take in relevant data that can be *recreated* and *re-presented* in dynamic solutions different from the ones provided by the lexicographical Model T Fords which link to specific and selected Web pages in order to reuse their data.
>
> (Tarp 2012a: 259)

It may be expected that with the development of new technologies, online dictionaries will go beyond individualized lexicographical solutions and head in the direction of dynamic recreation and re-presentation of data automatically absorbed from the Internet.

41.3 Core issues and topics

Much has been said about the advantages of electronic dictionaries over paper ones (e.g. Bergenholtz and Gouws 2007, De Schryver 2003, Dziemianko 2012a, 2012b, 2016, Lew 2011, 2012, Nesi 1999, 2015, Prinsloo 2005). The following are among the most widely recognized ones: easy and fast access, enhanced information retrieval with the help of hypertext, virtually unlimited storage space, less textual condensation, better readability of entries or links to external sources (like corpora or citation banks). Yet, despite the many unquestionable advantages of electronic dictionaries, their quality and actual usefulness cannot be simply taken for granted. Core issues related to electronic dictionaries are divided below into access on the one hand, and quality and usefulness – on the other.

41.3.1 Access

Electronic dictionaries facilitate both outer and inner access, that is finding the right entry and the desired information within the entry (Bergenholtz and Gouws 2007: 243). Accessing the headword in an electronic dictionary is a marked improvement on the search in a paper dictionary. Instead of turning pages, scanning running heads and finding a headword on a densely printed page, in the electronic medium it is now enough to enter the headword in the search window. Increasingly often, even this effort is not necessary. On the one hand, incremental search, also known as type ahead search, search-as-you-type, inline search, or instant search (Lew 2012: 351), makes the dictionary suggest possible headwords even after entering a few characters in the search window (see Figure 41.5). In this way the user is saved the effort of reproducing the spelling of the looked-up word, which users may not be sure of. Interestingly enough, in the *Merriam-Webster's Advanced Learner's English Dictionary*, it is enough to key in the initial letter to activate incremental search. Yet, such a "single-letter trigger" is considered to be excessively intrusive and needlessly distracting (Lew 2012: 351).

Another outer access enhancement offered by electronic dictionaries is the relatively robust approach to inflected forms. If an inflected form is entered in the search window, the system strips it of inflections and the canonical form is accessed (e.g. entering *taking* in the search window of MEDO immediately directs the user to the headword for the verb *take*). Even more conveniently, dictionary users may reach the right headword even if they misspell it. Dictionaries are increasingly often becoming able to arrive at the right spelling by advanced matching, that is "recognizing associations between non-identical but sufficiently close variants" (Lew 2012: 347). Figure 41.6 illustrates how CALD online deals with the misspelling *exagerate*.

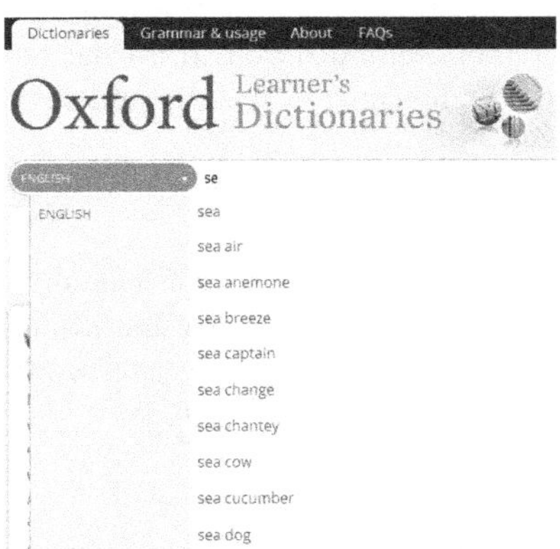

Figure 41.5 Incremental search in OALD online

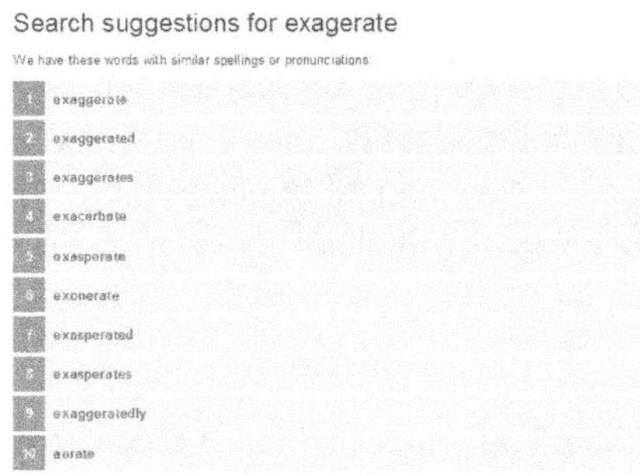

Figure 41.6 Handling misspellings by CALD online

Fuzzy matching is a notable achievement, considering the fact that many electronic dictionaries available globally are consulted by non-native speakers. It can be quite difficult to predict the misspellings of the words looked up, because such mistakes are to a large extent dependent on the native language of dictionary users. Besides, dictionary algorithms are not helped by the immediate textual context, which can perform an important disambiguating function (see Lew 2012). Overall, even though the "did you mean" function is now available in many dictionaries, there is still plenty of room for improving the accuracy of the suggestions offered for misspelt words, as recent research conducted on electronic versions of learners' dictionaries of English shows (Lew and Mitton 2013).

The orthographic form of a word is not the only way to arrive at the desired headword in an electronic dictionary. Sometimes, dictionary users may not know how to spell a word which they only heard but never saw written, and they may wish to take the pronunciation of the word as the outset of electronic dictionary search. Phonetic search, which consists in entering phonetic symbols rather than the letters of the alphabet in the search window (e.g., Sobkowiak 1999, 2003) is a spelling-independent access path which has been adopted in few dictionaries. The SoundSearch offered by the CD-ROM edition of MEDAL1 (2002) or the pronunciation search in LDOCE4 on CD-ROM are good examples of the idea put into practice. Obviously, such solutions are not commonly adopted in electronic dictionaries, presumably because of the rightly assumed unfamiliarity with phonetic symbols among regular dictionary users.

Fortunately, it is possible to use the audio channel to access headwords without resorting to phonetic symbols but just by uttering the unknown word to the device hosting a dictionary with a speech recognition system, a solution already offered by some dictionary applications for smartphones. Still, even though it seems that this access path cannot be easier, speech recognition systems should be robust enough to deal with non-native speech, idiosyncratic pronunciation of different dictionary users and accent variations.

It must also be noted that it is not only isolated words that dictionary users may need. Language is now viewed not as a basically atomic structure, composed of isolated words which can be inserted into specific slots according to predefined rules. Corpus evidence reveals the essentially phraseological nature of language (e.g., Sinclair 1991, Altenberg 1998); meaning is not decomposed into independent words, but rather comes in chunks which go beyond the boundaries of individual words. Unfortunately, language users, especially learners, often lack collocational and phraseological awareness, and fail to realize that they are dealing with multi-word units (Herbst 1996: 336, Scholfield 1999: 15). They might also have problems with delimiting the exact boundaries of a meaningful language chunk which goes beyond one word, especially considering the variable fixedness, or fuzziness, of multi-word lexical items (Moon 1998). Besides, the long lexicographic tradition of focusing on isolated words as building blocks of a language as well as users' experience in word-based search pose a serious challenge to lexicographers, who need to give longer expressions a prominent place in dictionaries (see Lew 2012, Dziemianko 2014). Naturally, this gives rise to the problem of accessing multi-word units. Today, many electronic dictionaries suggest possible multi-word expressions even if one constituent thereof is entered (see Figure 41.7.). Advanced matching mechanisms are employed so that a dictionary lists approximate matches of the looked-up expression spanning a few words, rather than only the exact sequence as entered into the search box. Yet, even more advantage could be taken of the electronic medium if dictionaries were context-sensitive. In other words, they should be able to examine the co-text of the text being read, provided that the text is in electronic form and is accessed on the same device. Then, even hovering the cursor at a single word or long-tapping a word on the touch screen could activate a pop-up window with the relevant multi-word expression, including the word in question. Importantly, the electronic format of the text does not have to be the necessary requirement for contextual sensitivity. It could also be applicable to printed, or even handwritten text, provided that the device hosting a dictionary is equipped with a camera and OCR technology. Then, it should be possible to take a picture of the unknown phrase in a foreign language and activate a context-sensitive dictionary entry on the device (Lew 2012: 351).

Finally, a word looked up may be homonymous, or represent a few grammatical categories (e.g., *average* as a noun, a verb and an adjective). In such situations, many electronic dictionaries offer layered, hierarchical or step-wise outer access – the information in the entry is presented in various phases – rather than flat access, typical of paper dictionaries. One example of such step-wise access to the desired entry is the situation where a dictionary offers a menu with a vertically arranged list of headwords, often along with derivatives and multi-word expressions (see Figure 41.7). The items on the list are hyperlinked, so a single click is enough to take the user to the right entry (for example for the adjective rather than the verb or the noun). Alternatively, the dictionary might still offer a menu with hyperlinks to specific entries, but also open the one which is considered to be the most likely to be chosen first (see Figure 41.8). Such a solution might save some of the clicking required by the first approach, but there is always the risk that the entry opened by default will not be the one that is needed, a fact that the user might be ignorant of and simply fail to notice. Another way of turning the outer access into a step-wise sequence consists in offering an overview of multiple entries for the looked up word in the form of a list featuring top sections of each entry followed by a link to the full content. Such an approach was adopted some time ago by myCOBUILD.com, but has not been implemented in any renowned online dictionary (cf. Lew 2011). Lew (2012: 357) rightly notes that this is somewhat surprising, considering the similarity of this interface to the format in which the output in Internet search is presented in many search engines, including Google.

Not only the outer access can be layered or hierarchical. The same applies to the inner access path, which takes the user from the headword to the needed information within the entry. The step-wise inner access is achieved by restricting the amount of information made available to the user at a time. In the case of polysemous entries, a list of senses can be first offered in the form of a menu, which consists of a hyperlinked set of sense indicators (see

Figure 41.7 Lookup results for *date* in LDOCE online

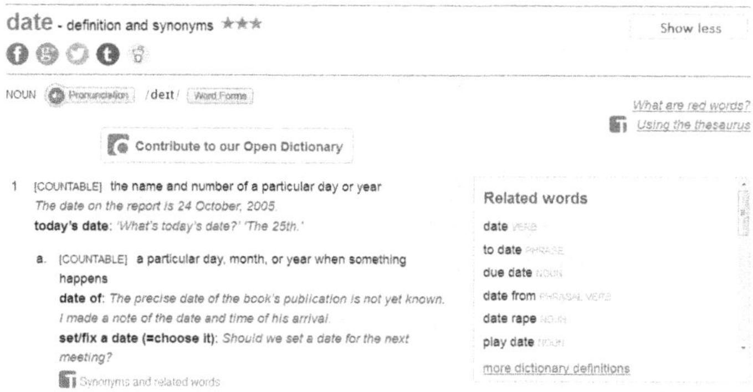

Figure 41.8 Lookup results for *date* in MEDO

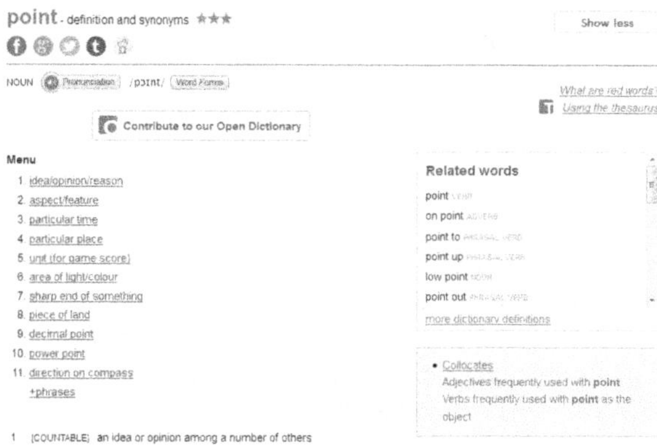

Figure 41.9 A menu of senses in the MEDO entry for *point*

Figure 41.9). The dictionary user may click on the sense which is most likely to meet the needs at a given moment, and the relevant information limited to the desired sense is displayed on the screen.

The menu of senses at the top of a polysemous entry appears to be quite attractive, considering the prominence of the menu in information technology as well as the largely menu-driven computer environment, which electronic dictionary users can be assumed to be familiar with (Lew 2012: 358). Besides, it appears to remedy, at least in part, the problem of overreliance on entry-initial senses, frequently noted in lexicographic research on the use of paper dictionaries (Bogaards 1998; Lew 2004; Nesi 1987; Nesi and Haill 2002; Nuccorini 1994; Tono 1984). It is worth noting that apart from the automatic scrolling to the sense selected from the menu in a polysemous entry, MEDO features additional temporary highlighting of the selected sense to immediately draw users' attention to the right place in the microstructure.

41.3.2 Quality and usefulness

Electronic dictionaries are expected to be fast, easy and accessible (Levy and Steel 2015: 11). Apart from the widespread availability, speed and ease of consultation, enhanced by the solutions described in Section 41.3.1, multimedia add to their attractiveness. Thanks to audio recordings of headwords, registering correct pronunciation could not be easier. Yet, it needs to be remembered that users hear foreign language sounds through the filter of their own language and are unable to identify sound distinctions not present in their mother tongue (Lew 2011). It has also been shown that animations in dictionaries do not enhance retention, despite the fact that they are frequently consulted (Lew and Doroszewska 2009). Overall, on the basis of current research, Lew (2012: 360) concludes that the existing "evidence invites optimism with respect to static pictures and audio recordings, but looks less optimistic when it comes to video and animation enhancements". However, video recordings now seem almost indispensable in sign language dictionaries (see Chapter 25 of this *Handbook*; users can see, also at various speeds, how a given sign is produced; Vale 2015).

Electronic dictionaries have largely reduced search-related lexicographic costs, which are connected with dictionary consultation (Nielsen 2008: 173). Even the additional amount of clicking and scrolling necessary to go through the hierarchical access structures of electronic dictionaries cannot be compared with the time-consuming access paths in traditional dictionaries. Yet, the quality of electronic dictionaries does not go hand in hand with the ease of access. Users themselves often consider them less reliable and accurate that those on paper. Koyama and Takeuchi (2003: 72) found that the portable electronic dictionary used in their study was considered to provide insufficient information, despite the fact that the content was the same as that of its paper counterpart. Although a possible explanation for that can be the layered interface of that specific electronic dictionary and its content segmentation, it is worth noting that electronic dictionaries are quite often regarded as inferior in quality (Chen 2010: Nesi 2012, Tono 2009). After all, they can be instantly produced, modified and published virtually by anybody without any supervision or quality control (Béjoint 2010: 375). Yet, dictionary users want a dictionary to be, above all, reliable. In a recent study by Müller-Spitzer et al. (2011), English and German dictionary users were requested to rank 10 aspects of online dictionary usability. The most appreciated features included: reliable and up-to-date content, clarity and speed. By contrast, links to other dictionaries, adaptability, suggestions for further browsing as well as multimedia proved to play only a minor role. The authors conclude that "the classical criteria of reference books (e.g. reliability, clarity) were both ranked and rated highest, whereas the unique characteristics of online dictionaries (e.g. multimedia, adaptability) were rated and ranked as (partly) unimportant" (Müller-Spitzer et al. 2011: 207). A possible reason for such scepticism about innovative features of online dictionaries may reside in their novelty value; users may not be used to them, or even realize that they exist. This hypothesis was tested in another study, which revealed a definite learning effect; acquainting users with innovative design features of online dictionaries increased the rating of those characteristics (Müller-Spitzer and Koplenig 2014).

Nonetheless, dictionary authority is fading away, especially among digital natives (Zaenen 2002, Rundell 2011). A possible reason for that may reside in user involvement. Collaboration on the creation of works of reference in the electronic format is inherent in the notion of collective intelligence, or the wisdom of crowds (Surowiecki 2005); it is assumed that experts are willing to share their knowledge in virtual reality for public benefit (Meyer and Gurevych 2012: 259). Collaboratively constructed encyclopaedias, such as *Wikipedia*, bear comparison with eminent published brands (Giles 2005). The beginning of the twenty-first century witnessed wiki software becoming an open-source tool, which boosted the development of collaborative lexicography (Nesi 2009: 475). Thus, users themselves, rather than professional lexicographers, started to contribute dictionary content. *Wiktionary* or *Urban Dictionary* are the classic examples of collaboratively produced dictionaries. This bottom-up approach to lexicography has unquestionable advantages. Apart from the steeply rising coverage of words and senses, including those which are not yet institutionalized, as well as cant, slang and jargon expressions, "the broad diversity of authors fosters the encoding of a vast amount of domain-specific knowledge" (Meyer and Gurevych 2012: 259). According to Rundell (2012a: 80), user involvement in lexicography can prove particularly valuable in the case of neologisms, technical language and regional varieties. Yet, it remains obvious that "serious lexicography requires specialized skills and expertise; for this reason, a large part of crowdsourced content is of questionable lexicographic value" (Lew 2014). Another reason for the scepticism towards electronic dictionary authority is that electronic dictionaries with reliable, licensed dictionary content are being supplanted by Wi-Fi connected mobile devices (Nesi 2015: 580). In the contemporary give-away culture, promoted by technology, dictionaries are increasingly often compiled by anonymous amateur editors and made available free of charge. It is sometimes even impossible to find information on the authorship and authorization, either individual or institutional, of a given reference work on its website. It thus seems only natural that users may grow doubtful about the quality of information which such sources share. Overall, in contrast to collaborative encyclopaedias, "good modern dictionaries cannot be created without corpus-derived insights into grammar and usage, and collaboratively produced dictionaries will always require additional lexicographical input in order to be really useful reference tools" (Nesi 2012: 377).

User involvement in electronic dictionaries can be seen to form a yet different perspective. Levy and Steel (2015: 15) point out the possibility of getting involved in a virtual conversation about the use and meaning of words that the electronic medium offers. *WordReference* or *Macmillan Dictionary Blog* are examples of such channels of communication between native speakers and learners, lexicographers and dictionary users. Such discussion forums are evaluated positively by users; they are claimed to improve the grasp of nuances of word meaning and use (Levy and Steel 2015: 15).

Another way of involving electronic dictionary users consists in complementary tools, ancillary to essential dictionary functions and functionalities. Some electronic dictionaries make it possible to create individual word lists, transform them into flash cards and create personalized learning tools, thereby developing learner autonomy. The sense of progress and achievement can be even stronger if users decide to take advantage of self-monitoring facilities that some dictionaries offer, such as a system of revisions built around personalized dictionary-based wordlists. Such functionalities are available, for example, in the premium version of OALD online. Users can create there their own wordlists and be tested by the system (see Figure 41.10).

Sometimes, it is even possible to turn individualized dictionaries into gamified tools which monitor progress (Levy and Steel 2015: 14). All in all, what Nesi (2012: 377) calls "peripheral e-dictionary facilities such as audio and video files, word-list creation tools, language tests, and language games, all popular with users and unique to the electronic medium" appear to improve the competitive edge of electronic dictionaries and, most importantly, give users greater autonomy in managing their learning process.

A discussion of the quality of electronic dictionaries also requires mentioning alternative dictionaries. Typically, they are a medley of

> diverse resources, some of which are up-to-date dictionaries from prestigious publishing houses, some of which are local dictionaries, often of old or uncertain provenance,

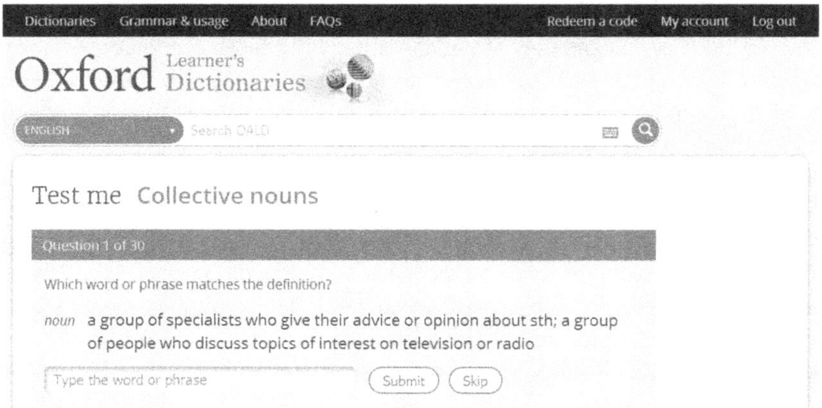

Figure 41.10 A test on a wordlist in OALD online (premium version)

> and some of which are not produced by lexicographers at all . . . bewilderingly subject to change.
>
> (Nesi 2012: 364)

Such dictionaries are largely appreciated by users for additional features such as wordlists, language tests, games and personal organizers, rather than the content (Nesi 2010). They quite often aggregate a number of different local dictionaries targeted at different user groups, compiled at various points of time and/or digitized, often with errors and mistranslations. Even though they boast a large number of lemma stock, many of their headwords are theoretically possible, but, in fact, unattested derivatives (e.g., *examinationism* or *examinationist*) (Nesi 2012: 372). The lack of labels does not warn users against obsolete or archaic words, included in such dictionaries only to blow up the wordlist. Another reason for the poor quality of alternative dictionaries rests in the lack of lexicographic intervention in the selection and editing of (some) lexicographic data. Examples happen to be automatically selected from websites, social portals or encyclopaedias. Automatic translation provides parallel example sentences in two languages. Apparently, then, users should be sensitized to the quality of electronic dictionaries. Nonetheless, alternative dictionaries should not be dismissed by metalexicographers as not good enough to be worthy of attention, but, considering their powerful appeal, they should be systematically described and reviewed in proper metalexicographic literature (cf. Nesi 2012: 376).

Unfortunately, empirical research into the actual usefulness of electronic dictionaries in reception, production and retention leads to divergent results. The medium (paper vs. electronic) did not exert any significant effect on language reception in the study by Nesi (2000), Kobayashi (2007), Koyama and Takeuchi (2007) and Chen (2010, 2012). The same variable proved to be important in the study by Osaki et al. (2003), Osaki and Nakayama (2004) and Dziemianko (2010). Conclusions from research into the usefulness of electronic dictionaries in language production are no less contradictory. Chen (2010) found that the medium does not play a role in encoding, while Dziemianko (2010) showed that the electronic dictionary stimulates more successful language production. Unfortunately, not much is known about the value of electronic dictionaries in language learning, either. Some research reveals that they have no effect on vocabulary retention (Chen 2010, 2012, Kobayashi 2007; Osaki et al. 2003; Osaki and Nakayama 2004; Xu 2010). Yet, in the study by Koyama and Takeuchi (2004), the electronic medium proved to be detrimental to learning words, whereas Dziemianko (2010) observed that it was beneficial. Even a replication of one study into the significance of dictionary medium produces different results. Dziemianko (2011 and 2012b) replicated her original 2010 study with all the experimental conditions retained apart from the dictionary. The traditional and electronic versions of COBUILD6 were employed in 2010, and in the consecutive replications – those of LDOCE5 and MEDO. As noted earlier, the earliest study revealed a positive influence of the electronic medium on language comprehension, production and retention, while no such effect was noted in the replications. Yet, reliance on real dictionaries, rather than purpose-built ones, must have introduced a number of variables which remained beyond the researcher's control such as different layouts, colours and typography, all of which might have affected the results.

41.4 Looking to the future

The future of electronic dictionaries has been a matter of much discussion recently. In his eLex 2015 plenary lecture with the telling title *Unlocking the Power of the Oxford Learners' Dictionaries*, Gorin echoes one of the conclusions reached at the eLex conference in 2013: the future of dictionaries does not concern dictionary products, but rather lexicographic assets integrated with other products to add value. The example which he gives, the *Oxford Vocabulary Trainer*, is an application designed as a blended learning product. It is aligned with coursebooks or traditional curricula, but also offers a number of related exercises and a dictionary. Its most intriguing feature seems to be the feedback butterfly, or *feebu*, which is a way of visualizing feedback – the four wings of a butterfly grow or shrink depending on the quality of answers with respect to grammar, spelling, meaning and word choice (see Figure 41.11). Another noteworthy feature of the application is a semi-trilingual dictionary designed to facilitate learning languages in a multicultural environment (Figure 41.12). This is just an instantiation of the direction in which electronic lexicography will probably develop. In Nielsen's (2013: 370) words, "dictionaries of the future will, to an increasing extent, be regarded as digital assistants".

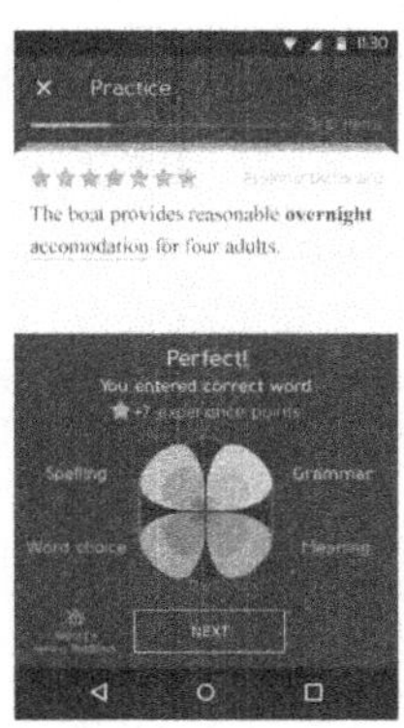

Figure 41.11 A screenshot of the *Oxford Vocabulary Trainer* with *feebu*

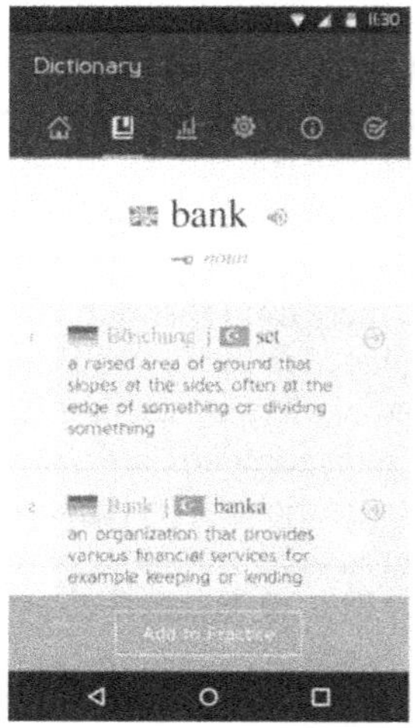

Figure 41.12 A screenshot of the semi-trilingual dictionary of the *Oxford Vocabulary Trainer*

One more example which proves that the predicted future of dictionaries is already materializing is provided by the *Cambridge English Write and Improve*, presented at the same eLexis 2015 conference (Briscoe 2015). This online software is designed, as the name itself suggests, to help learners of English hone their writing skills. It uses a great deal of lexical information. Having written or uploaded a text for assessment, the user waits under a minute to obtain feedback. This software tool involves a learner corpus, error-coded script, quite liberal parsing (which looks for some type of interpretation of users' sentences) and lemmatization. To assign a final grade (a numerical value) in next to no time, it trades off the richness of the submitted text against the number of errors, and relies on advanced statistics, including regression and classification (ranking algorithms). Considering the fact that the IT-enhanced environment has already become the standard working and learning environment for many, it is may indeed be expected that "electronic dictionaries have a chance to blend into that environment by discreetly staying in the background and coming to the rescue when needed" (Lew 2012: 361).

It may be expected that automatic lexicographic compilation will grow in strength in the future. Although automatically compiled dictionaries have been around for a while now (see Kompara 2012), the proportion of automatically compiled lexicographic content in electronic dictionaries may increase (see Klosa 2009). After all, "the role of the lexicographer and editor is moving away from the origination of dictionary text to the validation of decisions and selections made by the software" (Rundell 2012b: 28). Tickbox lexicography gives promising outcomes. In crude terms, the lexicographer ticks the options suggested by corpus software which appear to be relevant, and they automatically land in the proper sections in a dictionary writing system (Rundell 2012b: 23). The focus of the lexicographer's job will shift even more from identifying and selecting revenant data to reviewing and editing decisions made by software.

It can also be predicted that electronic dictionaries and corpora will be brought together to an even greater extent than is the case nowadays. There are already dictionaries which give links to corpora, show more corpus examples or feature customized tools which make to possible to explore corpora (Müller-Spitzer 2013: 378).

It is recommended that the integration of corpora with dictionaries be intelligent, so that users can find corpus examples for specific senses of the looked-up headword (Abel 2013: 1123). Klosa (2009) also sees the potential for including corpus metadata in electronic dictionaries to a larger extent to show users in how many different sources and in what years a word can be found, which might help them estimate the usefulness of the word on their own. Access to corpora granted in dictionaries resembles the methods of data-driven learning, whereby learners become investigators who discover facts about language of their own (see Flowerdew 2009: 339). This approach is considered more beneficial for language learning than exposing learners to ready rules (see Kilgarriff 2009).

There is a need for a lot of research into the usefulness of electronic dictionaries. One promising area of further investigation is electronic dictionary entry design. Electronic dictionary interface is extremely varied. As already noted in Section 40.3.1, content can be shown on one screen or on different screens. In the latter case, it can be book-like, with no segmentation of lexicographic data. Collapsible entries arranged vertically, on the other hand, make it possible to get a compact overview of the whole content, and access more information on demand. There can also be clickable tabs, where information is arranged horizontally. This layout saves dictionary users a lot of scrolling, which is usually indispensable in the vertical arrangement.

Koplenig and Müller-Spitzer (2014) tested the usefulness of four entry layouts: explorer view, panel view, tab view and print view. The explorer view has a tree-like structure with expandable content on demand. The explorer view has the structure of a chart with different information categories in each cell. Finally, the tab view has the horizontal structure which makes it possible to switch between information modules. The print view resembles a picture or scan of a paper dictionary, where the only advantage taken of the electronic medium is storage. The results point to the tab view as the unquestionable winner; it was appreciated for clarity, uncluttered look and navigation ease as well as adaptability. Yet, it seems to be necessary to do more research on the topic, involve more varied user groups in different situations of lexical deficit.

Another interesting research topic is the effect of advertising on retrieving information from dictionaries (Levy and Steel 2015: 17). Preliminary conclusions from existing research imply that electronic dictionaries may lose a lot of their appeal and usefulness because of obtrusive promotional material (Dziemianko 2012b: 210).

Despite the limitations of user-generated content, described in section 41.3.2, dictionaries of the future should stay in contact with users. Feedback forms, comments on entries and justified content contribution are worthy of attention, because the interaction between users and lexicographers is crucial for creating user-friendly dictionaries in the years to come. Indeed, although collaborative lexicography is not forecast to replace the more traditional approach to dictionary making, it is almost certain to throw a new light on electronic dictionaries, which can benefit lexicography in the future (Meyer and Gurevych 2012).

It is also recommendable to take even more advantage of the electronic medium to investigate the actual use that learners make of electronic dictionaries. In particular, eye tracking and log files should be employed to a larger extent in empirical research to automatically monitor the search process and users' decisions. Further research should also be directed at comparing the usefulness of various types of electronic dictionaries, that is, those online, on CD and on portable devices (Dziemianko 2012a: 336).

41.5 Conclusion

Electronic dictionaries come in various shapes and sizes, from those book-like to those which are truly advanced and interactive. It is obvious, though, that electronic lexicography is not just a continuation of print lexicography. Nor does it mean merely making print dictionaries available online or on some data carrier. The most obvious advantage of the electronic medium manifests itself in simplified access structures, which make the electronic dictionary look-up time-effective and accurate. The integration of electronic dictionaries into educational software tools as well as the potential for dictionary customization and personalization encourage autonomy in language learners. Gamification possibly adds an element of joy to the otherwise complex task of solving language problems. However, ease, speed and user-friendliness do not always go hand in hand with top quality. The electronic medium implies freedom and the (often false) sense of security and anonymity, which may prompt amateurish lexicographic contributions (or even creations). This, in turn, undermines dictionary authority and reliability. There is no denying that thanks to the electronic medium, the user has come to the fore. The user of the electronic dictionary is not merely the subject of research, but also the contributor of lexicographic content, commentator, critic and enquirer, whose voice is welcome and heard. There is a considerable need to discuss the quality of electronic dictionaries, decide on criteria for evaluating their functionalities and assess user-generated content (see Klosa 2009). These days, electronic dictionaries are not compiled only by teams of expert lexicographers; advanced and intelligent software, machines, web designers, corpus linguists and users are playing an increasingly important role. Besides, the underlying goal of creating dictionaries in the electronic form is not linguistic research, but actual usage, thanks to the Internet – on a global scale. Unfortunately, it is possible to venture a statement that not much is known for sure about the actual usefulness of dictionaries in the electronic medium (cf. Dziemianko 2012a). Admittedly, it might be increasingly difficult to examine the use of electronic dictionaries, advances in research methodology notwithstanding, because of the tendency to make dictionaries implicitly embedded into other software. Despite this obvious development, it seems quite unlikely that freestanding electronic dictionaries will shortly disappear.

Related topics

Dictionaries and access; innovations in online dictionaries; learner's dictionaries of English; domain ontologies; Wordnik.

Further reading

Dziemianko, A. (2015). "Colours in Online Dictionaries: A Case of Functional Labels", *International Journal of Lexicography* 28(1): 27–61.

This paper presents the results of an empirical study on the effect of colour on the speed and accuracy of retrieving grammatical information form electronic dictionaries. Another aspect discussed here is the significance of examples in entries.

Müller-Spitzer, C. (ed.) (2014). *Using Online Dictionaries*. Berlin/Boston: de Gruyter.

This book gives details on the latest research into digital dictionaries and suggests further directions in which it should develop.

Tono, Y. (2011). "Application of Eye-Tracking in EFL Learners' Dictionary Look-Up Process Research", *International Journal of Lexicography* 24(1): 124–153.

This paper reports on a study in which eye tracking was used to investigate how internal access facilitators such as menus and signposts help users navigate dictionary entries.

References

Dictionaries

DWDS = *Digitales Wörterbuch der deutschen Sprache:* www.dwds.de/ressourcen/woerterbuecher/
LDOCE = *Longman Dictionary of Contemporary English:* www.ldoceonline.com/
MEDAL1 = Rundell, Michael. (ed.) (2002) *Macmillan English Dictionary for Advanced Learners.* 1st edition. Oxford: Macmillan Education.
MEDAL2 = Rundell, Michael. (ed.) (2007) *Macmillan English Dictionary for Advanced Learners.* 2nd edition. Oxford: Macmillan Education.
MEDO = *Macmillan English Dictionary Online*: www.macmillandictionary.com
OALD = *Oxford Advanced Learner's Dictionary of Current English:* www.oxfordlearnersdictionaries.com/
OWID = *Online-Wortschatz-Informationssystem Deutsch:* www.owid.de/
American Heritage Dictionary: https://ahdictionary.com/
American Sign Language Dictionary: www.handspeak.com/
FreeDcitionary.com: www.thefreedictionary.com/
Macmillan Dictionary Blog: www.macmillandictionaryblog.com/
OneLook Dictionary Search: www.onelook.com/
Oxford English Dictionary: www.oed.com/ (available on subscription)
Sign Language dictionary: www.handspeak.com
Urban Dictionary: www.urbandictionary.com/
Wiktionary: www.wiktionary.org/
WordReference: www.wordreference.com/

Other literature

Abel, A. (2013) "Electronic Dictionaries for Computer-Assisted Language Learning", in R. H. Gouws, U. Heid, W. Schweickard and H. E. Wiegand (eds.), pp. 1115–1136.
Akkerman, E., H. Voogt-Van Zutphen and W. Meijs (1988) *A Computerized Lexicon for Word-level Tagging*. Amsterdam: Radopi.
Altenberg, B. (1998) "On the Phraseology of Spoken English: The Evidence of Recurrent Word-Combinations", in A. P. Cowie (ed.), *Phraseology. Theory, Analysis and Applications.* Oxford: Oxford University Press: pp. 101–124.
Béjoint, H. (2010) *The Lexicography of English.* Oxford: Oxford University Press.
Bergenholtz, H. and R. Gouws (2007) "The Access Process in Dictionaries for Fixed Expressions", *Lexicographica. International Annual for Lexicography* 23: 237–260.
Bogaards, P. (1998) "Scanning Long Entries in Learners' Dictionaries", in T. Fontenelle, P. Hiligsmann, A. Michiels, A. Moulin and S. Theissen (eds.), *EURALEX'98 Proceedings.* Liège: University of Liège, pp. 555–563.
Briscoe, T. (2015) "The Use of Lexical Resources in Cambridge English Write and Improve", eLex2013 conference videos. See at: https://youtu.be/AI_jhIDSMtM
Cambridge English Write and Improve (Beta). See at: https://sat.ilexir.co.uk/
Chen, Y. (2010) "Dictionary Use and EFL Learning: A Contrastive Study of Pocket Electronic Dictionaries and Paper Dictionaries", *International Journal of Lexicography* 23(3): 275–306.
Chen, Y. (2012) "Dictionary Use and Vocabulary Learning in the Context of Reading", *International Journal of Lexicography* 25(2): 216–247.
Cowie, A. P. (1999) *English Dictionaries for Foreign Learners: A History.* Oxford: Clarendon Press.

De Schryver, G.-M. (2003) "Lexicographers' Dreams in the Electronic-Dictionary Age", *International Journal of Lexicography* 16(2): 143–199.

Dziemianko, A. (2010) "Paper or Electronic? The Role of Dictionary Form in Language Reception, Production and the Retention of Meaning and Collocations", *International Journal of Lexicography* 23(3): 257–273.

Dziemianko, A. (2011) "Does Dictionary Form Really Matter?", in K. Akasu and U. Satoru (eds.) *ASIALEX2011 Proceedings. Lexicography: Theoretical and Practical Perspectives*. Kyoto: Asian Association for Lexicography, pp. 92–101.

Dziemianko, A. (2012a) "On the Use(Fulness) of Paper and Electronic Dictionaries", in S. Granger and M. Paquot (eds.), pp. 319–341.

Dziemianko, A. (2012b) "Why One and Two Do Not Make Three: Dictionary Form Revisited", *Lexikos* 22: 195–216.

Dziemianko, A. (2014) "On the Presentation and Placement of Collocations in Monolingual English Learners' Dictionaries: Insights Into Encoding and Retention", *International Journal of Lexicography* 27(3): 259–279.

Dziemianko, A. (2016) "An Insight into the Visual Presentation of Signposts in English Learners' Dictionaries Online", *International Journal of Lexicography* 29: 490–524.

Flowerdew, J. (2009) "Corpora in Language Teaching", in M. H. Long and C. J. Doughty (eds.), *The Handbook of Language Teaching*. Oxford: Wiley-Blackwell, pp. 327–350.

Fontenelle, T. (1997) *Turning a Bilingual Dictionary into a Lexical-Semantic Database*. Tübingen: Niemeyer.

Fuertes-Olivera, P. A. (2009) "The Function Theory of Lexicography and Electronic Dictionaries: Wiktionary as a Prototype of Collective Free Multiple-Language Internet Dictionary", in H. Bergenholtz, S. Nielsen and S. Tarp (eds.), *Lexicography at a Crossroads: Dictionaries and Encyclopedias Today, Lexicographical Tools Tomorrow*. Bern: Peter Lang, pp. 99–134.

Fuertes-Olivera, P. A. (2013) "e-Lexicography: The Continuing Challenge of Applying New Technology to Dictionary Making", in H. Jackson (ed.), *The Bloomsbury Companion to Lexicography*. London: Bloomsbury Publishing, pp. 323–340.

Fuertes-Olivera, P. A. and H. Bergenholtz (eds.) (2011) *e-Lexicography: The Internet, Digital Initiatives and Lexicography*. London and New York: Continuum.

Giles, J. (2005) "Internet Encyclopaedias Go Head to Head", *Nature* 438: 900–901.

Gorin, D. (2015) "Unlocking the Power of the Oxford Learners' Dictionaries", eLex2013 conference videos. See at: https://youtu.be/KlvcNKpvmUQ

Gouws, Rufus H., U. Heid, W. Schweickard, and H. E. Wiegand (eds.) (2013) *Dictionaries: An International Encyclopedia of Lexicography. Supplementary Volume: Recent Developments with Focus on Electronic and Computational Lexicography*. Berlin, Boston, MA: De Gruyter Mouton.

Granger, S. and M. Paquot (eds.) (2012) *Electronic Lexicography*. Oxford: Oxford University Press.

Herbst, T. (1996) "On the Way to the Perfect Learners' Dictionary: A First Comparison of OALD5, LDOCE3, COBUILD2 and CIDE", *International Journal of Lexicography* 8(4): 321–357.

Kilgarriff, A. (2009) "Corpora in the Classroom without Scaring the Students", in *Lexical Computing Ltd. Proceedings From the 18th International Symposium on English Teaching*. Taipei. www.kilgarriff.co.uk/Publications/2009-K-ETA-Taiwan-scaring.Doc.

Klosa, A. (2009) "Modern German Dictionaries and Their Impact on Linguistic Research", in: S. Bruti, R. Cella and M. Foschi Albert (eds.), *Perspectives on Lexicography in Italy and Europe*. Newcastle: Cambridge Scholars Publishing, pp. 175–199.

Klotz, M. and T. Herbst (2016) *English Dictionaries*. Berlin: Erich Schmidt Verlag.

Kobayashi, C. (2007) "Comparing Electronic and Printed Dictionaries: Their Effects on Lexical Processing Strategy Use, Word Retention and Reading Comprehension", in K. Bradford-Watts (ed.), *JALT2006 Conference Proceedings*. Tokyo: JALT: pp. 657–671.

Kompara, M. (2012) "The First Slovene Automatically Compiled Dictionary of Abbreviations", in R. Vatvedt Fjeld and J. M. Torjusen (eds.), *Proceedings of the 15th EURALEX International*

Congress. 7–11 August 2012. Oslo: Department of Linguistics and Scandinavian Studies, University of Oslo, pp. 304–309.

Koplenig, A. and C. Müller-Spitzer (2014) "Questions of Design", in C. Müller-Spitzer (ed.), pp. 189–206.

Koyama, T., and O. Takeuchi (2003) "Printed Dictionaries vs. Electronic Dictionaries: A Pilot Study on How Japanese EFL Learners Differ in Using Dictionaries", *Language Education and Technology* 40: 61–79.

Koyama, T. and O. Takeuchi (2004) "Comparing Electronic and Printed Dictionaries: How the Difference Affected EFL Learning", *JACET Bulletin* 38: 33–46.

Koyama, T. and O. Takeuchi (2007) "Does Look-Up Frequency Help Reading Comprehension of EFL Learners? Two Empirical Studies of Electronic Dictionaries", *CALICO Journal* 25(1): 110–125.

Levy, M. and C. H. Steel (2015) "Language Learner Perspectives on the Functionality and Use of Electronic Language Dictionaries", *ReCALL* 27(2): 177–196.

Lew, R. (2004). *Which Dictionary for Whom? Receptive Use of Bilingual, Monolingual and Semi-bilingual Dictionaries by Polish Learners of English*. Poznań: Motivex.

Lew, R. (2011) "Online Dictionaries of English", in P. A. Fuertes-Olivera and H. Bergenholtz (eds.), pp. 230–250.

Lew, R. (2012) "How Can We Make Electronic Dictionaries More Effective?", in S. Granger and M. Paquot (eds.), pp. 343–362.

Lew, R. (2014) "User-Generated Content (UGC) in Online English Dictionaries", *OPAL – Online publizierte Arbeiten zur Linguistik* 2014(4): 8–16.

Lew, R., and J. Doroszewska (2009) "Electronic Dictionary Entries with Animated Pictures: Lookup Preferences and Word Retention", *International Journal of Lexicography* 22(3): 239–257.

Lew, R. and R. Mitton (2013) "Online English Learners' Dictionaries and Misspellings: One Year On", *International Journal of Lexicography* 26(2): 219–233.

Li, L. (1998) "Cyberdictionaries", *English Today* 14: 21–24.

Meyer, C. M. and I. Gurevych (2012) "Wiktionary: A New Rival for Expert-Built Lexicons? Exploring the Possibilities of Collaborative Lexicography", in S. Granger and M. Paquot (eds.), pp. 259–291.

Moon, R. (1998) *Fixed Expressions and Idioms in English*. Oxford: Clarendon Press.

Müeller-Spitzer, C. (2013) "Textual Structures in Electronic Dictionaries Compared with Printed Dictionaries: A Short General Survey", in R. H. Gouws, U. Heid, W. Schweickard and H. E. Wiegand (eds.), pp. 367–381.

Müller-Spitzer, C. (ed.) (2014) *Using Online Dictionaries*. Berlin/Boston: de Gruyter.

Müller-Spitzer, C. and A. Koplenig (2014). "Online Dictionaries: Expectations and Demands", in C. Müller-Spitzer (ed.), pp. 143–188.

Müller-Spitzer, C., A. Koplenig, and A. Töpel (2011) "What Makes a Good Online Dictionary? Empirical Insights From an Interdisciplinary Research Project", in I. Kosem and K. Kosem, pp. 203–208. http://elex2011.trojina.si/Vsebine/proceedings/eLex2011–27.pdf.

Nesi, H. (1987) "Do Dictionaries Help Students Write?", in T. Bloor and J. Norrish (eds.), *Written Language*. London: CILT, pp. 85–97.

Nesi, H. (1999) "A User's Guide to Electronic Dictionaries for Language Learners", *International Journal of Lexicography* 12(1): 56–66.

Nesi, H. (2000) "On Screen or in Print? Students' Use of a Learner's Dictionary on CD-ROM and in Book Form", in P. Howarth and R. Herington (eds.), *EAP Learning Technologies*. Leeds: University Press, pp. 106–114.

Nesi, H. (2009) "Dictionaries in Electronic Form", in A. P. Cowie (ed.), *The Oxford History of English Lexicography*. Oxford: Oxford University Press, pp. 458–478.

Nesi, H. (2010) "The Virtual Vocabulary Notebook: The Electronic Dictionary as Vocabulary Learning Tool", in G. Blue (ed.), *Developing Academic Literacy*. Oxford: Peter Lang, pp. 213–226.

Nesi, H. (2012) "Alternative e-Dictionaries: Uncovering Dark Practices", in S. Granger and M. Paquot (eds.), pp. 363–378.

Nesi, H. (2015) "The Demands of Users and the Publishing World: Printed or Online, Free or Paid for?", in P. Durkin (ed.), *The Oxford Handbook of Lexicography*. Oxford: Oxford University Press, 579–589.

Nesi, H. and R. Haill (2002) "A Study of Dictionary Use by International Students at a British University", *International Journal of Lexicography* 15(4): 277–305.

Nielsen, S. (2008) "The Effect of Lexicographical Information Costs on Dictionary Making and Use", *Lexikos* 18: 170–189.

Nielsen, S. (2013) "The Future of Dictionaries, Dictionaries of the Future", in H. Jackson (ed.), *The Bloomsbury Companion to Lexicography*. London: Bloomsbury Academic, pp. 355–372.

Nuccorini, S. (1994) "On Dictionary Misuse", in M. Willy and W. Meijs (eds.), *EURALEX'94: Papers submitted to the 6th EURALEX International Congress on Lexicography in Amsterdam*. Amsterdam: Vrije Universiteit, pp. 586–597.

Osaki, S. and N. Nakayama (2004) "Denshijisyo vs. Insatujisyo: Yuyosei to jikkousei no chigainituiteno kosatu [Electronic Dictionary vs. Paper Dictionary: A Comparison of the Two Dictionary studies]", *Bulletin of Tokyo Denki University, Arts and Sciences* 2: 77–83.

Osaki, S., N. Ochiai, T. Iso and K. Aizawa (2003) "Electronic Dictionary vs. Printed Dictionary: Accessing the Appropriate Meaning, Reading Comprehension and Retention", in M. Murata, S. Yamada and Y. Tono (eds.), *Proceedings of ASIALEX '03 Tokyo*. Tokyo: Asialex, pp. 205–212.

Oxford Vocabulary Trainer https://elt.oup.com/catalogue/items/global/dictionaries/9780194705455?cc=global&selLanguage=en

Prinsloo, D. J. (2005) "Electronic Dictionaries Viewed from South Africa", *Hermes* 34: 11–35.

Rundell, M. (2011) "Many a Mickle Makes a Muckle." Round table talk at *Electronic Lexicography in the 21st Century: New Applications for New Users* (eLex2011). Published: 2 December 2011. Recorded: November 2011. Available online at: http://videolectures.net/ elex2011_rundell_table/

Rundell, M. (2012a) "It Works in Practice But Will It Work in Theory? The Uneasy Relationship Between Lexicography and Matters Theoretical", in R. Vatvedt Fjeld and J. M. Torjusen (eds.), *Proceedings of the 15th EURALEX International Congress. 7–11 August 2012*. Oslo: Department of Linguistics and Scandinavian Studies, University of Oslo, pp. 47–92.

Rundell, M. (2012b) "The Road to Automated Lexicography: An Editor's Viewpoint", in S. Granger and M. Paquot (eds.), pp. 15–30.

Scholfield, P. (1999) "Dictionary Use in Reception", *International Journal of Lexicography* 12(1): 13–34.

Sinclair, J. (1991) *Corpus, Concordance, Collocation*. Oxford: Oxford University Press.

Sobkowiak, W. (1999) *Pronunciation in EFL Machine-Readable Dictionaries*. Poznań: Motivex.

Sobkowiak, W. (2003) "Pronunciation in *Macmillan English Dictionary for Advanced Learners* on CD-ROM", *International Journal of Lexicography* 16(4): 423–441.

Surowiecki, J. (2005) *The Wisdom of Crowds*. New York: Anchor Books.

Tarp, S. (2012a) "Online Dictionaries: Today and Tomorrow", *Lexicographica* 28(1): 253–267.

Tarp, S. (2012b) "Theoretical Challenges in the Transition From Lexicographical P-Works to E-Tools", in S. Granger and M. Paquot (eds.), pp. 107–118.

Tono, Y. (1984) *On the Dictionary User's Reference Skills*. B.Ed. Dissertation, Tokyo: Gakugei Univeristy.

Tono, Y. (2009) "Pocket Electronic Dictionaries in Japan: User Perspectives", in H. Bergenholtz, S. Nielsen and S. Tarp (eds.), *Lexicography at a Crossroads: Dictionaries and Encyclopedias Today, Lexicographical Tools Tomorrow*. Bern: Peter Lang, pp. 33–67.

Vale, M. (2015) "A Study of the Users of an Online Sign Language Dictionary", in I. Kosem, M. Jakubiček, J. Kallas and S. Krek (eds.), *Electronic Lexicography in the 21st Century: Linking Lexical Data in the Digital Age: Proceedings of the eLex 2015 Conference, 11–13 August 2015,*

Herstmonceux Castle, United Kingdom. Ljubljana/Brighton: Trojina, Institute for Applied Slovene Studies/Lexical Computing Ltd., pp. 281–303.

Verlinde, S. and G. Peeters (2012) "Data Access Revisited: The Interactive Language Toolbox", in S. Granger and M. Paquot (eds.), pp. 147–162.

Verlinde, S., P. Leroyer and J. Binon (2010) "Search and You Will Find: From Standalone Lexicographic Tools to User Driven Task and Problem-Oriented Multifunctional Leximats", *International Journal of Lexicography* 23(1): 1–17.

Xu, X. (2010) "Study on the Effect of Dictionary Use on Second Language Incidental Vocabulary Acquisition: An Empirical Study of College English Vocabulary Learning Strategy", *Journal of Language Teaching and Research* 1(4): 519–523.

Zaenen, A. (2002) "Musings about the Impossible Electronic Dictionary", in M.-H. Corréard (ed.) *Lexicography and Natural Language Processing: A Festschrift in Honour of B.T.S. Atkins*. Stuttgart: Euralex, pp. 230–44.

42

Using the Web for lexicographic purposes

Vincent Ooi

42.1 Introduction

When Tim Berners-Lee proposed the World Wide Web in 1989, he envisaged a personal information system which people of "whatever size could easily express themselves, quickly acquire and convey knowledge, overcome misunderstandings, and reduce duplication of effort", that is, "a web of knowledge linked through hypertext that would contain a snapshot of their shared understanding" (Berners-Lee 1999: 162). Transposing the title of the Berners-Lee volume on the original design and rationale of the Web (as it is now known) to lexicography, this chapter could perhaps be alternatively known as 'Weaving lexicography in the Web' or a tad too boldly, 'The ultimate destiny of lexicography in the age of the World Wide Web'. Much more modestly, though, this chapter aims to explore the changing nature of the 'dictionary' to 'lexicographic tools' on the Web in terms of "user", "data" and "access" (Verlinde et al 2009). Given that the Web is an unprecedented and vast source of electronic linguistic data, it would be necessary to ask whether the Web can be treated as a 'corpus' for lexicographic purposes. In this chapter, I draw on English primarily (as it is the language that I know best) but common principles exist for their appropriate treatment in various languages.

In order to understand the remit of 'lexicographic purposes', we should first examine our 'shared understanding' of lexicography, one which first had its theoretical underpinnings in lexicology (in turn a sub-discipline of linguistics) but has now become a discipline on its own that draws not only on linguistics but also information science. In so doing, we shall also see that the line between 'word knowledge' (lexical/linguistic information) and 'world knowledge' (encyclopaedic information) has become increasingly blurred in the practice of lexicography.

Our 'shared understanding' of the lexicon vis-à-vis the dictionary can arguably be best explained by the theory of lexical priming (Hoey 2005, 2009, 2014). Adapting Hoey, each of us has a mental lexicon that engages with a published dictionary according to the sum total of our prior/previous experience with language and our socio-cultural environment. For the 40 percent of the world population that has Internet access, the layperson's first recourse nowadays is not to consult a print dictionary but to use a major search engine such as Google, Yahoo!, Bing or Baidu to search for lexical meaning, triangulate the various sources and arrive at the intended meaning. For the professional and commercial lexicographer, structuring dictionary entries for productive and/or receptive competence among general users and especially learners means that potentially conflicting lexical priming should be reconciled by using as much socio-cultural knowledge and corpus information as possible. Indeed, an examination of some lexical entries in existing English learner dictionaries shows that the information – when taken collectively – may be incomplete and confusing to the reader (Ooi 2016). Such confusion may exist because the evidence base or corpus which the lexical entry is drawn on is representative for that particular variety, or sub-variety, only. It becomes incumbent upon corpus linguists and lexicographers to draw on better and more representative corpora that will "advance a collective understanding of lexical priming" (Ooi 2014: 209). Also, the Web user need not totally rely on such 'ready-made' corpora but can actively collect their own data from the Web for investigating "whether the dynamics of the Web can engender different language patterning" (Ooi 2001: 177). In order to indicate further ideas for learning and research, the section will also briefly sketch a couple of specialized lexis projects undertaken by students.

Technological affordances continue to change, and a lexical resource on the Web is not only confined to the browser but gets mirrored as a smartphone App or integrated into word-processing software (e.g. Microsoft Word's Research and Thesaurus features are linked to the web browser). Such competitive lexicography goes together with cooperative lexicography, the latter being an invitation to the general public to contribute to lexicography. This means that anyone and everyone can potentially be a lexicographer either actively (through writing a lexical entry) or passively (through the use of their writing, e.g. Twitter data, in the example sentences). Beyond competitive and cooperative lexicography, though, access afforded by the lexicographic tool is only as good as the richness of the information coded in the first place. There is a current 'flux' in lexicography, as dictionaries gradually migrate from print to digital media on the Web; for the future, the organisation of the lexicon will also benefit from research into alternative and more computational methods afforded by the Web.

42.2 Historical perspectives: lexicography, lexicology and the remit of 'lexicographic purposes'

> We think of a dictionary as the repository of meaning, but it defines words only in terms of other words.
>
> (Berners-Lee 1999: 12)

Berners-Lee's notion of the dictionary as comprising only "word knowledge" has been the received wisdom for a long time: "word knowledge must be kept distinct from world knowledge" (Kegl 1987). *A fortiori*, some linguists such as Mel'čuk (1996, 2003) see the lexicon as the central repository of linguistic knowledge (with its attendant phonetic, phonological, morphological, syntactic, semantic, pragmatic and discoursal levels). Whereas lexicography is concerned with "the theory of dictionary compiling and use", lexicology is concerned with "the unified theoretical study of D(ictionaries) and of LUs (Lexical Units), considered on both semantic and grammatical levels" (Mel'čuk 2003: 454). An analogy of the relationship between lexicology and lexicography may be as follows: "lexicography is to dictionary-making what engineering is to industrial production; lexicology is to lexicography what physics is to engineering" (Mel'čuk 2003: 454).

However, such analogies do not appeal to everyone. For Hartmann and James (1999: 86), "the relationship between lexicology and lexicography cannot be reduced to theory versus practice: lexicography is not merely 'applied lexicology', but an autonomous field with its own premises (dictionary research), utilising the findings of other disciplines to its ends". Similarly, Bergenholtz and Gouws (2012) favour the Wikipedia entry on lexicography, with its division between 'practical lexicography' and 'theoretical lexicography'. Their caveat is that there should also be an emphasis on "dictionaries as practical tools". They further see lexicography as "a series of special types" that include the following: "linguistic lexicography", "subject field lexicography", "corpus lexicography" and "encyclopaedic lexicography". Similar to Bergenholtz and Gouws, Leroyer (2011: 125) says that lexicography is

> a modern, interdisciplinary and independent discipline whose subject field is not limited to lexicographic user-needs adapted information tools, but also encompasses all kinds of information tools and reference works that can be optimized with the very same user-needs adapted information and data access – from handbooks and manuals to dynamic information websites and web portal.

Leroyer's definition of lexicography as a discipline based on information science holds quite true in using the Web for lexicographic purposes. An example of Bergenholtz and Gouws's emphasis on dictionaries as *practical tools* can be illustrated by means of a typical search on Google, which not only has all the search examples but also its own dictionary. For example, in order to understand the word *discombobulate* in the following sentence (example 1):

(1)
I don't think so, I replied, by this time thoroughly discombobulated, which I now realise was his intention (*The Straits Times*, August 25, 2016, by Bilahari Kausikan, in a eulogy on the death of his mentor, Mr S R Nathan)

Google's dictionary indicates that it is a North American (i.e. U.S. and/or Canadian English) 'humorous' verb that means "to disconcert or confuse (someone)". In turn, one can get (pardon the pun) discombobulated by this marking of 'humorous', as the author is likely not to be inappropriately humorous on such a sombre occasion. Indeed, lexical knowledge for *discombobulate* is stored and hopefully *triangulated* on the Web by means of corroborating the various search references (Figure 42.1):

Discombobulated | Define Discombobulated at Dictionary.com[1]
to confuse or disconcert; upset; frustrate: The speaker was completely discombobulated by the hecklers. Origin of discombobulate Expand. 1825–1835. 1825–35, Americanism; fanciful alteration of discompose or discomfort.
Discombobulate | Definition of Discombobulate by Merriam-Webster[2]
verb dis·com·bob·u·late \ˌdis-kəm-ˈbä-b(y)ə-ˌlāt\. Definition of discombobulate. discombobulated. discombobulating. transitive verb. : upset, confuse. . .
discombobulate – Dictionary Definition : Vocabulary.com[3]
Discombobulate is a fun, fancy word for "confuse." If something has put you in a state where you don't know up from down and you can't spell your own name, . . .
discombobulate – definition of discombobulate in English from the Oxforddictionaries.com[4]
Disconcert or confuse (someone):. Meaning, pronunciation and example sentences, English to English reference content.

Figure 42.1 Partial Google search results for *discombobulate*

A check with *Oxforddictionaries.com* (the leading English dictionary) indicates the same meaning, 'humorous' label and example used in the *Google Dictionary* entry (leading to the suspicion that the former contributed to the latter). However, *Dictionary.com* just lists it as "to confuse or disconcert; upset; frustrate" without adding the 'humorous' label; this is similarly the case with the leading U.S. dictionary *Merriam-Webster.com* which just lists it as a transitive verb meaning 'upset' or 'confuse'. More confusingly, *Macmillandictionary.com* lists it as 'humorous' for both their British and American English versions.

In the next section, we explore the question of what it often means for the dictionary user to navigate the Web judiciously.

42.3 Core issues and topics

42.3.1 Lexical priming for Web dictionary users

> The Web becomes a much more powerful means for collaboration between people. I have always imagined the information space as something to which everyone has immediate and intuitive access, and not just to browse, but to create.
>
> (Berners-Lee 1999: 157)

The sketch of *discombobulate* in the preceding section makes different sense to users in various contexts, because people have varying "lexical frequencies" (see Section 42.3.2). In this regard, Hoey (2005: 8) postulates that the mental lexicon is probabilistic:

> As a word is acquired through encounters with it in speech and writing, it becomes cumulatively loaded with the contexts and co-texts in which it is encountered, and our knowledge of it includes the fact that it co-occurs with certain other words in certain kinds of context.

This process of subconsciously noticing – and storing – these observations of language is *lexical priming*. While lexical priming is indubitably part of psycholinguistic research, the wider agenda is to integrate such findings with those of corpus linguistics (Hoey 2014: 12). For Hoey, the types of information that get noticed include collocational, grammatical and semantic patterns, formal vs. informal style, speech vs. writing, sociocultural information about the speaker, whether the speaker who uses the word is being humorous or serious, the genres that the word or phrase is typically used in and even "whether it is associated with the beginnings or ends of sentences or with paragraph boundaries". (Hoey 2009: para. 10).

Thus, my first encounter of the term *discombobulate* in Singapore's leading broadsheet, *The Straits Times*, is through its use in a sombre context (a eulogy) by another person (Bilahari Kausikan) whose prior experience and storage of the term in his mental lexicon is definitely richer than mine. I begin to build up my knowledge of the word by noticing not only its definition in Google Dictionary but also its label as 'humorous'. Through the various search results, knowledge of the term is built up by consulting various dictionary definitions; conflicting information about its label remains that still needs to be resolved. Hoey's theory of lexical priming is thus very useful, as it accords with the way the Web works: the 'shared understanding' comes from triangulating the various types of (sometimes conflicting) information given. According to Hoey (2005), we are still able to communicate with one another and have a notion of standard English because conflicting primings are reconciled through such common factors as education, mass media, literary and religious traditions, grammars and dictionaries. Applying this observation to the Berners-Lee's saying in this section, recognising the fact that every person has the ability to create something on the Web extends not only to making web pages but also recognising that a person's distinctive lexical priming can be transposed anywhere on the Web: voicing comments on Facebook and other social media platforms, keeping personal blogs, contributing to the efficacy of a dictionary entry etc.

Lexical priming exists – and can conflict – for different varieties of a language. Thus, the mental lexicon of a Malaysian Malay speaker and that of an Indonesian Malay speaker can vary quite a bit in their storage of *banci*, a word whose two main meanings can be either 'population census' or 'transvestite/effeminate person'. In an online Indonesian Malay dictionary[5] the 'transvestite' meaning is listed first, and the 'census' meaning is given a 'Mal n' marker, that is, it is listed as a 'Malay noun' (non-Indonesian). On the other hand, the official Malay language dictionary[6] lists the 'census' version first before the 'transvestite version' (which it also intriguingly lists as a reference to the transgendered dressing of a male witch doctor (*bomoh*) in Sulawesi (an Indonesian province). The generalisation is that Indonesians are primed to think of *banci* as referring to a 'transvestite/effeminate person', whereas Malays in Malaysia are primed to go for the 'census' meaning first. Further corroboration can be found at the aggregator website *Lexilogos*.[7] This is listed as "a comprehensive set of resources for the study of the language of the world", for example, for standard Malay vis-à-vis standard Indonesian. On the other hand, electronic lexical tools and resources could do better in indicating preferred primings in various varieties of the same language for linguistic identity and sociocultural salience. A case in point is the Chinese term for *taxi*, which has at least four forms (which, for convenience, will be labelled A to D) (example 2):

(2)
A. 出租车 (Chūzū chē);
B. 的 士 (Dí / De shì)
C. 计程车 (Jìchéngchē)
D. 駕駛室 (Jiàshǐ shì).

If Google translate is customised for Hong Kong,[8] the translation for *taxi* is still invariably listed as Form A, without distinguishing the mainland Chinese residents living in Hong Kong from their Cantonese counterparts – who seem to prefer Form B (see Figure 42.2[9]). Also, while the *lexilogos* aggregator website generally prefers Form A,[10] this version is also intriguingly labelled on its associated website[11] as a "(Taiwan) rental car" and, besides Form A, has the variant 出租汽车 (chūzūqìchē) as the preferred form in mainland China (labelled 'PRC') (Figure 42.2):

出租车 chūzūchē taxi/(Taiwan) rental car
打的 dǎdī (coll.) to take a taxi/to go by taxi
打车 dǎchē to take a taxi (in town)/to hitch a lift
黑车 hēichē unlicensed or unofficial taxi/unlicensed motor vehicle
面的 miàndī abbr. of 麵包車的士｜面包车的士/minivan taxi
出租汽车 chūzūqìchē taxi/cab (PRC)/hire car (Tw)/CL: 輛｜辆
计程车 jìchéngchē taxi/cab (Tw)

Figure 42.2 Translation of *taxi* to its Chinese forms[12]

Aggregator websites require the user to run through each of their chosen websites: such consultation takes more time and effort. On the other hand, a website such as *wordreference.com* indicates the information quickly by listing Form A as the preferred choice in mainland China, Form B for Hong Kong, Form C for Taiwan and the variant '德士' for Singapore. However, wordreference.com also does not give a comprehensive picture of the usage of *taxi* in the Chinese language. As it is important to show the presence of *diglossia* (Ooi 2015, 2016) in a dictionary, consulting a native mainland Chinese informant yields the information that Form A (i.e. 出租车) tends to be used in formal (H-igh) situations, whereas Form B (i.e. 的 士) is preferred in informal (L-ow) situations (particularly by the younger generation) in mainland China.

What this exercise indicates, then, is that the value proposition of electronic dictionaries (whether online or stand-alone) increases by accounting for diglossia and other lexical priming information in varieties of the same language.

42.3.2 Using the Web as/for corpus

> "The Web, which I designed to be a medium for all sorts of information, from the very local to the very global, grew decidedly in the direction of the very global"
>
> (Berners-Lee 1999: 57).

As the preceding section has demonstrated, taking the lexical priming perspective leads to a better understanding among dictionary users. Such lexical priming information can be ordered in terms of frequency, collocational and sociocultural information that can be obtained from examining empirical linguistic evidence – one that a large and well-informed corpus can provide the lexicographer.

As "an unprecedented and virtually inexhaustible source of authentic natural language data . . . for researchers in [various fields]" (The Web as Corpus Community, 2016), it would seem attractive to use the Web as it is without doing any additional curation, that is, a Google, Baidu, Bing or Yahoo! search will provide us with adequate lexicographic evidence. However, John Sinclair – one of the pioneers of corpus linguistics – rightly warns us that

> The World Wide Web is not a corpus, because its dimensions are unknown and constantly changing, and because it has not been designed from a linguistic perspective. At present it is quite mysterious, because the search engines, through which the retrieval programs operate, are all different, none of them are comprehensive, and it is not at all clear what population is being sampled. Nevertheless, the WWW is a remarkable new resource for any worker in language.
>
> (Sinclair 2005a)

For Sinclair, it would be necessary to achieve a certain type of *curation*, that is, a corpus is filtered by means of "sampling", "representativeness", "balance", "external criteria" and "size" (Sinclair 2005a). Although "the Web is truly bountiful", a corpus

> expects documents (including transcripts) to be discrete, text to be linear and separable from non-text, and it expects documents to fall into recognisable sizings, similar to hard-copy documents. A *normal corpus* (emphasis mine) has no provision for hypertext, far less flashing text and animations.
>
> (Sinclair 2005b)

Thus, using Sinclair's strictures, taking data from the Web must be done with caution in terms of knowing "precisely what is actually copied or downloaded from a web page".

Indeed, the "cheerful anarchy of the Web thus places a burden of care on a user, and *slows down the process of corpus building* (emphasis mine)" (Sinclair 2005b: para 12). Reifying Sinclair's caution regarding what might be really considered a "linguistic corpus", Meyer et al (2003: 241) provide estimates of the size and composition of the Web because "we do not know, for instance, precisely how large it is or what kinds of texts are on it". They make the point that raw frequency information provided by search engines "must be interpreted with caution", but this information is also "suggestive" and "can give a sense of which linguistic usages are common and which are not".

In regard to Sinclair's point on the "cheerful anarchy of the Web", Berners-Lee's quotation listed in this section indicates that there is indeed "all sorts of information" on the Web – which I once characterised as "a monumental electronic resource" (Ooi 2001: 176). Nowadays, words such as *big data* and *data mining* come to mind: this monumental electronic resource has to be curated according to the (linguistic) purpose of the day. Thus, although "a [synchronic] corpus, like a dictionary, is a mere snapshot of the language at a certain point in time, and therefore may need to be continually updated for changing and new patterns of usage" (Ooi 1998: 55), the Web is unlike a conventional corpus and may be characterised as the unprecedented "most dynamic megacorpus of all time" (Ooi 2002: 103). Herein lies the key point: perhaps the definition for a conventional, "normal corpus" should not be applied to the Web. In this regard, Kilgarriff and Grefenstette (2003: 334) suggest that

> the definition of corpus should be broad. We define a corpus simply as a "collection of texts". If that seems too broad, the one qualification we allow relates to the domain and contexts in which the word is used, rather than its denotation: *A corpus is a collection of texts when considered as an object of language or literary study*. The answer to the question "Is the web a corpus?" is yes.

For Kilgarriff and Grefenstette, there is no need to mix the question "What is a corpus?" with "What is a good corpus (for certain kinds of linguistic study)?" Such mixing would "muddy" the question "Is corpus x good for task y?" with the distracting semantic question "Is x a corpus at all?" Examining Kilgarriff and Grefenstette's distinction, Gatto (2011: 38) says that their shift of "the notion of 'corpushood' to the intention of the researcher rather than seeing it as intrinsic to the text collection itself' has contributed to "the emergence of a scientific community determined to exploit the inestimable potential of the web" in light of "the specific features of the Web as a spontaneous, self-generating collection of texts".

In relation to Sinclair's point that the Web actually "slows down the process of corpus building", the re-definition of a corpus as "a collection of texts when considered as an object of language or literary study" has meant that (semi-) automatic software tools nowadays can build and curate texts on the Web for lexicographic purposes very fast. A salient example includes the building of the *TenTen corpora* by the Sketch Engine team. These range of corpora are in the order of billions of words: "the 'tenten-corpus' designates the target sizes of the corpora which is 1010 (10 billion) words":

> Corpora are crawled from the Internet by *Spiderling* (a web spider for linguistics). After downloading texts, they are first processed by *jusText* (a heuristic based boilerplate removal tool) for removing irrelevant content such as navigation links, advertisements, headers, and footers. Afterwards, *onion* (a tool for removing duplicate parts) performs deduplication on paragraph level – the ones consisting of more than 50% word 7-tuples

> encountered in previously processed data are removed. Then the corpus is tokenized into words, lemmatised (matching stemmed form of the word to the words), and part-of-speech tagged by suitable taggers.[13]

If we examine the English version of this corpus, that is, *enTenTen* (2013 version, 19 billion words), a *word sketch* of the nouns modified by *economy* (i.e. compound nouns) returns the following top 10 forms (ordered by frequency and 'salience'): *airfare* (316 times per million words for *economy airfare*), *rating* (1572 times), *seat* (1444 times), *cabin* (489 times), *passenger* (429 times), *fare* (471 times), *class* (3844 times), *hostage* (255 times), *car* (2342 times) and *plus* (415 times, as in *Economy Plus*). A word sketch is "a one-page, corpus-based summary of a word's grammatical and collocational behaviour" (Kilgarriff 2013: 84). Notwithstanding this, the collocations in the word sketch here suggest that flight aviation texts feature prominently in the *enTenTen corpus*. Compare this sketch with the one for *Skell* (Sketch Engine for Language Learning), which contains "more than one billion words from news, scientific papers, Wikipedia articles, fiction books, web pages, [and] blogs".[14] The top 10 nouns modified for *economy* in *Skell* include the following: *rating, fare, politics, seat, car, collapse, unemployment, overall, cabin* and *initiative*. Given that the two sketches are remarkably different, it would be useful to know both the proportions of genres/registers and the type(s) of English (British English, U.S. English, Australian English, etc.) that are sampled for the corpus. Also, what is presented to the Skell learner of English may vary with different educated varieties of English (other than British and U.S. English). For instance, speakers and learners of English in certain Southeast Asian contexts are lexically primed to expect *rice* to be modified by *economy*.[15] Further evidence of *economy rice* can be found in the *GloWbe corpus* (Ooi 2016: 10–11).

Other very recent Web-based corpora of English include the *Corpus of Contemporary American English* (*COCA Corpus*), *Corpus of Global Web-based English* (*GloWbe Corpus* – see Davies and Fuchs 2015), the *News on the Web Corpus* (*NOW Corpus*) and the *Corpus of Online Registers of English* (*CORE Corpus*). The well-motivated corpora mentioned here are notably the efforts of Mark Davies and his team at Brigham Young University. Returning to the earlier example of *discombobulate* (in Section 42.2), an examination of the *COCA corpus* indicates that term is not only used humorously but also seriously (Figure 42.3):

1	2015	MAG	SatEvenPost	A	B	C	ADD on crack "). In extreme cases, his thoughts can intensify and **discombobulate** to the point of physical tics like standing on his toes or pulling on his
2	2012	SPOK	PBS_NewsHour	A	B	C	they'd like to cause him some grief. I think they'd like to **discombobulate** the Michigan Republican Party. And there may be some angry independent and Democratic vo
3	2010	NEWS	NYTimes	A	B	C	too much of such imagery, which actually seems to demonstrate Houdini's ability to **discombobulate** rational thought, even after a century. # Far more intriguing are H
4	2007	ACAD	Poetry	A	B	C	having abdicated their role as loud-mouth rousers of weeping and gnashing. They won't **discombobulate** the young, especially young soldiers, whom Plato warned off (
5	2001	SPOK	NBC_Dateline	A	B	C	or 800... MURPHY: (Voiceover) But look at how the mental gymnastics **discombobulate** our drivers. (People-driving) Unidentified Man 5: 734. MURPHY: (Voiceover) And
6	2001	NEWS	NYTimes	A	B	C	entirely? # Part of the fun of new music is that it often does **discombobulate** us. New plays are allowed to be elusive and abstract, but new concert
7	2001	NEWS	CSMonitor	A	B	C	two different actresses, not to reveal different sides of her personality, but to **discombobulate** the notion that personalities can be comprehended in the first place. Thi
8	2000	MAG	SportingNews	A	B	C	wait is over. Like L.T, there simply are too many ways Kearse can **discombobulate** an offense. " He has some of the same qualities that Lawrence had-a fast
9	1995	SPOK	ABC_Brinkley	A	B	C	The economy is a $7-trillion economy. Do you think a $60-billion deficit reduction can **discombobulate** that economy? LEON PANETTA: Well, I think- I think the- the issue
10	1992	SPOK	ABC_Brinkley	A	B	C	" Mr. WILL: Forty-three governors have a line- item veto and it doesn't **discombobulate** the balance of power in those states. Neither does it balance the budget.

Figure 42.3 discombobulate, COCA Corpus

Given that the *COCA corpus* is "the only large and balanced corpus of American English" comprising 520 million words (at the time of writing), the 10 occurrences of *discombobulate* indicate that the term is not widespread in the United States; in particular, lines 9 and 10 indicate that there are speakers who use the term neutrally with serious subject matter. Thus, the 'humorous' impression suggested by Google Dictionary does not seem to hold water for all contexts. However, this term does seem to be largely a U.S. term, and nowadays (at least) not a Canadian one (despite the 'North American' label in Google Dictionary). A search shows that it occurs a total of only 33 times in the 1.9-billion-word *GloWbe corpus*, suggesting that the term is not used frequently: U.S. (9 times), Canada (1 time), United Kingdom (6 times), Ireland (2 times), Australia (2 times), New Zealand (1 time), India (1 time), Sri Lanka (1 time), Pakistan (2 times), South Africa (1 time), Nigeria (1 time), Tanzania (2 times) and Jamaica (4 times).

Our discussion regarding the use of Internet data for lexicographic purposes thus far may be usefully summed up in the distinction by De Schryver (2002: 266) between 'Web-as-corpus' and 'Web-for-corpus', that is, the idea of using Internet data without curating it for size, text types, genres etc (Web-as-corpus) and curating Internet data such that such vast bodies of data can be used for linguistic purposes (Web-for-corpus). Beyond this distinction, it is particularly useful to adopt the idea of a "lexicographical corpus" (Fuertes-Olivera 2012: 51) which is "any collection of texts where lexicographers can find inspiration for completing the dictionary structures they need when making a real dictionary". More precisely, to regard the Internet as a lexicographical corpus is to create "the virtual space in which lexicographers can easily access data they might need" (Fuertes-Olivera 2012: 51).

Web data need not be curated by the professional corpus linguist or professional lexicographer only. Given that the Web is a "virtually inexhaustible source of authentic language data", anyone can investigate its "myriad texts and discourses" (Ooi 2001: 175) and "multivariate electronic textualities" (Ooi 2002: 118). For instance, students who take my module on Lexicology and Lexicography are required to investigate the English lexis of interesting genres by collecting empirical data (including those on the Web). Intriguing project titles have included 'The English Lexis of 9gag' and 'The English Lexis of Game Talk'. Although 9gag is an alternative social media platform for primarily sharing humorous photos or videos, it has a fair bit of linguistic text generated by users in the comments section etc. As for 'Game Talk', electronic gaming is an ever popular genre which also has a fair bit of linguistic text (cf. Ooi 2008) and the students collected the data from popular gaming forums such as *playdota* and *piratekingonline*. First, let us consider the term *upvote* (Figure 42.4):

1 You **get an upvote** simply for your fabulous
2 home when 10pm **you deserve mi upvote**
3 you **deserve the Matrix and my upvote** You need 50 individual
4 t what? exactly I **took back my upvote** from that guy and gave
5 ere from oh well. Here **have my upvote** that was on the origin
6 e my upvote, sir Here, **have my upvote** So if you wear this sh
7 time, where are they!? **take my upvote** sir That was a strong
8 my upvote omg! XD **take my omg, upvote**! When you were afk for
9 ng *bows down* take it **take my upvote** VespTrap? Bee Mine ! O
10 pvote ? Cant afford it **Take my upvote** sir . . . now you can afford

Figure 42.4 A partial concordance of *upvote* (n), from the 'English Lexis of 9gag' corpus[16]

If we are interested in finding the kinds of verb that collocate with *upvote* as a noun, the concordance in Figure 40.4 suggests that the salient ones include *get*, *deserve*, *take*, and *have* – with *take* as the top verb. Such information can augment its entry in (i) WordNik.com, whose only noun example has the associated verb *garner*, and (ii) Wiktionary.com, which has no example sentences beyond the definition of "A vote for something that increases a cumulative tally of popularity". Turning to *nerf* as a noun (Figure 42.5), a similar analysis would indicate that the salient verbs that collocate with the term include *deserve*, *merit*, *need* and *stop* – with *need* as the top verb.

1 e the manacost. She **deserves a nerf** yes, not a remake or removal
2 ll. I don't think she **merits a nerf** though. Nerf the ms slightly.
3 that his Str gain **could need a nerf** (minus 0.2–0.3, he aint no tank anyway.
4 Her shield **DOES need a slight nerf**. Thus, nerf one and buff the other
5 und. I think he **needs a small nerf** to his agility, a small buff to his strength
6 fun hero and **doesn't need any "nerfs"** he had an very hard time nerfing him much.
7 ul enough to **deserve that much nerfs** anyway. Just nerf it so she becomes a glass cannon.
11 balanced now, please **stop the nerfs**. Would be nerfed straight away.

Figure 42.5 A partial concordance of *nerf* (n), from the 'English Lexis of Game Talk' corpus[17]

Such information can augment its entry in (i) WordNik.com, which has only two definitions for its verb form (including, "to water down, dumb down or especially weaken, particularly in video games") but none for the noun form. Interestingly enough, some Web examples have the nominal form; and (ii) Wiktionary.com, which also has only the verb definition: "(*slang, video games*) To weaken, deteriorate or debuff (a character, a weapon, a spell, etc. or make it worsen) between multiple installments of a series of games or versions of the same game".

Both these illustrations further indicate that online dictionaries – however vague – can improve their engagement with Web data for better lexical entries.

42.3.3 Competitive/cooperative lexicography and the rise of smartphone apps

> The recent moves to put the Web on everything from televisions to mobile phone screens have made the need for device dependence very clear.
>
> (Berners-Lee 1999: 166)

Lexical knowledge is stored on the Web in various forms, and not just by means of the traditional structure that we know as 'the dictionary'. This is evident in the preceding sections which have used various tools to extract lexicographic information, ranging from search engines to aggregator dictionary websites to concordance lines. For this reason, Verlinde et al (2009: 3) adopt H.E. Wiegand's suggestion to call all such structures *lexicographic tools:* this concept refers to "functional reference works, which should therefore be balanced in order to ensure fast and easy access to the data that users need in specific types of usage situations". Whether in traditional format or on the Web, such reference works can include the following: "general dictionaries, specialised dictionaries, encyclopaedias, terminological databases, lexical databases, glossaries, registers etc." For Verlinde et al (2009: 4), evaluating the performance of such lexicographic tools means a triangulation and balance between the parameters of "data", "access" and "user". Adapting Verlinde et al, the preceding sections may be said to have focused more on "data" and the "user", whereas this section will discuss the "access" component that involves technological affordances on the Web (see Chapter 3 of this *Handbook*).

In this regard, Berners-Lee's saying regarding "mobile phone screens" in this section is arguably "prescient" in foretelling the rise of 'apps' that mirror and extend their equivalents on the Web. According to Google Dictionary, an 'app' is "a self-contained program or piece of software designed to fulfil a particular purpose; an application, especially as downloaded by a user to a mobile device". Indeed, smartphones and tablets now have touchscreen technology such that highlighting a word on screen, and lightly tapping it will bring up the 'Define' and 'Share' features – on my iPhone (whose choice will both delight some and irk others), a touch on *discombobulate* (the example in Section 42.2) for 'Define' by default brings one to the *New Oxford American Dictionary* (a subsidiary of Oxford University Press, that produces *oxforddictionaries.com*) with the same Google Dictionary definition that has been discussed earlier. On the bottom left and right screens, there are 'Manage' and 'Search Web' features. Under 'Manage', there is a series of pre-defined dictionary apps that can be downloaded on the phone for English (*New Oxford American Dictionary* for 'American English', *Oxford Dictionary of English* for 'British English'), Dutch (*Prisma woordenboek Nederlands*), French (*Multidictionnaire de la langue francaise*) and currently thirteen other languages. The 'Search Web' feature will, of course, bring the user to the Google dictionary search partially listed in Figure 42.1. The 'share' feature is also interesting, which means that any series of text and lexical entries can be stored for reference in the 'Note' section, or sent by e-mail or instant messaging (Whatsapp, Wechat etc) and other social media platforms (e.g. Twitter, Facebook, Weibo and Tumblr) to oneself, family members and friends. It has really extended what I sketched in Ooi (1998: 119) regarding "the transfer, exchange, and study of lexicons . . . [in which] lexicons . . . can be created and e-mailed back to the end user". The end goals of this exercise are, of course, to enhance both receptive and productive linguistic competence by the user.

The choice of dictionary apps and languages that are available for selection and download to the user's phone on either the Android or iOS (Apple) platform has huge implications for competitive lexicography: this refers to the commercial and professional lexicographer's efforts and products alone, which are then passed on to the user as consumer. On the other hand, cooperative lexicography refers to the user as creator, suggesting and crafting lexical entries – a kind of 'crowdsourcing', as it were. However, the days of clearly delineating "competitive lexicography" from "cooperative lexicography" may be well over soon. For instance, the *Macmillan Dictionary* invites readers to help the dictionary stay "up to date" by contributing to its *Open Dictionary*; this is a form of crowdsourcing. Turning to *Wordnik*, which lists itself as a non-profit organisation that has "the world's biggest online English dictionary, by number of words", our favourite example *discombobulate* is listed as seen in Figure 42.6.

Wordnik has a novel and interesting structure. Besides aggregating the definition from various dictionaries (in which the 'humorous' element seems to missing), it also seems to automatically draw on various Web sources (whose 'humorous' use does not necessarily match with the aggregate definitions). In addition to 'define', it also has 'relate', 'list', 'discuss', 'see', 'hear' and 'love' sections for the entry. Besides input from professional lexicographers, *Wordnik* generally works by drawing on users' comments, tweets, lists and 'likes'/'dislikes' (similar to the Facebook function) – this is a well-motivated example of cooperative lexicography at work. However, although there is a section on audio, with links to their pronunciation in the *American Heritage Dictionary* and the *Macmillan Dictionary*, the audio links did not work at the time of writing, with the message that "recording pronunciations and sound effects is temporarily unavailable". As for visuals, photos of scenery and events are also associated with the word in the respective web pages. Once again, the

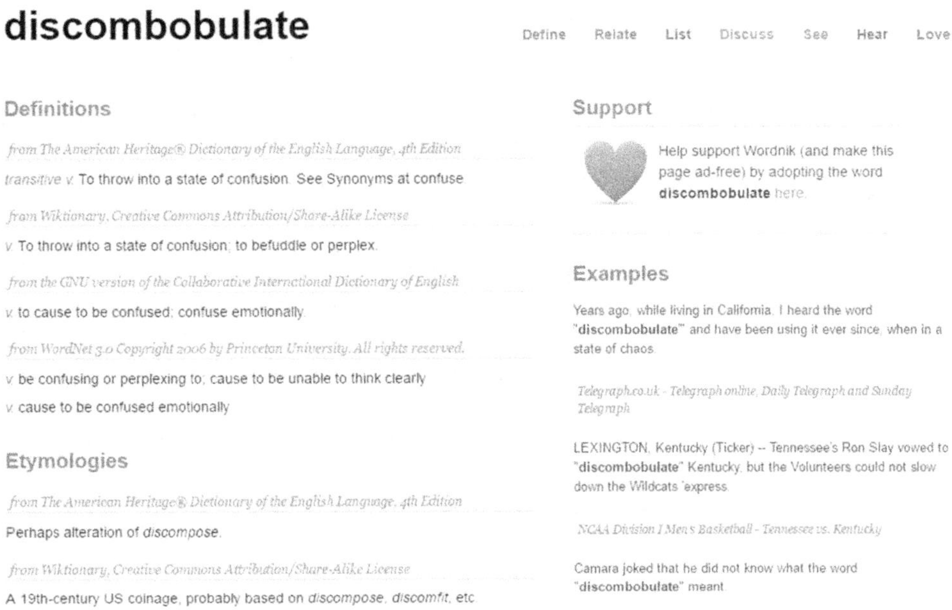
discombobulate

Define Relate List Discuss See Hear Love

Definitions

from The American Heritage® Dictionary of the English Language, 4th Edition

transitive v. To throw into a state of confusion. See Synonyms at confuse

from Wiktionary, Creative Commons Attribution/Share-Alike License

v. To throw into a state of confusion; to befuddle or perplex.

from the GNU version of the Collaborative International Dictionary of English

v. to cause to be confused; confuse emotionally

from WordNet 3.0 Copyright 2006 by Princeton University. All rights reserved.

v. be confusing or perplexing to; cause to be unable to think clearly

v. cause to be confused emotionally

Etymologies

from The American Heritage® Dictionary of the English Language, 4th Edition

Perhaps alteration of *discompose*.

from Wiktionary, Creative Commons Attribution/Share-Alike License

A 19th-century US coinage, probably based on *discompose*, *discomfit*, etc

Support

Help support Wordnik (and make this page ad-free) by adopting the word **discombobulate** here.

Examples

Years ago, while living in California, I heard the word "**discombobulate**" and have been using it ever since, when in a state of chaos.

Telegraph.co.uk - Telegraph online, Daily Telegraph and Sunday Telegraph

LEXINGTON, Kentucky (Ticker) -- Tennessee's Ron Slay vowed to "**discombobulate**" Kentucky, but the Volunteers could not slow down the Wildcats 'express.

NCAA Division I Men's Basketball - Tennessee vs. Kentucky

Camara joked that he did not know what the word "**discombobulate**" meant

Figure 42.6 Wordnik – partial entry for *discombobulate*[18]

incorporation of text, audio and visuals that reference the outside world all at once indicates that the line between word and world knowledge is nowadays quite seamless in the multimodal age that we are in.

Individual lexical priming is also encouraged by means of user contributions in a lexical resource such as *Urban Dictionary* (listed as a "crowdsourced online dictionary of slang words and phrases"). Using the same example (hopefully, not *ad nauseam*), the user can focus on the sense most relevant to the example sentence in Section 42.2. (Figure 42.7):

> Confused, messed up, not in place
> *I'm so discombobulated!*
> *My brain is very discombobulated*
> *These books are very discombobulated*
> #confused #disscombobulate #complex #understand #combobulate
> by Sammi Grantham March 13, 2006

Figure 42.7 A user lexical entry on *discombobulate*[19]

In Figure 42.7, we do not exactly know who 'Sammi Grantham' is, but there is a well-motivated use of the 'hashtag' which is a meme spread originally from the Twitter social media platform. The use of the hashtag goes beyond its similarity to functioning like keywords in scientific abstract articles, and arguably also provides an insight into the feelings of its author through the use of hashtags and (made-up) example sentences that do not really reflect their situational usage (compared with the *WordNik* examples). Other users also get to vote based on their feelings, and this entry has garnered 54 'likes' and 22 'dislikes' at the time of writing.

Adapting the title 'Search and you will find' from Verlinde et al (2009)'s paper, the converse situation 'Search and you will not find' is also all too familiar in dictionary use. In this regard, Ooi (2010) suggests the following to test the coverage of a dictionary (or "lexicographic tool"): i) how up-to-date the dictionary is with recent popular neologisms and computer-mediated words such as *google* (verb), *blog, Twitter, lol* (Laugh-Out-Loud emoticon) and *imma* ('I am going to', found in U.S. rap lyrics); ii) its inherent cultural bias (as in *durian* being a smelly fruit, because a number of people in Southeast Asia at least find it fragrant); iii) its coverage of the two main varieties, that is, British English and U.S. English, as in the pronunciation of *flautist* (British English)/*flutist* (U.S. English); iv) its coverage of other varieties (as in the case of the transitive verb *retrench* in Australian English to mean 'make redundant' or 'lay off'); v) the codification of a five-syllable word that indicates its coverage of *hard* words (as in the case of *pusillanimous*); and vi) its tolerance of misspellings (as in *recognisible*, instead of the standard spelling *recognizable*), for those dictionaries (e.g. *Wordnik*; see Chapter 29 of this *Handbook*) that draw material directly from the Web. Although no one set list may be comprehensive, higher standards of content that include not having "irrelevant and highly repetitive information" and restricted micro and macro-structures would be welcome (cf. Lew 2011: 238–249).

42.4 Looking to the future

In the preceding section, there is the tacit acknowledgement that the 'gatekeeper' role for the lexicographer has changed. If one gatekeeper will not include a word, then another one will somewhat do so on the Web. Besides being more willing to include terms quickly, various online dictionaries seek advertising revenue and vie for greater attention through the incorporation of crowdsourcing dictionary writing, word games, crossword puzzles, encyclopaedic information and tweeting dictionary teasers periodically (e.g. dictionary.com). More importantly, though, the all-but-inevitable move from print to digital format (whether on the Web or its mirror in apps) has meant that both cooperative and competitive lexicography are in a transitional phase. As Rundell (2015: 302–303) puts it, "lexicography is going through a turbulent phase" and, citing Patrick Hanks, "lexicographers . . . currently live in a sort of interregnum". Rundell (2015) examines how "long-outdated defining styles" and conventions suited for the print dictionary (constrained mainly by space) still exist in the online dictionary, but there are conscious efforts to take advantage of the unlimited space afforded by the digital medium. These concerns are earlier echoed by Fuertes-Olivera (2013), who traces the move from print to online dictionaries in terms of "printed online dictionaries", "replicated online dictionaries" and "functional online dictionaries".

Notwithstanding these challenges, Nielsen (2013: 370) suggests that "dictionaries do have a future and dictionaries of the future will, to an increasing extent, be regarded as 'digital assistants'". The dictionaries of the future will be "information tools which provide help to satisfy specific types of lexicographically relevant need of specific types of potential user in specific types of extra-lexicographic situation . . . databases will serve as bases for several dictionaries". Extending this vision, lexical knowledge on the Web will continue to exist at different levels of abstraction. Alternative and formal methods that continue to engage the attention of information scientists and those alike include, among others, the Webdante Lexical Database,[20] FrameNet Lexical Database,[21] and the WordNet Lexical Database[22] (see Chapters 12, 13 and 24 of this *Handbook*).

42.5 Conclusion

We have much to be grateful to Tim Berners-Lee for creating a free Web structure that echoes what Jones (1999: 2) has claimed: that the Internet has become "not only a technology but an engine of social change, one that has modified work habits, education, social relations generally, and maybe most important, our hopes and dreams". In everyday life, lexicography as information science helps us access those 'hopes' and 'dreams' through 'lexicographic tools' (Verlinde et al 2009: 4) which reformulate the notion of the traditional 'dictionary'. For Verlinde et al. (2009: 4), "the *user-adapted access to data* is the *raison d'être* of lexicography", i.e. lexicographic tools have to triangulate three parameters: 'user', 'data' and 'access'. Similarly, Fuertes-Olivera (2012: 49) reminds us that "the very essence of lexicography is its capacity to provide quick and easy access to dictionary data from which information needed by different types of users in different types of social situations can be retrieved." Adapting Verlinde et al.'s use of the term 'user', the theory of lexical priming (Hoey 2005, 2009, 2014) provides a coherent explanation of differing construals in the mental lexicon of various users for the same term in different situations. Our understanding of the term 'data' has meant revisiting the competing notions of 'Web-as-corpus' and 'Web-for-corpus' (De Schryver 2002) which in turn has helped in valorising the notion of the "lexicographical corpus" (Fuertes-Olivera 2012: 51). In addition, the use of web data for lexicographic purposes need not be restricted to the professional lexicographer; the student lexicographer has abundant new web genres and projects to engage in. In our use of the term 'access', we note the distinction between 'competitive lexicography' and 'cooperative lexicography', the rise of smartphone apps and issues in coverage as a result of the shift from the p(rinted) to the e(lectronic) format. The triangulation of such 'user', 'data' and 'access' parameters will continue to mediate our perspective of (online) dictionaries of the future.

Related topics

Dictionaries and culture; English lexicography in the Internet era; lexicography and corpus linguistics; lexicography and information science; using the Web for information retrieval.

Further reading

Fontenelle, T. (ed.) (2008). *Practical Lexicography: A Reader*. Oxford: Oxford University Press.
Despite the term 'practical' in the title, this volume is a well-chosen selection of the theoretically lexicographic and linguistic 'classic' articles by leading contributors. This volume is a must-read for greater understanding of the 'user', 'data' and 'access' content in the present chapter.

Fuertes-Olivera, P. A. (2012). "Lexicography and the Internet as a (Re-)source". *Lexicographica* 28(1): 49–70.
In this paper, the relation between the Web, (specialised) lexicography and corpus linguistics is directly elaborated on. In particular, it illustrates the vision of the Internet as a lexicographical corpus in terms of an example entry in an accounting dictionary.

Fuertes-Olivera, P. A. and H. Bergenholtz (eds.) (2011). *e-Lexicography: The Internet, Digital Initiatives and Lexicography*. London: Continuum.
In this volume, the contributors consider the rise of Internet dictionaries that change our conceptions of what the dictionary entails. In particular, read the editors' appropriate introduction on the change from p(rinted)-dictionaries to e(lectronic)-dictionaries; Lew's chapter for a survey of current online English dictionaries and relevant issues; Heid's chapter on the closer connection between lexicography and information science; and Verlinde's chapter on a more useful reading, translation and writing assistant that makes up the BLF lexical database.

Granger, S. and M. Paquot (eds.) (2013). *Electronic Lexicography*. Oxford Scholarship Online. DOI: 10.1093/acprof:oso/9780199654864.001.0001 [last accessed: 21 November 2016]

In this volume, leading contributors consider the rise of electronic lexicography which, while having its roots in the "late 1950s/early 1960s" (pre-Web), is blossoming in the Web age. As Granger (2013:6) puts it, hybridization is a hallmark of the new type of lexicography: "one of the most striking results of the electronic revolution in lexicography is that barriers between the different types of language resources – dictionaries, encyclopedias, term banks, lexical databases, vocabulary learning tools, writing aids, translation tools – are breaking down".

Jackson, H. (ed.) (2013). *The Bloomsbury Companion to Lexicography*. London: Bloomsbury.

In this volume, the contributors favour the term 'lexicography' (instead of 'lexicology') for a wider inclusion beyond linguistics. Lexicography has been advocated as an 'independent discipline', a branch of reference science or even information science. Leading topics include a "critique of dictionaries in the electronic medium, the future of historical lexicography in the electronic mode with special reference to the online Oxford English Dictionary, and e-lexicography in general".

Notes

1 See www.dictionary.com/browse/discombobulated
2 See www.merriam-webster.com/dictionary/discombobulate
3 See www.vocabulary.com/dictionary/discombobulate
4 See www.oxforddictionaries.com/definition/english/discombobulate
5 See kamusbahasaindonesia.org
6 See ekamus.dbp.gov.my
7 See www.lexilogos.com
8 See translate.google.com.hk
9 See www.lexilogos.com/english/chinese_dictionary.htm
10 See www.lexilogos.com/english/translation.htm
11 See www.mdbg.net
12 See www.lexilogos.com/english/chinese_dictionary.htm
13 See www.sketchengine.co.uk/documentation/tenten-corpora
14 See forbetterenglish.com/
15 See en.wikipedia.org/wiki/economy_rice
16 This corpus was compiled by Bei Qing, Charlotte, Khoon, and Olivia.
17 This corpus was compiled by the 'Caramelized Computer Chips' group.
18 See www.wordnik.com
19 See www.urbandictionary.com
20 See www.webdante.com
21 See www.framenet.icsi.berkeley.edu
22 See www.wordnet.princeton.edu

References

Bergenholtz, H. and R. Gouws (2012) "What Is Lexicography?", *Lexikos* 22: 31–42.

Berners-Lee, T. (1999) *Weaving the Web: The Original Design and Ultimate Destiny of the World Wide Web by Its Inventor*. New York: HarperCollins.

Davies, M. and R. Fuchs (2015) "Expanding Horizons in the Study of World Englishes with the 1.9 Billion Word Global Web-Based English Corpus (GloWbe)", *English World-Wide* 36(1): 1–29.

De Schryver, G. M. (2002) "Web for/as Corpus: A Perspective for the African Languages", *Nordic Journal of African Studies* 11(2): 266–282.

Fuertes-Olivera, P. A. (2012) "Lexicography and the Internet as a (Re-)Source", *Lexicographica* 28(1): 49–70.

Fuertes-Olivera, P. A. (2013) "e-Lexicography: The Continuing Challenge of Applying New Technology to Dictionary-Making", in Jackson, H. (ed.), *The Bloomsbury Companion to Lexicography*. London: Bloomsbury, pp. 323–340.

Fuertes-Olivera, P. A. and H. Bergenholtz (eds.) (2011) *e-Lexicography: The Internet, Digital Initiatives and Lexicography*. London: Continuum.

Gatto, M. (2011) "The 'body' and the 'web': The Web as Corpus Ten Years on", *ICAME Journal No.* 35: 35–58.

Gouws, R. H. (2014) "Article Structures: Moving from Printed to e-Dictionaries", *Lexikos* 24: 155–177.

Hartmann, R. and G. James (1998) *Dictionary of Lexicography*. London: Taylor and Francis.

Hoey, M. (2005) *Lexical Priming: A New Theory of Words and Language*. London: Routledge.

Hoey, M. (2009) "Lexical Priming", in *MED (Macmillan English Dictionaries) Magazine*, Issue 52. www.macmillandictionaries.com/MED-Magazine/January2009/52-LA-LexicalPriming.htm [last accessed: November 21 2016].

Hoey, M. (2014) "Words and Their Neighbours", in J. R. Taylor (ed.), *The Oxford Handbook of the Word*, Oxford Handbooks Online. DOI: 10.1093/oxfordhb/9780199641604.013.39

Jones, S. (ed.) (1999) *Doing Internet Research: Critical Issues and Methods for Examining the Net*. London: Sage.

Kegl, J. (1987) "The Boundary between Word Knowledge and World Knowledge", in *TINLAP '87: Proceedings of the 1987 workshop on Theoretical issues in natural language processing*, Stroudsburg, PA: Association for Computational Linguistics, pp. 28–33.

Kilgarriff, A. (2013) "Using Corpora as Data Sources for Dictionaries", in H. Jackson (ed.), *The Bloomsbury Companion to Lexicography*. London: Bloomsbury, pp. 77–96.

Kilgarriff, A. and G. Grefenstette (2003) "Introduction to the Special Issue on the Web as Corpus", *Computational Linguistics* 29(3): 333–347.

Leroyer, P. (2011) "Change of Paradigm: From Linguistics to Information Science and from Dictionaries to Lexicographic Information Tools, in Fuertes-Olivera and Bergenholtz (eds.), pp. 121–140.

Lew, R. (2011) "Online Dictionaries of English", in Fuertes-Olivera and Bergenholtz (eds.), pp. 230–250.

Mel'čuk, I. (1996) "Lexical Functions: A Tool for the Description of Lexical Relations in the Lexicon", in L. Wanner (ed.), *Lexical Functions in Lexicography and Natural Language Processing*. Amsterdam: John Benjamins, pp. 37–102.

Mel'čuk, I. (2003) "Lexicon", in *International Encyclopedia of Linguistics: AAVE-Esperanto* 1: 453–456.

Meyer, C. F., R. Grabowski, H-Y Han, K. Mantzouranis, and S. Moses (2003) "The World Wide Web as Linguistic Corpus", in P. Leistyna and C. F. Meyer (eds.), *Corpus Analysis: Language Structure and Language Use*. Amsterdam: Rodopi, pp. 241–254.

Nielsen, S. (2013) "The Future of Dictionaries, Dictionaries of the Future", in H. Jackson (ed.), *The Bloomsbury Companion to Lexicography*. London: Bloomsbury, pp. 355–372.

Ooi, V.B.Y. (1998) *Computer Corpus Lexicography*. Edinburgh: Edinburgh University Press.

Ooi, V.B.Y. (2001) "Investigating and Teaching Genres on the World Wide Web", in M. Ghadessy, A. Henry, and R. Roseberry (eds.), *Small Corpus Studies and ELT: Theory and Practice*. Amsterdam: John Benjamins, pp. 175–203.

Ooi, V.B.Y. (2002) "Aspects of Computer-Mediated Communication for Research in Corpus Linguistics", in P. Peters, P. Collins and A. Smith (eds.), *New Frontiers of Corpus Research*. Amsterdam-New York: Rodopi, pp. 91–104.

Ooi, V.B.Y. (2008) "The Lexis of Electronic Gaming on the Web: A Sinclairian Approach", *International Journal of Lexicography* 21(3): 311–323.

Ooi, V.B.Y. (2010) "English Internet Lexicography and Online Dictionaries", *Lexicographica* 26(1): 143–154.

Ooi, V.B.Y. (2014) "Examining Learner Strategies in a Facebook Corpus of Lexical Priming", in D. Qian and L. Li (eds.), *Teaching and Learning English in East Asian Universities: Global Visions and Local Practices*. Newcastle upon Tyne: Cambridge Scholars, pp. 209–224.

Ooi, V.B.Y. (2015) "A Dictionary of Hong Kong English vs The GloWbe Corpus? Triangulating Sources of Lexicographic Evidence", in L. Li, J. McKeown and L. M. Liu (eds.), *Words,*

Dictionaries and Corpora: Innovations in Reference Science (ASIALEX 2015). Hong Kong: Hong Kong Polytechnic University, pp. 80–89. See at: http://asialex.org/pdf/Asialex-Proceedings-2015.pdf [last accessed: November 21, 2016].

Ooi, V.B.Y. (2016) "Lexical Priming, Dictionaries and Asian Users of English", in S. N. Dita and D. W. Gonzales (eds.), *Advancing Language Teaching with Lexicography and Corpus-Building* (ASIALEX 2016), Manila, 1–11. http://asialex.org/pdf/Asialex-Proceedings-2016.pdf [last accessed: November 21, 2016].

Rundell, M. (2015) "From Print to Digital: Implications for Dictionary Policy and Lexicographic Conventions", *Lexikos* 25: 301–322.

Sinclair, J. (2005a) "Corpus and Text: Basic Principles", in M. Wynne (ed.), *Developing Linguistic Corpora: A Guide to Good Practice*. Oxford: Oxbrow Books. See at: http://ota.ox.ac.uk/documents/creating/dlc/chapter1.htm [last accessed: November 21, 2016].

Sinclair, J. (2005b) "Appendix: How to Build a Corpus", in M. Wynne (ed.), *Developing Linguistic Corpora: A Guide to Good Practice*, Oxford: Oxbrow Books. http://ota.ox.ac.uk/documents/creating/dlc/appendix.htm [last accessed: November 21, 2016].

Verlinde, S., P. Leroyer and J. Binon (2009) "Search and You Will Find: From Stand-Alone Lexicographic Tools to User Driven Task and Problem-Oriented Multifunctional Formats", *International Journal of Lexicography* 23(1): 1–17.

43

Information retrieval for lexicographic purposes

Orin Hargraves

43.1 Introduction

The availability of raw and summarized natural language databases for lexicographic use online and in other digital formats has been steadily increasing since the late twentieth century. The ease of access to such data and its abundance for the world's major languages make it easier for lexicographers today to take a fully evidential approach to the development of sense inventories, definitions and the selection of the most appropriate illustrative examples of usage. Dictionaries generally, and especially learner's and bilingual dictionaries, have benefited greatly from the more complete information about word behaviour that is now readily available. During this same period, a great deal of language reference in the form of dictionaries and other works has migrated from the printed page to the Internet, with its nearly limitless storage capacity. This in turn has given the lexicographer much more room to display the fruits of his labours.

Given this enhanced availability of linguistic data, the question for lexicographers now is not whether to use digitally formatted language samples for research, but how to use them most wisely and effectively; in other words, to learn to work efficiently with a glut, rather than a dearth, of lexical information. The tremendous growth of available data and the burgeoning of space to display it in has not been accompanied by a commensurate growth in the amount of time that lexicographers have to spend in developing entries and doing other dictionary-related tasks, so it is paramount for lexicographers to become experts at identifying and locating the best data available, and at retrieving and analysing it skilfully. Those skills are the focus of this chapter.

43.2 Historical perspective

Nearly all reputable dictionary publishers now make use of corpora, whether proprietary or publically available. Other chapters (notably Chapters 8, 19, 22, 24, 25, 33 and 35 of this *Handbook*) give some indication of the centrality of the use of corpora in modern lexicography, and that centrality is assumed here. The corpus represents the single most useful database of lexical information for modern lexicographic work. In combination with a well-developed user interface, a well-constructed corpus should be able to bring forth nearly all information that a lexicographer needs to make informed and confident decisions in the construction of dictionary entries.

The KWIC (key word in context) display of text (see Figure 43.1), allowing the lexicographer to examine dozens or hundreds of instances of the use of a word in context, was thought to be the ultimate lexicographer's tool when it first became available. Today, however, there are many other lexical resources that helpfully digest information about word meaning and behaviour. The application of traditional lexicographic skills to these new and emerging data sources, along with the greatly expanded possibilities of information provision that online lexical reference provides, enable lexicographers to craft extremely detailed and rich entries for dictionary consumers; entries that go far beyond the old-fashioned paradigm of a word followed by definitions of its senses and occasional examples.

43.3 Core issues and topics

The two electronic data sources that provide the most reliable information for the working lexicographer are a well-designed corpus and (especially for tracing historical patterns) the Google NGrams Viewer. For corpora, no commercially available product today competes with Sketch Engine. It is designed specifically for use by lexicographers working in any language and it is used by dictionary publishers around the world; facility with it is nearly essential for the twenty-first century lexicographer. Therefore, a tour of its main features will lay a foundation for the discussion of word-specific information retrieval that follows.

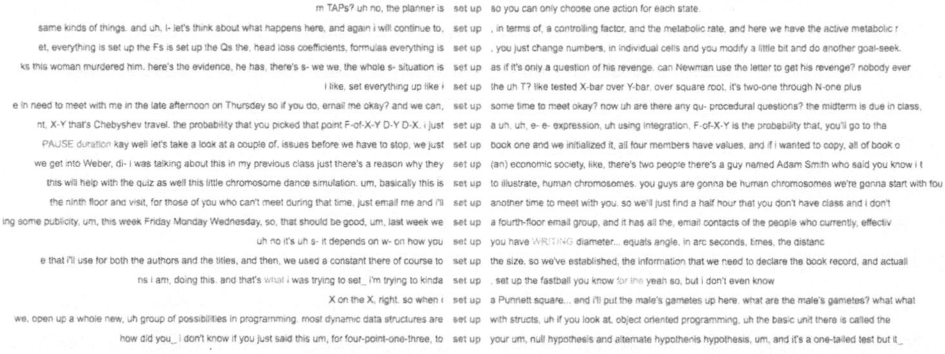

Figure 43.1 Screenshot of a concordance in KWIC format

43.3.1 *The Sketch Engine and word sketches*

This chapter cannot compete in depth of coverage and detail with the documentation provided by Sketch Engine for its use, and the reader is referred there for a more in-depth discussion.[1] All Sketch Engine user information is available free to the public. Many general features of Sketch Engine software are useful for the lexicographer, and they are discussed in appropriate places below. The central feature of the Sketch Engine, the Word Sketch, is where nearly all definitional tasks begin for any major part of speech (noun, verb, adjective, adverb), and so it is appropriate to discuss its principal features here. The Word Sketch is a statistical abstract of the collocational, syntactic and frequency information of a word in a corpus, presented in a table with hyperlinks to examples. Metadata in the corpus determines which and how much information appears in a Word Sketch. Figure 43.2 is a typical example, a portion of the sketch for the noun *patch* in a general English corpus (*LEXMCI*) of about 1.5 billion words.

The sketch (truncated in the figure) shows the collocational behaviour of *patch* (noun) organized by collocation and grammatical relation, listed within each category in descending order of salience. The online version includes hyperlinks (all underscored numbers in the figure), which take the user directly to examples of usage that exemplify the listed relation. The Word Sketch as shown is simply generated from a query to the corpus, and study of it provides the lexicographer with everything required to organize an entry for *patch*, including sense division, frequency of various senses and a selection of examples.

patch *(noun)* LEXMCI freq = 30,059 (17.47 per million)

Constructions		
wh	672	0.02
Vinf_to	485	0.02

object_of	9,495	0.32	AJ_premod	11,367	0.38	PP_X	8,826		SUPPREP	8,595	0.29
install +	362	6.44	**bald +**	235	8.94	PP_of-i	4,991	0.17	**through +**	413	3.47
sew	26	6.01	**purple +**	193	7.96	PP_on-i	928	0.03	across	77	2.52
download	97	5.90	**bare +**	193	7.76	PP_for-i	711	0.02	onto	25	2.33
downloading	26	5.69	transdermal	77	7.75	PP_in-i	572	0.02	**with +**	1,402	2.10
apply +	487	5.66	**damp +**	142	7.57	PP_to-i	324	0.01	once	9	1.85
release +	281	5.57	remnant	55	7.21	PP_from-i	295	0.01	out	18	1.84
downloaded	40	5.38	**rough +**	188	7.04	PP_at-i	198	0.01	via	25	1.82
fog	10	5.01	sticky	74	6.91	PP_with-i	165	0.01	although	23	1.66
wear +	149	5.00	scaly	41	6.77	PP_over-i	73	0.00	**over +**	131	1.57
discolour	10	4.95	muddy	60	6.61	PP_as-i	52	0.00	amongst	8	1.53
patch	13	4.93	boggy	35	6.47	PP_by-i	45	0.00	like	76	1.48
deploy	32	4.65	isoplanatic	24	6.10	PP_around-i	42	0.00	until	30	1.46
fertilise	9	4.64	icy	32	5.97	PP_into-i	33	0.00	**if +**	111	1.31
localise	12	4.56	**wet +**	118	5.95	PP_near-i	33	0.00	near	16	1.31
hit +	135	4.53	isolated	56	5.95	PP_within-i	32	0.00	above	11	1.25
weld	12	4.48	**dark +**	212	5.82	PP_against-i	29	0.00	around	36	1.23
damp	9	4.40	brown	91	5.77	PP_after-i	28	0.00	**into +**	152	1.12
thicken	8	4.38	rocky	40	5.76	PP_under-i	26	0.00	**on +**	744	1.07
embroider	8	4.34	grassy	28	5.75	PP_along-i	24	0.00	without	38	0.96
merge	17	4.34	dense	45	5.71	PP_through-i	23	0.00	**as +**	396	0.84
cultivate	14	4.27	**white +**	339	5.70	PP_behind-i	19	0.00	after	70	0.82
clear	40	4.08	sandy	47	5.65	PP_during-i	19	0.00	between	59	0.77
colonise	7	4.08	pale	42	5.52	PP_about-i	18	0.00	beyond	7	0.73
stitch	7	4.08	yellow	90	5.52	PP_between-i	18	0.00	though	10	0.69
overgrow	7	4.07	itchy	19	5.49	PP_before-i	17	0.00	despite	7	0.69

Figure 43.2 Word Sketch for *patch*

A common function of Sketch Engine that is nearly as useful as the Word Sketch is called SketchDiff, which compares the usage patterns and statistics of two words that share the same part of speech. This digested information can be extremely useful for distinguishing near synonyms, or words that are used in similar contexts, such as *smile* and *grin* (whether noun or verb), *slay* and *murder, happy* and *glad.*

Of course Sketch Engine allows for a simpler concordance search that immediately returns a KWIC display. Such searches can be qualified in advance according to various parameters (context, part of speech, genre, to name a few). Once a KWIC display has been returned, it is also possible to search within the results to filter or sort examples according to context, to generate a statistically ordered list of collocations, to determine relative frequencies of the various inflections of the target word, and to perform several other sub-searches.

43.3.2 The Google NGrams Viewer

Google's ongoing project of digitizing nearly every book ever published has resulted in a trove of lexical information that is happily only keystrokes away from the working lexicographer. An *NGram* is a phrase consisting of one to five words, where N stands for any digit in that range. 'Off the wall' is a 3-gram; 'paint chip' is a 2-gram, or in more traditional parlance, a bigram. For lexicographic purposes, 2-grams are probably of greatest interest because of their information richness in developing dictionary entries. The Google NGrams Viewer enables users to see in graphic format how the collocational behaviour of a word has changed over time. This sort of information can be of particular use when revisiting sense inventories ordered by frequency to note, for example, whether some newer sense has supplanted an older one in frequency. Historical NGram displays may also provide interesting and important connotative information, by showing how a word's most frequent companions have changed radically over time – a shift that may well also signal a shift in semantics. This involves the simple use of wildcard searches, which are explained in detail on the NGram help page.[2] Here is an NGram showing the relative frequencies of the 2-gram *adjective + silence* from the mid-eighteenth century to the early twenty-first century. Perhaps the most interesting feature is that the 2-gram 'profound silence', by far the most frequent for most of the nineteenth century, has now lost nearly all of its ground to 'long silence' (Figure 43.3).

At present the Google NGrams database defaults to searching on English books (both British and American, which can be searched separately) published between 1800 and 2000.

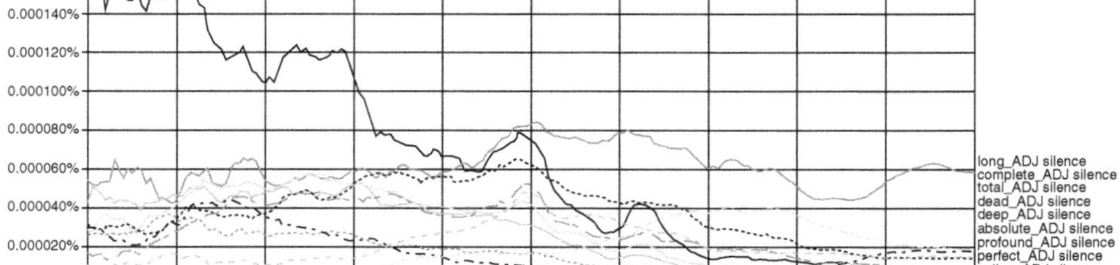

Figure 43.3 NGram of adjective + *silence* in Google Books

There are also significant corpora of books in French, German, Spanish, Russian, Hebrew and Chinese. The latest year for which book searches are available is 2008. The earliest year is 1500, but books published before the eighteenth century are generally of poor quality for scanning purposes and do not return reliable results.

An NGram-like search facility for much more contemporary language (namely, the language of the online forums collected at Reddit.com) is also available.[3] The search interface is not nearly as sophisticated as the one provided for Google Books and does not currently allow for searches on collocations or phrases, only on individual words. Its usefulness is in providing a more contemporary window on language use than can be found in books. Here you can search for trade jargon, slang or even conventional language to get a more up-to-date impression of usage than appears in the Google NGrams Viewer.

43.3.3 A Word about WordNet(s)

Since the introduction of English *WordNet* in the late 1980s, WordNets in dozens of other languages have been developed, and many are freely available online.[4] Since WordNets share characteristics and offer a variety of insights to the lexicographer, some discussion is in order here, centered on English *WordNet*.

A *WordNet* categorizes words (generally only the four major parts of speech, as noted above) into sets of synonyms called synsets and provides short definitions and usage examples. A *synset*, for practical purposes, can be thought of as an individual word sense. Importantly for computational linguistics, *WordNets* record a number of relations among the synonym sets or their members. *WordNet* is undoubtedly the single most-used lexical database in natural language processing (NLP) (see Chapters 12 and 14 of this *Handbook*). It combines features of a dictionary and a thesaurus but goes far beyond both of these traditional formats in ways that are conducive to use in computational linguistics. The quality of definitions and examples in English *WordNet* is often poor and uneven at best, and it is not recommended that *WordNet* ever be emulated with respect to those. However, *WordNet* has some useful features that are lacking from traditional print and electronic dictionaries and that would in some cases be desirable additions. For that reason, a quick look at a *WordNet* can often be helpful to the lexicographer working on a particular dictionary entry.

The principal virtue of *WordNets* is their ontological structure and the interrelatedness of their contents. Relations among words in *WordNet* include hypernymy, synonymy, meronymy, antonymy and others. These are accessible (in English *WordNet*) by clicking on the 'S' next to the bullet point in any displayed sense inventory in the online interface.

Why would a lexicographer wish to consult this information? The chief reason is to get a quick thumbnail impression of how a particular word fits into the lexicon of a language generally. Whereas the native speaker will often have an intuitive grasp of this, no one's intuition is ever complete, and a glance at the relations of a word in *WordNet* can be vital in filling in the blind spots in your personal lexical database of relations. It can also often help the lexicographer get past an instance of agonizing about a particular distinction by showing a time-tested configuration of how a word works in a language's network of words.

43.3.4 Some key lexicographic tasks

Traditionally, and still today, an essential task for the lexicographer organizing an entry must begin with the basic question 'what is it?' – meaning, what part of speech does the word at hand represent? (see Chapter 4 of this *Handbook*). The discussion following, therefore, is subdivided according to this traditional rubric. Dictionary publishers, in their style books, typically lay out specific guidelines or templates for what approach should be taken in the definition each part of speech, and that approach is followed here, with some generalization, and with a particular focus on maximum efficiency in information retrieval for the working lexicographer. In each of the sections below, useful electronic resources in addition to Sketch Engine, Google NGrams and *WordNets* are noted. For an electronic resource to be useful to a lexicographer it has to be both searchable and browsable, and freely available online; that is the case with all resources listed below, with the proviso that some resources have a much more intuitive and user-friendly interface than others. For resources whose usefulness is not immediately apparent to the lexicographer – as may be the case with *VerbNet* or *Just-the-Word*, for example – it is recommended that you spend enough time getting to know these resources in order to develop an idea of when they might be helpful to you. Once they become a part of your working knowledge, you will easily develop a sense of when it might be helpful to consult a particular resource to help you with the entry at hand.

I have generally listed electronic resources under the part of speech to which I think they lend the greatest usefulness for the lexicographer, but in doing this I do not mean to suggest that the resource is limited in application to that part of speech. Thus, *FrameNet* (discussed in Section 43.3.4.2; see also Chapter 24 of this *Handbook*) can be equally useful in working with nouns and adjectives, and *Just The Word* (discussed in Section 43.3.4.3) can be equally helpful for studying other parts of speech. The only resources that are quite part-of-speech specific in their helpfulness next are *VerbNet*, *PDEV* and *PDEP*.

43.3.4.1 Defining nouns

No other part of speech lends itself so easily to a traditional analytic, substitutable definition. For the lexicographer who is familiar with the thing being defined, there may be little need to examine corpus examples of usage to craft a definition. Electronic information for noun definitions is much more pertinent to the more refined tasks of noun definition: sense division in cases of polysemy, and ontological classification.

For sense division of polysemous nouns (and ranking by frequency when style requires that), there are several useful tools. Within Sketch Engine, the Cluster function (it appears in the left panel in a Word Sketch display) will give a computationally derived display of 'senses' of a word that appear to be distinct from each other. Outside of Sketch Engine, there are some other tools that provide the lexicographer a place to start on sense division. English *WordNet* is notorious for its glut of superfluous divisions of sense, but a human-curated version of *WordNet* is available at *Vocabulary.com*. There, an examination of the noun *floor* (for example), which appears in 10 synsets in *WordNet*, is reduced to five more intuitively useful ones.

The problem of classification of nouns is more nuanced but certainly worth the small amount of time that the lexicographer should spend on it with a view to getting it right. A long-standing criticism of traditional dictionaries in the NLP community is their ontological inconsistency, which results in their being unreliable for computational tasks. What, for example, is the generic term for a *bedpan*? It may be a vessel, a receptacle, a chamber pot, a container, a pan or a utensil, depending on which dictionary you consult. These generic terms are themselves inconsistent in their hypernyms across dictionaries, and even within a given dictionary is not difficult to discover instances of circularity in defining (where each of two terms is defined by the other, thereby negating any clear relation of hypernymy/hyponymy). Such problems can be largely avoided by putting in place a simple algorithm for lexicographers to follow in classifying nouns and then having them consult the same electronic source to determine the hypernym of a noun. The hierarchy of nouns in *WordNet* is more complete and robust than for any other part of speech, so looking there for a noun's hypernym is the easiest place to start. The distributional thesaurus function provided in Sketch Engine will also often give a hypernym as one of the word's highest scoring synonyms: thus, *car* is a kind of *vehicle*, *shrub* is a form of *vegetation*, a *rivulet* is a *watercourse*.

Noun *Word Sketches* are also very useful for identification of compound nouns that consist of noun + noun; the sketches give the lexicographer adequate data for determining whether frequent use of a noun attributively merits consideration of it as an adjective headword. The *Word Sketch* for the noun *root* in one corpus, for example, shows the frequent compounds *root cause, root directory, root vegetable* (for attributive/adjectival use) and *square root, deep roots, historical roots* (possible compounds, especially from a learner's perspective). For other compounds consisting of adjective + noun, see the discussion in Section 43.3.4.3.

NGram searches focused on noun use are a rich source of diachronic lexical information, and the challenge for the lexicographer is probably when to stop, not where to start. Various collocational searches in which an adjoining word is wildcarded show interesting patterns of change for many common nouns and are often worth studying for an original or a revised entry. See, for example, *work is *_ADJ, *_VERB clients, *_NOUN bed.*

43.3.4.2 Defining Verbs

The centrality of verbs in modern computational linguistics and in numerous important natural language processing (NLP) tasks has resulted in many more electronic resources for lexicographic consultation than is available for other parts of speech. Despite this rich data field, however, the *Word Sketch* is still the best source for one-stop information: it provides the basis for sense division, common syntactic patterns, grammatical relations, frequency and collocations.

As with other parts of speech, the Google NGrams viewer can easily alert the lexicographer to diachronic shifts in verb usage in meaning with the use of wildcard searches on parts of speech accompanying the target verb. See, for example, *attach a *_NOUN*, which shows the increasing recent use of *attach* as it applies to email, along with the sharply declining sense "bring (someone into association with)" as in "the ordinary tendency of a family is to attach a man more closely to his home". Other example wildcard searches for verbs can be patterned on, e.g., *receive_VERB *_NOUN*, where the addition of *_VERB* on the target verb returns results on all inflections of the verb, rather than just the input form.

Polysemy in verbs can be examined in the same ways as with nouns, noted above, but also with the help of many other readily available sources, for example:

- *FrameNet* (see Chapter 24 of this *Handbook*): *FrameNet*, despite being forever incomplete and lacking in coverage in some critical areas, gives an excellent coarse-grained division of senses for most common verbs. A thorough investigation of the lexicographic uses of *FrameNet* can be found in Rundell et al (2003: 333–357), who say that it "uncovers significant distinguishing features that might otherwise have remained buried in the mass of evidence" including semantic prosody; the disambiguating of near synonyms; and the disentangling of the semantic neighbours (e.g., *say* and *tell*) whose semantic similarity can be somewhat obscured by their contrasting argument structure.

- The *Pattern Dictionary of English Verbs* (PDEV): *PDEV* shows the principal syntactic and semantic patterns, ranked in order of frequency, for all the verbs it contains (about 1700 at this writing, with a goal of eventually reaching about 5400). The governing principle in *PDEV* is Corpus Pattern Analysis, which "aims to identify all normal patterns of use of English verbs by systematic analysis of evidence" (Hanks 2013: 404) and to distinguish norms (normal patterns of use) from exploitations (creative, original uses of words). *PDEV* is based on the British National Corpus.
- *VerbNet:* Of these three resources, *VerbNet* is the most complete in terms of coverage but perhaps least useful for lexicographic purposes since it is designed primarily as a tool for computational linguistics. Nevertheless, it classifies more than 4000 verbs into more than 500 classes, "based on commonalities in their semantic and syntactic behaviour" (Brown et al 2014: 203). The best place to get acquainted with it is by exploring its user interface, but it may also be helpful to read the book chapter by Brown et al. quoted here.

A question pertinent for all of these resources is this: how or when should they be used for lexicographic purposes? A reasonable suggestion is: not at all, if you are proceeding confidently in your defining and you feel that you have enough information at hand from corpora to complete the task. It is ever a danger for the modern lexicographer to inundate herself with so much information that it is suddenly not possible to draw a breath of inspiration or insight. All of these sources, however, are browsable or searchable online, and can be very helpful to consult in cases where the alternative seems to be agonizing about whether you have correctly distinguished a sense, whether two similar senses ought to be lumped, whether one even merits inclusion and the like. All three of these resources have received hundreds, even thousands, of person-hours of native-speaker attention, in many cases from trained lexicographers, and the distinctions drawn in them can be of great use in deciding how many and which senses of a verb merit coverage in a particular dictionary.

43.3.4.3 Defining Adjectives

The treatment of adjectives in *WordNet* is spotty and often poor, due to the unaccountable lack of connection between many adjectives that are in fact synonymous or antonymous, and so it is not recommended at all for consultation in adjective definition, except in one regard: antonymy provides a central organizing principle for the adjectives in *WordNet*, and research suggests that speakers of nearly all languages also use antonymy as an organizing principle for the qualities represented by adjectives in their lexicons. So it may be worth looking at *WordNet*'s antonymic schematization of a word if the lexicographer's intuition does not supply this.

NGrams utilizing a noun wildcard with an adjective preceding can often show in striking fashion when new or changed usages of adjectives became prominent, and they are worth consulting for patterns that do not occur intuitively to the lexicographer. The search *gay *_NOUN*, for example, shows the collocation *gay world* with elevated usage in the early nineteenth century, and still some contemporary usage, though the earlier gay world is surely not the same as the contemporary one. The same NGram shows a huge spike in *gay men* in the 1970s, corresponding to the gay liberation movement. The search *nuclear *_NOUN* shows that *nuclear* had very little to do before the mid-1940s, when nuclear weapons, power and war became part of everyone's lexicon.

The *Word Sketch* display for an adjective provides the most pertinent information for determining adjective polysemy, frequency of various senses and a snapshot of how (or if) attributive and predicative use may differ. For adjectives formed from participles (such as *abiding* or *bent*) it is always worth examining the *Word Sketch* of the underlying verb (i.e., *abide* or *bend*) in order to see if the tagging in the corpus you are consulting has camouflaged an important collocation by misidentifying the use of the modifier. Such errors are common in the computational tagging of text.

A typical feature of an adjective *Word Sketch* is the appearance of some adjective + noun compounds that far outnumber others, because they are effectively compound nouns that merit entry treatment in their own right. Examples include *yellow pages, cerebral palsy, striped bass* and *playing field.* Dictionaries can benefit tremendously by including such compounds that are more likely to come to notice in corpora than in the lexicographer's imagination.

More complex searches in Sketch Engine can bring to light extremely frequent compound adjectives that often escape the notice of headword list compilers. Although many such compounds are taken to be transparent and thus unworthy of separate treatment in a dictionary, usage shows that they are often more than the sum of their parts, and even polysemous. In addition, a sampling of compound adjectives that are defined in dictionaries often shows that their frequency does not merit the attention they have received, especially when other more frequent and less transparent compounds are overlooked. The frequent compound adjective *heart-shaped*, for example, appears in virtually no dictionary headword list, but a learner may be unaware that *heart* in this case refers to the shape ♥, not the internal organ. Examples of other compound adjectives needing definition but rarely receiving it include *natural-looking, sweet-smelling, full-fingered, slab-sided* and *well-used.* All of these, and hundreds of others, are easily discoverable using targeted searches in Sketch Engine or other corpora.

43.3.4.4 Defining adverbs

Of the 'big four' parts of speech for which *Word Sketches* are available, adverbs are as a class the least frequent. In cases where they are derived from a related adjective they are also the least likely to present defining challenges, and in fact many such adverbs are simply run on in dictionaries (e.g. *unquestionably* at the entry for *unquestionable*). Adverbs that require wider treatment and thus better evidential support from corpora are generally well served by the *Word Sketches* for them. Such adverbs fall into multiple classes: 1) those that enjoy similar use as another part of speech, usually either preposition or adjective (e.g., *out, up, down, back, fast, good*); 2) those that frequently serve as sentence adverbs (e.g., *unfortunately, hopefully, frankly, obviously*); and 3) high-frequency adverbs, often those signalling temporal relations (e.g., *then, now, just, still*), that are effectively function words. The tagsets in most corpora do not make distinctions among these adverb types and so *Word Sketches* give a relatively coarse-grained snapshot of adverb behaviour, one that is much less informative than sketches for the other main parts of speech. That said, it is rarely useful or necessary for lexicographers to rack their brains over adverb definitions; they are extremely well documented in existing dictionaries, especially in newer learner's dictionaries, and it is hard to imagine useful treatments of them that have not already been developed. No online source that I am aware of other than Sketch Engine provides easily accessible information specifically about adverb behaviour that would be of use in practical lexicography.

In the absence of adverb-specific databases for learning about word behaviour, this is a suitable place to mention *Just The Word*, a search interface based on the British National Corpus that enables the user to see at a glance a visual interpretation of a word's most frequent collocates. Entering *relatively*, for example, in the site's search window shows that the most frequent collocations are *relatively easy/low/simple/small/few/high*. All displayed collocations are hyperlinks that take the user to a KWIC display of the collocation in question, allowing for easy example selection. *Just The Word* is equally useful for other parts of speech and may be helpful to consult when you have the impression that Sketch Engine is giving you too much information to digest easily. One note of caution: the clustering of senses in *Just The Word* is generally not reliable for any lexicographic pursuit.

43.3.4.5 Defining prepositions

It is lamentable that *Word Sketches* are not available for prepositions, but that is the case as of this writing. It is also lamentable that lexicographers must often spend a good deal of time crafting difficult entries for preposition sense inventories that no one will ever read. They are treated at full length in all types of dictionaries in a remarkable range of approaches geared to each dictionary's main audience. Users of bilingual and learner's dictionaries are most likely to find preposition entries useful, but native speakers do not often have occasion to consult them.

The great disparity in sense inventories among prepositions in different dictionaries may suggest that no dictionary has got it quite right, but this is probably more due to the chameleon-like nature of prepositions than anything else. It is hard to make a case that lexicographers should exert great effort in locating sources about preposition information beyond what a sorted and refined corpus search provides (e.g., in order to determine collocations) because they are all already very well documented. The one online source that may provide interesting insight is the *Pattern Dictionary of English Prepositions (PDEP)*, which provides a wide-ranging analytical survey of preposition behaviour. Its user interface is not very intuitive, and mastery of it is recommended only for a lexicographer tasked with an instauration of preposition treatment.

43.3.4.6 Defining other function words

The remaining traditional English parts of speech (pronoun, conjunction and interjection), as well as newer or alternative designations (determiner, pre-determiner, quantifier, clitic, particle, etc.) are generally high frequency, and often highly context dependent for meaning. Although *Word Sketches* are not available for these, corpus querying software allows the isolation of syntactic patterns and collocational information by using other functions in Sketch Engine; in particular, the collocation search, using information to the left and right of the target word of one or two tokens, usually brings to light any patterns that will be of interest to the lexicographer. Using a combination of collocational an filter searches, a user can usually get rid of unwanted examples, or isolate desired ones, by using iterative searches. At present there are no online resources that provide more insight into the behaviour of these words more than corpora do.

43.3.5.7 Defining phrases, idioms and other multiword expressions

Modern computational attempts to crack the secrets of language have brought to light in many different ways the extent to which lexical analysis is insufficient for understanding how language works. To put it another way, knowing the dictionary meaning of every word in a sentence is only occasionally all that is required to understand what the sentence means.

Traditionally dictionaries were not seen as having a mission to explain the meaning of anything longer than a word, but beginning in the twentieth century there was a broadening of the scope of dictionaries and of kinds of dictionaries with a view of enabling the language user, and especially the language learner, to understand not only individual words but combinations and patterns of words. Corpora have been of tremendous benefit for this enterprise, both for language reference books and NLP.

The modern lexicographer in the world of globalization is likely to have the opportunity to compile reference works devoted to idioms and other multiword expressions (MWEs) because these are increasingly a part of the traffic in international translation, and often one of the slowest moving parts of it because of their noncompositionality and resistance to word-for-word translation methods. Corpora, and Sketch Engine in particular, are excellent electronic resources for the lexicographer to determine the best treatment for language units longer than the word.

One defining problem for which a statistical survey of examples is helpful is to determine whether a canonical form of an expression exists. What, for example, should be the canonical or lemmatized form of the idiom in these sentences?

- It is as if *the dirty linen has been washed in public*, as each day a new skeleton comes out of the cupboard with a fresh report of a gang-rape committed in some part of India.
- A party is like a family: it *does not wash its dirty linen in public.*
- You *can't have your dirty linen washed in public* every week of the year without it affecting the club.
- *Washing your dirty linen in public* does not put down only your partner, it also puts you down.
- It is not my goal *to wash our dirty linens in public*, but it is also not my desire to see false information disseminated.

A survey of examples can be generated with a contextual search, in which the search term is *linen* and the words *wash, dirty, public* are included in a context window of five tokens on either side of *linen*. In a sufficiently large corpus, this provides enough examples for the lexicographer to make an informed decision about how to treat the idiom and whether variants of it merit mention as well.

Corpora are also extremely useful for bringing to light semantic differences arising from seemingly small variation in phrasal syntax or inflection. Conventional dictionaries, for example, may not treat the phrase *nooks and crannies* at all, or if they do, they may overlook the considerable difference between "every nook and cranny" (typically used in expressions about penetrative searching) and the plural "nooks and crannies" (which usually refers to small, remote, or unconventional locations, independent of a specific activity). Similarly, there can be quite a semantic gap between *down and dirty* used attributively (*down-and-dirty details/work/politics/approaches*) and used predicatively (*One of these days Mal and Chrysabelle are gonna get down-and-dirty*). A survey of dictionaries suggests that even if such meanings are distinguished, no usage clues are given as to how this might be determined by the reader.

43.3.5 Electronic resources for bilingual lexicography

Today's lexicographer is spoiled for choice in the number of resources freely available for consultation in bilingual lexicography between major languages. There is a much greater danger of information overload for the working lexicographer than there is for a want of resources. Due to this surfeit of data, a sensible approach is one similar to what is suggested earlier for English-language resources: acquaint yourself with what is available to the degree that you have an instinctive sense of which resource will be useful for which particular lexicographic problem. Here is a list of resources that bilingual lexicographers will find useful, along with descriptions of each.

- The *parallel corpora in Sketch Engine* give a quick and easy way to see multiple examples of how a particular word or phrase has been translated by others. These corpora are accessed from the home page by clicking on the 'Parallel' link, from which corpora in one or more languages can be selected.
- *Google Image Search* can be of tremendous help to the lexicographer to confirm the meaning of a word or phrase in a target language, simply by searching on the word or phrase and studying the images returned. It is also extremely helpful for finding good translations for unfamiliar technical terms where a provided gloss doesn't quite bring to light what the thing is.
- *Word Reference.com* is a commercial website that is widely used by professional translators who query particular semantic nuances in the site's many forums. It is easy to get lost in the weeds, but with practice you will be able to determine quickly whether someone else has already struggled with (and perhaps found a solution to) your translation quandary.
- *BabelNet.org* is, in its own words, "both a multilingual encyclopaedic dictionary, with lexicographic and encyclopaedic coverage of terms, and a semantic network which connects concepts and named entities in a very large network of semantic relations, made up of about 14 million entries." It is particularly useful for phrases and proper nouns for which lexicographic information may be lacking in other more traditional resources.
- The *Surrey Deponency Databases*, although not very comprehensive at this writing, "looks at the presence of morphological mismatches in a controlled sample of genetically and geographically diverse languages" and may provide a basis for determining what features of a target L2 language may present special challenges for L1 learners and thus require expanded treatment in a dictionary.

43.4 Looking to the future

It is inevitable that as computational research into language and various digital humanities projects proliferate, the number of resources available to lexicographers for consultation about word meaning and behaviour will continue to multiply (see Chapters 13 and 29 of this *Handbook*). What is not likely to increase, however, is the amount of time that lexicographers are allotted to devote to the important tasks at hand, which are likely to be sense differentiation, defining and example selection for a given word. In light of that fact, it is imperative that lexicographers stay current with any new developments in computational semantics and digital humanities that are likely to be of use. It would also be greatly desirable for computationally minded lexicographers to develop, from emerging databases, the necessary digesting tools that will make the mining of such data feasible for working lexicographers. For language databases in particular there is currently a gap between the great availability of big data and the addressability of that data.

43.5 Conclusion

The richness of linguistic data currently available in electronic format would surely have been the envy of lexicographers even in the late twentieth century. Those who experienced the thrill of working with corpora for the first time were not deterred by the corpora being stored tediously on stacks of floppy disks that had to be laboriously loaded onto a desktop computer before they became usable. Now such data and more is only keystrokes away from the contemporary lexicographer, but the glut of it is not accompanied by a glut of time to exploit it, and as a result, lexicographers must become experts at becoming aware of the resources available in their target language(s) and adept at using these resources as efficiently as possible in order to craft the best dictionary entries, using the most complete, up-to-date and accurate linguistic information available.

Related topics

Dictionary management; FrameNet; lexicography and corpus linguistics; lexicography and information science; lexicography and natural language processing; terminological knowledge bases; using the Web for lexicographic purposes.

Further reading

Hanks, P. (2013). *Lexical Analysis: Norms and Exploitations*. Cambridge, MA: MIT Press.
Hardly a man now alive has thought longer and harder about lexical analysis from the lexicographer's point of view than Patrick Hanks, and his findings are beautifully laid out in this recent book, as good a companion for the lexicographer as any you will find.

Kilgarriff, A., V. Baisa, J. Bušta, M. Jakubíček, V. Kovář, J. Michelfeit, P. Rychlý and V.Suchomel. (2014). "The Sketch Engine: Ten Years on", *Lexicography* 1(1): 7–36.
This paper explores Sketch Engine in detail, providing a great deal more historical background and technical information than is pertinent in this chapter.

Rundell, M., S. Atkins and H. Sato. (2003). "The Contribution of FrameNet to Practical Lexicography", *International Journal of Lexicography* 16(3): 333–357.
In addition to a coherent presentation of what you would expect from the paper's title, this study lays out in interesting detail a good deal of what lexicographic work entails.

Notes

1 See at www.sketchengine.co.uk/documentation/
2 See at https://books.google.com/ngrams/info
3 See at http://projects.fivethirtyeight.com/reddit-ngram/
4 See a list at http://globalwordnet.org/wordnets-in-the-world/

References

Online resources [All accessed on September 22, 2016]

BabelNet: http://babelnet.org
FrameNet: https://framenet.icsi.berkeley.edu/fndrupal/
Google Image Search: https://images.google.com
Google NGrams Viewer: https://books.google.com/ngrams
Pattern Dictionary of English Verbs: http://pdev.org.uk

Sketch Engine: www.sketchengine.co.uk
Surrency Deponency Databases: www.smg.surrey.ac.uk/deponency/
VerbNet: http://verbs.colorado.edu/verb-index
WordNet: https://wordnet.princeton.edu/
WordReference: www.wordreference.com

Other literature

Brown, S. W., D. Dligach, and M. Palmer (2014) "VerbNet Class Assignment as a WSD task", in A. E. Bunt, H. E. Bos and J. E. Pulman (eds.), *Computing Meaning*. 4. Dordrecht: Springer, pp. 203–216. Also in *Proceedings of the 9th International Conference on Computational Semantics*, 2011. Oxford: Association for Computational Linguistics, pp. 85–94.

Hanks, P. (2013) *Lexical Analysis: Norms and Exploitations*. Cambridge, MA: MIT Press.

Miller, G. A., R. Beckwith, C. Fellbaum, D. Gross and K. J. Miller (1990) "Introduction to WordNet: An On-Line Lexical Database", *International Journal of Lexicography* 3(4): 235.

Rundell, M., S. Atkins and H. Sato (2003) "The Contribution of FrameNet to Practical Lexicography", *International Journal of Lexicography* 16(3): 333–357.

44

Dictionary usage research in the Internet era

Carolin Müller-Spitzer, Alexander Koplenig and Sascha Wolfer

44.1 Introduction

Linguistic dictionaries are usually compiled to support communication between speakers and writers of different languages or language varieties as well as to provide information on linguistic phenomena that might be of general interest for potential users. Therefore, dictionaries are regarded as tools. Their genuine purpose is to help solve language-related tasks. The use of lexicographic tools, and – more generally – finding solutions to language related tasks with reference works, is the topic of dictionary usage research (see e.g. Lew 2015a, Tarp 2009, Müller-Spitzer 2014a). The purpose and intent of research into dictionary use is to find out in which situations, how and, with which degree of success, etc., lexicographic tools are used. Insights based on such empirical user studies can then serve as a basis for improving future dictionaries and better adapting them to the needs of potential users. In an even broader sense, these findings can supply us with empirical data on how users try to solve language-related tasks with lexicographic aids. There are a number of diverse possibilities to collect empirical data on the use of dictionaries. We can, to name but a few, address potential users via questionnaires, we can observe users of online dictionaries via protocol data (log files) or we can track the interaction of a user with a digital dictionary in the lab.

The remainder of this article is structured as follows: In order to provide an insight into the field of dictionary usage research, we initially situate it historically (Section 44.2), and then focus on three different methods to collect empirical data on dictionary use: online questionnaires (Section 44.3.1), eye tracking (Section 44.3.2) and log files (Section 44.3.3). Each section begins with a brief explanation of the methodological basics, followed by an illustrating study on dictionary use that applied the respective method. All studies presented here were conducted at the Institute for the German Language in Mannheim and are focused on linguistic dictionaries, but are just as applicable for empirical studies on dictionaries for specific purposes.

44.2 Historical perspective

As mentioned earlier, dictionaries are usually designed as practical tools. However, until "fairly recently, dictionary users were not usually of central concern in the process of dictionary making, however strange it may sound today" (Lew 2015a: 1; see also Wiegand 1998: 259–60; Bogaards 2003: 26–33; Tarp 2008: 33–43; Wiegand et al. 2010: 680; Sharifi 2012: 626). The area explored best within this field is the usage of dictionaries of L2 users. There are also some studies on the use of printed vs. digital dictionaries (cf. e.g. Dziemanko 2012). Less well known is the use of monolingual dictionaries, especially in regard to L1 users (as an exception see Klosa, Koplenig and Töpel 2014), as well as the use of lexicographic tools by the general public. There are also very few studies on the use of online dictionaries in particular (see Töpel 2014). The studies in Müller-Spitzer (2014b) present a series of studies focused on online dictionaries (reviewed in Lew 2015b). However, there is still a great need for empirical research in this area (cf. e.g. Bowker 2012; Welker 2013).

One reason is that lexicography today is "at a turning point in its history" (Granger 2012: 10). Since the middle of the 1990s, the lexicographic landscape has changed radically. Especially the impressive success of the Internet and the related occurrence of free access dictionaries, which are not developed by established publishers, is a relatively new phenomenon, even if we take it for granted today. The many free-to-use dictionaries attract numerous users, though these dictionaries cannot always keep up with established dictionaries in terms of quality. As a consequence of the success of free-to-use dictionaries, the sales of publishers' dictionaries decreased significantly. It became very difficult for publishers to find adequate models to charge users for their dictionaries. Also, academic lexicography took a long time to adapt to the new media requirements. As a long-term effect, we find a fundamentally changed lexicographic landscape today. Many interesting and specialized dictionaries are easy to access. In addition, some reference works that could once only be found in special libraries are today sometimes just one click away (for an overview of online dictionaries from all over the world, see the online bibliography OBELEX^{dict}.[1] This is the positive aspect of the development. However, for professional lexicographers, there are also negative consequences. Numerous lexicographic teams are being downsized because the publishers are commercially less successful with their reference works. Apart from how to evaluate this development, the process of change is irreversible. Under these circumstances it is "better to embrace a future that will come anyway, than to hang grimly on to a way of doing things whose time is passing", as Rundell stated when Macmillan decided to stop printing dictionaries.[2] Within this changed lexicographic landscape, however, it is more important than ever to make the best use of limited personal and financial resources. Dictionary usage research can contribute empirical knowledge on how this can be achieved, without losing sight of the dictionary users' interests. That is why the relevance of dictionary usage research has increased in the last two decades.

44.3 Core issues and topics: methods used in dictionary usage research

44.3.1 Online questionnaires

Surveys – no matter whether administered in the form of a questionnaire or an interview, distributed online or as paper sheets to be filled out with paper and pencil – involve collecting data by asking questions. The collected answers of multiple respondents can then be analysed (statistically) in order to answer specific research questions or in an exploratory fashion, for example to gain first insights into a topic (Koplenig 2014). In the empirical social sciences, conducting a survey is the most commonly used data collection method.

44.3.1.1 Methodological basics

The frequent use of questionnaires is due to the fact that, in most cases, (basic) surveys are fairly easy to create and easy to administer, for example by using an online survey tool, such as SurveyMonkey or Unipark. In addition, collecting data through surveys is – in most cases – much cheaper than other methods such as laboratory tests or eye-tracking studies (see Section 44.3.2). In comparison to the analysis of log files (see Section 44.3.3), the researcher has much more control of the research process which makes it possible to collect data on the background of the observed users.

In the next section, we will present an example of an online questionnaire in which we tried to collect empirical data on questions regarding the design of an online dictionary.

44.3.1.2 Study: how do potential users assess different designs for online dictionaries?

Online dictionaries should not look like printed dictionaries on a computer screen. Instead of arranging the dictionary entries unidimensionally using typical conventions of printed dictionaries like compressions and common abbreviations, alternative ways of presenting word entries in online dictionaries can be and are already being used (see Lew 2012). However, there has been little empirical research into the basic design of dictionaries so far (for exceptions see Tono 2000; Lew 2010; Lew and Tokarek 2010; Nesi and Tan 2011; Dziemanko 2012). Therefore, lexicographers who do not wish to choose an established form of presentation, or simply have to present new kinds of data, are faced with the problem of what kind of arrangement is best suited to the intended users of the dictionary.

Therefore, we tried to collect empirical data on questions of design using an online questionnaire study (for a detailed description of the study see Koplenig and Müller-Spitzer 2014). We were interested not only in the assessment of different dictionary layouts but particularly in the reasons for this assessment. As a result, more general conclusions can be drawn about important aspects of design. The study ran from 11 August to 16 September 2010, and 390 participants took part.

In our study, we asked our participants to rate different basic alternatives of presenting word entries in an online dictionary and to decide which they preferred. All alternatives included in the survey illustrated the same word entry ("summer") covering (as far as possible) identical content (see Figure 44.1). By presenting these design options, we focused on academic dictionaries with a detailed microstructure.

We used the following procedure. First, every respondent was shown the four alternative views one after another. The order of presentation was randomized to avoid any order effects. After the respondents had the opportunity to look at and try out each alternative, they were asked to rate all four types of presentation with respect to the following characteristics, using 7-point Likert scales: Quality (1 = not good, 7 = very good); Arrangement (1 = not well arranged, 7 = very well arranged); Comprehensibility (1 = not comprehensible, 7 = very comprehensible). Then, we asked the participants to rank the options according to their preference. The best presentation type was ranked first, while the type of presentation the respondent liked second best was ranked second, etc. When the respondents had finished

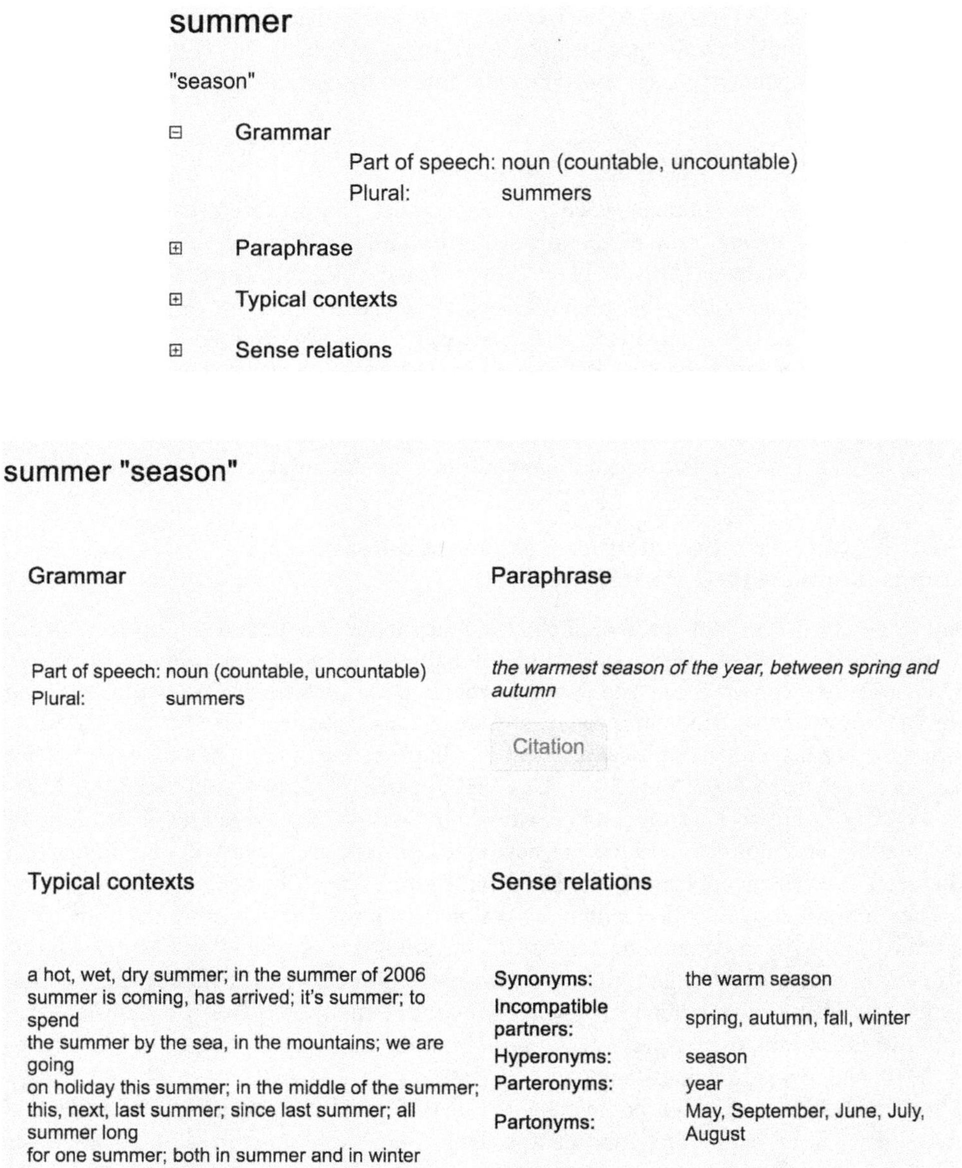

Figure 44.1 Four alternative designs for presenting word entries included in the questionnaire study (Explorer, Panel, Tab and Print)

the ranking task, they were shown the view they had rated best and asked what they particularly liked about it in an open-ended question. To identify potential user group differences, we used background variables similar to those in the last section: academic and professional background and the language version of the survey.

All the ratings of all four alternatives were averaged to form a reliable scale of ratings, with higher values indicating higher ratings. Table 44.1 summarizes the average ratings and first rank percentages for each alternative way of presenting word entries.

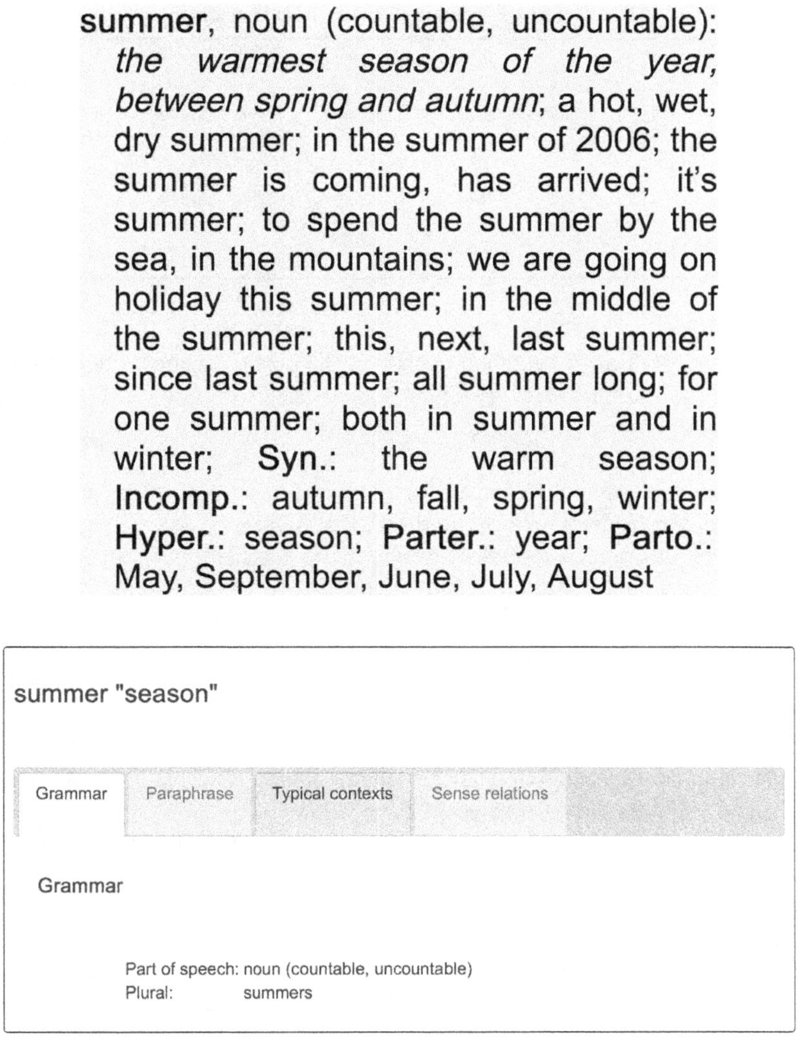

Figure 44.1 Continued

Table 44.1 Means and standard deviations of the ratings and first rank percentages for each tested view

Alternative	*Mean-rating*[a]	*SD*	*First rank percentage*
Tab View	5.43	1.39	42.82
Panel View	5.15	1.46	32.82
Explorer View	4.93	1.44	17.69
Print View	3.36	1.55	6.67

[a] All means are significantly different from each other as indicated by separate t-tests (p*s* < .05).

Table 44.2 Percentage of first ranks as a function of professional background

	Professional background		
First rank	*Non-translator*	*Translator*	*Total*
TAB VIEW	47.74	34.69	42.82
PANEL VIEW	30.04	37.41	32.82
EXPLORER VIEW	16.05	20.41	17.69
PRINT VIEW	6.17	7.48	6.67

The Tab View was both rated best, and chosen as the best view most often. Although the Panel View and the Explorer View received somewhat lower, but still high ratings, they were chosen less often as the favourite view. The Print View was rated worst, as well as chosen least often as the best view.

To analyse potential group differences, we conducted several X^2 difference tests. Neither language version nor academic background ($X^2(3) = 3.08$, $p = .38$) are significant predictors of preference for a screen format. However, there is a marginally significant relationship between professional background and preferred view ($X^2(3) = 6.38$, $p < .10$, see also Table 44.2): non-translators strongly prefer the Tab View – roughly one of two non-translators prefers this way of presenting word entries. Most translators prefer the Panel View (37.41 percent), although almost as many respondents in this group choose the Tab View (34.69 percent).

As an interim conclusion, two things can be said: first, the Tab View is – on average – the most popular; second, the subgroup analyses do not paint a clear picture; with the possible exception that translators seem to prefer the Panel View.

To explain why respondents preferred one type of presentation over the others, we manually inspected the answers to the open-ended question ("This is the view you rated best. What do you particularly like about it?"). Here, some participants explained their selection in some detail. To make this data analysable, several categories were created in a bottom-up process in order to summarise recurring arguments. Then, the data were coded according to the method of structuring (Diekmann 2010: 608–613; Mayring 2011; Müller-Spitzer 2014b).

In Table 44.3 the frequency distributions of the categories for each alternative are displayed. The three most frequently mentioned categories for each alternative are highlighted. All alternatives are preferred for being clear, as "clarity" is the most frequently mentioned criterion overall (57.18 percent), especially by respondents who favour the Tab View (63.64 percent). Compared to the Panel View (3.94 percent) and the Print View (8.00 percent), both the Tab View (32.12 percent) and the Explorer View (56.06 percent) stand out for being adaptable to the preferences of the user. This difference is highly significant ($X^2(3) = 71.68$, $p < .01$). A user interface that is easy to navigate also seems to be an important factor in the decision for respondents who chose the Tab View (36.12 percent), those who chose the Panel View (29.13 percent) and those who chose the Explorer View (25.76 percent). In relation to the three other ways of presenting word entries, the Panel View (76.38 percent) is preferred because it allows the user to access all information without clicking ($X^2(3) = 179.64$, $p < .01$). Unsurprisingly, the Print View is mostly chosen for its familiarity (40.00 percent). The contrast to the other three alternatives is highly significant ($X^2(3) = 49.28$, $p < .01$, see Table 44.3).

Table 44.3 Reason for preference (percentages) as a function of chosen alternative of presentation

	Preferred alternative of presentation					
Category	*TAB*	*PANEL*	*EXPLORER*	*PRINT*	*total*	*χ^2/p-value*
Clarity	**63.64**[a]	**55.12**	**56.06**	**28.00**	57.18	11.76 / 0.10
No need to click	5.45	**76.38**	16.67	16.00	31.59	179.64 / 0.00
Navigation	**36.12**	**29.13**	**25.76**	16.00	40.81	5.92 / 1.00
Adaptability/Selectivity	**32.12**	3.94	**56.06**	8.00	25.33	71.68 / 0.00
No information overload	24.24	8.66	16.70	**28.00**	18.54	13.30 / 0.05
Essential information	12.73	12.60	22.73	4.00	13.84	6.74 / 0.97
Efficiency	10.30	11.02	9.09	12.00	10.44	0.24 / 1.00
Look and feel	12.73	4.72	7.58	16.00	9.40	6.94 / 0 .89
Familiarity	12.12	0.79	1.52	**40.00**	8.36	49.28 / 0.00
Quickness	5.45	6.30	7.58	12.00	6.53	1.67 / 1.00
Others	3.03	3.15	0.00	0.00	2.35	2.88 / 1.00
No need to scroll	1.82	0.79	0.00	0.00	1.04	2.00 / 1.00
Total	220.00	212.60	222.73	180.0	215.40	

[a] The three most frequently mentioned categories for each alternative in bold.
[b] P values are Bonferroni adjusted.

Our analyses show that most of our respondents tended to prefer the Tab View. Potential group differences in this context only seem to play a minor role: in almost every subgroup, the Tab View receives the most first-place votes. The analyses of the open-ended responses show that the participants like this way of presenting word entries because it is clear, easy to navigate and adaptable. One exception is translators. They seem to prefer a view that provides all the data at a glance. The analysis of the open-ended question shows very clearly the reasons for the preferences. Surprisingly, adaptivity is a very frequently cited criterion. This came as a surprise because this criterion was evaluated as very unimportant for good online dictionaries in a preceding study (Müller-Spitzer and Koplenig 2014). One possible explanation, we assume, is the fact that respondents are not used to online dictionaries incorporating those features. Thus, the participants of the previous study had no basis on which to judge their potential usefulness. We confirmed this assumption in an experiment incorporated into a survey (Müller-Spitzer and Koplenig 2014: 170–179). We showed that respondents who were first presented with examples of possible innovative features of online dictionaries judged adaptability and multimedia to be more useful than participants who did not have this information. A similar phenomenon may also be observed here: as soon as subjects see the different ways in which entries can be presented, they see the possibility of an adaptive adjustment as an advantage.

In sum, the empirical data on questions of design collected from this study provide us with valuable information. Especially projects that use these or similar forms of presentation for their lexicographic data can profit from these results. In addition, the responses to the open-ended question show, detached from concrete design models, which criteria potential users particularly value in a good online representation: clarity, an uncluttered look and the possibility to customise, if the latter does not entail too complex a usability model.

This example study should also illustrate that we can evaluate relevant questions from the field of dictionary usage research empirically with questionnaire studies. The overall criticism of Bergenholtz and Johnson or Tarp (Bergenholtz and Johnsen 2005: 119–120; Tarp 2009: 285) is therefore not valid for questionnaire studies in general, but only for poorly prepared survey studies. Survey methods only deliver reliable information if the study is constructed in a comprehensible and precise way. Accordingly, there is a special branch of the social sciences that tries to evaluate the quality of survey questions and identifies potential flaws in experiments (Madans et al. 2011). Thus, the bottom line is that it is important, to keep in mind that "[c]onstructing a survey instrument is an art in itself" (Trochim 2006).

44.3.2 Eye tracking

With eye trackers, we are able to tell when (and how long) a participant looks at a specific location on a stimulus. By connecting eye movements to cognitive processes conceptually, we are relying on the *eye-mind assumption* formulated by Just and Carpenter (1980), which states that "there is no appreciable lag between what is being fixated and what is being processed" (*ibid.*: 331). The most commonly used eye-tracking systems present the visual stimulus on a computer screen and track the participants' gaze on the screen while the participant is sitting in front of the screen. For dictionary usage research, these stationary eye-tracking systems are an obvious choice. It is quite easy to present (parts of) dictionary entries on a computer screen, especially for electronic dictionary resources. For a comprehensive overview over several eye-tracking systems, methodology and analyses, please refer to the introductory textbook by Duchowski (2007). Also, for a more computational, language-oriented and human-computer interactional focus, see Hyönä, Radach and Deubel (2003).

It is worth pointing out that eye tracking is an *online* measurement, that is, the point in time when the data are collected is very near to the point in time when the relevant cognitive process is happening, which is an advantage when immediateness of process and measurement is important. This is in contrast to the type of data described in the previous section of this contribution. (Internet) Questionnaires are considered an *offline* measurement because the moment of data collection (choosing an answer option in the questionnaire) occurs some time after the actual cognitive process.

44.3.2.1 Methodological basics

Typically, when analysing eye-tracking data, we are interested in *fixations* and *saccades*. Fixations are time periods when the eyes are relatively stationary. Saccades are the quick movements of the eye between two fixations. Given the large number of fixations and saccades that occur while looking at visual stimuli, we arrive at a very large database that we have to manage in order to answer our research question(s). It is virtually impossible to analyse the fixation patterns of all participants and extract "typical" patterns in a qualitative manner. That is why we formulate hypotheses that we test with our empirical data, which is the standard approach in empirical research. For example, you could present two designs of an online dictionary to your participants. The differences in the two designs should be motivated by a certain hypothesis related to which of the two versions "works better" (e.g. enables the participants to extract the relevant information faster).

Most eye-tracking systems come with sophisticated software packages that provide a range of different variables to the researcher, for example, total fixation duration, first fixation duration, saccade amplitude (the speed at which the eye moves) and many more. However, just as specifying your hypotheses beforehand, you should also specify which variables you will take into consideration for your analyses before conducting your experiment and testing your hypothesis. "Cherry picking" the measures that best fit the hypothesis is not recommended.

44.3.2.2 Study: how do potential users cope with certain features of the relaunched dictionary portal OWID?

There are not many eye-tracking studies on dictionary usage. Lew, Grzelak and Leszkowicz (2013: 230ff) present one such study and also give an overview over the studies conducted so far. To our knowledge, the study we present here is the first to use eye tracking for research into a dictionary *portal* (see Chapter 46 of this *Handbook*). We will start by clarifying a few things regarding the dictionary portal OWID. Due to limited space, we will keep this rather short but refer readers to the more detailed descriptions in Müller-Spitzer et al. (2014). OWID is a lexicographic Internet portal for various electronic dictionary resources compiled at the Institute for the German Language (IDS).[3] In 2010, we planned a relaunch of the website. On the one hand, we wanted to increase the visibility of the individual dictionaries, that is, strengthen the character of OWID as a dictionary portal. On the other hand, we wanted a clearer and less cluttered web interface compared to the old version. One of the measures to achieve this was the introduction of colour codes for each of the dictionaries that are presented next to the names of the dictionaries, next to the headword of the entry in a lemma list and in the entry itself.

The study we will present in this section is rather exploratory, and we will discuss how this could constitute a problem. We conducted the study in mid-2011 when the relaunch of the web design was finished internally but had not yet been released externally.

Of the research questions that played a role in our study, we will focus on the following three in this section: (1) Is it easy to recognise that OWID is a dictionary *portal*? (2) Does the colour scheme work for the identification of the individual dictionaries, that is, is it easy to assign keywords to the individual dictionaries using the coloured boxes? (3) Do the comments in boxes distract users from the items themselves?

The apparatus and procedure were as follows: For this study, we used a remote eye tracker. Remote eye-tracking systems track the participant's gaze without any physical contact between the participant and the device. Hence, participants are free to move their head in a certain area which makes the setting more comfortable and naturalistic (see in contrast Tono 2011: 151). The participants of our study had several tasks that were divided into two recurring blocks. Both blocks consisted of an instruction, a presentation of the screenshot (where gaze patterns were tracked) and, in most cases, a question after the presentation of the screenshot.

For a more natural setting, a live version of the portal would be better suited. In our case, this was not possible because a usability study with a live website is much more demanding.[4]

Thirty-eight people between the ages of 20 and 30 participated in our study. Our first research question was whether participants recognised that OWID is a dictionary portal. The cumulated fixation data can be visualised as a heat map (Figure 44.2). The two panels show fixation data after the first and the second instruction in comparison. First, we instructed

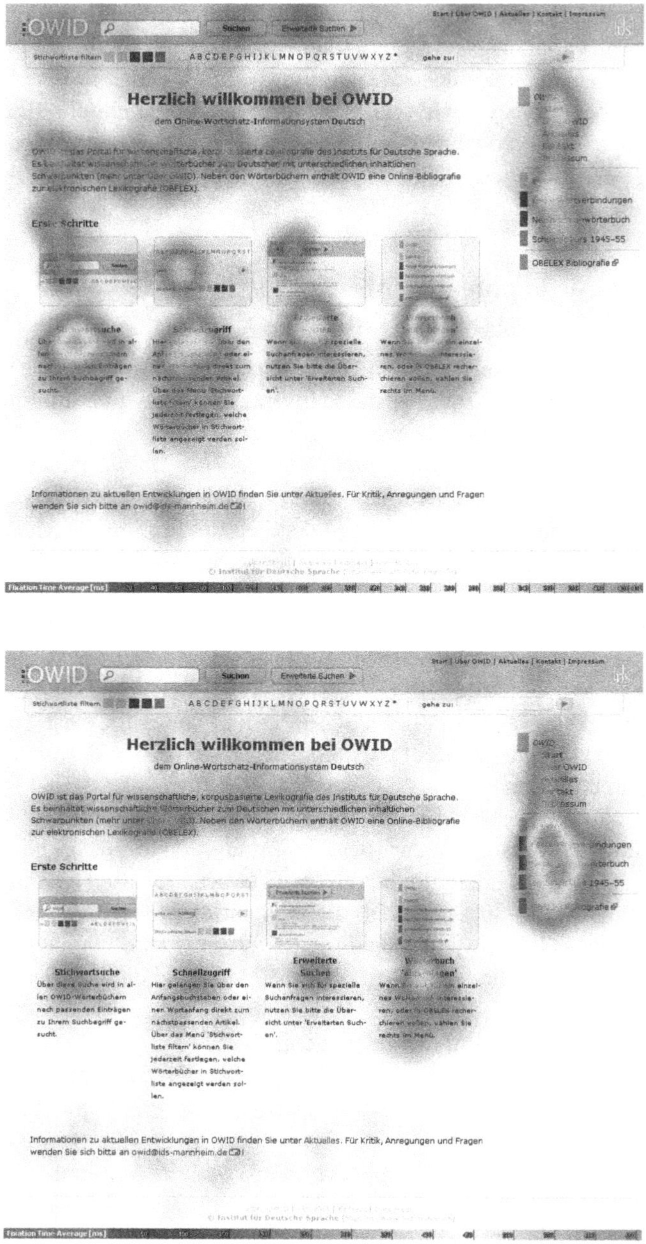

Figure 44.2 Heat map for all participants: (1) instruction: familiarise yourself with the homepage; (2) instruction: find out which dictionaries are included

participants to familiarise themselves with OWID. In the second step, we asked participants to find out which dictionaries are included in OWID. The difference between the fixation patterns in the left and the right panel suggests that participants recognised that the included dictionaries are listed on the right-hand side of the screen. From the first to second instruction, their attention shifts from the centre of the screen to the dictionary list on the right.

However, there would have been multiple possibilities to corroborate this interpretation. First, we could have added more variants of the screen layout with different arrangements and positions of the dictionary list. Second, the appearance of the dictionary list itself could have been altered in multiple ways to check whether the current design decision really is the most optimal. Third, the contrast to the old design would have been very interesting because it would have enabled us to evaluate whether the new design is truly beneficial.

The participants' second task was to identify which dictionary contains the presented article. This relates to our second research question: Are participants able to relate a headword to its respective dictionary? First, we instructed participants to identify the headword that is described in the article. In the second experimental block, we explicitly asked them to identify the dictionary containing the article. Figure 44.3 shows the contrast of these instructions by opposing two *scan paths* (sequence of fixations) of two participants to one another (heat maps are also available in Müller-Spitzer, Michaelis and Koplenig 2014). We can see how the participant in the second experimental block makes the connection between the headword and the respective dictionary. Also, the connection to the same-coloured words in the keyword list on the left can also be recognised in the scan path. This pattern is comparable across different dictionary entries. Again, the inclusion of other contrasts would have been desirable to achieve a more reliable interpretation of these results, but we did not compare these results with different screen layouts and also not with the old design.

The third research question was on whether users get distracted by the comments included in *elexiko*, one of the dictionaries that is integrated in OWID. These comments contain additional information which might be interesting to some users. The comments should be visible, but it would be counterproductive if they distracted the users' attention from the items themselves. The new OWID design therefore presents comments in a more subtle way (i.e. in lighter boxes). To evaluate the consequences of this style of comment, we presented two entries with items on word formation. The first item did not include a comment, the second did. This time, we varied the stimulus but used the same instruction in both experimental blocks: "Please determine which components the following word consists of".

The contrasting gaze patterns between the first (without comments) and second experimental block (with comments) are visualised in a heat map in Figure 44.4. Obviously, the comment did not attract that much attention. At least not to an extent that attention was drawn away from the information participants had to search for. Regarding this research question, our experimental design was more clear-cut than in previous experiments. We were interested in the contrast between entries with and without comments. Our choice of stimulus items reflects precisely this contrast. However, the contrast between different kinds of comment layout (e.g. lighter boxes vs. darker boxes) cannot be analysed with this experimental design.

As indicated earlier, our eye-tracking study was an exploratory attempt to investigate the new design of OWID. In retrospect, we should have integrated more contrastive views in order to check the positive consequences of our current design decisions. Contrasts might have been established to alternative design decisions and/or to the old design. The last analysis related to the comments in elexiko is one way of doing this. If the goal is a methodologically sound eye-tracking study, such contrasts are a good starting point.

44.3.3 Log files

Imagine a user typing a word or a phrase into the search bar of an online dictionary. In doing so, the user leaves a digital trace that contains different kinds of information: where the user

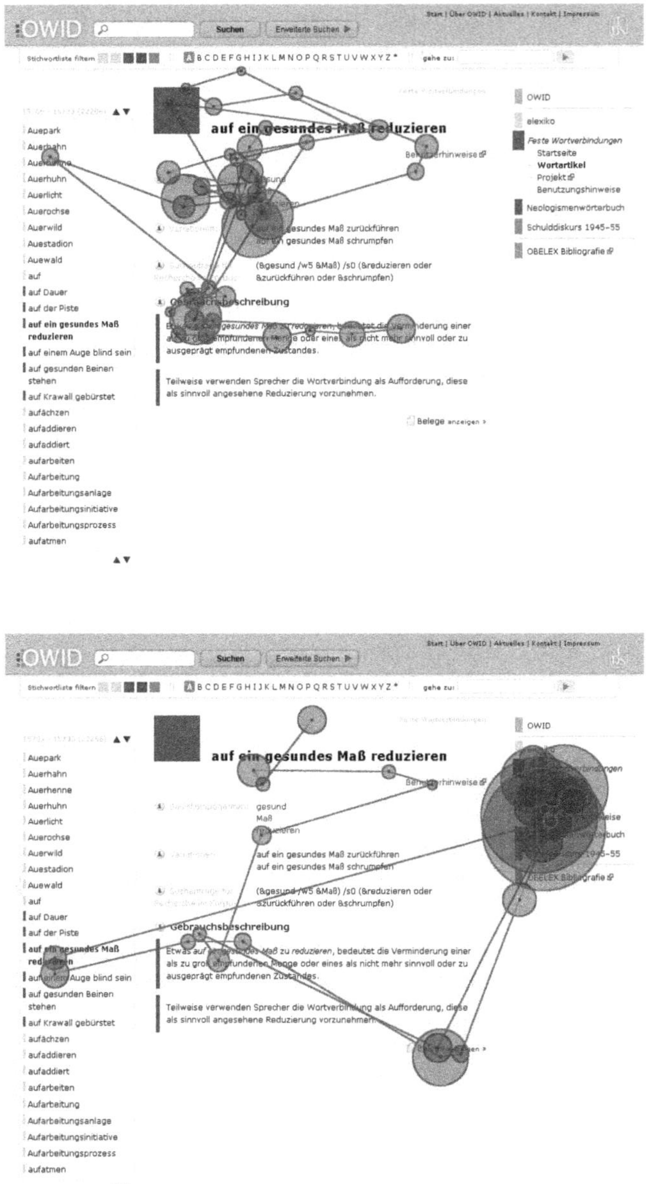

Figure 44.3 Scan paths of two participants: (1) instruction: which headword; (2) instruction: headword from which dictionary

comes from, how often she or he has already used the dictionary and, of course, what kind of word she or he was looking for and if the search was successful. A log file is a written record that contains the information associated with this event. Combining the log files from many such events is a special type of data collection method in dictionary usage research. These data are interesting as they arise directly from the normal use of online dictionaries

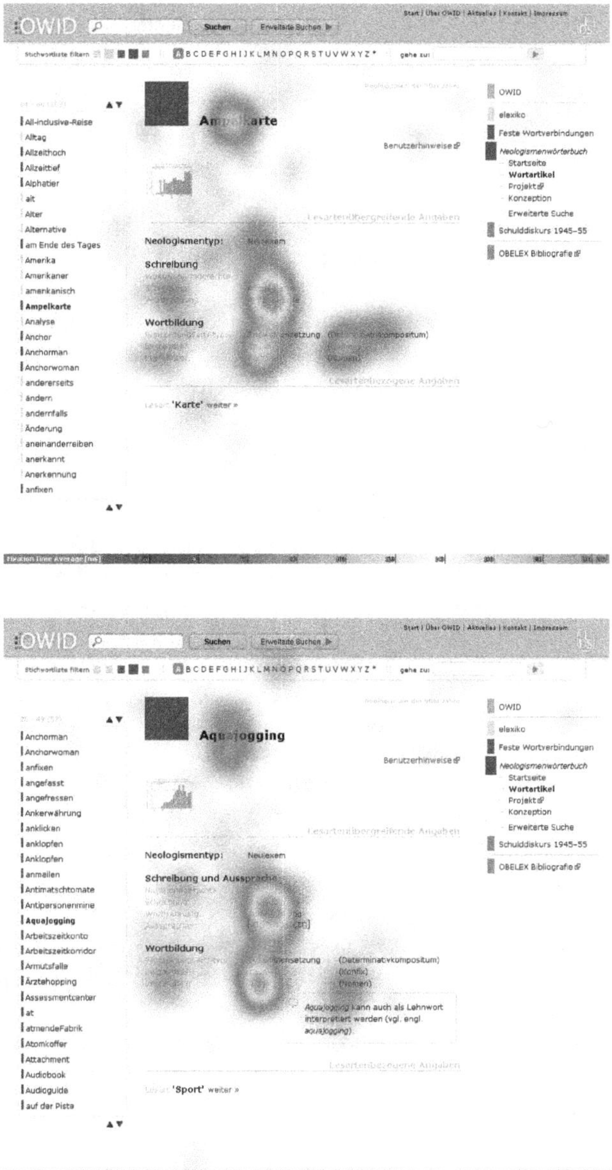

Figure 44.4 Heat map of all participants: items on word formation; (one with a comment on word formation, one without)

rather than within the context of a specifically designed test, for example, a survey or an eye-tracking study as described in the previous sections of this contribution. Those digital traces of the consultation behaviour of multiple users can be tracked and then analysed statistically over a long period, for example, in order to improve the dictionary (Bergenholtz and Johnsen 2005: 117).

44.3.3.1 Methodological basics

As indicated earlier, the analysis of log-file studies has the advantage that it enables the researcher to record real behaviour of dictionary users in a natural setting compared to the other two methods presented in this contribution (e.g. Bergenholtz and Johnsen 2005; De Schryver and Joffe 2006; De Schryver et al. 2006; Lew 2011; De Schryver 2013). Therefore, collecting log files can be considered as an unobtrusive method. In general, such a method can be understood as a method of data collection without the knowledge of the participant or the unit of interest. In contrast, obtrusive measurements are made when the researcher has "to intrude in the research context" (Trochim 2006). As survey participation or laboratory tests are also social interactions between the respondents and the researcher, respondents tend to present themselves in a favourable light. This is called *social desirability* (Diekmann 2002: 382–386). Furthermore, filling out a questionnaire or taking part in a laboratory test can be exhausting or boring, which may lead to biased results, too. Thus, the great advantage of unobtrusive methods, such as log-file analyses, is that the measurement does not influence what is measured. Without the knowledge of a participant, one can expect to measure his or her "actual behaviour as opposed to self-reported behaviour" (Kellehear 1993: 5).

In the next section, we will present an example of a log-file analysis in which we tried to answer the question of whether the inclusion of words in an online dictionary based on frequency of usage considerations (i.e. corpus frequency) makes sense.

44.3.3.2 Study: do dictionary users look up frequent words frequently?

As noted earlier, log files can be used to improve online dictionaries. For example, it is important for lexicographers to know which words are being looked up in dictionaries, as lexicographers usually want to satisfy the information needs of their users in the best way possible. It is also essential to know what users are interested in when a new dictionary is being compiled (in order to choose the right headwords for editing first). As most linguistic dictionaries today are corpus-based, one possible strategy for choosing the most important headwords could be to take the frequency of use in a corpus into account. To understand whether including words based on frequency of usage considerations makes sense for a new dictionary, it is a reasonable strategy to check whether dictionary users actually look up frequent words in other comparable dictionaries. Of course, in this specific case, it is not possible to design a survey (or an experiment) to ask potential users whether they prefer to look up frequent words or something similar. In this case, using log files as "the electronic trace of the dictionary user's consultation behaviour" (Lew 2011: 6) seems to be a promising research strategy. Therefore, our research question for this study was whether dictionary users look up frequent words frequently in a general linguistic dictionary. To conduct this study, we needed log-file data of a widely used dictionary (if a dictionary is used very sparsely, the log-file data does not have enough explanatory power for such a general research question). These criteria were met by the log files of the German *Wiktionary*.[5]

The Wikimedia Foundation publishes log files in the form of page-view statistics where all visits to any page are registered.[6] The log files contain information about all projects of the foundation (*Wikipedia*, *Wiktionary* and others). Here, we used the German *Wiktionary* log-file data from 2013; Table 44.4 gives an impression of the distribution. Almost two-thirds (65.44 percent) of all entries were visited once per 1 million visits during 2013. A quarter (26.75 percent) of the entries was visited between 2 and 10 times

Table 44.4 Distribution of the log-file data of the German *Wiktionary*

Category (visits per 1 million visits)	*Percentage in* Wiktionary *log files 2013*
1	65.44
2–10	26.75
11–49	6.70
50–500	1.10
500+	0.01
Total	*100 (abs. 163,100)*

per 1 million visits. Accordingly, only 7.81 percent were visited 11 times or more per 1 million visits.

This distributional profile is comparable to, for example, word lengths. Words that are very short are highly frequent in a language and make up the vast majority of all tokens within a language (Bentz and Ferrer-i-Cancho 2016). Longer words are very infrequent in comparison – just like entries in *Wiktionary* that are visited very often. In Koplenig et al. (2014), we argued that log-file and corpus-frequency data pose a serious challenge to standard statistical techniques, because of the unequal distribution of both log files (see Table 44.2) and word frequencies in corpora (Baayen 2008: 229). To answer our research question, we therefore employed something that we call a "simulation strategy". The idea is to compile several "imaginary dictionaries" that contain a specific number of words that are selected due to a certain criterion (e.g. corpus frequency) that we can control in detail. These dictionaries can then be compared to one another in terms of look-up frequency.

To further analyse the log-file data, we use the categories we introduced in Koplenig et al. (Koplenig, Meyer and Müller-Spitzer 2014: 240–242). If an entry was visited at least once per 1 million visits during 2013, we say it was visited "regularly". If it was visited at least twice per 1 million visits, we call it "frequently" visited. If it was visited at least 11 times per 1 million visits during 2013, we call it "very frequently" visited. Note that the boundaries and names of these categories are chosen arbitrarily and merely have an illustrative function.

Using the "simulation strategy" briefly introduced earlier, we now create several dictionaries, including more and more corpus frequency ranks based on *DeReKo* corpus data. This list contains frequency information for all spelled forms found in the German Reference Corpus (Kupietz et al. 2010: 1848). We then compare those dictionaries in terms of the proportion of entries visited regularly, frequently and very frequently. Table 44.5 clearly shows the relationship between the number of included *DeReKo* ranks and the number of visits. The "imaginary dictionaries" are represented in the left-most column in Table 44.5. The more corpus frequency ranks we include in our dictionary, the fewer proportions of entries are visited regularly, frequently and very frequently. Also, there are systematic differences between the look-up categories. In the first two tiny dictionaries with the first 10 and 50 most frequently described headwords, all entries are visited very frequently. If we consider the dictionary with the 2,000 most frequent headwords, there are already considerable differences between those categories. Still, almost all entries are visited regularly given the German *Wiktionary* log files of 2013. However, only 58 percent of all entries are visited very frequently. After a dictionary size of 500 entries, all categories diverge in terms

Table 44.5 Proportion of regularly, frequently and very frequently visited entries and their relationship to the number of included corpus frequency ranks

Included freq. Ranks	*% visited regularly*	*% visited frequently*	*% very frequently*
10	100	100	100
50	100	100	100
100	100	100	87.0
500	100	99.2	73.6
1000	99.9	97.0	65.7
2000	99.3	92.4	58.1
5000	97.2	82.2	45.5
10000	92.1	73.4	36.5
20000	83.4	64.5	27.9
30000	77.6	59.0	22.8
50000	69.2	51.2	17.2

of proportions. Finally, in the largest dictionary, which contains the first 50,000 frequency ranks, almost 70 percent of the entries are still visited regularly, but only roughly 17 percent are visited very frequently. So, obviously, there is a relationship between the number of corpus frequency ranks we include in our dictionary and the proportion of regularly, frequently and very frequently visited entries.

Based on this result, we can thus state that frequency information based on a corpus can be used fruitfully to decide which words to include in a general dictionary: frequent words in a corpus are indeed looked up frequently. The 2013 log files for the German *Wiktionary* support this statement as the 2012 data for *Wiktionary* and the *DWDS* dictionary did, too (Koplenig, Meyer and Müller-Spitzer 2014). However, we also want to emphasise that corpus frequency is not a cure-all or "magic answer" (as was pointed out by De Schryver et al. 2006: 78–79) when it comes to compiling dictionaries. If the aim of a lexicographical project is to provide a general description of a language's vocabulary, it simply is the best answer there is at the moment. If the aim is a specialised dictionary with a specific user group in mind, other criteria are relevant for selecting headword candidates (De Schryver and Prinsloo 2003; see e.g. Tarp 2008: 173–184; Granger and Paquot 2010; Bowker 2012).

Keep in mind though that log files are sensitive data that commercial publishers would never publish, because they are part of their business secrets. The Wikimedia products are therefore a valuable resource for research, because everyone can evaluate these resources for free and without copyright constraints. Generally, the analysis of log files does not permit any conclusions on an individual level if data privacy issues are taken seriously. We believe that this should always be the case. But also without this level of granularity, we hope that we have demonstrated that quantitative evaluations of log files can give profound insights into general patterns of look-up behaviour. Those evaluations can give "solid empirical evidence" (Lew 2011: 3) for questions such as the most frequently searched words in a dictionary or the connection between corpus frequency or grade of ambiguity and look-up frequency. In addition, social events and/or related linguistic discussions in social discourse can be observed by analysing log files beyond the intuitively expectable extent (Müller-Spitzer, Wolfer and Koplenig 2015). This makes it possible to draw conclusions on linguistic reflection, especially on the temporal relations between social events and look-up acts in dictionaries.

44.4 Conclusion

As mentioned in the beginning of this chapter, the situation for commercial dictionary publishers is difficult today because of the great success of free-to-use dictionaries on the Internet. At the same time, a myriad of lexical questions are researched on the Internet, presumably many more than ever in printed dictionaries. For example, we observed in the log-file data of the *German Wiktionary* that an uncommon word used in a sports commentary in a friendly match between the French and German football national team led to a sharp increase in look-ups within the same hour (Müller-Spitzer, Wolfer and Koplenig 2015: 21–22). Who would have used a printed dictionary in such a situation? However, the question is how these lexical needs and the questions people have can be most effectively united with existing lexicographic resources.

In our view, empirical data from dictionary usage studies can contribute essential data to analyse the needs of potential users, to bring them together with existing lexicographic tools and to point the way to future developments. The latter is particularly important, because the dictionary landscape will continue to change:

> While it is fairly uncontroversial that people will continue to have lexical needs in natural communication as well as in more or less artificial learning contexts, it is much less certain that dictionaries will persist for much longer, at least in the form as we know them today. Rather, it seems likely that dictionaries will increasingly become absorbed into more general digital tools designed to provide assistance with communication, expression, and information searching.
>
> (Lew 2015a: 7).

Therefore, dictionary usage research in the Internet era still has a lot of empirical work to do.

Related topics

Dictionary criticism; dictionary management; dictionaries and culture; user participation in the Internet era; Wordnik.

Further reading

Dziemanko, A. (2012). "On the Use(fulness) of Paper and Electronic Dictionaries", in S. Granger and M. Paquot (eds.), *Electronic Lexicography*. Oxford: Oxford University Press, pp. 320–341.
This work contains a good summary of user studies with the focus on printed vs. digital dictionaries, a topic which is not addressed in this chapter.

Tarp, S. (2009). "Reflections on Lexicographical User Research", *Lexikos* 19: 275–296.
This article also gives an introductory overview over the research field described in this chapter, but focuses more on the function theory of lexicography.

Töpel, A. (2014). "Review of Research Into the Use of Electronic Dictionaries", in C. Müller-Spitzer (ed.), *Using Online Dictionaries*, Berlin: De Gruyter, pp. 13–54.
This article provides a good overview on dictionary user studies already conducted within the context of digital lexicography.

Notes

1 See at www.owid.de/obelex/dict
2 Michael Rundell, Editor-in-chief, Macmillan Dictionaries, Euralex Mailing list, 11 June 2012.
3 See at www.owid.de
4 One reason why eye-tracking studies with live web pages are very time consuming is that the stimulus itself (the web page) is dynamic. Participants scroll, navigate to other pages and so on. If we want to map fixations on dynamic content, we have to annotate the stimulus with time information which has to be done mostly manually.
5 https://de.wiktionary.org
6 See at http://wikimediafoundation.org

References

Baayen, R.H. (2008) *Analyzing Linguistic Data. A Practical Introduction to Statistics*. Cambridge: Cambridge University Press.

Bentz, C. and R. Ferrer-i-Cancho (2016) "Zipf's Law of Abbreviation as a Language Universal", in C. Bentz, G. Jäger and I. Yanovich (eds.), *Proceedings of the Leiden Workshop on Capturing Phylogenetic Algorithms for Linguistics*. Tübingen: University of Tübingen. Available at: https://publikationen.uni-tuebingen.de/xmlui/handle/10900/68558.

Bergenholtz, H. and M. Johnsen (2005) "Log Files as a Tool for Improving Internet Dictionaries", *Hermes* 34: 117–141.

Bogaards, P. (2003) "Uses and Users of Dictionaries", in P. van Sterkenburg (ed.), *A Practical Guide to Lexikography*. Amsterdam/Philadelphia: John Benjamins Publishing Company, pp. 26–33.

Bowker, L. (2012) "Meeting the Needs of Translators in the Age of e-Lexicography: Exploring the Possibilities", in S. Granger and M. Paquot (eds.), pp. 379–397.

De Schryver, G.-M. de (2013) "Tools to Support the Design of a Macrostructure", in R. H. Gouws, U. Heid, W. Schweickard, and H. E. Wiegand (eds.), pp. 1384–1395.

De Schryver, G.-M. and D. Joffe (2006) "The Users and Uses of TshwaneLex One", in G.-M. De Schryver (ed.), *Fourth International Workshop on Dictionary Writing Systems*. Turin, 5 September, 2006. Pretoria: SF Press, pp. 41–46.

De Schryver, G.-M., D. Joffe, P. Joffe and S. Hillewaert (2006) "Do Dictionary Users Really Look Up Frequent Words? – on the Overestimation of the Value of Corpus-Based Lexicography", *Lexikos* 16: 67–83.

De Schryver, G.-M. and D. J. Prinsloo (2003) "Compiling a Lemma-Sign List for a Specific Target User Group: The Junior Dictionary as a Case in Point", *Dictionaries* 24: 28–58.

Diekmann, A. (2002) *Empirische Sozialforschung: Grundlagen, Methoden, Anwendungen*. 8th edition. Reinbek: Rowohlt Taschenbuch Verlag.

Diekmann, A. (2010) *Empirische Sozialforschung: Grundlagen, Methoden, Anwendungen*. 4th edition. Hamburg: Rowohlt.

Duchowski, A. (2007) *Eye Tracking Methodology: Theory and Practice*. London: Springer-Verlag London Limited. http://dx.doi.org/10.1007/978-1-84628-609-4 (Accessed 12 June 2013).

Dziemanko, A. (2012) "On the Use(fulness) of Paper and Electronic Dictionaries", in S. Granger and M. Paquot (eds.), pp. 320–341.

Granger, S. (2012) "Introduction: Electronic Lexicography – From Challenge to Opportunity", in S. Granger and M. Paquot (eds.), pp. 1–11.

Granger, S. and M. Paquot (2010) "The Louvain EAP Dictionary", in A. Dykstra and T. Schoonheim (eds.), *XIV EURALEX International Congress*. Leeuwarden/Ljouwert, pp. 321–326.

Granger, S. and M. Paquot (eds.) (2012) *Electronic Lexicography*. Oxford: Oxford University Press.

Gouws, R. H., U. Heid, W. Schweickard and H. E. Wiegand (eds.) (2013) *Dictionaries: An International Encyclopedia of Lexicography Supplementary Volume: Recent Developments with Focus on Electronic and Computational Lexicography*. Berlin, Boston, MA: Mouton de Gruyter.

Hyönä, J., R. Radach and H. Deubel (eds.) (2003) *The Mind's Eye: Cognitive and Applied Aspects of Eye Movement Research*. Amsterdam, Boston, MA: North-Holland.

Just, M. A. and P. A. Carpenter (1980) "A Theory of Reading: From Eye Fixations to Comprehension", *Psychological Review* 87(4): 329–354.

Kellehear, A. (1993) *The Unobtrusive Researcher: A Guide to Methods*. St. Leonards, NSW: Allen & Unwin Pty LTD.

Klosa, A., A. Koplenig and A. Töpel (2014) "Benutzerwünsche und -meinungen zu dem monolingualen deutschen Onlinewörterbuch elexiko", in C. Müller-Spitzer (ed.), pp. 281–384.

Koplenig, A. (2014) "Empirical Research into Dictionary Use", in C. Müller-Spitzer (ed.), pp. 55–76.

Koplenig, A., P. Meyer and C. Müller-Spitzer (2014) "Dictionary Users Do Look Up Frequent Words: A Log File Analysis", in C. Müller-Spitzer (ed.), pp. 229–250.

Koplenig, A. and C. Müller-Spitzer (2014) "Questions of Design", in C. Müller-Spitzer (ed.), pp. 189–204.

Kupietz, M., C. Belica, H. Keibel and A. Witt. (2010) "The German Reference Corpus ReReKo: A Primordial Sample for Linguistic Research", in N. Calzolari, K. Choukri, B. Maegaard, J. Mariani, J. Odijk, S. Piperidis, M. Rosner and D. Tapias (eds.), *Proceedings of the 7th Conference on International Language Resources and Evaluation (LREC 2010)*. Valetta: European Language Resources Association (ELRA), pp. 1848–1854.

Lew, R. (2010) "Users Take Shortcuts: Navigating Dictionary Entries", in A. Dykstra and T. Schoonheim (eds.) *Proceedings of the XIV Euralex International Congress*. Ljouwert: Afûk, pp. 1121–1132.

Lew, R. (2011) "Studies in Dictionary Use. Recent Developments", *International Journal of Lexicography* 26(4), 1-4.

Lew, R. (2012) "How Can We Make Electronic Dictionaries More Effective?", in S. Granger and M. Paquot (eds.), pp. 343–361.

Lew, R. (2015a) "Dictionaries and Their Users", in P. Hanks and G-M de Schryver (eds.) *International Handbook of Modern Lexis and Lexicography*. Berlin/Heidelberg: Springer. DOI 10.1007/978-3-642-45369-4_11-1

Lew, R. (2015b) "Research into the Use of Online Dictionaries", *International Journal of Lexicography*, 28(2): 232–253.

Lew, R., M. Grzelak and M. Leszkowicz (2013) "How Dictionary Users Choose Senses in Bilingual Dictionary Entries: An Eye-Tracking Study", *Lexikos* 23: 228–254.

Lew, R. and P. Tokarek (2010) "Entry Menus in Bilingual Electronic Dictionaries", in S. Granger and M. Paquot (eds.), *eLexicography in the 21st Century: New Challenges, New Applications*. Louvain-la-Neuve: Cahiers du CENTAL, pp. 145–146.

Madans, J., K. Miller, A. Maitland and G. Willis (eds.) (2011) *Experiments for Evaluating Survey Questions*. New York: John Wiley & Sons.

Mayring, P. (2011) *Qualitative Inhaltsanalyse: Grundlagen und Techniken*. 8th edition. Weinheim: Beltz.

Müller-Spitzer, C. (ed.) (2014a) *Using Online Dictionaries*. Berlin, New York: de Gruyter.

Müller-Spitzer, C. (2014b) "Empirical Data on Contexts of Dictionary Use", in C. Müller-Spitzer (ed.), pp. 85–126.

Müller-Spitzer, C. and A. Koplenig (2014) "Online Dictionaries: Expectations and Demands", in C. Müller-Spitzer (ed.), pp. 143–188.

Müller-Spitzer, C., F. Michaelis and A. Koplenig (2014) "Evaluation of a New Web Design for the Dictionary Portal OWID: An Attempt at Using Eye-Tracking Technology", in C. Müller-Spitzer (ed.), pp. 207–228.

Müller-Spitzer, C., S. Wolfer and A. Koplenig (2015) "Observing Online Dictionary Users: Studies Using Wiktionary Log Files", *International Journal of Lexicography* 28(1): 1–26. doi: 10.1093/ijl/ecu029.

Nesi, H. and K. H. Tan (2011) "The Effect of Menus and Signposting on the Speed and Accuracy of Sense Selection", *International Journal of Lexicography* 24(1): 79.

Sharifi, S. (2012) "General Monolingual Persian Dictionaries and Their Users: A Case Study", in J. M. Torjusen and R. V. Fjeld (eds.), *Proceedings of the 15th EURALEX International Congress 2012, Oslo, Norway, 7–11 August 2012*. Oslo: Universitetet i Oslo, Institutt for lingvistiske og nordiske studier, pp. 626–639. www.euralex.org/elx_proceedings/Euralex2012/pp626-639%20Sharifi.pdf.

Tarp, S. (2008) *Lexicography in the Borderland between Knowledge and Non-Knowledge: General Lexicographical Theory with Particular Focus on Learner's Lexicography*. Tübingen: Niemeyer.

Tarp, S. (2009) "Reflections on Lexicographical User Research", *Lexikos* 19: 275–296.

Tono, Y. (2000) "On the Effects of Different Types of Electronic Dictionary Interfaces on L 2 Learners' Reference Behaviour in Productive/Receptive Tasks", in U. Heid, S. Evert, E. Lehmann and C. Rohrer (eds.), *Proceedings of the Ninth EURALEX International Congress, Stuttgart, Germany, August 8th–12th*. Stuttgart: Universität Stuttgart, Institut für Maschinelle Sprachverarbeitung, pp. 855–861.

Tono, Y. (2011) "Application of Eye-Tracking in EFL Learners' Dictionary Look-Up Process Research", *International Journal of Lexicography* 24(1): 124–153.

Töpel, A. (2014) "Review of Research into the Use of Electronic Dictionaries", in C. Müller-Spitzer (ed.), pp. 13–54.

Trochim, W. (2006) *Design, Research Methods Knowledge Base*. www.socialresearchmethods.net/kb/design.php (Accessed 14 September 2011).

Welker, H. A. (2013) "Empirical Research into Dictionary Use since 1990", in R. H. Gouws, U. Heid, W. Schweickard and H. E. Wiegand (eds.), pp. 531–540.

Wiegand, H. E. (1998) *Wörterbuchforschung: Untersuchungen zur Wörterbuchbenutzung, zur Theorie, Geschichte, Kritik und Automatisierung der Lexikographie*. Berlin u.a.: Walter de Gruyter.

Wiegand, H. E., M. Beißwenger, R. H. Gouws, M. Kammerer, A. Storrer and W. Wolski (2010) *Wörterbuch zur Lexikographie und Wörterbuchforschung: mit englischen Übersetzungen der Umtexte und Definitionen sowie Äquivalenten in neuen Sprachen*. Berlin: de Gruyter.

45

User participation in the Internet era

Christian M. Meyer and Andrea Abel

45.1 Introduction

Online mass collaboration and user participation have been major driving forces in the development of the World Wide Web during the last fifteen years. The role of a web user has significantly changed from a passive consumer of carefully redacted content to an active *prosumer* (Lew 2014: 9), who contributes to the development of a website by producing new content or making revisions, while at the same time being interested in consuming information contributed by others.

This development also changed the relationship between any recent electronic reference work (i.e. dictionary or encyclopaedia) and its users. Both academic and commercial lexicographic publishers face the question of which types of user participation exist, which of them meet the needs of a given project, and how they affect the project's plan, implementation, and maintenance.

The emergence of the World Wide Web has not only changed the way humans deal with information and thus how dictionaries and encyclopaedias are made, but also the role and business models of major publishers and institutions. To date, the Web offers a plethora of data, and vast parts of the society expect to find answers to practically any question in real time and free of charge. This raises the important question to which extent novel types of user participation can benefit or inhibit the development of a reference work.

The case of the collaboratively created *Wikipedia* emphasizes the importance of this question: *Wikipedia* is by far the largest encyclopaedia worldwide with versions in almost 300 languages. It is among the most often visited websites in the world[1] and likely the most popular social web service (Weller et al. 2010).

At the same time, established publishers of expert-built encyclopaedias changed their strategies. The *Encyclopædia Britannica*, for example, invited users to write encyclopaedic articles.[2] The German *Brockhaus Enzyklopädie* reported severe economic loss and announced the end of direct sale, which was partly attributed to the development of *Wikipedia*.[3] For dictionaries, we can observe similar developments fostering the need for revised products, workflows, and business models (Pearsall 2013).

As a consequence, we find that the relation between a lexicographic reference work and its users is more important than ever, although this is yet only cursorily addressed in the metalexicographic research community as well as in practical guidelines for planning and implementing electronic reference works.

In this chapter, we first review previous works and comment on the historical perspective of user participation before the era of the World Wide Web. At the core of the chapter, we introduce user participation as a new field of metalexicographic research, and we present a unified framework covering the three major types of user participation methods, ranging from newly creating entire articles and giving feedback and correcting errors to discussing language- or subject-related questions beyond the actual lexicographic descriptions. We describe each method in detail and give numerous practical examples. Finally, we discuss quality issues and how the proposed classification of user participation methods helps when planning and developing a reference work. User participation research concerns dictionaries and encyclopaedias alike. In this chapter, we put a particular focus on dictionaries, but also reach out to encyclopaedic works at multiple occasions (see Chapter 15 of this *Handbook*, which deals with the concept of "dictionary").

45.2 Historical perspective and previous work

The compilation of dictionaries and encyclopaedias has traditionally been the profession of a single expert or small groups of professional lexicographers and subject specialists. However, there is a long tradition of incorporating feedback from users. The *Oxford English Dictionary*, for example, initiated reading programmes already in the nineteenth century, in which they asked volunteers to read books and submit evidence for a word's usage in a specific format. Thier (2014) gives a detailed overview about the history of involving users in the development of the *Oxford English Dictionary* (see Chapter 33 of this *Handbook*).

Prior to the invention of the World Wide Web, user participation was, however, mostly limited to giving feedback to an expert-built product and communicating with its publishers. Carr (1997: 214) introduces the term *bottom-up lexicography* as the "most significant transformation" of electronic lexicography. Instead of creating a dictionary "top-down", from editor, through publishers, to readers, the Web allows for "bottom-up" approaches yielding a dictionary composed of multiple individual user contributions.

Storrer and Freese (1996) and Storrer (1998) aim at a first classification by distinguishing error corrections, suggestions for new headwords, contributions by a domain expert, and contributions by lay users. Køhler Simonsen (2005) defines *active user involvement* as using surveys and test groups to collect user feedback during the development of a lexicographic product and *lexicographic democracy* as feedback on final articles (e.g. error corrections). Although this definition is limited to giving feedback to the editorial staff, Fuertes-Olivera (2009) uses the term *democratization* differently: He considers *collective free multiple-language Internet dictionaries* (ibid.: p. 101) such as *Wikipedia* and *Wiktionary*, which are compiled entirely by users. Storrer (2010) makes a similar distinction between user contributions carefully checked by professional editors and those that are the result of a collaborative effort in a self-organized product. Further works by Lew (2011 and 2014) suggest a more detailed classification of dictionaries that allow for direct user contributions, including *collaborative-institutional dictionaries* and dictionaries making use of external *user-generated content*. Melchior (2012 and 2014) introduced the term *semi-collaborative dictionary* as being supported by users rather than generated by users.

In a different strand of research, de Schryver and Prinsloo (2001) coined the term *fuzzy simultaneous feedback* to refer to user feedback available during the development of a lexicographic product. De Schryver and Joffe (2004) focus primarily on log-file analyses, which are a way to explore a user's behaviour and demands without additional effort by the users.

45.3 Core issues and topics: user participation research

Research into user participation in online dictionaries and encyclopaedias is a comparatively young topic area (Wiegand et al. 2010: 17). It has not developed as an own field of research yet, but has been rather selectively treated in a variety of different studies focusing on one specific type of user participation. Although those studies became increasingly detailed, the field is currently lacking a commonly agreed upon and consistent terminology.

Against this background, we face the challenge of integrating the isolated works on user participation as an independent field into the metalexicographic research environment. Research into dictionary use (see Müller-Spitzer 2014 and Chapter 44 of this *Handbook*) is closely linked to the analysis of user participation, because the publishers of a reference work can get valuable insights about designing and structuring a product based on how the users participate and how they interact with the user interface. Nonetheless, we consider user participation research as a separate field of metalexicography, because it raises new research questions regarding the analysis and development of user participation; the meaningful selection and implementation of suitable methods when planning a product; and the evaluation of motivational factors, quality, legal restrictions, and effectiveness of user participation methods, which yield a topic area in its own right. Besides the tight connection to dictionary usage research, we consider user participation research as a cross-cutting concern for almost all activities of the lexicographic process (Klosa and Tiberius 2016; Meyer 2013), because it affects a project's planning, implementation, and publication. Beyond the lexicographic community, we consider the social and cognitive sciences, as well as web engineering and human-computer interaction, as highly relevant neighbouring fields.

As a first milestone concerning the investigation of user participation, we bring together several previous works and introduce a unified framework for classifying user activities and contributions. We consider this framework to be especially helpful during the planning and development phases of a dictionary or encyclopaedia and for working towards a scientific community around user participation research. Our classification originates from Mann's (2010) criterion 4 of his analysis of 88 online dictionaries. He distinguishes *direct* from *indirect contributions* as well as dictionaries allowing for *an exchange with other dictionary users*.

Table 45.1 Top-level items of our unified framework for classifying user participation in electronic reference works

Direct user participation	*Indirect user participation*	*Accessory user participation*
• Contributions to open-collaborative dictionaries • Contributions to collaborative-institutional dictionaries • Contributions to semi-collaborative dictionaries	• Explicit feedback • Implicit feedback	• Exchange between publishers and users • Exchange among dictionary users

In Abel and Meyer (2013 and 2016), we substantially go beyond this work and suggest multiple fine-grained distinctions which we explain below using a wide range of practical examples. Table 45.1 shows an overview of our proposed unified framework.

Within the international 'Academic Network of Internet Lexicography'[4] we further developed this classification, which led to the organisation of a dedicated symposium entitled 'Your contribution, please! – The user contribution in the dictionary process' at the 2013 GAL conference 'Wörter – Wissen – Wörterbücher' (Abel and Klosa 2014) and a 2014 EURALEX pre-conference workshop[5] focussing on the quality of dictionaries in the digital age – including a strong focus on user participation and a debate of their strengths and weaknesses.

Our proposed framework was already fruitfully used for the pan-European survey 'Online Dictionaries, Dictionary Portals and their Users' (hereafter: ENeL survey) conducted 2015/2016 in the context of the COST Action 'European Network of e-Lexicography' (ENeL)[6] and for organising a respective workshop.[7] For the first time, an empirical study aimed at collecting information about user participation in scholarly dictionaries and dictionary portals throughout Europe. The results from 56 dictionary projects demonstrated, among other findings, that direct user contributions are usually checked before publishing. In the majority of cases, explicit feedback concerning dictionary content and technical issues was received by e-mail, phone, or letter and preferred over filling online forms with a predefined structure. Besides suggesting new content, some projects also asked their users to rate examples and translations. More than 90 percent of the dictionary projects gather implicit feedback, whereas the predominant case was the use of webserver log files yielding insight into dictionary use. The dictionary publishers additionally promote different types of interaction with dictionary users, e.g. using social media blogs and forums, online courses, and radio broadcasts. In general, the exploitation of user contributions is perceived as a (too) time-consuming task in current projects, which raises important questions for user participation research. For a better understanding of the characteristics of the different types of user participation, we introduce and exemplify them in more detail in the following sections.

45.3.1 Direct user participation

Direct user participation refers to all user contributions which directly affect the content of a lexicographic product. This ranges from making error corrections to writing entire articles. We distinguish contributions to open-collaborative, collaborative-institutional, and semi-collaborative products, which differ in the publisher's role and the users' scope of action.

Open-collaborative lexicographic products consist entirely of user-contributed content. The most prominent examples are *Wikipedia*, an open-collaborative encyclopaedia, and *Wiktionary*, its dictionary counterpart. In these products, there is no fixed group of experts monitoring the user contributions (i.e. no professional editors). Instead, any change becomes directly visible to other users, who may revise the article over again. Consequently, the contributions are not limited to writing entire articles, but also allow for starting a (yet incomplete) article, making minor or substantial revisions, correcting errors, and deleting content that does not fulfil certain quality constraints or contain copyright infringement.

Collaborative-institutional products are offered by established publishers or institutions, for example, the *Merriam-Webster Open Dictionary* and the *Macmillan Open Dictionary*. The user contributions to these products are usually complete lexicographic articles, which are checked for vandalism and offence by the publishers prior to being published. The content of the contributed articles remains, however, largely unedited, yielding a heterogeneous collection of lexicographic descriptions. Other users may browse the contributed articles but not revise or delete them as it is the case in open-collaborative products.

User contributions to *semi-collaborative products* are the third type of involving users directly in the lexicographic work. These contributions are collected at a large scale and carefully checked by experts before being integrated. The *TechDictionary* is, for example, based on user contributions of computer- and technology-related terminology. While the editors of a semi-collaborative work critically assess the user contributions, they typically do not extensively edit them as it is the case for *explicit feedback* discussed in the next section. There are multiple translation dictionaries, such as *LEO* and *dict.cc* that consist mostly of user-contributed translations and donated terminology and word lists.

In all three types of direct user participation, a contribution – if accepted – directly affects the dictionary content without being extensively edited by professional lexicographers. The *collective intelligence* of the contributing users – also called *human swarm intelligence* (Rosenberg 2015) or the *wisdom of crowds* (Surowiecki 2005) – is supposed to yield a group-dynamic process consolidating the subjective views and opinions of the participating users as a substitute for expert knowledge. Meyer and Gurevych (2012) propose the term *collaborative lexicography* to describe this novel paradigm of compiling dictionaries and encyclopaedias.

In the remaining section, we discuss the motivation, sources, and quality of direct user contributions as well as the lexicographic instructions, user interfaces, and input formats used.

A lexicographic work involving users directly can potentially benefit from a large diversity of users covering many different skills, domains, languages, etc. Meyer (2013) argues that this yields a particular added value for describing language varieties (e.g. dialect, jargon, technical terminology) as well as translations between infrequent language pairs.

Malone et al. (2010) investigate the motivation of the users to contribute to collaborative products. They distinguish *money* (immediate or delayed financial gain, training of personal skills), *love* (enjoyment, altruism, socialization), and *glory* (recognition by peers) as the major driving forces. Rafaeli and Ariel (2008) and Lampe et al. (2010) introduce additional motivational factors, such as obtaining and exchanging information, identification, and allegiance to a group.

The publishers of collaborative products typically follow a different motivation. In open-collaborative and semi-collaborative products, user contributions are the backbone of the lexicographic database, as little to no professional lexicographers are involved. Instead, collaborative-institutional products use the contributed articles to improve a professional lexicographic work offered by the publisher. Macmillan, for instance, added the article *hypocaust*[8] to the *Macmillan Dictionary Online* and attributed the description to a user of the *Macmillan Open Dictionary*. If a collaborative-institutional project accompanies a publisher's major lexicographic product, then there are typically fewer articles in the collaborative part, as users focus on articles which do not already exist in the professional work. In some cases, the publishers of a collaborative-institutional product aim at a specific vocabulary or language variety, such as young people's language (e.g. *Duden Szenesprachenwiki*).

Although collaborative products can attract a huge number of users, Naber (2005) finds for the semi-collaborative *OpenThesaurus*, a German synonymy dictionary, that only a small fraction of the registered users actively contribute to the dictionary and that a small group of users make the vast majority of contributions. Similar findings have been reported for *Wikipedia* (Javanmardi et al. 2009) and *Wiktionary* (Meyer 2013). The unequal distribution of the number of contributions per user is called *power law* or *long tail distribution* in statistics, which is known to hold for scale-free networks typically observed for the communities of online mass collaboration platforms.

Most user contributions to open-collaborative projects are published under open-content licenses, such as *Creative Commons* licenses.[9] Other than traditional copyright models, these licenses allow for reusing and sharing a user's contribution – depending on the license type even in commercial products (see Kreutzer 2014).

For contributions to collaborative-institutional and semi-collaborative products, the publishers often do not use open-content licenses, but the copyrights either remain by the users or are transferred to the publisher. The latter allows for integrating or reusing the contributed material in other lexicographic projects without having to negotiate with the contributors later on.

Apart from the license for the user contributions, the sources and the original ownership of the contributed content is a highly relevant question. Detecting and removing copyright infringements is a major challenge for the publishers of collaborative products. Although plagiarism is not a new phenomenon in lexicography (Hausmann 1989), the electronic means and the large number of users elevates this question to a new level. The large communities around *Wikipedia* and *Wiktionary*, for instance, defined extensive guidelines[10] for dealing with copyright issues. A crucial goal of these two projects is to provide references for most lexicographic descriptions, such that items of dubious origin can be discussed and, where necessary, deleted.

By the same token, open-collaborative products make use of copyright-free sources or sources whose copyright has expired. Some articles of the English *Wiktionary* are, for example, based on a digitized version of *Webster's Revised Unabridged Dictionary* from 1913, which is no longer protected by copyright. Although these imported articles should be revised by the community to adapt them to present-day language, Hanks (2012) and Lew (2014) notice multiple outdated sense descriptions and usage examples that do not reflect current language use, but originate from reusing copyright-expired material.

The quality of lexicographic descriptions in general and of those contributed by lay users in particular is a still cursorily researched topic. We can distinguish low-quality contributions containing spam and vandalism from contributions that are unspecific, wrong, outdated, or overly complex. Spam and vandalism are particular problems in open-collaborative products, as any changes are directly published and thus have to be cleaned up within a short time. In *Wikipedia* and *Wiktionary*, there are dedicated counter-vandalism units that aim at identifying and removing spam.[11] Though the publishers of collaborative-institutional and semi-collaborative products face similar problems, the corresponding contributions are not directly published. Thus, they can just ignore spam or use automatic prefiltering.

Assuring the correctness and usefulness of the lexicographic descriptions is an even more challenging task, because we lack operationalised quality criteria even for professional reference works (Kemmer 2010). In open-collaborative projects, the quality should be improved by iteratively revising an article. Because a user might not be capable of fixing every recognised issue, some projects allow for adding maintenance tags indicating a need to check, revise, extend, or delete a certain description. Meyer and Gurevych (2014) discuss quality assurance methods in *Wiktionary*.

A number of collaborative products enforce their lexicographic instructions by using a predefined setup of input boxes in the online user interface. The *Urban Dictionary*, for example, sets a clear focus on colloquial language and asks its users to submit a sense description, a usage example, and a number of tags for a new lemma. Many translation dictionaries follow the same principle, as they are based on a simple data model. *Glosbe*, for example, provides merely two input fields capturing a lemma and its translation. Similarly, the *Refugee Phrasebook* makes use of a spreadsheet that allows for adding phrase translations in multiple languages at the same time. Besides these simple user interfaces, there are reference works that use more complex data models distinguishing multiple item types (e.g. part of speech, pronunciation, multiple usage examples, citations). The *Kamusi Project* provides a complex user interface with multiple input fields and steps.

A different approach to collect direct user contributions is using *markup languages*. Instead of providing a fixed setup of input fields, users can change the entire article within a single text field. The different types of lexicographic items are distinguished using a specific syntax to express typographic formatting (e.g. italics) or complex logical units (e.g. a headword's pronunciation). Although professional reference works typically use XML-based markup languages (e.g. following TEI or LMF standards) and specialised XML editors, this setup is less suitable for collaborative products, because the XML syntax and the corresponding software may require extensive training. Instead, multiple collaborative projects use wikis. The wiki technology proved especially useful for encyclopaedic content (e.g. in *Wikipedia*), but it is also applied for compiling dictionaries (e.g. for the *Rap Dictionary*), because the wiki markup language is easy to learn and thus lowers the inhibition threshold.

Matuschek et al. (2013) compare the wiki-based *Wiktionary* with *OmegaWiki*, a dictionary with fixed data structure and a predefined set of input fields. They discuss the trade-off between achieving a consistent article layout when using a fixed data structure and allowing for a more expressive and flexible layout when using a wiki markup language. The former approach does not permit deviations and exceptions in an article's structure; however, the latter makes it possible to change the lexicographic instructions iteratively without breaking existing articles – albeit at the cost of an inconsistent article layout.

45.3.2 Indirect user participation

Indirect user participation refers to feedback given by users to existing or missing lexicographic content, to the reference work as a whole, or to its effective usage. It may include suggestions, corrections, supplementary material, external user-generated content, and usage data. Unlike for direct user participation methods, users cannot directly modify the content of a dictionary or encyclopaedia, but only induce changes indirectly. We discriminate between explicit and implicit feedback depending on whether users submit their contributions consciously.

By *explicit feedback* we refer to contributions intentionally submitted by a user to the publishers, including suggestions and error corrections of new content (e.g. to fill lemma gaps) and of already existing content (e.g. to provide illustrative usage examples, to indicate unclear definitions or erroneous entries, or to comment on the presentation of a lexicographic articles). Explicit feedback is widely used by established publishers and institutions, for example, for the *Oxford English Dictionary* or *Duden online*, and by different types of collaborative reference works, such as the *LEO* dictionaries.

In contrast to this first type of feedback, *implicit feedback* is generated without any user effort – often without their awareness. Implicit feedback is entirely based on a user's interaction with and usage of the reference work (e.g. used by *Duden online* or the *Base lexicale du français*) or on external user-generated content, such as images, which users originally created for another, typically non-lexicographic, purposes (e.g. used by *Wordnik*). In the remaining section, we will discuss these two types of indirect user participation in detail.

Users can give explicit feedback in different ways. At a general level, we distinguish between *form-based feedback*, which enforces a certain feedback structure by providing a predefined set of form fields, and *free form feedback*, which allows for submitting any text (e.g. by e-mail or using free text fields) as well as combinations of both. Using the example of the *LEO* dictionary portal and the online version of the *Oxford English Dictionary*, we discuss these two types of explicit feedback in more detail.

The use of form-based feedback has the advantage that the type, structure, and even quantity of the submissions can be controlled to some extent. The *LEO* dictionaries provide, for instance, different web forms for reporting errors and for suggesting new lemmas.[12] This automatically yields a presorting of the submissions. The web forms in *LEO* are characterised by providing only a few, but obligatory fields. In contrast, the *Oxford English Dictionary* provides a very detailed web form with multiple mandatory and optional fields.[13] As large forms may present a significant inhibition threshold for users, one can expect fewer, but more accurate, submissions (Thier 2014).

Publishers often react to free-form feedback submitted by letter or e-mail. As such free-form feedback might be much more diverse in terms of suggestions, structure, and extent, and publishers may provide guidelines about what to include or what is of interest or have their users presort their contributions (e.g. defining a certain mail address or subject). The *Oxford English Dictionary* aims at controlling for this type of feedback by initiating focused campaigns such as the search for science fiction citations, which ask participants to follow specific rules when submitting their free-form feedback.[14] The same holds for the 'Wordhunt' appeal aimed at the collection of verifiable evidence of a word's first usage (Thier 2014).[15]

In addition to the feedback to specific dictionary or encyclopaedic articles, users can comment on the reference work as a whole, including organisational, content-related, and design issues. Melchior (2012) discusses the conflicting opinions of different types of users regarding the content of the *LEO* dictionary German-Italian. Some users argue, for example, in favour of adding newly coined terms even though they might be used only for a short period of time. This conflicts with other users complaining about overfull search results.

These two dictionary examples show that there is a smooth transition between direct participation in semi-collaborative dictionaries and indirect contributions based on explicit feedback. In fact, a single reference work may utilise different types of user participation at the same time. Although the submission of a new translation to *LEO* (a contribution to a semi-collaborative dictionary) can be directly published as part of the dictionary (given that the editors agree on it), the citations sent to the *Oxford English Dictionary* (i.e. explicit feedback) represent supplementary material that require critical verification and revision.

A particular type of explicit feedback aims at user-driven quality assessment. There is, for example, a separate 'Contribute!' website in *dict.cc* which asks users to rate the quality of translations as correct or incorrect – or skip the decision.[16] In order to prior high-quality ratings, the correct button is labelled 'YES (100% correct)' indicating that it should only be used if a user is absolutely sure, whereas any doubts should trigger a negative decision, as indicated by the button label 'NO/MAYBE'.

We can find similar evaluation tasks in the context of (paid or unpaid) *crowdsourcing*, a common strategy used by companies and institutions to outsource small, so-called Human Intelligence Tasks (HITs) to a large number of participating users in the web, to benefit from the *wisdom of the crowd*.[17] As an example for a HIT consider the identification of the best suitable category for a newly developed product, which is a highly subjective decision relying on human intuition. For recruiting participating users, HITs are usually published at crowdsourcing platforms such as Crowdflower[18] or Amazon Mechanical Turk[19] and rewarded with a small amount (e.g. as low as 0.05 US dollars, see Fort et al. 2011). To the best of our knowledge, there are, however, no publications about using crowdsourcing platforms to compile a reference work.

As for explicit feedback, we can distinguish multiple different ways of gathering implicit feedback. Tracking how dictionaries are used is an important instrument for dictionary usage research (Chapter 44 of this *Handbook*). *Webserver log files* present a viable solution to analyse the users' access strategies to explore an online reference work. Aggregation and visualization tools, such as Google Analytics or Piwik,[20] enable publishers to identify often-accessed articles, an estimated duration of a stay, and potentially which navigational or search components were used to find the information. As for other types of implicit feedback, privacy is an important legal issue when using webserver log file analysis and recording a user's interaction with the website as, for example, revealed by the ENeL survey introduced earlier.

The *Duden online* publishers include, for example, the list of the most frequently accessed articles in a sidebar of their website. In addition to that, they analyse the users' search terms in order to spot lemma gaps in the dictionary and understand certain lookup strategies. For *Duden online*, it turned out that users often enter multiword expressions, such as *im Folgenden* (English: *hereafter*) or *des Weiteren* (*in addition*), into the search box. Therefore, the editors decided to add frequently searched multiword expressions as separate lemmas into the dictionary rather than treating them as a subentry of one of their constituents (Rautmann 2014).

However, the use of log-file analysis has also been criticized as yielding limited, superficial conclusions (Müller-Spitzer and Möhrs 2008; Verlinde and Binon 2010). A particular problem is the noise introduced by robots and scripts that automatically browse through the website and thus cause imprecise results. The relevant literature in lexicography is yet short on methods for properly cleaning webserver log files of online reference works (see Chapter 44 of this *Handbook*).

The use of *external user-generated content* is another type of implicit feedback. That is, publishers include text, images, videos, sound files, etc., created by the users of an external website or service into an online reference work. *Wordnik*, for instance, includes a great deal of user-contributed images from Flickr and short text messages from Twitter to describe word meanings and use (Davidson 2013). The users contributing to these external services implicitly contribute their content to the dictionary. An important consideration of using external user-generated content is dealing with inappropriate content.

Submitting feedback is quite popular among users and their motivation is similar to those discussed for direct user participation, whereas *love* and *glory* according to the distinction by Malone et al. (2010) are the most predominant factors.

The motivation for publishers to gather implicit or explicit feedback is, however, different. Their aim is to exploit feedback delivered via e-mail, web forms, webserver log files, etc. for improving single aspects of their products, sometimes even on the basis on beta versions. For example, a beta version of the *Digitales Wörterbuch der Deutschen Sprache* with multiple new features has been the subject of a call for explicit feedback (Klein and Geyken 2010). Implicit feedback may provide insights into strengths and weaknesses of a reference work, for example, on the basis of a log file analysis. But also the selection of articles as favourites by registered users (e.g. in *Merriam-Webster online*) might give useful hints on which articles may benefit from revision or extension.

To be maximally useful for publishers, the collected feedback may not contain material protected by copyright and ensure a high information quality. As for direct user participation, respecting copyright is an important factor for indirect user participation as well. This is especially true for including external user-generated content. *Wordnik*, for example, includes only Flickr images published under Creative Commons licenses.

The quality and usefulness of user feedback are important issues for the publishers of a dictionary or encyclopaediabecause because they have to decide to what extent the contributed material requires revision. Many reference works such as the *Oxford English Dictionary* or *Duden online* react to explicit feedback (e.g. e-mails containing propositions, suggestions via web forms). The user feedback to *Duden online* is, for instance, perceived as a valuable resource for the editors to improve the dictionary substance (Rautmann 2014).

Quality is also an issue with regard to the inclusion of external user-generated content. Lew (2014) discusses, for example, the use of embarrassing images in the former *Google Dictionary* which until 2011 automatically included pictures from Google Images in its articles. The vast amount of these constantly changing contents usually impedes checking the contents manually. Thus, publishers rather rely on disclaimers, collaborative spam filtering, or natural language processing systems (Wang and McKeown 2010).

45.3.3 Accessory user participation

We introduce the term *accessory user participation* as a third approach to involve users into the development of a lexicographic product. Accessory user participation goes beyond the direct and indirect contribution of lexicographic descriptions and materials, but addresses the general communication between publishers and users as well as between users themselves.

Perhaps the oldest form of communication between publishers and users is print advertisement. In the era of the World Wide Web, traditional means of print advertisement have largely been replaced or at least supplemented by electronic and online formats, such as e-mail newsletters. Because social media technologies are increasingly penetrating online communication, publishers also have new ways to inform users about their products, including blogs and microblogs, podcasts, video channels, and social networks. Typically, the communicated content goes far beyond a product presentation, but aims at interesting, useful, or humorous information about the compilation or usage of lexicographic products, adequate language use, the origin of words, noteworthy facts and trivia, etc. Macmillan, for instance, provides a dictionary blog[21] that features series such as 'stories behind words' and 'language tip of the week.' For interested users, these blog series can be a reason to return to a product's website on a recurring basis. Blog articles and other accessory content often contain hyperlinks to encyclopaedic or dictionary articles. For publishers, this is a major strategy to motivate users to lookup information in their products and to become actively involved in their development. For the *Oxford English Dictionary*, Thier (2014) reports that the publisher offers a large variety of services, including a language blog, Twitter and Facebook profiles, and a YouTube channel, for which both the marketing and the lexicographic department provide content.

In 2010, the Dutch *Instituut voor Nederlandse Lexicologie* published the language game 'Het Verloren Woord' (English: *the lost word*), in which users had to find a word based on a number of cryptic descriptions. To solve this task, the publishers recommended to use their dictionary, the *Algemeen Nederlands Woordenboek*. Schoonheim et al. (2012) note that – besides marketing the dictionary – they pursued a didactic goal allowing users to learn effective dictionary usage in a playful setting.

The aforementioned services are mostly targeted at communicating from publishers to users in a unidirectional way; however, there are also means of user participation that initiate a bidirectional exchange. In blogs and social networks, there are usually possibilities to comment on a posting and thus initiate an exchange between publishers and users (e.g. by suggesting new blog topics).

A particular type of bidirectional communication is language consultation services. The German publisher Duden offers a hotline for clarifying language-related questions since the 1960s. This is especially useful because users may ask questions for which they could not find an answer in one of the publisher's dictionaries, which complements the actual purpose of the lexicographic product. The *canoonet* language blog 'Fragen Sie Dr. Bopp' (English: *Ask Dr. Bopp*) provides a similar service: Users may send language-related questions by e-mail and receive a personalised answer. Interesting and recurring questions are additionally published as a blog article. Each blog post usually links to multiple lexicographic articles and thus naturally combines the language consultation service blog with an actual reference work.

Accessory user participation is not limited to the communication between a publisher and its users, but also addresses the communication between users themselves. The comment function of multiple websites is one option for users to respond to another user's contribution. *Wordnik*, for instance, allows users to comment the dictionary articles directly. Besides cases of explicit feedback (see Section 45.3.2), users pose and answer questions related to an article's lemma or discuss issues beyond the scope of a single article. Instead of a specific commenting function, wiki-based projects typically provide a separate discussion page, which can be freely edited by all users.

Although comments are usually sorted by date, it is hard to discuss multiple issues at the same time or respond to a question that has been posed some time ago. Discussion pages provide a viable solution, because users can add their response or comment at an arbitrary position within the page. In the open-collaborative *Wikipedia* and *Wiktionary*, discussion pages serve an additional purpose as they are also used to discuss and distribute the lexicographic work.

Another alternative is using an online forum, which allows for grouping the discussed issues in distinct threads. The *LEO* dictionary portal, for example, provides a large and frequently used online forum to discuss translations. For users, this is especially helpful if a certain translation is yet missing from the dictionary or if the descriptions are not sufficient to clarify a specific language question (e.g. whether a word is commonly used in a certain domain or register).

The main motivational factors of the publishers to initiate an exchange with their users include advertising own lexicographic products, engaging users in using and contributing to a product, and explaining how a product can be used effectively. To this end, publishers often provide online services to either disseminate information to their users in a unidirectional way (i.e. without reacting to their responses at a large scale) or initiate a bidirectional exchange between users and publishers or among the users themselves. The motivation for users to contribute to such services varies from informing oneself about a product and solving questions beyond the lexicographic descriptions to socialising with others. In addition to the users' motivation, their degree of experience varies, from novices who rarely use lexicographic products, to language enthusiasts who use reference works extensively.

Because user contributions created by one of these accessory services are often immediately published online, publishers have to effectively filter out inappropriate contributions, such as defamation, offence, and spam. Given the potentially huge number of contributions, publishers use either automatic filtering techniques or they rely on crowdsourcing. In

Wordnik, for instance, users can click on a thumbs-down button in order to bring an inappropriate comment to the publisher's attention.

45.4 Looking to the future

In the future, the participation of users might play an even bigger role for the compilation of dictionaries and encyclopaedias, which motivates multiple strands of further research (see Chapter 29 of this *Handbook*). Of particular interest is the question of how a certain project can benefit most from their users' contributions. At present, there is a broad diversity of methods to involve users in the development of a dictionary or encyclopaedia. Typically, a single work utilizes multiple user participation means in parallel. The *LEO* dictionary portal is a good example for this: As a semi-collaborative dictionary, *LEO* is largely based on translations submitted by its users (i.e. direct user participation), whereas users are also asked to give feedback about the quality of existing translations and the dictionary as a whole (i.e. indirect user participation). In addition to that, there is a large online forum in *LEO* facilitating an exchange between dictionary users and publishers and between the users themselves (i.e. accessory user participation). Therefore, a crucial question for planning an online reference work is often not if, but how the users can participate. In order to select user participation methods that fit the needs of a project, it is necessary to understand their individual strengths and weaknesses.

On the positive side, direct user participation and explicit feedback typically create an added value with respect to content. Allowing users to contribute directly and even take part in decision-making facilitates many successful revisions, error corrections, and filled gaps concerning missing lemmas or examples. The collaborative paradigm yields a continually growing reference work, and it has the potential to make lexicographic activities faster and cheaper by distributing tasks to a large number of often voluntary users. For encyclopaedias, the *Wikipedia* project demonstrates that the open-collaborative approach can yield a high-quality result (Giles 2005). A particular advantage is the diversity of the users. This enables a broad coverage of specialised domains and language varieties (e.g. dialects, slang, technical terminology) as well as multiple languages (Meyer 2013). Another advantage of the collaborative paradigm is the large number of users compared to the few editors of professional works. Besides individual opinions, collaborative approaches may consolidate the views of larger groups, yielding a more accurate or objective description. Error spotting and correction is an important pillar of collaborative quality assurance, which can further improve the quality of a reference work, which can be even formalised as *dict.cc*'s user ratings on the usefulness of translation equivalents demonstrate. But also with regard to the user contributions themselves, there are clear advantages of relying on collaborative quality assurance, because a single user is hardly able to check all contributions for being inappropriate or useful.

From the user's point of view, the open licences of most collaborative projects guarantee free access to lexicographic content. They generally benefit from direct and indirect participation methods in that they may actively shape "their" favourite reference work. Accessory user contributions additionally raise the awareness of different types of reference works or how they can be effectively used. By providing article comments, discussion pages, or online forums, a reference work can become a central platform to discuss language- and subject-related questions.

Besides explicit usage guidelines (e.g. in blogs), the close involvement of users has also an implicit educational facet, as users typically develop their usage skills by locating the article or item a new contribution belongs to. Accessory user participation offers can achieve this goal in a playful way by providing exciting blog entries or games that encourage users to lookup information in the reference work. Last but not least, the interaction between users and professional consulting services may help resolving language- or subject-related questions not covered by the reference work itself.

On the other hand, there are multiple challenges and weaknesses we face when using certain user participation methods. First of all, we cannot take the cost- and time-saving effect for granted. If user contributions are checked by editors, we need to plan additional editorial efforts that require additional time or budget. To what extent the usefulness of user contributions is higher than the time needed for their quality control may vary from project to project. In general, explicit feedback is considered rather positive (Rautmann 2014; Thier 2014), whereas the informative value of log file analysis is often limited (Müller-Spitzer and Möhrs 2008) and subject to ongoing discussion (see Chapter 44 of this *Handbook*).

A major challenge of direct user participation is dealing with plagiarism and copyright infringement. Identifying high-quality contributions as copies from secondary sources is a difficult task, which may require an even greater effort than the elaboration of a new lexicographic description on the basis of primary sources.

The quality of user contributions in contrast to professionally edited content needs a critical reflection. Collaborative dictionaries often contain information concerning very different language varieties and rare but easy-to-describe lemmas, whereas common and highly polysemous words might be missing (Meyer and Gurevych 2014).

The existence of unhelpful, inappropriate, or wrong descriptions in a user-supported reference work bears the risk that language- or subject-related questions cannot be reliably answered, which would make the entire product useless. Results from dictionary usage research suggest that reliability is one of the most important features for users (Müller-Spitzer and Koplenig 2014). To what extent user contributions really achieve an added value has yet only been cursorily explored. The publications by Fuertes-Olivera (2009), Meyer and Gurevych (2012), Hanks (2012), Rundell (2012), and Lew (2014) show qualitative shortcomings in collaborative dictionaries based on a number of erroneous, unspecified, archaic, or outdated descriptions. As a whole, user-supported dictionaries seem to have considerable gaps and quality deficits which may reduce their usefulness. Because most of these works are, however, in progress, it remains to be seen how they develop in the future. Interestingly, encyclopaedias come off well in comparison to dictionaries, which indicates that the compilation of encyclopaedias is more suitable for direct user participation than the compilation of dictionaries.

Particularly important is, however, the question whether collaborative approaches resemble actual lexicographic work at all. Meyer and Gurevych (2014) analyse the sources referenced in *Wiktionary* articles and find predominantly secondary sources (i.e., other editorial dictionaries). Rather than original lexicographic work resulting in newly worked out descriptions (e.g., based on a contemporary language corpus), this collaborative dictionary seems to concentrate on the collection and re-composition of existing data. Thus, drawing on expert knowledge of professional lexicographers seems still to be important with regard to the elaboration of high-quality lexicography products.

45.5 Conclusion

In this chapter, we introduced user participation research as a new field of metalexicography. Crucial research questions address the development and analysis of user participation methods and how they affect the planning, implementation, and evaluation of an online reference work. To this end, we reviewed a large body of previous work in which aspects of user participation have been discussed in isolation, and we propose a unified framework distinguishing three major types of user participation: direct, indirect, and accessory user participation.

Our classification framework serves as a tool for describing dictionaries and encyclopaedias as well as for exploring user participation systematically. We consider the knowledge, selection, and implementation of user participation methods as indispensable for properly planning new and revising existing lexicographic works. Our analysis has shown that user participation is anything but new, because especially explicit feedback has already been vastly used in the past, for example by the Oxford University Press. But what is new is the large-scale interaction by means of social media technologies, which paved the way for user participation to become a mass phenomenon. The predominant change is collaborative lexicography allowing users to modify a reference work directly. Analysing the user types and their motivation as well as the effectiveness and quality of their contributions is an important task in order to properly benefit from user participation methods. In the present chapter, we discussed multiple examples with a particular focus on dictionaries and language lexicography, for which we critically assess and organise studies and experiences reported in the recent literature.

For the future, we consider it important to combine the so far largely disjoined work within the emerging field of user participation research and work towards a research programme for effectively benefiting from user contributions and researching new ways of compiling reference works with the user in the loop.

Related topics

Dictionary management; dictionary usage research in the Internet era; explaining meaning in lexicographical information tools; using the Web for lexicographic purposes; the concept of dictionary; Wordnik.

Further reading

Abel, A. and C. M. Meyer. (2013). "The Dynamics Outside the Paper: User Contributions to Online Dictionaries", in *Proceedings of the 3rd eLex conference 'Electronic lexicography in the 21st century: thinking outside the paper'*. Tallinn: Estonia, pp. 179–194.
The fine-grained classification of user participation methods described in the present chapter is based on this eLex 2013 paper, which is the first attempt towards a comprehensive classification framework for user contributions to dictionaries.

Abel, A. and C. M. Meyer. (2016). "Nutzerbeteiligung", in A. Klosa and C. Müller-Spitzer (eds.), *Internetlexikografie. Ein Kompendium*. Berlin/Boston: de Gruyter, pp. 249–290.
This work contains a detailed discussion of the strengths and weaknesses of different means of user participation, which the present chapter builds upon.

Fuertes-Olivera, P. A. (2009). "The Function Theory of Lexicography and Electronic Dictionaries: Wiktionary as a Prototype of Collective Free Multiple-Language Internet Dictionary", in H. Bergenholtz, S. Nielsen, and S. Tarp (eds.), *Lexicography at a Crossroads: Dictionaries and Encyclopedias Today, Lexicographical Tools Tomorrow*. Linguistic Insights: Studies in Language and Communication. Bern: Peter Lang, pp. 99–134.

On the basis of the function theory of lexicography, this chapter describes the concept of collective free multiple-language Internet reference works such as Wiktionary, including a discussion of their reliability and concrete proposals for enhancing them.

Lew, R. (2014). "User-Generated Content (UGC) in English Online Dictionaries", in A. Abel and A. Klosa (eds.), *Ihr Beitrag bitte! – Der Nutzerbeitrag im Wörterbuchprozess. 3. Arbeitsbericht des wissenschaftlichen Netzwerks "Internetlexikografie"*. OPAL – Online publizierte Arbeiten zur Linguistik. Mannheim: Institut für Deutsche Sprache, pp. 9–30.
This contribution discusses multiple dictionary projects along the dimension of the degree of user-generated content they rely on. The author points out the potential of combining user-generated and professional content, especially for certain types of dictionaries, but also emphasises the importance of professional lexicographers for the development of high-quality dictionaries.

Melchior, L. (2014). "Ansätze einer halbkollaborativen Lexikographie", in A. Abel and A. Klosa (eds.), *Ihr Beitrag bitte! – Der Nutzerbeitrag im Wörterbuchprozess. 3. Arbeitsbericht des wissenschaftlichen Netzwerks "Internetlexikografie"*. OPAL – Online publizierte Arbeiten zur Linguistik. Mannheim: Institut für Deutsche Sprache, pp. 31–52.
This article describes different types of user contributions within the semi-collaborative paradigm, illustrating them using the LEO dictionary portal. It becomes apparent that users can, above all, contribute to a dictionary's outside matter without editorial control, whereas the whole macro- and microstructures are processed exclusively by the editors.

Meyer, C. M. and I. Gurevych. (2012). "Wiktionary: A New Rival for Expert-Built Lexicons? Exploring the Possibilities of Collaborative Lexicography", in S. Granger and M. Paquot (eds.), *Electronic Lexicography*. Oxford: Oxford University Press, pp. 259–291.
This chapter investigates the potential of collaborative lexicography through a comprehensive description of the open-collaborative Wiktionary. The authors identify different aspects of Wiktionary in comparison to expert-built lexicons and suggest a series of categories of users who can benefit from collaboratively constructed contents.

Notes

1 For example, according to the Alexa Top 500 Global Sites, www.alexa.com/topsites (accessed 2016–01–20).
2 Matthew Moore: Encyclopaedia Britannica fights back against Wikipedia. London: Telegraph.co.uk, 23 January 2009. www.telegraph.co.uk/culture/books/booknews/4318176/Encyclopaedia-Britannica-fights-back-against-Wikipedia.html (accessed 2016–01–20).
3 Bernd Graff: Wissen, das nie am rechten Ort ist. München: Süddeutsche Zeitung, 12 June 2013. www.sueddeutsche.de/kultur/brockhaus-am-ende-wissen-das-nie-am-rechten-ort-ist-1.1695116 (accessed 2016–01–20).
4 Academic Network of Internet Lexicography: www.internetlexikografie.de
5 EURALEX 2014 preconference workshop 'Was ist ein gutes (Internet-)Wörterbuch? – Alte und neue Fragen zur Qualität lexikographischer Produkte im digitalen Zeitalter,' Bolzano, Italy, July 2014. http://multimedia.ids-mannheim.de/mediawiki/web/index.php/EURALEX2014
6 European Network of e-Lexicography: www.elexicography.eu
7 COST ENeL WG3 meeting 'Online Dictionaries, Dictionary Protals and their Users,' Barcelona, Spain, March/April, 2016. www.elexicography.eu/working-groups/working-group-3/wg3-meetings/wg3-barcelona-2016/
8 www.macmillandictionary.com/dictionary/british/hypocaust (accessed 2016–06–08).
9 https://creativecommons.org (accessed 2016–06–08).
10 https://en.wikipedia.org/wiki/Wikipedia:Copyrights; https://en.wiktionary.org/wiki/Wiktionary:Copyrights (accessed 2016–06–08).
11 https://en.wikipedia.org/wiki/Wikipedia:Spam (accessed 2016–07–01).
12 https://dict.leo.org/forum/previewWrongentry.php?idForum=7&lp=ende&lang=de
13 www.oup.com/uk/oedsubform/
14 www.jessesword.com/sf/how_to_cite

15 http://public.oed.com/resources/for-students-and-teachers/balderdash-and-piffle
16 http://contribute.dict.cc/?action=wizard
17 However, crowdsourcing is not limited to paid evaluation tasks only. In the broadest sense, all types *of human swarm intelligence* can be subsumed under the term crowdsourcing, including especially user contributions to collaborative dictionaries.
18 www.crowdflower.com/
19 www.mturk.com/mturk/welcome
20 www.google.com/analytics/; https://piwik.org/
21 Macmillan Dictionary blog: www.macmillandictionaryblog.com (accessed 2016–07–04).

References

Dictionaries and encyclopaedias [All accessed on September 29, 2016]

Algemeen Nederlands Woordenboek. Leiden: Instituut voor Nederlandse Lexicologie. http://anw.inl.nl
Base lexicale du français. Leuven: Katholieke Universiteit. http://ilt.kuleuven.be/blf
Brockhaus Enzyklopädie. 20th edition, Leipzig/Mannheim: Brockhaus, 1996–1999.
Canoonet. Deutsche Wörterbücher und Grammatik. Basel: Canoo Engineering. www.canoo.net
dict.cc. Wien: dict.cc GmbH. www.dict.cc
Digitales Wörterbuch der Deutschen Sprache. Berlin: Berlin-Brandenburgischen Akademie der Wissenschaften. http://dwds.de
Duden online. Berlin: Bibliographisches Institut/Dudenverlag. www.duden.de
Duden Szenesprachenwiki. Mannheim: Bibliographisches Institut/Dudenverlag. http://szenesprachenwiki.de [offline]
Encyclopædia Britannica Online. Chicago: Encyclopædia Britannica, www.britannica.com
Glosbe. The multilingual online dictionary. Warschau: Cloud Inside. http://glosbe.com
Google Dictionary. Mountain View: Google. www.google.com/dictionary [offline]
Kamusi Project. Global Online Living Dictionary. Genf: Kamusi Project International/Delaware: Kamusi Project USA. http://kamusi.org
LEO. München: LEO. http://dict.leo.org
Macmillan Dictionary Online. Houndmills: Macmillan. www.macmillandictionary.com
Macmillan Open Dictionary. Houndmills: Macmillan. www.macmillandictionary.com/open-dictionary
Merriam-Webster online. Springfield, MA: Merriam-Webster. www.merriam-webster.com
Merriam-Webster Open Dictionary. Springfield, MA: Merriam-Webster. http://nws.merriam-webster.com/opendictionary
OmegaWiki. A dictionary in all languages. San Francisco: Wikimedia Foundation. www.omegawiki.org
OpenThesaurus. Synonyme und Assoziationen. Potsdam: Daniel Naber. www.openthesaurus.de
Oxford English Dictionary Online. Oxford: Oxford University Press. www.oed.com
Rap Dictionary. Nijmegen: Patrick Atoon. www.rapdict.org
Refugee Phrasebook. Berlin: Open Knowledge Foundation Deutschland. www.refugeephrasebook.de
TechDictionary. The Online Computer Dictionary. Chesterbrook: techdictionary.com. www.techdictionary.com
Urban Dictionary. San Francisco: Urban Dictionary. www.urbandictionary.com
Webster's Revised Unabridged Dictionary (Noah Porter, ed.). Springfield: G. & C. Merriam Co., 1913.
Wikipedia. San Francisco, CA: Wikimedia Foundation. www.wikipedia.org
Wiktionary. San Francisco, CA: Wikimedia Foundation. www.wiktionary.org
Wordnik. All the words. San Mateo, CA: Wordnik. Online: www.wordnik.com

Other literature

Abel, A. and A. Klosa (eds.) (2014) *Ihr Beitrag bitte! – Der Nutzerbeitrag im Wörterbuchprozess. 3. Arbeitsbericht des wissenschaftlichen Netzwerks "Internetlexikografie".* OPAL – Online publizierte Arbeiten zur Linguistik. Mannheim: Institut für Deutsche Sprache.

Abel, A. and C. M. Meyer (2013) "The Dynamics Outside the Paper: User Contributions to Online Dictionaries", in *Proceedings of the 3rd eLex Conference 'Electronic Lexicography in the 21st Century: Thinking Outside the Paper'*. Tallinn, Estonia, pp. 179–194.

Abel, A. and C. M. Meyer (2016) "Nutzerbeteiligung", in A. Klosa and C. Müller-Spitzer (eds.), *Internetlexikografie: Ein Kompendium*. Berlin/Boston: de Gruyter, pp. 249–290.

Carr, M. (1997) "Internet Dictionaries and Lexicography", *International Journal of Lexicography* 10(3): 209–230.

Davidson, S. (2013) "Wordnik", *The Charleston Advisor* 15(2): 54–58.

De Schryver, G.-M. and D. Joffe (2004) "On How Electronic Dictionaries Are Really Used", in *Proceedings of the 11th EURALEX International Congress*. Lorient, France, pp. 187–196.

De Schryver, G.-M. and D. J. Prinsloo (2001) "Fuzzy SF: Towards the Ultimate Customised Dictionary", *Studies in Lexicography* 11(1): 97–111.

Fort, K., G. Adda and K. B. Cohen (2011) "Last Words: Amazon Mechanical Turk: Gold Mine or Coal Mine?", *Computational Linguistics* 37(2): 413–420.

Fuertes-Olivera, P. A. (2009) "The Function Theory of Lexicography and Electronic Dictionaries: *Wiktionary* as a Prototype of Collective Free Multiple-Language Internet Dictionary", in H. Bergenholtz, S. Nielsen, and S. Tarp (eds.), *Lexicography at a Crossroads: Dictionaries and Encyclopedias Today, Lexicographical Tools Tomorrow*. Bern: Peter Lang, pp. 99–134.

Fuertes-Olivera, P. A. and H. Bergenholtz (eds.) (2011) *e-Lexicography: The Internet, Digital Initiatives and Lexicography*. London/New York: Continuum.

Giles, J. (2005) "Internet Encyclopaedias Go Head to Head", *Nature* 438(7070): 900–901.

Hanks, P. (2012) "Word Meaning and Word Use: Corpus Evidence and Electronic Lexicography", in S. Granger and M. Paquot (eds.), *Electronic Lexicography*. Oxford: Oxford University Press, pp. 57–82.

Hausmann, F. J. (1989) "Dictionary Criminality", in F. J. Hausmann O. Reichmann, H.E. Wiegand and L. Zgusta (eds.), *Wörterbücher: Ein internationales Handbuch zur Lexokographie*. Berlin/New York: de Gruyter, pp. 97–101.

Javanmardi, S., Y. Ganjisaffar, C. Lopes and P. Baldi (2009) "User Contribution and Trust in Wikipedia", in *Proceedings of the 5th International Conference on Collaborative Computing: Networking, Applications and Worksharing* (CollaborateCom), pp. 1–6.

Kemmer, K. (2010) *Onlinewörterbücher in der Wörterbuchkritik. Ein Evaluationsraster mit 39 Bewertungskriterien*. OPAL – Online publizierte Arbeiten zur Linguistik. Mannheim: Institut für Deutsche Sprache.

Klein, W. and A. Geyken (2010) "Das Digitale Wörterbuch der Deutschen Sprache (DWDS)", *Lexicographica* 26: 79–96.

Klosa, A. and C. Tiberius (2016) "Der lexikografische Prozess", in A. Klosa and C. Müller-Spitzer (eds.), *Internetlexikografie. Ein Kompendium*. Berlin/Boston, MA: de Gruyter, pp. 65–110.

Køhler Simonsen, H. (2005) "User Involvement in Corporate LSP Intranet Lexicography", in H. Gottlieb, J. E. Mogensen, and A. Zettersten (eds.), *Symposium on Lexicography XI: Proceedings of the Eleventh International Symposium on Lexicography*. Lexicographica Series Maior. Tübingen: Niemeyer, pp. 489–510.

Kreutzer, T. (2014) *Open Content – A Practical Guide to Using Creative Commons Licences*, Bonn: General Commission for UNESCO.

Lampe, C., R. Wash, A. Velasquez and E. Ozkaya (2010) "Motivations to Participate in Online Communities", in *Proceedings of the SIGCHI Conference on Human Factors in Computing Systems*. Atlanta, GA, pp. 1927–1936.

Lew, R. (2014) "User-Generated Content (UGC) in English Online Dictionaries", in A. Abel and A. Klosa (eds.), *Ihr Beitrag bitte! – Der Nutzerbeitrag im Wörterbuchprozess. 3. Arbeitsbericht des wissenschaftlichen Netzwerks "Internetlexikografie"*. OPAL – Online publizierte Arbeiten zur Linguistik. Mannheim: Institut für Deutsche Sprache, pp. 9–30.

Lew, R. (2011) "Online Dictionaries of English", in P. A. Fuertes-Olivera and H. Bergenholtz (eds.), pp. 230–250.

Malone, T. W., R. Laubacher and C. Dellarocas (2010) "Harnessing Crowds: Mapping the Genome of Collective Intelligence", MIT Sloan Research Paper No. 4732–09. http://ssrn.com/abstract=1381502

Mann, M. (2010) "Internet-Wörterbücher am Ende der 'Nullerjahre': Der Stand der Dinge. Eine vergleichende Untersuchung beliebter Angebote hinsichtlich formaler Kriterien", *Lexicographica* 26: 19–46.

Matuschek, M., C. M. Meyer and I. Gurevych (2013) "Multilingual Knowledge in Aligned Wiktionary and OmegaWiki for Translation Applications", *Translation: Computation, Corpora, Cognition: Special Issue "Language Technology for a Multilingual Europe"*, 3(1): 87–118.

Melchior, L. (2014) "Ansätze einer halbkollaborativen Lexikographie", in A. Abel and A. Klosa (eds.), *Ihr Beitrag bitte! – Der Nutzerbeitrag im Wörterbuchprozess. 3. Arbeitsbericht des wissenschaftlichen Netzwerks "Internetlexikografie"*. OPAL – Online publizierte Arbeiten zur Linguistik. Mannheim: Institut für Deutsche Sprache, pp. 31–52.

Melchior, L. (2012) "Halbkollaborativität und Online-Lexikographie. Ansätze und Überlegungen zu Wörterbuchredaktion und Wörterbuchforschung am Beispiel LEO Deutsch-Italienisch", *Lexicographica* 28: 337–372.

Meyer, C. M. (2013) *Wiktionary: The Metalexicographic and the Natural Language Processing Perspective*. Dissertation, Technische Universität Darmstadt. tuprints 3654. http://tuprints.ulb.tu-darmstadt.de/3654/

Meyer, C. M. and I. Gurevych (2012) "Wiktionary: A New Rival for Expert-Built Lexicons? Exploring the Possibilities of Collaborative Lexicography", in S. Granger and M. Paquot (eds.), *Electronic Lexicography*. Oxford: Oxford University Press, pp. 259–291.

Meyer, C. M. and I. Gurevych (2014) "Methoden bei kollaborativen Wörterbüchern", *Lexicographica* 30: 187–212.

Müller-Spitzer, C. (ed.) (2014) *Using Online Dictionaries*. Berlin/Boston: de Gruyter.

Müller-Spitzer, C. and A. Koplenig (2014) "Online Dictionaries: Expectations and Demands", in C. Müller-Spitzer (ed.), pp. 143–188.

Müller-Spitzer, C. and C. Möhrs (2008) "First Ideas of User-Adapted Views of Lexicographic Data Exemplified on OWID and Elexiko", in *Proceedings of the COLING Workshop on 'Cognitive Aspects on the Lexicon'*. Manchester, UK, pp. 39–46.

Naber, D. (2005) "OpenThesaurus: ein offenes deutsches Wortnetz", in B. Fisseni, H-C Schmitz, B. Schröeder and P. Wagner (eds.), *Sprachtechnologie, mobile Kommunikation und linguistische Ressourcen: Beiträge zur GLDV-Tagung*. Sprache, Sprechen, Computer. Frankfurt: Peter Lang, pp. 422–433.

Pearsall, J. (2013) "The Future of Dictionaries", in I. Kernerman (ed.), *Kernerman Dictionary News* 21: 2–4.

Rafaeli, S. and Y. Ariel (2008) "Online Motivational Factors: Incentives for Participation and Contribution in Wikipedia", in A. Barak (ed.), *Psychological Aspects of Cyberspace: Theory, Research, Applications*. Cambridge: Cambridge University Press, pp. 243–267.

Rautmann, K. (2014) "Duden online und seine Nutzer", in A. Abel and A. Klosa (eds.), *Ihr Beitrag bitte! – Der Nutzerbeitrag im Wörterbuchprozess. 3. Arbeitsbericht des wissenschaftlichen Netzwerks "Internetlexikografie"*. OPAL – Online publizierte Arbeiten zur Linguistik. Mannheim: Institut für Deutsche Sprache, pp. 53–66.

Rosenberg, L. B. (2015) "Human Swarms: A Real-Time Paradigm for Collective Intelligence", in P. Andrews, L. Caves, R. Doursat, S. Hickinbotham, F. Polack, S. Stepney, T. Taylor and J. Timmis (eds.), *Proceedings of the European Conference on Artificial Life 2015 (ECAL)*, pp. 658–659.

Rundell, M. (2012) "It Works in Practice But Will It Work in Theory? The Uneasy Relationship Between Lexicography and Matters Theoretical", in *Proceedings of the 15th EURALEX International Congress*. Oslo, Norway, pp. 47–92.

Schoonheim, T., C. Tiberius, J. Niestadt, and R. Tempelaars (2012) "Dictionary Use and Language Games: Getting to Know the Dictionary as Part of the Game", in *Proceedings of the 15th EURALEX International Congress*. Oslo, Norway, pp. 974–979.

Storrer, A. (1998) “Hypermedia-Wörterbücher: Perspektiven für eine neue Generation elektronischer Wörterbücher”, in H. E. Wiegand (ed.), *Wörterbücher in der Diskussion III*. Lexicographica Series Maior. Tübingen: Niemeyer, pp. 107–135.

Storrer, A. (2010) “Deutsche Internet-Wörterbücher: Ein Überblick”, *Lexicographica* 26: 155–164.

Storrer, A. and K. Freese (1996) “Wörterbücher im Internet”, *Deutsche Sprache* 24(2): 97–153.

Surowiecki, J. (2005) *The Wisdom of Crowds*, New York: Anchor Books.

Thier, K. (2014) “Das Oxford English Dictionary und seine Nutzer”, in A. Abel and A. Klosa (eds.), *Ihr Beitrag bitte! – Der Nutzerbeitrag im Wörterbuchprozess. 3. Arbeitsbericht des wissenschaftlichen Netzwerks “Internetlexikografie”*. OPAL – Online publizierte Arbeiten zur Linguistik. Mannheim: Institut für Deutsche Sprache, pp. 67–74.

Verlinde, S. and J. Binon (2010) “Monitoring Dictionary Use in the Electronic Age”, in *Proceedings of the 14th EURALEX International Congress*. Leeuwarden: The Netherlands, pp. 1144–1151.

Wang, W. Y. and K. McKeown (2010) “‘Got You!’: Automatic Vandalism Detection in Wikipedia With Web-Based Shallow Syntactic-Semantic Modeling”, in *Proceedings of the 23rd International Conference on Computational Linguistics*. Beijing, China, pp. 1146–1154.

Weller, K., R. Dornstädter, R. Freimanis, R. N. Klein and M. Perez (2010) “Social Software in Academia: Three Studies on Users’ Acceptance of Web 2.0 Services”, in *Proceedings of the WebSci10: Extending the Frontiers of Society On-Line, April 26–27th, 2010*, Raleigh, NC.

Wiegand, H. E., M. Beißwenger, R. H. Gouws, M. Kammerer, A. Storrer, and W. Wolski (eds.) (2010) *Wörterbuch zur Lexikographie und Wörterbuchforschung / Dictionary of Lexicography and Dictionary Research*. Berlin/New York: de Gruyter.

46
Dictionary portals

Bob Boelhouwer, Anne Dykstra and Hindrik Sijens

46.1 Introduction

Web portals have been one of the first web services that have helped users to find the information they need in the ever expanding World Wide Web. A web portal is basically a website that groups links to information available on the Web. These links are selected based on certain criteria. Some web portals group links that pertain to a certain interest (e.g. tennis). Such a portal is sometimes classified as a vertical portal because it may include several categories like history of tennis, biographies of players, manufacturers of sport attributes. Horizontal web portals, on the other hand, group links to a specific category of resources. Dictionary portals are a good example of that.

In this chapter we will describe the present landscape of dictionary portals. First, we will look at the typology of dictionary portals that has been offered by Engelberg and Müller-Spitzer (2013).[1] Then we present the results of a survey that has been conducted in the context of the COST Action 'European Network of e-Lexicography' (ENeL).[2] In that survey we made an inventory of dictionary portals presently in operation (see Section 46.2.3). Based on that survey, we will have a closer look at what dictionary portals have to offer to the user. Finally, we dwell on possible future developments of dictionary portals.

46.2 Core issues and topics

46.2.1 Typology of dictionary portals

Engelberg and Müller-Spitzer (2013: 1023) define the term dictionary portal as "a data structure that is presented as a page or set of interlinked pages on a computer screen and provides access to a set of electronic dictionaries, and where these dictionaries can also be consulted as standalone products".

Their "typology of dictionary portals" is based on the following four criteria: (1) types of access provided, (2) the implemented cross-reference structures between dictionaries, (3) the ownership relation between the portal and the available dictionaries and (4) the layout of the portal.

The types of access (1) pertain to the granularity of search, and differentiate among portals providing access to dictionaries (*external access*), access to the articles within the dictionaries (*outer access*) or access to elements within the articles (*inner access*). Criterion (2) refers to cross-referenced lemmas in different integrated dictionaries. Criterion (3) deals with "questions of the right of ownership." If both the portal and the dictionaries have the same owner, "it is easier to increase the interconnectedness between the dictionaries"(Engelberg and Müller-Spitzer 2013: 1026). Finally, criterion (4) is concerned with presenting the search results from individual dictionaries in a uniform fashion.

Based on those criteria they arrive at the following typology of prototype dictionary portals:

1 *Dictionary nets*, which provide inner, outer and external access to the dictionary content, contain a high degree of interdictionary cross-referencing and present the search results of the several dictionaries in a uniform way. Usually, the organisation responsible for the portals is also the owner of the dictionaries. Note that in those cases the dictionaries within the portal are complementary, portals of this type do not contain dictionaries of the same type. Examples are: *Owid*, *Canoonet* and *Wörterbuchnetz*.
2 *Dictionary search engines* provide outer and external access to dictionaries and do not exhibit interdictionary cross-referencing. Also, the results from several dictionaries are not presented in a uniform fashion. Examples are: *Dictionaryportal.eu.* and *Onelook.*
3 *Dictionary collections* only provide external access to dictionaries. They generally do not include a facility to search within dictionaries. Examples are: *Travlang* and *Slang Portal.*

46.2.2 Added value of dictionary portals

In this section we will focus on what extra functionality dictionary portals offer compared to plain online dictionaries. We will approach dictionary portals from the perspective of the user. What we will try to establish is if and why a dictionary portal is more useful to a user than individual online dictionaries.

Our analysis is based on Sijens' method (2015a and b). He compiled a list of dictionary portals in which he collected lexicographical features of the dictionaries in those portals. That list was used in the present desk-based research to investigate the additional features these portals have. Sijens also reported on some features that are not strictly related to lexicographical properties. So, there is some overlap between the features that are described in this report and that of Sijens. The results of our analysis are commented on next.

46.2.2.1 Discovery, selection and comparison

Three advantages of dictionary portals over single dictionary sites are quite obvious and reflect the purpose of Internet portals in general. First, a user can discover previously unknown dictionaries. Especially less known dictionaries might be difficult to find via general search tools like Google. Second, a portal can classify dictionaries according to type (e.g. learners' dictionaries, scholarly dictionaries). This makes it easier for the user to identify a dictionary that will most likely suits his purpose. Third, the portal can make it easier for the user to compare two or more dictionaries in order to find the one that best satisfies his requirements. To this purpose the portal might offer an option for federated search by which a word is looked up in several dictionaries simultaneously and the results are presented side by side.

46.2.2.2 Enhanced search

Besides these basic functions of a portal, namely discovery, selection and comparison, a dictionary portal can offer the user a better search experience. The results of a federated search by which the entries from several dictionaries are placed together might offer the user a more complete description of a word than a single dictionary might provide. Examples are: *Wordnik.*

46.2.2.3 Other features

Many dictionary portals provide additional features which might be of interest to the user. These features generally do not assist the user in the basic task of dictionaries, which is finding the meaning or translation of words. The type of additional features differs according to the 'business models' for the organisations deploying the portal. To classify these features it is useful to distinguish three types of organisations: commercial organisations, subsidized organisations and volunteer-based organisations.

Commercial organisations sometimes own and publish the dictionaries listed in their portal. In that case they might want to monetize the content directly and will place the most important part of it behind a paywall or try to sell hard copies of their dictionaries. Often they also gain income from advertisements on their website. Portal owners that do not own the dictionaries will rely mainly on advertisements. This means that they need to attract as many visitors as possible. To achieve this, they employ several strategies, like adding fast-changing content and word-related entertainment to the portal (blogs, word of the day, word games, etc.). Many will consider advertisements on a website rather as a nuisance than a feature, but it might still be useful if the advertisements pertain to related subjects like commercial dictionaries, translation software, etc.

Another way to monetize the portal is to provide (paid) services like travel information, money conversion (*Travelang*), language courses (*Leo*), translation services and OCR software. Portals are not typically established by commercial organizations. In addition, they show no sign of commercial intent (e.g. *Woxikon*). These portals might serve as a showcase for the organisation.

Subsidized organisations, like institutions that produce scholarly dictionaries, will usually make their content available for free. But they also want to attract as many users as possible in order to prove their relevance to their sponsor. The additions are mainly in the realm of scientific research and will probably not generate much interest from the general public (see Heid, Prinsloo and Bothma 2012). Examples are access to additional data like synonyms, metonyms, hyponyms, hypernyms, word profiles and corpora queries and adding content from several disciplines within humanities, like history, literature and poetry (*Portal for the Greek language*). Others provide access to specialised dictionaries of regional dictionaries (e.g. Wörterbuchnetz).

Volunteer-based organisations also make their content available for free, but strive after maximising the impact of their product in order to attract more and better authors. Because of the low expenses of these portals and possibly the objections voluntary contributors might have, they usually do not carry advertisements. One volunteer-based portal

(*Wiktionary*) sports fast-changing content like 'word-of-the-day' and community-oriented services. *Woordenboek.org* offers vocabulary training, a picture dictionary, and a phrases dictionary.

In our inventory of dictionary portals, we have also looked at additional, non-lexicographical features. Table 46.1 provides an overview of the number of portals per organization type.

It strikes the eye that more than half of the 37 portals are being managed by commercial organisations (21), subsidized organisations account for ten portals and six portals are being managed by volunteer-based organisations.

46.2.2.4 Content

Table 46.2 shows what organisations manage what kind of dictionary portals.

It is kind of unexpected that a commercial organisation (*Canoonet*) owns a dictionary net, because commercial organisations usually opt for a dictionary search engine (e.g. *Dictionary.com, Leo, Van dale*). Two dictionary collections (*Travlang* and *Slang Portal*) are owned by a commercial organisation.

Subsidized organisations manage in total ten portals, of which eight are dictionary nets (among others *Owid, Geïntegreerde, Taalbank* and *Wurdboekportaal*), one dictionary search engine (*Ortolang*) and one dictionary collection (*Ordnet.dk*).

Six portals have been established and are managed by volunteer-based organisations, namely four dictionary search engines and two dictionary collections (*Erlanger Liste, Lexilogos*).

46.2.2.5 Advertisements

As we have seen, dictionary portals may have advertisements as a source of revenue (Table 46.3). In this inventory, we also examined what portal sites display advertisements. It turns out that 13 portals have advertisements. Sometimes the owner of the portal places

Table 46.1 Organisation types and number of dictionary portals

Organisation Types	*Number*
commercial organisations	21
subsidized organisations	10
volunteer-based organisations	6

Table 46.2 Organisation in relation to portal type

	Dictionary net	*Dictionary search engine*	*Dictionary collections*
commercial organisations	1	18	2
subsidized organisations	8	1	1
volunteer-based organisations	0	4	2

Table 46.3 Ads on dictionary portals in relation to owner type

Owner type	*Ads*	*Ad free*
commercial organisations	13	7
subsidized organisations	0	0
volunteer-based organisations	0	0

Table 46.4 Type of content in relation to portal type

Portal type	*Lexical content only*	*Lexical content Encyclopaedic content*	*Lexical content*	*Other content*
dictionary net	9	0	0	0
dictionary search engine	16	2	4	5
dictionary collection	2	0	0	3

the advertisements; more often they come from third parties. It is remarkable that all the portals featuring advertisements are owned by commercial organisations. Maybe even more remarkable is that eight commercial portals do not contain advertisements. The latter portals may generate income by letting the user pay for access. Sometimes they offer free access to a part of the information and paid access to all the information they provide (*Oxford Dictionaries*, *Cambridge Dictionaries Online*).

The portals that have been developed and managed by subsidized organisations and volunteers are free of advertisements.

Finally, we looked at what content the portals contain. They contain lexical content, encyclopaedic content and other content, for example, games, puzzles, news, travel, languages, translation services and online Bibles (Table 46.4).

Most portals (27) contain only lexical content, whereas ten portals also offer additional content like encyclopaedic information or other services. What is striking is that all nine dictionary nets offer lexical content only. When we look at dictionary search engines, we see that there are seven that also provide other information. Three of the five dictionary collections also list online information channels other than lexical ones. The *Erlanger Liste*, for example, provides links to online encyclopaedias, databases with non-lexicographical content and online translation services.

Our previous analysis allows us to conclude that the main advantage of dictionary portals is helping the users find the dictionary they need. Sometimes they also provide a better search experience by enhanced querying in order to find wider results than a single dictionary might provide.

Beside discovery, selection, comparison and enhanced search, dictionary portals often provide additional features that are not directly related to the primary function of dictionaries: to find the meaning or translation of a word. These additional features differ according to the underlying 'business model' of the portal. Commercial portal owners offer advertising, entertainment and (paid) services. Subsidised organisations in general offer scientific facilities, and volunteer-based organisations very rarely offer additional features.

46.2.3 Inventory of dictionary portals

In this section we present an overview of the lexicographical properties of dictionary portals. We used the following method to find these portals: the starting point for the list of portals were the examples provided by Engelberg and Müller-Spitzer (2013). That list was augmented by using standard Internet search engines to look for terms like 'dictionary portal', 'lexicographic portal', 'English dictionary', 'Dutch dictionary', etc. The resulting list of 37 portals will certainly not be exhaustive. Nevertheless, it will give a good impression of the diversity and extent of the concept *dictionary portal*. For the survey presented in this section we have mainly investigated the lexicographical features of dictionary portals. The list of features included those used by Engelberg and Müller-Spitzer (2013) to establish a typology for dictionary portals. The full list is presented later (see References). The features discussed in this chapter are portal types, interface languages, number of dictionaries within in a portal, dictionaries available as standalone products, dictionary types, search options and display of search results.

46.2.3.1 Portal types

Engelberg and Müller-Spitzer (2013) distinguish three types of dictionary portals: dictionary collections, dictionary search engines and dictionary nets (see Section 46.1). Table 46.5 presents how many portals of each type we found.

The distinction between those types is not very strict – there are portals that have features of more than one type. An example is *Canoonet* that presents its own content like a dictionary net, but also provides an option to search through other dictionary portals. Therefore, *Canoonet* also resembles a dictionary search engine. For our inventory we allocated the portals to the type for which they carried most features.

46.2.3.2 Interface languages

The 37 portals sport together 22 interface languages: Afrikaans, Catalan, Chinese, Croatian, Danish, Dutch, English, Esperanto, French, Frisian, German, Hungarian, Italian, Modern Greek, Norwegian-Bokmål, Norwegian-Nynorsk, Polish, Portuguese, Romanian, Russian, Slovenian and Spanish.

Sixteen portals had an interface supporting more than one language. In all these cases, English was one of them. On the other hand, 11 portals do not offer an interface in English. There are seven portals with an interface in German and seven in French. Of interest are the five portals that offer a Russian language interface because these are all dictionary search engines for bilingual dictionaries that include at least one dictionary that has Russian as its source or target language.

Table 46.5 Portal types

Portal type	*Number*
dictionary collections	5
dictionary search engines	23
dictionary nets	9

There are 21 portals with only one interface language (Table 46.6). Among those are five dictionary nets. Of those dictionary nets three have only monolingual dictionaries and two also include a bilingual dictionary. The two dictionary nets with a single language interface and multilingual content both are from the Netherlands (*Geïntegreerde Taalbank* and *Wurdboekportaal*).

46.2.3.3 Dictionaries per portal

Every dictionary portal, by definition, includes at least two dictionaries. Dictionary nets contain on average fewer dictionaries than collections and search engines. The dictionary net with the largest number of integrated dictionaries is *Wörterbuchnetz* with 24 dictionaries, whereas the Norwegian dictionary net *Bokmålsordboka/Nynorskordboka* carries the minimal set of two dictionaries. The number of dictionaries indexed by dictionary search engines varies from three (*Wordsmyth*) to more than 1,000 (*Onelook*). Portals that include more than 30 dictionaries are generally dictionary collections or dictionary search engines. Finally, three out of five dictionary collections offer a list with more than 100 dictionaries. The Danish collection *Ordnet.dk* is an exception: it only contains two dictionaries (Table 46.7).

46.2.4 Dictionaries available as standalone products

Prototypic(al) for dictionary portals is that their dictionaries can also be consulted as standalone products (Engelberg and Müller-Spitzer 2013: 1024). In our inventory, we have investigated this feature for all 37 portals (Table 46.8).

Table 46.6 Interface language in relation to portal types

Portal Type	*1 language*	*2 languages*	*3 or more languages*
dictionary nets	5	4	0
dictionary search engines	13	3	7
dictionary collections	1	2	0

Table 46.7 Number of dictionaries per portal type

Portal type	*1–5*	*6–10*	*10–20*	*>20*
dictionary nets	5	2	2	0
dictionary search engines	2	4	4	13
dictionary collections	1	0	0	4

Table 46.8 Accessible as standalone product

Portal type	*Accessible as standalone*	*Not accessible as standalone*
dictionary nets	8	1
dictionary search engines	17	6
dictionary collections	5	0

Most of the dictionary portals (30) give access to individual dictionaries. Engelberg and Müller-Spitzer (2013) also indicate that not all dictionary portals share this feature. What stands out is that the dictionary net *Dwds* does not offer that possibility; the dictionaries in this portal are only accessible via a main screen and a single search box and not individually. Five dictionary search engines return only results and offer no access to individual dictionary sources. *The Free Dictionary* allows the user to consult some dictionaries as a standalone product.

46.2.5 Dictionary types

The portals accommodate a large variety of dictionary types. For the 37 portals in the present inventory we found in total 21 types of dictionaries: (1) monolingual synchronic/contemporary; (2) monolingual diachronic/historical; (3) bilingual (translation); (4) multilingual (translation); (5) dialect; (6) etymological; (7) rhyming; (8) proverbs; (9) pronunciation; (10) spelling; (11) special; (12) thesaurus; (13) acronyms; (14) idioms; (15) wordlist; (16) inflection; (17) morphology/word formation; (18) sign language; (19) neologisms; (20) synonyms; and (21) illustrated.

Of the 37 portals included in this survey one dictionary search engine and three dictionary collections present more than 100 dictionaries. For practical reasons, we did not attempt to analyse the types of dictionaries in those four portals. Of the 33 remaining portals, there were ten that contain only dictionaries of one type. Among those were two dictionary nets. One of them (*Bokmålsordboka/Nynorskordboka*) contains synchronic monolingual dictionaries, and the other one (*De Geïntegreerde Taalbank*) contains diachronic monolingual dictionaries. The eight other portals with only one dictionary type function as a multilingual dictionary search engine providing access to bilingual dictionaries exclusively. The lemmas of these dictionaries were often linked and the portals served more or less as a translation aid.

Most dictionary portals contain between two and five different dictionary types. Only five portals contain six or more dictionary types. Two of them are dictionary nets: *Canoonet* with nine dictionary types and *Owid* with six dictionary types. The remaining three are all dictionary search engines: *The First Dictionary* (seven types), *Ortolang* (seven types) and *Diccionarios.com* (eight types). Interestingly, the five portals with a large number of dictionary types do all contain a monolingual synchronic dictionary and an idioms dictionary. Also, four out of these five contain a special dictionary and an inflection dictionary.

46.2.6 Search options

The simplest search method to explore dictionary content is lemma search. All dictionary nets and dictionary search engines in our survey offer that possibility. Two dictionary collections only provide a list of links (*Slang Portal* and *Travlang*). Of the remaining dictionary collections, the Danish *Ordnet* offers a search option on its home page to both of its dictionaries, but they can only be searched one at a time. The *Erlanger Liste* and *Lexilogos* provide a search box for some of the included dictionaries, but a search action will lead to the website of the external dictionary in case. One out of nine dictionary nets offer but one search option (*Dwds*). Of the 23 dictionary search engines in our survey, nine limit themselves to lemma search. Among those are seven multilingual portals that provide access to mainly bilingual dictionaries.

Twenty-six portals offer more search options that provide access to the integrated dictionaries. Some portals make these options available at the opening page of the website, others only make them available after opening a tab or after navigating to another page. The most frequent search option after lemma search is full text search (10 of the 37 portals).

Five portals offer more than five search options, among them the Hungarian dictionary search engine *Szotar*; the other four are dictionary nets. The dictionary net with most search options is *Owid* since it offers next to lemma search nine other search options. However, not all dictionaries within *Owid* can be accessed with all search options. The *Owid*-dictionary *eLexiko* offers, among others, the option to search for parts of the lemma string. Further options are spelling variety, part of speech, semantic class, word relations and usage.

The Norwegian portal *Bokmålsordboka/Nynorskordboka* with two monolingual dictionaries offers seven search options, among which are the options to select the alphabet associated with each of the two Norwegian languages, free text search and searching with regular expressions.

Portals that offer inner access often provide additional search options to specify information at specific information positions within the microstructure.

Wörterbuchnetz and *De Geïntegreerde Taalbank*, both dictionary nets containing historical dictionaries and/or dialect dictionaries, allow searching multiple dictionaries by means of a super lemma. This concept allows linking lexical variants of dialect forms to a single standard form. A special feature of *De Geïntegreerde Taalbank* is that with the aid of Dutch super lemmas a dictionary in another language (Frisian) can be queried.

46.2.7 Display of search results

Portals display search results in several ways (Table 46.9). Some portals only present a lemma list. Clicking one of the lemmas brings the user to the content of the entry. Some other portals display a list of complete entries. Again, other portals limit themselves to returning only a list with the dictionaries which have been searched. Some dictionary collections do not provide a search option and therefore do not return search results.

Within portal types different approaches to displaying search results can be found. The dictionary nets *Taalweb Frysk Wurdboekportaal* and *De Geïntegreerde Taalbank* present the results as a lemma list, where *DWDS*, for example, offers complete entries as a result. *Canoonet* returns not only links to dictionaries that contain the queried term, but also displays full entries. Some dictionary nets (mostly multilingual portals) only return search results from their own content. *Canoonet* and *Pons* supplement this with results from external dictionaries or portals.

46.3 Looking to the future

Earlier we grouped dictionary portals in three classes, according to their properties: The traditional functions of portals (discovery, selection and comparison), search enhancement and other features like (paid) services, advertisements and lexicographical tools.

Table 46.9 Display search results in relation to portal types

	1 lemma list	*2 entire entries*	*3 list of links*	*2 + 3*	*4 no results*
dictionary nets	2	4	2	1	
dictionary search engines	0	19	1	3	
dictionary collections	0	2	0		3

In this section we will focus on how search enhancement might make dictionary portals more useful to the users. We will also dwell on the hurdles that need to be cleared in order to put these features into work.

46.3.1 Augmented search

We already mentioned that presenting the user with entries from several dictionaries simultaneously might present a richer description of the words and an increased number of examples of word uses. A disadvantage of presenting the user with multiple entries is that dictionaries tend to differ in the way the entries are structured, in typography, etc. The user has to glean the required information from several large and complex text areas. The user might be helped in that process if the information from the several sources is grouped (e.g. definitions, examples) and if the layout, typography and structure of the entries are harmonized (see Müller-Spitzer, Michaelis, Koplenig 2014 and Lew 2015). To realize this, a portal needs access to the dictionaries' data. A number of portals already support harmonised displays. Especially portals from organizations that only include their own dictionaries (e.g. *DWDS, Bokmålsordboka/Nynorskordboka*). These organisations, of course, have direct access to their own data. Other portals probably rely on reverse engineering to display formatting data in order to harmonise the entries (e.g. *Wordnik.com*).

It seems obvious that if dictionaries allow access to data that is structured according to standards (e.g. LMF, RDF), portals will be in a better position to harmonise content from different sources. A serious problem is that this requires a major effort of many producers of online dictionaries. Moreover, they have to relinquish control over the rendering of their data.

Portals might also provide augmented search options like lemmatisation, wild card search (partial strings), historical spelling forms, etc. Of course, single dictionaries can offer similar search options, but a portal might add this functionality to dictionaries that do not natively support them. The portal, therefore, has to provide a pre-process that expands the search from the user into (multiple) requests that can be digested by the individual dictionaries. The user is presented with the collected results from the individual dictionaries. We have only found very few portals that provide such a facility (e.g. *Dict.cc*). Augmented search is an option readily available for portals, because it does not depend on efforts from the side of dictionary makers. It requires additional data like word form lexicons and spelling databases, which exist for many languages.

46.3.2 Search in context

Online dictionaries in many ways are used like traditional printed dictionaries. A user encounters an unfamiliar word when reading a text. He stops reading the text and consults a dictionary to look up the word and to learn its meaning, and he continues reading the text. In this age of connected information it would be so much more convenient for a user if he would be able to tap or click on an unfamiliar word in a text in order to bring up a popup with the meaning of the word; close the popup with another tap or click and continue reading. There are basically two methods. One is to add a facility to the browser (e.g. in the form of an add-on). The other method is to add a facility to the server (e.g. in the form of JavaScript). In fact, these facilities are already available.[3] The existing tools are almost exclusively for English. Moreover, they include a single dictionary.

A very useful function of a dictionary portal could be to provide a facility that delivers the content for these tools. Admittedly, we have to extend the definition of a dictionary portal such that it not only provides dictionary information from several sources to a human user, but also makes that information available for machine processing.

Consider a library which displays historic documents at its website. These documents contain unfamiliar words, and the library wants to provide the user with an explanation of these words. The library might construct the website such that when the user hovers the mouse over a word, the website sends a message to the dictionary portal (over another channel and invisible to the user) requesting information about that word. The request might be extended with parameters which specify language, period, etc. The dictionary portal responds with data from one or more dictionaries which fit with the parameters provided. The website of the library uses the received data to display an unobtrusive popup with a number of glosses according to the number of meanings the word has next to the word in the document where the user held his mouse. Clicking one of the glosses will bring up further dictionary content, possibly tailored towards the context of use in order to prevent information overload (see Gouws and Tarp 2016).

For such a service the dictionary portal might require additional data and processes. In the simplest case, dictionaries are selected according to the language that was specified in the request. It will be more useful to extend the service with a lemmatizer to map the word form in the input on a lemma form. A further extension is providing a system for spelling normalization in order to map older spellings on the contemporary spelling used in the dictionary.

An important hurdle for this development is that organisations that produce dictionaries need to make their data available in a standard format (directly or through a dictionary portal) in order to allow third-party tool developers or content providers to transform it into a form that is not intrusive when displayed in the context of another web page. Generally subsidized organisations are reluctant to relinquish control over their data to other parties. Commercial organisations, of course, need to control their data in order to make money from it. Subsidized organisations need acknowledgement of the impact their products have in order to substantiate their relevance towards their sponsor.

Another hurdle is that professional content providers (e.g. national libraries) will only add external services to their website if the speed and reliability of the service adheres to industrial standards. This will be required for the portal service as well as for all dictionary providers that distribute their content through the portal. For subsidised institutions it generally is too costly to provide services at industrial strength.

Earlier we discussed possibilities for using dictionary content in context when decoding text. But also during encoding dictionaries are of use. When writing a user might feel the need to check the meaning of a word. It will also be useful if the user can look up synonyms of the present word in order to check if another word represents the intended meaning better.

Writing in a computational environment is usually done with proprietary software for text editing. Proprietary text editors usually already provide a set of proofing tools which assist the user during the process of encoding. In order to use dictionary content through a portal for encoding, special tools or plugins for office packages need to be developed by third parties. A complicating factor is that text editors are still often used offline with no access to dictionary portals.

Related topics

English lexicography in the Internet era; towards an international directory of lexicography; user participation in the Internet era; the concept of dictionary; lexicography and information science.

Further reading

Engelberg S. and Müller-Spitzer, C. (2013). "Dictionary Portals", in R. H. Gouws, U. Heid, W. Schweickard, and H. E. Wiegand (eds.), *Dictionaries: An International Encyclopedia of Lexicography. Supplementary Volume: Recent Developments With Focus on Electronic and Computational Lexicography*. Berlin/Boston: De Gruyter Mouton, pp. 1023–1035.

This article presents a typology of dictionary portals based on properties of interlinking and access. See Section 46.2.1 for a further description.

Notes

1 See also Engelberg and Storrer (2016).
2 http://www.elexicography.eu
3 For example, the plugin Instaword from AceKYD can be used in Opera, and thefreedictionary.com provides a basic JavaScript that adds a dictionary lookup function to a web page.

References

Dictionary portals (All accessed on June 15, 2016)

AllWords.com: www.allwords.com
Bokmålsordboka / Nynorskordboka: www.nob-ordbok.uio.no
Cambridge Dictionaries Online: http://dictionary.cambridge.org
Canoonet: www.canoo.net
Croatian Old Dictionary Portal: http://crodip.ffzg.hr/default_e.aspx
De Geïntegreerde Taalbank: http://gtb.inl.nl
diccionarios.com: www.diccionarios.com
dict.cc: www.dict.cc
Dictionary.com: http://dictionary.reference.com
dicts.info: www.dicts.info/
DWDS: www.dwds.de
Erlanger Liste: www.erlangerliste.de/ressourc/lex.html
Le Dictionaire: www.le-dictionnaire.com
Leo: www.leo.org
Lexilogos: www.lexilogos.com
Linguee: www.linguee.nl
Majstro: www.majstro.com/Web/Majstro/home.php
OneLook: www.onelook.com
Ordnet.dk: http://ordnet.dk
Ortolang: www.cnrtl.fr
Owid: www.owid.de
Oxford Dictionaries: www.oxforddictionaries.com
Pons: http://de.pons.com
Portal for the Greek Language: www.greek-language.gr/greekLang/index.html
Slang Portal: www.spraakservice.net/slangportal
szótár.net: www.szotar.net
Taalweb Frysk Wurdboekportaal: http://taalweb.frl/wurdboekportaal
Termania: www.termania.net
The Free Dictionary: www.thefreedictionary.com
Travlang: www.travlang.com
Tureng: http://tureng.com
Van Dale: www.vandale.nl

Wordnik: www.wordnik.com
Wordreference.com: www.wordreference.com
Wordsmyth: www.wordsmyth.net
Wörterbuchnetz: http://woerterbuchnetz.de
Woxikon: www.woxikon.co.nz

Other literature

Engelberg, S. and C. Müller-Spitzer (2013) "Dictionary Portals", in R. H. Gouws, U. Heid, W. Schweickard and H.E. Wiegand (eds.), *Dictionaries: An International Encyclopedia of Lexicography. Supplementary Volume: Recent Developments with Focus on Electronic and Computational Lexicography*. Berlin/Boston, MA: de Gruyter Mouton, pp. 1023–1035.

Engelberg, S. A. and A. Storrer (2016) "Typologie von Internetwőrterbüchern und-portalen", in A. Klosa and C. Müller-Spitzer (eds.), *Internetlexicografie*. Berlin/Boston: Walter de Gruyter, pp. 31–64.

Gouws, R. H. and S. Tarp (2016) "Information Overload and Data Overload in Lexicography", *International Journal of Lexicography*: ecw030. doi: 10.1093/ijl/ecw030

Heid, U., D. J. Prinsloo and T.D.J. Bothma (2012) "Dictionary and Corpus Data in a Common Portal: State of the Art and Requirements for the Future", *Lexicographica* 28: 269–291.

Lew, R. (2015) "Research Into the Online Use of Online Dictionaries", *International Journal of Lexicography* 28(4): 232–253.

Müller-Spitzer, C., F. Michaelis and A. Koplenig (2014) "Evaluation of a New Web Design for the Dictionary Portal ÒWID", in C. Müller-Spitzer (ed.), *Using Online Dictionaries*. Berlin: Walter de Gruyter, pp. 207–228.

Sijens, H. (2015a) "Inventory of Dictionary Portals", www.elexicography.eu/wp-content/uploads/2017/03/inventory-of-dictionary-portals-June-2016.xlsx [accessed July 3, 2017].

Sijens, H. (2015b) "List of Criteria", www.elexicography.eu/wp-content/uploads/2017/03/list-of-criteria-features-inventory-June-2016.docx [accessed July 3, 2017]

47

Towards an international directory of lexicography

Reinhard R. K. Hartmann

47.1 Introduction

Imagine the potentially frequent occasion when you are puzzled as to who exactly might be responsible for which entry in which dictionary. This potentially complex question might well lead to the realisation that what you need is a source book that could provide information of this kind, and – more specifically – which lexicographers have been involved in its making, which kind of reference work we are concerned with, which publishers have been responsible for its production, which kind of information has been treated, what makes it so special and how research could have contributed to improving the compilation process and its resulting text.

Over the years I have been through several experiences of this kind, which have led me to the opinion that what we need is one (or more) reference work(s) in which such details are presented. Indeed, other subject fields such as linguistics, literature and physical science are known to have such problems, too.

47.2 Approaches to documentation

47.2.1 Compilation practice and lexicographic theory

Practical and theoretical aspects of our discipline have been opposed to each other for a long time, but in recent years more efforts have been made to bring them together in more realistic and accurate descriptions, for example, by means of several influential textbooks such as the *Oxford Guide to Practical Lexicography* (edited by Atkins and Rundell 2008), the (*Cambridge*) *Handbook of Lexicography* (edited by Svensén 2009) and the *Bloomsbury Companion to Lexicography* (edited by Jackson 2013), all of which have managed to specify the essential elements of both practical 'dictionary-making' and theoretical 'dictionary research', first as part of the three main aspects of the compilation process, in terms of:

- collecting evidence (fieldwork to build up data corpora),
- editing the entries (descriptive activities to define and exemplify specific words/phrases) and
- formatting the text (efforts to present the material in a comprehensive manner),

and then, as part of the five or six aspects of their objective analysis, in terms of:

- pursuing their lexicographic traditions (dictionary history),
- classifying their reference genres (dictionary typology),
- evaluating their qualities (dictionary criticism),
- specifying their component parts (dictionary structure),
- observing the consultation of their contents (dictionary use) and
- applying the support of computing (information technology).

Most of these so-called "perspectives" (Hartmann 2003: Vol. I: 7 and Hartmann 2011: 38) will be discussed later in an attempt to show their relevance to analysing and codifying lexicographic activities.

The tensions between theory and practice have affected the often confused way in which research on the structure and compilation of dictionaries and other reference works has progressed. The term *metalexicography* can indicate a rather abstract approach to the way the basic information categories are described, for example, linguistic data and their classification (etymology, spelling, definition, et al.) in relation to aspects of their graphic, morphological, syntactic, semantic and encyclopedic features, but they are essential for the process of introducing the whole field to a new generation.

Relations with neighbouring subject fields (such as terminology, onomastics, dialectology, applied linguistics and computing) are not always acknowledged, although inherent complexities may be ignored if such an approach is not allowed and documented, as in Chapter 8 of this *Handbook* on the role of corpus linguistics in providing data and evidence on variable usage (see Part II of this *Handbook*).

47.2.2 Perspectives

So have any attempts been made to cover such needs for lexicography? I have offered an overview myself of some basic "resources" (Hartmann 2013b), which concentrates on the chief mutual contacts and collaboration activities between institutions like academic bodies and publishers through such means as societies, meetings and publications, presenting the information in the form of eight tables, each with 10 examples and all supplemented by additional details, for example, on Europe-wide and international developments:

- academies such as the *Accademia della Crusca* (founded in 1583 at Florence), the *Académie Française* (f. 1635 at Paris) and the *Akademie der Wissenschaften* (f. 1751 at Göttingen), together with overarching bodies like ALLEA at Berlin (*All-European Federation of Academies of Sciences and* Humanities)[1], IAC at Amsterdam (*InterAcademy* Council)[2] and UAI at Brussels (*International Union of* Academies)[3];
- associations such as AELex (*Asociación Española de Estudios Lexicográficos*), AFRILEX (*African Association for Lexicography*) and ASIALEX (*Asian Association for Lexicography*), together with international and interdisciplinary bodies like EAFT (*European Association for Terminology*)[4] and ICOS (*International Council of Onomastic Sciences*)[5];
- corpora/databases such as the *Base Lexicale du Française* at Leuven, the *British National Corpus* at Oxford and the *Bank of English* at Birmingham, together with regional and international developments like ICAME (*International Computer Archive of Modern and Medieval English*)[6] and ELRA (*European Language Resources Association*)[7];

- journals such as *Cahiers de Lexicologie*, *Cishu Yanjiu* and *Dictionaries. Journal of the DSNA*, together with lists like EBSCO (*EBSCO Journals*)[8] and JSTOR (*Scholarly Journal Archive*)[9];
- networks such as EFNIL (the *European Federation of National Institutions for Language*) based at the Hague, ELC (the *European Language Council*) at Berlin and NordTerm (*Network of Nordic Terminology Associations*) at Helsinki, together with unions like ENS (*Expert Group Nordic Language Council*)[10] and ICC (*International Celtic Congress*)[11];
- online dictionaries such as the *Algemeen Nederlands Woordenboek* (*ANW*) for Dutch, the *Collins* (*COBUILD*) *Dictionary* for English, and the *Elektronisches Lernerwörterbuch* (*ELDIT*) for German and Italian, together with Internet portals like CLRES (*CL Research*)[12] and FD (*Free Dictionary*)[13];
- publishers such as Benjamins in Amsterdam, Bibliographisches Institut/Duden in Mannheim and Larousse in Paris, together with groups like AAP (*Association of American Publishers*)[14] and FEP (*Federation of European Publishers*)[15]; and
- university research institutes such as the *Center for Lexikografi* at Aarhus, the *Dictionary Research Centre* at Birmingham and the *Forskargruppe for Leksikografi* at Oslo, together with directories like *UDW* (*University Directory Worldwide*)[16] and *EWL* (*Europa World of Learning* 2016).[17]

The idea was that such resources constitute important elements that we need to acknowledge in order to understand the complex interrelations between lexicographic theory and practice. They partly overlap with lists of perspectives mentioned earlier, such as the 10 in the following list:

1. compiler perspectives: the motivation and skills involved in dictionary making (e.g. recording/fieldwork, editing/description and publishing/presentation),
2. linguistic perspectives: the effect of different languages on reference works (e.g. classical and modern languages, leading and minority languages, pure and mixed languages, and languages in combination),
3. regional perspectives: the influence of different parts of the world on reference works (e.g. continents and their international and national subdivisions),
4. disciplinary perspectives: the subject fields that lexicographers interact with (e.g. dialectology, onomastics, terminology, and divisions and applications of linguistics such as grammar, semantics and contrastive studies),
5. dictionary history: the development of lexicographic traditions (e.g. the English dictionary from Cawdrey to Johnson),
6. dictionary criticism: the evaluation of the relative quality of reference works (e.g. the review of a particular dictionary),
7. dictionary typology: the classification of reference works into genres (e.g. alphabetical versus thematic, graphic versus pictorial, or monolingual versus bilingual),
8. dictionary structure: the description of the architectural complexity of reference works (e.g. front matter, macrostructure or sequence of entries, microstructure or internal design of entries, and back matter),
9. dictionary use: the observation of dictionary lookup processes (e.g. reference needs and skills of the dictionary user), and
10. dictionary IT: the application of computer techniques to the compilation of reference works (e.g. corpus linguistics, frequency listing, sense discrimination and pictorial illustration).

In a three-volume selection of important papers (ed. Hartmann 2003), I also took the chance to honour a range of famous dictionary compilers and theorists (from Samuel Johnson and Ladislav Zgusta to Olga Karpova and Rufus Gouws) by presenting their innovative publications in the form of 70 chapters (five of which are also written by authors of chapters in this *Handbook*), with particular attention to the first nine of these "branches", "components" or "perspectives" of lexicography.

47.2.3 Towards a directory

For several years since my retirement, I have been working on the idea of compiling a directory for our subject, defined in the *Dictionary of Lexicography* (1998: 44) as a "type of REFERENCE WORK which gives information, usually in alphabetical order of names, on contact addresses and specialisations of people, organisations or products listed". Examples of such guides from related fields are:

- the *Directory of Publishing* (*DoP* sponsored by the Publishers Association 37th edition 2014), with information on publishing bodies in the United Kingdom and the Republic of Ireland, their contact details, key personnel and fields of activity,
- the *Europa International Foundation Directory* (*EIFD* 25th edition 2016), with information on a wide range of institutions and subjects, from Albania to Zimbabwe, but although "reference and information science" is included, lexicography does not stand out,
- the directory of *Entities Involved in Terminology Activities* (*EITA* sponsored by EAFT 2004), with information on 73 national and international bodies (such as the Spanish Terminology Association AETER), their objectives, their description and their main activities,
- the *Europa World of Learning* handbook (*EWL* 66th edition 2016), with information – arranged in alphabetical order of countries – on regulatory and representative bodies, learned societies, research institutes, libraries and archives, museums and art galleries, universities and universities of applied sciences, together with their leading staff and specialisations as well as their postal and e-mail addresses and websites,
- the *Kenkyusha Biographical Dictionary of English Linguistics and Philology* (*KBDELP* ed. by Sasaki and Kihara since 1995), with information – in order of authors listed – on their names (including their pronunciation), their origin, their education, their training, their position, their field(s) of specialisation and (occasional details) on their hobbies and family links,
- the *Debrett's People of Today* (*DPoT* since 1982) and
- the *University Directory Worldwide* (*UDW* since 1995), with information on over 10,000 universities and similar institutions, their degree courses and partnerships.

However, there are two problems with these reference works: one is related to the fact that some of them – such as *EIFD*, *EWL* and *UDW* – are too general to include much information on lexicography; the other is caused by their subject fields – such as *DoP* for librarianship, *EITA* for terminology and *KBDELP* for English language and literature – which are too specific to cover all the overlaps with lexicography, and their relevance therefore remains marginal.

Specifically for the field of lexicography, an early directory forerunner was the *Who's Who in Lexicography* (*WWL* ed. by Steven McGill 1996), which provided professional details on EURALEX members at the time (157, from Abate to Zoefgen). A typical entry included:

- the full name of the person,
- his/her address,
- position(s) held,
- language(s) covered,
- current dictionary project(s),
- published dictionaries,
- specialisation(s),
- software of relevance and
- (optional) additional information.

It may be of interest to note that only four of the authors of the 47 chapters in this *Handbook* are included in this *WWL*, as most of them probably belong to a more recent generation. Thus one obvious conclusion is that a renewal of this *Who's Who* and/or the compilation of other directories like it are certainly desiderata.

Famous lexicographers are, of course, listed in encyclopaedic reference works such as *Wikipedia*, which offers us an alphabetical 10-page list of over 360 lexicographers from around the world (including names such as Jacob Grimm, Émile Littré and Konrad Duden) and informative entries on 79 specialising on English (from Robert Cawdrey and Samuel Johnson to Peter Mark Roget and Noah Webster). However, a full international register of practical dictionary makers and theoretical lexicographers is still missing.

There are several reasons why there is a shortage of such reference works for our field. As most of the chapters in Section 5 of this *Handbook* demonstrate, there are numerous diversities in the way lexicography has developed around the world in recent years, ranging from individual to joint production efforts, from local to national publication projects, from academic research to commercial practice, from conventional subject fields to interdisciplinary contacts, from monolingual to multilingual specialties, from general to special-terminological reference works, from traditional to computerised approaches, etc., making our mutual awareness between all these activities necessary, but extremely difficult to achieve.

47.2.4 Portals

To catalogue most of the basic institutions of relevance to the compilers of reference works, I provided a list of such essential "Reference Portals" on the website of the European Association for Lexicography/EURALEX (Hartmann 2010). The list is presented in the form of a table of over 50 pages, and it includes several types of entries based on the perspectives mentioned in previous sections:

1. Dictionaries and websites that provide lists of dictionaries, such as the *Free Dictionary* (*FD*) at Huntingdon Valley PA and the *Lexicons of Early Modern English* (*LEME*) at Toronto, as well as Internet links such as ASK.COM and MÉTADIF;
2. Publishers such as Oxford U.P., SHERPA (Securing a Hybrid Environment for Research Preservation and Access) in Nottingham and WBE (World Book Encyclopedia & Learning Resources) in Chicago;
3. Academies such as the *British Academy* in London, the *Académie Française* in Paris and the *Rossijskaja Akademija Nauk* in Moscow;

4 University research bodies such as the *Dictionary Research Centre*, which started at the University of Exeter and is now based at the University of Birmingham, the *Institut Universitari de Lingüística Aplicada* at the Universitat Pompeu Fabra in Barcelona and the *Centre for Lexicographical Studies* at Guangdong University in Guangzhou;
5 Funding bodies such as the *Consiglio Nazionale delle Ricerche* in Rome, the *European Research Council* (of the European Union) in Brussels and the *American Council of Learned Societies* in New York;
6 Associations/societies such as ABNT (Brazilian Association of Technical Standardisation) and EURALEX (European Association for Lexicography);
7 Conference series such as AELex (Asociación Española de Estudios Lexicográficos), DSNA (Dictionary Society of North America) and AUSTRALEX (Australasian Association for Lexicography);
8 Interdisciplinary links such as the *Chartered Institute of Library and Information Professionals* based in London, the *Research Network for Lexicology, Terminology and Translation* in Brussels and the *International Celtic Congress* in Dublin; and finally
9 Other links and search engines such as ACADEMIA (*Tree of Academics*, at Oxford), ASK.COM (*Tools and Resources*, at Oakland CA, U.S.A.) and COLOSSUS (*International Directory of Search Engines*, at Kamloops BC, Canada).

Table 47.1 shows a typical entry from this EURALEX-based list, which provides the name (or acronym) of each of these portals, their location and the kind of information they offer on their websites.

Table 47.1 Entry from a EURALEX-based list

DIALNET	*Location*	*Links*
Fundación Dialnet Plus http://dialnet.unirioja.es/	Universidad de la Rioja, Spain	Journals, Theses, Congresses, Register

47.3 Core issues and topics

47.3.1 Essential facts

The 10 core issues and topics listed next, which partly overlap with the "perspectives" mentioned in Section 47.2.2, need to be addressed to bring about further improvements. Some are also hinted at in earlier sections of this *Handbook*, particularly in Chapter 2 (on dictionary management), in Chapter 6 (on contacts with other disciplines), in Chapter 8 (on corpus linguistics), in Chapter 20 (on specialised dictionaries) and in Chapter 46 (on dictionary portals).

Although most of these specialisations have made significant contributions to lexicography as a field that deserves more elaborate treatment in the form of international directories, they are also still in need of a better overall treatment that would allow them to move forward. Sections 47.3.1.1 to 47.3.1.10 are intended to illustrate some of their inherent limitations.

47.3.1.1 Languages

Language and communication are certainly the most basic objects of the work of lexicographers, hence their initial position in this list of relevant facts. There are enormous diversities in

Table 47.2 Entry for a typical language board

Institut de Linguistique Française	*Location*	*Links offered*
(French Linguistic Institute) www.ilf.cnrs.fr/	Paris, France	Federation Units, Research Axes, Projects, Biennial Congresses

the way individual languages are used and treated in every country, for example, dialect(s) vs. standard language, mother tongue vs. foreign language(s), native vs. immigrant language(s), and general vs. special-purpose vocabulary, so their coverage in dictionaries and other reference works tends to vary considerably, which also leads to some of the reasons why lexicography has developed in so many different ways around the world (see Part V of this *Handbook*).

Some aspects of the treatment of information, especially in general-historical dictionaries, are handled in academies (see Section 47.3.1.4), but some of the leading languages are attributed special attention through "language boards" or "language institutes", such as the *Institut de Linguistique Française* for French at Paris, and sometimes in combination with academies, such as ILASS (*Institute of Linguistics of the Chinese Academy of Social Sciences* at Beijing in China). The *European Federation of National Institutions for Language* in the European Union at Den Haag[18] provides a useful account of the situation by listing relevant bodies in European countries as members. Table 47.2 shows a typical entry for one of the language boards (founded in 2008).

47.3.1.2 Dictionaries

An improved awareness of the wide range of publications is essential not only for the classification of reference works into genres, but also for the documentation of the lexicographic literature as a whole (see Section 47.3.1.8). Depending on the country, the language(s) and subject matter of concern, there are numerous dictionaries, some of which are documented in lists such as the *Dictionary of Dictionaries and Eminent Encyclopedias* (*DDEE* 1997) or my bibliography on the EURALEX website (Hartmann 2007). Table 47.3 shows a typical entry for an electronic guide to reference works.

47.3.1.3 Publishing Bodies

Several different types of bodies are responsible for the production of dictionaries, most notably commercial publishers. In one of my informal files of dictionary publishers, 19 of these are listed for the UK (from Blackwell to Routledge) and 10 for the United States (from Appleton-Century-Crofts to Wiley & Sons). Dictionary compilation and publication is also promoted by academies (see Section 47.3.1.4), university research centres (Section 47.3.1.5) and other organisations. Table 47.4 shows a typical entry for one of the most famous publishers in England (founded in 1633), with informal links to the University of Oxford.

Table 47.3 Entry for an electronic guide

YourDictionary	*The last word in words*	*Links*
Examples, www.yourdictionary.com/	LoveToKnow Corporation Burlingame CA, U.S.A.	Dictionaries, Thesaurus, Examples, Quotes, Word Lists, References, Word Finder

Table 47.4 Entry for a publisher

Oxford U. P.	*Location*	*Links*
www.oxforddictionaries.com/	Oxford University Press Oxford, U.K.	Dictionary, Synonyms, Grammar, Spelling, Writing, Usage, Premium Resources, Explore Word Origins

47.3.1.4 National academies

One of the first comparative attempts to describe the contribution of academies to lexicography, a topic neglected in the literature, was a description I attempted of 74 such "institutions of scholarship" in 50 countries (Hartmann 2012). Many of these have long histories, such as the *Académie Française* and other national academies in Romance-language countries, originally with reference to the Latin tradition, and more recently in countries with Germanic, Slavic and other Indo-European languages as well as non-Indo-European languages such as Finnish, Hungarian and Basque. Their work has been spearheaded by pioneers like Christopher Wren and Cardinal Richelieu, and patrons like King Christian VII of Denmark (1774).

Many of these bodies have been performing a wide range of functions which also vary from country to country, such as language, literature, science and the arts, and their structure very often differs according to how many subject fields are covered in how many sections. In countries with more than one academy, networks exist to coordinate their activities, for example, the *Union der deutschen Akademien der Wissenschaften* which links bodies in eight German provinces and the *Institut de France* which coordinates activities between five national academies. There are also international links through institutions like the IAC at Amsterdam and the UAI at Brussels.

Some of these academies can boast impressive achievements in the field of lexicography, such as language dictionaries and other reference works like the *Medieval Latin Dictionary* (at Brussels), the *Czech Historical Dictionary* (at Prague), the *Frisian Dictionary* (at Leeuwarden), the *Georgian Dictionary* (at Tbilisi), the *German Dictionary* (at Göttingen), the *Macedonian Dictionary* (at Skopje) and the *Turkish Dictionary of Scientific Terms* (at Ankara). Table 47.5 shows a typical entry for an academy, the Hungarian Academy of Sciences and Humanities (founded in 1825).

47.3.1.5 University centres

Other academic institutions such as colleges and universities specialising in lexicography are still relatively rare around the world, especially where training and instruction tend to be based on higher-degree diplomas, MA theses and doctoral dissertations.

Table 47.5 Entry for an academy

MTA	*Location*	*Links*
Magyar Tudományos Akadémia www.mta.hu/	Budapest, Hungary	Types of Academy, Hungarian Dictionaries, Corpus Linguistics, Language Technology, Dialectology, Journal: *Acta Linguistica Hungarica*

Table 47.6 Entry for a research unit

DRC	*Location*	*Links*
Dictionary Research Centre	University of Birmingham Edgbaston, Birmingham B15 2TT, U.K.	Research Activities, Research Degrees, Resources, Enquiries, Centre for Corpus Research
www.birmingham.ac.uk/schools/edacs/departments/englishlanguage/research/projects/drc.aspx		

Tensions are always experienced at such research centres, for example, between practice and theory, between the field of lexicography and neighbouring disciplines and between academic interests and commercial preferences. As they are typically minority units with a relatively rare subject specialisation and typically limited members of staff, their websites are often restricted and sometimes even out of date, so it is difficult to verify their current composition and their lexicographic achievements, for example, statistics on courses, numbers of students and data on postgraduate theses. (For more on such dictionary research centres in four European countries see Section 47.3.2.5) Table 47.6 shows a typical entry for a research unit at a British university (founded in 2001).

47.3.1.6 Conference series

The significance and predominance of one conference in my career has been the basis for several of my own publications, such as the proceedings of one of the first international meetings devoted entirely to the field of lexicography (Hartmann 1984), which not only provided an opportunity for many lexicographers from around the world to come together and exchange information, but also helped to establish the European Association for Lexicography as well as the book series *Lexicographica Series Maior* and the periodical *International Journal of Lexicography*.

The EURALEX conference series has increased to 17 biennial meetings by 2016, and others sponsored by new associations have followed this example (see Section 47.3.1.7). This has developed my interest in such new creations in the field of lexicography, as part of my 15 contributions to the *DSNA Newsletter* ("Reinhard's References", between 2006 and 2014, two of which were devoted to conferences) and eventually led to my regular column "Forthcoming Events" in the *EURALEX Newsletter* (Hartmann 2009–2016), with 30 "Lists" published over a seven-year period, ranging from 10+ conferences cited in Nos. 1 to 8 in the first two years (2009–2010) to 20+ conferences cited in Nos. 21 to 29 in the last two years (2015–2016), documenting over 420 conference series, some of which are repeated in several successive lists. Table 47.7 shows a typical entry, from List No. 28 of "Forthcoming Events" (which covered the period from January to September 2016).

Table 47.7 Entry for a listed event

EURALEX 17	*Location*	*Links*
Sep. 6–10 2016 http://euralex2016.tsu.ge/	L.J. Tbilisi State University Georgia	Topics, Speakers

In the final List of "Forthcoming Events" (No. 30) I summarised my approach and presented an overall website "*LINGUIST.List@*"[19] which will help readers of the *EURALEX Newsletter* to collect information on forthcoming events of relevance to lexicography and related subject fields in future.

The term *conference series* can of course cover quite a wide range of events, from small-scale local workshops and seminars to specialised symposia, national and international conferences and global congresses, and since the time of the LEXeter '83 conference quite an impressive range of such series have been developed for lexicography and related disciplines, such as those linked to professional associations (see Section 47.3.1.7).

47.3.1.6 Associations and societies

As we have already seen, one of the advantages of a conference meeting is the possibility of using it to create a professional society. This is exactly what happened at the LEXeter '83 Conference where EURALEX was founded, and the proceedings (ed. Hartmann 1984) were published in Vol. 1 of a new book series. It is also a useful way to indicate the reasons for starting such associations (e.g. the ever-increasing need to establish contacts and collaboration), to illustrate their various types (e.g. local, national, regional and international bodies) and to describe some of their main purposes and achievements (e.g. to promote get-togethers, publications such as newsletters and journals as well as other networks).

For lexicography, we now have several associations, ranging from continental ones like DSNA (founded 1975), EURALEX (f. 1983), AFRILEX (f. 1995) and ASIALEX (f. 1997) to regional ones like the Nordic NFL (f. 1991) and country-based ones like the Spanish AELex, the Bulgarian BLS, the Chinese ZCX, the Indian LxSI and the Korean KOREALEX; from small personal initiatives and local bodies like APLSPCA (for Chinese/English special-purpose communication), JACET (for Japanese English teachers) and SLD (for Scottish language dictionary-making) to interdisciplinary bodies like AILA (for applied linguistics) and EAFT (for terminology studies). Forty-six of these – several from neighbouring disciplines – are listed in my overview contribution to *DIEL* (Hartmann 2013a), most of them together with their websites, which document their achievements in terms of conference series held (see Section 47.3.1.6) and professional journals published (see Section 47.3.1.8). Table 47.8 shows a typical entry for one of the international associations (founded in 1995).

Table 47.8 Entry for an international association

AFRILEX	*Location*	*Links*
African Association for Lexicography www.afrilex.africanlanguages.com/	c/o University of Pretoria Pretoria, South Africa	Annual Conferences and Activities, Dictionaries by Members, Related Websites, Journal *Lexikos*

47.3.1.8 Periodicals

Publications of relevance to lexicography range from dictionaries and other reference works, textbooks and conference proceedings to readers, festschrift volumes and periodicals. One paper of mine (Hartmann in *Lexikos* 2009) presents a list of 40 representative periodicals from a number of countries and neighbouring subject fields, such as *Cahiers de Lexicologie* (2 issues p.a. since 1957), *Cishu Yanjiu* (6 issues p.a. since 1979), *Dictionaries. Journal of the DSNA* (1 issue p.a. since 1979), *Lexicographica. International Annual for Lexicography* (1 issue p.a. since 1985), *Reference Reviews* (8 issues p.a. since 1987), *International Journal of Lexicography* (4 issues p.a. since 1988), *LexicoNordica* (1 issue p.a. since 1994), *Lexikos* (1 issue p.a. since 1991), *Names. A Journal of Onomastics* (4 issues p.a. since 1953), *Revista de Lexicografía* (1 issue p.a. since 1995) and *Terminology* (2 issues p.a. since 1994). To these, we should add *Lexicography: Journal of ASIALEX* (2 issues p.a. since 2014).

Such journals have turned out to be effective tools for providing information on topics that would not be available in any other way, and they have increased our awareness of the achievements, links and limits of the whole field (see Section 47.3.1.9). Table 47.9 shows a typical entry on a worldwide periodical (founded in 1988).

47.3.1.9 Disciplinary connections

Links with other disciplines can be helpful to any academic and professional subject field. For lexicography, there have been long-term connections with traditional language-based disciplines such as literary studies, philology and dialectology, with modern applied linguistic specialisms such as language teaching and translation, with library science, onomastics and terminology, and most recently with information technology. The complexities can be worsened by the fact that some of these specialised fields are not widely taught in the academic context. Table 47.10 shows a typical entry on a particular interdisciplinary group (which was founded in 2010 to link lexicology, terminology and translation under the guidance of the *Agence Universitaire de la Francophonie*).

Table 47.9 Entry for a lexicographic periodical

IJL	*Location*	*Contents*
International Journal for Lexicography www.ijl.oxfordjournals.org/	Oxford U.P. Oxford, U.K.	Articles, Reviews, Archive, *EURALEX Newsletter*, Special issues

Table 47.10 Entry for an interdisciplinary research group

LTT	*Location*	*Links*
Lexicologie, Terminologie, Traduction www.ltt.auf.org/index.php/	c/o Institut Supérieur de Traducteurs et Interprètes H.E. de Bruxelles Brussels, Belgium	Institutions (AUF), Networks, Conferences Publications, Dictionaries, Journals, Web Portals, Databases

47.3.1.10 Networks

Collaboration is needed – both between disciplines and localities – to achieve progress. One pioneering forerunner in this group has been the *Thematic Network Project in the Area of Languages* sponsored by the *European Language Council* based in Berlin, for which I coordinated an empirical research project investigating dictionary use among language learners in 13 countries (Hartmann 1999).

Other examples of networks are sketched out in another paper (Hartmann 2011), which includes a list of collaborating languages, academies, universities, associations, dictionary publishers and journals/textbooks, with special attention to the situation in Europe. Table 47.11 shows an entry for the ELC (founded in 1997 to sponsor the TNP survey and other projects).

47.3.2 Comparative accounts

There are not only many overlaps between the perspectives listed earlier, but it is also obvious that the situation in different countries is sometimes comparable. Table 47.12 summarises the main points established in earlier sections, concentrating on 10 perspectives, from *Languages* to *Networks*, with special reference to four European countries: the United Kingdom of Great Britain (England, Scotland, Wales and Northern Ireland), France, Germany and Spain. Some representative international bodies are also referred to in the final column. Documentary evidence is still very limited, and some facts are not readily available, which is why the data presented here are restricted to a maximum of five items in each of the boxes.

Abbreviations used for relevant institutions can be found in lists quoted elsewhere in this chapter (e.g. EURALEX in Sections 47.3.1.6 and 47.3.1.7 or dictionary-like publications in the reference list at the end), or by doing a website search.

47.3.2.1 Languages and language boards

Topic No. 1 in Table 47.12 lists the most important languages in the countries documented (see also Chapters 33, 34, 35 and 40 of this *Handbook*). All four have a wide range of 'native' languages and dialects (such as English, Welsh and other Celtic languages as well as regional variants like Scots Gaelic) as well as popular 'foreign' languages (such as Hindi and Urdu) in Great Britain; French and Breton as well as Arabic in France; German as well as Turkish in Germany; and Spanish and Catalan as well as Arabic in Spain. And most have academy-like institutions devoted to the status of languages, such as (in Great Britain) the Grymraeg Canolfan Bedwyr/Welsh Language Board, (in France) the ILF, (in Germany) the IdS and (in Spain) the AALE.

Table 47.11 Entry for an international network

ELC	*Location*	*Links*
European Language Council www.celelc.org/	c/o Sprachenzentrum FU Berlin Germany	Projects (TNP), Conferences, Presentations (ELPHE)

Table 47.12 Summary of main "perspectives" in four selected countries and international bodies

Topics	*GREAT BRITAIN*	*FRANCE*	*GERMANY*	*SPAIN*	*INTER-NATIONAL BODIES*
1 *Languages* (approximate number of speakers) *and language boards*	English (60 m) Urdu (1 m) Welsh (0.6 m) GCB (Welsh) KTK (Cornish)	French (55 m) Arabic (2 m) German (1 m) ILF (French) IEO (Occitan) OLB (Breton)	German (78 m) Turkish (2 m) Serbian (0.6 m) IdS (German) RDR (German)	Spanish (38 m) Catalan (7 m) Arabic (4 m) AALE (Spanish) Euskaltzaindia (Basque) IEC (Catalan)	EFNIL ELC ICC ISO UL
2 *Dictionaries and other reference works*	*DDEE* *DoL* *DoP* *OED* *WWL*	*BCSI* *BTCM* *TLF*	*IBGLW* *LGL* *WDD* *WLWF*	*DBME* *DLP* *DSAL* *EITA* *NTLE*	*DIEL*
3 *Publishing bodies*	OUP Harper-Collins ICE NaCTeM NDWT	Didier-Larousse Gallimard Hachette Le Robert	Brockhaus Duden/BI Langenscheidt Klett/Pons Mouton/WdG	Anaya Espasa-Calpe Gredos SGEL VOXBiblograf	AAP FEP
4 *National academies*	BA GCB RSE	AF DGLF ILF IEO	AWG BAW BBAW	RAE RAG IEC	ALLEA IAC UAI
5 *University centres*	Birmingham Glasgow London Manchester Oxford	Lyon 2 Nancy 2 Paris 7 Rennes 2 Toulouse 2	Heidelberg München Erlangen-Nürnberg Tübingen	Alicante Barcelona Granada Madrid Valladolid	*EWL* *UDW*
6 *Conference series*	ATL EPNS LAGB SI SNSBI	AFNOR ATALA JdD ProTLS	GAL GSCL IGDD InternetLex	AESLA AETER AIETI	CICLing CILC EURALEX SoL *Linguist.List*
7 *Associations and societies*	BAAL EPNS SI SNSBI	AFLA AFNOR SFO SFT	DGI	AELex SCATERM	AFRILEX ALECSO ASIALEX DSNA EURALEX
8 *Periodicals*	*Corpora*, *The Indexer*, *Nomina*, *Journal of English for Academic Purposes*, *Reference Reviews*	*Cahiers de Lexicologie*, *Études Lexicographiques*, *Lexique*, *Neologica*, *Nouvelle Revue d'Onomastique*	*Beiträge zur Namenforschung*, *Deutsche Sprache*, *Lebende Sprachen*, *Lexicographica*	*Elhuyar Zientzia eta Teknika*, *Revista de Lexicografía*, *Terminalia*	*International Journal of Corpus Linguistics*, *International Journal of Lexicography*, *Lexicography*, *Onoma*, *Terminology*

(*Continued*)

Table 47.12 Continued

Topics	*GREAT BRITAIN*	*FRANCE*	*GERMANY*	*SPAIN*	*INTER-NATIONAL BODIES*
9 *Disciplinary connections*	Applied Linguistics, Information Technology	Corpus Linguistics, Dialectology, Onomastics	Terminology, Translation	Terminology	Linguistics, Terminology
10 *Networks*	BIG/WLB CLARET COLT ITI-TN SLD	CILF GERAS GLAT ProTLS TERMINALF	CiTaL DEBETERM DGI DTT ICLVCR	GLL IULMA LexiCom REDESTerm	ELRA ICAME ICOS LTT NordTerm

These language boards (sometimes part of academies) may claim 'regulatory' duties for certain aspects of language use, such as orthography, pronunciation and specialised vocabulary. Thus, the German *Rat für deutsche Rechtschreibung* at Mannheim is responsible for coordinating rules for spelling across German-speaking countries, and the *International Organization for Standardization* at Geneva is devoted to developing standards for technical terminology.

Other international bodies of relevance include the European Federation of National Institutions for Language, the European Language Council, the International Celtic Congress, the International Organization for Standardization and the Union Latine.

47.3.2.2 Dictionaries and other reference works

Topic No. 2 in Table 47.12 is devoted to publications like the *Lexikon der germanistischen Linguistik* (*LGL*), a rather groundbreaking attempt to provide a guide to Germanic language studies, in terms of specialisations within linguistics such as language structures, areal aspects and contrastive aspects, overlapping fields such as literature, lexicography and translation, or practical applications such as language teaching (Yamada 2014).

Many (series of) dictionaries have been produced around the world, but their archiving and documentation in the kinds of directories listed in the table – such as *DDEE* for English, *BCSI* for French, *IBGLW* for German and *NTLE* for Spanish – is not always easily available and fully elaborate.

47.3.2.3 Publishing bodies

As earlier sections have demonstrated, the tradition of publishing dictionaries and other reference works has been very strong in many countries. Examples from the four countries documented in the table include Oxford University Press in Great Britain (one of several publishers promoting personal contact with potential readers through their websites), Didier-Larousse in France, Duden/BI in Germany and Gredos in Spain.

There are also trends for some of these to join up with universities (such as OUP) and with companies in other countries; some even contribute to the development of international bodies such as the American AAP and the European FEP.

47.3.2.4 National academies

Section 47.3.1.4 referred to the contribution of national and locally based academies to dictionary making. Point 4 in Table 47.12 mentions several of these based in Great Britain, France, Germany and Spain, and the final column lists international bodies of relevance. Several academies elsewhere specialise in neighbouring fields like etymology (e.g. at Bratislava), terminology (e.g. at Minsk), dialectology (e.g. at Bern) and onomastics (e.g. at Vienna). Some have sponsored regular conference series, most notably the one coordinated by the UAI and held – 88 times between 1919 and 2015 – in various member countries. Many of them issue periodicals, for example, *Polonica Onomastica* (in Warsaw) and *Revue Euskara* (in Bilbao), and some provide academic training through higher degree programmes, such as the *Escuela de Lexicografía Hispánica*, which is based in Madrid and León.

Several academies have been involved in 'language regulation' (the example of the Chinese ILASS is mentioned in Section 47.3.1.1), which means that they may be referred to as 'language academies', as in the list provided by *Wikipedia* of 40+ bodies responsible for 70+ languages in over 70 countries, such as the *Accademia della Crusca* in Florence, which has been cited for an early attempt to compile a prescriptive (also called *puristic*) dictionary of Italian, and the *Asociación de Academias de la Lengua Española* which acts as a 'language board' for several Hispanic languages.

47.3.2.5 University centres

According to Hartmann (2013b), only 6 out of 117 universities in the United Kingdom, 6 out of 79 in France, 7 out of 83 in Germany, and 5 out of 62 in Spain can be proud of such research bodies concentrating on different aspects of lexicography, such as (for the United Kingdom) English dialectology and onomastics at Oxford and Glasgow, Celtic languages at Coleraine and Bangor, applied linguistics at Birmingham and Swansea and corpus technology at Manchester and Sheffield.

There is still a shortage of lists of such centres (by countries, institutions and departments as well as their leaders), with particular attention to dissertations submitted as part of postgraduate courses. One example of a relatively rare index to theses is the website offered by *Expert Information Ltd.* Occasionally cooperation exists between research centres, sponsored through bodies cited in such university directories as the European *EWL* and the universal *UDW*.

47.3.2.6 Conference series

My work on such meetings (see Section 47.3.1.6) has encouraged me to develop three basic lists: one in the form of an alphabetical table of over 40 pages (from AAAL to ZCX), the second in the form of a chronological list of over 50 pages (from 1952 to 2014) – citing more than 300 and 500 conference series, respectively – and the third as an overview of associations and institutions specialising in lexicography (limited to Europe in the first decade of the twentieth century).

To find upcoming conferences in various subfields of linguistics, the website *Linguist. List* could be a useful electronic source.

47.3.2.7 Associations and societies

It has become easier to pursue information on national societies on electronic sites (such as EPNS in Great Britain, AFLA in France, DGI in Germany and AELex in Spain) as well as those of international organisations (such as EURALEX, AFRILEX and ASIALEX). Some of these are responsible for the development of conference series (see Section 47.3.2.6) and the production of periodicals in the field of lexicography (see Section 47.3.2.8).

47.3.2.8 Periodicals and other publications

In Section 47.3.1.8 several text types have been cited, such as technical journals, introductory books and conference proceedings. Many of these have been listed in bibliographies, such as the one I compiled for the EURALEX website (Hartmann 2007), which also mentions monographs based on research dissertations and other collections. Several periodicals devoted to the field of lexicography have been started in the last few years, such as the *IJL* (promoted by EURALEX) and *Lexicography. Journal of ASIALEX.*

Other bibliographical guides of relevance to lexicography are the *Dictionary of Dictionaries and Eminent Encyclopedias* (*DDEE* 1997) for English, the *Bibliographie chronologique sommaire et indicative 1950–2000 des ouvrages utilisés relevant des domaines de la lexicologie, lexicographie, dictionnairique et métalexicographie* (*BCSI* 2000) and the *Bibliographie thématique et chronologique de métalexicographie 1950–2006* (*BTCM* 2007) for French, the *Internationale Bibliographie zur germanistischen Lexikographie und Wörterbuchforschung* (*IBGLW* 2006–2011) for German and the *Diccionario Bibliográfico de la Metalexicografía del Español* (*DBME* 2006–2009) for Spanish. More bibliographical details are provided in lexicographic reference works such as the *Dictionary of Lexicography* (*DoL* 1998) and the *Nuevo Tesoro Lexicográfico del Español* (*NTLE* 2007).

47.3.2.9 Disciplinary connections

As the 47 chapters of this *Handbook* demonstrate, lexicography is a relatively new and complex subject field, which is why its experts often have difficulties establishing themselves within the academic context. The study of national languages is one of the primary concerns, also the main reason for linguistics being one of the chief suppliers of basic data, on varieties such as dialects and technical terminology, and on language structures from graphology, phonetics and phonology to morphology, syntax and textology. Applied linguistics, language teaching, library science and cartography can sometimes be considered important *sister disciplines*, too (see Part II of this *Handbook*).

Information technology can also help in this complex process by providing computer corpus evidence (see *E-Lexicography* ed. by Fuertes-Olivera and Bergenholtz 2011), onomastics can support data on the study of names, and translation studies can supply additional details about contrasts between pairs of different languages. One particularly difficult area is the coverage of encyclopaedic knowledge and the often varying and open borders between dictionaries and more technical reference works.

All this makes our subject extremely hard to develop and to elaborate uniform approaches across continents, countries and institutions. An additional factor is the relatively difficult need for lexicographers to collaborate with publishers of dictionaries and other reference works. Topic No. 9 in Table 47.12 can merely hint at all these complexities.

47.3.2.10 Networks

The final topic in Table 47.12 is an attempt to provide a list of 'networks' that have been developed in the four countries selected as well as in the international context, such as CLARET for Corpus Linguistics (at Birmingham) and ITI-TN for Terminology and Translation (at Guildford) in Great Britain, GERAS for English LSP (at Toulouse) and GLAT for Telecommunication (at Brest) in France, CiTaL for International Terminology and Applied Linguistics (at Konstanz) and DGI for Information Science (at Frankfurt) in Germany, and IULMA for Modern Languages (at Alicante) and REDESTerm for Terminology (at Jaume I) in Spain.

Efforts elsewhere include ELRA for European Language Resources (at Paris), ICOS for Onomastic Science (at Bern), LTT for networking Lexicology, Terminology and Translation (at Brussels) and NordTerm for Nordic Terminology (at Oslo).

47.4 Conclusion

It might be interesting to pursue other perspectives here, but they do not fit in easily. Most notably:

- Who are the most leading lexicographers?
- Which are the most relevant dictionaries?
- Do we need to learn more about the methods used in the compiling process(es)?
- Do we have bibliographical details of the most relevant publications?
- Do we know enough abut interlingual connections, such as translation equivalents?
- Do we know enough about interdisciplinary links to further develop metalexicography?
- Do we agree on international training and teaching facilities?

So it is going to be a hard job to specify the significant factors that determine our knowledge about and control of the field of lexicography.

I hope that my survey has presented the main problems that still lie in our way of understanding the various issues we have to address, such as the compilation and publication of more complete directories of lexicographic information. The potential components of such an integrated approach are most likely to have to include the following information categories (some potential sample entries for these are provided in Sections 47.2 and 47.3):

- Languages by country, including their historical connections;
- Elements of the production process, including fieldwork, entry edition, and text formatting;
- Fields of specialisation, including graphology, phonology, grammar, and meaning;
- People responsible, including research students, editors, and compilers;
- Institutions involved, including publishers, university research centres, and academies;

- Higher-degree theses and dissertations of relevance;
- National and international associations and relevant networks;
- National and international conference series; and
- Bibliographies of relevant publications, including dictionaries and other reference works, textbooks and periodicals.

I trust that someone will be able to attempt and complete this worthwhile task to produce an international directory of lexicography for us.

Notes

1 See at www.allea.org/
2 See at www.interacademycouncil.net/
3 See at www.uai-iua.org/
4 See at www.eaft-aet.net/
5 See at www.icosweb.net/
6 See at http://icame.uib.no/
7 See at www.elra.info/
8 See at www.ebscohost.com/title-list/
9 See at www.jstor.org/
10 See at www.norden.org/en/
11 See at www.ccheilteach.ie/
12 See at www.clres.com/
13 See at www.thefreedictionary.com/
14 See at www.publishers.org/
15 See at www.fep-fee.eu/
16 See at www.university-directory.eu/
17 See at www.worldoflearning.com/
18 See at www.efnil.org/
19 See at www.linguistlist.org/callconf/

References

Dictionaries and other reference works

ANW = *Algemeen Nederlands Woordenboek* ed. by T. Schoonheim. Leiden: Instituut voor Nederlandse Lexicologie 1970–2019

BCSI = *Bibliographie chronologique sommaire et indicative 1950–2000 des ouvrages utilisés relevant des domaines de la lexicologie, lexicographie, dictionnairique et métalexicographie* ed. by J. Pruvost. Cergy: Musée Virtuel 2000

BTCM = *Bibliographie thématique et chronologique de métalexicographie 1950–2006* (Biblioteca della Ricerca 10) comp by C. Boccuzzi et al. Fasano: Schena Editore 2007

COBUILD = *Collins COBUILD [Birmingham University International Language Database] English Language Dictionary* ed. by J. Sinclair et al. London/Glasgow: Collins 1987

DBME 2006–2009 = *Diccionario Bibliográfico de la Metalexicografía del Español* comp. by I. Ahumada. Jaén: Publicaciones de la Universidad de Jaen

DDEE = *Dictionary of Dictionaries and Eminent Encyclopedias* comp. by T. Kabdebo and N. Armstrong. London: Bowker-Saur 1997

DIEL = *Dictionaries. An International Encyclopedia of Lexicography* ed. by R.H. Gouws, U. Heid, W. Schweickard and H.E. Wiegand. Supplementary Volume 5.4 (Recent Developments with Focus on

Electronic and Computational Lexicography) of *Handbücher zur Sprach- und Kommunikationswissenschaft*. Berlin: W. de Gruyter 2013

DLP = *Diccionario de lexicografía práctica* comp. by J. Martínez de Sousa. Barcelona: VOX-Biblograf 1995

DoL = *Dictionary of Lexicography* comp. by R.R.K. Hartmann and G. James. London: Routledge 1998 (paperback 2001)

DoP = *Directory of Publishing 2014: United Kingdom and Republic of Ireland* ed. by Continuum. London: Bloomsbury Academic (37th edition) 2013 www.bloomsbury.com/uk/directory-of-publishing-2014-9781472521910/

DPoT = *Debrett's People of Today*. London: Debrett's Ltd. (34th edition) 2016 www.debretts.com/people/people-today-0/

DSAL = *Diccionario Salamanca de la lengua española*. Madrid: Universidad de Salamanca-Santillana 1996

EIFD = *The Europa International Foundation Directory*. London: Europe Publications/Routledge (25th edition) 2016 www.routledge.com/series/EIFD

EITA = *(Directory of) Entities Involved in Terminology Activities*. Barcelona: EAFT Terminology Summit 2004 http://eaft-aet.net/fileadmin/files/Directory.pdf

ELDIT = *Elektronisches Lernerwörterbuch Deutsch-Italienisch*. Bolzano: Europäische Akademie 2002

EWL = *The Europa World of Learning. The International Guide to the Academic World*. London: Routledge (66th edition) 2016 www.worldoflearning.com/

FD = *The Free Dictionary*. Huntingdon Valley PA: Farlex Inc. (2004–2014) www.thefreedictionary.com/

IBGLW = *Internationale Bibliographie zur germanistischen Lexikographie und Wörterbuchforschung* comp. by H.E. Wiegand. Berlin: W. de Gruyter (4 volumes) 2006–2011

KBDELP = *The Kenkyusha Biographical Dictionary of English Linguistics and Philology* ed. by T. Sasaki and K. Kihara. Tokyo: Kenkyusha since 1995 www.worldcat.org/

LEME = *The Lexicons of Early Modern English* ed. by I. Lancashire. Toronto: Toronto U.P. (Database) 2003 http://lexicall.widged.com/

LGL = *Lexikon der germanistischen Linguistik* ed. by H.P. Althaus, H. Henne and H.E. Wiegand. Tübingen: M. Niemeyer Verlag (1st edition) 1973, (2nd edition) 1980

Linguist.List = *Calls for Papers by Linguistic Subfield*. Indiana University (since 2014) http://linguistlist.org/callconf/browse-current LF.cfm?type=Conf&subclassid=7411

NTLE = *Nuevo Tesoro Lexicográfico del Español* ed. by L.N. Jiménez and M.A. Ezquerra. Madrid: Arcos/Libros (11 volumes) 2007

OED = *Oxford English Dictionary* ed. J. Murray et al. (+ 2nd edition and additional/supplementary volumes). Oxford: Clarendon Press 1884–1928, 1933, 1972–1986, 1989 www.oed.com/

TLF = *Trésor de la langue française* ed. by P. Imbs. Nancy: Gallimard 1971–1994 www.inalf.fr/tlfi

UDW = *University Directory Worldwide* ed. by O. Vinzent. CEO @ eUni GmbH: Saarbrücken since 1995 www.university-directory.eu/

WDD = *Wörterbücher/Dictionaries/Dictionnaires. Ein internationales Handbuch zur Lexikographie* ed. by F.J. Hausmann, O. Reichmann, H.E. Wiegand and L. Zgusta. Berlin: W. de Gruyter (Volumes 5.1 to 5.3 of *Handbücher zur Sprach- und Kommunikationswissenschaft)* 1989–1991

Wikipedia = *Wikipedia, the Free Encyclopedia*. San Francisco: Wikimedia Foundation https://en.wikipedia.org/wiki/List_of_lexicographers https://en.wikipedia.org/wiki/List_of_language_regulators

WLWF = *Wörterbuch zur Lexikographie und Wörterbuchforschung/Dictionary of Lexicography and Dictionary Research* ed. by H.E. Wiegand et al. Berlin: W. de Gruyter (Vol. 1) 2010

WWL = *Who's Who in Lexicography. An International Directory of EURALEX Members* ed. by S. McGill. Exeter: University of Exeter, Dictionary Research Centre 1996

Other literature

Atkins, B.T.S. and M. Rundell (2008) *The Oxford Guide to Practical Lexicography*. Oxford: Oxford University Press

Fuertes-Olivera, P. A. and H. Bergenholtz (eds.) (2011) *E-Lexicography. The Internet, Digital Initiatives and Lexicography*. London and New York: Continuum

Hartmann, R.R.K. (ed.) (1984) *LEXeter '83 Proceedings. Papers from the International Conference on Lexicography at Exeter, 9–12 September 1983* (Lexicographica Series Maior 1). Tübingen: M. Niemeyer

Hartmann, R.R.K. (ed.) (1999) *Dictionaries in Language Learning: Recommendations, National Reports and Thematic Reports From the TNP Sub-Project 9: Dictionaries*. Berlin: Freie Universität Berlin (TNP in the Area of Languages) www.celelc.org/projects/Past_Projects/TNP_Languages/index.html

Hartmann, R.R.K. (2001) *Teaching and Researching Lexicography* (Applied Linguistics in Action Series). Harlow, Essex: Longman/Pearson Education.

Hartmann, R.R.K. (ed.) (2003) *Lexicography. Critical Concepts*. 3 Volumes. London: Routledge.

Hartmann, R.R.K. (2006–2014) "Reinhard's References (No. 1–15)", in *DSNA Newsletter* from Vol. 30/2 (p. 5) to Vol. 38/1–2 (pp. 15–17)

Hartmann, R.R.K. (2007) "Bibliography of Lexicography", on *EURALEX Website* http://euralex.pbworks.com/, c. 29 pp.

Hartmann, R.R.K. (2009) "Keeping in Touch: A Survey of Lexicographic Periodicals", *Lexikos AFRILEX-Reeks/Series* 19: 404–422

Hartmann, R.R.K. (2009–2016) "Forthcoming Events (No. 1–30)", *International Journal of Lexicography* from Vol. 22/1 (pp. 119–120) to Vol. 29/2 (pp. 266–267)

Hartmann, R.R.K. (2010) "Reference Portals to Internet Sources Relevant to Lexicography and Terminology", on *EURALEX Website* http://euralex.pbworks.com/, c. 58 pp.

Hartmann, R.R.K. (2011) "Linking Up: The Role of Networking in Disciplinary Contacts Within and Around Lexicography, With Special Reference to Four European Countries", *Dictionaries: Journal of the Dictionary Society of North America* 32: 33–65

Hartmann, R.R.K. (2012) "The Contribution of European Academies to Dictionary-Making, Lexicography and Reference Science", in K. P. Márkus, T. Pintér and D. Pödör (eds.), *Szavak Pásztora (Festschrift in Honour of Tamás Magay)*. Szeged: Grimm Publishing House, pp. 310–333

Hartmann, R.R.K. (2013a) "Lexicographic Associations", in *Dictionaries. An International Encyclopedia of Lexicography* Volume 5.4 of *WDD:* 580–586

Hartmann, R.R.K. (2013b) "Resources", in H. Jackson (ed.), *The Bloomsbury Companion to Lexicography*. London: Bloomsbury, pp. 373–390

Hartmann, R.R.K. and G. James (1998) *Dictionary of Lexicography*. London, New York: Routledge.

Jackson, H. ed. (2013) *The Bloomsbury Companion to Lexicography*. London: Bloomsbury.

Svensén, B. (2009) *A Handbook of Lexicography: The Theory and Practice of Dictionary-Making*. Cambridge: Cambridge University Press.

Yamada, S. (2014) *Guide to the Practical Usage of English Monolingual Learners' Dictionaries*. Tokyo: Oxford University Press. See at: www.oupjapan.co.jp/teachers/resources/oup_guide_to_dictionary_use_2014_E.pd

Index

Page numbers in italic indicate a figure on the corresponding page.

www.ingramcontent.com/pod-product-compliance
Lightning Source LLC
Chambersburg PA
CBHW080752150926
51501CB00045B/1222
* 9 7 8 1 0 3 2 0 9 6 2 6 1 *